BARRON'S

FOREIGN LANGUAGE GUIDES

D0019784

501
SPANISH
VERBS

SIXTH EDITION

**Fully conjugated in all the tenses in a new,
easy-to-learn format, alphabetically arranged**

by

Christopher Kendris
B.S., M.S., Columbia University
M.A., Ph.D., Northwestern University
Diplômé, Faculté des Lettres, Sorbonne

Former Chairman,
Department of Foreign Languages
Farmingdale High School,
Farmingdale, New York

and
Theodore Kendris
B.A., Union College
M.A., Northwestern University
Ph.D., Université Laval, Québec, Canada

Adjunct Instructor
Penn State University, Hazleton Campus

BARRON'S

All inquiries should be addressed to:
Barron's Educational Series, Inc.
250 Wireless Boulevard
Hauppauge, New York 11788
www.barronseduc.com

ISBN-13: 978-0-7641-3559-0 (Book)
ISBN-10: 0-7641-3559-7 (Book)

ISBN-13: 978-0-7641-7984-5 (Book/CD-Rom package)
ISBN-10: 0-7641-7984-6 (Book/CD-Rom package)

Library of Congress Catalog Card No. 2006025877

Library of Congress Cataloging-in-Publication Data

Kendris, Christopher.
    [501 Spanish verbs fully conjugated in all the tenses in a new easy-to-learn format, alphabetically arranged]
    501 Spanish verbs / by Christopher Kendris & Theodore Kendris.—6th ed.
       p.   cm.
    Includes indexes.
    ISBN-13: 978-0-7641-3559-0 (alk. paper)
    ISBN-10: 0-7641-3559-7 (alk. paper)
    ISBN-13: 978-0-7641-7984-5
    ISBN-10: 0-7641-7984-6
    1. Spanish language—Verb—Tables. I. Kendris, Theodore. II. Title.
III. Title: Five hundred and one Spanish verbs. IV. Title: Five hundred one Spanish verbs.

PC4271.K38 2006
468.2'421—dc22   2006025877

PRINTED IN CANADA
9 8 7 6 5

Contents

About the Authors

Dr. Christopher Kendris has worked as interpreter and translator of French for the U.S. State Department at the American Embassy in Paris. He earned his B.S. and M.S. degrees at Columbia University in the City of New York, where he held a New York State Scholarship, and his M.A. and Ph.D. degrees at Northwestern University in Evanston, Illinois, where he held a Teaching Assistantship and Tutorial Fellowship for four years. He also earned two diplomas with *Mention très Honorable* at the Université de Paris (en Sorbonne), Faculté des Lettres, École Supérieure de Préparation et de Perfectionnement des Professeurs de Français à l'Étranger, and at the Institut de Phonétique, Paris. In 1986, he was one of 95 teachers in the United States who was awarded a Rockefeller Foundation Fellowship for Teachers of Foreign Languages in American High Schools. He has taught French at the College of The University of Chicago as visiting summer lecturer, at Colby College, Duke University, Rutgers—The State University of New Jersey, and the State University of New York at Albany. He was Chairman of the Department of Foreign Languages and Supervisor of 16 foreign language teachers on the secondary level at Farmingdale High School, Farmingdale, New York, where he was also a teacher of all levels of French and Spanish, and prepared students for the New York State French and Spanish Regents, SAT exams, and AP tests. Dr. Kendris is the author of 22 school and college books, workbooks, and other language guides of French and Spanish. He is listed in *Contemporary Authors* and *Directory of American Scholars.*

Dr. Theodore Kendris earned his B.A. degree in Modern Languages at Union College, Schenectady, New York, where he received the Thomas J. Judson Memorial Book Prize for modern language study. He went on to earn his M.A. degree in French Language and Literature at Northwestern University, Evanston, Illinois, where he held a Teaching Assistantship. He earned his Ph.D. degree in French Literature at Université Laval in Quebec City, where he studied the Middle Ages and Renaissance. While at Université Laval, he taught French writing skills as a *chargé de cours* in the French as a Second Language program and, in 1997, he was awarded a doctoral scholarship by the *Fondation de l'Université Laval.* Dr. Kendris is coauthor of *Spanish Fundamentals,* published by Barron's in 1992. He has also taught in the Department of English and Foreign Languages at the University of St. Francis in Joliet, Illinois as well as at the Hazleton Campus of Penn State University.

Preface to the Sixth Edition

This new edition of *501 Spanish Verbs* has been updated so that it is easier to use than ever! All of the verb lists that you need are in the back pages of the book with handy tabs so that you can find the list you need quickly and easily. We hope that you will also take the time to practice your conjugations and grammar with the new verb drills and tests with answers explained on CD-ROM. The model verbs themselves have been revised and include extra material for certain Essential Verbs. These are verbs that we believe will be helpful to students because they represent an important conjugation group or because they are useful in many everyday situations and idiomatic expressions. We have also taken into account the many technological advances that have taken place over the past several years, as well as the increased globalization and social change in the 21st century. We hope that *501 Spanish Verbs* will continue to provide the guidance that students and travelers like you have come to expect over the years.

We have, therefore, added a number of related words and idiomatic expressions, along with English meanings, at the bottom of every verb page from 97 to 648. We also hope that you will take advantage of the section on verb drills and tests with answers explained, beginning on page 45. There, you will find a lot of practice in Spanish verb forms and tenses in a variety of tests and word games to determine your strengths and weaknesses yourself and to make some things clearer in your mind. Also, it would be a good idea to get acquainted with the section on definitions of basic grammatical terms. It's on page 33. Many students who study a foreign language have problems because they do not understand certain grammatical terms. If you know what they are, what they are called, and how they are used in the grammatical structure of a sentence, you will improve your skill in speaking and writing Spanish.

Don't miss the expanded Spanish-English index at the end of the book. There are now over 2,100 verbs—in addition to the 501 in the main listing. The English-Spanish list, which begins on page 682, is a handy tool if you can't remember the Spanish verb you need to use.

Have you ever wondered what preposition goes with what verb? Many people do. Check out page 669 for the section on verbs with prepositions. On page 666, there is a simple system of sound transcriptions to help you pronounce Spanish words effectively.

In this edition, we have put all the Defective and Impersonal Verbs in one convenient place, at the end of the main listing. This gave us room to give you more fully conjugated verbs in the main list.

We hope that you will make full use of all the features of this new edition of *501 Spanish Verbs* and that you will enjoy your exploration of Spanish language and culture.

Christopher Kendris and Theodore Kendris

To St. Sophia Greek Orthodox Church
of Albany, New York, our parish

and

To the eternal memory of our beloved
YOLANDA FENYO KENDRIS
who is always by our side

With love

Introduction

This self-teaching book of 501 commonly used Spanish verbs for students and travelers provides fingertip access to correct verb forms.

Verb conjugations are usually found scattered in Spanish grammar books and they are difficult to find quickly when needed. Verbs have always been a major problem for students no matter what system or approach the teacher uses. You will master Spanish verb forms if you study this book for a few minutes every day, especially the pages before and after the alphabetical listing of the 501 verbs.

This book will help make your work easier and at the same time will teach you Spanish verb forms systematically. It is a useful book because it provides a quick and easy way to find the full conjugation of many Spanish verbs.

The 501 verbs included here are arranged alphabetically by infinitive at the top of each page. The book contains many common verbs of high frequency, both reflexive and nonreflexive, which you need to know. It also contains many other frequently used verbs which are irregular in some way. Beginning on page 707, there are over 2,100 Spanish verbs that can be conjugated in the same way as model verbs among the 501. If the verb you have in mind is not given among the 501, consult this list.

The subject pronouns have been omitted from the conjugations in order to emphasize the verb forms. The subject pronouns are given on page 92. Turn to that page now and become acquainted with them.

The first thing to do when you use this book is to become familiar with it from cover to cover—in particular, the front and back pages, where you will find valuable and useful information to make your work easier and more enjoyable. Take a minute right now and turn to the table of contents at the beginning of this book as we guide you in the following way:

(a) Beginning on page 3, you can learn how to form a present participle regularly in Spanish with examples. There, you will find the common irregular present participles and the many uses of the present participle.

(b) Beginning on page 5, you can learn how to form a past participle regularly in Spanish with examples. There, you will find the common irregular past participles and the many uses of the past participle.

(c) On page 7, the Passive and Active voices are explained with numerous examples.

(d) Beginning on page 9, you will find the principal parts of some important Spanish verbs. This is useful because, if you know these, you are well on your way to mastering Spanish verb forms.

(e) Beginning on page 11, we give you a sample English verb conjugation so that you can get an idea of the way a verb is expressed in the English tenses. Many people do not know one tense from another because they have never learned the use of verb tenses in a systematic and organized way—not even in English! How can you, for example, know that you need the conditional form of a verb in Spanish when you want to say *"I would go* to the movies if . . ."* or the pluperfect tense in Spanish if you want to say *"I had gone* . . . ."*? The sample English verb conjugation with the names of the tenses and their numerical ranking will help you to distinguish one tense from another so that you will know what tense you need in order to express a verb in Spanish.

(f) On page 13, you will find a summary of meanings and uses of Spanish verb tenses and moods as related to English verb tenses and moods. That section is very important and useful because the seven simple tenses are separated from the seven compound tenses. You are given the name of each tense in Spanish and English starting with the present indicative, which we call tense number one because it is the tense most frequently used. We assign a number to each tense name so that you can fix each one in your mind and associate the tense names and numbers in their logical order. We explain briefly what each tense is, when you use it, and we give examples using verbs in sentences in Spanish and English. At the end of each tense, you are shown how to form that tense for regular verbs.

(g) Beginning on page 27, we explain the Imperative, which is a mood, not a tense, and give numerous examples using it.

(h) Beginning on page 4, the progressive forms of tenses are explained with examples. Also note the future subjunctive and the future perfect subjunctive on page 30. We explain how these two rarely used tenses are formed, and we give examples of what tenses are used in place of them in informal writing and in conversation.

(i) Beginning on page 14, we give you a summary of all of the fourteen tenses in Spanish with English equivalents, which we have divided into the seven simple tenses and the seven compound tenses. After referring to that summary frequently, you will soon know that tense number 1 is the present indicative, tense number 2 is the imperfect indicative, and so on. We also explain how each compound tense is based on each simple tense. Try to see these two divisions as two frames, two pictures, with the seven simple tenses in one frame and the seven compound tenses in another frame. Place them side by side in your mind, and you will see how tense number 8 is related to tense number 1, tense number 9 to tense number 2, and so on. If you study the numerical arrangement of each of the seven simple tenses and associate the tense number with the tense name, you will find it very easy to learn the names of the seven compound tenses, how they rank numerically according to use, how they are formed, and when they are used. Spend at least ten minutes every day studying these preliminary pages to help you better understand the fourteen tenses in Spanish.

Finally, in the back pages of this book, there are useful indexes: an index of English-Spanish verbs, an index of common irregular Spanish verb forms identified by infinitive, and a list of over 2,100 Spanish verbs that are conjugated like model verbs among the 501.

Note that each verb listed in the Alphabetical Listing of *501 Spanish Verbs* is followed by a number in parentheses. This number is the verb number for the purpose of easy cross-referencing in this book. If you refer to the many features of this book each time you look up verb tense forms for a particular verb, you will increase your knowledge of Spanish vocabulary and Spanish idioms by leaps and bounds.

We sincerely hope that this new edition of *501 Spanish Verbs* will be of great help to you in learning and using Spanish verbs.

Christopher Kendris and Theodore Kendris

Formation of the Present and Past Participles in Spanish

Formation of the present participle in Spanish

A present participle is a verb form which, in English, ends in *-ing*; for example, *singing, eating, receiving.* In Spanish, a present participle is regularly formed as follows:

drop the **ar** of an **-ar** ending verb, like **cantar,** and add **ando: cantando**/singing

drop the **er** of an **-er** ending verb, like **comer,** and add **iendo: comiendo**/eating

drop the **ir** of an **-ir** ending verb, like **recibir,** and add **iendo: recibiendo**/receiving

In English, a gerund also ends in **-ing**, but there is a distinct difference in use between a gerund and a present participle in English. In brief, it is this: in English, when a present participle is used as a noun it is called a gerund; for example, *Reading is good.* As a present participle in English, it would be used as follows: *While reading,* the boy fell asleep.

In the first example (*Reading is good*), *reading* is a gerund because it is the subject of the verb *is.* In Spanish, however, we do not use the present participle form as a noun to serve as a subject; we use the infinitive form of the verb: *Leer es bueno.*

Common irregular present participles

INFINITIVE	PRESENT PARTICIPLE
caer to fall	**cayendo** falling
conseguir to attain, to achieve	**consiguiendo** attaining, achieving
construir to construct	**construyendo** constructing
corregir to correct	**corrigiendo** correcting
creer to believe	**creyendo** believing
decir to say, to tell	**diciendo** saying, telling
despedirse to say good-bye	**despidiéndose** saying good-bye
destruir to destroy	**destruyendo** destroying
divertirse to enjoy oneself	**divirtiéndose** enjoying oneself
dormir to sleep	**durmiendo** sleeping
huir to flee	**huyendo** fleeing
ir to go	**yendo** going
leer to read	**leyendo** reading
mentir to lie (tell a falsehood)	**mintiendo** lying
morir to die	**muriendo** dying
oír to hear	**oyendo** hearing
pedir to ask (for), to request	**pidiendo** asking (for), requesting
poder to be able	**pudiendo** being able
reír to laugh	**riendo** laughing
repetir to repeat	**repitiendo** repeating
seguir to follow	**siguiendo** following
sentir to feel	**sintiendo** feeling

INFINITIVE	PRESENT PARTICIPLE
servir to serve	sirviendo serving
traer to bring	trayendo bringing
venir to come	viniendo coming
vestir to dress	vistiendo dressing
vestirse to dress oneself	vistiéndose dressing oneself

Uses of the present participle

1. To form the progressive tenses: **The Progressive Present** is formed by using **estar** in the present tense plus the present participle of the main verb you are using. **The Progressive Past** is formed by using **estar** in the imperfect indicative plus the present participle of the main verb you are using. (See below and on page 5 for a complete description of the uses and formation of the progressive tenses with examples.)

2. To express vividly an action that occurred (preterit + present participle):
   *El niño entró llorando en la casa/*The little boy came into the house crying.

3. To express the English use of *by* + present participle in Spanish, we use the gerund form, which has the same ending as a present participle explained above: *Trabajando, se gana dinero/*By working, one earns (a person earns) money; *Estudiando mucho, Pepe recibió buenas notas/*By studying hard, Joe received good grades.

   Note that no preposition is used in front of the present participle (the Spanish gerund) even though it is expressed in English as *by* + present participle.

   Note, too, that in Spanish we use **al** + inf. (not + present part.) to express *on* or *upon* + present part. in English: *Al entrar en la casa, el niño comenzó a llorar/*Upon entering the house, the little boy began to cry.

4. To form the Perfect Participle: **habiendo hablado**/having talked.

The Progressive forms of tenses

(1) In Spanish, there are progressive forms of tenses. They are the Progressive Present and the Progressive Past.

(2) The **Progressive Present** is formed by using *estar* in the present tense plus the present participle of your main verb; e.g., *Estoy hablando/*I am talking, i.e., I am (in the act of) talking (right now). Here is how you would form the progressive present of *hablar* (to talk) using *estar* in the present tense plus the present participle of **hablar**:

estoy hablando	estamos hablando
estás hablando	estáis hablando
está hablando	están hablando

(3) The **Progressive Past** is formed by using *estar* in the imperfect indicative plus the present participle of your main verb; e.g., *Estaba hablando*/I was talking, i.e., I was (in the act of) talking (right then). Here is how you would form the progressive past of *hablar* (to talk) using *estar* in the imperfect indicative plus the present participle of **hablar**:

estaba hablando   estábamos hablando
estabas hablando   estabais hablando
estaba hablando   estaban hablando

(4) The progressive forms are generally used when you want to emphasize or intensify an action; if you don't want to do that, then simply use the present or imperfect; e.g., say *Hablo*, not *Estoy hablando*; or *Hablaba*, not *Estaba hablando.*

(5) Sometimes *ir* is used instead of *estar* to form the progressive tenses; e.g., *Va hablando*/He (she) keeps right on talking, *Iba hablando*/He (she) kept right on talking. Note that they do not have the exact same meaning as *Está hablando* and *Estaba hablando*. See (2) and (3) above.

(6) Also, at times *andar, continuar, seguir,* and *venir* are used as helping verbs in the present or imperfect indicative tenses plus the present participle to express the progressive forms: *Los muchachos andaban cantando*/The boys were walking along singing; *La maestra seguía leyendo a la clase*/The teacher kept right on reading to the class.

Formation of the past participle in Spanish

A past participle is a verb form which, in English, usually ends in *-ed*: for example, *worked, talked, arrived,* as in *I have worked, I have talked, I have arrived.* There are many irregular past participles in English; for example, *gone, sung,* as in *She has gone, We have sung.* In Spanish, a past participle is regularly formed as follows:

drop the **ar** of an **-ar** ending verb, like **cantar,** and add **ado: cantado**/sung
drop the **er** of an **-er** ending verb, like **comer,** and add **ido: comido**/eaten
drop the **ir** of an **-ir** ending verb, like **recibir,** and add **ido: recibido**/received

Common irregular past participles

INFINITIVE	PAST PARTICIPLE
abrir to open	**abierto** opened
caer to fall	**caído** fallen
creer to believe	**creído** believed
cubrir to cover	**cubierto** covered
decir to say, to tell	**dicho** said, told
descubrir to discover	**descubierto** discovered
deshacer to undo	**deshecho** undone
devolver to return (something)	**devuelto** returned (something)
escribir to write	**escrito** written
hacer to do, to make	**hecho** done, made
imponer to impose	**impuesto** imposed
imprimir to print	**impreso** printed
ir to go	**ido** gone
leer to read	**leído** read
morir to die	**muerto** died
oír to hear	**oído** heard
poner to put	**puesto** put
poseer to possess	**poseído** possessed
rehacer to redo, to remake	**rehecho** redone, remade
reír to laugh	**reído** laughed
resolver to resolve, to solve	**resuelto** resolved, solved
romper to break	**roto** broken
sonreír to smile	**sonreído** smiled
traer to bring	**traído** brought
ver to see	**visto** seen
volver to return	**vuelto** returned

Uses of the past participle

1. To form the seven compound tenses

2. To form the Perfect Infinitive: *haber hablado*/to have spoken.

3. To form the Perfect Participle: *habiendo hablado*/having spoken.

4. To serve as an adjective, which must agree in gender and number with the noun it modifies: *El señor Molina es muy respetado por todos los alumnos*/Mr. Molina is very respected by all the students; *La señora González es muy conocida*/Mrs. González is very well known.

5. To express the result of an action with **estar** and sometimes with **quedar** or **quedarse:** *La puerta está abierta*/The door is open; *Las cartas están escritas*/The letters are written; *Los niños se quedaron asustados*/The children remained frightened.

6. To express the passive voice with **ser:** *La ventana fue abierta por el ladrón*/The window was opened by the robber.

Passive voice means that the action of the verb falls on the subject; in other words, the subject receives the action: *La ventana fue abierta por el ladrón*/The window was opened by the robber. Note that *abierta* (really a form of the past part. *abrir/abierto*) is used as an adjective and it must agree in gender and number with the subject that it describes.

Active voice means that the subject performs the action and the subject is always stated: *El ladrón abrió la ventana*/The robber opened the window.

To form the true passive, use **ser** + the past part. of the verb you have in mind; the past part. then serves as an adjective and it must agree in gender and number with the subject that it describes. In the true passive, the agent (the doer) is always expressed with the prep. **por** in front of it. The formula for the true passive construction is: subject + tense of **ser** + past part. + **por** + the agent (the doer): *Estas composiciones fueron escritas por Juan/*These compositions were written by John.

The reflexive pronoun **se** may be used to substitute for the true passive voice construction. When you use the **se** construction, the subject is a thing (not a person) and the doer (agent) is not stated: *Aquí se habla español*/Spanish is spoken here; *Aquí se hablan español e inglés*/Spanish and English are spoken here; *Se venden libros en esta tienda*/Books are sold in this store.

There are a few standard idiomatic expressions that are commonly used with the pronoun **se.** These expressions are not truly passive, the pronoun **se** is not truly a reflexive pronoun, and the verb form is in the 3rd pers. sing. only. In this construction, there is no subject expressed; the subject is contained in the use of **se** + the 3rd pers. sing. of the verb at all times and the common translations into English are: it is . . . , people . . . , they . . . , one . . .

Se cree que . . . It is believed that . . . , people believe that . . . , they believe that . . . , one believes that . . .

Se cree que este criminal es culpable. It is believed that this criminal is guilty.

Se dice que . . . It is said that . . . , people say that . . . , they say that . . . , one says that . . . , you say . . .

Se dice que va a nevar esta noche. They say that it's going to snow tonight.
¿Cómo se dice en español "ice cream"? How do you say *ice cream* in Spanish?

Se sabe que . . . It is known that . . . , people know that . . . , they know that . . . , one knows that . . .

*Se sabe que María va a casarse con Juan./*People know that Mary is going to marry John.

The **se** reflexive pronoun construction is avoided if the subject is a person because there can be ambiguity in meaning. For example, how would you translate the following into English? **Se da un regalo.** Which of the following two meanings is intended? She (he) is being given a present, *or* She (he) is giving a present to himself (to herself). In correct Spanish, you would have to say: **Le da** (a María, a Juan, etc.) un regalo/He (she) is giving a present to Mary (to John, etc.). Avoid using the se construction in the passive when the subject is a person; change your sentence around and state it in the active voice to make the meaning clear. Otherwise, the pronoun se seems to go with the verb, as if the verb is reflexive, which gives an entirely different meaning. Another example: Se miró would mean *He (she) looked at himself (herself)*, not *He (she) was looked at!* If you mean to say *He (she) looked at her*, say: La miró or, if in the plural, say: La miraron/They looked at her.

The Spanish Infinitive and Its Principal Uses

An infinitive is a verb that is not inflected; in other words, it does not change in form by inflection. In grammar, inflection takes place when a verb changes in form according to whether the subject of the sentence is singular in the 1st (yo), 2nd (tú), or 3rd (Ud., él, ella) person, or plural (nosotros, etc.), and according to the conjugated form of the verb in a particular tense, such as the present, preterit, imperfect, future, etc. An infinitive is generally considered to be a mood and it does not refer to a particular person, number, or tense. It is indeterminate and general. It is not conjugated in the tenses. The verb, however, is inflected because it is conjugated in the various tenses and changes in form. An infinitive remains in the same form: hablar, comer, vivir. In English, an infinitive is recognized by the preposition *to* in front of it, as in *to speak, to eat, to live.* When conjugated, *to speak* changes to *he, she speaks, I spoke, we have spoken,* etc. The change in the verb form is called inflection. The form of an infinitive is always the same because it is not conjugated and it is not inflected.

Here are three principal uses of the Spanish infinitive. For more examples in Spanish and English, please turn to page 669 where you will find an outline of what preposition (if any) goes with what verb plus an infinitive.

1. An infinitive can be used as a noun and it is masculine in gender. In English we use the present participle of a verb to function as a noun, in which case, we call it a *gerund.* In Spanish, however, the infinitive form of a verb is used. Examples:
   Leer es bueno/El leer es bueno/Reading is good.
   Fumar no es bueno para la salud/Smoking is not good for one's health.

2. An infinitive is used with some finite verbs (those that are conjugated in the various tenses) when affirmation or belief is conveyed. Examples:
   María siempre cree tener razón/Mary always believes she is right.
   Nosotros podemos venir a tu casa esta noche/We can come to your house tonight (this evening).

3. An infinitive can be used with idiomatic expressions that contain que or de. Examples:
   Tengo mucho que hacer esta mañana/I have a lot to do this morning.
   Mis amigos acaban de llegar/My friends have just arrived.

Principal Parts of Some Important Spanish Verbs

INFINITIVE	(GERUNDIO) PRESENT PARTICIPLE	PAST PARTICIPLE	PRESENT INDICATIVE	PRETERIT
abrir	abriendo	abierto	abro	abrí
andar	andando	andado	ando	anduve
caber	cabiendo	cabido	quepo	cupe
caer	cayendo	caído	caigo	caí
conseguir	consiguiendo	conseguido	consigo	conseguí
construir	construyendo	construido	construyo	construí
corregir	corrigiendo	corregido	corrijo	corregí
creer	creyendo	creído	creo	creí
cubrir	cubriendo	cubierto	cubro	cubrí
dar	dando	dado	doy	di
decir	diciendo	dicho	digo	dije
descubrir	descubriendo	descubierto	descubro	descubrí
deshacer	deshaciendo	deshecho	deshago	deshice
despedirse	despidiéndose	despedido	me despido	me despedí
destruir	destruyendo	destruido	destruyo	destruí
devolver	devolviendo	devuelto	devuelvo	devolví
divertirse	divirtiéndose	divertido	me divierto	me divertí
dormir	durmiendo	dormido	duermo	dormí
escribir	escribiendo	escrito	escribo	escribí
estar	estando	estado	estoy	estuve
haber	habiendo	habido	he	hube
hacer	haciendo	hecho	hago	hice
huir	huyendo	huido	huyo	huí
ir	yendo	ido	voy	fui
irse	yéndose	ido	me voy	me fui
leer	leyendo	leído	leo	leí
mentir	mintiendo	mentido	miento	mentí
morir	muriendo	muerto	muero	morí
oír	oyendo	oído	oigo	oí
oler	oliendo	olido	huelo	olí
pedir	pidiendo	pedido	pido	pedí
poder	pudiendo	podido	puedo	pude
poner	poniendo	puesto	pongo	puse
querer	queriendo	querido	quiero	quise
reír	riendo	reído	río	reí
repetir	repitiendo	repetido	repito	repetí
resolver	resolviendo	resuelto	resuelvo	resolví
romper	rompiendo	roto	rompo	rompí
saber	sabiendo	sabido	sé	supe
salir	saliendo	salido	salgo	salí

INFINITIVE	(GERUNDIO) PRESENT PARTICIPLE	PAST PARTICIPLE	PRESENT INDICATIVE	PRETERIT
seguir	siguiendo	seguido	sigo	seguí
sentir	sintiendo	sentido	siento	sentí
ser	siendo	sido	soy	fui
servir	sirviendo	servido	sirvo	serví
tener	teniendo	tenido	tengo	tuve
traer	trayendo	traído	traigo	traje
venir	viniendo	venido	vengo	vine
ver	viendo	visto	veo	vi
vestir	vistiendo	vestido	visto	vestí
volver	volviendo	vuelto	vuelvo	volví

TIP

In the present indicative and the preterit columns above, only the 1st person singular (**yo**) forms are given to get you started. If you cannot recall the remaining verb forms in the present indicative and the preterit tenses of the verbs listed above in the first column under **infinitive**, please practice them by looking them up in this book, where the infinitive form of the verb is listed alphabetically at the top of each model verb from 1 to 501. When you find them, say them aloud at the same time you practice writing them in Spanish. This is a very useful exercise.

Sample English Verb Conjugation

INFINITIVE **to eat**
PRESENT PARTICIPLE **eating**   *PAST PARTICIPLE* **eaten**

Tense no.	The seven simple tenses
1 *Present Indicative*	I eat, you eat, he (she, it) eats; we eat, you eat, they eat
	or: I do eat, you do eat, he (she, it) does eat; we do eat, you do eat, they do eat
	or: I am eating, you are eating, he (she, it) is eating; we are eating, you are eating, they are eating
2 *Imperfect Indicative*	I was eating, you were eating, he (she, it) was eating; we were eating, you were eating, they were eating
	or: I ate, you ate, he (she, it) ate; we ate, you ate, they ate
	or: I used to eat, you used to eat, he (she, it) used to eat: we used to eat, you used to eat, they used to eat
3 *Preterit*	I ate, you ate, he (she, it) ate; we ate, you ate, they ate
	or: I did eat, you did eat, he (she, it) did eat; we did eat, you did eat, they did eat
4 *Future*	I shall eat, you will eat, he (she, it) will eat; we shall eat, you will eat, they will eat
5 *Conditional*	I would eat, you would eat, he (she, it) would eat; we would eat, you would eat, they would eat
6 *Present Subjunctive*	that I may eat, that you may eat, that he (she, it) may eat; that we may eat, that you may eat, that they may eat
7 *Imperfect or Past Subjunctive*	that I might eat, that you might eat, that he (she, it) might eat; that we might eat, that you might eat, that they might eat

Tense no.	The seven compound tenses
8 *Present Perfect or Past Indefinite*	I have eaten, you have eaten, he (she, it) has eaten; we have eaten, you have eaten, they have eaten
9 *Pluperfect Indic. or Past Perfect*	I had eaten, you had eaten, he (she, it) had eaten; we had eaten, you had eaten, they had eaten
10 *Past Anterior or Preterit Perfect*	I had eaten, you had eaten, he (she, it) had eaten; we had eaten, you had eaten, they had eaten
11 *Future Perfect or Future Anterior*	I shall have eaten, you will have eaten, he (she, it) will have eaten; we shall have eaten, you will have eaten, they will have eaten
12 *Conditional Perfect*	I would have eaten, you would have eaten, he (she, it) would have eaten; we would have eaten, you would have eaten, they would have eaten
13 *Present Perfect or Past Subjunctive*	that I may have eaten, that you may have eaten, that he (she, it) may have eaten; that we may have eaten, that you may have eaten that they may have eaten
14 *Pluperfect or Past Perfect Subjunctive*	that I might have eaten, that you might have eaten, that he (she, it) might have eaten; that we might have eaten, that you might have eaten, that they might have eaten
Imperative or Command	—— eat, let him (her) eat; let us eat, eat, let them eat

A Summary of Meanings and Uses of Spanish Verb Tenses and Moods as Related to English Verb Tenses and Moods

A verb is where the action is! A verb is a word that expresses an action (like *go, eat, write*) or a state of being (like *think, believe, be*). Tense means time. Spanish and English verb tenses are divided into three main groups of time: past, present, and future. A verb tense shows if an action or state of being took place, is taking place, or will take place.

Spanish and English verbs are also used in moods, or modes. Mood has to do with the *way* a person regards an action or a state of being that he expresses. For example, a person may merely make a statement or ask a question—this is the Indicative Mood, which we use most of the time in Spanish and English. A person may say that he *would do* something if something else were possible or that he *would have* done something if something else had been possible—this is the Conditional. A person may use a verb *in such a way* that he indicates a wish, a fear, a regret, a joy, a request, a supposition, or something of this sort—this is the Subjunctive Mood. The Subjunctive Mood is used in Spanish much more than in English. Finally, a person may command someone to do something or demand that something be done—this is the Imperative Mood. English Conditional is not a mood. (There is also the Infinitive Mood, but we are not concerned with that here.)

There are six tenses in English: Present, Past, Future, Present Perfect, Past Perfect, and Future Perfect. The first three are simple tenses. The other three are compound tenses and are based on the simple tenses. In Spanish, however, there are fourteen tenses, seven of which are simple and seven of which are compound. The seven compound tenses are based on the seven simple tenses. In Spanish and English, a verb tense is simple if it consists of one verb form, e.g., *estudio.* A verb tense is compound if it consists of two parts—the auxiliary (or helping) verb plus the past participle, e.g., *he estudiado.* See the Summary of verb tenses and moods in Spanish with English equivalents on page 31. We have numbered each tense name for easy reference and recognition.

In Spanish, there is also another tense which is used to express an action in the present. It is called the Progressive Present. It is used only if an action is actually in progress at the time; for example, *Estoy leyendo*/I am reading (right now). It is formed by using the Present Indicative of *estar* plus the present participle of the verb. There is still another tense in Spanish which is used to express an action that was taking place in the past. It is called the Progressive Past. It is used if an action was actually in progress at a certain moment in the past; for example, *Estaba leyendo cuando mi hermano entró*/I was reading when my brother came in. The Progressive Past is formed by using the Imperfect Indicative of *estar* plus the present participle of the verb. See pages 4 and 5 for more on the Progressive forms.

In the pages that follow, the tenses and moods are given in Spanish and the equivalent name or names in English are given in parentheses. Although some of the names given in English are not considered to be tenses (there are only six), they are given for the purpose of identification as they are related to the Spanish names. The comparison includes only the essential points you need to know about the meanings and uses of Spanish verb tenses and moods as related to English usage. We shall use examples to illustrate their meanings and uses. This is not intended to be a detailed treatise. It is merely a summary. We hope you find it helpful.

THE SEVEN SIMPLE TENSES

Tense No. 1 Presente de Indicativo
(Present Indicative)

This tense is used most of the time in Spanish and English. It indicates:

(a) An action or a state of being at the present time.
EXAMPLES:
1. **Hablo** español. *I speak* Spanish.
I am speaking Spanish.
I do speak Spanish.
2. **Creo en** Dios. *I believe* in God.

(b) Habitual action.
EXAMPLE:
Voy a la biblioteca todos los días.
I go to the library every day.
I do go to the library every day.

(c) A general truth, something which is permanently true.
EXAMPLES:
1. Seis menos dos **son** cuatro.
Six minus two *are* four.
2. El ejercicio **hace** maestro al novicio.
Practice *makes* perfect.

(d) Vividness when talking or writing about past events.
EXAMPLE:
El asesino **se pone** pálido. **Tiene** miedo. **Sale** de la casa y **corre** a lo largo del río.
The murderer *turns* pale. *He is* afraid. *He goes out* of the house and *runs* along the river.

(e) A near future.
EXAMPLES:
1. Mi hermano **llega** mañana.
My brother *arrives* tomorrow.
2. ¿**Escuchamos** un disco ahora?
Shall we *listen* to a record now?

(f) An action or state of being that occurred in the past and *continues up to the present*. In Spanish, this is an idiomatic use of the present tense of a verb with **hace,** which is also in the present.
EXAMPLE:
Hace tres horas que **miro** la televisión.
I have been watching television for three hours.

(g) The meaning of *almost* or *nearly* when used with **por poco.**
EXAMPLE:
Por poco me **matan.**
They almost *killed* me.

This tense is regularly formed as follows:

Drop the **-ar** ending of an infinitive, like **hablar,** and add the following endings: **o, as, a; amos, áis, an.**
You then get: **hablo, hablas, habla;**
hablamos, habláis, hablan

Drop the **-er** ending of an infinitive, like **beber,** and add the following endings: **o, es, e; emos, éis, en.**
You then get: **bebo, bebes, bebe;**
bebemos, bebéis, beben

Drop the **-ir** ending of an infinitive, like **recibir,** and add the following endings: **o, es, e; imos, ís, en.**
You then get: **recibo, recibes, recibe;**
recibimos, recibís, reciben

Tense No. 2 Imperfecto de Indicativo
(Imperfect Indicative)

This is a past tense. Imperfect suggests incomplete. The imperfect tense expresses an action or a state of being that was continuous in the past and its completion is not indicated. This tense is used, therefore, to express:

(a) An action that was going on in the past at the same time as another action.
EXAMPLE:
Mi hermano **leía** y mi padre **hablaba.**
My brother *was reading* and my father *was talking*.

(b) An action that was going on in the past when another action occurred.
EXAMPLE:
Mi hermana **cantaba** cuando yo entré.
My sister *was singing* when I came in.

(c) A habitual action in the past.
EXAMPLE:
1. Cuando **estábamos** en Nueva York, **íbamos** al cine todos los sábados.
When *we were* in New York, *we went* to the movies every Saturday.
When *we were* in New York, *we used to go* to the movies every Saturday.
2. Cuando **vivíamos** en California, **íbamos** a la playa todos los días.
When *we used to live* in California, *we would go* to the beach every day.
NOTE: In this last example, *we would go* looks like the conditional, but it is not. It is the imperfect tense in this sentence because habitual action in the past is expressed.

(d) A description of a mental, emotional, or physical condition in the past.
EXAMPLES:
1. (mental condition) **Quería** ir al cine.
I *wanted* to go to the movies.
Common verbs in this use are **creer, desear, pensar, poder, preferir, querer, saber, sentir.**
2. (emotional condition) **Estaba** contento de verlo.
I *was* happy to see him.
3. (physical condition) Mi madre **era** hermosa cuando **era** pequeña.
My mother *was* beautiful when she *was* young.

(e) The time of day in the past.
   EXAMPLES:
   1. ¿Qué hora **era**?
      What time *was* it?
   2. **Eran** las tres.
      It *was* three o'clock.

(f) An action or state of being that occurred in the past and *lasted for a certain length of time* prior to another past action. In English it is usually translated as a pluperfect tense and is formed with *had been* plus the present participle of the verb you are using. It is like the special use of the presente de indicativo explained in the above section in paragraph (f), except that the action or state of being no longer exists at present. This is an idiomatic use of the imperfect tense of a verb with **hacía**, which is also in the imperfect.
   EXAMPLE:
   Hacía tres horas que **miraba** la televisión cuando mi hermano entró.
   I had been watching television for three hours when my brother came in.

(g) An indirect quotation in the past.
   EXAMPLE:
   Present: Dice que **quiere** venir a mi casa.
               He says *he wants* to come to my house.
   Past: Dijo que **quería** venir a mi casa.
               He said he wanted to come to my house.

This tense is regularly formed as follows:

Drop the -**ar** ending of an infinitive, like **hablar**, and add the following endings: **aba, abas, aba; ábamos, abais, aban.**
You then get: **hablaba, hablabas, hablaba;**
                hablábamos, hablabais, hablaban

The usual equivalent in English is: I was talking OR I used to talk OR I talked; you were talking OR you used to talk OR you talked, etc.

Drop the -**er** ending of an infinitive, like **beber,** or the -**ir** ending of an infinitive, like **recibir,** and add the following endings: **ía, ías, ía; íamos, íais, ían.**
You then get: **bebía, bebías, bebía;**
                bebíamos, bebíais, bebían

                recibía, recibías, recibía;
                recibíamos, recibíais, recibían

The usual equivalent in English is: I was drinking OR I used to drink OR I drank; you were drinking OR you used to drink OR you drank, etc.; I was receiving OR I used to receive OR I received; you were receiving OR you used to receive OR you received, etc.

Verbs irregular in the imperfect indicative:

ir/to go	**iba, ibas, iba;** (I was going, I used to go, etc.) **íbamos, ibais, iban**
ser/to be	**era, eras, era;** (I was, I used to be, etc.) **éramos, erais, eran**
ver/to see	**veía, veías, veía;** (I was seeing, I used to see, etc.) **veíamos, veíais, veían**

Tense No. 3 Pretérito
(Preterit)

This tense expresses an action that was completed at some time in the past.

EXAMPLES:

1. Mi padre **llegó** ayer.
   My father *arrived* yesterday.
   My father *did arrive* yesterday.
2. María **fue** a la iglesia esta mañana.
   Mary *went* to church this morning.
   Mary *did go* to church this morning.
3. ¿Qué **pasó?**
   What *happened*?
   What *did happen*?
4. **Tomé** el desayuno a las siete.
   I *had* breakfast at seven o'clock.
   I *did have* breakfast at seven o'clock.
5. **Salí** de casa, **tomé** el autobús y **llegué** a la escuela a las ocho.
   I *left* the house, *I took* the bus, and *I arrived* at school at eight o'clock.

In Spanish, some verbs that express a mental state have a different meaning when used in the preterit.

EXAMPLES:

1. La **conocí** la semana pasada en el baile.
   I *met* her last week at the dance.
   (**Conocer,** which means *to know* or *be acquainted with*, means *met*, that is, introduced to for the first time, in the preterit.)
2. **Pude** hacerlo.
   I *succeeded* in doing it.
   (**Poder,** which means *to be able*, means *succeeded* in the preterit.)
3. **No pude** hacerlo.
   I *failed* to do it.
   (**Poder,** when used in the negative in the preterit, means *failed* or *did not succeed*.)
4. **Quise** llamarle.
   I *tried* to call you.
   (**Querer,** which means *to wish* or *want,* means *tried* in the preterit.)
5. **No quise** hacerlo.
   I *refused* to do it.
   (**Querer,** when used in the negative in the preterit, means *refused*.)
6. **Supe** la verdad.
   I *found out* the truth.
   (**Saber,** which means *to know*, means *found out* in the preterit.)
7. **Tuve** una carta de mi amigo Roberto.
   I *received* a letter from my friend Robert.
   (**Tener,** which means *to have*, means *received* in the preterit.)

This tense is regularly formed as follows:

Drop the -**ar** ending of an infinitive, like **hablar,** and add the following endings: **é, aste, ó; amos, asteis, aron.**

You then get: **hablé, hablaste, habló;**
   hablamos, hablasteis, hablaron

The usual equivalent in English is: I talked OR I did talk; you talked OR you did talk, etc. OR I spoke OR I did speak; you spoke OR you did speak, etc.

Drop the **-er** ending of an infinitive, like **beber,** or the **-ir** ending of an infinitive, like **recibir,** and add the following endings: **í, iste, ió; imos, isteis, ieron.**

You then get: **bebí, bebiste, bebió;**
bebimos, bebisteis, bebieron

recibí, recibiste, recibió;
recibimos, recibisteis, recibieron

The usual equivalent in English is: I drank OR I did drink; you drank OR you did drink, etc.; I received OR I did receive, etc.

Tense No. 4   Futuro
(Future)

In Spanish and English, the future tense is used to express an action or a state of being that will take place at some time in the future.

EXAMPLES:
1. Lo **haré.**
   I shall do it.
   I will do it.
2. **Iremos** al campo la semana que viene.
   We shall go to the country next week.
   We will go to the country next week.

Also, in Spanish the future tense is used to indicate:

(a) Conjecture regarding the present.
EXAMPLES:
1. ¿Qué hora **será**?
   I wonder what time it is.
2. ¿Quién **será** a la puerta?
   Who can that be at the door?
   I wonder who is at the door.

(b) Probability regarding the present.
EXAMPLES:
1. **Serán** las cinco.
   It is probably five o'clock.
   It must be five o'clock.
2. **Tendrá** muchos amigos.
   He probably has many friends.
   He must have many friends.
3. María **estará** enferma.
   Mary *is probably* sick.
   Mary *must be* sick.

(c) An indirect quotation.
EXAMPLE:
María dice que **vendrá** mañana.
Mary says that she *will come* tomorrow.

Finally, remember that the future is never used in Spanish after *si* when *si* means *if*.

This tense is regularly formed as follows:

Add the following endings to the whole infinitive: **é, ás, á; emos, éis, án.**

Note that these Future endings happen to be the endings of **haber** in the present indicative: **he, has, ha; hemos, habéis, han.** Also note the accent marks on the Future endings, except for **emos.**

You then get: **hablaré, hablarás, hablará;**
hablaremos, hablaréis, hablarán

beberé, beberás, beberá;
beberemos, beberéis, beberán

recibiré, recibirás, recibirá;
recibiremos, recibiréis, recibirán

Tense No. 5 Potencial Simple
(Conditional)

The conditional is used in Spanish and in English to express:

(a) An action that you *would do* if something else were possible.
example:
Iría a España si tuviera dinero.
I would go to Spain if I had money.

(b) A conditional desire. This is a conditional of courtesy.
EXAMPLE:
Me **gustaría** tomar una limonada.
I would like (I should like) to have a lemonade . . . (if you are willing to let me have it).

(c) An indirect quotation.
EXAMPLES:
1. María **dijo** que **vendría** mañana.
Mary *said* that she *would come* tomorrow.
2. María **decía** que **vendría** mañana.
Mary *was saying* that she *would come* tomorrow.
3. María **había dicho** que **vendría** mañana.
Mary *had said* that she *would come* tomorrow.

(d) Conjecture regarding the past.
EXAMPLE:
¿Quién **sería?**
I wonder who that was.

(e) Probability regarding the past.
EXAMPLE:
Serían las cinco cuando salieron.
It was probably five o'clock when they went out.

This tense is regularly formed as follows:

Add the following endings to the whole infinitive:

ía, ías, ía; íamos, íais, ían

Note that these conditional endings are the same endings of the imperfect indicative for **-er** and **-ir** verbs.

You then get:	hablaría, hablarías, hablaría; hablaríamos, hablaríais, hablarían
	bebería, beberías, bebería; beberíamos, beberíais, beberían
	recibiría, recibirías, recibiría; recibiríamos, recibiríais, recibirían

The usual translation in English is: I would talk, you would talk, etc.; I would drink, you would drink, etc.; I would receive, you would receive, etc.

Tense No. 6   Presente de Subjuntivo
(Present Subjunctive)

The subjunctive mood is used in Spanish much more than in English. In Spanish, the present subjunctive is used:

(a) To express a command in the **usted** or **ustedes** form, either in the affirmative or negative.
EXAMPLES:
1. **Siéntese** Ud. *Sit down.*
2. **No se siente** Ud. *Don't sit down.*
3. **Cierren** Uds. la puerta. *Close the door.*
4. **No cierren** Uds. la puerta. *Don't close the door.*
5. **Dígame** Ud. la verdad. *Tell me the truth.*

(b) To express a negative command in the familiar form (**tú**).
EXAMPLES:

1. **No te sientes.** *Don't sit down.*
2. **No entres.** *Don't come in.*

3. **No duermas.** *Don't sleep.*
4. **No lo hagas.** *Don't do it.*

(c) To express a negative command in the second person plural (**vosotros**).
EXAMPLES:

1. **No os sentéis.** *Don't sit down.*
2. **No entréis.** *Don't come in.*

3. **No durmáis.** *Don't sleep.*
4. **No lo hagáis.** *Don't do it.*

(d) To express a command in the first person plural, either in the affirmative or negative (**nosotros**).
EXAMPLES:
1. **Sentémonos.** *Let's sit down.*
2. **No entremos.** *Let's not go in.*

See also **Imperativo** (Imperative) farther on.

(e) After a verb that expresses some kind of wish, insistence, preference, suggestion, or request.
EXAMPLES:
1. *Quiero* que María lo **haga.**
I want Mary to do it.
NOTE: In this example, English uses the infinitive form, *to do*. In Spanish, however, a new clause is needed introduced by *que* because there is a new subject, María. The present subjunctive of *hacer* is used *(haga)* because the main verb is *Quiero,* which indicates a wish. If there were no change in subject, Spanish would use the infinitive form, as we do in English, for example, *Quiero hacerlo*/I want to do it.

2. *Insisto* en que María lo **haga.**
   I insist that Mary *do* it.
3. *Prefiero* que María lo **haga.**
   I prefer that Mary *do* it.
4. *Pido* que María lo **haga.**
   I ask that Mary *do* it.
NOTE: In examples 2, 3, and 4 here, English also uses the subjunctive form *do*.
Not so in example no. 1, however.

(f) After a verb that expresses doubt, fear, joy, hope, sorrow, or some other emotion.
     Notice in the following examples, however, that the subjunctive is not used in English.
     EXAMPLES:
     1. *Dudo* que María lo **haga.**
        I doubt that Mary *is doing* it.
        I doubt that Mary *will do* it.
     2. *No creo* que María **venga.**
        I don't believe (I doubt) that Mary *is coming.*
        I don't believe (I doubt) that Mary *will come.*
     3. *Temo* que María **esté** enferma.
        I fear that Mary *is* ill.
     4. *Me alegro* de que **venga** María.
        I'm glad that Mary *is coming.*
        I'm glad that Mary *will come.*
     5. *Espero* que María no **esté** enferma.
        I hope that Mary *is* not ill.

(g) After certain impersonal expressions that show necessity, doubt, regret, impor-
     tance, urgency, or possibility. Notice, however, that the subjunctive is not used in
     English in some of the following examples.
     EXAMPLES:
     1. *Es necesario que* María lo **haga.**
        It is necessary for Mary to do it.
        It is necessary that Mary *do* it.
     2. *No es cierto que* María **venga.**
        It is doubtful (not certain) that Mary *is coming.*
        It is doubtful (not certain) that Mary *will come.*
     3. *Es lástima que* María no **venga.**
        It's too bad (a pity) that Mary *isn't coming.*
     4. *Es importante que* María **venga.**
        It is important for Mary to come.
        It is important that Mary *come.*
     5. *Es preciso que* María **venga.**
        It is necessary for Mary to come.
        It is necessary that Mary *come.*
     6. *Es urgente que* María **venga.**
        It is urgent for Mary to come.
        It is urgent that Mary *come.*

(h) After certain conjunctions of time, such as, **antes (de) que, cuando, en cuanto,
     después (de) que, hasta que, mientras,** and the like. The subjunctive form of the
     verb is used when introduced by any of these time conjunctions if the time
     referred to is either indefinite or is expected to take place in the future. However,
     if the action was completed in the past, the indicative mood is used.

EXAMPLES:

1. Le hablaré a María cuando **venga.**
   I shall talk to Mary when she *comes*.
2. Vámonos antes (de) que **llueva.**
   Let's go before *it rains*.
3. En cuanto la **vea** yo, le hablaré.
   As soon as *I see her*, I shall talk to her.
4. Me quedo aquí hasta que **vuelva.**
   I'm staying here until *he returns*.

NOTE: In the above examples, the subjunctive is not used in English.

(i) After certain conjunctions that express a condition, negation, purpose, such as **a menos que, con tal que, para que, a fin de que, sin que, en caso (de) que,** and the like. Notice, however, that the subjunctive is not used in English in the following examples.

EXAMPLES:

1. Démelo con tal que **sea** bueno.
   Give it to me provided that *it is* good.
2. Me voy a menos que **venga.**
   I'm leaving unless *he comes*.

(j) After certain adverbs, such as **acaso, quizá,** and **tal vez.**

EXAMPLE:

Acaso **venga** mañana.
Perhaps *he will come* tomorrow.
Perhaps *he is coming* tomorrow.

(k) After **aunque** if the action has not yet occurred.

EXAMPLE:

Aunque María **venga** esta noche, no me quedo.
Although Mary *may come* tonight, I'm not staying.
Although Mary *is coming* tonight, I'm not staying.

(l) In an adjectival clause if the antecedent is something or someone that is indefinite, negative, vague, or nonexistent.

EXAMPLES:

1. Busco un libro que **sea** interesante.
   I'm looking for a book that *is* interesting.
   NOTE: In this example, *que* (which is the relative pronoun) refers to *un libro* (which is the antecedent). Since *un libro* is indefinite, the verb in the following clause must be in the subjunctive *(sea)*. Notice, however, that the subjunctive is not used in English.
2. ¿Hay alguien aquí que **hable** francés?
   Is there anyone here who *speaks* French?
   NOTE: In this example, *que* (which is the relative pronoun) refers to *alguien* (which is the antecedent). Since *alguien* is indefinite and somewhat vague—we do not know who this anyone might be—the verb in the following clause must be in the subjunctive *(hable)*. Notice, however, that the subjunctive is not used in English.
3. No hay nadie que **pueda** hacerlo.
   There is no one who *can* do it.
   NOTE: In this example, *que* (which is the relative pronoun) refers to *nadie* (which is the antecedent). Since *nadie* is nonexistent, the verb in the following clause must be in the subjunctive *(pueda)*. Notice, however, that the subjunctive is not used in English.

(m) After **por más que** or **por mucho que.**

EXAMPLES:

1. **Por más que hable usted,** no quiero escuchar.
No matter how much you talk, I don't want to listen.
2. **Por mucho que se alegre,** no me importa.
No matter how glad he is, I don't care.

(n) After the expression **ojalá (que),** which expresses a great desire. This interjection means *would to God!* or *may God grant! . . .* It is derived from the Arabic, *ya Allah!* (Oh, God!)

EXAMPLE:

¡Ojalá que vengan mañana!
Would to God that they come tomorrow!
May God grant that they come tomorrow!
How I wish that they would come tomorrow!
If only they would come tomorrow!

Finally, remember that the present subjunctive is never used in Spanish after *si* when *si* means *if.*

The present subjunctive of regular verbs and many irregular verbs is normally formed as follows:

Go to the present indicative, 1st pers. sing., of the verb you have in mind, drop the ending **o,** and

for an **-ar** ending type, add: **e, es, e; emos, éis, en**
for an **-er** or **-ir** ending type, add: **a, as, a; amos, áis, an**

As you can see, the characteristic vowel in the present subjunctive endings for an **-ar** type verb is **e** in the six persons.

As you can see, the characteristic vowel in the present subjunctive endings for an **-er** or **-ir** type verb is **a** in the six persons.

Since the present subjunctive of some irregular verbs is not normally formed as stated above (*e.g.,* **dar, dormir, haber, ir, secar, sentir, ser, tocar**), you must look up the verb you have in mind in the alphabetical listing in this book.

Tense No. 7   Imperfecto de Subjuntivo
                (Imperfect Subjunctive)

This past tense is used for the same reasons as the presente de subjuntivo—that is, after certain verbs, conjunctions, impersonal expressions, etc., which were explained and illustrated above in tense no. 6. The main difference between these two tenses is the time of the action.

If the verb in the main clause is in the present indicative or future or present perfect indicative or imperative, the *present subjunctive* or the *present perfect subjunctive* is used in the dependent clause—provided, of course, that there is some element which requires the use of the subjunctive.

However, if the verb in the main clause is in the imperfect indicative, preterit, conditional, or pluperfect indicative, the *imperfect subjunctive* (this tense) or *pluperfect subjunctive* is ordinarily used in the dependent clause—provided, of course, that there is some element which requires the use of the subjunctive.

EXAMPLES:

1. *Insistí* en que María lo **hiciera.**
I insisted that Mary *do it.*
2. Se lo *explicaba* a María **para que lo comprendiera.**
I was explaining it to Mary *so that she might understand it.*

Note that the imperfect subjunctive is used after **como si** to express a condition contrary to fact.

EXAMPLE:
Me habla como si **fuera** un niño.
He speaks to me as if *I were* a child.
NOTE: In this last example, the subjunctive is used in English also for the same reason.

Finally, note that **quisiera** (the imperfect subjunctive of **querer**) can be used to express politely a wish or desire, as in *I should like:* **Quisiera hablar ahora**/I should like to speak now.

The imperfect subjunctive is regularly formed as follows:

For all verbs, drop the **ron** ending of the 3rd pers. pl. of the preterit and add the following endings:

ra, ras, ra;	OR	se, ses, se;
ramos, rais, ran		semos, seis, sen

The only accent mark on the forms of the imperfect subjunctive is on the 1st pers. pl. form (**nosotros**) and it is placed on the vowel which is right in front of the ending **ramos** or **semos.**

THE SEVEN COMPOUND TENSES

Tense No. 8   **Perfecto de Indicativo**
                     (Present Perfect Indicative)

This is the first of the seven compound tenses that follow here. This tense expresses an action that took place at no definite time in the past. It is also called the past indefinite. It is a compound tense because it is formed with the present indicative of **haber** (the auxiliary or helping verb) plus the past participle of your main verb. Note the translation into English in the examples that follow. Then compare this tense with the **perfecto de subjuntivo,** which is tense no. 13. For the seven simple tenses of **haber** (which you need to know to form these seven compound tenses), see **haber** listed alphabetically among the 501 verbs in this book.

EXAMPLES:
1. (Yo) **he hablado.**
   I have spoken.
2. (Tú) no **has venido** a verme.
   You have not come to see me.
3. Elena **ha ganado** el premio.
   Helen *has won* the prize.

Tense No. 9   **Pluscuamperfecto de Indicativo**
                     (Pluperfect *or* Past Perfect Indicative)

This is the second of the compound tenses. In Spanish and English, this past tense is used to express an action which happened in the past *before* another past action. Since it is used in relation to another past action, the other past action is ordinarily expressed in the preterit. However, it is not always necessary to have the other past action expressed, as in example 2 on the following page.

In English, this tense is formed with the past tense of *to have* (had) plus the past participle of your main verb. In Spanish, this tense is formed with the imperfect indicative of **haber** plus the past participle of the verb you have in mind. Note the translation into English in the examples that follow. Then compare this tense with the **pluscuamperfecto de subjuntivo,** which is tense no. 14. For the seven simples tenses of **haber** (which you need to know to form these seven compound tenses), see **haber** listed alphabetically among the 501 verbs in this book.

EXAMPLES:

1. Cuando **llegué a casa, mi hermano había salido.**
   When I *arrived* home, my brother *had gone out.*
   NOTE: *First,* my brother went out; *then,* I arrived home. Both actions happened in the past. The action that occurred in the past *before* the other past action is in the pluperfect, and, in this example, it is *my brother had gone out* (**mi hermano había salido).**
   NOTE also that **llegué** (*I arrived*) is in the preterit because it is an action that happened in the past and it was completed.

2. Juan lo **había perdido** en la calle.
   John *had lost* it in the street.
   NOTE: In this example, the pluperfect indicative is used even though no other past action is expressed. It is assumed that John *had lost* something *before* some other past action.

Tense No. 10   Pretérito Anterior or Pretérito Perfecto
                  (Past Anterior *or* Preterit Perfect)

This is the third of the compound tenses. This past tense is compound because it is formed with the preterit of **haber** plus the past participle of the verb you are using. It is translated into English like the pluperfect indicative, which is tense no. 9. This tense is not used much in spoken Spanish. Ordinarily, the pluperfect indicative is used in spoken Spanish (and sometimes even the simple preterit) in place of the past anterior.

This tense is ordinarily used in formal writing, such as history and literature. It is normally used after certain conjunctions of time, e.g., **después que, cuando, apenas, luego que, en cuanto.**

EXAMPLE:
Después que **hubo hablado,** salió.
After *he had spoken*, he left.

Tense No. 11   Futuro Perfecto
                  (Future Perfect *or* Future Anterior)

This is the fourth of the compound tenses. This compound tense is formed with the future of **haber** plus the past participle of the verb you have in mind. In Spanish and in English, this tense is used to express an action that will happen in the future *before* another future action. In English, this tense is formed by using *shall have* or *will have* plus the past participle of the verb you have in mind.

EXAMPLE:
María llegará mañana y **habré terminado** mi trabajo.
Mary will arrive tomorrow and *I shall have finished* my work.

NOTE: *First,* I shall finish my work; *then,* Mary will arrive. The action that will occur in the future *before* the other future action is in the **Futuro perfecto,** and in this example it is (yo) **habré terminado mi trabajo.**

Also, in Spanish, the future perfect is used to indicate conjecture or probability regarding recent past time.

EXAMPLES:

1. María **se habrá acostado.**
   Mary *has probably gone to bed.*
   Mary *must have gone to bed.*
2. José **habrá llegado.**
   Joseph *has probably arrived.*
   Joseph *must have arrived.*

Tense No. 12   **Potencial Compuesto**
                (Conditional Perfect)

This is the fifth of the compound tenses. It is formed with the conditional of **haber** plus the past participle of your main verb. It is used in Spanish and English to express an action that you *would have done* if something else had been possible; that is, you would have done something *on condition* that something else had been possible.

In English, it is formed by using *would have* plus the past participle of the verb you have in mind. Observe the difference between the following example and the one given for the use of the potencial simple.

EXAMPLE:

Habría ido a España si hubiera tenido dinero.
I would have gone to Spain if I had had money.

Also, in Spanish, the conditional perfect is used to indicate probability or conjecture in the past.

EXAMPLES:

1. **Habrían sido** las cinco cuando salieron.
   It must have been five o'clock when they went out.
   (Compare this with the example given for the simple conditional.)
2. ¿Quién **habría sido**?
   Who *could that have been*? (*or* I wonder *who that could have been*.)
   (Compare this with the example given for the simple conditional.)

Tense No. 13   **Perfecto de Subjuntivo**
                (Present Perfect *or* Past Subjunctive)

This is the sixth of the compound tenses. It is formed by using the present subjunctive of **haber** as the helping verb plus the past participle of the verb you have in mind.

If the verb in the main clause is in the present indicative, future, or present perfect tense, the present subjunctive is used *or* this tense is used in the dependent clause—provided, of course, that there is some element which requires the use of the subjunctive.

The present subjunctive is used if the action is not past. However, if the action is past, this tense (present perfect subjunctive) is used, as in the examples given below.

EXAMPLES:
1. María duda que yo le **haya hablado** al profesor.
   Mary doubts that *I have spoken* to the professor.
2. Siento que tú no **hayas venido** a verme.
   I am sorry that you *have not come* to see me.
3. Me alegro de que Elena **haya ganado** el premio.
   I am glad that Helen *has won* the prize.

In these three examples, the auxiliary verb **haber** is used in the present subjunctive because the main verb in the clause that precedes is one that requires the subjunctive mood of the verb in the dependent clause.

Tense No. 14   **Pluscuamperfecto de Subjuntivo**
               (Pluperfect *or* Past Perfect Subjunctive)

This is the seventh of the compound tenses. It is formed by using the imperfect subjunctive of **haber** as the helping verb plus the past participle of your main verb.

The translation of this tense into English is often like the pluperfect indicative.

If the verb in the main clause is in a past tense, this tense is used in the dependent clause—provided, of course, that there is some element which requires the use of the subjunctive.

EXAMPLES:
1. Sentí mucho que **no hubiera venido** María.
   I was very sorry that Mary *had not come*.
2. Me alegraba de que **hubiera venido** María.
   I was glad that Mary *had come*.
3. No creía que María **hubiera llegado.**
   I did not believe that Mary *had arrived*.

So much for the seven simple tenses and the seven compound tenses. Now, let's look at the Imperative Mood.

Imperativo
(Imperative *or* Command)

The imperative mood is used in Spanish and in English to express a command. We saw earlier that the subjunctive mood is used to express commands in the **Ud.** and **Uds.** forms, in addition to other uses of the subjunctive mood.

Here are other points you ought to know about the imperative.

(a) An indirect command or deep desire expressed in the third pers. sing. or pl. is in the subjunctive. Notice the use of *Let* or *May* in the English translations. **Que** introduces this kind of command.
     EXAMPLES:
     1. ¡Que lo **haga** Jorge!   4. ¡Que **entre** Roberto!
        Let George do it!   *Let* Robert enter!
     2. ¡Que Dios se lo **pague!**   5. ¡Que **salgan!**
        May God reward you!   *Let* them leave!
     3. ¡Que **vengan** pronto!   6. ¡Que **entren** las muchachas!
        Let them come quickly!   *Let* the girls come in!

(b) In some indirect commands, **que** is omitted. Here, too, the subjunctive is used.
EXAMPLE:
¡**Viva** el presidente!
Long live the president!

(c) The verb form of the affirmative sing. familiar (**tú**) is the same as the 3rd pers. sing. of the present indicative when expressing a command.
EXAMPLE:
1. ¡**Entra** pronto!
   Come in quickly!
2. ¡**Sigue** leyendo!
   Keep on reading!
   Continue reading!

(d) There are some exceptions, however, to (c) above. The following verb forms are irregular in the affirmative sing. imperative (**tú** form only).

di (decir)	**sal** (salir)	**val** (valer)
haz (hacer)	**sé** (ser)	**ve** (ir)
hé (haber)	**ten** (tener)	**ven** (venir)
pon (poner)		

(e) In the affirmative command, 1st pers. pl., instead of using the present subjunctive hortatory command, **vamos a** (*Let's* or *Let us*) + **inf.** may be used.
examples:
1. **Vamos a** comer/Let's eat.
   or: **Comamos** (1st pers. pl., present subj., hortatory command)
2. **Vamos a** cantar/Let's sing.
   or: **Cantemos** (1st pers. pl., present subj., hortatory command)

(f) In the affirmative command, 1st pers. pl., **vamos** may be used to mean *Let's go*:
Vamos al cine/Let's go to the movies.

(g) However, if in the negative (*Let's not go*), the present subjunctive of **ir** must be used: **No vayamos** al cine/Let's not go to the movies.

(h) Note that **vámonos** (1st pers. pl. of **irse,** imperative) means *Let's go*, or *Let's go away*, or *Let's leave*. See (m) below.

(i) Also note that **no nos vayamos** (1st pers. pl. of **irse,** present subjunctive) means *Let's not go*, or *Let's not go away*, or *Let's not leave*.

(j) The imperative in the affirmative familiar plural (**vosotros, vosotras**) is formed by dropping the final **r** of the inf. and adding **d.**
EXAMPLES:
1. ¡**Hablad!**/Speak!   3.¡**Id!**/Go!
2. ¡**Comed!**/Eat!   4.¡**Venid!**/Come!

(k) When forming the affirmative familiar plural (**vosotros, vosotras**) imperative of a reflexive verb, the final **d** on the inf. must be dropped before the reflexive pronoun **os** is added, and both elements are joined to make one word.
EXAMPLES:
1. ¡**Levantaos!**/Get up!   2.¡**Sentaos!**/Sit down!

(l) Referring to (k) above, when the final **d** is dropped in a reflexive verb ending in **-ir,** an accent mark must be written on the **i.**
examples:
1. ¡Vestíos!/Get dressed!   2.¡Divertíos!/Have a good time!

(m) When forming the 1st pers. pl. affirmative imperative of a reflexive verb, final **s** must drop before the reflexive pronoun **os** is added, and both elements are joined to make one word. This requires an accent mark on the vowel of the syllable that was stressed before **os** was added.
example:
Vamos + nos changes to: ¡**Vámonos!**/*Let's go!* or *Let's go away!* or *Let's leave!*
See (h) above.

(n) All negative imperatives in the familiar 2nd pers. sing. (**tú**) and plural (**vosotros, vosotras**) are expressed in the present subjunctive.
examples:
1. ¡**No corras (tú)!**/Don't run!
2. ¡**No corráis (vosotros** or **vosotras)!**/Don't run!
3. ¡**No vengas (tú)!**/Don't come!
4. ¡**No vengáis (vosotros** or **vosotras)!**/Don't come!

(o) Object pronouns (direct, indirect, or reflexive) with an imperative verb form in the **affirmative** are attached to the verb form.
EXAMPLES:
1. ¡**Hágalo (Ud.)!**/Do it!
2. ¡**Díganoslo (Ud.)!**/Tell it to us!
3. ¡**Dímelo (tú)!**/Tell it to me!
4. ¡Levántate (**tú)!**/Get up!
5. ¡**Siéntese (Ud.)!**/Sit down!
6. ¡**Hacedlo (vosotros, vosotras)!**/Do it!
7. ¡**Démelo (Ud.)!**/Give it to me!

(p) Object pronouns (direct, indirect, or reflexive) with an imperative verb form in the **negative** are placed in front of the verb form. Compare the following examples with those given in (o) above:
EXAMPLES:
1. ¡**No lo haga (Ud.)!**/Don't do it!
2. ¡**No nos lo diga (Ud.)!**/Don't tell it to us!
3. ¡**No me lo digas (tú)!**/Don't tell it to me!
4. ¡**No te levantes (tú)!**/Don't get up!
5. ¡**No se siente (Ud.)!**/Don't sit down!
6. ¡**No lo hagáis (vosotros, vosotras)!**/Don't do it!
7. ¡**No me lo dé (Ud.)!**/Don't give it to me!

(q) Note that in some Latin American countries, the 2nd pers. pl. familiar (**vosotros, vosotras**) forms are avoided. In place of them, the 3rd pers. pl. **Uds.** forms are customarily used.

The Future Subjunctive and the Future Perfect Subjunctive: A note

The future subjunctive and the future perfect subjunctive exist in Spanish, but they are rarely used. Nowadays, instead of using the future subjunctive, one uses the present subjunctive of the present indicative. Instead of using the future perfect subjunctive, one uses the future perfect indicative or the present perfect subjunctive. However, if you are curious to know how to form the future subjunctive and the future perfect subjunctive in Spanish, the following is offered:

(1) To form the future subjunctive, take the third person plural of the preterit of any Spanish verb and change the ending -ron to re, res, re; remos, reis, ren. An accent mark is needed as shown below on the first person plural form to preserve the stress.

EXAMPLES:

amar	amare, amares, amare; amáremos, amareis, amaren
comer	comiere, comieres, comiere; comiéremos, comiereis, comieren
dar	diere, dieres, diere; diéremos, diereis, dieren
haber	hubiere, hubieres, hubiere; hubiéremos, hubiereis, hubieren
hablar	hablare, hablares, hablare; habláremos, hablareis, hablaren
ir or ser	fuere, fueres, fuere; fuéremos, fuereis, fueren

(2) Let's look at the forms of amar above to see what the English translation is of this tense:

(que) yo amare, (that) I love . . .
(que) tú amares, (that) you love . . .
(que) Ud. (él, ella) amare, (that) you (he, she) love . . .
(que) nosotros (-tras) amáremos, (that) we love . . .
(que) vosotros (-tras) amareis, (that) you love . . .
(que) Uds. (ellos, ellas) amaren, (that) you (they) love . . .

(3) To form the future perfect subjunctive, use the future subjunctive form of haber (shown above) as your auxiliary plus the past participle of the verb you have in mind.

EXAMPLES:
(que) hubiere amado, hubieres amado, hubiere amado;
(que) hubiéremos amado, hubiereis amado, hubieren amado

English translation:
(that) I have or I shall have loved, (that) you have or will have loved, etc.

Summary of verb tenses and moods in Spanish with English equivalents

Los siete tiempos simples *The seven simple tenses*		Los siete tiempos compuestos *The seven compound tenses*	
Tense No.	Tense Name	Tense No.	Tense Name
1	**Presente de indicativo** *Present indicative*	8	**Perfecto de indicativo** *Present perfect indicative*
2	**Imperfecto de indicativo** *Imperfect indicative*	9	**Pluscuamperfecto de indicativo** *Pluperfect or Past perfect indicative*
3	**Pretérito** *Preterit*	10	**Pretérito anterior (Pret. perfecto)** *Past anterior or Preterit perfect*
4	**Futuro** *Future*	11	**Futuro perfecto** *Future perfect or Future anterior*
5	**Potencial simple** *Conditional*	12	**Potencial compuesto** *Conditional perfect*
6	**Presente de subjuntivo** *Present subjunctive*	13	**Perfecto de subjuntivo** *Present perfect or Past subjunctive*
7	**Imperfecto de subjuntivo** *Imperfect subjunctive*	14	**Pluscuamperfecto de subjuntivo** *Pluperfect or Past perfect subjunctive*

The imperative is not a tense; it is a mood.

In Spanish, there are 7 simple tenses and 7 compound tenses. A simple tense means that the verb form consists of one word. A compound tense means that the verb form consists of two words (the auxiliary verb and the past participle). The auxiliary verb is also called a helping verb and in Spanish, as you know, it is any of the 7 simple tenses of **haber** (*to have*).

Each compound tense is based on each simple tense. The 14 tenses given on the previous page are arranged in the following logical order:

Tense number 8 is based on Tense number 1 of **haber**; in other words, you form the **Perfecto de indicativo** by using the auxiliary **haber** in the **Presente de indicativo** plus the past participle of the verb you are dealing with.

Tense number 9 is based on Tense number 2 of **haber**; in other words, you form the **Pluscuamperfecto de indicativo** by using the auxiliary **haber** in the **Imperfecto de indicativo** plus the past participle of the verb you are dealing with.

Tense number 10 is based on Tense number 3 of **haber**; in other words, you form the **Pretérito anterior** by using the auxiliary **haber** in the **Pretérito** plus the past participle of the verb you are dealing with.

Tense number 11 is based on Tense number 4 of **haber**; in other words, you form the **Futuro perfecto** by using the auxiliary **haber** in the **Futuro** plus the past participle of the verb you are dealing with.

Tense number 12 is based on Tense number 5 of **haber**; in other words, you form the **Potencial compuesto** by using the auxiliary **haber** in the **Potencial simple** plus the past participle of the verb you are dealing with.

Tense number 13 is based on Tense number 6 of **haber**; in other words, you form the **Perfecto de subjuntivo** by using the auxiliary **haber** in the **Presente de subjuntivo** plus the past participle of the verb you are dealing with.

Tense number 14 is based on Tense number 7 of **haber**; in other words, you form the **Pluscuamperfecto de subjuntivo** by using the auxiliary **haber** in the **Imperfecto de subjuntivo** plus the past participle of the verb you are dealing with.

What does all the above mean? This: If you ever expect to know or even recognize the meaning of any of the 7 compound tenses, you certainly have to know **haber** in the 7 simple tenses. If you do not, you cannot form the 7 compound tenses. This is one perfect example to illustrate that learning Spanish verb forms is a cumulative experience. Look up **haber** where it is listed alphabetically among the 501 verbs in this book and study the 7 simple tenses.

active voice   When we speak or write in the active voice, the subject of the verb performs the action. The action falls on the direct object.

> *The robber opened the window/El ladrón abrió la ventana.*

The subject is *the robber.* The verb is *opened.* The direct object is *the window. See also passive voice* in this list. Compare the above sentence with the example in the passive voice. Review the section on passive voice and active voice on page 7. *See also* page 6, example 6.

adjective   An adjective is a word that modifies a noun or a pronoun. In grammar, to modify a word means to describe, limit, expand, or make the meaning particular.

> *a beautiful garden/un jardín hermoso; she is pretty/ella es bonita*

The adjective *beautiful/hermoso* modifies the noun *garden/jardín.* The adjective *pretty/bonita* modifies the pronoun *she/ella.* In Spanish, there are different kinds of adjectives. *See also* comparative adjective, demonstrative adjective, descriptive adjective, interrogative adjective, limiting adjective, possessive adjective, superlative adjective.

adverb   An adverb is a word that modifies a verb, an adjective, or another adverb. An adverb says something about how, when, where, to what extent, or in what way.

> *Mary runs swiftly/María corre rápidamente.*

The adverb *swiftly/rápidamente* modifies the verb *runs/corre.* The adverb shows *how* she runs.

> *John is very handsome/Juan es muy guapo.*

The adverb *very/muy* modifies the adjective *handsome/guapo.* The adverb shows *how* handsome he is.

> *The boy is talking very fast now/El muchacho habla muy rápidamente ahora.*

The adverb *very/muy* modifies the adverb *fast/rápidamente.* The adverb shows *to what extent* he is talking *fast.* The adverb *now/ahora* tells us *when.*

> *The post office is there/La oficina de correos está allá.*

The adverb *there/allá* modifies the verb *is/está.* It tells us *where* the post office is.

> *Mary writes meticulously/María escribe meticulosamente.*

The adverb *meticulously/meticulosamente* modifies the verb *writes/escribe.* It tells us *in what way* she writes.

affirmative statement, negative statement   A statement in the affirmative is the opposite of a statement in the negative. To negate an affirmative statement is to make it negative.

> Affirmative: *I like ice cream/Me gusta el helado.*
>
> Negative: *I do not like ice cream/No me gusta el helado.*

Review **gustar.**

agreement of adjective with noun   Agreement is made on the adjective with the noun it modifies in gender (masculine or feminine) and number (singular or plural).

> *a white house/una casa blanca.*

The adjective **blanca** is feminine singular because the noun **una casa** is feminine singular

> *many white houses/muchas casas blancas.*

The adjective **blancas** is feminine plural because the noun **casas** is feminine plural.

agreement of verb with its subject   A verb agrees in person (1st, 2nd, or 3rd) and in number (singular or plural) with its subject.

> *Paul tells the truth/Pablo dice la verdad.*

The verb **dice** (of **decir**) is 3rd person singular because the subject *Pablo/Paul* is 3rd person singular.

Where are the tourists going?/¿Adónde van los turistas?

The verb **van** (of **ir**) is 3rd person plural because the subject *los turistas/the tourists* is 3rd person plural. For subject pronouns in the singular and plural, review page 92.

antecedent An antecedent is a word to which a relative pronoun refers. It comes *before* the pronoun.

The girl who is laughing loudly is my sister/
La muchacha que está riendo a carcajadas es mi hermana.

The antecedent is *girl/la muchacha.* The relative pronoun *who/que* refers to the girl.

The car that I bought is very expensive/
El carro que yo compré es muy costoso.

The antecedent is *car/el carro.* The relative pronoun *that/que* refers to the car. Review **comprar** and **reír** among the 501 verbs in this book. Note that **está riendo** is the progressive present. Review example 1 in the section on uses of the present participle as well as examples 1 and 2 in the section on the Progressive forms of tenses. Both sections are on page 4. *See also* relative pronoun.

auxiliary verb An auxiliary verb is a helping verb. In English grammar it is *to have.* In Spanish grammar it is *haber/to have.* An auxiliary verb is used to help form the compound tenses.

I have eaten/(Yo) he comido.

Review the forms of **haber** (verb 257) in the seven simple tenses. You need to know them to form the seven compound tenses. Also, review **comer** among the 501 verbs in this book.

cardinal number A cardinal number is a number that expresses an amount, such as *one, two, three,* and so on. *See also* ordinal number.

clause A clause is a group of words that contains a subject and a predicate. A predicate may contain more than one word. A conjugated verb form is revealed in the predicate.

Mrs. Gómez lives in a large apartment/
La señora Gómez vive en un gran apartamento.

The subject is *Mrs. Gómez/la señora Gómez.* The predicate is *lives in a large apartment/vive en un gran apartamento.* The verb is *lives/vive.* Review **vivir** among the 501 verbs in this book. *See also* dependent clause, independent clause, predicate.

comparative adjective When making a comparison between two persons or things, an adjective is used to express the degree of comparison in the following ways.
Same degree of comparison:

Helen is as tall as Mary/Elena es tan alta como María.

Lesser degree of comparison

Jane is less intelligent than Eva/Juana es menos inteligente que Eva.

Higher degree of comparison:

This apple is more delicious than that one/Esta manzana es más deliciosa que ésa.

See also superlative adjective.

comparative adverb An adverb is compared in the same way as an adjective is compared. *See* comparative adjective above.
Same degree of comparison:

Mr. Robles speaks as well as Mr. Vega/
El señor Robles habla tan bien como el señor Vega.

Lesser degree of comparison:

> *Alice studies less diligently than her sister/*
> *Alicia estudia menos diligentemente que su hermana.*

Higher degree of comparison:

> *Albert works more slowly than his brother/*
> *Alberto trabaja más lentamente que su hermano.*

See also superlative adverb.

complex sentence   A complex sentence contains one independent clause and one or more dependent clauses.

One independent clause and one dependent clause:

> *Joseph works but his brother doesn't/*
> *José trabaja pero su hermano no trabaja.*

The independent clause is *Joseph works.* It makes sense when it stands alone because it expresses a complete thought. The dependent clause is *but his brother doesn't.* The dependent clause, which is introduced by the conjunction *but/pero,* does not make complete sense when it stands alone because it *depends* on the thought expressed in the independent clause.

One independent clause and two dependent clauses:

> *Anna is a good student because she studies but her sister never studies/*
> *Ana es una buena alumna porque estudia pero su hermana nunca estudia.*

The independent clause is *Anna is a good student.* It makes sense when it stands alone because it expresses a complete thought. The first dependent clause is *because she studies.* The dependent clause, which is introduced by the conjunction *because/porque,* does not make complete sense when it stands alone because it *depends* on the thought expressed in the independent clause. The second dependent clause is *but her sister never studies.* That dependent clause, which is introduced by the conjunction *but/pero,* does not make complete sense, either, when it stands alone because it *depends* on the thought expressed in the independent clause. *See also* dependent clause, independent clause.

compound sentence   A compound sentence contains two or more independent clauses.

> *Mrs. Fuentes went to the supermarket, she bought a few*
> *things, and then she went home/*
> *La señora Fuentes fue al supermercado, compró*
> *algunas cosas, y entonces fue a casa.*

This compound sentence contains three independent clauses. They are independent because they make sense when they stand alone. Review the explanation, uses, and examples of the **pretérito** (Tense No. 3) on page 17. Review **comprar** and **ir** among the 501 verbs in this book. *See also* independent clause.

conditional perfect tense   In Spanish grammar, the conditional **(el potencial)** is considered a mood. This tense is defined with examples on page 26.

conditional present tense   In Spanish grammar, the conditional **(el potencial)** is considered a mood. This tense is defined with examples on pages 19 and 20.

conjugation   The conjugation of a verb is the fixed order of all its forms showing their inflections (changes) in the three persons of the singular and plural in a particular tense. *See also* number and person (1st, 2nd, 3rd).

conjunction   A conjunction is a word that connects words or groups of words.

> *and/y, or/o, but/pero, because/porque*
> *Charles and Charlotte/Carlos y Carlota*

You can stay home or you can come with me/
(Tú) peudes quedarte en casa o venir conmigo.

contrary to fact This term refers to an "if" clause. *See* if (si) clause.

declarative sentence A declarative sentence makes a statement.
Review the **perfecto de indicativo** (Tense No. 8) on page 24 and **terminar** among the 501 verbs in this book.

definite article The definite article in Spanish has four forms and they all mean *the*. They are **el, la, los, las.**
el libro/the book, la casa/the house,
los libros/the books, las casas/the houses.
The definite articles **la, los, las** are also used as direct object pronouns. *See* direct object pronoun.

demonstrative adjective A demonstrative adjective is an adjective that points out. It is placed in front of a noun.
this book/este libro; these books/estos libros;
this cup/esta taza; these flowers/estas flores.

demonstrative pronoun A demonstrative pronoun is a pronoun that points out. It takes the place of a noun. It agrees in gender and number with the noun it replaces.
I have two oranges; do you prefer this one or that one?/
Tengo dos naranjas; ¿prefiere usted ésta o ésa?
I prefer those [over there]/Prefiero aquéllas.
For demonstrative pronouns that are neuter, *see* neuter.

dependent clause A dependent clause is a group of words that contains a subject and a predicate. It does not express a complete thought when it stands alone. It is called *dependent* because it depends on the independent clause for a complete meaning. Subordinate clause is another term for dependent clause.
Edward is absent today because he is sick/
Eduardo está ausente hoy porque está enfermo.
The independent clause is *Edward is absent today.* The dependent clause is *because he is sick. See also* clause, independent clause.

descriptive adjective A descriptive adjective is an adjective that describes a person, place, or thing.
a pretty girl/una muchacha bonita; a big house/una casa grande;
an expensive car/un carro costoso.
See also adjective.

direct object noun A direct object noun receives the action of the verb *directly*. That is why it is called a direct object, as opposed to an indirect object. A direct object noun is normally placed *after* the verb.
I am writing a letter/Escribo una carta.
The direct object is the noun *letter/una carta. See also* direct object pronoun.

direct object pronoun A direct object pronoun receives the action of the verb *directly*. It takes the place of a direct object noun. In Spanish, a pronoun that is a direct object of a verb is ordinarily placed *in front of* the verb.
I am writing it [the letter]/La escribo.

In the *affirmative imperative,* a direct object pronoun is placed *after* the verb and is joined to it, resulting in one word.

Write it [the letter] now!/¡Escríbala [Ud.] ahora!

An accent mark is added on the vowel **i** [**í**] in order to keep the emphasis on that vowel as it was in **escriba** before the direct object pronoun **la** was added to the verb form. Review the Imperative section (o) on page 29.

disjunctive pronoun   A disjunctive pronoun is a pronoun that is stressed; in other words, emphasis is placed on it. It is usually an object of a preposition. In Spanish usage, prepositional pronoun is another term for disjunctive pronoun.

for me/para mí; for you (fam.)/para ti;
con usted/with you; con él/with him; con ella/with her

Note the following exceptions with **con:**

conmigo/with me; contigo/with you (fam.);
consigo/with yourself (yourselves, himself, herself, themselves)

ending of a verb   In Spanish grammar, the ending of a verb form changes according to the person and number of the subject and the tense of the verb.

To form the present indicative tense of a regular **-ar** type verb like **hablar,** drop **ar** of the infinitive and add the following endings; **-o, -as, -a** for the 1st, 2nd, and 3rd persons of the singular; **-amos, -áis, -an** for the 1st, 2nd, and 3rd persons of the plural. You then get: **hablo, hablas, habla; hablamos, habláis, hablan.** Review at the top of page 15. *See also* stem of a verb.

feminine   In Spanish grammar, the gender of a noun, pronoun, or adjective is feminine or masculine, not male or female.

Masculine			Feminine		
noun	*pronoun*	*adjective*	*noun*	*pronoun*	*adjective*
el hombre	**él**	**guapo**	**la mujer**	**ella**	**hermosa**
the man	he	handsome	the woman	she	beautiful

See also gender.

future perfect tense   This tense is defined with examples on pages 25 and 26. It is also called the future anterior.

future tense   This tense is defined with examples on pages 18 and 19.

gender   Gender means masculine or feminine.

Masculine: *the boy/el muchacho; the book/el libro*
Feminine: *the girl/la muchacha; the house/la casa*

gerund   In English grammar, a gerund is a word formed from a verb. It ends in *ing.* Actually, it is the present participle of a verb. However, it is not used as a verb. It is used as a noun.

Seeing is believing/Ver es creer/[to see is to believe].

However, in Spanish grammar, the infinitive form of the verb is used, as in the above example, when the verb is used as a noun.

The Spanish gerund is also a word formed from a verb. It is the present participle of a verb. The Spanish gerund [**el gerundio**] regularly ends in **ando** for **ar** type verbs (of the 1st conjugation), in **iendo** for **er** type verbs (of the 2nd conjugation), and **iendo** for **ir** type verbs (of the 3rd conjugation). There are also irregular present participles that end in **yendo.**

hablando/talking   comiendo/eating   viviendo/living

See also present participle.

if (si) clause   An "if" clause is defined with an example at the top of page 24, where **como si** (as if) is used. Another term for an "if" clause is contrary to fact, as in English, if I were king . . ., if I were rich . . .

Si yo tuviera bastante dinreo, iría a España/
If I had enough money, I would go to Spain.

Review the **imperfecto de subjuntivo** (Tense No. 7) of **tener** (verb 468) and the **potencial simple** (Tense No. 5) of **ir** (verb 280). *See also* clause.

imperative   The imperative is a mood, not a tense. It is used to express a command. In Spanish it is used in the 2nd person of the singular (**tú**), the 3rd person of the singular (**usted**), the 1st person of the plural (**nosotros, nosotras**), the 2nd person of the plural (**vosotros, vosotras**), and in the 3rd person of the plural (**ustedes**). As an example, review the **imperativo** of **comer** among the 501 verbs in this book. Review the explanation of the **imperativo** with examples on pages 27 to 29. *See also* person (1st, 2nd, 3rd).

imperfect indicative tense   This tense is defined with examples on pages 15 and 16.

imperfect subjunctive tense   This tense is defined with examples on pages 23 and 24.

indefinite article   In English, the indefinite articles are *a, an,* as in *a book, an apple.* They are indefinite because they do not refer to any definite or particular noun.

In Spanish, there are two indefinite articles in the singular: one in the masculine form (**un**) and one in the feminine form (**una**).

Masculine singular: *un libro/a book*
Feminine singular: *una manzana/an apple*

In the plural they change to **unos** and **unas.**

unos libros/some books; unas manzanas/some apples

See also definite article.

indefinite pronoun   An indefinite pronoun is a pronoun that does not refer to any definite or particular noun.

something/algo; someone, somebody/alguien

independent clause   An independent clause is a group of words that contains a subject and a predicate. It expresses a complete thought when it stands alone.

The cat is sleeping on the bed/El gato está durmiendo sobre la cama.

See also clause, dependent clause, predicate.

indicative mood   The indicative mood is used in sentences that make a statement or ask a question. The indicative mood is used most of the time when we speak or write in English or Spanish.

I am going to the movies now/Voy al cine ahora.
When are you going?/¿Adónde vas?

indirect object noun   An indirect object noun receives the action of the verb *indirectly.*

I am writing a letter to Christine or *I am writing Christine a letter/*
Estoy escribiendo una carta a Cristina.

The verb is *am writing/estoy escribiendo.* The direct object noun is *a letter/una carta.* The indirect object noun is *Cristina/Christine. See also* indirect object pronoun.

indirect object pronoun   An indirect object pronoun takes the place of an indirect object noun. It receives the action of the verb *indirectly.*

I am writing a letter to her or *I am writing her a letter/*
Le escribo una carta (a ella).

The indirect object pronoun is *(to) her/le. See also* indirect object noun.

infinitive   An infinitive is a verb form. In English, it is normally stated with the preposition to, as in *to talk, to drink, to receive.* In Spanish, the infinitive form of a verb consists of three major types: those of the 1st conjugation that end in **-ar,** the 2nd conjugation that end in **-er,** and the 3rd conjugation that end in **-ir.** In Spanish grammar, the infinitive **(el infinitivo)** is considered a mood.

hablar/to talk, to speak; beber/to drink; recibir/to receive

All the verbs in this book on pages 97 to 648 are given in the infinitive form at the top of each page where they are arranged alphabetically.

interjection   An interjection is a word that expresses emotion, a feeling of joy, of sadness, an exclamation of surprise, and other exclamations consisting of one or two words.

Ah!/¡Ah! Ouch!/¡Ay! Darn it!/¡Caramba!! My God!/¡Dios mío!

interrogative adjective   In Spanish, an interrogative adjective is an adjective that is used in a question. As an adjective, it is placed in front of a noun.

What book do you want?/¿Qué libro desea usted?

What time is it?/¿Qué hora es?

interrogative adverb   In Spanish, an interrogative adverb is an adverb that introduces a question. As an adverb, it modifies the verb.

How are you?/¿Cómo está usted?

How much does this book cost?/¿Cuánto cuesta este libro?

When will you arrive?/¿Cuándo llegará usted?

interrogative pronoun   An interrogative pronoun is a pronoun that asks a question. There are interrogative pronouns that refer to persons and those that refer to things.

Who is it?/¿Quién es?

What are you saying?/¿Qué dice usted?

interrogative sentence   An interrogative sentence asks a question.

What are you doing?/¿Qué hace usted?

intransitive verb   An intransitive verb is a verb that does not take a direct object.

The professor is talking/El profesor habla.

An intransitive verb takes an indirect object.

The professor is talking to us/El profesor nos habla.

See also direct object pronoun, indirect object pronoun, transitive verb.

irregular verb   An irregular verb is a verb that does not follow a fixed pattern in its conjugation in the various verb tenses. Basic irregular verbs in Spanish:

estar/to be   hacer/to do, to make   ir/to go   ser/to be

See also conjugation, regular verb.

limiting adjective   A limiting adjective is an adjective that limits a quantity.

three lemons/tres limones; a few candies/ algunos dulces

main clause   Main clause is another term for independent clause. *See* independent clause.

masculine   In Spanish grammar, the gender of a noun, pronoun, or adjective is masculine or feminine, not male or female. *See also* feminine, gender.

mood of verbs   Some grammarians use the term *the mode* instead of *the mood* of a verb. Either term means *the manner or way* a verb is expressed. In English and Spanish grammar, a verb expresses an action or state of being in a particular mood. In Spanish grammar, there are five moods **(modos);** the infinitive **(el infinitivo),** the indicative **(el indicativo),** the imperative **(el imperativo),** the conditional **(el potencial),** and the subjunctive **(el subjuntivo).** In English grammar, there are three moods: the indicative mood, the imperative mood, and the subjunctive mood. Most of the time, in English and Spanish, we speak and write in the indicative mood.

negative statement, affirmative statement
See affirmative statement, negative statement.

neuter   A word that is neuter is neither masculine nor feminine. Common neuter demonstrative pronouns in Spanish are *esto/this, eso/that, aquello/that* [farther away].

What's this?/¿Qué es esto? What's that?/¿Qué es eso?

For demonstrative pronouns that are not neuter, *see* demonstrative pronoun. There is also the neuter pronoun **lo.** It usually refers to an idea or statement. It is not normally translated into English but often the translation is *so.*

¿Estás enferma, María?/Are you sick, Mary? Sí, lo estoy/Yes, I am.

No lo creo/I don't think so.

Lo parece/It seems so.

noun   A noun is a word that names a person, animal, place, thing, condition or state, or quality.

the man/el hombre, the woman/la mujer, the horse/el caballo,
the house/la casa, the pencil/el lápiz,
happiness/la felicidad, excellence/la excelencia

In Spanish the noun **el nombre** is the word for name and noun. Another word for noun in Spanish is *el sustantivo/substantive.*

number   In English and Spanish grammar, number means singular or plural.
Masc. sing.:

the boy/el muchacho; the pencil/el lápiz; the eye/el ojo

Masc. pl.:

the boys/los muchachos; the pencils/los lápices; the eyes/los ojos

Fem. sing.:

the girl/la muchacha; the house/la casa; the cow/la vaca

Fem. pl.:

the girls/las muchachas; the houses/las casas; the cows/las vacas

ordinal number   An ordinal number is a number that expresses position in a series, such as *first, second, third,* and so on. In English and Spanish grammar we talk about 1st person, 2nd person, 3rd person singular or plural regarding subjects and verbs. *See also* cardinal number and person (1st, 2nd, 3rd).

orthographical changes in verb forms   An orthographical change in a verb form is a change in spelling.

The verb *conocer/to know, to be acquainted with* changes in spelling in the 1st person singular of the present indicative. The letter **z** is inserted in front of the second **c.** When formed regularly, the ending **er** of the infinitive drops and **o** is added for the 1st person singular form of the present indicative. That would result in **conoco,** a peculiar sound to the Spanish ear for a verb form of **conocer.** The letter **z** is added to keep the sound of **s** as it is in the infinitive **conocer.** Therefore, the spelling changes and the form is **yo conozco.** In other forms of **conocer** in the present indicative, **z** is not inserted because the sound of **s** is retained.

There are many verb forms in Spanish that contain orthographical changes. Review the verb **conocer** in the present indicative tense among the 501 verbs.

passive voice   When we speak or write in the active voice and change to the passive voice, the direct object becomes the subject, the subject becomes the object of a preposition, and the verb becomes *to be* plus the past participle of the active verb. The past participle functions as an adjective.

The window was opened by the robber/La ventana fue abierta por el ladrón.
The subject is *la ventana*. The verb is *fue*. The word *abierta* is a feminine adjective agreeing with *la ventana*. Actually, it is the past participle of *abrir/to open* but here it serves as an adjective. The object of the preposition *by/por* is the *robber/el ladrón*. *See also* active voice in this list. Compare the above sentence with the examples in the active voice. Review the section on passive voice and active voice on pages 7 and 8. *See also* page 6, example 6.

past anterior tense This tense is defined with examples on page 25. It is also called the *preterit perfect.*

past participle A past participle is derived from a verb. It is used to form the compound tenses. Its auxiliary verb in English is *to have.* In Spanish, the auxiliary verb is *haber/to have.* It is part of the verb tense.

hablar/to speak, to talk	*I have spoken/he hablado*
comer/to eat	*I have eaten/he comido*
recibir/to receive	*I have received/he recibido*

Review pages 5 and 6 for the regular formation of a past participle and a list of common irregular past participles. *See also* auxiliary verb.

past perfect tense This tense is defined with examples on pages 24 and 25. It is also called the pluperfect indicative tense.

past subjunctive tense This tense is defined with examples on pages 26 and 27. It is also called the present perfect subjunctive.

person (1st, 2nd, 3rd) Verb forms in a particular tense are learned systematically according to person (1st, 2nd, 3rd) and number (singular, plural).
Example, showing the present indicative tense of the verb ir/to go:

Singular	Plural
1st person: *(yo) voy*	1st person: *(nosotros, nosotras) vamos*
2nd person: *(tú) vas*	2nd person: *(vosotros, vosotras) vais*
3rd person: *(Ud., él, ella) va*	3rd person: *(Uds., ellos, ellas) van*

personal pronoun A personal pronoun is a pronoun that refers to a person. Review the subject pronouns on page 92. For examples of other types of pronouns, *see also* demonstrative pronoun, direct object pronoun, disjunctive pronoun, indefinite pronoun, indirect object pronoun, interrogative pronoun, possessive pronoun, reflexive pronoun, relative pronoun.

pluperfect indicative tense This tense is defined with examples on pages 24 and 25. It is also called the past perfect indicative tense.

pluperfect subjunctive tense This tense is defined with examples on page 27. It is also called the past perfect subjunctive tense.

plural Plural means more than one. *See also* person (1st, 2nd, 3rd) and singular.

possessive adjective A possessive adjective is an adjective that is placed in front of a noun to show possession.

my book/mi libro my friend/mis amigos our school/nuestra escuela

possessive pronoun A possessive pronoun is a pronoun that shows possession. It takes the place of a possessive adjective with the noun. Its form agrees in gender (masculine or feminine) and number (singular or plural) with what it is replacing.
English:

mine, yours, his, hers, its, ours, theirs

Spanish:

Possessive Adjective	Possessive Pronoun
my book/mi libro	*mine/el mío*
my house/mi casa	*mine/la mía*
my shoes/mis zapatos	*mine/los míos*

predicate   The predicate is that part of the sentence that tells us something about the subject. The main word of the predicate is the verb.

Today the tourists are going to the Prado Museum/
Hoy los turistas van al Museo del Prado.

The subject is the *tourists/los turistas.* The predicate is *are going to the Prado Museum/ van al Museo del Prado.* The verb is *are going/van.*

preposition   A preposition is a word that establishes a rapport between words.

with, without, to, at, between

with her/con ella   without money/sin dinero   to Spain/a España
at six o'clock/a las seis   between you and me/entre tú y yo

Review verbs with prepositions beginning on page 669.

prepositional pronoun   A prepositional pronoun is a pronoun that is an object of a preposition. The term disjunctive pronoun is also used. For examples, *see* disjunctive pronoun.

present indicative tense   This tense is defined with examples on pages 14 and 15.

present participle   A present participle is derived from a verb form. In English a present participle ends in *ing*. In Spanish a present participle is called **un gerundio.**

cantando/singing   comiendo/eating   yendo/going

Review pages 3 and 4 for regular and irregular present participles and their uses. *See also* gerund.

present perfect indicative tense   This tense is defined with examples on page 24.

present subjunctive tense   This tense is defined with examples on pages 20 to 23.

preterit tense   This tense is defined with examples on pages 17 and 18.

preterit perfect tense   This tense is defined with examples on page 25. It is also called the past anterior.

pronoun   A pronoun is a word that takes the place of a noun.

el hombre/él   la mujer/ella
the man/he   the woman/she

reflexive pronoun and reflexive verb   In English, a reflexive pronoun is a personal pronoun that contains *self* or *selves*. In Spanish and English, a reflexive pronoun is used with a verb that is called reflexive because the action of the verb falls on the reflexive pronoun. In Spanish, there is a required set of reflexive pronouns for a reflexive verb.

lavarse	*(Yo) me lavo.*	*afeitarse*	*Pablo se ha afeitado.*
to wash oneself	*I wash myself.*	*to shave oneself*	*Paul has shaved himself.*

Review, for example, the reflexive verbs **afeitarse, lavarse, levantarse, llamarse** among the 501 verbs in this book to become familiar with the reflexive pronouns that go with reflexive verbs in the three persons of the singular and plural.

regular verb   A regular verb is a verb that is conjugated in the various tenses according to a fixed pattern. For examples, review page 15 at the top and page 16 at the bottom. *See also* conjugation, irregular verb.

relative pronoun   A relative pronoun is a pronoun that refers to its antecedent.

The girl who is talking with John is my sister/
La muchacha que está hablando con Juan es mi hermana.

The antecedent is *girl/la muchacha.* The relative pronoun *who/que* refers to the girl.
See also antecedent.

sentence   A sentence is a group of words that contains a subject and a predicate. The verb is contained in the predicate. A sentence expresses a complete thought.

The train leaves at two o'clock in the afternoon/
El tren sale a las dos de la tarde.

The subject is *train/el tren.* The predicate is *leaves at two o'clock in the afternoon/sale a las dos de la tarde.* The verb is *leaves/sale. See also* complex sentence, compound sentence, simple sentence.

simple sentence   A simple sentence is a sentence that contains one subject and one predicate. The verb is the core of the predicate. The verb is the most important word in a sentence because it tells us what the subject is doing.

Mary is eating an apple from her garden/
María está comiendo una manzana de su jardín.

The subject is *Mary/María.* The predicate is *is eating an apple from her garden/está comiendo una manzana de su jardín.* The verb is *is eating/está comiendo.* The direct object is *an apple/una manzana. From her garden/de su jardín* is an adverbial phrase. It tells you from where the apple came. *See also* complex sentence, compound sentence.

singular   Singular means one. *See also* plural.

stem of a verb   The stem of a verb is what is left after we drop the ending of its infinitive form. It is needed to add to it the required endings of a regular verb in a particular verb tense.

Infinitive	Stem	Ending of infinitive
hablar/to talk	*habl*	*ar*
comer/to eat	*com*	*er*
escribir/to write	*escrib*	*ir*

See also ending of a verb.

stem-changing verb   In Spanish, there are many verb forms that change in the stem. The verb *dormir/to sleep* changes the vowel o in the stem to **ue** when the stress (emphasis, accent) falls on that o; for example, **(yo) duermo.** When the stress does not fall on that **o,** it does not change; for example, **(nosotros) dormimos.** Here, the stress is on the vowel **i.**

Review the present indicative tense of **dormir** among the 501 verbs.

subject   A subject is that part of a sentence that is related to its verb. The verb says something about the subject.

Clara and Isabel are beautiful/Clara e Isabel son hermosas.

subjunctive mood   The subjunctive mood is the mood of a verb that is used in specific cases, e.g., after certain verbs expressing a wish, doubt, emotion, fear, joy, uncertainty, an indefinite expression, an indefinite antecedent, certain conjunctions, and others. The subjunctive mood is used more frequently in Spanish than in English. Review the uses of the subjunctive mood with examples on pages 20 to 23, pages 26 to 27, and page 30. *See also* mood of verbs.

subordinate clause   Subordinate clause is another term for dependent clause. *See* dependent clause.

superlative adjective A superlative adjective is an adjective that expresses the highest degree when making a comparison of more than two persons or things.

Adjective	Comparative	Superlative
bueno/good	*mejor/better*	*el mejor/best*
alto/tall	*más alto/taller*	*el más alto/tallest*

See also comparative adjective.

superlative adverb A superlative adverb is an adverb that expresses the highest degree when making a comparison of more than two persons or things.

Adjective	Comparative	Superlative
lentamente	*más lentamente*	*lo más lentamente*
slowly	*more slowly*	*most slowly*

See also comparative adverb.

tense of verb In English and Spanish grammar, tense means time. The tense of the verb indicates the time of the action or state of being. The three major segments of time are past, present, and future. In Spanish, there are fourteen major verb tenses, of which seven are simple tenses and seven are compound. Review pages 31 and 92 for the names of the fourteen tenses in Spanish and English.

transitive verb A transitive verb is a verb that takes a direct object.

> *I am closing the window/Cierro la ventana.*

The subject is *I/(Yo)*. The verb is *am closing/cierro*. The direct object is *the window/la ventana*. *See also* intransitive verb.

verb A verb is a word that expresses action or a state of being.

Action:

> *Los pájaros están volando/The birds are flying.*

The verb is *éstan volando/are flying.*

State of being:

> *La señora López está contenta/Mrs. López is happy.*

The verb is *está/is.*

The hundreds of verb forms in this part of the book will immerse you in the practice and improvement of your knowledge of Spanish verb forms, tenses, and uses. You will find a variety of types of questions to make your experience interesting, challenging, and rewarding. All verb forms used in the drills and tests are found in the preliminary pages, among the 501 verbs, and in the back pages of this book.

The answers and explanations begin on page 78. The explanations are brief and to the point, including references to pages in this book for study and review.

Tips: To figure out the correct verb form of the required tense, examine each sentence carefully. Take a good look at the subject of the verb. Is it 1st, 2nd, or 3rd person? Is it singular or plural? Is it masculine or feminine? Look for key elements that precede or follow the verb to determine the verb form and tense, for example, such words as yesterday, last week, today, at this moment, tomorrow, next year, a preposition, a certain conjunction, and other key words that indicate the need for an infinitive, present participle **(gerundio),** past participle, or the indicative or subjunctive moods in the required tense. The correct verb form depends on the sense and grammatical structure of the sentence.

The best way to learn irregular forms in the seven simple tenses is from study, practice, and experience. For the information of present and past participles, including irregulars, consult pages 3 to 6. As for the formation of regular verb forms, consult pages 14 to 32. For an easy way to form the seven compound tenses in Spanish, consult page 92 from time to time.

Verb Test 1

SENTENCE COMPLETION

Directions: Each of the following sentences contains a missing verb form. From the choices given, select the verb form of the tense that is required, according to the sense of the sentence, and write the letter of your choice on the line. At times, only the infinitive form is needed or a present or past participle. Answers and answer explanations begin on page 78.

1. Margarita acaba de _____ una falda.
   A. compró   B. compré   C. comprar   D. compraste

2. Aquel hombre no _____ nadar.
   A. supe   B. sepa   C. sé   D. sabe

3. Hace mal tiempo. Está _____ .
   A. llover   B. lloviendo   C. llorando   D. llovido

4. Te _____ mañana, José. ¡Adiós!
   A. verá   B. veré   C. ver   D. vi

5. Me parece que María _____ pálida hoy.
   A. está   B. es   C. estuve   D. fue

6. Ricardo y Dora _____ cansados.
   A. son   B. están   C. fueron   D. fuimos

7. Voy a _____ temprano porque tomo el tren a las seis de la mañana.
   A. acostarse   B. me acuesto   C. acostarme   D. se acuesta

8. No _____ ganas de comer porque no me gusta esta sopa.
   A. tengo   B. quiero   C. tuvo   D. pago

9. Tengo que _____ la cocina y necesito una escoba.
   A. limpiar   B. limpio   C. limpiara   D. limpie

10. La madre ha _____ el cabello de la niña.
   A. lavado   B. lavando   C. lavar   D. lava

11. Mi abuelito _____ anoche.
   A. muere   B. murió   C. morí   D. morir

12. Aquí tiene usted el dinero que le _____ .
   A. quiero   B. necesito   C. debo   D. conozco

13. No se olviden ustedes que mañana la tienda _____ cerrada.
   A. será   B. estará   C. es   D. estuve

14. La maestra dijo a los alumnos: "_____ los libros en la página diez, por favor."
   A. Abren   B. Abrid   C. Abrieron   d. Abrían

15. En la ciudad de Madrid _____ divertirme porque hay muchos teatros y cines.
   A. puedes   B. puede   C. puedo   D. podemos

16. Los Reyes Magos han _____ muchos regalos a los niños.
   A. traemos   B. traen   C. traído   D. trajeran

17. Miguel _____ de escribir una carta.
   A. acaba   B. acabé   C. acabaré   D. acabar

18. Hace tres horas que (yo) _____ la televisión.
   A. miré   B. miró   C. miro   D. miraré

19. Cuando yo entré en la sala de estar, mi madre _____ y mi padre escribía.
   A. leía   B. leí   C. leyó   D. lee

20. Esta mañana mi hermana _____ en el cuarto de baño cuando me desperté.
   A. canté   B. cantará   C. cantaría   D. cantaba

DIALOGUE

Directions: *In the following dialogue, there are blank spaces indicating missing verb forms. Select the appropriate verb form according to the sense of what the speakers are saying and write the letter of your choice on the line. The situation is given below. First, read the entire selection once. During the second reading, make your choices.*

Situation: You are on the telephone talking to a clerk at the Teatro Colón. You are asking about a ticket for a show.

La señorita: ¡Teatro Colón! ¡Información y reservas!
Usted: ¿ _____ entradas para el sábado?

1. A. Había   B. Haber   C. Hubo   D. Hay

La señorita: Sí. Hay entradas de varios precios.
Usted: _____ una por cien pesos, por favor.

2. A. Quise   B. Quiso   C. Quiera   D. Quisiera

La señorita: ¡Qué suerte tiene usted! Es la última entrada a este precio.
Usted: ¡Qué bueno! ¿Cómo _____ ?

3. A. pago   B. pagué   C. pagó   D. pagaba

La señorita: Si usted nos envía un cheque hoy, llegará mañana y le enviaremos la entrada.
Usted: ¿A qué hora _____ la función?

4. A. empecé   B. empezó   C. empieza   D. empiece

La señorita: A las dos y media de la tarde.
Usted: Muchas gracias. Usted _____ muy amable.

5. A. es   B. está   C. sea   D. fuera

PATTERN RESPONSES

Directions: *Answer the following questions in Spanish in complete sentences in the affirmative, using a pronoun for the subject. Add* **también** *(also). See page 678 for irregular verb forms that you cannot identify.*

Model: **Francisco comprende bien. ¿Y sus hermanos?**
                  (Francis understands well. And his brothers?)

You write: **Ellos comprenden bien, también.** (They understand well, also.)

1. Pedro estudia bien. ¿Y los otros alumnos?

    _____

2. Roberto escribe bien. ¿Y sus hermanas?

    _____

3. Sofía está leyendo un libro en la cama. ¿Y tú?

    _____

4. Isabel va de compras. ¿Y tus amigos?

    _____

5. Ricardo fue al cine. ¿Y tú?

    _____

6. Juan ha comido bien. ¿Y nosotros?

    _____

7. Ana está bien. ¿Y sus padres?

    _____

8. Juana se sentó. ¿Y las otras muchachas?

    _____

9. Mariana se lavó la cara. ¿Y tú?

    _____

10. Carlos sabe nadar. ¿Y tú?

    _____

11. Tú has cantado bien. ¿Y Luis?

    _____

12. El sénor Fuentes escogió un carro costoso. ¿Y usted?

    _____

13. Tú has terminado la lección. ¿Y los otros alumnos?

    _____

14. Yo escribí una carta. ¿Y Felipe?

    _____

15. Roberto tiene que estudiar. ¿Y tú?

_____

16. Yo he devuelto los libros a la biblioteca. ¿Y María?

_____

17. Manuel ha dicho la verdad. ¿Y nosotros?

_____

18. Tú te acuestas a las diez. ¿Y tus amigos?

_____

19. José ha leído un libro. ¿Y usted?

_____

20. Adolfo quiere hacerlo. ¿Y nosotros?

_____

Verb Test 4

SENTENCE COMPLETION

Directions: *Each of the following sentences contains a missing verb form. From the choices given, select the verb form of the tense that is required, according to the sense of the sentence, and write the letter of your choice on the line. At times, only the infinitive form is needed or a present or past participle.*

1. Cuando estábamos en Barcelona, _____ al cine todos los sábados.
A. vamos   B. iremos   C. vayamos   D. íbamos

2. Cuando _____ en Málaga, íbamos a la playa todos los días.
A. vivíamos   B. viviremos   C. vivamos   D. viviéramos

3. Mi madre era hermosa cuando _____ pequeña.
A. es   B. fui   C. fue   D. era

4. ¿Qué hora _____ cuando usted telefoneó?
A. era   B. fue   C. fuí   D. es

5. Cuando yo telefoneé, _____ las tres.
A. fue   B. fueron   C. eran   D. son

6. Hacía dos horas que yo _____ la televisión cuando mi hermano entró.
A. miraba   B. miró   C. miraré   D. miraría

7. Roberto dice que quiere _____ a mi casa.
A. venir   B. viene   C. vendrá   D. vendría

8. ¿Has _____ mis guantes?
   A. ve   B. ver   C. visto   D. veía

9. Casandra dijo que _____ venir a mi casa.
   A. quería   B. quise   C. querrá   D. quiera

10. Ayer mi amigo _____ de Madrid.
   A. llegué   B. llegaste   C. llegó   D. llegará

11. Anoche María _____ a la iglesia.
   A. fui   B. fue   C. irá   D. iría

12. ¿Qué _____ en la calle ayer por la tarde?
   A. pasa   B. pasó   C. pasé   D. pasará

13. Antes de salir de casa esta mañana, yo _____ un buen desayuno.
   A. tomó   B. tomé   C. tome   D. tomara

14. Esta mañana salí de casa, tomé el autobús, y _____ a la escuela a las ocho.
   A. llego   B. llegó   C. llegué   D. llegaré

15. Yo _____ a Elena la semana pasada en el baile.
   A. conozco   B. conocí   C. conoció   D. conocería

16. ¿Cuándo _____ la verdad, José?
   A. sepa   B. supe   C. supiste   D. supiera

17. ¿El trabajo? Yo lo _____ la semana que viene.
   A. haré   B. hará   C. hice   D. hizo

18. El verano que viene nosotros _____ al campo.
   A. iremos   B. fuimos   C. vayamos   D. íbamos

19. María dice que _____ mañana.
   A. vine   B. vino   C. vendrá   D. venga

20. Si Miguel tuviera dinero, _____ a España.
   A. irá   B. iría   C. iré   D. va

DIALOGUE

Directions: *In the following dialogue, there are blank spaces indicating missing verb forms. Select the appropriate verb form according to the sense of what the speakers are saying and write the letter of your choice on the line. The situation is given below. First, read the entire selection once. During the second reading, make your choices.*

Situation: **Dolores, an exchange student from Barcelona, is visiting your school. The school principal has asked you to accompany her as a guide.**

Dolores: ¡Qué escuela tan moderna! Me _____ mucho.
  1. A. gusto   B. gusta   C. gustaría   D. guste
Tú: Sí, es muy moderna.

Dolores: ¿Cuántos años hace que _____ (tú) a esta escuela?
  2. A. asistes   B. asiste   C. asistí   D. asistió

Tú: Ya _____ tres años.
  3. A. hace   B. hacen   C. haría   D. harían

Dolores: ¿A qué hora empieza y termina el día escolar?
Tú: _____ a las ocho y termina a las dos y media.
  4. A. Empieza   B. Empecé   C. Empezó   D. Empezará

Dolores: Me gustaría mucho asistir a unas clases.
Tú: Puedes _____ a mi clase de biología.
  5. A. viene   B. vine   C. venir   D. vino

Dolores: Me interesan más las lenguas extranjeras.
Tú: Entonces, _____ a mi clase de español.
  6. A. voy   B. vas   C. vamos   D. iríamos

CHANGING FROM ONE VERB TO ANOTHER

Directions: *The verb forms in the following statements are all in the imperative. Change each sentence by replacing the verb with the proper form of the verb in parentheses, keeping the imperative form. The verb form you write must be in the same person as the one you are replacing. In other words, you must recognize if the given verb form is 2nd person singular (tú), 3rd person singular (usted) or plural (ustedes), or 1st person plural (nosotros). See page 678 for irregular verb forms that you cannot identify.*

Model: **Lea la oración. (escribir)** (Read the sentence.)

You write: **Escriba la oración.** (Write the sentence.)

1. Lea la palabra. (decir)

_____

2. Toma la leche. (beber)

_____

3. Venga inmediatamente. (partir)

_____

4. Abre la ventana. (cerrar)

_____

5. Ponga la maleta sobre la cama. (tomar)

_____

6. Pronuncie la palabra. (escribir)

_____

7. Leamos la carta. (enviar)

_____

8. Aprendan el poema. (leer)

_____

9. Partamos ahora. (salir)

_____

10. Siéntese, por favor. (levantarse)

_____

11. Venda la casa. (comprar)

_____

12. Salgan ahora. (venir)

_____

13. Lávate. (secarse)

_____

14. Compre estos guantes. (escoger)

_____

15. Cómalo. (beber)

_____

CHANGING FROM ONE TENSE TO ANOTHER

Directions: _The following verb forms are all in the **future tense.** Change them to the **conditional,** keeping the same subject. See page 678 for irregular verb forms that you cannot identify._

Model: **Yo iré.**   **You write:**   **Yo iría.**

1. Yo saldré.

_____

2. Ud. tendrá.

_____

3. Nosotros seremos.

_____

4. Uds. estarán.

_____

5. María querrá.

_____

6. Tú ganarás.

_____

7. Ellos harán.

_____

8. Ella cantará.

_____

9. José bailará.

_____

10. Tú escribirás.

_____

11. Él será.

_____

12. Yo me lavaré.

_____

13. Alberto se sentará.

_____

14. Nosotros nos sentiremos.

_____

15. Nosotros nos sentaremos.

_____

16. Yo aprenderé.

_____

17. Tú beberás.

_____

18. Ud. sabrá.

_____

19. Miguel leerá.

_____

20. Nosotros iremos.

_____

21. Vosotros iréis.

_____

22. Uds. dirán.

_____

23. Ellos vendrán.

_____

24. Ellas venderán.

_____

25. José y Dora serán.

_____

26. Los chicos comerán.

_____

27. María y yo haremos.

_____

28. Elena y Ana pondrán.

_____

29. Vosotros veréis.

_____

30. Yo estudiaré.

_____

Verb Test 8

PATTERN RESPONSES

Directions: _Answer the following questions in the negative in complete Spanish sentences. In answer (a), use_ **No.** _In answer (b), use_ **tampoco** _(either). Study models (a) and (b) carefully. Use a pronoun as subject in your answers. Place_ **tampoco** _at the end of the sentence. See page 678 for irregular verb forms that you cannot identify._

Model:	(a) **¿Trabaja Ud.?**	You write:	(a) **No. Yo no trabajo.**
	(Do you work?)		(No. I don't work.)
	(b) **¿Y Carlos?**		(b) **Él no trabaja tampoco.**
	(And Charles?)		(He does not work, either.)

1. (a) ¿Saldrá Ud. de casa esta noche?

_____

(b) ¿Y sus amigos?

_____

2. (a) ¿Quieres venir a mi casa esta tarde?

_____

(b) ¿Y vosotros?

_____

3. (a) ¿Cantaste esta mañana?

_____

(b) ¿Y María y José?

_____

4. (a) ¿Dices mentiras?

_____

(b) ¿Y Francisca?

_____

5. (a) ¿Fue Ud. al cine ayer?

_____

(b) ¿Y sus padres?

_____

CHANGING FROM ONE TENSE TO ANOTHER

*Directions: The following verb forms are all in the **imperfect indicative tense**. Change them to the **preterit tense**, keeping the same subject. See page 678 for irregular verb forms that you cannot identify.*

Model: **Yo trabajaba.** (I was working *or* I used to work.)

You write: **Yo trabajé.** (I worked.)

1. Yo iba al parque.

2. Elisa miraba la televisión.

3. El niño bebía la leche.

4. Margarita hacía la lección.

5. José hablaba mucho.

6. Mi amigo pagaba la cuenta.

7. Nosotros tomábamos el desayuno a las ocho.

8. Luis escribía cartas.

9. Marta aprendía la lección.

10. Los Señores López vivían en esta casa.

11. Yo hacía el trabajo.

12. La señorita traía el plato.

13. Pablo leía el poema.

14. Carlota decía la verdad.

15. La profesora abría el libro.

SENTENCE COMPLETION

Directions: *Each of the following sentences contains a missing verb form. From the choices given, select the verb form of the tense that is required, according to the sense of the sentence, and write the letter of your choice on the line. At times, only the infinitive form is needed or a present or past participle.*

1. Me _____ tomar una limonada ahora.
   A. gustaría   B. gusto   C. gusté   D. guste

2. Si mis padres tuvieran dinero, _____ a Barcelona.
   A. irían   B. irán   C. fueron   D. iban

3. María había _____ que vendría mañana.
   A. dijo   B. dice   C. dicho   D. decir

4. Claudia decía que _____ a mi casa esta tarde.
   A. vendría   B. viene   C. vine   D. venir

5. No se _____ aquí, Señor Robles, por favor.
   A. siente   B. sientes   C. sienta   D. sentó

6. Quiero que Jorge lo _____.
   A. hace   B. hacía   C. haga   D. hizo

7. Yo voy a _____ un café.
   A. tomo   B. tomar   C. tomando   D. tomado

8. En este momento, estoy _____ mis lecciones.
   A. estudiar   B. estudio   C. estudié   D. estudiando

9. El niño entró _____ en la casa.
   A. llorando   B. llorar   C. lloré   D. lloró

10. Prefiero que Juan lo _____ .
    A. hace   B. hizo   C. hice   D. haga

11. Dudo que Julia _____ a verme.
    A. viene   B. venga   C. vino   D. vendrá

12. Es necesario que Inés _____ bien.
    A. come   B. coma   C. comer   D. comiera

13. Le hablaré a Juan cuando _____ .
    A. llega   B. llegará   C. llegó   D. llegue

14. Me quedo aquí hasta que el Señor Hildago _____ .
A. vuelve   B. volverá   C. vuelva   D. volvería

15. Démelo con tal que _____ bueno.
A. sea   B. es   C. era   D. fue

16. Aunque Pablo _____ esta noche, no me quedo.
A. viene   B. viniera   C. vendrá   D. venga

17. Busco un libro que _____ interesante.
A. es   B. sea   C. será   D. sería

18. ¿Hay alguien aquí que _____ francés?
A. hable   B. habla   C. hablara   D. hablaría

19. No hay nadie que _____ hacerlo.
A. poder   B. puede   C. pueda   D. podrá

20. Yo insistí en que María lo _____ .
A. hace   B. haga   C. hiciera   D. hará

Verb Test 11

CHANGING FROM ONE TENSE TO ANOTHER

*Directions: The following verb forms are all in the present indicative tense. Change them to the **pretérito**. Keep the same subject, of course. Consult page 678 for irregular verb forms that you cannot identify.*

Model: **Ella estudia.**

You write: **Ella estudió.**

1. Yo hablo.

_____

2. Tú aprendes.

_____

3. Ud. vive aquí.

_____

4. Él trabaja.

_____

5. Ella dice algo.

_____

6. Uds. van al cine.

_____

7. Vosotros pedís algo.

_____

8. Ellos son.

_____

9. Ellas beben café.

_____

10. Juana juega.

_____

11. Tú tocas.

_____

12. El perro muerde.

_____

13. Ellos oyen algo.

_____

14. Uds. escuchan.

_____

15. Yo estoy en casa.

_____

16. Gabriela viene.

_____

17. El niño duerme.

_____

18. Los alumnos leen.

_____

19. Nosotros comemos.

_____

20. Vosotros hacéis la lección.

_____

21. Nosotros vamos al teatro.

_____

22. Ellos piensan.

_____

23. Ellas tienen dinero.

_____

24. Alberto escribe.

_____

25. Ella muere.

_____

26. María y José comen.

_____

27. Yo oigo la música.

_____

28. Yo quiero comer.

_____

29. Ella está en la escuela.

_____

30. Yo voy a casa.

_____

Verb Test 12

COMPLETION OF VERB FORMS
(in the Seven Simple Tenses)

Directions: _Complete each verb form in the tenses indicated by writing the correct letter or letters on the blank lines._

Presente de indicativo (Tense No. 1)

1. (hablar) Yo habl ___
2. (beber) Tú beb ___
3. (recibir) Ud. recib ___
4. (abrir) Uds. abr ___
5. (hacer) Ellos hac ___
6. (aprender) Nostros aprend ___
7. (leer) María le ___
8. (aceptar) Ellos acept ___
9. (amar) Yo am ___
10. (escribir) Tú escrib ___

Imperfecto de indicativo (Tense No. 2)

1. (cantar) Yo cant ___
2. (dar) Uds. d ___
3. (bañarse) Tú te bañ ___
4. (hacer) Nosotros hac ___
5. (hablar) Ud. habl ___
6. (hallar) Nosotros hall ___
7. (comprender) Yo comprend ___
8. (comer) Uds. com ___
9. (levantarse) Yo me levant ___
10. (vivir) Ella viv ___

Pretérito (Tense No. 3)

1. (hablar) Yo habl ___
2. (comprar) Tú compr ___
3. (aprender) Ud. aprend ___
4. (correr) Nosotros corr ___
5. (recibir) Uds. recib ___

6. (cantar) Él cant ___
7. (apresurarse) Ellos se apresur ___
8. (traer) Uds. traj ___
9. (vivir) Ella viv ___
10. (lavarse) Ellas se lav ___

Futuro (Tense No. 4)

1. (bailar) Yo bailar ___
2. (aprender) Tú aprender ___
3. (ir) Ud. ir ___
4. (venir) Uds. vendr ___
5. (irse) Nosotros nos ir ___

6. (recibir) Ud. recibir ___
7. (dar) Yo dar ___
8. (cantar) Ellos cantar ___
9. (comprender) Ella comprender ___
10. (vivir) Uds. vivir ___

Potencial simple (Tense No. 5)

1. (comprender) Ella comprender ___
2. (vivir) Uds. vivir ___
3. (comprar) Ellos comprar ___
4. (dar) Yo dar ___
5. (recibir) Ud. recibir ___

6. (saltar) Nosotros saltar ___
7. (dormir) Ella dormir ___
8. (entender) Ellos entender ___
9. (estar) Yo estar ___
10. (ser) Yo ser ___

Presente de subjuntivo (Tense No. 6)

1. (hablar) que yo habl ___
2. (aprender) que tú aprend ___
3. (recibir) que Ud. recib ___
4. (tener) que él teng ___
5. (estar) que ella est ___

6. (ser) que Ud. se ___
7. (cantar) que Uds. cant ___
8. (casarse) que nosotros nos cas ___
9. (venir) que ella veng ___
10. (comprender) que yo comprend ___

Imperfecto de subjuntivo (Tense No. 7)

1. (hablar) que yo habla ___
2. (aprender) que él aprendie ___
3. (vivir) que Ud. vivie ___

4. (bailar) que nosotros bailá ___
5. (bajar) que ella baja ___
6. (comprender) que ellos comprendie ___

PAST PARTICIPLES

Directions: *In this acrostic* (***un acróstico***), *complete each word in Spanish by writing the past participle of the infinitive given for each row. When you write the past participles for the infinitives given below, write them across next to the numbers. The first letter of each past participle is given. If you read the printed letters down from 1 to 9, you will read the Spanish word* ***enamorado,*** *which means* in love.

1.	escribir	4.	morir	7. aprender
2.	nacer	5.	oír	8. decir
3.	abrir	6.	reír	9. obtener

DRILLING THE VERB HABER
(in the Seven Simple Tenses)

Note: You must know the verb **haber** (to have) in the seven simple tenses because they are needed to form the seven compound tenses, for example, the **perfecto de indicativo** (Tense No. 8), as in **yo he comido** (I have eaten). Practice these by writing them every day until you know them thoroughly. If you don't know them, see verb 257. Also, review pages 31 and 32.

Directions: *Write the verb forms of* **haber** *in the seven simple tenses indicated.*

1. Presente de indicativo (Tense No. 1)

Singular	*Plural*
yo _____	nosotros (nosotras)_____
tú _____	vosotros (vosotras) _____
Ud./él/ella/*(or a noun)* _____	Uds./ellos/ellas/*(or a noun)*_____

2. Imperfecto de indicativo (Tense No. 2)

yo _____   nosotros (nosotras)_____

tú _____   vosotros (vosotras) _____

Ud./él/ella/*(or a noun)* _____   Uds./ellos/ellas/*(or a noun)*_____

3. Pretérito (Tense No. 3)

yo _____   nosotros (nosotras)_____

tú _____   vosotros (vosotras) _____

Ud./él/ella/*(or a noun)* _____   Uds./ellos/ellas/*(or a noun)*_____

4. Futuro (Tense No. 4)

yo _____   nosotros (nosotras)_____

tú _____   vosotros (vosotras) _____

Ud./él/ella/*(or a noun)* _____   Uds./ellos/ellas/*(or a noun)*_____

5. Potencial simple (Tense No. 5)

yo _____   nosotros (nosotras)_____

tú _____   vosotros (vosotras) _____

Ud./él/ella/*(or a noun)* _____   Uds./ellos/ellas/*(or a noun)*_____

6. Presente de subjuntivo (Tense No. 6)

que yo_____   que nosotros (nosotras)_____

que tú _____   que vosotros (vosotras) _____

que Ud./él/ella/*(or a noun)*_____   que Uds./ellos/ellas/*(or a noun)*_____

7. Imperfecto de subjuntivo (Tense No. 7)

que yo_____   que nosotros (nosotras)_____

que tú _____   que vosotros (vosotras) _____

que Ud./él/ella/*(or a noun)*_____   que Uds./ellos/ellas/*(or a noun)*_____

DRILLING THE VERB ESTAR
(in the Seven Simple Tenses)

Note: You must know the verb **estar** (to be) in the seven simple tenses because it is a commonly used verb. Besides, the present indicative tense of **estar** is needed to form the progressive present, as in **estoy estudiando** (I am studying). The imperfect indicative tense of **estar** is needed to form the progressive past, as in **estaba estudiando** (I was studying). Review no. 1 at the top of page 4. Also, review the progressive forms of tenses on pages 4 and 5. Review the formation of the present participles on page 3 so that you may be able to form the progressive present and progressive past.

Directions: *Write the verb forms of* **estar** *in the seven simple tenses indicated.*

1. Presente de indicativo (Tense No. 1)

Singular	*Plural*
yo _____	nosotros (nosotras)_____
tú _____	vosotros (vosotras) _____
Ud./él/ella/*(or a noun)* _____	Uds./ellos/ellas/*(or a noun)*_____

2. Imperfecto de indicativo (Tense No. 2)

yo _____	nosotros (nosotras)_____
tú _____	vosotros (vosotras) _____
Ud./él/ella/*(or a noun)* _____	Uds./ellos/ellas/*(or a noun)*_____

3. Pretérito (Tense No. 3)

yo _____	nosotros (nosotras)_____
tú _____	vosotros (vosotras) _____
Ud./él/ella/*(or a noun)* _____	Uds./ellos/ellas/*(or a noun)*_____

4. Futuro (Tense No. 4)

yo _____	nosotros (nosotras)_____
tú _____	vosotros (vosotras) _____
Ud./él/ella/*(or a noun)* _____	Uds./ellos/ellas/*(or a noun)*_____

5. Potencial simple (Tense No. 5)

yo _____ nosotros (nosotras)_____

tú _____ vosotros (vosotras) _____

Ud./él/ella/*(or a noun)* _____ Uds./ellos/ellas/*(or a noun)*_____

6. Presente de subjuntivo (Tense No. 6)

que yo_____ que nosotros (nosotras)_____

que tú _____ que vosotros (vosotras) _____

que Ud./él/ella/*(or a noun)*_____ que Uds./ellos/ellas/*(or a noun)*_____

7. Imperfecto de subjuntivo (Tense No. 7)

que yo_____ que nosotros (nosotras)_____

que tú _____ que vosotros (vosotras) _____

que Ud./él/ella/*(or a noun)*_____ que Uds./ellos/ellas/*(or a noun)*_____

Verb Test 16

CHANGING FROM ONE TENSE TO ANOTHER

Directions: *The following verb forms are all in the **perfecto de indicativo** (Tense No. 8). Change them to the **pluscuamperfecto de indicativo** (Tense No. 9), keeping the same subject. Keep in mind that to form the **pluscuamperfecto de indicativo**, you need to use the imperfect indicative tense of **haber** plus the past participle of the verb you are working with. Review the formation of the past participles on pages 5 and 6. Also, review Verb Test 14.*

	Perfecto de indicativo	*Pluscuamperfecto de indicativo*
Model:	**María ha comido.**	You write: **María había comido.**
	(Mary has eaten.)	(Mary had eaten.)

1. Yo he hablado.

_____

2. Tú has aprendido.

_____

3. Ud. ha salido.

_____

4. Él ha comprendido.

_____

5. Ella ha comprado.

_____

6. El chico ha comido.

_____

7. Nosotros hemos ido.

_____

8. Yo he abierto.

_____

9. Uds. han hecho.

_____

10. Ellas han caído.

_____

11. Yo he llegado.

_____

12. Tú has escrito.

_____

13. Ud. ha creído.

_____

14. Él ha dicho.

_____

15. Ella ha dado.

_____

16. La chica ha bebido.

_____

17. Nosotros hemos oído.

_____

18. Uds. han tenido.

_____

19. Ellos han puesto.

_____

20. Ellas han cubierto.

_____

Verb Test 17

SENTENCE COMPLETION

**Directions:** Each of the following sentences contains a missing verb form. From the choices given, select the verb form of the tense that is required, according to the sense of the sentence, and write the letter of your choice on the line. At times, only the infinitive form is needed or a present or past participle.

1. ¡Ojalá que _____ los niños mañana!
   A. vienen　　　　　B. vendrán　　　　　C. vengan　　　　　D. vendrían

2. Yo se lo explicaba a Roberto para que lo _____ .
   A. comprender　　B. comprende　　C. comprenderá　　D. comprendiera

3. Sí, sí. Yo he _____ con ella.
   A. hablando　　　　B. hablado　　　　C. hablo　　　　　D. hablé

4. Este profesor me habla como si _____ un niño.
   A. soy　　　　　　B. fuera　　　　　C. fui　　　　　　D. fue

5. ¿Quién ha _____ el premio?
   A. ganado　　　　　B. ganando　　　　C. gana　　　　　D. ganó

6. No quiero _____ porque está lloviendo.
   A. salgo　　　　　B. salir　　　　　C. saliendo　　　　D. sale

7. Juanito, ¿cuándo vas a _____ el ruido?
   A. terminar　　　　B. terminando　　　C. terminas　　　D. terminado

8. ¿Qué quiere _____ este muchacho?
   A. dice　　　　　B. decir　　　　　C. diciendo　　　　D. dicho

9. ¡Qué tiempo espléndido! ¡Está _____ !
   A. nevar　　　　　B. nevando　　　　C. nevado　　　　D. nevó

10. Cuando llegué a casa, mi hermano había _____ .
    A. salir　　　　　B. salido　　　　C. saliendo　　　　D. salía

PRESENT PARTICIPLES

Directions: *In this word puzzle, find the present participle of each of the verbs listed below and draw a line around each one. To get you started, the first verb on the list (comer), whose present participle is comiendo, is already done. The present participles are written horizontally or vertically. If you need to, review page 3 before you start.*

```
H  A  B  L  A  N  D  O  D
C  V  S  E  C  O  M  I  I
O  I  I  Y  E  N  D  O  C
M  V  E  E  V  I  V  R  I
I  I  N  N  B  L  A  I  E
E  E  D  D  A  N  D  E  N
N  N  O  O  E  S  T  N  D
D  D  E  S  T  A  N  D  O
O  O  Y  E  S  A  D  O  H
```

comer	hablar	reír
decir	ir	ser
estar	leer	vivir

DIALOGUE

Directions: *In the following dialogue, there are blank spaces indicating missing verb forms. Select the appropriate verb form according to the sense of what the speakers are saying and write the letter of your choice on the line. The situation is given below.*

Situation: You and your sister Julia are in a veterinarian's waiting room because your dog, Rojo, needs a rabies shot.

Julia : ¡Diós mío! ¡Qué ruido! ¿Por qué ladran todos los perros a la vez?
Tú: Me parece que _____ miedo.

1. A. tiene   B. tienes   C. tienen   D. teniendo

| Julia : | Ese gatito precioso allí parece dormido. |
| Tú: | Verdad. Debe _____ enfermo. |

2. A. ser B. estar C. tener D. estando

| Julia : | Mira a aquel chico tan pequeño con el perro enorme. |
| Tú: | Sí. ¡ _____ muy cómico! |

3. A. Es B. Está C. Son D. Están

| Julia : | ¡Qué quieto está Rojo! En casa siempre salta por todas partes. |
| Tú: | _____ en un lugar extraño. |

4. A. Es B. Está C. Son D. Están

| Julia : | Ya nos llaman. Y ahora Rojo quiere correr como siempre. ¿Qué haremos? |
| Tú: | Yo lo _____ adentro. |

5. A. llevo B. llevaba C. llevé D. llevó

Verb Test 20

CHANGING FROM ONE VERB TO ANOTHER

*Directions: The verb forms in the following statements are all in the **pretérito**. Change each sentence by replacing the verb in the sentence with the proper form of the verb in parentheses, keeping the **pretérito**. Rewrite the statement in Spanish.*

| **Model:** | **Claudia habló. (cantar)** (Claudia spoke.) |
| **You write:** | **Claudia cantó.** (Claudia sang.) |

1. Roberto *aprendió* la lección. (escribir)

_____

2. La Señora Fuentes *se sentó.* (levantarse)

_____

3. Yo *recibí* un regalo. (ofrecer)

_____

4. María *pensó.* (trabajar)

_____

5. El alumno *escribió* una carta. (leer)

_____

6. El Señor Robles *llegó.* (morir)

_____

7. Margarita *entró.* (salir)

_____

8. Ricardo *cantó.* (hablar)

_____

9. Yo *vi* a María. (saludar)

_____

10. Mi padre *vio* un accidente. (tener)

_____

11. Mi hermana *comió* la comida. (hacer)

_____

12. ¿*Viajó* usted a España? (ir)

_____

13. ¿*Se levantaron* los chicos? (vestirse)

_____

14. Esta mañana yo *me apresuré.* (lavarse)

_____

15. Yo no *pude* hacerlo. (querer)

_____

MATCHING SPANISH VERB FORMS WITH ENGLISH VERB FORMS

Directions: *Match the following Spanish verb forms with the English equivalent verb forms by writing the number in column one on the blank line in column two.*

Column One	Column Two
1. Yo he comido	_____ I came
2. Ud. puso	_____ I have eaten
3. Ella quiere	_____ You said
4. Ellos hicieron	_____ You put
5. Tú ganas	_____ She wants
6. Yo me afeito	_____ You will buy
7. Nosotros dimos	_____ We give
8. Uds. dieron	_____ They made (did)
9. Está lloviendo	_____ He became frightened
10. Ellos murieron	_____ You win
11. Él se asustó	_____ We gave
12. Nosotros damos	_____ I am shaving myself
13. Uds. comprarán	_____ You gave
14. Tú dijiste	_____ It is raining
15. Yo vine	_____ They died

CHANGING FROM ONE TENSE TO ANOTHER

Directions: *The verb forms are all in the **presente de indicativo** (Tense No. 1). Change them to the **pretérito** (Tense No. 3), keeping the same subject.*

	Presente de indicativo		*Pretérito*
Model:	**Yo como bien.**	**You write:**	**Yo comí bien.**
	(I eat well.)		(I ate well.)

1. Yo cojo la pelota.

_____

2. Ud. duerme demasiado.

_____

3. Tú vas al cine.

_____

4. Él habla mucho.

_____

5. Ella escribe una tarjeta.

_____

6. Nosotros comemos en este restaurante.

_____

7. Vosotros aceptáis el dinero.

_____

8. Uds. dan de comer a los pájaros.

_____

9. Yo voy al teatro.

_____

10. Ellas van a casa.

_____

11. Ellos están en la piscina.

_____

12. Yo me siento cerca de la ventana.

_____

13. Ud. se levanta.

_____

14. Nosotros nos apresuramos.

_____

15. Los muchachos vienen a verme.

_____

16. Berta está enferma.

_____

17. Mi madre hace un bizcocho.

_____

18. Yo busco mis libros.

_____

19. La profesora abre la puerta.

_____

20. Me gusta el helado.

_____

PRETERIT PERFECT

Directions: _In this word puzzle, find the **pretérito perfecto** (also known as the **pretérito anterior**), which is Tense No. 10, of the three verbs given below. When you find those three verb forms, draw a line around each one. One is printed horizontally, another one is printed vertically, and another is printed backwards. To refresh your memory of what the **pretérito perfecto** is, review page 25._

```
B  U  H  O  H  B  U  T  O
H  B  U  A  G  I  R  O  T
H  U  B  E  V  I  S  T  O
R  I  O  E  S  C  I  R  T
H  U  E  B  I  M  O  E  S
O  R  S  E  I  B  U  I  H
E  S  C  R  I  O  T  B  U
V  I  R  T  O  A  B  A  E
H  A  I  B  A  B  I  E  R
I  S  T  O  V  H  U  B  E
R  O  O  T  R  O  T  U  I
R  C  S  E  E  B  U  H  O
```

abrir   escribir   ver

DRILLING AGAIN THE VERB HABER
(in the Seven Simple Tenses)

Note: In Test 14, you drilled the verb **haber** in the seven simple tenses. Now, do it again here because you must know those verb forms in order to form the seven compound tenses (Tense Nos. 8 to 14). Practice these by writing them every day until you know them thoroughly. If you don't know them yet, see verb 257. Also, review pages 24 to 27 and pages 31 and 32.

Directions: *Write the verb forms of* ***haber*** *in the seven simple tenses indicated.*

1. **Presente de indicativo** (Tense No. 1)

Singular	*Plural*
yo _____	nosotros (nosotras)_____
tú _____	vosotros (vosotras) _____
Ud./él/ella/*(or a noun)* _____	Uds./ellos/ellas/*(or a noun)*_____

2. **Imperfecto de indicativo** (Tense No. 2)

yo _____	nosotros (nosotras)_____
tú _____	vosotros (vosotras) _____
Ud./él/ella/*(or a noun)* _____	Uds./ellos/ellas/*(or a noun)*_____

3. **Pretérito** (Tense No. 3)

yo _____	nosotros (nosotras)_____
tú _____	vosotros (vosotras) _____
Ud./él/ella/*(or a noun)* _____	Uds./ellos/ellas/*(or a noun)*_____

4. **Futuro** (Tense No. 4)

yo _____	nosotros (nosotras)_____
tú _____	vosotros (vosotras) _____
Ud./él/ella/*(or a noun)* _____	Uds./ellos/ellas/*(or a noun)*_____

5. **Potencial simple** (Tense No. 5)

yo _____	nosotros (nosotras)_____
tú _____	vosotros (vosotras) _____
Ud./él/ella/*(or a noun)* _____	Uds./ellos/ellas/*(or a noun)*_____

6. Presente de subjuntivo (Tense No. 6)

que yo_____   que nosotros (nosotras)_____

que tú _____   que vosotros (vosotras) _____

que Ud./él/ella/*(or a noun)*_____   que Uds./ellos/ellas/*(or a noun)*_____

7. Imperfecto de subjuntivo (Tense No. 7)

que yo_____   que nosotros (nosotras)_____

que tú _____   que vosotros (vosotras) _____

que Ud./él/ella/*(or a noun)*_____   que Uds./ellos/ellas/*(or a noun)*_____

Verb Test 25

PATTERN RESPONSES

Directions: *Answer the following questions in Spanish in complete sentences in the affirmative, using a pronoun for the subject. Add **también** (also). See page 678 for irregular verb forms that you cannot identify.*

Model: **Pedro escribe bien. ¿Y los otros alumnos?**
              (Peter writes well. And the other students?)

You write: **Ellos escriben bien, también.**
              (They write well, also.)

  1. María sabe nadar. ¿Y tú?

    _____

  2. Tú sales de la escuela a las tres. ¿Y los profesores?

    _____

  3. Yo estoy sentado. ¿Y Juanita?

    _____

  4. Tú eres inteligente. ¿Y tus hermanos?

    _____

  5. Ud. sonríe de vez en cuando. ¿Y Pedro y Juana?

    _____

6. Isabel leyó el libro. ¿Y María y José?

_____

7. Ester recibió muchos regalos. ¿Y nosotros?

_____

8. Yo bebí café con leche. ¿Y Andrés?

_____

9. Los alumnos oyeron la música. ¿Y Ud.?

_____

10. Susana durmió mucho. ¿Y los niños?

_____

11. Pablo fue al cine. ¿Y tus amigos?

_____

12. Tú te acuestas a las diez. ¿Y tus padres?

_____

13. José ha dicho la verdad. ¿Y Gabriela y Margarita?

_____

14. Yo hice la lección. ¿Y los otros alumnos?

_____

15. Tú has cantado bien. ¿Y Luis?

_____

IDENTIFYING VERB FORMS IN A PASSAGE
FROM SPANISH LITERATURE

Directions: *Read the following literary passage twice. Then, identify the verb forms with their subjects printed in* **bold face** *by giving (a) the infinitive of the verb form, (b) the name of the tense in Spanish, and (c) the person and number of the verb form.*

Example: son   You write: **(a) ser**
                                        (b) presente de indicativo
                                        (c) 3rd person plural

Al ruido, **salió** Sancho, **diciendo:**

    —Señor don Quixote, bien **puede** entrar, que al punto que yo **llegué se direon todos** por vencidos. **Baje, baje,** que **todos son** amigos y **hemos echado** pelillos a la mar, y nos **están aguardando** con una muy gentil olla de vaca, tocino, carnero, nabos y berzas, que **está diciendo:** "¡Cómeme, cómeme!"

Selection from *Don Quixote de la Mancha,*
by Miguel de Cervantes

1. salió

(a) _____

(b) _____

(c) _____

2. diciendo

(a) _____

(b) _____

(c) _____

3. puede

(a) _____

(b) _____

(c) _____

4. llegué

(a) _____

(b) _____

(c) _____

5. se dieron

(a) _____

(b) _____

(c) _____

6. baje

(a) _____

(b) _____

(c) _____

7. son

(a) _____

(b) _____

(c) _____

8. hemos echado

(a) _____

(b) _____

(c) _____

9. están aguardando

    (a) _____

    (b) _____

    (c) _____

10. está diciendo

    (a) _____

    (b) _____

    (c) _____

11. come

    (a) _____

    (b) _____

    (c) _____

Answers to Verb Tests with Explanations

Test 1

1. C You need the infinitive form of the verb in C because of the preceding preposition **de.** Review section F on page 672. The forms of **comprar** (verb 130) in A, B, and D are in the preterit.

2. D You need the 3rd person singular, pres. ind. of the verb in D because the subject **hombre** is 3rd person singular. Review the other forms of **saber** (verb 423) in A, B, and C.

3. B You need to complete the progressive present with the present participle **lloviendo** in B. Review pages 4 and 5. Review **llorar** (verb 300) and **llover**, a defective verb on page 660.

4. B The 1st person singular, future, of **ver** is needed because future time is implied in the word **mañana.** You are telling José, "I will see you tomorrow." Choice A is 3rd person singular, future. Review the forms of **ver** (verb 489).

5. A A form of **estar** is needed because a temporary state or condition is indicated in the sentence: Mary is pale. Review the uses of **estar** on pages 345–347. As for the other choices, review the forms of **estar** (verb 230) and **ser** (verb 438).

6. B Here, too, a form of **estar** is needed because a temporary state or condition is indicated in the sentence: Ricardo and Dora are tired. Review the uses of **estar** beginning on page 346, specifically in (c) (1). Review the forms of **estar** (verb 230). Review the forms of **ser** (verb 438) in A, C, and D.

7. C You are dealing with the verb **acostarse.** You need the infinitive form **acostarme** in C because of the preceding preposition **a.** The **me** in **acostarme** is needed because **voy** (I am going) is stated. Review the examples in section A on page 669 where **ir**, a verb of motion, requires the preposition a + inf. Review the forms of **acostarse** (verb 21) in choices B and D.

8. A You must know the idiomatic expression **tener ganas de** + inf. As for **tuvo** in C, it is preterit, 3rd person singular. Study the forms of **tener** (verb 468). As for **quiero** in B, study **querer** (verb 390). Regarding choice D, **pago** is a form of **pagar** (verb 341).

9. A You need the infinitive form **limpiar** because of the idiomatic expression **tener que** + inf. See **tener** (verb 468). Review the other forms of **limpiar** (verb 293) in B, C, and D.

10. A You need to complete the **perfecto de indicativo** (Tense No. 8) because **ha** is given as the helping verb. Review this tense and the other forms of **lavar** (verb 288) in choices B, C, and D. Also, review the formation of the **perfecto de indicativo** on page 24.

11. B The subject is 3rd person singular. You need the 3rd person singular of **morir** in the preterit, which is in choice B, because **anoche** (last night) is stated. Review the other forms of **morir** (verb 319) in choices A, C, and D.

12. C According to the meaning of the sentence, you are dealing with the verb **deber** (verb 159). The other verbs in A, B, and D would make no sense in this sentence. Review verbs 134, 326, and 390.

13. B A form of **estar** is needed because a temporary state or condition is indicated in the sentence: the store will be closed. The future tense is needed because **mañana** (tomorrow) is stated. The subject **la tienda** is 3rd person singular and

so is the verb **estará**. Review the uses of **estar** (verb 230), in particular, the example in (d) (5). Review the preterit of **estar** in choice D and the forms of **ser** (verb 438) in choices A and C.

14. **B** You need the imperative of **abrir** because the teacher told the pupils, "Open" the books. The 2nd person plural familiar form of **vosotros** is needed because the teacher talked to her pupils in the familiar form. Review **abrid** in the imperative as well as the other forms of **abrir** (verb 4).

15. **C** The form **puedo** (1st person singular, pres. ind.) is the correct choice because right after it is **divertirme** and they must agree in person; in other words, the statement is saying, "I can enjoy myself." Review **poder** (verb 363) on pages 494 and 495 for the forms in choices A, B, C, and D.

16. **C** You need to complete the **perfecto de indicativo** (Tense No. 8) by selecting the past participle **traído** because **han** is given as the helping verb. The sentence is saying that The Three Wise Men *have brought* many presents to the children. Review the forms of **traer** (verb 477).

17. **A** You are dealing with the idiomatic expression **acabar de** + inf. Review the forms of **acabar** (verb 9).

18. **C** The sentence states **"hace tres horas"** and it requires the pres. ind. of **mirar**. Review the explanation in (f) on page 14. Review the other forms of **mirar** (verb 314) in A, B, and D.

19. **A** The sentence states that when I entered the living room, my mother *was reading* and my father *was writing*. Review the uses of the **imperfecto de indicativo** in such a sentence structure and the explanation in (b) on page 15. Review the other forms of **leer** (verb 290) in B, C, and D.

20. **D** The sentence states that this morning my sister *was singing* in the bathroom when I woke up. The explanation here is the same as in no. 19 above. Review the other forms of **cantar** (verb 109) in A, B, and C.

Test 2

1. **D** You are asking the clerk if *there are* tickets for Saturday. **Hay** is the word for *there are* or *there is*. Review the forms of **haber** (verb 257) in choices A, B, and C.

2. **D** The polite form of saying *I would like* or *I should like* is **quisiera,** which is the **imperfecto de subjuntivo** of **querer**. Review it at the top of page 24. Also, study the other forms of **querer** (verb 390) in choices A, B, and C.

3. **A** You are asking the clerk, *How do I pay?* That means you need the 1st person singular of the **presente de indicativo** in A. Review the other forms of **pagar** (verb 341) in choices B, C, and D.

4. **C** You need the 3rd pers. sing. **empieza** in C because the subject, **la función** (the performance) is 3rd pers. sing. Study the other forms of **empezar** (verb 205) in choices A, B, and D.

5. **A** Review the uses of **ser** (verb 438) and **estar** (verb 230) listed with those verbs. There is nothing in the sentence that requires a form of **estar** in B, or the presente de subjuntivo in C, and nothing that requires the **imperfecto de subjuntivo** in D. Review the forms of **estar** and **ser**.

Answers to Verb Tests with Explanations   **79**

Test 3

1. **Ellos estudian bien, también.** Study the **presente de indicativo** of estudiar (verb 232).
2. **Ellas escriben bien, también.** Study the **presente de indicativo** of escribir (verb 224).
3. **Yo estoy leyendo un libro en la cama, también.** Study the formation of the progressive present beginning on page 4. Note the irregular present participle **(gerundio)** of **leer** (leyendo; verb 290) on page 3.
4. **Ellos van de compras, también.** Study the **presente de indicativo** of ir on page 402 and the idiomatic expression **ir de compras** on the following page.
5. **Yo fui al cine, también.** Study the **pretérito** of ir (verb 280).
6. **Nosotros hemos comido bien, también.** Study the **perfecto de indicativo** (Tense No. 8) of **comer** (verb 128).
7. **Ellos están bien, también.** Study the **presente de indicativo** of estar (verb 230).
8. **Ellas se sentaron, también.** Study the **pretérito** of **sentarse** (verb 434).
9. **Yo me lavé la cara, también.** Study the **pretérito** of **lavarse** (verb 289).
10. **Yo sé nadar, también.** Study the **presente de indicativo** of saber (verb 423).
11. **Él ha cantado bien, también.** Study the **perfecto de indicativo** of cantar (verb 109).
12. **Yo escogí un carro costoso, también.** Study the **pretérito** of escoger (verb 223).
13. **Ellos han terminado la lección, también.** Study the **perfecto de indicativo** of terminar (verb 470).
14. **Él escribió una carta, también.** Study the **pretérito** of escribir (verb 224).
15. **Yo tengo que estudiar, también.** Study the **presente de indicativo** of tener (verb 468) and the idiomatic expression **tener que** + inf. on the following page.
16. **Ella ha devuelto los libros a la biblioteca, también.** Study the **perfecto de indicativo** of devolver (verb 186). Note on page 6 that the past participle is irregular.
17. **Nosotros hemos dicho la verdad, también.** Study the **perfecto de indicativo** of decir (verb 161) and the irregular past participle dicho on page 6.
18. **Ellos se acuestan a las diez, también.** Study the **presente de indicativo** of acostarse (verb 21) and note the change in spelling in the stem for o to ue when o in **acostarse** is stressed.
19. **Yo he leído un libro, también.** Study the **perfecto de indicativo** of leer (verb 290). Note the irregular past participle leído on page 6.
20. **Nosotros queremos hacerlo, también.** Study the **presente de indicativo** of querer (verb 390) and note the change in spelling in the stem of this verb when it is stressed.

Test 4

1. **D** You need the **imperfecto de indicativo** of ir because, according to the sense of the statement, the action was performed habitually in the past. Study the explanation and examples in (c) on page 15. Also, review the forms of ir (verb 280) in choices A, B, and C.
2. **A** You need the **imperfecto de indicativo** of vivir (verb 495) for the same reason and explanation given in the preceding statment no. 1 above. Review the forms of vivir in choices B, C, and D.
3. **D** You need the **imperfecto de indicativo** of ser (verb 438) because, according to the sense of the statement, there is a description of a physical condition in the past. Study the explanation and examples in (d) on page 15. Also, review the forms of ser in choices A, B, and C.
4. **A** You need the **imperfecto de indicativo** of ser (verb 438) because you are asking what time it was in the past. Study the explanation and examples in (e) at the top of page 16. Also, review the forms of ser.

5.   C   You need the **imperfecto de indicativo** of **ser** (verb 438) in the 3rd person plural because the time stated is plural (**tres**). Study again the explanation and examples in (e) at the top of page 16. Review the **pretérito** of **telefonear** (verb 463).

6.   A   And here, too, you need the **imperfecto de indicativo** of **mirar** (verb 314). Study the explanation and examples in (f) on page 16. Also, review the forms of **mirar** in choices B, C, and D.

7.   A   You need the infinitive form of **venir** (verb 488) because in front of it there is a verb form (**quiere**). Robert says that *he wants to come* to my house. Review verbs that take no preposition + infinitive in section K, beginning on page 676. On page 677 **querer** + inf. is listed. Also, review the other forms of **venir** in choices B, C, and D.

8.   C   You must complete the **perfecto de indicativo** tense by using the past participle **visto** because the helping verb **has** is stated in front of the missing verb form. Review this tense of **ver** (verb 489) and the choices in A, B, and D. Also study the irregular past participles on page 6.

9.   A   You need the **imperfecto de indicativo** of **querer** (verb 390) because you are dealing with an indirect quotation in the past. Casandra said that *she wanted* to come to my house. Compare this sentence with the one in number 7 above. Study the explanation and example in (g) on page 16. Also, review the other forms of **querer** in choices B, C, and D.

10. C   The adverb **ayer** (yesterday) tells us that the verb is in the past. The subject is **amigo** (friend), 3rd person singular; therefore, the verb must be 3rd person singular also. Choice C is 3rd person singular in the **pretérito** of **llegar** (verb 297). Review the other forms of **llegar** in choices A, B, and D.

11. B   The adverb **anoche** (last night) tells us that the verb is in the past. The subject is **María,** which is 3rd person singular; therefore, the verb must also be 3rd person singular. Choice B is 3rd person singular in the **pretérito** or **ir** (verb 280). Review the other forms of **ir** in choices A, C, and D.

12. B   **Ayer por la tarde** (yesterday afternoon) tells us that the verb is in the past. The statement asks *what happened* in the street. Review the forms of **pasar** (verb 347) in the **presente de indicativo** (choice A), the **pretérito** (choices B and C), and in the **futuro** (choice D). Also, check out example 3 at the top of page 17.

13. B   According to the sense of the sentence, the verb must be in the past. The subject is **yo,** 1st person singular; therefore, the verb must also be 1st person singular. Review the **pretérito** of **tomar** (verb 473) in choices A and B, as well as the choices in C and D.

14. C   The two verbs in the sentence (**salí** and **tomé**) are in the **pretérito**. The missing verb form must also be in the same tense and person because of the sense indicated in the statement. Review the forms of **llegar** (verb 297), **salir** (verb 426), and **tomar** (verb 473). Also, check out example 5 at the top of page 17.

15. B   Because of the subject **yo,** you need the 1st person singular of **conocer** (verb 134) in the **pretérito**. According to the sense of the statement, **la semana pasada** (last week) indicates a past tense. Review the other choices of verb forms of **conocer**. Also, examine example number 1 in the middle of page 17.

16. C   You are talking to José and are using the familiar **tú** form of the verb in the 2nd person singular. You are asking him when he found out the truth. The only **tú** form in the **pretérito** among the choices is in C. Review the other forms of **saber** (verb 423) in the other choices. Also, note the special use of **saber** in the **pretérito** in example number 6 on page 17.

17. A The subject is **yo**. You need the **futuro**, 1st person singular of **hacer** (verb 260) because **la semana que viene** (next week) is stated. Review the **futuro** and **pretérito** of **hacer**. Also, review the uses and formation of the future tense, with many examples, on pages 18 and 19.

18. A The subject is **nosotros**. You need the **futuro,** 1st person plural of **ir** (verb 280) because **el verano que viene** (next summer) is stated. Review the other forms of **ir** in choices B, C, and D.

19. C Mary say that she *will come* tomorrow. The **futuro** of **venir** (verb 488) is needed in the 3rd person singular because **María** is 3rd person singular. Review the forms of **venir** among the other choices. It would make no sense to use the **pretérito** of **venir** in A and B because **mañana** (tomorrow) implies future time. Also, review the uses of the future tense on page 18, in particular example (c), and the formation of that tense on page 19.

20. B If Miguel had money, he *would go* to Spain. The only conditional form of **ir** (verb 280) is in B. A and C are future tense. D is the present tense. Review the forms of **ir**. Also, review the uses of the **potencial simple** (conditional) with examples on page 19, in particular example (a).
Let's look at the dependent clause in this sentence: **Si Miguel** *tuviera* **dinero** . . . (If Miguel *had* money . . .). The form *tuviera* is the **imperfecto de subjuntivo** (Tense No. 7) of **tener** (verb 468). That form is used because si (if) introduces the clause. Typical examples in English of this sort of thing are the following: If *I were* king, if *I were* you, he talks to me as if *I were* a child. These are contrary to fact conditions. Review the uses and formation of the **imperfecto de subjuntivo,** with examples, on page 23, in particular, the example at the top of page 24.

Test 5

1. B Review the explanation and examples of the use of **gustar** (def. and imp.) and the usual forms of the verb, as well as the examples that follow.

2. A The subject **tú** agrees with the verb **asistes** because they are both 2nd person singular, present indicative. Review the other tenses of **asistir** (verb 74).

3. A Review the explanation and use of **hace** + length of time in example (f) on page 14, and with the verb **hacer** (verb 260).

4. A The use of **empieza** is in the question, as well as in the answer. Study the forms of **empezar** (verb 205) in choices A, B, C, and D. Note that the second e in this verb changes to **ie** when it is stressed. Also, **z** changes to **c** when the vowel **e** follows it.

5. C You need the infinitive form **venir** because a verb form (**puedes**) precedes it. Review verbs that take no preposition + infinitive in section K, beginning on page 676. On page 676, **poder** + inf. is listed. What you are saying to Dolores is "You can come" (You *are able to come*). Review the forms of **venir** (verb 488) in choices A, B, C, and D.

6. C You are telling Dolores, "Then, *let's go* to my Spanish class." Review the forms of **ir** (verb 280) in the four choices, giving special attention to **vamos** *(let's go)* in the imperative near the bottom of that page. When you are not sure of the translation into English of a Spanish verb tense, review pages 11 and 12 where there is a sample English verb conjugated in all the tenses.

Test 6

Note: In this test, the verb form given in each sentence is in the imperative (command) mood. You are also given a verb in parentheses to use in place of the one in the sentence. Review the **imperativo** on pages 27 to 29. If you had any difficulty with the imperative forms of the verbs used in this test, you must turn to the page in this book among the 501 verbs and review the forms that are given near the bottom of each page under **imperativo.**

1. Diga la palabra.
2. Bebe la leche.
3. Parta inmediatamente.
4. Cierra la ventana.
5. Tome la maleta sobre la cama.
6. Escriba la palabra.
7. Enviemos la carta.
8. Lean el poema.
9. Salgamos ahora.
10. Levántese, por favor.
11. Compre la casa.
12. Vengan ahora.
13. Sécate.
14. Escoja estos guantes.
15. Bébalo.

Test 7

Note: Review the formation of regular verbs in the future (futuro) (Tense No. 4) at the top of page 19 and the conditional (**potencial simple**) (Tense No. 5) at the bottom of page 19.

1. Yo saldría.
2. Ud. tendría.
3. Nosotros seríamos.
4. Uds. estarían.
5. María querría.
6. Tú ganarías.
7. Ellos harían.
8. Ella cantaría.
9. José bailaría.
10. Tú escribirías.
11. Él sería.
12. Yo me lavaría.
13. Alberto se sentaría.
14. Nosotros nos sentiríamos.
15. Nosotros nos sentaríamos.
16. Yo aprendería.
17. Tú beberías.
18. Ud. sabría.
19. Miguel leería.
20. Nosotros iríamos.
21. Vosotros iríais.
22. Uds. dirían.
23. Ellos vendrían.
24. Ellas venderían.
25. José y Dora serían.
26. Los chicos comerían.
27. María y yo haríamos.
28. Elena y Ana pondrían.
29. Vosotros veríais.
30. Yo estudiaría.

Test 8

1. (a) No. Yo no saldré de casa esta noche.
   (b) Ellos no saldrán de casa esta noche tampoco.
   Review the **futuro** of **salir** among the 501 verbs in this book.
2. (a) No. Yo no quiero venir a tu casa esta tarde.
   (b) Nosotros no queremos venir a tu casa esta tarde tampoco.
   Review the **presente de indicativo** of **querer** among the 501 verbs.
3. (a) No. Yo no canté esta mañana.
   (b) Ellos no cantaron esta mañana tampoco.
   Review the **pretérito** of **cantar** among the 501 verbs.
4. (a) No. Yo no digo mentiras.
   (b) Ella no dice mentiras tampoco.
   Review the **presente de indicativo** of **decir** among the 501 verbs.
5. (a) No. Yo no fui al cine ayer.
   (b) Ellos no fueron al cine ayer tampoco.
   Review the **pretérito** of **ir** among the 501 verbs.

Test 9

1.	Yo fui al parque.	**8.**	Luis escribió cartas.
2.	Elisa miró la televisión.	**9.**	Marta aprendió la lección.
3.	El niño bebió la leche.	**10.**	Los Señores López vivieron en esta casa.
4.	Margarita hizo la lección.	**11.**	Yo hice el trabajo.
5.	José habló mucho.	**12.**	La señorita trajo el plato.
6.	Mi amigo pagó la cuenta.	**13.**	Pablo leyó el poema.
7.	Nosotros tomamos el desayuno a las ocho.	**14.**	Carlota dijo la verdad.
		15.	La profesora abrió el libro.

Test 10

1. **A**   Review the explanations and examples of the **potencial simple** (Tense No. 5), in particular, example (b) on page 19. Review the other forms of **gustar** (def. and imp.) and the examples that follow. Also, review the explanations and examples of **gustar**.

2. **A**   Review the explanation and examples in question number 20 in **Test 4.** The idea is the same here.

3. **C**   You need to complete the **pluscuamperfecto de indicativo** (Tense No. 9) because **había** is given as the helping verb. Review this tense and the other forms of **decir** (verb 161) in choices A, B, and D. Also, review the formation of the **pluscuamperfecto de indicativo** on pages 24 and 25. From time to time, refer to the regular formation of past participles and the list of irregular past participles on pages 5 and 6 where you will find **dicho.** Study example (c) 3 on page 19.

4. **A**   Review the **potencial simple** (Tense No. 5) on page 19, in particular, example (c) 2. Review the other forms of **venir** among the 501 verbs.

5. **A**   Review the **imperativo** on pages 27 to 29 and at the bottom of the page where **sentarse** is listed among the 501 verbs.

6. **C**   Study the explanations and examples of the uses of the **presente de subjuntivo** (Tense No. 6) on pages 20 to 23. See example (e) on page 20. Review the other forms of **hacer** among the 501 verbs.

7. **B**   Review the verbs of motion that take the preposition **a** + infinitive in section A on page 669. Study the other forms of **tomar** among the 501 verbs.

8. **D**   Review the formation of the progressive present beginning at the bottom of page 4. Study the regular formation of present participles and irregular present participles on pages 3 and 4. Study the other forms of **estudiar** among the 501 verbs.

9. **A**   Review example 2 on page 4. Also, review the other forms of **llorar** among the 501 verbs.

10. **D**   Study the explanations and examples of the uses of the **presente de subjuntivo** (Tense No. 6) on pages 20 to 23. See statement (e) on page 20 and example 3 at the top of page 21.

11. **B**   See explanation (f), example 1 on page 21. Review the other forms of **venir** among the 501 verbs.

12. **B**   See explanation (g), example 1 on page 21. Review the other forms of **comer** among the 501 verbs.

13. **D**   See explanation (h) on page 21 and example 1 at the top of page 22. Review the other forms of **llegar** among the 501 verbs.

14. **C**   See explanation (h) on page 21 and example 4 at the top of page 22. Review the other forms of **volver** among the 501 verbs.

15. A   See explanation (i), example 1 on page 22. Review the other forms of
ser among the 501 verbs.
16. D   See explanation (k) and the example on page 22. Review the other forms of
venir among the 501 verbs.
17. B   See explanation (l), example 1 on page 22. Review the other forms of **ser**
among the 501 verbs.
18. A   See explanation (l), example 2 on page 22. Review the other forms of
hablar among the 501 verbs.
19. C   See explanation (l), example 3 on page 22. Review the other forms of
poder among the 501 verbs.
20. C   Review the explanation, formation, and uses of the **imperfecto de subjuntivo** (Tense No. 7) on pages 23 and 24. See example 1 at the bottom of
page 23. Review the other forms of **hacer** among the 501 verbs.

Test 11

Note: The infinitive form of the verb is given in parentheses in front of the following
answers in case you had difficulty identifying any of the irregular verb forms. They are given
so you may verify the forms in the **presente de indicativo** and the **pretérito** by turning to
the page where the verbs are arranged alphabetically among the 501 verbs in this book.

1. (hablar) Yo hablé.
2. (aprender) Tú aprendiste.
3. (vivir) Ud. vivió aquí.
4. (trabajar) Él trabajó.
5. (decir) Ella dijo algo.
6. (ir) Uds. fueron al cine.
7. (pedir) Vosotros pedisteis algo.
8. (ser) Ellos fueron.
9. (beber) Ellas bebieron café.
10. (jugar) Juana jugó.
11. (tocar) Tú tocaste.
12. (morder) El perro mordió.
13. (oír) Ellos oyeron algo.
14. (escuchar) Uds. escucharon.
15. (estar) Yo estuve en casa.

16. (venir) Gabriela vino.
17. (dormir) El niño durmió.
18. (leer) Los alumnos leyeron.
19. (comer) Nosotros comimos.
20. (hacer) Vosotros hicisteis la lección.
21. (ir) Nosotros fuimos al teatro.
22. (pensar) Ellos pensaron.
23. (tener) Ellos tuvieron dinero.
24. (escribir) Alberto escribió.
25. (morir) Ella murió.
26. (comer) María y José comieron.
27. (oír) Yo oí la música.
28. (querer) Yo quise comer.
29. (estar) Ella estuvo en la escuela.
30. (ir) Yo fui a casa.

Test 12

Presente de indicativo
1. Yo hablo.
2. Tú bebes.
3. Ud. recibe.
4. Uds. abren.
5. Ellos hacen.

6. Nosotros aprendemos.
7. María lee.
8. Ellos aceptan.
9. Yo amo.
10. Tú escribes.

Imperfecto de indicativo
1. Yo cantaba.
2. Uds. daban.
3. Tú te bañabas.
4. Nosotros hacíamos.
5. Ud. hablaba.

6. Nosotros hallábamos.
7. Yo comprendía.
8. Uds. comían.
9. Yo me levantaba.
10. Ella vivía.

Pretérito

1. Yo hablé.
2. Tú compraste.
3. Ud. aprendió.
4. Nosotros corrimos.
5. Uds. recibieron.

6. Él cantó.
7. Ellos se apresuraron.
8. Uds. trajeron.
9. Ella vivió.
10. Ellas se lavaron.

Futuro

1. Yo bailaré.
2. Tú aprenderás.
3. Ud. irá.
4. Uds. vendrán.
5. Nosotros nos iremos.

6. Ud. recibirá.
7. Yo daré.
8. Ellos cantarán.
9. Ella comprenderá.
10. Uds. vivirán.

Potencial simple

1. Ella comprendería.
2. Uds. vivirían.
3. Ellos comprarían.
4. Yo daría.
5. Ud. recibiría.

6. Nosotros saltaríamos.
7. Ella dormiría.
8. Ellos entenderían.
9. Yo estaría.
10. Yo sería.

Presente de subjuntivo

1. que yo hable
2. que tú aprendas
3. que Ud. reciba
4. que él tanga
5. que ella esté

6. que Ud. sea
7. que Uds. canten
8. que nosotros nos casemos
9. que ella venga
10. que yo comprenda

Imperfecto de subjuntivo

1. que yo hablara *or* hablase
2. que él aprendiera *or* aprendiese
3. que Ud. viviera *or* viviese

4. que nosotros bailáramos *or* bailásemos
5. que ella bajara *or* bajase
6. que ellos comprendieran *or* comprendiesen

Test 13

1.	E	S	C	R	I	T	O		
2.	N	A	C	I	D	O		
3.	A	B	I	E	R	T	O	
4.	M	U	E	R	T	O		
5.	O	Í	D	O				
6.	R	E	Í	D	O		
7.	A	P	R	E	N	D	I	D	O
8.	D	I	C	H	O			
9.	O	B	T	E	N	I	D	O	

Test 14

Note: All the forms of **haber** (verb 257) in the seven simple tenses are given in the book. Verify your work by consulting that page. Remember that these verb forms are needed to form the seven compound tenses that are also on that page.

Test 15

Note: All the forms of **estar** (verb 230) in the seven simple tenses are given in the book. Verify your work by consulting that page. Remember that the verb forms in the **presente de indicativo** (Tense No. 1) of **estar** are needed to form the progressive present, as in **estoy trabajando** (I am working). The verb forms in the **imperfecto de indicativo** (Tense No. 2) of **estar** are needed to form the progressive past, as in **estaba trabajando** (I was working). Review page 4 to page 5. Review the formation of the present participles on pages 3 and 4 so that you may be able to form the progressive present and progressive past.

Test 16

Note: Keep in mind that to form the **pluscuamperfecto de indicativo** (Tense No. 9), you need to use the **imperfecto de indicativo** (Tense No. 2) of **haber** plus the past participle of the verb you are working with. Review the formation of the past participles on pages 5 and 6. Also, review Test 14.

1.	Yo había hablado.	11.	Yo había llegado.
2.	Tú habías aprendido.	12.	Tú habías escrito.
3.	Ud. había salido.	13.	Ud. había creído.
4.	Él había comprendido.	14.	Él había dicho.
5.	Ella había comprado.	15.	Ella había dado.
6.	El chico había comido.	16.	La chica había bebido.
7.	Nosotros habíamos ido.	17.	Nosotros habíamos oído.
8.	Yo había abierto.	18.	Uds. habían tenido.
9.	Uds. habían hecho.	19.	Ellos habían puesto.
10.	Ellas habían caído.	20.	Ellas habían cubierto.

Test 17

1. **C** See explanation (n) and the example on page 23. Review the other forms of **venir** among the 501 verbs.

2. **D** See the explanation, examples, and regular formation of the **imperfecto de subjuntivo** (Tense No. 7) on pages 23 and 24. Review the other forms of **comprender** among the 501 verbs.

3. **B** You need to complete the **perfecto de indicativo** (Tense No. 8) by selecting the past participle **hablado** because **he** is given in front of the missing verb form. Review the other verb forms of **hablar** among the 501 verbs.

4. **B** See the explanation, examples, and regular formation of the **imperfecto de subjuntivo** (Tense No. 7) on pages 23 and 24, in particular, the example at the top of page 24. Review the other forms of **ser** among the 501 verbs.

5. **A** You need to complete the **perfecto de indicativo** (Tense No. 8) by selecting the past participle **ganado** because **ha** is given in front of the missing verb form. See the explanation, examples, and regular formation of the **perfecto de**

indicativo on page 24, in particular, example 3. Review the other forms of
ganar among the 501 verbs.

6. **B**   The infinitive form **salir** is needed because a verb form (**quiero**) precedes it.
Review section K on pages 676 and 677, where you will find **querer** + infinitive. Review the other forms of **salir** among the 501 verbs.

7. **A**   You need the infinitive form **terminar** because the preposition a precedes the
missing verb form. Review section A on page 669, where you will find **ir** and
other verbs of motion that take the preposition a + infinitive. Also, review the
other forms of **terminar** among the 501 verbs.

8. **B**   The infinitive form **decir** is needed because a verb form (**quiere**) precedes the
missing verb form. Review section K on pages 676 and 677 where you will
find **querer** + infinitive. See also the two examples given there. Review the
other forms of **decir** among the 501 verbs.

9. **B**   You need to complete the progressive present by selecting the present participle
nevando because **está** is given in front of the missing verb form. Review the
formation of the progressive forms on pages 4 and 5. Also, review the present
participles on pages 3 and 4. As for the other forms of **nevar** in the choices,
turn to the page where **nevar** is given among the 501 verbs.

10. **B**   The sentence means, *When I arrived home, my brother had gone out.* You need
to complete the **pluscuamperfecto de indicativo** (Tense No. 9) by selecting the
past participle **salido** because the helping verb **había** is given in front of the
missing verb form. Review the explanation, formation, and examples of this
tense on pages 24 and 25, in particular, example 1. As for the other forms of
salir in the choices, turn to the page where **salir** is given among the 501 verbs.

Test 18

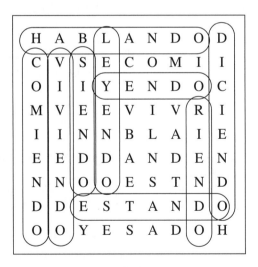

Test 19

1. **C**   You need the 3rd person plural, **presente de indicativo** of **tener** because you
are telling Julia it seems to you that *they* (the dogs/**los perros**) *are* afraid. Note
the idiomatic expression **tener miedo** (to be afraid), which is listed after **tener**.
Review the other forms of **tener** among the 501 verbs.

2. **B** You need **estar** because you are saying that the little cat must *be* sick. Review the uses of **estar** on the pages following that verb. Also, the infinitive form **estar** is needed because **debe** is a verb that precedes the missing verb form. Generally speaking, the infinitive form of a verb is used when it is preceded by a conjugated verb form. Review the forms of the verbs in the choices among the 501 verbs: **estar, ser, tener.**

3. **A** Review again the difference in the uses of **ser** and **estar**. See the pages that follow each verb. Also, review the forms of these two verbs among the 501 verbs.

4. **B** You are telling Julia that Rojo, the dog, is quiet because he *is* in a strange place. Review the reason for **estar** in (b) on the pages that follow the verb conjugation.

5. **A** You need the **presente de indicativo** of **llevar** because the situation is taking place at the present time. Review the other choices of forms and tenses of **llevar** where the verb appears among the 501 verbs.

Test 20

Note: If you are still not sure of verb forms in the **pretérito,** you must review all the verbs used in this test by turning to the page where they appear among the 501 verbs.

1. Roberto escribió la lección.
2. La Señora Fuentes se levantó.
3. Yo ofrecí un regalo.
4. María trabajó.
5. El alumno leyó una carta.
6. El Señor Robles murió.
7. Margarita salió.
8. Ricardo habló.
9. Yo saludé a María.
10. Mi padre tuvo un accidente.
11. Mi hermana hizo la comida.
12. ¿Fue usted a España?
13. ¿Se vistieron los chicos?
14. Esta mañana yo me lavé.
15. Yo no quise hacerlo.

Test 21

15, 1, 14, 2, 3, 13, 12, 4, 11, 5, 7, 6, 8, 9, 10

Test 22

Note: Review all the verbs used in the sentences in this test in the **presente de indicativo** (Tense No. 1) and in the **pretérito** (Tense No. 3) by turning to the page where they appear among the 501 verbs in this book. If you were not able to identify some of the irregular verb forms in the sentences, consult the index of common irregular Spanish verb forms identified by infinitive beginning on page 678. For example, in the first sentence, **cojo** is given as an irregular form of **coger.** Then, look up **coger** among the 501 verbs.

1. Yo cogí la pelota.
2. Ud. durmió demasiado.
3. Tú fuiste al cine.
4. Él habló mucho.
5. Ella escribió una tarjeta.
6. Nosotros comimos en este restaurante.
7. Vosotros aceptasteis el dinero.
8. Uds. dieron de comer a los pájaros.
9. Yo fui al teatro.
10. Ellas fueron a casa.
11. Ellos estuvieron en la piscina.
12. Yo me senté cerca de la ventana.
13. Ud. se levantó.
14. Nosotros nos apresuramos.
15. Los muchachos vinieron a verme.
16. Berta estuvo enferma.
17. Mi madre hizo un bizcocho.
18. Yo busqué mis libros.
19. La profesora brió la puerta.
20. Me gustó el helado. *[The subject in this sentence is el helado. See gustar.]*

Test 23

```
B  U  H  O  H  B  U  T  O
H  B  U  A  G  I  R  O  T
H  U  B  E  V  I  S  T  O
R  I  O  E  S  C  I  R  T
H  U  E  B  I  M  O  E  S
O  R  S  E  I  B  U  I  H
E  S  C  R  I  O  T  B  U
V  I  R  T  O  A  B  A  E
H  A  I  B  A  B  I  E  R
I  S  T  O  V  H  U  B  E
R  O  O  T  R  O  T  U  I
R  C  S  E  E  B  U  H  O
```

Test 24

Note: All the forms of **haber** (verb 257) in the seven simple tenses are given in the book. Verify your work by consulting that page. Remember that these verb forms are needed to form the seven compound tenses (Tense Nos. 8 to 14). Review again page 32.

Test 25

1. Yo sé nadar, también.
2. Ellos salen de la escuela a las tres, trambién.
3. Ella está sentada, también.
4. Ellos son inteligentes, también.
5. Ellos sonríen, también.
6. Ellos leyeron el libro, también.
7. Nosotros recibimos muchos regalos, también.
8. Él bebió café con leche, también.
9. Yo oí la música, también.
10. Ellos durmieron mucho, también.
11. Ellos fueron al cine, también.
12. Ellos se acuestan a las diez, también.
13. Ellas han dicho la verdad, también.
14. Ellos hicieron la lección, también.
15. Él ha cantado bien, también.

Test 26

Note: Turn to the page among the 501 verbs and verify the form of the verb given in (a) in the following answers. Also, consult the page references that are given here.

1. (a) **salir**
   (b) **pretérito**
   (c) 3rd pers., sing. (The subject is Sancho.)
2. (a) **decir**
   (b) **gerundio** (pres. part.)
   (c) Review present participles on page 3.

3. (a) **poder**
   (b) **presente de indicativo**
   (c) 3rd pers., sing. (**Ud.** understood. Sancho is talking to **Don Quixote.**)
4. (a) **llegar**
   (b) **pretérito**
   (c) 1st pers., sing.
5. (a) **darse**
   (b) **pretérito**
   (c) 3rd pers., pl. See **darse** on the page that follows **dar** (verb 158).
6. (a) **bajar**
   (b) **imperativo**
   (c) 3rd pers., sing. (**Ud.**) (**baje, baje**/come down, come down)
7. (a) **ser**
   (b) **presente de indicativo**
   (c) 3rd pers., pl.
8. (a) **echar**
   (b) **perfecto de indicativo**
   (c) 1st pers., pl. (we have thrown)
9. (a) **aguardar**
   (b) progressive present
   (c) Review example 1 in the section on uses of the present participle as well as examples 1 and 2 in the section on the Progressive forms of tenses. Both sections are on page 4. (**nos están aguardando**/they are waiting for us)
10. (a) **decir**
    (b) progressive present
    (c) Review example 1 in the section on uses of the present participle as well as examples 1 and 2 in the section on the Progressive forms of tenses. Both sections are on page 4. (**la olla que está diciendo**/the pot that is saying)
11. (a) **comer**
    (b) **imperativo**
    (c) 2nd pers., sing. (**tú**)
    (**come, come**/eat, eat; ¡**cóme**me, **cóme**me!/eat me! eat me!)

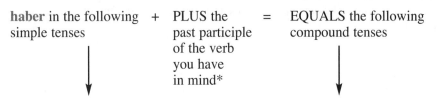

haber in the following + PLUS the = EQUALS the following
simple tenses   past participle   compound tenses
                   of the verb
                   you have
                   in mind*

1. Presente de indicativo	8. Perfecto de indicativo
2. Imperfecto de indicativo	9. Pluscuamperfecto de indicativo
3. Pretérito	10. Pretérito anterior (Pret. perfecto)
4. Futuro	11. Futuro perfecto
5. Potencial simple	12. Potencial compuesto
6. Presente de subjuntivo	13. Perfecto de subjuntivo
7. Imperfecto de subjuntivo	14. Pluscuamperfecto de subjuntivo

*To know how to form a past participle, see page 5.

Subject Pronouns

(a) The subject pronouns for all verb forms on the following pages have been omitted in order to emphasize the verb forms, which is what this book is all about.

(b) The subject pronouns that have been omitted are, as you know, as follows:

singular	*plural*
yo	nosotros (nosotras)
tú	vosotros (vosotras)
Ud. (él, ella)	Uds. (ellos, ellas)

The Spanish Alphabet and the New System of Alphabetizing

The Association of Spanish Language Academies met in Madrid for its 10th Annual Congress on April 27, 1994 and voted to eliminate **CH** and **LL** as separate letters of the Spanish alphabet.

Words beginning with **CH** will be listed alphabetically under the letter **C**. Words beginning with **LL** will be listed alphabetically under the letter **L**. The two separate letters historically have had separate headings in dictionaries and alphabetized word lists. Spanish words that contain the letter **ñ** are now alphabetized accordingly with words that do not contain the tilde over the **n**. For example, the Spanish system of alphabetizing used to place the word **andar** before **añadir** because the **ñ** would fall in after all words containing **n**. According to the new system, **añadir** is placed before **andar** because alphabetizing is now done letter by letter. The same applies to words containing **rr**.

The move was taken to simplify dictionaries, to make Spanish more compatible with English, and to aid translation and computer standardization. The vote was 17 in favor, 1 opposed, and 3 abstentions. Ecuador voted "no" and Panama, Nicaragua, and Uruguay abstained. (*The New York Times,* International Section, May 1, 1994, p. 16).

Essential 55 verb list

Beginning students should pay careful attention to the 55 verbs in this list. We have chosen them because they are useful for learning essential conjugations, tricky spelling changes, and common usage. We have also highlighted certain pairs of verbs to help you understand the difference between a reflexive and a nonreflexive verb. If you study the verbs on this list, you will be able to conjugate just about any verb you come across and you will be able to express yourself in correct idiomatic Spanish.

acabar	ir/irse
andar	*(Verb Pair)*
aprender	leer
caer/caerse	llamar/llamarse
(Verb Pair)	*(Verb Pair)*
cantar	llevar
comenzar	mirar/mirarse
comer	*(Verb Pair)*
comprar	oír
conducir	pagar
conocer	pensar
construir	perder
contar	poder
creer	poner/ponerse
dar	*(Verb Pair)*
deber	quedarse
decir	querer
dormir	saber
entrar	salir
escribir	sentir/sentirse
estar	*(Verb Pair)*
estudiar	ser
gustar *(See*	tener
Defective and	tomar
Impersonal	traer
Verbs)	venir
haber	ver
hablar	vivir
hacer	volver

Subject Pronouns

singular	plural
yo	nosotros (nosotras)
tú	vosotros (vosotras)
Ud. (él, ella)	Uds. (ellos, ellas)

Abbreviations

adj.   adjetivo (adjective)

ant.   anterior

comp.   compuesto (compound, perfect)

e.g.   for example

fut.   futuro (future)

i.e.   that is, that is to say

imp.   imperfecto (imperfect)

ind.   indicativo (indicative)

inf.   infinitivo (infinitive)

p.   página (page)

part.   participio (participle)

part. pas.   participio de pasado, participio pasivo (past participle)

part. pr.   participio de presente, participio activo, gerundio (present participle)

pas.   pasado, pasivo (past, passive)

perf.   perfecto (perfect)

perf. ind.   perfecto de indicativo (present perfect indicative)

perf. subj.   perfecto de subjuntivo (present perfect or past subjunctive)

plpf.   pluscuamperfecto (pluperfect)

pot.   potencial (conditional)

pot. comp.   potencial compuesto (conditional perfect)

pr. or *pres.*   presente (present)

prep.   preposición (preposition)

pres. or *pr.*   presente (present)

pret.   pretérito (preterit)

subj.   subjuntivo (subjunctive)

Alphabetical Listing of
501 Spanish Verbs
Fully Conjugated in
All the Tenses and Moods

Regular **-ir** verb   to knock down, to overthrow, to throw down

The Seven Simple Tenses		The Seven Compound Tenses	
Singular	Plural	Singular	Plural

1 presente de indicativo

abato	abatimos		
abates	abatís		
abate	abaten		

8 perfecto de indicativo

he abatido	hemos abatido		
has abatido	habéis abatido		
ha abatido	han abatido		

2 imperfecto de indicativo

abatía	abatíamos
abatías	abatíais
abatía	abatían

9 pluscuamperfecto de indicativo

había abatido	habíamos abatido
habías abatido	habíais abatido
había abatido	habían abatido

3 pretérito

abatí	abatimos
abatiste	abatisteis
abatió	abatieron

10 pretérito anterior

hube abatido	hubimos abatido
hubiste abatido	hubisteis abatido
hubo abatido	hubieron abatido

4 futuro

abatiré	abatiremos
abatirás	abatiréis
abatirá	abatirán

11 futuro perfecto

habré abatido	habremos abatido
habrás abatido	habréis abatido
habrá abatido	habrán abatido

5 potencial simple

abatiría	abatiríamos
abatirías	abatiríais
abatiría	abatirían

12 potencial compuesto

habría abatido	habríamos abatido
habrías abatido	habríais abatido
habría abatido	habrían abatido

6 presente de subjuntivo

abata	abatamos
abatas	abatáis
abata	abatan

13 perfecto de subjuntivo

haya abatido	hayamos abatido
hayas abatido	hayáis abatido
haya abatido	hayan abatido

7 imperfecto de subjuntivo

abatiera	abatiéramos
abatieras	abatierais
abatiera	abatieran
OR	
abatiese	abatiésemos
abatieses	abatieseis
abatiese	abatiesen

14 pluscuamperfecto de subjuntivo

hubiera abatido	hubiéramos abatido
hubieras abatido	hubierais abatido
hubiera abatido	hubieran abatido
OR	
hubiese abatido	hubiésemos abatido
hubieses abatido	hubieseis abatido
hubiese abatido	hubiesen abatido

imperativo

—	abatamos
abate; no abatas	abatid; no abatáis
abata	abatan

Words and expressions related to this verb

abatidamente dejectedly
el abatimiento abasement, depression, discouragement
abatir el ánimo to feel discouraged, low in spirit

batir to beat, strike
batir palmas to applaud, clap
abatido, abatida dejected

Can't find the verb you're looking for?
Check the back pages of this book for a list of over 2,100 additional verbs!

The subject pronouns are found on page 93.

abrasar (2)

to burn, to set on fire

Gerundio **abrasando** — Part. pas. **abrasado**

Regular **-ar** verb

The Seven Simple Tenses		The Seven Compound Tenses	
Singular	Plural	Singular	Plural
1 presente de indicativo		**8 perfecto de indicativo**	
abraso	abrasamos	he abrasado	hemos abrasado
abrasas	abrasáis	has abrasado	habéis abrasado
abrasa	abrasan	ha abrasado	han abrasado
2 imperfecto de indicativo		**9 pluscuamperfecto de indicativo**	
abrasaba	abrasábamos	había abrasado	habíamos abrasado
abrasabas	abrasabais	habías abrasado	habíais abrasado
abrasaba	abrasaban	había abrasado	habían abrasado
3 pretérito		**10 pretérito anterior**	
abrasé	abrasamos	hube abrasado	hubimos abrasado
abrasaste	abrasasteis	hubiste abrasado	hubisteis abrasado
abrasó	abrasaron	hubo abrasado	hubieron abrasado
4 futuro		**11 futuro perfecto**	
abrasaré	abrasaremos	habré abrasado	habremos abrasado
abrasarás	abrasaréis	habrás abrasado	habréis abrasado
abrasará	abrasarán	habrá abrasado	habrán abrasado
5 potencial simple		**12 potencial compuesto**	
abrasaría	abrasaríamos	habría abrasado	habríamos abrasado
abrasarías	abrasaríais	habrías abrasado	habríais abrasado
abrasaría	abrasarían	habría abrasado	habrían abrasado
6 presente de subjuntivo		**13 perfecto de subjuntivo**	
abrase	abrasemos	haya abrasado	hayamos abrasado
abrases	abraséis	hayas abrasado	hayáis abrasado
abrase	abrasen	haya abrasado	hayan abrasado
7 imperfecto de subjuntivo		**14 pluscuamperfecto de subjuntivo**	
abrasara	abrasáramos	hubiera abrasado	hubiéramos abrasado
abrasaras	abrasarais	hubieras abrasado	hubierais abrasado
abrasara	abrasaran	hubiera abrasado	hubieran abrasado
OR		OR	
abrasase	abrasásemos	hubiese abrasado	hubiésemos abrasado
abrasases	abrasaseis	hubieses abrasado	hubieseis abrasado
abrasase	abrasasen	hubiese abrasado	hubiesen abrasado

imperativo	
—	abrasemos
abrasa; no abrases	abrasad; no abraséis
abrase	abrasen

Words and expressions related to this verb

abrasadamente ardently, fervently
abrasado, abrasada burning; flushed with anger
el abrasamiento burning, excessive passion

abrasarse vivo to burn with passion
abrasarse de amor to be passionately in love
abrasarse en deseos to become full of desire

Get acquainted with what preposition goes with what verb on pages 669–677.

Regular **-ar** verb endings with spelling change: to embrace, to hug; to clamp
z becomes **c** before **e**

The Seven Simple Tenses		The Seven Compound Tenses	
Singular	Plural	Singular	Plural

A

1 presente de indicativo		8 perfecto de indicativo	
abrazo	**abrazamos**	**he abrazado**	**hemos abrazado**
abrazas	**abrazáis**	**has abrazado**	**habéis abrazado**
abraza	**abrazan**	**ha abrazado**	**han abrazado**

2 imperfecto de indicativo		9 pluscuamperfecto de indicativo	
abrazaba	**abrazábamos**	**había abrazado**	**habíamos abrazado**
abrazabas	**abrazabais**	**habías abrazado**	**habíais abrazado**
abrazaba	**abrazaban**	**había abrazado**	**habían abrazado**

3 pretérito		10 pretérito anterior	
abracé	**abrazamos**	**hube abrazado**	**hubimos ábrazado**
abrazaste	**abrazasteis**	**hubiste abrazado**	**hubisteis abrazado**
abrazó	**abrazaron**	**hubo abrazado**	**hubieron abrazado**

4 futuro		11 futuro perfecto	
abrazaré	**abrazaremos**	**habré abrazado**	**habremos abrazado**
abrazarás	**abrazaréis**	**habrás abrazado**	**habréis abrazado**
abrazará	**abrazarán**	**habrá abrazado**	**habrán abrazado**

5 potencial simple		12 potencial compuesto	
abrazaría	**abrazaríamos**	**habría abrazado**	**habríamos abrazado**
abrazarías	**abrazaríais**	**habrías abrazado**	**habríais abrazado**
abrazaría	**abrazarían**	**habría abrazado**	**habrían abrazado**

6 presente de subjuntivo		13 perfecto de subjuntivo	
abrace	**abracemos**	**haya abrazado**	**hayamos abrazado**
abraces	**abracéis**	**hayas abrazado**	**hayáis abrazado**
abrace	**abracen**	**haya abrazado**	**hayan abrazado**

7 imperfecto de subjuntivo		14 pluscuamperfecto de subjuntivo	
abrazara	**abrazáramos**	**hubiera abrazado**	**hubiéramos abrazado**
abrazaras	**abrazarais**	**hubieras abrazado**	**hubierais abrazado**
abrazara	**abrazaran**	**hubiera abrazado**	**hubieran abrazado**
OR		OR	
abrazase	**abrazásemos**	**hubiese abrazado**	**hubiésemos abrazado**
abrazases	**abrazaseis**	**hubieses abrazado**	**hubieseis abrazado**
abrazase	**abrazasen**	**hubiese abrazado**	**hubiesen abrazado**

imperativo

—	**abracemos**
abraza; no abraces	**abrazad; no abracéis**
abrace	**abracen**

Words related to this verb
un abrazo   embrace, hug
el abrazamiento   embracing
un abrazo de Juanita   Love, Juanita

una abrazada   embrace
una abrazadera   clamp, clasp

Don't forget to study the section on defective and impersonal verbs. It's right after this main list.

The subject pronouns are found on page 93.

abrir (4)   Gerundio **abriendo**   Part. pas. **abierto**

to open

Regular **-ir** verb endings with spelling change: irregular past participle

The Seven Simple Tenses		The Seven Compound Tenses	
Singular	Plural	Singular	Plural
1 presente de indicativo		**8 perfecto de indicativo**	
abro	abrimos	he abierto	hemos abierto
abres	abrís	has abierto	habéis abierto
abre	abren	ha abierto	han abierto
2 imperfecto de indicativo		**9 pluscuamperfecto de indicativo**	
abría	abríamos	había abierto	habíamos abierto
abrías	abríais	habías abierto	habíais abierto
abría	abrían	había abierto	habían abierto
3 pretérito		**10 pretérito anterior**	
abrí	abrimos	hube abierto	hubimos abierto
abriste	abristeis	hubiste abierto	hubisteis abierto
abrió	abrieron	hubo abierto	hubieron abierto
4 futuro		**11 futuro perfecto**	
abriré	abriremos	habré abierto	habremos abierto
abrirás	abriréis	habrás abierto	habréis abierto
abrirá	abrirán	habrá abierto	habrán abierto
5 potencial simple		**12 potencial compuesto**	
abriría	abriríamos	habría abierto	habríamos abierto
abrirías	abriríais	habrías abierto	habríais abierto
abriría	abrirían	habría abierto	habrían abierto
6 presente de subjuntivo		**13 perfecto de subjuntivo**	
abra	abramos	haya abierto	hayamos abierto
abras	abráis	hayas abierto	hayáis abierto
abra	abran	haya abierto	hayan abierto
7 imperfecto de subjuntivo		**14 pluscuamperfecto de subjuntivo**	
abriera	abriéramos	hubiera abierto	hubiéramos abierto
abrieras	abrierais	hubieras abierto	hubierais abierto
abriera	abrieran	hubiera abierto	hubieran abierto
OR		OR	
abriese	abriésemos	hubiese abierto	hubiésemos abierto
abrieses	abrieseis	hubieses abierto	hubieseis abierto
abriese	abriesen	hubiese abierto	hubiesen abierto

imperativo	
—	abramos
abre; no abras	abrid; no abráis
abra	abran

Sentences using this verb and words related to it

La maestra dijo a los alumnos: — Abrid los libros en la página diez, por favor.
Todos los alumnos abrieron los libros en la página diez y Pablo comenzó a leer la lectura.

un abrimiento   opening
abrir paso   to make way

La puerta está abierta.   The door is open.
Los libros están abiertos.   The books are open.
en un abrir y cerrar de ojos   in a wink

Gerundio **absolviendo**   Part. pas. **absuelto**   **absolver** (5)

Regular **-er** verb endings with spelling change: irregular   to absolve, to acquit
past participle; stem change: Tenses 1, 6, Imperative

The Seven Simple Tenses		The Seven Compound Tenses	
Singular	Plural	Singular	Plural
1 presente de indicativo		**8 perfecto de indicativo**	
absuelvo	absolvemos	he absuelto	hemos absuelto
absuelves	absolvéis	has absuelto	habéis absuelto
absuelve	absuelven	ha absuelto	han absuelto
2 imperfecto de indicativo		**9 pluscuamperfecto de indicativo**	
absolvía	absolvíamos	había absuelto	habíamos absuelto
absolvías	absolvíais	habías absuelto	habíais absuelto
absolvía	absolvían	había absuelto	habían absuelto
3 pretérito		**10 pretérito anterior**	
absolví	absolvimos	hube absuelto	hubimos absuelto
absolviste	absolvisteis	hubiste absuelto	hubisteis absuelto
absolvió	absolvieron	hubo absuelto	hubieron absuelto
4 futuro		**11 futuro perfecto**	
absolveré	absolveremos	habré absuelto	habremos absuelto
absolverás	absolveréis	habrás absuelto	habréis absuelto
absolverá	absolverán	habrá absuelto	habrán absuelto
5 potencial simple		**12 potencial compuesto**	
absolvería	absolveríamos	habría absuelto	habríamos absuelto
absolverías	absolveríais	habrías absuelto	habríais absuelto
absolvería	absolverían	habría absuelto	habrían absuelto
6 presente de subjuntivo		**13 perfecto de subjuntivo**	
absuelva	absolvamos	haya absuelto	hayamos absuelto
absuelvas	absolváis	hayas absuelto	hayáis absuelto
absuelva	absuelvan	haya absuelto	hayan absuelto
7 imperfecto de subjuntivo		**14 pluscuamperfecto de subjuntivo**	
absolviera	absolviéramos	hubiera absuelto	hubiéramos absuelto
absolvieras	absolvierais	hubieras absuelto	hubierais absuelto
absolviera	absolvieran	hubiera absuelto	hubieran absuelto
OR		OR	
absolviese	absolviésemos	hubiese absuelto	hubiésemos absuelto
absolvieses	absolvieseis	hubieses absuelto	hubieseis absuelto
absolviese	absolviesen	hubiese absuelto	hubiesen absuelto

imperativo

	absolvamos
absuelve; no absuelvas	absolved; no absolváis
absuelva	absuelvan

Words and expressions related to this verb
la absolución absolution, acquittal, pardon
absolutamente absolutely
absoluto, absoluta absolute, unconditional
en absoluto absolutely
nada en absoluto nothing at all

el absolutismo absolutism, despotism
la absolución libre not guilty verdict
salir absuelto to come out clear of any charges

The subject pronouns are found on page 93.

abstenerse (6)   Gerundio absteniéndose   Part. pas. abstenido

to abstain   Reflexive irregular verb

The Seven Simple Tenses | The Seven Compound Tenses

Singular — Plural | Singular — Plural

1 presente de indicativo

me abstengo	nos abstenemos
te abstienes	os abstenéis
se abstiene	se abstienen

8 perfecto de indicativo

me he abstenido	nos hemos abstenido
te has abstenido	os habéis abstenido
se ha abstenido	se han abstenido

2 imperfecto de indicativo

me abstenía	nos absteníamos
te abstenías	os absteníais
se abstenía	se abstenían

9 pluscuamperfecto de indicativo

me había abstenido	nos habíamos abstenido
te habías abstenido	os habíais abstenido
se había abstenido	se habían abstenido

3 pretérito

me abstuve	nos abstuvimos
te abstuviste	os abstuvisteis
se abstuvo	se abstuvieron

10 pretérito anterior

me hube abstenido	nos hubimos abstenido
te hubiste abstenido	os hubisteis abstenido
se hubo abstenido	se hubieron abstenido

4 futuro

me abstendré	nos abstendremos
te abstendrás	os abstendréis
se abstendrá	se abstendrán

11 futuro perfecto

me habré abstenido	nos habremos abstenido
te habrás abstenido	os habréis abstenido
se habrá abstenido	se habrán abstenido

5 potencial simple

me abstendría	nos abstendríamos
te abstendrías	os abstendríais
se abstendría	se abstendrían

12 potencial compuesto

me habría abstenido	nos habríamos abstenido
te habrías abstenido	os habríais abstenido
se habría abstenido	se habrían abstenido

6 presente de subjuntivo

me abstenga	nos abstengamos
te abstengas	os abstengáis
se abstenga	se abstengan

13 perfecto de subjuntivo

me haya abstenido	nos hayamos abstenido
te hayas abstenido	os hayáis abstenido
se haya abstenido	se hayan abstenido

7 imperfecto de subjuntivo

me abstuviera	nos abstuviéramos
te abstuvieras	os abstuvierais
se abstuviera	se abstuvieran
OR	
me abstuviese	nos abstuviésemos
te abstuvieses	os abstuvieseis
se abstuviese	se abstuviesen

14 pluscuamperfecto de subjuntivo

me hubiera abstenido	nos hubiéramos abstenido
te hubieras abstenido	os hubierais abstenido
se hubiera abstenido	se hubieran abstenido
OR	
me hubiese abstenido	nos hubiésemos abstenido
te hubieses abstenido	os hubieseis abstenido
se hubiese abstenido	se hubiesen abstenido

imperativo

—	abstengámonos
abstente; no te abstengas	absteneos; no os abstengáis
absténgase	absténganse

Words and expressions related to this verb
la abstención   abstention, forbearance
abstenerse de   to abstain from, to refrain from
la abstinencia   abstinence, fasting
hacer abstinencia   to fast

el, la abstencionista   abstentionist
el abstencionismo   abstentionism
el día de abstinencia   day of fasting

Regular **-ir** verb   to annoy, to bore, to vex

The Seven Simple Tenses		The Seven Compound Tenses	
Singular	Plural	Singular	Plural
1 presente de indicativo		8 perfecto de indicativo	
aburro	**aburrimos**	**he aburrido**	**hemos aburrido**
aburres	**aburrís**	**has aburrido**	**habéis aburrido**
aburre	**aburren**	**ha aburrido**	**han aburrido**
2 imperfecto de indicativo		9 pluscuamperfecto de indicativo	
aburría	**aburríamos**	**había aburrido**	**habíamos aburrido**
aburrías	**aburríais**	**habías aburrido**	**habíais aburrido**
aburría	**aburrían**	**había aburrido**	**habían aburrido**
3 pretérito		10 pretérito anterior	
aburrí	**aburrimos**	**hube aburrido**	**hubimos aburrido**
aburriste	**aburristeis**	**hubiste aburrido**	**hubisteis aburrido**
aburrió	**aburrieron**	**hubo aburrido**	**hubieron aburrido**
4 futuro		11 futuro perfecto	
aburriré	**aburriremos**	**habré aburrido**	**habremos aburrido**
aburrirás	**aburriréis**	**habrás aburrido**	**habréis aburrido**
aburrirá	**aburrirán**	**habrá aburrido**	**habrán aburrido**
5 potencial simple		12 potencial compuesto	
aburriría	**aburriríamos**	**habría aburrido**	**habríamos aburrido**
aburrirías	**aburriríais**	**habrías aburrido**	**habríais aburrido**
aburriría	**aburrirían**	**habría aburrido**	**habrían aburrido**
6 presente de subjuntivo		13 perfecto de subjuntivo	
aburra	**aburramos**	**haya aburrido**	**hayamos aburrido**
aburras	**aburráis**	**hayas aburrido**	**hayáis aburrido**
aburra	**aburran**	**haya aburrido**	**hayan aburrido**
7 imperfecto de subjuntivo		14 pluscuamperfecto de subjuntivo	
aburriera	**aburriéramos**	**hubiera aburrido**	**hubiéramos aburrido**
aburrieras	**aburrierais**	**hubieras aburrido**	**hubierais aburrido**
aburriera	**aburrieran**	**hubiera aburrido**	**hubieran aburrido**
OR		OR	
aburriese	**aburriésemos**	**hubiese aburrido**	**hubiésemos aburrido**
aburrieses	**aburrieseis**	**hubieses aburrido**	**hubieseis aburrido**
aburriese	**aburriesen**	**hubiese aburrido**	**hubiesen aburrido**

imperativo

—	**aburramos**
aburre; no aburras	**aburrid; no aburráis**
aburra	**aburran**

Sentences using this verb and words related to it
**El profesor de español cree que Pedro está aburrido, que María está aburrida, que todos los
alumnos en la clase están aburridos. Pero la verdad es que no se aburren.**
Todos los alumnos se interesan en aprender español.

el aburrimiento   boredom, weariness   **una cara de aburrimiento**   a bored look
un aburridor, una aburridora   boring person   **la aburrición**   annoyance, ennui
See also **aburrirse.**

The subject pronouns are found on page 93.

103

to be bored, to grow tired, to grow weary

The Seven Simple Tenses		The Seven Compound Tenses	
Singular	Plural	Singular	Plural
1 presente de indicativo		8 perfecto de indicativo	
me aburro	nos aburrimos	me he aburrido	nos hemos aburrido
te aburres	os aburrís	te has aburrido	os habéis aburrido
se aburre	se aburren	se ha aburrido	se han aburrido
2 imperfecto de indicativo		9 pluscuamperfecto de indicativo	
me aburría	nos aburríamos	me había aburrido	nos habíamos aburrido
te aburrías	os aburríais	te habías aburrido	os habíais aburrido
se aburría	se aburrían	se había aburrido	se habían aburrido
3 pretérito		10 pretérito anterior	
me aburrí	nos aburrimos	me hube aburrido	nos hubimos aburrido
te aburriste	os aburristeis	te hubiste aburrido	os hubisteis aburrido
se aburrió	se aburrieron	se hubo aburrido	se hubieron aburrido
4 futuro		11 futuro perfecto	
me aburriré	nos aburriremos	me habré aburrido	nos habremos aburrido
te aburrirás	os aburriréis	te habrás aburrido	os habréis aburrido
se aburrirá	se aburrirán	se habrá aburrido	se habrán aburrido
5 potencial simple		12 potencial compuesto	
me aburriría	nos aburriríamos	me habría aburrido	nos habríamos aburrido
te aburrirías	os aburriríais	te habrías aburrido	os habríais aburrido
se aburriría	se aburrirían	se habría aburrido	se habrían aburrido
6 presente de subjuntivo		13 perfecto de subjuntivo	
me aburra	nos aburramos	me haya aburrido	nos hayamos aburrido
te aburras	os aburráis	te hayas aburrido	os hayáis aburrido
se aburra	se aburran	se haya aburrido	se hayan aburrido
7 imperfecto de subjuntivo		14 pluscuamperfecto de subjuntivo	
me aburriera	nos aburriéramos	me hubiera aburrido	nos hubiéramos aburrido
te aburrieras	os aburrierais	te hubieras aburrido	os hubierais aburrido
se aburriera	se aburrieran	se hubiera aburrido	se hubieran aburrido
OR		OR	
me aburriese	nos aburriésemos	me hubiese aburrido	nos hubiésemos aburrido
te aburrieses	os aburrieseis	te hubieses aburrido	os hubieseis aburrido
se aburriese	se aburriesen	se hubiese aburrido	se hubiesen aburrido

imperativo	
—	aburrámonos
abúrrete; no te aburras	aburríos; no os aburráis
abúrrase	abúrranse

Words and expressions related to this verb
Hace treinta años que el profesor de español enseña la lengua en la misma escuela, pero no se aburre.

el aburrimiento	boredom, weariness	**aburrirse como una ostra**	to be bored stiff
aburridamente	tediously	(like an oyster)	
See also **aburrir.**		**¡Qué aburrimiento!** What a bore!	

Regular **-ar** verb   to finish, to end, to complete

The Seven Simple Tenses		The Seven Compound Tenses	
Singular	Plural	Singular	Plural
1 presente de indicativo		8 perfecto de indicativo	
acabo	acabamos	he acabado	hemos acabado
acabas	acabáis	has acabado	habéis acabado
acaba	acaban	ha acabado	han acabado
2 imperfecto de indicativo		9 pluscuamperfecto de indicativo	
acababa	acabábamos	había acabado	habíamos acabado
acababas	acababais	habías acabado	habíais acabado
acababa	acababan	había acabado	habían acabado
3 pretérito		10 pretérito anterior	
acabé	acabamos	hube acabado	hubimos acabado
acabaste	acabasteis	hubiste acabado	hubisteis acabado
acabó	acabaron	hubo acabado	hubieron acabado
4 futuro		11 futuro perfecto	
acabaré	acabaremos	habré acabado	habremos acabado
acabarás	acabaréis	habrás acabado	habréis acabado
acabará	acabarán	habrá acabado	habrán acabado
5 potencial simple		12 potencial compuesto	
acabaría	acabaríamos	habría acabado	habríamos acabado
acabarías	acabaríais	habrías acabado	habríais acabado
acabaría	acabarían	habría acabado	habrían acabado
6 presente de subjuntivo		13 perfecto de subjuntivo	
acabe	acabemos	haya acabado	hayamos acabado
acabes	acabéis	hayas acabado	hayáis acabado
acabe	acaben	haya acabado	hayan acabado
7 imperfecto de subjuntivo		14 pluscuamperfecto de subjuntivo	
acabara	acabáramos	hubiera acabado	hubiéramos acabado
acabaras	acabarais	hubieras acabado	hubierais acabado
acabara	acabaran	hubiera acabado	hubieran acabado
OR		OR	
acabase	acabásemos	hubiese acabado	hubiésemos acabado
acabases	acabaseis	hubieses acabado	hubieseis acabado
acabase	acabasen	hubiese acabado	hubiesen acabado

	imperativo	
—		acabemos
acaba; no acabes		acabad; no acabéis
acabe		acaben

AN ESSENTIAL
55 VERB

The subject pronouns are found on page 93.

Acabar

Acabar is an important verb to learn because it is a regular –ar verb and because there are many everyday expressions related to it.

The Spanish idiomatic expression **acabar de + inf.** is expressed in English as *to have just* + past participle.

Present Indicative:
When you use **acabar** in the present tense, it indicates that the action of the main verb (+ inf.) has just occurred now in the present. In English, we express this by using *have just* + the past participle of the main verb.

Examples:
María acaba de llegar.
Mary has just arrived.

Acabo de comer.
I have just eaten.

Acabamos de terminar la lección.
We have just finished the lesson.

Imperfect Indicative:
When you use **acabar** in the imperfect indicative, it indicates that the action of the main verb (+ inf.) had occurred at some time in the past when another action occurred in the past. In English, we express this by using *had just* + the past participle of the main verb.

María acababa de llegar.
Mary had just arrived.

Yo acababa de comer.
I had just eaten.

Acabábamos de terminar la lección.
We had just finished the lesson.

Words and expressions related to this verb

el acabamiento **completion**

acabar con **to put an end to**

acabar en **to end in**

acabar por **to end by, to ... finally**

acabado, acabada **finished**

Note: When **acabar** is used in the imperfect indicative + inf. (of the main verb being expressed), the verb in the other clause is usually in the preterit.

Example:
Acabábamos de entrar cuando el teléfono sonó.
We had just entered the house when the telephone rang.

Proverb

Bien está lo que bien acaba.
All's well that ends well.

Don't forget to study the section on defective and impersonal verbs. It's right after this main list.

Regular **-ar** verb   to accelerate, to speed, to hasten, to hurry

The Seven Simple Tenses		The Seven Compound Tenses	
Singular	Plural	Singular	Plural
1 presente de indicativo		**8 perfecto de indicativo**	
acelero	aceleramos	he acelerado	hemos acelerado
aceleras	aceleráis	has acelerado	habéis acelerado
acelera	aceleran	ha acelerado	han acelerado
2 imperfecto de indicativo		**9 pluscuamperfecto de indicativo**	
aceleraba	acelerábamos	había acelerado	habíamos acelerado
acelerabas	acelerabais	habías acelerado	habíais acelerado
aceleraba	aceleraban	había acelerado	habían acelerado
3 pretérito		**10 pretérito anterior**	
aceleré	aceleramos	hube acelerado	hubimos acelerado
aceleraste	acelerasteis	hubiste acelerado	hubisteis acelerado
aceleró	aceleraron	hubo acelerado	hubieron acelerado
4 futuro		**11 futuro perfecto**	
aceleraré	aceleraremos	habré acelerado	habremos acelerado
acelerarás	aceleraréis	habrás acelerado	habréis acelerado
acelerará	acelerarán	habrá acelerado	habrán acelerado
5 potencial simple		**12 potencial compuesto**	
aceleraría	aceleraríamos	habría acelerado	habríamos acelerado
acelerarías	aceleraríais	habrías acelerado	habríais acelerado
aceleraría	acelerarían	habría acelerado	habrían acelerado
6 presente de subjuntivo		**13 perfecto de subjuntivo**	
acelere	aceleremos	haya acelerado	hayamos acelerado
aceleres	acelereis	hayas acelerado	hayáis acelerado
acelere	aceleren	haya acelerado	hayan acelerado
7 imperfecto de subjuntivo		**14 pluscuamperfecto de subjuntivo**	
acelerara	aceleráramos	hubiera acelerado	hubiéramos acelerado
aceleraras	acelerarais	hubieras acelerado	hubierais acelerado
acelerara	aceleraran	hubiera acelerado	hubieran acelerado
OR		OR	
acelerase	acelerásemos	hubiese acelerado	hubiésemos acelerado
acelerases	aceleraseis	hubieses acelerado	hubieseis acelerado
acelerase	acelerasen	hubiese acelerado	hubiesen acelerado

	imperativo	
—		aceleremos
acelera; no aceleres		acelerad; no aceleréis
acelere		aceleren

Words related to this verb
aceleradamente   hastily, quickly, speedily   **acelerante**   accelerating
la aceleración   haste, acceleration   **el aceleramiento**   acceleration

Can't remember the Spanish verb you need?
Check the back pages of this book for the English-Spanish verb index!

The subject pronouns are found on page 93.

to accept   Regular **-ar** verb

The Seven Simple Tenses		The Seven Compound Tenses	
Singular	Plural	Singular	Plural
1 presente de indicativo		8 perfecto de indicativo	
acepto	aceptamos	he aceptado	hemos aceptado
aceptas	aceptáis	has aceptado	habéis aceptado
acepta	aceptan	ha aceptado	han aceptado
2 imperfecto de indicativo		9 pluscuamperfecto de indicativo	
aceptaba	aceptábamos	había aceptado	habíamos aceptado
aceptabas	aceptabais	habías aceptado	habíais aceptado
aceptaba	aceptaban	había aceptado	habían aceptado
3 pretérito		10 pretérito anterior	
acepté	aceptamos	hube aceptado	hubimos aceptado
aceptaste	aceptasteis	hubiste aceptado	hubisteis aceptado
aceptó	aceptaron	hubo aceptado	hubieron aceptado
4 futuro		11 futuro perfecto	
aceptaré	aceptaremos	habré aceptado	habremos aceptado
aceptarás	aceptaréis	habrás aceptado	habréis aceptado
aceptará	aceptarán	habrá aceptado	habrán aceptado
5 potencial simple		12 potencial compuesto	
aceptaría	aceptaríamos	habría aceptado	habríamos aceptado
aceptarías	aceptaríais	habrías aceptado	habríais aceptado
aceptaría	aceptarían	habría aceptado	habrían aceptado
6 presente de subjuntivo		13 perfecto de subjuntivo	
acepte	aceptemos	haya aceptado	hayamos aceptado
aceptes	aceptéis	hayas aceptado	hayáis aceptado
acepte	acepten	haya aceptado	hayan aceptado
7 imperfecto de subjuntivo		14 pluscuamperfecto de subjuntivo	
aceptara	aceptáramos	hubiera aceptado	hubiéramos aceptado
aceptaras	aceptarais	hubieras aceptado	hubierais aceptado
aceptara	aceptaran	hubiera aceptado	hubieran aceptado
OR		OR	
aceptase	aceptásemos	hubiese aceptado	hubiésemos aceptado
aceptases	aceptaseis	hubieses aceptado	hubieseis aceptado
aceptase	aceptasen	hubiese aceptado	hubiesen aceptado

	imperativo	
—		aceptemos
acepta; no aceptes		aceptad; no aceptéis
acepte		acepten

Words and expressions related to this verb

aceptable acceptable
el aceptador, la aceptadora acceptor
el aceptante, la aceptante accepter
la aceptación acceptance
la acepción acceptation, meaning (of a word)

aceptar + inf. to agree + inf.
aceptar empleo to take a job
acepto, acepta acceptable
aceptar o rechazar una oferta
    to accept or reject an offer

Regular **-ar** verb endings with spelling change: **c** becomes **qu** before **e**

to bring near, to place near

The Seven Simple Tenses

The Seven Compound Tenses

Singular	Plural	Singular	Plural
1 presente de indicativo		8 perfecto de indicativo	
acerco	acercamos	he acercado	hemos acercado
acercas	acercáis	has acercado	habéis acercado
acerca	acercan	ha acercado	han acercado
2 imperfecto de indicativo		9 pluscuamperfecto de indicativo	
acercaba	acercábamos	había acercado	habíamos acercado
acercabas	acercabais	habías acercado	habíais acercado
acercaba	acercaban	había acercado	habían acercado
3 pretérito		10 pretérito anterior	
acerqué	acercamos	hube acercado	hubimos acercado
acercaste	acercasteis	hubiste acercado	hubisteis acercado
acercó	acercaron	hubo acercado	hubieron acercado
4 futuro		11 futuro perfecto	
acercaré	acercaremos	habré acercado	habremos acercado
acercarás	acercaréis	habrás acercado	habréis acercado
acercará	acercarán	habrá acercado	habrán acercado
5 potencial simple		12 potencial compuesto	
acercaría	acercaríamos	habría acercado	habríamos acercado
acercarías	acercaríais	habrías acercado	habríais acercado
acercaría	acercarían	habría acercado	habrían acercado
6 presente de subjuntivo		13 perfecto de subjuntivo	
acerque	acerquemos	haya acercado	hayamos acercado
acerques	acerquéis	hayas acercado	hayáis acercado
acerque	acerquen	haya acercado	hayan acercado
7 imperfecto de subjuntivo		14 pluscuamperfecto de subjuntivo	
acercara	acercáramos	hubiera acercado	hubiéramos acercado
acercaras	acercarais	hubieras acercado	hubierais acercado
acercara	acercaran	hubiera acercado	hubieran acercado
OR		OR	
acercase	acercásemos	hubiese acercado	hubiésemos acercado
acercases	acercaseis	hubieses acercado	hubieseis acercado
acercase	acercasen	hubiese acercado	hubiesen acercado

imperativo

—	acerquemos
acerca; no acerques	acercad; no acerquéis
acerque	acerquen

Words and expressions related to this verb
acerca de   about, regarding, with regard to
el acercamiento   approaching, approximation
cerca de   near
de cerca   close at hand, closely

acerca de esto   hereof
la cerca   fence, hedge
el cercado   fenced in area
mis parientes cercanos   my close relatives

See also **acercarse.**

The subject pronouns are found on page 93.

to approach, to draw near

Reflexive verb; regular **-ar** verb endings with spelling change: **c** becomes **qu** before **e**

The Seven Simple Tenses		The Seven Compound Tenses	
Singular	Plural	Singular	Plural
1 presente de indicativo		**8 perfecto de indicativo**	
me acerco	nos acercamos	me he acercado	nos hemos acercado
te acercas	os acercáis	te has acercado	os habéis acercado
se acerca	se acercan	se ha acercado	se han acercado
2 imperfecto de indicativo		**9 pluscuamperfecto de indicativo**	
me acercaba	nos acercábamos	me había acercado	nos habíamos acercado
te acercabas	os acercabais	te habías acercado	os habíais acercado
se acercaba	se acercaban	se había acercado	se habían acercado
3 pretérito		**10 pretérito anterior**	
me acerqué	nos acercamos	me hube acercado	nos hubimos acercado
te acercaste	os acercasteis	te hubiste acercado	os hubisteis acercado
se acercó	se acercaron	se hubo acercado	se hubieron acercado
4 futuro		**11 futuro perfecto**	
me acercaré	nos acercaremos	me habré acercado	nos habremos acercado
te acercarás	os acercaréis	te habrás acercado	os habréis acercado
se acercará	se acercarán	se habrá acercado	se habrán acercado
5 potencial simple		**12 potencial compuesto**	
me acercaría	nos acercaríamos	me habría acercado	nos habríamos acercado
te acercarías	os acercaríais	te habrías acercado	os habríais acercado
se acercaría	se acercarían	se habría acercado	se habrían acercado
6 presente de subjuntivo		**13 perfecto de subjuntivo**	
me acerque	nos acerquemos	me haya acercado	nos hayamos acercado
te acerques	os acerquéis	te hayas acercado	os hayáis acercado
se acerque	se acerquen	se haya acercado	se hayan acercado
7 imperfecto de subjuntivo		**14 pluscuamperfecto de subjuntivo**	
me acercara	nos acercáramos	me hubiera acercado	nos hubiéramos acercado
te acercaras	os acercarais	te hubieras acercado	os hubierais acercado
se acercara	se acercaran	se hubiera acercado	se hubieran acercado
OR		OR	
me acercase	nos acercásemos	me hubiese acercado	nos hubiésemos acercado
te acercases	os acercaseis	te hubieses acercado	os hubieseis acercado
se acercase	se acercasen	se hubiese acercado	se hubiesen acercado

imperativo	
—	acerquémonos
acércate; no te acerques	acercaos; no os acerquéis
acérquese	acérquense

Words and expressions related to this verb

acerca de about, regarding, with regard to
el acercamiento approaching, approximation
cerca de near
de cerca close at hand, closely

cercanamente soon, shortly
cercano, cercana near, close
cercar to enclose, fence in
las cercanías neighborhood, suburbs

See also **acercar.**

Regular **-ar** verb endings with stem change: Tenses 1, 6, Imperative

to hit the mark, to hit upon, to do (something) right, to succeed in, to guess right

The Seven Simple Tenses		The Seven Compound Tenses	
Singular	Plural	Singular	Plural
1 presente de indicativo		**8 perfecto de indicativo**	
acierto	acertamos	he acertado	hemos acertado
aciertas	acertáis	has acertado	habéis acertado
acierta	aciertan	ha acertado	han acertado
2 imperfecto de indicativo		**9 pluscuamperfecto de indicativo**	
acertaba	acertábamos	había acertado	habíamos acertado
acertabas	acertabais	habías acertado	habíais acertado
acertaba	acertaban	había acertado	habían acertado
3 pretérito		**10 pretérito anterior**	
acerté	acertamos	hube acertado	hubimos acertado
acertaste	acertasteis	hubiste acertado	hubisteis acertado
acertó	acertaron	hubo acertado	hubieron acertado
4 futuro		**11 futuro perfecto**	
acertaré	acertaremos	habré acertado	habremos acertado
acertarás	acertaréis	habrás acertado	habréis acertado
acertará	acertarán	habrá acertado	habrán acertado
5 potencial simple		**12 potencial compuesto**	
acertaría	acertaríamos	habría acertado	habríamos acertado
acertarías	acertaríais	habrías acertado	habríais acertado
acertaría	acertarían	habría acertado	habrían acertado
6 presente de subjuntivo		**13 perfecto de subjuntivo**	
acierte	acertemos	haya acertado	hayamos acertado
aciertes	acertéis	hayas acertado	hayáis acertado
acierte	acierten	haya acertado	hayan acertado
7 imperfecto de subjuntivo		**14 pluscuamperfecto de subjuntivo**	
acertara	acertáramos	hubiera acertado	hubiéramos acertado
acertaras	acertarais	hubieras acertado	hubierais acertado
acertara	acertaran	hubiera acertado	hubieran acertado
OR		OR	
acertase	acertásemos	hubiese acertado	hubiésemos acertado
acertases	acertaseis	hubieses acertado	hubieseis acertado
acertase	acertasen	hubiese acertado	hubiesen acertado

imperativo	
—	acertemos
acierta; no aciertes	acertad; no acertéis
acierte	acierten

Words and expressions related to this verb
acertado, acertada proper, fit, sensible
el acertador, la acertadora good guesser
acertar a to happen to + inf.
acertar con to come across, to find

Es cierto. It's certain/sure.

el acertamiento tact, ability
el acertijo riddle
acertadamente opportunely, correctly
ciertamente certainly

Get acquainted with what preposition goes with what verb on pages 669–677.

The subject pronouns are found on page 93.

A

to acclaim, to applaud, to shout, to hail   Regular **-ar** verb

The Seven Simple Tenses		The Seven Compound Tenses	
Singular	Plural	Singular	Plural
1 presente de indicativo		8 perfecto de indicativo	
aclamo	aclamamos	he aclamado	hemos aclamado
aclamas	aclamáis	has aclamado	habéis aclamado
aclama	aclaman	ha aclamado	han aclamado
2 imperfecto de indicativo		9 pluscuamperfecto de indicativo	
aclamaba	aclamábamos	había aclamado	habíamos aclamado
aclamabas	aclamabais	habías aclamado	habíais aclamado
aclamaba	aclamaban	había aclamado	habían aclamado
3 pretérito		10 pretérito anterior	
aclamé	aclamamos	hube aclamado	hubimos aclamado
aclamaste	aclamasteis	hubiste aclamado	hubisteis aclamado
aclamó	aclamaron	hubo aclamado	hubieron aclamado
4 futuro		11 futuro perfecto	
aclamaré	aclamaremos	habré aclamado	habremos aclamado
aclamarás	aclamaréis	habrás aclamado	habréis aclamado
aclamará	aclamarán	habrá aclamado	habrán aclamado
5 potencial simple		12 potencial compuesto	
aclamaría	aclamaríamos	habría aclamado	habríamos aclamado
aclamarías	aclamaríais	habrías aclamado	habríais aclamado
aclamaría	aclamarían	habría aclamado	habrían aclamado
6 presente de subjuntivo		13 perfecto de subjuntivo	
aclame	aclamemos	haya aclamado	hayamos aclamado
aclames	aclaméis	hayas aclamado	hayáis aclamado
aclame	aclamen	haya aclamado	hayan aclamado
7 imperfecto de subjuntivo		14 pluscuamperfecto de subjuntivo	
aclamara	aclamáramos	hubiera aclamado	hubiéramos aclamado
aclamaras	aclamarais	hubieras aclamado	hubierais aclamado
aclamara	aclamaran	hubiera aclamado	hubieran aclamado
OR		OR	
aclamase	aclamásemos	hubiese aclamado	hubiésemos aclamado
aclamases	aclamaseis	hubieses aclamado	hubieseis aclamado
aclamase	aclamasen	hubiese aclamado	hubiesen aclamado

imperativo	
—	aclamemos
aclama; no aclames	aclamad; no aclaméis
aclame	aclamen

Words and expressions related to this verb

aclamado, aclamada acclaimed
la aclamación acclaim, acclamation
la reclamación claim, demand
reclamar en juicio to sue

aclamable laudable
por aclamación unanimously
reclamar to claim, to demand, to reclaim
reclamar por daños to claim damages

Regular **-ar** verb   to explain, to clarify, to make clear, to rinse, to clear

The Seven Simple Tenses		The Seven Compound Tenses	
Singular	Plural	Singular	Plural
1 presente de indicativo		8 perfecto de indicativo	
aclaro	aclaramos	he aclarado	hemos aclarado
aclaras	aclaráis	has aclarado	habéis aclarado
aclara	aclaran	ha aclarado	han aclarado
2 imperfecto de indicativo		9 pluscuamperfecto de indicativo	
aclaraba	aclarábamos	había aclarado	habíamos aclarado
aclarabas	aclarabais	habías aclarado	habíais aclarado
aclaraba	aclaraban	había aclarado	habían aclarado
3 pretérito		10 pretérito anterior	
aclaré	aclaramos	hube aclarado	hubimos aclarado
aclaraste	aclarasteis	hubiste aclarado	hubisteis aclarado
aclaró	aclararon	hubo aclarado	hubieron aclarado
4 futuro		11 futuro perfecto	
aclararé	aclararemos	habré aclarado	habremos aclarado
aclararás	aclararéis	habrás aclarado	habréis aclarado
aclarará	aclararán	habrá aclarado	habrán aclarado
5 potencial simple		12 potencial compuesto	
aclararía	aclararíamos	habría aclarado	habríamos aclarado
aclararías	aclararíais	habrías aclarado	habríais aclarado
aclararía	aclararían	habría aclarado	habrían aclarado
6 presente de subjuntivo		13 perfecto de subjuntivo	
aclare	aclaremos	haya aclarado	hayamos aclarado
aclares	aclaréis	hayas aclarado	hayáis aclarado
aclare	aclaren	haya aclarado	hayan aclarado
7 imperfecto de subjuntivo		14 pluscuamperfecto de subjuntivo	
aclarara	aclaráramos	hubiera aclarado	hubiéramos aclarado
aclararas	aclararais	hubieras aclarado	hubierais aclarado
aclarara	aclararan	hubiera aclarado	hubieran aclarado
OR		OR	
aclarase	aclarásemos	hubiese aclarado	hubiésemos aclarado
aclarases	aclaraseis	hubieses aclarado	hubieseis aclarado
aclarase	aclarasen	hubiese aclarado	hubiesen aclarado

imperativo

—	aclaremos
aclara; no aclares	aclarad; no aclaréis
aclare	aclaren

Words and expressions related to this verb
una aclaración   explanation
aclarado, aclarada   cleared, made clear; rinsed
aclarar la voz   to clear one's throat
poner en claro   to clarify

aclarecer   to make clear
¡Claro que sí!   Of course!
¡Claro que no!   Of course not!
¿Está claro?   Is that clear?

Review the principal parts of important Spanish verbs on pages 9–10.

The subject pronouns are found on page 93.

to accompany, to escort, to go with, to keep company   Regular **-ar** verb

The Seven Simple Tenses		The Seven Compound Tenses	
Singular	Plural	Singular	Plural
1 presente de indicativo		8 perfecto de indicativo	
acompaño	acompañamos	he acompañado	hemos acompañado
acompañas	acompañáis	has acompañado	habéis acompañado
acompaña	acompañan	ha acompañado	han acompañado
2 imperfecto de indicativo		9 pluscuamperfecto de indicativo	
acompañaba	acompañábamos	había acompañado	habíamos acompañado
acompañabas	acompañabais	habías acompañado	habíais acompañado
acompañaba	acompañaban	había acompañado	habían acompañado
3 pretérito		10 pretérito anterior	
acompañé	acompañamos	hube acompañado	hubimos acompañado
acompañaste	acompañasteis	hubiste acompañado	hubisteis acompañado
acompañó	acompañaron	hubo acompañado	hubieron acompañado
4 futuro		11 futuro perfecto	
acompañaré	acompañaremos	habré acompañado	habremos acompañado
acompañarás	acompañaréis	habrás acompañado	habréis acompañado
acompañará	acompañarán	habrá acompañado	habrán acompañado
5 potencial simple		12 potencial compuesto	
acompañaría	acompañaríamos	habría acompañado	habríamos acompañado
acompañarías	acompañaríais	habrías acompañado	habríais acompañado
acompañaría	acompañarían	habría acompañado	habrían acompañado
6 presente de subjuntivo		13 perfecto de subjuntivo	
acompañe	acompañemos	haya acompañado	hayamos acompañado
acompañes	acompañéis	hayas acompañado	hayáis acompañado
acompañe	acompañen	haya acompañado	hayan acompañado
7 imperfecto de subjuntivo		14 pluscuamperfecto de subjuntivo	
acompañara	acompañáramos	hubiera acompañado	hubiéramos acompañado
acompañaras	acompañarais	hubieras acompañado	hubierais acompañado
acompañara	acompañaran	hubiera acompañado	hubieran acompañado
OR		OR	
acompañase	acompañásemos	hubiese acompañado	hubiésemos acompañado
acompañases	acompañaseis	hubieses acompañado	hubieseis acompañado
acompañase	acompañasen	hubiese acompañado	hubiesen acompañado

imperativo	
—	acompañemos
acompaña; no acompañes	acompañad; no acompañéis
acompañe	acompañen

Words and expressions related to this verb
el acompañador, la acompañadora   companion, chaperon, accompanist
el acompañamiento   accompaniment
el acompañado, la acompañada   assistant
un compañero, una compañera   friend, mate, companion;
    compañero de cuarto   roommate; **compañero de juego**   playmate

Regular **-ar** verb   to advise, to counsel

The Seven Simple Tenses		The Seven Compound Tenses	
Singular	Plural	Singular	Plural
1 presente de indicativo		**8 perfecto de indicativo**	
aconsejo	aconsejamos	he aconsejado	hemos aconsejado
aconsejas	aconsejáis	has aconsejado	habéis aconsejado
aconseja	aconsejan	ha aconsejado	han aconsejado
2 imperfecto de indicativo		**9 pluscuamperfecto de indicativo**	
aconsejaba	aconsejábamos	había aconsejado	habíamos aconsejado
aconsejabas	aconsejabais	habías aconsejado	habíais aconsejado
aconsejaba	aconsejaban	había aconsejado	habían aconsejado
3 pretérito		**10 pretérito anterior**	
aconsejé	aconsejamos	hube aconsejado	hubimos aconsejado
aconsejaste	aconsejasteis	hubiste aconsejado	hubisteis aconsejado
aconsejó	aconsejaron	hubo aconsejado	hubieron aconsejado
4 futuro		**11 futuro perfecto**	
aconsejaré	aconsejaremos	habré aconsejado	habremos aconsejado
aconsejarás	aconsejaréis	habrás aconsejado	habréis aconsejado
aconsejará	aconsejarán	habrá aconsejado	habrán aconsejado
5 potencial simple		**12 potencial compuesto**	
aconsejaría	aconsejaríamos	habría aconsejado	habríamos aconsejado
aconsejarías	aconsejaríais	habrías aconsejado	habríais aconsejado
aconsejaría	aconsejarían	habría aconsejado	habrían aconsejado
6 presente de subjuntivo		**13 perfecto de subjuntivo**	
aconseje	aconsejemos	haya aconsejado	hayamos aconsejado
aconsejes	aconsejéis	hayas aconsejado	hayáis aconsejado
aconseje	aconsejen	haya aconsejado	hayan aconsejado
7 imperfecto de subjuntivo		**14 pluscuamperfecto de subjuntivo**	
aconsejara	aconsejáramos	hubiera aconsejado	hubiéramos aconsejado
aconsejaras	aconsejarais	hubieras aconsejado	hubierais aconsejado
aconsejara	aconsejaran	hubiera aconsejado	hubieran aconsejado
OR		OR	
aconsejase	aconsejásemos	hubiese aconsejado	hubiésemos aconsejado
aconsejases	aconsejaseis	hubieses aconsejado	hubieseis aconsejado
aconsejase	aconsejasen	hubiese aconsejado	hubiesen aconsejado

imperativo	
—	aconsejemos
aconseja; no aconsejes	aconsejad; aconsejéis
aconseje	aconsejen

Words and expressions related to this verb
el aconsejador, la aconsejadora adviser, counselor
aconsejar con to consult
el consejo advice, counsel
El tiempo da buen consejo. Time will tell.

aconsejarse to seek advice
aconsejarse de to consult with
el aconsejamiento counselling
desaconsejadamente ill-advisedly

Do you need more drills? Have fun with the *501 Spanish Verbs* CD-ROM!

The subject pronouns are found on page 93.

to agree (upon)

Regular **-ar** verb endings with stem change: Tenses 1, 6, Imperative

The Seven Simple Tenses		The Seven Compound Tenses	
Singular	Plural	Singular	Plural
1 presente de indicativo		8 perfecto de indicativo	
acuerdo	acordamos	he acordado	hemos acordado
acuerdas	acordáis	has acordado	habéis acordado
acuerda	acuerdan	ha acordado	han acordado
2 imperfecto de indicativo		9 pluscuamperfecto de indicativo	
acordaba	acordábamos	había acordado	habíamos acordado
acordabas	acordabais	habías acordado	habíais acordado
acordaba	acordaban	había acordado	habían acordado
3 pretérito		10 pretérito anterior	
acordé	acordamos	hube acordado	hubimos acordado
acordaste	acordasteis	hubiste acordado	hubisteis acordado
acordó	acordaron	hubo acordado	hubieron acordado
4 futuro		11 futuro perfecto	
acordaré	acordaremos	habré acordado	habremos acordado
acordarás	acordaréis	habrás acordado	habréis acordado
acordará	acordarán	habrá acordado	habrán acordado
5 potencial simple		12 potencial compuesto	
acordaría	acordaríamos	habría acordado	habríamos acordado
acordarías	acordaríais	habrías acordado	habríais acordado
acordaría	acordarían	habría acordado	habrían acordado
6 presente de subjuntivo		13 perfecto de subjuntivo	
acuerde	acordemos	haya acordado	hayamos acordado
acuerdes	acordéis	hayas acordado	hayáis acordado
acuerde	acuerden	haya acordado	hayan acordado
7 imperfecto de subjuntivo		14 pluscuamperfecto de subjuntivo	
acordara	acordáramos	hubiera acordado	hubiéramos acordado
acordaras	acordarais	hubieras acordado	hubierais acordado
acordara	acordaran	hubiera acordado	hubieran acordado
OR		OR	
acordase	acordásemos	hubiese acordado	hubiésemos acordado
acordases	acordaseis	hubieses acordado	hubieseis acordado
acordase	acordasen	hubiese acordado	hubiesen acordado

imperativo	
—	acordemos
acuerda; no acuerdes	acordad; no acordéis
acuerde	acuerden

Words and expressions related to this verb
la **acordada**   decision, resolution
acordadamente   jointly, by common consent
un **acuerdo**   agreement
de **acuerdo**   in agreement
de común **acuerdo**   unanimously,
   by mutual agreement

desacordar   to put out of tune
desacordante   discordant
desacordado, desacordada   out of tune (music)
estar de **acuerdo con**   to be in agreement with

See also **acordarse**.

Reflexive verb; regular **-ar** verb endings with   to remember, to agree
stem change: Tenses 1, 6, Imperative

The Seven Simple Tenses		The Seven Compound Tenses	
Singular	Plural	Singular	Plural
1 presente de indicativo		8 perfecto de indicativo	
me acuerdo	**nos acordamos**	**me he acordado**	**nos hemos acordado**
te acuerdas	**os acordáis**	**te has acordado**	**os habéis acordado**
se acuerda	**se acuerdan**	**se ha acordado**	**se han acordado**
2 imperfecto de indicativo		9 pluscuamperfecto de indicativo	
me acordaba	**nos acordábamos**	**me había acordado**	**nos habíamos acordado**
te acordabas	**os acordabais**	**te habías acordado**	**os habíais acordado**
se acordaba	**se acordaban**	**se había acordado**	**se habían acordado**
3 pretérito		10 pretérito anterior	
me acordé	**nos acordamos**	**me hube acordado**	**nos hubimos acordado**
te acordaste	**os acordasteis**	**te hubiste acordado**	**os hubisteis acordado**
se acordó	**se acordaron**	**se hubo acordado**	**se hubieron acordado**
4 futuro		11 futuro perfecto	
me acordaré	**nos acordaremos**	**me habré acordado**	**nos habremos acordado**
te acordarás	**os acordaréis**	**te habrás acordado**	**os habréis acordado**
se acordará	**se acordarán**	**se habrá acordado**	**se habrán acordado**
5 potencial simple		12 potencial compuesto	
me acordaría	**nos acordaríamos**	**me habría acordado**	**nos habríamos acordado**
te acordarías	**os acordaríais**	**te habrías acordado**	**os habríais acordado**
se acordaría	**se acordarían**	**se habría acordado**	**se habrían acordado**
6 presente de subjuntivo		13 perfecto de subjuntivo	
me acuerde	**nos acordemos**	**me haya acordado**	**nos hayamos acordado**
te acuerdes	**os acordéis**	**te hayas acordado**	**os hayáis acordado**
se acuerde	**se acuerden**	**se haya acordado**	**se hayan acordado**
7 imperfecto de subjuntivo		14 pluscuamperfecto de subjuntivo	
me acordara	**nos acordáramos**	**me hubiera acordado**	**nos hubiéramos acordado**
te acordaras	**os acordarais**	**te hubieras acordado**	**os hubierais acordado**
se acordara	**se acordaran**	**se hubiera acordado**	**se hubieran acordado**
OR		OR	
me acordase	**nos acordásemos**	**me hubiese acordado**	**nos hubiésemos acordado**
te acordases	**os acordaseis**	**te hubieses acordado**	**os hubieseis acordado**
se acordase	**se acordasen**	**se hubiese acordado**	**se hubiesen acordado**

	imperativo	
—		**acordémenos**
acuérdate; no te acuerdes		**acordaos; no os acordéis**
acuérdese		**acuérdense**

Words and expressions related to this verb
si mal no me acuerdo   if I remember correctly, if my memory does not fail me
un acuerdo   agreement
de acuerdo   in agreement
de común acuerdo   unanimously, by mutual agreement
desacordarse   to become forgetful

See also **acordar.**

The subject pronouns are found on page 93.

to go to bed, to lie down | Reflexive verb; regular **-ar** verb endings with stem change: Tenses 1, 6, Imperative

The Seven Simple Tenses		The Seven Compound Tenses	
Singular	Plural	Singular	Plural
1 presente de indicativo		8 perfecto de indicativo	
me acuesto	nos acostamos	me he acostado	nos hemos acostado
te acuestas	os acostáis	te has acostado	os habéis acostado
se acuesta	se acuestan	se ha acostado	se han acostado
2 imperfecto de indicativo		9 pluscuamperfecto de indicativo	
me acostaba	nos acostábamos	me había acostado	nos habíamos acostado
te acostabas	os acostabais	te habías acostado	os habíais acostado
se acostaba	se acostaban	se había acostado	se habían acostado
3 pretérito		10 pretérito anterior	
me acosté	nos acostamos	me hube acostado	nos hubimos acostado
te acostaste	os acostasteis	te hubiste acostado	os hubisteis acostado
se acostó	se acostaron	se hubo acostado	se hubieron acostado
4 futuro		11 futuro perfecto	
me acostaré	nos acostaremos	me habré acostado	nos habremos acostado
te acostarás	os acostaréis	te habrás acostado	os habréis acostado
se acostará	se acostarán	se habrá acostado	se habrán acostado
5 potencial simple		12 potencial compuesto	
me acostaría	nos acostaríamos	me habría acostado	nos habríamos acostado
te acostarías	os acostaríais	te habrías acostado	os habríais acostado
se acostaría	se acostarían	se habría acostado	se habrían acostado
6 presente de subjuntivo		13 perfecto de subjuntivo	
me acueste	nos acostemos	me haya acostado	nos hayamos acostado
te acuestes	os acostéis	te hayas acostado	os hayáis acostado
se acueste	se acuesten	se haya acostado	se hayan acostado
7 imperfecto de subjuntivo		14 pluscuamperfecto de subjuntivo	
me acostara	nos acostáramos	me hubiera acostado	nos hubiéramos acostado
te acostaras	os acostarais	te hubieras acostado	os hubierais acostado
se acostara	se acostaran	se hubiera acostado	se hubieran acostado
OR		OR	
me acostase	nos acostásemos	me hubiese acostado	nos hubiésemos acostado
te acostases	os acostaseis	te hubieses acostado	os hubieseis acostado
se acostase	se acostasen	se hubiese acostado	se hubiesen acostado

	imperativo
—	acostémonos; no nos acostemos
acuéstate; no te acuestes	acostaos; no os acostéis
acuéstese; no se acueste	acuéstense; no se acuesten

Sentences using this verb and words and expressions related to it
Todas las noches me acuesto a las diez, mi hermanito se acuesta a las ocho, y mis padres se acuestan a las once.

el acostamiento   lying down
acostado, acostada   in bed, lying down

acostar   to put to bed
acostarse con las gallinas   to go to bed very early (with the hens/chickens)

Regular **-ar** verb   to be accustomed, to be in the habit of

The Seven Simple Tenses		The Seven Compound Tenses	
Singular	Plural	Singular	Plural
1 presente de indicativo		8 perfecto de indicativo	
acostumbro	**acostumbramos**	**he acostumbrado**	**hemos acostumbrado**
acostumbras	**acostumbráis**	**has acostumbrado**	**habéis acostumbrado**
acostumbra	**acostumbran**	**ha acostumbrado**	**han acostumbrado**
2 imperfecto de indicativo		9 pluscuamperfecto de indicativo	
acostumbraba	**acostumbrábamos**	**había acostumbrado**	**habíamos acostumbrado**
acostumbrabas	**acostumbrabais**	**habías acostumbrado**	**habíais acostumbrado**
acostumbraba	**acostumbraban**	**había acostumbrado**	**habían acostumbrado**
3 pretérito		10 pretérito anterior	
acostumbré	**acostumbramos**	**hube acostumbrado**	**hubimos acostumbrado**
acostumbraste	**acostumbrasteis**	**hubiste acostumbrado**	**hubisteis acostumbrado**
acostumbró	**acostumbraron**	**hubo acostumbrado**	**hubieron acostumbrado**
4 futuro		11 futuro perfecto	
acostumbraré	**acostumbraremos**	**habré acostumbrado**	**habremos acostumbrado**
acostumbrarás	**acostumbraréis**	**habrás acostumbrado**	**habréis acostumbrado**
acostumbrará	**acostumbrarán**	**habrá acostumbrado**	**habrán acostumbrado**
5 potencial simple		12 potencial compuesto	
acostumbraría	**acostumbraríamos**	**habría acostumbrado**	**habríamos acostumbrado**
acostumbrarías	**acostumbraríais**	**habrías acostumbrado**	**habríais acostumbrado**
acostumbraría	**acostumbrarían**	**habría acostumbrado**	**habrían acostumbrado**
6 presente de subjuntivo		13 perfecto de subjuntivo	
acostumbre	**acostumbremos**	**haya acostumbrado**	**hayamos acostumbrado**
acostumbres	**acostumbréis**	**hayas acostumbrado**	**hayáis acostumbrado**
acostumbre	**acostumbren**	**haya acostumbrado**	**hayan acostumbrado**
7 imperfecto de subjuntivo		14 pluscuamperfecto de subjuntivo	
acostumbrara	**acostumbráramos**	**hubiera acostumbrado**	**hubiéramos acostumbrado**
acostumbraras	**acostumbrarais**	**hubieras acostumbrado**	**hubierais acostumbrado**
acostumbrara	**acostumbraran**	**hubiera acostumbrado**	**hubieran acostumbrado**
OR		OR	
acostumbrase	**acostumbrásemos**	**hubiese acostumbrado**	**hubiésemos acostumbrado**
acostumbrases	**acostumbraseis**	**hubieses acostumbrado**	**hubieseis acostumbrado**
acostumbrase	**acostumbrasen**	**hubiese acostumbrado**	**hubiesen acostumbrado**

imperativo

	—	**acostumbremos**
	acostumbra; no acostumbres	**acostumbrad; no acostumbréis**
	acostumbre	**acostumbren**

Words and expressions related to this verb

acostumbradamente   customarily
la costumbre   custom, habit
de costumbre   customary, usual
tener por costumbre   to be in the habit of

acostumbrado, acostumbrada   accustomed
acostumbrarse   to become accustomed,
   to get used to
acostumbrarse a algo   to become accustomed
   to something

Can't find the verb you're looking for?
Check the back pages of this book for a list of over 2,100 additional verbs!

The subject pronouns are found on page 93.   **119**

to knife, to cut, to slash, to cut open   Regular **-ar** verb

The Seven Simple Tenses		The Seven Compound Tenses	
Singular	Plural	Singular	Plural
1 presente de indicativo		8 perfecto de indicativo	
acuchillo	acuchillamos	he acuchillado	hemos acuchillado
acuchillas	acuchilláis	has acuchillado	habéis acuchillado
acuchilla	acuchillan	ha acuchillado	han acuchillado
2 imperfecto de indicativo		9 pluscuamperfecto de indicativo	
acuchillaba	acuchillábamos	había acuchillado	habíamos acuchillado
acuchillabas	acuchillabais	habías acuchillado	habíais acuchillado
acuchillaba	acuchillaban	había acuchillado	habían acuchillado
3 pretérito		10 pretérito anterior	
acuchillé	acuchillamos	hube acuchillado	hubimos acuchillado
acuchillaste	acuchillasteis	hubiste acuchillado	hubisteis acuchillado
acuchilló	acuchillaron	hubo acuchillado	hubieron acuchillado
4 futuro		11 futuro perfecto	
acuchillaré	acuchillaremos	habré acuchillado	habremos acuchillado
acuchillarás	acuchillaréis	habrás acuchillado	habréis acuchillado
acuchillará	acuchillarán	habrá acuchillado	habrán acuchillado
5 potencial simple		12 potencial compuesto	
acuchillaría	acuchillaríamos	habría acuchillado	habríamos acuchillado
acuchillarías	acuchillaríais	habrías acuchillado	habríais acuchillado
acuchillaría	acuchillarían	habría acuchillado	habrían acuchillado
6 presente de subjuntivo		13 perfecto de subjuntivo	
acuchille	acuchillemos	haya acuchillado	hayamos acuchillado
acuchilles	acuchilléis	hayas acuchillado	hayáis acuchillado
acuchille	acuchillen	haya acuchillado	hayan acuchillado
7 imperfecto de subjuntivo		14 pluscuamperfecto de subjuntivo	
acuchillara	acuchilláramos	hubiera acuchillado	hubiéramos acuchillado
acuchillaras	acuchillarais	hubieras acuchillado	hubierais acuchillado
acuchillara	acuchillaran	hubiera acuchillado	hubieran acuchillado
OR		OR	
acuchillase	acuchillásemos	hubiese acuchillado	hubiésemos acuchillado
acuchillases	acuchillaseis	hubieses acuchillado	hubieseis acuchillado
acuchillase	acuchillasen	hubiese acuchillado	hubiesen acuchillado

	imperativo	
—		acuchillemos
acuchilla; no acuchilles		acuchillad; no acuchilléis
acuchille		acuchillen

Words and expressions related to this verb
un cuchillo   knife
un cuchillo de monte   hunting knife
un cuchillo de cocina   kitchen knife
ser cuchillo de otro   to be a thorn in someone's side
un acuchillador, una acuchilladora   quarrelsome person; bully

acuchillado, acuchillada   knifed, slashed
las mangas acuchilladas   slashed sleeves
   (fashion, style)

Regular **-ir** verb

to attend, to be present frequently, to respond
(to a call), to come to the rescue

The Seven Simple Tenses		The Seven Compound Tenses	
Singular	Plural	Singular	Plural
1 presente de indicativo		8 perfecto de indicativo	
acudo	acudimos	he acudido	hemos acudido
acudes	acudís	has acudido	habéis acudido
acude	acuden	ha acudido	han acudido
2 imperfecto de indicativo		9 pluscuamperfecto de indicativo	
acudía	acudíamos	había acudido	habíamos acudido
acudías	acudíais	habías acudido	habíais acudido
acudía	acudían	había acudido	habían acudido
3 pretérito		10 pretérito anterior	
acudí	acudimos	hube acudido	hubimos acudido
acudiste	acudisteis	hubiste acudido	hubisteis acudido
acudió	acudieron	hubo acudido	hubieron acudido
4 futuro		11 futuro perfecto	
acudiré	acudiremos	habré acudido	habremos acudido
acudirás	acudiréis	habrás acudido	habréis acudido
acudirá	acudirán	habrá acudido	habrán acudido
5 potencial simple		12 potencial compuesto	
acudiría	acudiríamos	habría acudido	habríamos acudido
acudirías	acudiríais	habrías acudido	habríais acudido
acudiría	acudirían	habría acudido	habrían acudido
6 presente de subjuntivo		13 perfecto de subjuntivo	
acuda	acudamos	haya acudido	hayamos acudido
acudas	acudáis	hayas acudido	hayáis acudido
acuda	acudan	haya acudido	hayan acudido
7 imperfecto de subjuntivo		14 pluscuamperfecto de subjuntivo	
acudiera	acudiéramos	hubiera acudido	hubiéramos acudido
acudieras	acudierais	hubieras acudido	hubierais acudido
acudiera	acudieran	hubiera acudido	hubieran acudido
OR		OR	
acudiese	acudiésemos	hubiese acudido	hubiésemos acudido
acudieses	acudieseis	hubieses acudido	hubieseis acudido
acudiese	acudiesen	hubiese acudido	hubiesen acudido

imperativo	
—	acudamos
acude; no acudas	acudid; no acudáis
acuda	acudan

Words and expressions related to this verb

el acudimiento aid
acudir en socorro de to go to help
acudir con el remedio to get there with the remedy
acudir a los tribunales to go to court (law)

acudir a una cita to keep an appointment
acudir a un examen to take an exam
acudir a alguien to give help to someone
acudir en ayuda de alguien to come
to someone's rescue

The subject pronouns are found on page 93.

121

to accuse   Regular **-ar** verb

The Seven Simple Tenses		The Seven Compound Tenses	
Singular	Plural	Singular	Plural
1 presente de indicativo		8 perfecto de indicativo	
acuso	acusamos	he acusado	hemos acusado
acusas	acusáis	has acusado	habéis acusado
acusa	acusan	ha acusado	han acusado
2 imperfecto de indicativo		9 pluscuamperfecto de indicativo	
acusaba	acusábamos	había acusado	habíamos acusado
acusabas	acusabais	habías acusado	habíais acusado
acusaba	acusaban	había acusado	habían acusado
3 pretérito		10 pretérito anterior	
acusé	acusamos	hube acusado	hubimos acusado
acusaste	acusasteis	hubiste acusado	hubisteis acusado
acusó	acusaron	hubo acusado	hubieron acusado
4 futuro		11 futuro perfecto	
acusaré	acusaremos	habré acusado	habremos acusado
acusarás	acusaréis	habrás acusado	habréis acusado
acusará	acusarán	habrá acusado	habrán acusado
5 potencial simple		12 potencial compuesto	
acusaría	acusaríamos	habría acusado	habríamos acusado
acusarías	acusaríais	habrías acusado	habríais acusado
acusaría	acusarían	habría acusado	habrían acusado
6 presente de subjuntivo		13 perfecto de subjuntivo	
acuse	acusemos	haya acusado	hayamos acusado
acuses	acuséis	hayas acusado	hayáis acusado
acuse	acusen	haya acusado	hayan acusado
7 imperfecto de subjuntivo		14 pluscuamperfecto de subjuntivo	
acusara	acusáramos	hubiera acusado	hubiéramos acusado
acusaras	acusarais	hubieras acusado	hubierais acusado
acusara	acusaran	hubiera acusado	hubieran acusado
OR		OR	
acusase	acusásemos	hubiese acusado	hubiésemos acusado
acusases	acusaseis	hubieses acusado	hubieseis acusado
acusase	acusasen	hubiese acusado	hubiesen acusado

imperativo

—	acusemos
acusa; no acuses	acusad; no acuséis
acuse	acusen

Words and expressions related to this verb
el acusado, la acusada defendant, accused
la acusación accusation
el acusador, la acusadora accuser

acusar de robo to accuse of robbery
acusar recibo de una cosa to acknowledge
   receipt of something
acusarse de un pecado to confess a sin

Regular **-ar** verb   to advance, to keep on, to progress, to go ahead

The Seven Simple Tenses		The Seven Compound Tenses	
Singular	Plural	Singular	Plural

1   presente de indicativo

		8 perfecto de indicativo	
adelanto	adlenatamos	he adelantado	hemos adelantado
adelantas	adelantáis	has adelantado	habéis adelantado
adelanta	adelantan	ha adelantado	han adelantado

2   imperfecto de indicativo

		9 pluscuamperfecto de indicativo	
adelantaba	adelantábamos	había adelantado	habíamos adelantado
adelantabas	adelantabais	habías adelantado	habíais adelantado
adelantaba	adelantaban	había adelantado	habían adelantado

3   pretérito

		10 pretérito anterior	
adelanté	adelantamos	hube adelantado	hubimos adelantado
adelantaste	adelantasteis	hubiste adelantado	hubisteis adelantado
adelantó	adelantaron	hubo adelantado	hubieron adelantado

4   futuro

		11 futuro perfecto	
adelantaré	adelantaremos	habré adelantado	habremos adelantado
adelantarás	adelantaréis	habrás adelantado	habréis adelantado
adelantará	adelantarán	habrá adelantado	habrán adelantado

5   potencial simple

		12 potencial compuesto	
adelantaría	adelantaríamos	habría adelantado	habríamos adelantado
adelantarías	adelantaríais	habrías adelantado	habríais adelantado
adelantaría	adelantarían	habría adelantado	habrían adelantado

6   presente de subjuntivo

		13 perfecto de subjuntivo	
adelante	adelantemos	haya adelantado	hayamos adelantado
adelantes	adelantéis	hayas adelantado	hayáis adelantado
adelante	adelanten	haya adelantado	hayan adelantado

7   imperfecto de subjuntivo

		14 pluscuamperfecto de subjuntivo	
adelantara	adelantáramos	hubiera adelantado	hubiéramos adelantado
adelantaras	adelantarais	hubieras adelantado	hubierais adelantado
adelantara	adelantaran	hubiera adelantado	hubieran adelantado
OR		OR	
adelantase	adelantasemos	hubiese adelantado	hubiésemos adelantado
adelantases	adelantaseis	hubieses adelantado	hubieseis adelantado
adelantase	adelantasen	hubiese adelantado	hubiesen adelantado

imperativo

—	**adelantemos**
adelanta; no adelantes	**adelantad; no adelantéis**
adelante	**adelanten**

Words and expressions related to this verb
el adelantamiento   advance, growth, increase, progress
adelante   ahead, forward; **¡Adelante!**   Come in! Go ahead!
adelantar dinero   to advance money; **un adelanto**   advance payment
en lo adelante   in the future; **los adelantos tecnológicos**   technological advances, progress
de aquí en adelante   henceforth; **de hoy en adelante**   from now on

For other words and expressions related to this verb, see **adelantarse.**

The subject pronouns are found on page 93.

to go forward, to go ahead,   Reflexive regular **-ar** verb
to move ahead, to take the lead

The Seven Simple Tenses		The Seven Compound Tenses	
Singular	Plural	Singular	Plural
1 presente de indicativo		8 perfecto de indicativo	
me adelanto	nos adelantamos	me he adelantado	nos hemos adelantado
te adelantas	os adelantáis	te has adelantado	os habéis adelantado
se adelanta	se adelantan	se ha adelantado	se han adelantado
2 imperfecto de indicativo		9 pluscuamperfecto de indicativo	
me adelantaba	nos adelantábamos	me había adelantado	nos habíamos adelantado
te adelantabas	os adelantabais	te habías adelantado	os habíais adelantado
se adelantaba	se adelantaban	se había adelantado	se habían adelantado
3 pretérito		10 pretérito anterior	
me adelanté	nos adelantamos	me hube adelantado	nos hubimos adelantado
te adelantaste	os adelantasteis	te hubiste adelantado	os hubisteis adelantado
se adelantó	se adelantaron	se hubo adelantado	se hubieron adelantado
4 futuro		11 futuro perfecto	
me adelantaré	nos adelantaremos	me habré adelantado	nos habremos adelantado
te adelantarás	os adelantaréis	te habrás adelantado	os habréis adelantado
se adelantará	se adelantarán	se habrá adelantado	se habrán adelantado
5 potencial simple		12 potencial compuesto	
me adelantaría	nos adelantaríamos	me habría adelantado	nos habríamos adelantado
te adelantarías	os adelantaríais	te habrías adelantado	os habríais adelantado
se adelantaría	se adelantarían	se habría adelantado	se habrían adelantado
6 presente de subjuntivo		13 perfecto de subjuntivo	
me adelante	nos adelantemos	me haya adelantado	nos hayamos adelantado
te adelantes	os adelantéis	te hayas adelantado	os hayáis adelantado
se adelante	se adelanten	se haya adelantado	se hayan adelantado
7 imperfecto de subjuntivo		14 pluscuamperfecto de subjuntivo	
me adelantara	nos adelantáramos	me hubiera adelantado	nos hubiéramos adelantado
te adelantaras	os adelantarais	te hubieras adelantado	os hubierais adelantado
se adelantara	se adelantaran	se hubiera adelantado	se hubieran adelantado
OR		OR	
me adelantase	nos adelantásemos	me hubiese adelantado	nos hubiésemos adelantado
te adelantases	os adelantaseis	te hubieses adelantado	os hubieseis adelantado
se adelantase	se adelantasen	se hubiese adelantado	se hubiesen adelantado

	imperativo	
—		adelantémonos
adelántate; no te adelantes		adelantaos; no os adelantéis
adelántese		adelántense

Words and expressions related to this verb
adelantado, adelantada   bold; anticipated; fast (watch or clock)
adelantadamente   in anticipation, beforehand
más adelante   later on; farther on
llevar adelante   to carry on, to go ahead

For other words and expressions related to this verb, see **adelantar.**

Regular **-ar** verb   to divine, to foretell, to guess, to solve

The Seven Simple Tenses		The Seven Compound Tenses	
Singular	Plural	Singular	Plural
1 presente de indicativo		8 perfecto de indicativo	
adivino	adivinamos	he adivinado	hemos adivinado
adivinas	adivináis	has adivinado	habéis adivinado
adivina	adivinan	ha adivinado	han adivinado
2 imperfecto de indicativo		9 pluscuamperfecto de indicativo	
adivinaba	adivinábamos	había adivinado	habíamos adivinado
adivinabas	adivinabais	habías adivinado	habíais adivinado
adivinaba	adivinaban	había adivinado	habían adivinado
3 pretérito		10 pretérito anterior	
adiviné	adivinamos	hube adivinado	hubimos adivinado
adivinaste	adivinasteis	hubiste adivinado	hubisteis adivinado
adivinó	adivinaron	hubo adivinado	hubieron adivinado
4 futuro		11 futuro perfecto	
adivinaré	adivinaremos	habré adivinado	habremos adivinado
adivinarás	adivinaréis	habrás adivinado	habréis adivinado
adivinará	adivinarán	habrá adivinado	habrán adivinado
5 potencial simple		12 potencial compuesto	
adivinaría	adivinaríamos	habría adivinado	habríamos adivinado
adivinarías	adivinaríais	habrías adivinado	habríais adivinado
adivinaría	adivinarían	habría adivinado	habrían adivinado
6 presente de subjuntivo		13 perfecto de subjuntivo	
adivine	adivinemos	haya adivinado	hayamos adivinado
adivines	adivinéis	hayas adivinado	hayáis adivinado
adivine	adivinen	haya adivinado	hayan adivinado
7 imperfecto de subjuntivo		14 pluscuamperfecto de subjuntivo	
adivinara	adivináramos	hubiera adivinado	hubiéramos adivinado
adivinaras	adivinarais	hubieras adivinado	hubierais adivinado
adivinara	adivinaran	hubiera adivinado	hubieran adivinado
OR		OR	
adivinase	adivinásemos	hubiese adivinado	hubiésemos adivinado
adivinases	adivinaseis	hubieses adivinado	hubieseis adivinado
adivinase	adivinasen	hubiese adivinado	hubiesen adivinado

imperativo	
—	adivinemos
adivina; no adivines	adivinad; no adivinéis
adivine	adivinen

Words and expressions related to this verb

un adivino, una adivina   prophet; fortune teller; guesser

la adivinación del pensamiento   mind reading

¡Adivine quién soy!   Guess who (I am)!

una adivinanza   prophecy, prediction; enigma, riddle, puzzle
una adivinaja   riddle, puzzle
adivinar el pensamiento de alguien   to read a person's mind

Don't forget to study the section on defective and impersonal verbs. It's right after this main list.

The subject pronouns are found on page 93.

to admire   Regular **-ar** verb

The Seven Simple Tenses		The Seven Compound Tenses	
Singular	Plural	Singular	Plural
1 presente de indicativo		8 perfecto de indicativo	
admiro	admiramos	he admirado	hemos admirado
admiras	admiráis	has admirado	habéis admirado
admira	admiran	ha admirado	han admirado
2 imperfecto de indicativo		9 pluscuamperfecto de indicativo	
admiraba	admirábamos	había admirado	habíamos admirado
admirabas	admirabais	habías admirado	habíais admirado
admiraba	admiraban	había admirado	habían admirado
3 pretérito		10 pretérito anterior	
admiré	admiramos	hube admirado	hubimos admirado
admiraste	admirasteis	hubiste admirado	hubisteis admirado
admiró	admiraron	hubo admirado	hubieron admirado
4 futuro		11 futuro perfecto	
admiraré	admiraremos	habré admirado	habremos admirado
admirarás	admiraréis	habrás admirado	habréis admirado
admirará	admirarán	habrá admirado	habrán admirado
5 potencial simple		12 potencial compuesto	
admiraría	admiraríamos	habría admirado	habríamos admirado
admirarías	admiraríais	habrías admirado	habríais admirado
admiraría	admirarían	habría admirado	habrían admirado
6 presente de subjuntivo		13 perfecto de subjuntivo	
admire	admiremos	haya admirado	hayamos admirado
admires	admiréis	hayas admirado	hayáis admirado
admire	admiren	haya admirado	hayan admirado
7 imperfecto de subjuntivo		14 pluscuamperfecto de subjuntivo	
admirara	admiráramos	hubiera admirado	hubiéramos admirado
admiraras	admirarais	hubieras admirado	hubierais admirado
admirara	admiraran	hubiera admirado	hubieran admirado
OR		OR	
admirase	admirásemos	hubiese admirado	hubiésemos admirado
admirases	admiraseis	hubieses admirado	hubieseis admirado
admirase	admirasen	hubiese admirado	hubiesen admirado

imperativo

—	admiremos
admira; no admires	**admirad; no admiréis**
admire	**admiren**

Words and expressions related to this verb

el admirador, la admiradora admirer
la admiración admiration
admirable admirable
admirablemente admirably
admirativamente admiringly, with admiration

sentir admiración por alguien to feel admiration for someone
hablar en tono admirativo to speak in an admiring tone
causar admiración to inspire admiration

The Seven Simple Tenses		The Seven Compound Tenses	
Singular	Plural	Singular	Plural
1 presente de indicativo		**8 perfecto de indicativo**	
admito	admitimos	he admitido	hemos admitido
admites	admitís	has admitido	habéis admitido
admite	admiten	ha admitido	han admitido
2 imperfecto de indicativo		**9 pluscuamperfecto de indicativo**	
admitía	admitíamos	había admitido	habíamos admitido
admitías	admitíais	habías admitido	habíais admitido
admitía	admitían	había admitido	habían admitido
3 pretérito		**10 pretérito anterior**	
admití	admitimos	hube admitido	hubimos admitido
admitiste	admitisteis	hubiste admitido	hubisteis admitido
admitió	admitieron	hubo admitido	hubieron admitido
4 futuro		**11 futuro perfecto**	
admitiré	admitiremos	habré admitido	habremos admitido
admitirás	admitiréis	habrás admitido	habréis admitido
admitirá	admitirán	habrá admitido	habrán admitido
5 potencial simple		**12 potencial compuesto**	
admitiría	admitiríamos	habría admitido	habríamos admitido
admitirías	admitiríais	habrías admitido	habríais admitido
admitiría	admitirían	habría admitido	habrían admitido
6 presente de subjuntivo		**13 perfecto de subjuntivo**	
admita	admitamos	haya admitido	hayamos admitido
admitas	admitáis	hayas admitido	hayáis admitido
admita	admitan	haya admitido	hayan admitido
7 imperfecto de subjuntivo		**14 pluscuamperfecto de subjuntivo**	
admitiera	admitiéramos	hubiera admitido	hubiéramos admitido
admitieras	admitierais	hubieras admitido	hubierais admitido
admitiera	admitieran	hubiera admitido	hubieran admitido
OR		OR	
admitiese	admitiésemos	hubiese admitido	hubiésemos admitido
admitieses	admitieseis	hubieses admitido	hubieseis admitido
admitiese	admitiesen	hubiese admitido	hubiesen admitido

imperativo

—	**admitamos**
admite; no admitas	**admitid; no admitáis**
admita	**admitan**

Words and expressions related to this verb

la admisión acceptance, admission
admisible admissible

admitir una aclamación to accept a claim
el examen de admisión entrance exam

Can't remember the Spanish verb you need?
Check the back pages of this book for the English-Spanish verb index!

The subject pronouns are found on page 93.

adoptar (31)

Gerundio adoptando   Part. pas. **adoptado**

to adopt

The Seven Simple Tenses		The Seven Compound Tenses	
Singular	Plural	Singular	Plural
1 presente de indicativo		**8 perfecto de indicativo**	
adopto	adoptamos	he adoptado	hemos adoptado
adoptas	adoptáis	has adoptado	habéis adoptado
adopta	adoptan	ha adoptado	han adoptado
2 imperfecto de indicativo		**9 pluscuamperfecto de indicativo**	
adoptaba	adoptábamos	había adoptado	habíamos adoptado
adoptabas	adoptabais	habías adoptado	habíais adoptado
adaptaba	adoptaban	había adoptado	habían adoptado
3 pretérito		**10 pretérito anterior**	
adopté	adoptamos	hube adoptado	hubimos adoptado
adoptaste	adoptasteis	hubiste adoptado	hubisteis adoptado
adoptó	adoptaron	hubo adoptado	hubieron adoptado
4 futuro		**11 futuro perfecto**	
adoptaré	adoptaremos	habré adoptado	habremos adoptado
adoptarás	adoptaréis	habrás adoptado	habréis adoptado
adoptará	adoptarán	habrá adoptado	habrán adoptado
5 potencial simple		**12 potencial compuesto**	
adoptaría	adoptaríamos	habría adoptado	habríamos adoptado
adoptarías	adoptaríais	habrías adoptado	habríais adoptado
adoptaría	adoptarían	habría adoptado	habrían adoptado
6 presente de subjuntivo		**13 perfecto de subjuntivo**	
adopte	adoptemos	haya adoptado	hayamos adoptado
adoptes	adoptéis	hayas adoptado	hayáis adoptado
adopte	adopten	haya adoptado	hayan adoptado
7 imperfecto de subjuntivo		**14 pluscuamperfecto de subjuntivo**	
adoptara	adoptáramos	hubiera adoptado	hubiéramos adoptado
adoptaras	adoptarais	hubieras adoptado	hubierais adoptado
adoptara	adoptaran	hubiera adoptado	hubieran adoptado
OR		OR	
adoptase	adoptásemos	hubiese adoptado	hubiésemos adoptado
adoptases	adoptaseis	hubieses adoptado	hubieseis adoptado
adoptase	adoptasen	hubiese adoptado	hubiesen adoptado

imperativo	
—	adoptemos
adopta; no adoptes	adoptad; no adoptéis
adopte	adopten

Words and expressions related to this verb

la adopción adoption
el adopcionismo adoptionism
el, la adopcionista adoptionist

adoptable adoptable
adoptado, adoptada adopted
adoptivamente adoptively

Do you need more drills? Have fun with the *501 Spanish Verbs* CD-ROM!

Regular **-ar** verb   to adore, to worship

The Seven Simple Tenses		The Seven Compound Tenses	
Singular	Plural	Singular	Plural
1 presente de indicativo		**8 perfecto de indicativo**	
adoro	adoramos	he adorado	hemos adorado
adoras	adoráis	has adorado	habéis adorado
adora	adoran	ha adorado	han adorado
2 imperfecto de indicativo		**9 pluscuamperfecto de indicativo**	
adoraba	adorábamos	había adorado	habíamos adorado
adorabas	adorabais	habías adorado	habíais adorado
adoraba	adoraban	había adorado	habían adorado
3 pretérito		**10 pretérito anterior**	
adoré	adoramos	hube adorado	hubimos adorado
adoraste	adorasteis	hubiste adorado	hubisteis adorado
adoró	adoraron	hubo adorado	hubieron adorado
4 futuro		**11 futuro perfecto**	
adoraré	adoraremos	habré adorado	habremos adorado
adorarás	adoraréis	habrás adorado	habréis adorado
adorará	adorarán	habrá adorado	habrán adorado
5 potencial simple		**12 potencial compuesto**	
adoraría	adoraríamos	habría adorado	habríamos adorado
adorarías	adoraríais	habrías adorado	habríais adorado
adoraría	adorarían	habría adorado	habrían adorado
6 presente de subjuntivo		**13 perfecto de subjuntivo**	
adore	adoremos	haya adorado	hayamos adorado
adores	adoréis	hayas adorado	hayáis adorado
adore	adoren	haya adorado	hayan adorado
7 imperfecto de subjuntivo		**14 pluscuamperfecto de subjuntivo**	
adorara	adoráramos	hubiera adorado	hubiéramos adorado
adoraras	adorarais	hubieras adorado	hubierais adorado
adorara	adoraran	hubiera adorado	hubieran adorado
OR		OR	
adorase	adorásemos	hubiese adorado	hubiésemos adorado
adorases	adoraseis	hubieses adorado	hubieseis adorado
adorase	adorasen	hubiese adorado	hubiesen adorado

imperativo	
—	adoremos
adora; no adores	adorad; no adoréis
adore	adoren

Words and expressions related to this verb
el adorador, la adoradora adorer, worshipper
adorable adorable
la adoración adoration, worship, veneration
adorablemente adorably, adoringly
adorado, adorada adored

Get your feet wet with verbs used in weather expressions on page 668.

adquirir (33)

Gerundio **adquiriendo**   Part. pas. **adquirido**

to acquire, to get, to obtain

Regular **-ir** verb endings with stem change: Tenses 1, 6, Imperative

The Seven Simple Tenses		The Seven Compound Tenses	
Singular	Plural	Singular	Plural
1 presente de indicativo		**8 perfecto de indicativo**	
adquiero	adquirimos	he adquirido	hemos adquirido
adquieres	adquirís	has adquirido	habéis adquirido
adquiere	adquieren	ha adquirido	han adquirido
2 imperfecto de indicativo		**9 pluscuamperfecto de indicativo**	
adquiría	adquiríamos	había adquirido	habíamos adquirido
adquirías	adquiríais	habías adquirido	habíais adquirido
adquiría	adquirían	había adquirido	habían adquirido
3 pretérito		**10 pretérito anterior**	
adquirí	adquirimos	hube adquirido	hubimos adquirido
adquiriste	adquiristeis	hubiste adquirido	hubisteis adquirido
adquirió	adquirieron	hubo adquirido	hubieron adquirido
4 futuro		**11 futuro perfecto**	
adquiriré	adquiriremos	habré adquirido	habremos adquirido
adquirirás	adquiriréis	habrás adquirido	habréis adquirido
adquirirá	adquirirán	habrá adquirido	habrán adquirido
5 potencial simple		**12 potencial compuesto**	
adquiriría	adquiriríamos	habría adquirido	habríamos adquirido
adquirirías	adquiriríais	habrías adquirido	habríais adquirido
adquiriría	adquirirían	habría adquirido	habrían adquirido
6 presente de subjuntivo		**13 perfecto de subjuntivo**	
adquiera	adquiramos	haya adquirido	hayamos adquirido
adquieras	adquiráis	hayas adquirido	hayáis adquirido
adquiera	adquieran	haya adquirido	hayan adquirido
7 imperfecto de subjuntivo		**14 pluscuamperfecto de subjuntivo**	
adquiriera	adquiriéramos	hubiera adquirido	hubiéramos adquirido
adquirieras	adquirierais	hubieras adquirido	hubierais adquirido
adquiriera	adquirieran	hubiera adquirido	hubieran adquirido
OR		OR	
adquiriese	adquiriésemos	hubiese adquirido	hubiésemos adquirido
adquirieses	adquirieseis	hubieses adquirido	hubieseis adquirido
adquiriese	adquiriesen	hubiese adquirido	hubiesen adquirido

imperativo	
—	adquiramos
adquiere; no adquieras	adquirid; no adquiráis
adquiera	adquieran

Words and expressions related to this verb

el adquiridor, la adquiridora acquirer
el (la) adquirente, el (la) adquiriente
  acquirer
la adquisición acquisition, attainment

adquirir los bienes dotales to acquire a dowry
los bienes adquiridos acquired wealth
adquirible obtainable
adquirir un hábito to acquire a habit

Irregular verb   to advise, to give notice, to give warning,
                                              to take notice of, to warn

The Seven Simple Tenses		The Seven Compound Tenses	
Singular	Plural	Singular	Plural
1 presente de indicativo		**8 perfecto de indicativo**	
advierto	advertimos	he advertido	hemos advertido
adviertes	advertís	has advertido	habéis advertido
advierte	advierten	ha advertido	han advertido
2 imperfecto de indicativo		**9 pluscuamperfecto de indicativo**	
advertía	advertíamos	había advertido	habíamos advertido
advertías	advertíais	habías advertido	habíais advertido
advertía	advertían	había advertido	habían advertido
3 pretérito		**10 pretérito anterior**	
advertí	advertimos	hube advertido	hubimos advertido
advertiste	advertisteis	hubiste advertido	hubisteis advertido
advirtió	advirtieron	hubo advertido	hubieron advertido
4 futuro		**11 futuro perfecto**	
advertiré	advertiremos	habré advertido	habremos advertido
advertirás	advertiréis	habrás advertido	habréis advertido
advertirá	advertirán	habrá advertido	habrán advertido
5 potencial simple		**12 potencial compuesto**	
advertiría	advertiríamos	habría advertido	habríamos advertido
advertirías	advertiríais	habrías advertido	habríais advertido
advertiría	advertirían	habría advertido	habrían advertido
6 presente de subjuntivo		**13 perfecto de subjuntivo**	
advierta	advirtamos	haya advertido	hayamos advertido
adviertas	advirtáis	hayas advertido	hayáis advertido
advierta	adviertan	haya advertido	hayan advertido
7 imperfecto de subjuntivo		**14 pluscuamperfecto de subjuntivo**	
advirtiera	advirtiéramos	hubiera advertido	hubiéramos advertido
advirtieras	advirtierais	hubieras advertido	hubierais advertido
advirtiera	advirtieran	hubiera advertido	hubieran advertido
OR		OR	
advirtiese	advirtiésemos	hubiese advertido	hubiésemos advertido
advirtieses	advirtieseis	hubieses advertido	hubieseis advertido
advirtiese	advirtiesen	hubiese advertido	hubiesen advertido

imperativo	
—	advirtamos
advierte; no adviertas	advertid; no advirtáis
advierta	adviertan

Words and expressions related to this verb
advertido, advertida   skillful, clever
la advertencia   warning, notice, foreword
advertidamente   advisedly
un advertimiento   notice, warning

después de repetidas advertencias
   after repeated warnings
hacer una advertencia a un niño
   to correct a child's inappropriate behavior

Can't find the verb you're looking for?
Check the back pages of this book for a list of over 2,100 additional verbs!

The subject pronouns are found on page 93.   **131**

Gerundio **afeitándose**   Part. pas. **afeitado**

The Seven Simple Tenses		The Seven Compound Tenses	
Singular	Plural	Singular	Plural
1 presente de indicativo		**8 perfecto de indicativo**	
me afeito	nos afeitamos	me he afeitado	nos hemos afeitado
te afeitas	os afeitáis	te has afeitado	os habéis afeitado
se afeita	se afeitan	se ha afeitado	se han afeitado
2 imperfecto de indicativo		**9 pluscuamperfecto de indicativo**	
me afeitaba	nos afeitábamos	me había afeitado	nos habíamos afeitado
te afeitabas	os afeitabais	te habías afeitado	os habíais afeitado
se afeitaba	se afeitaban	se había afeitado	se habían afeitado
3 pretérito		**10 pretérito anterior**	
me afeité	nos afeitamos	me hube afeitado	nos hubimos afeitado
te afeitaste	os afeitasteis	te hubiste afeitado	os hubisteis afeitado
se afeitó	se afeitaron	se hubo afeitado	se hubieron afeitado
4 futuro		**11 futuro perfecto**	
me afeitaré	nos afeitaremos	me habré afeitado	nos habremos afeitado
te afeitarás	os afeitaréis	te habrás afeitado	os habréis afeitado
se afeitará	se afeitarán	se habrá afeitado	se habrán afeitado
5 potencial simple		**12 potencial compuesto**	
me afeitaría	nos afeitaríamos	me habría afeitado	nos habríamos afeitado
te afeitarías	os afeitaríais	te habrías afeitado	os habríais afeitado
se afeitaría	se afeitarían	se habría afeitado	se habrían afeitado
6 presente de subjuntivo		**13 perfecto de subjuntivo**	
me afeite	nos afeitemos	me haya afeitado	nos hayamos afeitado
te afeites	os afeitéis	te hayas afeitado	os hayáis afeitado
se afeite	se afeiten	se haya afeitado	se hayan afeitado
7 imperfecto de subjuntivo		**14 pluscuamperfecto de subjuntivo**	
me afeitara	nos afeitáramos	me hubiera afeitado	nos hubiéramos afeitado
te afeitaras	os afeitarais	te hubieras afeitado	os hubierais afeitado
se afeitara	se afeitaran	se hubiera afeitado	se hubieran afeitado
OR		OR	
me afeitase	nos afeitásemos	me hubiese afeitado	nos hubiésemos afeitado
te afeitases	os afeitaseis	te hubieses afeitado	os hubieseis afeitado
se afeitase	se afeitasen	se hubiese afeitado	se hubiesen afeitado

imperativo	
—	afeitémonos
aféitate; no te afeites	afeitaos; no os afeitéis
aféitese	aféitense

Words related to this verb

afeitar to shave	**afeitadamente** ornately
una afeitada a shave	**una afeitadora** shaving machine, shaver
el afeite cosmetic, makeup	**la maquinilla (de afeitar) eléctrica**
	electric shaver, razor

Get acquainted with what preposition goes with what verb on pages 669–677.

Regular **-ar** verb   to grasp, to obtain, to seize, to catch, to clutch, to come upon

The Seven Simple Tenses		The Seven Compound Tenses	
Singular	Plural	Singular	Plural
1 presente de indicativo		**8 perfecto de indicativo**	
agarro	agarramos	he agarrado	hemos agarrado
agarras	agarráis	has agarrado	habéis agarrado
agarra	agarran	ha agarrado	han agarrado
2 imperfecto de indicativo		**9 pluscuamperfecto de indicativo**	
agarraba	agarrábamos	había agarrado	habíamos agarrado
agarrabas	agarrabais	habías agarrado	habíais agarrado
agarraba	agarraban	había agarrado	habían agarrado
3 pretérito		**10 pretérito anterior**	
agarré	agarramos	hube agarrado	hubimos agarrado
agarraste	agarrasteis	hubiste agarrado	hubisteis agarrado
agarró	agarraron	hubo agarrado	hubieron agarrado
4 futuro		**11 futuro perfecto**	
agarraré	agarraremos	habré agarrado	habremos agarrado
agarrarás	agarraréis	habrás agarrado	habréis agarrado
agarrará	agarrarán	habrá agarrado	habrán agarrado
5 potencial simple		**12 potencial compuesto**	
agarraría	agarraríamos	habría agarrado	habríamos agarrado
agarrarías	agarraríais	habrías agarrado	habríais agarrado
agarraría	agarrarían	habría agarrado	habrían agarrado
6 presente de subjuntivo		**13 perfecto de subjuntivo**	
agarre	agarremos	haya agarrado	hayamos agarrado
agarres	agarréis	hayas agarrado	hayáis agarrado
agarre	agarren	haya agarrado	hayan agarrado
7 imperfecto de subjuntivo		**14 pluscuamperfecto de subjuntivo**	
agarrara	agarráramos	hubiera agarrado	hubiéramos agarrado
agarraras	agarrarais	hubieras agarrado	hubierais agarrado
agarrara	agarraran	hubiera agarrado	hubieran agarrado
OR		OR	
agarrase	agarrásemos	hubiese agarrado	hubiésemos agarrado
agarrases	agarraseis	hubieses agarrado	hubieseis agarrado
agarrase	agarrasen	hubiese agarrado	hubiesen agarrado

imperativo	
—	agarremos
agarra; no agarres	agarrad; no agarréis
agarre	agarren

Words and expressions related to this verb

el agarro grasp
la agarrada quarrel, scrap
agarrarse a *or* **de** to seize

agarrarse una fiebre to catch a fever
agarrar de un pelo to provide an excuse
desgarrar to rend, rip, tear

Do you need more drills? Have fun with the *501 Spanish Verbs* CD-ROM!

The subject pronouns are found on page 93.

agitar (37)

Gerundio **agitando**　　Part. pas. **agitado**

to agitate, to wave, to shake up, to stir

The Seven Simple Tenses		The Seven Compound Tenses	
Singular	Plural	Singular	Plural
1 presente de indicativo		**8 perfecto de indicativo**	
agito	agitamos	he agitado	hemos agitado
agitas	agitáis	has agitado	habéis agitado
agita	agitan	ha agitado	han agitado
2 imperfecto de indicativo		**9 pluscuamperfecto de indicativo**	
agitaba	agitábamos	había agitado	habíamos agitado
agitabas	agitabais	habías agitado	habíais agitado
agitaba	agitaban	había agitado	habían agitado
3 pretérito		**10 pretérito anterior**	
agité	agitamos	hube agitado	hubimos agitado
agitaste	agitasteis	hubiste agitado	hubisteis agitado
agitó	agitaron	hubo agitado	hubieron agitado
4 futuro		**11 futuro perfecto**	
agitaré	agitaremos	habré agitado	habremos agitado
agitarás	agitaréis	habrás agitado	habréis agitado
agitará	agitarán	habrá agitado	habrán agitado
5 potencial simple		**12 potencial compuesto**	
agitaría	agitaríamos	habría agitado	habríamos agitado
agitarías	agitaríais	habrías agitado	habríais agitado
agitaría	agitarían	habría agitado	habrían agitado
6 presente de subjuntivo		**13 perfecto de subjuntivo**	
agite	agitemos	haya agitado	hayamos agitado
agites	agitéis	hayas agitado	hayáis agitado
agite	agiten	haya agitado	hayan agitado
7 imperfecto de subjuntivo		**14 pluscuamperfecto de subjuntivo**	
agitara	agitáramos	hubiera agitado	hubiéramos agitado
agitaras	agitarais	hubieras agitado	hubierais agitado
agitara	agitaran	hubiera agitado	hubieran agitado
OR		OR	
agitase	agitásemos	hubiese agitado	hubiésemos agitado
agitases	agitaseis	hubieses agitado	hubieseis agitado
agitase	agitasen	hubiese agitado	hubiesen agitado

	imperativo	
—		**agitemos**
agita; no agites		**agitad; no agitéis**
agite		**agiten**

Words related to this verb
la agitación agitation, excitement
agitado, agitada agitated, excited
agitarse to fidget, to become agitated

agitable agitable
un agitador, una agitadora agitator, shaker

Don't miss the definitions of basic grammatical terms with examples
in English and Spanish on pages 33–44.

134

Regular **-ar** verb   to exhaust, to use up

The Seven Simple Tenses		The Seven Compound Tenses	
Singular	Plural	Singular	Plural

A

1 presente de indicativo		8 perfecto de indicativo	
agoto	agotamos	he agotado	hemos agotado
agotas	agotáis	has agotado	habéis agotado
agota	agotan	ha agotado	han agotado

2 imperfecto de indicativo		9 pluscuamperfecto de indicativo	
agotaba	agotábamos	había agotado	habíamos agotado
agotabas	agotabais	habías agotado	habíais agotado
agotaba	agotaban	había agotado	habían agotado

3 pretérito		10 pretérito anterior	
agoté	agotamos	hube agotado	hubimos agotado
agotaste	agotasteis	hubiste agotado	hubisteis agotado
agotó	agotaron	hubo agotado	hubieron agotado

4 futuro		11 futuro perfecto	
agotaré	agotaremos	habré agotado	habremos agotado
agotarás	agotaréis	habrás agotado	habréis agotado
agotará	agotarán	habrá agotado	habrán agotado

5 potencial simple		12 potencial compuesto	
agotaría	agotaríamos	habría agotado	habríamos agotado
agotarías	agotaríais	habrías agotado	habríais agotado
agotaría	agotarían	habría agotado	habrían agotado

6 presente de subjuntivo		13 perfecto de subjuntivo	
agote	agotemos	haya agotado	hayamos agotado
agotes	agotéis	hayas agotado	hayáis agotado
agote	agoten	haya agotado	hayan agotado

7 imperfecto de subjuntivo		14 pluscuamperfecto de subjuntivo	
agotara	agotáramos	hubiera agotado	hubiéramos agotado
agotaras	agotarais	hubieras agotado	hubierais agotado
agotara	agotaran	hubiera agotado	hubieran agotado
OR		OR	
agotase	agotásemos	hubiese agotado	hubiésemos agotado
agotases	agotaseis	hubieses agotado	hubieseis agotado
agotase	agotasen	hubiese agotado	hubiesen agotado

imperativo

—	agotemos
agota; no agotes	agotad; no agotéis
agote	agoten

Words related to this verb

agotador, agotadora exhausting
el agotamiento exhaustion

agotable exhaustible
agotado, agotada exhausted; out of print, out of stock, sold out

If you don't know the Spanish verb for the English verb you have in mind,
look it up in the index on pages 682–706.

The subject pronouns are found on page 93.

to please, to be pleasing   Regular **-ar** verb

The Seven Simple Tenses		The Seven Compound Tenses	
Singular	Plural	Singular	Plural
1 presente de indicativo		**8 perfecto de indicativo**	
agrado	agradamos	he agradado	hemos agradado
agradas	agradáis	has agradado	habéis agradado
agrada	agradan	ha agradado	han agradado
2 imperfecto de indicativo		**9 pluscuamperfecto de indicativo**	
agradaba	agradábamos	había agradado	habíamos agradado
agradabas	agradabais	habías agradado	habíais agradado
agradaba	agradaban	había agradado	habían agradado
3 pretérito		**10 pretérito anterior**	
agradé	agradamos	hube agradado	hubimos agradado
agradaste	agradasteis	hubiste agradado	hubisteis agradado
agradó	agradaron	hubo agradado	hubieron agradado
4 futuro		**11 futuro perfecto**	
agradaré	agradaremos	habré agradado	habremos agradado
agradarás	agradaréis	habrás agradado	habréis agradado
agradará	agradarán	habrá agradado	habrán agradado
5 potencial simple		**12 potencial compuesto**	
agradaría	agradaríamos	habría agradado	habríamos agradado
agradarías	agradaríais	habrías agradado	habríais agradado
agradaría	agradarían	habría agradado	habrían agradado
6 presente de subjuntivo		**13 perfecto de subjuntivo**	
agrade	agrademos	haya agradado	hayamos agradado
agrades	agradéis	hayas agradado	hayáis agradado
agrade	agraden	haya agradado	hayan agradado
7 imperfecto de subjuntivo		**14 pluscuamperfecto de subjuntivo**	
agradara	agradáramos	hubiera agradado	hubiéramos agradado
agradaras	agradarais	hubieras agradado	hubierais agradado
agradara	agradaran	hubiera agradado	hubieran agradado
OR		OR	
agradase	agradásemos	hubiese agradado	hubiésemos agradado
agradases	agradaseis	hubieses agradado	hubieseis agradado
agradase	agradasen	hubiese agradado	hubiesen agradado

imperativo	
—	agrademos
agrada; no agrades	agradad; no agradéis
agrade	agraden

Words and expressions related to this verb
agradable pleasing, pleasant, agreeable
agradablemente agreeably, pleasantly
el agrado pleasure, liking
Es de mi agrado. It's to my liking.
de su agrado to one's liking
ser del agrado de uno to be to one's taste (liking)

Pablo es un muchacho agradador.
   Paul is eager to please.
María es una muchacha agradadora.
   Mary is eager to please.
desagradable unpleasant, disagreeable

Regular **-er** verb endings with spelling   to thank, to be thankful for
change: **c** becomes **zc** before **a** or **o**

The Seven Simple Tenses		The Seven Compound Tenses	
Singular	Plural	Singular	Plural

1   presente de indicativo

agradezco	agradecemos
agradeces	agradecéis
agradece	agradecen

8   perfecto de indicativo

he agradecido	hemos agradecido
has agradecido	habéis agradecido
ha agradecido	han agradecido

2   imperfecto de indicativo

agradecía	agradecíamos
agradecías	agradecíais
agradecía	agradecían

9   pluscuamperfecto de indicativo

había agradecido	habíamos agradecido
habías agradecido	habíais agradecido
había agradecido	habían agradecido

3   pretérito

agradecí	agradecimos
agradeciste	agradecisteis
agradeció	agradecieron

10   pretérito anterior

hube agradecido	hubimos agradecido
hubiste agradecido	hubisteis agradecido
hubo agradecido	hubieron agradecido

4   futuro

agradeceré	agradeceremos
agradecerás	agradeceréis
agradecerá	agradecerán

11   futuro perfecto

habré agradecido	habremos agradecido
habrás agradecido	habréis agradecido
habrá agradecido	habrán agradecido

5   potencial simple

agradecería	agradeceríamos
agradecerías	agradeceríais
agradecería	agradecerían

12   potencial compuesto

habría agradecido	habríamos agradecido
habrías agradecido	habríais agradecido
habría agradecido	habrían agradecido

6   presente de subjuntivo

agradezca	agradezcamos
agradezcas	agradezcáis
agradezca	agradezcan

13   perfecto de subjuntivo

haya agradecido	hayamos agradecido
hayas agradecido	hayáis agradecido
haya agradecido	hayan agradecido

7   imperfecto de subjuntivo

agradeciera	agradeciéramos
agradecieras	agradecierais
agradeciera	agradecieran
OR	
agradeciese	agradeciésemos
agradecieses	agradecieseis
agradeciese	agradeciesen

14   pluscuamperfecto de subjuntivo

hubiera agradecido	hubiéramos agradecido
hubieras agradecido	hubierais agradecido
hubiera agradecido	hubieran agradecido
OR	
hubiese agradecido	hubiésemos agradecido
hubieses agradecido	hubieseis agradecido
hubiese agradecido	hubiesen agradecido

imperativo

—	agradezcamos
agradece; no agradezcas	agradeced; no agradezcáis
agradezca	agradezcan

Words and expressions related to this verb

agradecido, agradecida   thankful, grateful
el agradecimiento   gratitude, gratefulness
muy agradecido   much obliged

desagradecer   to be ungrateful
desagradecidamente   ungratefully

Don't miss the definitions of basic grammatical terms with examples
in English and Spanish on pages 33–44.

The subject pronouns are found on page 93.

to enlarge, to grow larger, to increase, to exaggerate   Regular **-ar** verb

The Seven Simple Tenses		The Seven Compound Tenses	
Singular	Plural	Singular	Plural
1 presente de indicativo		8 perfecto de indicativo	
agrando	agrandamos	he agrandado	hemos agrandado
agrandas	agrandáis	has agrandado	habéis agrandado
agranda	agrandan	ha agrandado	han agrandado
2 imperfecto de indicativo		9 pluscuamperfecto de indicativo	
agrandaba	agrandábamos	había agrandado	habíamos agrandado
agrandabas	agrandabais	habías agrandado	habíais agrandado
agrandaba	agrandaban	había agrandado	habían agrandado
3 pretérito		10 pretérito anterior	
agrandé	agrandamos	hube agrandado	hubimos agrandado
agrandaste	agrandasteis	hubiste agrandado	hubisteis agrandado
agrandó	agrandaron	hubo agrandado	hubieron agrandado
4 futuro		11 futuro perfecto	
agrandaré	agrandaremos	habré agrandado	habremos agrandado
agrandarás	agrandaréis	habrás agrandado	habréis agrandado
agrandará	agrandarán	habrá agrandado	habrán agrandado
5 potencial simple		12 potencial compuesto	
agrandaría	agrandaríamos	habría agrandado	habríamos agrandado
agrandarías	agrandaríais	habrías agrandado	habríais agrandado
agrandaría	agrandarían	habría agrandado	habrían agrandado
6 presente de subjuntivo		13 perfecto de subjuntivo	
agrande	agrandemos	haya agrandado	hayamos agrandado
agrandes	agrandéis	hayas agrandado	hayáis agrandado
agrande	agranden	haya agrandado	hayan agrandado
7 imperfecto de subjuntivo		14 pluscuamperfecto de subjuntivo	
agrandara	agrandáramos	hubiera agrandado	hubiéramos agrandado
agrandaras	agrandarais	hubieras agrandado	hubierais agrandado
agrandara	agrandaran	hubiera agrandado	hubieran agrandado
OR		OR	
agrandase	agrandásemos	hubiese agrandado	hubiésemos agrandado
agrandases	agrandaseis	hubieses agrandado	hubieseis agrandado
agrandase	agrandasen	hubiese agrandado	hubiesen agrandado

imperativo	
—	agrandemos
agranda; no agrandes	agrandad; no agrandéis
agrande	agranden

Words and expressions related to this verb
el agrandamiento aggrandizement, increase
en grande in a grand way
grandemente greatly

grande great, big, large, grand, huge
vivir a lo grande to live high (live it up)
dárselas de grande to swagger

The Seven Simple Tenses | The Seven Compound Tenses

Singular	Plural	Singular	Plural
1 presente de indicativo		**8 perfecto de indicativo**	
agravo	agravamos	he agravado	hemos agravado
agravas	agraváis	has agravado	habéis agravado
agrava	agravan	ha agravado	han agravado
2 imperfecto de indicativo		**9 pluscuamperfecto de indicativo**	
agravaba	agravábamos	había agravado	habíamos agravado
agravabas	agravabais	habías agravado	habíais agravado
agravaba	agravaban	había agravado	habían agravado
3 pretérito		**10 pretérito anterior**	
agravé	agravamos	hube agravado	hubimos agravado
agravaste	agravasteis	hubiste agravado	hubisteis agravado
agravó	agravaron	hubo agravado	hubieron agravado
4 futuro		**11 futuro perfecto**	
agravaré	agravaremos	habré agravado	habremos agravado
agravarás	agravaréis	habrás agravado	habréis agravado
agravará	agravarán	habrá agravado	habrán agravado
5 potencial simple		**12 potencial compuesto**	
agravaría	agravaríamos	habría agravado	habríamos agravado
agravarías	agravaríais	habrías agravado	habríais agravado
agravaría	agravarían	habría agravado	habrían agravado
6 presente de subjuntivo		**13 perfecto de subjuntivo**	
agrave	agravemos	haya agravado	hayamos agravado
agraves	agravéis	hayas agravado	hayáis agravado
agrave	agraven	haya agravado	hayan agravado
7 imperfecto de subjuntivo		**14 pluscuamperfecto de subjuntivo**	
agravara	agraváramos	hubiera agravado	hubiéramos agravado
agravaras	agravarais	hubieras agravado	hubierais agravado
agravara	agravaran	hubiera agravado	hubieran agravado
OR		OR	
agravase	agravásemos	hubiese agravado	hubiésemos agravado
agravases	agravaseis	hubieses agravado	hubieseis agravado
agravase	agravasen	hubiese agravado	hubiesen agravado

imperativo

—	agravemos
agrava; no agraves	agravad; no agravéis
agrave	agraven

Words related to this verb
agraviadamente offensively
agraviado, agraviada insulted
el agraviamiento offense, wrongful injury

agravante aggravating
una agravación, un agravamiento aggravation

Don't forget to study the section on defective and impersonal verbs. It's right after this main list.

The subject pronouns are found on page 93.

to add, to collect, to gather,
to aggregate, to collate

Regular **-ar** verb endings with spelling
change: **g** becomes **gu** before **e**

The Seven Simple Tenses		The Seven Compound Tenses	
Singular	Plural	Singular	Plural

1 presente de indicativo

		8 perfecto de indicativo	
agrego	agregamos	he agregado	hemos agregado
agregas	agregáis	has agregado	habéis agregado
agrega	agregan	ha agregado	han agregado

2 imperfecto de indicativo

		9 pluscuamperfecto de indicativo	
agregaba	agregábamos	había agregado	habíamos agregado
agregabas	agregabais	habías agregado	habíais agregado
agregaba	agregaban	había agregado	habían agregado

3 pretérito

		10 pretérito anterior	
agregué	agregamos	hube agregado	hubimos agregado
agregaste	agregasteis	hubiste agregado	hubisteis agregado
agregó	agregaron	hubo agregado	hubieron agregado

4 futuro

		11 futuro perfecto	
agregaré	agregaremos	habré agregado	habremos agregado
agregarás	agregaréis	habrás agregado	habréis agregado
agregará	agregarán	habrá agregado	habrán agregado

5 potencial simple

		12 potencial compuesto	
agregaría	agregaríamos	habría agregado	habríamos agregado
agregarías	agregaríais	habrías agregado	habríais agregado
agregaría	agregarían	habría agregado	habrían agregado

6 presente de subjuntivo

		13 perfecto de subjuntivo	
agregue	agreguemos	haya agregado	hayamos agregado
agregues	agreguéis	hayas agregado	hayáis agregado
agregue	agreguen	haya agregado	hayan agregado

7 imperfecto de subjuntivo

		14 pluscuamperfecto de subjuntivo	
agregara	agregáramos	hubiera agregado	hubiéramos agregado
agregaras	agregarais	hubieras agregado	hubierais agregado
agregara	agregaran	hubiera agregado	hubieran agregado
OR		OR	
agregase	agregásemos	hubiese agregado	hubiésemos agregado
agregases	agregaseis	hubieses agregado	hubieseis agregado
agregase	agregasen	hubiese agregado	hubiesen agregado

imperativo

—	agreguemos
agrega; no agregues	agregad; no agreguéis
agregue	agreguen

Words and expressions related to this verb
agregarse a   to join
un agregado comercial   commercial attaché

agregar dos a cinco   to add two to five

If you want to see a sample English verb fully conjugated in
all the tenses, check out pages 11 and 12.

The Seven Simple Tenses		The Seven Compound Tenses	
Singular	Plural	Singular	Plural

1 presente de indicativo

agrupo	agrupamos		
agrupas	agrupáis		
agrupa	agrupan		

8 perfecto de indicativo

he agrupado	hemos agrupado
has agrupado	habéis agrupado
ha agrupado	han agrupado

2 imperfecto de indicativo

agrupaba	agrupábamos
agrupabas	agrupabais
agrupaba	agrupaban

9 pluscuamperfecto de indicativo

había agrupado	habíamos agrupado
habías agrupado	habíais agrupado
había agrupado	habían agrupado

3 pretérito

agrupé	agrupamos
agrupaste	agrupasteis
agrupó	agruparon

10 pretérito anterior

hube agrupado	hubimos agrupado
hubiste agrupado	hubisteis agrupado
hubo agrupado	hubieron agrupado

4 futuro

agruparé	agruparemos
agruparás	agruparéis
agrupará	agruparán

11 futuro perfecto

habré agrupado	habremos agrupado
habrás agrupado	habréis agrupado
habrá agrupado	habrán agrupado

5 potencial simple

agruparía	agruparíamos
agruparías	agruparíais
agruparía	agruparían

12 potencial compuesto

habría agrupado	habríamos agrupado
habrías agrupado	habríais agrupado
habría agrupado	habrían agrupado

6 presente de subjuntivo

agrupe	agrupemos
agrupes	agrupéis
agrupe	agrupen

13 perfecto de subjuntivo

haya agrupado	hayamos agrupado
hayas agrupado	hayáis agrupado
haya agrupado	hayan agrupado

7 imperfecto de subjuntivo

agrupara	agrupáramos
agruparas	agruparais
agrupara	agruparan
OR	
agrupase	agrupásemos
agrupases	agrupaseis
agrupase	agrupasen

14 pluscuamperfecto de subjuntivo

hubiera agrupado	hubiéramos agrupado
hubieras agrupado	hubierais agrupado
hubiera agrupado	hubieran agrupado
OR	
hubiese agrupado	hubiésemos agrupado
hubieses agrupado	hubieseis agrupado
hubiese agrupado	hubiesen agrupado

imperativo

—	agrupemos
agrupa; no agrupes	agrupad; no agrupéis
agrupe	agrupen

Words related to this verb

una agrupación, un agrupamiento group   **un grupo** group
   (cluster)   **una agrupación coral** choral group
agrupado, agrupada grouped

Check out the verb drills and verb tests with answers explained on pages 45–91.

The subject pronouns are found on page 93.

to expect, to wait for   Regular **-ar** verb

The Seven Simple Tenses		The Seven Compound Tenses	
Singular	Plural	Singular	Plural
1 presente de indicativo		8 perfecto de indicativo	
aguardo	aguardamos	he aguardado	hemos aguardado
aguardas	aguardáis	has aguardado	habéis aguardado
aguarda	aguardan	ha aguardado	han aguardado
2 imperfecto de indicativo		9 pluscuamperfecto de indicativo	
aguardaba	aguardábamos	había aguardado	habíamos aguardado
aguardabas	aguardabais	habías aguardado	habíais aguardado
aguardaba	aguardaban	había aguardado	habían aguardado
3 pretérito		10 pretérito anterior	
aguardé	aguardamos	hube aguardado	hubimos aguardado
aguardaste	aguardasteis	hubiste aguardado	hubisteis aguardado
aguardó	aguardaron	hubo aguardado	hubieron aguardado
4 futuro		11 futuro perfecto	
aguardaré	aguardaremos	habré aguardado	habremos aguardado
aguardarás	aguardaréis	habrás aguardado	habréis aguardado
aguardará	aguardarán	habrá aguardado	habrán aguardado
5 potencial simple		12 potencial compuesto	
aguardaría	aguardaríamos	habría aguardado	habríamos aguardado
aguardarías	aguardaríais	habrías aguardado	habríais aguardado
aguardaría	aguardarían	habría aguardado	habrían aguardado
6 presente de subjuntivo		13 perfecto de subjuntivo	
aguarde	aguardemos	haya aguardado	hayamos aguardado
aguardes	aguardéis	hayas aguardado	hayáis aguardado
aguarde	aguarden	haya aguardado	hayan aguardado
7 imperfecto de subjuntivo		14 pluscuamperfecto de subjuntivo	
aguardara	aguardáramos	hubiera aguardado	hubiéramos aguardado
aguardaras	aguardarais	hubieras aguardado	hubierais aguardado
aguardara	aguardaran	hubiera aguardado	hubieran aguardado
OR		OR	
aguardase	aguardásemos	hubiese aguardado	hubiésemos aguardado
aguardases	aguardaseis	hubieses aguardado	hubieseis aguardado
aguardase	aguardasen	hubiese aguardado	hubiesen aguardado

	imperativo	
—		aguardemos
	aguarda; no aguardes	aguardad; no aguardéis
	aguarde	aguarden

Words and expressions related to this verb
la aguardada   expecting, waiting
guardar   to guard, to watch (over)

guardar silencio   to keep silent
¡Dios guarde al Rey!   God save the King!

Can't find the verb you're looking for?
Check the back pages of this book for a list of over 2,100 additional verbs!

Regular **-ar** verb

to economize, to save

A

The Seven Simple Tenses		The Seven Compound Tenses	
Singular	Plural	Singular	Plural
1 presente de indicativo		8 perfecto de indicativo	
ahorro	ahorramos	he ahorrado	hemos ahorrado
ahorras	ahorráis	has ahorrado	habéis ahorrado
ahorra	ahorran	ha ahorrado	han ahorrado
2 imperfecto de indicativo		9 pluscuamperfecto de indicativo	
ahorraba	ahorrábamos	había ahorrado	habíamos ahorrado
ahorrabas	ahorrabais	habías ahorrado	habíais ahorrado
ahorraba	ahorraban	había ahorrado	habían ahorrado
3 pretérito		10 pretérito anterior	
ahorré	ahorramos	hube ahorrado	hubimos ahorrado
ahorraste	ahorrasteis	hubiste ahorrado	hubisteis ahorrado
ahorró	ahorraron	hubo ahorrado	hubieron ahorrado
4 futuro		11 futuro perfecto	
ahorraré	ahorraremos	habré ahorrado	habremos ahorrado
ahorrarás	ahorraréis	habrás ahorrado	habréis ahorrado
ahorrará	ahorrarán	habrá ahorrado	habrán ahorrado
5 potencial simple		12 potencial compuesto	
ahorraría	ahorraríamos	habría ahorrado	habríamos ahorrado
ahorrarías	ahorraríais	habrías ahorrado	habríais ahorrado
ahorraría	ahorrarían	habría ahorrado	habrían ahorrado
6 presente de subjuntivo		13 perfecto de subjuntivo	
ahorre	ahorremos	haya ahorrado	hayamos ahorrado
ahorres	ahorréis	hayas ahorrado	hayáis ahorrado
ahorre	ahorren	haya ahorrado	hayan ahorrado
7 imperfecto de subjuntivo		14 pluscuamperfecto de subjuntivo	
ahorrara	ahorráramos	hubiera ahorrado	hubiéramos ahorrado
ahorraras	ahorrarais	hubieras ahorrado	hubierais ahorrado
ahorrara	ahorraran	hubiera ahorrado	hubieran ahorrado
OR		OR	
ahorrase	ahorrásemos	hubiese ahorrado	hubiésemos ahorrado
ahorrases	ahorraseis	hubieses ahorrado	hubieseis ahorrado
ahorrase	ahorrasen	hubiese ahorrado	hubiesen ahorrado

imperativo	
—	ahorremos
ahorra; no ahorres	ahorrad; no ahorréis
ahorre	ahorren

Words and expressions related to this verb

ahorrado, ahorrada thrifty
un ahorrador de tiempo time saver
ahorrador, ahorradora thrifty person, thrifty

el ahorramiento saving, economy
no ahorrarse con nadie not to be afraid
of anybody

> If you don't know the Spanish verb for an English verb you have in mind,
> try the index on pages 682–706.

The subject pronouns are found on page 93.

alcanzar (47)

Gerundio **alcanzando**   Part. pas. **alcanzado**

to reach, to overtake

Regular **-ar** verb endings with spelling change: **z** becomes **c** before **e**

The Seven Simple Tenses		The Seven Compound Tenses	
Singular	Plural	Singular	Plural
1 presente de indicativo		**8 perfecto de indicativo**	
alcanzo	alcanzamos	he alcanzado	hemos alcanzado
alcanzas	alcanzáis	has alcanzado	habéis alcanzado
alcanza	alcanzan	ha alcanzado	han alcanzado
2 imperfecto de indicativo		**9 pluscuamperfecto de indicativo**	
alcanzaba	alcanzábamos	había alcanzado	habíamos alcanzado
alcanzabas	alcanzabais	habías alcanzado	habíais alcanzado
alcanzaba	alcanzaban	había alcanzado	habían alcanzado
3 pretérito		**10 pretérito anterior**	
alcancé	alcanzamos	hube alcanzado	hubimos alcanzado
alcanzaste	alcanzasteis	hubiste alcanzado	hubisteis alcanzado
alcanzó	alcanzaron	hubo alcanzado	hubieron alcanzado
4 futuro		**11 futuro perfecto**	
alcanzaré	alcanzaremos	habré alcanzado	habremos alcanzado
alcanzarás	alcanzaréis	habrás alcanzado	habréis alcanzado
alcanzará	alcanzarán	habrá alcanzado	habrán alcanzado
5 potencial simple		**12 potencial compuesto**	
alcanzaría	alcanzaríamos	habría alcanzado	habríamos alcanzado
alcanzarías	alcanzaríais	habrías alcanzado	habríais alcanzado
alcanzaría	alcanzarían	habría alcanzado	habrían alcanzado
6 presente de subjuntivo		**13 perfecto de subjuntivo**	
alcance	alcancemos	haya alcanzado	hayamos alcanzado
alcances	alcancéis	hayas alcanzado	hayáis alcanzado
alcance	alcancen	haya alcanzado	hayan alcanzado
7 imperfecto de subjuntivo		**14 pluscuamperfecto de subjuntivo**	
alcanzara	alcanzáramos	hubiera alcanzado	hubiéramos alcanzado
alcanzaras	alcanzarais	hubieras alcanzado	hubierais alcanzado
alcanzara	alcanzaran	hubiera alcanzado	hubieran alcanzado
OR		OR	
alcanzase	alcanzásemos	hubiese alcanzado	hubiésemos alcanzado
alcanzases	alcanzaseis	hubieses alcanzado	hubieseis alcanzado
alcanzase	alcanzasen	hubiese alcanzado	hubiesen alcanzado

imperativo	
—	alcancemos
alcanza; no alcances	alcanzad; no alcancéis
alcance	alcancen

Words and expressions related to this verb

el alcance   overtaking, reach
al alcance de   within reach of
dar alcance a   to overtake

al alcance del oído   within earshot
alcanzable   attainable, reachable
el alcanzador, la alcanzadora   pursuer

If you want an explanation of meanings and uses of Spanish and English verb tenses and moods, see pages 13–32.

144

Reflexive regular **-ar** verb   to be glad, to rejoice, to be happy

The Seven Simple Tenses		The Seven Compound Tenses	
Singular	Plural	Singular	Plural

A

1 presente de indicativo

		8 perfecto de indicativo	
me alegro	nos alegramos	me he alegrado	nos hemos alegrado
te alegras	os alegráis	te has alegrado	os habéis alegrado
se alegra	se alegran	se ha alegrado	se han alegrado

2 imperfecto de indicativo   **9 pluscuamperfecto de indicativo**

me alegraba	nos alegrábamos	me había alegrado	nos habíamos alegrado
te alegrabas	os alegrabais	te habías alegrado	os habíais alegrado
se alegraba	se alegraban	se había alegrado	se habían alegrado

3 pretérito   **10 pretérito anterior**

me alegré	nos alegramos	me hube alegrado	nos hubimos alegrado
te alegraste	os alegrasteis	te hubiste alegrado	os hubisteis alegrado
se alegró	se alegraron	se hubo alegrado	se hubieron alegrado

4 futuro   **11 futuro perfecto**

me alegraré	nos alegraremos	me habré alegrado	nos habremos alegrado
te alegrarás	os alegraréis	te habrás alegrado	os habréis alegrado
se alegrará	se alegrarán	se habrá alegrado	se habrán alegrado

5 potencial simple   **12 potencial compuesto**

me alegraría	nos alegraríamos	me habría alegrado	nos habríamos alegrado
te alegrarías	os alegraríais	te habrías alegrado	os habríais alegrado
se alegraría	se alegrarían	se habría alegrado	se habrían alegrado

6 presente de subjuntivo   **13 perfecto de subjuntivo**

me alegre	nos alegremos	me haya alegrado	nos hayamos alegrado
te alegres	os alegréis	te hayas alegrado	os hayáis alegrado
se alegre	se alegren	se haya alegrado	se hayan alegrado

7 imperfecto de subjuntivo   **14 pluscuamperfecto de subjuntivo**

me alegrara	nos alegráramos	me hubiera alegrado	nos hubiéramos alegrado
te alegraras	os alegrarais	te hubieras alegrado	os hubierais alegrado
se alegrara	se alegraran	se hubiera alegrado	se hubieran alegrado
OR		OR	
me alegrase	nos alegrásemos	me hubiese alegrado	nos hubiésemos alegrado
te alegrases	os alegraseis	te hubieses alegrado	os hubieseis alegrado
se alegrase	se alegrasen	se hubiese alegrado	se hubiesen alegrado

imperativo

—	alegrémonos
alégrate; no te alegres	**alegraos; no os alegréis**
alégrese	**alégrense**

Words and expressions related to this verb

la alegría joy, rejoicing, mirth
alegro allegro
tener mucha alegría to be very glad
¡Qué alegría! What joy!

alegremente gladly, cheerfully
alegre happy, joyful, merry, bright (color)
alegrar la fiesta to liven up the party
saltar de alegría to jump for joy

The subject pronouns are found on page 93.

to lunch, to have lunch   Regular **-ar** verb endings with stem change: Tenses 1, 6, Imperative; spelling change: **z** becomes **c** before **e**

The Seven Simple Tenses		The Seven Compound Tenses	
Singular	Plural	Singular	Plural
1 presente de indicativo		**8 perfecto de indicativo**	
almuerzo	almorzamos	he almorzado	hemos almorzado
almuerzas	almorzáis	has almorzado	habéis almorzado
almuerza	almuerzan	ha almorzado	han almorzado
2 imperfecto de indicativo		**9 pluscuamperfecto de indicativo**	
almorzaba	almorzábamos	había almorzado	habíamos almorzado
almorzabas	almorzabais	habías almorzado	habíais almorzado
almorzaba	almorzaban	había almorzado	habían almorzado
3 pretérito		**10 pretérito anterior**	
almorcé	almorzamos	hube almorzado	hubimos almorzado
almorzaste	almorzasteis	hubiste almorzado	hubisteis almorzado
almorzó	almorzaron	hubo almorzado	hubieron almorzado
4 futuro		**11 futuro perfecto**	
almorzaré	almorzaremos	habré almorzado	habremos almorzado
almorzarás	almorzaréis	habrás almorzado	habréis almorzado
almorzará	almorzarán	habrá almorzado	habrán almorzado
5 potencial simple		**12 potencial compuesto**	
almorzaría	almorzaríamos	habría almorzado	habríamos almorzado
almorzarías	almorzaríais	habrías almorzado	habríais almorzado
almorzaría	almorzarían	habría almorzado	habrían almorzado
6 presente de subjuntivo		**13 perfecto de subjuntivo**	
almuerce	almorcemos	haya almorzado	hayamos almorzado
almuerces	almorcéis	hayas almorzado	hayáis almorzado
almuerce	almuercen	haya almorzado	hayan almorzado
7 imperfecto de subjuntivo		**14 pluscuamperfecto de subjuntivo**	
almorzara	almorzáramos	hubiera almorzado	hubiéramos almorzado
almorzaras	almorzarais	hubieras almorzado	hubierais almorzado
almorzara	almorzaran	hubiera almorzado	hubieran almorzado
OR		OR	
almorzase	almorzásemos	hubiese almorzado	hubiésemos almorzado
almorzases	almorzaseis	hubieses almorzado	hubieseis almorzado
almorzase	almorzasen	hubiese almorzado	hubiesen almorzado

imperativo	
—	almorcemos
almuerza; no almuerces	almorzad; no almorcéis
almuerce	almuercen

Sentences using this verb and words related to it
Todos los días tomo el desayuno en casa, tomo el almuerzo en la escuela con mis amigos, y ceno con mi familia a las ocho.

el desayuno breakfast   **cenar** to have dinner, supper
el almuerzo lunch   **una almorzada** handful
la cena dinner, supper

Use the guide to Spanish pronunciation on pages 665–667.

Gerundio alquilando   Part. pas. alquilado   alquilar (50)

Regular **-ar** verb

to hire, to rent

The Seven Simple Tenses		The Seven Compound Tenses	
Singular	Plural	Singular	Plural
1 presente de indicativo		**8 perfecto de indicativo**	
alquilo	alquilamos	he alquilado	hemos alquilado
alquilas	alquiláis	has alquilado	habéis alquilado
alauila	alquilan	ha alquilado	han alquilado
2 imperfecto de indicativo		**9 pluscuamperfecto de indicativo**	
alquilaba	alquilábamos	había alquilado	habíamos alquilado
alquilabas	alquilabais	habías alquilado	habíais alquilado
alquilaba	alquilaban	había alquilado	habían alquilado
3 pretérito		**10 pretérito anterior**	
alquilé	alquilamos	hube alquilado	hubimos alquilado
alquilaste	alquilasteis	hubiste alquilado	hubisteis alquilado
alquiló	alquilaron	hubo alquilado	hubieron alquilado
4 futuro		**11 futuro perfecto**	
alquilaré	alquilaremos	habré alquilado	habremos alquilado
alquilarás	alquilaréis	habrás alquilado	habréis alquilado
alquilará	alquilarán	habrá alquilado	habrán alquilado
5 potencial simple		**12 potencial compuesto**	
alquilaría	alquilaríamos	habría alquilado	habríamos alquilado
alquilarías	alquilaríais	habrías alquilado	habríais alquilado
alquilaría	alquilarían	habría alquilado	habrían alquilado
6 presente de subjuntivo		**13 perfecto de subjuntivo**	
alquile	alquilemos	haya alquilado	hayamos alquilado
alquiles	alquiléis	hayas alquilado	hayáis alquilado
alquile	alquilen	haya alquilado	hayan alquilado
7 imperfecto de subjuntivo		**14 pluscuamperfecto de subjuntivo**	
alquilara	alquiláramos	hubiera alquilado	hubiéramos alquilado
alquilaras	alquilarais	hubieras alquilado	hubierais alquilado
alquilara`	alquilaran	hubiera alquilado	hubieran alquilado
OR		OR	
alquilase	alquilásemos	hubiese alquilado	hubiésemos alquilado
alquilases	alquilaseis	hubieses alquilado	hubieseis alquilado
alquilase	alquilasen	hubiese alquilado	hubiesen alquilado

imperativo

—	alquilemos
alquila; no alquiles	alquilad; no alquiléis
alquile	alquilen

Words and expressions related to this verb

alquilable rentable
SE ALQUILA FOR RENT
ALQUILA AVAILABLE

desalquilar to vacate, stop renting
desalquilarse to become vacant, unrented
desalquilado, desalquilada unrented, unlet, vacant

> If you want to see a sample English verb fully conjugated
> in all the tenses, check out pages 11 and 12.

alumbrar (51)　　Gerundio **alumbrando**　Part. pas. **alumbrado**

to illuminate, to light, to enlighten　　Regular **-ar** verb

The Seven Simple Tenses		The Seven Compound Tenses	
Singular	Plural	Singular	Plural
1 presente de indicativo		**8 perfecto de indicativo**	
alumbro	alumbramos	he alumbrado	hemos alumbrado
alumbras	alumbráis	has alumbrado	habéis alumbrado
alumbra	alumbran	ha alumbrado	han alumbrado
2 imperfecto de indicativo		**9 pluscuamperfecto de indicativo**	
alumbraba	alumbrábamos	había alumbrado	habíamos alumbrado
alumbrabas	alumbrabais	habías alumbrado	habíais alumbrado
alumbraba	alumbraban	había alumbrado	habían alumbrado
3 pretérito		**10 pretérito anterior**	
alumbré	alumbramos	hube alumbrado	hubimos alumbrado
alumbraste	alumbrasteis	hubiste alumbrado	hubisteis alumbrado
alumbró	alumbraron	hubo alumbrado	hubieron alumbrado
4 futuro		**11 futuro perfecto**	
alumbraré	alumbraremos	habré alumbrado	habremos alumbrado
alumbrarás	alumbraréis	habrás alumbrado	habréis alumbrado
alumbrará	alumbrarán	habrá alumbrado	habrán alumbrado
5 potencial simple		**12 potencial compuesto**	
alumbraría	alumbraríamos	habría alumbrado	habríamos alumbrado
alumbrarías	alumbraríais	habrías alumbrado	habríais alumbrado
alumbraría	alumbrarían	habría alumbrado	habrían alumbrado
6 presente de subjuntivo		**13 perfecto de subjuntivo**	
alumbre	alumbremos	haya alumbrado	hayamos alumbrado
alumbres	alumbréis	hayas alumbrado	hayáis alumbrado
alumbre	alumbren	haya alumbrado	hayan alumbrado
7 imperfecto de subjuntivo		**14 pluscuamperfecto de subjuntivo**	
alumbrara	alumbráramos	hubiera alumbrado	hubiéramos alumbrado
alumbraras	alumbrarais	hubieras alumbrado	hubierais alumbrado
alumbrara	alumbraran	hubiera alumbrado	hubieran alumbrado
OR		OR	
alumbrase	alumbrásemos	hubiese alumbrado	hubiésemos alumbrado
alumbrases	alumbraseis	hubieses alumbrado	hubieseis alumbrado
alumbrase	alumbrasen	hubiese alumbrado	hubiesen alumbrado

imperativo	
—	alumbremos
alumbra; no alumbres	alumbrad; no alumbréis
alumbre	alumbren

Words and expressions related to this verb
alumbrante illuminating, enlightening
el **alumbramiento** lighting
el **alumbrado fluorescente** fluorescent lighting
el **alumbrado reflejado (indirecto)** indirect lighting
la **lumbre** fire, light; **calentarse a la lumbre** to warm oneself by the fire

Reflexive regular **-ar** verb

to be (get) high, to get tipsy,
to become lively (from liquor)

The Seven Simple Tenses | The Seven Compound Tenses

A

Singular	Plural

1 presente de indicativo

me alumbro	nos alumbramos
te alumbras	os alumbráis
se alumbra	se alumbran

2 imperfecto de indicativo

me alumbraba	nos alumbrábamos
te alumbrabas	os alumbrabais
se alumbraba	se alumbraban

3 pretérito

me alumbré	nos alumbramos
te alumbraste	os alumbrasteis
se alumbró	se alumbraron

4 futuro

me alumbraré	nos alumbraremos
te alumbrarás	os alumbraréis
se alumbrará	se alumbrarán

5 potencial simple

me alumbraría	nos alumbraríamos
te alumbrarías	os alumbraríais
se alumbraría	se alumbrarían

6 presente de subjuntivo

me alumbre	nos alumbremos
te alumbres	os alumbréis
se alumbre	se alumbren

7 imperfecto de subjuntivo

me alumbrara	nos alumbráramos
te alumbraras	os alumbrarais
se alumbrara	se alumbraran
OR	
me alumbrase	nos alumbrásemos
te alumbrases	os alumbraseis
se alumbrase	se alumbrasen

Singular	Plural

8 perfecto de indicativo

me he alumbrado	nos hemos alumbrado
te has alumbrado	os habéis alumbrado
se ha alumbrado	se han alumbrado

9 pluscuamperfecto de indicativo

me había alumbrado	nos habíamos alumbrado
te habías alumbrado	os habíais alumbrado
se había alumbrado	se habían alumbrado

10 pretérito anterior

me hube alumbrado	nos hubimos alumbrado
te hubiste alumbrado	os hubisteis alumbrado
se hubo alumbrado	se hubieron alumbrado

11 futuro perfecto

me habré alumbrado	nos habremos alumbrado
te habrás alumbrado	os habréis alumbrado
se habrá alumbrado	se habrán alumbrado

12 potencial compuesto

me habría alumbrado	nos habríamos alumbrado
te habrías alumbrado	os habríais alumbrado
se habría alumbrado	se habrían alumbrado

13 perfecto de subjuntivo

me haya alumbrado	nos hayamos alumbrado
te hayas alumbrado	os hayáis alumbrado
se haya alumbrado	se hayan alumbrado

14 pluscuamperfecto de subjuntivo

me hubiera alumbrado	nos hubiéramos alumbrado
te hubieras alumbrado	os hubierais alumbrado
se hubiera alumbrado	se hubieran alumbrado
OR	
me hubiese alumbrado	nos hubiésemos alumbrado
te hubieses alumbrado	os hubieseis alumbrado
se hubiese alumbrado	se hubiesen alumbrado

imperativo

—	alumbrémonos
alúmbrate; no te alumbres	**alumbraos, no os alumbréis**
alúmbrese	**alúmbrense**

For words and expressions related to this verb, see **alumbrar.**

Can't find the verb you're looking for?
Check the back pages of this book for a list of over 2,100 additional verbs!

Gerundio **alzando**   Part. pas. **alzado**

to heave, to lift, to pick up, to raise (prices)	Regular **-ar** verb endings with spelling change: **z** becomes **c** before **e**

The Seven Simple Tenses	The Seven Compound Tenses

Singular	Plural	Singular	Plural
1 presente de indicativo		**8 perfecto de indicativo**	
alzo	alzamos	he alzado	hemos alzado
alzas	alzáis	has alzado	habéis alzado
alza	alzan	ha alzado	han alzado
2 imperfecto de indicativo		**9 pluscuamperfecto de indicativo**	
alzaba	alzábamos	había alzado	habíamos alzado
alzabas	alzabais	habías alzado	habíais alzado
alzaba	alzaban	había alzado	habían alzado
3 pretérito		**10 pretérito anterior**	
alcé	alzamos	hube alzado	hubimos alzado
alzaste	alzasteis	hubiste alzado	hubisteis alzado
alzó	alzaron	hubo alzado	hubieron alzado
4 futuro		**11 futuro perfecto**	
alzaré	alzaremos	habré alzado	habremos alzado
alzarás	alzaréis	habrás alzado	habréis alzado
alzará	alzarán	habrá alzado	habrán alzado
5 potencial simple		**12 potencial compuesto**	
alzaría	alzaríamos	habría alzado	habríamos alzado
alzarías	alzaríais	habrías alzado	habríais alzado
alzaría	alzarían	habría alzado	habrían alzado
6 presente de subjuntivo		**13 perfecto de subjuntivo**	
alce	alcemos	haya alzado	hayamos alzado
alces	alcéis	hayas alzado	hayáis alzado
alce	alcen	haya alzado	hayan alzado
7 imperfecto de subjuntivo		**14 pluscuamperfecto de subjuntivo**	
alzara	alzáramos	hubiera alzado	hubiéramos alzado
alzaras	alzarais	hubieras alzado	hubierais alzado
alzara	alzaran	hubiera alzado	hubieran alzado
OR		OR	
alzase	alzásemos	hubiese alzado	hubiésemos alzado
alzases	alzaseis	hubieses alzado	hubieseis alzado
alzase	alzasen	hubiese alzado	hubiesen alzado

imperativo

—	alcemos
alza; no alces	alzad; no alcéis
alce	alcen

Words and expressions related to this verb
alzar velas   to set the sails, to hoist sail
alzar con   to run off with, to steal
la alzadura   elevation
el alzamiento   raising, lifting

el alzo   robbery, theft
alzar la mano   to threaten, to raise one's hand
alzar la voz   to raise one's voice
alzar el codo   to drink to excess (to raise one's elbow)

A

The Seven Simple Tenses		The Seven Compound Tenses	
Singular	Plural	Singular	Plural
1 presente de indicativo		8 perfecto de indicativo	
amo	amamos	he amado	hemos amado
amas	amáis	has amado	habéis amado
ama	aman	ha amado	han amado
2 imperfecto de indicativo		9 pluscuamperfecto de indicativo	
amaba	amábamos	había amado	habíamos amado
amabas	amabais	habías amado	habíais amado
amaba	amaban	había amado	habían amado
3 pretérito		10 pretérito anterior	
amé	amamos	hube amado	hubimos amado
amaste	amasteis	hubiste amado	hubisteis amado
amó	amaron	hubo amado	hubieron amado
4 futuro		11 futuro perfecto	
amaré	amaremos	habré amado	habremos amado
amarás	amaréis	habrás amado	habréis amado
amará	amarán	habrá amado	habrán amado
5 potencial simple		12 potencial compuesto	
amaría	amaríamos	habría amado	habríamos amado
amarías	amaríais	habrías amado	habríais amado
amaría	amarían	habría amado	habrían amado
6 presente de subjuntivo		13 perfecto de subjuntivo	
ame	amemos	haya amado	hayamos amado
ames	améis	hayas amado	hayáis amado
ame	amen	haya amado	hayan amado
7 imperfecto de subjuntivo		14 pluscuamperfecto de subjuntivo	
amara	amáramos	hubiera amado	hubiéramos amado
amaras	amarais	hubieras amado	hubierais amado
amara	amaran	hubiera amado	hubieran amado
OR		OR	
amase	amásemos	hubiese amado	hubiésemos amado
amases	amaseis	hubieses amado	hubieseis amado
amase	amasen	hubiese amado	hubiesen amado

	imperativo	
—		amemos
ama; no ames		amad; no améis
ame		amen

Words related to this verb
la amabilidad   amiability, kindness
amable   amiable, kind, affable

amablemente   amiably, kindly; **una carta amatoria**   love letter
el amor   love; **amante** lover

Do you need more drills? Have fun with the *501 Spanish Verbs* CD-ROM!

The subject pronouns are found on page 93.

151

añadir (55)
to add

Gerundio añadiendo **Part. pas. añadido**

Regular **-ir** verb

The Seven Simple Tenses		The Seven Compound Tenses	
Singular	Plural	Singular	Plural

1 presente de indicativo

añado	añadimos		
añades	añadís		
añade	añaden		

8 perfecto de indicativo

he añadido	hemos añadido
has añadido	habéis añadido
ha añadido	han añadido

2 imperfecto de indicativo

añadía	añadíamos
añadías	añadíais
añadía	añadían

9 pluscuamperfecto de indicativo

había añadido	habíamos añadido
habías añadido	habíais añadido
había añadido	habían añadido

3 pretérito

añadí	añadimos
añadiste	añadisteis
añadió	añadieron

10 pretérito anterior

hube añadido	hubimos añadido
hubiste añadido	hubisteis añadido
hubo añadido	hubieron añadido

4 futuro

añadiré	añadiremos
añadirás	añadiréis
añadirá	añadirán

11 futuro perfecto

habré añadido	habremos añadido
habrás añadido	habréis añadido
habrá añadido	habrán añadido

5 potencial simple

añadiría	añadiríamos
añadirías	añadiríais
añadiría	añadirían

12 potencial compuesto

habría añadido	habríamos añadido
habrías añadido	habríais añadido
habría añadido	habrían añadido

6 presente de subjuntivo

añada	añadamos
añadas	añadáis
añada	añadan

13 perfecto de subjuntivo

haya añadido	hayamos añadido
hayas añadido	hayáis añadido
haya añadido	hayan añadido

7 imperfecto de subjuntivo

añadiera	añadiéramos
añadieras	añadierais
añadiera	añadieran
OR	
añadiese	añadiésemos
añadieses	añadieseis
añadiese	añadiesen

14 pluscuamperfecto de subjuntivo

hubiera añadido	hubiéramos añadido
hubieras añadido	hubierais añadido
hubiera añadido	hubieran añadido
OR	
hubiese añadido	hubiésemos añadido
hubieses añadido	hubieseis añadido
hubiese añadido	hubiesen añadido

imperativo

—	añadamos
añade; no añadas	añadid; no añadáis
añada	añadan

Words and expressions related to this verb
la añadidura   increase, addition
por añadidura   in addition, besides
de añadidura   extra, for good measure
añadido, añadida   added, additional

Can't find the verb you're looking for?
Check the back pages of this book for a list of over 2,100 additional verbs!

The Seven Simple Tenses		The Seven Compound Tenses	
Singular	Plural	Singular	Plural
1 presente de indicativo		8 perfecto de indicativo	
ando	andamos	he andado	hemos andado
andas	andáis	has andado	habéis andado
anda	andan	ha andado	han andado
2 imperfecto de indicativo		9 pluscuamperfecto de indicativo	
andaba	andábamos	había andado	habíamos andado
andabas	andabais	habías andado	habíais andado
andaba	andaban	había andado	habían andado
3 pretérito		10 pretérito anterior	
anduve	anduvimos	hube andado	hubimos andado
anduviste	anduvisteis	hubiste andado	hubisteis andado
anduvo	anduvieron	hubo andado	hubieron andado
4 futuro		11 futuro perfecto	
andaré	andaremos	habré andado	habremos andado
andarás	andaréis	habrás andado	habréis andado
andará	andarán	habrá andado	habrán andado
5 potencial simple		12 potencial compuesto	
andaría	andaríamos	habría andado	habríamos andado
andarías	andaríais	habrías andado	habríais andado
andaría	andarían	habría andado	habrían andado
6 presente de subjuntivo		13 perfecto de subjuntivo	
ande	andemos	haya andado	hayamos andado
andes	andéis	hayas andado	hayáis andado
ande	anden	haya andado	hayan andado
7 imperfecto de subjuntivo		14 pluscuamperfecto de subjuntivo	
anduviera	anduviéramos	hubiera andado	hubiéramos andado
anduvieras	anduvierais	hubieras andado	hubierais andado
anduviera	anduvieran	hubiera andado	hubieran andado
OR		OR	
anduviese	anduviésemos	hubiese andado	hubiésemos andado
anduvieses	anduvieseis	hubieses andado	hubieseis andado
anduviese	anduviesen	hubiese andado	hubiesen andado

	imperativo	
—		andemos
anda; no andes		andad; no andéis
ande		anden

AN ESSENTIAL 55 VERB

The subject pronouns are found on page 93.

153

AN ESSENTIAL 55 VERB

Andar

Andar is a very useful verb for a beginning Spanish student. Pay special attention to the spelling change in Tenses 3 and 7.

Sentences using andar and related words

¿Cómo andan los negocios?
How's business?

Anda despacio que tengo prisa.
Make haste slowly.

Amadís de Gaula fue un caballero andante de la Edad Media.
Amadis of Gaul was a knight-errant of the Middle Ages.

¡Anda a pasear!
Take a walk! (Take a hike!)

Proverbs

Dime con quién andas y te diré quién eres.
Tell me who your friends are and I will tell you who you are.

Poco a poco se anda lejos.
One step at a time. (Little by little, one goes far away.)

Words and expressions related to this verb

andarse **to go away**

las andanzas **events**

buena andanza **good fortune**

mala andanza **bad fortune**

a todo andar **at full speed**

desandar **to retrace one's steps**

andante **errant**

un caballero andante **knight-errant**

Anda con Dios. **Go with God.**

andar con cien ojos **to be cautious (to have eyes on the back of one's head)**

el andar **gait (way of walking)**

andar a gatas **to crawl, to walk/on all fours**

andar a caballo **to ride a horse**

Can't find the verb you're looking for?
Check the back pages of this book for a list of over 2,100 additional verbs!

Regular **-ar** verb   to announce, to foretell, to proclaim

The Seven Simple Tenses | The Seven Compound Tenses

A

Singular	Plural	Singular	Plural
1 presente de indicativo		8 perfecto de indicativo	
anuncio	**anunciamos**	**he anunciado**	**hemos anunciado**
anuncias	**anunciáis**	**has anunciado**	**habéis anunciado**
anuncia	**anuncian**	**ha anunciado**	**han anunciado**
2 imperfecto de indicativo		9 pluscuamperfecto de indicativo	
anunciaba	**anunciábamos**	**había anunciado**	**habíamos anunciado**
anunciabas	**anunciabais**	**habías anunciado**	**habíais anunciado**
anunciaba	**anunciaban**	**había anunciado**	**habían anunciado**
3 pretérito		10 pretérito anterior	
anuncié	**anunciamos**	**hube anunciado**	**hubimos anunciado**
anunciaste	**anunciasteis**	**hubiste anunciado**	**hubisteis anunciado**
anunció	**anunciaron**	**hubo anunciado**	**hubieron anunciado**
4 futuro		11 futuro perfecto	
anunciaré	**anunciaremos**	**habré anunciado**	**habremos anunciado**
anunciarás	**anunciaréis**	**habrás anunciado**	**habréis anunciado**
anunciará	**anunciarán**	**habrá anunciado**	**habrán anunciado**
5 potencial simple		12 potencial compuesto	
anunciaría	**anunciaríamos**	**habría anunciado**	**habríamos anunciado**
anunciarías	**anunciaríais**	**habrías anunciado**	**habríais anunciado**
anunciaría	**anunciarían**	**habría anunciado**	**habrían anunciado**
6 presente de subjuntivo		13 perfecto de subjuntivo	
anuncie	**anunciemos**	**haya anunciado**	**hayamos anunciado**
anuncies	**anunciéis**	**hayas anunciado**	**hayáis anunciado**
anuncie	**anuncien**	**haya anunciado**	**hayan anunciado**
7 imperfecto de subjuntivo		14 pluscuamperfecto de subjuntivo	
anunciara	**anunciáramos**	**hubiera anunciado**	**hubiéramos anunciado**
anunciaras	**anunciarais**	**hubieras anunciado**	**hubierais anunciado**
anunciara	**anunciaran**	**hubiera anunciado**	**hubieran anunciado**
OR		OR	
anunciase	**anunciásemos**	**hubiese anunciado**	**hubiésemos anunciado**
anunciases	**anunciaseis**	**hubieses anunciado**	**hubieseis anunciado**
anunciase	**anunciasen**	**hubiese anunciado**	**hubiesen anunciado**

imperativo

—	**anunciemos**
anuncia; no anuncies	**anunciad; no anunciéis**
anuncie	**anuncien**

Words related to this verb

el, la anunciante   advertiser
la Anunciación   Annunciation
el anunciador, la anunciadora   advertiser, announcer

el anuncio   advertisement, announcement
el cartel anunciador   billboard
los anuncios por palabras   classified advertisements

Get your feet wet with verbs used in weather expressions on page 668.

The subject pronouns are found on page 93.

| to put out (flame, fire), to extinguish, to turn off (flame, fire, light) | Regular **-ar** verb endings with spelling change: **g** becomes **gu** before **e** |

The Seven Simple Tenses		The Seven Compound Tenses	
Singular	Plural	Singular	Plural
1 presente de indicativo		8 perfecto de indicativo	
apago	apagamos	he apagado	hemos apagado
apagas	apagáis	has apagado	habéis apagado
apaga	apagan	ha apagado	han apagado
2 imperfecto de indicativo		9 pluscuamperfecto de indicativo	
apagaba	apagábamos	había apagado	habíamos apagado
apagabas	apagabais	habías apagado	habíais apagado
apagaba	apagaban	había apagado	habían apagado
3 pretérito		10 pretérito anterior	
apagué	apagamos	hube apagado	hubimos apagado
apagaste	apagasteis	hubiste apagado	hubisteis apagado
apagó	apagaron	hubo apagado	hubieron apagado
4 futuro		11 futuro perfecto	
apagaré	apagaremos	habré apagado	habremos apagado
apagarás	apagaréis	habrás apagado	habréis apagado
apagará	apagarán	habrá apagado	habrán apagado
5 potencial simple		12 potencial compuesto	
apagaría	apagaríamos	habría apagado	habríamos apagado
apagarías	apagaríais	habrías apagado	habríais apagado
apagaría	apagarían	habría apagado	habrían apagado
6 presente de subjuntivo		13 perfecto de subjuntivo	
apague	apaguemos	haya apagado	hayamos apagado
apagues	apaguéis	hayas apagado	hayáis apagado
apague	apaguen	haya apagado	hayan apagado
7 imperfecto de subjuntivo		14 pluscuamperfecto de subjuntivo	
apagara	apagáramos	hubiera apagado	hubiéramos apagado
apagaras	apagarais	hubieras apagado	hubierais apagado
apagara	apagaran	hubiera apagado	hubieran apagado
OR		OR	
apagase	apagásemos	hubiese apagado	hubiésemos apagado
apagases	apagaseis	hubieses apagado	hubieseis apagado
apagase	apagasen	hubiese apagado	hubiesen apagado

	imperativo	
—	apaguemos
apaga; no apagues	apagad; no apaguéis
apague	apaguen

Words and expressions related to this verb
el apagafuegos, el apagaincendios   fire extinguisher
apagadizo, apagadiza   fire resistant
¡Apaga y vámonos!   Let's end this and let's go! Let's put an end to all this!

el apagavelas   candle extinguisher
el apagón   blackout (no electricity)

Do you need more drills? Have fun with the *501 Spanish Verbs* CD-ROM!

Regular **-er** verb endings with spelling change: **c**   to appear, to show up
becomes **zc** before **a** or **o**

The Seven Simple Tenses | The Seven Compound Tenses

Singular	Plural	Singular	Plural
1 presente de indicativo		8 perfecto de indicativo	
aparezco	**aparecemos**	**he aparecido**	**hemos aparecido**
apareces	**aparecéis**	**has aparecido**	**habéis aparecido**
aparece	**aparecen**	**ha aparecido**	**han aparecido**
2 imperfecto de indicativo		9 pluscuamperfecto de indicativo	
aparecía	**aparecíamos**	**había aparecido**	**habíamos aparecido**
aparecías	**aparecíais**	**habías aparecido**	**habíais aparecido**
aparecía	**aparecían**	**había aparecido**	**habían aparecido**
3 pretérito		10 pretérito anterior	
aparecí	**aparecimos**	**hube aparecido**	**hubimos aparecido**
apareciste	**aparecisteis**	**hubiste aparecido**	**hubisteis aparecido**
apareció	**aparecieron**	**hubo aparecido**	**hubieron aparecido**
4 futuro		11 futuro perfecto	
apareceré	**apareceremos**	**habré aparecido**	**habremos aparecido**
aparecerás	**apareceréis**	**habrás aparecido**	**habréis aparecido**
aparecerá	**aparecerán**	**habrá aparecido**	**habrán aparecido**
5 potencial simple		12 potencial compuesto	
aparecería	**apareceríamos**	**habría aparecido**	**habríamos aparecido**
aparecerías	**apareceríais**	**habrías aparecido**	**habríais aparecido**
aparecería	**aparecerían**	**habría aparecido**	**habrían aparecido**
6 presente de subjuntivo		13 perfecto de subjuntivo	
aparezca	**aparezcamos**	**haya aparecido**	**hayamos aparecido**
aparezcas	**aparezcáis**	**hayas aparecido**	**hayáis aparecido**
aparezca	**aparezcan**	**haya aparecido**	**hayan aparecido**
7 imperfecto de subjuntivo		14 pluscuamperfecto de subjuntivo	
apareciera	**apareciéramos**	**hubiera aparecido**	**hubiéramos aparecido**
aparecieras	**aparecierais**	**hubieras aparecido**	**hubierais aparecido**
apareciera	**aparecieran**	**hubiera aparecido**	**hubieran aparecido**
OR		OR	
apareciese	**apareciésemos**	**hubiese aparecido**	**hubiésemos aparecido**
aparecieses	**aparecieseis**	**hubieses aparecido**	**hubieseis aparecido**
apareciese	**apareciesen**	**hubiese aparecido**	**hubiesen aparecido**

imperativo

—	**aparezcamos**
aparece; no aparezcas	**apareced; no aparezcáis**
aparezca	**aparezcan**

Words and expressions related to this verb

un aparecimiento   apparition
un aparecido   ghost
una aparición   apparition, appearance
parecer   to seem, to appear
parecerse a   to look like

aparecerse en casa   to arrive home unexpectedly
aparecerse a alguno   to see a ghost
aparecerse entre sueños   to see someone in a dream

The subject pronouns are found on page 93.

The Seven Simple Tenses		The Seven Compound Tenses	
Singular	Plural	Singular	Plural
1　presente de indicativo		8　perfecto de indicativo	
aplaudo	aplaudimos	he aplaudido	hemos aplaudido
aplaudes	aplaudís	has aplaudido	habéis aplaudido
aplaude	aplauden	ha aplaudido	han aplaudido
2　imperfecto de indicativo		9　pluscuamperfecto de indicativo	
aplaudía	aplaudíamos	había aplaudido	habíamos aplaudido
aplaudías	aplaudíais	habías aplaudido	habíais aplaudido
aplaudía	aplaudían	había aplaudido	habían aplaudido
3　pretérito		10　pretérito anterior	
aplaudí	aplaudimos	hube aplaudido	hubimos aplaudido
aplaudiste	aplaudisteis	hubiste aplaudido	hubisteis aplaudido
aplaudió	aplaudieron	hubo aplaudido	hubieron aplaudido
4　futuro		11　futuro perfecto	
aplaudiré	aplaudiremos	habré aplaudido	habremos aplaudido
aplaudirás	aplaudiréis	habrás aplaudido	habréis aplaudido
aplaudirá	aplaudirán	habrá aplaudido	habrán aplaudido
5　potencial simple		12　potencial compuesto	
aplaudiría	aplaudiríamos	habría aplaudido	habríamos aplaudido
aplaudirías	aplaudiríais	habrías aplaudido	habríais aplaudido
aplaudiría	aplaudirían	habría aplaudido	habrían aplaudido
6　presente de subjuntivo		13　perfecto de subjuntivo	
aplauda	aplaudamos	haya aplaudido	hayamos aplaudido
aplaudas	aplaudáis	hayas aplaudido	hayáis aplaudido
aplauda	aplaudan	haya aplaudido	hayan aplaudido
7　imperfecto de subjuntivo		14　pluscuamperfecto de subjuntivo	
aplaudiera	aplaudiéramos	hubiera aplaudido	hubiéramos aplaudido
aplaudieras	aplaudierais	hubieras aplaudido	hubierais aplaudido
aplaudiera	aplaudieran	hubiera aplaudido	hubieran aplaudido
OR		OR	
aplaudiese	aplaudiésemos	hubiese aplaudido	hubiésemos aplaudido
aplaudieses	aplaudieseis	hubieses aplaudido	hubieseis aplaudido
aplaudiese	aplaudiesen	hubiese aplaudido	hubiesen aplaudido

imperativo

—	aplaudamos
aplaude; no aplaudas	aplaudid; no aplaudáis
aplauda	aplaudan

Words and expressions related to this verb

el aplauso　applause

el aplaudidor, la aplaudidora　applauder

con el aplauso de　to the applause of

una salva de aplausos　thunderous applause

Get acquainted with what preposition goes with what verb on pages 669–677.

Reflexive regular **-ar** verb   to take power, to take possession

The Seven Simple Tenses		The Seven Compound Tenses	
Singular	Plural	Singular	Plural

A

1   presente de indicativo

Singular	Plural
me apodero	nos apoderamos
te apoderas	os apoderáis
se apodera	se apoderan

8   perfecto de indicativo

Singular	Plural
me he apoderado	nos hemos apoderado
te has apoderado	os habéis apoderado
se ha apoderado	se han apoderado

2   imperfecto de indicativo

me apoderaba	nos apoderábamos
te apoderabas	os apoderabais
se apoderaba	se apoderaban

9   pluscuamperfecto de indicativo

me había apoderado	nos habíamos apoderado
te habías apoderado	os habíais apoderado
se había apoderado	se habían apoderado

3   pretérito

me apoderé	nos apoderamos
te apoderaste	os apoderasteis
se apoderó	se apoderaron

10   pretérito anterior

me hube apoderado	nos hubimos apoderado
te hubiste apoderado	os hubisteis apoderado
se hubo apoderado	se hubieron apoderado

4   futuro

me apoderaré	nos apoderaremos
te apoderarás	os apoderaréis
se apoderará	se apoderarán

11   futuro perfecto

me habré apoderado	nos habremos apoderado
te habrás apoderado	os habréis apoderado
se habrá apoderado	se habrán apoderado

5   potencial simple

me apoderaría	nos apoderaríamos
te apoderarías	os apoderaríais
se apoderaría	se apoderarían

12   potencial compuesto

me habría apoderado	nos habríamos apoderado
te habrías apoderado	os habríais apoderado
se habría apoderado	se habrían apoderado

6   presente de subjuntivo

me apodere	nos apoderemos
te apoderes	os apoderéis
se apodere	se apoderen

13   perfecto de subjuntivo

me haya apoderado	nos hayamos apoderado
te hayas apoderado	os hayáis apoderado
se haya apoderado	se hayan apoderado

7   imperfecto de subjuntivo

me apoderara	nos apoderáramos
te apoderaras	os apoderarais
se apoderara	se apoderaran
OR	
me apoderase	nos apoderásemos
te apoderases	os apoderaseis
se apoderase	se apoderasen

14   pluscuamperfecto de subjuntivo

me hubiera apoderado	nos hubiéramos apoderado
te hubieras apoderado	os hubierais apoderado
se hubiera apoderado	se hubieran apoderado
OR	
me hubiese apoderado	nos hubiésemos apoderado
te hubieses apoderado	os hubieseis apoderado
se hubiese apoderado	se hubiesen apoderado

imperativo

—	apoderémonos
apodérate; no te apoderes	apoderaos; no os apoderéis
apodérese	apodérense

Words and expressions related to this verb

poder   to be able
el poder   power
el apoderado   proxy

apoderarse de algo   to take possession of something
apoderado, apoderada   empowered
apoderar   to empower, to authorize

> Don't forget to study the section on defective and impersonal verbs. It's right after this main list.

The subject pronouns are found on page 93.

to appreciate, to appraise, to esteem   Regular **-ar** verb

The Seven Simple Tenses		The Seven Compound Tenses	
Singular	Plural	Singular	Plural
1 presente de indicativo		**8 perfecto de indicativo**	
aprecio	apreciamos	he apreciado	hemos apreciado
aprecias	apreciáis	has apreciado	habéis apreciado
aprecia	aprecian	ha apreciado	han apreciado
2 imperfecto de indicativo		**9 pluscuamperfecto de indicativo**	
apreciaba	apreciábamos	había apreciado	habíamos apreciado
apreciabas	apreciabais	habías apreciado	habíais apreciado
apreciaba	apreciaban	había apreciado	habían apreciado
3 pretérito		**10 pretérito anterior**	
aprecié	apreciamos	hube apreciado	hubimos apreciado
apreciaste	apreciasteis	hubiste apreciado	hubisteis apreciado
apreció	apreciaron	hubo apreciado	hubieron apreciado
4 futuro		**11 futuro perfecto**	
apreciaré	apreciaremos	habré apreciado	habremos apreciado
apreciarás	apreciaréis	habrás apreciado	habréis apreciado
apreciará	apreciarán	habrá apreciado	habrán apreciado
5 potencial simple		**12 potencial compuesto**	
apreciaría	apreciaríamos	habría apreciado	habríamos apreciado
apreciarías	apreciaríais	habrías apreciado	habríais apreciado
apreciaría	apreciarían	habría apreciado	habrían apreciado
6 presente de subjuntivo		**13 perfecto de subjuntivo**	
aprecie	apreciemos	haya apreciado	hayamos apreciado
aprecies	apreciéis	hayas apreciado	hayáis apreciado
aprecie	aprecien	haya apreciado	hayan apreciado
7 imperfecto de subjuntivo		**14 pluscuamperfecto de subjuntivo**	
apreciara	apreciáramos	hubiera apreciado	hubiéramos apreciado
apreciaras	apreciarais	hubieras apreciado	hubierais apreciado
apeciara	apreciaran	hubiera apreciado	hubieran apreciado
OR		OR	
apreciase	apreciásemos	hubiese apreciado	hubiésemos apreciado
apreciases	apreciaseis	hubieses apreciado	hubieseis apreciado
apreciase	apreciasen	hubiese apreciado	hubiesen apreciado

	imperativo	
—	apreciemos	
aprecia; no aprecies	apreciad; no apreciéis	
aprecie	aprecien	

Words and expressions related to this verb

el aprecio   appreciation, esteem
la apreciación   appreciation, estimation
apreciable   appreciable; worthy
la apreciabilidad   appreciability

preciar   to appraise, to estimate
el precio   price; **no tener precio** to be priceless
un precio fijo   set price

Can't remember the Spanish verb you need?
Check the back pages of this book for the English-Spanish verb index!

The Seven Simple Tenses		The Seven Compound Tenses	
Singular	Plural	Singular	Plural
1 presente de indicativo		8 perfecto de indicativo	
aprendo	aprendemos	he aprendido	hemos aprendido
aprendes	aprendéis	has aprendido	habéis aprendido
aprende	aprenden	ha aprendido	han aprendido
2 imperfecto de indicativo		9 pluscuamperfecto de indicativo	
aprendía	aprendíamos	había aprendido	habíamos aprendido
aprendías	aprendíais	habías aprendido	habíais aprendido
aprendía	aprendían	había aprendido	habían aprendido
3 pretérito		10 pretérito anterior	
aprendí	aprendimos	hube aprendido	hubimos aprendido
aprendiste	aprendisteis	hubiste aprendido	hubisteis aprendido
aprendió	aprendieron	hubo aprendido	hubieron aprendido
4 futuro		11 futuro perfecto	
aprenderé	aprenderemos	habré aprendido	habremos aprendido
aprenderás	aprenderéis	habrás aprendido	habréis aprendido
aprenderá	aprenderán	habrá aprendido	habrán aprendido
5 potencial simple		12 potencial compuesto	
aprendería	aprenderíamos	habría aprendido	habríamos aprendido
aprenderías	aprenderíais	habrías aprendido	habríais aprendido
aprendería	aprenderían	habría aprendido	habrían aprendido
6 presente de subjuntivo		13 perfecto de subjuntivo	
aprenda	aprendamos	haya aprendido	hayamos aprendido
aprendas	aprendáis	hayas aprendido	hayáis aprendido
aprenda	aprendan	haya aprendido	hayan aprendido
7 imperfecto de subjuntivo		14 pluscuamperfecto de subjuntivo	
aprendiera	aprendiéramos	hubiera aprendido	hubiéramos aprendido
aprendieras	aprendierais	hubieras aprendido	hubierais aprendido
aprendiera	aprendieran	hubiera aprendido	hubieran aprendido
OR		OR	
aprendiese	aprendiésemos	hubiese aprendido	hubiésemos aprendido
aprendieses	aprendieseis	hubieses aprendido	hubieseis aprendido
aprendiese	aprendiesen	hubiese aprendido	hubiesen aprendido

imperativo

—	aprendamos
aprende; no aprendas	aprended; no aprendáis
aprenda	aprendan

AN ESSENTIAL 55 VERB

The subject pronouns are found on page 93.

Aprender

Aprender is an important verb to learn because it is a regular –er verb and because there are many everyday expressions related to it.

Sentences using aprender **and related words**

En la clase de español estamos aprendiendo
a hablar, a leer, y a escribir en español.
In Spanish class we are learning to speak, to read,
and to write in Spanish.

Machacando se aprende el oficio.
Practice makes perfect.

Mi abuela aprendió a navegar en Internet.
My grandmother learned to surf the Internet.

Words and expressions related to this verb

el aprendedor, la aprendedora **learner**

el aprendizaje **apprenticeship**

el aprendiz, la aprendiza **apprentice**

aprender a + inf. **to learn + inf.**

aprender de memoria **to memorize**

aprender con **to study with**

desaprender **to unlearn**

aprendiz de todo (mucho), oficial
de nada **Jack of all trades, master
of none**

Proverbs

El que mucho duerme poco aprende.
Whoever sleeps a lot learns little.

Cada día se aprende algo nuevo.
You learn something new every day.

Don't forget to study the section on defective and impersonal verbs. It's right after this main list.

Reflexive regular **-ar** verb   to hasten, to hurry, to rush

| The Seven Simple Tenses | The Seven Compound Tenses |

A

Singular	Plural	Singular	Plural
1 presente de indicativo		8 perfecto de indicativo	
me apresuro	nos apresuramos	me he apresurado	nos hemos apresurado
te apresuras	os apresuráis	te has apresurado	os habéis apresurado
se apresura	se apresuran	se ha apresurado	se han apresurado
2 imperfecto de indicativo		9 pluscuamperfecto de indicativo	
me apresuraba	nos apresurábamos	me había apresurado	nos habíamos apresurado
te apresurabas	os apresurabais	te habías apresurado	os habíais apresurado
se apresuraba	se apresuraban	se había apresurado	se habían apresurado
3 pretérito		10 pretérito anterior	
me apresuré	nos apresuramos	me hube apresurado	nos hubimos apresurado
te apresuraste	os apresurasteis	te hubiste apresurado	os hubisteis apresurado
se apresuró	se apresuraron	se hubo apresurado	se hubieron apresurado
4 futuro		11 futuro perfecto	
me apresuraré	nos apresuraremos	me habré apresurado	nos habremos apresurado
te apresurarás	os apresuraréis	te habrás apresurado	os habréis apresurado
se apresurará	se apresurarán	se habrá apresurado	se habrán apresurado
5 potencial simple		12 potencial compuesto	
me apresuraría	nos apresuraríamos	me habría apresurado	nos habríamos apresurado
te apresurarías	os apresuraríais	te habrías apresurado	os habríais apresurado
se apresuraría	se apresurarían	se habría apresurado	se habrían apresurado
6 presente de subjuntivo		13 perfecto de subjuntivo	
me apresure	nos apresuremos	me haya apresurado	nos hayamos apresurado
te apresures	os apresuréis	te hayas apresurado	os hayáis apresurado
se apresure	se apresuren	se haya apresurado	se hayan apresurado
7 imperfecto de subjuntivo		14 pluscuamperfecto de subjuntivo	
me apresurara	nos apresuráramos	me hubiera apresurado	nos hubiéramos apresurado
te apresuraras	os apresurarais	te hubieras apresurado	os hubierais apresurado
se apresurara	se apresuraran	se hubiera apresurado	se hubieran apresurado
OR		OR	
me apresurase	nos apresurásemos	me hubiese apresurado	nos hubiésemos apresurado
te apresurases	os apresuraseis	te hubieses apresurado	os hubieseis apresurado
se apresurase	se apresurasen	se hubiese apresurado	se hubiesen apresurado

imperativo

—	apresurémonos
apresúrate; no te apresures	apresuraos; no os apresuréis
apresúrese	apresúrense

Words and expressions related to this verb

la apresuración haste	**el apresuramiento** hastiness
apresurado, apresurada hasty, quick	**apresurar** to accelerate
apresuradamente hastily	**apresurarse a + inf.** to hurry + inf.
la prisa haste	**tener prisa** to be in a hurry

Get acquainted with what preposition goes with what verb on pages 669–677.

The subject pronouns are found on page 93.   **163**

to approve, to pass a test | Regular **-ar** verb endings with stem change: Tenses 1, 6, Imperative

The Seven Simple Tenses		The Seven Compound Tenses	
Singular	Plural	Singular	Plural
1 presente de indicativo		8 perfecto de indicativo	
apruebo	**aprobamos**	**he aprobado**	**hemos aprobado**
apruebas	**aprobáis**	**has aprobado**	**habéis aprobado**
aprueba	**aprueban**	**ha aprobado**	**han aprobado**
2 imperfecto de indicativo		9 pluscuamperfecto de indicativo	
aprobaba	**aprobábamos**	**había aprobado**	**habíamos aprobado**
aprobabas	**aprobabais**	**habías aprobado**	**habíais aprobado**
aprobaba	**aprobaban**	**había aprobado**	**habían aprobado**
3 pretérito		10 pretérito anterior	
aprobé	**aprobamos**	**hube aprobado**	**hubimos aprobado**
aprobaste	**aprobasteis**	**hubiste aprobado**	**hubisteis aprobado**
aprobó	**aprobaron**	**hubo aprobado**	**hubieron aprobado**
4 futuro		11 futuro perfecto	
aprobaré	**aprobaremos**	**habré aprobado**	**habremos aprobado**
aprobarás	**aprobaréis**	**habrás aprobado**	**habréis aprobado**
aprobará	**aprobarán**	**habrá aprobado**	**habrán aprobado**
5 potencial simple		12 potencial compuesto	
aprobaría	**aprobaríamos**	**habría aprobado**	**habríamos aprobado**
aprobarías	**aprobaríais**	**habrías aprobado**	**habríais aprobado**
aprobaía	**aprobarían**	**habría aprobado**	**habrían aprobado**
6 presente de subjuntivo		13 perfecto de subjuntivo	
apruebe	**aprobemos**	**haya aprobado**	**hayamos aprobado**
apruebes	**aprobéis**	**hayas aprobado**	**hayáis aprobado**
apruebe	**aprueben**	**haya aprobado**	**hayan aprobado**
7 imperfecto de subjuntivo		14 pluscuamperfecto de subjuntivo	
aprobara	**aprobáramos**	**hubiera aprobado**	**hubiéramos aprobado**
aprobaras	**aprobarais**	**hubieras aprobado**	**hubierais aprobado**
aprobara	**aprobaran**	**hubiera aprobado**	**hubieran aprobado**
OR		OR	
aprobase	**aprobásemos**	**hubiese aprobado**	**hubiésemos aprobado**
aprobases	**aprobaseis**	**hubieses aprobado**	**hubieseis aprobado**
aprobase	**aprobasen**	**hubiese aprobado**	**hubiesen aprobado**

imperativo	
—	**aprobemos**
aprueba; no apruebes	**aprobad; no aprobéis**
apruebe	**aprueben**

Words and expressions related to this verb
la aprobación approbation, approval, consent
aprobatoriamente approvingly
el aprobado passing grade in an exam
aprobado, aprobada accepted, admitted, approved, passed (in an exam)
aprobado por mayoría accepted by a majority
comprobar to verify, compare, check prove; **desaprobar** to disapprove
la desaprobación disapproval

Reflexive regular **-ar** verb   to take advantage, to avail oneself

The Seven Simple Tenses		The Seven Compound Tenses	
Singular	Plural	Singular	Plural

A

1   presente de indicativo

me aprovecho	nos aprovechamos		
te aprovechas	os aprovecháis		
se aprovecha	se aprovechan		

8   perfecto de indicativo

me he aprovechado	nos hemos aprovechado
te has aprovechado	os habéis aprovechado
se ha aprovechado	se han aprovechado

2   imperfecto de indicativo

me aprovechaba	nos aprovechábamos
te aprovechabas	os aprovechabais
se aprovechaba	se aprovechaban

9   pluscuamperfecto de indicativo

me había aprovechado	nos habíamos aprovechado
te habías aprovechado	os habíais aprovechado
se había aprovechado	se habían aprovechado

3   pretérito

me aproveché	nos aprovechamos
te aprovechaste	os aprovechasteis
se aprovechó	se aprovecharon

10   pretérito anterior

me hube aprovechado	nos hubimos aprovechado
te hubiste aprovechado	os hubisteis aprovechado
se hubo aprovechado	se hubieron aprovechado

4   futuro

me aprovecharé	nos aprovecharemos
te aprovecharás	os aprovecharéis
se aprovechará	se aprovecharán

11   futuro perfecto

me habré aprovechado	nos habremos aprovechado
te habrás aprovechado	os habréis aprovechado
se habrá aprovechado	se habrán aprovechado

5   potencial simple

me aprovecharía	nos aprovecharíamos
te aprovecharías	os aprovecharíais
se aprovecharía	se aprovecharían

12   potencial compuesto

me habría aprovechado	nos habríamos aprovechado
te habrías aprovechado	os habríais aprovechado
se habría aprovechado	se habrían aprovechado

6   presente de subjuntivo

me aproveche	nos aprovechemos
te aproveches	os aprovechéis
se aproveche	se aprovechen

13   perfecto de subjuntivo

me haya aprovechado	nos hayamos aprovechado
te hayas aprovechado	os hayáis aprovechado
se haya aprovechado	se hayan aprovechado

7   imperfecto de subjuntivo

me aprovechara	nos aprovecháramos
te aprovecharas	os aprovecharais
se aprovechara	se aprovecharan
OR	
me aprovechase	nos aprovechásemos
te aprovechases	os aprovechaseis
se aprovechase	se aprovechasen

14   pluscuamperfecto de subjuntivo

me hubiera aprovechado	nos hubiéramos aprovechado
te hubieras aprovechado	os hubierais aprovechado
se hubiera aprovechado	se hubieran aprovechado
OR	
me hubiese aprovechado	nos hubiésemos aprovechado
te hubieses aprovechado	os hubieseis aprovechado
se hubiese aprovechado	se hubiesen aprovechado

imperativo

—	aprovechémonos
aprovéchate; no te aproveches	aprovechaos; no os aprovechéis
aprovéchese	aprovéchense

Words and expressions related to this verb
aprovechado, aprovechada   economical
aprovechable   available, profitable
aprovechamiento   use, utilization
aprovecharse de   to take advantage of

aprovechar   to make use of
aprovechar la ocasión   to take the opportunity
aprovechón, aprovechona   opportunist

Can't find the verb you're looking for?
Check the back pages of this book for a list of over 2,100 additional verbs!

to fret, to grieve, to worry   Reflexive regular **-ar** verb

The Seven Simple Tenses		The Seven Compound Tenses	
Singular	Plural	Singular	Plural
1 presente de indicativo		8 perfecto de indicativo	
me apuro	nos apuramos	me he apurado	nos hemos apurado
te apuras	os apuráis	te has apurado	os habéis apurado
se apura	se apuran	se ha apurado	se han apurado
2 imperfecto de indicativo		9 pluscuamperfecto de indicativo	
me apuraba	nos apurábamos	me había apurado	nos habíamos apurado
te apurabas	os apurabais	te habías apurado	os habíais apurado
se apuraba	se apuraban	se había apurado	se habían apurado
3 pretérito		10 pretérito anterior	
me apuré	nos apuramos	me hube apurado	nos hubimos apurado
te apuraste	os apurasteis	te hubiste apurado	os hubisteis apurado
se apuró	se apuraron	se hubo apurado	se hubieron apurado
4 futuro		11 futuro perfecto	
me apuraré	nos apuraremos	me habré apurado	nos habremos apurado
te apurarás	os apuraréis	te habrás apurado	os habréis apurado
se apurará	se apurarán	se habrá apurado	se habrán apurado
5 potencial simple		12 potencial compuesto	
me apuraría	nos apuraríamos	me habría apurado	nos habríamos apurado
te apurarías	os apuraríais	te habrías apurado	os habríais apurado
se apuraría	se apurarían	se habría apurado	se habrían apurado
6 presente de subjuntivo		13 perfecto de subjuntivo	
me apure	nos apuremos	me haya apurado	nos hayamos apurado
te apures	os apuréis	te hayas apurado	os hayáis apurado
se apure	se apuren	se haya apurado	se hayan apurado
7 imperfecto de subjuntivo		14 pluscuamperfecto de subjuntivo	
me apurara	nos apuráramos	me hubiera apurado	nos hubiéramos apurado
te apuraras	os apurarais	te hubieras apurado	os hubierais apurado
se apurara	se apuraran	se hubiera apurado	se hubieran apurado
OR		OR	
me apurase	nos apurásemos	me hubiese apurado	nos hubiésemos apurado
te apurases	os apuraseis	te hubieses apurado	os hubieseis apurado
se apurase	se apurasen	se hubiese apurado	se hubiesen apurado

	imperativo	
—		apurémonos
apúrate; no te apures		apuraos; no os apuréis
apúrese		apúrense

Words and expressions related to this verb
apurar   to purify; to exhaust, consume; to annoy, to tease
apurar todos los recursos   to exhaust every recourse, every means
apurar la paciencia de uno   to wear out one's patience
apurarse por poco   to worry over trivialities
el apuro   difficulty, trouble
estar en un apuro   to be in a fix

Regular **-ar** verb endings with spelling change: **c** becomes **qu** before **e**

to root up (out), to pull up (out), to tear off (away), to snatch, to start (a motor), to boot up (a computer)

The Seven Simple Tenses | The Seven Compound Tenses

Singular	Plural	Singular	Plural
1 presente de indicativo		**8 perfecto de indicativo**	
arranco	**arrancamos**	**he arrancado**	**hemos arrancado**
arrancas	**arrancáis**	**has arrancado**	**habéis arrancado**
arranca	**arrancan**	**ha arrancado**	**han arrancado**
2 imperfecto de indicativo		**9 pluscuamperfecto de indicativo**	
arrancaba	**arrancábamos**	**había arrancado**	**habíamos arrancado**
arrancabas	**arrancabais**	**habías arrancado**	**habíais arrancado**
arrancaba	**arrancaban**	**había arrancado**	**habían arrancado**
3 pretérito		**10 pretérito anterior**	
arranqué	**arrancamos**	**hube arrancado**	**hubimos arrancado**
arrancaste	**arancasteis**	**hubiste arrancado**	**hubisteis arrancado**
arrancó	**arrancaron**	**hubo arrancado**	**hubieron arrancado**
4 futuro		**11 futuro perfecto**	
arrancaré	**arrancaremos**	**habré arrancado**	**habremos arrancado**
arrancarás	**arancaréis**	**habrás arrancado**	**habréis arrancado**
arrancará	**arrancarán**	**habrá arrancado**	**habrán arrancado**
5 potencial simple		**12 potencial compuesto**	
arrancaría	**arrancaríamos**	**habría arrancado**	**habríamos arrancado**
arrancarías	**arrancaríais**	**habrías arrancado**	**habríais arrancado**
arrancaría	**arancarían**	**habría arrancado**	**habrían arrancado**
6 presente de subjuntivo		**13 perfecto de subjuntivo**	
arranque	**arranquemos**	**haya arrancado**	**hayamos arrancado**
arranques	**arranquéis**	**hayas arrancado**	**hayáis arrancado**
arranque	**arranquen**	**haya arrancado**	**hayan arrancado**
7 imperfecto de subjuntivo		**14 pluscuamperfecto de subjuntivo**	
arrancara	**arrancáramos**	**hubiera arrancado**	**hubiéramos arrancado**
arrancaras	**arrancarais**	**hubieras arrancado**	**hubierais arrancado**
arrancara	**arancaran**	**hubiera arrancado**	**hubieran arrancado**
OR		OR	
arrancase	**arrancásemos**	**hubiese arrancado**	**hubiésemos arrancado**
arrancases	**arrancaseis**	**hubieses arrancado**	**hubieseis arrancado**
arrancase	**arrancasen**	**hubiese arrancado**	**hubiesen arrancado**

imperativo

—	**arranquemos**
arranca; no arranques	**arrancad; no arranquéis**
arranque	**arranquen**

Words and expressions related to this verb

un arrancarraíces　tool to pull out roots
arrancar a　to snatch away from
arrancar de raíz　to cut up, to pull out by the root
arrancar el ordenador portátil　to turn on (boot up) the laptop computer

una arrancadora　tool for pulling out
la arrancadura　extraction
el arrancador　starter (engine)

Do you need more drills? Have fun with the *501 Spanish Verbs* CD-ROM!

arreglar (69)   Gerundio arreglando   Part. pas. arreglado

to fix, to arrange, to adjust, to regulate, to settle, to repair   Regular **-ar** verb

The Seven Simple Tenses		The Seven Compound Tenses	
Singular	Plural	Singular	Plural
1 presente de indicativo		8 perfecto de indicativo	
arreglo	**arreglamos**	**he arreglado**	**hemos arreglado**
arreglas	**arregláis**	**has arreglado**	**habéis arreglado**
arregla	**arreglan**	**ha arreglado**	**han arreglado**
2 imperfecto de indicativo		9 pluscuamperfecto de indicativo	
arreglaba	**arreglábamos**	**había arreglado**	**habíamos arreglado**
arreglabas	**arreglabais**	**habías arreglado**	**habíais arreglado**
arreglaba	**arreglaban**	**había arreglado**	**habían arreglado**
3 pretérito		10 pretérito anterior	
arreglé	**arreglamos**	**hube arreglado**	**hubimos arreglado**
arreglaste	**arreglasteis**	**hubiste arreglado**	**hubisteis arreglado**
arregló	**arreglaron**	**hubo arreglado**	**hubieron arreglado**
4 futuro		11 futuro perfecto	
arreglaré	**arreglaremos**	**habré arreglado**	**habremos arreglado**
arreglarás	**arrelgaréis**	**habrás arreglado**	**habréis arreglado**
arreglará	**arreglarán**	**habrá arreglado**	**habrán arreglado**
5 potencial simple		12 potencial compuesto	
arreglaría	**arreglaríamos**	**habría arreglado**	**habríamos arreglado**
arreglarías	**arreglaríais**	**habrías arreglado**	**habríais arreglado**
arreglaría	**arreglarían**	**habría arreglado**	**habrían arreglado**
6 presente de subjuntivo		13 perfecto de subjuntivo	
arregle	**arreglemos**	**haya arreglado**	**hayamos arreglado**
arregles	**arregléis**	**hayas arreglado**	**hayáis arreglado**
arregle	**arreglen**	**haya arreglado**	**hayan arreglado**
7 imperfecto de subjuntivo		14 pluscuamperfecto de subjuntivo	
arreglara	**arregláramos**	**hubiera arreglado**	**hubiéramos arreglado**
arreglaras	**arreglarais**	**hubieras arreglado**	**hubierais arreglado**
arreglara	**arreglaran**	**hubiera arreglado**	**hubieran arreglado**
OR		OR	
arreglase	**arreglásemos**	**hubiese arreglado**	**hubiésemos arreglado**
arreglases	**arreglaseis**	**hubieses arreglado**	**hubieseis arreglado**
arreglase	**arreglasen**	**hubiese arreglado**	**hubiesen arreglado**

	imperativo	
—		**arreglemos**
arregla; no arregles		**arreglad; no argleéis**
arregle		**arreglen**

Words and expressions related to this verb

arregladamente regularly
arreglarse con   to settle with, to reach an agreement with
arreglarse por las buenas   to settle a matter in a friendly way

arreglar una factura   to pay a bill
con arreglo a   according to
un reglamento   rule, regulation
un arreglo   agreement, solution
arreglado, arreglada   neat, orderly
arreglar una cuenta   to settle an account

The Seven Simple Tenses | The Seven Compound Tenses

A

Singular	Plural	Singular	Plural
1 presente de indicativo		8 perfecto de indicativo	
arrojo	**arrojamos**	**he arrojado**	**hemos arrojado**
arrojas	**arrojáis**	**has arrojado**	**habéis arrojado**
arroja	**arrojan**	**ha arrojado**	**han arrojado**
2 imperfecto de indicativo		9 pluscuamperfecto de indicativo	
arrojaba	**arrojábamos**	**había arrojado**	**habíamos arrojado**
arrojabas	**arrojabais**	**habías arrojado**	**habíais arrojado**
arrojaba	**arrojaban**	**había arrojado**	**habían arrojado**
3 pretérito		10 pretérito anterior	
arrojé	**arrojamos**	**hube arrojado**	**hubimos arrojado**
arrojaste	**arrojasteis**	**hubiste arrojado**	**hubisteis arrojado**
arrojó	**arrojaron**	**hubo arrojado**	**hubieron arrojado**
4 futuro		11 futuro perfecto	
arrojaré	**arrojaremos**	**habré arrojado**	**habremos arrojado**
arrojarás	**arrojaréis**	**habrás arrojado**	**habréis arrojado**
arrojará	**arrojarán**	**habrá arrojado**	**habrán arrojado**
5 potencial simple		12 potencial compuesto	
arrojaría	**arrojaríamos**	**habría arrojado**	**habríamos arrojado**
arrojarías	**arrojaríais**	**habrías arrojado**	**habríais arrojado**
arrojaría	**arrojarían**	**habría arrojado**	**habrían arrojado**
6 presente de subjuntivo		13 perfecto de subjuntivo	
arroje	**arrojemos**	**haya arrojado**	**hayamos arrojado**
arrojes	**arrojéis**	**hayas arrojado**	**hayáis arrojado**
arroje	**arrojen**	**haya arrojado**	**hayan arrojado**
7 imperfecto de subjuntivo		14 pluscuamperfecto de subjuntivo	
arrojara	**arrojáramos**	**hubiera arrojado**	**hubiéramos arrojado**
arrojaras	**arrojarais**	**hubieras arrojado**	**hubierais arrojado**
arrojara	**arrojaran**	**hubiera arrojado**	**hubieran arrojado**
OR		OR	
arrojase	**arrojásemos**	**hubiese arrojado**	**hubiésemos arrojado**
arrojases	**arrojaseis**	**hubieses arrojado**	**hubieseis arrojado**
arrojase	**arrojasen**	**hubiese arrojado**	**hubiesen arrojado**

imperativo

—	**arrojemos**
arroja; no arrojes	**arrojad; no arrojéis**
arroje	**arrojen**

Words and expressions related to this verb
el arrojador, la arrojadora   thrower
arrojado, arrojada   fearless
el arrojo   fearlessness

arrojar la esponja   to throw in the towel (sponge)
el arrojallamas   flame thrower (also **el lanzallamas**)

See also **lanzar.**

If you want an explanation of meanings and uses of Spanish and English verb tenses and moods, see pages 13–32.

to articulate, to pronounce distinctly   Regular **-ar** verb

The Seven Simple Tenses		The Seven Compound Tenses	
Singular	Plural	Singular	Plural
1 presente de indicativo		8 perfecto de indicativo	
articulo	articulamos	he articulado	hemos articulado
articulas	articuláis	has articulado	habéis articulado
articula	articulan	ha articulado	han articulado
2 imperfecto de indicativo		9 pluscuamperfecto de indicativo	
articulaba	articulábamos	había articulado	habíamos articulado
articulabas	articulabais	habías articulado	habíais articulado
articulaba	articulaban	había articulado	habían articulado
3 pretérito		10 pretérito anterior	
articulé	articulamos	hube articulado	hubimos articulado
articulaste	articulasteis	hubiste articulado	hubisteis articulado
articuló	articularon	hubo articulado	hubieron articulado
4 futuro		11 futuro perfecto	
articularé	articularemos	habré articulado	habremos articulado
articularás	articularéis	habrás articulado	habréis articulado
articulará	articularán	habrá articulado	habrán articulado
5 potencial simple		12 potencial compuesto	
articularía	artricularíamos	habría articulado	habríamos articulado
articularías	articularíais	habrías articulado	habríais articulado
articularía	articularían	habría articulado	habrían articulado
6 presente de subjuntivo		13 perfecto de subjuntivo	
articule	articulemos	haya articulado	hayamos articulado
articules	articuléis	hayas articulado	hayáis articulado
articule	articulen	haya articulado	hayan articulado
7 imperfecto de subjuntivo		14 pluscuamperfecto de subjuntivo	
articulara	articuláramos	hubiera articulado	hubiéramos articulado
articularas	articularais	hubieras articulado	hubierais articulado
articulara	articularan	hubiera articulado	hubieran articulado
OR		OR	
articulase	articulásemos	hubiese articulado	hubiésemos articulado
articulases	articulaseis	hubieses articulado	hubieseis articulado
articulase	articulasen	hubiese articulado	hubiesen articulado

imperativo

—	articulemos
articula; no articules	articulad; no articuléis
articule	articulen

Words related to this verb

articuladamente   clearly, distinctly   **articular claramente**   to articulate clearly
la articulación   articulation, pronunciation   **articular (expresar) las emociones claramente**
el, la articulista   someone who writes articles   to express emotions clearly

Consult the back pages for over 2,100 verbs conjugated like model verbs among the 501 in this book.

Regular **-ar** verb   to assure, to affirm, to assert, to insure

The Seven Simple Tenses		The Seven Compound Tenses	
Singular	Plural	Singular	Plural
1 presente de indicativo		**8 perfecto de indicativo**	
aseguro	**aseguramos**	**he asegurado**	**hemos asegurado**
aseguras	**aseguráis**	**has asegurado**	**habéis asegurado**
asegura	**aseguran**	**ha asegurado**	**han asegurado**
2 imperfecto de indicativo		**9 pluscuamperfecto de indicativo**	
aseguraba	**asegurábamos**	**había asegurado**	**habíamos asegurado**
asegurabas	**asegurabais**	**habías asegurado**	**habíais asegurado**
aseguraba	**aseguraban**	**había asegurado**	**habían asegurado**
3 pretérito		**10 pretérito anterior**	
aseguré	**aseguramos**	**hube asegurado**	**hubimos asegurado**
aseguraste	**asegurasteis**	**hubiste asegurado**	**hubisteis asegurado**
aseguró	**aseguraron**	**hubo asegurado**	**hubieron asegurado**
4 futuro		**11 futuro perfecto**	
aseguraré	**aseguraremos**	**habré asegurado**	**habremos asegurado**
asegurarás	**aseguraréis**	**habrás asegurado**	**habréis asegurado**
asegurará	**asegurarán**	**habrá asegurado**	**habrán asegurado**
5 potencial simple		**12 potencial compuesto**	
aseguraría	**aseguraríamos**	**habría asegurado**	**habríamos asegurado**
asegurarías	**aseguraríais**	**habrías asegurado**	**habríais asegurado**
aseguraría	**asegurarían**	**habría asegurado**	**habrían asegurado**
6 presente de subjuntivo		**13 perfecto de subjuntivo**	
asegure	**aseguremos**	**haya asegurado**	**hayamos asegurado**
asegures	**aseguréis**	**hayas asegurado**	**hayáis asegurado**
asegure	**aseguren**	**haya asegurado**	**hayan asegurado**
7 imperfecto de subjuntivo		**14 pluscuamperfecto de subjuntivo**	
asegurara	**aseguráramos**	**hubiera asegurado**	**hubiéramos asegurado**
aseguraras	**asegurarais**	**hubieras asegurado**	**hubierais asegurado**
asegurara	**aseguraran**	**hubiera asegurado**	**hubieran asegurado**
OR		OR	
asegurase	**asegurásemos**	**hubiese asegurado**	**hubiésemos asegurado**
asegurases	**aseguraseis**	**hubieses asegurado**	**hubieseis asegurado**
asegurase	**asegurasen**	**hubiese asegurado**	**hubiesen asegurado**

imperativo

—	**aseguremos**
asegura; no asegures	**asegurad; no aseguréis**
asegure	**aseguren**

Words and expressions related to this verb
la aseguración   insurance
asegurable   insurable
el asegurado, la asegurada   insured person
la seguridad   security, surety
seguramente   surely, securely

¡Ya puede usted asegurarlo!   You can
   be sure of it!
tener por seguro   for sure
de seguro   surely
el asegurador contra incendios   fire insurance
   underwriter

The subject pronouns are found on page 93.

to seize, to grasp Irregular **-ir** verb in Tenses 1, 6, and Imperative

The Seven Simple Tenses		The Seven Compound Tenses	
Singular	Plural	Singular	Plural
1 presente de indicativo		8 perfecto de indicativo	
asgo	**asimos**	**he asido**	**hemos asido**
ases	**asís**	**has asido**	**habéis asido**
ase	**asen**	**ha asido**	**han asido**
2 imperfecto de indicativo		9 pluscuamperfecto de indicativo	
asía	**asíamos**	**había asido**	**habíamos asido**
asías	**asíais**	**habías asido**	**habíais asido**
asía	**asían**	**había asido**	**habían asido**
3 pretérito		10 pretérito anterior	
así	**asimos**	**hube asido**	**hubimos asido**
asiste	**asisteis**	**hubiste asido**	**hubisteis asido**
asió	**asieron**	**hubo asido**	**hubieron asido**
4 futuro		11 futuro perfecto	
asiré	**asiremos**	**habré asido**	**habremos asido**
asirás	**asiréis**	**habrás asido**	**habréis asido**
asirá	**asirán**	**habrá asido**	**habrán asido**
5 potencial simple		12 potencial compuesto	
asiría	**asiríamos**	**habría asido**	**habríamos asido**
asirías	**asiríais**	**habrías asido**	**habríais asido**
asiría	**asirían**	**habría asido**	**habrían asido**
6 presente de subjuntivo		13 perfecto de subjuntivo	
asga	**asgamos**	**haya asido**	**hayamos asido**
asgas	**asgáis**	**hayas asido**	**hayáis asido**
asga	**asgan**	**haya asido**	**hayan asido**
7 imperfecto de subjuntivo		14 pluscuamperfecto de subjuntivo	
asiera	**asiéramos**	**hubiera asido**	**hubiéramos asido**
asieras	**asierais**	**hubieras asido**	**hubierais asido**
asiera	**asieran**	**hubiera asido**	**hubieran asido**
OR		OR	
asiese	**asiésemos**	**hubiese asido**	**hubiésemos asido**
asieses	**asieseis**	**hubieses asido**	**hubieseis asido**
asiese	**asiesen**	**hubiese asido**	**hubiesen asido**

	imperativo	
—		**asgamos**
ase; no asgas		**asid; no asgáis**
asga		**asgan**

Words and expressions related to this verb
asir de los cabellos   to grab by the hair
asirse a (or **de**)   to take hold of, to seize, grab
asirse con   to grapple with

asirse   to quarrel with each other
asir del brazo   to get hold of by the arm
asidos del brazo   arm in arm

Do you need more drills? Have fun with the *501 Spanish Verbs* CD-ROM!

The Seven Simple Tenses		The Seven Compound Tenses	
Singular	Plural	Singular	Plural
1 presente de indicativo		8 perfecto de indicativo	
asisto	asistimos	he asistido	hemos asistido
asistes	asistís	has asistido	habéis asistido
asiste	asisten	ha asistido	han asistido
2 imperfecto de indicativo		9 pluscuamperfecto de indicativo	
asistía	asistíamos	había asistido	habíamos asistido
asistías	asistíais	habías asistido	habíais asistido
asistía	asistían	había asistido	habían asistido
3 pretérito		10 pretérito anterior	
asistí	asistimos	hube asistido	hubimos asistido
asististe	asististeis	hubiste asistido	hubisteis asistido
asistió	asistieron	hubo asistido	hubieron asistido
4 futuro		11 futuro perfecto	
asistiré	asistiremos	habré asistido	habremos asistido
asistirás	asistiréis	habrás asistido	habréis asistido
asistirá	asistirán	habrá asistido	habrán asistido
5 potencial simple		12 potencial compuesto	
asistiría	asistiríamos	habría asistido	habríamos asistido
asistirías	asistiríais	habrías asistido	habríais asistido
asistiría	asistirían	habría asistido	habrían asistido
6 presente de subjuntivo		13 perfecto de subjuntivo	
asista	asistamos	haya asistido	hayamos asistido
asistas	asistáis	hayas asistido	hayáis asistido
asista	asistan	haya asistido	hayan asistido
7 imperfecto de subjuntivo		14 pluscuamperfecto de subjuntivo	
asistiera	asistiéramos	hubiera asistido	hubiéramos asistido
asistieras	asistierais	hubieras asistido	hubierais asistido
asistiera	asistieran	hubiera asistido	hubieran asistido
OR		OR	
asistiese	asistiésemos	hubiese asistido	hubiésemos asistido
asistieses	asistieseis	hubieses asistido	hubieseis asistido
asistiese	asistiesen	hubiese asistido	hubiesen asistido

imperativo	
—	**asistamos**
asiste; no asistas	**asistid; no asistáis**
asista	**asistan**

Words and expressions related to this verb
asistir a to attend, to be present at
la asistencia attendance, presence

la asistencia social social welfare
la asistencia técnica technical assistance

Don't miss the definitions of basic grammatical terms with examples
in English and Spanish on pages 33–44.

The subject pronouns are found on page 93.

to be frightened, to be scared   Reflexive regular **-ar** verb

The Seven Simple Tenses		The Seven Compound Tenses	
Singular	Plural	Singular	Plural
1 presente de indicativo		8 perfecto de indicativo	
me asusto	**nos asustamos**	**me he asustado**	**nos hemos asustado**
te asustas	**os asustáis**	**te has asustado**	**os habéis asustado**
se asusta	**se asustan**	**se ha asustado**	**se han asustado**
2 imperfecto de indicativo		9 pluscuamperfecto de indicativo	
me asustaba	**nos asustábamos**	**me había asustado**	**nos habíamos asustado**
te asustabas	**os asustabais**	**te habías asustado**	**os habíais asustado**
se asustaba	**se asustaban**	**se había asustado**	**se habían asustado**
3 pretérito		10 pretérito anterior	
me asusté	**nos asustamos**	**me hube asustado**	**nos hubimos asustado**
te asustaste	**os asustasteis**	**te hubiste asustado**	**os hubisteis asustado**
se asustó	**se asustaron**	**se hubo asustado**	**se hubieron asustado**
4 futuro		11 futuro perfecto	
me asustaré	**nos asustaremos**	**me habré asustado**	**nos habremos asustado**
te asustarás	**os asustaréis**	**te habrás asustado**	**os habréis asustado**
se asustará	**se asustarán**	**se habrá asustado**	**se habrán asustado**
5 potencial simple		12 potencial compuesto	
me asustaría	**nos asustaríamos**	**me habría asustado**	**nos habríamos asustado**
te asustarías	**os asustaríais**	**te habrías asustado**	**os habríais asustado**
se asustaría	**se asustarían**	**se habría asustado**	**se habrían asustado**
6 presente de subjuntivo		13 perfecto de subjuntivo	
me asuste	**nos asustemos**	**me haya asustado**	**nos hayamos asustado**
te asustes	**os asustéis**	**te hayas asustado**	**os hayáis asustado**
se asuste	**se asusten**	**se haya asustado**	**se hayan asustado**
7 imperfecto de subjuntivo		14 pluscuamperfecto de subjuntivo	
me asustara	**nos asustáramos**	**me hubiera asustado**	**nos hubiéramos asustado**
te asustaras	**os asustarais**	**te hubieras asustado**	**os hubierais asustado**
se asustara	**se asustaran**	**se hubiera asustado**	**se hubieran asustado**
OR		OR	
me asustase	**nos asustásemos**	**me hubiese asustado**	**nos hubiésemos asustado**
te asustases	**os asustaseis**	**te hubieses asustado**	**os hubieseis asustado**
se asustase	**se asustasen**	**se hubiese asustado**	**se hubiesen asustado**

imperativo

—	**asustémonos**
asústate; no te asustes	**asustaos; no os asustéis**
asústese	**asústense**

Words and expressions related to this verb

asustado, asustada   frightened, scared
asustadizo, asustadiza   easily frightened
asustador, asustadora   frightening
asustar   to frighten, to scare
Me asusto de pensarlo.   It frightens me
    to think about it.
un susto   a fright, scare

asustarse de + inf.   to be afraid + inf.
asustarse por nada   to be frightened by the
    slightest thing

Get acquainted with what preposition goes
with what verb on pages 669–677.

Regular **-ar** verb endings with spelling   to attack
change: **c** becomes **qu** before **e**

The Seven Simple Tenses | The Seven Compound Tenses

Singular	Plural	Singular	Plural
1 presente de indicativo		8 perfecto de indicativo	
ataco	**atacamos**	**he atacado**	**hemos atacado**
atacas	**atacáis**	**has atacado**	**habéis atacado**
ataca	**atacan**	**ha atacado**	**han atacado**
2 imperfecto de indicativo		9 pluscuamperfecto de indicativo	
atacaba	**atacábamos**	**había atacado**	**habíamos atacado**
atacabas	**atacabais**	**habías atacado**	**habíais atacado**
atacaba	**atacaban**	**había atacado**	**habían atacado**
3 pretérito		10 pretérito anterior	
ataqué	**atacamos**	**hube atacado**	**hubimos atacado**
atacaste	**atacasteis**	**hubiste atacado**	**hubisteis atacado**
atacó	**atacaron**	**hubo atacado**	**hubieron atacado**
4 futuro		11 futuro perfecto	
atacaré	**atacaremos**	**habré atacado**	**habremos atacado**
atacarás	**atacaréis**	**habrás atacado**	**habréis atacado**
atacará	**atacarán**	**habrá atacado**	**habrán atacado**
5 potencial simple		12 potencial compuesto	
atacaría	**atacaríamos**	**habría atacado**	**habríamos atacado**
atacarías	**atacaríais**	**habrías atacado**	**habríais atacado**
atacaría	**atacarían**	**habría atacado**	**habrían atacado**
6 presente de subjuntivo		13 perfecto de subjuntivo	
ataque	**ataquemos**	**haya atacado**	**hayamos atacado**
ataques	**ataquéis**	**hayas atacado**	**hayáis atacado**
ataque	**ataquen**	**haya atacado**	**hayan atacado**
7 imperfecto de subjuntivo		14 pluscuamperfecto de subjuntivo	
atacara	**atacáramos**	**hubiera atacado**	**hubiéramos atacado**
atacaras	**atacarais**	**hubieras atacado**	**hubierais atacado**
atacara	**atacaran**	**hubiera atacado**	**hubieran atacado**
OR		OR	
atacase	**atacásemos**	**hubiese atacado**	**hubiésemos atacado**
atacases	**atacaseis**	**hubieses atacado**	**hubieseis atacado**
atacase	**atacasen**	**hubiese atacado**	**hubiesen atacado**

imperativo

—	**ataquemos**
ataca; no ataques	**atacad; no ataquéis**
ataque	**ataquen**

Words related to this verb
el ataque attack   **el, la atacante** attacker
atacado, atacada attacked   **el atacador, la atacadora** aggressor

Check out the verb drills and verb tests with answers explained on pages 45–91.

The subject pronouns are found on page 93.

to rely on, to depend on

The Seven Simple Tenses		The Seven Compound Tenses	
Singular	Plural	Singular	Plural
1 presente de indicativo		8 perfecto de indicativo	
me atengo	**nos atenemos**	**me he atenido**	**nos hemos atenido**
te atienes	**os atenéis**	**te has atenido**	**os habéis atenido**
se atiene	**se atienen**	**se ha atenido**	**se han atenido**
2 imperfecto de indicativo		9 pluscuamperfecto de indicativo	
me atenía	**nos ateníamos**	**me había atenido**	**nos habíamos atenido**
te atenías	**os ateníais**	**te habías atenido**	**os habíais atenido**
se atenía	**se atenían**	**se había atenido**	**se habían atenido**
3 pretérito		10 pretérito anterior	
me atuve	**nos atuvimos**	**me hube atenido**	**nos hubimos atenido**
te atuviste	**os atuvisteis**	**te hubiste atenido**	**os hubisteis atenido**
se atuvo	**se atuvieron**	**se hubo atenido**	**se hubieron atenido**
4 futuro		11 futuro perfecto	
me atendré	**nos atendremos**	**me habré atenido**	**nos habremos atenido**
te atendrás	**os atendréis**	**te habrás atenido**	**os habréis atenido**
se atendrá	**se atendrán**	**se habrá atenido**	**se habrán atenido**
5 potencial simple		12 potencial compuesto	
me atendría	**nos atenderíamos**	**me habría atenido**	**nos habríamos atenido**
te atenderías	**os atenderíais**	**te habrías atenido**	**os habríais atenido**
se atendría	**se atenderían**	**se habría atenido**	**se habrían atenido**
6 presente de subjuntivo		13 perfecto de subjuntivo	
me atenga	**nos atengamos**	**me haya atenido**	**nos hayamos atenido**
te antengas	**os atengáis**	**te hayas atenido**	**os hayáis atenido**
se atenga	**se atengan**	**se haya atenido**	**se hayan atenido**
7 imperfecto de subjuntivo		14 pluscuamperfecto de subjuntivo	
me atuviera	**nos atuviéramos**	**me hubiera atenido**	**nos hubiéramos atenido**
te atuvieras	**os atuvierais**	**te hubieras atenido**	**os hubierais atenido**
se atuviera	**se atuvieran**	**se hubiera atenido**	**se hubieran atenido**
OR		OR	
me atuviese	**nos atuviésemos**	**me hubiese atenido**	**nos hubiésemos atenido**
te atuvieses	**os atuvieseis**	**te hubieses atenido**	**os hubieseis atenido**
se atuviese	**se atuviesen**	**se hubiese atenido**	**se hubiesen atenido**

imperativo

—	**atengámonos**
atente; no te atengas	**ateneos; no os atengáis**
aténgase	**aténganse**

Words and expressions related to this verb

mantener to maintain	**atenerse al convenio** to abide by the agreement
atenerse a to depend on, to rely on	**atenerse a las reglas** to abide by the rules

Irregular verb

to attract, to allure, to charm

The Seven Simple Tenses		The Seven Compound Tenses	
Singular	Plural	Singular	Plural

1 presente de indicativo

		8 perfecto de indicativo	
atraigo	atraemos	he atraído	hemos atraído
atraes	atraéis	has atraído	habéis atraído
atrae	atraen	ha atraído	han atraído

2 imperfecto de indicativo

		9 pluscuamperfecto de indicativo	
atraía	atraíamos	había atraído	habíamos atraído
atraías	atraíais	habías atraído	habíais atraído
atraía	atraían	había atraído	habían atraído

3 pretérito

		10 pretérito anterior	
atraje	atrajimos	hube atraído	hubimos atraído
atrajiste	atrajisteis	hubiste atraído	hubisteis atraído
atrajo	atrajeron	hubo atraído	hubieron atraído

4 futuro

		11 futuro perfecto	
atraeré	atraeremos	habré atraído	habremos atraído
atraerás	atraeréis	habrás atraído	habréis atraído
atraerá	atraerán	habrá atraído	habrán atraído

5 potencial simple

		12 potencial compuesto	
atraería	atraeríamos	habría atraído	habríamos atraído
atraerías	atraeríais	habrías atraído	habríais atraído
atraería	atraerían	habría atraído	habrían atraído

6 presente de subjuntivo

		13 perfecto de subjuntivo	
atraiga	atraigamos	haya atraído	hayamos atraído
atraigas	atraigáis	hayas atraído	hayáis atraído
atraiga	atraigan	haya atraído	hayan atraído

7 imperfecto de subjuntivo

		14 pluscuamperfecto de subjuntivo	
atrajera	atrajéramos	hubiera atraído	hubiéramos atraído
atrajeras	atrajerais	hubieras atraído	hubierais atraído
atrajera	atrajeran	hubiera atraído	hubieran atraído
OR		OR	
atrajese	atrajésemos	hubiese atraído	hubiésemos atraído
atrajeses	atrajeseis	hubieses atraído	hubieseis atraído
atrajese	atrajesen	hubiese atraído	hubiesen atraído

imperativo

—	atraigamos
atrae; no atraigas	atraed; no atraigáis
atraiga	atraigan

Words and expressions related to this verb

la atracción attraction; **atracción sexual**
sex appeal; **las atracciones** entertainment
atractivamente attractively
atractivo, atractiva attractive

atrayentemente attractively
atrayente appealing, attractive
el parque de atracciones amusement park
atraer las miradas to attract attention

Don't forget to study the section on defective and impersonal verbs. It's right after this main list.

The subject pronouns are found on page 93.

to cross, to go through, to run through   Regular **-ar** verb endings with stem change: Tenses 1, 6, Imperative

The Seven Simple Tenses		The Seven Compound Tenses	
Singular	Plural	Singular	Plural
1 presente de indicativo		**8 perfecto de indicativo**	
atravieso	atravesamos	he atravesado	hemos atravesado
atraviesas	atravesáis	has atravesado	habéis atravesado
atraviesa	atraviesan	ha atravesado	han atravesado
2 imperfecto de indicativo		**9 pluscuamperfecto de indicativo**	
atravesaba	atravesábamos	había atravesado	habíamos atravesado
atravesabas	atravesabais	habías atravesado	habíais atravesado
atravesaba	atravesaban	había atravesado	habían atravesado
3 pretérito		**10 pretérito anterior**	
atravesé	atravesamos	hube atravesado	hubimos atravesado
atravesaste	atravesasteis	hubiste atravesado	hubisteis atravesado
atravesó	atravesaron	hubo atravesado	hubieron atravesado
4 futuro		**11 futuro perfecto**	
atravesaré	atravesaremos	habré atravesado	habremos atravesado
atravesarás	atravesaréis	habrás atravesado	habréis atravesado
atravesará	atravesarán	habrá atravesado	habrán atravesado
5 potencial simple		**12 potencial compuesto**	
atravesaría	atravesaríamos	habría atravesado	habríamos atravesado
atravesarías	atravesaríais	habrías atravesado	habríais atravesado
atravesaría	atravesarían	habría atravesado	habrían atravesado
6 presente de subjuntivo		**13 perfecto de subjuntivo**	
atraviese	atravesemos	haya atravesado	hayamos atravesado
atravieses	atraveséis	hayas atravesado	hayáis atravesado
atraviese	atraviesen	haya atravesado	hayan atravesado
7 imperfecto de subjuntivo		**14 pluscuamperfecto de subjuntivo**	
atravesara	atravesáramos	hubiera atravesado	hubiéramos atravesado
atravesaras	atravesarais	hubieras atravesado	hubierais atravesado
atravesara	atravesaran	hubiera atravesado	hubieran atravesado
OR		OR	
atravesase	atravesásemos	hubiese atravesado	hubiésemos atravesado
atravesases	atravesaseis	hubieses atravesado	hubieseis atravesado
atravesase	atravesasen	hubiese atravesado	hubiesen atravesado

imperativo	
—	atravesemos
atraviesa; no atravieses	atravesad; no atraveséis
atraviese	atraviesen

Words and expressions related to this verb
atravesar con   to meet
travesar   to cross
mirar de través   to look out of the corner
   of one's eye

la travesía   crossing (sea), voyage
atravesado, atravesada   cross-eyed
atravesable   traversable
a través de   across, through

Can't remember the Spanish verb you need?
Check the back pages of this book for the English-Spanish verb index!

Reflexive regular **-er** verb   to dare, to venture

The Seven Simple Tenses		The Seven Compound Tenses	
Singular	Plural	Singular	Plural

A

1 presente de indicativo		8 perfecto de indicativo	
me atrevo	nos atrevemos	me he atrevido	nos hemos atrevido
te atreves	os atrevéis	te has atrevido	os habéis atrevido
se atreve	se atreven	se ha atrevido	se han atrevido
2 imperfecto de indicativo		9 pluscuamperfecto de indicativo	
me atrevía	nos atrevíamos	me había atrevido	nos habíamos atrevido
te atrevías	os atrevíais	te habías atrevido	os habíais atrevido
se atrevía	se atrevían	se había atrevido	se habían atrevido
3 pretérito		10 pretérito anterior	
me atreví	nos atrevimos	me hube atrevido	nos hubimos atrevido
te atreviste	os atrevisteis	te hubiste atrevido	os hubisteis atrevido
se atrevió	se atrevieron	se hubo atrevido	se hubieron atrevido
4 futuro		11 futuro perfecto	
me atreveré	nos atreveremos	me habré atrevido	nos habremos atrevido
te atreverás	os atreveréis	te habrás atrevido	os habréis atrevido
se atreverá	se atreverán	se habrá atrevido	se habrán atrevido
5 potencial simple		12 potencial compuesto	
me atrevería	nos atreveríamos	me habría atrevido	nos habríamos atrevido
te atreverías	os atreveríais	te habrías atrevido	os habríais atrevido
se atrevería	se atreverían	se habría atrevido	se habrían atrevido
6 presente de subjuntivo		13 perfecto de subjuntivo	
me atreva	nos atrevamos	me haya atrevido	nos hayamos atrevido
te atrevas	os atreváis	te hayas atrevido	os hayáis atrevido
se atreva	se atrevan	se haya atrevido	se hayan atrevido
7 imperfecto de subjuntivo		14 pluscuamperfecto de subjuntivo	
me atreviera	nos atreviéramos	me hubiera atrevido	nos hubiéramos atrevido
te atrevieras	os atrevierais	te hubieras atrevido	os hubierais atrevido
se atreviera	se atrevieran	se hubiera atrevido	se hubieran atrevido
OR		OR	
me atreviese	nos atreviésemos	me hubiese atrevido	nos hubiésemos atrevido
te atrevieses	os atrevieseis	te hubieses atrevido	os hubieseis atrevido
se atreviese	se atreviesen	se hubiese atrevido	se hubiesen atrevido

imperativo

—	atrevámonos
atrévete; no te atrevas	atreveos; no os atreváis
atrévase	atrévanse

Words and expressions related to this verb
atrevido, atrevida   daring, bold
el atrevimiento   audacity, boldness
atrevidamente   boldly, daringly
atreverse con *or* **contra**   to be insolent to,
  to be offensive toward

¡Atrévete!   You just dare!
Hazlo si te atreves.   Do it if you dare.
atreverse a decir mentiras   to dare to tell lies

Use the guide to Spanish
pronunciation on pages 665–667.

to advance

Regular **-ar** verb endings with spelling change: **z** becomes **c** before **e**

The Seven Simple Tenses		The Seven Compound Tenses	
Singular	Plural	Singular	Plural
1 presente de indicativo		**8 perfecto de indicativo**	
avanzo	avanzamos	he avanzado	hemos avanzado
avanzas	avanzáis	has avanzado	habéis avanzado
avanza	avanzan	ha avanzado	han avanzado
2 imperfecto de indicativo		**9 pluscuamperfecto de indicativo**	
avanzaba	avanzábamos	había avanzado	habíamos avanzado
avanzabas	avanzabais	habías avanzado	habíais avanzado
avanzaba	avanzaban	había avanzado	habían avanzado
3 pretérito		**10 pretérito anterior**	
avancé	avanzamos	hube avanzado	hubimos avanzado
avanzaste	avanzasteis	hubiste avanzado	hubisteis avanzado
avanzó	avanzaron	hubo avanzado	hubieron avanzado
4 futuro		**11 futuro perfecto**	
avanzaré	avanzaremos	habré avanzado	habremos avanzado
avanzarás	avanzaréis	habrás avanzado	habréis avanzado
avanzará	avanzarán	habrá avanzado	habrán avanzado
5 potencial simple		**12 potencial compuesto**	
avanzaría	avanzaríamos	habría avanzado	habríamos avanzado
avanzarías	avanzaríais	habrías avanzado	habríais avanzado
avanzaría	avanzarían	habría avanzado	habrían avanzado
6 presente de subjuntivo		**13 perfecto de subjuntivo**	
avance	avancemos	haya avanzado	hayamos avanzado
avances	avancéis	hayas avanzado	hayáis avanzado
avance	avancen	haya avanzado	hayan avanzado
7 imperfecto de subjuntivo		**14 pluscuamperfecto de subjuntivo**	
avanzara	avanzáramos	hubiera avanzado	hubiéramos avanzado
avanzaras	avanzarais	hubieras avanzado	hubierais avanzado
avanzara	avanzaran	hubiera avanzado	hubieran avanzado
OR		OR	
avanzase	avanzásemos	hubiese avanzado	hubiésemos avanzado
avanzases	avanzaseis	hubieses avanzado	hubieseis avanzado
avanzase	avanzasen	hubiese avanzado	hubiesen avanzado

imperativo

—	avancemos
avanza; no avances	avanzad; no avancéis
avance	avancen

Words and expressions related to this verb
avanzado, avanzada   advanced; **de edad avanzada**   advanced in years
la avanzada   advance guard, **los avances tecnológicos**   technological advances

> If you don't know the Spanish verb for the English verb you have in mind,
> look it up in the index on pages 682–706.

Regular **-ar** verb endings with spelling changes: to shame
z becomes **c** before **e**; **go** becomes **gü** before **e**.

The Seven Simple Tenses | The Seven Compound Tenses

Singular	Plural	Singular	Plural
1 presente de indicativo		8 perfecto de indicativo	
avergüenzo	**avergonzamos**	**he avergonzado**	**hemos avergonzado**
avergüenzas	**avergonzáis**	**has avergonzado**	**habéis avergonzado**
avergüenza	**avergüenzan**	**ha avergonzado**	**han avergonzado**
2 imperfecto de indicativo		9 pluscuamperfecto de indicativo	
avergonzaba	**avergonzábamos**	**había avergonzado**	**habíamos avergonzado**
avergonzabas	**avergonzabais**	**habías avergonzado**	**habíais avergonzado**
avergonzaba	**avergonzaban**	**había avergonzado**	**habían avergonzado**
3 pretérito		10 pretérito anterior	
avergoncé	**avergonzamos**	**hube avergonzado**	**hubimos avergonzado**
avergonzaste	**avergonzasteis**	**hubiste avergonzado**	**hubisteis avergonzado**
avergonzó	**avergonzaron**	**hubo avergonzado**	**hubieron avergonzado**
4 futuro		11 futuro perfecto	
avergonzaré	**avergonzaremos**	**habré avergonzado**	**habremos avergonzado**
avergonzarás	**avergonzaréis**	**habrás avergonzado**	**habréis avergonzado**
avergonzará	**avergonzarán**	**habrá avergonzado**	**habrán avergonzado**
5 potencial simple		12 potencial compuesto	
avergonzaría	**avergonzaríamos**	**habría avergonzado**	**habríamos avergonzado**
avergonzarías	**avergonzaríais**	**habrías avergonzado**	**habríais avergonzado**
avergonzaría	**avergonzarían**	**habría avergonzado**	**habrían avergonzado**
6 presente de subjuntivo		13 perfecto de subjuntivo	
avergüence	**avergoncemos**	**haya avergonzado**	**hayamos avergonzado**
avergüences	**avergoncéis**	**hayas avergonzado**	**hayáis avergonzado**
avergüence	**avergüencen**	**haya avergonzado**	**hayan avergonzado**
7 imperfecto de subjuntivo		14 pluscuamperfecto de subjuntivo	
avergonzara	**avergonzáramos**	**hubiera avergonzado**	**hubiéramos avergonzado**
avergonzaras	**avergonzarais**	**hubieras avergonzado**	**hubierais avergonzado**
avergonzara	**avergonzaran**	**hubiera avergonzado**	**hubieran avergonzado**
OR		**OR**	
avergonzase	**avergonzásemos**	**hubiese avergonzado**	**hubiésemos avergonzado**
avergonzases	**avergonzaseis**	**hubieses avergonzado**	**hubieseis avergonzado**
avergonzase	**avergonzasen**	**hubiese avergonzado**	**hubiesen avergonzado**

imperativo

—	**avergoncemos**
avergüenza; no avergüences	**avergonzad; no avergoncéis**
avergüence	**avergüencen**

Words and expressions related to this verb

avergonzado, avergonzada   ashamed
avergonzarse   to be ashamed
la vergüenza   shame, embarrassment
sin vergüenza   shameless

tener vergüenza   to be ashamed
la desvergüenza   shamelessness
desvergonzado, desvergonzada   shameless

Do you need more drills? Have fun with the *501 Spanish Verbs* CD-ROM!

The subject pronouns are found on page 93.

to find out, to inquire, to investigate	Regular **-ar** verb endings with spelling change: **gu** becomes **gü** before **e**
The Seven Simple Tenses	The Seven Compound Tenses

Singular	Plural	Singular	Plural
1 presente de indicativo		**8 perfecto de indicativo**	
averiguo	averiguamos	he averiguado	hemos averiguado
averiguas	averiguáis	has averiguado	habéis averiguado
averigua	averiguan	ha averiguado	han averiguado
2 imperfecto de indicativo		**9 pluscuamperfecto de indicativo**	
averiguaba	averiguábamos	había averiguado	habíamos averiguado
averiguabas	averiguabais	habías averiguado	habíais averiguado
averiguaba	averiguaban	había averiguado	habían averiguado
3 pretérito		**10 pretérito anterior**	
averigüé	averiguamos	hube averiguado	hubimos averiguado
averiguaste	averiguasteis	hubiste averiguado	hubisteis averiguado
averiguó	averiguaron	hubo averiguado	hubieron averiguado
4 futuro		**11 futuro perfecto**	
averiguaré	averiguaremos	habré averiguado	habremos averiguado
averiguarás	averiguaréis	habrás averiguado	habréis averiguado
averiguará	averiguarán	habrá averiguado	habrán averiguado
5 potencial simple		**12 potencial compuesto**	
averiguaría	averiguaríamos	habría averiguado	habríamos averiguado
averiguarías	averiguaríais	habrías averiguado	habríais averiguado
averiguaría	averiguarían	habría averiguado	habrían averiguado
6 presente de subjuntivo		**13 perfecto de subjuntivo**	
averigüe	averigüemos	haya averiguado	hayamos averiguado
averigües	averigüéis	hayas averiguado	hayáis averiguado
averigüe	averigüen	haya averiguado	hayan averiguado
7 imperfecto de subjuntivo		**14 pluscuamperfecto de subjuntivo**	
averiguara	averiguáramos	hubiera averiguado	hubiéramos averiguado
averiguaras	averiguarais	hubieras averiguado	hubierais averiguado
averiguara	averiguaran	hubiera averiguado	hubieran averiguado
OR		OR	
averiguase	averiguásemos	hubiese averiguado	hubiésemos averiguado
averiguases	averiguaseis	hubieses averiguado	hubieseis averiguado
averiguase	averiguasen	hubiese averiguado	hubiesen averiguado

imperativo	
—	averigüemos
averigua; no averigües	averiguad; no averigüéis
averigüe	averigüen

Words related to this verb

el averiguador, la averiguadora   investigator   averiguable   investigable, verifiable
la averiguación   inquiry, investigation   averiguadamente   surely, certainly

Don't miss the definitions of basic grammatical terms with examples
in English and Spanish on pages 33–44.

Regular **-ar** verb   to help, to aid, to assist

The Seven Simple Tenses		The Seven Compound Tenses	
Singular	Plural	Singular	Plural
1 presente de indicativo		**8 perfecto de indicativo**	
ayudo	ayudamos	he ayudado	hemos ayudado
ayudas	ayudáis	has ayudado	habéis ayudado
ayuda	ayudan	ha ayudado	han ayudado
2 imperfecto de indicativo		**9 pluscuamperfecto de indicativo**	
ayudaba	ayudábamos	había ayudado	habíamos ayudado
ayudabas	ayudabais	habías ayudado	habíais ayudado
ayudaba	ayudaban	había ayudado	habían ayudado
3 pretérito		**10 pretérito anterior**	
ayudé	ayudamos	hube ayudado	hubimos ayudado
ayudaste	ayudasteis	hubiste ayudado	hubisteis ayudado
ayudó	ayudaron	hubo ayudado	hubieron ayudado
4 futuro		**11 futuro perfecto**	
ayudaré	ayudaremos	habré ayudado	habremos ayudado
ayudarás	ayudaréis	habrás ayudado	habréis ayudado
ayudará	ayudarán	habrá ayudado	habrán ayudado
5 potencial simple		**12 potencial compuesto**	
ayudaría	ayudaríamos	habría ayudado	habríamos ayudado
ayudarías	ayudaríais	habrías ayudado	habríais ayudado
ayudaría	ayudarían	habría ayudado	habrían ayudado
6 presente de subjuntivo		**13 perfecto de subjuntivo**	
ayude	ayudemos	haya ayudado	hayamos ayudado
ayudes	ayudéis	hayas ayudado	hayáis ayudado
ayude	ayuden	haya ayudado	hayan ayudado
7 imperfecto de subjuntivo		**14 pluscuamperfecto de subjuntivo**	
ayudara	ayudáramos	hubiera ayudado	hubiéramos ayudado
ayudaras	ayudarais	hubieras ayudado	hubierais ayudado
ayudara	ayudaran	hubiera ayudado	hubieran ayudado
OR		OR	
ayudase	ayudásemos	hubiese ayudado	hubiésemos ayudado
ayudases	ayudaseis	hubieses ayudado	hubieseis ayudado
ayudase	ayudasen	hubiese ayudado	hubiesen ayudado

imperativo	
—	ayudemos
ayuda; no ayudes	ayudad; no ayudéis
ayude	ayuden

Words and expressions related to this verb
la ayuda aid, assistance, help
ayuda de cámara valet
un ayudador, una ayudadora helper
ayudante assistant

la ayuda financiera financial aid
A quien madruga, Dios le ayuda.
     The early bird catches the worm.

Can't find the verb you're looking for?
Check the back pages of this book for a list of over 2,100 additional verbs!

The subject pronouns are found on page 93.

bailar (85)

Gerundio bailando **Part. pas. bailado**

to dance

Regular **-ar** verb

The Seven Simple Tenses		The Seven Compound Tenses	
Singular	Plural	Singular	Plural
1 presente de indicativo		**8 perfecto de indicativo**	
bailo	bailamos	he bailado	hemos bailado
bailas	bailáis	has bailado	habéis bailado
baila	bailan	ha bailado	han bailado
2 imperfecto de indicativo		**9 pluscuamperfecto de indicativo**	
bailaba	bailábamos	había bailado	habíamos bailado
bailabas	bailabais	habías bailado	habíais bailado
bailaba	bailaban	había bailado	habían bailado
3 pretérito		**10 pretérito anterior**	
bailé	bailamos	hube bailado	hubimos bailado
bailaste	bailasteis	hubiste bailado	hubisteis bailado
bailó	bailaron	hubo bailado	hubieron bailado
4 futuro		**11 futuro perfecto**	
bailaré	bailaremos	habré bailado	habremos bailado
bailarás	bailaréis	habrás bailado	habréis bailado
bailará	bailarán	habrá bailado	habrán bailado
5 potencial simple		**12 potencial compuesto**	
bailaría	bailaríamos	habría bailado	habríamos bailado
bailarías	bailaríais	habrías bailado	habríais bailado
bailaría	bailarían	habría bailado	habrían bailado
6 presente de subjuntivo		**13 perfecto de subjuntivo**	
baile	bailemos	haya bailado	hayamos bailado
bailes	bailéis	hayas bailado	hayáis bailado
baile	bailen	haya bailado	hayan bailado
7 imperfecto de subjuntivo		**14 pluscuamperfecto de subjuntivo**	
bailara	bailáramos	hubiera bailado	hubiéramos bailado
bailaras	bailarais	hubieras bailado	hubierais bailado
bailara	bailaran	hubiera bailado	hubieran bailado
OR		OR	
bailase	bailásemos	hubiese bailado	hubiésemos bailado
bailases	bailaseis	hubieses bailado	hubieseis bailado
bailase	bailasen	hubiese bailado	hubiesen bailado

imperativo	
—	bailemos
baila; no bailes	bailad; no bailéis
baile	bailen

Sentences using this verb and words related to it

Cuando el gato va a sus devociones, bailan los ratones. When the cat is away, the mice will play.

un baile dance; **un bailete** ballet

un bailarín, una bailarina dancer (professional)

un bailador, una bailadora dancer

la música bailable dance music

Don't forget to study the section on defective and impersonal verbs. It's right after this main list.

184

Regular **-ar** verb   to lower, to let down, to come down, to go down, to descend

The Seven Simple Tenses		The Seven Compound Tenses	
Singular	Plural	Singular	Plural
1 presente de indicativo		**8 perfecto de indicativo**	
bajo	**bajamos**	**he bajado**	**hemos bajado**
bajas	**bajáis**	**has bajado**	**habéis bajado**
baja	**bajan**	**ha bajado**	**han bajado**
2 imperfecto de indicativo		**9 pluscuamperfecto de indicativo**	
bajaba	**bajábamos**	**había bajado**	**habíamos bajado**
bajabas	**bajabais**	**habías bajado**	**habíais bajado**
bajaba	**bajaban**	**había bajado**	**habían bajado**
3 pretérito		**10 pretérito anterior**	
bajé	**bajamos**	**hube bajado**	**hubimos bajado**
bajaste	**bajasteis**	**hubiste bajado**	**hubisteis bajado**
bajó	**bajaron**	**hubo bajado**	**hubieron bajado**
4 futuro		**11 futuro perfecto**	
bajaré	**bajaremos**	**habré bajado**	**habremos bajado**
bajarás	**bajaréis**	**habrás bajado**	**habréis bajado**
bajará	**bajarán**	**habrá bajado**	**habrán bajado**
5 potencial simple		**12 potencial compuesto**	
bajaría	**bajaríamos**	**habría bajado**	**habríamos bajado**
bajarías	**bajaríais**	**habrías bajado**	**habríais bajado**
bajaría	**bajarían**	**habría bajado**	**habrían bajado**
6 presente de subjuntivo		**13 perfecto de subjuntivo**	
baje	**bajemos**	**haya bajado**	**hayamos bajado**
bajes	**bajéis**	**hayas bajado**	**hayáis bajado**
baje	**bajen**	**haya bajado**	**hayan bajado**
7 imperfecto de subjuntivo		**14 pluscuamperfecto de subjuntivo**	
bajara	**bajáramos**	**hubiera bajado**	**hubiéramos bajado**
bajaras	**bajarais**	**hubieras bajado**	**hubierais bajado**
bajara	**bajaran**	**hubiera bajado**	**hubieran bajado**
OR		OR	
bajase	**bajásemos**	**hubiese bajado**	**hubiésemos bajado**
bajases	**bajaseis**	**hubieses bajado**	**hubieseis bajado**
bajase	**bajasen**	**hubiese bajado**	**hubiesen bajado**

	imperativo	
—		**bajemos**
baja; no bajes		**bajad; no bajéis**
baje		**bajen**

Words and expressions related to this verb
la baja reduction (fall) in prices
la bajada descent
bajamente basely
en voz baja in a low voice
bajo down, below
bajar/bajarse el correo electrónico to download e-mail

bajarse to download (Internet); **telecargar** and **descargar** are also used for "to download"
rebajar to reduce
bajar de to get off
bajar de valor to decline in value
el piso bajo ground floor
una rebaja rebate, discount
¿En qué estación debo bajar? At what station do I need to get off?

The subject pronouns are found on page 93.

to stammer, to hesitate (in speech)
Regular **-ar** verb

The Seven Simple Tenses		The Seven Compound Tenses	
Singular	Plural	Singular	Plural
1 presente de indicativo		8 perfecto de indicativo	
balbuceo	balbuceamos	he balbuceado	hemos balbuceado
balbuceas	balbuceáis	has balbuceado	habéis balbuceado
balbucea	balbucean	ha balbuceado	han balbuceado
2 imperfecto de indicativo		9 pluscuamperfecto de indicativo	
balbuceaba	balbuceábamos	había balbuceado	habíamos balbuceado
balbuceabas	balbuceabais	habías balbuceado	habíais balbuceado
balbuceaba	balbuceaban	había balbuceado	habían balbuceado
3 pretérito		10 pretérito anterior	
balbuceé	balbuceamos	hube balbuceado	hubimos balbuceado
babluceaste	balbuceasteis	hubiste balbuceado	hubisteis balbuceado
balbuceó	balbucearon	hubo balbuceado	hubieron balbuceado
4 futuro		11 futuro perfecto	
balbucearé	balbucearemos	habré balbuceado	habremos balbuceado
balbucearás	balbucearéis	habrás balbuceado	habréis balbuceado
balbuceará	balbucerán	habrá balbuceado	habrán balbuceado
5 potencial simple		12 potencial compuesto	
balbucearía	balbucearíamos	habría balbuceado	habríamos balbuceado
balbucearías	balbucearíais	habrías balbuceado	habríais balbuceado
balbucearía	balbucearían	habría balbuceado	habrían balbuceado
6 presente de subjuntivo		13 perfecto de subjuntivo	
balbucee	balbuceemos	haya balbuceado	hayamos balbuceado
balbucees	balbuceéis	hayas balbuceado	hayáis balbuceado
balbucee	balbuceen	haya balbuceado	hayan balbuceado
7 imperfecto de subjuntivo		14 pluscuamperfecto de subjuntivo	
balbuceara	balbuceáramos	hubiera balbuceado	hubiéramos balbuceado
balbucearas	balbucearais	hubieras balbuceado	hubierais balbuceado
balbuceara	balbucearan	hubiera balbuceado	hubieran balbuceado
OR		OR	
balbucease	balbuceásemos	hubiese balbuceado	hubiésemos balbuceado
balbuceases	balbuceaseis	hubieses balbuceado	hubieseis balbuceado
balbucease	balbuceasen	hubiese balbuceado	hubiesen balbuceado

	imperativo
—	balbuceemos
balbucea; no balbucees	balbucead; no balbuceéis
balbucee	balbuceen

Words related to this verb
balbuciente lisping, stammering
el balbuceo, la balbucencia stuttering, stammering, lisp

Can't remember the Spanish verb you need?
Check the back pages of this book for the English-Spanish verb index!

Reflexive regular **-ar** verb   to bathe oneself, to take a bath

The Seven Simple Tenses		The Seven Compound Tenses	
Singular	Plural	Singular	Plural
1 presente de indicativo		8 perfecto de indicativo	
me baño	nos bañamos	me he bañado	nos hemos bañado
te bañas	os bañáis	te has bañado	os habéis bañado
se baña	se bañan	se ha bañado	se han bañado
2 imperfecto de indicativo		9 pluscuamperfecto de indicativo	
me bañaba	nos bañábamos	me había bañado	nos habíamos bañado
te bañabas	os bañabais	te habías bañado	os habíais bañado
se bañaba	se bañaban	se había bañado	se habían bañado
3 pretérito		10 pretérito anterior	
me bañé	nos bañamos	me hube bañado	nos hubimos bañado
te bañaste	os bañasteis	te hubiste bañado	os hubisteis bañado
se bañó	se bañaron	se hubo bañado	se hubieron bañado
4 futuro		11 futuro perfecto	
me bañaré	nos bañaremos	me habré bañado	nos habremos bañado
te bañarás	os bañaréis	te habrás bañado	os habréis bañado
se bañará	se bañarán	se habrá bañado	se habrán bañado
5 potencial simple		12 potencial compuesto	
me bañaría	nos bañaríamos	me habría bañado	nos habríamos bañado
te bañarías	os bañaríais	te habrías bañado	os habríais bañado
se bañaría	se bañarían	se habría bañado	se habrían bañado
6 presente de subjuntivo		13 perfecto de subjuntivo	
me bañe	nos bañemos	me haya bañado	nos hayamos bañado
te bañes	os bañéis	te hayas bañado	os hayáis bañado
se bañe	se bañen	se haya bañado	se hayan bañado
7 imperfecto de subjuntivo		14 pluscuamperfecto de subjuntivo	
me bañara	nos bañáramos	me hubiera bañado	nos hubiéramos bañado
te bañaras	os bañarais	te hubieras bañado	os hubierais bañado
se bañara	se bañaran	se hubiera bañado	se hubieran bañado
OR		OR	
me bañase	nos bañásemos	me hubiese bañado	nos hubiésemos bañado
te bañases	os bañaseis	te hubieses bañado	os hubieseis bañado
se bañase	se bañasen	se hubiese bañado	se hubiesen bañado

imperativo

—	**bañémonos**
báñate; no te bañes	**bañaos; no os bañéis**
báñese	**báñense**

Words and expressions related to this verb

una bañera, una bañadera   bathtub
un bañador, una bañadora   bather
un baño   bath, bathing
un baño de vapor   steam bath

bañar un papel de lágrimas   to write a mournful letter
bañar a la luz   to light up, to illuminate
bañar   to bathe

The subject pronouns are found on page 93.

to sweep, to whisk   Regular **-er** verb

The Seven Simple Tenses		The Seven Compound Tenses	
Singular	Plural	Singular	Plural
1 presente de indicativo		8 perfecto de indicativo	
barro	barremos	he barrido	hemos barrido
barres	barréis	has barrido	habéis barrido
barre	barren	ha barrido	han barrido
2 imperfecto de indicativo		9 pluscuamperfecto de indicativo	
barría	barríamos	había barrido	habíamos barrido
barrías	barríais	habías barrido	habíais barrido
barria	barrían	había barrido	habían barrido
3 pretérito		10 pretérito anterior	
barrí	barrimos	hube barrido	hubimos barrido
barriste	barristeis	hubiste barrido	hubisteis barrido
barrió	barrieron	hubo barrido	hubieron barrido
4 futuro		11 futuro perfecto	
barreré	barreremos	habré barrido	habremos barrido
barrerás	barreréis	habrás barrido	habréis barrido
barrerá	barrerán	habrá barrido	habrán barrido
5 potencial simple		12 potencial compuesto	
barrería	barreríamos	habría barrido	habríamos barrido
barrerías	barreríais	habrías barrido	habríais barrido
barrería	barrerían	habría barrido	habrían barrido
6 presente de subjuntivo		13 perfecto de subjuntivo	
barra	barramos	haya barrido	hayamos barrido
barras	barráis	hayas barrido	hayáis barrido
barra	barran	haya barrido	hayan barrido
7 imperfecto de subjuntivo		14 pluscuamperfecto de subjuntivo	
barriera	barriéramos	hubiera barrido	hubiéramos barrido
barrieras	barrierais	hubieras barrido	hubierais barrido
barriera	barrieran	hubiera barrido	hubieran barrido
OR		OR	
barriese	barriésemos	hubiese barrido	hubiésemos barrido
barrieses	barrieseis	hubieses barrido	hubieseis barrido
barriese	barriesen	hubiese barrido	hubiesen barrido

	imperativo	
—		barramos
	barre; no barras	barred; no barráis
	barra	barran

Words and expressions related to this verb
la barredera   street sweeper machine
el barredero de alfombra   carpet sweeper
la barredura   sweeping
la barredora eléctrica (also **la aspiradora**)
   vacuum cleaner

Regular **-ar** verb endings with spelling
change: **z** becomes **c** before **e**

to baptize, to christen

The Seven Simple Tenses		The Seven Compound Tenses	
Singular	Plural	Singular	Plural

1   presente de indicativo

bautizo	bautizamos	
bautizas	bautizáis	
bautiza	bautizan	

8   perfecto de indicativo

he bautizado	hemos bautizado
has bautizado	habéis bautizado
ha bautizado	han bautizado

2   imperfecto de indicativo

bautizaba	bautizábamos
bautizabas	bautizabais
bautizaba	bautizaban

9   pluscuamperfecto de indicativo

había bautizado	habíamos bautizado
habías bautizado	habíais bautizado
había bautizado	habían bautizado

3   pretérito

bauticé	bautizamos
bautizaste	bautizasteis
bautizó	bautizaron

10   pretérito anterior

hube bautizado	hubimos bautizado
hubiste bautizado	hubisteis bautizado
hubo bautizado	hubieron bautizado

4   futuro

bautizaré	bautizaremos
bautizarás	bautizaréis
bautizará	bautizarán

11   futuro perfecto

habré bautizado	habremos bautizado
habrás bautizado	habréis bautizado
habrá bautizado	habrán bautizado

5   potencial simple

bautizaría	bautizaríamos
bautizarías	bautizaríais
bautizaría	bautizarían

12   potencial compuesto

habría bautizado	habríamos bautizado
habrías bautizado	habríais bautizado
habría bautizado	habrían bautizado

6   presente de subjuntivo

bautice	bauticemos
bautices	bauticéis
bautice	bauticen

13   perfecto de subjuntivo

haya bautizado	hayamos bautizado
hayas bautizado	hayáis bautizado
haya bautizado	hayan bautizado

7   imperfecto de subjuntivo

bautizara	bautizáramos
bautizaras	bautizarais
bautizara	bautizaran
OR	
bautizase	bautizásemos
bautizases	bautizaseis
bautizase	bautizasen

14   pluscuamperfecto de subjuntivo

hubiera bautizado	hubiéramos bautizado
hubieras bautizado	hubierais bautizado
hubiera bautizado	hubieran bautizado
OR	
hubiese bautizado	hubiésemos bautizado
hubieses bautizado	hubieseis bautizado
hubiese bautizado	hubiesen bautizado

imperativo

—	bauticemos
bautiza; no bautices	bautizad; no bauticéis
bautice	bauticen

Words and expressions related to this verb
el bautisterio   baptistery
el bautismo   baptism, christening
bautismal   baptismal

el, la Bautista   Baptist
bautizar una calle   to name a street

Get your feet wet with verbs used in weather expressions on page 668.

The subject pronouns are found on page 93.

beber (91)

Gerundio bebiendo **Part. pas.** bebido

to drink

Regular -er verb

The Seven Simple Tenses		The Seven Compound Tenses	
Singular	Plural	Singular	Plural
1 presente de indicativo		**8 perfecto de indicativo**	
bebo	bebemos	he bebido	hemos bebido
bebes	bebéis	has bebido	habéis bebido
bebe	beben	ha bebido	han bebido
2 imperfecto de indicativo		**9 pluscuamperfecto de indicativo**	
bebía	bebíamos	había bebido	habíamos bebido
bebías	bebíais	habías bebido	habíais bebido
bebía	bebían	había bebido	habían bebido
3 pretérito		**10 pretérito anterior**	
bebí	bebimos	hube bebido	hubimos bebido
bebiste	bebisteis	hubiste bebido	hubisteis bebido
bebió	bebieron	hubo bebido	hubieron bebido
4 futuro		**11 futuro perfecto**	
beberé	beberemos	habré bebido	habremos bebido
beberás	beberéis	habrás bebido	habréis bebido
beberá	beberán	habrá bebido	habrán bebido
5 potencial simple		**12 potencial compuesto**	
bebería	beberíamos	habría bebido	habríamos bebido
beberías	beberíais	habrías bebido	habríais bebido
bebería	beberían	habría bebido	habrían bebido
6 presente de subjuntivo		**13 perfecto de subjuntivo**	
beba	bebamos	haya bebido	hayamos bebido
bebas	bebáis	hayas bebido	hayáis bebido
beba	beban	haya bebido	hayan bebido
7 imperfecto de subjuntivo		**14 pluscuamperfecto de subjuntivo**	
bebiera	bebiéramos	hubiera bebido	hubiéramos bebido
bebieras	bebierais	hubieras bebido	hubierais bebido
bebiera	bebieran	hubiera bebido	hubieran bebido
OR		OR	
bebiese	bebiésemos	hubiese bebido	hubiésemos bebido
bebieses	bebieseis	hubieses bebido	hubieseis bebido
bebiese	bebiesen	hubiese bebido	hubiesen bebido

imperativo	
—	bebamos
bebe; no bebas	bebed; no bebáis
beba	beban

Words and expressions related to this verb
una bebida   drink, beverage
beber de   to drink from
beber a la salud   to drink to health
embeber   to soak in, soak up, imbibe
embeberse en   to absorb onself, to immerse
  oneself in
embebedor, embebedora   absorbent

beber como una cuba   to drink like a fish
querer beber la sangre a otro   to hate
  somebody bitterly

> Can't find the verb you're looking for?
> Check the back pages of this book for a list
> of over 2,100 additional verbs!

Irregular verb   to bless, to consecrate

The Seven Simple Tenses		The Seven Compound Tenses	
Singular	Plural	Singular	Plural
1 presente de indicativo		8 perfecto de indicativo	
bendigo	**bendecimos**	**he bendecido**	**hemos bendecido**
bendices	**bendecís**	**has bendecido**	**habéis bendecido**
bendice	**bendicen**	**ha bendecido**	**han bendecido**
2 imperfecto de indicativo		9 pluscuamperfecto de indicativo	
bendecía	**bendecíamos**	**había bendecido**	**habíamos bendecido**
bendecías	**bendecíais**	**habías bendecido**	**habíais bendecido**
bendecía	**bendecían**	**había bendecido**	**habían bendecido**
3 pretérito		10 pretérito anterior	
bendije	**bendijimos**	**hube bendecido**	**hubimos bendecido**
bendijiste	**bendijisteis**	**hubiste bendecido**	**hubisteis bendecido**
bendijo	**bendijeron**	**hubo bendecido**	**hubieron bendecido**
4 futuro		11 futuro perfecto	
bendeciré	**bendeciremos**	**habré bendecido**	**habremos bendecido**
bendecirás	**bendeciréis**	**habrás bendecido**	**habréis bendecido**
bendecirá	**bendecirán**	**habrá bendecido**	**habrán bendecido**
5 potencial simple		12 potencial compuesto	
bendeciría	**bendeciríamos**	**habría bendecido**	**habríamos bendecido**
bendecirías	**bendeciríais**	**habrías bendecido**	**habríais bendecido**
bendeciría	**bendecirían**	**habría bendecido**	**habrían bendecido**
6 presente de subjuntivo		13 perfecto de subjuntivo	
bendiga	**bendigamos**	**haya bendecido**	**hayamos bendecido**
bendigas	**bendigáis**	**hayas bendecido**	**hayáis bendecido**
bendiga	**bendigan**	**haya bendecido**	**hayan bendecido**
7 imperfecto de subjuntivo		14 pluscuamperfecto de subjuntivo	
bendijera	**bendijéramos**	**hubiera bendecido**	**hubiéramos bendecido**
bendijeras	**bendijerais**	**hubieras bendecido**	**hubierais bendecido**
bendijera	**bendijeran**	**hubiera bendecido**	**hubieran bendecido**
OR		OR	
bendijese	**bendijésemos**	**hubiese bendecido**	**hubiésemos bendecido**
bendijeses	**bendijeseis**	**hubieses bendecido**	**hubieseis bendecido**
bendijese	**bendijesen**	**hubiese bendecido**	**hubiesen bendecido**

imperativo

—	**bendigamos**
bendice; no bendigas	**bendecid; no bendigáis**
bendiga	**bendigan**

Words and expressions related to this verb
la bendición   benediction, blessing
las bendiciones nupciales   marriage
Dormí como un bendito   I slept like a baby/
like a log.

un bendecidor, una bendecidora   blesser
el pan bendito   communion bread (blessed)

See also **maldecir.**
See also the note on the bottom of verb 368.

The subject pronouns are found on page 93.

to erase, to cross out

The Seven Simple Tenses		The Seven Compound Tenses	
Singular	Plural	Singular	Plural
1 presente de indicativo		8 perfecto de indicativo	
borro	borramos	he borrado	hemos borrado
borras	borráis	has borrado	habéis borrado
borra	borran	ha borrado	han borrado
2 imperfecto de indicativo		9 pluscuamperfecto de indicativo	
borraba	borrábamos	había borrado	habíamos borrado
borrabas	borrabais	habías borrado	habíais borrado
borraba	borraban	había borrado	habían borrado
3 pretérito		10 pretérito anterior	
borré	borramos	hube borrado	hubimos borrado
borraste	borrasteis	hubiste borrado	hubisteis borrado
borró	borraron	hubo borrado	hubieron borrado
4 futuro		11 futuro perfecto	
borraré	borraremos	habré borrado	habremos borrado
borrarás	borraréis	habrás borrado	habréis borrado
borrará	borrarán	habrá borrado	habrán borrado
5 potencial simple		12 potencial compuesto	
borraría	borraríamos	habría borrado	habríamos borrado
borrarías	borraríais	habrías borrado	habríais borrado
borraría	borrarían	habría borrado	habrían borrado
6 presente de subjuntivo		13 perfecto de subjuntivo	
borre	borremos	haya borrado	hayamos borrado
borres	borréis	hayas borrado	hayáis borrado
borre	borren	haya borrado	hayan borrado
7 imperfecto de subjuntivo		14 pluscuamperfecto de subjuntivo	
borrara	borráramos	hubiera borrado	hubiéramos borrado
borraras	borrarais	hubieras borrado	hubierais borrado
borrara	borraran	hubiera borrado	hubieran borrado
OR		OR	
borrase	borrásemos	hubiese borrado	hubiésemos borrado
borrases	borraseis	hubieses borrado	hubieseis borrado
borrase	borrasen	hubiese borrado	hubiesen borrado

	imperativo	
—		borremos
borra; no borres		borrad; no borréis
borre		borren

Words and expressions related to this verb

la goma de borrar   rubber eraser

la borradura   erasure

el borrador   eraser (chalk), rough draft

la tecla de borrado   delete key (computer)

desborrar   to burl (to clean off the knots from cloth)

emborrar   to pad, to stuff, to wad; to gulp down food

Regular **-ar** verb endings with spelling
change: **z** becomes **c** before **e**

to yawn, to gape

The Seven Simple Tenses		The Seven Compound Tenses	
Singular	Plural	Singular	Plural
1　presente de indicativo		8　perfecto de indicativo	
bostezo	bostezamos	he bostezado	hemos bostezado
bostezas	bostezáis	has bostezado	habéis bostezado
bosteza	bostezan	ha bostezado	han bostezado
2　imperfecto de indicativo		9　pluscuamperfecto de indicativo	
bostezaba	bostezábamos	había bostezado	habíamos bostezado
bostezabas	bostezabais	habías bostezado	habíais bostezado
bostezaba	bostezeban	había bostezado	habían bostezado
3　pretérito		10　pretérito anterior	
bostecé	bostezamos	hube bostezado	hubimos bostezado
bostezaste	bostezasteis	hubiste bostezado	hubisteis bostezado
bostezó	bostezaron	hubo bostezado	hubieron bostezado
4　futuro		11　futuro perfecto	
bostezaré	bostezaremos	habré bostezado	habremos bostezado
bostezarás	bostezaréis	habrás bostezado	habréis bostezado
bostezará	bostezarán	habrá bostezado	habrán bostezado
5　potencial simple		12　potencial compuesto	
bostezaría	bostezaríamos	habría bostezado	habríamos bostezado
bostezarías	bostezaríais	habrías bostezado	habríais bostezado
bostezaría	bostezarían	habría bostezado	habrían bostezado
6　presente de subjuntivo		13　perfecto de subjuntivo	
bostece	bostecemos	haya bostezado	hayamos bostezado
bosteces	bostecéis	hayas bostezado	hayáis bostezado
bostece	bostecen	haya bostezado	hayan bostezado
7　imperfecto de subjuntivo		14　pluscuamperfecto de subjuntivo	
bostezara	bostezáramos	hubiera bostezado	hubiéramos bostezado
bostezaras	bostezarais	hubieras bostezado	hubierais bostezado
bostezara	bostezaran	hubiera bostezado	hubieran bostezado
OR		OR	
bostezase	bostezásemos	hubiese bostezado	hubiésemos bostezado
bostezases	bostezaseis	hubieses bostezado	hubieseis bostezado
bostezase	bostezasen	hubiese bostezado	hubiesen bostezado

imperativo	
—	bostecemos
bosteza; no bosteces	bostezad; no bostecéis
bostece	bostecen

Words related to this verb

un bostezo　yawn
bostezante　yawning, gaping

un bostezador, una bostezadora　a person
　who yawns frequently

Can't remember the Spanish verb you need?
Check the back pages of this book for the English-Spanish verb index!

The subject pronouns are found on page 93.

193

botar (95)

Gerundio botando   Part. pas. **botado**

to fling, to cast (away), to throw (away), to launch   Regular **-ar** verb

The Seven Simple Tenses		The Seven Compound Tenses	
Singular	Plural	Singular	Plural
1 presente de indicativo		**8 perfecto de indicativo**	
boto	botamos	he botado	hemos botado
botas	botáis	has botado	habéis botado
bota	botan	ha botado	han botado
2 imperfecto de indicativo		**9 pluscuamperfecto de indicativo**	
botaba	botábamos	había botado	habíamos botado
botabas	botabais	habías botado	habíais botado
botaba	botaban	había botado	habían botado
3 pretérito		**10 pretérito anterior**	
boté	botamos	hube botado	hubimos botado
botaste	botasteis	hubiste botado	hubisteis botado
botó	botaron	hubo botado	hubieron botado
4 futuro		**11 futuro perfecto**	
botaré	botaremos	habré botado	habremos botado
botarás	botaréis	habrás botado	habréis botado
botará	botarán	habrá botado	habrán botado
5 potencial simple		**12 potencial compuesto**	
botaría	botaríamos	habría botado	habríamos botado
botarías	botaríais	habrías botado	habríais botado
botaría	botarían	habría botado	habrían botado
6 presente de subjuntivo		**13 perfecto de subjuntivo**	
bote	botemos	haya botado	hayamos botado
botes	botéis	hayas botado	hayáis botado
bote	boten	haya botado	hayan botado
7 imperfecto de subjuntivo		**14 pluscuamperfecto de subjuntivo**	
botara	botáramos	hubiera botado	hubiéramos botado
botaras	botarais	hubieras botado	hubierais botado
botara	botaran	hubiera botado	hubieran botado
OR		OR	
botase	botásemos	hubiese botado	hubiésemos botado
botases	botaseis	hubieses botado	hubieseis botado
botase	botasen	hubiese botado	hubiesen botado

imperativo	
—	botemos
bota; no botes	botad; no botéis
bote	boten

Words and expressions related to this verb

un bote thrust, blow; boat; **un bote de remos** rowboat
rebotar to bend back; to repel; to bounce back, rebound
un rebote bounce, rebound; **de rebote** indirectly

dar bote to buck
el bote automóvil powerboat
el bote de salvavidas lifeboat

Don't forget to study the section on defective and impersonal verbs. It's right after this main list.

Regular **-ar** verb   to bronze, to tan

B

The Seven Simple Tenses		The Seven Compound Tenses	
Singular	Plural	Singular	Plural
1 presente de indicativo		8 perfecto de indicativo	
bronceo	bronceamos	he bronceado	hemos bronceado
bronceas	bronceáis	has bronceado	habéis bronceado
broncea	broncean	ha bronceado	han bronceado
2 imperfecto de indicativo		9 pluscuamperfecto de indicativo	
bronceaba	bronceábamos	había bronceado	habíamos bronceado
bronceabas	bronceabais	habías bronceado	habíais bronceado
bronceaba	bronceaban	había bronceado	habían bronceado
3 pretérito		10 pretérito anterior	
bronceé	bronceamos	hube bronceado	hubimos bronceado
bronceaste	bronceasteis	hubiste bronceado	hubisteis bronceado
bronceó	broncearon	hubo bronceado	hubieron bronceado
4 futuro		11 futuro perfecto	
broncearé	broncearemos	habré bronceado	habremos bronceado
broncearás	broncearéis	habrás bronceado	habréis bronceado
bronceará	broncearán	habrá bronceado	habrán bronceado
5 potencial simple		12 potencial compuesto	
broncearía	broncearíamos	habría bronceado	habríamos bronceado
broncearías	broncearíais	habrías bronceado	habríais bronceado
broncearía	broncearían	habría bronceado	habrían bronceado
6 presente de subjuntivo		13 perfecto de subjuntivo	
broncee	bronceemos	haya bronceado	hayamos bronceado
broncees	bronceéis	hayas bronceado	hayáis bronceado
broncee	bronceen	haya bronceado	hayan bronceado
7 imperfecto de subjuntivo		14 pluscuamperfecto de subjuntivo	
bronceara	bronceáramos	hubiera bronceado	hubiéramos bronceado
broncearas	broncearais	hubieras bronceado	hubierais bronceado
bronceara	broncearan	hubiera bronceado	hubieran bronceado
OR		OR	
broncease	bronceásemos	hubiese bronceado	hubiésemos bronceado
bronceases	bronceaseis	hubieses bronceado	hubieseis bronceado
broncease	bronceasen	hubiese bronceado	hubiesen bronceado

imperativo	
—	**bronceemos**
broncea; no broncees	**broncead; no bronceéis**
broncee	**bronceen**

Words related to this verb
el bronce bronze
bronceado, bronceada bronze colored, sunburned, tanned
broncearse to tan, bronze oneself (skin)

Do you need more drills? Have fun with the *501 Spanish Verbs* CD-ROM!

The subject pronouns are found on page 93.

to boil, to bustle, to hustle, to stir   Irregular verb (Tenses 3 and 7)

The Seven Simple Tenses		The Seven Compound Tenses	
Singular	Plural	Singular	Plural
1 presente de indicativo		8 perfecto de indicativo	
bullo	bullimos	he bullido	hemos bullido
bulles	bullís	has bullido	habéis bullido
bulle	bullen	ha bullido	han bullido
2 imperfecto de indicativo		9 pluscuamperfecto de indicativo	
bullía	bullíamos	había bullido	habíamos bullido
bullías	bullíais	habías bullido	habíais bullido
bullía	bullían	había bullido	habían bullido
3 pretérito		10 pretérito anterior	
bullí	bullimos	hube bullido	hubimos bullido
bulliste	bullisteis	hubiste bullido	hubisteis bullido
bulló	bulleron	hubo bullido	hubieron bullido
4 futuro		11 futuro perfecto	
bulliré	bulliremos	habré bullido	habremos bullido
bullirás	bulliréis	habrás bullido	habréis bullido
bullirá	bullirán	habrá bullido	habrán bullido
5 potencial simple		12 potencial compuesto	
bulliría	bulliríamos	habría bullido	habríamos bullido
bullirías	bulliríais	habrías bullido	habríais bullido
bulliría	bullirían	habría bullido	habrían bullido
6 presente de subjuntivo		13 perfecto de subjuntivo	
bulla	bullamos	haya bullido	hayamos bullido
bullas	bulláis	hayas bullido	hayáis bullido
bulla	bullan	haya bullido	hayan bullido
7 imperfecto de subjuntivo		14 pluscuamperfecto de subjuntivo	
bullera	bulléramos	hubiera bullido	hubiéramos bullido
bulleras	bullerais	hubieras bullido	hubierais bullido
bullera	bulleran	hubiera bullido	hubieran bullido
OR		OR	
bullese	bullésemos	hubiese bullido	hubiésemos bullido
bulleses	bulleseis	hubieses bullido	hubieseis bullido
bullese	bullesen	hubiese bullido	hubiesen bullido

imperativo	
—	bullamos
bulle; no bullas	bullid; no bulláis
bulla	bullan

Words related to this verb
un, una bullebulle busybody
el bullicio noise, bustle
bulliciosamente noisily

bullente bubbling
la bulla bustle, noise; mob
un bullaje noisy crowd

Review the principal parts of important Spanish verbs on pages 9 and 10.

Reflexive regular **-ar** verb   to make fun of, to poke fun at, to ridicule

The Seven Simple Tenses		The Seven Compound Tenses	
Singular	Plural	Singular	Plural
1 presente de indicativo		8 perfecto de indicativo	
me burlo	nos burlamos	me he burlado	nos hemos burlado
te burlas	os burláis	te has burlado	os habéis burlado
se burla	se burlan	se ha burlado	se han burlado
2 imperfecto de indicativo		9 pluscuamperfecto de indicativo	
me burlaba	nos burlábamos	me había burlado	nos habíamos burlado
te burlabas	os burlabais	te habías burlado	os habíais burlado
se burlaba	se burlaban	se había burlado	se habían burlado
3 pretérito		10 pretérito anterior	
me burlé	nos burlamos	me hube burlado	nos hubimos burlado
te burlaste	os burlasteis	te hubiste burlado	os hubisteis burlado
se burló	se burlaron	se hubo burlado	se hubieron burlado
4 futuro		11 futuro perfecto	
me burlaré	nos burlaremos	me habré burlado	nos habremos burlado
te burlarás	os burlaréis	te habrás burlado	os habréis burlado
se burlará	se burlarán	se habrá burlado	se habrán burlado
5 potencial simple		12 potencial compuesto	
me burlaría	nos burlaríamos	me habría burlado	nos habríamos burlado
te burlarías	os burlaríais	te habrías burlado	os habríais burlado
se burlaría	se burlarían	se habría burlado	se habrían burlado
6 presente de subjuntivo		13 perfecto de subjuntivo	
me burle	nos burlemos	me haya burlado	nos hayamos burlado
te burles	os burléis	te hayas burlado	os hayáis burlado
se burle	se burlen	se haya burlado	se hayan burlado
7 imperfecto de subjuntivo		14 pluscuamperfecto de subjuntivo	
me burlara	nos burláramos	me hubiera burlado	nos hubiéramos burlado
te burlaras	os burlarais	te hubieras burlado	os hubierais burlado
se burlara	se burlaran	se hubiera burlado	se hubieran burlado
OR		OR	
me burlase	nos burlásemos	me hubiese burlado	nos hubiésemos burlado
te burlases	os burlaseis	te hubieses burlado	os hubieseis burlado
se burlase	se burlasen	se hubiese burlado	se hubiesen burlado

imperativo	
—	**burlémonos**
búrlate; no te burles	**burlaos; no os burléis**
búrlese	**búrlense**

Words and expressions related to this verb

el burlador, la burladora   practical joker, jester, wag
burlescamente   comically
de burlas   for fun
la burlería   trick

burlesco, burlesca   burlesque
burlarase de alguien   to make fun of someone
burlar a alguien   to deceive someone
hacer burla de   to make fun of
una burla   jeer

The subject pronouns are found on page 93.

to look for, to seek   Regular **-ar** verb endings with spelling change: **c** becomes **qu** before **e**

The Seven Simple Tenses		The Seven Compound Tenses	
Singular	Plural	Singular	Plural
1 presente de indicativo		8 perfecto de indicativo	
busco	buscamos	he buscado	hemos buscado
buscas	buscáis	has buscado	habéis buscado
busca	buscan	ha buscado	han buscado
2 imperfecto de indicativo		9 pluscuamperfecto de indicativo	
buscaba	buscábamos	había buscado	habíamos buscado
buscabas	buscabais	habías buscado	habíais buscado
buscaba	buscaban	había buscado	habían buscado
3 pretérito		10 pretérito anterior	
busqué	buscamos	hube buscado	hubimos buscado
buscaste	buscasteis	hubiste buscado	hubisteis buscado
buscó	buscaron	hubo buscado	hubieron buscado
4 futuro		11 futuro perfecto	
buscaré	buscaremos	habré buscado	habremos buscado
buscarás	buscaréis	habrás buscado	habréis buscado
buscará	buscarán	habrá buscado	habrán buscado
5 potencial simple		12 potencial compuesto	
buscaría	buscaríamos	habría buscado	habríamos buscado
buscarías	buscaríais	habrías buscado	habríais buscado
buscaría	buscarían	habría buscado	habrían buscado
6 presente de subjuntivo		13 perfecto de subjuntivo	
busque	busquemos	haya buscado	hayamos buscado
busques	busquéis	hayas buscado	hayáis buscado
busque	busquen	haya buscado	hayan buscado
7 imperfecto de subjuntivo		14 pluscuamperfecto de subjuntivo	
buscara	buscáramos	hubiera buscado	hubiéramos buscado
buscaras	buscarais	hubieras buscado	hubierais buscado
buscara	buscaran	hubiera buscado	hubieran buscado
OR		OR	
buscase	buscásemos	hubiese buscado	hubiésemos buscado
buscases	buscaseis	hubieses buscado	hubieseis buscado
buscase	buscasen	hubiese buscado	hubiesen buscado

imperativo	
—	busquemos
busca; no busques	buscad; no busquéis
busque	busquen

Sentences using this verb and words related to it
¿Qué busca Ud.?   What are you looking for?
Busco mis libros.   I'm looking for my books.
la busca, la buscada   research, search

la búsqueda   search
rebuscar   to search into meticulously
el rebuscamiento   meticulous searching

Get acquainted with what preposition goes with what verb on pages 669–677.

Irregular verb   to be contained, to fit into

The Seven Simple Tenses		The Seven Compound Tenses	
Singular	Plural	Singular	Plural
1 presente de indicativo		**8 perfecto de indicativo**	
quepo	**cabemos**	**he cabido**	**hemos cabido**
cabes	**cabéis**	**has cabido**	**habéis cabido**
cabe	**caben**	**ha cabido**	**han cabido**
2 imperfecto de indicativo		**9 pluscuamperfecto de indicativo**	
cabía	**cabíamos**	**había cabido**	**habíamos cabido**
cabías	**cabíais**	**habías cabido**	**habíais cabido**
cabía	**cabían**	**había cabido**	**habían cabido**
3 pretérito		**10 pretérito anterior**	
cupe	**cupimos**	**hube cabido**	**hubimos cabido**
cupiste	**cupisteis**	**hubiste cabido**	**hubisteis cabido**
cupo	**cupieron**	**hubo cabido**	**hubieron cabido**
4 futuro		**11 futuro perfecto**	
cabré	**cabremos**	**habré cabido**	**habremos cabido**
cabrás	**cabréis**	**habrás cabido**	**habréis cabido**
cabrá	**cabrán**	**habrá cabido**	**habrán cabido**
5 potencial simple		**12 potencial compuesto**	
cabría	**cabríamos**	**habría cabido**	**habríamos cabido**
cabrías	**cabríais**	**habrías cabido**	**habríais cabido**
cabría	**cabrían**	**habría cabido**	**habrían cabido**
6 presente de subjuntivo		**13 perfecto de subjuntivo**	
quepa	**quepamos**	**haya cabido**	**hayamos cabido**
quepas	**quepáis**	**hayas cabido**	**hayáis cabido**
quepa	**quepan**	**haya cabido**	**hayan cabido**
7 imperfecto de subjuntivo		**14 pluscuamperfecto de subjuntivo**	
cupiera	**cupiéramos**	**hubiera cabido**	**hubiéramos cabido**
cupieras	**cupierais**	**hubieras cabido**	**hubierais cabido**
cupiera	**cupieran**	**hubiera cabido**	**hubieran cabido**
OR		OR	
cupiese	**cupiésemos**	**hubiese cabido**	**hubiésemos cabido**
cupieses	**cupieseis**	**hubieses cabido**	**hubieseis cabido**
cupiese	**cupiesen**	**hubiese cabido**	**hubiesen cabido**

imperativo	
—	**quepamos**
cabe; no quepas	**cabed; no quepáis**
quepa	**quepan**

Common idiomatic expressions using this verb

Pablo no cabe en sí. Paul has a swelled head.
No quepo aquí. I don't have enough room here.
No cabe duda de que ... There is no doubt that ...

No me cabe en la cabeza. I don't get (understand) it.
Todo cabe. All is possible. (It all fits.)

Can't recognize an irregular verb form? Check out pages 678–681.

The subject pronouns are found on page 93.

The Seven Simple Tenses		The Seven Compound Tenses	
Singular	Plural	Singular	Plural
1 presente de indicativo		**8 perfecto de indicativo**	
caigo	caemos	he caído	hemos caído
caes	caéis	has caído	habéis caído
cae	caen	ha caído	han caído
2 imperfecto de indicativo		**9 pluscuamperfecto de indicativo**	
caía	caíamos	había caído	habíamos caído
caías	caíais	habías caído	habíais caído
caía	caían	había caído	habían caído
3 pretérito		**10 pretérito anterior**	
caí	caímos	hube caído	hubimos caído
caíste	caísteis	hubiste caído	hubisteis caído
cayó	cayeron	hubo caído	hubieron caído
4 futuro		**11 futuro perfecto**	
caeré	caeremos	habré caído	habremos caído
caerás	caeréis	habrás caído	habréis caído
caerá	caerán	habrá caído	habrán caído
5 potencial simple		**12 potencial compuesto**	
caería	caeríamos	habría caído	habríamos caído
caerías	caeríais	habrías caído	habríais caído
caería	caerían	habría caído	habrían caído
6 presente de subjuntivo		**13 perfecto de subjuntivo**	
caiga	caigamos	haya caído	hayamos caído
caigas	caigáis	hayas caído	hayáis caído
caiga	caigan	haya caído	hayan caído
7 imperfecto de subjuntivo		**14 pluscuamperfecto de subjuntivo**	
cayera	cayéramos	hubiera caído	hubiéramos caído
cayeras	cayerais	hubieras caído	hubierais caído
cayera	cayeran	hubiera caído	hubieran caído
OR		OR	
cayese	cayésemos	hubiese caído	hubiésemos caído
cayeses	cayeseis	hubieses caído	hubieseis caído
cayese	cayesen	hubiese caído	hubiesen caído

imperativo

—	**caigamos**
cae; no caigas	**caed; no caigáis**
caiga	**caigan**

Caer and Caerse

C

Caer and caerse are an important pair of verbs for a beginning student. Both verbs are irregular and they are very useful in many everyday situations and expressions. Pay special attention when you use caer reflexively (caerse).

Sentences using caer, caerse, and related words

Mi madre cayó enferma en octubre.
My mother fell ill in October.

Yo me caí por la ventana. Por suerte, estuve
en la planta baja.
I fell out of the window. Luckily, I was on the
first floor.

El hombre que se levanta aún es más grande
que el que no ha caído. (Concepción Arenal)
The man who is still raising himself up is greater
than the one who hasn't fallen.

If you can conjugate caer, you can also
conjugate these verbs:

decaer to decay, decline

recaer to relapse, fall back

Words and expressions related to these verbs

la caída **the fall**

a la caída del sol **at sunset**

a la caída de la tarde **at the end of
the afternoon**

caer enfermo (enferma) **to fall sick**

dejar caer **to drop**

dejar caer la voz **to drop one's voice**

caer de espaldas **to fall backwards**

caer con **to come down with**

caer de lo alto **to fall from above**

caer de plano **to fall flat**

caer en la cuenta **to catch on, to
realize, to get the point**

caerse a pedazos **to fall to pieces**

caerse de risa **to roll (on the floor)
with laughter**

Can't find the verb you're looking for?
Check the back pages of this book for a list of over 2,100 additional verbs!

to fall, to fall down, to tumble   Reflexive irregular verb

The Seven Simple Tenses		The Seven Compound Tenses	
Singular	Plural	Singular	Plural
1 presente de indicativo		8 perfecto de indicativo	
me caigo	**nos caemos**	**me he caído**	**nos hemos caído**
te caes	**os caéis**	**te has caído**	**os habéis caído**
se cae	**se caen**	**se ha caído**	**se han caído**
2 imperfecto de indicativo		9 pluscuamperfecto de indicativo	
me caía	**nos caíamos**	**me había caído**	**nos habíamos caído**
te caías	**os caíais**	**te habías caído**	**os habíais caído**
se caía	**se caían**	**se había caído**	**se habían caído**
3 pretérito		10 pretérito anterior	
me caí	**nos caímos**	**me hube caído**	**nos hubimos caído**
te caíste	**os caísteis**	**te hubiste caído**	**os hubisteis caído**
se cayó	**se cayeron**	**se hubo caído**	**se hubieron caído**
4 futuro		11 futuro perfecto	
me caeré	**nos caeremos**	**me habré caído**	**nos habremos caído**
te caerás	**os caeréis**	**te habrás caído**	**os habréis caído**
se caerá	**se caerán**	**se habrá caído**	**se habrán caído**
5 potencial simple		12 potencial compuesto	
me caería	**nos caeríamos**	**me habría caído**	**nos habríamos caído**
te caerías	**os caeríais**	**te habrías caído**	**os habríais caído**
se caería	**se caerían**	**se habría caído**	**se habrían caído**
6 presente de subjuntivo		13 perfecto de subjuntivo	
me caiga	**nos caigamos**	**me haya caído**	**nos hayamos caído**
te caigas	**os caigáis**	**te hayas caído**	**os hayáis caído**
se caiga	**se caigan**	**se haya caído**	**se hayan caído**
7 imperfecto de subjuntivo		14 pluscuamperfecto de subjuntivo	
me cayera	**nos cayéramos**	**me hubiera caído**	**nos hubiéramos caído**
te cayeras	**os cayerais**	**te hubieras caído**	**os hubierais caído**
se cayera	**se cayeran**	**se hubiera caído**	**se hubieran caído**
OR		OR	
me cayese	**nos cayésemos**	**me hubiese caído**	**nos hubiésemos caído**
te cayeses	**os cayeseis**	**te hubieses caído**	**os hubieseis caído**
se cayese	**se cayesen**	**se hubiese caído**	**se hubiesen caído**

imperativo

—	**caigámonos**
cáete; no te caigas	**caeos; no os caigáis**
cáigase	**cáiganse**

Regular **-ar** verb endings with stem change: to heat (up), to warm (up)
Tenses 1, 6, Imperative

The Seven Simple Tenses		The Seven Compound Tenses	
Singular	Plural	Singular	Plural
1 presente de indicativo		8 perfecto de indicativo	
caliento	**calentamos**	**he calentado**	**hemos calentado**
calientas	**calentáis**	**has calentado**	**habéis calentado**
calienta	**calientan**	**ha calentado**	**han calentado**
2 imperfecto de indicativo		9 pluscuamperfecto de indicativo	
calentaba	**calentábamos**	**había calentado**	**habíamos calentado**
calentabas	**calentabais**	**habías calentado**	**habíais calentado**
calentaba	**calentaban**	**había calentado**	**habían calentado**
3 pretérito		10 pretérito anterior	
calenté	**calentamos**	**hube calentado**	**hubimos calentado**
calentaste	**calentasteis**	**hubiste calentado**	**hubisteis calentado**
calentó	**calentaron**	**hubo calentado**	**hubieron calentado**
4 futuro		11 futuro perfecto	
calentaré	**calentaremos**	**habré calentado**	**habremos calentado**
calentarás	**calentaréis**	**habrás calentado**	**habréis calentado**
calentará	**calentarán**	**habrá calentado**	**habrán calentado**
5 potencial simple		12 potencial compuesto	
calentaría	**calentaríamos**	**habría calentado**	**habríamos calentado**
calentarías	**calentaríais**	**habrías calentado**	**habríais calentado**
calentaría	**calentarían**	**habría calentado**	**habrían calentado**
6 presente de subjuntivo		13 perfecto de subjuntivo	
caliente	**calentemos**	**haya calentado**	**hayamos calentado**
calientes	**calentéis**	**hayas calentado**	**hayáis calentado**
caliente	**calienten**	**haya calentado**	**hayan calentado**
7 imperfecto de subjuntivo		14 pluscuamperfecto de subjuntivo	
calentara	**calentáramos**	**hubiera calentado**	**hubiéramos calentado**
calentaras	**calentarais**	**hubieras calentado**	**hubierais calentado**
calentara	**calentaran**	**hubiera calentado**	**hubieran calentado**
OR		OR	
calentase	**calentásemos**	**hubiese calentado**	**hubiésemos calentado**
calentases	**calentaseis**	**hubieses calentado**	**hubieseis calentado**
calentase	**calentasen**	**hubiese calentado**	**hubiesen calentado**

imperativo

—	**calentemos**
calienta; no calientes	**calentad; no calentéis**
caliente	**calienten**

Words and expressions related to this verb
calentar a uno las orejas   to reprimand (scold) a person
calentarse   to warm oneself
calentarse la cabeza   to rack one's brains
calentarse a la lumbre   to warm oneself by the fire
el calor   heat; **Hace calor esta noche.**   It is warm this evening.
recalentar   to warm over, reheat

The subject pronouns are found on page 93.

to be silent, to keep quiet   Reflexive regular **-ar** verb

The Seven Simple Tenses		The Seven Compound Tenses	
Singular	Plural	Singular	Plural
1 presente de indicativo		8 perfecto de indicativo	
me callo	**nos callamos**	**me he callado**	**nos hemos callado**
te callas	**os calláis**	**te has callado**	**os habéis callado**
se calla	**se callan**	**se ha callado**	**se han callado**
2 imperfecto de indicativo		9 pluscuamperfecto de indicativo	
me callaba	**nos callábamos**	**me había callado**	**nos habíamos callado**
te callabas	**os callabais**	**te habías callado**	**os habíais callado**
se callaba	**se callaban**	**se había callado**	**se habían callado**
3 pretérito		10 pretérito anterior	
me callé	**nos callamos**	**me hube callado**	**nos hubimos callado**
te callaste	**os callasteis**	**te hubiste callado**	**os hubisteis callado**
se calló	**se callaron**	**se hubo callado**	**se hubieron callado**
4 futuro		11 futuro perfecto	
me callaré	**nos callaremos**	**me habré callado**	**nos habremos callado**
te callarás	**os callaréis**	**te habrás callado**	**os habréis callado**
se callará	**se callarán**	**se habrá callado**	**se habrán callado**
5 potencial simple		12 potencial compuesto	
me callaría	**nos callaríamos**	**me habría callado**	**nos habríamos callado**
te callarías	**os callaríais**	**te habrías callado**	**os habríais callado**
se callaría	**se callarían**	**se habría callado**	**se habrían callado**
6 presente de subjuntivo		13 perfecto de subjuntivo	
me calle	**nos callemos**	**me haya callado**	**nos hayamos callado**
te calles	**os calléis**	**te hayas callado**	**os hayáis callado**
se calle	**se callen**	**se haya callado**	**se hayan callado**
7 imperfecto de subjuntivo		14 pluscuamperfecto de subjuntivo	
me callara	**nos calláramos**	**me hubiera callado**	**nos hubiéramos callado**
te callaras	**os callarais**	**te hubieras callado**	**os hubierais callado**
se callara	**se callaran**	**se hubiera callado**	**se hubieran callado**
OR		OR	
me callase	**nos callásemos**	**me hubiese callado**	**nos hubiésemos callado**
te callases	**os callaseis**	**te hubieses callado**	**os hubieseis callado**
se callase	**se callasen**	**se hubiese callado**	**se hubiesen callado**

imperativo	
—	**callémonos**
cállate; no te calles	**callaos; no os calléis**
cállese	**cállenese**

Common idiomatic expressions related to this verb
Quien calla, otorga. Silence means consent (**otorgar**/to grant, to consent)
¡Cállese Ud.! Keep quiet!
¡Cállate la boca! Shut your mouth!
callarse la boca to shut one's mouth

Don't miss the definitions of basic grammatical terms with examples in English and Spanish on pages 33–44.

Regular **-ar** verb endings with spelling change: **z** becomes **c** before **e**

to shoe, to wear (shoes), to put on (shoes)

C

The Seven Simple Tenses		The Seven Compound Tenses	
Singular	Plural	Singular	Plural
1 presente de indicativo		**8 perfecto de indicativo**	
calzo	calzamos	he calzado	hemos calzado
calzas	calzáis	has calzado	habéis calzado
calza	calzan	ha calzado	han calzado
2 imperfecto de indicativo		**9 pluscuamperfecto de indicativo**	
calzaba	calzábamos	había calzado	habíamos calzado
calzabas	calzabais	habías calzado	habíais calzado
calzaba	calzaban	había calzado	habían calzado
3 pretérito		**10 pretérito anterior**	
calcé	calzamos	hube calzado	hubimos calzado
calzaste	calzasteis	hubiste calzado	hubisteis calzado
calzó	calzaron	hubo calzado	hubieron calzado
4 futuro		**11 futuro perfecto**	
calzaré	calzaremos	habré calzado	habremos calzado
calzarás	calzaréis	habrás calzado	habréis calzado
calzará	calzarán	habrá calzado	habrán calzado
5 potencial simple		**12 potencial compuesto**	
calzaría	calzaríamos	habría calzado	habríamos calzado
calzarías	calzaríais	habrías calzado	habríais calzado
calzaría	calzarían	habría calzado	habrían calzado
6 presente de subjuntivo		**13 perfecto de subjuntivo**	
calce	calcemos	haya calzado	hayamos calzado
calces	calcéis	hayas calzado	hayáis calzado
calce	calcen	haya calzado	hayan calzado
7 imperfecto de subjuntivo		**14 pluscuamperfecto de subjuntivo**	
calzara	calzáramos	hubiera calzado	hubiéramos calzado
calzaras	calzarais	hubieras calzado	hubierais calzado
calzara	calzaran	hubiera calzado	hubieran calzado
OR		OR	
calzase	calzásemos	hubiese calzado	hubiésemos calzado
calzases	calzaseis	hubieses calzado	hubieseis calzado
calzase	calzasen	hubiese calzado	hubiesen calzado

	imperativo	
—	calcemos
calza; no calces	calzad; no calcéis
calce	calcen

Words related to this verb

la calza stocking
un calzadillo small shoe
un calzador shoehorn
un calcetín sock
la calceta stocking

medias calzas knee high stockings
las calzonarias suspenders
calcetar to knit stockings, socks
hacer calceta to knit

to change, to exchange   Regular **-ar** verb

The Seven Simple Tenses		The Seven Compound Tenses	
Singular	Plural	Singular	Plural
1 presente de indicativo		8 perfecto de indicativo	
cambio	cambiamos	he cambiado	hemos cambiado
cambias	cambiáis	has cambiado	habéis cambiado
cambia	cambian	ha cambiado	han cambiado
2 imperfecto de indicativo		9 pluscuamperfecto de indicativo	
cambiaba	cambiábamos	había cambiado	habíamos cambiado
cambiabas	cambiabais	habías cambiado	habíais cambiado
cambiaba	cambiaban	había cambiado	habían cambiado
3 pretérito		10 pretérito anterior	
cambié	cambiamos	hube cambiado	hubimos cambiado
cambiaste	cambiasteis	hubiste cambiado	hubisteis cambiado
cambió	cambiaron	hubo cambiado	hubieron cambiado
4 futuro		11 futuro perfecto	
cambiaré	cambiaremos	habré cambiado	habremos cambiado
cambiarás	cambiaréis	habrás cambiado	habréis cambiado
cambiará	cambiarán	habrá cambiado	habrán cambiado
5 potencial simple		12 potencial compuesto	
cambiaría	cambiaríamos	habría cambiado	habríamos cambiado
cambiarías	cambiaríais	habrías cambiado	habríais cambiado
cambiaría	cambiarían	habría cambiado	habrían cambiado
6 presente de subjuntivo		13 perfecto de subjuntivo	
cambie	cambiemos	haya cambiado	hayamos cambiado
cambies	cambiéis	hayas cambiado	hayáis cambiado
cambie	cambien	haya cambiado	hayan cambiado
7 imperfecto de subjuntivo		14 pluscuamperfecto de subjuntivo	
cambiara	cambiáramos	hubiera cambiado	hubiéramos cambiado
cambiaras	cambiarais	hubieras cambiado	hubierais cambiado
cambiara	cambiaran	hubiera cambiado	hubieran cambiado
OR		OR	
cambiase	cambiásemos	hubiese cambiado	hubiésemos cambiado
cambiases	cambiaseis	hubieses cambiado	hubieseis cambiado
cambiase	cambiasen	hubiese cambiado	hubiesen cambiado

imperativo	
—	cambiemos
cambia; no cambies	cambiad; no cambiéis
cambie	cambien

Common idiomatic expressions using this verb

cambiar de ropa   to change one's clothing

cambiar de opinión   to change one's mind

el cambio   exchange, change

el cambio de voz   change of voice

cambiar una rueda   to change a wheel

cambiar de costumbres   to change one's habits

cambiar de idea   to change one's mind

cambiar el horario   to change the timetable

Don't forget to study the section on defective and impersonal verbs. It's right after this main list.

Regular **-ar** verb   to walk, to move along

C

The Seven Simple Tenses		The Seven Compound Tenses	
Singular	Plural	Singular	Plural
1 presente de indicativo		8 perfecto de indicativo	
camino	caminamos	he caminado	hemos caminado
caminas	camináis	has caminado	habéis caminado
camina	caminan	ha caminado	han caminado
2 imperfecto de indicativo		9 pluscuamperfecto de indicativo	
caminaba	caminábamos	había caminado	habíamos caminado
caminabas	caminabais	habías caminado	habíais caminado
caminaba	caminaban	había caminado	habían caminado
3 pretérito		10 pretérito anterior	
caminé	caminamos	hube caminado	hubimos caminado
caminaste	caminasteis	hubiste caminado	hubisteis caminado
caminó	caminaron	hubo caminado	hubieron caminado
4 futuro		11 futuro perfecto	
caminaré	caminaremos	habré caminado	habremos caminado
caminarás	caminaréis	habrás caminado	habréis caminado
caminará	caminarán	habrá caminado	habrán caminado
5 potencial simple		12 potencial compuesto	
caminaría	caminaríamos	habría caminado	habríamos caminado
caminarías	caminaríais	habrías caminado	habríais caminado
caminaría	caminarían	habría caminado	habrían caminado
6 presente de subjuntivo		13 perfecto de subjuntivo	
camine	caminemos	haya caminado	hayamos caminado
camines	caminéis	hayas caminado	hayáis caminado
camine	caminen	haya caminado	hayan caminado
7 imperfecto de subjuntivo		14 pluscuamperfecto de subjuntivo	
caminara	camináramos	hubiera caminado	hubiéramos caminado
caminaras	caminarais	hubieras caminado	hubierais caminado
caminara	caminaran	hubiera caminado	hubieran caminado
OR		OR	
caminase	caminásemos	hubiese caminado	hubiésemos caminado
caminases	caminaseis	hubieses caminado	hubieseis caminado
caminase	caminasen	hubiese caminado	hubiesen caminado

imperativo	
—	caminemos
camina; no camines	caminad; no caminéis
camine	caminen

Words and expressions related to this verb
el camino   road, highway
el camino de hierro   railroad
en camino de   on the way to
una caminata   a long walk
hacer de un camino dos mandados   to kill
   two birds with one stone

el camino real   highway, high road
estar en camino   to be on one's way
quedarse a medio camino   to stop halfway
por buen camino   on the right road
al buen camino   on the right track
un camión   truck

The subject pronouns are found on page 93.

to become tired, to become weary, to get tired   Reflexive regular **-ar** verb

The Seven Simple Tenses		The Seven Compound Tenses	
Singular	Plural	Singular	Plural
1 presente de indicativo		8 perfecto de indicativo	
me canso	nos cansamos	me he cansado	nos hemos cansado
te cansas	os cansáis	te has cansado	os habéis cansado
se cansa	se cansan	se ha cansado	se han cansado
2 imperfecto de indicativo		9 pluscuamperfecto de indicativo	
me cansaba	nos cansábamos	me había cansado	nos habíamos cansado
te cansabas	os cansabais	te habías cansado	os habíais cansado
se cansaba	se cansaban	se había cansado	se habían cansado
3 pretérito		10 pretérito anterior	
me cansé	nos cansamos	me hube cansado	nos hubimos cansado
te cansaste	os cansasteis	te hubiste cansado	os hubisteis cansado
se cansó	se cansaron	se hubo cansado	se hubieron cansado
4 futuro		11 futuro perfecto	
me cansaré	nos cansaremos	me habré cansado	nos habremos cansado
te cansarás	os cansaréis	te habrás cansado	os habréis cansado
se cansará	se cansarán	se habrá cansado	se habrán cansado
5 potencial simple		12 potencial compuesto	
me cansaría	nos cansaríamos	me habría cansado	nos habríamos cansado
te cansarías	os cansaríais	te habrías cansado	os habríais cansado
se cansaría	se cansarían	se habría cansado	se habrían cansado
6 presente de subjuntivo		13 perfecto de subjuntivo	
me canse	nos cansemos	me haya cansado	nos hayamos cansado
te canses	os canséis	te hayas cansado	os hayáis cansado
se canse	se cansen	se haya cansado	se hayan cansado
7 imperfecto de subjuntivo		14 pluscuamperfecto de subjuntivo	
me cansara	nos cansáramos	me hubiera cansado	nos hubiéramos cansado
te cansaras	os cansarais	te hubieras cansado	os hubierais cansado
se cansara	se cansaran	se hubiera cansado	se hubieran cansado
OR		OR	
me cansase	nos cansásemos	me hubiese cansado	nos hubiésemos cansado
te cansases	os cansaseis	te hubieses cansado	os hubieseis cansado
se cansase	se cansasen	se hubiese cansado	se hubiesen cansado

imperativo	
—	cansémonos
cánsate; no te canses	cansaos; no os canséis
cánsese	cánsense

Sentences using this verb and words and expressions related to it
María se cansa, Pedro se cansa y yo me canso. Nosotros nos cansamos.

la cansera fatigue	cansarse de esperar to get tired of waiting
el cansancio fatigue, weariness	cansado, cansada tired, exhausted
cansar to fatigue, to tire, to weary	María está cansada. Mary is tired.
el descanso rest, relief; **el descansadero**	cansarse fácilmente to get tired easily
resting place	

Regular **-ar** verb   to sing

The Seven Simple Tenses		The Seven Compound Tenses	
Singular	Plural	Singular	Plural
1 presente de indicativo		8 perfecto de indicativo	
canto	cantamos	he cantado	hemos cantado
cantas	cantáis	has cantado	habéis cantado
canta	cantan	ha cantado	han cantado
2 imperfecto de indicativo		9 pluscuamperfecto de indicativo	
cantaba	cantábamos	había cantado	habíamos cantado
cantabas	cantabais	habías cantado	habíais cantado
cantaba	cantaban	había cantado	habían cantado
3 pretérito		10 pretérito anterior	
canté	cantamos	hube cantado	hubimos cantado
cantaste	cantasteis	hubiste cantado	hubisteis cantado
cantó	cantaron	hubo cantado	hubieron cantado
4 futuro		11 futuro perfecto	
cantaré	cantaremos	habré cantado	habremos cantado
cantarás	cantaréis	habrás cantado	habréis cantado
cantará	cantarán	habrá cantado	habrán cantado
5 potencial simple		12 potencial compuesto	
cantaría	cantaríamos	habría cantado	habríamos cantado
cantarías	cantaríais	habrías cantado	habríais cantado
cantaría	cantarían	habría cantado	habrían cantado
6 presente de subjuntivo		13 perfecto de subjuntivo	
cante	cantemos	haya cantado	hayamos cantado
cantes	cantéis	hayas cantado	hayáis cantado
cante	canten	haya cantado	hayan cantado
7 imperfecto de subjuntivo		14 pluscuamperfecto de subjuntivo	
cantara	cantáramos	hubiera cantado	hubiéramos cantado
cantaras	cantarais	hubieras cantado	hubierais cantado
cantara	cantaran	hubiera cantado	hubieran cantado
OR		OR	
cantase	cantásemos	hubiese cantado	hubiésemos cantado
cantases	cantaseis	hubieses cantado	hubieseis cantado
cantase	cantasen	hubiese cantado	hubiesen cantado

	imperativo	
—		cantemos
canta; no cantes		cantad; no cantéis
cante		canten

AN ESSENTIAL
55 VERB

The subject pronouns are found on page 93.

Cantar is a very important regular –ar verb that is used in numerous everyday expressions and situations.

Sentences using cantar and related words

Mi hermana canta muy bien.
My sister sings very well.

De vez en cuando, canto en la ducha.
Occasionally, I sing in the shower.

Words and expressions related to this verb

una canción **song;** dos canciones **two songs**

una cantata **cantata (music)**

encantar **to enchant, delight**

cantador, cantadora **singer**

una cantatriz **opera singer**

cantor, cantora, cantante **singer**

encantado, encantada **enchanted**

un canto **song**

el chantaje **blackmail**

hacer chantaje **to blackmail**

Proverbs

Quien canta su mal espanta.
When you sing, you drive away your grief.

El que mal canta, bien le suena.
He who sings badly likes what he hears.

Can't find the verb you're looking for?
Check the back pages of this book for a list of over 2,100 additional verbs!

Regular **-ar** verb endings with spelling   to characterize
change: **z** becomes **c** before **e**

The Seven Simple Tenses | The Seven Compound Tenses

C

Singular	Plural	Singular	Plural
1 presente de indicativo		8 perfecto de indicativo	
caracterizo	caracterizamos	he caracterizado	hemos caracterizado
caracterizas	caracterizáis	has caracterizado	habéis caracterizado
caracteriza	caracterizan	ha caracterizado	han caracterizado
2 imperfecto de indicativo		9 pluscuamperfecto de indicativo	
caracterizaba	caracterizábamos	había caracterizado	habíamos caracterizado
caracterizabas	caracterizabais	habías caracterizado	habíais caracterizado
caracterizaba	caracterizaban	había caracterizado	habían caracterizado
3 pretérito		10 pretérito anterior	
caractericé	caracterizamos	hube caracterizado	hubimos caracterizado
caracterizaste	caracterizasteis	hubiste caracterizado	hubisteis caracterizado
caracterizó	caracterizaron	hubo caracterizado	hubieron caracterizado
4 futuro		11 futuro perfecto	
caracterizaré	caracterizaremos	habré caracterizado	habremos caracterizado
caracterizarás	caracterizaréis	habrás caracterizado	habréis caracterizado
caracterizará	caracterizarán	habrá caracterizado	habrán caracterizado
5 potencial simple		12 potencial compuesto	
caracterizaría	caracterizaríamos	habría caracterizado	habríamos caracterizado
caracterizarías	caracterizaríais	habrías caracterizado	habríais caracterizado
caracterizaría	caracterizarían	habría caracterizado	habrían caracterizado
6 presente de subjuntivo		13 perfecto de subjuntivo	
caracterice	caractericemos	haya caracterizado	hayamos caracterizado
caracterices	caractericéis	hayas caracterizado	hayáis caracterizado
caracterice	caractericen	haya caracterizado	hayan caracterizado
7 imperfecto de subjuntivo		14 pluscuamperfecto de subjuntivo	
caracterizara	caracterizáramos	hubiera caracterizado	hubiéramos caracterizado
caracterizaras	caracterizarais	hubieras caracterizado	hubierais caracterizado
caracterizara	caracterizaran	hubiera caracterizado	hubieran caracterizado
OR		OR	
caracterizase	caracterizásemos	hubiese caracterizado	hubiésemos caracterizado
caracterizases	caracterizaseis	hubieses caracterizado	hubieseis caracterizado
caracterizase	caracterizasen	hubiese caracterizado	hubiesen caracterizado

imperativo

—	**caractericemos**
caracteriza; no caracterices	**caracterizad; no caractericéis**
caracterice	**caractericen**

Words related to this verb
el carácter   character (of a person); do not confuse with **personaje**   character (in a play)
característico, característica   characteristic; **tener buen (mal) carácter**
   to be good- (bad-) natured
característicamente   characteristically
la caracterización   characterization

Check out the verb drills and verb tests with answers explained on pages 45–91.

The subject pronouns are found on page 93.
                                                                                   211

to load, to burden, to charge (a battery)   Regular **-ar** verb endings with spelling
change: **g** becomes **gu** before **e**

The Seven Simple Tenses		The Seven Compound Tenses	
Singular	Plural	Singular	Plural
1 presente de indicativo		8 perfecto de indicativo	
cargo	**cargamos**	**he cargado**	**hemos cargado**
cargas	**cargáis**	**has cargado**	**habéis cargado**
carga	**cargan**	**ha cargado**	**han cargado**
2 imperfecto de indicativo		9 pluscuamperfecto de indicativo	
cargaba	**cargábamos**	**había cargado**	**habíamos cargado**
cargabas	**cargabais**	**habías cargado**	**habíais cargado**
cargaba	**cargaban**	**había cargado**	**habían cargado**
3 pretérito		10 pretérito anterior	
cargué	**cargamos**	**hube cargado**	**hubimos cargado**
cargaste	**cargasteis**	**hubiste cargado**	**hubisteis cargado**
cargó	**cargaron**	**hubo cargado**	**hubieron cargado**
4 futuro		11 futuro perfecto	
cargaré	**cargaremos**	**habré cargado**	**habremos cargado**
cargarás	**cargaréis**	**habrás cargado**	**habréis cargado**
cargará	**cargarán**	**habrá cargado**	**habrán cargado**
5 potencial simple		12 potencial compuesto	
cargaría	**cargaríamos**	**habría cargado**	**habríamos cargado**
cargarías	**cargaríais**	**habrías cargado**	**habríais cargado**
cargaría	**cargarían**	**habría cargado**	**habrían cargado**
6 presente de subjuntivo		13 perfecto de subjuntivo	
cargue	**carguemos**	**haya cargado**	**hayamos cargado**
cargues	**carguéis**	**hayas cargado**	**hayáis cargado**
cargue	**carguen**	**haya cargado**	**hayan cargado**
7 imperfecto de subjuntivo		14 pluscuamperfecto de subjuntivo	
cargara	**cargáramos**	**hubiera cargado**	**hubiéramos cargado**
cargaras	**cargarais**	**hubieras cargado**	**hubierais cargado**
cargara	**cargaran**	**hubiera cargado**	**hubieran cargado**
OR		OR	
cargase	**cargásemos**	**hubiese cargado**	**hubiésemos cargado**
cargases	**cargaseis**	**hubieses cargado**	**hubieseis cargado**
cargase	**cargasen**	**hubiese cargado**	**hubiesen cargado**

imperativo	
—	**carguemos**
carga; no cargues	**cargad; no carguéis**
cargue	**carguen**

Words and expressions related to this verb

cargoso, cargosa burdensome	una carga load, responsibility
la cargazón cargo	el telecarga download, upload (computer)
una cargazón de cabeza heaviness of the head	el cargador shipper
el cargamento shipment	

Review the principal parts of important Spanish verbs on pages 9 and 10.

Reflexive regular **-ar** verb   to get married, to marry

The Seven Simple Tenses		The Seven Compound Tenses	
Singular	Plural	Singular	Plural
1 presente de indicativo		8 perfecto de indicativo	
me caso	nos casamos	me he casado	nos hemos casado
te casas	os casáis	te has casado	os habéis casado
se casa	se casan	se ha casado	se han casado
2 imperfecto de indicativo		9 pluscuamperfecto de indicativo	
me casaba	nos casábamos	me había casado	nos habíamos casado
te casabas	os casabais	te habías casado	os habíais casado
se casaba	se casaban	se había casado	se habían casado
3 pretérito		10 pretérito anterior	
me casé	nos casamos	me hube casado	nos hubimos casado
te casaste	os casasteis	te hubiste casado	os hubisteis casado
se casó	se casaron	se hubo casado	se hubieron casado
4 futuro		11 futuro perfecto	
me casaré	nos casaremos	me habré casado	nos habremos casado
te casarás	os casaréis	te habrás casado	os habréis casado
se casará	se casarán	se habrá casado	se habrán casado
5 potencial simple		12 potencial compuesto	
me casaría	nos casaríamos	me habría casado	nos habríamos casado
te casarías	os casaríais	te habrías casado	os habríais casado
se casaría	se casarían	se habría casado	se habrían casado
6 presente de subjuntivo		13 perfecto de subjuntivo	
me case	nos casemos	me haya casado	nos hayamos casado
te cases	os caséis	te hayas casado	os hayáis casado
se case	se casen	se haya casado	se hayan casado
7 imperfecto de subjuntivo		14 pluscuamperfecto de subjuntivo	
me casara	nos casáramos	me hubiera casado	nos hubiéramos casado
te casaras	os casarais	te hubieras casado	os hubierais casado
se casara	se casaran	se hubiera casado	se hubieran casado
OR		OR	
me casase	nos casásemos	me hubiese casado	nos hubiésemos casado
te casases	os casaseis	te hubieses casado	os hubieseis casado
se casase	se casasen	se hubiese casado	se hubiesen casado

	imperativo	
—		casémonos
cásate; no te cases		casaos; no os caséis
cásese		cásense

Words and expressions related to this verb
Antes que te cases, mira lo que haces.   Look before you leap. (Before you get married, look
    at what you're doing); **un casamiento por amor**   a love marriage
un casamiento ventajoso   a marriage of convenience
casarse con alguien   to marry someone
los recién casados   newlyweds

Do you need more drills? Have fun with
the *501 Spanish Verbs* CD-ROM!

to celebrate, to praise   Regular -ar verb

The Seven Simple Tenses		The Seven Compound Tenses	
Singular	Plural	Singular	Plural
1 presente de indicativo		8 perfecto de indicativo	
celebro	celebramos	he celebrado	hemos celebrado
celebras	celebráis	has celebrado	habéis celebrado
celebra	celebran	ha celebrado	han celebrado
2 imperfecto de indicativo		9 pluscuamperfecto de indicativo	
celebraba	celebrábamos	había celebrado	habíamos celebrado
celebrabas	celebrabais	habías celebrado	habíais celebrado
celebraba	celebraban	había celebrado	habían celebrado
3 pretérito		10 pretérito anterior	
celebré	celebramos	hube celebrado	hubimos celebrado
celebraste	celebrasteis	hubiste celebrado	hubisteis celebrado
celebró	celebraron	hubo celebrado	hubieron celebrado
4 futuro		11 futuro perfecto	
celebraré	celebraremos	habré celebrado	habremos celebrado
celebrarás	celebraréis	habrás celebrado	habréis celebrado
celebrará	celebrarán	habrá celebrado	habrán celebrado
5 potencial simple		12 potencial compuesto	
celebraría	celebraríamos	habría celebrado	habríamos celebrado
celebrarías	celebraríais	habrías celebrado	habríais celebrado
celebraría	celebrarían	habría celebrado	habrían celebrado
6 presente de subjuntivo		13 perfecto de subjuntivo	
celebre	celebremos	haya celebrado	hayamos celebrado
celebres	celebréis	hayas celebrado	hayáis celebrado
celebre	celebren	haya celebrado	hayan celebrado
7 imperfecto de subjuntivo		14 pluscuamperfecto de subjuntivo	
celebrara	celebráramos	hubiera celebrado	hubiéramos celebrado
celebraras	celebrarais	hubieras celebrado	hubierais celebrado
celebrara	celebraran	hubiera celebrado	hubieran celebrado
OR		OR	
celebrase	celebrásemos	hubiese celebrado	hubiésemos celebrado
celebrases	celebraseis	hubieses celebrado	hubieseis celebrado
celebrase	celebrasen	hubiese celebrado	hubiesen celebrado

imperativo	
—	celebremos
celebra; no celebres	celebrad; no celebréis
celebre	celebren

Words and expressions related to this verb

célebre famous, celebrated, renowned
la celebridad fame, celebrity
la celebración celebration

celebrado, celebrada popular, celebrated
ganar celebridad to win fame
una persona célebre a celebrity

Check out the verb drills and verb tests with answers explained on pages 45–91.

Regular **-ar** verb   to have supper, to eat supper, to dine, to have dinner

The Seven Simple Tenses | The Seven Compound Tenses

Singular	Plural	Singular	Plural
1 presente de indicativo		8 perfecto de indicativo	
ceno	cenamos	he cenado	hemos cenado
cenas	cenáis	has cenado	habéis cenado
cena	cenan	ha cenado	han cenado
2 imperfecto de indicativo		9 pluscuamperfecto de indicativo	
cenaba	cenábamos	había cenado	habíamos cenado
cenabas	cenabais	habías cenado	habíais cenado
cenaba	cenaban	había cenado	habían cenado
3 pretérito		10 pretérito anterior	
cené	cenamos	hube cenado	hubimos cenado
cenaste	cenasteis	hubiste cenado	hubisteis cenado
cenó	cenaron	hubo cenado	hubieron cenado
4 futuro		11 futuro perfecto	
cenaré	cenaremos	habré cenado	habremos cenado
cenarás	cenaréis	habrás cenado	habréis cenado
cenará	cenarán	habrá cenado	habrán cenado
5 potencial simple		12 potencial compuesto	
cenaría	cenaríamos	habría cenado	habríamos cenado
cenarías	cenaríais	habrías cenado	habríais cenado
cenaría	cenarían	habría cenado	habrían cenado
6 presente de subjuntivo		13 perfecto de subjuntivo	
cene	cenemos	haya cenado	hayamos cenado
cenes	cenéis	hayas cenado	hayáis cenado
cene	cenen	haya cenado	hayan cenado
7 imperfecto de subjuntivo		14 pluscuamperfecto de subjuntivo	
cenara	cenáramos	hubiera cenado	hubiéramos cenado
cenaras	cenarais	hubieras cenado	hubierais cenado
cenara	cenaran	hubiera cenado	hubieran cenado
OR		OR	
cenase	cenásemos	hubiese cenado	hubiésemos cenado
cenases	cenaseis	hubieses cenado	hubieseis cenado
cenase	cenasen	hubiese cenado	hubiesen cenado

imperativo

—	cenemos
cena; no cenes	cenad; no cenéis
cene	cenen

Sentences using this verb and words related to it
—Carlos, ¿A qué hora cenas?
—Ceno a las ocho con mi familia en casa.

la cena   supper (dinner); **quedarse sin cenar**   to go (remain) without dinner
La última cena   (*The Last Supper,* fresco by Leonardo da Vinci)
la hora de cenar   dinnertime; suppertime; **una cena de despedida**   farewell dinner

Don't forget to study the section on defective and impersonal verbs. It's right after this main list.

to brush   Regular **-ar** verb

The Seven Simple Tenses		The Seven Compound Tenses	
Singular	Plural	Singular	Plural
1 presente de indicativo		8 perfecto de indicativo	
cepillo	cepillamos	he cepillado	hemos cepillado
capillas	cepilláis	has cepillado	habéis cepillado
capilla	cepillan	ha cepillado	han cepillado
2 imperfecto de indicativo		9 pluscuamperfecto de indicativo	
cepillaba	cepillábamos	había cepillado	habíamos cepillado
cepillabas	cepillabais	habías cepillado	habíais cepillado
cepillaba	cepillaban	había cepillado	habían cepillado
3 pretérito		10 pretérito anterior	
cepillé	cepillamos	hube cepillado	hubimos cepillado
cepillaste	cepillasteis	hubiste cepillado	hubisteis cepillado
cepilló	cepillaron	hubo cepillado	hubieron cepillado
4 futuro		11 futuro perfecto	
cepillaré	cepillaremos	habré cepillado	habremos cepillado
cepillarás	cepillaréis	habrás cepillado	habréis cepillado
cepillará	cepillarán	habrá cepillado	habrán cepillado
5 potencial simple		12 potencial compuesto	
cepillaría	cepillaríamos	habría cepillado	habríamos cepillado
cepillarías	cepillaríais	habrías cepillado	habríais cepillado
cepillaría	cepillarían	habría cepillado	habrían cepillado
6 presente de subjuntivo		13 perfecto de subjuntivo	
cepille	cepillemos	haya cepillado	hayamos cepillado
cepilles	cepilléis	hayas cepillado	hayáis cepillado
cepille	cepillen	haya cepillado	hayan cepillado
7 imperfecto de subjuntivo		14 pluscuamperfecto de subjuntivo	
cepillara	cepilláramos	hubiera cepillado	hubiéramos cepillado
cepillaras	cepillarais	hubieras cepillado	hubierais cepillado
cepillara	cepillaran	hubiera cepillado	hubieran cepillado
OR		OR	
cepillase	cepillásemos	hubiese cepillado	hubiésemos cepillado
cepillases	cepillaseis	hubieses cepillado	hubieseis cepillado
cepillase	cepillasen	hubiese cepillado	hubiesen cepillado

	imperativo	
—		cepillemos
cepilla; no cepilles		cepillad; no cepilléis
cepille		cepillen

Words and expressions related to this verb
un cepillo   brush
un cepillo para el cabello   hairbursh;
   un cepillo de cabeza   hairbrush
un buen cepillado   a good brushing
cepillarse   to brush oneself
Juanito, cepíllate los dientes.   Johnny, brush your teeth.

un cepillo de dientes   toothbrush
un cepillo para la ropa   clothesbrush;
   un cepillo de ropa   clothesbrush
Me cepillé el pelo/I brushed my hair

Regular **-ar** verb endings with stem change: Tenses 1, 6, Imperative

to close, to shut, to turn off

The Seven Simple Tenses		The Seven Compound Tenses	
Singular	Plural	Singular	Plural
1 presente de indicativo		8 perfecto de indicativo	
cierro	cerramos	he cerrado	hemos cerrado
cierras	cerráis	has cerrado	habéis cerrado
cierra	cierran	ha cerrado	han cerrado
2 imperfecto de indicativo		9 pluscuamperfecto de indicativo	
cerraba	cerrábamos	había cerrado	habíamos cerrado
cerrabas	cerrabais	habías cerrado	habíais cerrado
cerraba	cerraban	había cerrado	habían cerrado
3 pretérito		10 pretérito anterior	
cerré	cerramos	hube cerrado	hubimos cerrado
cerraste	cerrasteis	hubiste cerrado	hubisteis cerrado
cerró	cerraron	hubo cerrado	hubieron cerrado
4 futuro		11 futuro perfecto	
cerraré	cerraremos	habré cerrado	habremos cerrado
cerrarás	cerraréis	habrás cerrado	habréis cerrado
cerrará	cerrarán	habrá cerrado	habrán cerrado
5 potencial simple		12 potencial compuesto	
cerraría	cerraríamos	habría cerrado	habríamos cerrado
cerrarías	cerraríais	habrías cerrado	habríais cerrado
cerraría	cerrarían	habría cerrado	habrían cerrado
6 presente de subjuntivo		13 perfecto de subjuntivo	
cierre	cerremos	haya cerrado	hayamos cerrado
cierres	cerréis	hayas cerrado	hayáis cerrado
cierre	cierren	haya cerrado	hayan cerrado
7 imperfecto de subjuntivo		14 pluscuamperfecto de subjuntivo	
cerrara	cerráramos	hubiera cerrado	hubiéramos cerrado
cerraras	cerrarais	hubieras cerrado	hubierais cerrado
cerrara	cerraran	hubiera cerrado	hubieran cerrado
OR		OR	
cerrase	cerrásemos	hubiese cerrado	hubiésemos cerrado
cerrases	cerraseis	hubieses cerrado	hubieseis cerrado
cerrase	cerrasen	hubiese cerrado	hubiesen cerrado

imperativo	
—	cerremos
cierra; no cierres	cerrad; no cerréis
cierre	cierren

Words and expressions related to this verb

cerrar los ojos   to close one's eyes
cerrar los oídos   to turn a deaf ear
cerrar la boca   to shut up, to keep silent
la cerradura   lock
La puerta está cerrada.   The door is closed.
Las ventanas están cerradas.   The windows are closed.

encerrar   to lock up, to confine
encerrarse   to live in seclusion, to retire
cerrar con llave   to lock up (to close with a key)
una cerradura de combinación   combination lock
cerrar una cuenta   to close an account

The subject pronouns are found on page 93.

217

to certify, to register (a letter), to attest   Regular **-ar** verb endings with spelling change: **c** becomes **qu** before **e**

The Seven Simple Tenses		The Seven Compound Tenses	
Singular	Plural	Singular	Plural
1 presente de indicativo		8 perfecto de indicativo	
certifico	**certificamos**	**he certificado**	**hemos certificado**
certificas	**certificáis**	**has certificado**	**habéis certificado**
certifica	**certifican**	**ha certificado**	**han certificado**
2 imperfecto de indicativo		9 pluscuamperfecto de indicativo	
certificaba	**certificábamos**	**había certificado**	**habíamos certificado**
certificabas	**certificabais**	**habías certificado**	**habíais certificado**
certificaba	**certificaban**	**había certificado**	**habían certificado**
3 pretérito		10 pretérito anterior	
certifiqué	**certificamos**	**hube certificado**	**hubimos certificado**
certificaste	**certificasteis**	**hubiste certificado**	**hubisteis certificado**
certificó	**certificaron**	**hubo certificado**	**hubieron certificado**
4 futuro		11 futuro perfecto	
certificaré	**certificaremos**	**habré certificado**	**habremos certificado**
certificarás	**certificaréis**	**habrás certificado**	**habréis certificado**
certificará	**certificarán**	**habrá certificado**	**habrán certificado**
5 potencial simple		12 potencial compuesto	
certificaría	**certificaríamos**	**habría certificado**	**habríamos certificado**
certificarías	**certificaríais**	**habrías certificado**	**habríais certificado**
certificaría	**certificarían**	**habría certificado**	**habrían certificado**
6 presente de subjuntivo		13 perfecto de subjuntivo	
certifique	**certifiquemos**	**haya certificado**	**hayamos certificado**
certifiques	**certifiquéis**	**hayas certificado**	**hayáis certificado**
certifique	**certifiquen**	**haya certificado**	**hayan certificado**
7 imperfecto de subjuntivo		14 pluscuamperfecto de subjuntivo	
certificara	**certificáramos**	**hubiera certificado**	**hubiéramos certificado**
certificaras	**certificarais**	**hubieras certificado**	**hubierais certificado**
certificara	**certificaran**	**hubiera certificado**	**hubieran certificado**
OR		OR	
certificase	**certificásemos**	**hubiese certificado**	**hubiésemos certificado**
certificases	**certificaseis**	**hubieses certificado**	**hubieseis certificado**
certificase	**certificasen**	**hubiese certificado**	**hubiesen certificado**

imperativo	
—	**certifiquemos**
certifica; no certifiques	**certificad; no certifiquéis**
certifique	**certifiquen**

Words related to this verb
la **certificación** certificate, certification
certificador, certificadora certifier
la **certidumbre** certainty

la **certeza** certainty
la **certinidad** assurance, certainty
tener la certeza de que . . . to be sure that . . .

Get acquainted with what preposition goes with what verb on pages 669–677.

Regular **-ar** verb   to chat, to prattle

The Seven Simple Tenses | The Seven Compound Tenses

Singular	Plural	Singular	Plural
1 presente de indicativo		8 perfecto de indicativo	
charlo	charlamos	he charlado	hemos charlado
charlas	charláis	has charlado	habéis charlado
charla	charlan	ha charlado	han charlado
2 imperfecto de indicativo		9 pluscuamperfecto de indicativo	
charlaba	charlábamos	había charlado	habíamos charlado
charlabas	charlabais	habías charlado	habíais charlado
charlaba	charlaban	había charlado	habían charlado
3 pretérito		10 pretérito anterior	
charlé	charlamos	hube charlado	hubimos charlado
charlaste	charlasteis	hubiste charlado	hubisteis charlado
charló	charlaron	hubo charlado	hubieron charlado
4 futuro		11 futuro perfecto	
charlaré	charlaremos	habré charlado	habremos charlado
charlarás	charlaréis	habrás charlado	habréis charlado
charlará	charlarán	habrá charlado	habrán charlado
5 potencial simple		12 potencial compuesto	
charlaría	charlaríamos	habría charlado	habríamos charlado
charlarías	charlaríais	habrías charlado	habríais charlado
charlaría	charlarían	habría charlado	habrían charlado
6 presente de subjuntivo		13 perfecto de subjuntivo	
charle	charlemos	haya charlado	hayamos charlado
charles	charléis	hayas charlado	hayáis charlado
charle	charlen	haya charlado	hayan charlado
7 imperfecto de subjuntivo		14 pluscuamperfecto de subjuntivo	
charlara	charláramos	hubiera charlado	hubiéramos charlado
charlaras	charlarais	hubieras charlado	hubierais charlado
charlara	charlaran	hubiera charlado	hubieran charlado
OR		OR	
charlase	charlásemos	hubiese charlado	hubiésemos charlado
charlases	charlaseis	hubieses charlado	hubieseis charlado
charlase	charlasen	hubiese charlado	hubiesen charlado

imperativo

—	charlemos
charla; no charles	charlad; no charléis
charle	charlen

Words and expressions related to this verb
charlar por los codos   to talk one's head off; **una charla**   a talk, chat
la charladuría   chitchat, gossip, idle talk
un charlatán, una charlatana   chatterbox, charlatan, quack, talkative, gossip
charlatanear   to gossip; **charlador, charladora**   talkative, chatterbox
charlar en línea   to chat online
una charla en línea   an online chat

Get your feet wet with verbs used in weather expressions on page 668.

The subject pronouns are found on page 93.
                                                                    219

to mumble, to mutter   Regular -ar verb

The Seven Simple Tenses		The Seven Compound Tenses	
Singular	Plural	Singular	Plural
1 presente de indicativo		**8 perfecto de indicativo**	
chisto	chistamos	he chistado	hemos chistado
chistas	chistáis	has chistado	habéis chistado
chista	chistan	ha chistado	han chistado
2 imperfecto de indicativo		**9 pluscuamperfecto de indicativo**	
chistaba	chistábamos	había chistado	habíamos chistado
chistabas	chistabais	habías chistado	habíais chistado
chistaba	chistaban	había chistado	habían chistado
3 pretérito		**10 pretérito anterior**	
chisté	chistamos	hube chistado	hubimos chistado
chistaste	chistasteis	hubiste chistado	hubisteis chistado
chistó	chistaron	hubo chistado	hubieron chistado
4 futuro		**11 futuro perfecto**	
chistaré	chistaremos	habré chistado	habremos chistado
chistarás	chistaréis	habrás chistado	habréis chistado
chistará	chistarán	habrá chistado	habrán chistado
5 potencial simple		**12 potencial compuesto**	
chistaría	chistaríamos	habría chistado	habríamos chistado
chistarías	chistaríais	habrías chistado	habríais chistado
chistaría	chistarían	habría chistado	habrían chistado
6 presente de subjuntivo		**13 perfecto de subjuntivo**	
chiste	chistemos	haya chistado	hayamos chistado
chistes	chistéis	hayas chistado	hayáis chistado
chiste	chisten	haya chistado	hayan chistado
7 imperfecto de subjuntivo		**14 pluscuamperfecto de subjuntivo**	
chistara	chistáramos	hubiera chistado	hubiéramos chistado
chistaras	chistarais	hubieras chistado	hubierais chistado
chistara	chistaran	hubiera chistado	hubieran chistado
OR		OR	
chistase	chistásemos	hubiese chistado	hubiésemos chistado
chistases	chistaseis	hubieses chistado	hubieseis chistado
chistase	chistasen	hubiese chistado	hubiesen chistado

imperativo

—	chistemos
chista; no chistes	chistad; no chistéis
chiste	chisten

Words and expressions related to this verb

no chistar   to remain silent, not to say a word
un chiste   joke, witty saying
contar un chiste   to tell a joke
chistoso, chistosa   funny, witty

hacer chiste de una cosa   to make a joke of something
sin chistar ni mistar   without saying a word
caer en el chiste   to get the joke

Regular **-ar** verb   to suck

C

The Seven Simple Tenses		The Seven Compound Tenses	
Singular	Plural	Singular	Plural
1 presente de indicativo		8 perfecto de indicativo	
chupo	chupamos	he chupado	hemos chupado
chupas	chupáis	has chupado	habéis chupado
chupa	chupan	ha chupado	han chupado
2 imperfecto de indicativo		9 pluscuamperfecto de indicativo	
chupaba	chupábamos	había chupado	habíamos chupado
chupabas	chupabais	habías chupado	habíais chupado
chupaba	chupaban	había chupado	habían chupado
3 pretérito		10 pretérito anterior	
chupé	chupamos	hube chupado	hubimos chupado
chupaste	chupasteis	hubiste chupado	hubisteis chupado
chupó	chuparon	hubo chupado	hubieron chupado
4 futuro		11 futuro perfecto	
chuparé	chuparemos	habré chupado	habremos chupado
chuparás	chuparéis	habrás chupado	habréis chupado
chupará	chuparán	habrá chupado	habrán chupado
5 potencial simple		12 potencial compuesto	
chuparía	chuparíamos	habría chupado	habríamos chupado
chuparías	chuparíais	habrías chupado	habríais chupado
chuparía	chuparían	habría chupado	habrían chupado
6 presente de subjuntivo		13 perfecto de subjuntivo	
chupe	chupemos	haya chupado	hayamos chupado
chupes	chupéis	hayas chupado	hayáis chupado
chupe	chupen	haya chupado	hayan chupado
7 imperfecto de subjuntivo		14 pluscuamperfecto de subjuntivo	
chupara	chupáramos	hubiera chupado	hubiéramos chupado
chuparas	chuparais	hubieras chupado	hubierais chupado
chupara	chuparan	hubiera chupado	hubieran chupado
OR		OR	
chupase	chupásemos	hubiese chupado	hubiésemos chupado
chupases	chupaseis	hubieses chupado	hubieseis chupado
chupase	chupasen	hubiese chupado	hubiesen chupado

imperativo	
—	chupemos
chupa; no chupes	chupad; no chupéis
chupe	chupen

Words and expressions related to this verb
un chupadero, un chupaderito   teething ring
la chupada, la chupadura   suck, sucking
andarse en chupaderitos   to use ineffective
    means for a task
chuparse los dedos   to lick
    one's lips (fingers)

mejillas chupadas   hollow cheeks
está chupado   it's as easy as ABC
chupado, chupada   skinny
chupar un limón   to suck a lemon

If you don't know the Spanish verb for the English verb you have in mind, look it up in the index on pages 682–706.

The subject pronouns are found on page 93.

221

to to make an appointment, to cite, to quote, to summon   Regular **-ar** verb

The Seven Simple Tenses		The Seven Compound Tenses	
Singular	Plural	Singular	Plural
1 presente de indicativo		8 perfecto de indicativo	
cito	citamos	he citado	hemos citado
citas	citáis	has citado	habéis citado
cita	citan	ha citado	han citado
2 imperfecto de indicativo		9 pluscuamperfecto de indicativo	
citaba	citábamos	había citado	habíamos citado
citabas	citabais	habías citado	habíais citado
citaba	citaban	había citado	habían citado
3 pretérito		10 pretérito anterior	
cité	citamos	hube citado	hubimos citado
citaste	citasteis	hubiste citado	hubisteis citado
citó	citaron	hubo citado	hubieron citado
4 futuro		11 futuro perfecto	
citaré	citaremos	habré citado	habremos citado
citarás	citaréis	habrás citado	habréis citado
citará	citarán	habrá citado	habrán citado
5 potencial simple		12 potencial compuesto	
citaría	citaríamos	habría citado	habríamos citado
citarías	citaríais	habrías citado	habríais citado
citaría	citarían	habría citado	habrían citado
6 presente de subjuntivo		13 perfecto de subjuntivo	
cite	citemos	haya citado	hayamos citado
cites	citéis	hayas citado	hayáis citado
cite	citen	haya citado	hayan citado
7 imperfecto de subjuntivo		14 pluscuamperfecto de subjuntivo	
citara	citáramos	hubiera citado	hubiéramos citado
citaras	citarais	hubieras citado	hubierais citado
citara	citaran	hubiera citado	hubieran citado
OR		OR	
citase	citásemos	hubiese citado	hubiésemos citado
citases	citaseis	hubieses citado	hubieseis citado
citase	citasen	hubiese citado	hubiesen citado

imperativo	
—	citemos
cita; no cites	citad; no citéis
cite	citen

Words and expressions related to this verb
una cita appointment
tener cita (con) to have an appointment (with)
una citación quotation, citation

Can't find the verb you're looking for?
Check the back pages of this book for a list of over 2,100 additional verbs!

The Seven Simple Tenses		The Seven Compound Tenses	
Singular	Plural	Singular	Plural
1 presente de indicativo		**8 perfecto de indicativo**	
cocino	cocinamos	he cocinado	hemos cocinado
cocinas	cocináis	has cocinado	habéis cocinado
cocina	cocinan	ha cocinado	han cocinado
2 imperfecto de indicativo		**9 pluscuamperfecto de indicativo**	
cocinaba	cocinábamos	había cocinado	habíamos cocinado
cocinabas	cocinabais	habías cocinado	habíais cocinado
cocinaba	cocinaban	había cocinado	habían cocinado
3 pretérito		**10 pretérito anterior**	
cociné	cocinamos	hube cocinado	hubimos cocinado
cocinaste	cocinasteis	hubiste cocinado	hubisteis cocinado
cocinó	cocinaron	hubo cocinado	hubieron cocinado
4 futuro		**11 futuro perfecto**	
cocinaré	cocinaremos	habré cocinado	habremos cocinado
cocinarás	cocinaréis	habrás cocinado	habréis cocinado
cocinará	cocinarán	habrá cocinado	habrán cocinado
5 potencial simple		**12 potencial compuesto**	
cocinaría	cocinaríamos	habría cocinado	habríamos cocinado
cocinarías	cocinaríais	habrías cocinado	habríais cocinado
cocinaría	cocinarían	habría cocinado	habrían cocinado
6 presente de subjuntivo		**13 perfecto de subjuntivo**	
cocine	cocinemos	haya cocinado	hayamos cocinado
cocines	cocinéis	hayas cocinado	hayáis cocinado
cocine	cocinen	haya cocinado	hayan cocinado
7 imperfecto de subjuntivo		**14 pluscuamperfecto de subjuntivo**	
cocinara	cocináramos	hubiera cocinado	hubiéramos cocinado
cocinaras	cocinarais	hubieras cocinado	hubierais cocinado
cocinara	cocinaran	hubiera cocinado	hubieran cocinado
OR		OR	
cocinase	cocinásemos	hubiese cocinado	hubiésemos cocinado
cocinases	cocinaseis	hubieses cocinado	hubieseis cocinado
cocinase	cocinasen	hubiese cocinado	hubiesen cocinado

imperativo	
—	cocinemos
cocina; no cocines	cocinad; no cocinéis
cocine	cocinen

Words related to this verb
la cocina kitchen; cooking, cuisine
cocer to cook, to bake, to boil
el cocinero, la cocinera cook, kitchen chef
la cocinilla portable stove

el cocimiento cooking
el cocido plate of boiled meat and vegetables; stew
hacer la cocina to cook, do the cooking
un libro de cocina a cookbook

The subject pronouns are found on page 93.

coger (123) Gerundio cogiendo Part. pas. cogido

to seize, to take, to grasp, to grab,
to catch, to get (understand)

Regular **-er** verb endings with spelling
change: **g** becomes **j** before **a** or **o**

The Seven Simple Tenses		The Seven Compound Tenses	
Singular	Plural	Singular	Plural
1 presente de indicativo		8 perfecto de indicativo	
cojo	cogemos	he cogido	hemos cogido
coges	cogéis	has cogido	habéis cogido
coge	cogen	ha cogido	han cogido
2 imperfecto de indicativo		9 pluscuamperfecto de indicativo	
cogía	cogíamos	había cogido	habíamos cogido
cogías	cogíais	habías cogido	habíais cogido
cogía	cogían	había cogido	habían cogido
3 pretérito		10 pretérito anterior	
cogí	cogimos	hube cogido	hubimos cogido
cogiste	cogisteis	hubiste cogido	hubisteis cogido
cogió	cogieron	hubo cogido	hubieron cogido
4 futuro		11 futuro perfecto	
cogeré	cogeremos	habré cogido	habremos cogido
cogerás	cogeréis	habrás cogido	habréis cogido
cogerá	cogerán	habrá cogido	habrán cogido
5 potencial simple		12 potencial compuesto	
cogería	cogeríamos	habría cogido	habríamos cogido
cogerías	cogeríais	habrías cogido	habríais cogido
cogería	cogerían	habría cogido	habrían cogido
6 presente de subjuntivo		13 perfecto de subjuntivo	
coja	cojamos	haya cogido	hayamos cogido
cojas	cojáis	hayas cogido	hayáis cogido
coja	cojan	haya cogido	hayan cogido
7 imperfecto de subjuntivo		14 pluscuamperfecto de subjuntivo	
cogiera	cogiéramos	hubiera cogido	hubiéramos cogido
cogieras	cogierais	hubieras cogido	hubierais cogido
cogiera	cogieran	hubiera cogido	hubieran cogido
OR		OR	
cogiese	cogiésemos	hubiese cogido	hubiésemos cogido
cogieses	cogieseis	hubieses cogido	hubieseis cogido
cogiese	cogiesen	hubiese cogido	hubiesen cogido

imperativo	
—	cojamos
coge; no cojas	coged; no cojáis
coja	cojan

Sentences using this verb and words related to it
Quien siembra vientos recoge tempestades. If you sow the wind, you will reap the whirlwind.

la cogida gathering of fruits, a catch	**recoger** to pick (up), to gather, to reap
el cogedor collector, dustpan	**acoger** to greet, to receive, to welcome
escoger to choose, to select	**encoger** to shorten, to shrink
coger catarro (o resfriado) to catch cold	**descoger** to expand, to extend

224

Regular **-ir** verb endings with stem change: Tenses 1, 6, 7,   to collect
Imperative, Gerundio; spelling change: **g** becomes **j** before **a** or **o**

The Seven Simple Tenses		The Seven Compound Tenses	
Singular	Plural	Singular	Plural
1 presente de indicativo		8 perfecto de indicativo	
colijo	**colegimos**	**he colegido**	**hemos colegido**
coliges	**colegís**	**has colegido**	**habéis colegido**
colige	**coligen**	**ha colegido**	**han colegido**
2 imperfecto de indicativo		9 pluscuamperfecto de indicativo	
colegía	**colegíamos**	**había colegido**	**habíamos colegido**
colegias	**colegíais**	**habías colegido**	**habíais colegido**
colegía	**colegían**	**había colegido**	**habían colegido**
3 pretérito		10 pretérito anterior	
colegí	**colegimos**	**hube colegido**	**hubimos colegido**
colegiste	**colegisteis**	**hubiste colegido**	**hubisteis colegido**
coligió	**coligieron**	**hubo colegido**	**hubieron colegido**
4 futuro		11 futuro perfecto	
colegiré	**colegiremos**	**habré colegido**	**habremos colegido**
colegirás	**colegiréis**	**habrás colegido**	**habréis colegido**
colegirá	**colegirán**	**habrá colegido**	**habrán colegido**
5 potencial simple		12 potencial compuesto	
colegiría	**colegiríamos**	**habría colegido**	**habríamos colegido**
colegirías	**colegiríais**	**habrías colegido**	**habríais colegido**
colegiría	**colegirían**	**habría colegido**	**habrían colegido**
6 presente de subjuntivo		13 perfecto de subjuntivo	
colija	**colijamos**	**haya colegido**	**hayamos colegido**
colijas	**colijáis**	**hayas colegido**	**hayáis colegido**
colija	**colijan**	**haya colegido**	**hayan colegido**
7 imperfecto de subjuntivo		14 pluscuamperfecto de subjuntivo	
coligiera	**coligiéramos**	**hubiera colegido**	**hubiéramos colegido**
coligieras	**coligierais**	**hubieras colegido**	**hubierais colegido**
coligiera	**coligieran**	**hubiera colegido**	**hubieran colegido**
OR		OR	
coligiese	**coligiésemos**	**hubiese colegido**	**hubiésemos colegido**
coligieses	**coligieseis**	**hubieses colegido**	**hubieseis colegido**
coligiese	**coligiesen**	**hubiese colegido**	**hubiesen colegido**

	imperativo	
—		**colijamos**
colige; no colijas		**colegid; no colijáis**
colija		**colijan**

Words related to this verb
el colegio college, school
la colección collection

colectivo, colectiva collective
el colegio electoral electoral college

colgar (125)   Gerundio colgando   Part. pas. colgado

to hang (up)   Regular **-ar** verb endings with spelling change: **g** becomes
gu before **e**; stem change: Tenses 1, 6, Imperative

The Seven Simple Tenses		The Seven Compound Tenses	
Singular	Plural	Singular	Plural
1 presente de indicativo		8 perfecto de indicativo	
cuelgo	colgamos	he colgado	hemos colgado
cuelgas	colgáis	has colgado	habéis colgado
cuelga	cuelgan	ha colgado	han colgado
2 imperfecto de indicativo		9 pluscuamperfecto de indicativo	
colgaba	colgábamos	había colgado	habíamos colgado
colgabas	colgabais	habías colgado	habíais colgado
colgaba	colgaban	había colgado	habían colgado
3 pretérito		10 pretérito anterior	
colgué	colgamos	hube colgado	hubimos colgado
colgaste	colgasteis	hubiste colgado	hubisteis colgado
colgó	colgaron	hubo colgado	hubieron colgado
4 futuro		11 futuro perfecto	
colgaré	colgaremos	habré colgado	habremos colgado
colgarás	colgaréis	habrás colgado	habréis colgado
colgará	colgarán	habrá colgado	habrán colgado
5 potencial simple		12 potencial compuesto	
colgaría	colgaríamos	habría colgado	habríamos colgado
colgarías	colgaríais	habrías colgado	habríais colgado
colgaría	colgarían	habría colgado	habrían colgado
6 presente de subjuntivo		13 perfecto de subjuntivo	
cuelgue	colguemos	haya colgado	hayamos colgado
cuelgues	colguéis	hayas colgado	hayáis colgado
cuelgue	cuelguen	haya colgado	hayan colgado
7 imperfecto de subjuntivo		14 pluscuamperfecto de subjuntivo	
colgara	colgáramos	hubiera colgado	hubiéramos colgado
colgaras	colgarais	hubieras colgado	hubierais colgado
colgara	colgaran	hubiera colgado	hubieran colgado
OR		OR	
colgase	colgásemos	hubiese colgado	hubiésemos colgado
colgases	colgaseis	hubieses colgado	hubieseis colgado
colgase	colgasen	hubiese colgado	hubiesen colgado

	imperativo	
—		colguemos
cuelga; no cuelgues		colgad; no colguéis
cuelgue		cuelguen

Words related to this verb

el colgadero   hanger, hook on which to
hang things
dejar colgado (colgada)   to be left
disappointed
el puente colgante   suspension bridge
la colgadura   drapery, tapestry

colgar la ropa   to hang up the clothes
¡Cuelgue!   Hang up!
descolgar   to take down, to pick up
(a telephone receiver)
¡Descuelgue!   Pick up (the telephone receiver)!
colgar el teléfono   to hang up the telephone

> If you want to see a sample English verb fully conjugated
> in all the tenses, check out pages 11 and 12.

Regular **-ar** verb endings with spelling change: to put, to place
c becomes **qu** before **e**

The Seven Simple Tenses		The Seven Compound Tenses	
Singular	Plural	Singular	Plural
1 presente de indicativo		8 perfecto de indicativo	
coloco	**colocamos**	**he colocado**	**hemos colocado**
colocas	**colocáis**	**has colocado**	**habéis colocado**
coloca	**colocan**	**ha colocado**	**han colocado**
2 imperfecto de indicativo		9 pluscuamperfecto de indicativo	
colocaba	**colocábamos**	**había colocado**	**habíamos colocado**
colocabas	**colocabais**	**habías colocado**	**habíais colocado**
colocaba	**colocaban**	**había colocado**	**habían colocado**
3 pretérito		10 pretérito anterior	
coloqué	**colocamos**	**hube colocado**	**hubimos colocado**
colocaste	**colocasteis**	**hubiste colocado**	**hubisteis colocado**
colocó	**colocaron**	**hubo colocado**	**hubieron colocado**
4 futuro		11 futuro perfecto	
colocaré	**colocaremos**	**habré colocado**	**habremos colocado**
colocarás	**colocaréis**	**habrás colocado**	**habréis colocado**
colocará	**colocarán**	**habrá colocado**	**habrán colocado**
5 potencial simple		12 potencial compuesto	
colocaría	**colocaríamos**	**habría colocado**	**habríamos colocado**
colocarías	**colocaríais**	**habrías colocado**	**habríais colocado**
colocaría	**colocarían**	**habría colocado**	**habrían colocado**
6 presente de subjuntivo		13 perfecto de subjuntivo	
coloque	**coloquemos**	**haya colocado**	**hayamos colocado**
coloques	**coloquéis**	**hayas colocado**	**hayáis colocado**
coloque	**coloquen**	**haya colocado**	**hayan colocado**
7 imperfecto de subjuntivo		14 pluscuamperfecto de subjuntivo	
colocara	**colocáramos**	**hubiera colocado**	**hubiéramos colocado**
colocaras	**colocarais**	**hubieras colocado**	**hubierais colocado**
colocara	**colocaran**	**hubiera colocado**	**hubieran colocado**
OR		OR	
colocase	**colocásemos**	**hubiese colocado**	**hubiésemos colocado**
colocases	**colocaseis**	**hubieses colocado**	**hubieseis colocado**
colocase	**colocasen**	**hubiese colocado**	**hubiesen colocado**

imperativo	
—	**coloquemos**
coloca; no coloques	**colocad; no coloquéis**
coloque	**coloquen**

Words and expressions related to this verb
la colocación   job, employment, position
colocar dinero   to invest money

colocar un pedido   to place an order
la agencia de colocaciones   job placement
     agency

Can't recognize an irregular verb form? Check out pages 678–681.

The subject pronouns are found on page 93.

227

to begin, to start, to commence	Regular **-ar** verb endings with spelling change: **z** becomes **c** before **e**; stem change: Tenses 1, 6, Imperative

The Seven Simple Tenses		The Seven Compound Tenses	
Singular	Plural	Singular	Plural
1 presente de indicativo		8 perfecto de indicativo	
comienzo	comenzamos	he comenzado	hemos comenzado
comienzas	comenzáis	has comenzado	habéis comenzado
comienza	comienzan	ha comenzado	han comenzado
2 imperfecto de indicativo		9 pluscuamperfecto de indicativo	
comenzaba	comenzábamos	había comenzado	habíamos comenzado
comenzabas	comenzabais	habías comenzado	habíais comenzado
comenzaba	comenzaban	había comenzado	habían comenzado
3 pretérito		10 pretérito anterior	
comencé	comenzamos	hube comenzado	hubimos comenzado
comenzaste	comenzasteis	hubiste comenzado	hubisteis comenzado
comenzó	comenzaron	hubo comenzado	hubieron comenzado
4 futuro		11 futuro perfecto	
comenzaré	comenzaremos	habré comenzado	habremos comenzado
comenzarás	comenzaréis	habrás comenzado	habréis comenzado
comenzará	comenzarán	habrá comenzado	habrán comenzado
5 potencial simple		12 potencial compuesto	
comenzaría	comenzaríamos	habría comenzado	habríamos comenzado
comenzarías	comenzaríais	habrías comenzado	habríais comenzado
comenzaría	comenzarían	habría comenzado	habrían comenzado
6 presente de subjuntivo		13 perfecto de subjuntivo	
comience	comencemos	haya comenzado	hayamos comenzado
comiences	comencéis	hayas comenzado	hayáis comenzado
comience	comiencen	haya comenzado	hayan comenzado
7 imperfecto de subjuntivo		14 pluscuamperfecto de subjuntivo	
comenzara	comenzáramos	hubiera comenzado	hubiéramos comenzado
comenzaras	comenzarais	hubieras comenzado	hubierais comenzado
comenzara	comenzaran	hubiera comenzado	hubieran comenzado
OR		OR	
comenzase	comenzásemos	hubiese comenzado	hubiésemos comenzado
comenzases	comenzaseis	hubieses comenzado	hubieseis comenzado
comenzase	comenzasen	hubiese comenzado	hubiesen comenzado

imperativo

—	comencemos
comienza; no comiences	comenzad; no comencéis
comience	comiencen

AN ESSENTIAL 55 VERB

Comenzar is a useful verb for beginning Spanish students because it has an important stem change (in the imperative and in Tenses 1 and 6) and a spelling change from z to c before the letter e. It is also used in numerous everyday expressions and situations.

Sentences using comenzar and related words

–¿Qué tiempo hace?
—What is the weather like?

–Comienza a llover.
—It's starting to rain.

–Quiero comenzar al comienzo.
—I'd like to begin at the beginning.

–¡Comienza!
—Begin!

Words and expressions related to this verb

el comienzo **the beginning**

al comienzo **at the beginning, at first**

comenzar a + inf. **to begin + inf.**

comenzar por + inf. **to begin by + pres. part.**

comenzar por el principio **to begin at the beginning**

Proverb

Lo que mal comienza, mal acaba.
What starts badly ends badly.

Can't remember the Spanish verb you need?
Check the back pages of this book for the English-Spanish verb index!

The subject pronouns are found on page 93.

to eat   Regular **-er** verb

The Seven Simple Tenses		The Seven Compound Tenses	
Singular	Plural	Singular	Plural
1 presente de indicativo		**8 perfecto de indicativo**	
como	comemos	he comido	hemos comido
comes	coméis	has comido	habéis comido
come	comen	ha comido	han comido
2 imperfecto de indicativo		**9 pluscuamperfecto de indicativo**	
comía	comíamos	había comido	habíamos comido
comías	comíais	habías comido	habíais comido
comía	comían	había comido	habían comido
3 pretérito		**10 pretérito anterior**	
comí	comimos	hube comido	hubimos comido
comiste	comisteis	hubiste comido	hubisteis comido
comió	comieron	hubo comido	hubieron comido
4 futuro		**11 futuro perfecto**	
comeré	comeremos	habré comido	habremos comido
comerás	comeréis	habrás comido	habréis comido
comerá	comerán	habrá comido	habrán comido
5 potencial simple		**12 potencial compuesto**	
comería	comeríamos	habría comido	habríamos comido
comerías	comeríais	habrías comido	habríais comido
comería	comerían	habría comido	habrían comido
6 presente de subjuntivo		**13 perfecto de subjuntivo**	
coma	comamos	haya comido	hayamos comido
comas	comáis	hayas comido	hayáis comido
coma	coman	haya comido	hayan comido
7 imperfecto de subjuntivo		**14 pluscuamperfecto de subjuntivo**	
comiera	comiéramos	hubiera comido	hubiéramos comido
comieras	comierais	hubieras comido	hubierais comido
comiera	comieran	hubiera comido	hubieran comido
OR		OR	
comiese	comiésemos	hubiese comido	hubiésemos comido
comieses	comieseis	hubieses comido	hubieseis comido
comiese	comiesen	hubiese comido	hubiesen comido

imperativo

—	comamos
come; no comas	comed; no comáis
coma	coman

AN ESSENTIAL
55 VERB

Comer is a useful verb for you to know because it is a regular –er verb and because it is used in numerous everyday expressions and situations.

Sentences using comer and related words

Yo no quiero cocinar. Prefiero comer fuera de casa.
I don't want to cook. I'd rather eat out.

–¿Dónde está Miguel?
–Está en el comedor. Está comiendo su comida.
–Where is Michael?
–He's in the dining room. He's eating his meal.

¡A comer!
Come and get it!

Words and expressions related to this verb

ganar de comer **to earn a living**

la comida **meal**

el comedor **dining room**

cama y comida **bed and board**

comer fuera de casa **to eat out; dine out**

dar de comer a los niños **to feed the children**

comer con gana **to eat heartily**

comer con muchas ganas **to eat very heartily**

comer a todo correr **to eat quickly, wolf down**

comerse **to eat up**

comerse la risa **to stifle/hold back a laugh**

comer de todo **to eat everything**

comer para vivir **to eat to live**

comer como un pajarito **to eat like a little bird**

Proverbs

Dime qué comes y te diré quien eres.
Tell me what you eat and I'll tell you who you are.

Comer para vivir y no vivir para comer.
One should eat to live and not live to eat.

Don't forget to study the section on defective and impersonal verbs. It's right after this main list.

The Seven Simple Tenses		The Seven Compound Tenses	
Singular	Plural	Singular	Plural
1 presente de indicativo		8 perfecto de indicativo	
compongo	componemos	he compuesto	hemos compuesto
compones	componéis	has compuesto	habéis compuesto
compone	componen	ha compuesto	han compuesto
2 imperfecto de indicativo		9 pluscuamperfecto de indicativo	
componía	componíamos	había compuesto	habíamos compuesto
componías	componíais	habías compuesto	habíais compuesto
componía	componían	había compuesto	habían compuesto
3 pretérito		10 pretérito anterior	
compuse	compusimos	hube compuesto	hubimos compuesto
compusiste	compusisteis	hubiste compuesto	hubisteis compuesto
compuso	compusieron	hubo compuesto	hubieron compuesto
4 futuro		11 futuro perfecto	
compondré	compondremos	habré compuesto	habremos compuesto
compondrás	compondréis	habrás compuesto	habréis compuesto
compondrá	compondrán	habrá compuesto	habrán compuesto
5 potencial simple		12 potencial compuesto	
compondría	compondríamos	habría compuesto	habríamos compuesto
compondrías	compondríais	habrías compuesto	habríais compuesto
compondría	compondrían	habría compuesto	habrían compuesto
6 presente de subjuntivo		13 perfecto de subjuntivo	
componga	compongamos	haya compuesto	hayamos compuesto
compongas	compongáis	hayas compuesto	hayáis compuesto
componga	compongan	haya compuesto	hayan compuesto
7 imperfecto de subjuntivo		14 pluscuamperfecto de subjuntivo	
compusiera	compusiéramos	hubiera compuesto	hubiéramos compuesto
compusieras	compusierais	hubieras compuesto	hubierais compuesto
compusiera	compusieran	hubiera compuesto	hubieran compuesto
OR		OR	
compusiese	compusiésemos	hubiese compuesto	hubiésemos compuesto
compusieses	compusieseis	hubieses compuesto	hubieseis compuesto
compusiese	compusiesen	hubiese compuesto	hubiesen compuesto

imperativo

—	compongamos
compón; no compongas	componed; no compongáis
componga	compongan

Words and expressions related to this verb

el **compuesto** compound, mixture
compuestamente neatly, orderly
deponer to depose
imponer to impose
la **composición** composition

el **compositor,** la **compositora** composer
(music)
exponer to expose, to exhibit
indisponer to indispose

Don't miss the definitions of basic grammatical terms with examples in English and Spanish on pages 33–44.

Regular **-ar** verb   to buy, to purchase

The Seven Simple Tenses		The Seven Compound Tenses	
Singular	Plural	Singular	Plural
1 presente de indicativo		**8 perfecto de indicativo**	
compro	compramos	he comprado	hemos comprado
compras	compráis	has comprado	habéis comprado
compra	compran	ha comprado	han comprado
2 imperfecto de indicativo		**9 pluscuamperfecto de indicativo**	
compraba	comprábamos	había comprado	habíamos comprado
comprabas	comprabais	habías comprado	habíais comprado
compraba	compraban	había comprado	habían comprado
3 pretérito		**10 pretérito anterior**	
compré	compramos	hube comprado	hubimos comprado
compraste	comprasteis	hubiste comprado	hubisteis comprado
compró	compraron	hubo comprado	hubieron comprado
4 futuro		**11 futuro perfecto**	
compraré	compraremos	habré comprado	habremos comprado
comprarás	compraréis	habrás comprado	habréis comprado
comprará	comprarán	habrá comprado	habrán comprado
5 potencial simple		**12 potencial compuesto**	
compraría	compraríamos	habría comprado	habríamos comprado
comprarías	compraríais	habrías comprado	habríais comprado
compraría	comprarían	habría comprado	habrían comprado
6 presente de subjuntivo		**13 perfecto de subjuntivo**	
compre	compremos	haya comprado	hayamos comprado
compres	compréis	hayas comprado	hayáis comprado
compre	compren	haya comprado	hayan comprado
7 imperfecto de subjuntivo		**14 pluscuamperfecto de subjuntivo**	
comprara	compráramos	hubiera comprado	hubiéramos comprado
compraras	comprarais	hubieras comprado	hubierais comprado
comprara	compraran	hubiera comprado	hubieran comprado
OR		OR	
comprase	comprásemos	hubiese comprado	hubiésemos comprado
comprases	compraseis	hubieses comprado	hubieseis comprado
comprase	comprasen	hubiese comprado	hubiesen comprado

	imperativo
—	**compremos**
compra; no compres	**comprad; no compréis**
compre	**compren**

Comprar

Comprar is a useful verb for beginning students because it is a regular –ar verb. Comprar is used in numerous everyday expressions and situations, especially when you travel.

Sentences using comprar and related words

¿Dónde está la juguetería? Quisiera comprar juguetes.
Where is the toy store? I would like to buy some toys.

¡Cómprate un calvo y péinalo!
Beat it! (Literally: Buy a bald man and comb his hair.)

¿Qué piensas de mis zapatos? Yo los compré en el centro comercial.
What do you think of my shoes? I bought them at the shopping center.

Words and expressions related to this verb

la compra **purchase**

hacer compras **to shop**

ir de compras **to go shopping**

un comprador, una compradora **shopper, buyer**

comprar al contado **to buy for cash, to pay cash**

comprar al fiado, comprar a crédito **to buy on credit**

comprar con rebaja **to buy at a discount**

Proverb

La amistad no se compra.
Friendship cannot be bought (has no price).

Can't find the verb you're looking for?
Check the back pages of this book for a list of over 2,100 additional verbs!

The Seven Simple Tenses | The Seven Compound Tenses

Singular	Plural	Singular	Plural
1 presente de indicativo		8 perfecto de indicativo	
comprendo	**comprendemos**	**he comprendido**	**hemos comprendido**
comprendes	**comprendéis**	**has comprendido**	**habéis comprendido**
comprende	**comprenden**	**ha comprendido**	**han comprendido**
2 imperfecto de indicativo		9 pluscuamperfecto de indicativo	
comprendía	**comprendíamos**	**había comprendido**	**habíamos comprendido**
comprendías	**comprendíais**	**habías comprendido**	**habíais comprendido**
comprendía	**comprendían**	**había comprendido**	**habían comprendido**
3 pretérito		10 pretérito anterior	
comprendí	**comprendimos**	**hube comprendido**	**hubimos comprendido**
comprendiste	**comprendisteis**	**hubiste comprendido**	**hubisteis comprendido**
comprendió	**comprendieron**	**hubo comprendido**	**hubieron comprendido**
4 futuro		11 futuro perfecto	
comprenderé	**comprenderemos**	**habré comprendido**	**habremos comprendido**
comprenderás	**comprenderéis**	**habrás comprendido**	**habréis comprendido**
comprenderá	**comprenderán**	**habrá comprendido**	**habrán comprendido**
5 potencial simple		12 potencial compuesto	
comprendería	**comprenderíamos**	**habría comprendido**	**habríamos comprendido**
comprenderías	**comprenderíais**	**habrías comprendido**	**habríais comprendido**
comprendería	**comprenderían**	**habría comprendido**	**habrían comprendido**
6 presente de subjuntivo		13 perfecto de subjuntivo	
comprenda	**comprendamos**	**haya comprendido**	**hayamos comprendido**
comprendas	**comprendáis**	**hayas comprendido**	**hayáis comprendido**
comprenda	**comprendan**	**haya comprendido**	**hayan comprendido**
7 imperfecto de subjuntivo		14 pluscuamperfecto de subjuntivo	
comprendiera	**comprendiéramos**	**hubiera comprendido**	**hubiéramos comprendido**
comprendieras	**comprendierais**	**hubieras comprendido**	**hubierais comprendido**
comprendiera	**comprendieran**	**hubiera comprendido**	**hubieran comprendido**
OR		OR	
comprendiese	**comprendiésemos**	**hubiese comprendido**	**hubiésemos comprendido**
comprendieses	**comprendieseis**	**hubieses comprendido**	**hubieseis comprendido**
comprendiese	**comprendiesen**	**hubiese comprendido**	**hubiesen comprendido**

imperativo

—	**comprendamos**
comprende; no comprendas	**comprended; no comprendáis**
comprenda	**comprendan**

Words related to this verb

la comprensión   comprehension,
   understanding
la comprensibilidad   comprehensibility,
   intelligibility

comprensivo, comprensiva   comprehensive
comprensible   comprehensible, understandable
comprenderse   to understand one another
No comprendo.   I don't understand.
Sí, comprendo.   Yes, I understand.

Don't forget to study the section on defective and impersonal verbs. It's right after this main list.

The subject pronouns are found on page 93.
                                                                    235

to lead, to conduct, to drive | Irregular in Tenses 3 and 7, regular **-ir** endings in all others; spelling change: **c** becomes **zc** before **a** or **o**

The Seven Simple Tenses	The Seven Compound Tenses

Singular	Plural	Singular	Plural
1 presente de indicativo		8 perfecto de indicativo	
conduzco	conducimos	he conducido	hemos conducido
conduces	conducís	has conducido	habéis conducido
conduce	conducen	ha conducido	han conducido
2 imperfecto de indicativo		9 pluscuamperfecto de indicativo	
conducía	conducíamos	había conducido	habíamos conducido
conducías	conducíais	habías conducido	habíais conducido
conducía	conducían	había conducido	habían conducido
3 pretérito		10 pretérito anterior	
conduje	condujimos	hube conducido	hubimos conducido
condujiste	condujisteis	hubiste conducido	hubisteis conducido
condujo	condujeron	hubo conducido	hubieron conducido
4 futuro		11 futuro perfecto	
conduciré	conduciremos	habré conducido	habremos conducido
conducirás	conduciréis	habrás conducido	habréis conducido
conducirá	conducirán	habrá conducido	habrán conducido
5 potencial simple		12 potencial compuesto	
conduciría	conduciríamos	habría conducido	habríamos conducido
conducirías	conduciríais	habrías conducido	habríais conducido
conduciría	conducirían	habría conducido	habrían conducido
6 presente de subjuntivo		13 perfecto de subjuntivo	
conduzca	conduzcamos	haya conducido	hayamos conducido
conduzcas	conduzcáis	hayas conducido	hayáis conducido
conduzca	conduzcan	haya conducido	hayan conducido
7 imperfecto de subjuntivo		14 pluscuamperfecto de subjuntivo	
condujera	condujéramos	hubiera conducido	hubiéramos conducido
condujeras	condujerais	hubieras conducido	hubierais conducido
condujera	condujeran	hubiera conducido	hubieran conducido
OR		OR	
condujese	condujésemos	hubiese conducido	hubiésemos conducido
condujeses	condujeseis	hubieses conducido	hubieseis conducido
condujese	condujesen	hubiese conducido	hubiesen conducido

imperativo	
—	conduzcamos
conduce; no conduzcas	conducid; no conduzcáis
conduzca	conduzcan

AN ESSENTIAL
55 VERB

Conducir is an important verb for a beginning student to know because it has tricky spelling changes. Several other verbs are conjugated in the same way as **conducir**. This verb is also useful in numerous everyday expressions and situations.

Sentences using conducir and related words

¿Sabe Ud. conducir?
Do you know how to drive?

Sí, conduzco todos los días.
Yes, I drive every day.

Words and expressions related to this verb

el conductor, la conductora **driver, conductor**

el conducto **conduit, duct**

la conducta **conduct, behavior**

conducente **conducive**

la conducción **driving**

un permiso de conducir, un carnet de conducir **driver's license**

un permiso de conducción **driver's license**

conducir de prisa **to drive fast**

dar un paseo en coche **to go for a drive**

If you can conjugate **conducir**, you can also conjugate the following verbs:

abducir **to abduct**

inducir **to induce, lead**

introducir **to introduce**

producir **to produce**

traducir **to translate**

Do you need more drills? Have fun with the *501 Spanish Verbs* CD-ROM!

confesar (133)   Gerundio confesando   Part. pas. confesado

to confess

The Seven Simple Tenses		The Seven Compound Tenses	
Singular	Plural	Singular	Plural
1 presente de indicativo		8 perfecto de indicativo	
confieso	confesamos	he confesado	hemos confesado
confiesas	confesáis	has confesado	habéis confesado
confiesa	confiesan	ha confesado	han confesado
2 imperfecto de indicativo		9 pluscuamperfecto de indicativo	
confesaba	confesábamos	había confesado	habíamos confesado
confesabas	confesabais	habías confesado	habíais confesado
confesaba	confesaban	había confesado	habían confesado
3 pretérito		10 pretérito anterior	
confesé	confesamos	hube confesado	hubimos confesado
confesaste	confesasteis	hubiste confesado	hubisteis confesado
confesó	confesaron	hubo confesado	hubieron confesado
4 futuro		11 futuro perfecto	
confesaré	confesaremos	habré confesado	habremos confesado
confesarás	confesaréis	habrás confesado	habréis confesado
confesará	confesarán	habrá confesado	habrán confesado
5 potencial simple		12 potencial compuesto	
confesaría	confesaríamos	habría confesado	habríamos confesado
confesarías	confesaríais	habrías confesado	habríais confesado
confesaría	confesarían	habría confesado	habrían confesado
6 presente de subjuntivo		13 perfecto de subjuntivo	
confiese	confesemos	haya confesado	hayamos confesado
confieses	confeséis	hayas confesado	hayáis confesado
confiese	confiesen	haya confesado	hayan confesado
7 imperfecto de subjuntivo		14 pluscuamperfecto de subjuntivo	
confesara	confesáramos	hubiera confesado	hubiéramos confesado
confesaras	confesarais	hubieras confesado	hubierais confesado
confesara	confesaran	hubiera confesado	hubieran confesado
OR		OR	
confesase	confesásemos	hubiese confesado	hubiésemos confesado
confesases	confesaseis	hubieses confesado	hubieseis confesado
confesase	confesasen	hubiese confesado	hubiesen confesado

imperativo	
—	confesemos
confiesa; no confieses	confesad; no confeséis
confiese	confiesen

Words and expressions related to this verb

la confesión   confession
el confesionario   confessional (box)
el confesor   confessor

confesar de plano   to confess openly
un, una confesante   penitent
confesarse a Dios   to confess to God

Don't forget to study the section on defective and impersonal verbs. It's right after this main list.

Regular **-er** verb endings with spelling change: to know, to be acquainted with
c becomes **zc** before **a** or **o**

The Seven Simple Tenses		The Seven Compound Tenses	
Singular	Plural	Singular	Plural
1 presente de indicativo		8 perfecto de indicativo	
conozco	**conocemos**	**he conocido**	**hemos conocido**
conoces	**conocéis**	**has conocido**	**habéis conocido**
conoce	**conocen**	**ha conocido**	**han conocido**
2 imperfecto de indicativo		9 pluscuamperfecto de indicativo	
conocía	**conocíamos**	**había conocido**	**habíamos conocido**
conocías	**conocíais**	**habías conocido**	**habíais conocido**
conocía	**conocían**	**había conocido**	**habían conocido**
3 pretérito		10 pretérito anterior	
conocí	**conocimos**	**hube conocido**	**hubimos conocido**
conociste	**conocisteis**	**hubiste conocido**	**hubisteis conocido**
conoció	**conocieron**	**hubo conocido**	**hubieron conocido**
4 futuro		11 futuro perfecto	
conoceré	**conoceremos**	**habré conocido**	**habremos conocido**
conocerás	**conoceréis**	**habrás conocido**	**habréis conocido**
conocerá	**conocerán**	**habrá conocido**	**habrán conocido**
5 potencial simple		12 potencial compuesto	
conocería	**conoceríamos**	**habría conocido**	**habríamos conocido**
conocerías	**conoceríais**	**habrías conocido**	**habríais conocido**
conocería	**conocerían**	**habría conocido**	**habrían conocido**
6 presente de subjuntivo		13 perfecto de subjuntivo	
conozca	**conozcamos**	**haya conocido**	**hayamos conocido**
conozcas	**conozcáis**	**hayas conocido**	**hayáis conocido**
conozca	**conozcan**	**haya conocido**	**hayan conocido**
7 imperfecto de subjuntivo		14 pluscuamperfecto de subjuntivo	
conociera	**conociéramos**	**hubiera conocido**	**hubiéramos conocido**
conocieras	**conocierais**	**hubieras conocido**	**hubierais conocido**
conociera	**conocieran**	**hubiera conocido**	**hubieran conocido**
OR		OR	
conociese	**conociésemos**	**hubiese conocido**	**hubiésemos conocido**
conocieses	**conocieseis**	**hubieses conocido**	**hubieseis conocido**
conociese	**conociesen**	**hubiese conocido**	**hubiesen conocido**

	imperativo	
—	**conozcamos**
conoce; no conozcas	**conoced; no conozcáis**
conozca	**conozcan**

**AN ESSENTIAL
55 VERB**

AN ESSENTIAL 55 VERB

Conocer

Conocer is a verb that you should know! Pay special attention to the spelling change from **c** to **zc** before **a** or **o**. **Conocer** is useful in numerous everyday expressions and situations.

Be careful when choosing between **conocer** and **saber**, which also means *to know*.
(a) Generally speaking, **conocer** means to know in the sense of *being acquainted* with a person, a place, or a thing:

¿Conoce Ud. a María?
Do you know Mary?
¿Conoce Ud. bien los Estado Unidos?
Do you know the United States well?
¿Conoce Ud. este libro?
Do you know this book? (Are you acquainted with this book?)

In the preterit tense, **conocer** means *met* in the sense of *first met, first became acquainted with someone:*

¿Conoce Ud. a Elena?
Do you know Helen?
Sí, (yo) la conocí anoche en casa de un amigo mío.
Yes, I met her (for the first time) last night at the home of one of my friends.

Generally speaking, **saber** means to know a fact, to know something thoroughly: **¿Sabe Ud. qué hora es?** Do you know what time it is? (See **saber** for further examples.)

Sentences using conocer and related words

El árbol se conoce por su fruta.
The tree is known by its fruit. (You will be judged by your actions; the apple doesn't fall far from the tree.)

–**¿Conoce Ud. a esa mujer?**
–**Sí, la conozco.**
–Do you know that woman?
–Yes, I know her.

Words and expressions related to this verb

un conocido, una conocida an acquaintance

conocido, conocida known

conocidamente obviously

desconocido, desconocida unknown

un desconocido, una desconocida stranger, someone you don't know

un conocedor, una conocedora an expert

el conocimiento knowledge

el desconocimiento ignorance

poner en conocimiento de to inform (about)

muy conocido very well-known

reconocible recognizable

reconocido, reconocida grateful

If you can conjugate **conocer**, you can also conjugate the following verbs:

reconocer to recognize, to admit

desconocer to be ignorant of

Can't find the verb you're looking for?
Check the back pages of this book for a list of over 2,100 additional verbs!

Regular **-ir** verb endings with spelling change: **gu** becomes **g**   to attain, to get,
before **a** or **o**; stem change: Tenses 1, 6, Imperative, Gerundio   to obtain

The Seven Simple Tenses		The Seven Compound Tenses	
Singular	Plural	Singular	Plural
1 presente de indicativo		8 perfecto de indicativo	
consigo	conseguimos	he conseguido	hemos conseguido
consigues	conseguís	has conseguido	habéis conseguido
consigue	consiguen	ha conseguido	han conseguido
2 imperfecto de indicativo		9 pluscuamperfecto de indicativo	
conseguía	conseguíamos	había conseguido	habíamos conseguido
conseguías	conseguíais	habías conseguido	habíais conseguido
conseguía	conseguían	había conseguido	habían conseguido
3 pretérito		10 pretérito anterior	
conseguí	conseguimos	hube conseguido	hubimos conseguido
conseguiste	conseguisteis	hubiste conseguido	hubisteis conseguido
consiguió	consiguieron	hubo conseguido	hubieron conseguido
4 futuro		11 futuro perfecto	
conseguiré	conseguiremos	habré conseguido	habremos conseguido
conseguirás	conseguiréis	habrás conseguido	habréis conseguido
conseguirá	conseguirán	habrá conseguido	habrán conseguido
5 potencial simple		12 potencial compuesto	
conseguiría	conseguiríamos	habría conseguido	habríamos conseguido
conseguirías	conseguiríais	habrías conseguido	habríais conseguido
conseguiría	conseguirían	habría conseguido	habrían conseguido
6 presente de subjuntivo		13 perfecto de subjuntivo	
consiga	consigamos	haya conseguido	hayamos conseguido
consigas	consigáis	hayas conseguido	hayáis conseguido
consiga	consigan	haya conseguido	hayan conseguido
7 imperfecto de subjuntivo		14 pluscuamperfecto de subjuntivo	
consiguiera	consiguiéramos	hubiera conseguido	hubiéramos conseguido
consiguieras	consiguierais	hubieras conseguido	hubierais conseguido
consiguiera	consiguieran	hubiera conseguido	hubieran conseguido
OR		OR	
consiguiese	consiguiésemos	hubiese conseguido	hubiésemos conseguido
consiguieses	consiguieseis	hubieses conseguido	hubieseis conseguido
consiguiese	consiguiesen	hubiese conseguido	hubiesen conseguido

	imperativo	
—		consigamos
consigue; no consigas		conseguid; no consigáis
consiga		consigan

Words and expressions related to this verb
el conseguimiento   attainment
el consiguiente   consequent (syllogism)
de consiguiente, por consiguiente   consequently
consiguientemente   consequently

See also **seguir**.

dar por conseguido   to take for granted
conseguir un permiso   to get a permit
conseguir billetes   to get tickets
conseguir una buena colocación
   to get a good job

Don't forget to study the section on defective and impersonal verbs. It's right after this main list.

The subject pronouns are found on page 93.

to constitute, to make up   Regular **-ir** verb endings with spelling change: add **y** before **a**, **e**, or **o**

The Seven Simple Tenses | The Seven Compound Tenses

Singular	Plural	Singular	Plural
1 presente de indicativo		8 perfecto de indicativo	
constituyo	constituimos	he constituido	hemos constituido
constituyes	constituís	has constituido	habéis constituido
constituye	constituyen	ha constituido	han constituido
2 imperfecto de indicativo		9 pluscuamperfecto de indicativo	
constituía	constituíamos	había constituido	habíamos constituido
constituías	constituíais	habías constituido	habíais constituido
constituía	constituían	había constituido	habían constituido
3 pretérito		10 pretérito anterior	
constituí	constituimos	hube constituido	hubimos constituido
constituiste	constituisteis	hubiste constituido	hubisteis constituido
constituyó	constituyeron	hubo constituido	hubieron constituido
4 futuro		11 futuro perfecto	
constituiré	constituiremos	habré constituido	habremos constituido
constituirás	constituiréis	habrás constituido	habréis constituido
constituirá	constituirán	habrá constituido	habrán constituido
5 potencial simple		12 potencial compuesto	
constituiría	constituiríamos	habría constituido	habríamos constituido
constituirías	constituiríais	habrías constituido	habríais constituido
constituiría	constituirían	habría constituido	habrían constituido
6 presente de subjuntivo		13 perfecto de subjuntivo	
constituya	constituyamos	haya constituido	hayamos constituido
constituyas	constituyáis	hayas constituido	hayáis constituido
constituya	constituyan	haya constituido	hayan constituido
7 imperfecto de subjuntivo		14 pluscuamperfecto de subjuntivo	
constituyera	constituyéramos	hubiera constituido	hubiéramos constituido
constituyeras	constituyerais	hubieras constituido	hubierais constituido
constituyera	constituyeran	hubiera constituido	hubieran constituido
OR		OR	
constituyese	constituyésemos	hubiese constituido	hubiésemos constituido
constituyeses	constituyeseis	hubieses constituido	hubieseis constituido
constituyese	constituyesen	hubiese constituido	hubiesen constituido

imperativo

—	constituyamos
constituye; no constituyas	constituid; no constituyáis
constituya	constituyan

Words related to this verb

constitutivo, constitutiva   constitutive, essential   **constituyente**   constituent
la constitución   constitution   **instituir**   to institute, to instruct, to teach
el constitucionalismo   constitutionalism   **restituir**   to restore, to give back

If you don't know the Spanish verb for the English verb you have in mind,
look it up in the index on pages 682–706.

Regular **-ir** verb endings with spelling change: add **y** before **a**, **e**, or **o**

to construct, to build

C

The Seven Simple Tenses		The Seven Compound Tenses	
Singular	Plural	Singular	Plural

1   presente de indicativo

		8 perfecto de indicativo	
construyo	construimos	he construido	hemos construido
construyes	construís	has construido	habéis construido
construye	construyen	ha construido	han construido

2   imperfecto de indicativo

9   pluscuamperfecto de indicativo

construía	construíamos	había construido	habíamos construido
construías	construíais	habías construido	habíais construido
construía	construían	había construido	habían construido

3   pretérito

10   pretérito anterior

construí	construimos	hube construido	hubimos construido
construiste	construisteis	hubiste construido	hubisteis construido
construyó	construyeron	hubo construido	hubieron construido

4   futuro

11   futuro perfecto

construiré	construiremos	habré construido	habremos construido
construirás	construiréis	habrás construido	habréis construido
construirá	construirán	habrá construido	habrán construido

5   potencial simple

12   potencial compuesto

construiría	construiríamos	habría construido	habríamos construido
construirías	construiríais	habrías construido	habríais construido
construiría	construirían	habría construido	habrían construido

6   presente de subjuntivo

13   perfecto de subjuntivo

construya	construyamos	haya construido	hayamos construido
construyas	construyáis	hayas construido	hayáis construido
construya	construyan	haya construido	hayan construido

7   imperfecto de subjuntivo

14   pluscuamperfecto de subjuntivo

construyera	construyéramos	hubiera construido	hubiéramos construido
construyeras	construyerais	hubieras construido	hubierais construido
construyera	construyeran	hubiera construido	hubieran construido
OR		OR	
construyese	construyésemos	hubiese construido	hubiésemos construido
construyeses	construyeseis	hubieses construido	hubieseis construido
construyese	construyesen	hubiese construido	hubiesen construido

imperativo

—	**construyamos**
construye; no construyas	**construid; no construyáis**
construya	**construyan**

AN ESSENTIAL
55 VERB

The subject pronouns are found on page 93.

Construir

Construir is a useful verb, whether you're beginning to study Spanish or simply reviewing the language. Pay special attention to the added **y** before endings beginning with **a, e,** or **o**. **Construir** is used in numerous everyday expressions and situations.

Sentences using construir and related words

En la clase de carpintería, estoy construyendo una casita para pajaritos.
In woodworking class, I'm building a birdhouse.

Mi casa fue construida en 1889.
My house was built in 1889.

Words and expressions related to this verb

la construcción **construction**

el constructor, la constructora **builder**

la construcción naval **shipbuilding**

el edificio en construcción **building under construction**

constructivo, constructiva **constructive**

la crítica constructiva **constructive criticism**

reconstruir **to reconstruct, rebuild**

la reconstrucción **reconstruction**

reconstructivo, reconstructiva **reconstructive**

deconstruir **to deconstruct (analytical term)**

la deconstrucción **deconstruction (analytical term)**

Can't remember the Spanish verb you need?
Check the back pages of this book for the English-Spanish verb index!

Regular **-ar** verb endings with stem change: Tenses 1, 6, Imperative   to count, to relate, to tell

The Seven Simple Tenses		The Seven Compound Tenses	
Singular	Plural	Singular	Plural
1 presente de indicativo		**8 perfecto de indicativo**	
cuento	contamos	he contado	hemos contado
cuentas	contáis	has contado	habéis contado
cuenta	cuentan	ha contado	han contado
2 imperfecto de indicativo		**9 pluscuamperfecto de indicativo**	
contaba	contábamos	había contado	habíamos contado
contabas	contabais	habías contado	habíais contado
contaba	contaban	había contado	habían contado
3 pretérito		**10 pretérito anterior**	
conté	contamos	hube contado	hubimos contado
contaste	contasteis	hubiste contado	hubisteis contado
contó	contaron	hubo contado	hubieron contado
4 futuro		**11 futuro perfecto**	
contaré	contaremos	habré contado	habremos contado
contarás	contaréis	habrás contado	habréis contado
contará	contarán	habrá contado	habrán contado
5 potencial simple		**12 potencial compuesto**	
contaría	contaríamos	habría contado	habríamos contado
contarías	contaríais	habrías contado	habríais contado
contaría	contarían	habría contado	habrían contado
6 presente de subjuntivo		**13 perfecto de subjuntivo**	
cuente	contemos	haya contado	hayamos contado
cuentes	contéis	hayas contado	hayáis contado
cuente	cuenten	haya contado	hayan contado
7 imperfecto de subjuntivo		**14 pluscuamperfecto de subjuntivo**	
contara	contáramos	hubiera contado	hubiéramos contado
contaras	contarais	hubieras contado	hubierais contado
contara	contaran	hubiera contado	hubieran contado
OR		OR	
contase	contásemos	hubiese contado	hubiésemos contado
contases	contaseis	hubieses contado	hubieseis contado
contase	contasen	hubiese contado	hubiesen contado

imperativo

—	contemos
cuenta; no cuentes	contad; no contéis
cuente	cuenten

AN ESSENTIAL
55 VERB

245

Contar is a useful verb because it has an important stem change in Tenses 1 and 6, as well as in the imperative. It is helpful in a great number of everyday expressions and situations.

Sentences using contar and related words

Siéntate. Te contaré una historia maravillosa.
Sit down. I'll tell you a marvelous story.

Cuenta conmigo.
(You can) count on me.

¡Cuéntaselo a tu abuela!
I don't believe you! or You're pulling my leg!
(Literally: Tell it to your grandmother!)

Can't find the verb you're looking for?
Check the back pages of this book for a list of over 2,100 additional verbs!

Irregular verb   to contain, to hold, to restrain

The Seven Simple Tenses		The Seven Compound Tenses	
Singular	Plural	Singular	Plural
1 presente de indicativo		8 perfecto de indicativo	
contengo	**contenemos**	**he contenido**	**hemos contenido**
contienes	**contenéis**	**has contenido**	**habéis contenido**
contiene	**contienen**	**ha contenido**	**han contenido**
2 imperfecto de indicativo		9 pluscuamperfecto de indicativo	
contenía	**conteníamos**	**había contenido**	**habíamos contenido**
contenías	**conteníais**	**habías contenido**	**habíais contenido**
contenía	**contenían**	**había contenido**	**habían contenido**
3 pretérito		10 pretérito anterior	
contuve	**contuvimos**	**hube contenido**	**hubimos contenido**
contuviste	**contuvisteis**	**hubiste contenido**	**hubisteis contenido**
contuvo	**contuvieron**	**hubo contenido**	**hubieron contenido**
4 futuro		11 futuro perfecto	
contendré	**contendremos**	**habré contenido**	**habremos contenido**
contendrás	**contendréis**	**habrás contenido**	**habréis contenido**
contendrá	**contendrán**	**habrá contenido**	**habrán contenido**
5 potencial simple		12 potencial compuesto	
contendría	**contendríamos**	**habría contenido**	**habríamos contenido**
contendrías	**contendríais**	**habrías contenido**	**habríais contenido**
contendría	**contendrían**	**habría contenido**	**habrían contenido**
6 presente de subjuntivo		13 perfecto de subjuntivo	
contenga	**contengamos**	**haya contenido**	**hayamos contenido**
contengas	**contegáis**	**hayas contenido**	**hayáis contenido**
contenga	**contengan**	**haya contenido**	**hayan contenido**
7 imperfecto de subjuntivo		14 pluscuamperfecto de subjuntivo	
contuviera	**contuviéramos**	**hubiera contenido**	**hubiéramos contenido**
contuvieras	**contuvierais**	**hubieras contenido**	**hubierais contenido**
contuviera	**contuvieran**	**hubiera contenido**	**hubieran contenido**
OR		OR	
contuviese	**contuviésemos**	**hubiese contenido**	**hubiésemos contenido**
contuvieses	**contuvieseis**	**hubieses contenido**	**hubieseis contenido**
contuviese	**contuviesen**	**hubiese contenido**	**hubiesen contenido**

	imperativo	
—	**contengamos**
conten; no contengas	**contened; no contegáis**
contenga	**contengan**

Words related to this verb

el contenido content, contents	**contenerse** to contain oneself
conteniente containing	**contenible** containable
contenido, contenida contained	**contener la risa** to keep a straight face (to contain laughter)

See also **tener.**

Get your feet wet with verbs used in weather expressions on page 668.

The subject pronouns are found on page 93.
                                    247

to answer, to reply (to)   Regular **-ar** verb

The Seven Simple Tenses		The Seven Compound Tenses	
Singular	Plural	Singular	Plural
1 presente de indicativo		8 perfecto de indicativo	
contesto	contestamos	he contestado	hemos contestado
contestas	contestáis	has contestado	habéis contestado
contesta	contestan	ha contestado	han contestado
2 imperfecto de indicativo		9 pluscuamperfecto de indicativo	
contestaba	contestábamos	había contestado	habíamos contestado
contestabas	contestabais	habías contestado	habíais contestado
contestaba	contestaban	había contestado	habían contestado
3 pretérito		10 pretérito anterior	
contesté	contestamos	hube contestado	hubimos contestado
contestaste	contestasteis	hubiste contestado	hubisteis contestado
contestó	contestaron	hubo contestado	hubieron contestado
4 futuro		11 futuro perfecto	
contestaré	contestaremos	habré contestado	habremos contestado
contestarás	contestaréis	habrás contestado	habréis contestado
contestará	contestarán	habrá contestado	habrán contestado
5 potencial simple		12 potencial compuesto	
contestaría	contestaríamos	habría contestado	habríamos contestado
contestarías	contestaríais	habrías contestado	habríais contestado
contestaría	contestarían	habría contestado	habrían contestado
6 presente de subjuntivo		13 perfecto de subjuntivo	
conteste	contestemos	haya contestado	hayamos contestado
contestes	contestéis	hayas contestado	hayáis contestado
conteste	contesten	haya contestado	hayan contestado
7 imperfecto de subjuntivo		14 pluscuamperfecto de subjuntivo	
contestara	contestáramos	hubiera contestado	hubiéramos contestado
contestaras	contestarais	hubieras contestado	hubierais contestado
contestara	contestaran	hubiera contestado	hubieran contestado
OR		OR	
contestase	contestásemos	hubiese contestado	hubiésemos contestado
contestases	contestaseis	hubieses contestado	hubieseis contestado
contestase	contestasen	hubiese contestado	hubiesen contestado

	imperativo	
—		contestemos
contesta; no contestes		contestad; no contestéis
conteste		contesten

Words related to this verb
la contestación   answer, reply
contestable   contestable
protestar   to protest
contestar el teléfono   to answer the telephone

un contestador automático   an answering machine
contestar una pregunta   to answer a question

Check out the verb drills and verb tests with answers explained on pages 45–91.

Regular **-ar** verb endings with spelling change: **u** becomes   to continue
ú on stressed syllable (Tenses 1 and 6, Imperative)

The Seven Simple Tenses	The Seven Compound Tenses

Singular	Plural	Singular	Plural
1 presente de indicativo		8 perfecto de indicativo	
continúo	continuamos	he continuado	hemos continuado
continúas	continuáis	has continuado	habéis continuado
continúa	continúan	ha continuado	han continuado
2 imperfecto de indicativo		9 pluscuamperfecto de indicativo	
continuaba	continuábamos	había continuado	habíamos continuado
continuabas	continuabais	habías continuado	habíais continuado
continuaba	continuaban	había continuado	habían continuado
3 pretérito		10 pretérito anterior	
continué	continuamos	hube continuado	hubimos continuado
continuaste	continuasteis	hubiste continuado	hubisteis continuado
continuó	continuaron	hubo continuado	hubieron continuado
4 futuro		11 futuro perfecto	
continuaré	continuaremos	habré continuado	habremos continuado
continuarás	continuaréis	habrás continuado	habréis continuado
continuará	continuarán	habrá continuado	habrán continuado
5 potencial simple		12 potencial compuesto	
continuaría	continuaríamos	habría continuado	habríamos continuado
continuarías	continuaríais	habrías continuado	habríais continuado
continuaría	continuarían	habría continuado	habrían continuado
6 presente de subjuntivo		13 perfecto de subjuntivo	
continúe	continuemos	haya continuado	hayamos continuado
continúes	continuéis	hayas continuado	hayáis continuado
continúe	continúen	haya continuado	hayan continuado
7 imperfecto de subjuntivo		14 pluscuamperfecto de subjuntivo	
continuara	continuáramos	hubiera continuado	hubiéramos continuado
continuaras	continuarais	hubieras continuado	hubierais continuado
continuara	continuaran	hubiera continuado	hubieran continuado
OR		OR	
continuase	continuásemos	hubiese continuado	hubiésemos continuado
continusases	continuaseis	hubieses continuado	hubieseis continuado
continuase	continuasen	hubiese continuado	hubiesen continuado

	imperativo	
—		continuemos
continúa; no continúes		continuad; no continuéis
continúe		continúen

Words and expressions related to this verb

la continuación continuation	la descontinuación discontinuation
continuamente continually	continuo, continua continuous
a continuación following, next	la continuidad continuity
descontinuar to discontinue	

Review the principal parts of important Spanish verbs on pages 9 and 10.

The subject pronouns are found on page 93.   **249**

to contribute, to pay taxes   Regular **-ir** verb endings with spelling change: add **y** before **a**, **e**, or **o**

The Seven Simple Tenses		The Seven Compound Tenses	
Singular	Plural	Singular	Plural
1 presente de indicativo		8 perfecto de indicativo	
contribuyo	contribuimos	he contribuido	hemos contribuido
contribuyes	contribuís	has contribuido	habéis contribuido
contribuye	contribuyen	ha contribuido	han contribuido
2 imperfecto de indicativo		9 pluscuamperfecto de indicativo	
contribuía	contribuíamos	había contribuido	habíamos contribuido
contribuías	contribuíais	habías contribuido	habíais contribuido
contribuía	contribuían	había contribuido	habían contribuido
3 pretérito		10 pretérito anterior	
contribuí	contribuimos	hube contribuido	hubimos contribuido
contribuiste	contribuisteis	hubiste contribuido	hubisteis contribuido
contribuyó	contribuyeron	hubo contribuido	hubieron contribuido
4 futuro		11 futuro perfecto	
contribuiré	contribuiremos	habré contribuido	habremos contribuido
contribuirás	contribuiréis	habrás contribuido	habréis contribuido
contribuirá	contribuirán	habrá contribuido	habrán contribuido
5 potencial simple		12 potencial compuesto	
contribuiría	contribuiríamos	habría contribuido	habríamos contribuido
contribuirías	contribuiríais	habrías contribuido	habríais contribuido
contribuiría	contribuirían	habría contribuido	habrían contribuido
6 presente de subjuntivo		13 perfecto de subjuntivo	
contribuya	contribuyamos	haya contribuido	hayamos contribuido
contribuyas	contribuyáis	hayas contribuido	hayáis contribuido
contribuya	contribuyan	haya contribuido	hayan contribuido
7 imperfecto de subjuntivo		14 pluscuamperfecto de subjuntivo	
contribuyera	contribuyéramos	hubiera contribuido	hubiéramos contribuido
contribuyeras	contribuyerais	hubieras contribuido	hubierais contribuido
contribuyera	contribuyeran	hubiera contribuido	hubieran contribuido
OR		OR	
contribuyese	contribuyésemos	hubiese contribuido	hubiésemos contribuido
contribuyeses	contribuyeseis	hubieses contribuido	hubieseis contribuido
contribuyese	contribuyesen	hubiese contribuido	hubiesen contribuido

	imperativo	
—		contribuyamos
contribuye; no contribuyas		contribuid; no contribuyáis
contribuya		contribuyan

Words related to this verb

contribuidor, contribuidora   contributor
la contribución   contribution tax
contributario, contribuyente   taxpayer

la contribución directa   direct tax
la contribución de guerra   war tax (levy)

> If you want to see a sample English verb fully conjugated in all the tenses, check out pages 11 and 12.

Regular **-er** verb endings with spelling
change: **c** becomes **z** before **a** or **o**

to convince

The Seven Simple Tenses		The Seven Compound Tenses	
Singular	Plural	Singular	Plural
1 presente de indicativo		8 perfecto de indicativo	
convenzo	**convencemos**	**he convencido**	**hemos convencido**
convences	**convencéis**	**has convencido**	**habéis convencido**
convence	**convencen**	**ha convencido**	**han convencido**
2 imperfecto de indicativo		9 pluscuamperfecto de indicativo	
convencía	**convencíamos**	**había convencido**	**habíamos convencido**
convencías	**convencíais**	**habías convencido**	**habíais convencido**
convencía	**convencían**	**había convencido**	**habían convencido**
3 pretérito		10 pretérito anterior	
convencí	**convencimos**	**hube convencido**	**hubimos convencido**
convenciste	**convencisteis**	**hubiste convencido**	**hubisteis convencido**
convenció	**convencieron**	**hubo convencido**	**hubieron convencido**
4 futuro		11 futuro perfecto	
convenceré	**convenceremos**	**habré convencido**	**habremos convencido**
convencerás	**convenceréis**	**habrás convencido**	**habréis convencido**
convencerá	**convencerán**	**habrá convencido**	**habrán convencido**
5 potencial simple		12 potencial compuesto	
convencería	**convenceríamos**	**habría convencido**	**habríamos convencido**
convencerías	**convenceríais**	**habrías convencido**	**habríais convencido**
convencería	**convencerían**	**habría convencido**	**habrían convencido**
6 presente de subjuntivo		13 perfecto de subjuntivo	
convenza	**convenzamos**	**haya convencido**	**hayamos convencido**
convenzas	**convenzáis**	**hayas convencido**	**hayáis convencido**
convenza	**convenzan**	**haya convencido**	**hayan convencido**
7 imperfecto de subjuntivo		14 pluscuamperfecto de subjuntivo	
convenciera	**convenciéramos**	**hubiera convencido**	**hubiéramos convencido**
convencieras	**convencierais**	**hubieras convencido**	**hubierais convencido**
convenciera	**convencieran**	**hubiera convencido**	**hubieran convencido**
OR		OR	
convenciese	**convenciésemos**	**hubiese convencido**	**hubiésemos convencido**
convencieses	**convencieseis**	**hubieses convencido**	**hubieseis convencido**
convenciese	**convenciesen**	**hubiese convencido**	**hubiesen convencido**

imperativo	
—	**convenzamos**
convence; no convenzas	**convenced; no convenzáis**
convenza	**convenzan**

Words related to this verb

el convencimiento   conviction
convencido, convencida   convinced

convencible   convincible
convencedor, convencedora   convincing

For other words and expressions related to this verb, see **vencer.**

If you want an explanation of meanings and uses of
Spanish and English verb tenses and moods, see pages 13–32.

to agree, to convene, to be fitting　　　　　Irregular verb

The Seven Simple Tenses		The Seven Compound Tenses	
Singular	Plural	Singular	Plural
1　presente de indicativo		8　perfecto de indicativo	
convengo	convenimos	he convenido	hemos convenido
convienes	convenís	has convenido	habéis convenido
conviene	convienen	ha convenido	han convenido
2　imperfecto de indicativo		9　pluscuamperfecto de indicativo	
convenía	conveníamos	había convenido	habíamos convenido
convenías	conveníais	habías convenido	habíais convenido
convenía	convenían	había convenido	habían convenido
3　pretérito		10　pretérito anterior	
convine	convinimos	hube convenido	hubimos convenido
conviniste	convinisteis	hubiste convenido	hubisteis convenido
convino	convinieron	hubo convenido	hubieron convenido
4　futuro		11　futuro perfecto	
convendré	convendremos	habré convenido	habremos convenido
convendrás	convendréis	habrás convenido	habréis convenido
convendrá	convendrán	habrá convenido	habrán convenido
5　potencial simple		12　potencial compuesto	
convendría	convendríamos	habría convenido	habríamos convenido
convendrías	convendríais	habrías convenido	habríais convenido
convendría	convendrían	habría convenido	habrían convenido
6　presente de subjuntivo		13　perfecto de subjuntivo	
convenga	convengamos	haya convenido	hayamos convenido
convengas	convengáis	hayas convenido	hayáis convenido
convenga	convengan	haya convenido	hayan convenido
7　imperfecto de subjuntivo		14　pluscuamperfecto de subjuntivo	
conviniera	conviniéramos	hubiera convenido	hubiéramos convenido
convinieras	convinierais	hubieras convenido	hubierais convenido
conviniera	convinieran	hubiera convenido	hubieran convenido
OR		OR	
conviniese	conviniésemos	hubiese convenido	hubiésemos convenido
convinieses	convinieseis	hubieses convenido	hubieseis convenido
conviniese	conviniesen	hubiese convenido	hubiesen convenido

	imperativo	
—	convengamos
conven; no convengas	convenid; no convengáis
convenga	convengan

Words and expressions related to this verb

convenir + inf.　to be important + inf.　　　el convenio　agreement
convenir en + inf.　to agree + inf.　　　　conveniente　convenient
convenido, convenida　agreed　　　　　la convención　convention

For other words and expressions related to this verb, see **venir**.

Can't recognize an irregular verb form? Check out pages 678–681.

Regular **-ir** verb endings with stem change: to convert
Tenses 1, 3, 6, 7, Imperative, Gerundio

The Seven Simple Tenses		The Seven Compound Tenses	
Singular	Plural	Singular	Plural
1 presente de indicativo		8 perfecto de indicativo	
convierto	**convertimos**	**he convertido**	**hemos convertido**
conviertes	**convertís**	**has convertido**	**habéis convertido**
convierte	**convierten**	**ha convertido**	**han convertido**
2 imperfecto de indicativo		9 pluscuamperfecto de indicativo	
convertía	**convertíamos**	**había convertido**	**habíamos convertido**
convertías	**convertíais**	**habías convertido**	**habíais convertido**
convertía	**convertían**	**había convertido**	**habían convertido**
3 pretérito		10 pretérito anterior	
convertí	**convertimos**	**hube convertido**	**hubimos convertido**
convertiste	**convertisteis**	**hubiste convertido**	**hubisteis convertido**
convirtió	**convirtieron**	**hubo convertido**	**hubieron convertido**
4 futuro		11 futuro perfecto	
convertiré	**convertiremos**	**habré convertido**	**habremos convertido**
convertirás	**convertiréis**	**habrás convertido**	**habréis convertido**
convertirá	**convertirán**	**habrá convertido**	**habrán convertido**
5 potencial simple		12 potencial compuesto	
convertiría	**convertiríamos**	**habría convertido**	**habríamos convertido**
convertirías	**convertiríais**	**habrías convertido**	**habríais convertido**
convertiría	**convertirían**	**habría convertido**	**habrían convertido**
6 presente de subjuntivo		13 perfecto de subjuntivo	
convierta	**convirtamos**	**haya convertido**	**hayamos convertido**
conviertas	**convirtáis**	**hayas convertido**	**hayáis convertido**
convierta	**conviertan**	**haya convertido**	**hayan convertido**
7 imperfecto de subjuntivo		14 pluscuamperfecto de subjuntivo	
convirtiera	**convirtiéramos**	**hubiera convertido**	**hubiéramos convertido**
convirtieras	**convirtierais**	**hubieras convertido**	**hubierais convertido**
convirtiera	**convirtieran**	**hubiera convertido**	**hubieran convertido**
OR		OR	
convirtiese	**convirtiésemos**	**hubiese convertido**	**hubiésemos convertido**
convirtieses	**convirtieseis**	**hubieses convertido**	**hubieseis convertido**
convirtiese	**convirtiesen**	**hubiese convertido**	**hubiesen convertido**

imperativo	
—	**convirtamos**
convierte; no conviertas	**convertid; no convirtáis**
convierta	**conviertan**

Words and expressions related to this verb

convertir en dinero   to convert into cash
convertido, convertida   converted, changed
convertir el agua en vino   to turn water
   into wine

la conversión   conversion
convertible   convertible
convertirse   to convert (oneself), to be
   converted, to change religion

Can't find the verb you're looking for?
Check the back pages of this book for a list of over 2,100 additional verbs!

The subject pronouns are found on page 93.

to call together, to convene, to convoke, to summon

Regular **-ar** verb endings with spelling change: **c** becomes **qu** before **e**

The Seven Simple Tenses		The Seven Compound Tenses	
Singular	Plural	Singular	Plural
1 presente de indicativo		**8 perfecto de indicativo**	
convoco	convocamos	he convocado	hemos convocado
convocas	convocáis	has convocado	habéis convocado
convoca	convocan	ha convocado	han convocado
2 imperfecto de indicativo		**9 pluscuamperfecto de indicativo**	
convocaba	convocábamos	había convocado	habíamos convocado
convocabas	convocabais	habías convocado	habíais convocado
convocaba	convocaban	había convocado	habían convocado
3 pretérito		**10 pretérito anterior**	
convoqué	convocamos	hube convocado	hubimos convocado
convocaste	convocasteis	hubiste convocado	hubisteis convocado
convocó	convocaron	hubo convocado	hubieron convocado
4 futuro		**11 futuro perfecto**	
convocaré	convocaremos	habré convocado	habremos convocado
convocarás	convocaréis	habrás convocado	habréis convocado
convocará	convocarán	habrá convocado	habrán convocado
5 potencial simple		**12 potencial compuesto**	
convocaría	convocaríamos	habría convocado	habríamos convocado
convcoarías	convocaríais	habrías convocado	habríais convocado
convocaría	convocarían	habría convocado	habrían convocado
6 presente de subjuntivo		**13 perfecto de subjuntivo**	
convoque	convoquemos	haya convocado	hayamos convocado
convoques	convoquéis	hayas convocado	hayáis convocado
convoque	convoquen	haya convocado	hayan convocado
7 imperfecto de subjuntivo		**14 pluscuamperfecto de subjuntivo**	
convocara	convocáramos	hubiera convocado	hubiéramos convocado
convocaras	convocarais	hubieras convocado	hubierais convocado
convocara	convocaran	hubiera convocado	hubieran convocado
OR		OR	
convocase	convocásemos	hubiese convocado	hubiésemos convocado
convocases	convocaseis	hubieses convocado	hubieseis convocado
convocase	convocasen	hubiese convocado	hubiesen convocado

imperativo

—	**convoquemos**
convoca; no convoques	**convocad; no convoquéis**
convoque	**convoquen**

Words and expressions related to this verb

la **convocación**   convocation
la **vocación**   vocation, calling
el **vocabulario**   vocabulary

un **vocablo**   word, expression, term
jugar del vocablo   to pun, to make a pun
la **convocatoria**   convocation, calling together

Don't forget to study the section on defective and impersonal verbs. It's right after this main list.

Regular **-ir** verb endings with stem change: to correct
Tenses 1, 3, 6, 7, Imperative, Gerundio

The Seven Simple Tenses		The Seven Compound Tenses	
Singular	Plural	Singular	Plural
1 presente de indicativo		**8 perfecto de indicativo**	
corrijo	corregimos	he corregido	hemos corregido
corriges	corregís	has corregido	habéis corregido
corrige	corrigen	ha corregido	han corregido
2 imperfecto de indicativo		**9 pluscuamperfecto de indicativo**	
corregía	corregíamos	había corregido	habíamos corregido
corregías	corregíais	habías corregido	habíais corregido
corregía	corregían	había corregido	habían corregido
3 pretérito		**10 pretérito anterior**	
corregí	corregimos	hube corregido	hubimos corregido
corregiste	corregisteis	hubiste corregido	hubisteis corregido
corrigió	corrigieron	hubo corregido	hubieron corregido
4 futuro		**11 futuro perfecto**	
corregiré	corregiremos	habré corregido	habremos corregido
corregirás	corregiréis	habrás corregido	habréis corregido
corregirá	corregirán	habrá corregido	habrán corregido
5 potencial simple		**12 potencial compuesto**	
corregiría	corregiríamos	habría corregido	habríamos corregido
corregirías	corregiríais	habrías corregido	habríais corregido
corregiría	corregirían	habría corregido	habrían corregido
6 presente de subjuntivo		**13 perfecto de subjuntivo**	
corrija	corrijamos	haya corregido	hayamos corregido
corrijas	corrijáis	hayas corregido	hayáis corregido
corrija	corrijan	haya corregido	hayan corregido
7 imperfecto de subjuntivo		**14 pluscuamperfecto de subjuntivo**	
corrigiera	corrigiéramos	hubiera corregido	hubiéramos corregido
corrigieras	corrigierais	hubieras corregido	hubierais corregido
corrigiera	corrigieran	hubiera corregido	hubieran corregido
OR		OR	
corrigiese	corrigiésemos	hubiese corregido	hubiésemos corregido
corrigieses	corrigieseis	hubieses corregido	hubieseis corregido
corrigiese	corrigiesen	hubiese corregido	hubiesen corregido

	imperativo	
—		corrijamos
corrige; no corrijas		corregid; no corrijáis
corrija		corrijan

Words and expressions related to this verb

corregir pruebas to read proofs	**correcto, correcta** correct
corregible corrigible	**correctamente** correctly
incorregible incorrigible	**correccional** correctional
la corrección correction	**el correccional** reformatory

Can't recognize an irregular verb form? Check out pages 678–681.

The subject pronouns are found on page 93.

to run, to race, to flow   Regular **-er** verb

The Seven Simple Tenses		The Seven Compound Tenses	
Singular	Plural	Singular	Plural
1 presente de indicativo		8 perfecto de indicativo	
corro	corremos	he corrido	hemos corrido
corres	corréis	has corrido	habéis corrido
corre	corren	ha corrido	han corrido
2 imperfecto de indicativo		9 pluscuamperfecto de indicativo	
corría	corríamos	había corrido	habíamos corrido
corrías	corríais	habías corrido	habíais corrido
corría	corrían	había corrido	habían corrido
3 pretérito		10 pretérito anterior	
corrí	corrimos	hube corrido	hubimos corrido
corriste	corristeis	hubiste corrido	hubisteis corrido
corrió	corrieron	hubo corrido	hubieron corrido
4 futuro		11 futuro perfecto	
correré	correremos	habré corrido	habremos corrido
correrás	correréis	habrás corrido	habréis corrido
correrá	correrán	habrá corrido	habrán corrido
5 potencial simple		12 potencial compuesto	
correría	correríamos	habría corrido	habríamos corrido
correrías	correríais	habrías corrido	habríais corrido
correría	correrían	habría corrido	habrían corrido
6 presente de subjuntivo		13 perfecto de subjuntivo	
corra	corramos	haya corrido	hayamos corrido
corras	corráis	hayas corrido	hayáis corrido
corra	corran	haya corrido	hayan corrido
7 imperfecto de subjuntivo		14 pluscuamperfecto de subjuntivo	
corriera	corriéramos	hubiera corrido	hubiéramos corrido
corrieras	corrierais	hubieras corrido	hubierais corrido
corriera	corrieran	hubiera corrido	hubieran corrido
OR		OR	
corriese	corriésemos	hubiese corrido	hubiésemos corrido
corrieses	corrieseis	hubieses corrido	hubieseis corrido
corriese	corriesen	hubiese corrido	hubiesen corrido

	imperativo	
—		corramos
corre; no corras		corred; no corráis
corra		corran

Words and expressions related to this verb

el correo   mail, post
correo aéreo   air mail
echar una carta al correo   to mail (post) a letter
la corrida   race
de corrida   at full speed

descorrer   to flow (liquids); to draw a curtain or drape
por correo aparte   under separate cover (mail)
recorrer   to travel on, to go over

The Seven Simple Tenses		The Seven Compound Tenses	
Singular	Plural	Singular	Plural
1 presente de indicativo		8 perfecto de indicativo	
corto	cortamos	he cortado	hemos cortado
cortas	cortáis	has cortado	habéis cortado
corta	cortan	ha cortado	han cortado
2 imperfecto de indicativo		9 pluscuamperfecto de indicativo	
cortaba	cortábamos	había cortado	habíamos cortado
cortabas	cortabais	habías cortado	habíais cortado
cortaba	cortaban	había cortado	habían cortado
3 pretérito		10 pretérito anterior	
corté	cortamos	hube cortado	hubimos cortado
cortaste	cortasteis	hubiste cortado	hubisteis cortado
cortó	cortaron	hubo cortado	hubieron cortado
4 futuro		11 futuro perfecto	
cortaré	cortaremos	habré cortado	habremos cortado
cortarás	cortaréis	habrás cortado	habréis cortado
cortará	cortarán	habrá cortado	habrán cortado
5 potencial simple		12 potencial compuesto	
cortaría	cortaríamos	habría cortado	habríamos cortado
cortarías	cortaríais	habrías cortado	habríais cortado
cortaría	cortarían	habría cortado	habrían cortado
6 presente de subjuntivo		13 perfecto de subjuntivo	
corte	cortemos	haya cortado	hayamos cortado
cortes	cortéis	hayas cortado	hayáis cortado
corte	corten	haya cortado	hayan cortado
7 imperfecto de subjuntivo		14 pluscuamperfecto de subjuntivo	
cortara	cortáramos	hubiera cortado	hubiéramos cortado
cortaras	cortarais	hubieras cortado	hubierais cortado
cortara	cortaran	hubiera cortado	hubieran cortado
OR		OR	
cortase	cortásemos	hubiese cortado	hubiésemos cortado
cortases	cortaseis	hubieses cortado	hubieseis cortado
cortase	cortasen	hubiese cortado	hubiesen cortado

	imperativo	
—		cortemos
corta; no cortes		cortad; no cortéis
corte		corten

Words and expressions related to this verb
cortar el agua   to cut off the water
cortar las alas a uno   to cut a person down, "to cut off one's wings"
cortar el vino con agua   to dilute wine
corto, corta   short; **corto de oído**   hard of hearing
recortar   to trim, cut off, cut away; **un recorte**   clipping from a newspaper
un corte del pelo   haircut

The subject pronouns are found on page 93.

to create   Regular **-ar** verb

The Seven Simple Tenses		The Seven Compound Tenses	
Singular	Plural	Singular	Plural
1 presente de indicativo		8 perfecto de indicativo	
creo	creamos	he creado	hemos creado
creas	creáis	has creado	habéis creado
crea	crean	ha creado	han creado
2 imperfecto de indicativo		9 pluscuamperfecto de indicativo	
creaba	creábamos	había creado	habíamos creado
creabas	creabais	habías creado	habíais creado
creaba	creaban	había creado	habían creado
3 pretérito		10 pretérito anterior	
creé	creamos	hube creado	hubimos creado
creaste	creasteis	hubiste creado	hubisteis creado
creó	crearon	hubo creado	hubieron creado
4 futuro		11 futuro perfecto	
crearé	crearemos	habré creado	habremos creado
crearás	crearéis	habrás creado	habréis creado
creará	crearán	habrá creado	habrán creado
5 potencial simple		12 potencial compuesto	
crearía	crearíamos	habría creado	habríamos creado
crearías	crearíais	habrías creado	habríais creado
crearía	crearían	habría creado	habrían creado
6 presente de subjuntivo		13 perfecto de subjuntivo	
cree	creemos	haya creado	hayamos creado
crees	creéis	hayas creado	hayáis creado
cree	creen	haya creado	hayan creado
7 imperfecto de subjuntivo		14 pluscuamperfecto de subjuntivo	
creara	creáramos	hubiera creado	hubiéramos creado
crearas	crearais	hubieras creado	hubierais creado
creara	crearan	hubiera creado	hubieran creado
OR		OR	
crease	creásemos	hubiese creado	hubiésemos creado
creases	creaseis	hubieses creado	hubieseis creado
crease	creasen	hubiese creado	hubiesen creado

	imperativo
—	creemos
crea; no crees	cread; no creéis
cree	creen

Words and expressions related to this verb
la creación   creation
creador, creadora   creative
creativo, creativa   creative
la creatividad   creativeness, creativity

la facultad creadora   creativity
recrear   to recreate, entertain
la recreación   recreation

Do you need more drills? Have fun with the *501 Spanish Verbs* CD-ROM!

Regular **-er** verb endings with spelling   to grow
change: **c** becomes **zc** before **a** or **o**

The Seven Simple Tenses		The Seven Compound Tenses	
Singular	Plural	Singular	Plural
1 presente de indicativo		8 perfecto de indicativo	
crezco	**crecemos**	**he crecido**	**hemos crecido**
creces	**crecéis**	**has crecido**	**habéis crecido**
crece	**crecen**	**ha crecido**	**han crecido**
2 imperfecto de indicativo		9 pluscuamperfecto de indicativo	
crecía	**crecíamos**	**había crecido**	**habíamos crecido**
crecías	**crecíais**	**habías crecido**	**habíais crecido**
crecía	**crecían**	**había crecido**	**habían crecido**
3 pretérito		10 pretérito anterior	
crecí	**crecimos**	**hube crecido**	**hubimos crecido**
creciste	**crecisteis**	**hubiste crecido**	**hubisteis crecido**
creció	**crecieron**	**hubo crecido**	**hubieron crecido**
4 futuro		11 futuro perfecto	
creceré	**creceremos**	**habré crecido**	**habremos crecido**
crecerás	**creceréis**	**habrás crecido**	**habréis crecido**
crecerá	**crecerán**	**habrá crecido**	**habrán crecido**
5 potencial simple		12 potencial compuesto	
crecería	**creceríamos**	**habría crecido**	**habríamos crecido**
crecerías	**creceríais**	**habrías crecido**	**habríais crecido**
crecería	**crecerían**	**habría crecido**	**habrían crecido**
6 presente de subjuntivo		13 perfecto de subjuntivo	
crezca	**crezcamos**	**haya crecido**	**hayamos crecido**
crezcas	**crezcáis**	**hayas crecido**	**hayáis crecido**
crezca	**crezcan**	**haya crecido**	**hayan crecido**
7 imperfecto de subjuntivo		14 pluscuamperfecto de subjuntivo	
creciera	**creciéramos**	**hubiera crecido**	**hubiéramos crecido**
crecieras	**crecierais**	**hubieras crecido**	**hubierais crecido**
creciera	**crecieran**	**hubiera crecido**	**hubieran crecido**
OR		OR	
creciese	**creciésemos**	**hubiese crecido**	**hubiésemos crecido**
crecieses	**crecieseis**	**hubieses crecido**	**hubieseis crecido**
creciese	**creciesen**	**hubiese crecido**	**hubiesen crecido**

imperativo	
—	**crezcamos**
crece; no crezcas	**creced; no crezcáis**
crezca	**crezcan**

Words and expressions related to this verb

crecer como la mala hierba   to grow like a weed   **la luna creciente**   crescent moon
crecidamente   abundantly   **el crecimiento**   growth
el crescendo   crescendo (music)   **la crecida**   swelling of a river
     creciente   growing, increasing

Don't miss the definitions of basic grammatical terms
with examples in English and Spanish on pages 33–44.

The subject pronouns are found on page 93.
     259

to believe | Regular **-er** verb endings with spelling change: **i** becomes **y** in Tense 3 (3rd person) and Tense 7 (all)

The Seven Simple Tenses	The Seven Compound Tenses

Singular	Plural	Singular	Plural
1 presente de indicativo		8 perfecto de indicativo	
creo	creemos	he creído	hemos creído
crees	creéis	has creído	habéis creído
cree	creen	ha creído	han creído
2 imperfecto de indicativo		9 pluscuamperfecto de indicativo	
creía	creíamos	había creído	habíamos creído
creías	creíais	habías creído	habíais creído
creía	creían	había creído	habían creído
3 pretérito		10 pretérito anterior	
creí	creímos	hube creído	hubimos creído
creíste	creísteis	hubiste creído	hubisteis creído
creyó	creyeron	hubo creído	hubieron creído
4 futuro		11 futuro perfecto	
creeré	creeremos	habré creído	habremos creído
creerás	creeréis	habrás creído	habréis creído
creerá	creerán	habrá creído	habrán creído
5 potencial simple		12 potencial compuesto	
creería	creeríamos	habría creído	habríamos creído
creería	creeríais	habrías creído	habríais creído
creería	creerían	habría creído	habrían creído
6 presente de subjuntivo		13 perfecto de subjuntivo	
crea	creamos	haya creído	hayamos creído
creas	creáis	hayas creído	hayáis creído
crea	crean	haya creído	hayan creído
7 imperfecto de subjuntivo		14 pluscuamperfecto de subjuntivo	
creyera	creyéramos	hubiera creído	hubiéramos creído
creyeras	creyerais	hubieras creído	hubierais creído
creyera	creyeran	hubiera creído	hubieran creído
OR		OR	
creyese	creyésemos	hubiese creído	hubiésemos creído
creyeses	creyeseis	hubieses creído	hubieseis creído
creyese	creyesen	hubiese creído	hubiesen creído

imperativo

—	creamos
cree; no creas	creed; no creáis
crea	crean

AN ESSENTIAL 55 VERB

C

We believe that **creer** is a useful verb for you to learn because it has an important stem change in Tenses 3 and 7. This verb is helpful in a great number of everyday expressions and situations.

Sentences using creer and related words

Hasta que no lo veas, no lo creas.
Don't believe it until you see it.

Ver es creer.
Seeing is believing.

¡Ya lo creo!
Of course!

Creo que sí.
I think so.

Creo que no.
I don't think so.

No me lo creo.
I can't believe it.

Words and expressions related to this verb

crédulo, crédula **credulous, gullible**

la credulidad **credulity**

tener buenas creederas **to be credulous, very gullible**

crédulamente **credulously**

el credo **creed**

dar crédito **to believe**

descreer **to disbelieve**

incrédulo, incrédula **incredulous**

la incredulidad **incredulity, unbelief, disbelief**

increíble **incredible**

creíble **believable**

Can't remember the Spanish verb you need?
Check the back pages of this book for the English-Spanish verb index!

to breed, to raise, to bring up (rear)	Regular **-ar** verb endings with spelling change: **i** becomes **í** on stressed syllable (see Tenses 1, 6, Imperative)

The Seven Simple Tenses		The Seven Compound Tenses	
Singular	Plural	Singular	Plural
1 presente de indicativo		**8 perfecto de indicativo**	
crío	criamos	he criado	hemos criado
crías	criáis	has criado	habéis criado
cría	crían	ha criado	han criado
2 imperfecto de indicativo		**9 pluscuamperfecto de indicativo**	
criaba	criábamos	había criado	habíamos criado
criabas	criabais	habías criado	habíais criado
criaba	criaban	había criado	habían criado
3 pretérito		**10 pretérito anterior**	
crié	criamos	hube criado	hubimos criado
criaste	criasteis	hubiste criado	hubisteis criado
crió	criaron	hubo criado	hubieron criado
4 futuro		**11 futuro perfecto**	
criaré	criaremos	habré criado	habremos criado
criarás	criaréis	habrás criado	habréis criado
criará	criarán	habrá criado	habrán criado
5 potencial simple		**12 potencial compuesto**	
criaría	criaríamos	habría criado	habríamos criado
criarías	criaríais	habrías criado	habríais criado
criaría	criarían	habría criado	habrían criado
6 presente de subjuntivo		**13 perfecto de subjuntivo**	
críe	criemos	haya criado	hayamos criado
críes	criéis	hayas criado	hayáis criado
críe	críen	haya criado	hayan criado
7 imperfecto de subjuntivo		**14 pluscuamperfecto de subjuntivo**	
criara	criáramos	hubiera criado	hubiéramos criado
criaras	criarais	hubieras criado	hubierais criado
criara	criaran	hubiera criado	hubieran criado
OR		OR	
criase	criásemos	hubiese criado	hubiésemos criado
criases	criaseis	hubieses criado	hubieseis criado
criase	criasen	hubiese criado	hubiesen criado

imperativo	
—	criemos
cría; no críes	criad; no criéis
críe	críen

Words and expressions related to this verb

la criandera, la criadora   wet nurse
el criado, la criada   servant
la crianza   nursing
dar crianza   to educate, to bring up

mal crianza   bad manners, impoliteness
Dios los cría y ellos se juntan   Birds of a feather flock together.

Don't forget to study the section on defective and impersonal verbs. It's right after this main list.

Regular **-ar** verb endings with spelling change: to cross
z becomes **c** before **e**

The Seven Simple Tenses		The Seven Compound Tenses	
Singular	Plural	Singular	Plural
1 presente de indicativo		8 perfecto de indicativo	
cruzo	**cruzamos**	**he cruzado**	**hemos cruzado**
cruzas	**cruzáis**	**has cruzado**	**habéis cruzado**
cruza	**cruzan**	**ha cruzado**	**han cruzado**
2 imperfecto de indicativo		9 pluscuamperfecto de indicativo	
cruzaba	**cruzábamos**	**había cruzado**	**habíamos cruzado**
cruzabas	**cruzabais**	**habías cruzado**	**habíais cruzado**
cruzaba	**cruzaban**	**había cruzado**	**habían cruzado**
3 pretérito		10 pretérito anterior	
crucé	**cruzamos**	**hube cruzado**	**hubimos cruzado**
cruzaste	**cruzasteis**	**hubiste cruzado**	**hubisteis cruzado**
cruzó	**cruzaron**	**hubo cruzado**	**hubieron cruzado**
4 futuro		11 futuro perfecto	
cruzaré	**cruzaremos**	**habré cruzado**	**habremos cruzado**
cruzarás	**cruzaréis**	**habrás cruzado**	**habréis cruzado**
cruzará	**cruzarán**	**habrá cruzado**	**habrán cruzado**
5 potencial simple		12 potencial compuesto	
cruzaría	**cruzaríamos**	**habría cruzado**	**habríamos cruzado**
cruzarías	**cruzaríais**	**habrías cruzado**	**habríais cruzado**
cruzaría	**cruzarían**	**habría cruzado**	**habrían cruzado**
6 presente de subjuntivo		13 perfecto de subjuntivo	
cruce	**crucemos**	**haya cruzado**	**hayamos cruzado**
cruces	**crucéis**	**hayas cruzado**	**hayáis cruzado**
cruce	**crucen**	**haya cruzado**	**hayan cruzado**
7 imperfecto de subjuntivo		14 pluscuamperfecto de subjuntivo	
cruzara	**cruzáramos**	**hubiera cruzado**	**hubiéramos cruzado**
cruzaras	**cruzarais**	**hubieras cruzado**	**hubierais cruzado**
cruzara	**cruzaran**	**hubiera cruzado**	**hubieran cruzado**
OR		OR	
cruzase	**cruzásemos**	**hubiese cruzado**	**hubiésemos cruzado**
cruzases	**cruzaseis**	**hubieses cruzado**	**hubieseis cruzado**
cruzase	**cruzasen**	**hubiese cruzado**	**hubiesen cruzado**

imperativo

—	**crucemos**
cruza; no cruces	**cruzad; no crucéis**
cruce	**crucen**

Sentences using this verb and words related to it
El que no se aventura no cruza el mar.   Nothing ventured, nothing gained.

el cruzamiento   crossing   **la cruz**   cross
la cruzada   crusade, crossroads   **la Cruz de Malta**   Maltese Cross

Can't find the verb you're looking for?
Check the back pages of this book for a list of over 2,100 additional verbs!

The subject pronouns are found on page 93.

to cover   Regular **-ir** verb endings; note irregular spelling of past participle: **cubierto**

The Seven Simple Tenses		The Seven Compound Tenses	
Singular	Plural	Singular	Plural
1 presente de indicativo		8 perfecto de indicativo	
cubro	**cubrimos**	**he cubierto**	**hemos cubierto**
cubres	**cubrís**	**has cubierto**	**habéis cubierto**
cubre	**cubren**	**ha cubierto**	**han cubierto**
2 imperfecto de indicativo		9 pluscuamperfecto de indicativo	
cubría	**cubríamos**	**había cubierto**	**habíamos cubierto**
cubrías	**cubríais**	**habías cubierto**	**habíais cubierto**
cubría	**cubrían**	**había cubierto**	**habían cubierto**
3 pretérito		10 pretérito anterior	
cubrí	**cubrimos**	**hube cubierto**	**hubimos cubierto**
cubriste	**cubristeis**	**hubiste cubierto**	**hubisteis cubierto**
cubrió	**cubrieron**	**hubo cubierto**	**hubieron cubierto**
4 futuro		11 futuro perfecto	
cubriré	**cubriremos**	**habré cubierto**	**habremos cubierto**
cubrirás	**cubriréis**	**habrás cubierto**	**habréis cubierto**
cubrirá	**cubrirán**	**habrá cubierto**	**habrán cubierto**
5 potencial simple		12 potencial compuesto	
cubriría	**cubriríamos**	**habría cubierto**	**habríamos cubierto**
cubrirías	**cubriríais**	**habrías cubierto**	**habríais cubierto**
cubriría	**cubrirían**	**habría cubierto**	**habrían cubierto**
6 presente de subjuntivo		13 perfecto de subjuntivo	
cubra	**cubramos**	**haya cubierto**	**hayamos cubierto**
cubras	**cubráis**	**hayas cubierto**	**hayáis cubierto**
cubra	**cubran**	**haya cubierto**	**hayan cubierto**
7 imperfecto de subjuntivo		14 pluscuamperfecto de subjuntivo	
cubriera	**cubriéramos**	**hubiera cubierto**	**hubiéramos cubierto**
cubrieras	**cubrierais**	**hubieras cubierto**	**hubierais cubierto**
cubriera	**cubrieran**	**hubiera cubierto**	**hubieran cubierto**
OR		OR	
cubriese	**cubriésemos**	**hubiese cubierto**	**hubiésemos cubierto**
cubrieses	**cubrieseis**	**hubieses cubierto**	**hubieseis cubierto**
cubriese	**cubriesen**	**hubiese cubierto**	**hubiesen cubierto**

imperativo

—	**cubramos**
cubre; no cubras	**cubrid; no cubráis**
cubra	**cubran**

Words and expressions related to this verb

la **cubierta**   cover, wrapping
la **cubierta del motor**   hood of an automobile
el **cubrimiento**   covering
el **cubierto**   place setting (meal)
cubrir los gastos   to cover expenses
cubiertamente   covertly

encubrir   to hide, to conceal, to mask
el **encubrimiento**   hiding, concealment
descubrir   to discover
bajo cubierto   under cover
a cubierto de   under cover of
el **cielo está cubierto**   the sky is overcast

Get your feet wet with verbs used in weather expressions on page 668.

Reflexive regular **-ar** verb   to take care of oneself

The Seven Simple Tenses		The Seven Compound Tenses	
Singular	Plural	Singular	Plural
1 presente de indicativo		8 perfecto de indicativo	
me cuido	nos cuidamos	me he cuidado	nos hemos cuidado
te cuidas	os cuidáis	te has cuidado	os habéis cuidado
se cuida	se cuidan	se ha cuidado	se han cuidado
2 imperfecto de indicativo		9 pluscuamperfecto de indicativo	
me cuidaba	nos cuidábamos	me había cuidado	nos habíamos cuidado
te cuidabas	os cuidabais	te habías cuidado	os habíais cuidado
se cuidaba	se cuidaban	se había cuidado	se habían cuidado
3 pretérito		10 pretérito anterior	
me cuidé	nos cuidamos	me hube cuidado	nos hubimos cuidado
te cuidaste	os cuidasteis	te hubiste cuidado	os hubisteis cuidado
se cuidó	se cuidaron	se hubo cuidado	se hubieron cuidado
4 futuro		11 futuro perfecto	
me cuidaré	nos cuidaremos	me habré cuidado	nos habremos cuidado
te cuidarás	os cuidaréis	te habrás cuidado	os habréis cuidado
se cuidará	se cuidarán	se habrá cuidado	se habrán cuidado
5 potencial simple		12 potencial compuesto	
me cuidaría	nos cuidaríamos	me habría cuidado	nos habríamos cuidado
te cuidarías	os cuidaríais	te habrías cuidado	os habríais cuidado
se cuidaría	se cuidarían	se habría cuidado	se habrían cuidado
6 presente de subjuntivo		13 perfecto de subjuntivo	
me cuide	nos cuidemos	me haya cuidado	nos hayamos cuidado
te cuides	os cuidéis	te hayas cuidado	os hayáis cuidado
se cuide	se cuiden	se haya cuidado	se hayan cuidado
7 imperfecto de subjuntivo		14 pluscuamperfecto de subjuntivo	
me cuidara	nos cuidáramos	me hubiera cuidado	nos hubiéramos cuidado
te cuidaras	os cuidarais	te hubieras cuidado	os hubierais cuidado
se cuidara	se cuidaran	se hubiera cuidado	se hubieran cuidado
OR		OR	
me cuidase	nos cuidásemos	me hubiese cuidado	nos hubiésemos cuidado
te cuidases	os cuidaseis	te hubieses cuidado	os hubieseis cuidado
se cuidase	se cuidasen	se hubiese cuidado	se hubiesen cuidado

imperativo	
—	cuidémonos
cuídate; no te cuides	cuidaos; no os cuidéis
cuídese	cuídense

Words and expressions related to this verb

cuidar de to care for, to look after	**¡Cuidado!** Careful!
cuidarse de to care about, to be careful	**cuidadoso, cuidadosa** careful
el cuidado care, concern	**al cuidado de** under the care of
con cuidado with care	**tener cuidado** to be careful
descuidar to neglect, overlook	**descuidarse de** not to bother about
el descuido negligence, neglect	**descuidarse de + inf.** to neglect + inf.

The subject pronouns are found on page 93.

to fulfill, to keep (a promise), to reach   Regular **-ir** verb
one's birthday (use with **años**)

The Seven Simple Tenses		The Seven Compound Tenses	
Singular	Plural	Singular	Plural
1 presente de indicativo		8 perfecto de indicativo	
cumplo	cumplimos	he cumplido	hemos cumplido
cumples	cumplís	has cumplido	habéis cumplido
cumple	cumplen	ha cumplido	han cumplido
2 imperfecto de indicativo		9 pluscuamperfecto de indicativo	
cumplía	cumplíamos	había cumplido	habíamos cumplido
cumplías	cumplíais	habías cumplido	habíais cumplido
cumplía	cumplían	había cumplido	habían cumplido
3 pretérito		10 pretérito anterior	
cumplí	cumplimos	hube cumplido	hubimos cumplido
cumpliste	cumplisteis	hubiste cumplido	hubisteis cumplido
cumplió	cumplieron	hubo cumplido	hubieron cumplido
4 futuro		11 futuro perfecto	
cumpliré	cumpliremos	habré cumplido	habremos cumplido
cumplirás	cumpliréis	habrás cumplido	habréis cumplido
cumplirá	cumplirán	habrá cumplido	habrán cumplido
5 potencial simple		12 potencial compuesto	
cumpliría	cumpliríamos	habría cumplido	habríamos cumplido
cumplirías	cumpliríais	habrías cumplido	habríais cumplido
cumpliría	cumplirían	habría cumplido	habrían cumplido
6 presente de subjuntivo		13 perfecto de subjuntivo	
cumpla	cumplamos	haya cumplido	hayamos cumplido
cumplas	cumpláis	hayas cumplido	hayáis cumplido
cumpla	cumplan	haya cumplido	hayan cumplido
7 imperfecto de subjuntivo		14 pluscuamperfecto de subjuntivo	
cumpliera	cumpliéramos	hubiera cumplido	hubiéramos cumplido
cumplieras	cumplierais	hubieras cumplido	hubierais cumplido
cumpliera	cumplieran	hubiera cumplido	hubieran cumplido
OR		OR	
cumpliese	cumpliésemos	hubiese cumplido	hubiésemos cumplido
cumplieses	cumplieseis	hubieses cumplido	hubieseis cumplido
cumpliese	cumpliesen	hubiese cumplido	hubiesen cumplido

imperativo

—	cumplamos
cumple; no cumplas	cumplid; no cumpláis
cumpla	cumplan

Words and expressions related to this verb
el **cumpleaños**   birthday
cumplidamente   completely
el **cumplimiento**   completion
cumplir con   to fulfill one's obligations

cumplir . . . años   to reach the age of . . .
Hoy cumplo diez y siete años.   Today is my
     seventeenth birthday.
¡Feliz cumpleaños!   Happy birthday!

Use the guide to Spanish pronunciation on pages 665–667.

Irregular verb   to give

The Seven Simple Tenses		The Seven Compound Tenses	
Singular	Plural	Singular	Plural
1 presente de indicativo		8 perfecto de indicativo	
doy	**damos**	**he dado**	**hemos dado**
das	**dais**	**has dado**	**habéis dado**
da	**dan**	**ha dado**	**han dado**
2 imperfecto de indicativo		9 pluscuamperfecto de indicativo	
daba	**dábamos**	**había dado**	**habíamos dado**
dabas	**dabais**	**habías dado**	**habíais dado**
daba	**daban**	**había dado**	**habían dado**
3 pretérito		10 pretérito anterior	
di	**dimos**	**hube dado**	**hubimos dado**
diste	**disteis**	**hubiste dado**	**hubisteis dado**
dio	**dieron**	**hubo dado**	**hubieron dado**
4 futuro		11 futuro perfecto	
daré	**daremos**	**habré dado**	**habremos dado**
darás	**daréis**	**habrás dado**	**habréis dado**
dará	**darán**	**habrá dado**	**habrán dado**
5 potencial simple		12 potencial compuesto	
daría	**daríamos**	**habría dado**	**habríamos dado**
darías	**daríais**	**habrías dado**	**habríais dado**
daría	**darían**	**habría dado**	**habrían dado**
6 presente de subjuntivo		13 perfecto de subjuntivo	
dé	**demos**	**haya dado**	**hayamos dado**
des	**deis**	**hayas dado**	**hayáis dado**
dé	**den**	**haya dado**	**hayan dado**
7 imperfecto de subjuntivo		14 pluscuamperfecto de subjuntivo	
diera	**diéramos**	**hubiera dado**	**hubiéramos dado**
dieras	**dierais**	**hubieras dado**	**hubierais dado**
diera	**dieran**	**hubiera dado**	**hubieran dado**
OR		OR	
diese	**diésemos**	**hubiese dado**	**hubiésemos dado**
dieses	**dieseis**	**hubieses dado**	**hubieseis dado**
diese	**diesen**	**hubiese dado**	**hubiesen dado**

	imperativo	
—		**demos**
da; no des		**dad; no deis**
dé		**den**

AN ESSENTIAL
55 VERB

AN ESSENTIAL 55 VERB

Dar is useful in a vast number of everyday expressions and situations.

Sentences using dar and related words

El comedor da al jardín.
The dining room faces the garden.

Esta mañana di con dinero en la calle.
This morning, I found money in the street.

Anoche, di con mi amiga Elena en el cine.
Last night, I met my friend Helen at the movies.

El tiempo da buen consejo.
Time will tell.

Dame dineros y no consejos.
Give me money, and not advice.

Me gusta dar de comer a los pájaros en el parque.
I like to feed the birds in the park.

Lo doy por perdido.
I consider it lost.

Me doy por insultado.
I consider myself insulted.

Proverb

A Dios rogando y con el mazo dando.
Put your faith in God and keep your powder dry. (The Lord helps those who help themselves.)

Words and expressions related to this verb

dar a to face
dar cara a to face up to
dar con algo to find something, to come upon something
dar con alguien to meet someone, to run into someone, to come across someone, to find someone
dar cuerda al reloj to wind a watch
dar de beber a to give something to drink to
dar de comer a to feed, to give something to eat to
dar el primer paso to take the first step
dar en to hit against, to strike against
dar en el blanco to hit the target
dar gritos to shout
dar la bienvenida to welcome
dar la hora to strike the hour
dar la mano (las manos) a alguien to shake hands with someone
dar las buenas noches a alguien to say good evening (good night) to someone
dar las gracias a alguien to thank someone
dar los buenos días a alguien to say good morning (hello) to someone
dar por + past part. to consider
dar recuerdos a to give one's regards (best wishes) to
dar un abrazo to embrace
dar un paseo to take a walk
dar un paseo a caballo to go horseback riding
dar un paseo en automóvil to go for a drive
dar una vuelta to go for a short walk
dar voces to shout
darse to give oneself up, to give in
darse cuenta de to realize, to be aware of, to take into account
darse la mano to shake hands with each other
darse por + past part. to consider oneself
darse prisa to hurry

D

The Seven Simple Tenses		The Seven Compound Tenses	
Singular	Plural	Singular	Plural
1 presente de indicativo		8 perfecto de indicativo	
debo	debemos	he debido	hemos debido
debes	debéis	has debido	habéis debido
debe	deben	ha debido	han debido
2 imperfecto de indicativo		9 pluscuamperfecto de indicativo	
debía	debíamos	había debido	habíamos debido
debías	debíais	habías debido	habíais debido
debía	debían	había debido	habían debido
3 pretérito		10 pretérito anterior	
debí	debimos	hube debido	hubimos debido
debiste	debisteis	hubiste debido	hubisteis debido
debió	debieron	hubo debido	hubieron debido
4 futuro		11 futuro perfecto	
deberé	deberemos	habré debido	habremos debido
deberás	deberéis	habrás debido	habréis debido
deberá	deberán	habrá debido	habrán debido
5 potencial simple		12 potencial compuesto	
debería	deberíamos	habría debido	habríamos debido
deberías	deberíais	habrías debido	habríais debido
debería	deberían	habría debido	habrían debido
6 presente de subjuntivo		13 perfecto de subjuntivo	
deba	debamos	haya debido	hayamos debido
debas	debáis	hayas debido	hayáis debido
deba	deban	haya debido	hayan debido
7 imperfecto de subjuntivo		14 pluscuamperfecto de subjuntivo	
debiera	debiéramos	hubiera debido	hubiéramos debido
debieras	debierais	hubieras debido	hubierais debido
debiera	debieran	hubiera debido	hubieran debido
OR		OR	
debiese	debiésemos	hubiese debido	hubiésemos debido
debieses	debieseis	hubieses debido	hubieseis debido
debiese	debiesen	hubiese debido	hubiesen debido

	imperativo	
—	debamos
debe; no debas	debed; no debáis
deba	deban

AN ESSENTIAL 55 VERB

Deber is a verb that you ought to know! It is a regular –er verb that is used in a great number of everyday expressions and situations.

Generally speaking, use deber when you want to express a moral obligation, something you ought to do, but that you may or may not actually do:

Debo estudiar esta noche pero estoy cansado y no me siento bien.
I ought to study tonight, but I am tired and I do not feel well.

In general, **deber de + inf.** is used to express a supposition, something that is probable:

La señora Gómez debe de estar enferma porque sale de casa raramente.
Mrs. Gómez must be sick (is probably sick) because she rarely goes out of the house.

Sentences using deber and related words

José debe de haber llegado.
Joseph must have arrived.

¿Cuánto le debo?
How much do I owe you?

¿En qué estación debo bajar?
At what station do I need to get off?

Note: Generally speaking, use tener que when you want to say that you *have to* do something:

No puedo salir esta noche porque tengo que estudiar.
I cannot go out tonight because I have to study.

See tener.

Words and expressions related to this verb

el deber **duty, obligation**

los deberes **homework**

debido, debida **due**

debido a **due to**

la deuda **debt**

estar en deuda con **to be indebted to**

el deudor, la deudora **debtor**

Regular **-ir** verb   to decide

The Seven Simple Tenses		The Seven Compound Tenses	
Singular	Plural	Singular	Plural
1 presente de indicativo		**8 perfecto de indicativo**	
decido	decidimos	he decidido	hemos decidido
decides	decidís	has decidido	habéis decidido
decide	deciden	ha decidido	han decidido
2 imperfecto de indicativo		**9 pluscuamperfecto de indicativo**	
decidía	decidíamos	había decidido	habíamos decidido
decidías	decidíais	habías decidido	habíais decidido
decidía	decidían	había decidido	habían decidido
3 pretérito		**10 pretérito anterior**	
decidí	decidimos	hube decidido	hubimos decidido
decidiste	decidisteis	hubiste decidido	hubisteis decidido
decidió	decidieron	hubo decidido	hubieron decidido
4 futuro		**11 futuro perfecto**	
decidiré	decidiremos	habré decidido	habremos decidido
decidirás	decidiréis	habrás decidido	habréis decidido
decidirá	decidirán	habrá decidido	habrán decidido
5 potencial simple		**12 potencial compuesto**	
decidiría	decidiríamos	habría decidido	habríamos decidido
decidirías	decidiríais	habrías decidido	habríais decidido
decidiría	decidirían	habría decidido	habrían decidido
6 presente de subjuntivo		**13 perfecto de subjuntivo**	
decida	decidamos	haya decidido	hayamos decidido
decidas	decidáis	hayas decidido	hayáis decidido
decida	decidan	haya decidido	hayan decidido
7 imperfecto de subjuntivo		**14 pluscuamperfecto de subjuntivo**	
decidiera	decidiéramos	hubiera decidido	hubiéramos decidido
decidieras	decidierais	hubieras decidido	hubierais decidido
decidiera	decidieran	hubiera decidido	hubieran decidido
OR		OR	
decidiese	decidiésemos	hubiese decidido	hubiésemos decidido
decidieses	decidieseis	hubieses decidido	hubieseis decidido
decidiese	decidiesen	hubiese decidido	hubiesen decidido

imperativo	
—	decidamos
decide; no decidas	decidid; no decidáis
decida	decidan

Words and expressions related to this verb
la **decisión** decision
decididamente decidedly
decisivamente decisively
decisivo, decisiva decisive

decidir a + inf. to persuade + inf.; to decide + inf.
decidirse to make up one's mind, to be determined
estar decidido (decidida) a + inf.
    to make up one's mind

Can't find the verb you're looking for?
Check the back pages of this book for a list of over 2,100 additional verbs!

The subject pronouns are found on page 93.

to say, to tell   Irregular verb

The Seven Simple Tenses		The Seven Compound Tenses	
Singular	Plural	Singular	Plural
1 presente de indicativo		**8 perfecto de indicativo**	
digo	decimos	he dicho	hemos dicho
dices	decís	has dicho	habéis dicho
dice	dicen	ha dicho	han dicho
2 imperfecto de indicativo		**9 pluscuamperfecto de indicativo**	
decía	decíamos	había dicho	habíamos dicho
decías	decíais	habías dicho	habíais dicho
decía	decían	había dicho	habían dicho
3 pretérito		**10 pretérito anterior**	
dije	dijimos	hube dicho	hubimos dicho
dijiste	dijisteis	hubiste dicho	hubisteis dicho
dijo	dijeron	hubo dicho	hubieron dicho
4 futuro		**11 futuro perfecto**	
diré	diremos	habré dicho	habremos dicho
dirás	diréis	habrás dicho	habréis dicho
dirá	dirán	habrá dicho	habrán dicho
5 potencial simple		**12 potencial compuesto**	
diría	diríamos	habría dicho	habríamos dicho
dirías	diríais	habrías dicho	habríais dicho
diría	dirían	habría dicho	habrían dicho
6 presente de subjuntivo		**13 perfecto de subjuntivo**	
diga	digamos	haya dicho	hayamos dicho
digas	digáis	hayas dicho	hayáis dicho
diga	digan	haya dicho	hayan dicho
7 imperfecto de subjuntivo		**14 pluscuamperfecto de subjuntivo**	
dijera	dijéramos	hubiera dicho	hubiéramos dicho
dijeras	dijerais	hubieras dicho	hubierais dicho
dijera	dijeran	hubiera dicho	hubieran dicho
OR		OR	
dijese	dijésemos	hubiese dicho	hubiésemos dicho
dijeses	dijeseis	hubieses dicho	hubieseis dicho
dijese	dijesen	hubiese dicho	hubiesen dicho

	imperativo	
—		digamos
di; no digas		decid; no digáis
diga		digan

AN ESSENTIAL
55 VERB

Decir is an extremely useful irregular verb. You can use decir in many everyday situations and idiomatic expressions.

Sentences using decir and related words

Dígame, por favor, dónde está la sala de espera.
Tell me, please, where the waiting room is located.

¿Qué quiere decir esta palabra?
What does this word mean?

Words and expressions related to this verb

Dicho y hecho. **No sooner said than done.**

querer decir **to mean**

un decir **a familiar saying**

Diga **or** Dígame **Hello (on the telephone)**

decirle al oído **to whisper in one's ear**

no decir palabra **not to say a word**

Es decir... **That is to say...**

un dicho **a saying, expression**

dictar **to dictate**

el dictado **dictation**

el dictador **dictator**

Proverbs

Dime con quién andas y te diré quién eres.
Tell me who your friends are and I will tell you who you are.

Al decir las verdades se pierdan las amistades.
Friendships are lost when the truth is told.

De decir a hacer hay mucho que ver.
There is a great difference between saying and doing.

Don't forget to study the section on defective and impersonal verbs. It's right after this main list.

The subject pronouns are found on page 93.

declarar (162)
to declare

Gerundio **declarando**   Part. pas. **declarado**

Regular **-ar** verb

The Seven Simple Tenses		The Seven Compound Tenses	
Singular	Plural	Singular	Plural
1 presente de indicativo		8 perfecto de indicativo	
declaro	declaramos	he declarado	hemos declarado
declaras	declaráis	has declarado	habéis declarado
declara	declaran	ha declarado	han declarado
2 imperfecto de indicativo		9 pluscuamperfecto de indicativo	
declaraba	declarábamos	había declarado	habíamos declarado
declarabas	declarabais	habías declarado	habíais declarado
declaraba	declaraban	había declarado	habían declarado
3 pretérito		10 pretérito anterior	
declaré	declaramos	hube declarado	hubimos declarado
declaraste	declarasteis	hubiste declarado	hubisteis declarado
declaró	declararon	hubo declarado	hubieron declarado
4 futuro		11 futuro perfecto	
declararé	declararemos	habré declarado	habremos declarado
declararás	declararéis	habrás declarado	habréis declarado
declarará	declararán	habrá declarado	habrán declarado
5 potencial simple		12 potencial compuesto	
declararía	declararíamos	habría declarado	habríamos declarado
declararías	declararíais	habrías declarado	habríais declarado
declararía	declararían	habría declarado	habrían declarado
6 presente de subjuntivo		13 perfecto de subjuntivo	
declare	declaremos	haya declarado	hayamos declarado
declares	declaréis	hayas declarado	hayáis declarado
declare	declaren	haya declarado	hayan declarado
7 imperfecto de subjuntivo		14 pluscuamperfecto de subjuntivo	
declarara	declaráramos	hubiera declarado	hubiéramos declarado
declararas	declararais	hubieras declarado	hubierais declarado
declarara	declararan	hubiera declarado	hubieran declarado
OR		OR	
declarase	declarásemos	hubiese declarado	hubiésemos declarado
declarases	declaraseis	hubieses declarado	hubieseis declarado
declarase	declarasen	hubiese declarado	hubiesen declarado

imperativo	
—	declaremos
declara; no declares	declarad; no declaréis
declare	declaren

Words related to this verb
una **declaración** declaration
declarado, declarada declared

declarativo, declarativa declarative
una **declamación** declamation, recitation

If you want an explanation of meanings and uses of Spanish and English
verb tenses and moods, see pages 13–32.

Gerundio **dedicándose**   Part. pas. **dedicado**   **dedicarse (163)**

Reflexive verb; regular **-ar** verb endings with
spelling change: **c** becomes **qu** before **e**   to devote oneself

The Seven Simple Tenses | The Seven Compound Tenses

Singular	Plural	Singular	Plural
1 presente de indicativo		8 perfecto de indicativo	
me dedico	**nos dedicamos**	**me he dedicado**	**nos hemos dedicado**
te dedicas	**os dedicáis**	**te has dedicado**	**os habéis dedicado**
se dedica	**se dedican**	**se ha dedicado**	**se han dedicado**
2 imperfecto de indicativo		9 pluscuamperfecto de indicativo	
me dedicaba	**nos dedicábamos**	**me había dedicado**	**nos habíamos dedicado**
te dedicabas	**os dedicabais**	**te habías dedicado**	**os habíais dedicado**
se dedicaba	**se dedicaban**	**se había dedicado**	**se habían dedicado**
3 pretérito		10 pretérito anterior	
me dediqué	**nos dedicamos**	**me hube dedicado**	**nos hubimos dedicado**
te dedicaste	**os dedicasteis**	**te hubiste dedicado**	**os hubisteis dedicado**
se dedicó	**se dedicaron**	**se hubo dedicado**	**se hubieron dedicado**
4 futuro		11 futuro perfecto	
me dedicaré	**nos dedicaremos**	**me habré dedicado**	**nos habremos dedicado**
te dedicarás	**os dedicaréis**	**te habrás dedicado**	**os habréis dedicado**
se dedicará	**se dedicarán**	**se habrá dedicado**	**se habrán dedicado**
5 potencial simple		12 potencial compuesto	
me dedicaría	**nos dedicaríamos**	**me habría dedicado**	**nos habríamos dedicado**
te dedicarías	**os dedicaríais**	**te habrías dedicado**	**os habríais dedicado**
se dedicaría	**se dedicarían**	**se habría dedicado**	**se habrían dedicado**
6 presente de subjuntivo		13 perfecto de subjuntivo	
me dedique	**nos dediquemos**	**me haya dedicado**	**nos hayamos dedicado**
te dediques	**os dediquéis**	**te hayas dedicado**	**os hayáis dedicado**
se dedique	**se dediquen**	**se haya dedicado**	**se hayan dedicado**
7 imperfecto de subjuntivo		14 pluscuamperfecto de subjuntivo	
me dedicara	**nos dedicáramos**	**me hubiera dedicado**	**nos hubiéramos dedicado**
te dedicaras	**os dedicarais**	**te hubieras dedicado**	**os hubierais dedicado**
se dedicara	**se dedicaran**	**se hubiera dedicado**	**se hubieran dedicado**
OR		OR	
me dedicase	**nos dedicásemos**	**me hubiese dedicado**	**nos hubiésemos dedicado**
te dedicases	**os dedicaseis**	**te hubieses dedicado**	**os hubieseis dedicado**
se dedicase	**se dedicasen**	**se hubiese dedicado**	**se hubiesen dedicado**

imperativo

—	**dediquémonos**
dedícate; no te dediques	**dedicaos; no os dediquéis**
dedíquese	**dedíquense**

Words related to this verb

predicar   to preach, predicate   **dedicado, dedicada**   dedicated
dedicarse a   to devote oneself to   **una dedicación**   dedication
dedicar   to dedicate, consecrate   **dedicar algo a**   to dedicate something to

Get acquainted with what preposition goes with what verb on pages 669–677.

The subject pronouns are found on page 93.

to defend | Regular **-er** verb endings with stem change: Tenses 1, 6, Imperative

The Seven Simple Tenses | The Seven Compound Tenses

Singular	Plural	Singular	Plural
1 presente de indicativo		**8 perfecto de indicativo**	
defiendo	defendemos	he defendido	hemos defendido
defiendes	defendéis	has defendido	habéis defendido
defiende	defienden	ha defendido	han defendido
2 imperfecto de indicativo		**9 pluscuamperfecto de indicativo**	
defendía	defendíamos	había defendido	habíamos defendido
defendías	defendíais	habías defendido	habíais defendido
defendía	defendían	había defendido	habían defendido
3 pretérito		**10 pretérito anterior**	
defendí	defendimos	hube defendido	hubimos defendido
defendiste	defendisteis	hubiste defendido	hubisteis defendido
defendió	defendieron	hubo defendido	hubieron defendido
4 futuro		**11 futuro perfecto**	
defenderé	defenderemos	habré defendido	habremos defendido
defenderás	defenderéis	habrás defendido	habréis defendido
defenderá	defenderán	habrá defendido	habrán defendido
5 potencial simple		**12 potencial compuesto**	
defendería	defenderíamos	habría defendido	habríamos defendido
defenderías	defenderíais	habrías defendido	habríais defendido
defendería	defenderían	habría defendido	habrían defendido
6 presente de subjuntivo		**13 perfecto de subjuntivo**	
defienda	defendamos	haya defendido	hayamos defendido
defiendas	defendáis	hayas defendido	hayáis defendido
defienda	defiendan	haya defendido	hayan defendido
7 imperfecto de subjuntivo		**14 pluscuamperfecto de subjuntivo**	
defendiera	defendiéramos	hubiera defendido	hubiéramos defendido
defendieras	defendierais	hubieras defendido	hubierais defendido
defendiera	defendieran	hubiera defendido	hubieran defendido
OR		OR	
defendiese	defendiésemos	hubiese defendido	hubiésemos defendido
defendieses	defendieseis	hubieses defendido	hubieseis defendido
defendiese	defendiesen	hubiese defendido	hubiesen defendido

imperativo

—	defendamos
defiende; no defiendas	defended; no defendáis
defienda	defiendan

Words related to this verb

defendible   defensible
la defensa   defense
defensivo, defensiva   defensive
defensor, defensora   defender, supporter, protector

el defensorio   defense, plea
estar a la defensiva   to be on the defensive
en defensa propia   in self-defense
defender la patria contra el enemigo   to defend one's country against the enemy

Regular **-ar** verb   to let, to permit, to allow, to leave

The Seven Simple Tenses		The Seven Compound Tenses	
Singular	Plural	Singular	Plural
1 presente de indicativo		8 perfecto de indicativo	
dejo	dejamos	he dejado	hemos dejado
dejas	dejáis	has dejado	habéis dejado
deja	dejan	ha dejado	han dejado
2 imperfecto de indicativo		9 pluscuamperfecto de indicativo	
dejaba	dejábamos	había dejado	habíamos dejado
dejabas	dejabais	habías dejado	habíais dejado
dejaba	dejaban	había dejado	habían dejado
3 pretérito		10 pretérito anterior	
dejé	dejamos	hube dejado	hubimos dejado
dejaste	dejasteis	hubiste dejado	hubisteis dejado
dejó	dejaron	hubo dejado	hubieron dejado
4 futuro		11 futuro perfecto	
dejaré	dejaremos	habré dejado	habremos dejado
dejarás	dejaréis	habrás dejado	habréis dejado
dejará	dejarán	habrá dejado	habrán dejado
5 potencial simple		12 potencial compuesto	
dejaría	dejaríamos	habría dejado	habríamos dejado
dejarías	dejaríais	habrías dejado	habríais dejado
dejaría	dejarían	habría dejado	habrían dejado
6 presente de subjuntivo		13 perfecto de subjuntivo	
deje	dejemos	haya dejado	hayamos dejado
dejes	dejéis	hayas dejado	hayáis dejado
deje	dejen	haya dejado	hayan dejado
7 imperfecto de subjuntivo		14 pluscuamperfecto de subjuntivo	
dejara	dejáramos	hubiera dejado	hubiéramos dejado
dejaras	dejarais	hubieras dejado	hubierais dejado
dejara	dejaran	hubiera dejado	hubieran dejado
OR		OR	
dejase	dejásemos	hubiese dejado	hubiésemos dejado
dejases	dejaseis	hubieses dejado	hubieseis dejado
dejase	dejasen	hubiese dejado	hubiesen dejado

imperativo

—	dejemos
deja; no dejes	dejad; no dejéis
deje	dejen

Words and expressions related to this verb
dejar caer   to drop (to let fall)
el dejo   abandonment
dejado, dejada   dejected
El alumno dejó sus libros en la sala de clase.
  The pupil left his books in the classroom.
dejar de + inf.   to stop, to fail to

Los alumnos dejaron de hablar cuando la profesora entró en la sala de clase.   The students stopped talking when the teacher came into the classroom.
¡No deje Ud. de llamarme!   Don't fail to call me!
dejarse   to abandon (neglect) oneself
dejar atrás   to leave behind
¡Déjelo!   Let It! (Leave it!)

The subject pronouns are found on page 93.

to be delinquent, to violate the law | Regular **-ir** verb endings with spelling change: **qu** becomes **c** before **a** or **o**

The Seven Simple Tenses		The Seven Compound Tenses	
Singular	Plural	Singular	Plural
1 presente de indicativo		8 perfecto de indicativo	
delinco	delinquimos	he delinquido	hemos delinquido
delinques	delinquís	has delinquido	habéis delinquido
delinque	delinquen	ha delinquido	han delinquido
2 imperfecto de indicativo		9 pluscuamperfecto de indicativo	
delinquía	delinquíamos	había delinquido	habíamos delinquido
delinquías	delinquíais	habías delinquido	habíais delinquido
delinquía	delinquían	había delinquido	habían delinquido
3 pretérito		10 pretérito anterior	
delinquí	delinquimos	hube delinquido	hubimos delinquido
delinquiste	delinquisteis	hubiste delinquido	hubisteis delinquido
delinquió	delinquieron	hubo delinquido	hubieron delinquido
4 futuro		11 futuro perfecto	
delinquiré	delinquiremos	habré delinquido	habremos delinquido
delinquirás	delinquiréis	habrás delinquido	habréis delinquido
delinquirá	delinquirán	habrá delinquido	habrán delinquido
5 potencial simple		12 potencial compuesto	
delinquiría	delinquiríamos	habría delinquido	habríamos delinquido
delinquirías	delinquiríais	habrías delinquido	habríais delinquido
delinquiría	delinquirían	habría delinquido	habrían delinquido
6 presente de subjuntivo		13 perfecto de subjuntivo	
delinca	delincamos	haya delinquido	hayamos delinquido
delincas	delincáis	hayas delinquido	hayáis delinquido
delinca	delincan	haya delinquido	hayan delinquido
7 imperfecto de subjuntivo		14 pluscuamperfecto de subjuntivo	
delinquiera	delinquiéramos	hubiera delinquido	hubiéramos delinquido
delinquieras	delinquierais	hubieras delinquido	hubierais delinquido
delinquiera	delinquieran	hubiera delinquido	hubieran delinquido
OR		OR	
delinquiese	delinquiésemos	hubiese delinquido	hubiésemos delinquido
delinquieses	delinquieseis	hubieses delinquido	hubieseis delinquido
delinquiese	delinquiesen	hubiese delinquido	hubiesen delinquido

imperativo	
—	delincamos
delinque; no delincas	delinquid; no delincáis
delinca	delincan

Words related to this verb
el delinquimiento, la delincuencia delinquency
delincuente   delinquent

la delincuencia juvenil   juvenile delinquency
delincuente habitual   habitual offender

Review the principal parts of important Spanish verbs on pages 9 and 10.

Regular **-ar** verb endings with stem change: Tenses 1, 6, Imperative

to demonstrate, to prove

The Seven Simple Tenses		The Seven Compound Tenses	
Singular	Plural	Singular	Plural

1 presente de indicativo

demuestro	demostramos	
demuestras	demostráis	
demuestra	demuestran	

8 perfecto de indicativo

he demostrado	hemos demostrado
has demostrado	habéis demostrado
ha demostrado	han demostrado

2 imperfecto de indicativo

demostraba	demostrábamos
demostrabas	demostrabais
demostraba	demostraban

9 pluscuamperfecto de indicativo

había demostrado	habíamos demostrado
habías demostrado	habíais demostrado
había demostrado	habían demostrado

3 pretérito

demostré	demostramos
demostraste	demostrasteis
demostró	demostraron

10 pretérito anterior

hube demostrado	hubimos demostrado
hubiste demostrado	hubisteis demostrado
hubo demostrado	hubieron demostrado

4 futuro

demostraré	demostraremos
demostrarás	demostraréis
demostrará	demostrarán

11 futuro perfecto

habré demostrado	habremos demostrado
habrás demostrado	habréis demostrado
habrá demostrado	habrán demostrado

5 potencial simple

demostraría	demostraríamos
demostrarías	demostraríais
demostraría	demostrarían

12 potencial compuesto

habría demostrado	habríamos demostrado
habrías demostrado	habríais demostrado
habría demostrado	habrían demostrado

6 presente de subjuntivo

demuestre	demostremos
demuestres	demostréis
demuestre	demuestren

13 perfecto de subjuntivo

haya demostrado	hayamos demostrado
hayas demostrado	hayáis demostrado
haya demostrado	hayan demostrado

7 imperfecto de subjuntivo

demostrara	demostráramos
demostraras	demostrarais
demostrara	demostraran
OR	
demostrase	demostrásemos
demostrases	demostraseis
demostrase	demostrasen

14 pluscuamperfecto de subjuntivo

hubiera demostrado	hubiéramos demostrado
hubieras demostrado	hubierais demostrado
hubiera demostrado	hubieran demostrado
OR	
hubiese demostrado	hubiésemos demostrado
hubieses demostrado	hubieseis demostrado
hubiese demostrado	hubiesen demostrado

imperativo

—	demostremos
demuestra; no demuestres	demostrad; no demostréis
demuestre	demuestren

Words related to this verb

demostrativo, demostrativa demonstrative
la demostración demonstration, proof
demostrador, demostradora demonstrator

demostrable demonstrable
mostrar to show, to exhibit
la demostración de cariño show of affection

If you want to see a sample English verb fully conjugated in
all the tenses, check out pages 11 and 12.

The subject pronouns are found on page 93.

The Seven Simple Tenses		The Seven Compound Tenses	
Singular	Plural	Singular	Plural
1 presente de indicativo		**8 perfecto de indicativo**	
denuncio	denunciamos	he denunciado	hemos denunciado
denuncias	denunciáis	has denunciado	habéis denunciado
denuncia	denuncian	ha denunciado	han denunciado
2 imperfecto de indicativo		**9 pluscuamperfecto de indicativo**	
denunciaba	denunciábamos	había denunciado	habíamos denunciado
denunciabas	denunciabais	habías denunciado	habíais denunciado
denunciaba	denunciaban	había denunciado	habían denunciado
3 pretérito		**10 pretérito anterior**	
denuncié	denunciamos	hube denunciado	hubimos denunciado
denunciaste	denunciasteis	hubiste denunciado	hubisteis denunciado
denunció	denunciaron	hubo denunciado	hubieron denunciado
4 futuro		**11 futuro perfecto**	
denunciaré	denunciaremos	habré denunciado	habremos denunciado
denunciarás	denunciaréis	habrás denunciado	habréis denunciado
denunciará	denunciarán	habrá denunciado	habrán denunciado
5 potencial simple		**12 potencial compuesto**	
denunciaría	denunciaríamos	habría denunciado	habríamos denunciado
denunciarías	denunciaríais	habrías denunciado	habríais denunciado
denunciaría	denunciarían	habría denunciado	habrían denunciado
6 presente de subjuntivo		**13 perfecto de subjuntivo**	
denuncie	denunciemos	haya denunciado	hayamos denunciado
denuncies	denunciéis	hayas denunciado	hayáis denunciado
denuncie	denuncien	haya denunciado	hayan denunciado
7 imperfecto de subjuntivo		**14 pluscuamperfecto de subjuntivo**	
denunciara	denunciáramos	hubiera denunciado	hubiéramos denunciado
denunciaras	denunciarais	hubieras denunciado	hubierais denunciado
denunciara	denunciaran	hubiera denunciado	hubieran denunciado
OR		OR	
denunciase	denunciásemos	hubiese denunciado	hubiésemos denunciado
denunciases	denunciaseis	hubieses denunciado	hubieseis denunciado
denunciase	denunciasen	hubiese denunciado	hubiesen denunciado

imperativo	
—	denunciemos
denuncia; no denuncies	denunciad; no denunciéis
denuncie	denuncien

Words and expressions related to this verb
una denuncia, una denunciación denunciation   **denunciar un robo**   to report a theft
un denuncio denouncement   **una denuncia falsa**   a false accusation

---

If you want an explanation of meanings and uses of Spanish and
English verb tenses and moods, see pages 13–32.

Regular **-er** verb   to depend

D

The Seven Simple Tenses

Singular	Plural
1 presente de indicativo	
dependo	dependemos
dependes	dependéis
depende	dependen
2 imperfecto de indicativo	
dependía	dependíamos
dependías	dependíais
dependía	dependían
3 pretérito	
dependí	dependimos
dependiste	dependisteis
dependió	dependieron
4 futuro	
dependeré	dependeremos
dependerás	dependeréis
dependerá	dependerán
5 potencial simple	
dependería	dependeríamos
dependerías	dependeríais
dependería	dependerían
6 presente de subjuntivo	
dependa	dependamos
dependas	dependáis
dependa	dependan
7 imperfecto de subjuntivo	
dependiera	dependiéramos
dependieras	dependierais
dependiera	dependieran
OR	
dependiese	dependiésemos
dependieses	dependieseis
dependiese	dependiesen

The Seven Compound Tenses

Singular	Plural
8 perfecto de indicativo	
he dependido	hemos dependido
has dependido	habéis dependido
ha dependido	han dependido
9 pluscuamperfecto de indicativo	
había dependido	habíamos dependido
habías dependido	habíais dependido
había dependido	habían dependido
10 pretérito anterior	
hube dependido	hubimos dependido
hubiste dependido	hubisteis dependido
hubo dependido	hubieron dependido
11 futuro perfecto	
habré dependido	habremos dependido
habrás dependido	habréis dependido
habrá dependido	habrán dependido
12 potencial compuesto	
habría dependido	habríamos dependido
habrías dependido	habríais dependido
habría dependido	habrían dependido
13 perfecto de subjuntivo	
haya dependido	hayamos dependido
hayas dependido	hayáis dependido
haya dependido	hayan dependido
14 pluscuamperfecto de subjuntivo	
hubiera dependido	hubiéramos dependido
hubieras dependido	hubierais dependido
hubiera dependido	hubieran dependido
OR	
hubiese dependido	hubiésemos dependido
hubieses dependido	hubieseis dependido
hubiese dependido	hubiesen dependido

imperativo

—	dependamos
depende; no dependas	depended; no dependáis
dependa	dependan

Words and expressions related to this verb
depender de   to depend on, to rely on
no depender de nadie   to stand on one's own two feet
un dependiente, una dependienta   dependent, employee, clerk
la dependencia   dependence, dependency
pender   to dangle, hang, to be pending
suspender   to suspend, hang, hang up; **suspender pagos**   to stop payment

The subject pronouns are found on page 93.

derribar (170)

Gerundio derribando   **Part. pas. derribado**

to knock down, to overthrow, to tear down, to throw down   Regular **-ar** verb

The Seven Simple Tenses		The Seven Compound Tenses	
Singular	Plural	Singular	Plural
1 presente de indicativo		**8 perfecto de indicativo**	
derribo	derribamos	he derribado	hemos derribado
derribas	derribáis	has derribado	habéis derribado
derriba	derriban	ha derribado	han derribado
2 imperfecto de indicativo		**9 pluscuamperfecto de indicativo**	
derribaba	derribábamos	había derribado	habíamos derribado
derribabas	derribabais	habías derribado	habíais derribado
derribaba	derribaban	había derribado	habían derribado
3 pretérito		**10 pretérito anterior**	
derribé	derribamos	hube derribado	hubimos derribado
derribaste	derribasteis	hubiste derribado	hubisteis derribado
derribó	derribaron	hubo derribado	hubieron derribado
4 futuro		**11 futuro perfecto**	
derribaré	derribaremos	habré derribado	habremos derribado
derribarás	derribaréis	habrás derribado	habréis derribado
derribará	derribarán	habrá derribado	habrán derribado
5 potencial simple		**12 potencial compuesto**	
derribaría	derribaríamos	habría derribado	habríamos derribado
derribarías	derribaríais	habrías derribado	habríais derribado
derribaría	derribarían	habría derribado	habrían derribado
6 presente de subjuntivo		**13 perfecto de subjuntivo**	
derribe	derribemos	haya derribado	hayamos derribado
derribes	derribéis	hayas derribado	hayáis derribado
derribe	derriben	haya derribado	hayan derribado
7 imperfecto de subjuntivo		**14 pluscuamperfecto de subjuntivo**	
derribara	derribáramos	hubiera derribado	hubiéramos derribado
derribaras	derribarais	hubieras derribado	hubierais derribado
derribara	derribaran	hubiera derribado	hubieran derribado
OR		OR	
derribase	derribásemos	hubiese derribado	hubiésemos derribado
derribases	derribaseis	hubieses derribado	hubieseis derribado
derribase	derribasen	hubiese derribado	hubiesen derribado

imperativo	
—	**derribemos**
derriba; no derribes	**derribad; no derribéis**
derribe	**derriben**

Words and expressions related to this verb

derribar a tiros   to shoot down
derribado, derribada   demolished, humiliated
el derribador, la derribadora   overthrower

los derribos   rubble
derribar al criminal   to bring the criminal down

If you don't know the Spanish verb for an English verb you have in mind, look it up in the index on pages 682–706.

Reflexive regular **-ar** verb   to breakfast, to have breakfast

The Seven Simple Tenses		The Seven Compound Tenses	
Singular	Plural	Singular	Plural
1 presente de indicativo		8 perfecto de indicativo	
me desayuno	nos desayunamos	me he desayunado	nos hemos desayunado
te desayunas	os desayunáis	te has desayunado	os habéis desayunado
se desayuna	se desayunan	se ha desayunado	se han desayunado
2 imperfecto de indicativo		9 pluscuamperfecto de indicativo	
me desayunaba	nos desayunábamos	me había desayunado	nos habíamos desayunado
te desayunabas	os desayunabais	te habías desayunado	os habíais desayunado
se desayunaba	se desayunaban	se había desayunado	se habían desayunado
3 pretérito		10 pretérito anterior	
me desayuné	nos desayunamos	me hube desayunado	nos hubimos desayunado
te desayunaste	os desayunasteis	te hubiste desayunado	os hubisteis desayunado
se desayunó	se desayunaron	se hubo desayunado	se hubieron desayunado
4 futuro		11 futuro perfecto	
me desayunaré	nos desayunaremos	me habré desayunado	nos habremos desayunado
te desayunarás	os desayunaréis	te habrás desayunado	os habréis desayunado
se desayunará	se desayunarán	se habrá desayunado	se habrán desayunado
5 potencial simple		12 potencial compuesto	
me desayunaría	nos desayunaríamos	me habría desayunado	nos habríamos desayunado
te desayunarías	os desayunaríais	te habrías desayunado	os habríais desayunado
se desayunaría	se desayunarían	se habría desayunado	se habrían desayunado
6 presente de subjuntivo		13 perfecto de subjuntivo	
me desayune	nos desayunemos	me haya desayunado	nos hayamos desayunado
te desayunes	os desayunéis	te hayas desayunado	os hayáis desayunado
se desayune	se desayunen	se haya desayunado	se hayan desayunado
7 imperfecto de subjuntivo		14 pluscuamperfecto de subjuntivo	
me desayunara	nos desayunáramos	me hubiera desayunado	nos hubiéramos desayunado
te desayunaras	os desayunarais	te hubieras desayunado	os hubierais desayunado
se desayunara	se desayunaran	se hubiera desayunado	se hubieran desayunado
OR		OR	
me desayunase	nos desayunásemos	me hubiese desayunado	nos hubiésemos desayunado
te desayunases	os desayunaseis	te hubieses desayunado	os hubieseis desayunado
se desayunase	se desayunasen	se hubiese desayunado	se hubiesen desayunado

imperativo	
—	desayunémonos
desayúnate; no te desayunes	desayunaos; no os desayunéis
desayúnese	desayúnense

Sentences using this verb and words related to it
—¿Qué toma Ud. en el desayuno todas las mañanas?
—Tomo leche, café con crema, pan tostado y un huevo.

desayunar	to breakfast	ayunar	to fast (not to eat)
el desayuno	breakfast	el ayuno	fast, fasting

Get your feet wet with verbs used in weather expressions on page 668.

The subject pronouns are found on page 93.

to rest　　　　　　　　　　　　　　　　　Regular **-ar** verb

The Seven Simple Tenses		The Seven Compound Tenses	
Singular	Plural	Singular	Plural
1　presente de indicativo		8　perfecto de indicativo	
descanso	descansamos	he descansado	hemos descansado
descansas	descansáis	has descansado	habéis descansado
descansa	descansan	ha descansado	han descansado
2　imperfecto de indicativo		9　pluscuamperfecto de indicativo	
descansaba	descansábamos	había descansado	habíamos descansado
descansabas	descansabais	habías descansado	habíais descansado
descansaba	descansaban	había descansado	habían descansado
3　pretérito		10　pretérito anterior	
descansé	descansamos	hube descansado	hubimos descansado
descansaste	descansasteis	hubiste descansado	hubisteis descansado
descansó	descansaron	hubo descansado	hubieron descansado
4　futuro		11　futuro perfecto	
descansaré	descansaremos	habré descansado	habremos descansado
descansarás	descansaréis	habrás descansado	habréis descansado
descansará	descansarán	habrá descansado	habrán descansado
5　potencial simple		12　potencial compuesto	
descansaría	descansaríamos	habría descansado	habríamos descansado
descansarías	descansaríais	habrías descansado	habríais descansado
descansaría	descansarían	habría descansado	habrían descansado
6　presente de subjuntivo		13　perfecto de subjuntivo	
descanse	descansemos	haya descansado	hayamos descansado
descanses	descanséis	hayas descansado	hayáis descansado
descanse	descansen	haya descansado	hayan descansado
7　imperfecto de subjuntivo		14　pluscuamperfecto de subjuntivo	
descansara	descansáramos	hubiera descansado	hubiéramos descansado
descansaras	descansarais	hubieras descansado	hubierais descansado
descansara	descansaran	hubiera descansado	hubieran descansado
OR		OR	
descansase	descansásemos	hubiese descansado	hubiésemos descansado
descansases	descansaseis	hubieses descansado	hubieseis descansado
descansase	descansasen	hubiese descansado	hubiesen descansado

imperativo	
—	descansemos
descansa; no descanses	descansad; no descanséis
descanse	descansen

Words and expressions related to this verb

el descanso　rest, relief, break
el descansadero　resting place
la cansera　fatigue
cansar　to fatigue, to tire, to weary

el descansillo　landing on a staircase
el descanso a discreción　at ease (military)
cansarse de esperar　to be tired of waiting
el descanso por enfermedad　sick leave

Regular **-ir** verb endings, note irregular   to describe, to delineate
spelling of past participle: **descrito**

The Seven Simple Tenses		The Seven Compound Tenses	
Singular	Plural	Singular	Plural
1 presente de indicativo		8 perfecto de indicativo	
describo	**describimos**	**he descrito**	**hemos descrito**
describes	**describís**	**has descrito**	**habéis descrito**
describe	**describen**	**ha descrito**	**han descrito**
2 imperfecto de indicativo		9 pluscuamperfecto de indicativo	
describía	**describíamos**	**había descrito**	**habíamos descrito**
describías	**describíais**	**habías descrito**	**habíais descrito**
describía	**describían**	**había descrito**	**habían descrito**
3 pretérito		10 pretérito anterior	
describí	**describimos**	**hube descrito**	**hubimos descrito**
describiste	**describisteis**	**hubiste descrito**	**hubisteis descrito**
describió	**describieron**	**hubo descrito**	**hubieron descrito**
4 futuro		11 futuro perfecto	
describiré	**describiremos**	**habré descrito**	**habremos descrito**
describirás	**describiréis**	**habrás descrito**	**habréis descrito**
describirá	**describirán**	**habrá descrito**	**habrán descrito**
5 potencial simple		12 potencial compuesto	
describiría	**describiríamos**	**habría descrito**	**habríamos descrito**
describirías	**describiríais**	**habrías descrito**	**habríais descrito**
describiría	**describirían**	**habría descrito**	**habrían descrito**
6 presente de subjuntivo		13 perfecto de subjuntivo	
describa	**describamos**	**haya descrito**	**hayamos descrito**
describas	**describáis**	**hayas descrito**	**hayáis descrito**
describa	**describan**	**haya descrito**	**hayan descrito**
7 imperfecto de subjuntivo		14 pluscuamperfecto de subjuntivo	
describiera	**describiéramos**	**hubiera descrito**	**hubiéramos descrito**
describieras	**describierais**	**hubieras descrito**	**hubierais descrito**
describiera	**describieran**	**hubiera descrito**	**hubieran descrito**
OR		OR	
describiese	**describiésemos**	**hubiese descrito**	**hubiésemos descrito**
describieses	**describieseis**	**hubieses descrito**	**hubieseis descrito**
describiese	**describiesen**	**hubiese descrito**	**hubiesen descrito**

imperativo

—	**describamos**
describe; no describas	**describid; no describáis**
describa	**describan**

Words and expressions related to this verb

la descripción description
descriptor, descriptora describer
descriptivo, descriptiva descriptive

escribir to write
escribir a mano to write by hand
escribir a máquina to typewrite

For other words and expressions related to this verb, see **escribir** and **subscribir.**

> Don't miss the definitions of basic grammatical terms with
> examples in English and Spanish on pages 33–44.

The subject pronouns are found on page 93.

to discover, to reveal,
to uncover, to unveil

Regular **-ir** verb endings; note irregular
spelling of past participle: **descubierto**

The Seven Simple Tenses		The Seven Compound Tenses	
Singular	Plural	Singular	Plural
1　presente de indicativo		8　perfecto de indicativo	
descubro	**descubrimos**	**he descubierto**	**hemos descubierto**
descubres	**descubrís**	**has descubierto**	**habéis descubierto**
descubre	**descubren**	**ha descubierto**	**han descubierto**
2　imperfecto de indicativo		9　pluscuamperfecto de indicativo	
descubría	**descubríamos**	**había descubierto**	**habíamos descubierto**
descubrías	**descubríais**	**habías descubierto**	**habíais descubierto**
descubría	**descubrían**	**había descubierto**	**habían descubierto**
3　pretérito		10　pretérito anterior	
descubrí	**descubrimos**	**hube descubierto**	**hubimos descubierto**
descubriste	**descubristeis**	**hubiste descubierto**	**hubisteis descubierto**
descubrió	**descubrieron**	**hubo descubierto**	**hubieron descubierto**
4　futuro		11　futuro perfecto	
descubriré	**descubriremos**	**habré descubierto**	**habremos descubierto**
descubrirás	**descubriréis**	**habrás descubierto**	**habréis descubierto**
descubrirá	**descubrirán**	**habrá descubierto**	**habrán descubierto**
5　potencial simple		12　potencial compuesto	
descubriría	**descubriríamos**	**habría descubierto**	**habríamos descubierto**
descubrirías	**descubriríais**	**habrías descubierto**	**habríais descubierto**
descubriría	**descubrirían**	**habría descubierto**	**habrían descubierto**
6　presente de subjuntivo		13　perfecto de subjuntivo	
descubra	**descubramos**	**haya descubierto**	**hayamos descubierto**
descubras	**descubráis**	**hayas descubierto**	**hayáis descubierto**
descubra	**descubran**	**haya descubierto**	**hayan descubierto**
7　imperfecto de subjuntivo		14　pluscuamperfecto de subjuntivo	
descubriera	**descubriéramos**	**hubiera descubierto**	**hubiéramos descubierto**
descubrieras	**descubrierais**	**hubieras descubierto**	**hubierais descubierto**
descubriera	**descubrieran**	**hubiera descubierto**	**hubieran descubierto**
OR		OR	
descubriese	**descubriésemos**	**hubiese descubierto**	**hubiésemos descubierto**
descubrieses	**descubrieseis**	**hubieses descubierto**	**hubieseis descubierto**
descubriese	**descubriesen**	**hubiese descubierto**	**hubiesen descubierto**

	imperativo	
—	**descubramos**
descubre; no descubras	**descubrid; no descubráis**
descubra	**descubran**

Words and expressions related to this verb
descubrirse　to take off one's hat
el descubrimiento　discovery
descubridor, descubridora　discoverer
a la descubierta　clearly, openly

cubrir　to cover
cubrir el costo　to cover the cost
cubrir la mesa　to cover the table
descubrir un nuevo antibiótico　to discover
　a new antibiotic

Regular **-ar** verb

to desire, to wish, to want

The Seven Simple Tenses		The Seven Compound Tenses	
Singular	Plural	Singular	Plural
1 presente de indicativo		8 perfecto de indicativo	
deseo	**deseamos**	**he deseado**	**hemos deseado**
deseas	**deseáis**	**has deseado**	**habéis deseado**
desea	**desean**	**ha deseado**	**han deseado**
2 imperfecto de indicativo		9 pluscuamperfecto de indicativo	
deseaba	**deseábamos**	**había deseado**	**habíamos deseado**
deseabas	**deseabais**	**habías deseado**	**habíais deseado**
deseaba	**deseaban**	**había deseado**	**habían deseado**
3 pretérito		10 pretérito anterior	
deseé	**deseamos**	**hube deseado**	**hubimos deseado**
deseaste	**deseasteis**	**hubiste deseado**	**hubisteis deseado**
deseó	**desearon**	**hubo deseado**	**hubieron deseado**
4 futuro		11 futuro perfecto	
desearé	**desearemos**	**habré deseado**	**habremos deseado**
desearás	**desaréis**	**habrás deseado**	**habréis deseado**
deseará	**desearán**	**habrá deseado**	**habrán deseado**
5 potencial simple		12 potencial compuesto	
desearía	**desearíamos**	**habría deseado**	**habríamos deseado**
desearías	**desearíais**	**habrías deseado**	**habríais deseado**
desearía	**desearían**	**habría deseado**	**habrían deseado**
6 presente de subjuntivo		13 perfecto de subjuntivo	
desee	**deseemos**	**haya deseado**	**hayamos deseado**
desees	**deseéis**	**hayas deseado**	**hayáis deseado**
desee	**deseen**	**haya deseado**	**hayan deseado**
7 imperfecto de subjuntivo		14 pluscuamperfecto de subjuntivo	
deseara	**deseáramos**	**hubiera deseado**	**hubiéramos deseado**
desearas	**desearais**	**hubieras deseado**	**hubierais deseado**
deseara	**desearan**	**hubiera deseado**	**hubieran deseado**
OR		OR	
desease	**deseásemos**	**hubiese deseado**	**hubiésemos deseado**
deseases	**deseaseis**	**hubieses deseado**	**hubieseis deseado**
desease	**deseasen**	**hubiese deseado**	**hubiesen deseado**

imperativo	
—	**deseemos**
desea; no desees	**desead; no deseéis**
desee	**deseen**

Words and expressions related to this verb

el deseo   desire
deseoso, deseosa   desirous
tener deseo de + inf.   to be eager + inf.
deseable   desirable

el deseador, la deseadora   desirer, wisher
deseablemente   desirably
poco deseable   undesirable
desear hacer algo   to wish to do something

The subject pronouns are found on page 93.

desempeñar (176)   Gerundio **desempeñando**   Part. pas. **desempeñado**

to play (a part), to act (a part), to discharge,   Regular **-ar** verb
to perform (a duty), to take out of pawn

The Seven Simple Tenses		The Seven Compound Tenses	
Singular	Plural	Singular	Plural
1 presente de indicativo		8 perfecto de indicativo	
desempeño	desempeñamos	he desempeñado	hemos desempeñado
desempeñas	desempeñáis	has desempeñado	habéis desempeñado
desempeña	desempeñan	ha desempeñado	han desempeñado
2 imperfecto de indicativo		9 pluscuamperfecto de indicativo	
desempeñaba	desempeñábamos	había desempeñado	habíamos desempeñado
desempeñabas	desempeñabais	habías desempeñado	habíais desempeñado
desempeñaba	desempeñaban	había desempeñado	habían desempeñado
3 pretérito		10 pretérito anterior	
desempeñé	desempeñamos	hube desempeñado	hubimos desempeñado
desempeñaste	desempeñasteis	hubiste desempeñado	hubisteis desempeñado
desempeñó	desempeñaron	hubo desempeñado	hubieron desempeñado
4 futuro		11 futuro perfecto	
desempeñaré	desempeñaremos	habré desempeñado	habremos desempeñado
desempeñarás	desempeñaréis	habrás desempeñado	habréis desempeñado
desempeñará	desempeñarán	habrá desempeñado	habrán desempeñado
5 potencial simple		12 potencial compuesto	
desempeñaría	desempeñaríamos	habría desempeñado	habríamos desempeñado
desempeñarías	desempeñaríais	habrías desempeñado	habríais desempeñado
desempeñaría	desempeñarían	habría desempeñado	habrían desempeñado
6 presente de subjuntivo		13 perfecto de subjuntivo	
desempeñe	desempeñemos	haya desempeñado	hayamos desempeñado
desempeñes	desempeñéis	hayas desempeñado	hayáis desempeñado
desempeñe	desempeñen	haya desempeñado	hayan desempeñado
7 imperfecto de subjuntivo		14 pluscuamperfecto de subjuntivo	
desempeñara	desempeñáramos	hubiera desempeñado	hubiéramos desempeñado
desempeñaras	desempeñarais	hubieras desempeñado	hubierais desempeñado
desempeñara	desempeñaran	hubiera desempeñado	hubieran desempeñado
OR		OR	
desempeñase	desempeñásemos	hubiese desempeñado	hubiésemos desempeñado
desempeñases	desempeñaseis	hubieses desempeñado	hubieseis desempeñado
desempeñase	desempeñasen	hubiese desempeñado	hubiesen desempeñado

imperativo	
—	desempeñemos
desempeña; no desempeñes	desempeñad; no desempeñéis
desempeñe	desempeñen

Words and expressions related to this verb
desempeñado, desempeñada   out of debt
el desempeño   payment of a debt
desempeñar un cargo   to take a job

empeñar   to pawn, to pledge
una casa de empeños   pawnshop
el empeño   pawn, pledge, obligation

Check out the verb drills and verb tests with answers explained on pages 45–91.

Irregular verb   to undo, to destroy, to take apart

The Seven Simple Tenses		The Seven Compound Tenses	
Singular	Plural	Singular	Plural
1 presente de indicativo		**8 perfecto de indicativo**	
deshago	**deshacemos**	**he deshecho**	**hemos deshecho**
deshaces	**deshacéis**	**has deshecho**	**habéis deshecho**
deshace	**deshacen**	**ha deshecho**	**han deshecho**
2 imperfecto de indicativo		**9 pluscuamperfecto de indicativo**	
deshacía	**deshacíamos**	**había deshecho**	**habíamos deshecho**
deshacías	**deshacíais**	**habías deshecho**	**habíais deshecho**
deshacía	**deshacían**	**había deshecho**	**habían deshecho**
3 pretérito		**10 pretérito anterior**	
deshice	**deshicimos**	**hube deshecho**	**hubimos deshecho**
deshiciste	**deshicisteis**	**hubiste deshecho**	**hubisteis deshecho**
deshizo	**deshicieron**	**hubo deshecho**	**hubieron deshecho**
4 futuro		**11 futuro perfecto**	
desharé	**desharemos**	**habré deshecho**	**habremos deshecho**
desharás	**desharéis**	**habrás deshecho**	**habréis deshecho**
deshará	**desharán**	**habrá deshecho**	**habrán deshecho**
5 potencial simple		**12 potencial compuesto**	
desharía	**desharíamos**	**habría deshecho**	**habríamos deshecho**
desharías	**desharíais**	**habrías deshecho**	**habríais deshecho**
desharía	**desharían**	**habría deshecho**	**habrían deshecho**
6 presente de subjuntivo		**13 perfecto de subjuntivo**	
deshaga	**deshagamos**	**haya deshecho**	**hayamos deshecho**
deshagas	**deshagáis**	**hayas deshecho**	**hayáis deshecho**
deshaga	**deshagan**	**haya deshecho**	**hayan deshecho**
7 imperfecto de subjuntivo		**14 pluscuamperfecto de subjuntivo**	
deshiciera	**deshiciéramos**	**hubiera deshecho**	**hubiéramos deshecho**
deshicieras	**deshicierais**	**hubieras deshecho**	**hubierais deshecho**
deshiciera	**deshicieran**	**hubiera deshecho**	**hubieran deshecho**
OR		OR	
deshiciese	**deshiciésemos**	**hubiese deshecho**	**hubiésemos deshecho**
deshicieses	**deshicieseis**	**hubieses deshecho**	**hubieseis deshecho**
deshiciese	**deshiciesen**	**hubiese deshecho**	**hubiesen deshecho**

imperativo	
—	**deshagamos**
deshaz; no deshagas	**deshaced; no deshagáis**
deshaga	**deshagan**

Words and expressions related to this verb
deshecho, deshecha   destroyed, wasted, undone
el deshechizo   breaking off a magic spell
hacer la deshecha   to pretend, to feign

Can't find the verb you're looking for?
Check the back pages of this book for a list of over 2,100 additional verbs!

The subject pronouns are found on page 93.

despedirse (178)
Gerundio **despidiéndose**   Part. pas. **despedido**

to take leave of,
to say good-bye to

Reflexive verb; regular **-ir** verb endings with stem
change: Tenses 1, 3, 6, 7, Imperative, Gerundio

The Seven Simple Tenses

The Seven Compound Tenses

Singular	Plural	Singular	Plural
1 presente de indicativo		**8 perfecto de indicativo**	
me despido	nos despedimos	me he despedido	nos hemos despedido
te despides	os despedís	te has despedido	os habéis despedido
se despide	se despiden	se ha despedido	se han despedido
2 imperfecto de indicativo		**9 pluscuamperfecto de indicativo**	
me despedía	nos despedíamos	me había despedido	nos habíamos despedido
te despedías	os despedíais	te habías despedido	os habíais despedido
se despedía	se despedían	se había despedido	se habían despedido
3 pretérito		**10 pretérito anterior**	
me despedí	nos despedimos	me hube despedido	nos hubimos despedido
te despediste	os despedisteis	te hubiste despedido	os hubisteis despedido
se despidió	se despidieron	se hubo despedido	se hubieron despedido
4 futuro		**11 futuro perfecto**	
me despediré	nos despediremos	me habré despedido	nos habremos despedido
te despedirás	os despediréis	te habrás despedido	os habréis despedido
se despedirá	se despedirán	se habrá despedido	se habrán despedido
5 potencial simple		**12 potencial compuesto**	
me despediría	nos despediríamos	me habría despedido	nos habríamos despedido
te despedirías	os despediríais	te habrías despedido	os habríais despedido
se despediría	se despedirían	se habría despedido	se habrían despedido
6 presente de subjuntivo		**13 perfecto de subjuntivo**	
me despida	nos despidamos	me haya despedido	nos hayamos despedido
te despidas	os despidáis	te hayas despedido	os hayáis despedido
se despida	se despidan	se haya despedido	se hayan despedido
7 imperfecto de subjuntivo		**14 pluscuamperfecto de subjuntivo**	
me despidiera	nos despidiéramos	me hubiera despedido	nos hubiéramos despedido
te despidieras	os despidierais	te hubieras despedido	os hubierais despedido
se despidiera	se despidieran	se hubiera despedido	se hubieran despedido
OR		OR	
me despidiese	nos despidiésemos	me hubiese despedido	nos hubiésemos despedido
te despidieses	os despidieseis	te hubieses despedido	os hubieseis despedido
se despidiese	se despidiesen	se hubiese despedido	se hubiesen despedido

imperativo

—	despidámonos
despídete; no te despidas	despedíos; nos despidáis
despídase	despídanse

Words and expressions related to this verb
despedirse a la francesa   to take French leave
despedir   to dismiss
un despedimiento, una despedida   dismissal, discharge, farewell
despedirse de   to take leave of, to say good-bye to

Get acquainted with what preposition goes with what verb on pages 669–677.

Regular **-ar** verb endings with spelling
change: **g** becomes **gu** before **e**

to detach, to unglue, to unstick,
to take off (airplane)

The Seven Simple Tenses | The Seven Compound Tenses

Singular	Plural	Singular	Plural
1 presente de indicativo		**8 perfecto de indicativo**	
despego	**despegamos**	**he despegado**	**hemos despegado**
despegas	**despegáis**	**has despegado**	**habéis despegado**
despega	**despegan**	**ha despegado**	**han despegado**
2 imperfecto de indicativo		**9 pluscuamperfecto de indicativo**	
despegaba	**despegábamos**	**había despegado**	**habíamos despegado**
despegabas	**despegabais**	**habías despegado**	**habíais despegado**
despegaba	**despegaban**	**había despegado**	**habían despegado**
3 pretérito		**10 pretérito anterior**	
despegué	**despegamos**	**hube despegado**	**hubimos despegado**
despegaste	**despegasteis**	**hubiste despegado**	**hubisteis despegado**
despegó	**despegaron**	**hubo despegado**	**hubieron despegado**
4 futuro		**11 futuro perfecto**	
despegaré	**despegaremos**	**habré despegado**	**habremos despegado**
despegarás	**despergaréis**	**habrás despegado**	**habréis despegado**
despegará	**despegarán**	**habrá despegado**	**habrán despegado**
5 potencial simple		**12 potencial compuesto**	
despegaría	**despegaríamos**	**habría despegado**	**habríamos despegado**
despegarías	**despegaríais**	**habrías despegado**	**habríais despegado**
despegaría	**despegarían**	**habría despegado**	**habrían despegado**
6 presente de subjuntivo		**13 perfecto de subjuntivo**	
despegue	**despeguemos**	**haya despegado**	**hayamos despegado**
despegues	**despeguéis**	**hayas despegado**	**hayáis despegado**
despegue	**despeguen**	**haya despegado**	**hayan despegado**
7 imperfecto de subjuntivo		**14 pluscuamperfecto de subjuntivo**	
despegara	**despegáramos**	**hubiera despegado**	**hubiéramos despegado**
despegaras	**despegarais**	**hubieras despegado**	**hubierais despegado**
despegara	**despegaran**	**hubiera despegado**	**hubieran despegado**
OR		OR	
despegase	**despegásemos**	**hubiese despegado**	**hubiésemos despegado**
despegases	**despegaseis**	**hubieses despegado**	**hubieseis despegado**
despegase	**despegasen**	**hubiese despegado**	**hubiesen despegado**

	imperativo
—	**despeguemos**
despega; no despegues	**despegad; no despeguéis**
despegue	**despeguen**

Words and expressions related to this verb

despegar los labios   to speak
el despegue   take-off (airplane)
despegadamente   without concern

despegarse   to become distant, indifferent; to
   grow displeased
el despego, el despegamiento   aversion,
   indifference

For other words and expressions related to this verb, see **pegar.**

The subject pronouns are found on page 93.

desperezarse (180) Gerundio desperezándose Part. pas. desperezado

to stretch oneself, to stretch one's arms and legs

Reflexive verb; regular -ar verb endings with spelling change: z becomes c before e

The Seven Simple Tenses		The Seven Compound Tenses	
Singular	Plural	Singular	Plural
1 presente de indicativo		**8 perfecto de indicativo**	
me desperezo	nos desperezamos	me he desperezado	nos hemos desperezado
te desperezas	os desperezáis	te has desperezado	os habéis desperezado
se despereza	se desperezan	se ha desperezado	se han desperezado
2 imperfecto de indicativo		**9 pluscuamperfecto de indicativo**	
me desperezaba	nos desperezábamos	me había desperezado	nos habíamos desperezado
te desperezabas	os desperezabais	te habías desperezado	os habíais desperezado
se desperezaba	se desperezaban	se había desperezado	se habían desperezado
3 pretérito		**10 pretérito anterior**	
me desperecé	nos desperezamos	me hube desperezado	nos hubimos desperezado
te desperezaste	os desperezasteis	te hubiste desperezado	os hubisteis desperezado
se desperezó	se desperezaron	se hubo desperezado	se hubieron desperezado
4 futuro		**11 futuro perfecto**	
me desperezaré	nos desperezaremos	me habré desperezado	nos habremos desperezado
te desperezarás	os desperezaréis	te habrás desperezado	os habréis desperezado
se desperezará	se desperezarán	se habrá desperezado	se habrán desperezado
5 potencial simple		**12 potencial compuesto**	
me desperezaría	nos desperezaríamos	me habría desperezado	nos habríamos desperezado
te desperezarías	os desperezaríais	te habrías desperezado	os habríais desperezado
se desperezaría	se desperezarían	se habría desperezado	se habrían desperezado
6 presente de subjuntivo		**13 perfecto de subjuntivo**	
me desperece	nos desperecemos	me haya desperezado	nos hayamos desperezado
te despereces	os desperecéis	te hayas desperezado	os hayáis desperezado
se desperece	se desperecen	se haya desperezado	se hayan desperezado
7 imperfecto de subjuntivo		**14 pluscuamperfecto de subjuntivo**	
me desperezara	nos desperezáramos	me hubiera desperezado	nos hubiéramos desperezado
te desperezaras	os desperezarais	te hubieras desperezado	os hubierais desperezado
se desperezara	se desperezaran	se hubiera desperezado	se hubieran desperezado
OR		OR	
me desperezase	nos desperezásemos	me hubiese desperezado	nos hubiésemos desperezado
te desperezases	os desperezaseis	te hubieses desperezado	os hubieseis desperezado
se desperezase	se desperezasen	se hubiese desperezado	se hubiesen desperezado

imperativo	
—	desperecémonos
desperézate; no te despereces	desperezaos; no os desperecéis
desperécese	desperécense

Words related to this verb
el desperezo stretching one's arms and legs
perezoso, perezosa lazy
perezosamente lazily
la pereza laziness

Do you need more drills? Have fun with the *501 Spanish Verbs* CD-ROM!

Reflexive verb; regular -ar verb endings   to wake up oneself
with stem change: Tenses 1, 6, Imperative

The Seven Simple Tenses		The Seven Compound Tenses	
Singular	Plural	Singular	Plural
1 presente de indicativo		8 perfecto de indicativo	
me despierto	**nos despertamos**	**me he despertado**	**nos hemos despertado**
te despiertas	**os despertáis**	**te has despertado**	**os habéis despertado**
se despierta	**se despiertan**	**se ha despertado**	**se han despertado**
2 imperfecto de indicativo		9 pluscuamperfecto de indicativo	
me despertaba	**nos despertábamos**	**me había despertado**	**nos habíamos despertado**
te despertabas	**os despertabais**	**te habías despertado**	**os habíais despertado**
se despertaba	**se despertaban**	**se había despertado**	**se habían despertado**
3 pretérito		10 pretérito anterior	
me desperté	**nos despertamos**	**me hube despertado**	**nos hubimos despertado**
te despertaste	**os despertasteis**	**te hubiste despertado**	**os hubisteis despertado**
se despertó	**se despertaron**	**se hubo despertado**	**se hubieron despertado**
4 futuro		11 futuro perfecto	
me despertaré	**nos despertaremos**	**me habré despertado**	**nos habremos despertado**
te despertarás	**os despertaréis**	**te habrás despertado**	**os habréis despertado**
se despertará	**se despertarán**	**se habrá despertado**	**se habrán despertado**
5 potencial simple		12 potencial compuesto	
me despertaría	**nos despertaríamos**	**me habría despertado**	**nos habríamos despertado**
te despertarías	**os despertaríais**	**te habrías despertado**	**os habríais despertado**
se despertaría	**se despertarían**	**se habría despertado**	**se habrían despertado**
6 presente de subjuntivo		13 perfecto de subjuntivo	
me despierte	**nos despertemos**	**me haya despertado**	**nos hayamos despertado**
te despiertes	**os despertéis**	**te hayas despertado**	**os hayáis despertado**
se despierte	**se despierten**	**se haya despertado**	**se hayan despertado**
7 imperfecto de subjuntivo		14 pluscuamperfecto de subjuntivo	
me despertara	**nos despertáramos**	**me hubiera despertado**	**nos hubiéramos despertado**
te despertaras	**os despertarais**	**te hubieras despertado**	**os hubierais despertado**
se despertara	**se despertaran**	**se hubiera despertado**	**se hubieran despertado**
OR		OR	
me despertase	**nos despertásemos**	**me hubiese despertado**	**nos hubiésemos despertado**
te despertases	**os despertaseis**	**te hubieses despertado**	**os hubieseis despertado**
se despertase	**se despertasen**	**se hubiese despertado**	**se hubiesen despertado**

imperativo	
—	**despertémonos**
despiértate; no te despiertes	**despertaos; no os despertéis**
despiértese	**despiértense**

Words and expressions related to this verb

despertar   to awaken (someone), to enliven
un despertador   alarm clock
el despertamiento   awakening, arousal

despierto, despierta   wide awake, alert
María sueña despierta.   Mary daydreams.
despertarse a las siete de la mañana   to wake up at seven in the morning

If you want an explanation of meanings and uses of
Spanish and English verb tenses and moods, see pages 13–32.

The subject pronouns are found on page 93.

to destroy | Regular **-ir** verb endings with spelling change: add **y** before **a**, **e**, or **o**

The Seven Simple Tenses | The Seven Compound Tenses

Singular	Plural	Singular	Plural
1 presente de indicativo		**8 perfecto de indicativo**	
destruyo	destruimos	he destruido	hemos destruido
destruyes	destruís	has destruido	habéis destruido
destruye	destruyen	ha destruido	han destruido
2 imperfecto de indicativo		**9 pluscuamperfecto de indicativo**	
destruía	destruíamos	había destruido	habíamos destruido
destruías	destruíais	habías destruido	habíais destruido
destruía	destruían	había destruido	habían destruido
3 pretérito		**10 pretérito anterior**	
destruí	destruimos	hube destruido	hubimos destruido
destruiste	destruisteis	hubiste destruido	hubisteis destruido
destruyó	destruyeron	hubo destruido	hubieron destruido
4 futuro		**11 futuro perfecto**	
destruiré	destruiremos	habré destruido	habremos destruido
destruirás	destruiréis	habrás destruido	habréis destruido
destruirá	destruirán	habrá destruido	habrán destruido
5 potencial simple		**12 potencial compuesto**	
destruiría	destruiríamos	habría destruido	habríamos destruido
destruirías	destruiríais	habrías destruido	habríais destruido
destruiría	destruirían	habría destruido	habrían destruido
6 presente de subjuntivo		**13 perfecto de subjuntivo**	
destruya	destruyamos	haya destruido	hayamos destruido
destruyas	destruyáis	hayas destruido	hayáis destruido
destruya	destruyan	haya destruido	hayan destruido
7 imperfecto de subjuntivo		**14 pluscuamperfecto de subjuntivo**	
destruyera	destruyéramos	hubiera destruido	hubiéramos destruido
destruyeras	destruyerais	hubieras destruido	hubierais destruido
destruyera	destruyeran	hubiera destruido	hubieran destruido
OR		OR	
destruyese	destruyésemos	hubiese destruido	hubiésemos destruido
destruyeses	destruyeseis	hubieses destruido	hubieseis destruido
destruyese	destruyesen	hubiese destruido	hubiesen destruido

imperativo

—	destruyamos
destruye; no destruyas	destruid; no destruyáis
destruya	destruyan

Words and expressions related to this verb

destructor, destructora   destructor, destroyer
la destrucción   destruction
destruíble   destructible

destructivo, destructiva   destructive
destruidor, destruidora   destroyer
destructivamente   destructively

Don't forget to study the section on defective and impersonal verbs. It's right after this main list.

Regular **-ir** verb endings with stem change: to undress oneself, to get undressed
Tenses 1, 3, 6, 7, Imperative, Gerundio

The Seven Simple Tenses		The Seven Compound Tenses	
Singular	Plural	Singular	Plural
1 presente de indicativo		8 perfecto de indicativo	
me desvisto	**nos desvestimos**	**me he desvestido**	**nos hemos desvestido**
te desvistes	**os desvestís**	**te has desvestido**	**os habéis desvestido**
se desviste	**se desvisten**	**se ha desvestido**	**se han desvestido**
2 imperfecto de indicativo		9 pluscuamperfecto de indicativo	
me desvestía	**nos desvestíamos**	**me había desvestido**	**nos habíamos desvestido**
te desvestías	**os desvestíais**	**te habías desvestido**	**os habíais desvestido**
se desvestía	**se desvestían**	**se había desvestido**	**se habían desvestido**
3 pretérito		10 pretérito anterior	
me desvestí	**nos desvestimos**	**me hube desvestido**	**nos hubimos desvestido**
te desvestiste	**os desvestisteis**	**te hubiste desvestido**	**os hubisteis desvestido**
se desvistió	**se desvistieron**	**se hubo desvestido**	**se hubieron desvestido**
4 futuro		11 futuro perfecto	
me desvestiré	**nos desvestiremos**	**me habré desvestido**	**nos habremos desvestido**
te desvestirás	**os desvestiréis**	**te habrás desvestido**	**os habréis desvestido**
se desvestirá	**se desvestirán**	**se habrá desvestido**	**se habrán desvestido**
5 potencial simple		12 potencial compuesto	
me desvestiría	**nos desvestiríamos**	**me habría desvestido**	**nos habríamos desvestido**
te desvestirías	**os desvestiríais**	**te habrías desvestido**	**os habríais desvestido**
se desvestiría	**se desvestirían**	**se habría desvestido**	**se habrían desvestido**
6 presente de subjuntivo		13 perfecto de subjuntivo	
me desvista	**nos desvistamos**	**me haya desvestido**	**nos hayamos desvestido**
te desvistas	**os desvistáis**	**te hayas desvestido**	**os hayáis desvestido**
se desvista	**se desvistan**	**se haya desvestido**	**se hayan desvestido**
7 imperfecto de subjuntivo		14 pluscuamperfecto de subjuntivo	
me desvistiera	**nos desvistiéramos**	**me hubiera desvestido**	**nos hubiéramos desvestido**
te desvistieras	**os desvistierais**	**te hubieras desvestido**	**os hubierais desvestido**
se desvistiera	**se desvistieran**	**se hubiera desvestido**	**se hubieran desvestido**
OR		OR	
me desvistiese	**nos desvistiésemos**	**me hubiese desvestido**	**nos hubiésemos desvestido**
te desvistieses	**os desvistieseis**	**te hubieses desvestido**	**os hubieseis desvestido**
se desvistiese	**se desvistiesen**	**se hubiese desvestido**	**se hubiesen desvestido**

	imperativo
—	**desvistámonos**
desvístete; no te desvistas	**desvestíos; no os desvistáis**
desvístase	**desvístanse**

Words and expressions related to this verb

vestir to clothe, to dress	**bien vestido** well-dressed
vestirse to clothe oneself, to dress oneself	**vestir de blanco** to dress in white
el vestido clothing, clothes, dress	**vestir de uniforme** to dress in uniform
vestidos usados secondhand clothing	**el vestido de etiqueta** evening clothes

Don't miss the definitions of basic grammatical terms with examples
in English and Spanish on pages 33–44.

to stop (someone or something), to detain   Irregular verb

The Seven Simple Tenses		The Seven Compound Tenses	
Singular	Plural	Singular	Plural
1 presente de indicativo		**8 perfecto de indicativo**	
detengo	detenemos	he detenido	hemos detenido
detienes	detenéis	has detenido	habéis detenido
detiene	detienen	ha detenido	han detenido
2 imperfecto de indicativo		**9 pluscuamperfecto de indicativo**	
detenía	deteníamos	había detenido	habíamos detenido
detenías	deteníais	habías detenido	habíais detenido
detenía	detenían	había detenido	habían detenido
3 pretérito		**10 pretérito anterior**	
detuve	detuvimos	hube detenido	hubimos detenido
detuviste	detuvisteis	hubiste detenido	hubisteis detenido
detuvo	detuvieron	hubo detenido	hubieron detenido
4 futuro		**11 futuro perfecto**	
detendré	detendremos	habré detenido	habremos detenido
detendrás	detendréis	habrás detenido	habréis detenido
detendrá	detendrán	habrá detenido	habrán detenido
5 potencial simple		**12 potencial compuesto**	
detendría	detendríamos	habría detenido	habríamos detenido
detendrías	detendríais	habrías detenido	habríais detenido
detendría	detendrían	habría detenido	habrían detenido
6 presente de subjuntivo		**13 perfecto de subjuntivo**	
detenga	detengamos	haya detenido	hayamos detenido
detengas	detengáis	hayas detenido	hayáis detenido
detenga	detengan	haya detenido	hayan detenido
7 imperfecto de subjuntivo		**14 pluscuamperfecto de subjuntivo**	
detuviera	detuviéramos	hubiera detenido	hubiéramos detenido
detuvieras	detuvierais	hubieras detenido	hubierais detenido
detuviera	detuvieran	hubiera detenido	hubieran detenido
OR		OR	
detuviese	detuviésemos	hubiese detenido	hubiésemos detenido
detuvieses	detuvieseis	hubieses detenido	hubieseis detenido
detuviese	detuviesen	hubiese detenido	hubiesen detenido

imperativo

—	detengamos
detén; no detengas	detened; no detengáis
detenga	detengan

Words related to this verb

el detenimiento   delay
detenidamente   cautiously
sostener   to support, to sustain
la detención   detention, detainment

detenerse a + inf.   to stop + inf.
el sostenimiento   support, sustenance
el detenido, la detenida   person under arrest
sin detención   without delay

See also **tener.**

The Seven Simple Tenses		The Seven Compound Tenses	
Singular	Plural	Singular	Plural
1 presente de indicativo		8 perfecto de indicativo	
me detengo	**nos detenemos**	**me he detenido**	**nos hemos detenido**
te detienes	**os detenéis**	**te has detenido**	**os habéis detenido**
se detiene	**se detienen**	**se ha detenido**	**se han detenido**
2 imperfecto de indicativo		9 pluscuamperfecto de indicativo	
me detenía	**nos deteníamos**	**me había detenido**	**nos habíamos detenido**
te detenías	**os deteníais**	**te habías detenido**	**os habíais detenido**
se detenía	**se detenían**	**se había detenido**	**se habían detenido**
3 pretérito		10 pretérito anterior	
me detuve	**nos detuvimos**	**me hube detenido**	**nos hubimos detenido**
te detuviste	**os detuvisteis**	**te hubiste detenido**	**os hubisteis detenido**
se detuvo	**se detuvieron**	**se hubo detenido**	**se hubieron detenido**
4 futuro		11 futuro perfecto	
me detendré	**nos detendremos**	**me habré detenido**	**nos habremos detenido**
te detendrás	**os detendréis**	**te habrás detenido**	**os habréis detenido**
se detendrá	**se detendrán**	**se habrá detenido**	**se habrán detenido**
5 potencial simple		12 potencial compuesto	
me detendría	**nos detendríamos**	**me habría detenido**	**nos habríamos detenido**
te detendrías	**os detendríais**	**te habrías detenido**	**os habríais detenido**
se detendría	**se detendrían**	**se habría detenido**	**se habrían detenido**
6 presente de subjuntivo		13 perfecto de subjuntivo	
me detenga	**nos detengamos**	**me haya detenido**	**nos hayamos detenido**
te detengas	**os detangáis**	**te hayas detenido**	**os hayáis detenido**
se detenga	**se detengan**	**se haya detenido**	**se hayan detenido**
7 imperfecto de subjuntivo		14 pluscuamperfecto de subjuntivo	
me detuviera	**nos detuviéramos**	**me hubiera detenido**	**nos hubiéramos detenido**
te detuvieras	**os detuvierais**	**te hubieras detenido**	**os hubierais detenido**
se detuviera	**se detuvieran**	**se hubiera detenido**	**se hubieran detenido**
OR		OR	
me detuviese	**nos detuviésemos**	**me hubiese detenido**	**nos hubiésemos detenido**
te detuvieses	**os detuvieseis**	**te hubieses detenido**	**os hubieseis detenido**
se detuviese	**se detuviesen**	**se hubiese detenido**	**se hubiesen detenido**

imperativo

—	**detengámonos**
detente; no te detengas	**deteneos; no os detengáis**
deténgase	**deténganse**

Words and expressions related to this verb

detener   to stop (someone or something), to detain

detenedor, detenedora   detainer

See also **detener**.

detenerse en una idea   to dwell on an idea

If you don't know the Spanish verb for an English verb you have in mind, try the index on pages 682–706.

devolver (186)

Gerundio **devolviendo**   Part. pas. **devuelto**

to return (an object),
to refund, to give back

Regular **-er** verb endings with stem change:
Tenses 1, 6, Imperative, Part. pas.

The Seven Simple Tenses | The Seven Compound Tenses

Singular	Plural	Singular	Plural
1 presente de indicativo		**8 perfecto de indicativo**	
devuelvo	devolvemos	he devuelto	hemos devuelto
devuelves	devolvéis	has devuelto	habéis devuelto
devuelve	devuelven	ha devuelto	han devuelto
2 imperfecto de indicativo		**9 pluscuamperfecto de indicativo**	
devolvía	devolvíamos	había devuelto	habíamos devuelto
devolvías	devolvíais	habías devuelto	habíais devuelto
devolvía	devolvían	había devuelto	habían devuelto
3 pretérito		**10 pretérito anterior**	
devolví	devolvimos	hube devuelto	hubimos devuelto
devolviste	devolvisteis	hubiste devuelto	hubisteis devuelto
devolvió	devolvieron	hubo devuelto	hubieron devuelto
4 futuro		**11 futuro perfecto**	
devolveré	devolveremos	habré devuelto	habremos devuelto
devolverás	devolveréis	habrás devuelto	habréis devuelto
devolverá	devolverán	habrá devuelto	habrán devuelto
5 potencial simple		**12 potencial compuesto**	
devolvería	devolveríamos	habría devuelto	habríamos devuelto
devolverías	devolveríais	habrías devuelto	habríais devuelto
devolvería	devolverían	habría devuelto	habrían devuelto
6 presente de subjuntivo		**13 perfecto de subjuntivo**	
devuelva	devolvamos	haya devuelto	hayamos devuelto
devuelvas	devolváis	hayas devuelto	hayáis devuelto
devuelva	devuelvan	haya devuelto	hayan devuelto
7 imperfecto de subjuntivo		**14 pluscuamperfecto de subjuntivo**	
devolviera	devolviéramos	hubiera devuelto	hubiéramos devuelto
devolvieras	devolvierais	hubieras devuelto	hubierais devuelto
devolviera	devolvieran	hubiera devuelto	hubieran devuelto
OR		OR	
devolviese	devolviésemos	hubiese devuelto	hubiésemos devuelto
devolvieses	devolvieseis	hubieses devuelto	hubieseis devuelto
devolviese	devolviesen	hubiese devuelto	hubiesen devuelto

imperativo

—	devolvamos
devuelve; no devuelvas	devolved; no devolváis
devuelva	devuelvan

Words and expressions related to this verb
—¿Ha devuelto Ud. los libros a la biblioteca?
devolutivo, devolutiva returnable
volver to return, to go back

—Sí, señora, los devolví ayer.
devolver to vomit
la devolución return, giving back

For other words and expressions related to this verb, see **revolver** and **volver**.

See also **devolver**.

298

Regular **-ar** verb   to design, to draw, to sketch

The Seven Simple Tenses		The Seven Compound Tenses	
Singular	Plural	Singular	Plural
1 presente de indicativo		**8 perfecto de indicativo**	
dibujo	dibujamos	he dibujado	hemos dibujado
dibujas	dibujáis	has dibujado	habéis dibujado
dibuja	dibujan	ha dibujado	han dibujado
2 imperfecto de indicativo		**9 pluscuamperfecto de indicativo**	
dibujaba	dibujábamos	había dibujado	habíamos dibujado
dibujabas	dibujabais	habías dibujado	habíais dibujado
dibujaba	dibujaban	había dibujado	habían dibujado
3 pretérito		**10 pretérito anterior**	
dibujé	dibujamos	hube dibujado	hubimos dibujado
dibujaste	dibujasteis	hubiste dibujado	hubisteis dibujado
dibujó	dibujaron	hubo dibujado	hubieron dibujado
4 futuro		**11 futuro perfecto**	
dibujaré	dibujaremos	habré dibujado	habremos dibujado
dibujarás	dibujaréis	habrás dibujado	habréis dibujado
dibujará	dibujarán	habrá dibujado	habrán dibujado
5 potencial simple		**12 potencial compuesto**	
dibujaría	dibujaríamos	habría dibujado	habríamos dibujado
dibujarías	dibujaríais	habrías dibujado	habríais dibujado
dibujaría	dibujarían	habría dibujado	habrían dibujado
6 presente de subjuntivo		**13 perfecto de subjuntivo**	
dibuje	dibujemos	haya dibujado	hayamos dibujado
dibujes	dibujéis	hayas dibujado	hayáis dibujado
dibuje	dibujen	haya dibujado	hayan dibujado
7 imperfecto de subjuntivo		**14 pluscuamperfecto de subjuntivo**	
dibujara	dibujáramos	hubiera dibujado	hubiéramos dibujado
dibujaras	dibujarais	hubieras dibujado	hubierais dibujado
dibujara	dibujaran	hubiera dibujado	hubieran dibujado
OR		OR	
dibujase	dibujásemos	hubiese dibujado	hubiésemos dibujado
dibujases	dibujaseis	hubieses dibujado	hubieseis dibujado
dibujase	dibujasen	hubiese dibujado	hubiesen dibujado

	imperativo	
—		dibujemos
dibuja; no dibujes		dibujad; no dibujéis
dibuje		dibujen

Words and expressions related to this verb
un dibujo drawing, design, sketch   **dibujo a la pluma** pen and ink drawing
el, la dibujante designer, illustrator, sketcher   **dibujos animados** (animated) cartoons
dibujos humorísticos comics
el dibujo asistido por ordenador computer-assisted drawing

The subject pronouns are found on page 93.

to direct

Regular **-ir** verb endings with spelling change: **g** becomes **j** before **a** or **o**

The Seven Simple Tenses		The Seven Compound Tenses	
Singular	Plural	Singular	Plural
1 presente de indicativo		8 perfecto de indicativo	
dirijo	dirigimos	he dirigido	hemos dirigido
diriges	dirigís	has dirigido	habéis dirigido
dirige	dirigen	ha dirigido	han dirigido
2 imperfecto de indicativo		9 pluscuamperfecto de indicativo	
dirigía	dirigíamos	había dirigido	habíamos dirigido
dirigías	dirigíais	habías dirigido	habíais dirigido
dirigía	dirigían	había dirigido	habían dirigido
3 pretérito		10 pretérito anterior	
dirigí	dirigimos	hube dirigido	hubimos dirigido
dirigiste	dirigisteis	hubiste dirigido	hubisteis dirigido
dirigió	dirigieron	hubo dirigido	hubieron dirigido
4 futuro		11 futuro perfecto	
dirigiré	dirigiremos	habré dirigido	habremos dirigido
dirigirás	dirigiréis	habrás dirigido	habréis dirigido
dirigirá	dirigirán	habrá dirigido	habrán dirigido
5 potencial simple		12 potencial compuesto	
dirigiría	dirigiríamos	habría dirigido	habríamos dirigido
dirigirías	dirigiríais	habrías dirigido	habríais dirigido
dirigiría	dirigirían	habría dirigido	habrían dirigido
6 presente de subjuntivo		13 perfecto de subjuntivo	
dirija	dirijamos	haya dirigido	hayamos dirigido
dirijas	dirijáis	hayas dirigido	hayáis dirigido
dirija	dirijan	haya dirigido	hayan dirigido
7 imperfecto de subjuntivo		14 pluscuamperfecto de subjuntivo	
dirigiera	dirigiéramos	hubiera dirigido	hubiéramos dirigido
dirigieras	dirigierais	hubieras dirigido	hubierais dirigido
dirigiera	dirigieran	hubiera dirigido	hubieran dirigido
OR		OR	
dirigiese	dirigiésemos	hubiese dirigido	hubiésemos dirigido
dirigieses	dirigieseis	hubieses dirigido	hubieseis dirigido
dirigiese	dirigiesen	hubiese dirigido	hubiesen dirigido

imperativo

—	dirijamos
dirige; no dirijas	dirigid; no dirijáis
dirija	dirijan

Words and expressions related to this verb

el director, la directora director
director de orquesta orchestra conductor
el dirigente, la dirigente leader
dirigir la palabra a to address, to speak to

dirigible manageable
el dirigible dirigible, blimp (aviation)
dirigirse a to make one's way to, to go to
dirigir el baile to run the show

Can't recognize an irregular verb form? Check out pages 678–681.

Reflexive regular **-ar** verb   to apologize, to excuse (oneself)

The Seven Simple Tenses		The Seven Compound Tenses	
Singular	Plural	Singular	Plural
1 presente de indicativo		8 perfecto de indicativo	
me disculpo	nos disculpamos	me he disculpado	nos hemos disculpado
te disculpas	os disculpáis	te has disculpado	os habéis disculpado
se disculpa	se disculpan	se ha disculpado	se han disculpado
2 imperfecto de indicativo		9 pluscuamperfecto de indicativo	
me disculpaba	nos disculpábamos	me había disculpado	nos habíamos disculpado
te disculpabas	os disculpabais	te habías disculpado	os habíais disculpado
se disculpaba	se disculpaban	se había disculpado	se habían disculpado
3 pretérito		10 pretérito anterior	
me disculpé	nos disculpamos	me hube disculpado	nos hubimos disculpado
te disculpaste	os disculpasteis	te hubiste disculpado	os hubisteis disculpado
se disculpó	se disculparon	se hubo disculpado	se hubieron disculpado
4 futuro		11 futuro perfecto	
me disculparé	nos disculparemos	me habré disculpado	nos habremos disculpado
te disculparás	os disculparéis	te habrás disculpado	os habréis disculpado
se disculpará	se disculparán	se habrá disculpado	se habrán disculpado
5 potencial simple		12 potencial compuesto	
me disculparía	nos disculparíamos	me habría disculpado	nos habríamos disculpado
te disculparías	os disculparíais	te habrías disculpado	os habríais disculpado
se disculparía	se disculparían	se habría disculpado	se habrían disculpado
6 presente de subjuntivo		13 perfecto de subjuntivo	
me disculpe	nos disculpemos	me haya disculpado	nos hayamos disculpado
te disculpes	os disculpéis	te hayas disculpado	os hayáis disculpado
se disculpe	se disculpen	se haya disculpado	se hayan disculpado
7 imperfecto de subjuntivo		14 pluscuamperfecto de subjuntivo	
me disculpara	nos disculpáramos	me hubiera disculpado	nos hubiéramos disculpado
te disculparas	os disculparais	te hubieras disculpado	os hubierais disculpado
se disculpara	se disculparan	se hubiera disculpado	se hubieran disculpado
OR		OR	
me disculpase	nos disculpásemos	me hubiese disculpado	nos hubiésemos disculpado
te disculpases	os disculpaseis	te hubieses disculpado	os hubieseis disculpado
se disculpase	se disculpasen	se hubiese disculpado	se hubiesen disculpado

imperativo

—	disculpémonos
discúlpate; no te disculpes	disculpaos; no os disculpéis
discúlpese	discúlpense

Words and expressions related to this verb
disculpar   to excuse, to pardon (someone)
disculparse con   to apologize to, to make
  excuses to
disculparse de   to apologize for, to make
  excuses for

una disculpa   excuse, apology
la culpa   fault, blame, guilt
tener la culpa   to be guilty
culpar   to blame, to accuse
culparse   to blame oneself
dar disculpas   to make excuses

The subject pronouns are found on page 93.

discutir (190)

Gerundio **discutiendo**   Part. pas. **discutido**

to discuss, to debate

The Seven Simple Tenses		The Seven Compound Tenses	
Singular	Plural	Singular	Plural
1 presente de indicativo		**8 perfecto de indicativo**	
discuto	discutimos	he discutido	hemos discutido
discutes	discutís	has discutido	habéis discutido
discute	discuten	ha discutido	han discutido
2 imperfecto de indicativo		**9 pluscuamperfecto de indicativo**	
discutía	discutíamos	había discutido	habíamos discutido
discutías	discutíais	habías discutido	habíais discutido
discutía	discutían	había discutido	habían discutido
3 pretérito		**10 pretérito anterior**	
discutí	discutimos	hube discutido	hubimos discutido
discutiste	discutisteis	hubiste discutido	hubisteis discutido
discutió	discutieron	hubo discutido	hubieron discutido
4 futuro		**11 futuro perfecto**	
discutiré	discutiremos	habré discutido	habremos discutido
discutirás	discutiréis	habrás discutido	habréis discutido
discutirá	discutirán	habrá discutido	habrán discutido
5 potencial simple		**12 potencial compuesto**	
discutiría	discutiríamos	habría discutido	habríamos discutido
discutirías	discutiríais	habrías discutido	habríais discutido
discutiría	discutirían	habría discutido	habrían discutido
6 presente de subjuntivo		**13 perfecto de subjuntivo**	
discuta	discutamos	haya discutido	hayamos discutido
discutas	discutáis	hayas discutido	hayáis discutido
discuta	discutan	haya discutido	hayan discutido
7 imperfecto de subjuntivo		**14 pluscuamperfecto de subjuntivo**	
discutiera	discutiéramos	hubiera discutido	hubiéramos discutido
discutieras	discutierais	hubieras discutido	hubierais discutido
discutiera	discutieran	hubiera discutido	hubieran discutido
OR		OR	
discutiese	discutiésemos	hubiese discutido	hubiésemos discutido
discutieses	discutieseis	hubieses discutido	hubieseis discutido
discutiese	discutiesen	hubiese discutido	hubiesen discutido

imperativo	
—	discutamos
discute; no discutas	discutid; no discutáis
discuta	discutan

Words and expressions related to this verb

discutir sobre   to argue about
discutible   debatable, disputable
la discusión   discussion, argument

un discurso   discourse, speech
el discurso de la corona   King (Queen's) speech
discutir el precio   to argue over the price

Do you need more drills? Have fun with the *501 Spanish Verbs* CD-ROM!

Regular **-ar** verb   to enjoy, to enjoy oneself

The Seven Simple Tenses		The Seven Compound Tenses	
Singular	Plural	Singular	Plural
1 presente de indicativo		8 perfecto de indicativo	
disfruto	**disfrutamos**	**he disfrutado**	**hemos disfrutado**
disfrutas	**disfrutáis**	**has disfrutado**	**habéis disfrutado**
disfruta	**disfrutan**	**ha disfrutado**	**han disfrutado**
2 imperfecto de indicativo		9 pluscuamperfecto de indicativo	
disfrutaba	**disfrutábamos**	**había disfrutado**	**habíamos disfrutado**
disfrutabas	**disfrutabais**	**habías disfrutado**	**habíais disfrutado**
disfrutaba	**disfrutaban**	**había disfrutado**	**habían disfrutado**
3 pretérito		10 pretérito anterior	
disfruté	**disfrutamos**	**hube disfrutado**	**hubimos disfrutado**
disfrutaste	**disfrutasteis**	**hubiste disfrutado**	**hubisteis disfrutado**
disfrutó	**disfrutaron**	**hubo disfrutado**	**hubieron disfrutado**
4 futuro		11 futuro perfecto	
disfrutaré	**disfrutaremos**	**habré disfrutado**	**habremos disfrutado**
disfrutarás	**disfrutaréis**	**habrás disfrutado**	**habréis disfrutado**
disfrutará	**disfrutarán**	**habrá disfrutado**	**habrán disfrutado**
5 potencial simple		12 potencial compuesto	
disfrutaría	**disfrutaríamos**	**habría disfrutado**	**habríamos disfrutado**
disfrutarías	**disfrutaríais**	**habrías disfrutado**	**habríais disfrutado**
disfrutaría	**disfrutarían**	**habría disfrutado**	**habrían disfrutado**
6 presente de subjuntivo		13 perfecto de subjuntivo	
disfrute	**disfrutemos**	**haya disfrutado**	**hayamos disfrutado**
disfrutes	**disfrutéis**	**hayas disfrutado**	**hayáis disfrutado**
disfrute	**disfruten**	**haya disfrutado**	**hayan disfrutado**
7 imperfecto de subjuntivo		14 pluscuamperfecto de subjuntivo	
disfrutara	**disfrutáramos**	**hubiera disfrutado**	**hubiéramos disfrutado**
disfrutaras	**disfrutarais**	**hubieras disfrutado**	**hubierais disfrutado**
disfrutara	**disfrutaran**	**hubiera disfrutado**	**hubieran disfrutado**
OR		OR	
disfrutase	**disfrutásemos**	**hubiese disfrutado**	**hubiésemos disfrutado**
disfrutases	**disfrutaseis**	**hubieses disfrutado**	**hubieseis disfrutado**
disfrutase	**disfrutasen**	**hubiese disfrutado**	**hubiesen disfrutado**

	imperativo	
—		**disfrutemos**
disfruta; no disfrutes		**disfrutad; no disfrutéis**
disfrute		**disfruten**

Words and expressions related to this verb
el disfrute   enjoyment
disfrutar de   to enjoy

**Después de cenar, Magdalena disfrutó de
un baño caliente.**   After dinner, Magdalen
enjoyed a warm bath.

Don't forget to study the section on defective and impersonal verbs. It's right after this main list.

The subject pronouns are found on page 93.

to excuse, to dispense, to distribute, to exempt   Regular **-ar** verb

The Seven Simple Tenses		The Seven Compound Tenses	
Singular	Plural	Singular	Plural
1 presente de indicativo		8 perfecto de indicativo	
dispenso	dispensamos	he dispensado	hemos dispensado
dispensas	dispensáis	has dispensado	habéis dispensado
dispensa	dispensan	ha dispensado	han dispensado
2 imperfecto de indicativo		9 pluscuamperfecto de indicativo	
dispensaba	dispensábamos	había dispensado	habíamos dispensado
dispensabas	dispensabais	habías dispensado	habíais dispensado
dispensaba	dispensaban	había dispensado	habían dispensado
3 pretérito		10 pretérito anterior	
dispensé	dispensamos	hube dispensado	hubimos dispensado
dispensaste	dispensasteis	hubiste dispensado	hubisteis dispensado
dispensó	dispensaron	hubo dispensado	hubieron dispensado
4 futuro		11 futuro perfecto	
dispensaré	dispensaremos	habré dispensado	habremos dispensado
dispensarás	dispensaréis	habrás dispensado	habréis dispensado
dispensará	dispensarán	habrá dispensado	habrán dispensado
5 potencial simple		12 potencial compuesto	
dispensaría	dispensaríamos	habría dispensado	habríamos dispensado
dispensarías	dispensaríais	habrías dispensado	habríais dispensado
dispensaría	dispensarían	habría dispensado	habrían dispensado
6 presente de subjuntivo		13 perfecto de subjuntivo	
dispense	dispensemos	haya dispensado	hayamos dispensado
dispenses	dispenséis	hayas dispensado	hayáis dispensado
dispense	dispensen	haya dispensado	hayan dispensado
7 imperfecto de subjuntivo		14 pluscuamperfecto de subjuntivo	
dispensara	dispensáramos	hubiera dispensado	hubiéramos dispensado
dispensaras	dispensarais	hubieras dispensado	hubierais dispensado
dispensara	dispensaran	hubiera dispensado	hubieran dispensado
OR		OR	
dispensase	dispensásemos	hubiese dispensado	hubiésemos dispensado
dispensases	dispensaseis	hubieses dispensado	hubieseis dispensado
dispensase	dispensasen	hubiese dispensado	hubiesen dispensado

	imperativo	
—		dispensemos
dispensa; no dispenses		dispensad; no dispenséis
dispense		dispensen

Words and expressions related to this verb
¡**Dispénseme!**   Excuse me!   **dispensar de + inf.**   to excuse from + pres. part.
la **dispensación**   dispensation   la **dispensa**   privilege, exemption
el **dispensario**   dispensary, clinic

Can't find the verb you're looking for?
Check the back pages of this book for a list of over 2,100 additional verbs!

Regular **-ir** verb endings with spelling   to distinguish
change: **gu** becomes **g** before **a** or **o**

The Seven Simple Tenses | The Seven Compound Tenses

Singular	Plural	Singular	Plural
1 presente de indicativo		8 perfecto de indicativo	
distingo	**distinguimos**	**he distinguido**	**hemos distinguido**
distingues	**distinguís**	**has distinguido**	**habéis distinguido**
distingue	**distinguen**	**ha distinguido**	**han distinguido**
2 imperfecto de indicativo		9 pluscuamperfecto de indicativo	
distinguía	**distinguíamos**	**había distinguido**	**habíamos distinguido**
distinguías	**distinguíais**	**habías distinguido**	**habíais distinguido**
distinguía	**distinguían**	**había distinguido**	**habían distinguido**
3 pretérito		10 pretérito anterior	
distinguí	**distinguimos**	**hube distinguido**	**hubimos distinguido**
distinguiste	**distinguisteis**	**hubiste distinguido**	**hubisteis distinguido**
distinguió	**distinguieron**	**hubo distinguido**	**hubieron distinguido**
4 futuro		11 futuro perfecto	
distinguiré	**distinguiremos**	**habré distinguido**	**habremos distinguido**
distinguirás	**distinguiréis**	**habrás distinguido**	**habréis distinguido**
distinguirá	**distinguirán**	**habrá distinguido**	**habrán distinguido**
5 potencial simple		12 potencial compuesto	
distinguiría	**distinguiríamos**	**habría distinguido**	**habríamos distinguido**
distinguirías	**distinguiríais**	**habrías distinguido**	**habríais distinguido**
distinguiría	**distinguirían**	**habría distinguido**	**habrían distinguido**
6 presente de subjuntivo		13 perfecto de subjuntivo	
distinga	**distingamos**	**haya distinguido**	**hayamos distinguido**
distingas	**distingáis**	**hayas distinguido**	**hayáis distinguido**
distinga	**distingan**	**haya distinguido**	**hayan distinguido**
7 imperfecto de subjuntivo		14 pluscuamperfecto de subjuntivo	
distinguiera	**distinguiéramos**	**hubiera distinguido**	**hubiéramos distinguido**
distinguieras	**distinguierais**	**hubieras distinguido**	**hubierais distinguido**
distinguiera	**distinguieran**	**hubiera distinguido**	**hubieran distinguido**
OR		OR	
distinguiese	**distinguiésemos**	**hubiese distinguido**	**hubiésemos distinguido**
distinguieses	**distinguieseis**	**hubieses distinguido**	**hubieseis distinguido**
distinguiese	**distinguiesen**	**hubiese distinguido**	**hubiesen distinguido**

imperativo

—	**distingamos**
distingue; no distingas	**distinguid; no distingáis**
distinga	**distingan**

Words related to this verb

distinguirse   to distinguish oneself   **a distinción de**   as distinct from
distintivo, distintiva   distinctive   **distinto, distinta**   different, distinct, clear
el distingo   restriction   **la distinción**   distinction

> If you want to see a sample English verb fully conjugated in
> all the tenses, check out pages 11 and 12.

The subject pronouns are found on page 93.

to have a good time, to enjoy oneself, to amuse oneself	Reflexive verb; regular **-ir** verb endings with stem change: Tenses 1, 3, 6, 7, Imperative, Gerundio
The Seven Simple Tenses	The Seven Compound Tenses

Singular	Plural	Singular	Plural
1 presente de indicativo		**8 perfecto de indicativo**	
me divierto	nos divertimos	me he divertido	nos hemos divertido
te diviertes	os divertís	te has divertido	os habéis divertido
se divierte	se divierten	se ha divertido	se han divertido
2 imperfecto de indicativo		**9 pluscuamperfecto de indicativo**	
me divertía	nos divertíamos	me había divertido	nos habíamos divertido
te divertías	os divertíais	te habías divertido	os habíais divertido
se divertía	se divertían	se había divertido	se habían divertido
3 pretérito		**10 pretérito anterior**	
me divertí	nos divertimos	me hube divertido	nos hubimos divertido
te divertiste	os divertisteis	te hubiste divertido	os hubisteis divertido
se divirtió	se divirtieron	se hubo divertido	se hubieron divertido
4 futuro		**11 futuro perfecto**	
me divertiré	nos divertiremos	me habré divertido	nos habremos divertido
te divertirás	os divertiréis	te habrás divertido	os habréis divertido
se divertirá	se divertirán	se habrá divertido	se habrán divertido
5 potencial simple		**12 potencial compuesto**	
me divertiría	nos divertiríamos	me habría divertido	nos habríamos divertido
te divertirías	os divertiríais	te habrías divertido	os habríais divertido
se divertiría	se divertirían	se habría divertido	se habrían divertido
6 presente de subjuntivo		**13 perfecto de subjuntivo**	
me divierta	nos divirtamos	me haya divertido	nos hayamos divertido
te diviertas	os divirtáis	te hayas divertido	os hayáis divertido
se divierta	se diviertan	se haya divertido	se hayan divertido
7 imperfecto de subjuntivo		**14 pluscuamperfecto de subjuntivo**	
me divirtiera	nos divirtiéramos	me hubiera divertido	nos hubiéramos divertido
te divirtieras	os divirtierais	te hubieras divertido	os hubierais divertido
se divirtiera	se divirtieran	se hubiera divertido	se hubieran divertido
OR		OR	
me divirtiese	nos divirtiésemos	me hubiese divertido	nos hubiésemos divertido
te divirtieses	os divirtieseis	te hubieses divertido	os hubieseis divertido
se divirtiese	se divirtiesen	se hubiese divertido	se hubiesen divertido

imperativo	
—	divirtámonos; no nos divirtamos
diviértete; no te diviertas	divertíos; no os divirtáis
diviértase; no se divierta	diviértanse; no se diviertan

Words related to this verb

el divertimiento amusement, diversion
diverso, diversa diverse, different
la diversión entertainment, pastime

divertir to entertain
divertido, divertida amusing, entertaining
una película divertida an entertaining film

Don't forget to study the section on defective and impersonal verbs. It's right after this main list.

Reflexive regular **-ar** verb   to be (get) divorced

The Seven Simple Tenses | The Seven Compound Tenses

Singular	Plural	Singular	Plural
1 presente de indicativo		8 perfecto de indicativo	
me divorcio	**nos divorciamos**	**me he divorciado**	**nos hemos divorciado**
te divorcias	**os divorciáis**	**te has divorciado**	**os habéis divorciado**
se divorcia	**se divorcian**	**se ha divorciado**	**se han divorciado**
2 imperfecto de indicativo		9 pluscuamperfecto de indicativo	
me divorciaba	**nos divorciábamos**	**me había divorciado**	**nos habíamos divorciado**
te divorciabas	**os divorciabais**	**te habías divorciado**	**os habíais divorciado**
se divorciaba	**se divorciaban**	**se había divorciado**	**se habían divorciado**
3 pretérito		10 pretérito anterior	
me divorcié	**nos divorciamos**	**me hube divorciado**	**nos hubimos divorciado**
te divorciaste	**os divorciasteis**	**te hubiste divorciado**	**os hubisteis divorciado**
se divorció	**se divorciaron**	**se hubo divorciado**	**se hubieron divorciado**
4 futuro		11 futuro perfecto	
me divorciaré	**nso divorciaremos**	**me habré divorciado**	**nos habremos divorciado**
te divorciarás	**os divorciaréis**	**te habrás divorciado**	**os habréis divorciado**
se divoricará	**se divorciarán**	**se habrá divorciado**	**se habrán divorciado**
5 potencial simple		12 potencial compuesto	
me divorciaría	**nos divorciaríamos**	**me habría divorciado**	**nos habríamos divorciado**
te divorciarías	**os divorciaríais**	**te habrías divorciado**	**os habríais divorciado**
se divoricaría	**se divorciarían**	**se habría divorciado**	**se habrían divorciado**
6 presente de subjuntivo		13 perfecto de subjuntivo	
me divorcie	**nos divorciemos**	**me haya divorciado**	**nos hayamos divorciado**
te divorcies	**os divorciéis**	**te hayas divorciado**	**os hayáis divorciado**
se divorcie	**se divorcien**	**se haya divorciado**	**se hayan divorciado**
7 imperfecto de subjuntivo		14 pluscuamperfecto de subjuntivo	
me divorciara	**nos divorciáramos**	**me hubiera divorciado**	**nos hubiéramos divorciado**
te divorciaras	**os divorciarais**	**te hubieras divorciado**	**os hubierais divorciado**
se divorciara	**se divorciaran**	**se hubiera divorciado**	**se hubieran divorciado**
OR		OR	
me divorciase	**nos divorciásemos**	**me hubiese divorciado**	**nos hubiésemos divorciado**
te divorciases	**os divorciaseis**	**te hubieses divorciado**	**os hubieseis divorciado**
se divorciase	**se divorciasen**	**se hubiese divorciado**	**se hubiesen divorciado**

imperativo

—	**divorciémonos**
divórciate; no te divorcies	**divorciaos; no os divorciéis**
divórciese	**divórciense**

Words related to this verb
divorciarse de   to get a divorce from
el divorcio   divorce, separation
una mujer divorciada, un hombre divorciado   divorced woman, man

Check out the verb drills and verb tests with answers explained on pages 45–91.

The subject pronouns are found on page 93.

doler (196)

Gerundio **doliendo**   Part. pas. **dolido**

to ache, to pain, to hurt, to cause
grief, to cause regret

Regular **-er** verb endings with stem
change: Tenses 1, 6, Imperative

The Seven Simple Tenses		The Seven Compound Tenses	
Singular	Plural	Singular	Plural
1 presente de indicativo		**8 perfecto de indicativo**	
duelo	dolemos	he dolido	hemos dolido
dueles	doléis	has dolido	habéis dolido
duele	duelen	ha dolido	han dolido
2 imperfecto de indicativo		**9 pluscuamperfecto de indicativo**	
dolía	dolíamos	había dolido	habíamos dolido
dolías	dolíais	habías dolido	habíais dolido
dolía	dolían	había dolido	habían dolido
3 pretérito		**10 pretérito anterior**	
dolí	dolimos	hube dolido	hubimos dolido
doliste	dolisteis	hubiste dolido	hubisteis dolido
dolió	dolieron	hubo dolido	hubieron dolido
4 futuro		**11 futuro perfecto**	
doleré	doleremos	habré dolido	habremos dolido
dolerás	doleréis	habrás dolido	habréis dolido
dolerá	dolerán	habrá dolido	habrán dolido
5 potencial simple		**12 potencial compuesto**	
dolería	doleríamos	habría dolido	habríamos dolido
dolerías	doleríais	habrías dolido	habríais dolido
dolería	dolerían	habría dolido	habrían dolido
6 presente de subjuntivo		**13 perfecto de subjuntivo**	
duela	dolamos	haya dolido	hayamos dolido
duelas	doláis	hayas dolido	hayáis dolido
duela	duelan	haya dolido	hayan dolido
7 imperfecto de subjuntivo		**14 pluscuamperfecto de subjuntivo**	
doliera	doliéramos	hubiera dolido	hubiéramos dolido
dolieras	dolierais	hubieras dolido	hubierais dolido
doliera	dolieran	hubiera dolido	hubieran dolido
OR		OR	
doliese	doliésemos	hubiese dolido	hubiésemos dolido
dolieses	dolieseis	hubieses dolido	hubieseis dolido
doliese	doliesen	hubiese dolido	hubiesen dolido

imperativo

—	dolamos
duele; no duelas	doled; no doláis
duela	duelan

Words and expressions related to this verb

dolerse de   to complain about, to regret
un dolor   ache, hurt, pain, regret
causar dolor   to pain
estar con dolores   to be in labor
Me duelo de haber dicho tales cosas.
   I regret having said such things.

tener dolor de cabeza   to have a headache
tener dolor de muelas   to have a toothache
tener dolor do oído   to have an earache
un dolor sordo   dull nagging pain
dolerse de sus pecados   to repent of one's sins
José se duele de sus pecados.
   José repents of his sins.

Doler is usually conjugated in the third person (sing. and pl.) with an indirect object pronoun
(me, te, le, nos, os, les): **Me duele el pie**/My foot hurts.

Regular **-ir** verb endings with stem change: to sleep
Tenses 1, 3, 6, 7, Imperative, Gerundio

The Seven Simple Tenses		The Seven Compound Tenses	
Singular	Plural	Singular	Plural
1 presente de indicativo		8 perfecto de indicativo	
duermo	**dormimos**	**he dormido**	**hemos dormido**
duermes	**dormís**	**has dormido**	**habéis dormido**
duerme	**duermen**	**ha dormido**	**han dormido**
2 imperfecto de indicativo		9 pluscuamperfecto de indicativo	
dormía	**dormíamos**	**había dormido**	**habíamos dormido**
dormías	**dormíais**	**habías dormido**	**habíais dormido**
dormía	**dormían**	**había dormido**	**habían dormido**
3 pretérito		10 pretérito anterior	
dormí	**dormimos**	**hube dormido**	**hubimos dormido**
dormiste	**dormisteis**	**hubiste dormido**	**hubisteis dormido**
durmió	**durmieron**	**hubo dormido**	**hubieron dormido**
4 futuro		11 futuro perfecto	
dormiré	**dormiremos**	**habré dormido**	**habremos dormido**
dormirás	**dormiréis**	**habrás dormido**	**habréis dormido**
dormirá	**dormirán**	**habrá dormido**	**habrán dormido**
5 potencial simple		12 potencial compuesto	
dormiría	**dormiríamos**	**habría dormido**	**habríamos dormido**
dormirías	**dormiríais**	**habrías dormido**	**habríais dormido**
dormiría	**dormirían**	**habría dormido**	**habrían dormido**
6 presente de subjuntivo		13 perfecto de subjuntivo	
duerma	**durmamos**	**haya dormido**	**hayamos dormido**
duermas	**durmáis**	**hayas dormido**	**hayáis dormido**
duerma	**duerman**	**haya dormido**	**hayan dormido**
7 imperfecto de subjuntivo		14 pluscuamperfecto de subjuntivo	
durmiera	**durmiéramos**	**hubiera dormido**	**hubiéramos dormido**
durmieras	**durmierais**	**hubieras dormido**	**hubierais dormido**
durmiera	**durmieran**	**hubiera dormido**	**hubieran dormido**
OR		OR	
durmiese	**durmiésemos**	**hubiese dormido**	**hubiésemos dormido**
durmieses	**durmieseis**	**hubieses dormido**	**hubieseis dormido**
durmiese	**durmiesen**	**hubiese dormido**	**hubiesen dormido**

imperativo

—	**durmamos**
duerme; no duermas	**dormid; no durmáis**
duerma	**duerman**

AN ESSENTIAL
55 VERB

The subject pronouns are found on page 93.

Dormir is an extremely useful verb for beginning students of Spanish. Note the tricky stem change in Tenses 1, 3, 6, 7, as well as the imperative and gerundio.

Sentences using **dormir** and related words

Yo duermo mal.
I don't sleep well.

El que mucho duerme poco aprende.
Whoever sleeps a lot learns little.

Gato que duerme no caza ratónes.
A sleeping cat doesn't catch mice. (You snooze, you lose.)

Words and expressions related to this verb

dormir a pierna suelta **to sleep soundly**

dormir como una piedra **to sleep like a log** (piedra/**stone**)

pasar la noche en vela **to have a sleepless night**

dormir la siesta **to take an afternoon nap**

dormir la mona **to sleep off a hangover**

el dormitorio **bedroom, dormitory**

dormilón, dormilona **lazy**

un dormilón, una dormilona **sleepyhead**

la dormición **dormition**

dormitar **to doze**

dormirse **to fall asleep; (pres. part.: durmiéndose)**

tener la pierna dormida **to have one's leg fall asleep**

dormidero, dormidera **causing sleep**

Do you need more drills? Have fun with the *501 Spanish Verbs* CD-ROM!

Reflexive regular **-ar** verb   to take a shower, to shower oneself

The Seven Simple Tenses		The Seven Compound Tenses	
Singular	Plural	Singular	Plural
1 presente de indicativo		8 perfecto de indicativo	
me ducho	**nos duchamos**	**me he duchado**	**nos hemos duchado**
te duchas	**os ducháis**	**te has duchado**	**os habéis duchado**
se ducha	**se duchan**	**se ha duchado**	**se han duchado**
2 imperfecto de indicativo		9 pluscuamperfecto de indicativo	
me duchaba	**nos duchábamos**	**me había duchado**	**nos habíamos duchado**
te duchabas	**os duchabais**	**te habías duchado**	**os habíais duchado**
se duchaba	**se duchaban**	**se había duchado**	**se habían duchado**
3 pretérito		10 pretérito anterior	
me duché	**nos duchamos**	**me hube duchado**	**nos hubimos duchado**
te duchaste	**os duchasteis**	**te hubiste duchado**	**os hubisteis duchado**
se duchó	**se ducharon**	**se hubo duchado**	**se hubieron duchado**
4 futuro		11 futuro perfecto	
me ducharé	**nos ducharemos**	**me habré duchado**	**nos habremos duchado**
te ducharás	**os ducharéis**	**te habrás duchado**	**os habréis duchado**
se duchará	**se ducharán**	**se habrá duchado**	**se habrán duchado**
5 potencial simple		12 potencial compuesto	
me ducharía	**nos ducharíamos**	**me habría duchado**	**nos habríamos duchado**
te ducharías	**os ducharíais**	**te habrías duchado**	**os habríais duchado**
se ducharía	**se ducharían**	**se habría duchado**	**se habrían duchado**
6 presente de subjuntivo		13 perfecto de subjuntivo	
me duche	**nos duchemos**	**me haya duchado**	**nos hayamos duchado**
te duches	**os duchéis**	**te hayas duchado**	**os hayáis duchado**
se duche	**se duchen**	**se haya duchado**	**se hayan duchado**
7 imperfecto de subjuntivo		14 pluscuamperfecto de subjuntivo	
me duchara	**nos ducháramos**	**me hubiera duchado**	**nos hubiéramos duchado**
te ducharas	**os ducharais**	**te hubieras duchado**	**os hubierais duchado**
se duchara	**se ducharan**	**se hubiera duchado**	**se hubieran duchado**
OR		OR	
me duchase	**nos duchásemos**	**me hubiese duchado**	**nos hubiésemos duchado**
te duchases	**os duchaseis**	**te hubieses duchado**	**os hubieseis duchado**
se duchase	**se duchasen**	**se hubiese duchado**	**se hubiesen duchado**

imperativo

—	**duchémonos**
dúchate; no te duches	**duchaos; no os duchéis**
dúchese	**dúchense**

Sentences using this verb and words related to it
**Por lo general, me ducho todas las mañanas, pero esta mañana no me duché y mi padre me dijo:
—¡Dúchate!**

una ducha   shower, douche
tomar una ducha   to take a shower   **darse una ducha**   to have a shower

Use the guide to Spanish pronunciation on pages 665–667.

The subject pronouns are found on page 93.

to doubt   Regular **-ar** verb

The Seven Simple Tenses		The Seven Compound Tenses	
Singular	Plural	Singular	Plural
1 presente de indicativo		8 perfecto de indicativo	
dudo	dudamos	he dudado	hemos dudado
dudas	dudáis	has dudado	habéis dudado
duda	dudan	ha dudado	han dudado
2 imperfecto de indicativo		9 pluscuamperfecto de indicativo	
dudaba	dudábamos	había dudado	habíamos dudado
dudabas	dudabais	habías dudado	habíais dudado
dudaba	dudaban	había dudado	habían dudado
3 pretérito		10 pretérito anterior	
dudé	dudamos	hube dudado	hubimos dudado
dudaste	dudasteis	hubiste dudado	hubisteis dudado
dudó	dudaron	hubo dudado	hubieron dudado
4 futuro		11 futuro perfecto	
dudaré	dudaremos	habré dudado	habremos dudado
dudarás	dudaréis	habrás dudado	habréis dudado
dudará	dudarán	habrá dudado	habrán dudado
5 potencial simple		12 potencial compuesto	
dudaría	dudaríamos	habría dudado	habríamos dudado
dudarías	dudaríais	habrías dudado	habríais dudado
dudaría	dudarían	habría dudado	habrían dudado
6 presente de subjuntivo		13 perfecto de subjuntivo	
dude	dudemos	haya dudado	hayamos dudado
dudes	dudéis	hayas dudado	hayáis dudado
dude	duden	haya dudado	hayan dudado
7 imperfecto de subjuntivo		14 pluscuamperfecto de subjuntivo	
dudara	dudáramos	hubiera dudado	hubiéramos dudado
dudaras	dudarais	hubieras dudado	hubierais dudado
dudara	dudaran	hubiera dudado	hubieran dudado
OR		OR	
dudase	dudásemos	hubiese dudado	hubiésemos dudado
dudases	dudaseis	hubieses dudado	hubieseis dudado
dudase	dudasen	hubiese dudado	hubiesen dudado

imperativo	
—	dudemos
duda; no dudes	dudad; no dudéis
dude	duden

Words and expressions related to this verb
la duda doubt
sin duda undoubtedly, without a doubt
dudoso, dudosa doubtful
dudosamente doubtfully, hesitantly
dudar haber dicho eso to doubt having
  said that

poner en duda to doubt, to question
No cabe duda. There is no doubt.
No lo dudo. I don't doubt it.
dudar de algo to doubt something
dudar entre los dos to be unable to decide
  between the two

Regular **-ar** verb   to cast, to fling, to hurl, to pitch, to throw

The Seven Simple Tenses		The Seven Compound Tenses	
Singular	Plural	Singular	Plural
1 presente de indicativo		8 perfecto de indicativo	
echo	echamos	he echado	hemos echado
echas	echáis	has echado	habéis echado
echa	echan	ha echado	han echado
2 imperfecto de indicativo		9 pluscuamperfecto de indicativo	
echaba	echábamos	había echado	habíamos echado
echabas	echabais	habías echado	habíais echado
echaba	echaban	había echado	habían echado
3 pretérito		10 pretérito anterior	
eché	echamos	hube echado	hubimos echado
echaste	echasteis	hubiste echado	hubisteis echado
echó	echaron	hubo echado	hubieron echado
4 futuro		11 futuro perfecto	
echaré	echaremos	habré echado	habremos echado
echarás	echaréis	habrás echado	habréis echado
echará	echarán	habrá echado	habrán echado
5 potencial simple		12 potencial compuesto	
echaría	echaríamos	habría echado	habríamos echado
echarías	echaríais	habrías echado	habríais echado
echaría	echarían	habría echado	habrían echado
6 presente de subjuntivo		13 perfecto de subjuntivo	
eche	echemos	haya echado	hayamos echado
eches	echéis	hayas echado	hayáis echado
eche	echen	haya echado	hayan echado
7 imperfecto de subjuntivo		14 pluscuamperfecto de subjuntivo	
echara	echáramos	hubiera echado	hubiéramos echado
echaras	echarais	hubieras echado	hubierais echado
echara	echaran	hubiera echado	hubieran echado
OR		OR	
echase	echásemos	hubiese echado	hubiésemos echado
echases	echaseis	hubieses echado	hubieseis echado
echase	echasen	hubiese echado	hubiesen echado

	imperativo	
—		echemos
echa; no eches		echad; no echéis
eche		echen

Words and expressions related to this verb
echar mano a   to grab; **echar de menos a una persona**   to miss a person
echar una carta al correo   to mail (post) a letter; **echar raíces**   to take root
una echada, un echamiento   cast, throw, casting, throwing
echarse   to lie down, rest, stretch out (oneself)
desechar   to reject

The subject pronouns are found on page 93.
       313

to execute, to carry out, to perform　　　　Regular **-ar** verb

The Seven Simple Tenses		The Seven Compound Tenses	
Singular	Plural	Singular	Plural
1　presente de indicativo		8　perfecto de indicativo	
ejecuto	ejecutamos	he ejecutado	hemos ejecutado
ejecutas	ejecutáis	has ejecutado	habéis ejecutado
ejecuta	ejecutan	ha ejecutado	han ejecutado
2　imperfecto de indicativo		9　pluscuamperfecto de indicativo	
ejecutaba	ejecutábamos	había ejecutado	habíamos ejecutado
ejecutabas	ejecutabais	habías ejecutado	habíais ejecutado
ejecutaba	ejecutaban	había ejecutado	habían ejecutado
3　pretérito		10　pretérito anterior	
ejecuté	ejecutamos	hube ejecutado	hubimos ejecutado
ejecutaste	ejecutasteis	hubiste ejecutado	hubisteis ejecutado
ejecutó	ejecutaron	hubo ejecutado	hubieron ejecutado
4　futuro		11　futuro perfecto	
ejecutaré	ejecutaremos	habré ejecutado	habremos ejecutado
ejecutarás	ejecutaréis	habrás ejecutado	habréis ejecutado
ejecutará	ejecutarán	habrá ejecutado	habrán ejecutado
5　potencial simple		12　potencial compuesto	
ejecutaría	ejecutaríamos	habría ejecutado	habríamos ejecutado
ejecutarías	ejecutaríais	habrías ejecutado	habríais ejecutado
ejecutaría	ejecutarían	habría ejecutado	habrían ejecutado
6　presente de subjuntivo		13　perfecto de subjuntivo	
ejecute	ejecutemos	haya ejecutado	hayamos ejecutado
ejecutes	ejecutéis	hayas ejecutado	hayáis ejecutado
ejecute	ejecuten	haya ejecutado	hayan ejecutado
7　imperfecto de subjuntivo		14　pluscuamperfecto de subjuntivo	
ejecutara	ejecutáramos	hubiera ejecutado	hubiéramos ejecutado
ejecutaras	ejecutarais	hubieras ejecutado	hubierais ejecutado
ejecutara	ejecutaran	hubiera ejecutado	hubieran ejecutado
OR		OR	
ejecutase	ejecutásemos	hubiese ejecutado	hubiésemos ejecutado
ejecutases	ejecutaseis	hubieses ejecutado	hubieseis ejecutado
ejecutase	ejecutasen	hubiese ejecutado	hubiesen ejecutado

imperativo	
—	ejecutemos
ejecuta; no ejecutes	ejecutad; no ejecutéis
ejecute	ejecuten

Words and expressions related to this verb
un ejecutivo, una ejecutiva　executive
un ejecutor de la justicia　executioner
ejecutor, ejecutora　executor, executant

ejecutar un ajuste　to make an agreement
ejecutar un contrato　to carry out a contract
la ejecución　execution of a murderer, condemned person; execution of a plan, of a theatrical performance

Regular **-er** verb endings with spelling   to exercise, to practice (a profession)
change: **c** becomes **z** before **a** or **o**

The Seven Simple Tenses | The Seven Compound Tenses

E

Singular	Plural	Singular	Plural
1 presente de indicativo		8 perfecto de indicativo	
ejerzo	**ejercemos**	**he ejercido**	**hemos ejercido**
ejerces	**ejercéis**	**has ejercido**	**habéis ejercido**
ejerce	**ejercen**	**ha ejercido**	**han ejercido**
2 imperfecto de indicativo		9 pluscuamperfecto de indicativo	
ejercía	**ejercíamos**	**había ejercido**	**habíamos ejercido**
ejercías	**ejercíais**	**habías ejercido**	**habíais ejercido**
ejercía	**ejercían**	**había ejercido**	**habían ejercido**
3 pretérito		10 pretérito anterior	
ejercí	**ejercimos**	**hube ejercido**	**hubimos ejercido**
ejerciste	**ejercisteis**	**hubiste ejercido**	**hubisteis ejercido**
ejerció	**ejercieron**	**hubo ejercido**	**hubieron ejercido**
4 futuro		11 futuro perfecto	
ejerceré	**ejerceremos**	**habré ejercido**	**habremos ejercido**
ejercerás	**ejerceréis**	**habrás ejercido**	**habréis ejercido**
ejercerá	**ejercerán**	**habrá ejercido**	**habrán ejercido**
5 potencial simple		12 potencial compuesto	
ejercería	**ejerceríamos**	**habría ejercido**	**habríamos ejercido**
ejercerías	**ejerceríais**	**habrías ejercido**	**habríais ejercido**
ejercería	**ejercerían**	**habría ejercido**	**habrían ejercido**
6 presente de subjuntivo		13 perfecto de subjuntivo	
ejerza	**ejerzamos**	**haya ejercido**	**hayamos ejercido**
ejerzas	**ejerzáis**	**hayas ejercido**	**hayáis ejercido**
ejerza	**ejerzan**	**haya ejercido**	**hayan ejercido**
7 imperfecto de subjuntivo		14 pluscuamperfecto de subjuntivo	
ejerciera	**ejerciéramos**	**hubiera ejercido**	**hubiéramos ejercido**
ejercieras	**ejercierais**	**hubieras ejercido**	**hubierais ejercido**
ejerciera	**ejercieran**	**hubiera ejercido**	**hubieran ejercido**
OR		OR	
ejerciese	**ejerciésemos**	**hubiese ejercido**	**hubiésemos ejercido**
ejercieses	**ejercieseis**	**hubieses ejercido**	**hubieseis ejercido**
ejerciese	**ejerciesen**	**hubiese ejercido**	**hubiesen ejercido**

	imperativo
—	**ejerzamos**
ejerce; no ejerzas	**ejerced; no ejerzáis**
ejerza	**ejerzan**

Words and expressions related to this verb

el ejercicio   exercise
hacer ejercicios   to drill, to exercise
el ejército   army
ejercitar   to drill, to exercise, to train
ejercer la medicina   to practice medicine

los ejercicios escritos   written exercises (tests)
ejercer el derecho de voto   to exercise (use)
   one's right to vote
ejercitar a un estudiante en inglés   to drill
   a student in English

The subject pronouns are found on page 93.

to elect, to select,   Regular **-ir** verb endings with spelling change: **g** becomes **j**
to choose   before **a** or **o**; stem change: Tenses 1, 6, Imperative, Gerundio

The Seven Simple Tenses		The Seven Compound Tenses	
Singular	Plural	Singular	Plural
1 presente de indicativo		8 perfecto de indicativo	
elijo	**elegimos**	**he elegido**	**hemos elegido**
eliges	**elegís**	**has elegido**	**habéis elegido**
elige	**eligen**	**ha elegido**	**han elegido**
2 imperfecto de indicativo		9 pluscuamperfecto de indicativo	
elegía	**elegíamos**	**había elegido**	**habíamos elegido**
elegías	**elegíais**	**habías elegido**	**habíais elegido**
elegía	**elegían**	**había elegido**	**habían elegido**
3 pretérito		10 pretérito anterior	
elegí	**elegimos**	**hube elegido**	**hubimos elegido**
elegiste	**elegisteis**	**hubiste elegido**	**hubisteis elegido**
eligió	**eligieron**	**hubo elegido**	**hubieron elegido**
4 futuro		11 futuro perfecto	
elegiré	**elegiremos**	**habré elegido**	**habremos elegido**
elegirás	**elegiréis**	**habrás elegido**	**habréis elegido**
elegirá	**elegirán**	**habrá elegido**	**habrán elegido**
5 potencial simple		12 potencial compuesto	
elegiría	**elegiríamos**	**habría elegido**	**habríamos elegido**
elegirías	**elegiríais**	**habrías elegido**	**habríais elegido**
elegiría	**elegirían**	**habría elegido**	**habrían elegido**
6 presente de subjuntivo		13 perfecto de subjuntivo	
elija	**elijamos**	**haya elegido**	**hayamos elegido**
elijas	**elijáis**	**hayas elegido**	**hayáis elegido**
elija	**elijan**	**haya elegido**	**hayan elegido**
7 imperfecto de subjuntivo		14 pluscuamperfecto de subjuntivo	
eligiera	**eligiéramos**	**hubiera elegido**	**hubiéramos elegido**
eligieras	**eligierais**	**hubieras elegido**	**hubierais elegido**
eligiera	**eligieran**	**hubiera elegido**	**hubieran elegido**
OR		OR	
eligiese	**eligiésemos**	**hubiese elegido**	**hubiésemos elegido**
eligieses	**eligieseis**	**hubieses elegido**	**hubieseis elegido**
eligiese	**eligiesen**	**hubiese elegido**	**hubiesen elegido**

imperativo

—	**elijamos**
elige; no elijas	**elegid; no elijáis**
elija	**elijan**

Words related to this verb
elegible eligible   **elegir + inf.** to choose + inf.
la elegibilidad eligibility   **reelegir** to reelect
la elección election   **el elector, la electora** elector, voter

Get acquainted with what preposition goes with what verb on pages 669–677.

Regular **-er** verb   to soak in, to soak up, to suck in, to imbibe

The Seven Simple Tenses		The Seven Compound Tenses	
Singular	Plural	Singular	Plural
1 presente de indicativo		8 perfecto de indicativo	
embebo	embebemos	he embebido	hemos embebido
embebes	embebéis	has embebido	habéis embebido
embebe	embeben	ha embebido	han embebido
2 imperfecto de indicativo		9 pluscuamperfecto de indicativo	
embebía	embebíamos	había embebido	habíamos embebido
embebía	embebíais	habías embebido	habíais embebido
embebía	embebían	había embebido	habían embebido
3 pretérito		10 pretérito anterior	
embebí	embebimos	hube embebido	hubimos embebido
embebiste	embebisteis	hubiste embebido	hubisteis embebido
embebió	embebieron	hubo embebido	hubieron embebido
4 futuro		11 futuro perfecto	
embeberé	embeberemos	habré embebido	habremos embebido
embeberás	embeberéis	habrás embebido	habréis embebido
embeberá	embeberán	habrá embebido	habrán embebido
5 potencial simple		12 potencial compuesto	
embebería	embeberíamos	habría embebido	habríamos embebido
embeberías	embeberíais	habrías embebido	habríais embebido
embebería	embeberían	habría embebido	habrían embebido
6 presente de subjuntivo		13 perfecto de subjuntivo	
embeba	embebamos	haya embebido	hayamos embebido
embebas	embebáis	hayas embebido	hayáis embebido
embeba	embeban	haya embebido	hayan embebido
7 imperfecto de subjuntivo		14 pluscuamperfecto de subjuntivo	
embebiera	embebiéramos	hubiera embebido	hubiéramos embebido
embebieras	embebierais	hubieras embebido	hubierais embebido
embebiera	embebieran	hubiera embebido	hubieran embebido
OR		OR	
embebiese	embebiésemos	hubiese embebido	hubiésemos embebido
embebieses	embebieseis	hubieses embebido	hubieseis embebido
embebiese	embebiesen	hubiese embebido	hubiesen embebido

imperativo	
—	embebamos
embebe; no embebas	embebed; no embebáis
embeba	embeban

Words related to this verb

una columna embebida   imbedded column
 (architecture)
embebedor, embebedora   absorbent, imbibing
beber   to drink
una bebida   drink, beverage
embeber algo en agua   to soak something in water

embeberse en   to absorb oneself, to
 immerse oneself in
embeberse en un libro   to absorb oneself
 in a book, to become absorbed in a book

The subject pronouns are found on page 93.

empezar (205)　　　Gerundio empezando　　Part. pas. empezado

to begin, to start | Regular **-ar** verb endings with spelling change: **z** becomes **c** before **e**; stem change: Tenses 1, 6, Imperative

The Seven Simple Tenses | The Seven Compound Tenses

Singular	Plural	Singular	Plural
1 presente de indicativo		**8 perfecto de indicativo**	
empiezo	empezamos	he empezado	hemos empezado
empiezas	empezáis	has empezado	habéis empezado
empieza	empiezan	ha empezado	han empezado
2 imperfecto de indicativo		**9 pluscuamperfecto de indicativo**	
empezaba	empezábamos	había empezado	habíamos empezado
empezabas	empezabais	habías empezado	habíais empezado
empezaba	empezaban	había empezado	habían empezado
3 pretérito		**10 pretérito anterior**	
empecé	empezamos	hube empezado	hubimos empezado
empezaste	empezasteis	hubiste empezado	hubisteis empezado
empezó	empezaron	hubo empezado	hubieron empezado
4 futuro		**11 futuro perfecto**	
empezaré	empezaremos	habré empezado	habremos empezado
empezarás	empezaréis	habrás empezado	habréis empezado
empezará	empezarán	habrá empezado	habrán empezado
5 potencial simple		**12 potencial compuesto**	
empezaría	empezaríamos	habría empezado	habríamos empezado
empezarías	empezaríais	habrías empezado	habríais empezado
empezaría	empezarían	habría empezado	habrían empezado
6 presente de subjuntivo		**13 perfecto de subjuntivo**	
empiece	empecemos	haya empezado	hayamos empezado
empieces	empecéis	hayas empezado	hayáis empezado
empiece	empiecen	haya empezado	hayan empezado
7 imperfecto de subjuntivo		**14 pluscuamperfecto de subjuntivo**	
empezara	empezáramos	hubiera empezado	hubiéramos empezado
empezaras	empezarais	hubieras empezado	hubierais empezado
empezara	empezaran	hubiera empezado	hubieran empezado
OR		OR	
empezase	empezásemos	hubiese empezado	hubiésemos empezado
empezases	empezaseis	hubieses empezado	hubieseis empezado
empezase	empezasen	hubiese empezado	hubiesen empezado

imperativo

—	empecemos
empieza; no empieces	empezad; no empecéis
empiece	empiecen

Common idiomatic expressions using this verb
empezar por + inf.　to begin by + pres. part.
empezar a + inf.　to begin + inf.; **Ricardo empieza a escribir en inglés.**
par empezar　to begin with

Get acquainted with what preposition goes with what verb on pages 669–677.

Gerundio **empleando**   Part. pas. **empleado**   **emplear (206)**
Regular **-ar** verb   to employ, to use

The Seven Simple Tenses		The Seven Compound Tenses

Singular	Plural	Singular	Plural
1 presente de indicativo		**8 perfecto de indicativo**	
empleo	empleamos	he empleado	hemos empleado
empleas	empleáis	has empleado	habéis empleado
emplea	emplean	ha empleado	han empleado
2 imperfecto de indicativo		**9 pluscuamperfecto de indicativo**	
empleaba	empleábamos	había empleado	habíamos empleado
empleabas	empleabais	habías empleado	habíais empleado
empleaba	empleaban	había empleado	habían empleado
3 pretérito		**10 pretérito anterior**	
empleé	empleamos	hube empleado	hubimos empleado
empleaste	empleasteis	hubiste empleado	hubisteis empleado
empleó	emplearon	hubo empleado	hubieron empleado
4 futuro		**11 futuro perfecto**	
emplearé	emplearemos	habré empleado	habremos empleado
emplearás	emplearéis	habrás empleado	habréis empleado
empleará	emplearán	habrá empleado	habrán empleado
5 potencial simple		**12 potencial compuesto**	
emplearía	emplearíamos	habría empleado	habríamos empleado
emplearías	emplearíais	habrías empleado	habríais empleado
emplearía	emplearían	habría empleado	habrían empleado
6 presente de subjuntivo		**13 perfecto de subjuntivo**	
emplee	empleemos	haya empleado	hayamos empleado
emplees	empleéis	hayas empleado	hayáis empleado
emplee	empleen	haya empleado	hayan empleado
7 imperfecto de subjuntivo		**14 pluscuamperfecto de subjuntivo**	
empleara	empleáramos	hubiera empleado	hubiéramos empleado
emplearas	emplearais	hubieras empleado	hubierais empleado
empleara	emplearan	hubiera empleado	hubieran empleado
OR		OR	
emplease	empleásemos	hubiese empleado	hubiésemos empleado
empleases	empleaseis	hubieses empleado	hubieseis empleado
emplease	empleasen	hubiese empleado	hubiesen empleado

imperativo

—	empleemos
emplea; no emplees	emplead; no empleéis
emplee	empleen

Words and expressions related to this verb
un empleado, una empleada   employee
el empleo   job, employment, occupation, use
un empleador, una empleadora   employer
EMPLEO SOLICITADO   POSITION WANTED

Don't forget to study the section on defective and impersonal verbs. It's right after this main list.

The subject pronouns are found on page 93.

319

to incite, to inflame, to kindle, to light

Regular **-er** verb endings with stem change: Tenses 1, 6, Imperative

The Seven Simple Tenses	The Seven Compound Tenses

Singular	Plural	Singular	Plural
1 presente de indicativo		**8 perfecto de indicativo**	
enciendo	encendemos	he encendido	hemos encendido
enciendes	encendéis	has encendido	habéis encendido
enciende	encienden	ha encendido	han encendido
2 imperfecto de indicativo		**9 pluscuamperfecto de indicativo**	
encendía	encendíamos	había encendido	habíamos encendido
encendías	encendíais	habías encendido	habíais encendido
encendía	encendían	había encendido	habían encendido
3 pretérito		**10 pretérito anterior**	
encendí	encendimos	hube encendido	hubimos encendido
encendiste	encendisteis	hubiste encendido	hubisteis encendido
encendió	encendieron	hubo encendido	hubieron encendido
4 futuro		**11 futuro perfecto**	
encenderé	encenderemos	habré encendido	habremos encendido
encenderás	encenderéis	habrás encendido	habréis encendido
encenderá	encenderán	habrá encendido	habrán encendido
5 potencial simple		**12 potencial compuesto**	
encendería	encenderíamos	habría encendido	habríamos encendido
encenderías	encenderíais	habrías encendido	habríais encendido
encendería	encenderían	habría encendido	habrían encendido
6 presente de subjuntivo		**13 perfecto de subjuntivo**	
encienda	encendamos	haya encendido	hayamos encendido
enciendas	encendáis	hayas encendido	hayáis encendido
encienda	enciendan	haya encendido	hayan encendido
7 imperfecto de subjuntivo		**14 pluscuamperfecto de subjuntivo**	
encendiera	encendiéramos	hubiera encendido	hubiéramos encendido
encendieras	encendierais	hubieras encendido	hubierais encendido
encendiera	encendieran	hubiera encendido	hubieran encendido
OR		OR	
encendiese	encendiésemos	hubiese encendido	hubiésemos encendido
encendieses	encendieseis	hubieses encendido	hubieseis encendido
encendiese	encendiesen	hubiese encendido	hubiesen encendido

imperativo

—	**encendamos**
enciende; no enciendas	**encended; no encendáis**
encienda	**enciendan**

Words and expressions related to this verb

encenderse en ira   to burn up with anger
encendido, encendida   inflamed; **encendido de color**   highly colored
incendiar   to set on fire; **incendiarse**   to catch fire
un incendio   fire; **un extintor de incendio**   fire extinguisher

Regular **-ar** verb endings with stem change: Tenses 1, 6, Imperative

to enclose, to lock up, to confine

The Seven Simple Tenses		The Seven Compound Tenses	
Singular	Plural	Singular	Plural
1 presente de indicativo		8 perfecto de indicativo	
encierro	**encerramos**	**he encerrado**	**hemos encerrado**
encierras	**encerráis**	**has encerrado**	**habéis encerrado**
encierra	**encierran**	**ha encerrado**	**han encerrado**
2 imperfecto de indicativo		9 pluscuamperfecto de indicativo	
encerraba	**encerrábamos**	**había encerrado**	**habíamos encerrado**
encerrabas	**encerrabais**	**habías encerrado**	**habíais encerrado**
encerraba	**encerraban**	**había encerrado**	**habían encerrado**
3 pretérito		10 pretérito anterior	
encerré	**encerramos**	**hube encerrado**	**hubimos encerrado**
encerraste	**encerrasteis**	**hubiste encerrado**	**hubisteis encerrado**
encerró	**encerraron**	**hubo encerrado**	**hubieron encerrado**
4 futuro		11 futuro perfecto	
encerraré	**encerraremos**	**habré encerrado**	**habremos encerrado**
encerrarás	**encerraréis**	**habrás encerrado**	**habréis encerrado**
encerrará	**encerrarán**	**habrá encerrado**	**habrán encerrado**
5 potencial simple		12 potencial compuesto	
encerraría	**encerraríamos**	**habría encerrado**	**habríamos encerrado**
encerrarías	**encerraríais**	**habrías encerrado**	**habríais encerrado**
encerraría	**encerrarían**	**habría encerrado**	**habrían encerrado**
6 presente de subjuntivo		13 perfecto de subjuntivo	
encierre	**encerremos**	**haya encerrado**	**hayamos encerrado**
encierres	**encerréis**	**hayas encerrado**	**hayáis encerrado**
encierre	**encierren**	**haya encerrado**	**hayan encerrado**
7 imperfecto de subjuntivo		14 pluscuamperfecto de subjuntivo	
encerrara	**encerráramos**	**hubiera encerrado**	**hubiéramos encerrado**
encerraras	**encerrarais**	**hubieras encerrado**	**hubierais encerrado**
encerrara	**encerraran**	**hubiera encerrado**	**hubieran encerrado**
OR		OR	
encerrase	**encerrásemos**	**hubiese encerrado**	**hubiésemos encerrado**
encerrases	**encerraseis**	**hubieses encerrado**	**hubieseis encerrado**
encerrase	**encerrasen**	**hubiese encerrado**	**hubiesen encerrado**

imperativo

—	**encerremos**
encierra; no encierres	**encerrad; no encerréis**
encierre	**encierren**

Words related to this verb
encerrado, encerrada   closed, locked, shut
encerrarse   to live in seclusion; to be locked up, closeted, shut in

For other words and expressions related to this verb, see **cerrar.**

The subject pronouns are found on page 93.

encontrar (209) Gerundio encontrando Part. pas. encontrado

to meet, to
encounter, to find

Regular **-ar** verb endings with stem change:
Tenses 1, 6, Imperative

The Seven Simple Tenses

The Seven Compound Tenses

Singular	Plural	Singular	Plural
1 presente de indicativo		8 perfecto de indicativo	
encuentro	encontramos	he encontrado	hemos encontrado
encuentras	encontráis	has encontrado	habéis encontrado
encuentra	encuentran	ha encontrado	han encontrado
2 imperfecto de indicativo		9 pluscuamperfecto de indicativo	
encontraba	encontrábamos	había encontrado	habíamos encontrado
encontrabas	encontrabais	habías encontrado	habíais encontrado
encontraba	encontraban	había encontrado	habían encontrado
3 pretérito		10 pretérito anterior	
encontré	encontramos	hube encontrado	hubimos encontrado
encontraste	encontrasteis	hubiste encontrado	hubisteis encontrado
encontró	encontraron	hubo encontrado	hubieron encontrado
4 futuro		11 futuro perfecto	
encontraré	encontraremos	habré encontrado	habremos encontrado
encontrarás	encontraréis	habrás encontrado	habréis encontrado
encontrará	encontrarán	habrá encontrado	habrán encontrado
5 potencial simple		12 potencial compuesto	
encontraría	encontraríamos	habría encontrado	habríamos encontrado
encontrarías	encontraríais	habrías encontrado	habríais encontrado
encontraría	encontrarían	habría encontrado	habrían encontrado
6 presente de subjuntivo		13 perfecto de subjuntivo	
encuentre	encontremos	haya encontrado	hayamos encontrado
encuentres	encontréis	hayas encontrado	hayáis encontrado
encuentre	encuentren	haya encontrado	hayan encontrado
7 imperfecto de subjuntivo		14 pluscuamperfecto de subjuntivo	
encontrara	encontráramos	hubiera encontrado	hubiéramos encontrado
encontraras	encontrarais	hubieras encontrado	hubierais encontrado
encontrara	encontraran	hubiera encontrado	hubieran encontrado
OR		OR	
encontrase	encontrásemos	hubiese encontrado	hubiésemos encontrado
encontrases	encontraseis	hubieses encontrado	hubieseis encontrado
encontrase	encontrasen	hubiese encontrado	hubiesen encontrado

imperativo

—	encontremos
encuentra; no encuentres	encontrad; no encontréis
encuentre	encuentren

Words and expressions related to this verb
un encuentro   encounter, meeting
salir al encuentro de   to go to meet
encontrarse con alguien   to meet someone, to run across someone
   (pres. part.: **encontrándose**)

Can't recognize an irregular verb form? Check out pages 678–681.

Reflexive regular **-ar** verb   to become angry, annoyed, irritated

The Seven Simple Tenses		The Seven Compound Tenses	
Singular	Plural	Singular	Plural
1 presente de indicativo		8 perfecto de indicativo	
me enfado	**nos enfadamos**	**me he enfadado**	**nos hemos enfadado**
te enfadas	**os enfadáis**	**te has enfadado**	**os habéis enfadado**
se enfada	**se enfadan**	**se ha enfadado**	**se han enfadado**
2 imperfecto de indicativo		9 pluscuamperfecto de indicativo	
me enfadaba	**nos enfadábamos**	**me había enfadado**	**nos habíamos enfadado**
te enfadabas	**os enfadabais**	**te habías enfadado**	**os habíais enfadado**
se enfadaba	**se enfadaban**	**se había enfadado**	**se habían enfadado**
3 pretérito		10 pretérito anterior	
me enfadé	**nos enfadamos**	**me hube enfadado**	**nos hubimos enfadado**
te enfadaste	**os enfadasteis**	**te hubiste enfadado**	**os hubisteis enfadado**
se enfadó	**se enfadaron**	**se hubo enfadado**	**se hubieron enfadado**
4 futuro		11 futuro perfecto	
me enfadaré	**nos enfadaremos**	**me habré enfadado**	**nos habremos enfadado**
te enfadarás	**os enfadaréis**	**te habrás enfadado**	**os habréis enfadado**
se enfadará	**se enfadarán**	**se habrá enfadado**	**se habrán enfadado**
5 potencial simple		12 potencial compuesto	
me enfadaría	**nos enfadaríamos**	**me habría enfadado**	**nos habríamos enfadado**
te enfadarías	**os enfadaríais**	**te habrías enfadado**	**os habríais enfadado**
se enfadaría	**se enfadarían**	**se habría enfadado**	**se habrían enfadado**
6 presente de subjuntivo		13 perfecto de subjuntivo	
me enfade	**nos enfademos**	**me haya enfadado**	**nos hayamos enfadado**
te enfades	**os enfadéis**	**te hayas enfadado**	**os hayáis enfadado**
se enfade	**se enfaden**	**se haya enfadado**	**se hayan enfadado**
7 imperfecto de subjuntivo		14 pluscuamperfecto de subjuntivo	
me enfadara	**nos enfadáramos**	**me hubiera enfadado**	**nos hubiéramos enfadado**
te enfadaras	**os enfadarais**	**te hubieras enfadado**	**os hubierais enfadado**
se enfadara	**se enfadaran**	**se hubiera enfadado**	**se hubieran enfadado**
OR		OR	
me enfadase	**nos enfadásemos**	**me hubiese enfadado**	**nos hubiésemos enfadado**
te enfadases	**os enfadaseis**	**te hubieses enfadado**	**os hubieseis enfadado**
se enfadase	**se enfadasen**	**se hubiese enfadado**	**se hubiesen enfadado**

	imperativo	
—		**enfadémonos**
enfádate; no te enfades		**enfadaos; no os enfadéis**
enfádese		**enfádense**

Words related to this verb

enfadoso, enfadosa   annoying
el enfado   anger, vexation
enfadadizo, enfadadiza   irritable

enfadosamente   annoyingly, angrily
enfadar   to anger, to annoy, to irritate
enfadarse por cualquier   to get angry about anything

If you don't know the Spanish verb for the English verb
you have in mind, look it up in the index on pages 682–706.

The subject pronouns are found on page 93.   **323**

enfermarse (211) Gerundio enfermándose Part. pas. enfermado

to get sick, to fall sick, to become
sick, to fall ill, to become ill

Reflexive regular -ar verb

The Seven Simple Tenses		The Seven Compound Tenses	
Singular	Plural	Singular	Plural
1 presente de indicativo		8 perfecto de indicativo	
me enfermo	nos enfermamos	me he enfermado	nos hemos enfermado
te enfermas	os enfermáis	te has enfermado	os habéis enfermado
se enferma	se enferman	se ha enfermado	se han enfermado
2 imperfecto de indicativo		9 pluscuamperfecto de indicativo	
me enfermaba	nos enfermábamos	me había enfermado	nos habíamos enfermado
te enfermabas	os enfermabais	te habías enfermado	os habíais enfermado
se enfermaba	se enfermaban	se había enfermado	se habían enfermado
3 pretérito		10 pretérito anterior	
me enfermé	nos enfermamos	me hube enfermado	nos hubimos enfermado
te enfermaste	os enfermasteis	te hubiste enfermado	os hubisteis enfermado
se enfermó	se enfermaron	se hubo enfermado	se hubieron enfermado
4 futuro		11 futuro perfecto	
me enfermaré	nos enfermaremos	me habré enfermado	nos habremos enfermado
te enfermarás	os enfermaréis	te habrás enfermado	os habréis enfermado
se enfermará	se enfermarán	se habrá enfermado	se habrán enfermado
5 potencial simple		12 potencial compuesto	
me enfermaría	nos enfermaríamos	me habría enfermado	nos habríamos enfermado
te enfermarías	os enfermaríais	te habrías enfermado	os habríais enfermado
se enfermaría	se enfermarían	se habría enfermado	se habrían enfermado
6 presente de subjuntivo		13 perfecto de subjuntivo	
me enferme	nos enfermemos	me haya enfermado	nos hayamos enfermado
te enfermes	os enferméis	te hayas enfermado	os hayáis enfermado
se enferme	se enfermen	se haya enfermado	se hayan enfermado
7 imperfecto de subjuntivo		14 pluscuamperfecto de subjuntivo	
me enfermara	nos enfermáramos	me hubiera enfermado	nos hubiéramos enfermado
te enfermaras	os enfermarais	te hubieras enfermado	os hubierais enfermado
se enfermara	se enfermaran	se hubiera enfermado	se hubieran enfermado
OR		OR	
me enfermase	nos enfermásemos	me hubiese enfermado	nos hubiésemos enfermado
te enfermases	os enfermaseis	te hubieses enfermado	os hubieseis enfermado
se enfermase	se enfermasen	se hubiese enfermado	se hubiesen enfermado

	imperativo	
—		enfermémonos
enférmate; no te enfermes		enfermaos; no os enferméis
enférmese		enférmense

Words and expressions related to this verb

la enfermedad   illness, sickness
la enfermería   infirmary
enfermo de amor   lovesick
enfermar   to fall sick, to make sick
un enfermo, una enferma   patient
enfermoso, enfermosa   sickly
un enfermero, una enfermera   nurse

enfermero (enfermera) ambulante   visiting
  nurse
caer enfermo (enferma)   to get sick, to fall
  sick
enfermizo, enfermiza   sickly, ailing, unhealthy
enfermo interno   in-patient
estar enfermo (enferma)   to be sick

Reflexive regular **-ar** verb   to become angry, to get angry, to get cross

The Seven Simple Tenses		The Seven Compound Tenses	
Singular	Plural	Singular	Plural
1 presente de indicativo		8 perfecto de indicativo	
me enojo	nos enojamos	me he enojado	nos hemos enojado
te enojas	os enojáis	te has enojado	os habéis enojado
se enoja	se enojan	se ha enojado	se han enojado
2 imperfecto de indicativo		9 pluscuamperfecto de indicativo	
me enojaba	nos enojábamos	me había enojado	nos habíamos enojado
te enojabas	os enojabais	te habías enojado	os habíais enojado
se enojaba	se enojaban	se había enojado	se habían enojado
3 pretérito		10 pretérito anterior	
me enojé	nos enojamos	me hube enojado	nos hubimos enojado
te enojaste	os enojasteis	te hubiste enojado	os hubisteis enojado
se enojó	se enojaron	se hubo enojado	se hubieron enojado
4 futuro		11 futuro perfecto	
me enojaré	nos enojaremos	me habré enojado	nos habremos enojado
te enojarás	os enojaréis	te habrás enojado	os habréis enojado
se enojará	se enojarán	se habrá enojado	se habrán enojado
5 potencial simple		12 potencial compuesto	
me enojaría	nos enojaríamos	me habría enojado	nos habríamos enojado
te enojarías	os enojaríais	te habrías enojado	os habríais enojado
se enojaría	se enojarían	se habría enojado	se habrían enojado
6 presente de subjuntivo		13 perfecto de subjuntivo	
me enoje	nos enojemos	me haya enojado	nos hayamos enojado
te enojes	os enojéis	te hayas enojado	os hayáis enojado
se enoje	se enojen	se haya enojado	se hayan enojado
7 imperfecto de subjuntivo		14 pluscuamperfecto de subjuntivo	
me enojara	nos enojáramos	me hubiera enojado	nos hubiéramos enojado
te enojaras	os enojarais	te hubieras enojado	os hubierais enojado
se enojara	se enojaran	se hubiera enojado	se hubieran enojado
OR		OR	
me enojase	nos enojásemos	me hubiese enojado	nos hubiésemos enojado
te enojases	os enojaseis	te hubieses enojado	os hubieseis enojado
se enojase	se enojasen	se hubiese enojado	se hubiesen enojado

E

imperativo	
—	enojémonos
enójate; no te enojes	enojaos; no os enojéis
enójese	enójense

Words and expressions related to this verb
enojar   to annoy, to irritate, to make angry, to vex; **enojarse de**   to become angry at someone
el enojo   anger, annoyance; **enojadizo, enojadiza**   ill-tempered, irritable
enojoso, enojosa   irritating, troublesome
enojosamente   angrily
enojado, enojada   angry; **una enojada**   fit of anger
enojarse con (contra) alguien   to become angry with someone

The subject pronouns are found on page 93.

to teach, to show, to point out

Regular **-ar** verb

The Seven Simple Tenses		The Seven Compound Tenses	
Singular	Plural	Singular	Plural
1 presente de indicativo		8 perfecto de indicativo	
enseño	enseñamos	he enseñado	hemos enseñado
enseñas	enseñáis	has enseñado	habéis enseñado
enseña	enseñan	ha enseñado	han enseñado
2 imperfecto de indicativo		9 pluscuamperfecto de indicativo	
enseñaba	enseñábamos	había enseñado	habíamos enseñado
enseñabas	enseñabais	habías enseñado	habíais enseñado
enseñaba	enseñaban	había enseñado	habían enseñado
3 pretérito		10 pretérito anterior	
enseñé	enseñamos	hube enseñado	hubimos enseñado
enseñaste	enseñasteis	hubiste enseñado	hubisteis enseñado
enseñó	enseñaron	hubo enseñado	hubieron enseñado
4 futuro		11 futuro perfecto	
enseñaré	enseñaremos	habré enseñado	habremos enseñado
enseñarás	enseñaréis	habrás enseñado	habréis enseñado
enseñará	enseñarán	habrá enseñado	habrán enseñado
5 potencial simple		12 potencial compuesto	
enseñaría	enseñaríamos	habría enseñado	habríamos enseñado
enseñarías	enseñaríais	habrías enseñado	habríais enseñado
enseñaría	enseñarían	habría enseñado	habrían enseñado
6 presente de subjuntivo		13 perfecto de subjuntivo	
enseñe	enseñemos	haya enseñado	hayamos enseñado
enseñes	enseñéis	hayas enseñado	hayáis enseñado
enseñe	enseñen	haya enseñado	hayan enseñado
7 imperfecto de subjuntivo		14 pluscuamperfecto de subjuntivo	
enseñara	enseñáramos	hubiera enseñado	hubiéramos enseñado
enseñaras	enseñarais	hubieras enseñado	hubierais enseñado
enseñara	enseñaran	hubiera enseñado	hubieran enseñado
OR		OR	
enseñase	enseñásemos	hubiese enseñado	hubiésemos enseñado
enseñases	enseñaseis	hubieses enseñado	hubieseis enseñado
enseñase	enseñasen	hubiese enseñado	hubiesen enseñado

imperativo	
—	enseñemos
enseña; no enseñes	enseñad; no enseñéis
enseñe	enseñen

Words and expressions related to this verb

enseñarse   to teach oneself
enseñar a + inf.   to teach + inf.
el enseñamiento, la enseñanza   teaching, education
　la enseñanza primaria   primary education
　la enseñanza secundaria   secondary (high school)
　　education
　la enseñanza superior   higher education

diseñar   to design
el diseño   design
la enseña   emblem, standard
bien enseñado   well-bred
mal enseñado   ill-bred
un perro bien enseñado   a house-trained
　dog

Regular **-er** verb endings with stem   to understand
change: Tenses 1, 6, Imperative

The Seven Simple Tenses		The Seven Compound Tenses	
Singular	Plural	Singular	Plural
1 presente de indicativo		**8 perfecto de indicativo**	
entiendo	entendemos	he entendido	hemos entendido
entiendes	entendéis	has entendido	habéis entendido
entiende	entienden	ha entendido	han entendido
2 imperfecto de indicativo		**9 pluscuamperfecto de indicativo**	
entendía	entendíamos	había entendido	habíamos entendido
entendías	entendíais	habías entendido	habíais entendido
entendía	entendían	había entendido	habían entendido
3 pretérito		**10 pretérito anterior**	
entendí	entendimos	hube entendido	hubimos entendido
entendiste	entendisteis	hubiste entendido	hubisteis entendido
entendió	entendieron	hubo entendido	hubieron entendido
4 futuro		**11 futuro perfecto**	
entenderé	entenderemos	habré entendido	habremos entendido
entenderás	entenderéis	habrás entendido	habréis entendido
entenderá	entenderán	habrá entendido	habrán entendido
5 potencial simple		**12 potencial compuesto**	
entendería	entenderíamos	habría entendido	habríamos entendido
entenderías	entenderíais	habrías entendido	habríais entendido
entendería	entenderían	habría entendido	habrían entendido
6 presente de subjuntivo		**13 perfecto de subjuntivo**	
entienda	entendamos	haya entendido	hayamos entendido
entiendas	entendáis	hayas entendido	hayáis entendido
entienda	entiendan	haya entendido	hayan entendido
7 imperfecto de subjuntivo		**14 pluscuamperfecto de subjuntivo**	
entendiera	entendiéramos	hubiera entendido	hubiéramos entendido
entendieras	entendierais	hubieras entendido	hubierais entendido
entendiera	entendieran	hubiera entendido	hubieran entendido
OR		OR	
entendiese	entendiésemos	hubiese entendido	hubiésemos entendido
entendieses	entendieseis	hubieses entendido	hubieseis entendido
entendiese	entendiesen	hubiese entendido	hubiesen entendido

	imperativo	
—		entendamos
entiende; no entiendas		entended; no entendáis
entienda		entiendan

Words and expressions related to this verb
dar a entender to insinuate, to hint
Yo me entiendo. I have my reasons.
según mi entender according to my opinion
el entendimiento comprehension,
  understanding

¿Qué entiende Ud. por eso? What do you
  mean by that?
entenderse bien to get along well with
  each other
desentenderse de to have nothing to do with

327

The subject pronouns are found on page 93.

entrar (215)

Gerundio **entrando**

Part. pas. **entrado**

to enter, to go (in), to come (in)

Regular **-ar** verb

The Seven Simple Tenses		The Seven Compound Tenses	
Singular	Plural	Singular	Plural
1 presente de indicativo		**8 perfecto de indicativo**	
entro	entramos	he entrado	hemos entrado
entras	entráis	has entrado	habéis entrado
entra	entran	ha entrado	han entrado
2 imperfecto de indicativo		**9 pluscuamperfecto de indicativo**	
entraba	entrábamos	había entrado	habíamos entrado
entrabas	entrabais	habías entrado	habíais entrado
entraba	entraban	había entrado	habían entrado
3 pretérito		**10 pretérito anterior**	
entré	entramos	hube entrado	hubimos entrado
entraste	entrasteis	hubiste entrado	hubisteis entrado
entró	entraron	hubo entrado	hubieron entrado
4 futuro		**11 futuro perfecto**	
entraré	entraremos	habré entrado	habremos entrado
entrarás	entraréis	habrás entrado	habréis entrado
entrará	entrarán	habrá entrado	habrán entrado
5 potencial simple		**12 potencial compuesto**	
entraría	entraríamos	habría entrado	habríamos entrado
entrarías	entraríais	habrías entrado	habríais entrado
entraría	entrarían	habría entrado	habrían entrado
6 presente de subjuntivo		**13 perfecto de subjuntivo**	
entre	entremos	haya entrado	hayamos entrado
entres	entréis	hayas entrado	hayáis entrado
entre	entren	haya entrado	hayan entrado
7 imperfecto de subjuntivo		**14 pluscuamperfecto de subjuntivo**	
entrara	entráramos	hubiera entrado	hubiéramos entrado
entraras	entrarais	hubieras entrado	hubierais entrado
entrara	entraran	hubiera entrado	hubieran entrado
OR		OR	
entrase	entrásemos	hubiese entrado	hubiésemos entrado
entrases	entraseis	hubieses entrado	hubieseis entrado
entrase	entrasen	hubiese entrado	hubiesen entrado

imperativo	
—	entremos
entra; no entres	entrad; no entréis
entre	entren

Entrar is an essential regular –ar verb for beginning students of Spanish. It is used in many everyday expressions and situations.

E

Sentences using entrar and related words

Yo estudiaba cuando mi hermana entró en mi cuarto.
I was studying when my sister entered my room.

¿Dónde está la entrada?
Where is the entrance?

Words and expressions related to this verb

la entrada **entrance**

la entrada de datos **data entry**

entrada gratis **free admission**

entrada general **standing room (theater)**

entrado (entrada) en años **advanced in years**

entrar por la puerta **to enter through the door**

entrar en órbita **to go into orbit**

entrar en **to enter, to go in**

entrar en un club **to join a club**

entrar en una profesión **to enter into (take up) a profession**

volver a entrar **to reenter**

Proverb

En boca cerrada no entran moscas.
Flies do not enter a closed mouth. (Silence is golden.)

Can't find the verb you're looking for?
Check the back pages of this book for a list of over 2,100 additional verbs!

The subject pronouns are found on page 93.

to deliver, to hand over, to give

Regular **-ar** verb endings with spelling change: **g** becomes **gu** before **e**

The Seven Simple Tenses		The Seven Compound Tenses	
Singular	Plural	Singular	Plural

1 presente de indicativo

		8 perfecto de indicativo	
entrego	entregamos	he entregado	hemos entregado
entregas	entregáis	has entregado	habéis entregado
entrega	entregan	ha entregado	han entregado

2 imperfecto de indicativo

		9 pluscuamperfecto de indicativo	
entregaba	entregábamos	había entregado	habíamos entregado
entregabas	entregabais	habías entregado	habíais entregado
entregaba	entregaban	había entregado	habían entregado

3 pretérito

		10 pretérito anterior	
entregué	entregamos	hube entregado	hubimos entregado
entregaste	entregasteis	hubiste entregado	hubisteis entregado
entregó	entregaron	hubo entregado	hubieron entregado

4 futuro

		11 futuro perfecto	
entregaré	entregaremos	habré entregado	habremos entregado
entregarás	entregaréis	habrás entregado	habréis entregado
entregará	entregarán	habrá entregado	habrán entregado

5 potencial simple

		12 potencial compuesto	
entregaría	entregaríamos	habría entregado	habríamos entregado
entregarías	entregaríais	habrías entregado	habríais entregado
entregaría	entregarían	habría entregado	habrían entregado

6 presente de subjuntivo

		13 perfecto de subjuntivo	
entregue	entreguemos	haya entregado	hayamos entregado
entregues	entreguéis	hayas entregado	hayáis entregado
entregue	entreguen	haya entregado	hayan entregado

7 imperfecto de subjuntivo

		14 pluscuamperfecto de subjuntivo	
entregara	entregáramos	hubiera entregado	hubiéramos entregado
entregaras	entregarais	hubieras entregado	hubierais entregado
entregara	entregaran	hubiera entregado	hubieran entregado
OR		OR	
entregase	entregásemos	hubiese entregado	hubiésemos entregado
entregases	entregaseis	hubieses entregado	hubieseis entregado
entregase	entregasen	hubiese entregado	hubiesen entregado

imperativo	
—	entreguemos
entrega; no entregues	entregad; no entreguéis
entregue	entreguen

Words and expressions related to this verb

entregarse   to surrender, to give in
entragarse en brazos de uno   to trust someone completely
entregado, entregada   delivered
la entrega   delivery, installment, handing over

entregar al profesor los ejercicios   to hand in the exercises to the teacher
entregar a domicilio   to deliver to a residence (home delivery)

Regular **-ar** verb   to enunciate, to state

The Seven Simple Tenses		The Seven Compound Tenses	
Singular	Plural	Singular	Plural
1 presente de indicativo		8 perfecto de indicativo	
enuncio	enunciamos	he enunciado	hemos enunciado
enuncias	enunciáis	has enunciado	habéis enunciado
enuncia	enuncian	ha enunciado	han enunciado
2 imperfecto de indicativo		9 pluscuamperfecto de indicativo	
enunciaba	enunciábamos	había enunciado	habíamos enunciado
enunciabas	enunciabais	habías enunciado	habíais enunciado
enunciaba	enunciaban	había enunciado	habían enunciado
3 pretérito		10 pretérito anterior	
enuncié	enunciamos	hube enunciado	hubimos enunciado
enunciaste	enunciasteis	hubiste enunciado	hubisteis enunciado
enunció	enunciaron	hubo enunciado	hubieron enunciado
4 futuro		11 futuro perfecto	
enunciaré	enunciaremos	habré enunciado	habremos enunciado
enunciarás	enunciaréis	habrás enunciado	habréis enunciado
enunciará	enunciarán	habrá enunciado	habrán enunciado
5 potencial simple		12 potencial compuesto	
enunciaría	enunciaríamos	habría enunciado	habríamos enunciado
enunciarías	enunciaríais	habrías enunciado	habríais enunciado
enunciaría	enunciarían	habría enunciado	habrían enunciado
6 presente de subjuntivo		13 perfecto de subjuntivo	
enuncie	enunciemos	haya enunciado	hayamos enunciado
enuncies	enunciéis	hayas enunciado	hayáis enunciado
enuncie	enuncien	haya enunciado	hayan enunciado
7 imperfecto de subjuntivo		14 pluscuamperfecto de subjuntivo	
enunciara	enunciáramos	hubiera enunciado	hubiéramos enunciado
enunciaras	enunciarais	hubieras enunciado	hubierais enunciado
enunciara	enunciaran	hubiera enunciado	hubieran enunciado
OR		OR	
enunciase	enunciásemos	hubiese enunciado	hubiésemos enunciado
enunciases	enunciaseis	hubieses enunciado	hubieseis enunciado
enunciase	enunciasen	hubiese enunciado	hubiesen enunciado

	imperativo	
—		enunciemos
enuncia; no enuncies		enunciad; no enunciéis
enuncie		enuncien

Words related to this verb
la enunciación   enunciation, statement, declaration
enunciativo, enunciativa   enunciative

The subject pronouns are found on page 93.

to send	Regular **-ar** verb endings with spelling change: **i** becomes **í** on stressed syllable (see Tenses 1, 6, Imperative)

The Seven Simple Tenses		The Seven Compound Tenses	
Singular	Plural	Singular	Plural
1 presente de indicativo		8 perfecto de indicativo	
envío	enviamos	he enviado	hemos enviado
envías	enviáis	has enviado	habéis enviado
envía	envían	ha enviado	han enviado
2 imperfecto de indicativo		9 pluscuamperfecto de indicativo	
enviaba	enviábamos	había enviado	habíamos enviado
enviabas	enviabais	habías enviado	habíais enviado
enviaba	enviaban	había enviado	habían enviado
3 pretérito		10 pretérito anterior	
envié	enviamos	hube enviado	hubimos enviado
enviaste	enviasteis	hubiste enviado	hubisteis enviado
envió	enviaron	hubo enviado	hubieron enviado
4 futuro		11 futuro perfecto	
enviaré	enviaremos	habré enviado	habremos enviado
enviarás	enviaréis	habrás enviado	habréis enviado
enviará	enviarán	habrá enviado	habrán enviado
5 potencial simple		12 potencial compuesto	
enviaría	enviaríamos	habría enviado	habríamos enviado
enviarías	enviaríais	habrías enviado	habríais enviado
enviaría	enviarían	habría enviado	habrían enviado
6 presente de subjuntivo		13 perfecto de subjuntivo	
envíe	enviemos	haya enviado	hayamos enviado
envíes	enviéis	hayas enviado	hayáis enviado
envíe	envíen	haya enviado	hayan enviado
7 imperfecto de subjuntivo		14 pluscuamperfecto de subjuntivo	
enviara	enviáramos	hubiera enviado	hubiéramos enviado
enviaras	enviarais	hubieras enviado	hubierais enviado
enviara	enviaran	hubiera enviado	hubieran enviado
OR		OR	
enviase	enviásemos	hubiese enviado	hubiésemos enviado
enviases	enviaseis	hubieses enviado	hubieseis enviado
enviase	enviasen	hubiese enviado	hubiesen enviado

imperativo	
—	enviemos
envía; no envíes	enviad; no enviéis
envíe	envíen

Words and expressions related to this verb

enviar a alguien a pasear   to send someone to take a walk
el envío   dispatch; **un enviado**   envoy
la enviada   shipment
reenviar   to send back; to forward
enviar un mensaje de texto   to send a text message, to text

un enviado especial   special newspaper correspondent
enviar un fax   to send a fax
enviar por correo electrónico   to e-mail, send by e-mail

Review the principal parts of important Spanish verbs on pages 9 and 10.

Regular **-er** verb endings with stem change: to wrap up
Tenses 1, 6, Imperative, past participle

The Seven Simple Tenses		The Seven Compound Tenses	
Singular	Plural	Singular	Plural
1 presente de indicativo		8 perfecto de indicativo	
envuelvo	**envolvemos**	**he envuelto**	**hemos envuelto**
envuelves	**envolvéis**	**has envuelto**	**habéis envuelto**
envuelve	**envuelven**	**ha envuelto**	**han envuelto**
2 imperfecto de indicativo		9 pluscuamperfecto de indicativo	
envolvía	**envolvíamos**	**había envuelto**	**habíamos envuelto**
envolvías	**envolvíais**	**habías envuelto**	**habíais envuelto**
envolvía	**envolvían**	**había envuelto**	**habían envuelto**
3 pretérito		10 pretérito anterior	
envolví	**envolvimos**	**hube envuelto**	**hubimos envuelto**
envolviste	**envolvisteis**	**hubiste envuelto**	**hubisteis envuelto**
envolvió	**envolvieron**	**hubo envuelto**	**hubieron envuelto**
4 futuro		11 futuro perfecto	
envolveré	**envolveremos**	**habré envuelto**	**habremos envuelto**
envolverás	**envolveréis**	**habrás envuelto**	**habréis envuelto**
envolverá	**envolverán**	**habrá envuelto**	**habrán envuelto**
5 potencial simple		12 potencial compuesto	
envolvería	**envolveríamos**	**habría envuelto**	**habríamos envuelto**
envolverías	**envolveríais**	**habrías envuelto**	**habríais envuelto**
envolvería	**envolverían**	**habría envuelto**	**habrían envuelto**
6 presente de subjuntivo		13 perfecto de subjuntivo	
envuelva	**envolvamos**	**haya envuelto**	**hayamos envuelto**
envuelvas	**envolváis**	**hayas envuelto**	**hayáis envuelto**
envuelva	**envuelvan**	**haya envuelto**	**hayan envuelto**
7 imperfecto de subjuntivo		14 pluscuamperfecto de subjuntivo	
envolviera	**envolviéramos**	**hubiera envuelto**	**hubiéramos envuelto**
envolvieras	**envolvierais**	**hubieras envuelto**	**hubierais envuelto**
envolviera	**envolvieran**	**hubiera envuelto**	**hubieran envuelto**
OR		OR	
envolviese	**envolviésemos**	**hubiese envuelto**	**hubiésemos envuelto**
envolvieses	**envolvieseis**	**hubieses envuelto**	**hubieseis envuelto**
envolviese	**envolviesen**	**hubiese envuelto**	**hubiesen envuelto**

	imperativo	
—		**envolvamos**
envuele; no envuelvas		**envolved; no envolváis**
envuelva		**envuelvan**

Words related to this verb

envolverse   to have an affair, to become involved   **envuelto, envuelta**   wrapped
el envolvimiento   wrapping; involvement   **una envoltura**   wrapping, wrapper, cover

> Check out the verb drills and verb tests with answers explained on pages 45–91.

The subject pronouns are found on page 93.

equivocarse (220)

Gerundio **equivocándose**   Part. pas. **equivocado**

to be mistaken, to make a mistake

Regular **-ar** verb endings with spelling change: **c** becomes **qu** before **e**

The Seven Simple Tenses		The Seven Compound Tenses	
Singular	Plural	Singular	Plural
1 presente de indicativo		8 perfecto de indicativo	
me equivoco	nos equivocamos	me he equivocado	nos hemos equivocado
te equivocas	os equivocáis	te has equivocado	os habéis equivocado
se equivoca	se equivocan	se ha equivocado	se han equivocado
2 imperfecto de indicativo		9 pluscuamperfecto de indicativo	
me equivocaba	nos equivocábamos	me había equivocado	nos habíamos equivocado
te equivocabas	os equivocabais	te habías equivocado	os habíais equivocado
se equivocaba	se equivocaban	se había equivocado	se habían equivocado
3 pretérito		10 pretérito anterior	
me equivoqué	nos equivocamos	me hube equivocado	nos hubimos equivocado
te equivocaste	os equivocasteis	te hubiste equivocado	os hubisteis equivocado
se equivocó	se equivocaron	se hubo equivocado	se hubieron equivocado
4 futuro		11 futuro perfecto	
me equivocaré	nos equivocaremos	me habré equivocado	nos habremos equivocado
te equivocarás	os equivocaréis	te habrás equivocado	os habréis equivocado
se equivocará	se equivocarán	se habrá equivocado	se habrán equivocado
5 potencial simple		12 potencial compuesto	
me equivocaría	nos equivocaríamos	me habría equivocado	nos habríamos equivocado
te equivocarías	os equivocaríais	te habrías equivocado	os habríais equivocado
se equivocaría	se equivocarían	se habría equivocado	se habrían equivocado
6 presente de subjuntivo		13 perfecto de subjuntivo	
me equivoque	nos equivoquemos	me haya equivocado	nos hayamos equivocado
te equivoques	os equivoquéis	te hayas equivocado	os hayáis equivocado
se equivoque	se equivoquen	se haya equivocado	se hayan equivocado
7 imperfecto de subjuntivo		14 pluscuamperfecto de subjuntivo	
me equivocara	nos equivocáramos	me hubiera equivocado	nos hubiéramos equivocado
te equivocaras	os equivocarais	te hubieras equivocado	os hubierais equivocado
se equivocara	se equivocaran	se hubiera equivocado	se hubieran equivocado
OR		OR	
me equivocase	nos equivocásemos	me hubiese equivocado	nos hubiésemos equivocado
te equivocases	os equivocaseis	te hubieses equivocado	os hubieseis equivocado
se equivocase	se equivocasen	se hubiese equivocado	se hubiesen equivocado

imperativo

—	equivoquémonos
equivócate; no te equivoques	equivocaos; no os equivoquéis
equivóquese	equivóquense

Words and expressions related to this verb

equivoquista quibbler
equivocado, equivocada mistaken
una equivocación error, mistake, equivocation
equivocarse de fecha to be mistaken about the date

estar equivocado (equivocada) to be mistaken
cometer una equivocación to make a mistake

Gerundio **irguiendo**   Part. pas. **erguido**   **erguir (221)**

Regular **-ir** verb endings with stem change: to raise, to stand up straight
Tenses 1, 3, 6, 7, Imperative, Gerundio

The Seven Simple Tenses		The Seven Compound Tenses	
Singular	Plural	Singular	Plural
1 presente de indicativo		8 perfecto de indicativo	
irgo (yergo)	**erguimos**	**he erguido**	**hemos erguido**
irgues (yergues)	**erguís**	**has erguido**	**habéis erguido**
irgue (yergue)	**irguen (yerguen)**	**ha erguido**	**han erguido**
2 imperfecto de indicativo		9 pluscuamperfecto de indicativo	
erguía	**erguíamos**	**había erguido**	**habíamos erguido**
erguías	**erguíais**	**habías erguido**	**habíais erguido**
erguía	**erguían**	**había erguido**	**habían erguido**
3 pretérito		10 pretérito anterior	
erguí	**erguimos**	**hube erguido**	**hubimos erguido**
erguiste	**erguisteis**	**hubiste erguido**	**hubisteis erguido**
irguió	**irguieron**	**hubo erguido**	**hubieron erguido**
4 futuro		11 futuro perfecto	
erguiré	**erguiremos**	**habré erguido**	**habremos erguido**
erguirás	**erguiréis**	**habrás erguido**	**habréis erguido**
erguirá	**erguirán**	**habrá erguido**	**habrán erguido**
5 potencial simple		12 potencial compuesto	
erguiría	**erguiríamos**	**habría erguido**	**habríamos erguido**
erguirías	**erguiríais**	**habrías erguido**	**habríais erguido**
erguiría	**erguirían**	**habría erguido**	**habrían erguido**
6 presente de subjuntivo		13 perfecto de subjuntivo	
irga (yerga)	**irgamos (yergamos)**	**haya erguido**	**hayamos erguido**
irgas (yergas)	**irgáis (yergáis)**	**hayas erguido**	**hayáis erguido**
irga (yerga)	**irgan (yergan)**	**haya erguido**	**hayan erguido**
7 imperfecto de subjuntivo		14 pluscuamperfecto de subjuntivo	
irguiera	**irguiéramos**	**hubiera erguido**	**hubiéramos erguido**
irguieras	**irguierais**	**hubieras erguido**	**hubierais erguido**
irguiera	**irguieran**	**hubiera erguido**	**hubieran erguido**
OR		OR	
irguiese	**irguiésemos**	**hubiese erguido**	**hubiésemos erguido**
irguieses	**irguieseis**	**hubieses erguido**	**hubieseis erguido**
irguiese	**irguiesen**	**hubiese erguido**	**hubiesen erguido**

imperativo

—	**irgamos (yergamos)**
irgue (yergue); no irgas (yergas)	**erguid; no irgáis (yergáis)**
irga (yerga)	**irgan (yergan)**

Words and expressions related to this verb

enguirse to swell up with pride; to stiffen
un erguimiento straightening, raising,
  erection

erguido, erguida erect, proud
erguir las orejas to prick up one's ears
erguirse de repente to stand up suddenly

Can't recognize an irregular verb form? Check out pages 678–681.

The subject pronouns are found on page 93.   **335**

to err, to wander, to roam, to miss

Regular -ar verb endings with stem change: Tenses 1, 6, Imperative

The Seven Simple Tenses		The Seven Compound Tenses	
Singular	Plural	Singular	Plural
1 presente de indicativo		8 perfecto de indicativo	
yerro	**erramos**	**he errado**	**hemos errado**
yerras	**erráis**	**has errado**	**habéis errado**
yerra	**yerran**	**ha errado**	**han errado**
2 imperfecto de indicativo		9 pluscuamperfecto de indicativo	
erraba	**errábamos**	**había errado**	**habíamos errado**
errabas	**errabais**	**habías errado**	**habíais errado**
erraba	**erraban**	**había errado**	**habían errado**
3 pretérito		10 pretérito anterior	
erré	**erramos**	**hube errado**	**hubimos errado**
erraste	**errasteis**	**hubiste errado**	**hubisteis errado**
erró	**erraron**	**hubo errado**	**hubieron errado**
4 futuro		11 futuro perfecto	
erraré	**erraremos**	**habré errado**	**habremos errado**
errarás	**erraréis**	**habrás errado**	**habréis errado**
errará	**errarán**	**habrá errado**	**habrán errado**
5 potencial simple		12 potencial compuesto	
erraría	**erraríamos**	**habría errado**	**habríamos errado**
errarías	**erraríais**	**habrías errado**	**habríais errado**
erraría	**errarían**	**habría errado**	**habrían errado**
6 presente de subjuntivo		13 perfecto de subjuntivo	
yerre	**erremos**	**haya errado**	**hayamos errado**
yerres	**erréis**	**hayas errado**	**hayáis errado**
yerre	**yerren**	**haya errado**	**hayan errado**
7 imperfecto de subjuntivo		14 pluscuamperfecto de subjuntivo	
errara	**erráramos**	**hubiera errado**	**hubiéramos errado**
erraras	**errarais**	**hubieras errado**	**hubierais errado**
errara	**erraran**	**hubiera errado**	**hubieran errado**
OR		OR	
errase	**errásemos**	**hubiese errado**	**hubiésemos errado**
errases	**erraseis**	**hubieses errado**	**hubieseis errado**
errase	**errasen**	**hubiese errado**	**hubiesen errado**

imperativo		
—		**erremos**
yerra; no yerres		**errad; no erréis**
yerre		**yerren**

Words and expressions related to this verb

una errata   erratum, typographical error
errante   errant, wandering
un error   error, mistake

deshacer un yerro   to amend an error
un error de imprenta   misprint
un yerro   error, fault, mistake

Can't recognize an irregular verb form? Check out pages 678–681.

Regular **-er** verb endings with spelling change: **g** becomes **j** before **a** or **o**

to choose, to select, to pick

The Seven Simple Tenses		The Seven Compound Tenses	
Singular	Plural	Singular	Plural
1 presente de indicativo		8 perfecto de indicativo	
escojo	**escogemos**	**he escogido**	**hemos escogido**
escoges	**escogéis**	**has escogido**	**habéis escogido**
escoge	**escogen**	**ha escogido**	**han escogido**
2 imperfecto de indicativo		9 pluscuamperfecto de indicativo	
escogía	**escogíamos**	**había escogido**	**habíamos escogido**
escogías	**escogíais**	**habías escogido**	**habíais escogido**
escogía	**escogían**	**había escogido**	**habían escogido**
3 pretérito		10 pretérito anterior	
escogí	**escogimos**	**hube escogido**	**hubimos escogido**
escogiste	**escogisteis**	**hubiste escogido**	**hubisteis escogido**
escogió	**escogieron**	**hubo escogido**	**hubieron escogido**
4 futuro		11 futuro perfecto	
escogeré	**escogeremos**	**habré escogido**	**habremos escogido**
escogerás	**escogeréis**	**habrás escogido**	**habréis escogido**
escogerá	**escogerán**	**habrá escogido**	**habrán escogido**
5 potencial simple		12 potencial compuesto	
escogería	**escogeríamos**	**habría escogido**	**habríamos escogido**
escogerías	**escogeríais**	**habrías escogido**	**habríais escogido**
escogería	**escogerían**	**habría escogido**	**habrían escogido**
6 presente de subjuntivo		13 perfecto de subjuntivo	
escoja	**escojamos**	**haya escogido**	**hayamos escogido**
escojas	**escojáis**	**hayas escogido**	**hayáis escogido**
escoja	**escojan**	**haya escogido**	**hayan escogido**
7 imperfecto de subjuntivo		14 pluscuamperfecto de subjuntivo	
escogiera	**escogiéramos**	**hubiera escogido**	**hubiéramos escogido**
escogieras	**escogierais**	**hubieras escogido**	**hubierais escogido**
escogiera	**escogieran**	**hubiera escogido**	**hubieran escogido**
OR		OR	
escogiese	**escogiésemos**	**hubiese escogido**	**hubiésemos escogido**
escogieses	**escogieseis**	**hubieses escogido**	**hubieseis escogido**
escogiese	**escogiesen**	**hubiese escogido**	**hubiesen escogido**

imperativo	
—	**escojamos**
escoge; no escojas	**escoged; no escojáis**
escoja	**escojan**

Words and expressions related to this verb
un escogimiento   choice, selection
escogedor, escogedora   chooser
escogido, escogida   chosen

escoger entre dos colores   to choose between two colors
las obras escogidas   the selected works

See also **coger.**

Can't recognize an irregular verb form? Check out pages 678–681.

The subject pronouns are found on page 93.

to write

Regular **-ir** verb endings; note irregular
spelling of past participle: **escrito**

The Seven Simple Tenses		The Seven Compound Tenses	
Singular	Plural	Singular	Plural
1 presente de indicativo		8 perfecto de indicativo	
escribo	**escribimos**	**he escrito**	**hemos escrito**
escribes	**escribís**	**has escrito**	**habéis escrito**
escribe	**escriben**	**ha escrito**	**han escrito**
2 imperfecto de indicativo		9 pluscuamperfecto de indicativo	
escribía	**escribíamos**	**había escrito**	**habíamos escrito**
escribías	**escribíais**	**habías escrito**	**habíais escrito**
escribía	**escribían**	**había escrito**	**habían escrito**
3 pretérito		10 pretérito anterior	
escribí	**escribimos**	**hube escrito**	**hubimos escrito**
escribiste	**escribisteis**	**hubiste escrito**	**hubisteis escrito**
escribió	**escribieron**	**hubo escrito**	**hubieron escrito**
4 futuro		11 futuro perfecto	
escribiré	**escribiremos**	**habré escrito**	**habremos escrito**
escribirás	**escribiréis**	**habrás escrito**	**habréis escrito**
escribirá	**escribirán**	**habrá escrito**	**habrán escrito**
5 potencial simple		12 potencial compuesto	
escribiría	**escribiríamos**	**habría escrito**	**habríamos escrito**
escribirías	**escribiríais**	**habrías escrito**	**habríais escrito**
escribiría	**escribirían**	**habría escrito**	**habrían escrito**
6 presente de subjuntivo		13 perfecto de subjuntivo	
escriba	**escribamos**	**haya escrito**	**hayamos escrito**
escribas	**escribáis**	**hayas escrito**	**hayáis escrito**
escriba	**escriban**	**haya escrito**	**hayan escrito**
7 imperfecto de subjuntivo		14 pluscuamperfecto de subjuntivo	
escribiera	**escribiéramos**	**hubiera escrito**	**hubiéramos escrito**
escribieras	**escribierais**	**hubieras escrito**	**hubierais escrito**
escribiera	**escribieran**	**hubiera escrito**	**hubieran escrito**
OR		OR	
escribiese	**escribiésemos**	**hubiese escrito**	**hubiésemos escrito**
escribieses	**escribieseis**	**hubieses escrito**	**hubieseis escrito**
escribiese	**escribiesen**	**hubiese escrito**	**hubiesen escrito**

imperativo	
—	**escribamos**
escribe; no escribas	**escribid; no escribáis**
escriba	**escriban**

AN ESSENTIAL
55 VERB

AN ESSENTIAL 55 VERB

Escribir is an essential –**ir** verb for beginning students of Spanish. It is used in many everyday expressions and situations. Pay attention to the irregular past participle!

E

Sentences using escribir and related words

Mi padre está escribiendo una novela.
My father is writing a novel.

Por favor, responda por escrito a las preguntas siguientes.
Please answer the following questions in writing.

Words and expressions related to this verb

la escritura **writing**

un escritorio **writing desk**

un escriba **scribe**

escribir a máquina **to typewrite**

una máquina de escribir **typewriter**

un escritor, una escritora **writer, author**

el escribano **secretary, clerk**

por escrito **in writing**

escribir a mano **to write by hand**

describir **to describe**

describible **describable**

la descripción **description**

descriptivo, descriptiva **descriptive**

descriptor, descriptora **descriptive**

el examen escrito **written exam**

Proverb

El mal escribano le echa la culpa a la pluma.
The bad writer blames his pen.

Do you need more drills? Have fun with the *501 Spanish Verbs* CD-ROM!

The subject pronouns are found on page 93.

to listen (to)   Regular **-ar** verb

The Seven Simple Tenses		The Seven Compound Tenses	
Singular	Plural	Singular	Plural
1 presente de indicativo		8 perfecto de indicativo	
escucho	escuchamos	he escuchado	hemos escuchado
escuchas	escucháis	has escuchado	habéis escuchado
escucha	escuchan	ha escuchado	han escuchado
2 imperfecto de indicativo		9 pluscuamperfecto de indicativo	
escuchaba	escuchábamos	había escuchado	habíamos escuchado
escuchabas	escuchabais	habías escuchado	habíais escuchado
escuchaba	escuchaban	había escuchado	habían escuchado
3 pretérito		10 pretérito anterior	
escuché	escuchamos	hube escuchado	hubimos escuchado
escuchaste	escuchasteis	hubiste escuchado	hubisteis escuchado
escuchó	escucharon	hubo escuchado	hubieron escuchado
4 futuro		11 futuro perfecto	
escucharé	escucharemos	habré escuchado	habremos escuchado
escucharás	escucharéis	habrás escuchado	habréis escuchado
escuchará	escucharán	habrá escuchado	habrán escuchado
5 potencial simple		12 potencial compuesto	
escucharía	escucharíamos	habría escuchado	habríamos escuchado
escucharías	escucharíais	habrías escuchado	habríais escuchado
escucharía	escucharían	habría escuchado	habrían escuchado
6 presente de subjuntivo		13 perfecto de subjuntivo	
escuche	escuchemos	haya escuchado	hayamos escuchado
escuches	escuchéis	hayas escuchado	hayáis escuchado
escuche	escuchen	haya escuchado	hayan escuchado
7 imperfecto de subjuntivo		14 pluscuamperfecto de subjuntivo	
escuchara	escucháramos	hubiera escuchado	hubiéramos escuchado
escucharas	escucharais	hubieras escuchado	hubierais escuchado
escuchara	escucharan	hubiera escuchado	hubieran escuchado
OR		OR	
escuchase	escuchásemos	hubiese escuchado	hubiésemos escuchado
escuchases	escuchaseis	hubieses escuchado	hubieseis escuchado
escuchase	escuchasen	hubiese escuchado	hubiesen escuchado

imperativo	
—	escuchemos
escucha; no escuches	escuchad; no escuchéis
escuche	escuchen

Words and expressions related to this verb

escuchar + noun   to listen to + noun
  Escucho un disco compacto.   I'm listening
  to a CD.
escuchador, escuchadora, escuchante   listener
Para saber hablar, hay que saber escuchar.
  In order to know how to talk, one must know
  how to listen.

escuchar música   to listen to music
escuchar detrás de las puertas   to listen
behind doors

Regular **-ir** verb endings with spelling   to scatter, to spread
change: **c** becomes **z** before **a** or **o**

The Seven Simple Tenses		The Seven Compound Tenses	
Singular	Plural	Singular	Plural
1 presente de indicativo		8 perfecto de indicativo	
esparzo	**esparcimos**	**he esparcido**	**hemos esparcido**
esparces	**esparcís**	**has esparcido**	**habéis esparcido**
esparce	**esparcen**	**ha esparcido**	**han esparcido**
2 imperfecto de indicativo		9 pluscuamperfecto de indicativo	
esparcía	**esparcíamos**	**había esparcido**	**habíamos esparcido**
esparcías	**esparcíais**	**habías esparcido**	**habíais esparcido**
esparcía	**esparcían**	**había esparcido**	**habían esparcido**
3 pretérito		10 pretérito anterior	
esparcí	**esparcimos**	**hube esparcido**	**hubimos esparcido**
esparciste	**esparcisteis**	**hubiste esparcido**	**hubisteis esparcido**
esparció	**esparcieron**	**hubo esparcido**	**hubieron esparcido**
4 futuro		11 futuro perfecto	
esparciré	**esparciremos**	**habré esparcido**	**habremos esparcido**
esparcirás	**esparciréis**	**habrás esparcido**	**habréis esparcido**
esparcirá	**esparcirán**	**habrá esparcido**	**habrán esparcido**
5 potencial simple		12 potencial compuesto	
esparciría	**esparciríamos**	**habría esparcido**	**habríamos esparcido**
esparcirías	**esparciríais**	**habrías esparcido**	**habríais esparcido**
esparciría	**esparcirían**	**habría esparcido**	**habrían esparcido**
6 presente de subjuntivo		13 perfecto de subjuntivo	
esparza	**esparzamos**	**haya esparcido**	**hayamos esparcido**
esparzas	**esparzáis**	**hayas esparcido**	**hayáis esparcido**
esparza	**esparzan**	**haya esparcido**	**hayan esparcido**
7 imperfecto de subjuntivo		14 pluscuamperfecto de subjuntivo	
esparciera	**esparciéramos**	**hubiera esparcido**	**hubiéramos esparcido**
esparcieras	**esparcierais**	**hubieras esparcido**	**hubierais esparcido**
esparciera	**esparcieran**	**hubiera esparcido**	**hubieran esparcido**
OR		OR	
esparciese	**esparciésemos**	**hubiese esparcido**	**hubiésemos esparcido**
esparcieses	**esparcieseis**	**hubieses esparcido**	**hubieseis esparcido**
esparciese	**esparciesen**	**hubiese esparcido**	**hubiesen esparcido**

imperativo

—	**esparzamos**
esparce; no esparzas	**esparcid; no esparzáis**
esparza	**esparzan**

Words and expressions related to this verb
el esparcimiento scattering, spreading
esparcidamente separately, sparsely
el esparcidor, la esparcidora spreader, scatterer

flores esparcidas por las calles flowers
    scattered over the streets

Get your feet wet with verbs used in weather expressions on page 668.

The subject pronouns are found on page 93.

to expect, to hope, to wait (for)   Regular **-ar** verb

The Seven Simple Tenses		The Seven Compound Tenses	
Singular	Plural	Singular	Plural
1 presente de indicativo		8 perfecto de indicativo	
espero	esperamos	he esperado	hemos esperado
esperas	esperáis	has esperado	habéis esperado
espera	esperan	ha esperado	han esperado
2 imperfecto de indicativo		9 pluscuamperfecto de indicativo	
esperaba	esperábamos	había esperado	habíamos esperado
esperabas	esperabais	habías esperado	habíais esperado
esperaba	esperaban	había esperado	habían esperado
3 pretérito		10 pretérito anterior	
esperé	esperamos	hube esperado	hubimos esperado
esperaste	esperasteis	hubiste esperado	hubisteis esperado
esperó	esperaron	hubo esperado	hubieron esperado
4 futuro		11 futuro perfecto	
esperaré	esperaremos	habré esperado	habremos esperado
esperarás	esperaréis	habrás esperado	habréis esperado
esperará	esperarán	habrá esperado	habrán esperado
5 potencial simple		12 potencial compuesto	
esperaría	esperaríamos	habría esperado	habríamos esperado
esperarías	esperaríais	habrías esperado	habríais esperado
esperaría	esperarían	habría esperado	habrían esperado
6 presente de subjuntivo		13 perfecto de subjuntivo	
espere	esperemos	haya esperado	hayamos esperado
esperes	esperéis	hayas esperado	hayáis esperado
espere	esperen	haya esperado	hayan esperado
7 imperfecto de subjuntivo		14 pluscuamperfecto de subjuntivo	
esperara	esperáramos	hubiera esperado	hubiéramos esperado
esperaras	esperarais	hubieras esperado	hubierais esperado
esperara	esperaran	hubiera esperado	hubieran esperado
OR		OR	
esperase	esperásemos	hubiese esperado	hubiésemos esperado
esperases	esperaseis	hubieses esperado	hubieseis esperado
esperase	esperasen	hubiese esperado	hubiesen esperado

imperativo	
—	esperemos
espera; no esperes	esperad; no esperéis
espere	esperen

Words and expressions related to this verb
Mientras hay vida hay esperanza.
   When there is life, there is hope.
la esperanza hope
No hay esperanza. There is no hope.

dar esperanzas to give encouragement
desesperar to despair

Can't remember the Spanish verb you need?
Check the back pages of this book for the English-Spanish verb index!

Regular **-ar** verb endings with spelling change: **i** becomes   to ski
í on stressed syllable (see Tenses 1, 6, Imperative)

The Seven Simple Tenses		The Seven Compound Tenses	
Singular	Plural	Singular	Plural
1 presente de indicativo		8 perfecto de indicativo	
esquío	esquiamos	he esquiado	hemos esquiado
esquías	esquiáis	has esquiado	habéis esquiado
esquía	esquían	ha esquiado	han esquiado
2 imperfecto de indicativo		9 pluscuamperfecto de indicativo	
esquiaba	esquiábamos	había esquiado	habíamos esquiado
esquiabas	esquiabais	habías esquiado	habíais esquiado
esquiaba	esquiaban	había esquiado	habían esquiado
3 pretérito		10 pretérito anterior	
esquié	esquiamos	hube esquiado	hubimos esquiado
esquiaste	esquiasteis	hubiste esquiado	hubisteis esquiado
esquió	esquiaron	hubo esquiado	hubieron esquiado
4 futuro		11 futuro perfecto	
esquiaré	esquiaremos	habré esquiado	habremos esquiado
esquiarás	esquiaréis	habrás esquiado	habréis esquiado
esquiará	esquiarán	habrá esquiado	habrán esquiado
5 potencial simple		12 potencial compuesto	
esquiaría	esquiaríamos	habría esquiado	habríamos esquiado
esquiarías	esquiaríais	habrías esquiado	habríais esquiado
esquiaría	esquiarían	habría esquiado	habrían esquiado
6 presente de subjuntivo		13 perfecto de subjuntivo	
esquíe	esquiemos	haya esquiado	hayamos esquiado
esquíes	esquiéis	hayas esquiado	hayáis esquiado
esquíe	esquíen	haya esquiado	hayan esquiado
7 imperfecto de subjuntivo		14 pluscuamperfecto de subjuntivo	
esquiara	esquiáramos	hubiera esquiado	hubiéramos esquiado
esquiaras	esquiarais	hubieras esquiado	hubierais esquiado
esquiara	esquiaran	hubiera esquiado	hubieran esquiado
OR		OR	
esquiase	esquiásemos	hubiese esquiado	hubiésemos esquiado
esquiases	esquiaseis	hubieses esquiado	hubieseis esquiado
esquiase	esquiasen	hubiese esquiado	hubiesen esquiado

imperativo	
—	esquiemos
esquía; no esquíes	esquiad; no esquiéis
esquíe	esquíen

Sentences using this verb and words and expressions related to it

el esquí ski, skiing   **Me gusta el esquí.** I like skiing.
un esquiador, una esquiadora skier   **Me gusta esquiar.** I like to ski.
el esquí alpino Alpine skiing   **el esquí de fondo** cross-country skiing
el esquí acuático water-skiing

Can't find the verb you're looking for?
Check the back pages of this book for a list of over 2,100 additional verbs!

The subject pronouns are found on page 93.

E

establecer (229)   Gerundio estableciendo   Part. pas. establecido

to establish, to set up

Regular -er verb endings with spelling change: c becomes zc before a or o

The Seven Simple Tenses		The Seven Compound Tenses	
Singular	Plural	Singular	Plural
1 presente de indicativo		**8 perfecto de indicativo**	
establezco	establecemos	he establecido	hemos establecido
estableces	establecéis	has establecido	habéis establecido
establece	establecen	ha establecido	han establecido
2 imperfecto de indicativo		**9 pluscuamperfecto de indicativo**	
establecía	establecíamos	había establecido	habíamos establecido
establecías	establecíais	habías establecido	habíais establecido
establecía	establecían	había establecido	habían establecido
3 pretérito		**10 pretérito anterior**	
establecí	establecimos	hube establecido	hubimos establecido
estableciste	establecisteis	hubiste establecido	hubisteis establecido
estableció	establecieron	hubo establecido	hubieron establecido
4 futuro		**11 futuro perfecto**	
estableceré	estableceremos	habré establecido	habremos establecido
establecerás	estableceréis	habrás establecido	habréis establecido
establecerá	establecerán	habrá establecido	habrán establecido
5 potencial simple		**12 potencial compuesto**	
establecería	estableceríamos	habría establecido	habríamos establecido
establecerías	estableceríais	habrías establecido	habríais establecido
establecería	establecerían	habría establecido	habrían establecido
6 presente de subjuntivo		**13 perfecto de subjuntivo**	
establezca	establezcamos	haya establecido	hayamos establecido
establezcas	establezcáis	hayas establecido	hayáis establecido
establezca	establezcan	haya establecido	hayan establecido
7 imperfecto de subjuntivo		**14 pluscuamperfecto de subjuntivo**	
estableciera	estableciéramos	hubiera establecido	hubiéramos establecido
establecieras	establecierais	hubieras establecido	hubierais establecido
estableciera	establecieran	hubiera establecido	hubieran establecido
OR		OR	
estableciese	estableciésemos	hubiese establecido	hubiésemos establecido
establecieses	establecieseis	hubieses establecido	hubieseis establecido
estableciese	estableciesen	hubiese establecido	hubiesen establecido

imperativo	
—	establezcamos
establece; no establezcas	estableced; no establezcáis
establezca	establezcan

Words and expressions related to this verb
establecer normas to set up standards
un establecedor, una establecedora founder
un establecimiento establishment
establemente firmly, stably
establecerse to set oneself up, as in business; to settle down

establecer un campamento to set up camp
un establecimiento comercial commercial establishment

The Seven Simple Tenses		The Seven Compound Tenses	
Singular	Plural	Singular	Plural
1 presente de indicativo		8 perfecto de indicativo	
estoy	estamos	he estado	hemos estado
estás	estáis	has estado	habéis estado
está	están	ha estado	han estado
2 imperfecto de indicativo		9 pluscuamperfecto de indicativo	
estaba	estábamos	había estado	habíamos estado
estabas	estabais	habías estado	habíais estado
estaba	estaban	había estado	habían estado
3 pretérito		10 pretérito anterior	
estuve	estuvimos	hube estado	hubimos estado
estuviste	estuvisteis	hubiste estado	hubisteis estado
estuvo	estuvieron	hubo estado	hubieron estado
4 futuro		11 futuro perfecto	
estaré	estaremos	habré estado	habremos estado
estarás	estaréis	habrás estado	habréis estado
estará	estarán	habrá estado	habrán estado
5 potencial simple		12 potencial compuesto	
estaría	estaríamos	habría estado	habríamos estado
estarías	estaríais	habrías estado	habríais estado
estaría	estarían	habría estado	habrían estado
6 presente de subjuntivo		13 perfecto de subjuntivo	
esté	estemos	haya estado	hayamos estado
estés	estéis	hayas estado	hayáis estado
esté	estén	haya estado	hayan estado
7 imperfecto de subjuntivo		14 pluscuamperfecto de subjuntivo	
estuviera	estuviéramos	hubiera estado	hubiéramos estado
estuvieras	estuvierais	hubieras estado	hubierais estado
estuviera	estuvieran	hubiera estado	hubieran estado
OR		OR	
estuviese	estuviésemos	hubiese estado	hubiésemos estado
estuvieses	estuvieseis	hubieses estado	hubieseis estado
estuviese	estuviesen	hubiese estado	hubiesen estado

imperativo

—	estemos
está; no estés	estad; no estéis
esté	estén

AN ESSENTIAL
55 VERB

The subject pronouns are found on page 93.

345

Estar is one of the most important verbs for a beginning student to learn. In addition to the countless expressions that use **estar**, there is a distinction that you must make between **estar** and **ser**, which also means *to be*.

Generally speaking, use **ser** when you want to express *to be*. Use **estar** when *to be* is used in the following ways:

(a) Health:

1. **¿Cómo está Ud.?** How are you?
2. **Estoy bien.** I am well.
3. **Estoy enfermo (enferma).** I am sick.

(b) Location: persons, places, things

1. **Estoy en la sala de clase.** I am in the classroom.
2. **La escuela está lejos.** The school is far.
3. **Barcelona está en España.** Barcelona is (located) in Spain.
4. **Los libros están en la mesa.** The books are on the table.

(c) State or condition: persons

1. **Estoy contento (contenta).** I am happy.
2. **Los alumnos están cansados. (Las alumnas están cansadas.)** The students are tired.
3. **María está triste hoy.** Mary is sad today.
4. **Estoy listo (lista).** I am ready.
5. **Estoy pálido (pálida).** I am pale.
6. **Estoy ocupado (ocupada).** I am busy.
7. **Estoy seguro (segura).** I am sure.
8. **Este hombre está vivo.** This man is alive.
9. **Ese hombre está muerto.** That man is dead.
10. **Este hombre está borracho.** This man is drunk.

(d) State or condition: things and places

1. **La ventana está abierta.** The window is open.
2. **La taza está llena.** The cup is full.
3. **El té está caliente.** The tea is hot.
4. **La limonada está fría.** The lemonade is cold.
5. **La biblioteca está cerrada los domingos.** The library is closed on Sundays.

Can't remember the Spanish verb you need?
Check the back pages of this book for the English-Spanish verb index!

(e) To form the progressive present of a verb, use the present tense of estar **+ the present participle of the main verb:**

Estoy estudiando en mi cuarto y no puedo salir esta noche.
I am studying in my room and I cannot go out tonight.

(f) To form the progressive past of a verb, use the imperfect tense of estar **+ the present participle of the main verb:**

Mi hermano estaba leyendo cuando (yo) entré en el cuarto.
My brother was reading when I entered (came into) the room.

E

Sentences using estar **and related words**

Dígame, por favor, dónde está la sala de espera.
Tell me, please, where the waiting room is located.

¿Cuándo estará todo listo?
When will it all be ready?

Está lloviendo ahora.
It's raining now.

Estoy a punto de salir./Estoy para salir.
I am about to go out.

Words and expressions related to this verb

está bien **all right, okay**

estar a punto de + inf. **to be about + inf.**

estar a sus anchas **to be comfortable**

estar aburrido (aburrida) **to be bored**

estar al día **to be up to date**

estar bien **to be well**

estar conforme con **to be in agreement with**

estar de acuerdo **to agree**

estar de acuerdo con **to be in agreement with**

estar de boga **to be in fashion**

estar de buenas **to be lucky**

estar de más **to be unnecessary**

estar de pie **to be standing**

estar de vuelta **to be back**

estar listo (lista) **to be ready**

estar mal **to be ill**

estar para + inf. **to be about to**

estar por **to be in favor of**

no estar para bromas **not to be in the mood for jokes**

The subject pronouns are found on page 93.

to estimate, to esteem, to respect, to value   Regular **-ar** verb

The Seven Simple Tenses		The Seven Compound Tenses	
Singular	Plural	Singular	Plural
1 presente de indicativo		**8 perfecto de indicativo**	
estimo	estimamos	he estimado	hemos estimado
estimas	estimáis	has estimado	habéis estimado
estima	estiman	ha estimado	han estimado
2 imperfecto de indicativo		**9 pluscuamperfecto de indicativo**	
estimaba	estimábamos	había estimado	habíamos estimado
estimabas	estmabais	habías estimado	habíais estimado
estimaba	estimaban	había estimado	habían estimado
3 pretérito		**10 pretérito anterior**	
estimé	estimamos	hube estimado	hubimos estimado
estimaste	estimasteis	hubiste estimado	hubisteis estimado
estimó	estimaron	hubo estimado	hubieron estimado
4 futuro		**11 futuro perfecto**	
estimaré	estimaremos	habré estimado	habremos estimado
estimarás	estimaréis	habrás estimado	habréis estimado
estimará	estimarán	habrá estimado	habrán estimado
5 potencial simple		**12 potencial compuesto**	
estimaría	estimaríamos	habría estimado	habríamos estimado
estimarías	estimaríais	habrías estimado	habríais estimado
estimaría	estimarían	habría estimado	habrían estimado
6 presente de subjuntivo		**13 perfecto de subjuntivo**	
estime	estimemos	haya estimado	hayamos estimado
estimes	estiméis	hayas estimado	hayáis estimado
estime	estimen	haya estimado	hayan estimado
7 imperfecto de subjuntivo		**14 pluscuamperfecto de subjuntivo**	
estimara	estimáramos	hubiera estimado	hubiéramos estimado
estimaras	estimarais	hubieras estimado	hubierais estimado
estimara	estimaran	hubiera estimado	hubieran estimado
OR		OR	
estimase	estimásemos	hubiese estimado	hubiésemos estimado
estimases	estimaseis	hubieses estimado	hubieseis estimado
estimase	estimasen	hubiese estimado	hubiesen estimado

imperativo

—	estimemos
estima; no estimes	estimad; no estiméis
estime	estimen

Words and expressions related to this verb

la estima esteem, respect	estimar con exceso to overestimate
la estimabilidad worthiness, worth	estimar en menos to underestimate
la estimación estimation, esteem	estimar oportuno to deem (see) fit

Can't find the verb you're looking for?
Check the back pages of this book for a list of over 2,100 additional verbs!

The Seven Simple Tenses		The Seven Compound Tenses	
Singular	Plural	Singular	Plural
1 presente de indicativo		8 perfecto de indicativo	
estudio	**estudiamos**	**he estudiado**	**hemos estudiado**
estudias	**estudiáis**	**has estudiado**	**habéis estudiado**
estudia	**estudian**	**ha estudiado**	**han estudiado**
2 imperfecto de indicativo		9 pluscuamperfecto de indicativo	
estudiaba	**estudiábamos**	**había estudiado**	**habíamos estudiado**
estudiabas	**estudiabais**	**habías estudiado**	**habíais estudiado**
estudiaba	**estudiaban**	**había estudiado**	**habían estudiado**
3 pretérito		10 pretérito anterior	
estudié	**estudiamos**	**hube estudiado**	**hubimos estudiado**
estudiaste	**estudiasteis**	**hubiste estudiado**	**hubisteis estudiado**
estudió	**estudiaron**	**hubo estudiado**	**hubieron estudiado**
4 futuro		11 futuro perfecto	
estudiaré	**estudiaremos**	**habré estudiado**	**habremos estudiado**
estudiarás	**estudiaréis**	**habrás estudiado**	**habréis estudiado**
estudiará	**estudiarán**	**habrá estudiado**	**habrán estudiado**
5 potencial simple		12 potencial compuesto	
estudiaría	**estudiaríamos**	**habría estudiado**	**habríamos estudiado**
estudiarías	**estudiaríais**	**habrías estudiado**	**habríais estudiado**
estudiaría	**estudiarían**	**habría estudiado**	**habrían estudiado**
6 presente de subjuntivo		13 perfecto de subjuntivo	
estudie	**estudiemos**	**haya estudiado**	**hayamos estudiado**
estudies	**estudiéis**	**hayas estudiado**	**hayáis estudiado**
estudie	**estudien**	**haya estudiado**	**hayan estudiado**
7 imperfecto de subjuntivo		14 pluscuamperfecto de subjuntivo	
estudiara	**estudiáramos**	**hubiera estudiado**	**hubiéramos estudiado**
estudiaras	**estudiarais**	**hubieras estudiado**	**hubierais estudiado**
estudiara	**estudiaran**	**hubiera estudiado**	**hubieran estudiado**
OR		OR	
estudiase	**estudiásemos**	**hubiese estudiado**	**hubiésemos estudiado**
estudiases	**estudiaseis**	**hubieses estudiado**	**hubieseis estudiado**
estudiase	**estudiasen**	**hubiese estudiado**	**hubiesen estudiado**

imperativo	
—	**estudiemos**
estudia; no estudies	**estudiad; no estudiéis**
estudie	**estudien**

AN ESSENTIAL
55 VERB

The subject pronouns are found on page 93.

349

Estudiar

Estudiar is an essential regular –ar verb for beginning students of Spanish. It is used in many everyday expressions and situations.

Sentences using estudiar and related words

Estudio mis lecciones de español todos los días.
I study my Spanish lessons every day.

Es necesario estudiar para aprender.
It is necessary to study in order to learn.

Estudiamos español porque es un idioma muy hermoso.
We are studying Spanish because it is a very beautiful language.

Estoy estudiando en mi cuarto y no puedo mirar la televisión.
I am studying in my room and I cannot watch television.

Words and expressions related to this verb

un, una estudiante **student**

el estudio **study, studio, study room**

estudioso, estudiosa **studious**

un estudioso **a scholar**

estudiado, estudiada **studied, mannered**

los altos estudios **advanced studies**

hacer estudios **to study**

estudiosamente **studiously**

estudiante de intercambio **exchange student**

Do you need more drills? Have fun with the *501 Spanish Verbs* CD-ROM!

Regular **-ir** verb endings with spelling   to demand, to urge, to require
change: **g** becomes **j** before **a** or **o**

The Seven Simple Tenses		The Seven Compound Tenses	
Singular	Plural	Singular	Plural
1 presente de indicativo		8 perfecto de indicativo	
exijo	exigimos	he exigido	hemos exigido
exiges	exigís	has exigido	habéis exigido
exige	exigen	ha exigido	han exigido
2 imperfecto de indicativo		9 pluscuamperfecto de indicativo	
exigía	exigíamos	había exigido	habíamos exigido
exigías	exigíais	habías exigido	habíais exigido
exigía	exigían	había exigido	habían exigido
3 pretérito		10 pretérito anterior	
exigí	exigimos	hube exigido	hubimos exigido
exigiste	exigisteis	hubiste exigido	hubisteis exigido
exigió	exigieron	hubo exigido	hubieron exigido
4 futuro		11 futuro perfecto	
exigiré	exigiremos	habré exigido	habremos exigido
exigirás	exigiréis	habrás exigido	habréis exigido
exigirá	exigirán	habrá exigido	habrán exigido
5 potencial simple		12 potencial compuesto	
exigiría	exigiríamos	habría exigido	habríamos exigido
exigirías	exigiríais	habrías exigido	habríais exigido
exigiría	exigirían	habría exigido	habrían exigido
6 presente de subjuntivo		13 perfecto de subjuntivo	
exija	exijamos	haya exigido	hayamos exigido
exijas	exijáis	hayas exigido	hayáis exigido
exija	exijan	haya exigido	hayan exigido
7 imperfecto de subjuntivo		14 pluscuamperfecto de subjuntivo	
exigiera	exigiéramos	hubiera exigido	hubiéramos exigido
exigieras	exigierais	hubieras exigido	hubierais exigido
exigiera	exigieran	hubiera exigido	hubieran exigido
OR		OR	
exigiese	exigiésemos	hubiese exigido	hubiésemos exigido
exigieses	exigieseis	hubieses exigido	hubieseis exigido
exigiese	exigiesen	hubiese exigido	hubiesen exigido

imperativo	
—	exijamos
exige; no exijas	exigid; no exijáis
exija	exijan

Words and expressions related to this verb
exigente   exacting, demanding
la exigencia   exigency, requirement
exigible   demanding, payable on demand
exigir el pago   to demand payment

una persona muy exigente   a very demanding
  person
exigir algo de buena calidad   to insist upon
  something of good quality

Can't recognize an irregular verb form? Check out pages 678–681.

The subject pronouns are found on page 93.

to explain | Regular **-ar** verb endings with spelling change: **c** becomes **qu** before **e**

| The Seven Simple Tenses | The Seven Compound Tenses |

Singular	Plural	Singular	Plural
1　presente de indicativo		8　perfecto de indicativo	
explico	explicamos	he explicado	hemos explicado
explicas	explicáis	has explicado	habéis explicado
explica	explican	ha explicado	han explicado
2　imperfecto de indicativo		9　pluscuamperfecto de indicativo	
explicaba	explicábamos	había explicado	habíamos explicado
explicabas	explicabais	habías explicado	habíais explicado
explicaba	explicaban	había explicado	habían explicado
3　pretérito		10　pretérito anterior	
expliqué	explicamos	hube explicado	hubimos explicado
explicaste	explicasteis	hubiste explicado	hubisteis explicado
explicó	explicaron	hubo explicado	hubieron explicado
4　futuro		11　futuro perfecto	
explicaré	explicaremos	habré explicado	habremos explicado
explicarás	explicaréis	habrás explicado	habréis explicado
explicará	explicarán	habrá explicado	habrán explicado
5　potencial simple		12　potencial compuesto	
explicaría	explicaríamos	habría explicado	habríamos explicado
explicarías	explicaríais	habrías explicado	habríais explicado
explicaría	explicarían	habría explicado	habrían explicado
6　presente de subjuntivo		13　perfecto de subjuntivo	
explique	expliquemos	haya explicado	hayamos explicado
expliques	expliquéis	hayas explicado	hayáis explicado
explique	expliquen	haya explicado	hayan explicado
7　imperfecto de subjuntivo		14　pluscuamperfecto de subjuntivo	
explicara	explicáramos	hubiera explicado	hubiéramos explicado
explicaras	explicarais	hubieras explicado	hubierais explicado
explicara	explicaran	hubiera explicado	hubieran explicado
OR		OR	
explicase	explicásemos	hubiese explicado	hubiésemos explicado
explicases	explicaseis	hubieses explicado	hubieseis explicado
explicase	explicasen	hubiese explicado	hubiesen explicado

	imperativo	
—	expliquemos
explica; no expliques	explicad; no expliquéis
explique	expliquen

Words and expressions related to this verb
una **explicación**　explanation
explícito, explícita　explicit
explícitamente　explicitly

explicativo, explicativa　explanatory
pedir explicaciones　to ask for an explanation

Check out the verb drills and verb tests with answers explained on pages 45–91.

The Seven Simple Tenses | The Seven Compound Tenses

Singular	Plural	Singular	Plural
1 presente de indicativo		8 perfecto de indicativo	
expreso	**expresamos**	**he expresado**	**hemos expresado**
expresas	**expresáis**	**has expresado**	**habéis expresado**
expresa	**expresan**	**ha expresado**	**han expresado**
2 imperfecto de indicativo		9 pluscuamperfecto de indicativo	
expresaba	**expresábamos**	**había expresado**	**habíamos expresado**
expresabas	**expresabais**	**habías expresado**	**habíais expresado**
expresaba	**expresaban**	**había expresado**	**habían expresado**
3 pretérito		10 pretérito anterior	
expresé	**expresamos**	**hube expresado**	**hubimos expresado**
expresaste	**expresasteis**	**hubiste expresado**	**hubisteis expresado**
expresó	**expresaron**	**hubo expresado**	**hubieron expresado**
4 futuro		11 futuro perfecto	
expresaré	**expresaremos**	**habré expresado**	**habremos expresado**
expresarás	**expresaréis**	**habrás expresado**	**habréis expresado**
expresará	**expresarán**	**habrá expresado**	**habrán expresado**
5 potencial simple		12 potencial compuesto	
expresaría	**expresaríamos**	**habría expresado**	**habríamos expresado**
expresarías	**expresaríais**	**habrías expresado**	**habríais expresado**
expresaría	**expresarían**	**habría expresado**	**habrían expresado**
6 presente de subjuntivo		13 perfecto de subjuntivo	
exprese	**expresemos**	**haya expresado**	**hayamos expresado**
expreses	**expreséis**	**hayas expresado**	**hayáis expresado**
exprese	**expresen**	**haya expresado**	**hayan expresado**
7 imperfecto de subjuntivo		14 pluscuamperfecto de subjuntivo	
expresara	**expresáramos**	**hubiera expresado**	**hubiéramos expresado**
expresaras	**expresarais**	**hubieras expresado**	**hubierais expresado**
expresara	**expresaran**	**hubiera expresado**	**hubieran expresado**
OR		OR	
expresase	**expresásemos**	**hubiese expresado**	**hubiésemos expresado**
expresases	**expresaseis**	**hubieses expresado**	**hubieseis expresado**
expresase	**expresasen**	**hubiese expresado**	**hubiesen expresado**

imperativo

—	**expresemos**
expresa; no expreses	**expresad; no expreséis**
exprese	**expresen**

Words and expressions related to this verb

expresarse   to express oneself
una expresión   expression, phrase
expresamente   expressly, on purpose
expresivamente   expressively

el expresionismo   expressionism (art)
expreso   express (train, etc.)
una expresión idiomática   idiomatic expression
expresiones de mi parte   regards from me,
   kindest regards

The subject pronouns are found on page 93.

fabricar (236)

Gerundio fabricando **Part. pas. fabricado**

to fabricate, to manufacture

Regular **-ar** verb endings with spelling change: **c** becomes **qu** before **e**

The Seven Simple Tenses		The Seven Compound Tenses	
Singular	Plural	Singular	Plural
1 presente de indicativo		8 perfecto de indicativo	
fabrico	fabricamos	he fabricado	hemos fabricado
fabricas	fabricáis	has fabricado	habéis fabricado
fabrica	fabrican	ha fabricado	han fabricado
2 imperfecto de indicativo		9 pluscuamperfecto de indicativo	
fabricaba	fabricábamos	había fabricado	habíamos fabricado
fabricabas	fabricabais	habías fabricado	habíais fabricado
fabricaba	fabricaban	había fabricado	habían fabricado
3 pretérito		10 pretérito anterior	
fabriqué	fabricamos	hube fabricado	hubimos fabricado
fabricaste	fabricasteis	hubiste fabricado	hubisteis fabricado
fabricó	fabricaron	hubo fabricado	hubieron fabricado
4 futuro		11 futuro perfecto	
fabricaré	fabricaremos	habré fabricado	habremos fabricado
fabricarás	fabricaréis	habrás fabricado	habréis fabricado
fabricará	fabricarán	habrá fabricado	habrán fabricado
5 potencial simple		12 potencial compuesto	
fabricaría	fabricaríamos	habría fabricado	habríamos fabricado
fabricarías	fabricaríais	habrías fabricado	habríais fabricado
fabricaría	fabricarían	habría fabricado	habrían fabricado
6 presente de subjuntivo		13 perfecto de subjuntivo	
fabrique	fabriquemos	haya fabricado	hayamos fabricado
fabriques	fabriquéis	hayas fabricado	hayáis fabricado
fabrique	fabriquen	haya fabricado	hayan fabricado
7 imperfecto de subjuntivo		14 pluscuamperfecto de subjuntivo	
fabricara	fabricáramos	hubiera fabricado	hubiéramos fabricado
fabricaras	fabricarais	hubieras fabricado	hubierais fabricado
fabricara	fabricaran	hubiera fabricado	hubieran fabricado
OR		OR	
fabricase	fabricásemos	hubiese fabricado	hubiésemos fabricado
fabricases	fabricaseis	hubieses fabricado	hubieseis fabricado
fabricase	fabricasen	hubiese fabricado	hubiesen fabricado

imperativo	
—	fabriquemos
fabrica; no fabriques	fabricad; no fabriquéis
fabrique	fabriquen

Words and expressions related to this verb
la **fábrica** factory
la **fabricación** fabrication, manufacturing
de **fabricación casera** homemade

el **fabricante** manufacturer
fabricación en serie mass production
prefabricar to prefabricate

Get acquainted with what preposition goes with what verb on pages 669–677.

Regular **-ar** verb   to be lacking, to be wanting, to lack, to miss, to need

The Seven Simple Tenses		The Seven Compound Tenses	
Singular	Plural	Singular	Plural
1 presente de indicativo		8 perfecto de indicativo	
falto	faltamos	he faltado	hemos faltado
faltas	faltáis	has faltado	habéis faltado
falta	faltan	ha faltado	han faltado
2 imperfecto de indicativo		9 pluscuamperfecto de indicativo	
faltaba	faltábamos	había faltado	habíamos faltado
faltabas	faltabais	habías faltado	habíais faltado
faltaba	faltaban	había faltado	habían faltado
3 pretérito		10 pretérito anterior	
falté	faltamos	hube faltado	hubimos faltado
faltaste	faltasteis	hubiste faltado	hubisteis faltado
faltó	faltaron	hubo faltado	hubieron faltado
4 futuro		11 futuro perfecto	
faltaré	faltaremos	habré faltado	habremos faltado
faltarás	faltaréis	habrás faltado	habréis faltado
faltará	faltarán	habrá faltado	habrán faltado
5 potencial simple		12 potencial compuesto	
faltaría	faltaríamos	habría faltado	habríamos faltado
faltarías	faltaríais	habrías faltado	habríais faltado
faltaría	faltarían	habría faltado	habrían faltado
6 presente de subjuntivo		13 perfecto de subjuntivo	
falte	faltemos	haya faltado	hayamos faltado
faltes	faltéis	hayas faltado	hayáis faltado
falte	falten	haya faltado	hayan faltado
7 imperfecto de subjuntivo		14 pluscuamperfecto de subjuntivo	
faltara	faltáramos	hubiera faltado	hubiéramos faltado
faltaras	faltarais	hubieras faltado	hubierais faltado
faltara	faltaran	hubiera faltado	hubieran faltado
OR		OR	
faltase	faltásemos	hubiese faltado	hubiésemos faltado
faltases	faltaseis	hubieses faltado	hubieseis faltado
faltase	faltasen	hubiese faltado	hubiesen faltado

imperativo

—	faltemos
falta; no faltes	faltad; no faltéis
falte	falten

Common idiomatic expressions using this verb
a falta de for lack of
sin falta without fail, without fault
la falta lack, want
faltante lacking, wanting

¡No faltaba más! That's the limit!
faltar poco para + inf. not to be long before
hacer falta to be necessary
poner faltas a to find fault with

Get your feet wet with verbs used in weather expressions on page 668.

The subject pronouns are found on page 93.   **355**

to congratulate, to felicitate   Regular **-ar** verb

The Seven Simple Tenses		The Seven Compound Tenses	
Singular	Plural	Singular	Plural
1 presente de indicativo		8 perfecto de indicativo	
felicito	**felicitamos**	**he felicitado**	**hemos felicitado**
felicitas	**felicitáis**	**has felicitado**	**habéis felicitado**
felicita	**felicitan**	**ha felicitado**	**han felicitado**
2 imperfecto de indicativo		9 pluscuamperfecto de indicativo	
felicitaba	**felicitábamos**	**había felicitado**	**habíamos felicitado**
felicitabas	**felicitabais**	**habías felicitado**	**habíais felicitado**
felicitaba	**felicitaban**	**había felicitado**	**habían felicitado**
3 pretérito		10 pretérito anterior	
felicité	**felicitamos**	**hube felicitado**	**hubimos felicitado**
felicitaste	**felicitasteis**	**hubiste felicitado**	**hubisteis felicitado**
felicitó	**felicitaron**	**hubo felicitado**	**hubieron felicitado**
4 futuro		11 futuro perfecto	
felicitaré	**felicitaremos**	**habré felicitado**	**habremos felicitado**
felicitarás	**felicitaréis**	**habrás felicitado**	**habréis felicitado**
felicitará	**felicitarán**	**habrá felicitado**	**habrán felicitado**
5 potencial simple		12 potencial compuesto	
felicitaría	**felicitaríamos**	**habría felicitado**	**habríamos felicitado**
felicitarías	**felicitaríais**	**habrías felicitado**	**habríais felicitado**
felicitaría	**felicitarían**	**habría felicitado**	**habrían felicitado**
6 presente de subjuntivo		13 perfecto de subjuntivo	
felicite	**felicitemos**	**haya felicitado**	**hayamos felicitado**
felicites	**felicitéis**	**hayas felicitado**	**hayáis felicitado**
felicite	**feliciten**	**haya felicitado**	**hayan felicitado**
7 imperfecto de subjuntivo		14 pluscuamperfecto de subjuntivo	
felicitara	**felicitáramos**	**hubiera felicitado**	**hubiéramos felicitado**
felicitaras	**felicitarais**	**hubieras felicitado**	**hubierais felicitado**
felicitara	**felicitaran**	**hubiera felicitado**	**hubieran felicitado**
OR		OR	
felicitase	**felicitásemos**	**hubiese felicitado**	**hubiésemos felicitado**
felicitases	**felicitaseis**	**hubieses felicitado**	**hubieseis felicitado**
felicitase	**felicitasen**	**hubiese felicitado**	**hubiesen felicitado**

imperativo	
—	**felicitemos**
felicita; no felicites	**felicitad; no felicitéis**
felicite	**feliciten**

Words and expressions related to this verb

la felicitación, las felicitaciones
  congratulations
la felicidad   happiness, good fortune
felizmente   happily, fortunately

feliz   happy, fortunate, lucky (*pl.* **felices**)
felice   happy (in poetry)
¡Feliz Año Nuevo!   Happy New Year!
¡Feliz Cumpleaños!   Happy Birthday!

If you want to see a sample English verb fully conjugated
in all the tenses, check out pages 11 and 12.

Regular **-ar** verb   to feast, to entertain, to celebrate

The Seven Simple Tenses		The Seven Compound Tenses	
Singular	Plural	Singular	Plural
1 presente de indicativo		8 perfecto de indicativo	
festejo	festejamos	he festejado	hemos festejado
festejas	festejáis	has festejado	habéis festejado
festeja	festejan	ha festejado	han festejado
2 imperfecto de indicativo		9 pluscuamperfecto de indicativo	
festejaba	festejábamos	había festejado	habíamos festejado
festejabas	festejabais	habías festejado	habíais festejado
fetsejaba	festejaban	había festejado	habían festejado
3 pretérito		10 pretérito anterior	
festejé	fetejamos	hube festejado	hubimos festejado
festejaste	festejasteis	hubiste festejado	hubisteis festejado
festejó	festejaron	hubo festejado	hubieron festejado
4 futuro		11 futuro perfecto	
festejaré	festejaremos	habré festejado	habremos festejado
festejarás	festejaréis	habrás festejado	habréis festejado
festejará	festejarán	habrá festejado	habrán festejado
5 potencial simple		12 potencial compuesto	
festejaría	festejaríamos	habría festejado	habríamos festejado
festejarías	festejaríais	habrías festejado	habríais festejado
festejaría	festejarían	habría festejado	habrían festejado
6 presente de subjuntivo		13 perfecto de subjuntivo	
festeje	festejemos	haya festejado	hayamos festejado
festejes	festejéis	hayas festejado	hayáis festejado
festeje	festejen	haya festejado	hayan festejado
7 imperfecto de subjuntivo		14 pluscuamperfecto de subjuntivo	
festejara	festejáramos	hubiera festejado	hubiéramos festejado
festejaras	festejarais	hubieras festejado	hubierais festejado
festejara	festejaran	hubiera festejado	hubieran festejado
OR		OR	
festejase	festejásemos	hubiese festejado	hubiésemos festejado
festejases	festejaseis	hubieses festejado	hubieseis festejado
festejase	festejasen	hubiese festejado	hubiesen festejado

	imperativo	
—		festejemos
festeja; no festejes		festejad; no festejéis
festeje		festejen

Words and expressions related to this verb

un festejo banquet, feast, celebration	**la fiesta nacional** national holiday
una fiesta feast, holy day, festivity	**la fiesta de todos los santos** All Saints' Day
la Fiesta de la Raza Columbus Day	**la fiesta de cumpleaños** birthday party

> If you want an explanation of meanings and uses of Spanish and
> English verb tenses and moods, see pages 13–32.

The subject pronouns are found on page 93.

to confide, to trust	Regular **-ar** verb endings with spelling change: **i** becomes **í** on stressed syllable (see Tenses 1, 6, Imperative)

The Seven Simple Tenses	The Seven Compound Tenses

Singular	Plural	Singular	Plural
1 presente de indicativo		8 perfecto de indicativo	
fío	fiamos	he fiado	hemos fiado
fías	fiáis	has fiado	habéis fiado
fía	fían	ha fiado	han fiado
2 imperfecto de indicativo		9 pluscuamperfecto de indicativo	
fiaba	fiábamos	había fiado	habíamos fiado
fiabas	fiabais	habías fiado	habíais fiado
fiaba	fiaban	había fiado	habían fiado
3 pretérito		10 pretérito anterior	
fié	fiamos	hube fiado	hubimos fiado
fiaste	fiasteis	hubiste fiado	hubisteis fiado
fió	fiaron	hubo fiado	hubieron fiado
4 futuro		11 futuro perfecto	
fiaré	fiaremos	habré fiado	habremos fiado
fiarás	fiaréis	habrás fiado	habréis fiado
fiará	fiarán	habrá fiado	habrán fiado
5 potencial simple		12 potencial compuesto	
fiaría	fiaríamos	habría fiado	habríamos fiado
fiarías	fiaríais	habrías fiado	habríais fiado
fiaría	fiarían	habría fiado	habrían fiado
6 presente de subjuntivo		13 perfecto de subjuntivo	
fíe	fiemos	haya fiado	hayamos fiado
fíes	fiéis	hayas fiado	hayáis fiado
fíe	fíen	haya fiado	hayan fiado
7 imperfecto de subjuntivo		14 pluscuamperfecto de subjuntivo	
fiara	fiáramos	hubiera fiado	hubiéramos fiado
fiaras	fiarais	hubieras fiado	hubierais fiado
fiara	fiaran	hubiera fiado	hubieran fiado
OR		OR	
fiase	fiásemos	hubiese fiado	hubiésemos fiado
fiases	fiaseis	hubieses fiado	hubieseis fiado
fiase	fiasen	hubiese fiado	hubiesen fiado

	imperativo	
—		fiemos
fía; no fíes		fiad; no fiéis
fíe		fíen

Words and expressions related to this verb

fiarse de   to have confidence in, to trust
la fianza   security, surety, guarantee
al fiado   on credit, on trust
fiable   trustworthy

fiar en   to trust in
comprar al fiado   to buy on credit
en libertad bajo fianza   free on bail
no se fía   no credit

If you don't know the Spanish verb for the English verb you have in mind, look it up in the index on pages 682–706.

Reflexive regular **-ar** verb   to take notice, to pay attention, to settle

The Seven Simple Tenses		The Seven Compound Tenses	
Singular	Plural	Singular	Plural
1 presente de indicativo		**8 perfecto de indicativo**	
me fijo	nos fijamos	me he fijado	nos hemos fijado
te fijas	os fijáis	te has fijado	os habéis fijado
se fija	se fijan	se ha fijado	se han fijado
2 imperfecto de indicativo		**9 pluscuamperfecto de indicativo**	
me fijaba	nos fijábamos	me había fijado	nos habíamos fijado
te fijabas	os fijabais	te habías fijado	os habíais fijado
se fijaba	se fijaban	se había fijado	se habían fijado
3 pretérito		**10 pretérito anterior**	
me fijé	nos fijamos	me hube fijado	nos hubimos fijado
te fijaste	os fijasteis	te hubiste fijado	os hubisteis fijado
se fijó	se fijaron	se hubo fijado	se hubieron fijado
4 futuro		**11 futuro perfecto**	
me fijaré	nos fijaremos	me habré fijado	nos habremos fijado
te fijarás	os fijaréis	te habrás fijado	os habréis fijado
se fijará	se fijarán	se habrá fijado	se habrán fijado
5 potencial simple		**12 potencial compuesto**	
me fijaría	nos fijaríamos	me habría fijado	nos habríamos fijado
te fijarías	os fijaríais	te habrías fijado	os habríais fijado
se fijaría	se fijarían	se habría fijado	se habrían fijado
6 presente de subjuntivo		**13 perfecto de subjuntivo**	
me fije	nos fijemos	me haya fijado	nos hayamos fijado
te fijes	os fijéis	te hayas fijado	os hayáis fijado
se fije	se fijen	se haya fijado	se hayan fijado
7 imperfecto de subjuntivo		**14 pluscuamperfecto de subjuntivo**	
me fijara	nos fijáramos	me hubiera fijado	nos hubiéramos fijado
te fijaras	os fijarais	te hubieras fijado	os hubierais fijado
se fijara	se fijaran	se hubiera fijado	se hubieran fijado
OR		OR	
me fijase	nos fijásemos	me hubiese fijado	nos hubiésemos fijado
te fijases	os fijaseis	te hubieses fijado	os hubieseis fijado
se fijase	se fijasen	se hubiese fijado	se hubiesen fijado

imperativo	
—	fijémonos
fíjate; no te fijes	fijaos; no os fijéis
fíjese	fíjense

Words and expressions related to this verb
fijar to clinch, to fasten, to fix; **fijo** (when used as an adj.)
fijarse en to take notice of, to pay attention to, to settle in
hora fija set time, set hour, time agreed on; **de fijo** surely
fijamente fixedly, assuredly; **fijar el precio** to fix the price
una fija door hinge; **una fijación** fixation *PROHIBIDO FIJAR CARTELES* POST NO BILLS
la fijación de precios price fixing

The subject pronouns are found on page 93.

359

fingir (242)

Gerundio fingiendo　　Part. pas. **fingido**

to feign, to pretend

Regular **-ir** verb endings with spelling change: **g** becomes **j** before **a** or **o**

The Seven Simple Tenses		The Seven Compound Tenses	
Singular	Plural	Singular	Plural
1　presente de indicativo		8　perfecto de indicativo	
finjo	fingimos	he fingido	hemos fingido
finges	fingís	has fingido	habéis fingido
finge	fingen	ha fingido	han fingido
2　imperfecto de indicativo		9　pluscuamperfecto de indicativo	
fingía	fingíamos	había fingido	habíamos fingido
fingías	fingíais	habías fingido	habíais fingido
fingía	fingían	había fingido	habían fingido
3　pretérito		10　pretérito anterior	
fingí	fingimos	hube fingido	hubimos fingido
fingiste	finisteis	hubiste fingido	hubisteis fingido
fingió	fingieron	hubo fingido	hubieron fingido
4　futuro		11　futuro perfecto	
fingiré	fingiremos	habré fingido	habremos fingido
fingirás	fingiréis	habrás fingido	habréis fingido
fingirá	fingirán	habrá fingido	habrán fingido
5　potencial simple		12　potencial compuesto	
fingiría	fingiríamos	habría fingido	habríamos fingido
fingirías	fingiríais	habrías fingido	habríais fingido
fingiría	fingirían	habría fingido	habrían fingido
6　presente de subjuntivo		13　perfecto de subjuntivo	
finja	finjamos	haya fingido	hayamos fingido
finjas	finjáis	hayas fingido	hayáis fingido
finja	finjan	haya fingido	hayan fingido
7　imperfecto de subjuntivo		14　pluscuamperfecto de subjuntivo	
fingiera	fingiéramos	hubiera fingido	hubiéramos fingido
fingieras	fingierais	hubieras fingido	hubierais fingido
fingiera	fingieran	hubiera fingido	hubieran fingido
OR		OR	
fingiese	fingiésemos	hubiese fingido	hubiésemos fingido
fingieses	fingieseis	hubieses fingido	hubieseis fingido
fingiese	fingiesen	hubiese fingido	hubiesen fingido

	imperativo	
—		finjamos
finge; no finjas		fingid; no finjáis
finja		finjan

Words and expressions related to this verb

fingir + inf.　to pretend + inf.
el fingimiento　deceit, pretense, feigning
un fingidor, una fingidora　faker, feigner
fingidamente　fictitiously
fingir sorpresa　to fake surprise

fingirse amigos　to pretend to be friends
nombre fingido　assumed (fake) name
fingir alegría　to fake happiness

Can't recognize an irregular verb form? Check out pages 678–681.

Regular **-ar** verb   to sign

The Seven Simple Tenses		The Seven Compound Tenses	
Singular	Plural	Singular	Plural
1 presente de indicativo		8 perfecto de indicativo	
firmo	**firmamos**	**he firmado**	**hemos firmado**
firmas	**firmáis**	**has firmado**	**habéis firmado**
firma	**firman**	**ha firmado**	**han firmado**
2 imperfecto de indicativo		9 pluscuamperfecto de indicativo	
firmaba	**firmábamos**	**había firmado**	**habíamos firmado**
firmabas	**firmabais**	**habías firmado**	**habíais firmado**
firmaba	**firmaban**	**había firmado**	**habían firmado**
3 pretérito		10 pretérito anterior	
firmé	**firmamos**	**hube firmado**	**hubimos firmado**
firmaste	**firmasteis**	**hubiste firmado**	**hubisteis firmado**
firmó	**firmaron**	**hubo firmado**	**hubieron firmado**
4 futuro		11 futuro perfecto	
firmaré	**firmaremos**	**habré firmado**	**habremos firmado**
firmarás	**firmaréis**	**habrás firmado**	**habréis firmado**
firmará	**firmarán**	**habrá firmado**	**habrán firmado**
5 potencial simple		12 potencial compuesto	
firmaría	**firmaríamos**	**habría firmado**	**habríamos firmado**
firmarías	**firmaríais**	**habrías firmado**	**habríais firmado**
firmaría	**firmarían**	**habría firmado**	**habrían firmado**
6 presente de subjuntivo		13 perfecto de subjuntivo	
firme	**firmemos**	**haya firmado**	**hayamos firmado**
firmes	**firméis**	**hayas firmado**	**hayáis firmado**
firme	**firmen**	**haya firmado**	**hayan firmado**
7 imperfecto de subjuntivo		14 pluscuamperfecto de subjuntivo	
firmara	**firmáramos**	**hubiera firmado**	**hubiéramos firmado**
firmaras	**firmarais**	**hubieras firmado**	**hubierais firmado**
firmara	**firmaran**	**hubiera firmado**	**hubieran firmado**
OR		OR	
firmase	**firmásemos**	**hubiese firmado**	**hubiésemos firmado**
firmases	**firmaseis**	**hubieses firmado**	**hubieseis firmado**
firmase	**firmasen**	**hubiese firmado**	**hubiesen firmado**

imperativo	
—	**firmemos**
firma; no firmes	**firmad; no firméis**
firme	**firmen**

Words and expressions related to this verb
firmar y sellar   to sign and seal
el, la firmante   signer
confirmar   to confirm

de firme   steadily
en lo firme   in the right
color firme   fast color

Check out the verb drills and verb tests with answers explained on pages 45–91.

to form, to shape   Regular **-ar** verb

The Seven Simple Tenses		The Seven Compound Tenses	
Singular	Plural	Singular	Plural
1 presente de indicativo		8 perfecto de indicativo	
formo	**formamos**	**he formado**	**hemos formado**
formas	**formáis**	**has formado**	**habéis formado**
forma	**forman**	**ha formado**	**han formado**
2 imperfecto de indicativo		9 pluscuamperfecto de indicativo	
formaba	**formábamos**	**había formado**	**habíamos formado**
formabas	**formabais**	**habías formado**	**habíais formado**
formaba	**formaban**	**había formado**	**habían formado**
3 pretérito		10 pretérito anterior	
formé	**formamos**	**hube formado**	**hubimos formado**
formaste	**formasteis**	**hubiste formado**	**hubisteis formado**
formó	**formaron**	**hubo formado**	**hubieron formado**
4 futuro		11 futuro perfecto	
formaré	**formaremos**	**habré formado**	**habremos formado**
formarás	**formaréis**	**habrás formado**	**habréis formado**
formará	**formarán**	**habrá formado**	**habrán formado**
5 potencial simple		12 potencial compuesto	
formaría	**formaríamos**	**habría formado**	**habríamos formado**
formarías	**formaríais**	**habrías formado**	**habríais formado**
formaría	**formarían**	**habría formado**	**habrían formado**
6 presente de subjuntivo		13 perfecto de subjuntivo	
forme	**formemos**	**haya formado**	**hayamos formado**
formes	**forméis**	**hayas formado**	**hayáis formado**
forme	**formen**	**haya formado**	**hayan formado**
7 imperfecto de subjuntivo		14 pluscuamperfecto de subjuntivo	
formara	**formáramos**	**hubiera formado**	**hubiéramos formado**
formaras	**formarais**	**hubieras formado**	**hubierais formado**
formara	**formaran**	**hubiera formado**	**hubieran formado**
OR		OR	
formase	**formásemos**	**hubiese formado**	**hubiésemos formado**
formases	**formaseis**	**hubieses formado**	**hubieseis formado**
formase	**formasen**	**hubiese formado**	**hubiesen formado**

imperativo	
—	**formemos**
forma; no formes	**formad; no forméis**
forme	**formen**

Words and expressions related to this verb
formativo, formativa formative
formante forming
transformar to transform
la forma form, shape
de esta forma in this way

la formación formation
formalmente formally
la formalidad formality
de forma que . . . so that . . .
de una forma o de otra somehow or other, one way or another

Regular **-ar** verb endings with stem change: to wash dishes, to scrub
Tenses 1, 6, Imperative

The Seven Simple Tenses		The Seven Compound Tenses	
Singular	Plural	Singular	Plural
1 presente de indicativo		8 perfecto de indicativo	
friego	**fregamos**	**he fregado**	**hemos fregado**
friegas	**fregáis**	**has fregado**	**habéis fregado**
friega	**friegan**	**ha fregado**	**han fregado**
2 imperfecto de indicativo		9 pluscuamperfecto de indicativo	
fregaba	**fregábamos**	**había fregado**	**habíamos fregado**
fregabas	**fregabais**	**habías fregado**	**habíais fregado**
fregaba	**fregaban**	**había fregado**	**habían fregado**
3 pretérito		10 pretérito anterior	
fregué	**fregamos**	**hube fregado**	**hubimos fregado**
fregaste	**fregasteis**	**hubiste fregado**	**hubisteis fregado**
fregó	**fregaron**	**hubo fregado**	**hubieron fregado**
4 futuro		11 futuro perfecto	
fregaré	**fregaremos**	**habré fregado**	**habremos fregado**
fregarás	**fregaréis**	**habrás fregado**	**habréis fregado**
fregará	**fregarán**	**habrá fregado**	**habrán fregado**
5 potencial simple		12 potencial compuesto	
fregaría	**fregaríamos**	**habría fregado**	**habríamos fregado**
fregarías	**fregaríais**	**habrías fregado**	**habríais fregado**
fregaría	**fregarían**	**habría fregado**	**habrían fregado**
6 presente de subjuntivo		13 perfecto de subjuntivo	
friegue	**freguemos**	**haya fregado**	**hayamos fregado**
friegues	**freguéis**	**hayas fregado**	**hayáis fregado**
friegue	**frieguen**	**haya fregado**	**hayan fregado**
7 imperfecto de subjuntivo		14 pluscuamperfecto de subjuntivo	
fregara	**fregáramos**	**hubiera fregado**	**hubiéramos fregado**
fregaras	**fregarais**	**hubieras fregado**	**hubierais fregado**
fregara	**fregaran**	**hubiera fregado**	**hubieran fregado**
OR		OR	
fregase	**fregásemos**	**hubiese fregado**	**hubiésemos fregado**
fregases	**fregaseis**	**hubieses fregado**	**hubieseis fregado**
fregase	**fregasen**	**hubiese fregado**	**hubiesen fregado**

imperativo	
—	**freguemos**
friega; no friegues	**fregad; no freguéis**
friegue	**frieguen**

Words and expressions related to this verb

el fregador   sink; dish mop, scrubbing brush   **la fregadura**   scouring, mopping, scrubbing
el fregadero   kitchen sink   **refregar**   to rub; **el refregamiento**   rubbing, scrubbing

Can't recognize an irregular verb form? Check out pages 678–681.

The subject pronouns are found on page 93.

to fry　　　　　　　　　　　　　　　　　　　　Irregular verb

The Seven Simple Tenses | The Seven Compound Tenses

Singular	Plural	Singular	Plural
1　presente de indicativo		8　perfecto de indicativo	
frío	freímos	he frito	hemos frito
fríes	freís	has frito	habéis frito
fríe	fríen	ha frito	han frito
2　imperfecto de indicativo		9　pluscuamperfecto de indicativo	
freía	freíamos	había frito	habíamos frito
freías	freíais	habías frito	habíais frito
freía	freían	había frito	habían frito
3　pretérito		10　pretérito anterior	
freí	freímos	hube frito	hubimos frito
freíste	freísteis	hubiste frito	hubisteis frito
frió	frieron	hubo frito	hubieron frito
4　futuro		11　futuro perfecto	
freiré	freiremos	habré frito	habremos frito
freirás	freiréis	habrás frito	habréis frito
freirá	freirán	habrá frito	habrán frito
5　potencial simple		12　potencial compuesto	
freiría	freiríamos	habría frito	habríamos frito
freirías	freiríais	habrías frito	habríais frito
freiría	freirían	habría frito	habrían frito
6　presente de subjuntivo		13　perfecto de subjuntivo	
fría	friamos	haya frito	hayamos frito
frías	friáis	hayas frito	hayáis frito
fría	frían	haya frito	hayan frito
7　imperfecto de subjuntivo		14　pluscuamperfecto de subjuntivo	
friera	friéramos	hubiera frito	hubiéramos frito
frieras	frierais	hubieras frito	hubierais frito
friera	frieran	hubiera frito	hubieran frito
OR		OR	
friese	friésemos	hubiese frito	hubiésemos frito
frieses	frieseis	hubieses frito	hubieseis frito
friese	friesen	hubiese frito	hubiesen frito

imperativo

—	friamos
fríe; no frías	freíd; no friáis
fría	frían

Words and expressions related to this verb
patatas fritas　fried potatoes, French fries
patatas fritas a la inglesa　potato chips
las fritillas　fritters
frito, frita　fried

la fritada　fried food
la fritura　fry
el pescado frito　fried fish
los huevos fritos　fried eggs

Can't find the verb you're looking for?
Check the back pages of this book for a list of over 2,100 additional verbs!

The Seven Simple Tenses		The Seven Compound Tenses	
Singular	Plural	Singular	Plural
1 presente de indicativo		8 perfecto de indicativo	
fumo	**fumamos**	**he fumado**	**hemos fumado**
fumas	**fumáis**	**has fumado**	**habéis fumado**
fuma	**fuman**	**ha fumado**	**han fumado**
2 imperfecto de indicativo		9 pluscuamperfecto de indicativo	
fumaba	**fumábamos**	**había fumado**	**habíamos fumado**
fumabas	**fumabais**	**habías fumado**	**habíais fumado**
fumaba	**fumaban**	**había fumado**	**habían fumado**
3 pretérito		10 pretérito anterior	
fumé	**fumamos**	**hube fumado**	**hubimos fumado**
fumaste	**fumasteis**	**hubiste fumado**	**hubisteis fumado**
fumó	**fumaron**	**hubo fumado**	**hubieron fumado**
4 futuro		11 futuro perfecto	
fumaré	**fumaremos**	**habré fumado**	**habremos fumado**
fumarás	**fumaréis**	**habrás fumado**	**habréis fumado**
fumará	**fumarán**	**habrá fumado**	**habrán fumado**
5 potencial simple		12 potencial compuesto	
fumaría	**fumaríamos**	**habría fumado**	**habríamos fumado**
fumarías	**fumaríais**	**habrías fumado**	**habríais fumado**
fumaría	**fumarían**	**habría fumado**	**habrían fumado**
6 presente de subjuntivo		13 perfecto de subjuntivo	
fume	**fumemos**	**haya fumado**	**hayamos fumado**
fumes	**fuméis**	**hayas fumado**	**hayáis fumado**
fume	**fumen**	**haya fumado**	**hayan fumado**
7 imperfecto de subjuntivo		14 pluscuamperfecto de subjuntivo	
fumara	**fumáramos**	**hubiera fumado**	**hubiéramos fumado**
fumaras	**fumarais**	**hubieras fumado**	**hubierais fumado**
fumara	**fumaran**	**hubiera fumado**	**hubieran fumado**
OR		OR	
fumase	**fumásemos**	**hubiese fumado**	**hubiésemos fumado**
fumases	**fumaseis**	**hubieses fumado**	**hubieseis fumado**
fumase	**fumasen**	**hubiese fumado**	**hubiesen fumado**

imperativo	
—	**fumemos**
fuma; no fumes	**fumad; no fuméis**
fume	**fumen**

Words and expressions related to this verb

un fumador, una fumadora   smoker

una fumada, una fumarada   puff of smoke

fumar como una chimenea   to smoke like a chimney

un fumadero   smoking room

SE PROHIBE FUMAR   NO SMOKING

fumarse una clase   to cut (skip) a class

Fumar no es bueno para la salud/Smoking is not good for one's health.

(see page 8, *Spanish infinitive and its principal uses*)

The subject pronouns are found on page 93.

to function, to run (machine)   Regular **-ar** verb

The Seven Simple Tenses		The Seven Compound Tenses	
Singular	Plural	Singular	Plural
1 presente de indicativo		8 perfecto de indicativo	
funciono	**funcionamos**	**he funcionado**	**hemos funcionado**
funcionas	**funcionáis**	**has funcionado**	**habéis funcionado**
funciona	**funcionan**	**ha funcionado**	**han funcionado**
2 imperfecto de indicativo		9 pluscuamperfecto de indicativo	
funcionaba	**funcionábamos**	**había funcionado**	**habíamos funcionado**
funcionabas	**funcionabais**	**habías funcionado**	**habíais funcionado**
funcionaba	**funcionaban**	**había funcionado**	**habían funcionado**
3 pretérito		10 pretérito anterior	
funcioné	**funcionamos**	**hube funcionado**	**hubimos funcionado**
funcionaste	**funcionasteis**	**hubiste funcionado**	**hubisteis funcionado**
funcionó	**funcionaron**	**hubo funcionado**	**hubieron funcionado**
4 futuro		11 futuro perfecto	
funcionaré	**funcionaremos**	**habré funcionado**	**habremos funcionado**
funcionarás	**funcionaréis**	**habrás funcionado**	**habréis funcionado**
funcionará	**funcionarán**	**habrá funcionado**	**habrán funcionado**
5 potencial simple		12 potencial compuesto	
funcionaría	**funcionaríamos**	**habría funcionado**	**habríamos funcionado**
funcionarías	**funcionaríais**	**habrías funcionado**	**habríais funcionado**
funcionaría	**funcionarían**	**habría funcionado**	**habrían funcionado**
6 presente de subjuntivo		13 perfecto de subjuntivo	
funcione	**funcionemos**	**haya funcionado**	**hayamos funcionado**
funciones	**funcionéis**	**hayas funcionado**	**hayáis funcionado**
funcione	**funcionen**	**haya funcionado**	**hayan funcionado**
7 imperfecto de subjuntivo		14 pluscuamperfecto de subjuntivo	
funcionara	**funcionáramos**	**hubiera funcionado**	**hubiéramos funcionado**
funcionaras	**funcionarais**	**hubieras funcionado**	**hubierais funcionado**
funcionara	**funcionaran**	**hubiera funcionado**	**hubieran funcionado**
OR		OR	
funcionase	**funcionásemos**	**hubiese funcionado**	**hubiésemos funcionado**
funcionases	**funionaseis**	**hubieses funcionado**	**hubieseis funcionado**
funcionase	**funcionasen**	**hubiese funcionado**	**hubiesen funcionado**

imperativo	
—	**funcionemos**
funciona; no funciones	**funcionad; no funcionéis**
funcione	**funcionen**

Words and expressions related to this verb
una función function
función de títeres puppet show
un funcionario de aduanas customs official

el funcionado, la funcionada civil servant
un funcionario público public official

If you want to see a sample English verb fully conjugated in
all the tenses, check out pages 11 and 12.

Regular **-ar** verb   to earn, to gain, to win

The Seven Simple Tenses		The Seven Compound Tenses	
Singular	Plural	Singular	Plural
1 presente de indicativo		8 perfecto de indicativo	
gano	**ganamos**	**he ganado**	**hemos ganado**
ganas	**ganáis**	**has ganado**	**habéis ganado**
gana	**ganan**	**ha ganado**	**han ganado**
2 imperfecto de indicativo		9 pluscuamperfecto de indicativo	
ganaba	**ganábamos**	**había ganado**	**habíamos ganado**
ganabas	**ganabais**	**habías ganado**	**habíais ganado**
ganaba	**ganaban**	**había ganado**	**habían ganado**
3 pretérito		10 pretérito anterior	
gané	**ganamos**	**hube ganado**	**hubimos ganado**
ganaste	**ganasteis**	**hubiste ganado**	**hubisteis ganado**
ganó	**ganaron**	**hubo ganado**	**hubieron ganado**
4 futuro		11 futuro perfecto	
ganaré	**ganaremos**	**habré ganado**	**habremos ganado**
ganarás	**ganaréis**	**habrás ganado**	**habréis ganado**
ganará	**ganarán**	**habrá ganado**	**habrán ganado**
5 potencial simple		12 potencial compuesto	
ganaría	**ganaríamos**	**habría ganado**	**habríamos ganado**
ganarías	**ganaríais**	**habrías ganado**	**habríais ganado**
ganaría	**ganarían**	**habría ganado**	**habrían ganado**
6 presente de subjuntivo		13 perfecto de subjuntivo	
gane	**ganemos**	**haya ganado**	**hayamos ganado**
ganes	**ganéis**	**hayas ganado**	**hayáis ganado**
gane	**ganen**	**haya ganado**	**hayan ganado**
7 imperfecto de subjuntivo		14 pluscuamperfecto de subjuntivo	
ganara	**ganáramos**	**hubiera ganado**	**hubiéramos ganado**
ganaras	**ganarais**	**hubieras ganado**	**hubierais ganado**
ganara	**ganaran**	**hubiera ganado**	**hubieran ganado**
OR		OR	
ganase	**ganásemos**	**hubiese ganado**	**hubiésemos ganado**
ganases	**ganaseis**	**hubieses ganado**	**hubieseis ganado**
ganase	**ganasen**	**hubiese ganado**	**hubiesen ganado**

G

	imperativo	
—		**ganemos**
gana; no ganes		**ganad; no ganéis**
gane		**ganen**

Words and expressions related to this verb

ganar el pan, ganar la vida   to earn a living
la ganancia   profit, gain
ganador, ganadora   winner
ganar dinero   to earn (make) money
ganar a uno en inteligencia   to surpass
   someone in intelligence

desganar   to dissuade
desganarse   to lose one's appetite; to be bored
ganar el premio gordo   to win first prize
ir ganando   to be winning, to be in the lead

The subject pronouns are found on page 93.

to spend (money), to wear out, to waste   Regular **-ar** verb

The Seven Simple Tenses		The Seven Compound Tenses	
Singular	Plural	Singular	Plural
1 presente de indicativo		**8 perfecto de indicativo**	
gasto	gastamos	he gastado	hemos gastado
gastas	gastáis	has gastado	habéis gastado
gasta	gastan	ha gastado	han gastado
2 imperfecto de indicativo		**9 pluscuamperfecto de indicativo**	
gastaba	gastábamos	había gastado	habíamos gastado
gastabas	gastabais	habías gastado	habíais gastado
gastaba	gastaban	había gastado	habían gastado
3 pretérito		**10 pretérito anterior**	
gasté	gastamos	hube gastado	hubimos gastado
gastaste	gastasteis	hubiste gastado	hubisteis gastado
gastó	gastaron	hubo gastado	hubieron gastado
4 futuro		**11 futuro perfecto**	
gastaré	gastaremos	habré gastado	habremos gastado
gastarás	gastaréis	habrás gastado	habréis gastado
gastará	gastarán	habrá gastado	habrán gastado
5 potencial simple		**12 potencial compuesto**	
gastaría	gastaríamos	habría gastado	habríamos gastado
gastarías	gastaríais	habrías gastado	habríais gastado
gastaría	gastarían	habría gastado	habrían gastado
6 presente de subjuntivo		**13 perfecto de subjuntivo**	
gaste	gastemos	haya gastado	hayamos gastado
gastes	gastéis	hayas gastado	hayáis gastado
gaste	gasten	haya gastado	hayan gastado
7 imperfecto de subjuntivo		**14 pluscuamperfecto de subjuntivo**	
gastara	gastáramos	hubiera gastado	hubiéramos gastado
gastaras	gastarais	hubieras gastado	hubierais gastado
gastara	gastaran	hubiera gastado	hubieran gastado
OR		OR	
gastase	gastásemos	hubiese gastado	hubiésemos gastado
gastases	gastaseis	hubieses gastado	hubieseis gastado
gastase	gastasen	hubiese gastado	hubiesen gastado

imperativo	
—	gastemos
gasta; no gastes	gastad; no gastéis
gaste	gasten

Words and expressions related to this verb

el gasto expense, expenditure
cubrir gastos to cover expenses
un gastador, una gastadora spendthrift, wasteful
pagar los gastos to foot the bill, to pay the tab
malgastar to squander, misspend, waste

gastar el tiempo to waste time
con poco gasto at little cost (expense)
el dinero para gastos menudos pocket money

Use **gastar** when you spend money: **No me gusta gastar mucho dinero.**/I do not like to spend much money. (See **pasar**.)

Regular **-ir** verb endings with stem change: to grieve, to groan,
Tenses 1, 3, 6, 7, Imperative, Gerundio   to moan, to howl

The Seven Simple Tenses		The Seven Compound Tenses	
Singular	Plural	Singular	Plural
1 presente de indicativo		8 perfecto de indicativo	
gimo	gemimos	he gemido	hemos gemido
gimes	gemís	has gemido	habéis gemido
gime	gimen	ha gemido	han gemido
2 imperfecto de indicativo		9 pluscuamperfecto de indicativo	
gemía	gemíamos	había gemido	habíamos gemido
gemías	gemíais	habías gemido	habíais gemido
gemía	gemían	había gemido	habían gemido
3 pretérito		10 pretérito anterior	
gemí	gemimos	hube gemido	hubimos gemido
gemiste	gemisteis	hubiste gemido	hubisteis gemido
gimió	gimieron	hubo gemido	hubieron gemido
4 futuro		11 futuro perfecto	
gemiré	gemiremos	habré gemido	habremos gemido
gemirás	gemiréis	habrás gemido	habréis gemido
gemirá	gemirán	habrá gemido	habrán gemido
5 potencial simple		12 potencial compuesto	
gemiría	gemiríamos	habría gemido	habríamos gemido
gemirías	gemiríais	habrías gemido	habríais gemido
gemiría	gemirían	habría gemido	habrían gemido
6 presente de subjuntivo		13 perfecto de subjuntivo	
gima	gimamos	haya gemido	hayamos gemido
gimas	gimáis	hayas gemido	hayáis gemido
gima	giman	haya gemido	hayan gemido
7 imperfecto de subjuntivo		14 pluscuamperfecto de subjuntivo	
gimiera	gimiéramos	hubiera gemido	hubiéramos gemido
gimieras	gimierais	hubieras gemido	hubierais gemido
gimiera	gimieran	hubiera gemido	hubieran gemido
OR		OR	
gimiese	gimiésemos	hubiese gemido	hubiésemos gemido
gimieses	gimieseis	hubieses gemido	hubieseis gemido
gimiese	gimiesen	hubiese gemido	hubiesen gemido

G

imperativo	
—	gimamos
gime; no gimas	gemid; no gimáis
gima	giman

Words related to this verb
gemidor, gemidora   lamenter, griever   **gemiquear**   to whine, to blubber
el gemido   lamentation, howl, groan, moan   **el gemiqueo**   whining, blubbering

Don't miss the definitions of basic grammatical terms with examples
in English and Spanish on pages 33–44.

The subject pronouns are found on page 93.

gobernar (252)

Gerundio gobernando   **Part. pas. gobernado**

to govern, to rule

Regular **-ar** verb endings with stem change:
Tenses 1, 6, Imperative

The Seven Simple Tenses | The Seven Compound Tenses

Singular	Plural	Singular	Plural
1 presente de indicativo		**8 perfecto de indicativo**	
gobierno	gobernamos	he gobernado	hemos gobernado
gobiernas	gobernáis	has gobernado	habéis gobernado
gobierna	gobiernan	ha gobernado	han gobernado
2 imperfecto de indicativo		**9 pluscuamperfecto de indicativo**	
gobernaba	gobernábamos	había gobernado	habíamos gobernado
gobernabas	gobernabais	habías gobernado	habíais gobernado
gobernaba	gobernaban	había gobernado	habían gobernado
3 pretérito		**10 pretérito anterior**	
goberné	gobernamos	hube gobernado	hubimos gobernado
gobernaste	gobernasteis	hubiste gobernado	hubisteis gobernado
gobernó	gobernaron	hubo gobernado	hubieron gobernado
4 futuro		**11 futuro perfecto**	
gobernaré	gobernaremos	habré gobernado	habremos gobernado
gobernarás	gobernaréis	habrás gobernado	habréis gobernado
gobernará	gobernarán	habrá gobernado	habrán gobernado
5 potencial simple		**12 potencial compuesto**	
gobernaría	gobernaríamos	habría gobernado	habríamos gobernado
gobernarías	gobernaríais	habrías gobernado	habríais gobernado
gobernaría	gobernarían	habría gobernado	habrían gobernado
6 presente de subjuntivo		**13 perfecto de subjuntivo**	
gobierne	gobernemos	haya gobernado	hayamos gobernado
gobiernes	gobernéis	hayas gobernado	hayáis gobernado
gobierne	gobiernen	haya gobernado	hayan gobernado
7 imperfecto de subjuntivo		**14 pluscuamperfecto de subjuntivo**	
gobernara	gobernáramos	hubiera gobernado	hubiéramos gobernado
gobernaras	gobernarais	hubieras gobernado	hubierais gobernado
gobernara	gobernaran	hubiera gobernado	hubieran gobernado
OR		OR	
gobernase	gobernásemos	hubiese gobernado	hubiésemos gobernado
gobernases	gobernaseis	hubieses gobernado	hubieseis gobernado
gobernase	gobernasen	hubiese gobernado	hubiesen gobernado

imperativo	
—	gobernemos
gobierna; no gobiernes	gobernad; no gobernéis
gobierne	gobiernen

Words and expressions related to this verb

un gobernador, una gobernadora governor
el gobierno government
el gobierno central central government
el gobierno de la casa home management,
  housekeeping

un gobierno fantoche puppet government
la gobernación governing
el gobierno parlamentario parliamentary
  government
el gobierno militar military government

370

Regular **-ar** verb endings with spelling change: to enjoy
z becomes **c** before **e**

The Seven Simple Tenses		The Seven Compound Tenses	
Singular	Plural	Singular	Plural
1 presente de indicativo		8 perfecto de indicativo	
gozo	gozamos	he gozado	hemos gozado
gozas	gozáis	has gozado	habéis gozado
goza	gozan	ha gozado	han gozado
2 imperfecto de indicativo		9 pluscuamperfecto de indicativo	
gozaba	gozábamos	había gozado	habíamos gozado
gozabas	gozabais	habías gozado	habíais gozado
gozaba	gozaban	había gozado	habían gozado
3 pretérito		10 pretérito anterior	
gocé	gozamos	hube gozado	hubimos gozado
gozaste	gozasteis	hubiste gozado	hubisteis gozado
gozó	gozaron	hubo gozado	hubieron gozado
4 futuro		11 futuro perfecto	
gozaré	gozaremos	habré gozado	habremos gozado
gozarás	gozaréis	habrás gozado	habréis gozado
gozará	gozarán	habrá gozado	habrán gozado
5 potencial simple		12 potencial compuesto	
gozaría	gozaríamos	habría gozado	habríamos gozado
gozarías	gozaríais	habrías gozado	habríais gozado
gozaría	gozarían	habría gozado	habrían gozado
6 presente de subjuntivo		13 perfecto de subjuntivo	
goce	gocemos	haya gozado	hayamos gozado
goces	gocéis	hayas gozado	hayáis gozado
goce	gocen	haya gozado	hayan gozado
7 imperfecto de subjuntivo		14 pluscuamperfecto de subjuntivo	
gozara	gozáramos	hubiera gozado	hubiéramos gozado
gozaras	gozarais	hubieras gozado	hubierais gozado
gozara	gozaran	hubiera gozado	hubieran gozado
OR		OR	
gozase	gozásemos	hubiese gozado	hubiésemos gozado
gozases	gozaseis	hubieses gozado	hubieseis gozado
gozase	gozasen	hubiese gozado	hubiesen gozado

imperativo

—	gocemos
goza; no goces	gozad; no gocéis
goce	gocen

Words and expressions related to this verb
el goce   enjoyment
gozador, gozadora, gozante   enjoyer
el gozo   joy, pleasure
saltar de gozo   to jump with joy
gozosamente   joyfully

gozarla   to have a good time
gozar de buena salud   to enjoy good health
gozoso, gozosa   joyful

The subject pronouns are found on page 93.

to shout, to scream, to shriek, to cry out   Regular **-ar** verb

The Seven Simple Tenses		The Seven Compound Tenses	
Singular	Plural	Singular	Plural
1 presente de indicativo		8 perfecto de indicativo	
grito	gritamos	he gritado	hemos gritado
gritas	gritáis	has gritado	habéis gritado
grita	gritan	ha gritado	han gritado
2 imperfecto de indicativo		9 pluscuamperfecto de indicativo	
gritaba	gritábamos	había gritado	habíamos gritado
gritabas	gritabais	habías gritado	habíais gritado
gritaba	gritaban	había gritado	habían gritado
3 pretérito		10 pretérito anterior	
grité	gritamos	hube gritado	hubimos gritado
gritaste	gritasteis	hubiste gritado	hubisteis gritado
gritó	gritaron	hubo gritado	hubieron gritado
4 futuro		11 futuro perfecto	
gritaré	gritaremos	habré gritado	habremos gritado
gritarás	gritaréis	habrás gritado	habréis gritado
gritará	gritarán	habrá gritado	habrán gritado
5 potencial simple		12 potencial compuesto	
gritaría	gritaríamos	habría gritado	habríamos gritado
gritarías	gritaríais	habrías gritado	habríais gritado
gritaría	gritarían	habría gritado	habrían gritado
6 presente de subjuntivo		13 perfecto de subjuntivo	
grite	gritemos	haya gritado	hayamos gritado
grites	gritéis	hayas gritado	hayáis gritado
grite	griten	haya gritado	hayan gritado
7 imperfecto de subjuntivo		14 pluscuamperfecto de subjuntivo	
gritara	gritáramos	hubiera gritado	hubiéramos gritado
gritaras	gritarais	hubieras gritado	hubierais gritado
gritara	gritaran	hubiera gritado	hubieran gritado
OR		OR	
gritase	gritásemos	hubiese gritado	hubiésemos gritado
gritases	gritaseis	hubieses gritado	hubieseis gritado
gritase	gritasen	hubiese gritado	hubiesen gritado

imperativo	
—	gritemos
grita; no grites	gritad; no gritéis
grite	griten

Words and expressions related to this verb
el grito   cry, scream, shout
a gritos   at the top of one's voice, loudly
la grita, la gritería   outcry, shouting

un gritón, una gritona   screamer
dar grita a   to hoot at
gritar a un actor   to boo an actor

Can't remember the Spanish verb you need?
Check the back pages of this book for the English-Spanish verb index!

Regular **-ir** verb endings in all tenses
except Tenses 3 and 7; Note present participle

to grumble, to grunt,
to growl, to creak

The Seven Simple Tenses		The Seven Compound Tenses	
Singular	Plural	Singular	Plural
1 presente de indicativo		8 perfecto de indicativo	
gruño	**gruñimos**	**he gruñido**	**hemos gruñido**
gruñes	**gruñís**	**has gruñido**	**habéis gruñido**
gruñe	**gruñen**	**ha gruñido**	**han gruñido**
2 imperfecto de indicativo		9 pluscuamperfecto de indicativo	
gruñía	**gruñíamos**	**había gruñido**	**habíamos gruñido**
gruñías	**gruñíais**	**habías gruñido**	**habíais gruñido**
gruñía	**gruñían**	**había gruñido**	**habían gruñido**
3 pretérito		10 pretérito anterior	
gruñí	**gruñimos**	**hube gruñido**	**hubimos gruñido**
gruñiste	**gruñisteis**	**hubiste gruñido**	**hubisteis gruñido**
gruñó	**gruñeron**	**hubo gruñido**	**hubieron gruñido**
4 futuro		11 futuro perfecto	
gruñiré	**gruñiremos**	**habré gruñido**	**habremos gruñido**
gruñirás	**gruñiréis**	**habrás gruñido**	**habréis gruñido**
gruñirá	**gruñirán**	**habrá gruñido**	**habrán gruñido**
5 potencial simple		12 potencial compuesto	
gruñiría	**gruñiríamos**	**habría gruñido**	**habríamos gruñido**
gruñirías	**gruñiríais**	**habrías gruñido**	**habríais gruñido**
gruñiría	**gruñirían**	**habría gruñido**	**habrían gruñido**
6 presente de subjuntivo		13 perfecto de subjuntivo	
gruña	**gruñamos**	**haya gruñido**	**hayamos gruñido**
gruñas	**gruñáis**	**hayas gruñido**	**hayáis gruñido**
gruña	**gruñan**	**haya gruñido**	**hayan gruñido**
7 imperfecto de subjuntivo		14 pluscuamperfecto de subjuntivo	
gruñera	**gruñéramos**	**hubiera gruñido**	**hubiéramos gruñido**
gruñeras	**gruñerais**	**hubieras gruñido**	**hubierais gruñido**
gruñera	**gruñeran**	**hubiera gruñido**	**hubieran gruñido**
OR		OR	
gruñese	**gruñésemos**	**hubiese gruñido**	**hubiésemos gruñido**
gruñeses	**gruñeseis**	**hubieses gruñido**	**hubieseis gruñido**
gruñese	**gruñesen**	**hubiese gruñido**	**hubiesen gruñido**

imperativo	
—	**gruñamos**
gruñe; no gruñas	**gruñid; no gruñáis**
gruña	**gruñan**

Words related to this verb
gruñón, gruñona cranky, grumpy, grouchy
el gruñido, el gruñimiento grunting, grunt, growling, growl
gruñidor, gruñidora growler, grumbler

Use the guide to Spanish pronunciation on pages 665–667.

The subject pronouns are found on page 93.

to lead, to guide   Regular **-ar** verb endings with spelling change: **i** becomes **í** on stressed syllable (see Tenses 1, 6, Imperative)

The Seven Simple Tenses	The Seven Compound Tenses

Singular	Plural	Singular	Plural
1 presente de indicativo		**8 perfecto de indicativo**	
guío	guiamos	he guiado	hemos guiado
guías	guiáis	has guiado	habéis guiado
guía	guían	ha guiado	han guiado
2 imperfecto de indicativo		**9 pluscuamperfecto de indicativo**	
guiaba	guiábamos	había guiado	habíamos guiado
guiabas	guiabais	habías guiado	habíais guiado
guiaba	guiaban	había guiado	habían guiado
3 pretérito		**10 pretérito anterior**	
guié	guiamos	hube guiado	hubimos guiado
guiaste	guiasteis	hubiste guiado	hubisteis guiado
guió	guiaron	hubo guiado	hubieron guiado
4 futuro		**11 futuro perfecto**	
guiaré	guiaremos	habré guiado	habremos guiado
guiarás	guiaréis	habrás guiado	habréis guiado
guiará	guiarán	habrá guiado	habrán guiado
5 potencial simple		**12 potencial compuesto**	
guiaría	guiaríamos	habría guiado	habríamos guiado
guiarías	guiaríais	habrías guiado	habríais guiado
guiaría	guiarían	habría guiado	habrían guiado
6 presente de subjuntivo		**13 perfecto de subjuntivo**	
guíe	guiemos	haya guiado	hayamos guiado
guíes	guiéis	hayas guiado	hayáis guiado
guíe	guíen	haya guiado	hayan guiado
7 imperfecto de subjuntivo		**14 pluscuamperfecto de subjuntivo**	
guiara	guiáramos	hubiera guiado	hubiéramos guiado
guiaras	guiarais	hubieras guiado	hubierais guiado
guiara	guiaran	hubiera guiado	hubieran guiado
OR		OR	
guiase	guiásemos	hubiese guiado	hubiésemos guiado
guiases	guiaseis	hubieses guiado	hubieseis guiado
guiase	guiasen	hubiese guiado	hubiesen guiado

imperativo

—	guiemos
guía; no guíes	guiad; no guiéis
guíe	guíen

Words and expressions related to this verb
el guía guide, leader
la guía guidebook
guiarse por to be guided by, to be governed by
guiar a alguien en los estudios to guide
   (direct) someone in studies

la guía de teléfonos telephone directory
la guía de bicicleta handlebar of a bicycle
la guía turística tourist guidebook

Irregular verb

to have (as an auxiliary, helping verb to form the compound tenses)

The Seven Simple Tenses		The Seven Compound Tenses	
Singular	Plural	Singular	Plural
1 presente de indicativo		8 perfecto de indicativo	
he	hemos	he habido	hemos habido
has	habéis	has habido	habéis habido
ha	han	ha habido	han habido
2 imperfecto de indicativo		9 pluscuamperfecto de indicativo	
había	habíamos	había habido	habíamos habido
habías	habíais	habías habido	habíais habido
había	habían	había habido	habían habido
3 pretérito		10 pretérito anterior	
hube	hubimos	hube habido	hubimos habido
hubiste	hubisteis	hubiste habido	hubisteis habido
hubo	hubieron	hubo habido	hubieron habido
4 futuro		11 futuro perfecto	
habré	habremos	habré habido	habremos habido
habrás	habréis	habrás habido	habréis habido
habrá	habrán	habrá habido	habrán habido
5 potencial simple		12 potencial compuesto	
habría	habríamos	habría habido	habríamos habido
habrías	habríais	habrías habido	habríais habido
habría	habrían	habría habido	habrían habido
6 presente de subjuntivo		13 perfecto de subjuntivo	
haya	hayamos	haya habido	hayamos habido
hayas	hayáis	hayas habido	hayáis habido
haya	hayan	haya habido	hayan habido
7 imperfecto de subjuntivo		14 pluscuamperfecto de subjuntivo	
hubiera	hubiéramos	hubiera habido	hubiéramos habido
hubieras	hubierais	hubieras habido	hubierais habido
hubiera	hubieran	hubiera habido	hubieran habido
OR		OR	
hubiese	hubiésemos	hubiese habido	hubiésemos habido
hubieses	hubieseis	hubieses habido	hubieseis habido
hubiese	hubiesen	hubiese habido	hubiesen habido

H

imperativo	
—	hayamos
hé; no hayas	habed; no hayáis
haya	hayan

AN ESSENTIAL 55 VERB

The subject pronouns are found on page 93.

Haber is an essential verb for beginning students of Spanish. You need to be able to conjugate **haber** in order to form the compound tenses. In other words, if you can conjugate **haber** in the simple tenses, you can form any other verb in the compound tenses! The verb **haber** is used as an auxiliary (helping) verb as follows:

Compound tenses	Example (in the 1st person sing.)
Present Perfect (or Perfect) Indicative	**he hablado** (I have spoken)
Pluperfect (or Past Perfect) Indicative	**había hablado** (I had spoken)
Preterit Perfect (or Past Anterior)	**hube hablado** (I had spoken)
Future Perfect (or Future Anterior)	**habré hablado** (I will have spoken)
Conditional Perfect	**habría hablado** (I would have spoken)
Present Perfect (or Past) Subjunctive	**haya hablado** (I may have spoken)
Pluperfect (or Past Perfect) Subjunctive	**hubiera hablado** *or* **hubiese hablado** (I might have spoken)

For an explanation of the formation of these tenses, see pages 31, 32, and page 92.

The verb **haber** is also used to form the perfect (or past) infinitive: **haber hablado** (to have spoken). As you can see, this is formed by using the infinitive form of **haber** + the past participle of the main verb.

The verb **haber** is also used to form the perfect participle: **habiendo hablado** (having spoken). This is formed by using the present participle of **haber** + the past participle of the main verb.

The verb **haber** + **de** + **inf.** is equivalent to the English use of "to be supposed to..." or "to be to...": **María ha de traer un pastel, yo he de traer el helado, y mis amigos han de traer sus discos compactos**/Mary is supposed to bring a cake, I am supposed to bring the ice cream, and my friends are supposed to bring their CDs.

Note on hay and hay que + inf.
The word **hay** is not a verb. You might look at it as an impersonal irregular form of **haber.** Actually, the word is composed of **ha** + the archaic **y**, meaning *there*. It is generally seen as an adverbial expression because it points out that something or someone "is there." Its English equivalent is *There is...* or *There are...* For example: **Hay muchos libros en la mesa**/There are many books on the table; **Hay veinte alumnos en esta clase**/There are twenty students in this class.

Hay que + inf. is an impersonal expression that denotes an obligation and it is commonly translated into English as: *One must...* or *It is necessary to...* Examples: **Hay que estudiar para aprender**/It is necessary to study in order to learn; **Hay que comer para vivir**/One must eat in order to live.

Sentences using haber and related words

No hay rosa sin espina.
Every rose has its thorn. (There is no rose without a thorn.)

Donde hay humo, hay fuego.
Where there's smoke, there's fire.

Expressions related to this verb

ha habido... there has been..., there have been...
había... there was..., there were...
habrá... there will be...
habría... there would be...
hubo... there was..., there were...

Regular **-ar** verb to inhabit, to dwell, to live, to reside

The Seven Simple Tenses		The Seven Compound Tenses	
Singular	Plural	Singular	Plural
1 presente de indicativo		8 perfecto de indicativo	
habito	**habitamos**	**he habitado**	**hemos habitado**
habitas	**habitáis**	**has habitado**	**habéis habitado**
habita	**habitan**	**ha habitado**	**han habitado**
2 imperfecto de indicativo		9 pluscuamperfecto de indicativo	
habitaba	**habitábamos**	**había habitado**	**habíamos habitado**
habitabas	**habitabais**	**habías habitado**	**habíais habitado**
habitaba	**habitaban**	**había habitado**	**habían habitado**
3 pretérito		10 pretérito anterior	
habité	**habitamos**	**hube habitado**	**hubimos habitado**
habitaste	**habitasteis**	**hubiste habitado**	**hubisteis habitado**
habitó	**habitaron**	**hubo habitado**	**hubieron habitado**
4 futuro		11 futuro perfecto	
habitaré	**habitaremos**	**habré habitado**	**habremos habitado**
habitarás	**habitaréis**	**habrás habitado**	**habréis habitado**
habitará	**habitarán**	**habrá habitado**	**habrán habitado**
5 potencial simple		12 potencial compuesto	
habitaría	**habitaríamos**	**habría habitado**	**habríamos habitado**
habitarías	**habitaríais**	**habrías habitado**	**habríais habitado**
habitaría	**habitarían**	**habría habitado**	**habrían habitado**
6 presente de subjuntivo		13 perfecto de subjuntivo	
habite	**habitemos**	**haya habitado**	**hayamos habitado**
habites	**habitéis**	**hayas habitado**	**hayáis habitado**
habite	**habiten**	**haya habitado**	**hayan habitado**
7 imperfecto de subjuntivo		14 pluscuamperfecto de subjuntivo	
habitara	**habitáramos**	**hubiera habitado**	**hubiéramos habitado**
habitaras	**habitarais**	**hubieras habitado**	**hubierais habitado**
habitara	**habitaran**	**hubiera habitado**	**hubieran habitado**
OR		OR	
habitase	**habitásemos**	**hubiese habitado**	**hubiésemos habitado**
habitases	**habitaseis**	**hubieses habitado**	**hubieseis habitado**
habitase	**habitasen**	**hubiese habitado**	**hubiesen habitado**

imperativo	
—	**habitemos**
habita; no habites	**habitad; no habitéis**
habite	**habiten**

Words related to this verb
la habitación habitation, residence, dwelling, abode
habitador, habitadora inhabitant
la habitabilidad habitability
el, la habitante inhabitant

la habitación individual single room
la habitación doble double room
el piso con tres habitaciones apartment with three rooms

Get your feet wet with verbs used in weather expressions on page 668.

The subject pronouns are found on page 93.

The Seven Simple Tenses		The Seven Compound Tenses	
Singular	Plural	Singular	Plural
1 presente de indicativo		8 perfecto de indicativo	
hablo	**hablamos**	**he hablado**	**hemos hablado**
hablas	**habláis**	**has hablado**	**habéis hablado**
habla	**hablan**	**ha hablado**	**han hablado**
2 imperfecto de indicativo		9 pluscuamperfecto de indicativo	
hablaba	**hablábamos**	**había hablado**	**habíamos hablado**
hablabas	**hablabais**	**habías hablado**	**habíais hablado**
hablaba	**hablaban**	**había hablado**	**habían hablado**
3 pretérito		10 pretérito anterior	
hablé	**hablamos**	**hube hablado**	**hubimos hablado**
hablaste	**hablasteis**	**hubiste hablado**	**hubisteis hablado**
habló	**hablaron**	**hubo hablado**	**hubieron hablado**
4 futuro		11 futuro perfecto	
hablaré	**hablaremos**	**habré hablado**	**habremos hablado**
hablarás	**hablaréis**	**habrás hablado**	**habréis hablado**
hablará	**hablarán**	**habrá hablado**	**habrán hablado**
5 potencial simple		12 potencial compuesto	
hablaría	**hablaríamos**	**habría hablado**	**habríamos hablado**
hablarías	**hablaríais**	**habrías hablado**	**habríais hablado**
hablaría	**hablarían**	**habría hablado**	**habrían hablado**
6 presente de subjuntivo		13 perfecto de subjuntivo	
hable	**hablemos**	**haya hablado**	**hayamos hablado**
hables	**habléis**	**hayas hablado**	**hayáis hablado**
hable	**hablen**	**haya hablado**	**hayan hablado**
7 imperfecto de subjuntivo		14 pluscuamperfecto de subjuntivo	
hablara	**habláramos**	**hubiera hablado**	**hubiéramos hablado**
hablaras	**hablarais**	**hubieras hablado**	**hubierais hablado**
hablara	**hablaran**	**hubiera hablado**	**hubieran hablado**
OR		OR	
hablase	**hablásemos**	**hubiese hablado**	**hubiésemos hablado**
hablases	**hablaseis**	**hubieses hablado**	**hubieseis hablado**
hablase	**hablasen**	**hubiese hablado**	**hubiesen hablado**

	imperativo	
—		**hablemos**
habla; no hables		**hablad; no habléis**
hable		**hablen**

AN ESSENTIAL 55 VERB

Hablar is an essential regular –ar verb for beginning students of Spanish. It is used in many everyday situations and idiomatic expressions.

Sentences using hablar and related words

Aquí se habla español.
Spanish is spoken here.

No me gusta hablar a gritos.
I don't like to shout.

Antes de hablar es bueno pensar.
(It's good to) think before you speak.

El dinero habla.
Money talks.

Hable más despacio, por favor.
Speak more slowly, please.

Words and expressions related to this verb

la habladuría **gossip, idle rumor**

hispanohablante **Spanish-speaking**

de habla española **Spanish-speaking**

de habla inglesa **English-speaking**

hablador, habladora **talkative**

hablar a gritos **to shout**

hablar entre dientes **to mumble**

hablar al oído **to whisper in someone's ear**

H

Proverb

Para saber hablar, hay que saber escuchar.
In order to know how to talk, one must know how to listen.

Can't remember the Spanish verb you need?
Check the back pages of this book for the English-Spanish verb index!

The subject pronouns are found on page 93.

The Seven Simple Tenses		The Seven Compound Tenses	
Singular	Plural	Singular	Plural
1 presente de indicativo		8 perfecto de indicativo	
hago	hacemos	he hecho	hemos hecho
haces	hacéis	has hecho	habéis hecho
hace	hacen	ha hecho	han hecho
2 imperfecto de indicativo		9 pluscuamperfecto de indicativo	
hacía	hacíamos	había hecho	habíamos hecho
hacías	hacíais	habías hecho	habíais hecho
hacía	hacían	había hecho	habían hecho
3 pretérito		10 pretérito anterior	
hice	hicimos	hube hecho	hubimos hecho
hiciste	hicisteis	hubiste hecho	hubisteis hecho
hizo	hicieron	hubo hecho	hubieron hecho
4 futuro		11 futuro perfecto	
haré	haremos	habré hecho	habremos hecho
harás	haréis	habrás hecho	habréis hecho
hará	harán	habrá hecho	habrán hecho
5 potencial simple		12 potencial compuesto	
haría	haríamos	habría hecho	habríamos hecho
harías	haríais	habrías hecho	habríais hecho
haría	harían	habría hecho	habrían hecho
6 presente de subjuntivo		13 perfecto de subjuntivo	
haga	hagamos	haya hecho	hayamos hecho
hagas	hagáis	hayas hecho	hayáis hecho
haga	hagan	haya hecho	hayan hecho
7 imperfecto de subjuntivo		14 pluscuamperfecto de subjuntivo	
hiciera	hiciéramos	hubiera hecho	hubiéramos hecho
hicieras	hicierais	hubieras hecho	hubierais hecho
hiciera	hicieran	hubiera hecho	hubieran hecho
OR		OR	
hiciese	hiciésemos	hubiese hecho	hubiésemos hecho
hicieses	hicieseis	hubieses hecho	hubieseis hecho
hiciese	hiciesen	hubiese hecho	hubiesen hecho

imperativo	
—	hagamos
haz; no hagas	haced; no hagáis
haga	hagan

Hacer is an essential irregular verb for beginning students of Spanish. It is used in many everyday situations and idiomatic expressions. **Hacer** is especially important for weather expressions.

¿Cuánto tiempo hace que + present tense...?
(a) Use this formula when you want to ask *How long + the present perfect tense in English:*

H

¿Cuánto tiempo hace que Ud. estudia español?
How long have you been studying Spanish?

(b) When this formula is used, you generally expect the person to tell you how long a time it has been, e.g., one year, two months, a few minutes.

(c) This is used when the action began at some time in the past and continues up to the present moment. That is why you must use the present tense of the verb—the action of studying, waiting, etc., is still going on at the present.

¿Hace + length of time + que + present tense
(a) This formula is the usual answer to the question ¿Cuánto tiempo hace que + present tense...?

(b) Since the question is asked in terms of *how long,* the usual answer is in terms of time: a year, two years, a few days, months, minutes, etc.:

Hace tres años que estudio español.
I have been studying Spanish for three years.

(c) The same formula is used if you want to ask *how many weeks, how many months, how many minutes, etc.*:

¿Cuántos años hace que Ud. estudia español?
How many years have you been studying Spanish?

¿Desde cuándo + present tense...?
¿Desde cuándo estudia Ud. español?
How long have you been studying Spanish?

Present tense + desde hace + length of time
Estudio español desde hace tres años.
I have been studying Spanish for three years.

Proverbs
─────────────

De decir a hacer hay mucho
   que ver.
**There is a great difference between
   saying and doing.**

El ejercicio hace al maestro.
Practice makes perfect.

No dejes para mañana lo que
   puedes hacer hoy.
**Don't put off until tomorrow what
   you can do today.**

Don't forget to study the section on defective and impersonal verbs. It's right after this main list.

The subject pronouns are found on page 93.

¿Cuánto tiempo hacía que + imperfect tense?
(a) If the action of the verb began in the past and ended in the past, use the imperfect tense.

(b) This formula is equivalent to the English *How long + past perfect tense:*

¿Cuánto tiempo hacía que Ud. hablaba cuando entré en la sala de clase?
How long had you been talking when I entered the classroom?

(c) Note that the action of talking in this example began in the past and ended in the past when I entered the classroom.

Hacía + length of time + que + imperfect tense
The imperfect tense of the verb is used here because the action began in the past and ended in the past; it is not going on at the present moment.

Hacía una hora que yo hablaba cuando Ud. entró en la sala de clase.
I had been talking for one hour when you entered the classroom.

¿Desde cuándo + imperfect tense...?

¿Desde cuándo hablaba Ud. cuando yo entré en la sala de clase?
How long had you been talking when I entered the classroom?

Imperfect tense + desde hacía + length of time

(Yo) hablaba desde hacía una hora cuando
Ud. entró en la sala de clase.
I had been talking for one hour when you entered the classroom.

Weather expressions related to this verb

hace buen tiempo **the weather is good**
hace calor **it's warm (hot)**
hace fresco hoy **it's cool today**
hace frío **it's cold**
hace mal tiempo **the weather is bad**
hace sol **it's sunny**
hace viento **it's windy**

Sentences using hacer and related words

Hace un mes que partió el señor Molina.
Mr. Molina left one month ago.

¿Puede ayudarme a hacer una llamada?
Can you help me make a telephone call?

El señor González siempre hace de jefe.
Mr. González always acts as boss.

A Juan le hace falta un lápiz.
John needs a pencil.

Elena se hizo dentista.
Helen became a dentist.

¡Vámonos! Se hace tarde.
Let's leave! It's getting late.

Words and expressions related to this verb

hace poco **a little while ago**
hace un año **a year ago**
hace una hora **an hour ago**
hacer cara a **to face**
hacer caso de **to pay attention to**
hacer clic **to click (on an Internet link)**
hacer daño a algo **to harm something**
hacer daño a alguien **to harm someone**
hacer de **to act as**
hacer el baúl **to pack one's trunk**
hacer el favor de + inf. **please**
(Haga Ud. el favor de entrar/
Please come in.)
hacer el papel de **to play the role of**
hacer la maleta **to pack one's suitcase**
hacer pedazos **to smash, to break, to tear into pieces**
hacer un viaje **to take a trip**
hacer una broma **to play a joke**
hacer una pregunta **to ask a question**
hacer una visita **to pay a visit**
hacerle falta **to need**
hacerse **to become**
hacerse daño **to hurt oneself, to harm oneself**
hacerse tarde **to be getting late**

Regular **-ar** verb   to find, to discover, to locate

The Seven Simple Tenses		The Seven Compound Tenses	
Singular	Plural	Singular	Plural
1 presente de indicativo		8 perfecto de indicativo	
hallo	**hallamos**	**he hallado**	**hemos hallado**
hallas	**halláis**	**has hallado**	**habéis hallado**
halla	**hallan**	**ha hallado**	**han hallado**
2 imperfecto de indicativo		9 pluscuamperfecto de indicativo	
hallaba	**hallábamos**	**había hallado**	**habíamos hallado**
hallabas	**hallabais**	**habías hallado**	**habíais hallado**
hallaba	**hallaban**	**había hallado**	**habían hallado**
3 pretérito		10 pretérito anterior	
hallé	**hallamos**	**hube hallado**	**hubimos hallado**
hallaste	**hallasteis**	**hubiste hallado**	**hubisteis hallado**
halló	**hallaron**	**hubo hallado**	**hubieron hallado**
4 futuro		11 futuro perfecto	
hallaré	**hallaremos**	**habré hallado**	**habremos hallado**
hallarás	**hallaréis**	**habrás hallado**	**habréis hallado**
hallará	**hallarán**	**habrá hallado**	**habrán hallado**
5 potencial simple		12 potencial compuesto	
hallaría	**hallaríamos**	**habría hallado**	**habríamos hallado**
hallarías	**hallaríais**	**habrías hallado**	**habríais hallado**
hallaría	**hallarían**	**habría hallado**	**habrían hallado**
6 presente de subjuntivo		13 perfecto de subjuntivo	
halle	**hallemos**	**haya hallado**	**hayamos hallado**
halles	**halléis**	**hayas hallado**	**hayáis hallado**
halle	**hallen**	**haya hallado**	**hayan hallado**
7 imperfecto de subjuntivo		14 pluscuamperfecto de subjuntivo	
hallara	**halláramos**	**hubiera hallado**	**hubiéramos hallado**
hallaras	**hallarais**	**hubieras hallado**	**hubierais hallado**
hallara	**hallaran**	**hubiera hallado**	**hubieran hallado**
OR		OR	
hallase	**hallásemos**	**hubiese hallado**	**hubiésemos hallado**
hallases	**hallaseis**	**hubieses hallado**	**hubieseis hallado**
hallase	**hallasen**	**hubiese hallado**	**hubiesen hallado**

imperativo

—	**hallemos**
halla; no halles	**hallad; no halléis**
halle	**hallen**

Words and expressions related to this verb
hallar bien con to be well pleased with
un hallazgo a find, something found
hallador, halladora discoverer, finder

la hallada discovery, find
bien hallado at ease
mal hallado uneasy, ill at ease

Can't find the verb you're looking for?
Check the back pages of this book for a list of over 2,100 additional verbs!

The subject pronouns are found on page 93.
                                                                383

heredar (262)

Gerundio **heredando** Part. pas. **heredado**

to inherit

Regular **-ar** verb

The Seven Simple Tenses		The Seven Compound Tenses	
Singular	Plural	Singular	Plural
1 presente de indicativo		8 perfecto de indicativo	
heredo	heredamos	he heredado	hemos heredado
heredas	heredáis	has heredado	habéis heredado
hereda	heredan	ha heredado	han heredado
2 imperfecto de indicativo		9 pluscuamperfecto de indicativo	
heredaba	heredábamos	había heredado	habíamos heredado
heredabas	heredabais	habías heredado	habíais heredado
heredaba	heredaban	había heredado	habían heredado
3 pretérito		10 pretérito anterior	
heredé	heredamos	hube heredado	hubimos heredado
heredaste	heredasteis	hubiste heredado	hubisteis heredado
heredó	heredaron	hubo heredado	hubieron heredado
4 futuro		11 futuro perfecto	
heredaré	heredaremos	habré heredado	habremos heredado
heredarás	heredaréis	habrás heredado	habréis heredado
heredará	heredarán	habrá heredado	habrán heredado
5 potencial simple		12 potencial compuesto	
heredaría	heredaríamos	habría heredado	habríamos heredado
heredarías	heredaríais	habrías heredado	habríais heredado
heredaría	heredarían	habría heredado	habrían heredado
6 presente de subjuntivo		13 perfecto de subjuntivo	
herede	heredemos	haya heredado	hayamos heredado
heredes	heredéis	hayas heredado	hayáis heredado
herede	hereden	haya heredado	hayan heredado
7 imperfecto de subjuntivo		14 pluscuamperfecto de subjuntivo	
heredara	heredáramos	hubiera heredado	hubiéramos heredado
heredaras	heredarais	hubieras heredado	hubierais heredado
heredara	heredaran	hubiera heredado	hubieran heredado
OR		OR	
heredase	heredásemos	hubiese heredado	hubiésemos heredado
heredases	heredaseis	hubieses heredado	hubieseis heredado
heredase	heredasen	hubiese heredado	hubiesen heredado

imperativo	
—	heredemos
hereda; no heredes	heredad; no heredéis
herede	hereden

Words and expressions related to this verb

el heredero heir; **la heredera** heiress
heredable inheritable
hereditario, hereditaria hereditary
la herencia inheritance

la enfermedad hereditaria hereditary disease
heredar una fortuna de sus padres to inherit
a fortune from one's parents

Regular **-ir** verb endings with stem change: to harm, to hurt, to wound
Tenses 1, 3, 6, 7, Imperative, Gerundio

The Seven Simple Tenses		The Seven Compound Tenses	
Singular	Plural	Singular	Plural
1 presente de indicativo		8 perfecto de indicativo	
hiero	**herimos**	**he herido**	**hemos herido**
hieres	**herís**	**has herido**	**habéis herido**
hiere	**hieren**	**ha herido**	**han herido**
2 imperfecto de indicativo		9 pluscuamperfecto de indicativo	
hería	**heríamos**	**había herido**	**habíamos herido**
herías	**heríais**	**habías herido**	**habíais herido**
hería	**herían**	**había herido**	**habían herido**
3 pretérito		10 pretérito anterior	
herí	**herimos**	**hube herido**	**hubimos herido**
heriste	**heristeis**	**hubiste herido**	**hubisteis herido**
hirió	**hirieron**	**hubo herido**	**hubieron herido**
4 futuro		11 futuro perfecto	
heriré	**heriremos**	**habré herido**	**habremos herido**
herirás	**heriréis**	**habrás herido**	**habréis herido**
herirá	**herirán**	**habrá herido**	**habrán herido**
5 potencial simple		12 potencial compuesto	
heriría	**heriríamos**	**habría herido**	**habríamos herido**
herirías	**heriríais**	**habrías herido**	**habríais herido**
heriría	**herirían**	**habría herido**	**habrían herido**
6 presente de subjuntivo		13 perfecto de subjuntivo	
hiera	**hiramos**	**haya herido**	**hayamos herido**
hieras	**hiráis**	**hayas herido**	**hayáis herido**
hiera	**hieran**	**haya herido**	**hayan herido**
7 imperfecto de subjuntivo		14 pluscuamperfecto de subjuntivo	
hiriera	**hiriéramos**	**hubiera herido**	**hubiéramos herido**
hirieras	**hirierais**	**hubieras herido**	**hubierais herido**
hiriera	**hirieran**	**hubiera herido**	**hubieran herido**
OR		OR	
hiriese	**hiriésemos**	**hubiese herido**	**hubiésemos herido**
hirieses	**hirieseis**	**hubieses herido**	**hubieseis herido**
hiriese	**hiriesen**	**hubiese herido**	**hubiesen herido**

	imperativo	
—		**hiramos**
hiere; no hieras		**herid; no hiráis**
hiera		**hieran**

Words and expressions related to this verb

la herida   wound
mal herido, mal herida   seriously wounded

una herida abierta   open wound
a grito herido   in loud cries

Can't recognize an irregular verb form? Check out pages 678–681.

The subject pronouns are found on page 93.

to escape, to flee, to run away, to slip away

Regular **-ir** verb endings with spelling change: add **y** before **a**, **e**, or **o**

The Seven Simple Tenses		The Seven Compound Tenses	
Singular	Plural	Singular	Plural
1 presente de indicativo		8 perfecto de indicativo	
huyo	huimos	he huido	hemos huido
huyes	huís	has huido	habéis huido
huye	huyen	ha huido	han huido
2 imperfecto de indicativo		9 pluscuamperfecto de indicativo	
huía	huíamos	había huido	habíamos huido
huías	huíais	habías huido	habíais huido
huía	huían	había huido	habían huido
3 pretérito		10 pretérito anterior	
huí	huimos	hube huido	hubimos huido
huiste	huisteis	hubiste huido	hubisteis huido
huyó	huyeron	hubo huido	hubieron huido
4 futuro		11 futuro perfecto	
huiré	huiremos	habré huido	habremos huido
huirás	huiréis	habrás huido	habréis huido
huirá	huirán	habrá huido	habrán huido
5 potencial simple		12 potencial compuesto	
huiría	huiríamos	habría huido	habríamos huido
huirías	huiríais	habrías huido	habríais huido
huiría	huirían	habría huido	habrían huido
6 presente de subjuntivo		13 perfecto de subjuntivo	
huya	huyamos	haya huido	hayamos huido
huyas	huyáis	hayas huido	hayáis huido
huya	huyan	haya huido	hayan huido
7 imperfecto de subjuntivo		14 pluscuamperfecto de subjuntivo	
huyera	huyéramos	hubiera huido	hubiéramos huido
huyeras	huyerais	hubieras huido	hubierais huido
huyera	huyeran	hubiera huido	hubieran huido
OR		OR	
huyese	huyésemos	hubiese huido	hubiésemos huido
huyeses	huyeseis	hubieses huido	hubieseis huido
huyese	huyesen	hubiese huido	hubiesen huido

imperativo

—	huyamos
huye; no huyas	huid; no huyáis
huya	huyan

Words and expressions related to this verb

huir de to keep away from
la huida escape, flight
huidizo, huidiza fugitive, evasive
huir del vicio to flee from vice

huidor, huidora fleeing, fugitive
rehuir to avoid, refuse, shun (**yo rehúyo**)
¡Huye! Run! Flee!
¡Cómo huyen las horas! How time flies!
  (**las horas**/the hours)

The Seven Simple Tenses		The Seven Compound Tenses	
Singular	Plural	Singular	Plural
1 presente de indicativo		**8 perfecto de indicativo**	
ignoro	ignoramos	he ignorado	hemos ignorado
ignoras	ignoráis	has ignorado	habéis ignorado
ignora	ignoran	ha ignorado	han ignorado
2 imperfecto de indicativo		**9 pluscuamperfecto de indicativo**	
ignoraba	ignorábamos	había ignorado	habíamos ignorado
ignorabas	ignorabais	habías ignorado	habíais ignorado
ignoraba	ignoraban	había ignorado	habían ignorado
3 pretérito		**10 pretérito anterior**	
ignoré	ignoramos	hube ignorado	hubimos ignorado
ignoraste	ignorasteis	hubiste ignorado	hubisteis ignorado
ignoró	ignoraron	hubo ignorado	hubieron ignorado
4 futuro		**11 futuro perfecto**	
ignoraré	ignoraremos	habré ignorado	habremos ignorado
ignorarás	ignoraréis	habrás ignorado	habréis ignorado
ignorará	ignorarán	habrá ignorado	habrán ignorado
5 potencial simple		**12 potencial compuesto**	
ignoararía	ignoraríamos	habría ignorado	habríamos ignorado
ignoararías	ignoraríais	habrías ignorado	habríais ignorado
ignoraría	ignorarían	habría ignorado	habrían ignorado
6 presente de subjuntivo		**13 perfecto de subjuntivo**	
ignore	ignoremos	haya ignorado	hayamos ignorado
ignores	ignoréis	hayas ignorado	hayáis ignorado
ignore	ignoren	haya ignorado	hayan ignorado
7 imperfecto de subjuntivo		**14 pluscuamperfecto de subjuntivo**	
ignorara	ignoráramos	hubiera ignorado	hubiéramos ignorado
ignoraras	ignorarais	hubieras ignorado	hubierais ignorado
ignorara	ignoraran	hubiera ignorado	hubieran ignorado
OR		OR	
ignorase	ignorásemos	hubiese ignorado	hubiésemos ignorado
ignorases	ignoraseis	hubieses ignorado	hubieseis ignorado
ignorase	ignorasen	hubiese ignorado	hubiesen ignorado

imperativo	
—	ignoremos
ignora; no ignores	ignorad; no ignoréis
ignore	ignoren

Words and expressions related to this verb
la ignorancia ignorance
ignorante ignorant
ignoto, ignota unknown
no ignorar que . . . to be well aware that . . .
ignorantemente ignorantly
ignominioso, ignominiosa disgraceful, ignominious
la ignominia disgrace, infamy, ignominy
un ignorantón, una ignorantona an ignoramus

The subject pronouns are found on page 93.

387

to hinder, to impede, to prevent | Regular **-ir** verb endings with stem change: Tenses 1, 3, 6, 7, Imperative, Gerundio

The Seven Simple Tenses | The Seven Compound Tenses

Singular	Plural	Singular	Plural
1 presente de indicativo		8 perfecto de indicativo	
impido	impedimos	he impedido	hemos impedido
impides	impedís	has impedido	habéis impedido
impide	impiden	ha impedido	han impedido
2 imperfecto de indicativo		9 pluscuamperfecto de indicativo	
impedía	impedíamos	había impedido	habíamos impedido
impedías	impedíais	habías impedido	habíais impedido
impedía	impedían	había impedido	habían impedido
3 pretérito		10 pretérito anterior	
impedí	impedimos	hube impedido	hubimos impedido
impediste	impedisteis	hubiste impedido	hubisteis impedido
impidió	impidieron	hubo impedido	hubieron impedido
4 futuro		11 futuro perfecto	
impediré	impediremos	habré impedido	habremos impedido
impedirás	impediréis	habrás impedido	habréis impedido
impedirá	impedirán	habrá impedido	habrán impedido
5 potencial simple		12 potencial compuesto	
impediría	impediríamos	habría impedido	habríamos impedido
impedirías	impediríais	habrías impedido	habríais impedido
impediría	impedirían	habría impedido	habrían impedido
6 presente de subjuntivo		13 perfecto de subjuntivo	
impida	impidamos	haya impedido	hayamos impedido
impidas	impidáis	hayas impedido	hayáis impedido
impida	impidan	haya impedido	hayan impedido
7 imperfecto de subjuntivo		14 pluscuamperfecto de subjuntivo	
impidiera	impidiéramos	hubiera impedido	hubiéramos impedido
impidieras	impidierais	hubieras impedido	hubierais impedido
impidiera	impidieran	hubiera impedido	hubieran impedido
OR		OR	
impidiese	impidiésemos	hubiese impedido	hubiésemos impedido
impidieses	impidieseis	hubieses impedido	hubieseis impedido
impidiese	impidiesen	hubiese impedido	hubiesen impedido

imperativo

—	impidamos
impide; no impidas	impedid; no impidáis
impida	impidan

Words and expressions related to this verb
impediente impeding, hindering
un impedimento impediment, hindrance
impedir algo a uno to prevent somebody from doing something

impeditivo, impeditiva hindering, preventive
un impedido, una impedida disabled, handicapped person

See also **pedir.**

The Seven Simple Tenses		The Seven Compound Tenses	
Singular	Plural	Singular	Plural
1 presente de indicativo		8 perfecto de indicativo	
imprimo	**imprimimos**	**he impreso**	**hemos impreso**
imprimes	**imprimís**	**has impreso**	**habéis impreso**
imprime	**imprimen**	**ha impreso**	**han impreso**
2 imperfecto de indicativo		9 pluscuamperfecto de indicativo	
imprimía	**imprimíamos**	**había impreso**	**habíamos impreso**
imprimías	**imprimíais**	**habías impreso**	**habíais impreso**
imprimía	**imprimían**	**había impreso**	**habían impreso**
3 pretérito		10 pretérito anterior	
imprimí	**imprimimos**	**hube impreso**	**hubimos impreso**
imprimiste	**imprimisteis**	**hubiste impreso**	**hubisteis impreso**
imprimió	**imprimieron**	**hubo impreso**	**hubieron impreso**
4 futuro		11 futuro perfecto	
imprimiré	**imprimiremos**	**habré impreso**	**habremos impreso**
imprimirás	**imprimiréis**	**habrás impreso**	**habréis impreso**
imprimirá	**imprimirán**	**habrá impreso**	**habrán impreso**
5 potencial simple		12 potencial compuesto	
imprimiría	**imprimiríamos**	**habría impreso**	**habríamos impreso**
imprimirías	**imprimiríais**	**habrías impreso**	**habríais impreso**
imprimiría	**imprimirían**	**habría impreso**	**habrían impreso**
6 presente de subjuntivo		13 perfecto de subjuntivo	
imprima	**imprimamos**	**haya impreso**	**hayamos impreso**
imprimas	**imprimáis**	**hayas impreso**	**hayáis impreso**
imprima	**impriman**	**haya impreso**	**hayan impreso**
7 imperfecto de subjuntivo		14 pluscuamperfecto de subjuntivo	
imprimiera	**imprimiéramos**	**hubiera impreso**	**hubiéramos impreso**
imprimieras	**imprimierais**	**hubieras impreso**	**hubierais impreso**
imprimiera	**imprimieran**	**hubiera impreso**	**hubieran impreso**
OR		OR	
imprimiese	**imprimiésemos**	**hubiese impreso**	**hubiésemos impreso**
imprimieses	**imprimieseis**	**hubieses impreso**	**hubieseis impreso**
imprimiese	**imprimiesen**	**hubiese impreso**	**hubiesen impreso**

imperativo

—	**imprimamos**
imprime; no imprimas	**imprimid; no imprimáis**
imprima	**impriman**

Words and expressions related to this verb
imprimible printable
el imprimátur imprimatur
impreso, impresa printed, stamped

impresos printed matter
el impresor, la impresora printer, owner
of a printing shop

Don't forget to study the section on defective and impersonal verbs. It's right after this main list.

The subject pronouns are found on page 93.

incluir (268)   Gerundio **incluyendo**   Part. pas. **incluido** (**incluso**, when used as an *adj.*)
to include, to enclose

The Seven Simple Tenses

The Seven Compound Tenses

Singular	Plural	Singular	Plural
1 presente de indicativo		8 perfecto de indicativo	
incluyo	**incluimos**	**he incluido**	**hemos incluido**
incluyes	**incluís**	**has incluido**	**habéis incluido**
incluye	**incluyen**	**ha incluido**	**han incluido**
2 imperfecto de indicativo		9 pluscuamperfecto de indicativo	
incluía	**incluíamos**	**había incluido**	**habíamos incluido**
incluías	**incluíais**	**habías incluido**	**habíais incluido**
incluía	**incluían**	**había incluido**	**habían incluido**
3 pretérito		10 pretérito anterior	
incluí	**incluimos**	**hube incluido**	**hubimos incluido**
incluiste	**incluisteis**	**hubiste incluido**	**hubisteis incluido**
incluyó	**incluyeron**	**hubo incluido**	**hubieron incluido**
4 futuro		11 futuro perfecto	
incluiré	**incluiremos**	**habré incluido**	**habremos incluido**
incluirás	**incluiréis**	**habrás incluido**	**habréis incluido**
incluirá	**incluirán**	**habrá incluido**	**habrán incluido**
5 potencial simple		12 potencial compuesto	
incluiría	**incluiríamos**	**habría incluido**	**habríamos incluido**
incluirías	**incluiríais**	**habrías incluido**	**habríais incluido**
incluiría	**incluirían**	**habría incluido**	**habrían incluido**
6 presente de subjuntivo		13 perfecto de subjuntivo	
incluya	**incluyamos**	**haya incluido**	**hayamos incluido**
incluyas	**incluyáis**	**hayas incluido**	**hayáis incluido**
incluya	**incluyan**	**haya incluido**	**hayan incluido**
7 imperfecto de subjuntivo		14 pluscuamperfecto de subjuntivo	
incluyera	**incluyéramos**	**hubiera incluido**	**hubiéramos incluido**
incluyeras	**incluyerais**	**hubieras incluido**	**hubierais incluido**
incluyera	**incluyeran**	**hubiera incluido**	**hubieran incluido**
OR		OR	
incluyese	**incluyésemos**	**hubiese incluido**	**hubiésemos incluido**
incluyeses	**incluyeseis**	**hubieses incluido**	**hubieseis incluido**
incluyese	**incluyesen**	**hubiese incluido**	**hubiesen incluido**

imperativo

—	**incluyamos**
incluye; no incluyas	**incluid; no incluyáis**
incluya	**incluyan**

Words and expressions related to this verb
inclusivo, inclusiva   inclusive, including
la inclusión   inclusion
una inclusa   foundling home
el dinero incluso   the money enclosed,
   included
¿La propina está incluida?   Is the tip included?

la carta inclusa   the letter enclosed, included
inclusivamente   inclusively
sin incluir   not including
con inclusión de   including
todo incluido   everything included

Regular **-ar** verb endings with spelling change: **c** becomes **qu** before **e**

to indicate, to point out

The Seven Simple Tenses		The Seven Compound Tenses	
Singular	Plural	Singular	Plural
1 presente de indicativo		8 perfecto de indicativo	
indico	**indicamos**	**he indicado**	**hemos indicado**
indicas	**indicáis**	**has indicado**	**habéis indicado**
indica	**indican**	**ha indicado**	**han indicado**
2 imperfecto de indicativo		9 pluscuamperfecto de indicativo	
indicaba	**indicábamos**	**había indicado**	**habíamos indicado**
indicabas	**indicabais**	**habías indicado**	**habíais indicado**
indicaba	**indicaban**	**había indicado**	**habían indicado**
3 pretérito		10 pretérito anterior	
indiqué	**indicamos**	**hube indicado**	**hubimos indicado**
indicaste	**indicasteis**	**hubiste indicado**	**hubisteis indicado**
indicó	**indicaron**	**hubo indicado**	**hubieron indicado**
4 futuro		11 futuro perfecto	
indicaré	**indicaremos**	**habré indicado**	**habremos indicado**
indicarás	**indicaréis**	**habrás indicado**	**habréis indicado**
indicará	**indicarán**	**habrá indicado**	**habrán indicado**
5 potencial simple		12 potencial compuesto	
indicaría	**indicaríamos**	**habría indicado**	**habríamos indicado**
indicarías	**indicaríais**	**habrías indicado**	**habríais indicado**
indicaría	**indicarían**	**habría indicado**	**habrían indicado**
6 presente de subjuntivo		13 perfecto de subjuntivo	
indique	**indiquemos**	**haya indicado**	**hayamos indicado**
indiques	**indiquéis**	**hayas indicado**	**hayáis indicado**
indique	**indiquen**	**haya indicado**	**hayan indicado**
7 imperfecto de subjuntivo		14 pluscuamperfecto de subjuntivo	
indicara	**indicáramos**	**hubiera indicado**	**hubiéramos indicado**
indicaras	**indicarais**	**hubieras indicado**	**hubierais indicado**
indicara	**indicaran**	**hubiera indicado**	**hubieran indicado**
OR		OR	
indicase	**indicásemos**	**hubiese indicado**	**hubiésemos indicado**
indicases	**indicaseis**	**hubieses indicado**	**hubieseis indicado**
indicase	**indicasen**	**hubiese indicado**	**hubiesen indicado**

imperativo	
—	**indiquemos**
indica; no indiques	**indicad; no indiquéis**
indique	**indiquen**

Words and expressions related to this verb

indicativo, indicativa   indicative
la indicación   indication
el indicador   indicator; **el indicador de humo**   smoke detector

una falsa indicación   a wrong direction
el indicador de horarios   travel timetable (trains, *etc.*)
el indicador de velocidad   speedometer

The subject pronouns are found on page 93.

inducir (270)

Gerundio **induciendo**   Part. pas. **inducido**

to induce, to influence,
to persuade, to lead

Irregular in Tenses 3 and 7, regular **-ir** endings in all
others; spelling change: **c** becomes **zc** before **a** or **o**

The Seven Simple Tenses

The Seven Compound Tenses

Singular	Plural	Singular	Plural
1 presente de indicativo		8 perfecto de indicativo	
induzco	inducimos	he inducido	hemos inducido
induces	inducís	has inducido	habéis inducido
induce	inducen	ha inducido	han inducido
2 imperfecto de indicativo		9 pluscuamperfecto de indicativo	
inducía	inducíamos	había inducido	habíamos inducido
inducías	inducíais	habías inducido	habíais inducido
inducía	inducían	había inducido	habían inducido
3 pretérito		10 pretérito anterior	
induje	indujimos	hube inducido	hubimos inducido
indujiste	indujisteis	hubiste inducido	hubisteis inducido
indujo	indujeron	hubo inducido	hubieron inducido
4 futuro		11 futuro perfecto	
induciré	induciremos	habré inducido	habremos inducido
inducirás	induciréis	habrás inducido	habréis inducido
inducirá	inducirán	habrá inducido	habrán inducido
5 potencial simple		12 potencial compuesto	
induciría	induciríamos	habría inducido	habríamos inducido
inducirías	induciríais	habrías inducido	habríais inducido
induciría	inducirían	habría inducido	habrían inducido
6 presente de subjuntivo		13 perfecto de subjuntivo	
induzca	induzcamos	haya inducido	hayamos inducido
induzcas	induzcáis	hayas inducido	hayáis inducido
induzca	induzcan	haya inducido	hayan inducido
7 imperfecto de subjuntivo		14 pluscuamperfecto de subjuntivo	
indujera	indujéramos	hubiera inducido	hubiéramos inducido
indujeras	indujerais	hubieras inducido	hubierais inducido
indujera	indujeran	hubiera inducido	hubieran inducido
OR		OR	
indujese	indujésemos	hubiese inducido	hubiésemos inducido
indujeses	indujeseis	hubieses inducido	hubieseis inducido
indujese	indujesen	hubiese inducido	hubiesen inducido

imperativo

—	induzcamos
induce; no induzcas	inducid; no induzcáis
induzca	induzcan

Words and expressions related to this verb
inducidor, inducidora   inducer
el inducimiento   inducement

la inducción   induction
inducir a + inf.   to persuade to + inf.

Can't recognize an irregular verb form? Check out pages 678–681.

Regular **-ir** verb endings with spelling change: add **y** before **a**, **e**, or **o**

to influence, have influence on

The Seven Simple Tenses		The Seven Compound Tenses	
Singular	Plural	Singular	Plural
1 presente de indicativo		8 perfecto de indicativo	
influyo	**influimos**	**he influido**	**hemos influido**
influyes	**influís**	**has influido**	**habéis influido**
influye	**influyen**	**ha influido**	**han influido**
2 imperfecto de indicativo		9 pluscuamperfecto de indicativo	
influía	**influíamos**	**había influido**	**habíamos influido**
influías	**influíais**	**habías influido**	**habíais influido**
influía	**influían**	**había influido**	**habían influido**
3 pretérito		10 pretérito anterior	
influí	**influimos**	**hube influido**	**hubimos influido**
influiste	**influisteis**	**hubiste influido**	**hubisteis influido**
influyó	**influyeron**	**hubo influido**	**hubieron influido**
4 futuro		11 futuro perfecto	
influiré	**influiremos**	**habré influido**	**habremos influido**
influirás	**influiréis**	**habrás influido**	**habréis influido**
influirá	**influirán**	**habrá influido**	**habrán influido**
5 potencial simple		12 potencial compuesto	
influiría	**influiríamos**	**habría influido**	**habríamos influido**
influirías	**influiríais**	**habrías influido**	**habríais influido**
influiría	**influirían**	**habría influido**	**habrían influido**
6 presente de subjuntivo		13 perfecto de subjuntivo	
influya	**influyamos**	**haya influido**	**hayamos influido**
influyas	**influyáis**	**hayas influido**	**hayáis influido**
influya	**influyan**	**haya influido**	**hayan influido**
7 imperfecto de subjuntivo		14 pluscuamperfecto de subjuntivo	
influyera	**influyéramos**	**hubiera influido**	**hubiéramos influido**
influyeras	**influyerais**	**hubieras influido**	**hubierais influido**
influyera	**influyeran**	**hubiera influido**	**hubieran influido**
OR		OR	
influyese	**influyésemos**	**hubiese influido**	**hubiésemos influido**
influyeses	**influyeseis**	**hubieses influido**	**hubieseis influido**
influyese	**influyesen**	**hubiese influido**	**hubiesen influido**

imperativo	
—	**influyamos**
influye; no influyas	**influid; no influyáis**
influya	**influyan**

Words and expressions related to this verb
la influencia   influence
influente   influential, influencing
influir en   to affect, to have an influence on, upon
influir sobre alguien para que + subjunctive   to influence someone to + inf.
(Check out the subjunctive on pages 20 to 24.)

> If you want an explanation of meanings and uses of Spanish and
> English verb tenses and moods, see pages 13–32.

The Seven Simple Tenses		The Seven Compound Tenses	
Singular	Plural	Singular	Plural
1 presente de indicativo		8 perfecto de indicativo	
me informo	nos informamos	me he informado	nos hemos informado
te informas	os informáis	te has informado	os habéis informado
se informa	se informan	se ha informado	se han informado
2 imperfecto de indicativo		9 pluscuamperfecto de indicativo	
me informaba	nos informábamos	me había informado	nos habíamos informado
te informabas	os informabais	te habías informado	os habíais informado
se informaba	se informaban	se había informado	se habían informado
3 pretérito		10 pretérito anterior	
me informé	nos informamos	me hube informado	nos hubimos informado
te informaste	os informasteis	te hubiste informado	os hubisteis informado
se informó	se informaron	se hubo informado	se hubieron informado
4 futuro		11 futuro perfecto	
me informaré	nos informaremos	me habré informado	nos habremos informado
te informarás	os informaréis	te habrás informado	os habréis informado
se informará	se informarán	se habrá informado	se habrán informado
5 potencial simple		12 potencial compuesto	
me informaría	nos informaríamos	me habría informado	nos habríamos informado
te informarías	os informaríais	te habrías informado	os habríais informado
se informaría	se informarían	se habría informado	se habrían informado
6 presente de subjuntivo		13 perfecto de subjuntivo	
me informe	nos informemos	me haya informado	nos hayamos informado
te informes	os informéis	te hayas informado	os hayáis informado
se informe	se informen	se haya informado	se hayan informado
7 imperfecto de subjuntivo		14 pluscuamperfecto de subjuntivo	
me informara	nos informáramos	me hubiera informado	nos hubiéramos informado
te informaras	os informarais	te hubieras informado	os hubierais informado
se informara	se informaran	se hubiera informado	se hubieran informado
OR		OR	
me informase	nos informásemos	me hubiese informado	nos hubiésemos informado
te informases	os informaseis	te hubieses informado	os hubieseis informado
se informáse	se informasen	se hubiese informado	se hubiesen informado

imperativo

—	**informémonos**
infórmate; no te informes	**informaos; no os informéis**
infórmese	**infórmense**

Words and expressions related to this verb

el informe, los informes   information
un informe en confianza   confidential report
informativo, informativa   informative, informational
informarse de   to find out about

el, la informante   informant
informar   to inform, report
informar contra   to inform against
la información   information, report
información económica   financial news

The Seven Simple Tenses		The Seven Compound Tenses	
Singular	Plural	Singular	Plural
1 presente de indicativo		8 perfecto de indicativo	
inmigro	inmigramos	he inmigrado	hemos inmigrado
inmigras	inmigráis	has inmigrado	habéis inmigrado
inmigra	inmigran	ha inmigrado	han inmigrado
2 imperfecto de indicativo		9 pluscuamperfecto de indicativo	
inmigraba	inmigrábamos	había inmigrado	habíamos inmigrado
inmigrabas	inmigrabais	habías inmigrado	habíais inmigrado
inmigraba	inmigraban	había inmigrado	habían inmigrado
3 pretérito		10 pretérito anterior	
inmigré	inmigramos	hube inmigrado	hubimos inmigrado
inmigraste	inmigrasteis	hubiste inmigrado	hubisteis inmigrado
inmigró	inmigraron	hubo inmigrado	hubieron inmigrado
4 futuro		11 futuro perfecto	
inmigraré	inmigraremos	habré inmigrado	habremos inmigrado
inmigrarás	inmigraréis	habrás inmigrado	habréis inmigrado
inmigrará	inmigrarán	habrá inmigrado	habrán inmigrado
5 potencial simple		12 potencial compuesto	
inmigraría	inmigraríamos	habría inmigrado	habríamos inmigrado
inmigrarías	inmigraríais	habrías inmigrado	habríais inmigrado
inmigraría	inmigrarían	habría inmigrado	habrían inmigrado
6 presente de subjuntivo		13 perfecto de subjuntivo	
inmigre	inmigremos	haya inmigrado	hayamos inmigrado
inmigres	inmigréis	hayas inmigrado	hayáis inmigrado
inmigre	inmigren	haya inmigrado	hayan inmigrado
7 imperfecto de subjuntivo		14 pluscuamperfecto de subjuntivo	
inmigrara	inmigráramos	hubiera inmigrado	hubiéramos inmigrado
inmigraras	inmigrarais	hubieras inmigrado	hubierais inmigrado
inmigrara	inmigraran	hubiera inmigrado	hubieran inmigrado
OR		OR	
inmigrase	inmigrásemos	hubiese inmigrado	hubiésemos inmigrado
inmigrases	inmigraseis	hubieses inmigrado	hubieseis inmigrado
inmigrase	inmigrasen	hubiese inmigrado	hubiesen inmigrado

	imperativo
—	inmigremos
inmigra; no inmigres	inmigrad; no inmigréis
inmigre	inmigren

Words and expressions related to this verb

la **inmigración** immigration
inmigrado, inmigrada *adj.* immigrant
inmigrante *adj.* immigrant

inmigratorio, inmigratoria immigratory
emigrar to emigrate
un **emigrado, una emigrada** an émigré

The subject pronouns are found on page 93.

395

inscribir (274) Gerundio inscribiendo Part. pas. inscrito (inscripto, *as an adj.*)

to inscribe, to record, to register

Regular **-ir** verb

The Seven Simple Tenses		The Seven Compound Tenses	
Singular	Plural	Singular	Plural
1 presente de indicativo		**8 perfecto de indicativo**	
inscribo	inscribimos	he inscrito	hemos inscrito
inscribes	inscribís	has inscrito	habéis inscrito
inscribe	inscriben	ha inscrito	han inscrito
2 imperfecto de indicativo		**9 pluscuamperfecto de indicativo**	
inscribía	inscribíamos	había inscrito	habíamos inscrito
inscribías	inscribíais	habías inscrito	habíais inscrito
inscribía	inscribían	había inscrito	habían inscrito
3 pretérito		**10 pretérito anterior**	
inscribí	inscribimos	hube inscrito	hubimos inscrito
inscribiste	inscribisteis	hubiste inscrito	hubisteis inscrito
inscribió	inscribieron	hubo inscrito	hubieron inscrito
4 futuro		**11 futuro perfecto**	
inscribiré	inscribiremos	habré inscrito	habremos inscrito
inscribirás	inscribiréis	habrás inscrito	habréis inscrito
inscribirá	inscribirán	habrá inscrito	habrán inscrito
5 potencial simple		**12 potencial compuesto**	
inscribiría	inscribiríamos	habría inscrito	habríamos inscrito
inscribirías	inscribiríais	habrías inscrito	habríais inscrito
inscribiría	inscribirían	habría inscrito	habrían inscrito
6 presente de subjuntivo		**13 perfecto de subjuntivo**	
inscriba	inscribamos	haya inscrito	hayamos inscrito
inscribas	inscribáis	hayas inscrito	hayáis inscrito
inscriba	inscriban	haya inscrito	hayan inscrito
7 imperfecto de subjuntivo		**14 pluscuamperfecto de subjuntivo**	
inscribiera	inscribiéramos	hubiera inscrito	hubiéramos inscrito
inscribieras	inscribierais	hubieras inscrito	hubierais inscrito
inscribiera	inscribieran	hubiera inscrito	hubieran inscrito
OR		OR	
inscribiese	inscribiésemos	hubiese inscrito	hubiésemos inscrito
inscribieses	inscribieseis	hubieses inscrito	hubieseis inscrito
inscribiese	inscribiesen	hubiese inscrito	hubiesen inscrito

imperativo	
—	**inscribamos**
inscribe; no inscribas	**inscribid; no inscribáis**
inscriba	**inscriban**

Words and expressions related to this verb
la inscripción   inscription, registration
inscripto, inscripta   inscribed, registered
escribir   to write

describir   to describe, to sketch
la descripción   description
inscribirse en un concurso   to register one's name (to sign up) in a competition

If you don't know the Spanish verb for the English verb you have in mind, look it up in the index on pages 682–706.

Reflexive regular **-ir** verb   to enroll, to register, to sign up

The Seven Simple Tenses		The Seven Compound Tenses	
Singular	Plural	Singular	Plural
1 presente de indicativo		8 perfecto de indicativo	
me inscribo	**nos inscribimos**	**me he inscrito**	**nos hemos inscrito**
te inscribes	**os inscribís**	**te has inscrito**	**os habéis inscrito**
se inscribe	**se inscriben**	**se ha inscrito**	**se han inscrito**
2 imperfecto de indicativo		9 pluscuamperfecto de indicativo	
me inscribía	**nos inscribíamos**	**me había inscrito**	**nos habíamos inscrito**
te inscribías	**os inscribíais**	**te habías inscrito**	**os habíais inscrito**
se inscribía	**se inscribían**	**se había inscrito**	**se habían inscrito**
3 pretérito		10 pretérito anterior	
me inscribí	**nos inscribimos**	**me hube inscrito**	**nos hubimos inscrito**
te inscribiste	**os inscribisteis**	**te hubiste inscrito**	**os hubisteis inscrito**
se inscribió	**se inscribieron**	**se hubo inscrito**	**se hubieron inscrito**
4 futuro		11 futuro perfecto	
me inscribiré	**nos inscribiremos**	**me habré inscrito**	**nos habremos inscrito**
te inscribirás	**os inscribiréis**	**te habrás inscrito**	**os habréis inscrito**
se inscribirá	**se inscribirán**	**se habrá inscrito**	**se habrán inscrito**
5 potencial simple		12 potencial compuesto	
me inscribiría	**nos inscribiríamos**	**me habría inscrito**	**nos habríamos inscrito**
te inscribirías	**os inscribiríais**	**te habrías inscrito**	**os habríais inscrito**
se inscribiría	**se inscribirían**	**se habría inscrito**	**se habrían inscrito**
6 presente de subjuntivo		13 perfecto de subjuntivo	
me inscriba	**nos inscribamos**	**me haya inscrito**	**nos hayamos inscrito**
te inscribas	**os inscribáis**	**te hayas inscrito**	**os hayáis inscrito**
se inscriba	**se inscriban**	**se haya inscrito**	**se hayan inscrito**
7 imperfecto de subjuntivo		14 pluscuamperfecto de subjuntivo	
me inscribiera	**nos inscribiéramos**	**me hubiera inscrito**	**nos hubiéramos inscrito**
te inscribieras	**os inscribierais**	**te hubieras inscrito**	**os hubierais inscrito**
se inscribiera	**se inscribieran**	**se hubiera inscrito**	**se hubieran inscrito**
OR		OR	
me inscribiese	**nos inscribiésemos**	**me hubiese inscrito**	**nos hubiésemos inscrito**
te inscribieses	**os inscribieseis**	**te hubieses inscrito**	**os hubieseis inscrito**
se inscribiese	**se inscribiesen**	**se hubiese inscrito**	**se hubiesen inscrito**

imperativo

—	**inscribámonos**
inscríbete; no te inscribas	**inscribíos; no os inscribáis**
inscríbase	**inscríbanse**

For words and expressions related to this verb, see **inscribir**.

Don't miss the definitions of basic grammatical terms with examples
in English and Spanish on pages 33–44.

The subject pronouns are found on page 93.

to insist, to persist, to stress   Regular **-ir** verb

The Seven Simple Tenses		The Seven Compound Tenses	
Singular	Plural	Singular	Plural
1 presente de indicativo		8 perfecto de indicativo	
insisto	insistimos	he insistido	hemos insistido
insistes	insistís	has insistido	habéis insistido
insiste	insisten	ha insistido	han insistido
2 imperfecto de indicativo		9 pluscuamperfecto de indicativo	
insistía	insistíamos	había insistido	habíamos insistido
insistías	insistíais	habías insistido	habíais insistido
insistía	insistían	había insistido	habían insistido
3 pretérito		10 pretérito anterior	
insistí	insistimos	hube insistido	hubimos insistido
insististe	insististeis	hubiste insistido	hubisteis insistido
insistió	insistieron	hubo insistido	hubieron insistido
4 futuro		11 futuro perfecto	
insistiré	insistiremos	habré insistido	habremos insistido
insistirás	insistiréis	habrás insistido	habréis insistido
insistirá	insistirán	habrá insistido	habrán insistido
5 potencial simple		12 potencial compuesto	
insistiría	insistiríamos	habría insistido	habríamos insistido
insistirías	insistiríais	habrías insistido	habríais insistido
insistiría	insistirían	habría insistido	habrían insistido
6 presente de subjuntivo		13 perfecto de subjuntivo	
insista	insistamos	haya insistido	hayamos insistido
insistas	insistáis	hayas insistido	hayáis insistido
insista	insistan	haya insistido	hayan insistido
7 imperfecto de subjuntivo		14 pluscuamperfecto de subjuntivo	
insistiera	insistiéramos	hubiera insistido	hubiéramos insistido
insistieras	insistierais	hubieras insistido	hubierais insistido
insistiera	insistieran	hubiera insistido	hubieran insistido
OR		OR	
insistiese	insistiésemos	hubiese insistido	hubiésemos insistido
insistieses	insistieseis	hubieses insistido	hubieseis insistido
insistiese	insistiesen	hubiese insistido	hubiesen insistido

imperativo	
—	insistamos
insiste; no insistas	insistid; no insistáis
insista	insistan

Words related to this verb
insistir en to insist on, to persist in
la insistencia insistence, persistence

insistente insistent
insistir en la importancia de to stress the importance of

If you want to see a sample English verb fully conjugated in all the tenses, check out pages 11 and 12.

Reflexive regular **-ar** verb   to be interested in

The Seven Simple Tenses		The Seven Compound Tenses	
Singular	Plural	Singular	Plural
1 presente de indicativo		**8 perfecto de indicativo**	
me intereso	**nos interesamos**	**me he interesado**	**nos hemos interesado**
te interesas	**os interesáis**	**te has interesado**	**os habéis interesado**
se interesa	**se interesan**	**se ha interesado**	**se han interesado**
2 imperfecto de indicativo		**9 pluscuamperfecto de indicativo**	
me interesaba	**nos interesábamos**	**me había interesado**	**nos habíamos interesado**
te interesabas	**os interesabais**	**te habías interesado**	**os habíais interesado**
se interesaba	**se interesaban**	**se había interesado**	**se habían interesado**
3 pretérito		**10 pretérito anterior**	
me interesé	**nos interesamos**	**me hube interesado**	**nos hubimos interesado**
te interesaste	**os interesasteis**	**te hubiste interesado**	**os hubisteis interesado**
se interesó	**se interesaron**	**se hubo interesado**	**se hubieron interesado**
4 futuro		**11 futuro perfecto**	
me interesaré	**nos interesaremos**	**me habré interesado**	**nos habremos interesado**
te interesarás	**os interesaréis**	**te habrás interesado**	**os habréis interesado**
se interesará	**se interesarán**	**se habrá interesado**	**se habrán interesado**
5 potencial simple		**12 potencial compuesto**	
me interesaría	**nos interesaríamos**	**me habría interesado**	**nos habríamos interesado**
te interesarías	**os interesaríais**	**te habrías interesado**	**os habríais interesado**
se interesaría	**se interesarían**	**se habría interesado**	**se habrían interesado**
6 presente de subjuntivo		**13 perfecto de subjuntivo**	
me interese	**nos interesemos**	**me haya interesado**	**nos hayamos interesado**
te intereses	**os intereséis**	**te hayas interesado**	**os hayáis interesado**
se interese	**se interesen**	**se haya interesado**	**se hayan interesado**
7 imperfecto de subjuntivo		**14 pluscuamperfecto de subjuntivo**	
me interesara	**nos interesáramos**	**me hubiera interesado**	**nos hubiéramos interesado**
te interesaras	**os interesarais**	**te hubieras interesado**	**os hubierais interesado**
se interesara	**se interesaran**	**se hubiera interesado**	**se hubieran interesado**
OR		OR	
me interesase	**nos interesásemos**	**me hubiese interesado**	**nos hubiésemos interesado**
te interesases	**os interesaseis**	**te hubieses interesado**	**os hubieseis interesado**
se interesase	**se interesasen**	**se hubiese interesado**	**se hubiesen interesado**

	imperativo	
—		**interesémonos**
interésate; no te intereses		**interesaos; no os intereséis**
interésese		**interésense**

Words and expressions related to this verb

interesarse en to be interested in	**interesante** interesting
interesar to interest	**interesado, interesada** interested
el interés interest	**sin interés** uninteresting
en interés de on behalf of	**desinteresar** to disinterest
desinteresarse to become disinterested;	**desinteresado, desinteresada** disinterested
to lose interest	**el desinterés** disinterest

The subject pronouns are found on page 93.

introducir (278)
Gerundio **introduciendo**

Part. pas. **introducido**

to introduce

Regular **-ir** endings in all tenses except Tenses 3 and 7; spelling change: **c** becomes **zc** before **a** or **o**

The Seven Simple Tenses		The Seven Compound Tenses	
Singular	Plural	Singular	Plural
1 presente de indicativo		8 perfecto de indicativo	
introduzco	introducimos	he introducido	hemos introducido
introduces	introducís	has introducido	habéis introducido
introduce	introducen	ha introducido	han introducido
2 imperfecto de indicativo		9 pluscuamperfecto de indicativo	
introducía	introducíamos	había introducido	habíamos introducido
introducías	introducíais	habías introducido	habíais introducido
introducía	introducían	había introducido	habían introducido
3 pretérito		10 pretérito anterior	
introduje	introdujimos	hube introducido	hubimos introducido
introdujiste	introdujisteis	hubiste introducido	hubisteis introducido
introdujo	introdujeron	hubo introducido	hubieron introducido
4 futuro		11 futuro perfecto	
introduciré	introduciremos	habré introducido	habremos introducido
introducirás	introduciréis	habrás introducido	habréis introducido
introducirá	introducirán	habrá introducido	habrán introducido
5 potencial simple		12 potencial compuesto	
introduciría	introduciríamos	habría introducido	habríamos introducido
introducirías	introduciríais	habrías introducido	habríais introducido
introduciría	introducirían	habría introducido	habrían introducido
6 presente de subjuntivo		13 perfecto de subjuntivo	
introduzca	introduzcamos	haya introducido	hayamos introducido
introduzcas	introduzcáis	hayas introducido	hayáis introducido
introduzca	introduzcan	haya introducido	hayan introducido
7 imperfecto de subjuntivo		14 pluscuamperfecto de subjuntivo	
introdujera	introdujéramos	hubiera introducido	hubiéramos introducido
introdujeras	introdujerais	hubieras introducido	hubierais introducido
introdujera	introdujeran	hubiera introducido	hubieran introducido
OR		OR	
introdujese	introdujésemos	hubiese introducido	hubiésemos introducido
introdujeses	introdujeseis	hubieses introducido	hubieseis introducido
introdujese	introdujesen	hubiese introducido	hubiesen introducido

	imperativo	
—		introduzcamos
	introduce; no introduzcas	introducid; no introduzcáis
	introduzca	introduzcan

Words related to this verb

la introducción introduction
introductor, introductora introducer
introducir a una persona en la oficina
to show a person into the office

introductivo, introductiva introductive, introductory

Use the guide to Spanish pronunciation on pages 665–667.

400

The Seven Simple Tenses		The Seven Compound Tenses	
Singular	Plural	Singular	Plural
1 presente de indicativo		8 perfecto de indicativo	
invito	**invitamos**	**he invitado**	**hemos invitado**
invitas	**invitáis**	**has invitado**	**habéis invitado**
invita	**invitan**	**ha invitado**	**han invitado**
2 imperfecto de indicativo		9 pluscuamperfecto de indicativo	
invitaba	**invitábamos**	**había invitado**	**habíamos invitado**
invitabas	**invitabais**	**habías invitado**	**habíais invitado**
invitaba	**invitaban**	**había invitado**	**habían invitado**
3 pretérito		10 pretérito anterior	
invité	**invitamos**	**hube invitado**	**hubimos invitado**
invitaste	**invitasteis**	**hubiste invitado**	**hubisteis invitado**
invitó	**invitaron**	**hubo invitado**	**hubieron invitado**
4 futuro		11 futuro perfecto	
invitaré	**invitaremos**	**habré invitado**	**habremos invitado**
invitarás	**invitaréis**	**habrás invitado**	**habréis invitado**
invitará	**invitarán**	**habrá invitado**	**habrán invitado**
5 potencial simple		12 potencial compuesto	
invitaría	**invitaríamos**	**habría invitado**	**habríamos invitado**
invitarías	**invitaríais**	**habrías invitado**	**habríais invitado**
invitaría	**invitarían**	**habría invitado**	**habrían invitado**
6 presente de subjuntivo		13 perfecto de subjuntivo	
invite	**invitemos**	**haya invitado**	**hayamos invitado**
invites	**invitéis**	**hayas invitado**	**hayáis invitado**
invite	**inviten**	**haya invitado**	**hayan invitado**
7 imperfecto de subjuntivo		14 pluscuamperfecto de subjuntivo	
invitara	**invitáramos**	**hubiera invitado**	**hubiéramos invitado**
invitaras	**invitarais**	**hubieras invitado**	**hubierais invitado**
invitara	**invitaran**	**hubiera invitado**	**hubieran invitado**
OR		OR	
invitase	**invitásemos**	**hubiese invitado**	**hubiésemos invitado**
invitases	**invitaseis**	**hubieses invitado**	**hubieseis invitado**
invitase	**invitasen**	**hubiese invitado**	**hubiesen invitado**

	imperativo	
—		**invitemos**
invita; no invites		**invitad; no invitéis**
invite		**inviten**

Words related to this verb
invitar a + inf.   to invite + inf.
la invitación   invitation
un invitado, una invitada   guest

el invitador   host
la invitadora   hostess
evitar   to avoid

Can't find the verb you're looking for?
Check the back pages of this book for a list of over 2,100 additional verbs!

The subject pronouns are found on page 93.   **401**

The Seven Simple Tenses		The Seven Compound Tenses	
Singular	Plural	Singular	Plural
1 presente de indicativo		8 perfecto de indicativo	
voy	**vamos**	**he ido**	**hemos ido**
vas	**vais**	**has ido**	**habéis ido**
va	**van**	**ha ido**	**han ido**
2 imperfecto de indicativo		9 pluscuamperfecto de indicativo	
iba	**íbamos**	**había ido**	**habíamos ido**
ibas	**ibais**	**habías ido**	**habíais ido**
iba	**iban**	**había ido**	**habían ido**
3 pretérito		10 pretérito anterior	
fui	**fuimos**	**hube ido**	**hubimos ido**
fuiste	**fuisteis**	**hubiste ido**	**hubisteis ido**
fue	**fueron**	**hubo ido**	**hubieron ido**
4 futuro		11 futuro perfecto	
iré	**iremos**	**habré ido**	**habremos ido**
irás	**iréis**	**habrás ido**	**habréis ido**
irá	**irán**	**habrá ido**	**habrán ido**
5 potencial simple		12 potencial compuesto	
iría	**iríamos**	**habría ido**	**habríamos ido**
irías	**iríais**	**habrías ido**	**habríais ido**
iría	**irían**	**habría ido**	**habrían ido**
6 presente de subjuntivo		13 perfecto de subjuntivo	
vaya	**vayamos**	**haya ido**	**hayamos ido**
vayas	**vayáis**	**hayas ido**	**hayáis ido**
vaya	**vayan**	**haya ido**	**hayan ido**
7 imperfecto de subjuntivo		14 pluscuamperfecto de subjuntivo	
fuera	**fuéramos**	**hubiera ido**	**hubiéramos ido**
fueras	**fuerais**	**hubieras ido**	**hubierais ido**
fuera	**fueran**	**hubiera ido**	**hubieran ido**
OR		OR	
fuese	**fuésemos**	**hubiese ido**	**hubiésemos ido**
fueses	**fueseis**	**hubieses ido**	**hubieseis ido**
fuese	**fuesen**	**hubiese ido**	**hubiesen ido**

imperativo

—	**vamos (no vayamos)**
ve; no vayas	**id; no vayáis**
vaya	**vayan**

Ir and **irse** are a very important pair of verbs for a beginning student. In the following examples, note the difference in meaning between **ir** and the reflexive form **irse**.

Use **ir** when you simply mean *to go:*

> **Voy al cine**/I am going to the movies.

Use **irse** when you mean *to leave* in the sense of *to go away:*

> **Mis padres se fueron al campo para visitar a mis abuelos/**
> My parents left for (went away to) the country to visit my grandparents.

Sentences using ir and irse

Voy a pagar al contado.
I'm going to pay in cash.

¡Qué va! Nonsense!

¡Vámonos! Let's go! Let's leave!

¡Vete! Go away!

¡Váyase! Go away!

¿Cómo le va? How goes it? How are you?

Vaya con Dios.
Go with God. (God be with you.)

Words and expressions related to these verbs

ir de compras to go shopping

ir de brazo to walk arm in arm

ir a caballo to go on horseback

ir a medias to go halves

ir a pie to walk (to go on foot)

ir bien to get along well

ir con tiento to go quietly, softly

ir por to go for, to go ahead

irse de prisa to rush away

un billete de ida y vuelta return ticket

Proverb

Cuando el gato va a sus devociones, bailan los ratones.
When the cat is away, the mice will play.

to go away   Reflexive irregular verb

The Seven Simple Tenses		The Seven Compound Tenses	
Singular	Plural	Singular	Plural

1 presente de indicativo

		8 perfecto de indicativo	
me voy	nos vamos	me he ido	nos hemos ido
te vas	os vais	te has ido	os habéis ido
se va	se van	se ha ido	se han ido

2 imperfecto de indicativo

		9 pluscuamperfecto de indicativo	
me iba	nos íbamos	me había ido	nos habíamos ido
te ibas	os ibais	te habías ido	os habíais ido
se iba	se iban	se había ido	se habían ido

3 pretérito

		10 pretérito anterior	
me fui	nos fuimos	me hube ido	nos hubimos ido
te fuiste	os fuisteis	te hubiste ido	os hubisteis ido
se fue	se fueron	se hubo ido	se hubieron ido

4 futuro

		11 futuro perfecto	
me iré	nos iremos	me habré ido	nos habremos ido
te irás	os iréis	te habrás ido	os habréis ido
se irá	se irán	se habrá ido	se habrán ido

5 potencial simple

		12 potencial compuesto	
me iría	nos iríamos	me habría ido	nos habríamos ido
te irías	os iríais	te habrías ido	os habríais ido
se iría	se irían	se habría ido	se habrían ido

6 presente de subjuntivo

		13 perfecto de subjuntivo	
me vaya	nos vayamos	me haya ido	nos hayamos ido
te vayas	os vayáis	te hayas ido	os hayáis ido
se vaya	se vayan	se haya ido	se hayan ido

7 imperfecto de subjuntivo

		14 pluscuamperfecto de subjuntivo	
me fuera	nos fuéramos	me hubiera ido	nos hubiéramos ido
te fueras	os fuerais	te hubieras ido	os hubierais ido
se fuera	se fueran	se hubiera ido	se hubieran ido
OR		OR	
me fuese	nos fuésemos	me hubiese ido	nos hubiésemos ido
te fueses	os fueseis	te hubieses ido	os hubieseis ido
se fuese	se fuesen	se hubiese ido	se hubiesen ido

imperativo

—	vámonos; no nos vayamos
vete; no te vayas	idos; no os vayáis
váyase; no se vaya	váyanse; no se vayan

AN ESSENTIAL
55 VERB

Regular **-ar** verb endings with stem change: Tenses 1, 6;   to play (a game,
Imperative and spelling change: **g** becomes **gu** before **e**   sport)

The Seven Simple Tenses		The Seven Compound Tenses	
Singular	Plural	Singular	Plural
1 presente de indicativo		8 perfecto de indicativo	
juego	**jugamos**	**he jugado**	**hemos jugado**
juegas	**jugáis**	**has jugado**	**habéis jugado**
juega	**juegan**	**ha jugado**	**han jugado**
2 imperfecto de indicativo		9 pluscuamperfecto de indicativo	
jugaba	**jugábamos**	**había jugado**	**habíamos jugado**
jugabas	**jugabais**	**habías jugado**	**habíais jugado**
jugaba	**jugaban**	**había jugado**	**habían jugado**
3 pretérito		10 pretérito anterior	
jugué	**jugamos**	**hube jugado**	**hubimos jugado**
jugaste	**jugasteis**	**hubiste jugado**	**hubisteis jugado**
jugó	**jugaron**	**hubo jugado**	**hubieron jugado**
4 futuro		11 futuro perfecto	
jugaré	**jugaremos**	**habré jugado**	**habremos jugado**
jugarás	**jugaréis**	**habrás jugado**	**habréis jugado**
jugará	**jugarán**	**habrá jugado**	**habrán jugado**
5 potencial simple		12 potencial compuesto	
jugaría	**jugaríamos**	**habría jugado**	**habríamos jugado**
jugarías	**jugaríais**	**habrías jugado**	**habríais jugado**
jugaría	**jugarían**	**habría jugado**	**habrían jugado**
6 presente de subjuntivo		13 perfecto de subjuntivo	
juegue	**juguemos**	**haya jugado**	**hayamos jugado**
juegues	**juguéis**	**hayas jugado**	**hayáis jugado**
juegue	**jueguen**	**haya jugado**	**hayan jugado**
7 imperfecto de subjuntivo		14 pluscuamperfecto de subjuntivo	
jugara	**jugáramos**	**hubiera jugado**	**hubiéramos jugado**
jugaras	**jugarais**	**hubieras jugado**	**hubierais jugado**
jugara	**jugaran**	**hubiera jugado**	**hubieran jugado**
OR		OR	
jugase	**jugásemos**	**hubiese jugado**	**hubiésemos jugado**
jugases	**jugaseis**	**hubieses jugado**	**hubieseis jugado**
jugase	**jugasen**	**hubiese jugado**	**hubiesen jugado**

J

	imperativo	
—		**juguemos**
juega; no juegues		**jugad; no juguéis**
juegue		**jueguen**

Words and expressions related to this verb

un juguete toy, plaything	**jugar a los naipes** to play cards
jugador, jugadora player	**jugar al tenis** to play tennis
un juego game	**jugar al béisbol** to play baseball
la casa de juego gambling house	**hacer doble juego** to be two-faced
el juego de té tea set (service)	**¡Hagan juego!** Place your bets!
juego sucio foul (dishonest) play	**el juego de palabras** play on words, pun

The subject pronouns are found on page 93.

to join, to unite, to connect   Regular **-ar** verb

The Seven Simple Tenses		The Seven Compound Tenses	
Singular	Plural	Singular	Plural
1 presente de indicativo		8 perfecto de indicativo	
junto	juntamos	he juntado	hemos juntado
juntas	juntáis	has juntado	habéis juntado
junta	juntan	ha juntado	han juntado
2 imperfecto de indicativo		9 pluscuamperfecto de indicativo	
juntaba	juntábamos	había juntado	habíamos juntado
juntabas	juntabais	habías juntado	habíais juntado
juntaba	juntaban	había juntado	habían juntado
3 pretérito		10 pretérito anterior	
junté	juntamos	hube juntado	hubimos juntado
juntaste	juntasteis	hubiste juntado	hubisteis juntado
juntó	juntaron	hubo juntado	hubieron juntado
4 futuro		11 futuro perfecto	
juntaré	juntaremos	habré juntado	habremos juntado
juntarás	juntaréis	habrás juntado	habréis juntado
juntará	juntarán	habrá juntado	habrán juntado
5 potencial simple		12 potencial compuesto	
juntaría	juntaríamos	habría juntado	habríamos juntado
juntarías	juntaríais	habrías juntado	habríais juntado
juntaría	juntarían	habría juntado	habrían juntado
6 presente de subjuntivo		13 perfecto de subjuntivo	
junte	juntemos	haya juntado	hayamos juntado
juntes	juntéis	hayas juntado	hayáis juntado
junte	junten	haya juntado	hayan juntado
7 imperfecto de subjuntivo		14 pluscuamperfecto de subjuntivo	
juntara	juntáramos	hubiera juntado	hubiéramos juntado
juntaras	juntarais	hubieras juntado	hubierais juntado
juntara	juntaran	hubiera juntado	hubieran juntado
OR		OR	
juntase	juntásemos	hubiese juntado	hubiésemos juntado
juntases	juntaseis	hubieses juntado	hubieseis juntado
juntase	juntasen	hubiese juntado	hubiesen juntado

imperativo

—	juntemos
junta; no juntes	juntad; no juntéis
junte	junten

Words and expressions related to this verb
juntar con to associate with
juntarse to assemble, gather together
la junta junta, conference, convention, meeting
juntar meriendas to join forces
vivir juntos to live together

Can't find the verb you're looking for?
Check the back pages of this book for a list of over 2,100 additional verbs!

Regular **-ar** verb   to swear, to take an oath

The Seven Simple Tenses		The Seven Compound Tenses	
Singular	Plural	Singular	Plural
1 presente de indicativo		8 perfecto de indicativo	
juro	juramos	he jurado	hemos jurado
juras	juráis	has jurado	habéis jurado
jura	juran	ha jurado	han jurado
2 imperfecto de indicativo		9 pluscuamperfecto de indicativo	
juraba	jurábamos	había jurado	habíamos jurado
jurabas	jurabais	habías jurado	habíais jurado
juraba	juraban	había jurado	habían jurado
3 pretérito		10 pretérito anterior	
juré	juramos	hube jurado	hubimos jurado
juraste	jurasteis	hubiste jurado	hubisteis jurado
juró	juraron	hubo jurado	hubieron jurado
4 futuro		11 futuro perfecto	
juraré	juraremos	habré jurado	habremos jurado
jurarás	juraréis	habrás jurado	habréis jurado
jurará	jurarán	habrá jurado	habrán jurado
5 potencial simple		12 potencial compuesto	
juraría	juraríamos	habría jurado	habríamos jurado
jurarías	juraríais	habrías jurado	habríais jurado
juraría	jurarían	habría jurado	habrían jurado
6 presente de subjuntivo		13 perfecto de subjuntivo	
jure	juremos	haya jurado	hayamos jurado
jures	juréis	hayas jurado	hayáis jurado
jure	juren	haya jurado	hayan jurado
7 imperfecto de subjuntivo		14 pluscuamperfecto de subjuntivo	
jurara	juráramos	hubiera jurado	hubiéramos jurado
juraras	jurarais	hubieras jurado	hubierais jurado
jurara	juraran	hubiera jurado	hubieran jurado
OR		OR	
jurase	jurásemos	hubiese jurado	hubiésemos jurado
jurases	juraseis	hubieses jurado	hubieseis jurado
jurase	jurasen	hubiese jurado	hubiesen jurado

imperativo	
—	**juremos**
jura; no jures	**jurad; no juréis**
jure	**juren**

Words and expressions related to this verb
jurar en falso   to commit perjury
jurar decir la verdad   to swear to tell the
  truth
un juramento   oath; **juramento falso**
  perjury

juramentarse   to take an oath, to be sworn in
jurar como un carretero   to swear like a
  trooper
bajo juramento   under oath

The subject pronouns are found on page 93.

to judge

Regular **-ar** verb endings with spelling
change: **g** becomes **gu** before **e**

The Seven Simple Tenses		The Seven Compound Tenses	
Singular	Plural	Singular	Plural
1 presente de indicativo		8 perfecto de indicativo	
juzgo	juzgamos	he juzgado	hemos juzgado
juzgas	juzgáis	has juzgado	habéis juzgado
juzga	juzgan	ha juzgado	han juzgado
2 imperfecto de indicativo		9 pluscuamperfecto de indicativo	
juzgaba	juzgábamos	había juzgado	habíamos juzgado
juzgabas	juzgabais	habías juzgado	habíais juzgado
juzgaba	juzgaban	había juzgado	habían juzgado
3 pretérito		10 pretérito anterior	
juzgué	juzgamos	hube juzgado	hubimos juzgado
juzgaste	juzgasteis	hubiste juzgado	hubisteis juzgado
juzgó	juzgaron	hubo juzgado	hubieron juzgado
4 futuro		11 futuro perfecto	
juzgaré	juzgaremos	habré juzgado	habremos juzgado
juzgarás	juzgaréis	habrás juzgado	habréis juzgado
juzgará	juzgarán	habrá juzgado	habrán juzgado
5 potencial simple		12 potencial compuesto	
juzgaría	juzgaríamos	habría juzgado	habríamos juzgado
juzgarías	juzgaríais	habrías juzgado	habríais juzgado
juzgaría	juzgarían	habría juzgado	habrían juzgado
6 presente de subjuntivo		13 perfecto de subjuntivo	
juzgue	juzguemos	haya juzgado	hayamos juzgado
juzgues	juzguéis	hayas juzgado	hayáis juzgado
juzgue	juzguen	haya juzgado	hayan juzgado
7 imperfecto de subjuntivo		14 pluscuamperfecto de subjuntivo	
juzgara	juzgáramos	hubiera juzgado	hubiéramos juzgado
juzgaras	juzgarais	hubieras juzgado	hubierais juzgado
juzgara	juzgaran	hubiera juzgado	hubieran juzgado
OR		OR	
juzgase	juzgásemos	hubiese juzgado	hubiésemos juzgado
juzgases	juzgaseis	hubieses juzgado	hubieseis juzgado
juzgase	juzgasen	hubiese juzgado	hubiesen juzgado

imperativo	
—	juzguemos
juzga; no juzgues	juzgad; no juzguéis
juzgue	juzguen

Words and expressions related to this verb

a juzgar por   judging by
juzgar de   to pass judgment on
el juzgado   court of justice
el juez   judge (los jueces)
juzgar mal   to misjudge
juzgado, juzgada   judged

juez de paz, juez municipal   justice of the peace
prejuzgar   to prejudge
juzgar a un asesino   to judge a murderer
no poderse juzgar por las apariencias   not to
be able to judge by appearances

Regular **-ar** verb endings with spelling change: **z** becomes **c** before **e**

to throw, to hurl, to fling, to launch

The Seven Simple Tenses		The Seven Compound Tenses	
Singular	Plural	Singular	Plural
1 presente de indicativo		8 perfecto de indicativo	
lanzo	**lanzamos**	**he lanzado**	**hemos lanzado**
lanzas	**lanzáis**	**has lanzado**	**habéis lanzado**
lanza	**lanzan**	**ha lanzado**	**han lanzado**
2 imperfecto de indicativo		9 pluscuamperfecto de indicativo	
lanzaba	**lanzábamos**	**había lanzado**	**habíamos lanzado**
lanzabas	**lanzabais**	**habías lanzado**	**habíais lanzado**
lanzaba	**lanzaban**	**había lanzado**	**habían lanzado**
3 pretérito		10 pretérito anterior	
lancé	**lanzamos**	**hube lanzado**	**hubimos lanzado**
lanzaste	**lanzasteis**	**hubiste lanzado**	**hubisteis lanzado**
lanzó	**lanzaron**	**hubo lanzado**	**hubieron lanzado**
4 futuro		11 futuro perfecto	
lanzaré	**lanzaremos**	**habré lanzado**	**habremos lanzado**
lanzarás	**lanzaréis**	**habrás lanzado**	**habréis lanzado**
lanzará	**lanzarán**	**habrá lanzado**	**habrán lanzado**
5 potencial simple		12 potencial compuesto	
lanzaría	**lanzaríamos**	**habría lanzado**	**habríamos lanzado**
lanzarías	**lanzaríais**	**habrías lanzado**	**habríais lanzado**
lanzaría	**lanzarían**	**habría lanzado**	**habrían lanzado**
6 presente de subjuntivo		13 perfecto de subjuntivo	
lance	**lancemos**	**haya lanzado**	**hayamos lanzado**
lances	**lancéis**	**hayas lanzado**	**hayáis lanzado**
lance	**lancen**	**haya lanzado**	**hayan lanzado**
7 imperfecto de subjuntivo		14 pluscuamperfecto de subjuntivo	
lanzara	**lanzáramos**	**hubiera lanzado**	**hubiéramos lanzado**
lanzaras	**lanzarais**	**hubieras lanzado**	**hubierais lanzado**
lanzara	**lanzaran**	**hubiera lanzado**	**hubieran lanzado**
OR		OR	
lanzase	**lanzásemos**	**hubiese lanzado**	**hubiésemos lanzado**
lanzases	**lanzaseis**	**hubieses lanzado**	**hubieseis lanzado**
lanzase	**lanzasen**	**hubiese lanzado**	**hubiesen lanzado**

L

imperativo

—	**lancemos**
lanza; no lances	**lanzad; no lancéis**
lance	**lancen**

Words and expressions related to this verb

la lanza   lance, spear
el lanzamiento   casting, throwing, launching
el lanzador, la lanzadora   thrower, pitcher
  (sports)
lanzarse   to throw oneself
See also **arrojar.**

quebrar lanzas   to quarrel
ser una lanza   to be an expert
la plataforma de lanzamiento   launching pad
lanzarse al agua   to jump into the water

The subject pronouns are found on page 93.

to hurt oneself, to feel sorry
for, to complain, to regret

The Seven Simple Tenses		The Seven Compound Tenses	
Singular	Plural	Singular	Plural
1 presente de indicativo		8 perfecto de indicativo	
me lastimo	nos lastimamos	me he lastimado	nos hemos lastimado
te lastimas	os lastimáis	te has lastimado	os habéis lastimado
se lastima	se lastiman	se ha lastimado	se han lastimado
2 imperfecto de indicativo		9 pluscuamperfecto de indicativo	
me lastimaba	nos lastimábamos	me había lastimado	nos habíamos lastimado
te lastimabas	os lastimabais	te habías lastimado	os habíais lastimado
se lastimaba	se lastimaban	se había lastimado	se habían lastimado
3 pretérito		10 pretérito anterior	
me lastimé	nos lastimamos	me hube lastimado	nos hubimos lastimado
te lastimaste	os lastimasteis	te hubiste lastimado	os hubisteis lastimado
se lastimó	se lastimaron	se hubo lastimado	se hubieron lastimado
4 futuro		11 futuro perfecto	
me lastimaré	nos lastimaremos	me habré lastimado	nos habremos lastimado
te lastimarás	os lastimaréis	te habrás lastimado	os habréis lastimado
se lastimará	se lastimarán	se habrá lastimado	se habrán lastimado
5 potencial simple		12 potencial compuesto	
me lastimaría	nos lastimaríamos	me habría lastimado	nos habríamos lastimado
te lastimarías	os lastimaríais	te habrías lastimado	os habríais lastimado
se lastimaría	se lastimarían	se habría lastimado	se habrían lastimado
6 presente de subjuntivo		13 perfecto de subjuntivo	
me lastime	nos lastimemos	me haya lastimado	nos hayamos lastimado
te lastimes	os lastiméis	te hayas lastimado	os hayáis lastimado
se lastime	se lastimen	se haya lastimado	se hayan lastimado
7 imperfecto de subjuntivo		14 pluscuamperfecto de subjuntivo	
me lastimara	nos lastimáramos	me hubiera lastimado	nos hubiéramos lastimado
te lastimaras	os lastimarais	te hubieras lastimado	os hubierais lastimado
se lastimara	se lastimaran	se hubiera lastimado	se hubieran lastimado
OR		OR	
me lastimase	nos lastimásemos	me hubiese lastimado	nos hubiésemos lastimado
te lastimases	os lastimaseis	te hubieses lastimado	os hubieseis lastimado
se lastimase	se lastimasen	se hubiese lastimado	se hubiesen lastimado

imperativo	
—	**lastimémonos**
lastímate; no te lastimes	**lastimaos; no os lastiméis**
lastímese	**lastímense**

Words and expressions related to this verb
lastimar   to hurt, damage, injure, offend
lastimarse de   to feel sorry for, to complain about
una lástima   pity; **¡Qué lástima!**   What a pity! What a shame!
tener lástima   to feel sorry

Consult pages 669–677 for the section on verbs with prepositions.

Gerundio **lavando**   Part. pas. **lavado**   **lavar (288)**

Regular **-ar** verb   to wash

The Seven Simple Tenses | The Seven Compound Tenses

Singular	Plural	Singular	Plural
1 presente de indicativo		8 perfecto de indicativo	
lavo	**lavamos**	**he lavado**	**hemos lavado**
lavas	**laváis**	**has lavado**	**habéis lavado**
lava	**lavan**	**ha lavado**	**han lavado**
2 imperfecto de indicativo		9 pluscuamperfecto de indicativo	
lavaba	**lavábamos**	**había lavado**	**habíamos lavado**
lavabas	**lavabais**	**habías lavado**	**habíais lavado**
lavaba	**lavaban**	**había lavado**	**habían lavado**
3 pretérito		10 pretérito anterior	
lavé	**lavamos**	**hube lavado**	**hubimos lavado**
lavaste	**lavasteis**	**hubiste lavado**	**hubisteis lavado**
lavó	**lavaron**	**hubo lavado**	**hubieron lavado**
4 futuro		11 futuro perfecto	
lavaré	**lavaremos**	**habré lavado**	**habremos lavado**
lavarás	**lavaréis**	**habrás lavado**	**habréis lavado**
lavará	**lavarán**	**habrá lavado**	**habrán lavado**
5 potencial simple		12 potencial compuesto	
lavaría	**lavaríamos**	**habría lavado**	**habríamos lavado**
lavarías	**lavaríais**	**habrías lavado**	**habríais lavado**
lavaría	**lavarían**	**habría lavado**	**habrían lavado**
6 presente de subjuntivo		13 perfecto de subjuntivo	
lave	**lavemos**	**haya lavado**	**hayamos lavado**
laves	**lavéis**	**hayas lavado**	**hayáis lavado**
lave	**laven**	**haya lavado**	**hayan lavado**
7 imperfecto de subjuntivo		14 pluscuamperfecto de subjuntivo	
lavara	**laváramos**	**hubiera lavado**	**hubiéramos lavado**
lavaras	**lavarais**	**hubieras lavado**	**hubierais lavado**
lavara	**lavaran**	**hubiera lavado**	**hubieran lavado**
OR		OR	
lavase	**lavásemos**	**hubiese lavado**	**hubiésemos lavado**
lavases	**lavaseis**	**hubieses lavado**	**hubieseis lavado**
lavase	**lavasen**	**hubiese lavado**	**hubiesen lavado**

imperativo

—	**lavemos**
lava; no laves	**lavad; no lavéis**
lave	**laven**

Words and expressions related to this verb

el lavatorio, el lavabo   lavatory, washroom, washstand
lavandero, lavandera   launderer
la lavandería   laundry shop

el lavamanos   washstand, washbowl
lavar en seco   to dry clean
la máquina de lavar ropa   clothes washing machine

See also **lavarse**.

The subject pronouns are found on page 93.   **411**

to wash oneself

The Seven Simple Tenses		The Seven Compound Tenses	
Singular	Plural	Singular	Plural
1 presente de indicativo		**8 perfecto de indicativo**	
me lavo	nos lavamos	me he lavado	nos hemos lavado
te lavas	os laváis	te has lavado	os habéis lavado
se lava	se lavan	se ha lavado	se han lavado
2 imperfecto de indicativo		**9 pluscuamperfecto de indicativo**	
me lavaba	nos lavábamos	me había lavado	nos habíamos lavado
te lavabas	os lavabais	te habías lavado	os habíais lavado
se lavaba	se lavaban	se había lavado	se habían lavado
3 pretérito		**10 pretérito anterior**	
me lavé	nos lavamos	me hube lavado	nos hubimos lavado
te lavaste	os lavasteis	te hubiste lavado	os hubisteis lavado
se lavó	se lavaron	se hubo lavado	se hubieron lavado
4 futuro		**11 futuro perfecto**	
me lavaré	nos lavaremos	me habré lavado	nos habremos lavado
te lavarás	os lavaréis	te habrás lavado	os habréis lavado
se lavará	se lavarán	se habrá lavado	se habrán lavado
5 potencial simple		**12 potencial compuesto**	
me lavaría	nos lavaríamos	me habría lavado	nos habríamos lavado
te lavarías	os lavaríais	te habrías lavado	os habríais lavado
se lavaría	se lavarían	se habría lavado	se habrían lavado
6 presente de subjuntivo		**13 perfecto de subjuntivo**	
me lave	nos lavemos	me haya lavado	nos hayamos lavado
te laves	os lavéis	te hayas lavado	os hayáis lavado
se lave	se laven	se haya lavado	se hayan lavado
7 imperfecto de subjuntivo		**14 pluscuamperfecto de subjuntivo**	
me lavara	nos laváramos	me hubiera lavado	nos hubiéramos lavado
te lavaras	os lavarais	te hubieras lavado	os hubierais lavado
se lavara	se lavaran	se hubiera lavado	se hubieran lavado
OR		OR	
me lavase	nos lavásemos	me hubiese lavado	nos hubiésemos lavado
te lavases	os lavaseis	te hubieses lavado	os hubieseis lavado
se lavase	se lavasen	se hubiese lavado	se hubiesen lavado

imperativo

—	lavémonos; no nos lavemos
lávate; no te laves	lavaos; no os lavéis
lávese; no se lave	lávense; no se laven

Words and expressions related to this verb

el lavatorio, el lavabo   lavatory, washroom, washstand
lavandero, lavandera   launderer

la lavandería   laundry shop
la lavativa   enema
la lavadora de vajilla   dishwashing machine

For other words and expressions related to this verb, see **lavar.**

Irregular verb   to read

The Seven Simple Tenses		The Seven Compound Tenses	
Singular	Plural	Singular	Plural
1 presente de indicativo		8 perfecto de indicativo	
leo	leemos	he leído	hemos leído
lees	leéis	has leído	habéis leído
lee	leen	ha leído	han leído
2 imperfecto de indicativo		9 pluscuamperfecto de indicativo	
leía	leíamos	había leído	habíamos leído
leías	leíais	habías leído	habíais leído
leía	leían	había leído	habían leído
3 pretérito		10 pretérito anterior	
leí	leímos	hube leído	hubimos leído
leíste	leísteis	hubiste leído	hubisteis leído
leyó	leyeron	hubo leído	hubieron leído
4 futuro		11 futuro perfecto	
leeré	leeremos	habré leído	habremos leído
leerás	leeréis	habrás leído	habréis leído
leerá	leerán	habrá leído	habrán leído
5 potencial simple		12 potencial compuesto	
leería	leeríamos	habría leído	habríamos leído
leerías	leeríais	habrías leído	habríais leído
leería	leerían	habría leído	habrían leído
6 presente de subjuntivo		13 perfecto de subjuntivo	
lea	leamos	haya leído	hayamos leído
leas	leáis	hayas leído	hayáis leído
lea	lean	haya leído	hayan leído
7 imperfecto de subjuntivo		14 pluscuamperfecto de subjuntivo	
leyera	leyéramos	hubiera leído	hubiéramos leído
leyeras	leyerais	hubieras leído	hubierais leído
leyera	leyeran	hubiera leído	hubieran leído
OR		OR	
leyese	leyésemos	hubiese leído	hubiésemos leído
leyeses	leyeseis	hubieses leído	hubieseis leído
leyese	leyesen	hubiese leído	hubiesen leído

	imperativo
—	leamos
lee; no leas	leed; no leáis
lea	lean

AN ESSENTIAL
55 VERB

Leer is an essential verb for beginning students of Spanish. It is used in many idiomatic expressions and everyday situations.

Sentences using leer and related words

Estoy leyendo un libro de Borges.
I'm reading a book by Borges.

Me gusta leer.
I like to read.

Cuando lees entre líneas, corres el riesgo de cometer un error.
When you read between the lines, you run the risk of making a mistake.

Words and expressions related to this verb

la lectura **reading**

la lección **lesson**

lector, lectora **reader**

leer mal **to misread**

releer **to read again, to reread**

leer entre líneas **to read between the lines**

un, una leccionista **private tutor**

leer para sí **to read to oneself**

leer en voz baja **to read quietly**

leer pruebas de imprenta **to proofread**

Proverb

Después de comer, ni un sobre escrito leer.
After eating, don't even read an envelope.

Do you need more drills? Have fun with the *501 Spanish Verbs* CD-ROM!

Regular **-ar** verb to lift, to raise

The Seven Simple Tenses		The Seven Compound Tenses	
Singular	Plural	Singular	Plural
1 presente de indicativo		8 perfecto de indicativo	
levanto	**levantamos**	**he levantado**	**hemos levantado**
levantas	**levantáis**	**has levantado**	**habéis levantado**
levanta	**levantan**	**ha levantado**	**han levantado**
2 imperfecto de indicativo		9 pluscuamperfecto de indicativo	
levantaba	**levantábamos**	**había levantado**	**habíamos levantado**
levantabas	**levantabais**	**habías levantado**	**habíais levantado**
levantaba	**levantaban**	**había levantado**	**habían levantado**
3 pretérito		10 pretérito anterior	
levanté	**levantamos**	**hube levantado**	**hubimos levantado**
levantaste	**levantasteis**	**hubiste levantado**	**hubisteis levantado**
levantó	**levantaron**	**hubo levantado**	**hubieron levantado**
4 futuro		11 futuro perfecto	
levantaré	**levantaremos**	**habré levantado**	**habremos levantado**
levantarás	**levantaréis**	**habrás levantado**	**habréis levantado**
levantará	**levantarán**	**habrá levantado**	**habrán levantado**
5 potencial simple		12 potencial compuesto	
levantaría	**levantaríamos**	**habría levantado**	**habríamos levantado**
levantarías	**levantaríais**	**habrías levantado**	**habríais levantado**
levantaría	**levantarían**	**habría levantado**	**habrían levantado**
6 presente de subjuntivo		13 perfecto de subjuntivo	
levante	**levantemos**	**haya levantado**	**hayamos levantado**
levantes	**levantéis**	**hayas levantado**	**hayáis levantado**
levante	**levanten**	**haya levantado**	**hayan levantado**
7 imperfecto de subjuntivo		14 pluscuamperfecto de subjuntivo	
levantara	**levantáramos**	**hubiera levantado**	**hubiéramos levantado**
levantaras	**levantarais**	**hubieras levantado**	**hubierais levantado**
levantara	**levantaran**	**hubiera levantado**	**hubieran levantado**
OR		OR	
levantase	**levantásemos**	**hubiese levantado**	**hubiésemos levantado**
levantases	**levantaseis**	**hubieses levantado**	**hubieseis levantado**
levantase	**levantasen**	**hubiese levantado**	**hubiesen levantado**

imperativo	
—	**levantemos**
levanta; no levantes	**levantad; no levantéis**
levante	**levanten**

Words and expressions related to this verb

levantar los manteles   to clear the table
levantar con algo   to get away with
  something
el Levante   Levant, East

el levantamiento   elevation, raising
levantar fuego   to make a disturbance
levantar la cabeza   to take heart (courage)
levantar la voz   to raise one's voice

See also **levantarse.**

The subject pronouns are found on page 93.

The Seven Simple Tenses		The Seven Compound Tenses	
Singular	Plural	Singular	Plural
1 presente de indicativo		**8 perfecto de indicativo**	
me levanto	nos levantamos	me he levantado	nos hemos levantado
te levantas	os levantáis	te has levantado	os habéis levantado
se levanta	se levantan	se ha levantado	se han levantado
2 imperfecto de indicativo		**9 pluscuamperfecto de indicativo**	
me levantaba	nos levantábamos	me había levantado	nos habíamos levantado
te levantabas	os levantabais	te habías levantado	os habíais levantado
se levantaba	se levantaban	se había levantado	se habían levantado
3 pretérito		**10 pretérito anterior**	
me levanté	nos levantamos	me hube levantado	nos hubimos levantado
te levantaste	os levantasteis	te hubiste levantado	os hubisteis levantado
se levantó	se levantaron	se hubo levantado	se hubieron levantado
4 futuro		**11 futuro perfecto**	
me levantaré	nos levantaremos	me habré levantado	nos habremos levantado
te levantarás	os levantaréis	te habrás levantado	os habréis levantado
se levantará	se levantarán	se habrá levantado	se habrán levantado
5 potencial simple		**12 potencial compuesto**	
me levantaría	nos levantaríamos	me habría levantado	nos habríamos levantado
te levantarías	os levantaríais	te habrías levantado	os habríais levantado
se levantaría	se levantarían	se habría levantado	se habrían levantado
6 presente de subjuntivo		**13 perfecto de subjuntivo**	
me levante	nos levantemos	me haya levantado	nos hayamos levantado
te levantes	os levantéis	te hayas levantado	os hayáis levantado
se levante	se levanten	se haya levantado	se hayan levantado
7 imperfecto de subjuntivo		**14 pluscuamperfecto de subjuntivo**	
me levantara	nos levantáramos	me hubiera levantado	nos hubiéramos levantado
te levantaras	os levantarais	te hubieras levantado	os hubierais levantado
se levantara	se levantaran	se hubiera levantado	se hubieran levantado
OR		OR	
me levantase	nos levantásemos	me hubiese levantado	nos hubiésemos levantado
te levantases	os levantaseis	te hubieses levantado	os hubieseis levantado
se levantase	se levantasen	se hubiese levantado	se hubiesen levantado

	imperativo	
—	levantémonos; no nos levantemos	
levántate; no te levantes	levantaos; no os levantéis	
levántese; no se levante	levántense; no se levanten	

Words and expressions related to this verb

levantar los manteles to clear the table
levantar con algo to get away with something
el Levante Levant, East
el levantamiento elevation, raising

See also **levantar.**

levantar la sesión to adjourn
levantar la voz to raise one's voice
levantarse de la cama to get out of bed
El hombre que se levanta aún es más grande que el que no ha caído. (Concepción Arenal)
The man who is still raising himself up is greater than the one who hasn't fallen.

The Seven Simple Tenses		The Seven Compound Tenses	
Singular	Plural	Singular	Plural
1 presente de indicativo		8 perfecto de indicativo	
limpio	**limpiamos**	**he limpiado**	**hemos limpiado**
limpias	**limpiáis**	**has limpiado**	**habéis limpiado**
limpia	**limpian**	**ha limpiado**	**han limpiado**
2 imperfecto de indicativo		9 pluscuamperfecto de indicativo	
limpiaba	**limpiábamos**	**había limpiado**	**habíamos limpiado**
limpiabas	**limpiabais**	**habías limpiado**	**habíais limpiado**
limpiaba	**limpiaban**	**había limpiado**	**habían limpiado**
3 pretérito		10 pretérito anterior	
limpié	**limpiamos**	**hube limpiado**	**hubimos limpiado**
limpiaste	**limpiasteis**	**hubiste limpiado**	**hubisteis limpiado**
limpió	**limpiaron**	**hubo limpiado**	**hubieron limpiado**
4 futuro		11 futuro perfecto	
limpiaré	**limpiaremos**	**habré limpiado**	**habremos limpiado**
limpiarás	**limpiaréis**	**habrás limpiado**	**habréis limpiado**
llimpiará	**limpiarán**	**habrá limpiado**	**habrán limpiado**
5 potencial simple		12 potencial compuesto	
limpiaría	**limpiaríamos**	**habría limpiado**	**habríamos limpiado**
limpiarías	**limpiaríais**	**habrías limpiado**	**habríais limpiado**
limpiaría	**limpiarían**	**habría limpiado**	**habrían limpiado**
6 presente de subjuntivo		13 perfecto de subjuntivo	
limpie	**limpiemos**	**haya limpiado**	**hayamos limpiado**
limpies	**limpiéis**	**hayas limpiado**	**hayáis limpiado**
limpie	**limpien**	**haya limpiado**	**hayan limpiado**
7 imperfecto de subjuntivo		14 pluscuamperfecto de subjuntivo	
limpiara	**limiáramos**	**hubiera limpiado**	**hubiéramos limpiado**
limpiaras	**limpiarais**	**hubieras limpiado**	**hubierais limpiado**
limpiara	**limpiaran**	**hubiera limpiado**	**hubieran limpiado**
OR		OR	
limpiase	**limpiásemos**	**hubiese limpiado**	**hubiésemos limpiado**
limpiases	**limpiaseis**	**hubieses limpiado**	**hubieseis limpiado**
limpiase	**limpiasen**	**hubiese limpiado**	**hubiesen limpiado**

imperativo

—	**limpiemos**
limpia; no limpies	**limpiad; no limpiéis**
limpie	**limpien**

Words and expressions related to this verb
limpiar en seco   to dry clean; **limpiar las faltriqueras a uno**   to pick someone's pocket
la limpieza   cleaning, cleanliness; **limpieza de manos**   integrity
jugar limpio   to play fair

For other words and expressions related to this verb, see **limpiarse.**

The subject pronouns are found on page 93.

The Seven Simple Tenses		The Seven Compound Tenses	
Singular	Plural	Singular	Plural
1 presente de indicativo		8 perfecto de indicativo	
me limpio	nos limpiamos	me he limpiado	nos hemos limpiado
te limpias	os limpiáis	te has limpiado	os habéis limpiado
se limpia	se limpian	se ha limpiado	se han limpiado
2 imperfecto de indicativo		9 pluscuamperfecto de indicativo	
me limpiaba	nos limpiábamos	me había limpiado	nos habíamos limpiado
te limpiabas	os limpiabais	te habías limpiado	os habíais limpiado
se limpiaba	se limpiaban	se había limpiado	se habían limpiado
3 pretérito		10 pretérito anterior	
me limpié	nos limpiamos	me hube limpiado	nos hubimos limpiado
te limpiaste	os limpiasteis	te hubiste limpiado	os hubisteis limpiado
se limpió	se limpiaron	se hubo limpiado	se hubieron limpiado
4 futuro		11 futuro perfecto	
me limpiaré	nos limpiaremos	me habré limpiado	nos habremos limpiado
te limpiarás	os limpiaréis	te habrás limpiado	os habréis limpiado
se limpiará	se limpiarán	se habrá limpiado	se habrán limpiado
5 potencial simple		12 potencial compuesto	
me limpiaría	nos limpiaríamos	me habría limpiado	nos habríamos limpiado
te limpiarías	os limpiaríais	te habrías limpiado	os habríais limpiado
se limpiaría	se limpiarían	se habría limpiado	se habrían limpiado
6 presente de subjuntivo		13 perfecto de subjuntivo	
me limpie	nos limpiemos	me haya limpiado	nos hayamos limpiado
te limpies	os limpiéis	te hayas limpiado	os hayáis limpiado
se limpie	se limpien	se haya limpiado	se hayan limpiado
7 imperfecto de subjuntivo		14 pluscuamperfecto de subjuntivo	
me limpiara	nos limpiáramos	me hubiera limpiado	nos hubiéramos limpiado
te limpiaras	os limpiarais	te hubieras limpiado	os hubierais limpiado
se limpiara	se limpiaran	se hubiera limpiado	se hubieran limpiado
OR		OR	
me limpiase	nos limpiásemos	me hubiese limpiado	nos hubiésemos limpiado
te limpiases	os limpiaseis	te hubieses limpiado	os hubieseis limpiado
se limpiase	se limpiasen	se hubiese limpiado	se hubiesen limpiado

imperativo	
—	**limpiémonos**
límpiate; no te limpies	**limpiaos; no os limpiéis**
límpiese	**límpiense**

Words related to this verb
un limpiapipas   pipe cleaner   **un limpiadientes**   toothpick
un limpianieve   snowplow   **un limpiachimeneas**   chimney sweep

For other words and expressions related to this verb, see **limpiar.**

Don't forget to study the section on defective and impersonal verbs. It's right after this main list.

Regular **-ar** verb   to call, to name

The Seven Simple Tenses		The Seven Compound Tenses	
Singular	Plural	Singular	Plural
1 presente de indicativo		8 perfecto de indicativo	
llamo	llamamos	he llamado	hemos llamado
llamas	llamáis	has llamado	habéis llamado
llama	llaman	ha llamado	han llamado
2 imperfecto de indicativo		9 pluscuamperfecto de indicativo	
llamaba	llamábamos	había llamado	habíamos llamado
llamabas	llamabais	habías llamado	habíais llamado
llamaba	llamaban	había llamado	habían llamado
3 pretérito		10 pretérito anterior	
llamé	llamamos	hube llamado	hubimos llamado
llamaste	llamasteis	hubiste llamado	hubisteis llamado
llamó	llamaron	hubo llamado	hubieron llamado
4 futuro		11 futuro perfecto	
llamaré	llamaremos	habré llamado	habremos llamado
llamarás	llamaréis	habrás llamado	habréis llamado
llamará	llamarán	habrá llamado	habrán llamado
5 potencial simple		12 potencial compuesto	
llamaría	llamaríamos	habría llamado	habríamos llamado
llamarías	llamaríais	habrías llamado	habríais llamado
llamaría	llamarían	habría llamado	habrían llamado
6 presente de subjuntivo		13 perfecto de subjuntivo	
llame	llamemos	haya llamado	hayamos llamado
llames	llaméis	hayas llamado	hayáis llamado
llame	llamen	haya llamado	hayan llamado
7 imperfecto de subjuntivo		14 pluscuamperfecto de subjuntivo	
llamara	llamáramos	hubiera llamado	hubiéramos llamado
llamaras	llamarais	hubieras llamado	hubierais llamado
llamara	llamaran	hubiera llamado	hubieran llamado
OR		OR	
llamase	llamásemos	hubiese llamado	hubiésemos llamado
llamases	llamaseis	hubieses llamado	hubieseis llamado
llamase	llamasen	hubiese llamado	hubiesen llamado

	imperativo	
—		llamemos
llama; no llames		llamad; no llaméis
llame		llamen

AN ESSENTIAL
55 VERB

The subject pronouns are found on page 93.

Llamar and llamarse are essential verbs for beginning students of Spanish. They are used in many idiomatic expressions and everyday situations. As you study the following sentences and expressions, pay attention to the differences in use between llamar and the reflexive verb llamarse.

Sentences using llamar and llamarse

—¿Cómo se llama usted?
—Me llamo Juan Morales.
—¿Y cómo se llaman sus hermanos?
—Se llaman Teresa y Pedro.
—What is your name? (How do you call yourself?)
—My name is Juan Morales.
—And what are your siblings' names?
—Their names are Teresa and Peter.

¿Puede llamar a un médico, por favor?
Can you call a doctor, please?

Words and expressions related to these verbs

llamar al doctor **to call the doctor**

llamar por teléfono **to telephone, to call**

llamar la atención sobre **to call attention to**

llamar por los nombres **to call the roll**

llamar un taxi **to call a taxi**

una llamada **call, knock, ring**

hacer una llamada telefónica **to make a phone call**

un llamador, una llamadora **caller**

Mi nombre es... **My name is...**

Can't find the verb you're looking for?
Check the back pages of this book for a list of over 2,100 additional verbs!

Reflexive regular **-ar** verb   to be called, to be named

The Seven Simple Tenses		The Seven Compound Tenses	
Singular	Plural	Singular	Plural
1 presente de indicativo		**8 perfecto de indicativo**	
me llamo	nos llamamos	me he llamado	nos hemos llamado
te llamas	os llamáis	te has llamado	os habéis llamado
se llama	se llaman	se ha llamado	se han llamado
2 imperfecto de indicativo		**9 pluscuamperfecto de indicativo**	
me llamaba	nos llamábamos	me había llamado	nos habíamos llamado
te llamabas	os llamabais	te habías llamado	os habíais llamado
se llamaba	se llamaban	se había llamado	se habían llamado
3 pretérito		**10 pretérito anterior**	
me llamé	nos llamamos	me hube llamado	nos hubimos llamado
te llamaste	os llamasteis	te hubiste llamado	os hubisteis llamado
se llamó	se llamaron	se hubo llamado	se hubieron llamado
4 futuro		**11 futuro perfecto**	
me llamaré	nos llamaremos	me habré llamado	nos habremos llamado
te llamarás	os llamaréis	te habrás llamado	os habréis llamado
se llamará	se llamarán	se habrá llamado	se habrán llamado
5 potencial simple		**12 potencial compuesto**	
me llamaría	nos llamaríamos	me habría llamado	nos habríamos llamado
te llamarías	os llamaríais	te habrías llamado	os habríais llamado
se llamaría	se llamarían	se habría llamado	se habrían llamado
6 presente de subjuntivo		**13 perfecto de subjuntivo**	
me llame	nos llamemos	me haya llamado	nos hayamos llamado
te llames	os llaméis	te hayas llamado	os hayáis llamado
se llame	se llamen	se haya llamado	se hayan llamado
7 imperfecto de subjuntivo		**14 pluscuamperfecto de subjuntivo**	
me llamara	nos llamáramos	me hubiera llamado	nos hubiéramos llamado
te llamaras	os llamarais	te hubieras llamado	os hubierais llamado
se llamara	se llamaran	se hubiera llamado	se hubieran llamado
OR		OR	
me llamase	nos llamásemos	me hubiese llamado	nos hubiésemos llamado
te llamases	os llamaseis	te hubieses llamado	os hubieseis llamado
se llamase	se llamasen	se hubiese llamado	se hubiesen llamado

L

imperativo

—	llamémonos; no nos llamemos
llámate; no te llames	llamaos; no os llaméis
llámese; no se llame	llámense; no se llamen

AN ESSENTIAL
55 VERB

The subject pronouns are found on page 93.

llegar (297)

to arrive

Regular **-ar** verb endings with spelling
change: **g** becomes **gu** before **e**

The Seven Simple Tenses		The Seven Compound Tenses	
Singular	Plural	Singular	Plural
1 presente de indicativo		**8 perfecto de indicativo**	
llego	llegamos	he llegado	hemos llegado
llegas	llegáis	has llegado	habéis llegado
llega	llegan	ha llegado	han llegado
2 imperfecto de indicativo		**9 pluscuamperfecto de indicativo**	
llegaba	llegábamos	había llegado	habíamos llegado
llegabas	llegabais	habías llegado	habíais llegado
llegaba	llegaban	había llegado	habían llegado
3 pretérito		**10 pretérito anterior**	
llegué	llegamos	hube llegado	hubimos llegado
llegaste	llegasteis	hubiste llegado	hubisteis llegado
llegó	llegaron	hubo llegado	hubieron llegado
4 futuro		**11 futuro perfecto**	
llegaré	llegaremos	habré llegado	habremos llegado
llegarás	llegaréis	habrás llegado	habréis llegado
llegará	llegarán	habrá llegado	habrán llegado
5 potencial simple		**12 potencial compuesto**	
llegaría	llegaríamos	habría llegado	habríamos llegado
llegarías	llegaríais	habrías llegado	habríais llegado
llegaría	llegarían	habría llegado	habrían llegado
6 presente de subjuntivo		**13 perfecto de subjuntivo**	
llegue	lleguemos	haya llegado	hayamos llegado
llegues	lleguéis	hayas llegado	hayáis llegado
llegue	lleguen	haya llegado	hayan llegado
7 imperfecto de subjuntivo		**14 pluscuamperfecto de subjuntivo**	
llegara	llegáramos	hubiera llegado	hubiéramos llegado
llegaras	llegarais	hubieras llegado	hubierais llegado
llegara	llegaran	hubiera llegado	hubieran llegado
OR		OR	
llegase	llegásemos	hubiese llegado	hubiésemos llegado
llegases	llegaseis	hubieses llegado	hubieseis llegado
llegase	llegasen	hubiese llegado	hubiesen llegado

imperativo	
—	lleguemos
llega; no llegues	llegad; no lleguéis
llegue	lleguen

Words and expressions related to this verb
llegar a ser   to become
  Luis y Luisa quieren llegar a ser médicos.   Louis and Louise want to become doctors.
llegar a saber   to find out   **llegar a**   to reach
la llegada   arrival   **al llegar**   on arrival, upon arriving
llegar tarde   to arrive late

Can't find the verb you're looking for?
Check the back pages of this book for a list of over 2,100 additional verbs!

Regular **-ar** verb   to fill

The Seven Simple Tenses		The Seven Compound Tenses	
Singular	Plural	Singular	Plural
1 presente de indicativo		**8 perfecto de indicativo**	
lleno	llenamos	he llenado	hemos llenado
llenas	llenáis	has llenado	habéis llenado
llena	llenan	ha llenado	han llenado
2 imperfecto de indicativo		**9 pluscuamperfecto de indicativo**	
llenaba	llenábamos	había llenado	habíamos llenado
llenabas	llenabais	habías llenado	habíais llenado
llenaba	llenaban	había llenado	habían llenado
3 pretérito		**10 pretérito anterior**	
llené	llenamos	hube llenado	hubimos llenado
llenaste	llenasteis	hubiste llenado	hubisteis llenado
llenó	llenaron	hubo llenado	hubieron llenado
4 futuro		**11 futuro perfecto**	
llenaré	llenaremos	habré llenado	habremos llenado
llenarás	llenaréis	habrás llenado	habréis llenado
llenará	llenarán	habrá llenado	habrán llenado
5 potencial simple		**12 potencial compuesto**	
llenaría	llenaríamos	habría llenado	habríamos llenado
llenarías	llenaríais	habrías llenado	habríais llenado
llenaría	llenarían	habría llenado	habrían llenado
6 presente de subjuntivo		**13 perfecto de subjuntivo**	
llene	llenemos	haya llenado	hayamos llenado
llenes	llenéis	hayas llenado	hayáis llenado
llene	llenen	haya llenado	hayan llenado
7 imperfecto de subjuntivo		**14 pluscuamperfecto de subjuntivo**	
llenara	llenáramos	hubiera llenado	hubiéramos llenado
llenaras	llenarais	hubieras llenado	hubierais llenado
llenara	llenaran	hubiera llenado	hubieran llenado
OR		OR	
llenase	llenásemos	hubiese llenado	hubiésemos llenado
llenases	llenaseis	hubieses llenado	hubieseis llenado
llenase	llenasen	hubiese llenado	hubiesen llenado

imperativo

—	**llenemos**
llena; no llenes	**llenad; no llenéis**
llene	**llenen**

Words and expressions related to this verb

lleno, llena full, filled   **lleno de bote a bote** full to the brim
la llenura abundance, fullness   **llenar un pedido** to fill an order
llenamente fully   **llenar un formulario** to fill out a form

Use the guide to Spanish pronunciation on pages 665–667.

423

The subject pronouns are found on page 93.

to carry (away), to take (away), to wear   Regular **-ar** verb

The Seven Simple Tenses		The Seven Compound Tenses	
Singular	Plural	Singular	Plural
1 presente de indicativo		8 perfecto de indicativo	
llevo	llevamos	he llevado	hemos llevado
llevas	lleváis	has llevado	habéis llevado
lleva	llevan	ha llevado	han llevado
2 imperfecto de indicativo		9 pluscuamperfecto de indicativo	
llevaba	llevábamos	había llevado	habíamos llevado
llevabas	llevabais	habías llevado	habíais llevado
llevaba	llevaban	había llevado	habían llevado
3 pretérito		10 pretérito anterior	
llevé	llevamos	hube llevado	hubimos llevado
llevaste	llevasteis	hubiste llevado	hubisteis llevado
llevó	llevaron	hubo llevado	hubieron llevado
4 futuro		11 futuro perfecto	
llevaré	llevaremos	habré llevado	habremos llevado
llevarás	llevaréis	habrás llevado	habréis llevado
llevará	llevarán	habrá llevado	habrán llevado
5 potencial simple		12 potencial compuesto	
llevaría	llevaríamos	habría llevado	habríamos llevado
llevarías	llevaríais	habrías llevado	habríais llevado
llevaría	llevarían	habría llevado	habrían llevado
6 presente de subjuntivo		13 perfecto de subjuntivo	
lleve	llevemos	haya llevado	hayamos llevado
lleves	llevéis	hayas llevado	hayáis llevado
lleve	lleven	haya llevado	hayan llevado
7 imperfecto de subjuntivo		14 pluscuamperfecto de subjuntivo	
llevara	lleváramos	hubiera llevado	hubiéramos llevado
llevaras	llevarais	hubieras llevado	hubierais llevado
llevara	llevaran	hubiera llevado	hubieran llevado
OR		OR	
llevase	llevásemos	hubiese llevado	hubiésemos llevado
llevases	llevaseis	hubieses llevado	hubieseis llevado
llevase	llevasen	hubiese llevado	hubiesen llevado

	imperativo
—	llevemos
lleva; no lleves	llevad; no llevéis
lleve	lleven

Llevar is an essential regular –ar verb for beginning students of Spanish. It is used in many idiomatic expressions and everyday situations.

Llevar means *to take* in the sense of carry or transport from place to place:

> José llevó la silla de la cocina al comedor/ Joseph took the chair from the kitchen to the dining room.

The verb llevar is also used when you *take someone somewhere:*

> Pedro llevó a María al baile anoche/Peter took Mary to the dance last night.

Llevar also means *to wear:*

> María, ¿por qué llevas la falda nueva?/ Mary, why are you wearing your new skirt?

Sentences using llevar

Lo llevo conmigo.
I'll take it with me.

Aquel hombre lleva una vida de perros.
That man leads a dog's life.

Words and expressions related to this verb

llevar a cabo **to carry through, to accomplish**

llevar una caída **to have a fall**

llevar una vida de perros **to lead a dog's life**

llevar conmigo **to take with me**

un llevador, una llevadora **carrier**

llevarse **to take away, carry off**

llevarse algo de alguien **to take something from someone**

llevarse bien con alguien **to get along well with someone**

L

Can't remember the Spanish verb you need?
Check the back pages of this book for the English-Spanish verb index!

The subject pronouns are found on page 93.

to weep, to cry, to whine   Regular -ar verb

The Seven Simple Tenses		The Seven Compound Tenses	
Singular	Plural	Singular	Plural
1 presente de indicativo		**8 perfecto de indicativo**	
lloro	lloramos	he llorado	hemos llorado
lloras	lloráis	has llorado	habéis llorado
llora	lloran	ha llorado	han llorado
2 imperfecto de indicativo		**9 pluscuamperfecto de indicativo**	
lloraba	llorábamos	había llorado	habíamos llorado
llorabas	llorabais	habías llorado	habíais llorado
lloraba	lloraban	había llorado	habían llorado
3 pretérito		**10 pretérito anterior**	
lloré	lloramos	hube llorado	hubimos llorado
lloraste	llorasteis	hubiste llorado	hubisteis llorado
lloró	lloraron	hubo llorado	hubieron llorado
4 futuro		**11 futuro perfecto**	
lloraré	lloraremos	habré llorado	habremos llorado
llorarás	lloraréis	habrás llorado	habréis llorado
llorará	llorarán	habrá llorado	habrán llorado
5 potencial simple		**12 potencial compuesto**	
lloraría	lloraríamos	habría llorado	habríamos llorado
llorarías	lloraríais	habrías llorado	habríais llorado
lloraría	llorarían	habría llorado	habrían llorado
6 presente de subjuntivo		**13 perfecto de subjuntivo**	
llore	lloremos	haya llorado	hayamos llorado
llores	lloréis	hayas llorado	hayáis llorado
llore	lloren	haya llorado	hayan llorado
7 imperfecto de subjuntivo		**14 pluscuamperfecto de subjuntivo**	
llorara	lloráramos	hubiera llorado	hubiéramos llorado
lloraras	llorarais	hubieras llorado	hubierais llorado
llorara	lloraran	hubiera llorado	hubieran llorado
OR		OR	
llorase	llorásemos	hubiese llorado	hubiésemos llorado
llorases	lloraseis	hubieses llorado	hubieseis llorado
llorase	llorasen	hubiese llorado	hubiesen llorado

imperativo

—	lloremos
llora; no llores	llorad; no lloréis
llore	lloren

Words and expressions related to this verb
lloroso, llorosa   tearful, sorrowful
el lloro   weeping, crying
llorador, lloradora   weeper
lloriquear   to whimper, to whine
llorar con un ojo   to shed crocodile tears

llorar por   to weep (cry) for
llorar por cualquier cosa   to cry about anything
llorar a lágrima viva   to cry one's eyes out
romper a llorar   to burst into tears

Regular **-ar** verb   to fight, to strive, to struggle, to wrestle

The Seven Simple Tenses		The Seven Compound Tenses	
Singular	Plural	Singular	Plural
1 presente de indicativo		8 perfecto de indicativo	
lucho	luchamos	he luchado	hemos luchado
luchas	lucháis	has luchado	habéis luchado
lucha	luchan	ha luchado	han luchado
2 imperfecto de indicativo		9 pluscuamperfecto de indicativo	
luchaba	luchábamos	había luchado	habíamos luchado
luchabas	luchabais	habías luchado	habíais luchado
luchaba	luchaban	había luchado	habían luchado
3 pretérito		10 pretérito anterior	
luché	luchamos	hube luchado	hubimos luchado
luchaste	luchasteis	hubiste luchado	hubisteis luchado
luchó	lucharon	hubo luchado	hubieron luchado
4 futuro		11 futuro perfecto	
lucharé	lucharemos	habré luchado	habremos luchado
lucharás	lucharéis	habrás luchado	habréis luchado
luchará	lucharán	habrá luchado	habrán luchado
5 potencial simple		12 potencial compuesto	
lucharía	lucharíamos	habría luchado	habríamos luchado
lucharías	lucharíais	habrías luchado	habríais luchado
lucharía	lucharían	habría luchado	habrían luchado
6 presente de subjuntivo		13 perfecto de subjuntivo	
luche	luchemos	haya luchado	hayamos luchado
luches	luchéis	hayas luchado	hayáis luchado
luche	luchen	haya luchado	hayan luchado
7 imperfecto de subjuntivo		14 pluscuamperfecto de subjuntivo	
luchara	lucháramos	hubiera luchado	hubiéramos luchado
lucharas	lucharais	hubieras luchado	hubierais luchado
luchara	lucharan	hubiera luchado	hubieran luchado
OR		OR	
luchase	luchásemos	hubiese luchado	hubiésemos luchado
luchases	luchaseis	hubieses luchado	hubieseis luchado
luchase	luchasen	hubiese luchado	hubiesen luchado

	imperativo	
—	luchemos
lucha; no luches	luchad; no luchéis
luche	luchen

Words and expressions related to this verb

luchar por + inf.   to struggle + inf.
un luchador, una luchadora   wrestler, fighter
la lucha   battle, combat, fight, struggle, quarrel

la lucha cuerpo a cuerpo   hand-to-hand fighting
luchar por la libertad   to struggle for freedom

Get acquainted with what preposition goes with what verb on pages 669–677.

The subject pronouns are found on page 93.

maldecir (302)   Gerundio **maldiciendo**
Part. pas. **maldecido** (**maldito,** *when used as an adj. with* **estar**)

to curse   Irregular verb

The Seven Simple Tenses		The Seven Compound Tenses	
Singular	Plural	Singular	Plural
1 presente de indicativo		**8 perfecto de indicativo**	
maldigo	maldecimos	he maldecido	hemos maldecido
maldices	maldecís	has maldecido	habéis maldecido
maldice	maldicen	ha maldecido	han maldecido
2 imperfecto de indicativo		**9 pluscuamperfecto de indicativo**	
maldecía	maldecíamos	había maldecido	habíamos maldecido
maldecías	maldecíais	habías maldecido	habíais maldecido
maldecía	maldecían	había maldecido	habían maldecido
3 pretérito		**10 pretérito anterior**	
maldije	maldijimos	hube maldecido	hubimos maldecido
maldijiste	maldijisteis	hubiste maldecido	hubisteis maldecido
maldijo	maldijeron	hubo maldecido	hubieron maldecido
4 futuro		**11 futuro perfecto**	
maldeciré	maldeciremos	habré maldecido	habremos maldecido
maldecirás	maleciréis	habrás maldecido	habréis maldecido
maldecirá	maldecirán	habrá maldecido	habrán maldecido
5 potencial simple		**12 potencial compuesto**	
maldeciría	maldeciríamos	habría maldecido	habríamos maldecido
maldecirías	maldeciríais	habrías maldecido	habríais maldecido
maldeciría	maldecirían	habría maldecido	habrían maldecido
6 presente de subjuntivo		**13 perfecto de subjuntivo**	
maldiga	maldigamos	haya maldecido	hayamos maldecido
maldigas	maldigáis	hayas maldecido	hayáis maldecido
maldiga	maldigan	haya maldecido	hayan maldecido
7 imperfecto de subjuntivo		**14 pluscuamperfecto de subjuntivo**	
maldijera	maldijéramos	hubiera maldecido	hubiéramos maldecido
maldijeras	maldijerais	hubieras maldecido	hubierais maldecido
maldijera	maldijeran	hubiera maldecido	hubieran maldecido
OR		OR	
maldijese	maldijésemos	hubiese maldecido	hubiésemos maldecido
maldijeses	maldijeseis	hubieses maldecido	hubieseis maldecido
maldijese	maldijesen	hubiese maldecido	hubiesen maldecido

imperativo	
—	maldigamos
maldice; no maldigas	maldecid; no maldigáis
maldiga	maldigan

Words and expressions related to this verb
maldecir de to speak ill of
una maldición curse, malediction
maldiciente slanderous
maldito, maldita damned

un, una maldiciente slanderer
maldecido, maldecida wicked
maldispuesto, maldispuesta ill-disposed
los malditos the damned

See also **bendecir.** See also note on the bottom of verb 368.

The Seven Simple Tenses		The Seven Compound Tenses	
Singular	Plural	Singular	Plural
1 presente de indicativo		8 perfecto de indicativo	
manejo	**manejamos**	**he manejado**	**hemos manejado**
manejas	**manejáis**	**has manejado**	**habéis manejado**
maneja	**manejan**	**ha manejado**	**han manejado**
2 imperfecto de indicativo		9 pluscuamperfecto de indicativo	
manejaba	**manejábamos**	**había manejado**	**habíamos manejado**
manejabas	**manejabais**	**habías manejado**	**habíais manejado**
manejaba	**manejaban**	**había manejado**	**habían manejado**
3 pretérito		10 pretérito anterior	
manejé	**manejamos**	**hube manejado**	**hubimos manejado**
manejaste	**manejasteis**	**hubiste manejado**	**hubisteis manejado**
manejó	**manejaron**	**hubo manejado**	**hubieron manejado**
4 futuro		11 futuro perfecto	
manejaré	**manejaremos**	**habré manejado**	**habremos manejado**
manejarás	**manejaréis**	**habrás manejado**	**habréis manejado**
manejará	**manejarán**	**habrá manejado**	**habrán manejado**
5 potencial simple		12 potencial compuesto	
manejaría	**manejaríamos**	**habría manejado**	**habríamos manejado**
manejarías	**manejaríais**	**habrías manejado**	**habríais manejado**
manejaría	**manejarían**	**habría manejado**	**habrían manejado**
6 presente de subjuntivo		13 perfecto de subjuntivo	
maneje	**manejemos**	**haya manejado**	**hayamos manejado**
manejes	**manejéis**	**hayas manejado**	**hayáis manejado**
maneje	**manejen**	**haya manejado**	**hayan manejado**
7 imperfecto de subjuntivo		14 pluscuamperfecto de subjuntivo	
manejara	**manejáramos**	**hubiera manejado**	**hubiéramos manejado**
manejaras	**manejarais**	**hubieras manejado**	**hubierais manejado**
manejara	**manejaran**	**hubiera manejado**	**hubieran manejado**
OR		OR	
manejase	**manejásemos**	**hubiese manejado**	**hubiésemos manejado**
manejases	**manejaseis**	**hubieses manejado**	**hubieseis manejado**
manejase	**manejasen**	**hubiese manejado**	**hubiesen manejado**

imperativo	
—	**manejemos**
maneja; no manejes	**manejad; no manejéis**
maneje	**manejen**

Words and expressions related to this verb

el manejo management; driving	**manejable** manageable
el manejo doméstico housekeeping	**la manejabilidad** manageability
el manejo a distancia remote control	**la mano** hand

If you want an explanation of meanings and uses of Spanish
and English verb tenses and moods, see pages 13–32.

The subject pronouns are found on page 93.

mantener (304)　　Gerundio **manteniendo**　　Part. pas. **mantenido**

to maintain, to keep up, to support, to provide for　　Irregular verb

The Seven Simple Tenses		The Seven Compound Tenses	
Singular	Plural	Singular	Plural
1　presente de indicativo		8　perfecto de indicativo	
mantengo	mantenemos	he mantenido	hemos mantenido
mantienes	mantenéis	has mantenido	habéis mantenido
mantiene	mantienen	ha mantenido	han mantenido
2　imperfecto de indicativo		9　pluscuamperfecto de indicativo	
mantenía	manteníamos	había mantenido	habíamos mantenido
mantenías	manteníais	habías mantenido	habíais mantenido
mantenía	mantenían	había mantenido	habían mantenido
3　pretérito		10　pretérito anterior	
mantuve	mantuvimos	hube mantenido	hubimos mantenido
mantuviste	mantuvisteis	hubiste mantenido	hubisteis mantenido
mantuvo	mantuvieron	hubo mantenido	hubieron mantenido
4　futuro		11　futuro perfecto	
mantendré	mantendremos	habré mantenido	habremos mantenido
mantendrás	mantendréis	habrás mantenido	habréis mantenido
mantendrá	mantendrán	habrá mantenido	habrán mantenido
5　potencial simple		12　potencial compuesto	
mantendría	mantendríamos	habría mantenido	habríamos mantenido
mantendrías	mantendríais	habrías mantenido	habríais mantenido
mantendría	mantendrían	habría mantenido	habrían mantenido
6　presente de subjuntivo		13　perfecto de subjuntivo	
mentenga	mantengamos	haya mantenido	hayamos mantenido
mantengas	mantengáis	hayas mantenido	hayáis mantenido
mantenga	mantengan	haya mantenido	hayan mantenido
7　imperfecto de subjuntivo		14　pluscuamperfecto de subjuntivo	
mantuviera	mantuviéramos	hubiera mantenido	hubiéramos mantenido
mantuvieras	mantuvierais	hubieras mantenido	hubierais mantenido
mantuviera	mantuvieran	hubiera mantenido	hubieran mantenido
OR		OR	
mantuviese	mantuviésemos	hubiese mantenido	hubiésemos mantenido
mantuvieses	mantuvieseis	hubieses mantenido	hubieseis mantenido
mantuviese	mantuviesen	hubiese mantenido	hubiesen mantenido

imperativo	
—	mantengamos
manten; no mantengas	mantened; no mantengáis
mantenga	mantengan

Words and expressions related to this verb
mantener el orden　to keep (maintain) order
el mantenimiento, la mantenencia
　maintenance, support
mantener la palabra　to keep one's word
mantenerse　to support oneself

mantener su opinión　to maintain one's
　opinion
mantener a distancia　to keep at a distance

Regular **-ar** verb endings with spelling change: **c** becomes **qu** before **e**   to mark, to note, to observe

The Seven Simple Tenses		The Seven Compound Tenses	
Singular	Plural	Singular	Plural
1 presente de indicativo		**8 perfecto de indicativo**	
marco	marcamos	he marcado	hemos marcado
marcas	marcáis	has marcado	habéis marcado
marca	marcan	ha marcado	han marcado
2 imperfecto de indicativo		**9 pluscuamperfecto de indicativo**	
marcaba	marcábamos	había marcado	habíamos marcado
marcabas	marcabais	habías marcado	habíais marcado
marcaba	marcaban	había marcado	habían marcado
3 pretérito		**10 pretérito anterior**	
marqué	marcamos	hube marcado	hubimos marcado
marcaste	marcasteis	hubiste marcado	hubisteis marcado
marcó	marcaron	hubo marcado	hubieron marcado
4 futuro		**11 futuro perfecto**	
marcaré	marcaremos	habré marcado	habremos marcado
marcarás	marcaréis	habrás marcado	habréis marcado
marcará	marcarán	habrá marcado	habrán marcado
5 potencial simple		**12 potencial compuesto**	
marcaría	marcaríamos	habría marcado	habríamos marcado
marcarías	marcaríais	habrías marcado	habríais marcado
marcaría	marcarían	habría marcado	habrían marcado
6 presente de subjuntivo		**13 perfecto de subjuntivo**	
marque	marquemos	haya marcado	hayamos marcado
marques	marquéis	hayas marcado	hayáis marcado
marque	marquen	haya marcado	hayan marcado
7 imperfecto de subjuntivo		**14 pluscuamperfecto de subjuntivo**	
marcara	marcáramos	hubiera marcado	hubiéramos marcado
marcaras	marcarais	hubieras marcado	hubierais marcado
marcara	marcaran	hubiera marcado	hubieran marcado
OR		OR	
marcase	marcásemos	hubiese marcado	hubiésemos marcado
marcases	marcaseis	hubieses marcado	hubieseis marcado
marcase	marcasen	hubiese marcado	hubiesen marcado

imperativo	
—	marquemos
marca; no marques	marcad; no marquéis
marque	marquen

Words and expressions related to this verb

marcar un número de teléfono   to dial a telephone number
marcado, marcada   marked, remarkable
marcadamente   markedly, notably

marcar una canasta   to score a basket (basketball)
marcar las cartas   to mark the cards
marcar un gol   to score a goal

Review the principal parts of important Spanish verbs on pages 9–10.

The subject pronouns are found on page 93.

marchar (306)   Gerundio **marchando**   Part. pas. **marchado**

to walk, to march, to function (machine), to run (machine)   Regular **-ar** verb

The Seven Simple Tenses		The Seven Compound Tenses	
Singular	Plural	Singular	Plural
1 presente de indicativo		8 perfecto de indicativo	
marcho	marchamos	he marchado	hemos marchado
marchas	marcháis	has marchado	habéis marchado
marcha	marchan	ha marchado	han marchado
2 imperfecto de indicativo		9 pluscuamperfecto de indicativo	
marchaba	marchábamos	había marchado	habíamos marchado
marchabas	marchabais	habías marchado	habíais marchado
marchaba	marchaban	había marchado	habían marchado
3 pretérito		10 pretérito anterior	
marché	marchamos	hube marchado	hubimos marchado
marchaste	marchasteis	hubiste marchado	hubisteis marchado
marchó	marcharon	hubo marchado	hubieron marchado
4 futuro		11 futuro perfecto	
marcharé	marcharemos	habré marchado	habremos marchado
marcharás	marcharéis	habrás marchado	habréis marchado
marchará	marcharán	habrá marchado	habrán marchado
5 potencial simple		12 potencial compuesto	
marcharía	marcharíamos	habría marchado	habríamos marchado
marcharías	marcharíais	habrías marchado	habríais marchado
marcharía	marcharían	habría marchado	habrían marchado
6 presente de subjuntivo		13 perfecto de subjuntivo	
marche	marchemos	haya marchado	hayamos marchado
marches	marchéis	hayas marchado	hayáis marchado
marche	marchen	haya marchado	hayan marchado
7 imperfecto de subjuntivo		14 pluscuamperfecto de subjuntivo	
marchara	marcháramos	hubiera marchado	hubiéramos marchado
marcharas	marcharais	hubieras marchado	hubierais marchado
marchara	marcharan	hubiera marchado	hubieran marchado
OR		OR	
marchase	marchásemos	hubiese marchado	hubiésemos marchado
marchases	marchaseis	hubieses marchado	hubieseis marchado
marchase	marchasen	hubiese marchado	hubiesen marchado

	imperativo	
—		marchemos
marcha; no marches		marchad; no marchéis
marche		marchen

Words and expressions related to this verb
la marcha   march
a largas marchas   speedily, with speed
¡En marcha!   Forward march!
poner en marcha   to put in motion, to start
Esto no marcha   This won't work; This will not do.

Todo marcha bien.   Everything is going okay.
marcharse   to go away, to leave
marcharse por las buenas   to leave for good, never to return

432

Reflexive regular **-ar** verb   to go away, to leave

The Seven Simple Tenses		The Seven Compound Tenses	
Singular	Plural	Singular	Plural
1 presente de indicativo		8 perfecto de indicativo	
me marcho	nos marchamos	me he marchado	nos hemos marchado
te marchas	os marcháis	te has marchado	os habéis marchado
se marcha	se marchan	se ha marchado	se han marchado
2 imperfecto de indicativo		9 pluscuamperfecto de indicativo	
me marchaba	nos marchábamos	me había marchado	nos habíamos marchado
te marchabas	os marchabais	te habías marchado	os habíais marchado
se marchaba	se marchaban	se había marchado	se habían marchado
3 pretérito		10 pretérito anterior	
me marché	nos marchamos	me hube marchado	nos hubimos marchado
te marchaste	os marchasteis	te hubiste marchado	os hubisteis marchado
se marchó	se marcharon	se hubo marchado	se hubieron marchado
4 futuro		11 futuro perfecto	
me marcharé	nos marcharemos	me habré marchado	nos habremos marchado
te marcharás	os marcharéis	te habrás marchado	os habréis marchado
se marchará	se marcharán	se habrá marchado	se habrán marchado
5 potencial simple		12 potencial compuesto	
me marcharía	nos marcharíamos	me habría marchado	nos habríamos marchado
te marcharías	os marcharíais	te habrías marchado	os habríais marchado
se marcharía	se marcharían	se habría marchado	se habrían marchado
6 presente de subjuntivo		13 perfecto de subjuntivo	
me marche	nos marchemos	me haya marchado	nos hayamos marchado
te marches	os marchéis	te hayas marchado	os hayáis marchado
se marche	se marchen	se haya marchado	se hayan marchado
7 imperfecto de subjuntivo		14 pluscuamperfecto de subjuntivo	
me marchara	nos marcháramos	me hubiera marchado	nos hubiéramos marchado
te marcharas	os marcharais	te hubieras marchado	os hubierais marchado
se marchara	se marcharan	se hubiera marchado	se hubieran marchado
OR		OR	
me marchase	nos marchásemos	me hubiese marchado	nos hubiésemos marchado
te marchases	os marchaseis	te hubieses marchado	os hubieseis marchado
se marchase	se marchasen	se hubiese marchado	se hubiesen marchado

imperativo	
—	marchémonos
márchate; no te marches	marchaos; no os marchéis
márchese	márchense

For words and expressions related to this verb, see **marchar** which is related to it.

Can't find the verb you're looking for?
Check the back pages of this book for a list of over 2,100 additional verbs!

The subject pronouns are found on page 93.

The Seven Simple Tenses		The Seven Compound Tenses	
Singular	Plural	Singular	Plural
1 presente de indicativo		**8 perfecto de indicativo**	
mato	matamos	he matado	hemos matado
matas	matáis	has matado	habéis matado
mata	matan	ha matado	han matado
2 imperfecto de indicativo		**9 pluscuamperfecto de indicativo**	
mataba	matábamos	había matado	habíamos matado
matabas	matabais	habías matado	habíais matado
mataba	mataban	había matado	habían matado
3 pretérito		**10 pretérito anterior**	
maté	matamos	hube matado	hubimos matado
mataste	matasteis	hubiste matado	hubisteis matado
mató	mataron	hubo matado	hubieron matado
4 futuro		**11 futuro perfecto**	
mataré	mataremos	habré matado	habremos matado
matarás	mataréis	habrás matado	habréis matado
matará	matarán	habrá matado	habrán matado
5 potencial simple		**12 potencial compuesto**	
mataría	mataríamos	habría matado	habríamos matado
matarías	mataríais	habrías matado	habríais matado
mataría	matarían	habría matado	habrían matado
6 presente de subjuntivo		**13 perfecto de subjuntivo**	
mate	matemos	haya matado	hayamos matado
mates	matéis	hayas matado	hayáis matado
mate	maten	haya matado	hayan matado
7 imperfecto de subjuntivo		**14 pluscuamperfecto de subjuntivo**	
matara	matáramos	hubiera matado	hubiéramos matado
mataras	matarais	hubieras matado	hubierais matado
matara	mataran	hubiera matado	hubieran matado
OR		OR	
matase	matásemos	hubiese matado	hubiésemos matado
matases	mataseis	hubieses matado	hubieseis matado
matase	matasen	hubiese matado	hubiesen matado

imperativo

—	matemos
mata; no mates	matad; no matéis
mate	maten

Words and expressions related to this verb
el mate checkmate (chess)
dar jaque mate to checkmate (chess)
dar mate a to checkmate (chess)
matador, matadora killer; **el matador** bullfighter (kills the bull)

matar el tiempo to kill time
estar a matar con alguien to be angry at someone
matar a preguntas to bombard with questions

Gerundio **midiendo**   Part. pas. **medido**   **medir (309)**

Regular **-ir** verb endings with stem change: to measure, to weigh,
Tenses 1, 3, 6, 7; Imperative, Gerundio   to scan (verses)

The Seven Simple Tenses | The Seven Compound Tenses

Singular	Plural	Singular	Plural
1 presente de indicativo		8 perfecto de indicativo	
mido	medimos	he medido	hemos medido
mides	medís	has medido	habéis medido
mide	miden	ha medido	han medido
2 imperfecto de indicativo		9 pluscuamperfecto de indicativo	
medía	medíamos	había medido	habíamos medido
medías	medíais	habías medido	habíais medido
medía	medían	había medido	habían medido
3 pretérito		10 pretérito anterior	
medí	medimos	hube medido	hubimos medido
mediste	medisteis	hubiste medido	hubisteis medido
midió	midieron	hubo medido	hubieron medido
4 futuro		11 futuro perfecto	
mediré	mediremos	habré medido	habremos medido
medirás	mediréis	habrás medido	habréis medido
medirá	medirán	habrá medido	habrán medido
5 potencial simple		12 potencial compuesto	
mediría	mediríamos	habría medido	habríamos medido
medirías	mediríais	habrías medido	habríais medido
mediría	medirían	habría medido	habrían medido
6 presente de subjuntivo		13 perfecto de subjuntivo	
mida	midamos	haya medido	hayamos medido
midas	midáis	hayas medido	hayáis medido
mida	midan	haya medido	hayan medido
7 imperfecto de subjuntivo		14 pluscuamperfecto de subjuntivo	
midiera	midiéramos	hubiera medido	hubiéramos medido
midieras	midierais	hubieras medido	hubierais medido
midiera	midieran	hubiera medido	hubieran medido
OR		OR	
midiese	midiésemos	hubiese medido	hubiésemos medido
midieses	midieseis	hubieses medido	hubieseis medido
midiese	midiesen	hubiese medido	hubiesen medido

imperativo

—	midamos
mide; no midas	medid; no midáis
mida	midan

Common idiomatic expressions using this verb
medir las calles   to walk the streets out of a job   **medir sus pasos**   to watch one's step
medir el suelo   to fall flat on the ground   **medir las palabras**   to weigh one's words
la medida   measurement   **medirse con alguien**   to measure oneself
pesos y medidas   weights and measurements   against someone

Don't forget to study the section on defective and impersonal verbs. It's right after this main list.

The subject pronouns are found on page 93.   **435**

Gerundio **mejorando** Part. pas. **mejorado**

to improve

Regular **-ar** verb

The Seven Simple Tenses		The Seven Compound Tenses	
Singular	Plural	Singular	Plural
1 presente de indicativo		8 perfecto de indicativo	
mejoro	mejoramos	he mejorado	hemos mejorado
mejoras	mejoráis	has mejorado	habéis mejorado
mejora	mejoran	ha mejorado	han mejorado
2 imperfecto de indicativo		9 pluscuamperfecto de indicativo	
mejoraba	mejorábamos	había mejorado	habíamos mejorado
mejorabas	mejorabais	habías mejorado	habíais mejorado
mejoraba	mejoraban	había mejorado	habían mejorado
3 pretérito		10 pretérito anterior	
mejoré	mejoramos	hube mejorado	hubimos mejorado
mejoraste	mejorasteis	hubiste mejorado	hubisteis mejorado
mejoró	mejoraron	hubo mejorado	hubieron mejorado
4 futuro		11 futuro perfecto	
mejoraré	mejoraremos	habré mejorado	habremos mejorado
mejorarás	mejoraréis	habrás mejorado	habréis mejorado
mejorará	mejorarán	habrá mejorado	habrán mejorado
5 potencial simple		12 potencial compuesto	
mejoraría	mejoraríamos	habría mejorado	habríamos mejorado
mejorarías	mejoraríais	habrías mejorado	habríais mejorado
mejoraría	mejorarían	habría mejorado	habrían mejorado
6 presente de subjuntivo		13 perfecto de subjuntivo	
mejore	mejoremos	haya mejorado	hayamos mejorado
mejores	mejoréis	hayas mejorado	hayáis mejorado
mejore	mejoren	haya mejorado	hayan mejorado
7 imperfecto de subjuntivo		14 pluscuamperfecto de subjuntivo	
mejorara	mejoráramos	hubiera mejorado	hubiéramos mejorado
mejoraras	mejorarais	hubieras mejorado	hubierais mejorado
mejorara	mejoraran	hubiera mejorado	hubieran mejorado
OR		OR	
mejorase	mejorásemos	hubiese mejorado	hubiésemos mejorado
mejorases	mejoraseis	hubieses mejorado	hubieseis mejorado
mejorase	mejorasen	hubiese mejorado	hubiesen mejorado

imperativo	
—	mejoremos
mejora; no mejores	mejorad; no mejoréis
mejore	mejoren

Words and expressions related to this verb

la **mejora, la mejoría** improvement, betterment

mejor better, best

tanto mejor so much the better

desmejorar to spoil, make worse

mejorarse to get well, recover, improve oneself

mejor dicho rather

mejor que mejor even better

lo mejor the best

desmejorarse to decay, decline, get worse; lose one's health

The Seven Simple Tenses		The Seven Compound Tenses	
Singular	Plural	Singular	Plural
1 presente de indicativo		8 perfecto de indicativo	
menciono	mencionamos	he mencionado	hemos mencionado
mencionas	mencionáis	has mencionado	habéis mencionado
menciona	mencionan	ha mencionado	han mencionado
2 imperfecto de indicativo		9 pluscuamperfecto de indicativo	
mencionaba	mencionábamos	había mencionado	habíamos mencionado
mencionabas	mencionabais	habías mencionado	habíais mencionado
mencionaba	mencionaban	había mencionado	habían mencionado
3 pretérito		10 pretérito anterior	
mencioné	mencionamos	hube mencionado	hubimos mencionado
mencionaste	mencionasteis	hubiste mencionado	hubisteis mencionado
mencionó	mencionaron	hubo mencionado	hubieron mencionado
4 futuro		11 futuro perfecto	
mencionaré	mencionaremos	habré mencionado	habremos mencionado
mencionarás	mencionaréis	habrás mencionado	habréis mencionado
mencionará	mencionarán	habrá mencionado	habrán mencionado
5 potencial simple		12 potencial compuesto	
mencionaría	mencionaríamos	habría mencionado	habríamos mencionado
mencionarías	mencionaríais	habrías mencionado	habríais mencionado
mencionaría	mencionarían	habría mencionado	habrían mencionado
6 presente de subjuntivo		13 perfecto de subjuntivo	
mencione	mencionemos	haya mencionado	hayamos mencionado
menciones	mencionéis	hayas mencionado	hayáis mencionado
mencione	mencionen	haya mencionado	hayan mencionado
7 imperfecto de subjuntivo		14 pluscuamperfecto de subjuntivo	
mencionara	mencionáramos	hubiera mencionado	hubiéramos mencionado
mencionaras	mencionarais	hubieras mencionado	hubierais mencionado
mencionara	mencionaran	hubiera mencionado	hubieran mencionado
OR		OR	
mencionase	mencionásemos	hubiese mencionado	hubiésemos mencionado
mencionases	mencionaseis	hubieses mencionado	hubieseis mencionado
mencionase	mencionasen	hubiese mencionado	hubiesen mencionado

imperativo	
—	mencionemos
menciona; no menciones	mencionad; no mencionéis
mencione	mencionen

Words and expressions related to this verb
la mención   mention   **en mención**   under discussion
mención honorífica   honorable mention   **hacer mención de**   to make mention of
digno de mención   worthy of mention   **sin mencionar a**   not to mention

Review the principal parts of important Spanish verbs on pages 9–10.

The subject pronouns are found on page 93.

mentir (312)

Gerundio **mintiendo**   Part. pas. **mentido**

to lie, to tell a lie

Regular **-ir** verb endings with stem change:
Tenses 1, 3, 6, 7, Imperative, Gerundio

The Seven Simple Tenses		The Seven Compound Tenses	
Singular	Plural	Singular	Plural
1 presente de indicativo		8 perfecto de indicativo	
miento	mentimos	he mentido	hemos mentido
mientes	mentís	has mentido	habéis mentido
miente	mienten	ha mentido	han mentido
2 imperfecto de indicativo		9 pluscuamperfecto de indicativo	
mentía	mentíamos	había mentido	habíamos mentido
mentías	mentíais	habías mentido	habíais mentido
mentía	mentían	había mentido	habían mentido
3 pretérito		10 pretérito anterior	
mentí	mentimos	hube mentido	hubimos mentido
mentiste	mentisteis	hubiste mentido	hubisteis mentido
mintió	mintieron	hubo mentido	hubieron mentido
4 futuro		11 futuro perfecto	
mentiré	mentiremos	habré mentido	habremos mentido
mentirás	mentiréis	habrás mentido	habréis mentido
mentirá	mentirán	habrá mentido	habrán mentido
5 potencial simple		12 potencial compuesto	
mentiría	mentiríamos	habría mentido	habríamos mentido
mentirías	mentiríais	habrías mentido	habríais mentido
mentiría	mentirían	habría mentido	habrían mentido
6 presente de subjuntivo		13 perfecto de subjuntivo	
mienta	mintamos	haya mentido	hayamos mentido
mientas	mintáis	hayas mentido	hayáis mentido
mienta	mientan	haya mentido	hayan mentido
7 imperfecto de subjuntivo		14 pluscuamperfecto de subjuntivo	
mintiera	mintiéramos	hubiera mentido	hubiéramos mentido
mintieras	mintierais	hubieras mentido	hubierais mentido
mintiera	mintieran	hubiera mentido	hubieran mentido
OR		OR	
mintiese	mintiésemos	hubiese mentido	hubiésemos mentido
mintieses	mintieseis	hubieses mentido	hubieseis mentido
mintiese	mintiesen	hubiese mentido	hubiesen mentido

imperativo	
—	mintamos
miente; no mientas	mentid; no mintáis
mienta	mientan

Words and expressions related to this verb
una mentira a lie
un mentirón a great lie
una mentirilla a fib

mentido, mentida deceptive, false
mentirosamente falsely
¡Parece mentira! I just don't believe it!

Can't recognize an irregular verb form? Check out pages 678–681.

Regular **-er** verb endings with spelling change: **c** becomes **zc** before **a** or **o**   to merit, to deserve

The Seven Simple Tenses		The Seven Compound Tenses	
Singular	Plural	Singular	Plural
1 presente de indicativo		**8 perfecto de indicativo**	
merezco	merecemos	he merecido	hemos merecido
mereces	merecéis	has merecido	habéis merecido
merece	merecen	ha merecido	han merecido
2 imperfecto de indicativo		**9 pluscuamperfecto de indicativo**	
merecía	merecíamos	había merecido	habíamos merecido
merecías	merecíais	habías merecido	habíais merecido
merecía	merecían	había merecido	habían merecido
3 pretérito		**10 pretérito anterior**	
merecí	merecimos	hube merecido	hubimos merecido
mereciste	merecisteis	hubiste merecido	hubisteis merecido
mereció	merecieron	hubo merecido	hubieron merecido
4 futuro		**11 futuro perfecto**	
mereceré	mereceremos	habré merecido	habremos merecido
merecerás	mereceréis	habrás merecido	habréis merecido
merecerá	merecerán	habrá merecido	habrán merecido
5 potencial simple		**12 potencial compuesto**	
merecería	mereceríamos	habría merecido	habríamos merecido
merecerías	mereceríais	habrías merecido	habríais merecido
merecería	merecerían	habría merecido	habrían merecido
6 presente de subjuntivo		**13 perfecto de subjuntivo**	
merezca	merezcamos	haya merecido	hayamos merecido
merezcas	merezcáis	hayas merecido	hayáis merecido
merezca	merezcan	haya merecido	hayan merecido
7 imperfecto de subjuntivo		**14 pluscuamperfecto de subjuntivo**	
mereciera	mereciéramos	hubiera merecido	hubiéramos merecido
merecieras	merecierais	hubieras merecido	hubierais merecido
mereciera	merecieran	hubiera merecido	hubieran merecido
OR		OR	
mereciese	mereciésemos	hubiese merecido	hubiésemos merecido
merecieses	merecieseis	hubieses merecido	hubieseis merecido
mereciese	mereciesen	hubiese merecido	hubiesen merecido

imperativo	
—	merezcamos
merece; no merezcas	mereced; no merezcáis
merezca	merezcan

Words and expressions related to this verb

merecer la pena   to be worth the trouble
el merecimiento, el mérito   merit
meritísimo, meritísima   most deserving
merced a ...   thanks to ...
merecidamente   deservedly

por sus propios méritos   on one's own merits
hacer mérito de   to make mention of
vuestra merced   your honor, your grace; sir
merecer una bofetada   to deserve a slap (in the face)

The subject pronouns are found on page 93.

439

to look, to look at, to watch   Regular **-ar** verb

The Seven Simple Tenses		The Seven Compound Tenses	
Singular	Plural	Singular	Plural
1 presente de indicativo		8 perfecto de indicativo	
miro	miramos	he mirado	hemos mirado
miras	miráis	has mirado	habéis mirado
mira	miran	ha mirado	han mirado
2 imperfecto de indicativo		9 pluscuamperfecto de indicativo	
miraba	mirábamos	había mirado	habíamos mirado
mirabas	mirabais	habías mirado	habíais mirado
miraba	miraban	había mirado	habían mirado
3 pretérito		10 pretérito anterior	
miré	miramos	hube mirado	hubimos mirado
miraste	mirasteis	hubiste mirado	hubisteis mirado
miró	miraron	hubo mirado	hubieron mirado
4 futuro		11 futuro perfecto	
miraré	miraremos	habré mirado	habremos mirado
mirarás	miraréis	habrás mirado	habréis mirado
mirará	mirarán	habrá mirado	habrán mirado
5 potencial simple		12 potencial compuesto	
miraría	miraríamos	habría mirado	habríamos mirado
mirarías	miraríais	habrías mirado	habríais mirado
miraría	mirarían	habría mirado	habrían mirado
6 presente de subjuntivo		13 perfecto de subjuntivo	
mire	miremos	haya mirado	hayamos mirado
mires	miréis	hayas mirado	hayáis mirado
mire	miren	haya mirado	hayan mirado
7 imperfecto de subjuntivo		14 pluscuamperfecto de subjuntivo	
mirara	miráramos	hubiera mirado	hubiéramos mirado
miraras	mirarais	hubieras mirado	hubierais mirado
mirara	miraran	hubiera mirado	hubieran mirado
OR		OR	
mirase	mirásemos	hubiese mirado	hubiésemos mirado
mirases	miraseis	hubieses mirado	hubieseis mirado
mirase	mirasen	hubiese mirado	hubiesen mirado

imperativo	
—	miremos
mira; no mires	mirad; no miréis
mire	miren

AN ESSENTIAL
55 VERB

Mirar and mirarse are essential verbs for beginning students of Spanish. They are used in many idiomatic expressions and everyday situations. As you study the following sentences and expressions, pay attention to the differences in use between mirar and the reflexive verb mirarse.

Sentences using mirar and mirarse

¡Mira!
Look! Look out! See here! Listen!

Cuando me afeito, me miro en el espejo.
When I shave, I look (at myself) in the mirror.

Proverb

Antes que te cases, mira lo que haces.
Look before you leap. (Before you get married, look at what you are doing.)

Words and expressions related to these verbs

una mirada **a look**

echar una mirada a **to take a look at**

mirar alrededor **to look around**

mirar la televisión **to watch television**

mirar por **to look after**

mirar a **to face, to look out on**

mirar por encima del hombro **to look down one's nose at** (el hombro = shoulder)

mirarse las uñas **to twiddle one's thumbs, to be idle** (las uñas = fingernails)

mirarse unos a otros **to look at each other in awe**

mirarse al espejo, mirarse en el espejo **to look at oneself in the mirror**

M

Can't find the verb you're looking for?
Check the back pages of this book for a list of over 2,100 additional verbs!

The subject pronouns are found on page 93.

to look at oneself, to look at each other   Reflexive regular **-ar** verb
(**uno a otro; unos a otros**)

The Seven Simple Tenses		The Seven Compound Tenses	
Singular	Plural	Singular	Plural
1 presente de indicativo		8 perfecto de indicativo	
me miro	nos miramos	me he mirado	nos hemos mirado
te miras	os miráis	te has mirado	os habéis mirado
se mira	se miran	se ha mirado	se han mirado
2 imperfecto de indicativo		9 pluscuamperfecto de indicativo	
me miraba	nos mirábamos	me había mirado	nos habíamos mirado
te mirabas	os mirabais	te habías mirado	os habíais mirado
se miraba	se miraban	se había mirado	se habían mirado
3 pretérito		10 pretérito anterior	
me miré	nos miramos	me hube mirado	nos hubimos mirado
te miraste	os mirasteis	te hubiste mirado	os hubisteis mirado
se miró	se miraron	se hubo mirado	se hubieron mirado
4 futuro		11 futuro perfecto	
me miraré	nos miraremos	me habré mirado	nos habremos mirado
te mirarás	os miraréis	te habrás mirado	os habréis mirado
se mirará	se mirarán	se habrá mirado	se habrán mirado
5 potencial simple		12 potencial compuesto	
me miraría	nos miraríamos	me habría mirado	nos habríamos mirado
te mirarías	os miraríais	te habrías mirado	os habríais mirado
se miraría	se mirarían	se habría mirado	se habrían mirado
6 presente de subjuntivo		13 perfecto de subjuntivo	
me mire	nos miremos	me haya mirado	nos hayamos mirado
te mires	os miréis	te hayas mirado	os hayáis mirado
se mire	se miren	se haya mirado	se hayan mirado
7 imperfecto de subjuntivo		14 pluscuamperfecto de subjuntivo	
me mirara	nos miráramos	me hubiera mirado	nos hubiéramos mirado
te miraras	os mirarais	te hubieras mirado	os hubierais mirado
se mirara	se miraran	se hubiera mirado	se hubieran mirado
OR		OR	
me mirase	nos mirásemos	me hubiese mirado	nos hubiésemos mirado
te mirases	os miraseis	te hubieses mirado	os hubieseis mirado
se mirase	se mirasen	se hubiese mirado	se hubiesen mirado

imperativo

—	mirémonos
mírate; no te mires	miraos; no os miréis
mírese	mírense

Reflexive regular **-ar** verb   to get wet, to wet oneself

The Seven Simple Tenses		The Seven Compound Tenses	
Singular	Plural	Singular	Plural
1 presente de indicativo		8 perfecto de indicativo	
me mojo	**nos mojamos**	**me he mojado**	**nos hemos mojado**
te mojas	**os mojáis**	**te has mojado**	**os habéis mojado**
se moja	**se mojan**	**se ha mojado**	**se han mojado**
2 imperfecto de indicativo		9 pluscuamperfecto de indicativo	
me mojaba	**nos mojábamos**	**me había mojado**	**nos habíamos mojado**
te mojabas	**os mojabais**	**te habías mojado**	**os habíais mojado**
se mojaba	**se mojaban**	**se había mojado**	**se habían mojado**
3 pretérito		10 pretérito anterior	
me mojé	**nos mojamos**	**me hube mojado**	**nos hubimos mojado**
te mojaste	**os mojasteis**	**te hubiste mojado**	**os hubisteis mojado**
se mojó	**se mojaron**	**se hubo mojado**	**se hubieron mojado**
4 futuro		11 futuro perfecto	
me mojaré	**nos mojaremos**	**me habré mojado**	**nos habremos mojado**
te mojarás	**os mojaréis**	**te habrás mojado**	**os habréis mojado**
se mojará	**se mojarán**	**se habrá mojado**	**se habrán mojado**
5 potencial simple		12 potencial compuesto	
me mojaría	**nos mojaríamos**	**me habría mojado**	**nos habríamos mojado**
te mojarías	**os mojaríais**	**te habrías mojado**	**os habríais mojado**
se mojaría	**se mojarían**	**se habría mojado**	**se habrían mojado**
6 presente de subjuntivo		13 perfecto de subjuntivo	
me moje	**nos mojemos**	**me haya mojado**	**nos hayamos mojado**
te mojes	**os mojéis**	**te hayas mojado**	**os hayáis mojado**
se moje	**se mojen**	**se haya mojado**	**se hayan mojado**
7 imperfecto de subjuntivo		14 pluscuamperfecto de subjuntivo	
me mojara	**nos mojáramos**	**me hubiera mojado**	**nos hubiéramos mojado**
te mojaras	**os mojarais**	**te hubieras mojado**	**os hubierais mojado**
se mojara	**se mojaran**	**se hubiera mojado**	**se hubieran mojado**
OR		OR	
me mojase	**nos mojásemos**	**me hubiese mojado**	**nos hubiésemos mojado**
te mojases	**os mojaseis**	**te hubieses mojado**	**os hubieseis mojado**
se mojase	**se mojasen**	**se hubiese mojado**	**se hubiesen mojado**

	imperativo	
—		**mojémonos**
mójate; no te mojes		**mojaos; no os mojéis**
mójese		**mójense**

Words and expressions related to this verb

mojado, mojada   wet, drenched, soaked   **mojarse por la lluvia**   to get wet from the rain
mojar   to wet, to moisten; to interfere, to meddle   **¡Cuidado! Piso mojado.**   Caution! Wet floor.
mojar en   to get mixed up in
remojar   to soak; **remojar el gaznate**   to wet one's whistle (to drink something)

The subject pronouns are found on page 93.
                                                                    443

montar (317)   Gerundio montando   Part. pas. montado

to mount, to go up, to climb, to get on, to wind (a watch)   Regular -ar verb

The Seven Simple Tenses		The Seven Compound Tenses	
Singular	Plural	Singular	Plural
1 presente de indicativo		8 perfecto de indicativo	
monto	montamos	he montado	hemos montado
montas	montáis	has montado	habéis montado
monta	montan	ha montado	han montado
2 imperfecto de indicativo		9 pluscuamperfecto de indicativo	
montaba	montábamos	había montado	habíamos montado
montabas	montabais	habías montado	habíais montado
montaba	montaban	había montado	habían montado
3 pretérito		10 pretérito anterior	
monté	montamos	hube montado	hubimos montado
montaste	montasteis	hubiste montado	hubisteis montado
montó	montaron	hubo montado	hubieron montado
4 futuro		11 futuro perfecto	
montaré	montaremos	habré montado	habremos montado
montarás	montaréis	habrás montado	habréis montado
montará	montarán	habrá montado	habrán montado
5 potencial simple		12 potencial compuesto	
montaría	montaríamos	habría montado	habríamos montado
montarías	montaríais	habrías montado	habríais montado
montaría	montarían	habría montado	habrían montado
6 presente de subjuntivo		13 perfecto de subjuntivo	
monte	montemos	haya montado	hayamos montado
montes	montéis	hayas montado	hayáis montado
monte	monten	haya montado	hayan montado
7 imperfecto de subjuntivo		14 pluscuamperfecto de subjuntivo	
montara	montáramos	hubiera montado	hubiéramos montado
montaras	montarais	hubieras montado	hubierais montado
montara	montaran	hubiera montado	hubieran montado
OR		OR	
montase	montásemos	hubiese montado	hubiésemos montado
montases	montaseis	hubieses montado	hubieseis montado
montase	montasen	hubiese montado	hubiesen montado

imperativo

—	montemos
monta; no montes	montad; no montéis
monte	monten

Words and expressions related to this verb
montar a caballo   to ride horseback
montar en pelo   to ride bareback
montar a horcajadas   to straddle
el monte   mount, mountain
la montaña   mountain

montarse   to mount, to get on top
remontar   to frighten away, to scare away, to
  go back up, to get back on; to go back (in time)
trasmontar   to go over mountains
montar a   to amount to

Regular **-er** verb endings with stem   to bite
change: Tenses 1, 6, Imperative

The Seven Simple Tenses		The Seven Compound Tenses	
Singular	Plural	Singular	Plural
1 presente de indicativo		8 perfecto de indicativo	
muerdo	**mordemos**	**he mordido**	**hemos mordido**
muerdes	**mordéis**	**has mordido**	**habéis mordido**
muerde	**muerden**	**ha mordido**	**han mordido**
2 imperfecto de indicativo		9 pluscuamperfecto de indicativo	
mordía	**mordíamos**	**había mordido**	**habíamos mordido**
mordías	**mordíais**	**habías mordido**	**habíais mordido**
mordía	**mordían**	**había mordido**	**habían mordido**
3 pretérito		10 pretérito anterior	
mordí	**mordimos**	**hube mordido**	**hubimos mordido**
mordiste	**mordisteis**	**hubiste mordido**	**hubisteis mordido**
mordió	**mordieron**	**hubo mordido**	**hubieron mordido**
4 futuro		11 futuro perfecto	
morderé	**morderemos**	**habré mordido**	**habremos mordido**
morderás	**morderéis**	**habrás mordido**	**habréis mordido**
morderá	**morderán**	**habrá mordido**	**habrán mordido**
5 potencial simple		12 potencial compuesto	
mordería	**morderíamos**	**habría mordido**	**habríamos mordido**
morderías	**morderíais**	**habrías mordido**	**habríais mordido**
mordería	**morderían**	**habría mordido**	**habrían mordido**
6 presente de subjuntivo		13 perfecto de subjuntivo	
muerda	**mordamos**	**haya mordido**	**hayamos mordido**
muerdas	**mordáis**	**hayas mordido**	**hayáis mordido**
muerda	**muerdan**	**haya mordido**	**hayan mordido**
7 imperfecto de subjuntivo		14 pluscuamperfecto de subjuntivo	
mordiera	**mordiéramos**	**hubiera mordido**	**hubiéramos mordido**
mordieras	**mordierais**	**hubieras mordido**	**hubierais mordido**
mordiera	**mordieran**	**hubiera mordido**	**hubieran mordido**
OR		OR	
mordiese	**mordiésemos**	**hubiese mordido**	**hubiésemos mordido**
mordieses	**mordieseis**	**hubieses mordido**	**hubieseis mordido**
mordiese	**mordiesen**	**hubiese mordido**	**hubiesen mordido**

M

imperativo

—	**mordamos**
muerde; no muerdas	**morded; no mordáis**
muerda	**muerdan**

Words and expressions related to this verb

Perro que ladra no muerde.   A barking dog
   does not bite.
una mordaza   gag
la mordacidad   mordancy

mordazmente   bitingly
una mordedura   a bite
morderse   to bite oneself
Me mordí el labio.   I bit my lip.

The subject pronouns are found on page 93.

to die

Regular **-ir** verb endings with stem change:
Tenses 1, 3, 6, 7, Imperative, Gerundio, Part. pas.

The Seven Simple Tenses		The Seven Compound Tenses	
Singular	Plural	Singular	Plural
1　presente de indicativo		8　perfecto de indicativo	
muero	morimos	he muerto	hemos muerto
mueres	morís	has muerto	habéis muerto
muere	mueren	ha muerto	han muerto
2　imperfecto de indicativo		9　pluscuamperfecto de indicativo	
moría	moríamos	había muerto	habíamos muerto
morías	moríais	habías muerto	habíais muerto
moría	morían	había muerto	habían muerto
3　pretérito		10　pretérito anterior	
morí	morimos	hube muerto	hubimos muerto
moriste	moristeis	hubiste muerto	hubisteis muerto
murió	murieron	hubo muerto	hubieron muerto
4　futuro		11　futuro perfecto	
moriré	moriremos	habré muerto	habremos muerto
morirás	moriréis	habrás muerto	habréis muerto
morirá	morirán	habrá muerto	habrán muerto
5　potencial simple		12　potencial compuesto	
moriría	moriríamos	habría muerto	habríamos muerto
morirías	moriríais	habrías muerto	habríais muerto
moriría	morirían	habría muerto	habrían muerto
6　presente de subjuntivo		13　perfecto de subjuntivo	
muera	muramos	haya muerto	hayamos muerto
mueras	muráis	hayas muerto	hayáis muerto
muera	mueran	haya muerto	hayan muerto
7　imperfecto de subjuntivo		14　pluscuamperfecto de subjuntivo	
muriera	muriéramos	hubiera muerto	hubiéramos muerto
murieras	murierais	hubieras muerto	hubierais muerto
muriera	murieran	hubiera muerto	hubieran muerto
OR		OR	
muriese	muriésemos	hubiese muerto	hubiésemos muerto
murieses	murieseis	hubieses muerto	hubieseis muerto
muriese	muriesen	hubiese muerto	hubiesen muerto

imperativo	
—	**muramos**
muere; no mueras	**morid; no muráis**
muera	**mueran**

Words and expressions related to this verb

la muerte　death
mortal　fatal, mortal
la mortalidad　mortality
morir de risa　to die laughing
morirse de hambre　to starve to death (to
　die of hunger)

entremorir　to burn out, to flicker
morir de repente　to drop dead
hasta morir　until death
morirse de miedo　to be scared to death
morirse de frío　to freeze to death (to die
　of freezing cold)

Regular **-ar** verb endings with stem change: to show, to point out, to display
Tenses 1, 6, Imperative

The Seven Simple Tenses		The Seven Compound Tenses	
Singular	Plural	Singular	Plural
1 presente de indicativo		8 perfecto de indicativo	
muestro	**mostramos**	**he mostrado**	**hemos mostrado**
muestras	**mostráis**	**has mostrado**	**habéis mostrado**
muestra	**muestran**	**ha mostrado**	**han mostrado**
2 imperfecto de indicativo		9 pluscuamperfecto de indicativo	
mostraba	**mostrábamos**	**había mostrado**	**habíamos mostrado**
mostrabas	**mostrabais**	**habías mostrado**	**habíais mostrado**
mostraba	**mostraban**	**había mostrado**	**habían mostrado**
3 pretérito		10 pretérito anterior	
mostré	**mostramos**	**hube mostrado**	**hubimos mostrado**
mostraste	**mostrasteis**	**hubiste mostrado**	**hubisteis mostrado**
mostró	**mostraron**	**hubo mostrado**	**hubieron mostrado**
4 futuro		11 futuro perfecto	
mostraré	**mostraremos**	**habré mostrado**	**habremos mostrado**
mostrarás	**mostraréis**	**habrás mostrado**	**habréis mostrado**
mostrará	**mostrarán**	**habrá mostrado**	**habrán mostrado**
5 potencial simple		12 potencial compuesto	
mostraría	**mostraríamos**	**habría mostrado**	**habríamos mostrado**
mostrarías	**mostraríais**	**habrías mostrado**	**habríais mostrado**
mostraría	**mostrarían**	**habría mostrado**	**habrían mostrado**
6 presente de subjuntivo		13 perfecto de subjuntivo	
muestre	**mostremos**	**haya mostrado**	**hayamos mostrado**
muestres	**mostréis**	**hayas mostrado**	**hayáis mostrado**
muestre	**muestren**	**haya mostrado**	**hayan mostrado**
7 imperfecto de subjuntivo		14 pluscuamperfecto de subjuntivo	
mostrara	**mostráramos**	**hubiera mostrado**	**hubiéramos mostrado**
mostraras	**mostrarais**	**hubieras mostrado**	**hubierais mostrado**
mostrara	**mostraran**	**hubiera mostrado**	**hubieran mostrado**
OR		OR	
mostrase	**mostrásemos**	**hubiese mostrado**	**hubiésemos mostrado**
mostrases	**mostraseis**	**hubieses mostrado**	**hubieseis mostrado**
mostrase	**mostrasen**	**hubiese mostrado**	**hubiesen mostrado**

M

imperativo	
—	**mostremos**
muestra; no muestres	**mostrad; no mostréis**
muestre	**muestren**

Words and expressions related to this verb

mostrador   counter (in a store where merchandise is displayed under a glass case)
mostrarse   to show oneself, to appear
Muéstreme.   Show me.

See also **demostrar**.

Check out the verb drills and verb tests with answers explained on pages 45–91.

The subject pronouns are found on page 93.

to move, to persuade, to excite | Regular **-er** verb endings with stem change: Tenses 1, 6, Imperative

The Seven Simple Tenses | The Seven Compound Tenses

Singular	Plural	Singular	Plural
1 presente de indicativo		8 perfecto de indicativo	
muevo	movemos	he movido	hemos movido
mueves	movéis	has movido	habéis movido
mueve	mueven	ha movido	han movido
2 imperfecto de indicativo		9 pluscuamperfecto de indicativo	
movía	movíamos	había movido	habíamos movido
movías	movíais	habías movido	habíais movido
movía	movían	había movido	habían movido
3 pretérito		10 pretérito anterior	
moví	movimos	hube movido	hubimos movido
moviste	movisteis	hubiste movido	hubisteis movido
movió	movieron	hubo movido	hubieron movido
4 futuro		11 futuro perfecto	
moveré	moveremos	habré movido	habremos movido
moverás	moveréis	habrás movido	habréis movido
moverá	moverán	habrá movido	habrán movido
5 potencial simple		12 potencial compuesto	
movería	moveríamos	habría movido	habríamos movido
moverías	moveríais	habrías movido	habríais movido
movería	moverían	habría movido	habrían movido
6 presente de subjuntivo		13 perfecto de subjuntivo	
mueva	movamos	haya movido	hayamos movido
muevas	mováis	hayas movido	hayáis movido
mueva	muevan	haya movido	hayan movido
7 imperfecto de subjuntivo		14 pluscuamperfecto de subjuntivo	
moviera	moviéramos	hubiera movido	hubiéramos movido
movieras	movierais	hubieras movido	hubierais movido
moviera	movieran	hubiera movido	hubieran movido
OR		OR	
moviese	moviésemos	hubiese movido	hubiésemos movido
movieses	movieseis	hubieses movido	hubieseis movido
moviese	moviesen	hubiese movido	hubiesen movido

imperativo

—	movamos
mueve; no muevas	moved; no mováis
mueva	muevan

Words and expressions related to this verb
mover a alguien a + inf. to move someone + inf.
la movilidad mobility
el movimiento movement, motion
mover cielo y tierra to move heaven and earth
remover to move, transfer, remove; **removerse** to move away

conmover to move (one's emotions), to touch, stir, upset, shake
conmoverse to be moved, touched
promover to promote, to further

Reflexive regular **-ar** verb

to change one's clothes, to change
one's place of residence, to move

The Seven Simple Tenses		The Seven Compound Tenses	
Singular	Plural	Singular	Plural

1   presente de indicativo

me mudo	nos mudamos
te mudas	os mudáis
se muda	se mudan

8   perfecto de indicativo

me he mudado	nos hemos mudado
te has mudado	os habéis mudado
se ha mudado	se han mudado

2   imperfecto de indicativo

me mudaba	nos mudábamos
te mudabas	os mudabais
se mudaba	se mudaban

9   pluscuamperfecto de indicativo

me había mudado	nos habíamos mudado
te habías mudado	os habíais mudado
se había mudado	se habían mudado

3   pretérito

me mudé	nos mudamos
te mudaste	os mudasteis
se mudó	se mudaron

10   pretérito anterior

me hube mudado	nos hubimos mudado
te hubiste mudado	os hubisteis mudado
se hubo mudado	se hubieron mudado

4   futuro

me mudaré	nos mudaremos
te mudarás	os mudaréis
se mudará	se mudarán

11   futuro perfecto

me habré mudado	nos habremos mudado
te habrás mudado	os habréis mudado
se habrá mudado	se habrán mudado

5   potencial simple

me mudaría	nos mudaríamos
te mudarías	os mudaríais
se mudaría	se mudarían

12   potencial compuesto

me habría mudado	nos habríamos mudado
te habrías mudado	os habríais mudado
se habría mudado	se habrían mudado

6   presente de subjuntivo

me mude	nos mudemos
te mudes	os mudéis
se mude	se muden

13   perfecto de subjuntivo

me haya mudado	nos hayamos mudado
te hayas mudado	os hayáis mudado
se haya mudado	se hayan mudado

7   imperfecto de subjuntivo

me mudara	nos mudáramos
te mudaras	os mudarais
se mudara	se mudaran
OR	
me mudase	nos mudásemos
te mudases	os mudaseis
se mudase	se mudasen

14   pluscuamperfecto de subjuntivo

me hubiera mudado	nos hubiéramos mudado
te hubieras mudado	os hubierais mudado
se hubiera mudado	se hubieran mudado
OR	
me hubiese mudado	nos hubiésemos mudado
te hubieses mudado	os hubieseis mudado
se hubiese mudado	se hubiesen mudado

M

imperativo

—	mudémonos
múdate; no te mudes	mudaos; no os mudéis
múdese	múdense

Words and expressions related to this verb

transmudar, trasmudar   to transmute
la mudanza   moving (change)
un carro de mudanzas   moving van
demudar   to change facial expression
mudar   to change

mudarse de casa   to move from one house
     to another
mudarse de ropa   to change clothes
demudarse   to be changed (face)

Do you need more drills? Have fun with the *501 Spanish Verbs* CD-ROM!

The subject pronouns are found on page 93.

nacer (323)   Gerundio **naciendo**   Part. pas. **nacido**

to be born | Regular **-er** verb endings with spelling change: **c** becomes **zc** before **a** or **o**

The Seven Simple Tenses | The Seven Compound Tenses

Singular	Plural	Singular	Plural
1 presente de indicativo		**8 perfecto de indicativo**	
nazco	nacemos	he nacido	hemos nacido
naces	nacéis	has nacido	habéis nacido
nace	nacen	ha nacido	han nacido
2 imperfecto de indicativo		**9 pluscuamperfecto de indicativo**	
nacía	nacíamos	había nacido	habíamos nacido
nacías	nacíais	habías nacido	habíais nacido
nacía	nacían	había nacido	habían nacido
3 pretérito		**10 pretérito anterior**	
nací	nacimos	hube nacido	hubimos nacido
naciste	nacisteis	hubiste nacido	hubisteis nacido
nació	nacieron	hubo nacido	hubieron nacido
4 futuro		**11 futuro perfecto**	
naceré	naceremos	habré nacido	habremos nacido
nacerás	naceréis	habrás nacido	habréis nacido
nacerá	nacerán	habrá nacido	habrán nacido
5 potencial simple		**12 potencial compuesto**	
nacería	naceríamos	habría nacido	habríamos nacido
nacerías	naceríais	habrías nacido	habríais nacido
nacería	nacerían	habría nacido	habrían nacido
6 presente de subjuntivo		**13 perfecto de subjuntivo**	
nazca	nazcamos	haya nacido	hayamos nacido
nazcas	nazcáis	hayas nacido	hayáis nacido
nazca	nazcan	haya nacido	hayan nacido
7 imperfecto de subjuntivo		**14 pluscuamperfecto de subjuntivo**	
naciera	naciéramos	hubiera nacido	hubiéramos nacido
nacieras	nacierais	hubieras nacido	hubierais nacido
naciera	nacieran	hubiera nacido	hubieran nacido
OR		OR	
naciese	naciésemos	hubiese nacido	hubiésemos nacido
nacieses	nacieseis	hubieses nacido	hubieseis nacido
naciese	naciesen	hubiese nacido	hubiesen nacido

imperativo

—	nazcamos
nace; no nazcas	naced; no nazcáis
nazca	nazcan

Words and expressions related to this verb
bien nacido (nacida) well-bred; **mal nacido (nacida)** ill-bred
el nacimiento birth
renacer to be born again, to be reborn

nacer tarde to be born yesterday (not much intelligence)
nacer de pies to be born with a silver spoon in one's mouth

Don't forget to study the section on defective and impersonal verbs. It's right after this main list.

450

The Seven Simple Tenses		The Seven Compound Tenses	
Singular	Plural	Singular	Plural
1 presente de indicativo		8 perfecto de indicativo	
nado	**nadamos**	**he nadado**	**hemos nadado**
nadas	**nadáis**	**has nadado**	**habéis nadado**
nada	**nadan**	**ha nadado**	**han nadado**
2 imperfecto de indicativo		9 pluscuamperfecto de indicativo	
nadaba	**nadábamos**	**había nadado**	**habíamos nadado**
nadabas	**nadabais**	**habías nadado**	**habíais nadado**
nadaba	**nadaban**	**había nadado**	**habían nadado**
3 pretérito		10 pretérito anterior	
nadé	**nadamos**	**hube nadado**	**hubimos nadado**
nadaste	**nadasteis**	**hubiste nadado**	**hubisteis nadado**
nadó	**nadaron**	**hubo nadado**	**hubieron nadado**
4 futuro		11 futuro perfecto	
nadaré	**nadaremos**	**habré nadado**	**habremos nadado**
nadarás	**nadaréis**	**habrás nadado**	**habréis nadado**
nadará	**nadarán**	**habrá nadado**	**habrán nadado**
5 potencial simple		12 potencial compuesto	
nadaría	**nadaríamos**	**habría nadado**	**habríamos nadado**
nadarías	**nadaríais**	**habrías nadado**	**habríais nadado**
nadaría	**nadarían**	**habría nadado**	**habrían nadado**
6 presente de subjuntivo		13 perfecto de subjuntivo	
nade	**nademos**	**haya nadado**	**hayamos nadado**
nades	**nadéis**	**hayas nadado**	**hayáis nadado**
nade	**naden**	**haya nadado**	**hayan nadado**
7 imperfecto de subjuntivo		14 pluscuamperfecto de subjuntivo	
nadara	**nadáramos**	**hubiera nadado**	**hubiéramos nadado**
nadaras	**nadarais**	**hubieras nadado**	**hubierais nadado**
nadara	**nadaran**	**hubiera nadado**	**hubieran nadado**
OR		OR	
nadase	**nadásemos**	**hubiese nadado**	**hubiésemos nadado**
nadases	**nadaseis**	**hubieses nadado**	**hubieseis nadado**
nadase	**nadasen**	**hubiese nadado**	**hubiesen nadado**

	imperativo	
—		**nademos**
nada; no nades		**nadad; no nadéis**
nade		**naden**

Words and expressions related to this verb

nadador, nadadora   swimmer

la natación   swimming

nadar entre dos aguas   to be undecided

nadar en   to revel in, to delight in, to take great pleasure in

Consult page 668 for weather expressions using verbs.

The subject pronouns are found on page 93.   **451**

to navigate, to sail

The Seven Simple Tenses		The Seven Compound Tenses	
Singular	Plural	Singular	Plural
1 presente de indicativo		8 perfecto de indicativo	
navego	**navegamos**	**he navegado**	**hemos navegado**
navegas	**navegáis**	**has navegado**	**habéis navegado**
navega	**navegan**	**ha navegado**	**han navegado**
2 imperfecto de indicativo		9 pluscuamperfecto de indicativo	
navegaba	**navegábamos**	**había navegado**	**habíamos navegado**
navegabas	**navegabais**	**habías navegado**	**habíais navegado**
navegaba	**navegaban**	**había navegado**	**habían navegado**
3 pretérito		10 pretérito anterior	
navegué	**navegamos**	**hube navegado**	**hubimos navegado**
navegaste	**navegasteis**	**hubiste navegado**	**hubisteis navegado**
navegó	**navegaron**	**hubo navegado**	**hubieron navegado**
4 futuro		11 futuro perfecto	
navegaré	**navegaremos**	**habré navegado**	**habremos navegado**
navegarás	**navegaréis**	**habrás navegado**	**habréis navegado**
navegará	**navegarán**	**habrá navegado**	**habrán navegado**
5 potencial simple		12 potencial compuesto	
navegaría	**navegaríamos**	**habría navegado**	**habríamos navegado**
navegarías	**navegaríais**	**habrías navegado**	**habríais navegado**
navegaría	**navegarían**	**habría navegado**	**habrían navegado**
6 presente de subjuntivo		13 perfecto de subjuntivo	
navegue	**naveguemos**	**haya navegado**	**hayamos navegado**
navegues	**naveguéis**	**hayas navegado**	**hayáis navegado**
navegue	**naveguen**	**haya navegado**	**hayan navegado**
7 imperfecto de subjuntivo		14 pluscuamperfecto de subjuntivo	
navegara	**navegáramos**	**hubiera navegado**	**hubiéramos navegado**
navegaras	**navegarais**	**hubieras navegado**	**hubierais navegado**
navegara	**navegaran**	**hubiera navegado**	**hubieran navegado**
OR		OR	
navegase	**navegásemos**	**hubiese navegado**	**hubiésemos navegado**
navegases	**navegaseis**	**hubieses navegado**	**hubieseis navegado**
navegase	**navegasen**	**hubiese navegado**	**hubiesen navegado**

imperativo	
—	**naveguemos**
navega; no navegues	**navegad; no naveguéis**
navegue	**naveguen**

Words and expressions related to this verb
la navegación navigation
navegación de ultramar overseas shipping
navegar a distancia de to steer clear away
la nave ship
saber navegar to know how to navigate
navegar a la vela to sail

naval naval, nautical
navegable navigable
una naveta, una navecilla small ship
una nave cósmica spaceship
navegar los mares to sail the seas
la navegación fluvial river navigation

The Seven Simple Tenses		The Seven Compound Tenses	
Singular	Plural	Singular	Plural
1 presente de indicativo		**8 perfecto de indicativo**	
necesito	necesitamos	he necesitado	hemos necesitado
necesitas	necesitáis	has necesitado	habéis necesitado
necesita	necesitan	ha necesitado	han necesitado
2 imperfecto de indicativo		**9 pluscuamperfecto de indicativo**	
necesitaba	necesitábamos	había necesitado	habíamos necesitado
necesitabas	necesitabais	habías necesitado	habíais necesitado
necesitaba	necesitaban	había necesitado	habían necesitado
3 pretérito		**10 pretérito anterior**	
necesité	necesitamos	hube necesitado	hubimos necesitado
necesitaste	necesitasteis	hubiste necesitado	hubisteis necesitado
necesitó	necesitaron	hubo necesitado	hubieron necesitado
4 futuro		**11 futuro perfecto**	
necesitaré	necesitaremos	habré necesitado	habremos necesitado
necesitarás	necesitaréis	habrás necesitado	habréis necesitado
necesitará	necesitarán	habrá necesitado	habrán necesitado
5 potencial simple		**12 potencial compuesto**	
necesitaría	necesitaríamos	habría necesitado	habríamos necesitado
necesitarías	necesitaríais	habrías necesitado	habríais necesitado
necesitaría	necesitarían	habría necesitado	habrían necesitado
6 presente de subjuntivo		**13 perfecto de subjuntivo**	
necesite	necesitemos	haya necesitado	hayamos necesitado
necesites	necesitéis	hayas necesitado	hayáis necesitado
necesite	necesiten	haya necesitado	hayan necesitado
7 imperfecto de subjuntivo		**14 pluscuamperfecto de subjuntivo**	
necesitara	necesitáramos	hubiera necesitado	hubiéramos necesitado
necesitaras	necesitarais	hubieras necesitado	hubierais necesitado
necesitara	necesitaran	hubiera necesitado	hubieran necesitado
OR		OR	
necesitase	necesitásemos	hubiese necesitado	hubiésemos necesitado
necesitases	necesitaseis	hubieses necesitado	hubieseis necesitado
necesitase	necesitasen	hubiese necesitado	hubiesen necesitado

	imperativo	
—		necesitemos
necesita; no necesites		necesitad; no necesitéis
necesite		necesiten

Words and expressions related to this verb
la necesidad necessity
por necesidad from necessity
necesario, necesaria necessary
necesitar + inf. to have + inf., to need + inf.

un necesitado, una necesitada needy person
necesariamente necessarily
Necesito un cuaderno, por favor. I need
  a notebook, please.

Can't find the verb you're looking for?
Check the back pages of this book for a list of over 2,100 additional verbs!

The subject pronouns are found on page 93.

to deny

Regular **-ar** verb endings with spelling change: **g** becomes **gu** before **e**; stem change: Tenses 1, 6, Imperative

The Seven Simple Tenses		The Seven Compound Tenses	
Singular	Plural	Singular	Plural
1 presente de indicativo		8 perfecto de indicativo	
niego	negamos	he negado	hemos negado
niegas	negáis	has negado	habéis negado
niega	niegan	ha negado	han negado
2 imperfecto de indicativo		9 pluscuamperfecto de indicativo	
negaba	negábamos	había negado	habíamos negado
negabas	negabais	habías negado	habíais negado
negaba	negaban	había negado	habían negado
3 pretérito		10 pretérito anterior	
negué	negamos	hube negado	hubimos negado
negaste	negasteis	hubiste negado	hubisteis negado
negó	negaron	hubo negado	hubieron negado
4 futuro		11 futuro perfecto	
negaré	negaremos	habré negado	habremos negado
negarás	negaréis	habrás negado	habréis negado
negará	negarán	habrá negado	habrán negado
5 potencial simple		12 potencial compuesto	
negaría	negaríamos	habría negado	habríamos negado
negarías	negaríais	habrías negado	habríais negado
negaría	negarían	habría negado	habrían negado
6 presente de subjuntivo		13 perfecto de subjuntivo	
niegue	neguemos	haya negado	hayamos negado
niegues	neguéis	hayas negado	hayáis negado
niegue	nieguen	haya negado	hayan negado
7 imperfecto de subjuntivo		14 pluscuamperfecto de subjuntivo	
negara	negáramos	hubiera negado	hubiéramos negado
negaras	negarais	hubieras negado	hubierais negado
negara	negaran	hubiera negado	hubieran negado
OR		OR	
negase	negásemos	hubiese negado	hubiésemos negado
negases	negaseis	hubieses negado	hubieseis negado
negase	negasen	hubiese negado	hubiesen negado

	imperativo	
—		neguemos
niega; no niegues		negad; no neguéis
niegue		nieguen

Words and expressions related to this verb

negador, negadora denier
negativo, negativa negative
la negación denial, negation
negable deniable

negar haber + past part. to deny having + past part.
negarse a to refuse
renegar to abhor, to deny vehemently

Can't recognize an irregular verb form? Check out pages 678–681.

Regular **-er** verb endings with spelling　　　　　　　　　　to obey
change: **c** becomes **zc** before **a** or **o**

The Seven Simple Tenses		The Seven Compound Tenses	
Singular	Plural	Singular	Plural
1　presente de indicativo		8　perfecto de indicativo	
obedezco	**obedecemos**	**he obedecido**	**hemos obedecido**
obedeces	**obedecéis**	**has obedecido**	**habéis obedecido**
obedece	**obedecen**	**ha obedecido**	**han obedecido**
2　imperfecto de indicativo		9　pluscuamperfecto de indicativo	
obedecía	**obedecíamos**	**había obedecido**	**habíamos obedecido**
obedecías	**obedecíais**	**habías obedecido**	**habíais obedecido**
obedecía	**obedecían**	**había obedecido**	**habían obedecido**
3　pretérito		10　pretérito anterior	
obedecí	**obedecimos**	**hube obedecido**	**hubimos obedecido**
obedeciste	**obedecisteis**	**hubiste obedecido**	**hubisteis obedecido**
obedeció	**obedecieron**	**hubo obedecido**	**hubieron obedecido**
4　futuro		11　futuro perfecto	
obedeceré	**obedeceremos**	**habré obedecido**	**habremos obedecido**
obedecerás	**obedeceréis**	**habrás obedecido**	**habréis obedecido**
obedecerá	**obedecerán**	**habrá obedecido**	**habrán obedecido**
5　potencial simple		12　potencial compuesto	
obedecería	**obedeceríamos**	**habría obedecido**	**habríamos obedecido**
obedecerías	**obedeceríais**	**habrías obedecido**	**habríais obedecido**
obedecería	**obedecerían**	**habría obedecido**	**habrían obedecido**
6　presente de subjuntivo		13　perfecto de subjuntivo	
obedezca	**obedezcamos**	**haya obedecido**	**hayamos obedecido**
obedezcas	**obedezcáis**	**hayas obedecido**	**hayáis obedecido**
obedezca	**obedezcan**	**haya obedecido**	**hayan obedecido**
7　imperfecto de subjuntivo		14　pluscuamperfecto de subjuntivo	
obedeciera	**obedeciéramos**	**hubiera obedecido**	**hubiéramos obedecido**
obedecieras	**obedecierais**	**hubieras obedecido**	**hubierais obedecido**
obedeciera	**obedecieran**	**hubiera obedecido**	**hubieran obedecido**
OR		OR	
obedeciese	**obedeciésemos**	**hubiese obedecido**	**hubiésemos obedecido**
obedecieses	**obedecieseis**	**hubieses obedecido**	**hubieseis obedecido**
obedeciese	**obedeciesen**	**hubiese obedecido**	**hubiesen obedecido**

O

imperativo	
—	**obedezcamos**
obedece; no obedezcas	**obedeced; no obedezcáis**
obedezca	**obedezcan**

Words related to this verb
el obedecimiento, la obediencia　obedience
obediente　obedient
obedecer las leyes　to obey the law
desobediente　disobedient

obedientemente　obediently
desobedecer　to disobey
obedecer a sus padres　to obey one's parents
la desobediencia　disobedience

The subject pronouns are found on page 93.

to observe, to notice   Regular **-ar** verb

The Seven Simple Tenses		The Seven Compound Tenses	
Singular	Plural	Singular	Plural
1 presente de indicativo		8 perfecto de indicativo	
observo	observamos	he observado	hemos observado
observas	observáis	has observado	habéis observado
observa	observan	ha observado	han observado
2 imperfecto de indicativo		9 pluscuamperfecto de indicativo	
observaba	observábamos	había observado	habíamos observado
observabas	observabais	habías observado	habíais observado
osbervaba	observaban	había observado	habían observado
3 pretérito		10 pretérito anterior	
observé	observamos	hube observado	hubimos observado
observaste	observasteis	hubiste observado	hubisteis observado
observó	observaron	hubo observado	hubieron observado
4 futuro		11 futuro perfecto	
observaré	observaremos	habré observado	habremos observado
observarás	observaréis	habrás observado	habréis observado
observará	observarán	habrá observado	habrán observado
5 potencial simple		12 potencial compuesto	
observaría	observaríamos	habría observado	habríamos observado
observarías	observaríais	habrías observado	habríais observado
observaría	observarían	habría observado	habrían observado
6 presente de subjuntivo		13 perfecto de subjuntivo	
observe	observemos	haya observado	hayamos observado
observes	observéis	hayas observado	hayáis observado
observe	observen	haya observado	hayan observado
7 imperfecto de subjuntivo		14 pluscuamperfecto de subjuntivo	
observara	observáramos	hubiera observado	hubiéramos observado
observaras	observarais	hubieras observado	hubierais observado
observara	observaran	hubiera observado	hubieran observado
OR		OR	
observase	observásemos	hubiese observado	hubiésemos observado
observases	observaseis	hubieses observado	hubieseis observado
observase	observasen	hubiese observado	hubiesen observado

	imperativo	
—	observemos	
observa; no observes	observad; no observéis	
observe	observen	

Words and expressions related to this verb
el observatorio observatory   **la observancia** observance
la observación observation   **observante** observant

Can't remember the Spanish verb you need?
Check the back pages of this book for the English-Spanish verb index!

Irregular verb   to obtain, to get

The Seven Simple Tenses | The Seven Compound Tenses

Singular	Plural	Singular	Plural
1 presente de indicativo		8 perfecto de indicativo	
obtengo	**obtenemos**	**he obtenido**	**hemos obtenido**
obtienes	**obtenéis**	**has obtenido**	**habéis obtenido**
obtiene	**obtienen**	**ha obtenido**	**han obtenido**
2 imperfecto de indicativo		9 pluscuamperfecto de indicativo	
obtenía	**obteníamos**	**había obtenido**	**habíamos obtenido**
obtenías	**obteníais**	**habías obtenido**	**habíais obtenido**
obtenía	**obtenían**	**había obtenido**	**habían obtenido**
3 pretérito		10 pretérito anterior	
obtuve	**obtuvimos**	**hube obtenido**	**hubimos obtenido**
obtuviste	**obtuvisteis**	**hubiste obtenido**	**hubisteis obtenido**
obtuvo	**obtuvieron**	**hubo obtenido**	**hubieron obtenido**
4 futuro		11 futuro perfecto	
obtendré	**obtendremos**	**habré obtenido**	**habremos obtenido**
obtendrás	**obtendréis**	**habrás obtenido**	**habréis obtenido**
obtendrá	**obtendrán**	**habrá obtenido**	**habrán obtenido**
5 potencial simple		12 potencial compuesto	
obtendría	**obtendríamos**	**habría obtenido**	**habríamos obtenido**
obtendrías	**obtendríais**	**habrías obtenido**	**habríais obtenido**
obtendría	**obtendrían**	**habría obtenido**	**habrían obtenido**
6 presente de subjuntivo		13 perfecto de subjuntivo	
obtenga	**obtengamos**	**haya obtenido**	**hayamos obtenido**
obtengas	**obtengáis**	**hayas obtenido**	**hayáis obtenido**
obtenga	**obtengan**	**haya obtenido**	**hayan obtenido**
7 imperfecto de subjuntivo		14 pluscuamperfecto de subjuntivo	
obtuviera	**obtuviéramos**	**hubiera obtenido**	**hubiéramos obtenido**
obtuvieras	**obtuvierais**	**hubieras obtenido**	**hubierais obtenido**
obtuviera	**obtuvieran**	**hubiera obtenido**	**hubieran obtenido**
OR		OR	
obtuviese	**obtuviésemos**	**hubiese obtenido**	**hubiésemos obtenido**
obtuvieses	**obtuvieseis**	**hubieses obtenido**	**hubieseis obtenido**
obtuviese	**obtuviesen**	**hubiese obtenido**	**hubiesen obtenido**

O

imperativo

—	**obtengamos**
obtén; no obtengas	**obtened; obtengáis**
obtenga	**obtengan**

Words related to this verb
obtenible   obtainable, available
obtener una colocación   to get a job
la obtención   obtainment

obtener buenos resultados   to get good results
obtener malos resultados   to get bad results

See also the verb **tener.**

The subject pronouns are found on page 93.

to hide oneself   Reflexive regular **-ar** verb

The Seven Simple Tenses		The Seven Compound Tenses	
Singular	Plural	Singular	Plural
1 presente de indicativo		8 perfecto de indicativo	
me oculto	nos ocultamos	me he ocultado	nos hemos ocultado
te ocultas	os ocultáis	te has ocultado	os habéis ocultado
se oculta	se ocultan	se ha ocultado	se han ocultado
2 imperfecto de indicativo		9 pluscuamperfecto de indicativo	
me ocultaba	nos ocultábamos	me había ocultado	nos habíamos ocultado
te ocultabas	os ocultabais	te habías ocultado	os habíais ocultado
se ocultaba	se ocultaban	se había ocultado	se habían ocultado
3 pretérito		10 pretérito anterior	
me oculté	nos ocultamos	me hube ocultado	nos hubimos ocultado
te ocultaste	os ocultasteis	te hubiste ocultado	os hubisteis ocultado
se ocultó	se ocultaron	se hubo ocultado	se hubieron ocultado
4 futuro		11 futuro perfecto	
me ocultaré	nos ocultaremos	me habré ocultado	nos habremos ocultado
te ocultarás	os ocultaréis	te habrás ocultado	os habréis ocultado
se ocultará	se ocultarán	se habrá ocultado	se habrán ocultado
5 potencial simple		12 potencial compuesto	
me ocultaría	nos ocultaríamos	me habría ocultado	nos habríamos ocultado
te ocultarías	os ocultaríais	te habrías ocultado	os habríais ocultado
se ocultaría	se ocultarían	se habría ocultado	se habrían ocultado
6 presente de subjuntivo		13 perfecto de subjuntivo	
me oculte	nos ocultemos	me haya ocultado	nos hayamos ocultado
te ocultes	os ocultéis	te hayas ocultado	os hayáis ocultado
se oculte	se oculten	se haya ocultado	se hayan ocultado
7 imperfecto de subjuntivo		14 pluscuamperfecto de subjuntivo	
me ocultara	nos ocultáramos	me hubiera ocultado	nos hubiéramos ocultado
te ocultaras	os ocultarais	te hubieras ocultado	os hubierais ocultado
se ocultara	se ocultaran	se hubiera ocultado	se hubieran ocultado
OR		OR	
me ocultase	nos ocultásemos	me hubiese ocultado	nos hubiésemos ocultado
te ocultases	os ocultaseis	te hubieses ocultado	os hubieseis ocultado
se ocultase	se ocultasen	se hubiese ocultado	se hubiesen ocultado

imperativo	
—	ocultémonos
ocúltate; no te ocultes	ocultaos; no os ocultéis
ocúltese	ocúltense

Words and expressions related to this verb
ocultar to hide, conceal
ocultar una cosa de una persona to hide something from someone
ocultarsele a uno to hide oneself from someone
oculto, oculta occult; hidden, concealed; **en oculto** secretly
las Ciencias ocultas the Occult Sciences

The Seven Simple Tenses		The Seven Compound Tenses	
Singular	Plural	Singular	Plural
1 presente de indicativo		8 perfecto de indicativo	
ocupo	ocupamos	he ocupado	hemos ocupado
ocupas	ocupáis	has ocupado	habéis ocupado
ocupa	ocupan	ha ocupado	han ocupado
2 imperfecto de indicativo		9 pluscuamperfecto de indicativo	
ocupaba	ocupábamos	había ocupado	habíamos ocupado
ocupabas	ocupabais	habías ocupado	habíais ocupado
ocupaba	ocupaban	había ocupado	habían ocupado
3 pretérito		10 pretérito anterior	
ocupé	ocupamos	hube ocupado	hubimos ocupado
ocupaste	ocupasteis	hubiste ocupado	hubisteis ocupado
ocupó	ocuparon	hubo ocupado	hubieron ocupado
4 futuro		11 futuro perfecto	
ocuparé	ocuparemos	habré ocupado	habremos ocupado
ocuparás	ocuparéis	habrás ocupado	habréis ocupado
ocupará	ocuparán	habrá ocupado	habrán ocupado
5 potencial simple		12 potencial compuesto	
ocuparía	ocuparíamos	habría ocupado	habríamos ocupado
ocuparías	ocuparíais	habrías ocupado	habríais ocupado
ocuparía	ocuparían	habría ocupado	habrían ocupado
6 presente de subjuntivo		13 perfecto de subjuntivo	
ocupe	ocupemos	haya ocupado	hayamos ocupado
ocupes	ocupéis	hayas ocupado	hayáis ocupado
ocupe	ocupen	haya ocupado	hayan ocupado
7 imperfecto de subjuntivo		14 pluscuamperfecto de subjuntivo	
ocupara	ocupáramos	hubiera ocupado	hubiéramos ocupado
ocuparas	ocuparais	hubieras ocupado	hubierais ocupado
ocupara	ocuparan	hubiera ocupado	hubieran ocupado
OR		OR	
ocupase	ocupasemos	hubiese ocupado	hubiésemos ocupado
ocupases	ocupaseis	hubieses ocupado	hubieseis ocupado
ocupase	ocupasen	hubiese ocupado	hubiesen ocupado

imperativo	
—	ocupemos
ocupa; no ocupes	ocupad; no ocupéis
ocupe	ocupen

Words and expressions related to this verb

ocupado, ocupada busy, occupied
la ocupación occupation
ocuparse de (en) to be busy with, in, to be engaged in
un, una ocupante occupant

See also **preocuparse**.

desocupar to vacate
ocuparse con algo to be busy with something

The subject pronouns are found on page 93.

to offer

Regular **-er** verb endings with spelling
change: **c** becomes **zc** before **a** or **o**

The Seven Simple Tenses		The Seven Compound Tenses	
Singular	Plural	Singular	Plural
1　presente de indicativo		8　perfecto de indicativo	
ofrezco	**ofrecemos**	**he ofrecido**	**hemos ofrecido**
ofreces	**ofrecéis**	**has ofrecido**	**habéis ofrecido**
ofrece	**ofrecen**	**ha ofrecido**	**han ofrecido**
2　imperfecto de indicativo		9　pluscuamperfecto de indicativo	
ofrecía	**ofrecíamos**	**había ofrecido**	**habíamos ofrecido**
ofrecías	**ofrecíais**	**habías ofrecido**	**habíais ofrecido**
ofrecía	**ofrecían**	**había ofrecido**	**habían ofrecido**
3　pretérito		10　pretérito anterior	
ofrecí	**ofrecimos**	**hube ofrecido**	**hubimos ofrecido**
ofreciste	**ofrecisteis**	**hubiste ofrecido**	**hubisteis ofrecido**
ofreció	**ofrecieron**	**hubo ofrecido**	**hubieron ofrecido**
4　futuro		11　futuro perfecto	
ofreceré	**ofreceremos**	**habré ofrecido**	**habremos ofrecido**
ofrecerás	**ofreceréis**	**habrás ofrecido**	**habréis ofrecido**
ofrecerá	**ofrecerán**	**habrá ofrecido**	**habrán ofrecido**
5　potencial simple		12　potencial compuesto	
ofrecería	**ofreceríamos**	**habría ofrecido**	**habríamos ofrecido**
ofrecerías	**ofreceríais**	**habrías ofrecido**	**habríais ofrecido**
ofrecería	**ofrecerían**	**habría ofrecido**	**habrían ofrecido**
6　presente de subjuntivo		13　perfecto de subjuntivo	
ofrezca	**ofrezcamos**	**haya ofrecido**	**hayamos ofrecido**
ofrezcas	**ofrezcáis**	**hayas ofrecido**	**hayáis ofrecido**
ofrezca	**ofrezcan**	**haya ofrecido**	**hayan ofrecido**
7　imperfecto de subjuntivo		14　pluscuamperfecto de subjuntivo	
ofreciera	**ofreciéramos**	**hubiera ofrecido**	**hubiéramos ofrecido**
ofrecieras	**ofrecierais**	**hubieras ofrecido**	**hubierais ofrecido**
ofreciera	**ofrecieran**	**hubiera ofrecido**	**hubieran ofrecido**
OR		OR	
ofreciese	**ofreciésemos**	**hubiese ofrecido**	**hubiésemos ofrecido**
ofrecieses	**ofrecieseis**	**hubieses ofrecido**	**hubieseis ofrecido**
ofreciese	**ofreciesen**	**hubiese ofrecido**	**hubiesen ofrecido**

imperativo

—	**ofrezcamos**
ofrece; no ofrezcas	**ofreced; no ofrezcáis**
ofrezca	**ofrezcan**

Words related to this verb
ofreciente　offering
el ofrecimiento　offer, offering
la ofrenda　gift
ofrecer + inf.　to offer + inf.
el ofrecedor, la ofrecedora　offerer

ofrecer el brazo　to offer one's arm
ofrecerse　to offer oneself
ofrecerse para hacer un trabajo　to offer
　oneself to do a job
ofrecer su ayuda　to offer your help
ofrecer ventajas　to offer advantages

The Seven Simple Tenses		The Seven Compound Tenses	
Singular	Plural	Singular	Plural
1 presente de indicativo		**8 perfecto de indicativo**	
oigo	**oímos**	**he oído**	**hemos oído**
oyes	**oís**	**has oído**	**habéis oído**
oye	**oyen**	**ha oído**	**han oído**
2 imperfecto de indicativo		**9 pluscuamperfecto de indicativo**	
oía	**oíamos**	**había oído**	**habíamos oído**
oías	**oíais**	**habías oído**	**habíais oído**
oía	**oían**	**había oído**	**habían oído**
3 pretérito		**10 pretérito anterior**	
oí	**oímos**	**hube oído**	**hubimos oído**
oíste	**oísteis**	**hubiste oído**	**hubisteis oído**
oyó	**oyeron**	**hubo oído**	**hubieron oído**
4 futuro		**11 futuro perfecto**	
oiré	**oiremos**	**habré oído**	**habremos oído**
oirás	**oiréis**	**habrás oído**	**habréis oído**
oirá	**oirán**	**habrá oído**	**habrán oído**
5 potencial simple		**12 potencial compuesto**	
oiría	**oiríamos**	**habría oído**	**habríamos oído**
oirías	**oiríais**	**habrías oído**	**habríais oído**
oiría	**oirían**	**habría oído**	**habrían oído**
6 presente de subjuntivo		**13 perfecto de subjuntivo**	
oiga	**oigamos**	**haya oído**	**hayamos oído**
oigas	**oigáis**	**hayas oído**	**hayáis oído**
oiga	**oigan**	**haya oído**	**hayan oído**
7 imperfecto de subjuntivo		**14 pluscuamperfecto de subjuntivo**	
oyera	**oyéramos**	**hubiera oído**	**hubiéramos oído**
oyeras	**oyerais**	**hubieras oído**	**hubierais oído**
oyera	**oyeran**	**hubiera oído**	**hubieran oído**
OR		OR	
oyese	**oyésemos**	**hubiese oído**	**hubiésemos oído**
oyeses	**oyeseis**	**hubieses oído**	**hubieseis oído**
oyese	**oyesen**	**hubiese oído**	**hubiesen oído**

O

	imperativo	
—		**oigamos**
oye; no oigas		**oíd; no oigáis**
oiga		**oigan**

AN ESSENTIAL 55 VERB

The subject pronouns are found on page 93.

Oír

Oír is a very important irregular verb for you to learn. It is used in a great number of idiomatic expressions and everyday situations.

Sentences using oír and related words

¡Déme oídos, por favor!
Lend me an ear, please!

Oigo la voz de un amigo.
I hear the voice of a friend.

Words and expressions related to this verb

la oída **hearing**

de oídas **by hearsay**

dar oídos **to lend an ear**

oír decir **to hear tell, to hear say**

oír hablar de **to hear of, to hear talk of**

por oídos, de oídos **by hearing**

al oído **confidentially**

el oído **hearing (sense)**

desoír **to ignore, to be deaf to**

Can't find the verb you're looking for?
Check the back pages of this book for a list of over 2,100 additional verbs!

Regular **-er** verb endings with   to smell, to scent
stem change: Tenses 1, 6, Imperative

The Seven Simple Tenses		The Seven Compound Tenses	
Singular	Plural	Singular	Plural
1 presente de indicativo		8 perfecto de indicativo	
huelo	**olemos**	**he olido**	**hemos olido**
hueles	**oléis**	**has olido**	**habéis olido**
huele	**huelen**	**ha olido**	**han olido**
2 imperfecto de indicativo		9 pluscuamperfecto de indicativo	
olía	**olíamos**	**había olido**	**habíamos olido**
olías	**olíais**	**habías olido**	**habíais olido**
olía	**olían**	**había olido**	**habían olido**
3 pretérito		10 pretérito anterior	
olí	**olimos**	**hube olido**	**hubimos olido**
oliste	**olisteis**	**hubiste olido**	**hubisteis olido**
olió	**olieron**	**hubo olido**	**hubieron olido**
4 futuro		11 futuro perfecto	
oleré	**oleremos**	**habré olido**	**habremos olido**
olerás	**oleréis**	**habrás olido**	**habréis olido**
olerá	**olerán**	**habrá olido**	**habrán olido**
5 potencial simple		12 potencial compuesto	
olería	**oleríamos**	**habría olido**	**habríamos olido**
olerías	**oleríais**	**habrías olido**	**habríais olido**
olería	**olerían**	**habría olido**	**habrían olido**
6 presente de subjuntivo		13 perfecto de subjuntivo	
huela	**olamos**	**haya olido**	**hayamos olido**
huelas	**oláis**	**hayas olido**	**hayáis olido**
huela	**huelan**	**haya olido**	**hayan olido**
7 imperfecto de subjuntivo		14 pluscuamperfecto de subjuntivo	
oliera	**oliéramos**	**hubiera olido**	**hubiéramos olido**
olieras	**olierais**	**hubieras olido**	**hubierais olido**
oliera	**olieran**	**hubiera olido**	**hubieran olido**
OR		OR	
oliese	**oliésemos**	**hubiese olido**	**hubiésemos olido**
olieses	**olieseis**	**hubieses olido**	**hubieseis olido**
oliese	**oliesen**	**hubiese olido**	**hubiesen olido**

	imperativo	
—		**olamos**
huele; no huelas		**oled; no oláis**
huela		**huelan**

Words and expressions related to this verb
el olfato, la olfacción   olfaction (the sense of smelling, act of smelling)
olfatear   to sniff
oler a   to smell of; **oler a rosa**   to smell like a rose
No huele bien   It looks fishy. (It doesn't smell good.)

Can't recognize an irregular verb form? Check out pages 678–681.

The subject pronouns are found on page 93.   **463**

olvidar (336)   Gerundio **olvidando**   Part. pas. **olvidado**

to forget   Regular **-ar** verb

The Seven Simple Tenses		The Seven Compound Tenses	
Singular	Plural	Singular	Plural
1 presente de indicativo		8 perfecto de indicativo	
olvido	olvidamos	he olvidado	hemos olvidado
olvidas	olvidáis	has olvidado	habéis olvidado
olvida	olvidan	ha olvidado	han olvidado
2 imperfecto de indicativo		9 pluscuamperfecto de indicativo	
olvidaba	olvidábamos	había olvidado	habíamos olvidado
olvidabas	olvidabais	habías olvidado	habíais olvidado
olvidaba	olvidaban	había olvidado	habían olvidado
3 pretérito		10 pretérito anterior	
olvidé	olvidamos	hube olvidado	hubimos olvidado
olvidaste	olvidasteis	hubiste olvidado	hubisteis olvidado
olvidó	olvidaron	hubo olvidado	hubieron olvidado
4 futuro		11 futuro perfecto	
olvidaré	olvidaremos	habré olvidado	habremos olvidado
olvidarás	olvidaréis	habrás olvidado	habréis olvidado
olvidará	olvidarán	habrá olvidado	habrán olvidado
5 potencial simple		12 potencial compuesto	
olvidaría	olvidaríamos	habría olvidado	habríamos olvidado
olvidarías	olvidaríais	habrías olvidado	habríais olvidado
olvidaría	olvidarían	habría olvidado	habrían olvidado
6 presente de subjuntivo		13 perfecto de subjuntivo	
olvide	olvidemos	haya olvidado	hayamos olvidado
olvides	olvidéis	hayas olvidado	hayáis olvidado
olvide	olviden	haya olvidado	hayan olvidado
7 imperfecto de subjuntivo		14 pluscuamperfecto de subjuntivo	
olvidara	olvidáramos	hubiera olvidado	hubiéramos olvidado
olvidaras	olvidarais	hubieras olvidado	hubierais olvidado
olvidara	olvidaran	hubiera olvidado	hubieran olvidado
OR		OR	
olvidase	olvidásemos	hubiese olvidado	hubiésemos olvidado
olvidases	olvidaseis	hubieses olvidado	hubieseis olvidado
olvidase	olvidasen	hubiese olvidado	hubiesen olvidado

imperativo	
—	olvidemos
olvida; no olvides	olvidad; no olvidéis
olvide	olviden

Words and expressions related to this verb

olvidado, olvidada forgotten
olvidadizo, olvidadiza forgetful
el olvido forgetfulness, oblivion
Se me olvidó It slipped my mind.

olvidar + inf. to forget + inf.
olvidarse de to forget
olvidarse de + inf. to forget + inf.
olvidar la hora to forget the time

The Seven Simple Tenses		The Seven Compound Tenses	
Singular	Plural	Singular	Plural
1 presente de indicativo		8 perfecto de indicativo	
opongo	oponemos	he opuesto	hemos opuesto
opones	oponéis	has opuesto	habéis opuesto
opone	oponen	ha opuesto	han opuesto
2 imperfecto de indicativo		9 pluscuamperfecto de indicativo	
oponía	oponíamos	había opuesto	habíamos opuesto
oponías	oponíais	habías opuesto	habíais opuesto
oponía	oponían	había opuesto	habían opuesto
3 pretérito		10 pretérito anterior	
opuse	opusimos	hube opuesto	hubimos opuesto
opusiste	opusisteis	hubiste opuesto	hubisteis opuesto
opuso	opusieron	hubo opuesto	hubieron opuesto
4 futuro		11 futuro perfecto	
opondré	opondremos	habré opuesto	habremos opuesto
opondrás	opondréis	habrás opuesto	habréis opuesto
opondrá	opondrán	habrá opuesto	habrán opuesto
5 potencial simple		12 potencial compuesto	
opondría	opondríamos	habría opuesto	habríamos opuesto
opondrías	opondríais	habrías opuesto	habríais opuesto
opondría	opondrían	habría opuesto	habrían opuesto
6 presente de subjuntivo		13 perfecto de subjuntivo	
oponga	opongamos	haya opuesto	hayamos opuesto
opongas	opongáis	hayas opuesto	hayáis opuesto
oponga	opongan	haya opuesto	hayan opuesto
7 imperfecto de subjuntivo		14 pluscuamperfecto de subjuntivo	
opusiera	opusiéramos	hubiera opuesto	hubiéramos opuesto
opusieras	opusierais	hubieras opuesto	hubierais opuesto
opusiera	opusieran	hubiera opuesto	hubieran opuesto
OR		OR	
opusiese	opusiésemos	hubiese opuesto	hubiésemos opuesto
opusieses	opusieseis	hubieses opuesto	hubieseis opuesto
opusiese	opusiesen	hubiese opuesto	hubiesen opuesto

O

imperativo

—	opongamos
opón; no opongas	oponed; no opongáis
oponga	opongan

Words related to this verb
oponerse a   to be against
oponible   opposable
oponerse   to oppose each other
el, la oponente   opponent

la oposición   opposition
el, la oposicionista   oppositionist
oponerse a una moción   to oppose a motion

The subject pronouns are found on page 93.
                                                                    465

to order, to command, to put in order, to arrange   Regular **-ar** verb

The Seven Simple Tenses		The Seven Compound Tenses	
Singular	Plural	Singular	Plural
1 presente de indicativo		8 perfecto de indicativo	
ordeno	ordenamos	he ordenado	hemos ordenado
ordenas	ordenáis	has ordenado	habéis ordenado
ordena	ordenan	ha ordenado	han ordenado
2 imperfecto de indicativo		9 pluscuamperfecto de indicativo	
ordenaba	ordenábamos	había ordenado	habíamos ordenado
ordenabas	ordenabais	habías ordenado	habíais ordenado
ordenaba	ordenaban	había ordenado	habían ordenado
3 pretérito		10 pretérito anterior	
ordené	ordenamos	hube ordenado	hubimos ordenado
ordenaste	ordenasteis	hubiste ordenado	hubisteis ordenado
ordenó	ordenaron	hubo ordenado	hubieron ordenado
4 futuro		11 futuro perfecto	
ordenaré	ordenaremos	habré ordenado	habremos ordenado
ordenarás	ordenaréis	habrás ordenado	habréis ordenado
ordenará	ordenarán	habrá ordenado	habrán ordenado
5 potencial simple		12 potencial compuesto	
ordenaría	ordenaríamos	habría ordenado	habríamos ordenado
ordenarías	ordenaríais	habrías ordenado	habríais ordenado
ordenaría	ordenarían	habría ordenado	habrían ordenado
6 presente de subjuntivo		13 perfecto de subjuntivo	
ordene	ordenemos	haya ordenado	hayamos ordenado
ordenes	ordenéis	hayas ordenado	hayáis ordenado
ordene	ordenen	haya ordenado	hayan ordenado
7 imperfecto de subjuntivo		14 pluscuamperfecto de subjuntivo	
ordenara	ordenáramos	hubiera ordenado	hubiéramos ordenado
ordenaras	ordenarais	hubieras ordenado	hubierais ordenado
ordenara	ordenaran	hubiera ordenado	hubieran ordenado
OR		OR	
ordenase	ordenásemos	hubiese ordenado	hubiésemos ordenado
ordenases	ordenaseis	hubieses ordenado	hubieseis ordenado
ordenase	ordenasen	hubiese ordenado	hubiesen ordenado

imperativo

—	ordenemos
ordena; no ordenes	ordenad; no ordenéis
ordene	ordenen

Words and expressions related to this verb
el orden, los órdenes   order, orders
el orden del día   order of the day
ordenadamente   in order, orderly,
  methodically

ordenarse   to become ordained, to take
  holy orders
llamar al orden   to call to order

Regular **-ar** verb endings with spelling change: **z** becomes **c** before **e**

to organize, to arrange, to set up

The Seven Simple Tenses		The Seven Compound Tenses	
Singular	Plural	Singular	Plural
1 presente de indicativo		8 perfecto de indicativo	
organizo	organizamos	he organizado	hemos organizado
organizas	organizáis	has organizado	habéis organizado
organiza	organizan	ha organizado	han organizado
2 imperfecto de indicativo		9 pluscuamperfecto de indicativo	
organizaba	organizábamos	había organizado	habíamos organizado
organizabas	organizabais	habías organizado	habíais organizado
organizaba	organizaban	había organizado	habían organizado
3 pretérito		10 pretérito anterior	
organicé	organizamos	hube organizado	hubimos organizado
organizaste	organizasteis	hubiste organizado	hubisteis organizado
organizó	organizaron	hubo organizado	hubieron organizado
4 futuro		11 futuro perfecto	
organizaré	organizaremos	habré organizado	habremos organizado
organizarás	organizaréis	habrás organizado	habréis organizado
organizará	organizarán	habrá organizado	habrán organizado
5 potencial simple		12 potencial compuesto	
organizaría	organizaríamos	habría organizado	habríamos organizado
organizarías	organizaríais	habrías organizado	habríais organizado
organizaría	organizarían	habría organizado	habrían organizado
6 presente de subjuntivo		13 perfecto de subjuntivo	
organice	organicemos	haya organizado	hayamos organizado
organices	organicéis	hayas organizado	hayáis organizado
organice	organicen	haya organizado	hayan organizado
7 imperfecto de subjuntivo		14 pluscuamperfecto de subjuntivo	
organizara	organizáramos	hubiera organizado	hubiéramos organizado
organizaras	organizarais	hubieras organizado	hubierais organizado
organizara	organizaran	hubiera organizado	hubieran organizado
OR		OR	
organizase	organizásemos	hubiese organizado	hubiésemos organizado
organizases	organizaseis	hubieses organizado	hubieseis organizado
organizase	organizasen	hubiese organizado	hubiesen organizado

imperativo	
—	organicemos
organiza; no organices	organizad; no organicéis
organice	organicen

Words and expressions related to this verb

organizado, organizada organized
la organización organization
organizar una fiesta to organize a party

el organizador, la organizadora organizer
organizable organizable
la Organización de las Naciones Unidas (ONU) the United Nations Organization (UNO, UN)

The subject pronouns are found on page 93.

467

to dare, to venture　　　　　　　　　　　　　　　　　Regular **-ar** verb

The Seven Simple Tenses		The Seven Compound Tenses	
Singular	Plural	Singular	Plural
1　presente de indicativo		8　perfecto de indicativo	
oso	osamos	he osado	hemos osado
osas	osáis	has osado	habéis osado
osa	osan	ha osado	han osado
2　imperfecto de indicativo		9　pluscuamperfecto de indicativo	
osaba	osábamos	había osado	habíamos osado
osabas	osabais	habías osado	habíais osado
osaba	osaban	había osado	habían osado
3　pretérito		10　pretérito anterior	
osé	osamos	hube osado	hubimos osado
osaste	osasteis	hubiste osado	hubisteis osado
osó	osaron	hubo osado	hubieron osado
4　futuro		11　futuro perfecto	
osaré	osaremos	habré osado	habremos osado
osarás	osaréis	habrás osado	habréis osado
osará	osarán	habrá osado	habrán osado
5　potencial simple		12　potencial compuesto	
osaría	osaríamos	habría osado	habríamos osado
osarías	osaríais	habrías osado	habríais osado
osaría	osarían	habría osado	habrían osado
6　presente de subjuntivo		13　perfecto de subjuntivo	
ose	osemos	haya osado	hayamos osado
oses	oséis	hayas osado	hayáis osado
ose	osen	haya osado	hayan osado
7　imperfecto de subjuntivo		14　pluscuamperfecto de subjuntivo	
osara	osáramos	hubiera osado	hubiéramos osado
osaras	osarais	hubieras osado	hubierais osado
osara	osaran	hubiera osado	hubieran osado
OR		OR	
osase	osásemos	hubiese osado	hubiésemos osado
osases	osaseis	hubieses osado	hubieseis osado
osase	osasen	hubiese osado	hubiesen osado

	imperativo	
—		osemos
osa; no oses		osad; no oséis
ose		osen

Words and expressions related to this verb
osado, osada　audacious, bold, daring　　　　**la osadía**　audacity, boldness
osadamente　boldly, daringly

Check out the verb drills and verb tests with answers explained on pages 45–91.

Regular **-ar** verb endings with spelling change: **g** becomes **gu** before **e** to pay (for)

The Seven Simple Tenses		The Seven Compound Tenses	
Singular	Plural	Singular	Plural
1 presente de indicativo		8 perfecto de indicativo	
pago	pagamos	he pagado	hemos pagado
pagas	pagáis	has pagado	habéis pagado
paga	pagan	ha pagado	han pagado
2 imperfecto de indicativo		9 pluscuamperfecto de indicativo	
pagaba	pagábamos	había pagado	habíamos pagado
pagabas	pagabais	habías pagado	habíais pagado
pagaba	pagaban	había pagado	habían pagado
3 pretérito		10 pretérito anterior	
pagué	pagamos	hube pagado	hubimos pagado
pagaste	pagasteis	hubiste pagado	hubisteis pagado
pagó	pagaron	hubo pagado	hubieron pagado
4 futuro		11 futuro perfecto	
pagaré	pagaremos	habré pagado	habremos pagado
pagarás	pagaréis	habrás pagado	habréis pagado
pagará	pagarán	habrá pagado	habrán pagado
5 potencial simple		12 potencial compuesto	
pagaría	pagaríamos	habría pagado	habríamos pagado
pagarías	pagaríais	habrías pagado	habríais pagado
pagaría	pagarían	habría pagado	habrían pagado
6 presente de subjuntivo		13 perfecto de subjuntivo	
pague	paguemos	haya pagado	hayamos pagado
pagues	paguéis	hayas pagado	hayáis pagado
pague	paguen	haya pagado	hayan pagado
7 imperfecto de subjuntivo		14 pluscuamperfecto de subjuntivo	
pagara	pagáramos	hubiera pagado	hubiéramos pagado
pagaras	pagarais	hubieras pagado	hubierais pagado
pagara	pagaran	hubiera pagado	hubieran pagado
OR		OR	
pagase	pagásemos	hubiese pagado	hubiésemos pagado
pagases	pagaseis	hubieses pagado	hubieseis pagado
pagase	pagasen	hubiese pagado	hubiesen pagado

imperativo	
—	paguemos
paga; no pagues	pagad; no paguéis
pague	paguen

**AN ESSENTIAL
55 VERB**

Pagar

Pagar is an essential verb to learn because it is a regular –ar verb with an important spelling change. This verb is useful in many everyday expressions, especially when traveling.

Sentences using pagar

¿Dónde se paga la cuenta?
Where is the bill paid? Where can one pay the bill?

¿Cuánto le debo? Voy a pagar al contado.
How much do I owe you? I'm going to pay in cash.

Words and expressions related to this verb

la paga **pay**

el pago, el pagamiento **payment**

pagable **payable**

pagador, pagadora **payer**

el pagaré **promissory note, IOU**

pagar un crimen **to pay for a crime**

pagar las culpas **to pay for one's sins**

pagar al contado **to pay in cash**

pagar contra entrega **C.O.D. (Collect on delivery)**

pagar la cuenta **to pay the bill**

pagar un ojo de la cara **to pay an arm and a leg; to pay through your nose**

pagar los platos rotos **to pay the cost (pay for the damage)**

Proverbs

Paga lo que debes y sabrás lo que tienes.
Pay what you owe and you'll know what you have.

Él que la hace la paga.
You have to pay the consequences. (You made your bed, now sleep in it.)

Can't remember the Spanish verb you need?
Check the back pages of this book for the English-Spanish verb index!

Regular **-ar** verb   to stop (someone or something)

The Seven Simple Tenses		The Seven Compound Tenses	
Singular	Plural	Singular	Plural
1 presente de indicativo		8 perfecto de indicativo	
paro	**paramos**	**he parado**	**hemos parado**
paras	**paráis**	**has parado**	**habéis parado**
para	**paran**	**ha parado**	**han parado**
2 imperfecto de indicativo		9 pluscuamperfecto de indicativo	
paraba	**parábamos**	**había parado**	**habíamos parado**
parabas	**parabais**	**habías parado**	**habíais parado**
paraba	**paraban**	**había parado**	**habían parado**
3 pretérito		10 pretérito anterior	
paré	**paramos**	**hube parado**	**hubimos parado**
paraste	**parasteis**	**hubiste parado**	**hubisteis parado**
paró	**pararon**	**hubo parado**	**hubieron parado**
4 futuro		11 futuro perfecto	
pararé	**pararemos**	**habré parado**	**habremos parado**
pararás	**pararéis**	**habrás parado**	**habréis parado**
parará	**pararán**	**habrá parado**	**habrán parado**
5 potencial simple		12 potencial compuesto	
pararía	**pararíamos**	**habría parado**	**habríamos parado**
pararías	**pararíais**	**habrías parado**	**habríais parado**
pararía	**pararían**	**habría parado**	**habrían parado**
6 presente de subjuntivo		13 perfecto de subjuntivo	
pare	**paremos**	**haya parado**	**hayamos parado**
pares	**paréis**	**hayas parado**	**hayáis parado**
pare	**paren**	**haya parado**	**hayan parado**
7 imperfecto de subjuntivo		14 pluscuamperfecto de subjuntivo	
parara	**paráramos**	**hubiera parado**	**hubiéramos parado**
pararas	**pararais**	**hubieras parado**	**hubierais parado**
parara	**pararan**	**hubiera parado**	**hubieran parado**
OR		OR	
parase	**parásemos**	**hubiese parado**	**hubiésemos parado**
parases	**paraseis**	**hubieses parado**	**hubieseis parado**
parase	**parasen**	**hubiese parado**	**hubiesen parado**

	imperativo	
—	**paremos**	
para; no pares	**parad; no paréis**	
pare	**paren**	

Words and expressions related to this verb
parar en mal   to end badly   **la parada del autobús**   bus stop
PARADA   STOP   **parar en seco**   dead stop
la parada de coches   taxi stand   **una paradeta**   short stop
pararse en   to pay attention to   **sin parar**   right away (without stopping)

For other words and expressions related to this verb, see **pararse.**

The subject pronouns are found on page 93.   **471**

to stop (oneself)   Reflexive regular **-ar** verb

The Seven Simple Tenses		The Seven Compound Tenses	
Singular	Plural	Singular	Plural
1 presente de indicativo		8 perfecto de indicativo	
me paro	nos paramos	me he parado	nos hemos parado
te paras	os paráis	te has parado	os habéis parado
se para	se paran	se ha parado	se han parado
2 imperfecto de indicativo		9 pluscuamperfecto de indicativo	
me paraba	nos parábamos	me había parado	nos habíamos parado
te parabas	os parabais	te habías parado	os habíais parado
se paraba	se paraban	se había parado	se habían parado
3 pretérito		10 pretérito anterior	
me paré	nos paramos	me hube parado	nos hubimos parado
te paraste	os parasteis	te hubiste parado	os hubisteis parado
se paró	se pararon	se hubo parado	se hubieron parado
4 futuro		11 futuro perfecto	
me pararé	nos pararemos	me habré parado	nos habremos parado
te pararás	os pararéis	te habrás parado	os habréis parado
se parará	se pararán	se habrá parado	se habrán parado
5 potencial simple		12 potencial compuesto	
me pararía	nos pararíamos	me habría parado	nos habríamos parado
te pararías	osараríais	te habrías parado	os habríais parado
se pararía	se pararían	se habría parado	se habrían parado
6 presente de subjuntivo		13 perfecto de subjuntivo	
me pare	nos paremos	me haya parado	nos hayamos parado
te pares	os paréis	te hayas parado	os hayáis parado
se pare	se paren	se haya parado	se hayan parado
7 imperfecto de subjuntivo		14 pluscuamperfecto de subjuntivo	
me parara	nos paráramos	me hubiera parado	nos hubiéramos parado
te pararas	os pararais	te hubieras parado	os hubierais parado
se parara	se pararan	se hubiera parado	se hubieran parado
OR		OR	
me parase	nos parásemos	me hubiese parado	nos hubiésemos parado
te parases	os paraseis	te hubieses parado	os hubieseis parado
se parase	se parasen	se hubiese parado	se hubiesen parado

imperativo

—	parémonos
párate; no te pares	paraos; no os paréis
párese	párense

Words and expressions related to this verb

la parada   stop

una paradeta, una paradilla   pause

una parada en seco   dead stop

parar   to stop (someone or something)

no poder parar   to be restless

parar en mal   to end badly

For other words and expressions related to this verb, see **parar**.

Get acquainted with what preposition goes with what verb on pages 669–677.

Regular **-er** verb endings with spelling   to seem, to appear
change: **c** becomes **zc** before **a** or **o**

The Seven Simple Tenses		The Seven Compound Tenses	
Singular	Plural	Singular	Plural
1 presente de indicativo		8 perfecto de indicativo	
parezco	**parecemos**	**he parecido**	**hemos parecido**
pareces	**parecéis**	**has parecido**	**habéis parecido**
parece	**parecen**	**ha parecido**	**han parecido**
2 imperfecto de indicativo		9 pluscuamperfecto de indicativo	
parecía	**parecíamos**	**había parecido**	**habíamos parecido**
parecías	**parecíais**	**habías parecido**	**habíais parecido**
parecía	**parecían**	**había parecido**	**habían parecido**
3 pretérito		10 pretérito anterior	
parecí	**parecimos**	**hube parecido**	**hubimos parecido**
pareciste	**parecisteis**	**hubiste parecido**	**hubisteis parecido**
pareció	**parecieron**	**hubo parecido**	**hubieron parecido**
4 futuro		11 futuro perfecto	
pareceré	**pareceremos**	**habré parecido**	**habremos parecido**
parecerás	**pareceréis**	**habrás parecido**	**habréis parecido**
parecerá	**parecerán**	**habrá parecido**	**habrán parecido**
5 potencial simple		12 potencial compuesto	
parecería	**pareceríamos**	**habría parecido**	**habríamos parecido**
parecerías	**pareceríais**	**habrías parecido**	**habríais parecido**
parecería	**parecerían**	**habría parecido**	**habrían parecido**
6 presente de subjuntivo		13 perfecto de subjuntivo	
parezca	**parezcamos**	**haya parecido**	**hayamos parecido**
parezcas	**parezcáis**	**hayas parecido**	**hayáis parecido**
parezca	**parezcan**	**haya parecido**	**hayan parecido**
7 imperfecto de subjuntivo		14 pluscuamperfecto de subjuntivo	
pareciera	**pareciéramos**	**hubiera parecido**	**hubiéramos parecido**
parecieras	**parecierais**	**hubieras parecido**	**hubierais parecido**
pareciera	**parecieran**	**hubiera parecido**	**hubieran parecido**
OR		OR	
pareciese	**pareciésemos**	**hubiese parecido**	**hubiésemos parecido**
parecieses	**parecieseis**	**hubieses parecido**	**hubieseis parecido**
pareciese	**pareciesen**	**hubiese parecido**	**hubiesen parecido**

imperativo

—	**parezcamos**
parece; no parezcas	**pareced; no parezcáis**
parezca	**parezcan**

Words and expressions related to this verb
a lo que parece   according to what it seems
al parecer   seemingly, apparently
pareciente   similar
parecerse a   to resemble each other, to look alike
María parece contenta.   Maria seems happy.

Me parece . . .   It seems to me . . .
por el bien parecer   for the sake of
   appearances
parecer cansado (cansada)   to look (seem) tired

See also **parecerse.**

The subject pronouns are found on page 93.

473

parecerse (345) Gerundio **pareciéndose** Part. pas. **parecido**

to resemble each other,
to look alike

Reflexive verb; regular **-er** verb endings with
spelling change: **c** becomes **zc** before **a** or **o**

The Seven Simple Tenses

The Seven Compound Tenses

Singular	Plural	Singular	Plural
1 presente de indicativo		8 perfecto de indicativo	
me parezco	nos parecemos	me he parecido	nos hemos parecido
te pareces	os parecéis	te has parecido	os habéis parecido
se parece	se parecen	se ha parecido	se han parecido
2 imperfecto de indicativo		9 pluscuamperfecto de indicativo	
me parecía	nos parecíamos	me había parecido	nos habíamos parecido
te parecías	os parecíais	te habías parecido	os habíais parecido
se parecía	se parecían	se había parecido	se habían parecido
3 pretérito		10 pretérito anterior	
me parecí	nos parecimos	me hube parecido	nos hubimos parecido
te pareciste	os parecisteis	te hubiste parecido	os hubisteis parecido
se pareció	se parecieron	se hubo parecido	se hubieron parecido
4 futuro		11 futuro perfecto	
me pareceré	nos pareceremos	me habré parecido	nos habremos parecido
te parecerás	os pareceréis	te habrás parecido	os habréis parecido
se parecerá	se parecerán	se habrá parecido	se habrán parecido
5 potencial simple		12 potencial compuesto	
me parecería	nos pareceríamos	me habría parecido	nos habríamos parecido
te parecerías	os pareceríais	te habrías parecido	os habríais parecido
se parecería	se parecerían	se habría parecido	se habrían parecido
6 presente de subjuntivo		13 perfecto de subjuntivo	
me parezca	nos parezcamos	me haya parecido	nos hayamos parecido
te parezcas	os parezcáis	te hayas parecido	os hayáis parecido
se parezca	se parezcan	se haya parecido	se hayan parecido
7 imperfecto de subjuntivo		14 pluscuamperfecto de subjuntivo	
me pareciera	nos pareciéramos	me hubiera parecido	nos hubiéramos parecido
te parecieras	os parecierais	te hubieras parecido	os hubierais parecido
se pareciera	se parecieran	se hubiera parecido	se hubieran parecido
OR		OR	
me pareciese	nos pareciésemos	me hubiese parecido	nos hubiésemos parecido
te parecieses	os parecieseis	te hubieses parecido	os hubieseis parecido
se pareciese	se pareciesen	se hubiese parecido	se hubiesen parecido

imperativo

—	parezcámonos
parécete; no te parezcas	pareceos; no os parezcáis
parézcase	parézcanse

Words and expressions related to this verb
parecer   to seem, to appear
a lo que parece   according to what it seems

al parecer   seemingly, apparently
pareciente   similar

See also **parecer.**

Can't find the verb you're looking for?
Check the back pages of this book for a list of over 2,100 additional verbs!

Regular **-ir** verb   to leave, to depart, to divide, to split

The Seven Simple Tenses		The Seven Compound Tenses	
Singular	Plural	Singular	Plural
1 presente de indicativo		8 perfecto de indicativo	
parto	**partimos**	**he partido**	**hemos partido**
partes	**partís**	**has partido**	**habéis partido**
parte	**parten**	**ha partido**	**han partido**
2 imperfecto de indicativo		9 pluscuamperfecto de indicativo	
partía	**partíamos**	**había partido**	**habíamos partido**
partías	**partíais**	**habías partido**	**habíais partido**
partía	**partían**	**había partido**	**habían partido**
3 pretérito		10 pretérito anterior	
partí	**partimos**	**hube partido**	**hubimos partido**
partiste	**partisteis**	**hubiste partido**	**hubisteis partido**
partió	**partieron**	**hubo partido**	**hubieron partido**
4 futuro		11 futuro perfecto	
partiré	**partiremos**	**habré partido**	**habremos partido**
partirás	**partiréis**	**habrás partido**	**habréis partido**
partirá	**partirán**	**habrá partido**	**habrán partido**
5 potencial simple		12 potencial compuesto	
partiría	**partiríamos**	**habría partido**	**habríamos partido**
partirías	**partiríais**	**habrías partido**	**habríais partido**
partiría	**partirían**	**habría partido**	**habrían partido**
6 presente de subjuntivo		13 perfecto de subjuntivo	
parta	**partamos**	**haya partido**	**hayamos partido**
partas	**partáis**	**hayas partido**	**hayáis partido**
parta	**partan**	**haya partido**	**hayan partido**
7 imperfecto de subjuntivo		14 pluscuamperfecto de subjuntivo	
partiera	**partiéramos**	**hubiera partido**	**hubiéramos partido**
partieras	**partierais**	**hubieras partido**	**hubierais partido**
partiera	**partieran**	**hubiera partido**	**hubieran partido**
OR		OR	
partiese	**partiésemos**	**hubiese partido**	**hubiésemos partido**
partieses	**partieseis**	**hubieses partido**	**hubieseis partido**
partiese	**partiesen**	**hubiese partido**	**hubiesen partido**

P

	imperativo	
—		**partamos**
parte; no partas		**partid; no partáis**
parta		**partan**

Words and expressions related to this verb
a partir de   beginning with, starting from
tomar partido   to take sides, to make up
   one's mind
la partida   departure

partirse   to become divided
repartir   to distribute
partir algo en dos   to divide something
   in two

See also **repartir**.

The subject pronouns are found on page 93.

to pass (by), to happen, to spend (time)   Regular **-ar** verb

The Seven Simple Tenses		The Seven Compound Tenses	
Singular	Plural	Singular	Plural
1 presente de indicativo		8 perfecto de indicativo	
paso	pasamos	he pasado	hemos pasado
pasas	pasáis	has pasado	habéis pasado
pasa	pasan	ha pasado	han pasado
2 imperfecto de indicativo		9 pluscuamperfecto de indicativo	
pasaba	pasábamos	había pasado	habíamos pasado
pasabas	pasabais	habías pasado	habíais pasado
pasaba	pasaban	había pasado	habían pasado
3 pretérito		10 pretérito anterior	
pasé	pasamos	hube pasado	hubimos pasado
pasaste	pasasteis	hubiste pasado	hubisteis pasado
pasó	pasaron	hubo pasado	hubieron pasado
4 futuro		11 futuro perfecto	
pasaré	pasaremos	habré pasado	habremos pasado
pasarás	pasaréis	habrás pasado	habréis pasado
pasará	pasarán	habrá pasado	habrán pasado
5 potencial simple		12 potencial compuesto	
pasaría	pasaríamos	habría pasado	habríamos pasado
pasarías	pasaríais	habrías pasado	habríais pasado
pasaría	pasarían	habría pasado	habrían pasado
6 presente de subjuntivo		13 perfecto de subjuntivo	
pase	pasemos	haya pasado	hayamos pasado
pases	paséis	hayas pasado	hayáis pasado
pase	pasen	haya pasado	hayan pasado
7 imperfecto de subjuntivo		14 pluscuamperfecto de subjuntivo	
pasara	pasáramos	hubiera pasado	hubiéramos pasado
pasaras	pasarais	hubieras pasado	hubierais pasado
pasara	pasaran	hubiera pasado	hubieran pasado
OR		OR	
pasase	pasásemos	hubiese pasado	hubiésemos pasado
pasases	pasaseis	hubieses pasado	hubieseis pasado
pasase	pasasen	hubiese pasado	hubiesen pasado

imperativo		
—		pasemos
pasa; no pases		pasad; no paséis
pase		pasen

Words and expressions related to this verb
pasajero, pasajera passenger, traveler
¡Que lo pase Ud. bien! Good luck, good bye!
¿Qué pasa? What's happening? What's going on?

el pasatiempo amusement, pastime
¿Qué te pasa? What's the matter with you?
¡Pase un buen día! Have a nice day!
pasar un examen to take an exam

Use **pasar** when you spend time: **Me gustaría pasar un año en Costa Rica**/I would like to spend a year in Costa Rica. (See **gastar**.)

Reflexive regular **-ar** verb   to take a walk, to parade

The Seven Simple Tenses		The Seven Compound Tenses	
Singular	Plural	Singular	Plural
1 presente de indicativo		8 perfecto de indicativo	
me paseo	nos paseamos	me he paseado	nos hemos paseado
te paseas	os paseáis	te has paseado	os habéis paseado
se pasea	se pasean	se ha paseado	se han paseado
2 imperfecto de indicativo		9 pluscuamperfecto de indicativo	
me paseaba	nos paseábamos	me había paseado	nos habíamos paseado
te paseabas	os paseabais	te habías paseado	os habíais paseado
se paseaba	se paseaban	se había paseado	se habían paseado
3 pretérito		10 pretérito anterior	
me paseé	nos paseamos	me hube paseado	nos hubimos paseado
te paseaste	os paseasteis	te hubiste paseado	os hubisteis paseado
se paseó	se pasearon	se hubo paseado	se hubieron paseado
4 futuro		11 futuro perfecto	
me pasearé	nos pasearemos	me habré paseado	nos habremos paseado
te pasearás	os pasearéis	te habrás paseado	os habréis paseado
se paseará	se pasearán	se habrá paseado	se habrán paseado
5 potencial simple		12 potencial compuesto	
me pasearía	nos pasearíamos	me habría paseado	nos habríamos paseado
te pasearías	os pasearíais	te habrías paseado	os habríais paseado
se pasearía	se pasearían	se habría paseado	se habrían paseado
6 presente de subjuntivo		13 perfecto de subjuntivo	
me pasee	nos paseemos	me haya paseado	nos hayamos paseado
te pasees	os paseéis	te hayas paseado	os hayáis paseado
se pasee	se paseen	se haya paseado	se hayan paseado
7 imperfecto de subjuntivo		14 pluscuamperfecto de subjuntivo	
me paseara	nos paseáramos	me hubiera paseado	nos hubiéramos paseado
te pasearas	os pasearais	te hubieras paseado	os hubierais paseado
se paseara	se pasearan	se hubiera paseado	se hubieran paseado
OR		OR	
me pasease	nos paseásemos	me hubiese paseado	nos hubiésemos paseado
te paseases	os paseaseis	te hubieses paseado	os hubieseis paseado
se pasease	se paseasen	se hubiese paseado	se hubiesen paseado

imperativo	
—	paseémonos
paséate; no te pasees	paseaos; no os paseéis
paséese	paséense

Words and expressions related to this verb

un pase pass, permit	**un paseo campestre** picnic
un, una paseante stroller	**sacar a paseo** to take out for a walk
un paseo a walk, a promenade	**pasear** to walk (a child, a dog, etc.)
dar un paseo to take a walk	**pasear en bicicleta** to go bicycling
ir de paseo to go out for a walk	**el paseíllo** opening parade at bullfight

Proverb: **Cuando el gato no está, el ratón se pasea.** When the cat's away, the mice will play. (When the cat's away, the mouse takes a walk.)

The subject pronouns are found on page 93.

to ask for, to request

The Seven Simple Tenses		The Seven Compound Tenses	

Singular	Plural	Singular	Plural
1 presente de indicativo		8 perfecto de indicativo	
pido	pedimos	he pedido	hemos pedido
pides	pedís	has pedido	habéis pedido
pide	piden	ha pedido	han pedido
2 imperfecto de indicativo		9 pluscuamperfecto de indicativo	
pedía	pedíamos	había pedido	habíamos pedido
pedías	pedíais	habías pedido	habíais pedido
pedía	pedían	había pedido	habían pedido
3 pretérito		10 pretérito anterior	
pedí	pedimos	hube pedido	hubimos pedido
pediste	pedisteis	hubiste pedido	hubisteis pedido
pidió	pidieron	hubo pedido	hubieron pedido
4 futuro		11 futuro perfecto	
pediré	pediremos	habré pedido	habremos pedido
pedirás	pediréis	habrás pedido	habréis pedido
pedirá	pedirán	habrá pedido	habrán pedido
5 potencial simple		12 potencial compuesto	
pediría	pediríamos	habría pedido	habríamos pedido
pedirías	pediríais	habrías pedido	habríais pedido
pediría	pedirían	habría pedido	habrían pedido
6 presente de subjuntivo		13 perfecto de subjuntivo	
pida	pidamos	haya pedido	hayamos pedido
pidas	pidáis	hayas pedido	hayáis pedido
pida	pidan	haya pedido	hayan pedido
7 imperfecto de subjuntivo		14 pluscuamperfecto de subjuntivo	
pidiera	pidiéramos	hubiera pedido	hubiéramos pedido
pidieras	pidierais	hubieras pedido	hubierais pedido
pidiera	pidieran	hubiera pedido	hubieran pedido
OR		OR	
pidiese	pidiésemos	hubiese pedido	hubiésemos pedido
pidieses	pidieseis	hubieses pedido	hubieseis pedido
pidiese	pidiesen	hubiese pedido	hubiesen pedido

imperativo

—	pidamos
pide; no pidas	pedid; no pidáis
pida	pidan

Words and expressions related to this verb
un pedimento petition
hacer un pedido to place an order
un pedido request, order
colocar un pedido to place an order
pedir prestado to borrow
una petición petition, request
un pedidor, una pedidora client, petitioner
pedir socorro to ask for help

Pedir means *to ask for something* or *to request*:
El alumno pidió un lápiz al profesor/The
pupil asked the teacher for a pencil.
When you want to say *to inquire, to ask a question,* use **preguntar**: **La alumna preguntó a
la profesora cómo estaba**/The pupil asked
the teacher how she was.
See also **despedirse**.

Regular **-ar** verb endings with spelling
change: **g** becomes **gu** before **e**

to beat, to hit, to slap, to stick,
to glue, to paste

The Seven Simple Tenses		The Seven Compound Tenses	
Singular	Plural	Singular	Plural
1 presente de indicativo		8 perfecto de indicativo	
pego	**pegamos**	**he pegado**	**hemos pegado**
pegas	**pegáis**	**has pegado**	**habéis pegado**
pega	**pegan**	**ha pegado**	**han pegado**
2 imperfecto de indicativo		9 pluscuamperfecto de indicativo	
pegaba	**pebábamos**	**había pegado**	**habíamos pegado**
pegabas	**pegabais**	**habías pegado**	**habíais pegado**
pegaba	**pegaban**	**había pegado**	**habían pegado**
3 pretérito		10 pretérito anterior	
pegué	**pegamos**	**hube pegado**	**hubimos pegado**
pegaste	**pesgasteis**	**hubiste pegado**	**hubisteis pegado**
pegó	**pegaron**	**hubo pegado**	**hubieron pegado**
4 futuro		11 futuro perfecto	
pegaré	**pegaremos**	**habré pegado**	**habremos pegado**
pegarás	**pegaréis**	**habrás pegado**	**habréis pegado**
pegará	**pegarán**	**habrá pegado**	**habrán pegado**
5 potencial simple		12 potencial compuesto	
pegaría	**pegaríamos**	**habría pegado**	**habríamos pegado**
pegarías	**pegaríais**	**habrías pegado**	**habríais pegado**
pegaría	**pegarían**	**habría pegado**	**habrían pegado**
6 presente de subjuntivo		13 perfecto de subjuntivo	
pegue	**peguemos**	**haya pegado**	**hayamos pegado**
pegues	**peguéis**	**hayas pegado**	**hayáis pegado**
pegue	**peguen**	**haya pegado**	**hayan pegado**
7 imperfecto de subjuntivo		14 pluscuamperfecto de subjuntivo	
pegara	**pegáramos**	**hubiera pegado**	**hubiéramos pegado**
pegaras	**pegarais**	**hubieras pegado**	**hubierais pegado**
pegara	**pegaran**	**hubiera pegado**	**hubieran pegado**
OR		OR	
pegase	**pegásemos**	**hubiese pegado**	**hubiésemos pegado**
pegases	**pegaseis**	**hubieses pegado**	**hubieseis pegado**
pegase	**pegasen**	**hubiese pegado**	**hubiesen pegado**

imperativo	
—	**peguemos**
pega; no pegues	**pegad; no peguéis**
pegue	**peguen**

Words and expressions related to this verb

pegar fuego   to set fire to
pegar saltos   to jump
pegar voces   to shout
el pegamento glue

pegarse las sábanas   to sleep late in the morning
pegársele a uno   to deceive someone
no pegar los ojos   to spend a sleepless night
una pegatina   sticker

For other words and expressions related to this verb, see **despegar.**

The subject pronouns are found on page 93.

to comb one's hair   Reflexive regular **-ar** verb

The Seven Simple Tenses		The Seven Compound Tenses	
Singular	Plural	Singular	Plural
1 presente de indicativo		**8 perfecto de indicativo**	
me peino	nos peinamos	me he peinado	nos hemos peinado
te peinas	os peináis	te has peinado	os habéis peinado
se peina	se peinan	se ha peinado	se han peinado
2 imperfecto de indicativo		**9 pluscuamperfecto de indicativo**	
me peinaba	nos peinábamos	me había peinado	nos habíamos peinado
te peinabas	os peinabais	te habías peinado	os habíais peinado
se peinaba	se peinaban	se había peinado	se habían peinado
3 pretérito		**10 pretérito anterior**	
me peiné	nos peinamos	me hube peinado	nos hubimos peinado
te peinaste	os peinasteis	te hubiste peinado	os hubisteis peinado
se peinó	se peinaron	se hubo peinado	se hubieron peinado
4 futuro		**11 futuro perfecto**	
me peinaré	nos peinaremos	me habré peinado	nos habremos peinado
te peinarás	os peinaréis	te habrás peinado	os habréis peinado
se peinará	se peinarán	se habrá peinado	se habrán peinado
5 potencial simple		**12 potencial compuesto**	
me peinaría	nos peinaríamos	me habría peinado	nos habríamos peinado
te peinarías	os peinaríais	te habrías peinado	os habríais peinado
se peinaría	se peinarían	se habría peinado	se habrían peinado
6 presente de subjuntivo		**13 perfecto de subjuntivo**	
me peine	nos peinemos	me haya peinado	nos hayamos peinado
te peines	os peinéis	te hayas peinado	os hayáis peinado
se peine	se peinen	se haya peinado	se hayan peinado
7 imperfecto de subjuntivo		**14 pluscuamperfecto de subjuntivo**	
me peinara	nos peináramos	me hubiera peinado	nos hubiéramos peinado
te peinaras	os peinarais	te hubieras peinado	os hubierais peinado
se peinara	se peinaran	se hubiera peinado	se hubieran peinado
OR		OR	
me peinase	nos peinásemos	me hubiese peinado	nos hubiésemos peinado
te peinases	os peinaseis	te hubieses peinado	os hubieseis peinado
se peinase	se peinasen	se hubiese peinado	se hubiesen peinado

	imperativo	
—		peinémonos
péinate; no te peines		peinaos; no os peinéis
péinese		péinense

Words and expressions related to this verb

un peine a comb
una peineta shell comb (used by women as an ornament in the hair)
un peinado hairdo, hair style

un peinador dressing gown
peinar to comb; **peinarse** to comb one's hair
despeinarse to dishevel, to take down one's hair

Can't find the verb you're looking for?
Check the back pages of this book for a list of over 2,100 additional verbs!

Regular **-ar** verb endings with stem   to think
change: Tenses 1, 6, Imperative

The Seven Simple Tenses		The Seven Compound Tenses	
Singular	Plural	Singular	Plural
1 presente de indicativo		8 perfecto de indicativo	
pienso	**pensamos**	**he pensado**	**hemos pensado**
piensas	**pensáis**	**has pensado**	**habéis pensado**
piensa	**piensan**	**ha pensado**	**han pensado**
2 imperfecto de indicativo		9 pluscuamperfecto de indicativo	
pensaba	**pensábamos**	**había pensado**	**habíamos pensado**
pensabas	**pensabais**	**habías pensado**	**habíais pensado**
pensaba	**pensaban**	**había pensado**	**habían pensado**
3 pretérito		10 pretérito anterior	
pensé	**pensamos**	**hube pensado**	**hubimos pensado**
pensaste	**pensasteis**	**hubiste pensado**	**hubisteis pensado**
pensó	**pensaron**	**hubo pensado**	**hubieron pensado**
4 futuro		11 futuro perfecto	
pensaré	**pensaremos**	**habré pensado**	**habremos pensado**
pensarás	**pensaréis**	**habrás pensado**	**habréis pensado**
pensará	**pensarán**	**habrá pensado**	**habrán pensado**
5 potencial simple		12 potencial compuesto	
pensaría	**pensaríamos**	**habría pensado**	**habríamos pensado**
pensarías	**pensaríais**	**habrías pensado**	**habríais pensado**
pensaría	**pensarían**	**habría pensado**	**habrían pensado**
6 presente de subjuntivo		13 perfecto de subjuntivo	
piense	**pensemos**	**haya pensado**	**hayamos pensado**
pienses	**penséis**	**hayas pensado**	**hayáis pensado**
piense	**piensen**	**haya pensado**	**hayan pensado**
7 imperfecto de subjuntivo		14 pluscuamperfecto de subjuntivo	
pensara	**pensáramos**	**hubiera pensado**	**hubiéramos pensado**
pensaras	**pensarais**	**hubieras pensado**	**hubierais pensado**
pensara	**pensaran**	**hubiera pensado**	**hubieran pensado**
OR		OR	
pensase	**pensásemos**	**hubiese pensado**	**hubiésemos pensado**
pensases	**pensaseis**	**hubieses pensado**	**hubieseis pensado**
pensase	**pensasen**	**hubiese pensado**	**hubiesen pensado**

imperativo

—	**pensemos**
piensa; no pienses	**pensad; no penséis**
piense	**piensen**

P

**AN ESSENTIAL
55 VERB**

Pensar

We think that **pensar** is a very useful verb for you to learn. It is used in a great number of idiomatic expressions and everyday situations. Pay attention to the stem change in Tenses 1 and 6 and in the imperative mood.

Pensar is used with the preposition **de** when you ask someone what he/she thinks of someone or something, i.e., when you ask for someone's opinion: **¿Qué piensa Ud. de este libro?**/What do you think of this book? **Pienso que es bueno**/I think that it is good.

Pensar is used with the preposition **en** when you ask someone what or whom he/she is thinking about: **Miguel, no hablas mucho; ¿en qué piensas?**/Michael, you are not talking much; what are you thinking of? (of what are you thinking?); **Pienso en las vacaciones de verano**/I'm thinking of summer vacation.

Sentences using pensar and related words

¿Qué piensa Ud. de eso?
What do you think of that?

¿En qué piensa Ud.?
What are you thinking of?

Pensamos comprar una casa.
We intend to buy a house.

Words and expressions related to this verb

pensativo, pensativa **thoughtful, pensive**

un pensador, una pensadora **a thinker**

pensar + inf. **to intend + inf.**

pensar en **to think of, about**

sin pensar **thoughtlessly**

repensar **to think over (again)**

Proverb

Antes de hablar es bueno pensar.
(It's good to) think before you speak.

Don't forget to study the section on defective and impersonal verbs. It's right after this main list.

The Seven Simple Tenses		The Seven Compound Tenses	
Singular	Plural	Singular	Plural
1 presente de indicativo		8 perfecto de indicativo	
percibo	**percibimos**	**he percibido**	**hemos percibido**
percibes	**percibís**	**has percibido**	**habéis percibido**
percibe	**perciben**	**ha percibido**	**han percibido**
2 imperfecto de indicativo		9 pluscuamperfecto de indicativo	
percibía	**percibíamos**	**había percibido**	**habíamos percibido**
percibías	**percibíais**	**habías percibido**	**habíais percibido**
percibía	**percibían**	**había percibido**	**habían percibido**
3 pretérito		10 pretérito anterior	
percibí	**percibimos**	**hube percibido**	**hubimos percibido**
percibiste	**percibisteis**	**hubiste percibido**	**hubisteis percibido**
percibió	**percibieron**	**hubo percibido**	**hubieron percibido**
4 futuro		11 futuro perfecto	
percibiré	**percibiremos**	**habré percibido**	**habremos percibido**
percibirás	**percibiréis**	**habrás percibido**	**habréis percibido**
percibirá	**percibirán**	**habrá percibido**	**habrán percibido**
5 potencial simple		12 potencial compuesto	
percibiría	**percibiríamos**	**habría percibido**	**habríamos percibido**
percibirías	**percibiríais**	**habrías percibido**	**habríais percibido**
percibiría	**percibirían**	**habría percibido**	**habrían percibido**
6 presente de subjuntivo		13 perfecto de subjuntivo	
perciba	**percibamos**	**haya percibido**	**hayamos percibido**
percibas	**percibáis**	**hayas percibido**	**hayáis percibido**
perciba	**perciban**	**haya percibido**	**hayan percibido**
7 imperfecto de subjuntivo		14 pluscuamperfecto de subjuntivo	
percibiera	**percibiéramos**	**hubiera percibido**	**hubiéramos percibido**
percibieras	**percibierais**	**hubieras percibido**	**hubierais percibido**
percibiera	**percibieran**	**hubiera percibido**	**hubieran percibido**
OR		OR	
percibiese	**percibiésemos**	**hubiese percibido**	**hubiésemos percibido**
percibieses	**percibieseis**	**hubieses percibido**	**hubieseis percibido**
percibiese	**percibiesen**	**hubiese percibido**	**hubiesen percibido**

	imperativo	
—		**percibamos**
percibe; no percibas		**percibid; no percibáis**
perciba		**perciban**

Words and expressions related to this verb

la percepción   perception   **perceptiblemente**   perceptibly
la perceptibilidad   perceptibility   **perceptivo, perceptiva**   perceptive
perceptible   perceptible, perceivable   **imperceptible**   imperceptible

Check out the verb drills and verb tests with answers explained on pages 45–91.

The subject pronouns are found on page 93.

to lose

Regular **-er** verb endings with stem
change: Tenses 1, 6, Imperative

The Seven Simple Tenses		The Seven Compound Tenses	
Singular	Plural	Singular	Plural
1 presente de indicativo		8 perfecto de indicativo	
pierdo	perdemos	he perdido	hemos perdido
pierdes	perdéis	has perdido	habéis perdido
pierde	pierden	ha perdido	han perdido
2 imperfecto de indicativo		9 pluscuamperfecto de indicativo	
perdía	perdíamos	había perdido	habíamos perdido
perdías	perdíais	habías perdido	habíais perdido
perdía	perdían	había perdido	habían perdido
3 pretérito		10 pretérito anterior	
perdí	perdimos	hube perdido	hubimos perdido
perdiste	perdisteis	hubiste perdido	hubisteis perdido
perdió	perdieron	hubo perdido	hubieron perdido
4 futuro		11 futuro perfecto	
perderé	perderemos	habré perdido	habremos perdido
perderás	perderéis	habrás perdido	habréis perdido
perderá	perderán	habrá perdido	habrán perdido
5 potencial simple		12 potencial compuesto	
perdería	perderíamos	habría perdido	habríamos perdido
perderías	perderíais	habrías perdido	habríais perdido
perdería	perderían	habría perdido	habrían perdido
6 presente de subjuntivo		13 perfecto de subjuntivo	
pierda	perdamos	haya perdido	hayamos perdido
pierdas	perdáis	hayas perdido	hayáis perdido
pierda	pierdan	haya perdido	hayan perdido
7 imperfecto de subjuntivo		14 pluscuamperfecto de subjuntivo	
perdiera	perdiéramos	hubiera perdido	hubiéramos perdido
perdieras	perdierais	hubieras perdido	hubierais perdido
perdiera	perdieran	hubiera perdido	hubieran perdido
OR		OR	
perdiese	perdiésemos	hubiese perdido	hubiésemos perdido
perdieses	perdieseis	hubieses perdido	hubieseis perdido
perdiese	perdiesen	hubiese perdido	hubiesen perdido

imperativo

—	perdamos
pierde; no pierdas	perded; no perdáis
pierda	pierdan

Perder is a very useful verb for a beginning student. It is used in a great number of idiomatic expressions and everyday situations. Pay attention to the stem change in Tenses 1 and 6 and in the imperative mood.

Sentences using perder and related words

El señor Santiago pierde mucho dinero.
Mr. Santiago loses a lot of money.

Este chico está perdido.
This boy is lost.

Proverbs

El que todo lo quiere, todo lo pierde.
Whoever wants everything loses everything.

El tiempo perdido no se recobra.
One can never get back lost time.

Lo que hoy se pierde, se gana mañana.
What is lost today is won tomorrow.

Words and expressions related to this verb

un perdedor, una perdedora **loser**

la pérdida **loss**

perdidamente enamorado (enamorada) **passionately in love**

perder de vista a (alguien) **to lose sight of (someone)**

estar perdido (perdida) **to be lost**

perder el juicio **to go mad (crazy)**

perder los estribos **to lose self-control**

perderse **to lose one's way, to get lost**

la perdición **loss, ruin, perdition**

P

Can't remember the Spanish verb you need?
Check the back pages of this book for the English-Spanish verb index!

The subject pronouns are found on page 93.

to pardon, to forgive, to excuse   Regular **-ar** verb

The Seven Simple Tenses		The Seven Compound Tenses	
Singular	Plural	Singular	Plural
1 presente de indicativo		8 perfecto de indicativo	
perdono	perdonamos	he perdonado	hemos perdonado
perdonas	perdonáis	has perdonado	habéis perdonado
perdona	perdonan	ha perdonado	han perdonado
2 imperfecto de indicativo		9 pluscuamperfecto de indicativo	
perdonaba	perdonábamos	había perdonado	habíamos perdonado
perdonabas	perdonabais	habías perdonado	habíais perdonado
perdonaba	perdonaban	había perdonado	habían perdonado
3 pretérito		10 pretérito anterior	
perdoné	perdonamos	hube perdonado	hubimos perdonado
perdonaste	perdonasteis	hubiste perdonado	hubisteis perdonado
perdonó	perdonaron	hubo perdonado	hubieron perdonado
4 futuro		11 futuro perfecto	
perdonaré	perdonaremos	habré perdonado	habremos perdonado
perdonarás	perdonaréis	habrás perdonado	habréis perdonado
perdonará	perdonarán	habrá perdonado	habrán perdonado
5 potencial simple		12 potencial compuesto	
perdonaría	perdonaríamos	habría perdonado	habríamos perdonado
perdonarías	perdonaríais	habrías perdonado	habríais perdonado
perdonaría	perdonarían	habría perdonado	habrían perdonado
6 presente de subjuntivo		13 perfecto de subjuntivo	
perdone	perdonemos	haya perdonado	hayamos perdonado
perdones	perdonéis	hayas perdonado	hayáis perdonado
perdone	perdonen	haya perdonado	hayan perdonado
7 imperfecto de subjuntivo		14 pluscuamperfecto de subjuntivo	
perdonara	perdonáramos	hubiera perdonado	hubiéramos perdonado
perdonaras	perdonarais	hubieras perdonado	hubierais perdonado
perdonara	perdonaran	hubiera perdonado	hubieran perdonado
OR		OR	
perdonase	perdonásemos	hubiese perdonado	hubiésemos perdonado
perdonases	perdonaseis	hubieses perdonado	hubieseis perdonado
perdonase	perdonasen	hubiese perdonado	hubiesen perdonado

imperativo	
—	perdonemos
perdona; no perdones	perdonad; no perdonéis
perdone	perdonen

Words and expressions related to this verb
el perdón pardon, forgiveness
perdonable pardonable, forgivable
imperdonable unpardonable

Perdóneme Pardon me.
donar to donate; **el don** gift
¡Perdón! I'm sorry!

If you want to see a sample English verb fully conjugated
in all the tenses, check out pages 11 and 12.

Regular **-ir** verb   to permit, to admit, to allow, to grant

The Seven Simple Tenses		The Seven Compound Tenses	
Singular	Plural	Singular	Plural
1 presente de indicativo		8 perfecto de indicativo	
permito	permitimos	he permitido	hemos permitido
permites	permitís	has permitido	habéis permitido
permite	permiten	ha permitido	han permitido
2 imperfecto de indicativo		9 pluscuamperfecto de indicativo	
permitía	permitíamos	había permitido	habíamos permitido
permitías	permitíais	habías permitido	habíais permitido
permitía	permitían	había permitido	habían permitido
3 pretérito		10 pretérito anterior	
permití	permitimos	hube permitido	hubimos permitido
permitiste	permitisteis	hubiste permitido	hubisteis permitido
permitió	permitieron	hubo permitido	hubieron permitido
4 futuro		11 futuro perfecto	
permitiré	permitiremos	habré permitido	habremos permitido
permitirás	permitiréis	habrás permitido	habréis permitido
permitirá	permitirán	habrá permitido	habrán permitido
5 potencial simple		12 potencial compuesto	
permitiría	permitiríamos	habría permitido	habríamos permitido
permitirías	permitiríais	habrías permitido	habríais permitido
permitiría	permitirían	habría permitido	habrían permitido
6 presente de subjuntivo		13 perfecto de subjuntivo	
permita	permitamos	haya permitido	hayamos permitido
permitas	permitáis	hayas permitido	hayáis permitido
permita	permitan	haya permitido	hayan permitido
7 imperfecto de subjuntivo		14 pluscuamperfecto de subjuntivo	
permitiera	permitiéramos	hubiera permitido	hubiéramos permitido
permitieras	permitierais	hubieras permitido	hubierais permitido
permitiera	permitieran	hubiera permitido	hubieran permitido
OR		OR	
permitiese	permitiésemos	hubiese permitido	hubiésemos permitido
permitieses	permitieseis	hubieses permitido	hubieseis permitido
permitiese	permitiesen	hubiese permitido	hubiesen permitido

P

imperativo

—	permitamos
permite; no permitas	permitid; no permitáis
permita	permitan

Words and expressions related to this verb
el permiso permit, permission
¡Con permiso! Excuse me!
la permisión permission
emitir to emit
No se permite + inf. It is not permitted to + inf.

admitir to admit
permitirse + inf. to take the liberty + inf.
el permiso de conducir driver's license
transmitir to transmit

The subject pronouns are found on page 93.

to pertain, to appertain, to belong   Regular **-er** verb endings with spelling change: **c** becomes **zc** before **a** or **o**

The Seven Simple Tenses | The Seven Compound Tenses

Singular	Plural	Singular	Plural
1 presente de indicativo		**8 perfecto de indicativo**	
pertenezco	pertenecemos	he pertenecido	hemos pertenecido
perteneces	pertenecéis	has pertenecido	habéis pertenecido
pertenece	pertenecen	ha pertenecido	han pertenecido
2 imperfecto de indicativo		**9 pluscuamperfecto de indicativo**	
pertenecía	pertenecíamos	había pertenecido	habíamos pertenecido
pertenecías	pertenecíais	habías pertenecido	habíais pertenecido
pertenecía	pertenecían	había pertenecido	habían pertenecido
3 pretérito		**10 pretérito anterior**	
pertenecí	pertenecimos	hube pertenecido	hubimos pertenecido
perteneciste	pertenecisteis	hubiste pertenecido	hubisteis pertenecido
perteneció	pertenecieron	hubo pertenecido	hubieron pertenecido
4 futuro		**11 futuro perfecto**	
perteneceré	perteneceremos	habré pertenecido	habremos pertenecido
pertenecerás	perteneceréis	habrás pertenecido	habréis pertenecido
pertenecerá	pertenecerán	habrá pertenecido	habrán pertenecido
5 potencial simple		**12 potencial compuesto**	
pertenecería	perteneceríamos	habría pertenecido	habríamos pertenecido
pertenecerías	perteneceríais	habrías pertenecido	habríais pertenecido
pertenecería	pertenecerían	habría pertenecido	habrían pertenecido
6 presente de subjuntivo		**13 perfecto de subjuntivo**	
pertenezca	pertenezcamos	haya pertenecido	hayamos pertenecido
pertenezcas	pertenezcáis	hayas pertenecido	hayáis pertenecido
pertenezca	pertenezcan	haya pertenecido	hayan pertenecido
7 imperfecto de subjuntivo		**14 pluscuamperfecto de subjuntivo**	
perteneciera	perteneciéramos	hubiera pertenecido	hubiéramos pertenecido
pertenecieras	pertenecierais	hubieras pertenecido	hubierais pertenecido
perteneciera	pertenecieran	hubiera pertenecido	hubieran pertenecido
OR		OR	
perteneciese	perteneciésemos	hubiese pertenecido	hubiésemos pertenecido
pertenecieses	pertenecieseis	hubieses pertenecido	hubieseis pertenecido
perteneciese	perteneciesen	hubiese pertenecido	hubiesen pertenecido

imperativo

—	**pertenezcamos**
pertenece; no pertenezcas	**perteneced; no pertenezcáis**
pertenezca	**pertenezcan**

Words and expressions related to this verb
el pertenecido ownership, proprietorship
perteneciente belonging, pertaining
la pertinencia pertinence, relevance
pertinente pertinent, relevant

la pertenencia right of possession, ownership
ser de la pertenencia de to be in the domain of
la tenencia ilícita illegal possession

If you want an explanation of meanings and uses of Spanish and English verb tenses and moods, see pages 13–32.

Regular **-ar** verb   to paint

The Seven Simple Tenses		The Seven Compound Tenses	
Singular	Plural	Singular	Plural

1 presente de indicativo / **8 perfecto de indicativo**

pinto	pintamos	he pintado	hemos pintado
pintas	pintáis	has pintado	habéis pintado
pinta	pintan	ha pintado	han pintado

2 imperfecto de indicativo / **9 pluscuamperfecto de indicativo**

pintaba	pintábamos	había pintado	habíamos pintado
pintabas	pintabais	habías pintado	habíais pintado
pintaba	pintaban	había pintado	habían pintado

3 pretérito / **10 pretérito anterior**

pinté	pintamos	hube pintado	hubimos pintado
pintaste	pintasteis	hubiste pintado	hubisteis pintado
pintó	pintaron	hubo pintado	hubieron pintado

4 futuro / **11 futuro perfecto**

pintaré	pintaremos	habré pintado	habremos pintado
pintarás	pintaréis	habrás pintado	habréis pintado
pintará	pintarán	habrá pintado	habrán pintado

5 potencial simple / **12 potencial compuesto**

pintaría	pintaríamos	habría pintado	habríamos pintado
pintarías	pintaríais	habrías pintado	habríais pintado
pintaría	pintarían	habría pintado	habrían pintado

6 presente de subjuntivo / **13 perfecto de subjuntivo**

pinte	pintemos	haya pintado	hayamos pintado
pintes	pintéis	hayas pintado	hayáis pintado
pinte	pinten	haya pintado	hayan pintado

7 imperfecto de subjuntivo / **14 pluscuamperfecto de subjuntivo**

pintara	pintáramos	hubiera pintado	hubiéramos pintado
pintaras	pintarais	hubieras pintado	hubierais pintado
pintara	pintaran	hubiera pintado	hubieran pintado
OR		OR	
pintase	pintásemos	hubiese pintado	hubiésemos pintado
pintases	pintaseis	hubieses pintado	hubieseis pintado
pintase	pintasen	hubiese pintado	hubiesen pintado

imperativo

—	pintemos
pinta; no pintes	pintad; no pintéis
pinte	pinten

Words and expressions related to this verb

un pintor, una pintora   painter (artist)
una pintura   painting (picture)
un pintor de brocha gorda   house (sign) painter
una pintura al fresco   fresco painting

una pintura al óleo   oil painting
una pintura al pastel   pastel painting
pinturero, pinturera   conceited person
pintoresco, pintoresca   picturesque

The subject pronouns are found on page 93.   **489**

to make up (one's face), to tint,   Reflexive regular **-ar** verb
to color (one's hair, lips, etc.)

The Seven Simple Tenses		The Seven Compound Tenses	
Singular	Plural	Singular	Plural
1 presente de indicativo		8 perfecto de indicativo	
me pinto	nos pintamos	me he pintado	nos hemos pintado
te pintas	os pintáis	te has pintado	os habéis pintado
se pinta	se pintan	se ha pintado	se han pintado
2 imperfecto de indicativo		9 pluscuamperfecto de indicativo	
me pintaba	nos pintábamos	me había pintado	nos habíamos pintado
te pintabas	os pintabais	te habías pintado	os habíais pintado
se pintaba	se pintaban	se había pintado	se habían pintado
3 pretérito		10 pretérito anterior	
me pinté	nos pintamos	me hube pintado	nos hubimos pintado
te pintaste	os pintasteis	te hubiste pintado	os hubisteis pintado
se pintó	se pintaron	se hubo pintado	se hubieron pintado
4 futuro		11 futuro perfecto	
me pintaré	nos pintaremos	me habré pintado	nos habremos pintado
te pintarás	os pintaréis	te habrás pintado	os habréis pintado
se pintará	se pintarán	se habrá pintado	se habrán pintado
5 potencial simple		12 potencial compuesto	
me pintaría	nos pintaríamos	me habría pintado	nos habríamos pintado
te pintarías	os pintaríais	te habrías pintado	os habríais pintado
se pintaría	se pintarían	se habría pintado	se habrían pintado
6 presente de subjuntivo		13 perfecto de subjuntivo	
me pinte	nos pintemos	me haya pintado	nos hayamos pintado
te pintes	os pintéis	te hayas pintado	os hayáis pintado
se pinte	se pinten	se haya pintado	se hayan pintado
7 imperfecto de subjuntivo		14 pluscuamperfecto de subjuntivo	
me pintara	nos pintáramos	me hubiera pintado	nos hubiéramos pintado
te pintaras	os pintarais	te hubieras pintado	os hubierais pintado
se pintara	se pintaran	se hubiera pintado	se hubieran pintado
OR		OR	
me pintase	nos pintásemos	me hubiese pintado	nos hubiésemos pintado
te pintases	os pintaseis	te hubieses pintado	os hubieseis pintado
se pintase	se pintasen	se hubiese pintado	se hubiesen pintado

	imperativo	
—		pintémonos
píntate; no te pintes		pintaos; no os pintéis
píntese		píntense

When using this verb to mean to color one's hair, lips, etc., you must mention **el pelo,
los labios,** etc.

For words related to this verb, see the verb **pintar.**

Get acquainted with what preposition goes with what verb on pages 669–677.

Regular **-ar** verb   to tread (on), to step on, to trample

The Seven Simple Tenses		The Seven Compound Tenses	
Singular	Plural	Singular	Plural
1 presente de indicativo		8 perfecto de indicativo	
piso	pisamos	he pisado	hemos pisado
pisas	pisáis	has pisado	habéis pisado
pisa	pisan	ha pisado	han pisado
2 imperfecto de indicativo		9 pluscuamperfecto de indicativo	
pisaba	pisábamos	había pisado	habíamos pisado
pisabas	pisabais	habías pisado	habíais pisado
pisaba	pisaban	había pisado	habían pisado
3 pretérito		10 pretérito anterior	
pisé	pisamos	hube pisado	hubimos pisado
pisaste	pisasteis	hubiste pisado	hubisteis pisado
pisó	pisaron	hubo pisado	hubieron pisado
4 futuro		11 futuro perfecto	
pisaré	pisaremos	habré pisado	habremos pisado
pisarás	pisaréis	habrás pisado	habréis pisado
pisará	pisarán	habrá pisado	habrán pisado
5 potencial simple		12 potencial compuesto	
pisaría	pisaríamos	habría pisado	habríamos pisado
pisarías	pisaríais	habrías pisado	habríais pisado
pisaría	pisarían	habría pisado	habrían pisado
6 presente de subjuntivo		13 perfecto de subjuntivo	
pise	pisemos	haya pisado	hayamos pisado
pises	piséis	hayas pisado	hayáis pisado
pise	pisen	haya pisado	hayan pisado
7 imperfecto de subjuntivo		14 pluscuamperfecto de subjuntivo	
pisara	pisáramos	hubiera pisado	hubiéramos pisado
pisaras	pisarais	hubieras pisado	hubierais pisado
pisara	pisaran	hubiera pisado	hubieran pisado
OR		OR	
pisase	pisásemos	hubiese pisado	hubiésemos pisado
pisases	pisaseis	hubieses pisado	hubieseis pisado
pisase	pisasen	hubiese pisado	hubiesen pisado

imperativo	
—	pisemos
pisa; no pises	pisad; no piséis
pise	pisen

Words and expressions related to this verb

la pisa   kicking
el piso   floor, story (of a building)
el piso alto   top floor
repisar   to pack down
pisotear   to trample

el piso principal   main floor
el piso bajo   ground floor
el pisoteo   abuse, trampling
la repisa   shelf; repisa de ventana   windowsill
¡Piso mojado!   Wet floor!

The subject pronouns are found on page 93.

491

to gratify, to humor, to please

Regular **-er** verb endings with spelling change: **c** becomes **zc** before **a** or **o**

The Seven Simple Tenses		The Seven Compound Tenses	
Singular	Plural	Singular	Plural
1 presente de indicativo		8 perfecto de indicativo	
plazco	placemos	he placido	hemos placido
places	placéis	has placido	habéis placido
place	placen	ha placido	han placido
2 imperfecto de indicativo		9 pluscuamperfecto de indicativo	
placía	placíamos	había placido	habíamos placido
placías	placíais	habías placido	habíais placido
placía	placían	había placido	habían placido
3 pretérito		10 pretérito anterior	
plací	placimos	hube placido	hubimos placido
placiste	placisteis	hubiste placido	hubisteis placido
plació	placieron	hubo placido	hubieron placido
4 futuro		11 futuro perfecto	
placeré	placeremos	habré placido	habremos placido
placerás	placeréis	habrás placido	habréis placido
placerá	placerán	habrá placido	habrán placido
5 potencial simple		12 potencial compuesto	
placería	placeríamos	habría placido	habríamos placido
placerías	placeríais	habrías placido	habríais placido
placería	placerían	habría placido	habrían placido
6 presente de subjuntivo		13 perfecto de subjuntivo	
plazca	plazcamos	haya placido	hayamos placido
plazcas	plazcáis	hayas placido	hayáis placido
plazca	plazcan	haya placido	hayan placido
7 imperfecto de subjuntivo		14 pluscuamperfecto de subjuntivo	
placiera	placiéramos	hubiera placido	hubiéramos placido
placieras	placierais	hubieras placido	hubierais placido
placiera	placieran	hubiera placido	hubieran placido
OR		OR	
placiese	placiésemos	hubiese placido	hubiésemos placido
placieses	placieseis	hubieses placido	hubieseis placido
placiese	placiesen	hubiese placido	hubiesen placido

imperativo

—	plazcamos
place; no plazcas	placed; no plazcáis
plazca	plazcan

Words related to this verb
el placer pleasure
la placidez contentment
placenteramente joyfully
el placero, la placera market merchant

placentero, placentera agreeable, pleasant
placible agreeable, placid; **plácido** placid, pleasant
implacable implacable, inexorable

In poetry, **plugo** is sometimes used instead of **plació, pluguieron** instead of **placieron, plegue** instead of **plazca, pluguiera** instead of **placiera,** and **pluguiese** instead of **placiese.**

Regular **-ar** verb endings with spelling change: **c** becomes **qu** before **e**

to chat, to talk over, to discuss

The Seven Simple Tenses		The Seven Compound Tenses	
Singular	Plural	Singular	Plural
1 presente de indicativo		8 perfecto de indicativo	
platico	platicamos	he platicado	hemos platicado
platicas	platicáis	has platicado	habéis platicado
platica	platican	ha platicado	han platicado
2 imperfecto de indicativo		9 pluscuamperfecto de indicativo	
platicaba	platicábamos	había platicado	habíamos platicado
platicabas	platicabais	habías platicado	habíais platicado
platicaba	platicaban	había platicado	habían platicado
3 pretérito		10 pretérito anterior	
platiqué	platicamos	hube platicado	hubimos platicado
platicaste	platicasteis	hubiste platicado	hubisteis platicado
platicó	platicaron	hubo platicado	hubieron platicado
4 futuro		11 futuro perfecto	
platicaré	platicaremos	habré platicado	habremos platicado
platicarás	platicaréis	habrás platicado	habréis platicado
platicará	platicarán	habrá platicado	habrán platicado
5 potencial simple		12 potencial compuesto	
platicaría	platicaríamos	habría platicado	habríamos platicado
platicarías	platicaríais	habrías platicado	habríais platicado
platicaría	platicarían	habría platicado	habrían platicado
6 presente de subjuntivo		13 perfecto de subjuntivo	
platique	platiquemos	haya platicado	hayamos platicado
platiques	platiquéis	hayas platicado	hayáis platicado
platique	platiquen	haya platicado	hayan platicado
7 imperfecto de subjuntivo		14 pluscuamperfecto de subjuntivo	
platicara	platicáramos	hubiera platicado	hubiéramos platicado
platicaras	platicarais	hubieras platicado	hubierais platicado
platicara	platicaran	hubiera platicado	hubieran platicado
OR		OR	
platicase	platicásemos	hubiese platicado	hubiésemos platicado
platicases	platicaseis	hubieses platicado	hubieseis platicado
platicase	platicasen	hubiese platicado	hubiesen platicado

imperativo	
—	platiquemos
platica; no platiques	platicad; no platiquéis
platique	platiquen

Words related to this verb
una plática chat, talk, conversation
un platicador, una platicadora talker; *as an adj.,* talkative

Don't forget to study the section on defective and impersonal verbs. It's right after this main list.

The subject pronouns are found on page 93.

493

to be able, can　　　　　　　　　　　　　　　　　　Irregular verb

The Seven Simple Tenses		The Seven Compound Tenses	
Singular	Plural	Singular	Plural
1 presente de indicativo		8 perfecto de indicativo	
puedo	**podemos**	**he podido**	**hemos podido**
puedes	**podéis**	**has podido**	**habéis podido**
puede	**pueden**	**ha podido**	**han podido**
2 imperfecto de indicativo		9 pluscuamperfecto de indicativo	
podía	**podíamos**	**había podido**	**habíamos podido**
podías	**podíais**	**habías podido**	**habíais podido**
podía	**podían**	**había podido**	**habían podido**
3 pretérito		10 pretérito anterior	
pude	**pudimos**	**hube podido**	**hubimos podido**
pudiste	**pudisteis**	**hubiste podido**	**hubisteis podido**
pudo	**pudieron**	**hubo podido**	**hubieron podido**
4 futuro		11 futuro perfecto	
podré	**podremos**	**habré podido**	**habremos podido**
podrás	**podréis**	**habrás podido**	**habréis podido**
podrá	**podrán**	**habrá podido**	**habrán podido**
5 potencial simple		12 potencial compuesto	
podría	**podríamos**	**habría podido**	**habríamos podido**
podrías	**podríais**	**habrías podido**	**habríais podido**
podría	**podrían**	**habría podido**	**habrían podido**
6 presente de subjuntivo		13 perfecto de subjuntivo	
pueda	**podamos**	**haya podido**	**hayamos podido**
puedas	**podáis**	**hayas podido**	**hayáis podido**
pueda	**puedan**	**haya podido**	**hayan podido**
7 imperfecto de subjuntivo		14 pluscuamperfecto de subjuntivo	
pudiera	**pudiéramos**	**hubiera podido**	**hubiéramos podido**
pudieras	**pudierais**	**hubieras podido**	**hubierais podido**
pudiera	**pudieran**	**hubiera podido**	**hubieran podido**
OR		OR	
pudiese	**pudiésemos**	**hubiese podido**	**hubiésemos podido**
pudieses	**pudieseis**	**hubieses podido**	**hubieseis podido**
pudiese	**pudiesen**	**hubiese podido**	**hubiesen podido**

	imperativo	
—		**podamos**
puede; no puedas		**poded; no podáis**
pueda		**puedan**

Poder

Poder is a very useful verb for a beginning student. You can use it in a vast number of idiomatic expressions and everyday situations.

Poder means *can* in the sense of *ability:*
No puedo ayudarle; lo siento/I cannot (am unable to) help you; I'm sorry.

In the preterit tense poder has the special meaning of *succeeded:* Después de algunos minutos, Juan pudo abrir la puerta/After a few minutes, John succeeded in opening the door.

Sentences using poder **and related words**

No dejes para mañana lo que puedes hacer hoy.
Don't put off until tomorrow what you can do today.

Sí, sí, se puede muy fácilmente.
Yes, yes, it can be done very easily.

La jaula nunca puede ser nido.
(Alí Vanegas)
The cage can never be a nest.

¿Me puedo probar este vestido?
May I try on this dress?

No podemos nadar aquí. Es peligroso.
We can't swim here. It's dangerous.

Words and expressions related to this verb

el poder **power**

el poder absoluto **absolute power**

apoderar **to empower**

apoderarse de **to take possession, to take over**

poderoso, poderosa **powerful**

poderosamente **powerfully**

el poderío **power, strength**

estar en el poder **to be in power**

¿Puede usted...? **Can you...?**

¿Puede ayudarme? **Can you help me?**

No se puede. **It can't be done.**

No puede ser. **It's impossible. (It can't be.)**

no poder más **to be exhausted**

P

Proverbs

Querer es poder.
Where there's a will there's a way.

Saber es poder.
Knowledge is power.

Can't find the verb you're looking for?
Check the back pages of this book for a list of over 2,100 additional verbs!

poner (364)　　　Gerundio **poniendo**　　　Part. pas. **puesto**

to put, to place, to turn on (TV, radio)　　　Irregular verb

The Seven Simple Tenses		The Seven Compound Tenses	
Singular	Plural	Singular	Plural
1　presente de indicativo		8　perfecto de indicativo	
pongo	**ponemos**	**he puesto**	**hemos puesto**
pones	**ponéis**	**has puesto**	**habéis puesto**
pone	**ponen**	**ha puesto**	**han puesto**
2　imperfecto de indicativo		9　pluscuamperfecto de indicativo	
ponía	**poníamos**	**había puesto**	**habíamos puesto**
ponías	**poníais**	**habías puesto**	**habíais puesto**
ponía	**ponían**	**había puesto**	**habían puesto**
3　pretérito		10　pretérito anterior	
puse	**pusimos**	**hube puesto**	**hubimos puesto**
pusiste	**pusisteis**	**hubiste puesto**	**hubisteis puesto**
puso	**pusieron**	**hubo puesto**	**hubieron puesto**
4　futuro		11　futuro perfecto	
pondré	**pondremos**	**habré puesto**	**habremos puesto**
pondrás	**pondréis**	**habrás puesto**	**habréis puesto**
pondrá	**pondrán**	**habrá puesto**	**habrán puesto**
5　potencial simple		12　potencial compuesto	
pondría	**pondríamos**	**habría puesto**	**habríamos puesto**
pondrías	**pondríais**	**habrías puesto**	**habríais puesto**
pondría	**pondrían**	**habría puesto**	**habrían puesto**
6　presente de subjuntivo		13　perfecto de subjuntivo	
ponga	**pongamos**	**haya puesto**	**hayamos puesto**
pongas	**pongáis**	**hayas puesto**	**hayáis puesto**
ponga	**pongan**	**haya puesto**	**hayan puesto**
7　imperfecto de subjuntivo		14　pluscuamperfecto de subjuntivo	
pusiera	**pusiéramos**	**hubiera puesto**	**hubiéramos puesto**
pusieras	**pusierais**	**hubieras puesto**	**hubierais puesto**
pusiera	**pusieran**	**hubiera puesto**	**hubieran puesto**
OR		OR	
pusiese	**pusiésemos**	**hubiese puesto**	**hubiésemos puesto**
pusieses	**pusieseis**	**hubieses puesto**	**hubieseis puesto**
pusiese	**pusiesen**	**hubiese puesto**	**hubiesen puesto**

imperativo

—	**pongamos**
pon; no pongas	**poned; no pongáis**
ponga	**pongan**

AN ESSENTIAL
55 VERB

Poner/Ponerse

Poner and ponerse are very useful irregular verbs for beginning students. They are used in many idiomatic expressions and everyday situations. As you study the following sentences and expressions, pay attention to the differences in use between **poner** and the reflexive verb **ponerse**.

Sentences using poner **and** ponerse

Magdalena puso el papel en la papelera.
Magdalene put the paper in the wastebasket.

Cuando vi el accidente, me puse pálido.
When I saw the accident, I became pale.

Mi madre se puso triste al oír la noticia desgraciada.
My mother became sad upon hearing the unfortunate news.

Can't find the verb you're looking for?
Check the back pages of this book for a list
of over 2,100 additional verbs!

Words and expressions related to these verbs

poner fin a **to put a stop to**
poner coto a **to put a stop to**
poner la mesa **to set the table**
poner de acuerdo **to reach an agreement**
poner el dedo en la llaga **to hit the nail right on the head**
poner en claro **to explain clearly**
poner en marcha **to set in motion**
poner en ridículo **to ridicule**
poner los puntos sobre las íes **to dot the i's, to mind one's p's and q's**
poner por escrito **to put in writing**
posponer **to postpone**
la puesta de/del sol **sunset**
al poner del sol **at sunset**
bien puesto, bien puesta **well placed**
reponer **to replace, to put back**
poner una duda en claro **to clear up a doubt**
ponerse el abrigo **to put on one's overcoat**
ponerse de acuerdo **to reach an agreement**
ponerse cómodo **to make oneself at home**
ponerse en marcha **to start (out)**
ponerse mal **to get sick**
ponerse a + inf. **to begin, to start + inf.**
ponerse a dieta **to go on a diet**
reponerse **to calm down, to recover (one's health)**
indisponerse **to become ill**
ponerse + adj. **to become; the adjective indicates the state or condition (physical or mental) that you have become.**

P

The subject pronouns are found on page 93.

497

ponerse (365)

Gerundio **poniéndose**

Part. pas. **puesto**

to put on (clothing), to become, to set (of sun)

The Seven Simple Tenses		The Seven Compound Tenses	
Singular	Plural	Singular	Plural
1 presente de indicativo		8 perfecto de indicativo	
me pongo	nos ponemos	me he puesto	nos hemos puesto
te pones	os ponéis	te has puesto	os habéis puesto
se pone	se ponen	se ha puesto	se han puesto
2 imperfecto de indicativo		9 pluscuamperfecto de indicativo	
me ponía	nos poníamos	me había puesto	nos habíamos puesto
te ponías	os poníais	te habías puesto	os habíais puesto
se ponía	se ponían	se había puesto	se habían puesto
3 pretérito		10 pretérito anterior	
me puse	nos pusimos	me hube puesto	nos hubimos puesto
te pusiste	os pusisteis	te hubiste puesto	os hubisteis puesto
se puso	se pusieron	se hubo puesto	se hubieron puesto
4 futuro		11 futuro perfecto	
me pondré	nos pondremos	me habré puesto	nos habremos puesto
te pondrás	os pondréis	te habrás puesto	os habréis puesto
se pondrá	se pondrán	se habrá puesto	se habrán puesto
5 potencial simple		12 potencial compuesto	
me pondría	nos pondríamos	me habría puesto	nos habríamos puesto
te pondrías	os pondríais	te habrías puesto	os habríais puesto
se pondría	se pondrían	se habría puesto	se habrían puesto
6 presente de subjuntivo		13 perfecto de subjuntivo	
me ponga	nos pongamos	me haya puesto	nos hayamos puesto
te pongas	os pongáis	te hayas puesto	os hayáis puesto
se ponga	se pongan	se haya puesto	se hayan puesto
7 imperfecto de subjuntivo		14 pluscuamperfecto de subjuntivo	
me pusiera	nos pusiéramos	me hubiera puesto	nos hubiéramos puesto
te pusieras	os pusierais	te hubieras puesto	os hubierais puesto
se pusiera	se pusieran	se hubiera puesto	se hubieran puesto
OR		OR	
me pusiese	nos pusiésemos	me hubiese puesto	nos hubiésemos puesto
te pusieses	os pusieseis	te hubieses puesto	os hubieseis puesto
se pusiese	se pusiesen	se hubiese puesto	se hubiesen puesto

imperativo	
—	pongámonos
ponte; no te pongas	poneos; no os pongáis
póngase	pónganse

AN ESSENTIAL
55 VERB

Regular **-er** verb endings with stem change: Tenses 3 and 7, Gerundio

to possess, to own

The Seven Simple Tenses		The Seven Compound Tenses	
Singular	Plural	Singular	Plural
1 presente de indicativo		8 perfecto de indicativo	
poseo	poseemos	he poseído	hemos poseído
posees	poseéis	has poseído	habéis poseído
posee	poseen	ha poseído	han poseído
2 imperfecto de indicativo		9 pluscuamperfecto de indicativo	
poseía	poseíamos	había poseído	habíamos poseído
poseías	poseíais	habías poseído	habíais poseído
poseía	poseían	había poseído	habían poseído
3 pretérito		10 pretérito anterior	
poseí	poseímos	hube poseído	hubimos poseído
poseiste	poseísteis	hubiste poseído	hubisteis poseído
poseyó	poseyeron	hubo poseído	hubieron poseído
4 futuro		11 futuro perfecto	
poseeré	poseeremos	habré poseído	habremos poseído
poseerás	poseeréis	habrás poseído	habréis poseído
poseerá	poseerán	habrá poseído	habrán poseído
5 potencial simple		12 potencial compuesto	
poseería	poseeríamos	habría poseído	habríamos poseído
poseerías	poseeríais	habrías poseído	habríais poseído
poseería	poseerían	habría poseído	habrían poseído
6 presente de subjuntivo		13 perfecto de subjuntivo	
posea	poseamos	haya poseído	hayamos poseído
poseas	poseáis	hayas poseído	hayáis poseído
posea	posean	haya poseído	hayan poseído
7 imperfecto de subjuntivo		14 pluscuamperfecto de subjuntivo	
poseyera	poseyéramos	hubiera poseído	hubiéramos poseído
poseyeras	poseyerais	hubieras poseído	hubierais poseído
poseyera	poseyeran	hubiera poseído	hubieran poseído
OR		OR	
poseyese	poseyésemos	hubiese poseído	hubiésemos poseído
poseyeses	poseyeseis	hubieses poseído	hubieseis poseído
poseyese	poseyesen	hubiese poseído	hubiesen poseído

imperativo	
—	poseamos
posee; no poseas	poseed; no poseáis
posea	posean

Words related to this verb
el poseedor, la poseedora   owner, possessor
la posesión   possession
poseerse   to control oneself
dar posesión de   to give possession of
el posesor, la posesora   owner, possessor
desposeer   to dispossess

Review the principal parts of important Spanish verbs on pages 9–10.

The subject pronouns are found on page 93.

to practice

Regular **-ar** verb endings with spelling
change: **c** becomes **qu** before **e**

The Seven Simple Tenses		The Seven Compound Tenses	
Singular	Plural	Singular	Plural
1 presente de indicativo		8 perfecto de indicativo	
practico	practicamos	he practicado	hemos practicado
practicas	practicáis	has practicado	habéis practicado
practica	practican	ha practicado	han practicado
2 imperfecto de indicativo		9 pluscuamperfecto de indicativo	
practicaba	practicábamos	había practicado	habíamos practicado
practicabas	practicabais	habías practicado	habíais practicado
practicaba	practicaban	había practicado	habían practicado
3 pretérito		10 pretérito anterior	
practiqué	practicamos	hube practicado	hubimos practicado
practicaste	practicasteis	hubiste practicado	hubisteis practicado
practicó	practicaron	hubo practicado	hubieron practicado
4 futuro		11 futuro perfecto	
practicaré	practicaremos	habré practicado	habremos practicado
practicarás	practicaréis	habrás practicado	habréis practicado
practicará	practicarán	habrá practicado	habrán practicado
5 potencial simple		12 potencial compuesto	
practicaría	practicaríamos	habría practicado	habríamos practicado
practicarías	practicaríais	habrías practicado	habríais practicado
practicaría	practicarían	habría practicado	habrían practicado
6 presente de subjuntivo		13 perfecto de subjuntivo	
practique	practiquemos	haya practicado	hayamos practicado
practiques	practiquéis	hayas practicado	hayáis practicado
practique	practiquen	haya practicado	hayan practicado
7 imperfecto de subjuntivo		14 pluscuamperfecto de subjuntivo	
practicara	practicáramos	hubiera practicado	hubiéramos practicado
practicaras	practicarais	hubieras practicado	hubierais practicado
practicara	practicaran	hubiera practicado	hubieran practicado
OR		OR	
practicase	practicásemos	hubiese practicado	hubiésemos practicado
practicases	practicaseis	hubieses practicado	hubieseis practicado
practicase	practicasen	hubiese practicado	hubiesen practicado

imperativo	
—	practiquemos
practica; no practiques	practicad; no practiquéis
practique	practiquen

Words and expressions related to this verb

práctico, práctica practical
la práctica practice, habit
en la práctica in practice
practicar investigaciones to look into,
  to investigate

practicar un informe to make a report
practicar una buena acción to do a good deed
practicar el fútbol to play soccer
practicar las artes marciales to practice
  martial arts

The Seven Simple Tenses		The Seven Compound Tenses	
Singular	Plural	Singular	Plural
1 presente de indicativo		**8 perfecto de indicativo**	
predigo	predecimos	he predicho	hemos predicho
predices	predecís	has predicho	habéis predicho
predice	predicen	ha predicho	han predicho
2 imperfecto de indicativo		**9 pluscuamperfecto de indicativo**	
predecía	predecíamos	había predicho	habíamos predicho
predecías	predecíais	habías predicho	habíais predicho
predecía	predecían	había predicho	habían predicho
3 pretérito		**10 pretérito anterior**	
predije	predijimos	hube predicho	hubimos predicho
predijiste	predijisteis	hubiste predicho	hubisteis predicho
predijo	predijeron	hubo predicho	hubieron predicho
4 futuro		**11 futuro perfecto**	
predeciré	predeciremos	habré predicho	habremos predicho
predecirás	predeciréis	habrás predicho	habréis predicho
predecirá	predecirán	habrá predicho	habrán predicho
5 potencial simple		**12 potencial compuesto**	
predeciría	predeciríamos	habría predicho	habríamos predicho
predecirías	predeciríais	habrías predicho	habríais predicho
predeciría	predecirían	habría predicho	habrían predicho
6 presente de subjuntivo		**13 perfecto de subjuntivo**	
prediga	predigamos	haya predicho	hayamos predicho
predigas	predigáis	hayas predicho	hayáis predicho
prediga	predigan	haya predicho	hayan predicho
7 imperfecto de subjuntivo		**14 pluscuamperfecto de subjuntivo**	
predijera	predijéramos	hubiera predicho	hubiéramos predicho
perdijeras	predijerais	hubieras predicho	hubierais predicho
predijera	predijeran	hubiera predicho	hubieran predicho
OR		OR	
predijese	predijésemos	hubiese predicho	hubiésemos predicho
predijeses	predijeseis	hubieses predicho	hubieseis predicho
predijese	predijesen	hubiese predicho	hubiesen predicho

imperativo	
—	predigamos
predice; no predigas	predecid; no predigáis
prediga	predigan

Words and expressions related to this verb

decir   to say, to tell

una predicción   prediction

la predicción del tiempo   weather forecasting

la dicción   diction

This verb is conjugated like the irregular verb **decir,** except in the future and conditional (Tense Nos. 4 and 5), and in the 2nd person., sing. (**tú**) of the imperative, which are regular.

to preach

Regular **-ar** verb endings with spelling
change: **c** becomes **qu** before **e**

The Seven Simple Tenses		The Seven Compound Tenses	
Singular	Plural	Singular	Plural
1 presente de indicativo		8 perfecto de indicativo	
predico	**predicamos**	**he predicado**	**hemos predicado**
predicas	**predicáis**	**has predicado**	**habéis predicado**
predica	**predican**	**ha predicado**	**han predicado**
2 imperfecto de indicativo		9 pluscuamperfecto de indicativo	
predicaba	**predicábamos**	**había predicado**	**habíamos predicado**
predicabas	**predicabais**	**habías predicado**	**habíais predicado**
predicaba	**predicaban**	**había predicado**	**habían predicado**
3 pretérito		10 pretérito anterior	
prediqué	**predicamos**	**hube predicado**	**hubimos predicado**
predicaste	**predicasteis**	**hubiste predicado**	**hubisteis predicado**
predicó	**predicaron**	**hubo predicado**	**hubieron predicado**
4 futuro		11 futuro perfecto	
predicaré	**predicaremos**	**habré predicado**	**habremos predicado**
predicarás	**predicaréis**	**habrás predicado**	**habréis predicado**
predicará	**predicarán**	**habrá predicado**	**habrán predicado**
5 potencial simple		12 potencial compuesto	
predicaría	**predicaríamos**	**habría predicado**	**habríamos predicado**
predicarías	**predicaríais**	**habrías predicado**	**habríais predicado**
predicaría	**predicarían**	**habría predicado**	**habrían predicado**
6 presente de subjuntivo		13 perfecto de subjuntivo	
predique	**prediquemos**	**haya predicado**	**hayamos predicado**
prediques	**prediquéis**	**hayas predicado**	**hayáis predicado**
predique	**prediquen**	**haya predicado**	**hayan predicado**
7 imperfecto de subjuntivo		14 pluscuamperfecto de subjuntivo	
predicara	**predicáramos**	**hubiera predicado**	**hubiéramos predicado**
predicaras	**predicarais**	**hubieras predicado**	**hubierais predicado**
predicara	**predicaran**	**hubiera predicado**	**hubieran predicado**
OR		OR	
predicase	**predicásemos**	**hubiese predicado**	**hubiésemos predicado**
predicases	**predicaseis**	**hubieses predicado**	**hubieseis predicado**
predicase	**predicasen**	**hubiese predicado**	**hubiesen predicado**

imperativo	
—	**prediquemos**
predica; no prediques	**predicad; no prediquéis**
predique	**prediquen**

Words related to this verb
la predicación   preaching
un predicador   preacher

una prédica   sermon
predicativo, predicativa   predicative

> If you don't know the Spanish verb for the English verb you have
> in mind, look it up in the index on pages 682–706.

Regular **-ir** verb endings with stem change: to prefer
Tenses 1, 3, 6, 7, Imperative, Gerundio

The Seven Simple Tenses		The Seven Compound Tenses	
Singular	Plural	Singular	Plural
1 presente de indicativo		8 perfecto de indicativo	
prefiero	**preferimos**	**he preferido**	**hemos preferido**
prefieres	**preferís**	**has preferido**	**habéis preferido**
prefiere	**prefieren**	**ha preferido**	**han preferido**
2 imperfecto de indicativo		9 pluscuamperfecto de indicativo	
prefería	**preferíamos**	**había preferido**	**habíamos preferido**
preferías	**preferíais**	**habías preferido**	**habíais preferido**
prefería	**preferían**	**había preferido**	**habían preferido**
3 pretérito		10 pretérito anterior	
preferí	**preferimos**	**hube preferido**	**hubimos preferido**
preferiste	**preferisteis**	**hubiste preferido**	**hubisteis preferido**
prefirió	**prefirieron**	**hubo preferido**	**hubieron preferido**
4 futuro		11 futuro perfecto	
preferiré	**preferiremos**	**habré preferido**	**habremos preferido**
preferirás	**preferiréis**	**habrás preferido**	**habréis preferido**
preferirá	**preferirán**	**habrá preferido**	**habrán preferido**
5 potencial simple		12 potencial compuesto	
preferiría	**preferiríamos**	**habría preferido**	**habríamos preferido**
preferirías	**preferiríais**	**habrías preferido**	**habríais preferido**
preferiría	**preferirían**	**habría preferido**	**habrían preferido**
6 presente de subjuntivo		13 perfecto de subjuntivo	
prefiera	**prefiramos**	**haya preferido**	**hayamos preferido**
prefieras	**prefiráis**	**hayas preferido**	**hayáis preferido**
prefiera	**prefieran**	**haya preferido**	**hayan preferido**
7 imperfecto de subjuntivo		14 pluscuamperfecto de subjuntivo	
prefiriera	**prefiriéramos**	**hubiera preferido**	**hubiéramos preferido**
prefirieras	**prefirierais**	**hubieras preferido**	**hubierais preferido**
prefiriera	**prefirieran**	**hubiera preferido**	**hubieran preferido**
OR		OR	
prefiriese	**prefiriésemos**	**hubiese preferido**	**hubiésemos preferido**
prefirieses	**prefirieseis**	**hubieses preferido**	**hubieseis preferido**
prefiriese	**prefiriesen**	**hubiese preferido**	**hubiesen preferido**

P

imperativo	
—	**prefiramos**
prefiere; no prefieras	**preferid; no prefiráis**
prefiera	**prefieran**

Words related to this verb
preferiblemente   preferably
preferible   preferable
la preferencia   preference
preferido, preferida   preferred, favorite
de preferencia   preferably
preferentemente   preferably

referir   to refer, to relate
**Preferimos una habitación tranquila con
   un cuarto de baño privado, por favor.**
We prefer a quiet room with a private
bathroom, please.

The subject pronouns are found on page 93.

preguntar (371) Gerundio **preguntando** Part. pas. **preguntado**

to ask, to inquire, to question

Regular **-ar** verb

The Seven Simple Tenses		The Seven Compound Tenses	
Singular	Plural	Singular	Plural
1 presente de indicativo		**8 perfecto de indicativo**	
pregunto	preguntamos	he preguntado	hemos preguntado
preguntas	preguntáis	has preguntado	habéis preguntado
pregunta	preguntan	ha preguntado	han preguntado
2 imperfecto de indicativo		**9 pluscuamperfecto de indicativo**	
preguntaba	preguntábamos	había preguntado	habíamos preguntado
preguntabas	preguntabais	habías preguntado	habíais preguntado
preguntaba	preguntaban	había preguntado	habían preguntado
3 pretérito		**10 pretérito anterior**	
pregunté	preguntamos	hube preguntado	hubimos preguntado
preguntaste	preguntasteis	hubiste preguntado	hubisteis preguntado
preguntó	preguntaron	hubo preguntado	hubieron preguntado
4 futuro		**11 futuro perfecto**	
preguntaré	preguntaremos	habré preguntado	habremos preguntado
preguntarás	preguntaréis	habrás preguntado	habréis preguntado
preguntará	preguntarán	habrá preguntado	habrán preguntado
5 potencial simple		**12 potencial compuesto**	
preguntaría	preguntaríamos	habría preguntado	habríamos preguntado
preguntarías	preguntaríais	habrías preguntado	habríais preguntado
preguntaría	preguntarían	habría preguntado	habrían preguntado
6 presente de subjuntivo		**13 perfecto de subjuntivo**	
pregunte	preguntemos	haya preguntado	hayamos preguntado
preguntes	preguntéis	hayas preguntado	hayáis preguntado
pregunte	pregunten	haya preguntado	hayan preguntado
7 imperfecto de subjuntivo		**14 pluscuamperfecto de subjuntivo**	
preguntara	preguntáramos	hubiera preguntado	hubiéramos preguntado
preguntaras	preguntarais	hubieras preguntado	hubierais preguntado
preguntara	preguntaran	hubiera preguntado	hubieran preguntado
OR		OR	
preguntase	preguntásemos	hubiese preguntado	hubiésemos preguntado
preguntases	preguntaseis	hubieses preguntado	hubieseis preguntado
preguntase	preguntasen	hubiese preguntado	hubiesen preguntado

	imperativo	
—	preguntemos	
pregunta; no preguntes	preguntad; no preguntéis	
pregunte	pregunten	

Words and expressions related to this verb

una pregunta question
hacer una pregunta to ask a question
un preguntón, una preguntona
  inquisitive individual

preguntarse to wonder, to ask oneself
preguntante inquiring
preguntador, preguntadora inquisitive

Don't confuse **pedir** and **preguntar**. **Pedir** means *to ask for something* or *to request*. **Preguntar** means *to inquire, to ask a question:* **La alumna preguntó a la profesora cómo estaba**/The pupil asked the teacher how she was.

Reflexive regular **-ar** verb   to be concerned, to worry, to be worried

The Seven Simple Tenses		The Seven Compound Tenses	
Singular	Plural	Singular	Plural
1 presente de indicativo		8 perfecto de indicativo	
me preocupo	nos preocupamos	me he preocupado	nos hemos preocupado
te preocupas	os preocupáis	te has preocupado	os habéis preocupado
se preocupa	se preocupan	se ha preocupado	se han preocupado
2 imperfecto de indicativo		9 pluscuamperfecto de indicativo	
me preocupaba	nos preocupábamos	me había preocupado	nos habíamos preocupado
te preocupabas	os preocupabais	te habías preocupado	os habíais preocupado
se preocupaba	se preocupaban	se había preocupado	se habían preocupado
3 pretérito		10 pretérito anterior	
me preocupé	nos preocupamos	me hube preocupado	nos hubimos preocupado
te preocupaste	os preocupasteis	te hubiste preocupado	os hubisteis preocupado
se preocupó	se preocuparon	se hubo preocupado	se hubieron preocupado
4 futuro		11 futuro perfecto	
me preocuparé	nos preocuparemos	me habré preocupado	nos habremos preocupado
te preocuparás	os preocuparéis	te habrás preocupado	os habréis preocupado
se preocupará	se preocuparán	se habrá preocupado	se habrán preocupado
5 potencial simple		12 potencial compuesto	
me preocuparía	nos preocuparíamos	me habría preocupado	nos habríamos preocupado
te preocuparías	os preocuparíais	te habrías preocupado	os habríais preocupado
se preocuparía	se preocuparían	se habría preocupado	se habrían preocupado
6 presente de subjuntivo		13 perfecto de subjuntivo	
me preocupe	nos preocupemos	me haya preocupado	nos hayamos preocupado
te preocupes	os preocupéis	te hayas preocupado	os hayáis preocupado
se preocupe	se preocupen	se haya preocupado	se hayan preocupado
7 imperfecto de subjuntivo		14 pluscuamperfecto de subjuntivo	
me preocupara	nos preocupáramos	me hubiera preocupado	nos hubiéramos preocupado
te preocuparas	os preocuparais	te hubieras preocupado	os hubierais preocupado
se preocupara	se preocuparan	se hubiera preocupado	se hubieran preocupado
OR		OR	
me preocupase	nos preocupásemos	me hubiese preocupado	nos hubiésemos preocupado
te preocupases	os preocupaseis	te hubieses preocupado	os hubieseis preocupado
se preocupase	se preocupasen	se hubiese preocupado	se hubiesen preocupado

	imperativo	
—		preocupémonos
preocúpate; no te preocupes		preocupaos; no os preocupéis
preocúpese		preocúpense

Words related to this verb

preocupar to preoccupy, to worry
la preocupación preoccupation, worry
¡no se preocupe! don't worry

preocuparse de to take care of, to worry about; **estar preocupado** to be worried
ocupar to occupy

For other words and expressions related to this verb, see **ocupar.**

The subject pronouns are found on page 93.

The Seven Simple Tenses		The Seven Compound Tenses	
Singular	Plural	Singular	Plural
1 presente de indicativo		8 perfecto de indicativo	
preparo	**preparamos**	**he preparado**	**hemos preparado**
preparas	**preparáis**	**has preparado**	**habéis preparado**
prepara	**preparan**	**ha preparado**	**han preparado**
2 imperfecto de indicativo		9 pluscuamperfecto de indicativo	
preparaba	**preparábamos**	**había preparado**	**habíamos preparado**
preparabas	**preparabais**	**habías preparado**	**habíais preparado**
preparaba	**preparaban**	**había preparado**	**habían preparado**
3 pretérito		10 pretérito anterior	
preparé	**preparamos**	**hube preparado**	**hubimos preparado**
preparaste	**preparasteis**	**hubiste preparado**	**hubisteis preparado**
preparó	**prepararon**	**hubo preparado**	**hubieron preparado**
4 futuro		11 futuro perfecto	
prepararé	**prepararemos**	**habré preparado**	**habremos preparado**
prepararás	**prepararéis**	**habrás preparado**	**habréis preparado**
preparará	**prepararán**	**habrá preparado**	**habrán preparado**
5 potencial simple		12 potencial compuesto	
prepararía	**prepararíamos**	**habría preparado**	**habríamos preparado**
prepararías	**prepararíais**	**habrías preparado**	**habríais preparado**
prepararía	**prepararían**	**habría preparado**	**habrían preparado**
6 presente de subjuntivo		13 perfecto de subjuntivo	
prepare	**preparemos**	**haya preparado**	**hayamos preparado**
prepares	**preparéis**	**hayas preparado**	**hayáis preparado**
prepare	**preparen**	**haya preparado**	**hayan preparado**
7 imperfecto de subjuntivo		14 pluscuamperfecto de subjuntivo	
preparara	**preparáramos**	**hubiera preparado**	**hubiéramos preparado**
prepararas	**prepararais**	**hubieras preparado**	**hubierais preparado**
preparara	**prepararan**	**hubiera preparado**	**hubieran preparado**
OR		OR	
preparase	**preparásemos**	**hubiese preparado**	**hubiésemos preparado**
preparases	**preparaseis**	**hubieses preparado**	**hubieseis preparado**
preparase	**preparasen**	**hubiese preparado**	**hubiesen preparado**

	imperativo	
—		**preparemos**
prepara; no prepares		**preparad; no preparéis**
prepare		**preparen**

Words related to this verb

preparatorio, preparatoria preparatory   **la preparación** preparation
el preparativo preparation, preparative   **prepararse** to prepare oneself

Get your feet wet with verbs used in weather expressions on page 668.

Reflexive regular **-ar** verb   to be prepared, to get ready, to prepare oneself

The Seven Simple Tenses		The Seven Compound Tenses	
Singular	Plural	Singular	Plural
1 presente de indicativo		8 perfecto de indicativo	
me preparo	nos preparamos	me he preparado	nos hemos preparado
te preparas	os preparáis	te has preparado	os habéis preparado
se prepara	se preparan	se ha preparado	se han preparado
2 imperfecto de indicativo		9 pluscuamperfecto de indicativo	
me preparaba	nos preparábamos	me había preparado	nos habíamos preparado
te preparabas	os preparabais	te habías preparado	os habíais preparado
se preparaba	se preparaban	se había preparado	se habían preparado
3 pretérito		10 pretérito anterior	
me preparé	nos preparamos	me hube preparado	nos hubimos preparado
te preparaste	os preparasteis	te hubiste preparado	os hubisteis preparado
se preparó	se prepararon	se hubo preparado	se hubieron preparado
4 futuro		11 futuro perfecto	
me prepararé	nos prepararemos	me habré preparado	nos habremos preparado
te prepararás	os prepararéis	te habrás preparado	os habréis preparado
se preparará	se prepararán	se habrá preparado	se habrán preparado
5 potencial simple		12 potencial compuesto	
me prepararía	nos prepararíamos	me habría preparado	nos habríamos preparado
te prepararías	os prepararíais	te habrías preparado	os habríais preparado
se prepararía	se prepararían	se habría preparado	se habrían preparado
6 presente de subjuntivo		13 perfecto de subjuntivo	
me prepare	nos preparemos	me haya preparado	nos hayamos preparado
te prepares	os preparéis	te hayas preparado	os hayáis preparado
se prepare	se preparen	se haya preparado	se hayan preparado
7 imperfecto de subjuntivo		14 pluscuamperfecto de subjuntivo	
me preparara	nos preparáramos	me hubiera preparado	nos hubiéramos preparado
te prepararas	os prepararais	te hubieras preparado	os hubierais preparado
se preparara	se prepararan	se hubiera preparado	se hubieran preparado
OR		OR	
me preparase	nos preparásemos	me hubiese preparado	nos hubiésemos preparado
te preparases	os preparaseis	te hubieses preparado	os hubieseis preparado
se preparase	se preparasen	se hubiese preparado	se hubiesen preparado

imperativo	
—	preparémonos
prepárate; no te prepares	preparaos; no os preparéis
prepárese	preparense

Words related to this verb
preparar   to prepare   **el preparamiento, la preparación**   preparation

> Can't find the verb you're looking for?
> Check the back pages of this book for a list of over 2,100 additional verbs!

The subject pronouns are found on page 93.

to present, to display, to show, to introduce   Regular **-ar** verb

The Seven Simple Tenses		The Seven Compound Tenses	
Singular	Plural	Singular	Plural
1 presente de indicativo		8 perfecto de indicativo	
presento	**presentamos**	**he presentado**	**hemos presentado**
presentas	**presentáis**	**has presentado**	**habéis presentado**
presenta	**presentan**	**ha presentado**	**han presentado**
2 imperfecto de indicativo		9 pluscuamperfecto de indicativo	
presentaba	**presentábamos**	**había presentado**	**habíamos presentado**
presentabas	**presentabais**	**habías presentado**	**habíais presentado**
presentaba	**presentaban**	**había presentado**	**habían presentado**
3 pretérito		10 pretérito anterior	
presenté	**presentamos**	**hube presentado**	**hubimos presentado**
presentaste	**presentasteis**	**hubiste presentado**	**hubisteis presentado**
presentó	**presentaron**	**hubo presentado**	**hubieron presentado**
4 futuro		11 futuro perfecto	
presentaré	**presentaremos**	**habré presentado**	**habremos presentado**
presentarás	**presentaréis**	**habrás presentado**	**habréis presentado**
presentará	**presentarán**	**habrá presentado**	**habrán presentado**
5 potencial simple		12 potencial compuesto	
presentaría	**presentaríamos**	**habría presentado**	**habríamos presentado**
presentarías	**presentaríais**	**habrías presentado**	**habríais presentado**
presentaría	**presentarían**	**habría presentado**	**habrían presentado**
6 presente de subjuntivo		13 perfecto de subjuntivo	
presente	**presentemos**	**haya presentado**	**hayamos presentado**
presentes	**presentéis**	**hayas presentado**	**hayáis presentado**
presente	**presenten**	**haya presentado**	**hayan presentado**
7 imperfecto de subjuntivo		14 pluscuamperfecto de subjuntivo	
presentara	**presentáramos**	**hubiera presentado**	**hubiéramos presentado**
presentaras	**presentarais**	**hubieras presentado**	**hubierais presentado**
presentara	**presentaran**	**hubiera presentado**	**hubieran presentado**
OR		OR	
presentase	**presentásemos**	**hubiese presentado**	**hubiésemos presentado**
presentases	**presentaseis**	**hubieses presentado**	**hubieseis presentado**
presentase	**presentasen**	**hubiese presentado**	**hubiesen presentado**

	imperativo	
—		**presentemos**
presenta; no presentes		**presentad; no presentéis**
presente		**presenten**

Words and expressions related to this verb

representar   to represent
presentarse   to introduce oneself
el presente   present; present tense
por lo presente   for the present

al presente, de presente   at present
presentar armas   to present arms
la presentación   presentation
presentable   presentable

Can't find the verb you're looking for?
Check the back pages of this book for a list of over 2,100 additional verbs!

Regular **-ar** verb   to lend

The Seven Simple Tenses		The Seven Compound Tenses	
Singular	Plural	Singular	Plural
1 presente de indicativo		**8 perfecto de indicativo**	
presto	prestamos	he prestado	hemos prestado
prestas	prestáis	has prestado	habéis prestado
presta	prestan	ha prestado	han prestado
2 imperfecto de indicativo		**9 pluscuamperfecto de indicativo**	
prestaba	prestábamos	había prestado	habíamos prestado
prestabas	prestabais	habías prestado	habíais prestado
prestaba	prestaban	había prestado	habían prestado
3 pretérito		**10 pretérito anterior**	
presté	prestamos	hube prestado	hubimos prestado
prestaste	prestasteis	hubiste prestado	hubisteis prestado
prestó	prestaron	hubo prestado	hubieron prestado
4 futuro		**11 futuro perfecto**	
prestaré	prestaremos	habré prestado	habremos prestado
prestarás	prestaréis	habrás prestado	habréis prestado
prestará	prestarán	habrá prestado	habrán prestado
5 potencial simple		**12 potencial compuesto**	
prestaría	prestaríamos	habría prestado	habríamos prestado
prestarías	prestaríais	habrías prestado	habríais prestado
prestaría	prestarían	habría prestado	habrían prestado
6 presente de subjuntivo		**13 perfecto de subjuntivo**	
preste	prestemos	haya prestado	hayamos prestado
prestes	prestéis	hayas prestado	hayáis prestado
preste	presten	haya prestado	hayan prestado
7 imperfecto de subjuntivo		**14 pluscuamperfecto de subjuntivo**	
prestara	prestáramos	hubiera prestado	hubiéramos prestado
prestaras	prestarais	hubieras prestado	hubierais prestado
prestara	prestaran	hubiera prestado	hubieran prestado
OR		OR	
prestase	prestásemos	hubiese prestado	hubiésemos prestado
prestases	prestaseis	hubieses prestado	hubieseis prestado
prestase	prestasen	hubiese prestado	hubiesen prestado

imperativo	
—	prestemos
presta; no prestes	prestad; no prestéis
preste	presten

Words and expressions related to this verb

pedir prestado   to borrow
tomar prestado   to borrow
prestador, prestadora   lender
un préstamo   loan

prestar atención   to pay attention
una casa de préstamos   pawn shop
un, una prestamista   money lender
la prestación   benefit, contribution

The subject pronouns are found on page 93.

to begin   Regular **-ar** verb

The Seven Simple Tenses		The Seven Compound Tenses	
Singular	Plural	Singular	Plural
1 presente de indicativo		8 perfecto de indicativo	
principio	**principiamos**	**he principiado**	**hemos principiado**
principias	**principiáis**	**has principiado**	**habéis principiado**
principia	**principian**	**ha principiado**	**han principiado**
2 imperfecto de indicativo		9 pluscuamperfecto de indicativo	
principiaba	**principiábamos**	**había principiado**	**habíamos principiado**
principiabas	**principiabais**	**habías principiado**	**habíais principiado**
principiaba	**principiaban**	**había principiado**	**habían principiado**
3 pretérito		10 pretérito anterior	
principié	**principiamos**	**hube principiado**	**hubimos principiado**
principiaste	**principiasteis**	**hubiste principiado**	**hubisteis principiado**
principió	**principiaron**	**hubo principiado**	**hubieron principiado**
4 futuro		11 futuro perfecto	
principiaré	**principiaremos**	**habré principiado**	**habremos principiado**
principiarás	**principiaréis**	**habrás principiado**	**habréis principiado**
principiará	**principiarán**	**habrá principiado**	**habrán principiado**
5 potencial simple		12 potencial compuesto	
principiaría	**principiaríamos**	**habría principiado**	**habríamos principiado**
principiarías	**principiaríais**	**habrías principiado**	**habríais principiado**
principiaría	**principiarían**	**habría principiado**	**habrían principiado**
6 presente de subjuntivo		13 perfecto de subjuntivo	
principie	**principiemos**	**haya principiado**	**hayamos principiado**
principies	**principiéis**	**hayas principiado**	**hayáis principiado**
principie	**principien**	**haya principiado**	**hayan principiado**
7 imperfecto de subjuntivo		14 pluscuamperfecto de subjuntivo	
principiara	**principiáramos**	**hubiera principiado**	**hubiéramos principiado**
principiaras	**principiarais**	**hubieras principiado**	**hubierais principiado**
principiara	**principiaran**	**hubiera principiado**	**hubieran principiado**
OR		OR	
principiase	**principiásemos**	**hubiese principiado**	**hubiésemos principiado**
principiases	**principiaseis**	**hubieses principiado**	**hubieseis principiado**
principiase	**principiasen**	**hubiese principiado**	**hubiesen principiado**

	imperativo	
—		**principiemos**
principia; no principies		**principiad; no principiéis**
principie		**principien**

Words and expressions related to this verb
el principio beginning, start; principle
a principios de at the beginning of
desde el principio from the beginning
principio de admiración inverted
  exclamation point (¡)

en principio in principle
el, la principiante beginner
principio de interrogación inverted question
  mark (¿)
al principio (a los principios) at first, in
  the beginning
la edición principe first edition (*editio princeps*)

Regular **-ar** verb endings with stem
change: Tenses 1, 6, Imperative

to test, to prove, to try, to try on

The Seven Simple Tenses		The Seven Compound Tenses	
Singular	Plural	Singular	Plural
1 presente de indicativo		8 perfecto de indicativo	
pruebo	**probamos**	**he probado**	**hemos probado**
pruebas	**probáis**	**has probado**	**habéis probado**
prueba	**prueban**	**ha probado**	**han probado**
2 imperfecto de indicativo		9 pluscuamperfecto de indicativo	
probaba	**probábamos**	**había probado**	**habíamos probado**
probabas	**probabais**	**habías probado**	**habíais probado**
probaba	**probaban**	**había probado**	**habían probado**
3 pretérito		10 pretérito anterior	
probé	**probamos**	**hube probado**	**hubimos probado**
probaste	**probasteis**	**hubiste probado**	**hubisteis probado**
probó	**probaron**	**hubo probado**	**hubieron probado**
4 futuro		11 futuro perfecto	
probaré	**probaremos**	**habré probado**	**habremos probado**
probarás	**probaréis**	**habrás probado**	**habréis probado**
probará	**probarán**	**habrá probado**	**habrán probado**
5 potencial simple		12 potencial compuesto	
probaría	**probaríamos**	**habría probado**	**habríamos probado**
probarías	**probaríais**	**habrías probado**	**habríais probado**
probaría	**probarían**	**habría probado**	**habrían probado**
6 presente de subjuntivo		13 perfecto de subjuntivo	
pruebe	**probemos**	**haya probado**	**hayamos probado**
pruebes	**probéis**	**hayas probado**	**hayáis probado**
pruebe	**prueben**	**haya probado**	**hayan probado**
7 imperfecto de subjuntivo		14 pluscuamperfecto de subjuntivo	
probara	**probáramos**	**hubiera probado**	**hubiéramos probado**
probaras	**probarais**	**hubieras probado**	**hubierais probado**
probara	**probaran**	**hubiera probado**	**hubieran probado**
OR		OR	
probase	**probásemos**	**hubiese probado**	**hubiésemos probado**
probases	**probaseis**	**hubieses probado**	**hubieseis probado**
probase	**probasen**	**hubiese probado**	**hubiesen probado**

imperativo	
—	**probemos**
prueba; no pruebes	**probad; no probéis**
pruebe	**prueben**

Words and expressions related to this verb
la prueba   proof, evidence, test
poner a prueba   to put to the test, to try out
probable   probable
probablemente   probably
el probador   fitting room, dressing room
probar de   to taste, to take a taste of
la probatura   test, experiment
la probación   proof, probation
la probabilidad   probability
probatorio, probatoria   probative
¿Me puedo probar este traje?   May I try on this suit?

The subject pronouns are found on page 93.

to try on (clothes)

Reflexive verb; regular **-ar** verb endings
with stem change: Tenses 1, 6, Imperative

The Seven Simple Tenses | The Seven Compound Tenses

Singular	Plural	Singular	Plural
1 presente de indicativo		**8 perfecto de indicativo**	
me pruebo	nos probamos	me he probado	nos hemos probado
te pruebas	os probáis	te has probado	os habéis probado
se prueba	se prueban	se ha probado	se han probado
2 imperfecto de indicativo		**9 pluscuamperfecto de indicativo**	
me probaba	nos probábamos	me había probado	nos habíamos probado
te probabas	os probabais	te habías probado	os habíais probado
se probaba	se probaban	se había probado	se habían probado
3 pretérito		**10 pretérito anterior**	
me probé	nos probamos	me hube probado	nos hubimos probado
te probaste	os probasteis	te hubiste probado	os hubisteis probado
se probó	se probaron	se hubo probado	se hubieron probado
4 futuro		**11 futuro perfecto**	
me probaré	nos probaremos	me habré probado	nos habremos probado
te probarás	os probaréis	te habrás probado	os habréis probado
se probará	se probarán	se habrá probado	se habrán probado
5 potencial simple		**12 potencial compuesto**	
me probaría	nos probaríamos	me habría probado	nos habríamos probado
te probarías	os probaríais	te habrías probado	os habríais probado
se probaría	se probarían	se habría probado	se habrían probado
6 presente de subjuntivo		**13 perfecto de subjuntivo**	
me pruebe	nos probemos	me haya probado	nos hayamos probado
te pruebes	os probéis	te hayas probado	os hayáis probado
se pruebe	se prueben	se haya probado	se hayan probado
7 imperfecto de subjuntivo		**14 pluscuamperfecto de subjuntivo**	
me probara	nos probáramos	me hubiera probado	nos hubiéramos probado
te probaras	os probarais	te hubieras probado	os hubierais probado
se probara	se probaran	se hubiera probado	se hubieran probado
OR		OR	
me probase	nos probásemos	me hubiese probado	nos hubiésemos probado
te probases	os probaseis	te hubieses probado	os hubieseis probado
se probase	se probasen	se hubiese probado	se hubiesen probado

imperativo

—	probémonos
pruébate; no te pruebes	probaos; no os probéis
pruébese	pruébense

For words and expressions related to this verb, see **probar.**

Can't recognize an irregular verb form? Check out pages 678–681.

Regular **-ar** verb   to proclaim, to promulgate

The Seven Simple Tenses		The Seven Compound Tenses	
Singular	Plural	Singular	Plural
1 presente de indicativo		8 perfecto de indicativo	
proclamo	**proclamamos**	**he proclamado**	**hemos proclamado**
proclamas	**proclamáis**	**has proclamado**	**habéis proclamado**
proclama	**proclaman**	**ha proclamado**	**han proclamado**
2 imperfecto de indicativo		9 pluscuamperfecto de indicativo	
proclamaba	**proclamábamos**	**había proclamado**	**habíamos proclamado**
proclamabas	**proclamabais**	**habías proclamado**	**habíais proclamado**
proclamaba	**proclamaban**	**había proclamado**	**habían proclamado**
3 pretérito		10 pretérito anterior	
proclamé	**proclamamos**	**hube proclamado**	**hubimos proclamado**
proclamaste	**proclamasteis**	**hubiste proclamado**	**hubisteis proclamado**
proclamó	**proclamaron**	**hubo proclamado**	**hubieron proclamado**
4 futuro		11 futuro perfecto	
proclamaré	**proclamaremos**	**habré proclamado**	**habremos proclamado**
proclamarás	**proclamaréis**	**habrás proclamado**	**habréis proclamado**
proclamará	**proclamarán**	**habrá proclamado**	**habrán proclamado**
5 potencial simple		12 potencial compuesto	
proclamaría	**proclamaríamos**	**habría proclamado**	**habríamos proclamado**
proclamarías	**proclamaríais**	**habrías proclamado**	**habríais proclamado**
proclamaría	**proclamarían**	**habría proclamado**	**habrían proclamado**
6 presente de subjuntivo		13 perfecto de subjuntivo	
proclame	**proclamemos**	**haya proclamado**	**hayamos proclamado**
proclames	**proclaméis**	**hayas proclamado**	**hayáis proclamado**
proclame	**proclamen**	**haya proclamado**	**hayan proclamado**
7 imperfecto de subjuntivo		14 pluscuamperfecto de subjuntivo	
proclamara	**proclamáramos**	**hubiera proclamado**	**hubiéramos proclamado**
proclamaras	**proclamaras**	**hubieras proclamado**	**hubierais proclamado**
proclamara	**proclamaran**	**hubiera proclamado**	**hubieran proclamado**
OR		OR	
proclamase	**proclamásemos**	**hubiese proclamado**	**hubiésemos proclamado**
proclamases	**proclamaseis**	**hubieses proclamado**	**hubieseis proclamado**
proclamase	**proclamasen**	**hubiese proclamado**	**hubiesen proclamado**

imperativo	
—	**proclamemos**
proclama; no proclames	**proclamad; no proclaméis**
proclame	**proclamen**

Words related to this verb
la proclamación, la proclama   proclamation   **clamar**   to cry out, to beseech
clamoroso, clamorosa   loud, resounding   **el clamor**   shout

Use the guide to Spanish pronunciation on pages 665–667.

The subject pronouns are found on page 93.   **513**

producir (381)　　　Gerundio **produciendo**　　　Part. pas. **producido**

to produce, to cause | Irregular in Tenses 3 and 7, regular **-ir** endings in all others; spelling change: **c** becomes **zc** before **a** or **o**

The Seven Simple Tenses | The Seven Compound Tenses

Singular	Plural	Singular	Plural
1 presente de indicativo		**8 perfecto de indicativo**	
produzco	producimos	he producido	hemos producido
produces	producís	has producido	habéis producido
produce	producen	ha producido	han producido
2 imperfecto de indicativo		**9 pluscuamperfecto de indicativo**	
producía	producíamos	había producido	habíamos producido
producías	producíais	habías producido	habíais producido
producía	producían	había producido	habían producido
3 pretérito		**10 pretérito anterior**	
produje	produjimos	hube producido	hubimos producido
produjiste	produjisteis	hubiste producido	hubisteis producido
produjo	produjeron	hubo producido	hubieron producido
4 futuro		**11 futuro perfecto**	
produciré	produciremos	habré producido	habremos producido
producirás	produciréis	habrás producido	habréis producido
producirá	producirán	habrá producido	habrán producido
5 potencial simple		**12 potencial compuesto**	
produciría	produciríamos	habría producido	habríamos producido
producirías	produciríais	habrías producido	habríais producido
produciría	producirían	habría producido	habrían producido
6 presente de subjuntivo		**13 perfecto de subjuntivo**	
produzca	produzcamos	haya producido	hayamos producido
produzcas	produzcáis	hayas producido	hayáis producido
produzca	produzcan	haya producido	hayan producido
7 imperfecto de subjuntivo		**14 pluscuamperfecto de subjuntivo**	
produjera	produjéramos	hubiera producido	hubiéramos producido
produjeras	produjerais	hubieras producido	hubierais producido
produjera	produjeran	hubiera producido	hubieran producido
OR		OR	
produjese	produjésemos	hubiese producido	hubiésemos producido
produjeses	produjeseis	hubieses producido	hubieseis producido
produjese	produjesen	hubiese producido	hubiesen producido

imperativo

—	produzcamos
produce; no produzcas	producid; no produzcáis
produzca	produzcan

Words and expressions related to this verb
la **productividad** productivity
productivo, productiva productive
el **producto** product, produce; proceeds
productos de belleza cosmetics
reproducir to reproduce
la **producción** production

productos de aguja needlework
productos de consumo consumer goods
productos de tocador toilet articles
un productor, una productora producer
reproducir asexualmente to clone

Regular **-ir** verb endings with spelling change: **i** becomes   to prohibit, to forbid
í on stressed syllable (see Tenses 1, 6, Imperative)

The Seven Simple Tenses		The Seven Compound Tenses	
Singular	Plural	Singular	Plural
1 presente de indicativo		8 perfecto de indicativo	
prohíbo	**prohibimos**	**he prohibido**	**hemos prohibido**
prohíbes	**prohibís**	**has prohibido**	**habéis prohibido**
prohíbe	**prohíben**	**ha prohibido**	**han prohibido**
2 imperfecto de indicativo		9 pluscuamperfecto de indicativo	
prohibía	**prohibíamos**	**había prohibido**	**habíamos prohibido**
prohibías	**prohibíais**	**habías prohibido**	**habíais prohibido**
prohibía	**prohibían**	**había prohibido**	**habían prohibido**
3 pretérito		10 pretérito anterior	
prohibí	**prohibimos**	**hube prohibido**	**hubimos prohibido**
prohibiste	**prohibisteis**	**hubiste prohibido**	**hubisteis prohibido**
prohibió	**prohibieron**	**hubo prohibido**	**hubieron prohibido**
4 futuro		11 futuro perfecto	
prohibiré	**prohibiremos**	**habré prohibido**	**habremos prohibido**
prohibirás	**prohibiréis**	**habrás prohibido**	**habréis prohibido**
prohibirá	**prohibirán**	**habrá prohibido**	**habrán prohibido**
5 potencial simple		12 potencial compuesto	
prohibirá	**prohibiríamos**	**habría prohibido**	**habríamos prohibido**
prohibirías	**prohibiríais**	**habrías prohibido**	**habríais prohibido**
prohibiría	**prohibirían**	**habría prohibido**	**habrían prohibido**
6 presente de subjuntivo		13 perfecto de subjuntivo	
prohíba	**prohibamos**	**haya prohibido**	**hayamos prohibido**
prohíbas	**prohibáis**	**hayas prohibido**	**hayáis prohibido**
prohíba	**prohíban**	**haya prohibido**	**hayan prohibido**
7 imperfecto de subjuntivo		14 pluscuamperfecto de subjuntivo	
prohibiera	**prohibiéramos**	**hubiera prohibido**	**hubiéramos prohibido**
prohibieras	**prohibierais**	**hubieras prohibido**	**hubierais prohibido**
prohibiera	**prohibieran**	**hubiera prohibido**	**hubieran prohibido**
OR		OR	
prohibiese	**prohibiésemos**	**hubiese prohibido**	**hubiésemos prohibido**
prohibieses	**prohibieseis**	**hubieses prohibido**	**hubieseis prohibido**
prohibiese	**prohibiesen**	**hubiese prohibido**	**hubiesen prohibido**

imperativo

—	**prohibamos**
prohíbe; no prohíbas	**prohibid; no prohibáis**
prohíba	**prohíban**

Words and expressions related to this verb
la prohibición   prohibition
el, la prohibicionista   prohibitionist
SE PROHIBE EL ESTACIONAMIENTO
   NO PARKING
SE PROHIBE FUMAR   NO SMOKING
No podemos nadar aquí. Es prohibido.
   We can't swim here. It's forbidden.

prohibitivo, prohibitiva   prohibitive
prohibitorio, prohibitoria   prohibitory
SE PROHIBE LA ENTRADA   KEEP OUT
SE PROHIBE ESCUPIR   NO SPITTING
SE PROHIBE FIJAR CARTELES
   POST NO BILLS

to pronounce   Regular **-ar** verb

The Seven Simple Tenses		The Seven Compound Tenses	
Singular	Plural	Singular	Plural
1 presente de indicativo		8 perfecto de indicativo	
pronuncio	pronunciamos	he pronunciado	hemos pronunciado
pronuncias	pronunciáis	has pronunciado	habéis pronunciado
pronuncia	pronuncian	ha pronunciado	han pronunciado
2 imperfecto de indicativo		9 pluscuamperfecto de indicativo	
pronunciaba	pronunciábamos	había pronunciado	habíamos pronunciado
pronunciabas	pronunciabais	habías pronunciado	habíais pronunciado
pronunciaba	pronunciaban	había pronunciado	habían pronunciado
3 pretérito		10 pretérito anterior	
pronuncié	pronunciamos	hube pronunciado	hubimos pronunciado
pronunciaste	pronunciasteis	hubiste pronunciado	hubisteis pronunciado
pronunció	pronunciaron	hubo pronunciado	hubieron pronunciado
4 futuro		11 futuro perfecto	
pronunciaré	pronunciaremos	habré pronunciado	habremos pronunciado
pronunciarás	pronunciaréis	habrás pronunciado	habréis pronunciado
pronunciará	pronunciarán	habrá pronunciado	habrán pronunciado
5 potencial simple		12 potencial compuesto	
pronunciaría	pronunciaríamos	habría pronunciado	habríamos pronunciado
pronunciarías	pronunciaríais	habrías pronunciado	habríais pronunciado
pronunciaría	pronunciarían	habría pronunciado	habrían pronunciado
6 presente de subjuntivo		13 perfecto de subjuntivo	
pronuncie	pronunciemos	haya pronunciado	hayamos pronunciado
pronuncies	pronunciéis	hayas pronunciado	hayáis pronunciado
pronuncie	pronuncien	haya pronunciado	hayan pronunciado
7 imperfecto de subjuntivo		14 pluscuamperfecto de subjuntivo	
pronunciara	pronunciáramos	hubiera pronunciado	hubiéramos pronunciado
pronunciaras	pronunciarais	hubieras pronunciado	hubierais pronunciado
pronunciara	pronunciaran	hubiera pronunciado	hubieran pronunciado
OR		OR	
pronunciase	pronunciásemos	hubiese pronunciado	hubiésemos pronunciado
pronunciases	pronunciaseis	hubieses pronunciado	hubieseis pronunciado
pronunciase	pronunciasen	hubiese pronunciado	hubiesen pronunciado

imperativo

—	**pronunciemos**
pronuncia; no pronuncies	**pronunciad; no pronunciéis**
pronuncie	**pronuncien**

Words and expressions related to this verb
la pronunciación   pronunciation
pronunciado, pronunciada   pronounced
pronunciar un discurso   to make
  a speech
enunciar   to enunciate

pronunciar una conferencia   to deliver a lecture
anunciar   to announce
denunciar   to denounce
renunciar   to renounce
el nuncio   omen
impronunciable   unpronounceable

Gerundio **protegiendo**   Part. pas. **protegido**   **proteger (384)**

Regular **-er** verb endings with spelling   to protect
change: **g** becomes **j** before **a** or **o**

The Seven Simple Tenses | The Seven Compound Tenses

Singular	Plural	Singular	Plural
1 presente de indicativo		**8 perfecto de indicativo**	
protejo	protegemos	he protegido	hemos protegido
proteges	protegéis	has protegido	habéis protegido
protege	protegen	ha protegido	han protegido
2 imperfecto de indicativo		**9 pluscuamperfecto de indicativo**	
protegía	protegíamos	había protegido	habíamos protegido
protegías	protegíais	habías protegido	habíais protegido
protegía	protegían	había protegido	habían protegido
3 pretérito		**10 pretérito anterior**	
protegí	protegimos	hube protegido	hubimos protegido
protegiste	protegisteis	hubiste protegido	hubisteis protegido
protegió	protegieron	hubo protegido	hubieron protegido
4 futuro		**11 futuro perfecto**	
protegeré	protegeremos	habré protegido	habremos protegido
protegerás	protegeréis	habrás protegido	habréis protegido
protegerá	protegerán	habrá protegido	habrán protegido
5 potencial simple		**12 potencial compuesto**	
protegería	protegeríamos	habría protegido	habríamos protegido
protegerías	protegeríais	habrías protegido	habríais protegido
protegería	protegerían	habría protegido	habrían protegido
6 presente de subjuntivo		**13 perfecto de subjuntivo**	
proteja	protejamos	haya protegido	hayamos protegido
protejas	protejáis	hayas protegido	hayáis protegido
proteja	protejan	haya protegido	hayan protegido
7 imperfecto de subjuntivo		**14 pluscuamperfecto de subjuntivo**	
protegiera	protegiéramos	hubiera protegido	hubiéramos protegido
protegieras	protegierais	hubieras protegido	hubierais protegido
protegiera	protegieran	hubiera protegido	hubieran protegido
OR		OR	
protegiese	protegiésemos	hubiese protegido	hubiésemos protegido
protegieses	protegieseis	hubieses protegido	hubieseis protegido
protegiese	protegiesen	hubiese protegido	hubiesen protegido

imperativo

—	protejamos
protege; no protejas	proteged; no protejáis
proteja	protejan

Words related to this verb
la protección protection
protegido, protegida protected, favorite, protégé
el protector, la protectriz protector, protectress
protectorio, protectoria protective

proteger contra to protect against
proteger de to protect from
sin protección unprotected
excesivamente protector, protectora overprotective

The subject pronouns are found on page 93.

to putrefy, to rot (Inf. can also be **podrir**)　　　　Irregular verb

The Seven Simple Tenses		The Seven Compound Tenses	
Singular	Plural	Singular	Plural
1 presente de indicativo		**8 perfecto de indicativo**	
pudro	**pudrimos**	**he podrido**	**hemos podrido**
pudres	**pudrís**	**has podrido**	**habéis podrido**
pudre	**pudren**	**ha podrido**	**han podrido**
2 inperfecto de indicativo		**9 pluscuamperfecto de indicativo**	
pudría	**pudríamos**	**había podrido**	**habíamos podrido**
pudrías	**pudríais**	**habías podrido**	**habíais podrido**
pudría	**pudrían**	**había podrido**	**habían podrido**
3 pretérito		**10 pretérito anterior**	
pudrí or **podrí**	**pudrimos**	**hube podrido**	**hubimos podrido**
pudriste	**pudristeis**	**hubiste podrido**	**hubisteis podrido**
pudrió	**pudrieron**	**hubo podrido**	**hubieron podrido**
4 futuro		**11 futuro perfecto**	
pudriré or **podriré**	**pudriremos**	**habré podrido**	**habremos podrido**
pudrirás	**pudriréis**	**habrás podrido**	**habréis podrido**
pudrirá	**pudrirán**	**habrá podrido**	**habrán podrido**
5 potencial simple		**12 potencial compuesto**	
pudriría or **podriría**	**pudriríamos**	**habría podrido**	**habríamos podrido**
pudrirías	**pudriríais**	**habrías podrido**	**habríais podrido**
pudriría	**pudrirían**	**habría podrido**	**habrían podrido**
6 presente de subjuntivo		**13 perfecto de subjuntivo**	
pudra	**pudramos**	**haya podrido**	**hayamos podrido**
pudras	**pudráis**	**hayas podrido**	**hayáis podrido**
pudra	**pudran**	**haya podrido**	**hayan podrido**
7 imperfecto de subjuntivo		**14 pluscuamperfecto de subjuntivo**	
pudriera	**pudriéramos**	**hubiera podrido**	**hubiéramos podrido**
pudrieras	**pudrierais**	**hubieras podrido**	**hubierais podrido**
pudriera	**pudrieran**	**hubiera podrido**	**hubieran podrido**
OR		OR	
pudriese	**pudriésemos**	**hubiese podrido**	**hubiésemos podrido**
pudrieses	**pudrieseis**	**hubieses podrido**	**hubieseis podrido**
pudriese	**pudriesen**	**hubiese podrido**	**hubiesen podrido**

imperativo	
—	**pudramos**
pudre; no pudras	**pudrid; no pudráis**
pudra	**pudran**

Words and expressions related to this verb

la pudrición rotting　　　　**podrido, podrida** rotten
el podridero compost heap　　　　**una olla podrida** a heavily seasoned stew
el pudrimiento rotting

Don't forget to study the section on defective and impersonal verbs. It's right after this main list.

The Seven Simple Tenses		The Seven Compound Tenses	
Singular	Plural	Singular	Plural

1   presente de indicativo

		8 perfecto de indicativo	
pulo	pulimos	he pulido	hemos pulido
pules	pulís	has pulido	habéis pulido
pule	pulen	ha pulido	han pulido

2   imperfecto de indicativo

		9 pluscuamperfecto de indicativo	
pulía	pulíamos	había pulido	habíamos pulido
pulías	pulíais	habías pulido	habíais pulido
pulía	pulían	había pulido	habían pulido

3   pretérito

		10 pretérito anterior	
pulí	pulimos	hube pulido	hubimos pulido
puliste	pulisteis	hubiste pulido	hubisteis pulido
pulió	pulieron	hubo pulido	hubieron pulido

4   futuro

		11 futuro perfecto	
puliré	puliremos	habré pulido	habremos pulido
pulirás	puliréis	habrás pulido	habréis pulido
pulirá	pulirán	habrá pulido	habrán pulido

5   potencial simple

		12 potencial compuesto	
puliría	puliríamos	habría pulido	habríamos pulido
pulirías	puliríais	habrías pulido	habríais pulido
puliría	pulirían	habría pulido	habrían pulido

6   presente de subjuntivo

		13 perfecto de subjuntivo	
pula	pulamos	haya pulido	hayamos pulido
pulas	puláis	hayas pulido	hayáis pulido
pula	pulan	haya pulido	hayan pulido

7   imperfecto de subjuntivo

		14 pluscuamperfecto de subjuntivo	
puliera	puliéramos	hubiera pulido	hubiéramos pulido
pulieras	pulierais	hubieras pulido	hubierais pulido
puliera	pulieran	hubiera pulido	hubieran pulido
OR		OR	
puliese	puliésemos	hubiese pulido	hubiésemos pulido
pulieses	pulieseis	hubieses pulido	hubieseis pulido
puliese	puliesen	hubiese pulido	hubiesen pulido

	imperativo	
—		pulamos
pule; no pulas		pulid; no puláis
pula		pulan

Words related to this verb
el pulimento   polish, gloss   **pulimentar**   to polish; **la pulidez**   polish, elegance, shine
una pulidora   polishing machine   **pulidamente**   neatly

Can't remember the Spanish verb you need?
Check the back pages of this book for the English-Spanish verb index!

The Seven Simple Tenses		The Seven Compound Tenses	
Singular	Plural	Singular	Plural
1 presente de indicativo		8 perfecto de indicativo	
me quedo	nos quedamos	me he quedado	nos hemos quedado
te quedas	os quedáis	te has quedado	os habéis quedado
se queda	se quedan	se ha quedado	se han quedado
2 imperfecto de indicativo		9 pluscuamperfecto de indicativo	
me quedaba	nos quedábamos	me había quedado	nos habíamos quedado
te quedabas	os quedabais	te habías quedado	os habíais quedado
se quedaba	se quedaban	se había quedado	se habían quedado
3 pretérito		10 pretérito anterior	
me quedé	nos quedamos	me hube quedado	nos hubimos quedado
te quedaste	os quedasteis	te hubiste quedado	os hubisteis quedado
se quedó	se quedaron	se hubo quedado	se hubieron quedado
4 futuro		11 futuro perfecto	
me quedaré	nos quedaremos	me habré quedado	nos habremos quedado
te quedarás	os quedaréis	te habrás quedado	os habréis quedado
se quedará	se quedarán	se habrá quedado	se habrán quedado
5 potencial simple		12 potencial compuesto	
me quedaría	nos quedaríamos	me habría quedado	nos habríamos quedado
te quedarías	os quedaríais	te habrías quedado	os habríais quedado
se quedaría	se quedarían	se habría quedado	se habrían quedado
6 presente de subjuntivo		13 perfecto de subjuntivo	
me quede	nos quedemos	me haya quedado	nos hayamos quedado
te quedes	os quedéis	te hayas quedado	os hayáis quedado
se quede	se queden	se haya quedado	se hayan quedado
7 imperfecto de subjuntivo		14 pluscuamperfecto de subjuntivo	
me quedara	nos quedáramos	me hubiera quedado	nos hubiéramos quedado
te quedaras	os quedarais	te hubieras quedado	os hubierais quedado
se quedara	se quedaran	se hubiera quedado	se hubieran quedado
OR		OR	
me quedase	nos quedásemos	me hubiese quedado	nos hubiésemos quedado
te quedases	os quedaseis	te hubieses quedado	os hubieseis quedado
se quedase	se quedasen	se hubiese quedado	se hubiesen quedado

	imperativo	
—		quedémonos
quédate; no te quedes		quedaos; no os quedéis
quédese		quédense

Quedarse is a very important reflexive verb for a beginning student. It is used in a great number of idiomatic expressions and everyday situations.

Sentences using quedarse and related words

El año pasado, me quedé dos semanas en San José.
Last year, I stayed two weeks in San José.

Quédate aquí conmigo.
Stay here with me.

¿Cuánto dinero queda?
How much money is left?

Me quedan dos dólares.
I have two dollars left (remaining).

Words and expressions related to this verb

la quedada residence, stay

quedar to remain, to be left

quedar limpio to clean out (of money); to be broke

quedar bien to turn out well

quedar mal to turn out badly

quedar de acuerdo to reach an agreement

quedarse ciego to go (be left) blind

quedarse muerto (muerta) to be speechless, dumbfounded

quedarse con la boca abierta to be left open-mouthed

Q

Do you need more drills? Have fun with the *501 Spanish Verbs* CD-ROM!

to complain, to grumble

The Seven Simple Tenses		The Seven Compound Tenses	
Singular	Plural	Singular	Plural
1 presente de indicativo		8 perfecto de indicativo	
me quejo	nos quejamos	me he quejado	nos hemos quejado
te quejas	os quejáis	te has quejado	os habéis quejado
se queja	se quejan	se ha quejado	se han quejado
2 imperfecto de indicativo		9 pluscuamperfecto de indicativo	
me quejaba	nos quejábamos	me había quejado	nos habíamos quejado
te quejabas	os quejabais	te habías quejado	os habíais quejado
se quejaba	se quejaban	se había quejado	se habían quejado
3 pretérito		10 pretérito anterior	
me quejé	nos quejamos	me hube quejado	nos hubimos quejado
te quejaste	os quejasteis	te hubiste quejado	os hubisteis quejado
se quejó	se quejaron	se hubo quejado	se hubieron quejado
4 futuro		11 futuro perfecto	
me quejaré	nos quejaremos	me habré quejado	nos habremos quejado
te quejarás	os quejaréis	te habrás quejado	os habréis quejado
se quejará	se quejarán	se habrá quejado	se habrán quejado
5 potencial simple		12 potencial compuesto	
me quejaría	nos quejaríamos	me habría quejado	nos habríamos quejado
te quejarías	os quejaríais	te habrías quejado	os habríais quejado
se quejaría	se quejarían	se habría quejado	se habrían quejado
6 presente de subjuntivo		13 perfecto de subjuntivo	
me queje	nos quejemos	me haya quejado	nos hayamos quejado
te quejes	os quejéis	te hayas quejado	os hayáis quejado
se queje	se quejen	se haya quejado	se hayan quejado
7 imperfecto de subjuntivo		14 pluscuamperfecto de subjuntivo	
me quejara	nos quejáramos	me hubiera quejado	nos hubiéramos quejado
te quejaras	os quejarais	te hubieras quejado	os hubierais quejado
se quejara	se quejaran	se hubiera quejado	se hubieran quejado
OR		OR	
me quejase	nos quejásemos	me hubiese quejado	nos hubiésemos quejado
te quejases	os quejaseis	te hubieses quejado	os hubieseis quejado
se quejase	se quejasen	se hubiese quejado	se hubiesen quejado

	imperativo	
—		quejémonos
quéjate; no te quejes		quejaos; no os quejéis
quéjese		quéjense

Words and expressions related to this verb
quejarse de   to complain about
la queja   complaint
el quejido   groan, moan

quejoso, quejosa   annoyed
un quejumbrón, una quejumbrona   whiner
dar quejidos   to moan, groan

Get acquainted with what preposition goes with what verb on pages 669–677.

Regular **-ar** verb

to burn, to fire

The Seven Simple Tenses		The Seven Compound Tenses	
Singular	Plural	Singular	Plural
1 presente de indicativo		8 perfecto de indicativo	
quemo	quemamos	he quemado	hemos quemado
quemas	quemáis	has quemado	habéis quemado
quema	queman	ha quemado	han quemado
2 imperfecto de indicativo		9 pluscuamperfecto de indicativo	
quemaba	quemábamos	había quemado	habíamos quemado
quemabas	quemabais	habías quemado	habíais quemado
quemaba	quemaban	había quemado	habían quemado
3 pretérito		10 pretérito anterior	
quemé	quemamos	hube quemado	hubimos quemado
quemaste	quemasteis	hubiste quemado	hubisteis quemado
quemó	quemaron	hubo quemado	hubieron quemado
4 futuro		11 futuro perfecto	
quemaré	quemaremos	habré quemado	habremos quemado
quemarás	quemaréis	habrás quemado	habréis quemado
quemará	quemarán	habrá quemado	habrán quemado
5 potencial simple		12 potencial compuesto	
quemaría	quemaríamos	habría quemado	habríamos quemado
quemarías	quemaríais	habrías quemado	habríais quemado
quemaría	quemarían	habría quemado	habrían quemado
6 presente de subjuntivo		13 perfecto de subjuntivo	
queme	quememos	haya quemado	hayamos quemado
quemes	queméis	hayas quemado	hayáis quemado
queme	quemen	haya quemado	hayan quemado
7 imperfecto de subjuntivo		14 pluscuamperfecto de subjuntivo	
quemara	quemáramos	hubiera quemado	hubiéramos quemado
quemaras	quemarais	hubieras quemado	hubierais quemado
quemara	quemaran	hubiera quemado	hubieran quemado
OR		OR	
quemase	quemásemos	hubiese quemado	hubiésemos quemado
quemases	quemaseis	hubieses quemado	hubieseis quemado
quemase	quemasen	hubiese quemado	hubiesen quemado

imperativo	
—	quememos
quema; no quemes	quemad; no queméis
queme	quemen

Words and expressions related to this verb

la quemadura   burn, scald, sunburn
el quemador de gas   gas burner
la quema   fire

quemarse las cejas   to burn the midnight oil
huir de la quema   to run away from trouble
quemado   burned, burned out (emotionally, physically)

The subject pronouns are found on page 93.

The Seven Simple Tenses		The Seven Compound Tenses	
Singular	Plural	Singular	Plural
1 presente de indicativo		8 perfecto de indicativo	
quiero	queremos	he querido	hemos querido
quieres	queréis	has querido	habéis querido
quiere	quieren	ha querido	han querido
2 imperfecto de indicativo		9 pluscuamperfecto de indicativo	
quería	queríamos	había querido	habíamos querido
querías	queríais	habías querido	habíais querido
quería	querían	había querido	habían querido
3 pretérito		10 pretérito anterior	
quise	quisimos	hube querido	hubimos querido
quisiste	quisisteis	hubiste querido	hubisteis querido
quiso	quisieron	hubo querido	hubieron querido
4 futuro		11 futuro perfecto	
querré	querremos	habré querido	habremos querido
querrás	querréis	habrás querido	habréis querido
querrá	querrán	habrá querido	habrán querido
5 potencial simple		12 potencial compuesto	
querría	querríamos	habría querido	habríamos querido
querrías	querríais	habrías querido	habríais querido
querría	querrían	habría querido	habrían querido
6 presente de subjuntivo		13 perfecto de subjuntivo	
quiera	queramos	haya querido	hayamos querido
quieras	queráis	hayas querido	hayáis querido
quiera	quieran	haya querido	hayan querido
7 imperfecto de subjuntivo		14 pluscuamperfecto de subjuntivo	
quisiera	quisiéramos	hubiera querido	hubiéramos querido
quisieras	quisierais	hubieras querido	hubierais querido
quisiera	quisieran	hubiera querido	hubieran querido
OR		OR	
quisiese	quisiésemos	hubiese querido	hubiésemos querido
quisieses	quisieseis	hubieses querido	hubieseis querido
quisiese	quisiesen	hubiese querido	hubiesen querido

imperativo

—	queramos
quiere; no quieras	quered; no queráis
quiera	quieran

AN ESSENTIAL
55 VERB

Querer is a very important irregular verb for a beginning student. It is used in a great number of idiomatic expressions and everyday situations.

Sentences using querer and related words

¿Qué quiere Ud. beber?
What do you want to drink?

¿Qué quiere decir esto?
What does this mean?

Quisiera un café, por favor.
I would like a coffee, please.

Yo quisiera saber a qué hora el avión sale para Miami.
I would like to know at what time the plane leaves for Miami.

Queremos alquilar un coche, por favor.
We want to rent a car, please.

Words and expressions related to this verb

querer decir **to mean**

querido, querida **dear**

querido amigo, querida amiga **dear friend**

querido mío, querida mía **my dear**

querer bien a **to love**

Querer es poder. **Where there's a will, there's a way.**

Q

Proverbs

El que más tiene más quiere.
The more one has, the more one wants.

El que todo lo quiere, todo lo pierde.
Whoever wants everything loses everything.

Can't find the verb you're looking for?
Check the back pages of this book for a list of over 2,100 additional verbs!

The subject pronouns are found on page 93.

to take off (clothing), to remove oneself, to withdraw   Reflexive regular **-ar** verb

The Seven Simple Tenses		The Seven Compound Tenses	
Singular	Plural	Singular	Plural
1 presente de indicativo		8 perfecto de indicativo	
me quito	nos quitamos	me he quitado	nos hemos quitado
te quitas	os quitáis	te has quitado	os habéis quitado
se quita	se quitan	se ha quitado	se han quitado
2 imperfecto de indicativo		9 pluscuamperfecto de indicativo	
me quitaba	nos quitábamos	me había quitado	nos habíamos quitado
te quitabas	os quitabais	te habías quitado	os habíais quitado
se quitaba	se quitaban	se había quitado	se habían quitado
3 pretérito		10 pretérito anterior	
me quité	nos quitamos	me hube quitado	nos hubimos quitado
te quitaste	os quitasteis	te hubiste quitado	os hubisteis quitado
se quitó	se quitaron	se hubo quitado	se hubieron quitado
4 futuro		11 futuro perfecto	
me quitaré	nos quitaremos	me habré quitado	nos habremos quitado
te quitarás	os quitaréis	te habrás quitado	os habréis quitado
se quitará	se quitarán	se habrá quitado	se habrán quitado
5 potencial simple		12 potencial compuesto	
me quitaría	nos quitaríamos	me habría quitado	nos habríamos quitado
te quitarías	os quitaríais	te habrías quitado	os habríais quitado
se quitaría	se quitarían	se habría quitado	se habrían quitado
6 presente de subjuntivo		13 perfecto de subjuntivo	
me quite	nos quitemos	me haya quitado	nos hayamos quitado
te quites	os quitéis	te hayas quitado	os hayáis quitado
se quite	se quiten	se haya quitado	se hayan quitado
7 imperfecto de subjuntivo		14 pluscuamperfecto de subjuntivo	
me quitara	nos quitáramos	me hubiera quitado	nos hubiéramos quitado
te quitaras	os quitarais	te hubieras quitado	os hubierais quitado
se quitara	se quitaran	se hubiera quitado	se hubieran quitado
OR		OR	
me quitase	nos quitásemos	me hubiese quitado	nos hubiésemos quitado
te quitases	os quitaseis	te hubieses quitado	os hubieseis quitado
se quitase	se quitasen	se hubiese quitado	se hubiesen quitado

imperativo	
—	quitémonos
quítate; no te quites	quitaos; no os quitéis
quítese	quítense

Words and expressions related to this verb
la quita   release (from owing money), acquittance
¡Quita de ahí!   Get away from here!
quitar   to remove, to take away; to rob, to strip

una quitanieves   snowplow
la quitación   salary
el quitasol   parasol (sunshade)

Check out the verb drills and verb tests with answers explained on pages 45–91.

Irregular verb   to scrape, to rub off, to erase, to wipe out, to fray

The Seven Simple Tenses		The Seven Compound Tenses	
Singular	Plural	Singular	Plural
1 presente de indicativo		8 perfecto de indicativo	
raigo	**raemos**	**he raído**	**hemos raído**
raes	**raéis**	**has raído**	**habéis raído**
rae	**raen**	**ha raído**	**han raído**
2 imperfecto de indicativo		9 pluscuamperfecto de indicativo	
raía	**raíamos**	**había raído**	**habíamos raído**
raías	**raíais**	**habías raído**	**habíais raído**
raía	**raían**	**había raído**	**habían raído**
3 pretérito		10 pretérito anterior	
raí	**raímos**	**hube raído**	**hubimos raído**
raíste	**raísteis**	**hubiste raído**	**hubisteis raído**
rayó	**rayeron**	**hubo raído**	**hubieron raído**
4 futuro		11 futuro perfecto	
raeré	**raeremos**	**habré raído**	**habremos raído**
raerás	**raeréis**	**habrás raído**	**habréis raído**
raerá	**raerán**	**habrá raído**	**habrán raído**
5 potencial simple		12 potencial compuesto	
raería	**raeríamos**	**habría raído**	**habríamos raído**
raerías	**raeríais**	**habrías raído**	**habríais raído**
rearía	**raerían**	**habría raído**	**habrían raído**
6 presente de subjuntivo		13 perfecto de subjuntivo	
raiga	**raigamos**	**haya raído**	**hayamos raído**
raigas	**raigáis**	**hayas raído**	**hayáis raído**
raiga	**raigan**	**haya raído**	**hayan raído**
7 imperfecto de subjuntivo		14 pluscuamperfecto de subjuntivo	
rayera	**rayéramos**	**hubiera raído**	**hubiéramos raído**
rayeras	**rayerais**	**hubieras raído**	**hubierais raído**
rayera	**rayeran**	**hubiera raído**	**hubieran raído**
OR		OR	
rayese	**rayésemos**	**hubiese raído**	**hubiésemos raído**
rayeses	**rayeseis**	**hubieses raído**	**hubieseis raído**
rayese	**rayesen**	**hubiese raído**	**hubiesen raído**

imperativo	
—	**raigamos**
rae; no raigas	**raed; no raigáis**
raiga	**raigan**

Words related to this verb
la raedura scraping
el raedor, la raedora scraper

raerse to wear away, become threadbare
raedizo, raediza easily scraped or scratched
raído, raída worn, frayed

Do you need more drills? Have fun with the *501 Spanish Verbs* CD-ROM!

The subject pronouns are found on page 93.

realizar (393)

Gerundio **realizando** Part. pas. **realizado**

to realize, to carry out, to fulfill

Regular **-ar** verb endings with spelling change: **z** becomes **c** before **e**

The Seven Simple Tenses		The Seven Compound Tenses	
Singular	Plural	Singular	Plural
1 presente de indicativo		8 perfecto de indicativo	
realizo	realizamos	he realizado	hemos realizado
realizas	realizáis	has realizado	habéis realizado
realiza	realizan	ha realizado	han realizado
2 imperfecto de indicativo		9 pluscuamperfecto de indicativo	
realizaba	realizábamos	había realizado	habíamos realizado
realizabas	realizabais	habías realizado	habíais realizado
realizaba	realizaban	había realizado	habían realizado
3 pretérito		10 pretérito anterior	
realicé	realizamos	hube realizado	hubimos realizado
realizaste	realizasteis	hubiste realizado	hubisteis realizado
realizó	realizaron	hubo realizado	hubieron realizado
4 futuro		11 futuro perfecto	
realizaré	realizaremos	habré realizado	habremos realizado
realizarás	realizaréis	habrás realizado	habréis realizado
realizará	realizarán	habrá realizado	habrán realizado
5 potencial simple		12 potencial compuesto	
realizaría	realizaríamos	habría realizado	habríamos realizado
realizarías	realizaríais	habrías realizado	habríais realizado
realizaría	realizarían	habría realizado	habrían realizado
6 presente de subjuntivo		13 perfecto de subjuntivo	
realice	realicemos	haya realizado	hayamos realizado
realices	realicéis	hayas realizado	hayáis realizado
realice	realicen	haya realizado	hayan realizado
7 imperfecto de subjuntivo		14 pluscuamperfecto de subjuntivo	
realizara	realizáramos	hubiera realizado	hubiéramos realizado
realizaras	realizarais	hubieras realizado	hubierais realizado
realizara	realizaran	hubiera realizado	hubieran realizado
OR		OR	
realizase	realizásemos	hubiese realizado	hubiésemos realizado
realizases	realizaseis	hubieses realizado	hubieseis realizado
realizase	realizasen	hubiese realizado	hubiesen realizado

imperativo	
—	realicemos
realiza; no realices	realizad; no realicéis
realice	realicen

Words and expressions related to this verb

realizar su deseo to have one's wish
la realización fulfillment, realization, production
realizarse to become fulfilled, to be carried out
realizable practical

el, la realista realist
la realidad reality
el realismo realism
realmente really

The Seven Simple Tenses		The Seven Compound Tenses	
Singular	Plural	Singular	Plural
1 presente de indicativo		8 perfecto de indicativo	
recibo	**recibimos**	**he recibido**	**hemos recibido**
recibes	**recibís**	**has recibido**	**habéis recibido**
recibe	**reciben**	**ha recibido**	**han recibido**
2 imperfecto de indicativo		9 pluscuamperfecto de indicativo	
recibía	**recibíamos**	**había recibido**	**habíamos recibido**
recibías	**recibíais**	**habías recibido**	**habíais recibido**
recibía	**recibían**	**había recibido**	**habían recibido**
3 pretérito		10 pretérito anterior	
recibí	**recibimos**	**hube recibido**	**hubimos recibido**
recibiste	**recibisteis**	**hubiste recibido**	**hubisteis recibido**
recibió	**recibieron**	**hubo recibido**	**hubieron recibido**
4 futuro		11 futuro perfecto	
recibiré	**recibiremos**	**habré recibido**	**habremos recibido**
recibirás	**recibiréis**	**habrás recibido**	**habréis recibido**
recibirá	**recibirán**	**habrá recibido**	**habrán recibido**
5 potencial simple		12 potencial compuesto	
recibiría	**recibiríamos**	**habría recibido**	**habríamos recibido**
recibirías	**recibiríais**	**habrías recibido**	**habríais recibido**
recibiría	**recibirían**	**habría recibido**	**habrían recibido**
6 presente de subjuntivo		13 perfecto de subjuntivo	
reciba	**recibamos**	**haya recibido**	**hayamos recibido**
recibas	**recibáis**	**hayas recibido**	**hayáis recibido**
reciba	**reciban**	**haya recibido**	**hayan recibido**
7 imperfecto de subjuntivo		14 pluscuamperfecto de subjuntivo	
recibiera	**recibiéramos**	**hubiera recibido**	**hubiéramos recibido**
recibieras	**recibierais**	**hubieras recibido**	**hubierais recibido**
recibiera	**recibieran**	**hubiera recibido**	**hubieran recibido**
OR		OR	
recibiese	**recibiésemos**	**hubiese recibido**	**hubiésemos recibido**
recibieses	**recibieseis**	**hubieses recibido**	**hubieseis recibido**
recibiese	**recibiesen**	**hubiese recibido**	**hubiesen recibido**

R

imperativo	
—	**recibamos**
recibe; no recibas	**recibid; no recibáis**
reciba	**reciban**

Words and expressions related to this verb

un recibo   receipt
acusar recibo   to acknowledge receipt
la recepción   reception
recibir a cuenta   to receive on account

de recibo   acceptable; **ser de recibo**   to be acceptable
recibirse   to be admitted, to be received, to graduate

Don't miss the definitions of basic grammatical terms with
examples in English and Spanish on pages 33–44.

The subject pronouns are found on page 93.

to pick (up), to gather,
to harvest, to collect

Regular **-er** verb endings with spelling
change: **g** becomes **j** before **a** or **o**

The Seven Simple Tenses		The Seven Compound Tenses	
Singular	Plural	Singular	Plural
1 presente de indicativo		8 perfecto de indicativo	
recojo	recogemos	he recogido	hemos recogido
recoges	recogéis	has recogido	habéis recogido
recoge	recogen	ha recogido	han recogido
2 imperfecto de indicativo		9 pluscuamperfecto de indicativo	
recogía	recogíamos	había recogido	habíamos recogido
recogías	recogíais	habías recogido	habíais recogido
recogía	recogían	había recogido	habían recogido
3 pretérito		10 pretérito anterior	
recogí	recogimos	hube recogido	hubimos recogido
recogiste	recogisteis	hubiste recogido	hubisteis recogido
recogió	recogieron	hubo recogido	hubieron recogido
4 futuro		11 futuro perfecto	
recogeré	recogeremos	habré recogido	habremos recogido
recogerás	recogeréis	habrás recogido	habréis recogido
recogerá	recogerán	habrá recogido	habrán recogido
5 potencial simple		12 potencial compuesto	
recogería	recogeríamos	habría recogido	habríamos recogido
recogerías	recogeríais	habrías recogido	habríais recogido
recogería	recogerían	habría recogido	habrían recogido
6 presente de subjuntivo		13 perfecto de subjuntivo	
recoja	recojamos	haya recogido	hayamos recogido
recojas	recojáis	hayas recogido	hayáis recogido
recoja	recojan	haya recogido	hayan recogido
7 imperfecto de subjuntivo		14 pluscuamperfecto de subjuntivo	
recogiera	recogiéramos	hubiera recogido	hubiéramos recogido
recogieras	recogierais	hubieras recogido	hubierais recogido
recogiera	recogieran	hubiera recogido	hubieran recogido
OR		OR	
recogiese	recogiésemos	hubiese recogido	hubiésemos recogido
recogieses	recogieseis	hubieses recogido	hubieseis recogido
recogiese	recogiesen	hubiese recogido	hubiesen recogido

imperativo	
—	recojamos
recoge; no recojas	recoged; no recojáis
recoja	recojan

Words and expressions related to this verb
la recogida harvest; **la recogida de
basuras** garbage collection
un recogegotas drip pan

un recogedor dustpan
recogerse to be withdrawn, isolated
recoger datos to gather information, data

For other words related to this verb, see **coger.**

Regular -ar verb endings with stem change: Tenses 1, 6, Imperative

to recommend, to commend, to advise

The Seven Simple Tenses		The Seven Compound Tenses	
Singular	Plural	Singular	Plural
1 presente de indicativo		8 perfecto de indicativo	
recomiendo	recomendamos	he recomendado	hemos recomendado
recomiendas	recomendáis	has recomendado	habéis recomendado
recomienda	recomiendan	ha recomendado	han recomendado
2 imperfecto de indicativo		9 pluscuamperfecto de indicativo	
recomendaba	recomendábamos	había recomendado	habíamos recomendado
recomendabas	recomendabais	habías recomendado	habíais recomendado
recomendaba	recomendaban	había recomendado	habían recomendado
3 pretérito		10 pretérito anterior	
recomendé	recomendamos	hube recomendado	hubimos recomendado
recomendaste	recomendasteis	hubiste recomendado	hubisteis recomendado
recomendó	recomendaron	hubo recomendado	hubieron recomendado
4 futuro		11 futuro perfecto	
recomendaré	recomendaremos	habré recomendado	habremos recomendado
recomendarás	recomendaréis	habrás recomendado	habréis recomendado
recomendará	recomendarán	habrá recomendado	habrán recomendado
5 potencial simple		12 potencial compuesto	
recomendaría	recomendaríamos	habría recomendado	habríamos recomendado
recomendarías	recomendaríais	habrías recomendado	habríais recomendado
recomendará	recomendarían	habría recomendado	habrían recomendado
6 presente de subjuntivo		13 perfecto de subjuntivo	
recomiende	recomendemos	haya recomendado	hayamos recomendado
recomiendes	recomendéis	hayas recomendado	hayáis recomendado
recomiende	recomienden	haya recomendado	hayan recomendado
7 imperfecto de subjuntivo		14 pluscuamperfecto de subjuntivo	
recomendara	recomendáramos	hubiera recomendado	hubiéramos recomendado
recomendaras	recomendarais	hubieras recomendado	hubierais recomendado
recomendara	recomendaran	hubiera recomendado	hubieran recomendado
OR		OR	
recomendase	recomendásemos	hubiese recomendado	hubiésemos recomendado
recomendases	recomendaseis	hubieses recomendado	hubieseis recomendado
recomendase	recomendasen	hubiese recomendado	hubiesen recomendado

R

imperativo	
—	recomendemos
recomienda; no recomiendes	recomendad; no recomendéis
recomiende	recomienden

Words related to this verb
la recomendación   recommendation
recomendablemente   commendably

recomendable   commendable, praiseworthy
recomendar + inf.   to urge + inf.

If you want an explanation of meanings and uses of Spanish
and English verb tenses and moods, see pages 13–32.

The subject pronouns are found on page 93.

reconocer (397)   Gerundio **reconociendo**   Part. pas. **reconocido**

to recognize, to acknowledge,
to be grateful for

Regular **-er** verb endings with spelling
change: **c** becomes **zc** before **a** or **o**

The Seven Simple Tenses		The Seven Compound Tenses	
Singular	Plural	Singular	Plural
1 presente de indicativo		8 perfecto de indicativo	
reconozco	reconocemos	he reconocido	hemos reconocido
reconoces	reconocéis	has reconocido	habéis reconocido
reconoce	reconocen	ha reconocido	han reconocido
2 imperfecto de indicativo		9 pluscuamperfecto de indicativo	
reconocía	reconocíamos	había reconocido	habíamos reconocido
reconocías	reconocíais	habías reconocido	habíais reconocido
reconocía	reconocían	había reconocido	habían reconocido
3 pretérito		10 pretérito anterior	
reconocí	reconocimos	hube reconocido	hubimos reconocido
reconociste	reconocisteis	hubiste reconocido	hubisteis reconocido
reconoció	reconocieron	hubo reconocido	hubieron reconocido
4 futuro		11 futuro perfecto	
reconoceré	reconoceremos	habré reconocido	habremos reconocido
reconocerás	reconoceréis	habrás reconocido	habréis reconocido
reconocerá	reconocerán	habrá reconocido	habrán reconocido
5 potencial simple		12 potencial compuesto	
reconocería	reconoceríamos	habría reconocido	habríamos reconocido
reconocerías	reconoceríais	habrías reconocido	habríais reconocido
reconocería	reconocerían	habría reconocido	habrían reconocido
6 presente de subjuntivo		13 perfecto de subjuntivo	
reconozca	reconozcamos	haya reconocido	hayamos reconocido
reconozcas	reconozcáis	hayas reconocido	hayáis reconocido
reconozca	reconozcan	haya reconocido	hayan reconocido
7 imperfecto de subjuntivo		14 pluscuamperfecto de subjuntivo	
reconociera	reconociéramos	hubiera reconocido	hubiéramos reconocido
reconocieras	reconocierais	hubieras reconocido	hubierais reconocido
reconociera	reconocieran	hubiera reconocido	hubieran reconocido
OR		OR	
reconociese	reconociésemos	hubiese reconocido	hubiésemos reconocido
reconocieses	reconocieseis	hubieses reconocido	hubieseis reconocido
reconociese	reconociesen	hubiese reconocido	hubiesen reconocido

imperativo	
—	reconozcamos
reconoce; no reconozcas	reconoced; no reconozcáis
reconozca	reconozcan

Words related to this verb
reconocible recognizable
el reconocimiento recognition, gratitude
el reconocimiento de la voz voice recognition

reconocimiento médico medical examination
reconocidamente gratefully

For other words and expressions related to this verb, see **conocer.**

Regular **-ar** verb endings with stem   to remember, to recall, to remind
change: Tenses 1, 6, Imperative

The Seven Simple Tenses		The Seven Compound Tenses	
Singular	Plural	Singular	Plural
1 presente de indicativo		8 perfecto de indicativo	
recuerdo	**recordamos**	**he recordado**	**hemos recordado**
recuerdas	**recordáis**	**has recordado**	**habéis recordado**
recuerda	**recuerdan**	**ha recordado**	**han recordado**
2 imperfecto de indicativo		9 pluscuamperfecto de indicativo	
recordaba	**recordábamos**	**había recordado**	**habíamos recordado**
recordabas	**recordabais**	**habías recordado**	**habíais recordado**
recordaba	**recordaban**	**había recordado**	**habían recordado**
3 pretérito		10 pretérito anterior	
recordé	**recordamos**	**hube recordado**	**hubimos recordado**
recordaste	**recordasteis**	**hubiste recordado**	**hubisteis recordado**
recordó	**recordaron**	**hubo recordado**	**hubieron recordado**
4 futuro		11 futuro perfecto	
recordaré	**recordaremos**	**habré recordado**	**habremos recordado**
recordarás	**recordaréis**	**habrás recordado**	**habréis recordado**
recordará	**recordarán**	**habrá recordado**	**habrán recordado**
5 potencial simple		12 potencial compuesto	
recordaría	**recordaríamos**	**habría recordado**	**habríamos recordado**
recordarías	**recordaríais**	**habrías recordado**	**habríais recordado**
recordaría	**recordarían**	**habría recordado**	**habrían recordado**
6 presente de subjuntivo		13 perfecto de subjuntivo	
recuerde	**recordemos**	**haya recordado**	**hayamos recordado**
recuerdes	**recordéis**	**hayas recordado**	**hayáis recordado**
recuerde	**recuerden**	**haya recordado**	**hayan recordado**
7 imperfecto de subjuntivo		14 pluscuamperfecto de subjuntivo	
recordara	**recordáramos**	**hubiera recordado**	**hubiéramos recordado**
recordaras	**recordarais**	**hubieras recordado**	**hubierais recordado**
recordara	**recordaran**	**hubiera recordado**	**hubieran recordado**
OR		OR	
recordase	**recordásemos**	**hubiese recordado**	**hubiésemos recordado**
recordases	**recordaseis**	**hubieses recordado**	**hubieseis recordado**
recordase	**recordasen**	**hubiese recordado**	**hubiesen recordado**

R

imperativo	
—	**recordemos**
recuerda; no recuerdes	**recordad; no recordéis**
recuerde	**recuerden**

Words and expressions related to this verb
el recuerdo memory, recollection
los recuerdos regards, compliments
recordable memorable
el récord record
una tienda de recuerdos souvenir shop

recordar algo a uno to remind someone of
  something
un recordatorio memento, reminder
cuerdo rational, sensible
cuerdamente sensibly

The subject pronouns are found on page 93.   **533**

to reduce	Irregular in Tenses 3 and 7, regular **-ir** verb endings in all others; spelling change: **c** becomes **zc** before **a** or **o**

The Seven Simple Tenses		The Seven Compound Tenses	
Singular	Plural	Singular	Plural
1 presente de indicativo		8 perfecto de indicativo	
reduzco	reducimos	he reducido	hemos reducido
reduces	reducís	has reducido	habéis reducido
reduce	reducen	ha reducido	han reducido
2 imperfecto de indicativo		9 pluscuamperfecto de indicativo	
reducía	reducíamos	había reducido	habíamos reducido
reducías	reducíais	habías reducido	habíais reducido
reducía	reducían	había reducido	habían reducido
3 pretérito		10 pretérito anterior	
reduje	redujimos	hube reducido	hubimos reducido
redujiste	redujisteis	hubiste reducido	hubisteis reducido
redujo	redujeron	hubo reducido	hubieron reducido
4 futuro		11 futuro perfecto	
reduciré	reduciremos	habré reducido	habremos reducido
reducirás	reduciréis	habrás reducido	habréis reducido
reducirá	reducirán	habrá reducido	habrán reducido
5 potencial simple		12 potencial compuesto	
reduciría	reduciríamos	habría reducido	habríamos reducido
reducirías	reduciríais	habrías reducido	habríais reducido
reduciría	reducirían	habría reducido	habrían reducido
6 presente de subjuntivo		13 perfecto de subjuntivo	
reduzca	reduzcamos	haya reducido	hayamos reducido
reduzcas	reduzcáis	hayas reducido	hayáis reducido
reduzca	reduzcan	haya reducido	hayan reducido
7 imperfecto de subjuntivo		14 pluscuamperfecto de subjuntivo	
redujera	redujéramos	hubiera reducido	hubiéramos reducido
redujeras	redujerais	hubieras reducido	hubierais reducido
redujera	redujeran	hubiera reducido	hubieran reducido
OR		OR	
redujese	redujésemos	hubiese reducido	hubiésemos reducido
redujeses	redujeseis	hubieses reducido	hubieseis reducido
redujese	redujesen	hubiese reducido	hubiesen reducido

imperativo	
—	reduzcamos
reduce; no reduzcas	reducid; no reduzcáis
reduzca	reduzcan

Words and expressions related to this verb

reducido, reducida reduced	**la reducción** reduction
reducible reducible	**reducirse** to be reduced
la reducibilidad reducibility	**la reductibilidad** reductibility

| Gerundio **refiriendo** | Part. pas. **referido** | **referir (400)** |

Regular -ir verb endings with stem change: to refer, to relate
Tenses 1, 3, 6, 7, Imperative, Gerundio

The Seven Simple Tenses		The Seven Compound Tenses	
Singular	Plural	Singular	Plural
1 presente de indicativo		8 perfecto de indicativo	
refiero	referimos	he referido	hemos referido
refieres	referís	has referido	habéis referido
refiere	refieren	ha referido	han referido
2 imperfecto de indicativo		9 pluscuamperfecto de indicativo	
refería	referíamos	había referido	habíamos referido
referías	referíais	habías referido	habíais referido
refería	referían	había referido	habían referido
3 pretérito		10 pretérito anterior	
referí	referimos	hube referido	hubimos referido
referiste	referisteis	hubiste referido	hubisteis referido
refirió	refirieron	hubo referido	hubieron referido
4 futuro		11 futuro perfecto	
referiré	referiremos	habré referido	habremos referido
referirás	referiréis	habrás referido	habréis referido
referirá	referirán	habrá referido	habrán referido
5 potencial simple		12 potencial compuesto	
referiría	referiríamos	habría referido	habríamos referido
referirías	referiríais	habrías referido	habríais referido
referiría	referirían	habría referido	habrían referido
6 presente de subjuntivo		13 perfecto de subjuntivo	
refiera	refiramos	haya referido	hayamos referido
refieras	refiráis	hayas referido	hayáis referido
refiera	refieran	haya referido	hayan referido
7 imperfecto de subjuntivo		14 pluscuamperfecto de subjuntivo	
refiriera	refiriéramos	hubiera referido	hubiéramos referido
refirieras	refirieras	hubieras referido	hubierais referido
refiriera	refirieran	hubiera referido	hubieran referido
OR		OR	
refiriese	refiriésemos	hubiese referido	hubiésemos referido
refirieses	refirieseis	hubieses referido	hubieseis referido
refiriese	refiriesen	hubiese referido	hubiesen referido

imperativo

—	refiramos
refiere; no refieras	referid; no refiráis
refiera	refieran

Words related to this verb
la referencia   reference, account (narration)
referente   concerning, referring, relating (to)
el referéndum   referendum
transferir   to transfer

preferir   to prefer
el referido; la referida   the person referred to
conferir   to confer, to grant

The subject pronouns are found on page 93.

to give as a present, to make a   Regular **-ar** verb
present of, to give as a gift

The Seven Simple Tenses		The Seven Compound Tenses	
Singular	Plural	Singular	Plural
1 presente de indicativo		8 perfecto de indicativo	
regalo	regalamos	he regalado	hemos regalado
regalas	regaláis	has regalado	habéis regalado
regala	regalan	ha regalado	han regalado
2 imperfecto de indicativo		9 pluscuamperfecto de indicativo	
regalaba	regalábamos	había regalado	habíamos regalado
regalabas	regalabais	habías regalado	habíais regalado
regalaba	regalaban	había regalado	habían regalado
3 pretérito		10 pretérito anterior	
regalé	regalamos	hube regalado	hubimos regalado
regalaste	regalasteis	hubiste regalado	hubisteis regalado
regaló	regalaron	hubo regalado	hubieron regalado
4 futuro		11 futuro perfecto	
regalaré	regalaremos	habré regalado	habremos regalado
regalarás	regalaréis	habrás regalado	habréis regalado
regalará	regalarán	habrá regalado	habrán regalado
5 potencial simple		12 potencial compuesto	
regalaría	regalaríamos	habría regalado	habríamos regalado
regalarías	regalaríais	habrías regalado	habríais regalado
regalaría	regalarían	habría regalado	habrían regalado
6 presente de subjuntivo		13 perfecto de subjuntivo	
regale	regalemos	haya regalado	hayamos regalado
regales	regaléis	hayas regalado	hayáis regalado
regale	regalen	haya regalado	hayan regalado
7 imperfecto de subjuntivo		14 pluscuamperfecto de subjuntivo	
regalara	regaláramos	hubiera regalado	hubiéramos regalado
regalaras	regalarais	hubieras regalado	hubierais regalado
regalara	regalaran	hubiera regalado	hubieran regalado
OR		OR	
regalase	regalásemos	hubiese regalado	hubiésemos regalado
regalases	regalaseis	hubieses regalado	hubieseis regalado
regalase	regalasen	hubiese regalado	hubiesen regalado

imperativo	
—	regalemos
regala; no regales	regalad; no regaléis
regale	regalen

Words and expressions related to this verb
regalar el oído to flatter
un regalo gift, present
regaladamente comfortably

un regalejo small gift
de regalo free, gratis, complimentary

Get acquainted with what preposition goes with what verb on pages 669–677.

Regular **-ar** verb endings with spelling change: **g** becomes   to water, to irrigate,
gu before **e**; stem change: Tense 1, 6, Imperative   to sprinkle

The Seven Simple Tenses		The Seven Compound Tenses	
Singular	Plural	Singular	Plural
1 presente de indicativo		8 perfecto de indicativo	
riego	regamos	he regado	hemos regado
riegas	regáis	has regado	habéis regado
riega	riegan	ha regado	han regado
2 imperfecto de indicativo		9 pluscuamperfecto de indicativo	
regaba	regábamos	había regado	habíamos regado
regabas	regabais	habías regado	habíais regado
regaba	regaban	había regado	habían regado
3 pretérito		10 pretérito anterior	
regué	regamos	hube regado	hubimos regado
regaste	regasteis	hubiste regado	hubisteis regado
regó	regaron	hubo regado	hubieron regado
4 futuro		11 futuro perfecto	
regaré	regaremos	habré regado	habremos regado
regarás	regaréis	habrás regado	habréis regado
regará	regarán	habrá regado	habrán regado
5 potencial simple		12 potencial compuesto	
regaría	regaríamos	habría regado	habríamos regado
regarías	regaríais	habrías regado	habríais regado
regaría	regarían	habría regado	habrían regado
6 presente de subjuntivo		13 perfecto de subjuntivo	
riegue	reguemos	haya regado	hayamos regado
riegues	reguéis	hayas regado	hayáis regado
riegue	rieguen	haya regado	hayan regado
7 imperfecto de subjuntivo		14 pluscuamperfecto de subjuntivo	
regara	regáramos	hubiera regado	hubiéramos regado
regaras	regarais	hubieras regado	hubierais regado
regara	regaran	hubiera regado	hubieran regado
OR		OR	
regase	regásemos	hubiese regado	hubiésemos regado
regases	regaseis	hubieses regado	hubieseis regado
regase	regasen	hubiese regado	hubiesen regado

R

imperativo

—	reguemos
riega; no riegues	**regad; no reguéis**
riegue	**rieguen**

Words and expressions related to this verb

una regata regatta, boat race; irrigation ditch	**boca de riego** hydrant
el riego irrigation, sprinkling, watering	**una regadora** water sprinkler
irrigar to irrigate	**una regadura** sprinkling, watering
la irrigación irrigation	

The subject pronouns are found on page 93.

to return, to go back, to regress

The Seven Simple Tenses		The Seven Compound Tenses	
Singular	Plural	Singular	Plural
1 presente de indicativo		8 perfecto de indicativo	
regreso	**regresamos**	**he regresado**	**hemos regresado**
regresas	**regresáis**	**has regresado**	**habéis regresado**
regresa	**regresan**	**ha regresado**	**han regresado**
2 imperfecto de indicativo		9 pluscuamperfecto de indicativo	
regresaba	**regresábamos**	**había regresado**	**habíamos regresado**
regresabas	**regresabais**	**habías regresado**	**habíais regresado**
regresaba	**regresaban**	**había regresado**	**habían regresado**
3 pretérito		10 pretérito anterior	
regresé	**regresamos**	**hube regresado**	**hubimos regresado**
regresaste	**regresasteis**	**hubiste regresado**	**hubisteis regresado**
regresó	**regresaron**	**hubo regresado**	**hubieron regresado**
4 futuro		11 futuro perfecto	
regresaré	**regesaremos**	**habré regresado**	**habremos regresado**
regresarás	**regresaréis**	**habrás regresado**	**habréis regresado**
regresará	**regresarán**	**habrá regresado**	**habrán regresado**
5 potencial simple		12 potencial compuesto	
regresaría	**regresaríamos**	**habría regresado**	**habríamos regresado**
regresarías	**regresaríais**	**habrías regresado**	**habríais regresado**
regresaría	**regresarían**	**habría regresado**	**habrían regresado**
6 presente de subjuntivo		13 perfecto de subjuntivo	
regrese	**regresemos**	**haya regresado**	**hayamos regresado**
regreses	**regreséis**	**hayas regresado**	**hayáis regresado**
regrese	**regresen**	**haya regresado**	**hayan regresado**
7 imperfecto de subjuntivo		14 pluscuamperfecto de subjuntivo	
regresara	**regresáramos**	**hubiera regresado**	**hubiéramos regresado**
regresaras	**regresarais**	**hubieras regresado**	**hubierais regresado**
regresara	**regresaran**	**hubiera regresado**	**hubieran regresado**
OR		OR	
regresase	**regresásemos**	**hubiese regresado**	**hubiésemos regresado**
regreases	**regresaseis**	**hubieses regresado**	**hubieseis regresado**
regresase	**regresasen**	**hubiese regresado**	**hubiesen regresado**

	imperativo	
—		**regresemos**
regresa; no regreses		**regresad; no regreséis**
regrese		**regresen**

Words and expressions related to this verb

progresar to progress
la regresión regression
regresivo, regresiva regressive
progresar to advance, to progress

el regreso return
estar de regreso to be back (from a trip)
egresado, egresada graduate
egresar to graduate

Regular **-ir** verb endings with stem change: to laugh
Tenses 1, 3, 6, 7, Imperative, Gerundio

The Seven Simple Tenses		The Seven Compound Tenses	
Singular	Plural	Singular	Plural
1 presente de indicativo		8 perfecto de indicativo	
río	**reímos**	**he reído**	**hemos reído**
ríes	**reís**	**has reído**	**habéis reído**
ríe	**ríen**	**ha reído**	**han reído**
2 imperfecto de indicativo		9 pluscuamperfecto de indicativo	
reía	**reíamos**	**había reído**	**habíamos reído**
reías	**reíais**	**habías reído**	**habíais reído**
reía	**reían**	**había reído**	**habían reído**
3 pretérito		10 pretérito anterior	
reí	**reímos**	**hube reído**	**hubimos reído**
reíste	**reísteis**	**hubiste reído**	**hubisteis reído**
rió	**rieron**	**hubo reído**	**hubieron reído**
4 futuro		11 futuro perfecto	
reiré	**reiremos**	**habré reído**	**habremos reído**
reirás	**reiréis**	**habrás reído**	**habréis reído**
reirá	**reirán**	**habrá reído**	**habrán reído**
5 potencial simple		12 potencial compuesto	
reiría	**reiríamos**	**habría reído**	**habríamos reído**
reirías	**reiríais**	**habrías reído**	**habríais reído**
reiría	**reirían**	**habría reído**	**habrían reído**
6 presente de subjuntivo		13 perfecto de subjuntivo	
ría	**riamos**	**haya reído**	**hayamos reído**
rías	**riáis**	**hayas reído**	**hayáis reído**
ría	**rían**	**haya reído**	**hayan reído**
7 imperfecto de subjuntivo		14 pluscuamperfecto de subjuntivo	
riera	**riéramos**	**hubiera reído**	**hubiéramos reído**
rieras	**rierais**	**hubieras reído**	**hubierais reído**
riera	**rieran**	**hubiera reído**	**hubieran reído**
OR		OR	
riese	**riésemos**	**hubiese reído**	**hubiésemos reído**
rieses	**rieseis**	**hubieses reído**	**hubieseis reído**
riese	**riesen**	**hubiese reído**	**hubiesen reído**

	imperativo	
—		**riamos**
ríe; no rías		**reíd; no riáis**
ría		**rían**

Common idiomatic expressions using this verb
reír a carcajadas to laugh loudly   **risible** laughable
reír de to laugh at, to make fun of   **risueño, risueña** smiling
la risa laugh, laughter   **soltar la risa** to burst out in laughter

For additional words and expressions related to this verb, see **sonreír** and **reírse.**

to laugh

Reflexive verb; regular **-ir** verb endings with stem change: Tenses 1, 3, 6, 7, Imperative, Gerundio

The Seven Simple Tenses		The Seven Compound Tenses	
Singular	Plural	Singular	Plural
1 presente de indicativo		8 perfecto de indicativo	
me río	nos reímos	me he reído	nos hemos reído
te ríes	os reís	te has reído	os habéis reído
se ríe	se ríen	se ha reído	se han reído
2 imperfecto de indicativo		9 pluscuamperfecto de indicativo	
me reía	nos reíamos	me había reído	nos habíamos reído
te reías	os reíais	te habías reído	os habíais reído
se reía	se reían	se había reído	se habían reído
3 pretérito		10 pretérito anterior	
me reí	nos reímos	me hube reído	nos hubimos reído
te reíste	os reísteis	te hubiste reído	os hubisteis reído
se rió	se rieron	se hubo reído	se hubieron reído
4 futuro		11 futuro perfecto	
me reiré	nos reiremos	me habré reído	nos habremos reído
te reirás	os reiréis	te habrás reído	os habréis reído
se reirá	se reirán	se habrá reído	se habrán reído
5 potencial simple		12 potencial compuesto	
me reiría	nos reiríamos	me habría reído	nos habríamos reído
te reirías	os reiríais	te habrías reído	os habríais reído
se reiría	se reirían	se habría reído	se habrían reído
6 presente de subjuntivo		13 perfecto de subjuntivo	
me ría	nos riamos	me haya reído	nos hayamos reído
te rías	os riáis	te hayas reído	os hayáis reído
se ría	se rían	se haya reído	se hayan reído
7 imperfecto de subjuntivo		14 pluscuamperfecto de subjuntivo	
me riera	nos riéramos	me hubiera reído	nos hubiéramos reído
te rieras	os rierais	te hubieras reído	os hubierais reído
se riera	se rieran	se hubiera reído	se hubieran reído
OR		OR	
me riese	nos riésemos	me hubiese reído	nos hubiésemos reído
te rieses	os rieseis	te hubieses reído	os hubieseis reído
se riese	se riesen	se hubiese reído	se hubiesen reído

imperativo

—	riámonos
ríete; no te rías	reíos; no os riáis
ríase	ríanse

Words and expressions related to this verb

reírse de to laugh at, to make fun of
reírse de uno en sus propias barbas
  to laugh up one's sleeve
una cosa de risa a laughing matter

reír a carcajadas to laugh loudly
la risa laughter; **¡Qué risa!** What a laugh!
reírse en las barbas de alguien to laugh in
  someone's face

For other words related to this verb, see **sonreír** and **reír**.

Regular **-ar** verb   to refill, to fill again, to stuff

The Seven Simple Tenses		The Seven Compound Tenses	
Singular	Plural	Singular	Plural
1 presente de indicativo		8 perfecto de indicativo	
relleno	rellenamos	he rellenado	hemos rellenado
rellenas	rellenáis	has rellenado	habéis rellenado
rellena	rellenan	ha rellenado	han rellenado
2 imperfecto de indicativo		9 pluscuamperfecto de indicativo	
rellenaba	rellenábamos	había rellenado	habíamos rellenado
rellenabas	rellenabais	habías rellenado	habíais rellenado
rellenaba	rellenaban	había rellenado	habían rellenado
3 pretérito		10 pretérito anterior	
rellené	rellenamos	hube rellenado	hubimos rellenado
rellenaste	rellenasteis	hubiste rellenado	hubisteis rellenado
rellenó	rellenaron	hubo rellenado	hubieron rellenado
4 futuro		11 futuro perfecto	
rellenaré	rellenaremos	habré rellenado	habremos rellenado
rellenarás	rellenaréis	habrás rellenado	habréis rellenado
rellenará	rellenarán	habrá rellenado	habrán rellenado
5 potencial simple		12 potencial compuesto	
rellenaría	rellenaríamos	habría rellenado	habríamos rellenado
rellenarías	rellenaríais	habrías rellenado	habríais rellenado
rellenaría	rellenarían	habría rellenado	habrían rellenado
6 presente de subjuntivo		13 perfecto de subjuntivo	
rellene	rellenemos	haya rellenado	hayamos rellenado
rellenes	rellenéis	hayas rellenado	hayáis rellenado
rellene	rellenen	haya rellenado	hayan rellenado
7 imperfecto de subjuntivo		14 pluscuamperfecto de subjuntivo	
rellenara	rellenáramos	hubiera rellenado	hubiéramos rellenado
rellenaras	rellenarais	hubieras rellenado	hubierais rellenado
rellenara	rellenaran	hubiera rellenado	hubieran rellenado
OR		OR	
rellenase	rellenásemos	hubiese rellenado	hubiésemos rellenado
rellenases	rellenaseis	hubieses rellenado	hubieseis rellenado
rellenase	rellenasen	hubiese rellenado	hubiesen rellenado

R

	imperativo	
—		rellenemos
rellena; no rellenes		rellenad; no rellenéis
rellene		rellenen

Words and expressions related to this verb
el relleno   filling, stuffing   **rellenable**   refillable
relleno, rellena   stuffed, filled   **rellenarse**   to stuff oneself with food
For other words and expressions related to this verb, see **llenar.**

Don't miss the definitions of basic grammatical terms with examples
in English and Spanish on pages 33–44.

Gerundio remitiendo

Part. pas. remitido

to remit, to forward, to transmit

Regular -ir verb

The Seven Simple Tenses		The Seven Compound Tenses	
Singular	Plural	Singular	Plural
1 presente de indicativo		8 perfecto de indicativo	
remito	remitimos	he remitido	hemos remitido
remites	remitís	has remitido	habéis remitido
remite	remiten	ha remitido	han remitido
2 imperfecto de indicativo		9 pluscuamperfecto de indicativo	
remitía	remitíamos	había remitido	habíamos remitido
remitías	remitíais	habías remitido	habíais remitido
remitía	remitían	había remitido	habían remitido
3 pretérito		10 pretérito anterior	
remití	remitimos	hube remitido	hubimos remitido
remitise	remitisteis	hubiste remitido	hubisteis remitido
remitió	remitieron	hubo remitido	hubieron remitido
4 futuro		11 futuro perfecto	
remitiré	remitiremos	habré remitido	habremos remitido
remitirás	remitiréis	habrás remitido	habréis remitido
remitirá	remitirán	habrá remitido	habrán remitido
5 potencial simple		12 potencial compuesto	
remitiría	remitiríamos	habría remitido	habríamos remitido
remitirías	remitiríais	habrías remitido	habríais remitido
remitiría	remitirían	habría remitido	habrían remitido
6 presente de subjuntivo		13 perfecto de subjuntivo	
remita	remitamos	haya remitido	hayamos remitido
remitas	remitáis	hayas remitido	hayáis remitido
remita	remitan	haya remitido	hayan remitido
7 imperfecto de subjuntivo		14 pluscuamperfecto de subjuntivo	
remitiera	remitiéramos	hubiera remitido	hubiéramos remitido
remitieras	remitierais	hubieras remitido	hubierais remitido
remitiera	remitieran	hubiera remitido	hubieran remitido
OR		OR	
remitiese	remitiésemos	hubiese remitido	hubiésemos remitido
remitieses	remitieseis	hubieses remitido	hubieseis remitido
remitiese	remitiesen	hubiese remitido	hubiesen remitido

imperativo	
—	remitamos
remite; no remitas	remitid; no remitáis
remita	remitan

Words and expressions related to this verb

remitirse a   to refer oneself to

el, la remitente   sender, shipper

la remisión   remission

la remisión de los pecados   remission of sins

If you want an explanation of meanings and uses of Spanish and
English verb tenses and moods, see pages 13–32.

Regular **-ir** verb endings in all tenses except Tenses 3 and   to scold, to quarrel
7; stem change: Tenses 1, 3, 6, 7, Imperative, Gerundio

The Seven Simple Tenses		The Seven Compound Tenses	
Singular	Plural	Singular	Plural
1 presente de indicativo		**8 perfecto de indicativo**	
riño	reñimos	he reñido	hemos reñido
riñes	reñís	has reñido	habéis reñido
riñe	riñen	ha reñido	han reñido
2 imperfecto de indicativo		**9 pluscuamperfecto de indicativo**	
reñía	reñíamos	había reñido	habíamos reñido
reñías	reñíais	habías reñido	habíais reñido
reñía	reñían	había reñido	habían reñido
3 pretérito		**10 pretérito anterior**	
reñí	reñimos	hube reñido	hubimos reñido
reñiste	reñisteis	hubiste reñido	hubisteis reñido
riñó	riñeron	hubo reñido	hubieron reñido
4 futuro		**11 futuro perfecto**	
reñiré	reñiremos	habré reñido	habremos reñido
reñirás	reñiréis	habrás reñido	habréis reñido
reñirá	reñirán	habrá reñido	habrán reñido
5 potencial simple		**12 potencial compuesto**	
reñiría	reñiríamos	habría reñido	habríamos reñido
reñirías	reñiríais	habrías reñido	habríais reñido
reñiría	reñirían	habría reñido	habrían reñido
6 presente de subjuntivo		**13 perfecto de subjuntivo**	
riña	riñamos	haya reñido	hayamos reñido
riñas	riñáis	hayas reñido	hayáis reñido
riña	riñan	haya reñido	hayan reñido
7 imperfecto de subjuntivo		**14 pluscuamperfecto de subjuntivo**	
riñera	riñéramos	hubiera reñido	hubiéramos reñido
riñeras	riñerais	hubieras reñido	hubierais reñido
riñera	riñeran	hubiera reñido	hubieran reñido
OR		OR	
riñese	riñésemos	hubiese reñido	hubiésemos reñido
riñeses	riñeseis	hubieses reñido	hubieseis reñido
riñese	riñesen	hubiese reñido	hubiesen reñido

imperativo	
—	riñamos
riñe; no riñas	reñid; no riñáis
riña	riñan

Words and expressions related to this verb

reñidor, reñidora   quarreller
reñidamente   stubbornly
reñir por   to fight over

la riña   quarrel, fight
reñir a alguien   to tell someone off
una reñidura   scolding

> If you don't know the Spanish verb for the English verb you have
> in mind, look it up in the index on pages 682–706.

The subject pronouns are found on page 93.

R

to mend, to repair, to notice, to observe   Regular **-ar** verb

The Seven Simple Tenses		The Seven Compound Tenses	
Singular	Plural	Singular	Plural
1 presente de indicativo		8 perfecto de indicativo	
reparo	reparamos	he reparado	hemos reparado
reparas	reparáis	has reparado	habéis reparado
repara	reparan	ha reparado	han reparado
2 imperfecto de indicativo		9 pluscuamperfecto de indicativo	
reparaba	reparábamos	había reparado	habíamos reparado
reparabas	reparabais	habías reparado	habíais reparado
reparaba	reparaban	había reparado	habían reparado
3 pretérito		10 pretérito anterior	
reparé	reparamos	hube reparado	hubimos reparado
reparaste	reparasteis	hubiste reparado	hubisteis reparado
reparó	repararon	hubo reparado	hubieron reparado
4 futuro		11 futuro perfecto	
repararé	repararemos	habré reparado	habremos reparado
repararás	repararéis	habrás reparado	habréis reparado
reparará	repararán	habrá reparado	habrán reparado
5 potencial simple		12 potencial compuesto	
repararía	repararíamos	habría reparado	habríamos reparado
repararías	repararíais	habrías reparado	habríais reparado
repararía	repararían	habría reparado	habrían reparado
6 presente de subjuntivo		13 perfecto de subjuntivo	
repare	reparemos	haya reparado	hayamos reparado
repares	reparéis	hayas reparado	hayáis reparado
repare	reparen	haya reparado	hayan reparado
7 imperfecto de subjuntivo		14 pluscuamperfecto de subjuntivo	
reparara	reparáramos	hubiera reparado	hubiéramos reparado
repararas	repararais	hubieras reparado	hubierais reparado
reparara	repararan	hubiera reparado	hubieran reparado
OR		OR	
reparase	reparásemos	hubiese reparado	hubiésemos reparado
reparases	reparaseis	hubieses reparado	hubieseis reparado
reparase	reparasen	hubiese reparado	hubiesen reparado

	imperativo	
—		reparemos
repara; no repares		reparad; no reparéis
repare		reparen

Words and expressions related to this verb
reparar en   to notice, to pay attention to
un reparo   repairs, repairing; notice
una reparación   repairing, reparation

reparaciones provisionales   temporary repairs
reparable   reparable; noteworthy
un reparador, una reparadora   repairer

Can't find the verb you're looking for?
Check the back pages of this book for a list of over 2,100 additional verbs!

The Seven Simple Tenses		The Seven Compound Tenses	
Singular	Plural	Singular	Plural
1 presente de indicativo		8 perfecto de indicativo	
reparto	**repartimos**	**he repartido**	**hemos repartido**
repartes	**repartís**	**has repartido**	**habéis repartido**
reparte	**reparten**	**ha repartido**	**han repartido**
2 imperfecto de indicativo		9 pluscuamperfecto de indicativo	
repartía	**repartíamos**	**había repartido**	**habíamos repartido**
repartías	**repartíais**	**habías repartido**	**habíais repartido**
repartía	**repartían**	**había repartido**	**habían repartido**
3 pretérito		10 pretérito anterior	
repartí	**repartimos**	**hube repartido**	**hubimos repartido**
repartiste	**repartisteis**	**hubiste repartido**	**hubisteis repartido**
repartió	**repartieron**	**hubo repartido**	**hubieron repartido**
4 futuro		11 futuro perfecto	
repartiré	**repartiremos**	**habré repartido**	**habremos repartido**
repartirás	**repartiréis**	**habrás repartido**	**habréis repartido**
repartirá	**repartirán**	**habrá repartido**	**habrán repartido**
5 potencial simple		12 potencial compuesto	
repartiría	**repartiríamos**	**habría repartido**	**habríamos repartido**
repartirías	**repartiríais**	**habrías repartido**	**habríais repartido**
repartiría	**repartirían**	**habría repartido**	**habrían repartido**
6 presente de subjuntivo		13 perfecto de subjuntivo	
reparta	**repartamos**	**haya repartido**	**hayamos repartido**
repartas	**repartáis**	**hayas repartido**	**hayáis repartido**
reparta	**repartan**	**haya repartido**	**hayan repartido**
7 imperfecto de subjuntivo		14 pluscuamperfecto de subjuntivo	
repartiera	**repartiéramos**	**hubiera repartido**	**hubiéramos repartido**
repartieras	**repartierais**	**hubieras repartido**	**hubierais repartido**
repartiera	**repartieran**	**hubiera repartido**	**hubieran repartido**
OR		OR	
repartiese	**repartiésemos**	**hubiese repartido**	**hubiésemos repartido**
repartieses	**repartieseis**	**hubieses repartido**	**hubieseis repartido**
repartiese	**repartiesen**	**hubiese repartido**	**hubiesen repartido**

imperativo	
—	**repartamos**
reparte; no repartas	**repartid; no repartáis**
reparta	**repartan**

Words and expressions related to this verb
repartir un dividendo   to declare a dividend   **el reparto**   distribution, cast (of actors)
la repartición, el repartimiento   distribution   **repartible**   distributable

See also **partir.**

The subject pronouns are found on page 93.

to repeat | Regular **-ir** verb endings with stem change: Tenses 1, 3, 6, 7, Imperative, Gerundio

The Seven Simple Tenses		The Seven Compound Tenses	
Singular	Plural	Singular	Plural
1 presente de indicativo		8 perfecto de indicativo	
repito	repetimos	he repetido	hemos repetido
repites	repetís	has repetido	habéis repetido
repite	repiten	ha repetido	han repetido
2 imperfecto de indicativo		9 pluscuamperfecto de indicativo	
repetía	repetíamos	había repetido	habíamos repetido
repetías	repetíais	habías repetido	habíais repetido
repetía	repetían	había repetido	habían repetido
3 pretérito		10 pretérito anterior	
repetí	repetimos	hube repetido	hubimos repetido
repetiste	repetisteis	hubiste repetido	hubisteis repetido
repitió	repitieron	hubo repetido	hubieron repetido
4 futuro		11 futuro perfecto	
repetiré	repetiremos	habré repetido	habremos repetido
repetirás	repetiréis	habrás repetido	habréis repetido
repetirá	repetirán	habrá repetido	habrán repetido
5 potencial simple		12 potencial compuesto	
repetiría	repetiríamos	habría repetido	habríamos repetido
repetirías	repetiríais	habrías repetido	habríais repetido
repetiría	repetirían	habría repetido	habrían repetido
6 presente de subjuntivo		13 perfecto de subjuntivo	
repita	repitamos	haya repetido	hayamos repetido
repitas	repitáis	hayas repetido	hayáis repetido
repita	repitan	haya repetido	hayan repetido
7 imperfecto de subjuntivo		14 pluscuamperfecto de subjuntivo	
repitiera	repitiéramos	hubiera repetido	hubiéramos repetido
repitieras	repitierais	hubieras repetido	hubierais repetido
repitiera	repitieran	hubiera repetido	hubieran repetido
OR		OR	
repitiese	repitiésemos	hubiese repetido	hubiésemos repetido
repitieses	repitieseis	hubieses repetido	hubieseis repetido
repitiese	repitiesen	hubiese repetido	hubiesen repetido

	imperativo	
—		**repitamos**
repite; no repitas		**repetid; no repitáis**
repita		**repitan**

Words related to this verb
la repetición repetition
repetidamente repeatedly
repetidor, repetidora repeating

repetidas veces over and over again
repetido, repetida repeated
¡Que se repita! Encore!

Review the principal parts of important Spanish verbs on pages 9–10.

Regular **-er** verb endings with stem change: to resolve, to solve (a problem)
Tenses 1, 6, Imperative, Past Participle

The Seven Simple Tenses		The Seven Compound Tenses	
Singular	Plural	Singular	Plural
1 presente de indicativo		8 perfecto de indicativo	
resuelvo	**resolvemos**	**he resuelto**	**hemos resuelto**
resuelves	**resolvéis**	**has resuelto**	**habéis resuelto**
resuelve	**resuelven**	**ha resuelto**	**han resuelto**
2 imperfecto de indicativo		9 pluscuamperfecto de indicativo	
resolvía	**resolvíamos**	**había resuelto**	**habíamos resuelto**
resolvías	**resolvíais**	**habías resuelto**	**habíais resuelto**
resolvía	**resolvían**	**había resuelto**	**habían resuelto**
3 pretérito		10 pretérito anterior	
resolví	**resolvimos**	**hube resuelto**	**hubimos resuelto**
resolviste	**resolvisteis**	**hubiste resuelto**	**hubisteis resuelto**
resolvió	**resolvieron**	**hubo resuelto**	**hubieron resuelto**
4 futuro		11 futuro perfecto	
resolveré	**resolveremos**	**habré resuelto**	**habremos resuelto**
resolverás	**resolveréis**	**habrás resuelto**	**habréis resuelto**
resolverá	**resolverán**	**habrá resuelto**	**habrán resuelto**
5 potencial simple		12 potencial compuesto	
resolvería	**resolveríamos**	**habría resuelto**	**habríamos resuelto**
resolverías	**resolveríais**	**habrías resuelto**	**habríais resuelto**
resolvería	**resolverían**	**habría resuelto**	**habrían resuelto**
6 presente de subjuntivo		13 perfecto de subjuntivo	
resuelva	**resolvamos**	**haya resuelto**	**hayamos resuelto**
resuelvas	**resolváis**	**hayas resuelto**	**hayáis resuelto**
resuelva	**resuelvan**	**haya resuelto**	**hayan resuelto**
7 imperfecto de subjuntivo		14 pluscuamperfecto de subjuntivo	
resolviera	**resolviéramos**	**hubiera resuelto**	**hubiéramos resuelto**
resolvieras	**resolvierais**	**hubieras resuelto**	**hubierais resuelto**
resolviera	**resolvieran**	**hubiera resuelto**	**hubieran resuelto**
OR		OR	
resolviese	**resolviésemos**	**hubiese resuelto**	**hubiésemos resuelto**
resolvieses	**resolvieseis**	**hubieses resuelto**	**hubieseis resuelto**
resolviese	**resolviesen**	**hubiese resuelto**	**hubiesen resuelto**

imperativo

—	**resolvamos**
resuelve; no resuelvas	**resolved; no resolváis**
resuelva	**resuelvan**

Words and expressions related to this verb
resolver un conflicto   to settle a dispute
resolverse   to resolve (oneself)
resolverse a + inf.   to resolve + inf.
una resolución   resolution

una resolución definitiva   final decision
resolutivamente   resolutely
resoluto, resoluta   resolute
resuelto, resuelta   firm, resolute

The subject pronouns are found on page 93.

to answer, to reply, to respond   Regular **-er** verb

The Seven Simple Tenses		The Seven Compound Tenses	
Singular	Plural	Singular	Plural
1 presente de indicativo		8 perfecto de indicativo	
respondo	respondemos	he respondido	hemos respondido
respondes	respondéis	has respondido	habéis respondido
responde	responden	ha respondido	han respondido
2 imperfecto de indicativo		9 pluscuamperfecto de indicativo	
respondía	respondíamos	había respondido	habíamos respondido
respondías	respondíais	habías respondido	habíais respondido
respondía	respondían	había respondido	habían respondido
3 pretérito		10 pretérito anterior	
respondí	respondimos	hube respondido	hubimos respondido
respondiste	respondisteis	hubiste respondido	hubisteis respondido
respondió	respondieron	hubo respondido	hubieron respondido
4 futuro		11 futuro perfecto	
responderé	responderemos	habré respondido	habremos respondido
responderás	responderéis	habrás respondido	habréis respondido
responderá	responderán	habrá respondido	habrán respondido
5 potencial simple		12 potencial compuesto	
respondería	responderíamos	habría respondido	habríamos respondido
responderías	responderíais	habrías respondido	habríais respondido
respondería	responderían	habría respondido	habrían respondido
6 presente de subjuntivo		13 perfecto de subjuntivo	
responda	respondamos	haya respondido	hayamos respondido
respondas	respondáis	hayas respondido	hayáis respondido
responda	respondan	haya respondido	hayan respondido
7 imperfecto de subjuntivo		14 pluscuamperfecto de subjuntivo	
respondiera	respondiéramos	hubiera respondido	hubiéramos respondido
respondieras	respondierais	hubieras respondido	hubierais respondido
respondiera	respondieran	hubiera respondido	hubieran respondido
OR		OR	
respondiese	respondiésemos	hubiese respondido	hubiésemos respondido
respondieses	respondieseis	hubieses respondido	hubieseis respondido
respondiese	respondiesen	hubiese respondido	hubiesen respondido

imperativo	
—	respondamos
responde; no respondas	responded; no respondáis
responda	respondan

Words and expressions related to this verb

una respuesta answer, reply, response
respondiente respondent
la correspondencia correspondence
correspondientemente correspondingly
responsivo, responsiva responsive

corresponder to correspond
corresponder a to reciprocate
responder a la pregunta to answer the
   question, to respond to the question

Don't forget to study the section on defective and impersonal verbs. It's right after this main list.

The Seven Simple Tenses		The Seven Compound Tenses	
Singular	Plural	Singular	Plural
1 presente de indicativo		**8 perfecto de indicativo**	
retiro	retiramos	he retirado	hemos retirado
retiras	retiráis	has retirado	habéis retirado
retira	retiran	ha retirado	han retirado
2 imperfecto de indicativo		**9 pluscuamperfecto de indicativo**	
retiraba	retirábamos	había retirado	habíamos retirado
retirabas	retirabais	habías retirado	habíais retirado
retiraba	retiraban	había retirado	habían retirado
3 pretérito		**10 pretérito anterior**	
retiré	retiramos	hube retirado	hubimos retirado
retiraste	retirasteis	hubiste retirado	hubisteis retirado
retiró	retiraron	hubo retirado	hubieron retirado
4 futuro		**11 futuro perfecto**	
retiraré	retiraremos	habré retirado	habremos retirado
retirarás	retiraréis	habrás retirado	habréis retirado
retirará	retirarán	habrá retirado	habrán retirado
5 potencial simple		**12 potencial compuesto**	
retiraría	retiraríamos	habría retirado	habríamos retirado
retirarías	retiraríais	habrías retirado	habríais retirado
retiraría	retirarían	habría retirado	habrían retirado
6 presente de subjuntivo		**13 perfecto de subjuntivo**	
retire	retiremos	haya retirado	hayamos retirado
retires	retiréis	hayas retirado	hayáis retirado
retire	retiren	haya retirado	hayan retirado
7 imperfecto de subjuntivo		**14 pluscuamperfecto de subjuntivo**	
retirara	retiráramos	hubiera retirado	hubiéramos retirado
retiraras	retirarais	hubieras retirado	hubierais retirado
retirara	retiraran	hubiera retirado	hubieran retirado
OR		OR	
retirase	retirásemos	hubiese retirado	hubiésemos retirado
retirases	retiraseis	hubieses retirado	hubieseis retirado
retirase	retirasen	hubiese retirado	hubiesen retirado

R

imperativo

—	retiremos
retira; no retires	**retirad; no retiréis**
retire	**retiren**

Words and expressions related to this verb

retirarse to retire
retirarse a dormir to turn in (go to bed)
el retiro retirement, withdrawal
El Retiro (El Buen Retiro) name of a
  famous beautiful park in Madrid

la retirada retirement, retreat
el retiramiento retirement
pasar al retiro to go into retirement
retirar dinero (del banco) to make a
  withdrawal (from the bank)

The subject pronouns are found on page 93.

549

The Seven Simple Tenses		The Seven Compound Tenses	
Singular	Plural	Singular	Plural
1　presente de indicativo		8　perfecto de indicativo	
retraso	retrasamos	he retrasado	hemos retrasado
retrasas	retrasáis	has retrasado	habéis retrasado
retrasa	retrasan	ha retrasado	han retrasado
2　imperfecto de indicativo		9　pluscuamperfecto de indicativo	
retrasaba	retrasábamos	había retrasado	habíamos retrasado
retrasabas	retrasabais	habías retrasado	habíais retrasado
retrasaba	retrasaban	había retrasado	habían retrasado
3　pretérito		10　pretérito anterior	
retrasé	retrasamos	hube retrasado	hubimos retrasado
retrasaste	retrasasteis	hubiste retrasado	hubisteis retrasado
retrasó	retrasaron	hubo retrasado	hubieron retrasado
4　futuro		11　futuro perfecto	
retrasaré	retrasaremos	habré retrasado	habremos retrasado
retrasarás	retrasaréis	habrás retrasado	habréis retrasado
retrasará	retrasarán	habrá retrasado	habrán retrasado
5　potencial simple		12　potencial compuesto	
retrasaría	retrasaríamos	habría retrasado	habríamos retrasado
retrasarías	retrasaríais	habrías retrasado	habríais retrasado
retrasaría	retrasarían	habría retrasado	habrían retrasado
6　presente de subjuntivo		13　perfecto de subjuntivo	
retrase	retrasemos	haya retrasado	hayamos retrasado
retrases	retraséis	hayas retrasado	hayáis retrasado
retrase	retrasen	haya retrasado	hayan retrasado
7　imperfecto de subjuntivo		14　pluscuamperfecto de subjuntivo	
retrasara	retrasáramos	hubiera retrasado	hubiéramos retrasado
retrasaras	retrasarais	hubieras retrasado	hubierais retrasado
retrasara	retrasaran	hubiera retrasado	hubieran retrasado
OR		OR	
retrasase	retrasásemos	hubiese retrasado	hubiésemos retrasado
retrasases	retrasaseis	hubieses retrasado	hubieseis retrasado
retrasase	retrasasen	hubiese retrasado	hubiesen retrasado

	imperativo	
—		retrasemos
retrasa; no retrases		retrasad; no retraséis
retrase		retrasen

Words and expressions related to this verb
retrasarse en + inf.　to be slow in, to be late + pres. part.
el retraso　delay, lag, slowness
con retraso　late (behind time)
atrasar　to be slow, slow down (watch, clock); **el atraso**　delay, tardiness; **en atraso**　in arrears
atrás　backward, back; **atrás de**　behind, back of; **días atrás**　days ago; **hacia atrás**
backwards; **quedarse atrás**　to lag behind

Gerundio **reuniéndose**   Part. pas. **reunido**   **reunirse (416)**

Reflexive verb; regular **-ir** verb endings with spelling change: **u** becomes **ú** on stressed syllable in Tenses 1, 6, Imperative

to assemble, to get together, to meet, to gather

The Seven Simple Tenses		The Seven Compound Tenses	
Singular	Plural	Singular	Plural
1 presente de indicativo		8 perfecto de indicativo	
me reúno	nos reunimos	me he reunido	nos hemos reunido
te reúnes	os reunís	te has reunido	os habéis reunido
se reúne	se reúnen	se ha reunido	se han reunido
2 imperfecto de indicativo		9 pluscuamperfecto de indicativo	
me reunía	nos reuníamos	me había reunido	nos habíamos reunido
te reunías	os reuníais	te habías reunido	os habíais reunido
se reunía	se reunían	se había reunido	se habían reunido
3 pretérito		10 pretérito anterior	
me reuní	nos reunimos	me hube reunido	nos hubimos reunido
te reuniste	os reunisteis	te hubiste reunido	os hubisteis reunido
se reunió	se reunieron	se hubo reunido	se hubieron reunido
4 futuro		11 futuro perfecto	
me reuniré	nos reuniremos	me habré reunido	nos habremos reunido
te reunirás	os reuniréis	te habrás reunido	os habréis reunido
se reunirá	se reunirán	se habrá reunido	se habrán reunido
5 potencial simple		12 potencial compuesto	
me reuniría	nos reuniríamos	me habría reunido	nos habríamos reunido
te reunirías	os reuniríais	te habrías reunido	os habríais reunido
se reuniría	se reunirían	se habría reunido	se habrían reunido
6 presente de subjuntivo		13 perfecto de subjuntivo	
me reúna	nos reunamos	me haya reunido	nos hayamos reunido
te reúnas	os reunáis	te hayas reunido	os hayáis reunido
se reúna	se reúnan	se haya reunido	se hayan reunido
7 imperfecto de subjuntivo		14 pluscuamperfecto de subjuntivo	
me reuniera	nos reuniéramos	me hubiera reunido	nos hubiéramos reunido
te reunieras	os reunierais	te hubieras reunido	os hubierais reunido
se reuniera	se reunieran	se hubiera reunido	se hubieran reunido
OR		OR	
me reuniese	nos reuniésemos	me hubiese reunido	nos hubiésemos reunido
te reunieses	os reunieseis	te hubieses reunido	os hubieseis reunido
se reuniese	se reuniesen	se hubiese reunido	se hubiesen reunido

imperativo	
—	reunámonos
reúnete; no te reúnas	reuníos; no os reunáis
reúnase	reúnanse

Words and expressions related to this verb
reunirse con   to meet with
la reunión   reunion, meeting, gathering
una reunión en masa   mass meeting

una reunión plenaria   full meeting
la libertad de reunión   free assemblage
una reunión extraordinaria   special meeting

For other words related to this verb, see **unir**.

The subject pronouns are found on page 93.

to revoke, to repeal

Regular **-ar** verb endings with
spelling change: **c** becomes **qu** before **e**

The Seven Simple Tenses		The Seven Compound Tenses	
Singular	Plural	Singular	Plural
1 presente de indicativo		8 perfecto de indicativo	
revoco	revocamos	he revocado	hemos revocado
revocas	revocáis	has revocado	habéis revocado
revoca	revocan	ha revocado	han revocado
2 imperfecto de indicativo		9 pluscuamperfecto de indicativo	
revocaba	revocábamos	había revocado	habíamos revocado
revocabas	revocabais	habías revocado	habíais revocado
revocaba	revocaban	había revocado	habían revocado
3 pretérito		10 pretérito anterior	
revoqué	revocamos	hube revocado	hubimos revocado
revocaste	revocasteis	hubiste revocado	hubisteis revocado
revocó	revocaron	hubo revocado	hubieron revocado
4 futuro		11 futuro perfecto	
revocaré	revocaremos	habré revocado	habremos revocado
revocarás	revocaréis	habrás revocado	habréis revocado
revocará	revocarán	habrá revocado	habrán revocado
5 potencial simple		12 potencial compuesto	
revocaría	revocaríamos	habría revocado	habríamos revocado
revocarías	revocaríais	habrías revocado	habríais revocado
revocaría	revocarían	habría revocado	habrían revocado
6 presente de subjuntivo		13 perfecto de subjuntivo	
revoque	revoquemos	haya revocado	hayamos revocado
revoques	revoquéis	hayas revocado	hayáis revocado
revoque	revoquen	haya revocado	hayan revocado
7 imperfecto de subjuntivo		14 pluscuamperfecto de subjuntivo	
revocara	revocáramos	hubiera revocado	hubiéramos revocado
revocaras	revocarais	hubieras revocado	hubierais revocado
revocara	revocaran	hubiera revocado	hubieran revocado
OR		OR	
revocase	revocásemos	hubiese revocado	hubiésemos revocado
revocases	revocaseis	hubieses revocado	hubieseis revocado
revocase	revocasen	hubiese revocado	hubiesen revocado

imperativo

—	revoquemos
revoca; no revoques	revocad; no revoquéis
revoque	revoquen

Words and expressions related to this verb
la **revocación**   revocation
revocable   revocable, reversible
revocablemente   revocably

irrevocabilidad   irrevocability
irrevocable   irrevocable, irreversible
irrevocablemente   irrevocably

If you want to see a sample English verb fully conjugated in
all the tenses, check out pages 11 and 12.

Regular **-er** verb endings with stem change: to revolve, to turn around, to
Tenses 1, 6, Imperative, Past Participle   turn over, to turn upside down

The Seven Simple Tenses | The Seven Compound Tenses

Singular	Plural	Singular	Plural
1 presente de indicativo		8 perfecto de indicativo	
revuelvo	**revolvemos**	**he revuelto**	**hemos revuelto**
revuelves	**revolvéis**	**has revuelto**	**habéis revuelto**
revuelve	**revuelven**	**ha revuelto**	**han revuelto**
2 imperfecto de indicativo		9 pluscuamperfecto de indicativo	
revolvía	**revolvíamos**	**había revuelto**	**habíamos revuelto**
revolvías	**revolvíais**	**habías revuelto**	**habíais revuelto**
revolvía	**revolvían**	**había revuelto**	**habían revuelto**
3 pretérito		10 pretérito anterior	
revolví	**revolvimos**	**hube revuelto**	**hubimos revuelto**
revolviste	**revolvisteis**	**hubiste revuelto**	**hubisteis revuelto**
revolvió	**revolvieron**	**hubo revuelto**	**hubieron revuelto**
4 futuro		11 futuro perfecto	
revolveré	**revolveremos**	**habré revuelto**	**habremos revuelto**
revolverás	**revolveréis**	**habrás revuelto**	**habréis revuelto**
revolverá	**revolverán**	**habrá revuelto**	**habrán revuelto**
5 potencial simple		12 potencial compuesto	
revolvería	**revolveríamos**	**habría revuelto**	**habríamos revuelto**
revolverías	**revolveríais**	**habrías revuelto**	**habríais revuelto**
revolvería	**revolverían**	**habría revuelto**	**habrían revuelto**
6 presente de subjuntivo		13 perfecto de subjuntivo	
revuelva	**revolvamos**	**haya revuelto**	**hayamos revuelto**
revuelvas	**revolváis**	**hayas revuelto**	**hayáis revuelto**
revuelva	**revuelvan**	**haya revuelto**	**hayan revuelto**
7 imperfecto de subjuntivo		14 pluscuamperfecto de subjuntivo	
revolviera	**revolviéramos**	**hubiera revuelto**	**hubiéramos revuelto**
revolvieras	**revolvierais**	**hubieras revuelto**	**hubierais revuelto**
revolviera	**revolvieran**	**hubiera revuelto**	**hubieran revuelto**
OR		OR	
revolviese	**revolviésemos**	**hubiese revuelto**	**hubiésemos revuelto**
revolvieses	**revolvieseis**	**hubieses revuelto**	**hubieseis revuelto**
revolviese	**revolviesen**	**hubiese revuelto**	**hubiesen revuelto**

R

imperativo

—	**revolvamos**
revuelve; no revuelvas	**revolved; no revolváis**
revuelva	**revuelvan**

Words and expressions related to this verb
huevos revueltos   scrambled eggs   **el revolvimiento**   revolving, revolution
la revolución   revolution   **revueltamente**   confusedly

For other words and expressions related to this verb, see **devolver** and **volver**.

Try a few of the verb tests on pages 45–91 with answers explained.

The subject pronouns are found on page 93.   **553**

to rob, to steal   Regular **-ar** verb

The Seven Simple Tenses		The Seven Compound Tenses	
Singular	Plural	Singular	Plural
1 presente de indicativo		8 perfecto de indicativo	
robo	**robamos**	he robado	hemos robado
robas	**robáis**	has robado	habéis robado
roba	**roban**	ha robado	han robado
2 imperfecto de indicativo		9 pluscuamperfecto de indicativo	
robaba	**robábamos**	había robado	habíamos robado
robabas	**robabais**	habías robado	habíais robado
robaba	**robaban**	había robado	habían robado
3 pretérito		10 pretérito anterior	
robé	**robamos**	hube robado	hubimos robado
robaste	**robasteis**	hubiste robado	hubisteis robado
robó	**robaron**	hubo robado	hubieron robado
4 futuro		11 futuro perfecto	
robaré	**robaremos**	habré robado	habremos robado
robarás	**robaréis**	habrás robado	habréis robado
robará	**robarán**	habrá robado	habrán robado
5 potencial simple		12 potencial compuesto	
robaría	**robaríamos**	habría robado	habríamos robado
robarías	**robaríais**	habrías robado	habríais robado
robaría	**robarían**	habría robado	habrían robado
6 presente de subjuntivo		13 perfecto de subjuntivo	
robe	**robemos**	haya robado	hayamos robado
robes	**robéis**	hayas robado	hayáis robado
robe	**roben**	haya robado	hayan robado
7 imperfecto de subjuntivo		14 pluscuamperfecto de subjuntivo	
robara	**robáramos**	hubiera robado	hubiéramos robado
robaras	**robarais**	hubieras robado	hubierais robado
robara	**robaran**	hubiera robado	hubieran robado
OR		OR	
robase	**robásemos**	hubiese robado	hubiésemos robado
robases	**robaseis**	hubieses robado	hubieseis robado
robase	**robasen**	hubiese robado	hubiesen robado

imperativo

—	**robemos**
roba; no robes	**robad; no robéis**
robe	**roben**

Words and expressions related to this verb

robarle algo a alguien   to rob somebody of something   **un antirrobo**   theft protection device,
robado, robada   stolen   burglar alarm
un robador, una robadora   robber, thief   **el robo**   robbery, theft

> If you want to see a sample English verb fully conjugated in
> all the tenses, check out pages 11 and 12.

Regular **-er** verb endings with stem change: to nibble, to gnaw
Tenses 1, 3, 6, 7, Imperative, irreg. participles

The Seven Simple Tenses		The Seven Compound Tenses	
Singular	Plural	Singular	Plural
1 presente de indicativo		8 perfecto de indicativo	
roo *or* **roigo** *or* **royo**	**roemos**	**he roído**	**hemos roído**
roes	**roéis**	**has roído**	**habéis roído**
roe	**roen**	**ha roído**	**han roído**
2 imperfecto de indicativo		9 pluscuamperfecto de indicativo	
roía	**roíamos**	**había roído**	**habíamos roído**
roías	**roíais**	**habías roído**	**habíais roído**
roía	**roían**	**había roído**	**habían roído**
3 pretérito		10 pretérito anterior	
roí	**roímos**	**hube roído**	**hubimos roído**
roíste	**roísteis**	**hubiste roído**	**hubisteis roído**
royó	**royeron**	**hubo roído**	**hubieron roído**
4 futuro		11 futuro perfecto	
roeré	**roeremos**	**habré roído**	**habremos roído**
roerás	**roeréis**	**habrás roído**	**habréis roído**
roerá	**roerán**	**habrá roído**	**habrán roído**
5 potencial simple		12 potencial compuesto	
roería	**roeríamos**	**habría roído**	**habríamos roído**
roerías	**roeríais**	**habrías roído**	**habríais roído**
roería	**roerían**	**habría roído**	**habrían roído**
6 presente de subjuntivo		13 perfecto de subjuntivo	
roa *or* **roiga**	**roamos** *or* **roigamos**	**haya roído**	**hayamos roído**
or **roya**	*or* **royamos**	**hayas roído**	**hayáis roído**
roas *or* **roigas**	**roáis** *or* **roigáis**	**haya roído**	**hayan roído**
or **royas**	*or* **royáis**		
roa *or* **roiga**	**roan** *or* **roigan**	14 pluscuamperfecto de subjuntivo	
or **roya**	*or* **royan**	**hubiera roído**	**hubiéramos roído**
		hubieras roído	**hubierais roído**
7 imperfecto de subjuntivo		**hubiera roído**	**hubieran roído**
royera	**royéramos**	OR	
royeras	**royerais**	**hubiese roído**	**hubiésemos roído**
royera	**royeran**	**hubieses roído**	**hubieseis roído**
OR		**hubiese roído**	**hubiesen roído**
royese	**royésemos**		
royeses	**royeseis**		
royese	**royesen**		

	imperativo	
—		**roamos** *or* **roigamos** *or* **royamos**
roe		**roed**
roa *or* **roiga** *or* **roya**		**roan** *or* **roigan** *or* **royan**

Words and expressions related to this verb
un roedor   a rodent
roedor, roedora   gnawing
la roedura   gnawing, mark made by gnawing

roerse   to bite
roerse las uñas   to bite one's nails

R

The subject pronouns are found on page 93.

Gerundio **rogando**   Part. pas. **rogado**

to supplicate, to ask, to ask for, to request, to beg, to pray

Regular **-ar** verb endings with stem change: Tenses 1, 6, Imperative; spelling change: **g** becomes **gu** before **e**

The Seven Simple Tenses		The Seven Compound Tenses	
Singular	Plural	Singular	Plural
1 presente de indicativo		8 perfecto de indicativo	
ruego	rogamos	he rogado	hemos rogado
ruegas	rogáis	has rogado	habéis rogado
ruega	ruegan	ha rogado	han rogado
2 imperfecto de indicativo		9 pluscuamperfecto de indicativo	
rogaba	rogábamos	había rogado	habíamos rogado
rogabas	rogabais	habías rogado	habíais rogado
rogaba	rogaban	había rogado	habían rogado
3 pretérito		10 pretérito anterior	
rogué	rogamos	hube rogado	hubimos rogado
rogaste	rogasteis	hubiste rogado	hubisteis rogado
rogó	rogaron	hubo rogado	hubieron rogado
4 futuro		11 futuro perfecto	
rogaré	rogaremos	habré rogado	habremos rogado
rogarás	rogaréis	habrás rogado	habréis rogado
rogará	rogarán	habrá rogado	habrán rogado
5 potencial simple		12 potencial compuesto	
rogaría	rogaríamos	habría rogado	habríamos rogado
rogarías	rogaríais	habrías rogado	habríais rogado
rogaría	rogarían	habría rogado	habrían rogado
6 presente de subjuntivo		13 perfecto de subjuntivo	
ruegue	roguemos	haya rogado	hayamos rogado
ruegues	roguéis	hayas rogado	hayáis rogado
ruegue	rueguen	haya rogado	hayan rogado
7 imperfecto de subjuntivo		14 pluscuamperfecto de subjuntivo	
rogara	rogáramos	hubiera rogado	hubiéramos rogado
rogaras	rogarais	hubieras rogado	hubierais rogado
rogara	rogaran	hubiera rogado	hubieran rogado
OR		OR	
rogase	rogásemos	hubiese rogado	hubiésemos rogado
rogases	rogaseis	hubieses rogado	hubieseis rogado
rogase	rogasen	hubiese rogado	hubiesen rogado

imperativo	
—	roguemos
ruega; no ruegues	rogad; no roguéis
ruegue	rueguen

Sentences using this verb and words related to it
A Dios rogando y con el mazo dando.   Put your faith in God and keep your powder dry.
rogador, rogadora   suppliant, requester
rogativo, rogativa   supplicatory
rogar por   to plead for
derogar   to abolish, to repeal
una prerrogativa   prerogative

Regular **-er** verb with spelling   to break, to shatter, to tear
change: irregular past participle

The Seven Simple Tenses | The Seven Compound Tenses

Singular	Plural	Singular	Plural
1 presente de indicativo		8 perfecto de indicativo	
rompo	**rompemos**	**he roto**	**hemos roto**
rompes	**rompéis**	**has roto**	**habéis roto**
rompe	**rompen**	**ha roto**	**han roto**
2 imperfecto de indicativo		9 pluscuamperfecto de indicativo	
rompía	**rompíamos**	**había roto**	**habíamos roto**
rompías	**rompíais**	**habías roto**	**habíais roto**
rompía	**rompían**	**había roto**	**habían roto**
3 pretérito		10 pretérito anterior	
rompí	**rompimos**	**hube roto**	**hubimos roto**
rompiste	**rompisteis**	**hubiste roto**	**hubisteis roto**
rompió	**rompieron**	**hubo roto**	**hubieron roto**
4 futuro		11 futuro perfecto	
romperé	**romperemos**	**habré roto**	**habremos roto**
romperás	**romperéis**	**habrás roto**	**habréis roto**
romperá	**romperán**	**habrá roto**	**habrán roto**
5 potencial simple		12 potencial compuesto	
rompería	**romperíamos**	**habría roto**	**habríamos roto**
romperías	**romperíais**	**habrías roto**	**habríais roto**
rompería	**romperían**	**habría roto**	**habrían roto**
6 presente de subjuntivo		13 perfecto de subjuntivo	
rompa	**rompamos**	**haya roto**	**hayamos roto**
rompas	**rompáis**	**hayas roto**	**hayáis roto**
rompa	**rompan**	**haya roto**	**hayan roto**
7 imperfecto de subjuntivo		14 pluscuamperfecto de subjuntivo	
rompiera	**rompiéramos**	**hubiera roto**	**hubiéramos roto**
rompieras	**rompierais**	**hubieras roto**	**hubierais roto**
rompiera	**rompieran**	**hubiera roto**	**hubieran roto**
OR		OR	
rompiese	**rompiésemos**	**hubiese roto**	**hubiésemos roto**
rompieses	**rompieseis**	**hubieses roto**	**hubieseis roto**
rompiese	**rompiesen**	**hubiese roto**	**hubiesen roto**

imperativo

—	**rompamos**
rompe; no rompas	**romped; no rompáis**
rompa	**rompan**

Words and expressions related to this verb
un rompenueces   nutcracker
una rompedura   breakage, rupture
romperse la cabeza   to rack one's brains
romper con   to break relations with
romper a + inf.   to start suddenly + inf.

romper a llorar   to break into tears
romper las relaciones   to break off relations,
   an engagement
romper el hielo   to break the ice
romperse la pierna (el brazo)   to break a leg
   (an arm) [on oneself]
roto, rota   broken

The subject pronouns are found on page 93.   **557**

The Seven Simple Tenses		The Seven Compound Tenses	
Singular	Plural	Singular	Plural
1 presente de indicativo		8 perfecto de indicativo	
sé	sabemos	he sabido	hemos sabido
sabes	sabéis	has sabido	habéis sabido
sabe	saben	ha sabido	han sabido
2 imperfecto de indicativo		9 pluscuamperfecto de indicativo	
sabía	sabíamos	había sabido	habíamos sabido
sabías	sabíais	habías sabido	habíais sabido
sabía	sabían	había sabido	habían sabido
3 pretérito		10 pretérito anterior	
supe	supimos	hube sabido	hubimos sabido
supiste	supisteis	hubiste sabido	hubisteis sabido
supo	supieron	hubo sabido	hubieron sabido
4 futuro		11 futuro perfecto	
sabré	sabremos	habré sabido	habremos sabido
sabrás	sabréis	habrás sabido	habréis sabido
sabrá	sabrán	habrá sabido	habrán sabido
5 potencial simple		12 potencial compuesto	
sabría	sabríamos	habría sabido	habríamos sabido
sabrías	sabríais	habrías sabido	habríais sabido
sabría	sabrían	habría sabido	habrían sabido
6 presente de subjuntivo		13 perfecto de subjuntivo	
sepa	sepamos	haya sabido	hayamos sabido
sepas	sepáis	hayas sabido	hayáis sabido
sepa	sepan	haya sabido	hayan sabido
7 imperfecto de subjuntivo		14 pluscuamperfecto de subjuntivo	
supiera	supiéramos	hubiera sabido	hubiéramos sabido
supieras	supierais	hubieras sabido	hubierais sabido
supiera	supieran	hubiera sabido	hubieran sabido
OR		OR	
supiese	supiésemos	hubiese sabido	hubiésemos sabido
supieses	supieseis	hubieses sabido	hubieseis sabido
supiese	supiesen	hubiese sabido	hubiesen sabido

imperativo

—	sepamos
sabe; no sepas	sabed; no sepáis
sepa	sepan

AN ESSENTIAL 55 VERB

Saber is a very useful irregular verb for you to know. It is used in a great number of idiomatic expressions and everyday situations. Don't confuse saber with conocer (verb 134).

Generally speaking, saber means to know a fact, to know something thoroughly:

¿Sabe Ud. qué hora es?/Do you know what time it is?
¿Sabe Ud. la lección?/Do you know the lesson?

When you use saber + inf., it means *to know how:*

¿Sabe Ud. nadar?/Do you know how to swim?
Sí, (yo) sé nadar/Yes, I know how to swim.

In the preterit tense, saber means *to find out:*

¿Lo sabe Ud.?/Do you know it?
Sí, lo supe ayer/Yes, I found it out yesterday.

Sentences using saber and related words

Este niño no sabe contar.
This child can't (does not know how to) count.

No sé nada de este asunto.
I don't know anything about this matter.

¿Sabe usted si hay una farmacia por aquí?
Do you know if there is a pharmacy around here?

Words and expressions related to this verb

sabio, sabia wise, learned

un sabidillo, una sabidilla **a know-it-all**

la sabiduría **knowledge, learning, wisdom**

Que yo sepa... **As far as I know...**

¡Quién sabe! **Who knows! Perhaps! Maybe!**

la señorita Sabelotodo **Miss Know-It-All**

el señor Sabelotodo **Mr. Know-It-All**

sabido, sabida **known**

el saber **knowledge**

saber por experiencia **to learn from experience**

saber algo como el avemaría **to know something like the back of one's hand**

S

Proverbs

Saber es poder.
Knowledge is power.

Más vale saber que haber.
Knowing is better than having. (Knowledge is worth more than possessions/things.)

to take out, to get

Regular -ar verb endings with spelling change: c becomes qu before e

The Seven Simple Tenses

The Seven Compound Tenses

Singular	Plural	Singular	Plural
1 presente de indicativo		8 perfecto de indicativo	
saco	sacamos	he sacado	hemos sacado
sacas	sacáis	has sacado	habéis sacado
saca	sacan	ha sacado	han sacado
2 imperfecto de indicativo		9 pluscuamperfecto de indicativo	
sacaba	sacábamos	había sacado	habíamos sacado
sacabas	sacabais	habías sacado	habíais sacado
sacaba	sacaban	había sacado	habían sacado
3 pretérito		10 pretérito anterior	
saqué	sacamos	hube sacado	hubimos sacado
sacaste	sacasteis	hubiste sacado	hubisteis sacado
sacó	sacaron	hubo sacado	hubieron sacado
4 futuro		11 futuro perfecto	
sacaré	sacaremos	habré sacado	habremos sacado
sacarás	sacaréis	habrás sacado	habréis sacado
sacará	sacarán	habrá sacado	habrán sacado
5 potencial simple		12 potencial compuesto	
sacaría	sacaríamos	habría sacado	habríamos sacado
sacarías	sacaríais	habrías sacado	habríais sacado
sacaría	sacarían	habría sacado	habrían sacado
6 presente de subjuntivo		13 perfecto de subjuntivo	
saque	saquemos	haya sacado	hayamos sacado
saques	saquéis	hayas sacado	hayáis sacado
saque	saquen	haya sacado	hayan sacado
7 imperfecto de subjuntivo		14 pluscuamperfecto de subjuntivo	
sacara	sacáramos	hubiera sacado	hubiéramos sacado
sacaras	sacarais	hubieras sacado	hubierais sacado
sacara	sacaran	hubiera sacado	hubieran sacado
OR		OR	
sacase	sacásemos	hubiese sacado	hubiésemos sacado
sacases	sacaseis	hubieses sacado	hubieseis sacado
sacase	sacasen	hubiese sacado	hubiesen sacado

imperativo

—	saquemos
saca; no saques	sacad; no saquéis
saque	saquen

Words and expressions related to this verb

sacar agua   to draw water

sacar a paseo   to take out for a walk; ensacar   to put in a bag, to bag

un saco   bag, sack; saco de noche   overnight bag; un saco de dormir   sleeping bag

un sacapuntas   pencil sharpener

una saca   withdrawal; un sacacorchos   corkscrew

The Seven Simple Tenses		The Seven Compound Tenses	
Singular	Plural	Singular	Plural
1 presente de indicativo		8 perfecto de indicativo	
sacudo	sacudimos	he sacudido	hemos sacudido
sacudes	sacudís	has sacudido	habéis sacudido
sacude	sacuden	ha sacudido	han sacudido
2 imperfecto de indicativo		9 pluscuamperfecto de indicativo	
sacudía	sacudíamos	había sacudido	habíamos sacudido
sacudías	sacudíais	habías sacudido	habíais sacudido
sacudía	sacudían	había sacudido	habían sacudido
3 pretérito		10 pretérito anterior	
sacudí	sacudimos	hube sacudido	hubimos sacudido
sacudiste	sacudisteis	hubiste sacudido	hubisteis sacudido
sacudió	sacudieron	hubo sacudido	hubieron sacudido
4 futuro		11 futuro perfecto	
sacudiré	sacudiremos	habré sacudido	habremos sacudido
sacudirás	sacudiréis	habrás sacudido	habréis sacudido
sacudirá	sacudirán	habrá sacudido	habrán sacudido
5 potencial simple		12 potencial compuesto	
sacudiría	sacudiríamos	habría sacudido	habríamos sacudido
sacudirías	sacudiríais	habrías sacudido	habríais sacudido
sacudiría	sacudirían	habría sacudido	habrían sacudido
6 presente de subjuntivo		13 perfecto de subjuntivo	
sacuda	sacudamos	haya sacudido	hayamos sacudido
sacudas	sacudáis	hayas sacudido	hayáis sacudido
sacuda	sacudan	haya sacudido	hayan sacudido
7 imperfecto de subjuntivo		14 pluscuamperfecto de subjuntivo	
sacudiera	sacudiéramos	hubiera sacudido	hubiéramos sacudido
sacudieras	sacudierais	hubieras sacudido	hubierais sacudido
sacudiera	sacudieran	hubiera sacudido	hubieran sacudido
OR		OR	
sacudiese	sacudiésemos	hubiese sacudido	hubiésemos sacudido
sacudieses	sacudieseis	hubieses sacudido	hubieseis sacudido
sacudiese	sacudiesen	hubiese sacudido	hubiesen sacudido

S

imperativo	
—	sacudamos
sacude; no sacudas	sacudid; no sacudáis
sacuda	sacudan

Words and expressions related to this verb
un sacudimiento shaking, jolt, jerk
un sacudión violent jolt
una sacudida jerk, jolt, shake

sacudir el yugo to shake off the yoke (to become independent)
a sacudidas in jerks

Can't find the verb you're looking for?
Check the back pages of this book for a list of over 2,100 additional verbs!

The subject pronouns are found on page 93.

to go out, to leave   Irregular verb

The Seven Simple Tenses		The Seven Compound Tenses	
Singular	Plural	Singular	Plural
1 presente de indicativo		8 perfecto de indicativo	
salgo	salimos	he salido	hemos salido
sales	salís	has salido	habéis salido
sale	salen	ha salido	han salido
2 imperfecto de indicativo		9 pluscuamperfecto de indicativo	
salía	salíamos	había salido	habíamos salido
salías	salíais	habías salido	habíais salido
salía	salían	había salido	habían salido
3 pretérito		10 pretérito anterior	
salí	salimos	hube salido	hubimos salido
saliste	salisteis	hubiste salido	hubisteis salido
salió	salieron	hubo salido	hubieron salido
4 futuro		11 futuro perfecto	
saldré	saldremos	habré salido	habremos salido
saldrás	saldréis	habrás salido	habréis salido
saldrá	saldrán	habrá salido	habrán salido
5 potencial simple		12 potencial compuesto	
saldría	saldríamos	habría salido	habríamos salido
saldrías	saldríais	habrías salido	habríais salido
saldría	saldrían	habría salido	habrían salido
6 presente de subjuntivo		13 perfecto de subjuntivo	
salga	salgamos	haya salido	hayamos salido
salgas	salgáis	hayas salido	hayáis salido
salga	salgan	haya salido	hayan salido
7 imperfecto de subjuntivo		14 pluscuamperfecto de subjuntivo	
saliera	saliéramos	hubiera salido	hubiéramos salido
salieras	salierais	hubieras salido	hubierais salido
saliera	salieran	hubiera salido	hubieran salido
OR		OR	
saliese	saliésemos	hubiese salido	hubiésemos salido
salieses	salieseis	hubieses salido	hubieseis salido
saliese	saliesen	hubiese salido	hubiesen salido

imperativo	
—	salgamos
sal; no salgas	salid; no salgáis
salga	salgan

Salir is a very useful irregular verb for you to learn. It is used in a great number of idiomatic expressions and everyday situations.

Be careful not to confuse **salir** and **dejar** (verb 165). Use **salir de** when you mean *to leave* in the sense of *to go out of* (a place):

El alumno salió de la sala de clase.
The pupil left the classroom

Sentences using salir and related words

¿A qué hora sale el tren para San José?
At what time does the train leave for San José?

—**¿Dónde está su madre?**
—**Mi madre salió.**
—Where is your mother?
—My mother went out.

Words and expressions related to this verb

la salida **exit, departure**

la salida de emergencia **emergency exit**

sin salida **no exit, dead-end street**

salir de compras **to go out shopping**

salir mal **to go wrong, to do badly**

saliente **salient, prominent**

salir al encuentro de **to go to meet**

salir de **to leave from, to get out of**

salga lo que salga **come what may**

salir disparado **to take off like a shot, like an arrow**

S

Can't find the verb you're looking for?
Check the back pages of this book for a list of over 2,100 additional verbs!

The subject pronouns are found on page 93.

to jump, to leap, to hop, to spring   Regular -ar verb

The Seven Simple Tenses		The Seven Compound Tenses	
Singular	Plural	Singular	Plural
1 presente de indicativo		8 perfecto de indicativo	
salto	saltamos	he saltado	hemos saltado
saltas	saltáis	has saltado	habéis saltado
salta	saltan	ha saltado	han saltado
2 imperfecto de indicativo		9 pluscuamperfecto de indicativo	
saltaba	saltábamos	había saltado	habíamos saltado
saltabas	saltabais	habías saltado	habíais saltado
saltaba	saltaban	había saltado	habían saltado
3 pretérito		10 pretérito anterior	
salté	saltamos	hube saltado	hubimos saltado
saltaste	saltasteis	hubiste saltado	hubisteis saltado
saltó	saltaron	hubo saltado	hubieron saltado
4 futuro		11 futuro perfecto	
saltaré	saltaremos	habré saltado	habremos saltado
saltarás	saltaréis	habrás saltado	habréis saltado
saltará	saltarán	habrá saltado	habrán saltado
5 potencial simple		12 potencial compuesto	
saltaría	saltaríamos	habría saltado	habríamos saltado
saltarías	saltaríais	habrías saltado	habríais saltado
saltaría	saltarían	habría saltado	habrían saltado
6 presente de subjuntivo		13 perfecto de subjuntivo	
salte	saltemos	haya saltado	hayamos saltado
saltes	saltéis	hayas saltado	hayáis saltado
salte	salten	haya saltado	hayan saltado
7 imperfecto de subjuntivo		14 pluscuamperfecto de subjuntivo	
saltara	saltáramos	hubiera saltado	hubiéramos saltado
saltaras	saltarais	hubieras saltado	hubierais saltado
saltara	saltaran	hubiera saltado	hubieran saltado
OR		OR	
saltase	saltásemos	hubiese saltado	hubiésemos saltado
saltases	saltaseis	hubieses saltado	hubieseis saltado
saltase	saltasen	hubiese saltado	hubiesen saltado

imperativo	
—	saltemos
salta; no saltes	saltad; no saltéis
salte	salten

Words and expressions related to this verb

hacer saltar la banca   to break the bank (in gambling)
saltar de gozo   to jump with joy
saltar por   to jump over
el saltimbanqui   acrobat

un salto   jump, leap
un salto de esquí   ski jump
un salto de cisne   swan dive
un salto mortal   somersault
saltear   to sauté

The Seven Simple Tenses | The Seven Compound Tenses

Singular	Plural	Singular	Plural
1 presente de indicativo		**8 perfecto de indicativo**	
saludo	saludamos	he saludado	hemos saludado
saludas	saludáis	has saludado	habéis saludado
saluda	saludan	ha saludado	han saludado
2 imperfecto de indicativo		**9 pluscuamperfecto de indicativo**	
saludaba	saludábamos	había saludado	habíamos saludado
saludabas	saludabais	habías saludado	habíais saludado
saludaba	saludaban	había saludado	habían saludado
3 pretérito		**10 pretérito anterior**	
saludé	saludamos	hube saludado	hubimos saludado
saludaste	saludasteis	hubiste saludado	hubisteis saludado
saludó	saludaron	hubo saludado	hubieron saludado
4 futuro		**11 futuro perfecto**	
saludaré	saludaremos	habré saludado	habremos saludado
saludarás	saludaréis	habrás saludado	habréis saludado
saludará	saludarán	habrá saludado	habrán saludado
5 potencial simple		**12 potencial compuesto**	
saludaría	saludaríamos	habría saludado	habríamos saludado
saludarías	saludaríais	habrías saludado	habríais saludado
saludaría	saludarían	habría saludado	habrían saludado
6 presente de subjuntivo		**13 perfecto de subjuntivo**	
salude	saludemos	haya saludado	hayamos saludado
saludes	saludéis	hayas saludado	hayáis saludado
salude	saluden	haya saludado	hayan saludado
7 imperfecto de subjuntivo		**14 pluscuamperfecto de subjuntivo**	
saludara	saludáramos	hubiera saludado	hubiéramos saludado
saludaras	saludarais	hubieras saludado	hubierais saludado
saludara	saludaran	hubiera saludado	hubieran saludado
OR		OR	
saludase	saludásemos	hubiese saludado	hubiésemos saludado
saludases	saludaseis	hubieses saludado	hubieseis saludado
saludase	saludasen	hubiese saludado	hubiesen saludado

imperativo	
—	**saludemos**
saluda; no saludes	**saludad; no saludéis**
salude	**saluden**

S

Words and expressions related to this verb

la salutación   greeting, salutation
el saludo   salutation, greeting, salute
el saludo final   closing (of a letter)
saludarse uno a otro   to greet each other

la salud   health; **¡A su salud!**   To your health!
estar bien de salud   to be in good health
estar mal de salud   to be in bad health
¡Salud!   Bless you! (to someone who sneezes)

Consult the back pages for the section on verbs with prepositions.

The subject pronouns are found on page 93.

to satisfy

The Seven Simple Tenses		The Seven Compound Tenses	
Singular	Plural	Singular	Plural
1 presente de indicativo		**8 perfecto de indicativo**	
satisfago	satisfacemos	he satisfecho	hemos satisfecho
satisfaces	satisfacéis	has satisfecho	habéis satisfecho
satisface	satisfacen	ha satisfecho	han satisfecho
2 imperfecto de indicativo		**9 pluscuamperfecto de indicativo**	
satisfacía	satisfacíamos	había satisfecho	habíamos satisfecho
satisfacías	satisfacíais	habías satisfecho	habíais satisfecho
satisfacía	satisfacían	había satisfecho	habían satisfecho
3 pretérito		**10 pretérito anterior**	
satisfice	satisficimos	hube satisfecho	hubimos satisfecho
satisficiste	satisficisteis	hubiste satisfecho	hubisteis satisfecho
satisfizo	satisficieron	hubo satisfecho	hubieron satisfecho
4 futuro		**11 futuro perfecto**	
satisfaré	satisfaremos	habré satisfecho	habremos satisfecho
satisfarás	satisfaréis	habrás satisfecho	habréis satisfecho
satisfará	satisfarán	habrá satisfecho	habrán satisfecho
5 potencial simple		**12 potencial compuesto**	
satisfaría	satisfaríamos	habría satisfecho	habríamos satisfecho
satisfarías	satisfaríais	habrías satisfecho	habríais satisfecho
satisfaría	satisfarían	habría satisfecho	habrían satisfecho
6 presente de subjuntivo		**13 perfecto de subjuntivo**	
satisfaga	satisfagamos	haya satisfecho	hayamos satisfecho
satisfagas	satisfagáis	hayas satisfecho	hayáis satisfecho
satisfaga	satisfagan	haya satisfecho	hayan satisfecho
7 imperfecto de subjuntivo		**14 pluscuamperfecto de subjuntivo**	
satisficiera	satisficiéramos	hubiera satisfecho	hubiéramos satisfecho
satisficieras	satisficierais	hubieras satisfecho	hubierais satisfecho
satisficiera	satisficieran	hubiera satisfecho	hubieran satisfecho
OR		OR	
satisficiese	satisficiésemos	hubiese satisfecho	hubiésemos satisfecho
satisficieses	satisficieseis	hubieses satisfecho	hubieseis satisfecho
satisficiese	satisficiesen	hubiese satisfecho	hubiesen satisfecho

imperativo	
—	satisfagamos
satisfaz (satisface); no satisfagas	satisfaced; no satisfagáis
satisfaga	satisfagan

Words and expressions related to this verb

la **satisfacción** satisfaction
a **satisfacción** satisfactorily
a **satisfacción de** to the satisfaction of
insatisfecho, insatisfecha dissatisfied
insaciable insatiable

satisfecho, satisfecha satisfied
satisfactorio, satisfactoria satisfactory
satisfaciente satisfying
saciar to satisfy, to satiate
la **saciedad** satiety, satiation

Regular **-ar** verb endings with spelling change: **c** becomes **qu** before **e**   to dry, to wipe dry

The Seven Simple Tenses		The Seven Compound Tenses	
Singular	Plural	Singular	Plural
1 presente de indicativo		8 perfecto de indicativo	
seco	secamos	he secado	hemos secado
secas	secáis	has secado	habéis secado
seca	secan	ha secado	han secado
2 imperfecto de indicativo		9 pluscuamperfecto de indicativo	
secaba	secábamos	había secado	habíamos secado
secabas	secabais	habías secado	habíais secado
secaba	secaban	había secado	habían secado
3 pretérito		10 pretérito anterior	
sequé	secamos	hube secado	hubimos secado
secaste	secasteis	hubiste secado	hubisteis secado
secó	secaron	hubo secado	hubieron secado
4 futuro		11 futuro perfecto	
secaré	secaremos	habré secado	habremos secado
secarás	secaréis	habrás secado	habréis secado
secará	secarán	habrá secado	habrán secado
5 potencial simple		12 potencial compuesto	
secaría	secaríamos	habría secado	habríamos secado
secarías	secaríais	habrías secado	habríais secado
secaría	secarían	habría secado	habrían secado
6 presente de subjuntivo		13 perfecto de subjuntivo	
seque	sequemos	haya secado	hayamos secado
seques	sequéis	hayas secado	hayáis secado
seque	sequen	haya secado	hayan secado
7 imperfecto de subjuntivo		14 pluscuamperfecto de subjuntivo	
secara	secáramos	hubiera secado	hubiéramos secado
secaras	secarais	hubieras secado	hubierais secado
secara	secaran	hubiera secado	hubieran secado
OR		OR	
secase	secásemos	hubiese secado	hubiésemos secado
secases	secaseis	hubieses secado	hubieseis secado
secase	secasen	hubiese secado	hubiesen secado

imperativo	
—	sequemos
seca; no seques	secad; no sequéis
seque	sequen

Words and expressions related to this verb

seco, seca dry, dried up
la seca drought
secado al sol sun dried

limpiar en seco to dry-clean
en seco high and dry
¡Seco y volteado! Bottoms up!

For other words and expressions related to this verb, see **secarse.**

Use the guide to Spanish pronunciation on pages 665–667.

The subject pronouns are found on page 93.

secarse (431)   Gerundio **secándose**   Part. pas. **secado**

to dry oneself

Reflexive verb; regular **-ar** verb endings with spelling change: **c** becomes **qu** before **e**

The Seven Simple Tenses	The Seven Compound Tenses

Singular	Plural	Singular	Plural
1 presente de indicativo		**8 perfecto de indicativo**	
me seco	nos secamos	me he secado	nos hemos secado
te secas	os secáis	te has secado	os habéis secado
se seca	se secan	se ha secado	se han secado
2 imperfecto de indicativo		**9 pluscuamperfecto de indicativo**	
me secaba	nos secábamos	me había secado	nos habíamos secado
te secabas	os secabais	te habías secado	os habíais secado
se secaba	se secaban	se había secado	se habían secado
3 pretérito		**10 pretérito anterior**	
me sequé	nos secamos	me hube secado	nos hubimos secado
te secaste	os secasteis	te hubiste secado	os hubisteis secado
se secó	se secaron	se hubo secado	se hubieron secado
4 futuro		**11 futuro perfecto**	
me secaré	nos secaremos	me habré secado	nos habremos secado
te secarás	os secaréis	te habrás secado	os habréis secado
se secará	se secarán	se habrá secado	se habrán secado
5 potencial simple		**12 potencial compuesto**	
me secaría	nos secaríamos	me habría secado	nos habríamos secado
te secarías	os secaríais	te habrías secado	os habríais secado
se secaría	se secarían	se habría secado	se habrían secado
6 presente de subjuntivo		**13 perfecto de subjuntivo**	
me seque	nos sequemos	me haya secado	nos hayamos secado
te seques	os sequéis	te hayas secado	os hayáis secado
se seque	se sequen	se haya secado	se hayan secado
7 imperfecto de subjuntivo		**14 pluscuamperfecto de subjuntivo**	
me secara	nos secáramos	me hubiera secado	nos hubiéramos secado
te secaras	os secarais	te hubieras secado	os hubierais secado
se secara	se secaran	se hubiera secado	se hubieran secado
OR		OR	
me secase	nos secásemos	me hubiese secado	nos hubiésemos secado
te secases	os secaseis	te hubieses secado	os hubieseis secado
se secase	se secasen	se hubiese secado	se hubiesen secado

imperativo	
—	sequémonos
sécate; no te seques	secaos; no os sequéis
séquese	séquense

Words and expressions related to this verb

la secadora dryer	**a secas** plainly, simply
secado, secada dried	**el vino seco** dry wine

For other words and expressions related to this verb, see **secar**.

Don't forget to study the section on defective and impersonal verbs. It's right after this main list.

Regular **-ir** verb endings with stem change: to follow, to pursue, to continue
Tenses 1, 3, 6, 7, Imperative, Gerundio

The Seven Simple Tenses		The Seven Compound Tenses	
Singular	Plural	Singular	Plural
1 presente de indicativo		8 perfecto de indicativo	
sigo	seguimos	he seguido	hemos seguido
sigues	seguís	has seguido	habéis seguido
sigue	siguen	ha seguido	han seguido
2 imperfecto de indicativo		9 pluscuamperfecto de indicativo	
seguía	seguíamos	había seguido	habíamos seguido
seguías	seguíais	habías seguido	habíais seguido
seguía	seguían	había seguido	habían seguido
3 pretérito		10 pretérito anterior	
seguí	seguimos	hube seguido	hubimos seguido
seguiste	seguisteis	hubiste seguido	hubisteis seguido
siguió	siguieron	hubo seguido	hubieron seguido
4 futuro		11 futuro perfecto	
seguiré	seguiremos	habré seguido	habremos seguido
seguirás	seguiréis	habrás seguido	habréis seguido
seguirá	seguirán	habrá seguido	habrán seguido
5 potencial simple		12 potencial compuesto	
seguiría	seguiríamos	habría seguido	habríamos seguido
seguirías	seguiríais	habrías seguido	habríais seguido
seguiría	seguirían	habría seguido	habrían seguido
6 presente de subjuntivo		13 perfecto de subjuntivo	
siga	sigamos	haya seguido	hayamos seguido
sigas	sigáis	hayas seguido	hayáis seguido
siga	sigan	haya seguido	hayan seguido
7 imperfecto de subjuntivo		14 pluscuamperfecto de subjuntivo	
siguiera	siguiéramos	hubiera seguido	hubiéramos seguido
siguieras	siguierais	hubieras seguido	hubierais seguido
siguiera	siguieran	hubiera seguido	hubieran seguido
OR		OR	
siguiese	siguiésemos	hubiese seguido	hubiésemos seguido
siguieses	siguieseis	hubieses seguido	hubieseis seguido
siguiese	siguiesen	hubiese seguido	hubiesen seguido

S

	imperativo	
—		**sigamos**
sigue; no sigas		**seguid; no sigáis**
siga		**sigan**

Words and expressions related to this verb

según   according to
al día siguiente   on the following day
las frases siguientes   the following sentences
seguir + pres. part.   to keep on + pres. part.;
   Siga leyendo   Keep on reading.
seguido, seguida   continuous

conseguir   to attain, to get, to obtain
proseguir   to continue, proceed
perseguir   to pursue
seguirle los pasos a uno   to keep one's eye
   on someone
un seguidor, una seguidora   follower

The subject pronouns are found on page 93.

569

to signal, to indicate, to point out, to show   Regular **-ar** verb

The Seven Simple Tenses		The Seven Compound Tenses	
Singular	Plural	Singular	Plural
1 presente de indicativo		8 perfecto de indicativo	
señalo	señalamos	he señalado	hemos señalado
señalas	señaláis	has señalado	habéis señalado
señala	señalan	ha señalado	han señalado
2 imperfecto de indicativo		9 pluscuamperfecto de indicativo	
señalaba	señalábamos	había señalado	habíamos señalado
señalabas	señalabais	habías señalado	habíais señalado
señalaba	señalaban	había señalado	habían señalado
3 pretérito		10 pretérito anterior	
señalé	señalamos	hube señalado	hubimos señalado
señalaste	señalasteis	hubiste señalado	hubisteis señalado
señaló	señalaron	hubo señalado	hubieron señalado
4 futuro		11 futuro perfecto	
señalaré	señalaremos	habré señalado	habremos señalado
señalarás	señalaréis	habrás señalado	habréis señalado
señalará	señalarán	habrá señalado	habrán señalado
5 potencial simple		12 potencial compuesto	
señalaría	señalaríamos	habría señalado	habríamos señalado
señalarías	señalaríais	habrías señalado	habríais señalado
señalaría	señalarían	habría señalado	habrían señalado
6 presente de subjuntivo		13 perfecto de subjuntivo	
señale	señalemos	haya señalado	hayamos señalado
señales	señaléis	hayas señalado	hayáis señalado
señale	señalen	haya señalado	hayan señalado
7 imperfecto de subjuntivo		14 pluscuamperfecto de subjuntivo	
señalara	señaláramos	hubiera señalado	hubiéramos señalado
señalaras	señalarais	hubieras señalado	hubierais señalado
señalara	señalaran	hubiera señalado	hubieran señalado
OR		OR	
señalase	señalásemos	hubiese señalado	hubiésemos señalado
señalases	señalaseis	hubieses señalado	hubieseis señalado
señalase	señalasen	hubiese señalado	hubiesen señalado

imperativo	
—	señalemos
señala; no señales	señalad; no señaléis
señale	señalen

Words and expressions related to this verb

señalar un día   to set a day
señalar una fecha   to set a date
señalar con el dedo   to point out, to
    indicate (with your finger)

una seña   mark, sign, signal
por señas   by signs
dar señas de   to show signs of
una señal   sign, mark; señal de parada   stop sign

Can't find the verb you're looking for?
Check the back pages of this book for a list of over 2,100 additional verbs!

Reflexive verb; regular **-ar** verb endings   to sit down
with stem change: Tenses 1, 6, Imperative

The Seven Simple Tenses | | The Seven Compound Tenses

Singular	Plural	Singular	Plural
1 presente de indicativo		8 perfecto de indicativo	
me siento	nos sentamos	me he sentado	nos hemos sentado
te sientas	os sentáis	te has sentado	os habéis sentado
se sienta	se sientan	se ha sentado	se han sentado
2 imperfecto de indicativo		9 pluscuamperfecto de indicativo	
me sentaba	nos sentábamos	me había sentado	nos habíamos sentado
te sentabas	os sentabais	te habías sentado	os habíais sentado
se sentaba	se sentaban	se había sentado	se habían sentado
3 pretérito		10 pretérito anterior	
me senté	nos sentamos	me hube sentado	nos hubimos sentado
te sentaste	os sentasteis	te hubiste sentado	os hubisteis sentado
se sentó	se sentaron	se hubo sentado	se hubieron sentado
4 futuro		11 futuro perfecto	
me sentaré	nos sentaremos	me habré sentado	nos habremos sentado
te sentarás	os sentaréis	te habrás sentado	os habréis sentado
se sentará	se sentarán	se habrá sentado	se habrán sentado
5 potencial simple		12 potencial compuesto	
me sentaría	nos sentaríamos	me habría sentado	nos habríamos sentado
te sentarías	os sentaríais	te habrías sentado	os habríais sentado
se sentaría	se sentarían	se habría sentado	se habrían sentado
6 presente de subjuntivo		13 perfecto de subjuntivo	
me siente	nos sentemos	me haya sentado	nos hayamos sentado
te sientes	os sentéis	te hayas sentado	os hayáis sentado
se siente	se sienten	se haya sentado	se hayan sentado
7 imperfecto de subjuntivo		14 pluscuamperfecto de subjuntivo	
me sentara	nos sentáramos	me hubiera sentado	nos hubiéramos sentado
te sentaras	os sentarais	te hubieras sentado	os hubierais sentado
se sentara	se sentaran	se hubiera sentado	se hubieran sentado
OR		OR	
me sentase	nos sentásemos	me hubiese sentado	nos hubiésemos sentado
te sentases	os sentaseis	te hubieses sentado	os hubieseis sentado
se sentase	se sentasen	se hubiese sentado	se hubiesen sentado

imperativo

—	sentémonos; no nos sentemos
siéntate; no te sientes	sentaos; no os sentéis
siéntese; no se siente	siéntense; no se sienten

Words and expressions related to this verb
un asiento   a seat
sentado, sentada   seated
¡Siéntese Ud.!   Sit down!

sentar, asentar   to seat
una sentada   a sitting; **de una sentada**
   in one sitting
¡Vamos a sentarnos!   Let's sit down!

Can't recognize an irregular verb form? Check out pages 678–681.

The subject pronouns are found on page 93.   **571**

sentir (435)　　Gerundio sintiendo　　Part. pas. sentido

to feel sorry, to regret, to feel

The Seven Simple Tenses | The Seven Compound Tenses

Singular	Plural	Singular	Plural
1 presente de indicativo		**8 perfecto de indicativo**	
siento	sentimos	he sentido	hemos sentido
sientes	sentís	has sentido	habéis sentido
siente	sienten	ha sentido	han sentido
2 imperfecto de indicativo		**9 pluscuamperfecto de indicativo**	
sentía	sentíamos	había sentido	habíamos sentido
sentías	sentíais	habías sentido	habíais sentido
sentía	sentían	había sentido	habían sentido
3 pretérito		**10 pretérito anterior**	
sentí	sentimos	hube sentido	hubimos sentido
sentiste	sentisteis	hubiste sentido	hubisteis sentido
sintió	sintieron	hubo sentido	hubieron sentido
4 futuro		**11 futuro perfecto**	
sentiré	sentiremos	habré sentido	habremos sentido
sentirás	sentiréis	habrás sentido	habréis sentido
sentirá	sentirán	habrá sentido	habrán sentido
5 potencial simple		**12 potencial compuesto**	
sentiría	sentiríamos	habría sentido	habríamos sentido
sentirías	sentiríais	habrías sentido	habríais sentido
sentiría	sentirían	habría sentido	habrían sentido
6 presente de subjuntivo		**13 perfecto de subjuntivo**	
sienta	sintamos	haya sentido	hayamos sentido
sientas	sintáis	hayas sentido	hayáis sentido
sienta	sientan	haya sentido	hayan sentido
7 imperfecto de subjuntivo		**14 pluscuamperfecto de subjuntivo**	
sintiera	sintiéramos	hubiera sentido	hubiéramos sentido
sintieras	sintierais	hubieras sentido	hubierais sentido
sintiera	sintieran	hubiera sentido	hubieran sentido
OR		OR	
sintiese	sintiésemos	hubiese sentido	hubiésemos sentido
sintieses	sintieseis	hubieses sentido	hubieseis sentido
sintiese	sintiesen	hubiese sentido	hubiesen sentido

imperativo

—	sintamos
siente; no sientas	sentid; no sintáis
sienta	sientan

**AN ESSENTIAL
55 VERB**

Sentir/Sentirse

Sentir and sentirse are an essential pair of **-ir** verbs for you to learn. They are used in a great number of idiomatic expressions and everyday situations. Pay attention to the stem change in Tenses 1, 3, 6, and 7, as well as in the imperative and present participle (Gerundio).

Sentences using sentir and sentirse

La semana pasada sentimos un fuerte terremoto.
Last week we felt a powerful earthquake.

El chico sintió la muerte de su perro.
The boy felt very sorry about the death of his dog.

Lo siento mucho.
I regret it very much. I'm very sorry.

¿Cómo se siente Ud.?
How do you feel?

Me siento mal.
I feel sick.

Words and expressions related to these verbs

el sentimiento **feeling, sentiment**

sentimentalmente **sentimentally**

el sentir **feeling, judgment**

el sentido **sense, meaning, feeling**

los sentidos **the senses**

una persona sentimental **sentimentalist**

el sentimentalismo **sentimentalism**

sentir admiración por alguien **to feel admiration for someone**

sentir en el alma **to feel/regret deeply**

sentido, sentida **sincere, sensitive**

resentirse **to feel the effects**

resentirse de algo **to resent something**

S

Can't remember the Spanish verb you need?
Check the back pages of this book for the English-Spanish verb index!

The subject pronouns are found on page 93.

sentirse (436)   Gerundio **sintiéndose**   Part. pas. **sentido**

to feel (well, ill) | Reflexive verb; regular **-ir** verb endings with stem change: Tenses 1, 3, 6, 7, Imperative, Gerundio

The Seven Simple Tenses | The Seven Compound Tenses

Singular	Plural	Singular	Plural
1 presente de indicativo		**8 perfecto de indicativo**	
me siento	nos sentimos	me he sentido	nos hemos sentido
te sientes	os sentís	te has sentido	os habéis sentido
se siente	se sienten	se ha sentido	se han sentido
2 imperfecto de indicativo		**9 pluscuamperfecto de indicativo**	
me sentía	nos sentíamos	me había sentido	nos habíamos sentido
te sentías	os sentíais	te habías sentido	os habíais sentido
se sentía	se sentían	se había sentido	se habían sentido
3 pretérito		**10 pretérito anterior**	
me sentí	nos sentimos	me hube sentido	nos hubimos sentido
te sentiste	os sentisteis	te hubiste sentido	os hubisteis sentido
se sintió	se sintieron	se hubo sentido	se hubieron sentido
4 futuro		**11 futuro perfecto**	
me sentiré	nos sentiremos	me habré sentido	nos habremos sentido
te sentirás	os sentiréis	te habrás sentido	os habréis sentido
se sentirá	se sentirán	se habrá sentido	se habrán sentido
5 potencial simple		**12 potencial compuesto**	
me sentiría	nos sentiríamos	me habría sentido	nos habríamos sentido
te sentirías	os sentiríais	te habrías sentido	os habríais sentido
se sentiría	se sentirían	se habría sentido	se habrían sentido
6 presente de subjuntivo		**13 perfecto de subjuntivo**	
me sienta	nos sintamos	me haya sentido	nos hayamos sentido
te sientas	os sintáis	te hayas sentido	os hayáis sentido
se sienta	se sientan	se haya sentido	se hayan sentido
7 imperfecto de subjuntivo		**14 pluscuamperfecto de subjuntivo**	
me sintiera	nos sintiéramos	me hubiera sentido	nos hubiéramos sentido
te sintieras	os sintierais	te hubieras sentido	os hubierais sentido
se sintiera	se sintieran	se hubiera sentido	se hubieran sentido
OR		OR	
me sintiese	nos sintiésemos	me hubiese sentido	nos hubiésemos sentido
te sintieses	os sintieseis	te hubieses sentido	os hubieseis sentido
se sintiese	se sintiesen	se hubiese sentido	se hubiesen sentido

imperativo

—	**sintámonos**
siéntete; no te sientas	**sentíos; no os sintáis**
siéntase	**siéntanse**

AN ESSENTIAL 55 VERB

Regular **-ar** verb to separate, to detach, to sort, to set apart

The Seven Simple Tenses		The Seven Compound Tenses	
Singular	Plural	Singular	Plural
1 presente de indicativo		8 perfecto de indicativo	
separo	separamos	he separado	hemos separado
separas	separáis	has separado	habéis separado
separa	separan	ha separado	han separado
2 imperfecto de indicativo		9 pluscuamperfecto de indicativo	
separaba	separábamos	había separado	habíamos separado
separabas	separabais	habías separado	habíais separado
separaba	separaban	había separado	habían separado
3 pretérito		10 pretérito anterior	
separé	separamos	hube separado	hubimos separado
separaste	separasteis	hubiste separado	hubisteis separado
separó	separaron	hubo separado	hubieron separado
4 futuro		11 futuro perfecto	
separaré	separaremos	habré separado	habremos separado
separarás	separaréis	habrás separado	habréis separado
separará	separarán	habrá separado	habrán separado
5 potencial simple		12 potencial compuesto	
separaría	separaríamos	habría separado	habríamos separado
separarías	separaríais	habrías separado	habríais separado
separaría	separarían	habría separado	habrían separado
6 presente de subjuntivo		13 perfecto de subjuntivo	
separe	separemos	haya separado	hayamos separado
separes	separéis	hayas separado	hayáis separado
separe	separen	haya separado	hayan separado
7 imperfecto de subjuntivo		14 pluscuamperfecto de subjuntivo	
separara	separáramos	hubiera separado	hubiéramos separado
separaras	separarais	hubieras separado	hubierais separado
separara	separaran	hubiera separado	hubieran separado
OR		OR	
separase	separásemos	hubiese separado	hubiésemos separado
separases	separaseis	hubieses separado	hubieseis separado
separase	separasen	hubiese separado	hubiesen separado

imperativo	
—	separemos
separa; no separes	separad; no separéis
separe	separen

Words and expressions related to this verb
la separación separation
separante separating
separar un asiento to reserve a seat
por separado separately

una separata reprint
separativo, separativa separative
separado, separada separate, separated
separadamente separately

Use the guide to Spanish pronunciation on pages 665–667.

The subject pronouns are found on page 93.

The Seven Simple Tenses		The Seven Compound Tenses	
Singular	Plural	Singular	Plural

1 presente de indicativo

		8 perfecto de indicativo	
soy	somos	he sido	hemos sido
eres	sois	has sido	habéis sido
es	son	ha sido	han sido

2 imperfecto de indicativo

		9 pluscuamperfecto de indicativo	
era	éramos	había sido	habíamos sido
eras	erais	habías sido	habíais sido
era	eran	había sido	habían sido

3 pretérito

		10 pretérito anterior	
fui	fuimos	hube sido	hubimos sido
fuiste	fuisteis	hubiste sido	hubisteis sido
fue	fueron	hubo sido	hubieron sido

4 futuro

		11 futuro perfecto	
seré	seremos	habré sido	habremos sido
serás	seréis	habrás sido	habréis sido
será	serán	habrá sido	habrán sido

5 potencial simple

		12 potencial compuesto	
sería	seríamos	habría sido	habríamos sido
serías	seríais	habrías sido	habríais sido
sería	serían	habría sido	habrían sido

6 presente de subjuntivo

		13 perfecto de subjuntivo	
sea	seamos	haya sido	hayamos sido
seas	seáis	hayas sido	hayáis sido
sea	sean	haya sido	hayan sido

7 imperfecto de subjuntivo

		14 pluscuamperfecto de subjuntivo	
fuera	fuéramos	hubiera sido	hubiéramos sido
fueras	fuerais	hubieras sido	hubierais sido
fuera	fueran	hubiera sido	hubieran sido
OR		OR	
fuese	fuésemos	hubiese sido	hubiésemos sido
fueses	fueseis	hubieses sido	hubieseis sido
fuese	fuesen	hubiese sido	hubiesen sido

imperativo

—	seamos
sé; no seas	sed; no seáis
sea	sean

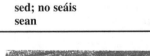

Ser is one of the most important irregular verbs for beginning students. It is used in a vast number of idiomatic expressions and everyday situations. Be careful when you need to choose between ser and estar (verb 230). You should study the special rules for the use of estar. They're listed with that verb.

Sentences using ser and related words

¿Qué hora es?
What time is it?

Es la una.
It's one o'clock.

Son las dos.
It's two o'clock.

Será un regalo.
It will be a gift.

Para ser tan viejo, él es muy ágil.
In spite of being so old, he is very nimble.

Soy aficionado al béisbol.
I'm a baseball fan.

Mi profesora de español es amable conmigo.
My Spanish teacher is kind to me.

Te escucho. Soy de todo oídos.
I'm listening to you. I'm all ears.

Este libro es de María.
This book is Mary's.

Proverb

Dime con quién andas y te diré quién eres.
Tell me who your friends are and I will tell you who you are.

Words and expressions related to this verb

Debe de ser... **It is probably...**

Debe ser... **It ought to be...**

Es de lamentar. **It's too bad.**

Es de mi agrado. **It's to my liking.**

Es hora de... **It is time to...**

Es (una) lástima. **It's a pity. It's too bad.**

Es que... **The fact is...**

para ser... **in spite of being...**

sea lo que sea **whatever it may be**

ser aburrido **to be boring**

ser aficionado a **to be a fan of**

ser amable con **to be kind to**

ser de **to belong to**

ser de rigor **to be indispensable**

ser de ver **to be worth seeing**

ser listo/lista **to be clever**

ser todo oídos **to be all ears**

si no fuera por... **if it were not for...**

Si yo fuera usted... **If I were you...**

S

Can't find the verb you're looking for?
Check the back pages of this book for a list of over 2,100 additional verbs!

The subject pronouns are found on page 93.

to serve

Regular **-ir** verb endings with stem change:
Tenses 1, 3, 6, 7, Imperative, Gerundio

The Seven Simple Tenses		The Seven Compound Tenses	
Singular	Plural	Singular	Plural
1 presente de indicativo		8 perfecto de indicativo	
sirvo	servimos	he servido	hemos servido
sirves	servís	has servido	habéis servido
sirve	sirven	ha servido	han servido
2 imperfecto de indicativo		9 pluscuamperfecto de indicativo	
servía	servíamos	había servido	habíamos servido
servías	servíais	habías servido	habíais servido
servía	servían	había servido	habían servido
3 pretérito		10 pretérito anterior	
serví	servimos	hube servido	hubimos servido
serviste	servisteis	hubiste servido	hubisteis servido
sirvió	sirvieron	hubo servido	hubieron servido
4 futuro		11 futuro perfecto	
serviré	serviremos	habré servido	habremos servido
servirás	serviréis	habrás servido	habréis servido
servirá	servirán	habrá servido	habrán servido
5 potencial simple		12 potencial compuesto	
serviría	serviríamos	habría servido	habríamos servido
servirías	serviríais	habrías servido	habríais servido
serviría	servirían	habría servido	habrían servido
6 presente de subjuntivo		13 perfecto de subjuntivo	
sirva	sirvamos	haya servido	hayamos servido
sirvas	sirváis	hayas servido	hayáis servido
sirva	sirvan	haya servido	hayan servido
7 imperfecto de subjuntivo		14 pluscuamperfecto de subjuntivo	
sirviera	sirviéramos	hubiera servido	hubiéramos servido
sirvieras	sirvierais	hubieras servido	hubierais servido
sirviera	sirvieran	hubiera servido	hubieran servido
OR		OR	
sirviese	sirviésemos	hubiese servido	hubiésemos servido
sirvieses	sirvieseis	hubieses servido	hubieseis servido
sirviese	sirviesen	hubiese servido	hubiesen servido

imperativo	
—	sirvamos
sirve; no sirvas	servid; no sirváis
sirva	sirvan

Words and expressions related to this verb

servidor, servidora servant, waiter, waitress
el servicio service
una servilleta table napkin
servirse to serve oneself
¡Sírvase usted! Help yourself!
el servicio de soporte técnico technical support service

Esto no sirve para nada This serves no
purpose; This is good for nothing.
servir para to be good for, to be used for

Regular **-ar** verb endings with spelling
change: **c** becomes **qu** before **e**

to mean, to signify

The Seven Simple Tenses		The Seven Compound Tenses	
Singular	Plural	Singular	Plural
1 presente de indicativo		8 perfecto de indicativo	
significo	**significamos**	**he significado**	**hemos significado**
significas	**significáis**	**has significado**	**habéis significado**
significa	**significan**	**ha significado**	**han significado**
2 imperfecto de indicativo		9 pluscuamperfecto de indicativo	
significaba	**significábamos**	**había significado**	**habíamos significado**
significabas	**significabais**	**habías significado**	**habíais significado**
significaba	**significaban**	**había significado**	**habían significado**
3 pretérito		10 pretérito anterior	
signifiqué	**significamos**	**hube significado**	**hubimos significado**
significaste	**significasteis**	**hubiste significado**	**hubisteis significado**
significó	**significaron**	**hubo significado**	**hubieron significado**
4 futuro		11 futuro perfecto	
significaré	**significaremos**	**habré significado**	**habremos significado**
significarás	**significaréis**	**habrás significado**	**habréis significado**
significará	**significarán**	**habrá significado**	**habrán significado**
5 potencial simple		12 potencial compuesto	
significaría	**significaríamos**	**habría significado**	**habríamos significado**
significarías	**significaríais**	**habrías significado**	**habríais significado**
significaría	**significarían**	**habría significado**	**habrían significado**
6 presente de subjuntivo		13 perfecto de subjuntivo	
signifique	**signifiquemos**	**haya significado**	**hayamos significado**
signifiques	**signifiquéis**	**hayas significado**	**hayáis significado**
signifique	**signifiquen**	**haya significado**	**hayan significado**
7 imperfecto de subjuntivo		14 pluscuamperfecto de subjuntivo	
significara	**significáramos**	**hubiera significado**	**hubiéramos significado**
significaras	**significarais**	**hubieras significado**	**hubierais significado**
significara	**significaran**	**hubiera significado**	**hubieran significado**
OR		OR	
significase	**significásemos**	**hubiese significado**	**hubiésemos significado**
significases	**significaseis**	**hubieses significado**	**hubieseis significado**
significase	**significasen**	**hubiese significado**	**hubiesen significado**

S

imperativo	
—	**signifiquemos**
significa; no signifiques	**significad; no signifiquéis**
signifique	**signifiquen**

Words and expressions related to this verb
la **significación** significance, meaning
significado, significada signified
el **significado** meaning
el **signo** sign

significante significant
significativo, significativa significative,
  meaningful

Review the principal parts of important Spanish verbs on pages 9–10.

The subject pronouns are found on page 93.

to help, to aid, to assist, to succor   Regular **-er** verb

The Seven Simple Tenses		The Seven Compound Tenses	
Singular	Plural	Singular	Plural
1 presente de indicativo		8 perfecto de indicativo	
socorro	**socorremos**	**he socorrido**	**hemos socorrido**
socorres	**socorréis**	**has socorrido**	**habéis socorrido**
socorre	**socorren**	**ha socorrido**	**han socorrido**
2 imperfecto de indicativo		9 pluscuamperfecto de indicativo	
socorría	**socorríamos**	**había socorrido**	**habíamos socorrido**
soccorrías	**socorríais**	**habías socorrido**	**habíais socorrido**
socorría	**socorrían**	**había socorrido**	**habían socorrido**
3 pretérito		10 pretérito anterior	
socorrí	**socorrimos**	**hube socorrido**	**hubimos socorrido**
socorriste	**socorristeis**	**hubiste socorrido**	**hubisteis socorrido**
socorrió	**socorrieron**	**hubo socorrido**	**hubieron socorrido**
4 futuro		11 futuro perfecto	
socorreré	**socorreremos**	**habré socorrido**	**habremos socorrido**
socorrerás	**socorreréis**	**habrás socorrido**	**habréis socorrido**
socorrerá	**socorrerán**	**habrá socorrido**	**habrán socorrido**
5 potencial simple		12 potencial compuesto	
socorrería	**socorreríamos**	**habría socorrido**	**habríamos socorrido**
socorrerías	**socorreríais**	**habrías socorrido**	**habríais socorrido**
socorrería	**socorrerían**	**habría socorrido**	**habrían socorrido**
6 presente de subjuntivo		13 perfecto de subjuntivo	
socorra	**socorramos**	**haya socorrido**	**hayamos socorrido**
socorras	**socorráis**	**hayas socorrido**	**hayáis socorrido**
socorra	**socorran**	**haya socorrido**	**hayan socorrido**
7 imperfecto de subjuntivo		14 pluscuamperfecto de subjuntivo	
socorriera	**socorriéramos**	**hubiera socorrido**	**hubiéramos socorrido**
socorrieras	**socorrierais**	**hubieras socorrido**	**hubierais socorrido**
socorriera	**socorrieran**	**hubiera socorrido**	**hubieran socorrido**
OR		OR	
socorriese	**socorriésemos**	**hubiese socorrido**	**hubiésemos socorrido**
socorrieses	**socorrieseis**	**hubieses socorrido**	**hubieseis socorrido**
socorriese	**socorriesen**	**hubiese socorrido**	**hubiesen socorrido**

imperativo

—	**socorramos**
socorre; no socorras	**socorred; no socorráis**
socorra	**socorran**

Words and expressions related to this verb
el socorro help; **¡Socorro! ¡Socorro!** Help! Help!   **socorrido, socorrida** helpful
un puesto de socorro first-aid station   **socorrista** first-aid provider

Check out the verb drills and verb tests with answers explained on pages 45–91.

Regular **-ar** verb endings with spelling change: **c** becomes **qu** before **e**

to choke, to smother, to suffocate, to stifle

The Seven Simple Tenses		The Seven Compound Tenses	
Singular	Plural	Singular	Plural
1 presente de indicativo		8 perfecto de indicativo	
sofoco	sofocamos	he sofocado	hemos sofocado
sofocas	sofocáis	has sofocado	habéis sofocado
sofoca	sofocan	ha sofocado	han sofocado
2 imperfecto de indicativo		9 pluscuamperfecto de indicativo	
sofocaba	sofocábamos	había sofocado	habíamos sofocado
sofocabas	sofocabais	habías sofocado	habíais sofocado
sofocaba	sofocaban	había sofocado	habían sofocado
3 pretérito		10 pretérito anterior	
sofoqué	sofocamos	hube sofocado	hubimos sofocado
sofocaste	sofocasteis	hubiste sofocado	hubisteis sofocado
sofocó	sofocaron	hubo sofocado	hubieron sofocado
4 futuro		11 futuro perfecto	
sofocaré	sofocaremos	habré sofocado	habremos sofocado
sofocarás	sofocaréis	habrás sofocado	habréis sofocado
sofocará	sofocarán	habrá sofocado	habrán sofocado
5 potencial simple		12 potencial compuesto	
sofocaría	sofocaríamos	habría sofocado	habríamos sofocado
sofocarías	sofocaríais	habrías sofocado	habríais sofocado
sofocaría	sofocarían	habría sofocado	habrían sofocado
6 presente de subjuntivo		13 perfecto de subjuntivo	
sofoque	sofoquemos	haya sofocado	hayamos sofocado
sofoques	sofoquéis	hayas sofocado	hayáis sofocado
sofoque	sofoquen	haya sofocado	hayan sofocado
7 imperfecto de subjuntivo		14 pluscuamperfecto de subjuntivo	
sofocara	sofocáramos	hubiera sofocado	hubiéramos sofocado
sofocaras	sofocarais	hubieras sofocado	hubierais sofocado
sofocara	sofocaran	hubiera sofocado	hubieran sofocado
OR		OR	
sofocase	sofocásemos	hubiese sofocado	hubiésemos sofocado
sofocases	sofocaseis	hubieses sofocado	hubieseis sofocado
sofocase	sofocasen	hubiese sofocado	hubiesen sofocado

S

imperativo	
—	sofoquemos
sofoca; no sofoques	sofocad; no sofoquéis
sofoque	sofoquen

Words and expressions related to this verb
sofocarse   to get out of breath
sofocarse por   to get excited over
sofocador, sofocadora   stifling, stuffy

la sofocación   suffocation, choking
sofocante   suffocating, stifling
el sofoco   suffocation

Review the principal parts of important Spanish verbs on pages 9–10.

The subject pronouns are found on page 93.

to sob, to whimper

Regular **-ar** verb endings with spelling change: **z** becomes **c** before **e**

The Seven Simple Tenses		The Seven Compound Tenses	
Singular	Plural	Singular	Plural
1 presente de indicativo		8 perfecto de indicativo	
sollozo	sollozamos	he sollozado	hemos sollozado
sollozas	sollozáis	has sollozado	habéis sollozado
solloza	sollozan	ha sollozado	han sollozado
2 imperfecto de indicativo		9 pluscuamperfecto de indicativo	
sollozaba	sollozábamos	había sollozado	habíamos sollozado
sollozabas	sollozabais	habías sollozado	habíais sollozado
sollozaba	sollozaban	había sollozado	habían sollozado
3 pretérito		10 pretérito anterior	
sollocé	sollozamos	hube sollozado	hubimos sollozado
sollozaste	sollozasteis	hubiste sollozado	hubisteis sollozado
sollozó	sollozaron	hubo sollozado	hubieron sollozado
4 futuro		11 futuro perfecto	
sollozaré	sollozaremos	habré sollozado	habremos sollozado
sollozarás	sollozaréis	habrás sollozado	habréis sollozado
sollozará	sollozarán	habrá sollozado	habrán sollozado
5 potencial simple		12 potencial compuesto	
sollozaría	sollozaríamos	habría sollozado	habríamos sollozado
sollozarías	sollozaríais	habrías sollozado	habríais sollozado
sollozaría	sollozarían	habría sollozado	habrían sollozado
6 presente de subjuntivo		13 perfecto de subjuntivo	
solloce	sollocemos	haya sollozado	hayamos sollozado
solloces	sollocéis	hayas sollozado	hayáis sollozado
solloce	sollocen	haya sollozado	hayan sollozado
7 imperfecto de subjuntivo		14 pluscuamperfecto de subjuntivo	
sollozara	sollozáramos	hubiera sollozado	hubiéramos sollozado
sollozaras	sollozarais	hubieras sollozado	hubierais sollozado
sollozara	sollozaran	hubiera sollozado	hubieran sollozado
OR		OR	
sollozase	sollozásemos	hubiese sollozado	hubiésemos sollozado
sollozases	sollozaseis	hubieses sollozado	hubieseis sollozado
sollozase	sollozasen	hubiese sollozado	hubiesen sollozado

imperativo	
—	sollocemos
solloza; no solloces	sollozad; no sollocéis
solloce	sollocen

Words related to this verb
un sollozo   sob
estallar en sollozos   to burst into sobs

sollozante   sobbing

Can't find the verb you're looking for?
Check the back pages of this book for a list of over 2,100 additional verbs!

Regular **-er** verb   to subdue, to subject, to surrender, to submit

The Seven Simple Tenses		The Seven Compound Tenses	
Singular	Plural	Singular	Plural
1 presente de indicativo		**8 perfecto de indicativo**	
someto	**sometemos**	**he sometido**	**hemos sometido**
sometes	**sometéis**	**has sometido**	**habéis sometido**
somete	**someten**	**ha sometido**	**han sometido**
2 imperfecto de indicativo		**9 pluscuamperfecto de indicativo**	
sometía	**sometíamos**	**había sometido**	**habíamos sometido**
sometías	**sometíais**	**habías sometido**	**habíais sometido**
sometía	**sometían**	**había sometido**	**habían sometido**
3 pretérito		**10 pretérito anterior**	
sometí	**sometimos**	**hube sometido**	**hubimos sometido**
sometiste	**sometisteis**	**hubiste sometido**	**hubisteis sometido**
sometió	**sometieron**	**hubo sometido**	**hubieron sometido**
4 futuro		**11 futuro perfecto**	
someteré	**someteremos**	**habré sometido**	**habremos sometido**
someterás	**someteréis**	**habrás sometido**	**habréis sometido**
someterá	**someterán**	**habrá sometido**	**habrán sometido**
5 potencial simple		**12 potencial compuesto**	
sometería	**someteríamos**	**habría sometido**	**habríamos sometido**
someterías	**someteríais**	**habrías sometido**	**habríais sometido**
sometería	**someterían**	**habría sometido**	**habrían sometido**
6 presente de subjuntivo		**13 perfecto de subjuntivo**	
someta	**sometamos**	**haya sometido**	**hayamos sometido**
sometas	**sometáis**	**hayas sometido**	**hayáis sometido**
someta	**sometan**	**haya sometido**	**hayan sometido**
7 imperfecto de subjuntivo		**14 pluscuamperfecto de subjuntivo**	
sometiera	**sometiéramos**	**hubiera sometido**	**hubiéramos sometido**
sometieras	**sometierais**	**hubieras sometido**	**hubierais sometido**
sometiera	**sometieran**	**hubiera sometido**	**hubieran sometido**
OR		OR	
sometiese	**sometiésemos**	**hubiese sometido**	**hubiésemos sometido**
sometieses	**sometieseis**	**hubieses sometido**	**hubieseis sometido**
sometiese	**sometiesen**	**hubiese sometido**	**hubiesen sometido**

S

imperativo

—	**sometamos**
somete; no sometas	**someted; no sometáis**
someta	**sometan**

Words and expressions related to this verb

someterse   to surrender, to humble oneself
sometido, sometida   submissive, docile
la sumisión   submission

el sometimiento   submission
someter la renuncia   to resign
someter a prueba   to put to the test

Don't forget to study the section on defective and impersonal verbs. It's right after this main list.

The subject pronouns are found on page 93.   **583**

to ring, to echo, to resound, to sound Regular **-ar** verb endings with stem change: Tenses 1, 6, Imperative

The Seven Simple Tenses		The Seven Compound Tenses	
Singular	Plural	Singular	Plural
1 presente de indicativo		8 perfecto de indicativo	
sueno	sonamos	he sonado	hemos sonado
suenas	sonáis	has sonado	habéis sonado
suena	suenan	ha sonado	han sonado
2 imperfecto de indicativo		9 pluscuamperfecto de indicativo	
sonaba	sonábamos	había sonado	habíamos sonado
sonabas	sonabais	habías sonado	habíais sonado
sonaba	sonaban	había sonado	habían sonado
3 pretérito		10 pretérito anterior	
soné	sonamos	hube sonado	hubimos sonado
sonaste	sonasteis	hubiste sonado	hubisteis sonado
sonó	sonaron	hubo sonado	hubieron sonado
4 futuro		11 futuro perfecto	
sonaré	sonaremos	habré sonado	habremos sonado
sonarás	sonaréis	habrás sonado	habréis sonado
sonará	sonarán	habrá sonado	habrán sonado
5 potencial simple		12 potencial compuesto	
sonaría	sonaríamos	habría sonado	habríamos sonado
sonarías	sonaríais	habrías sonado	habríais sonado
sonaría	sonarían	habría sonado	habrían sonado
6 presente de subjuntivo		13 perfecto de subjuntivo	
suene	sonemos	haya sonado	hayamos sonado
suenes	sonéis	hayas sonado	hayáis sonado
suene	suenen	haya sonado	hayan sonado
7 imperfecto de subjuntivo		14 pluscuamperfecto de subjuntivo	
sonara	sonáramos	hubiera sonado	hubiéramos sonado
sonaras	sonarais	hubieras sonado	hubierais sonado
sonara	sonaran	hubiera sonado	hubieran sonado
OR		OR	
sonase	sonásemos	hubiese sonado	hubiésemos sonado
sonases	sonaseis	hubieses sonado	hubieseis sonado
sonase	sonasen	hubiese sonado	hubiesen sonado

	imperativo	
—		sonemos
suena; no suenes		sonad; no sonéis
suene		suenen

Words and expressions related to this verb
sonar a to seem like
sonarse (las narices) to blow one's nose
sonante sonant, sonorous, sounding
el sonar sonar

una sonata sonata
una sonatina sonatina
sonar la alarma to ring the alarm
el sonido sound

Check out the verb drills and verb tests with answers explained on pages 45–91.

Regular **-ar** verb endings with stem　　　　　　　　to dream
change: Tenses 1, 6, Imperative

The Seven Simple Tenses		The Seven Compound Tenses	
Singular	Plural	Singular	Plural
1　presente de indicativo		8　perfecto de indicativo	
sueño	soñamos	he soñado	hemos soñado
sueñas	soñáis	has soñado	habéis soñado
sueña	sueñan	ha soñado	han soñado
2　imperfecto de indicativo		9　pluscuamperfecto de indicativo	
soñaba	soñábamos	había soñado	habíamos soñado
soñabas	soñabais	habías soñado	habíais soñado
soñaba	soñaban	había soñado	habían soñado
3　pretérito		10　pretérito anterior	
soñé	soñamos	hube soñado	hubimos soñado
soñaste	soñasteis	hubiste soñado	hubisteis soñado
soñó	soñaron	hubo soñado	hubieron soñado
4　futuro		11　futuro perfecto	
soñaré	soñaremos	habré soñado	habremos soñado
soñarás	soñaréis	habrás soñado	habréis soñado
soñará	soñarán	habrá soñado	habrán soñado
5　potencial simple		12　potencial compuesto	
soñaría	soñaríamos	habría soñado	habríamos soñado
soñarías	soñaríais	habrías soñado	habríais soñado
soñaría	soñarían	habría soñado	habrían soñado
6　presente de subjuntivo		13　perfecto de subjuntivo	
sueñe	soñemos	haya soñado	hayamos soñado
sueñes	soñéis	hayas soñado	hayáis soñado
sueñe	sueñen	haya soñado	hayan soñado
7　imperfecto de subjuntivo		14　pluscuamperfecto de subjuntivo	
soñara	soñáramos	hubiera soñado	hubiéramos soñado
soñaras	soñarais	hubieras soñado	hubierais soñado
soñara	soñaran	hubiera soñado	hubieran soñado
OR		OR	
soñase	soñásemos	hubiese soñado	hubiésemos soñado
soñases	soñaseis	hubieses soñado	hubieseis soñado
soñase	soñasen	hubiese soñado	hubiesen soñado

imperativo

—	soñemos
sueña; no sueñes	soñad; no soñéis
sueñe	sueñen

Words and expressions related to this verb

soñar con　to dream of
soñar despierto　to daydream
soñador, soñadora　dreamer
el sueño　sleep, dream
el insomnio　insomnia

tener sueño　to be sleepy
un sueño hecho realidad　a dream come true
sueño pesado　sound sleep
echar un sueño　to take a nap
el sonámbulo (somnámbulo)　sleepwalker

Get acquainted with what preposition goes with what verb on pages 669–677.

The subject pronouns are found on page 93.
585

sonreír (447)

Gerundio sonriendo **Part. pas. sonreído**

to smile

The Seven Simple Tenses

The Seven Compound Tenses

Singular	Plural	Singular	Plural
1 presente de indicativo		**8 perfecto de indicativo**	
sonrío	sonreímos	he sonreído	hemos sonreído
sonríes	sonreís	has sonreído	habéis sonreído
sonríe	sonríen	ha sonreído	han sonreído
2 imperfecto de indicativo		**9 pluscuamperfecto de indicativo**	
sonreía	sonreíamos	había sonreído	habíamos sonreído
sonreías	sonreíais	habías sonreído	habíais sonreído
sonreía	sonreían	había sonreído	habían sonreído
3 pretérito		**10 pretérito anterior**	
sonreí	sonreímos	hube sonreído	hubimos sonreído
sonreíste	sonreísteis	hubiste sonreído	hubisteis sonreído
sonrió	sonrieron	hubo sonreído	hubieron sonreído
4 futuro		**11 futuro perfecto**	
sonreiré	sonreiremos	habré sonreído	habremos sonreído
sonreirás	sonreiréis	habrás sonreído	habréis sonreído
sonreirá	sonreirán	habrá sonreído	habrán sonreído
5 potencial simple		**12 potencial compuesto**	
sonreiría	sonreiríamos	habría sonreído	habríamos sonreído
sonreirías	sonreiríais	habrías sonreído	habríais sonreído
sonreiría	sonreirían	habría sonreído	habrían sonreído
6 presente de subjuntivo		**13 perfecto de subjuntivo**	
sonría	sonriamos	haya sonreído	hayamos sonreído
sonrías	sonriáis	hayas sonreído	hayáis sonreído
sonría	sonrían	haya sonreído	hayan sonreído
7 imperfecto de subjuntivo		**14 pluscuamperfecto de subjuntivo**	
sonriera	sonriéramos	hubiera sonreído	hubiéramos sonreído
sonrieras	sonrierais	hubieras sonreído	hubierais sonreído
sonriera	sonrieran	hubiera sonreído	hubieran sonreído
OR		OR	
sonriese	sonriésemos	hubiese sonreído	hubiésemos sonreído
sonrieses	sonrieseis	hubieses sonreído	hubieseis sonreído
sonriese	sonriesen	hubiese sonreído	hubiesen sonreído

	imperativo
—	sonriamos
sonríe; no sonrías	sonreíd; no sonriáis
sonría	sonrían

Words and expressions related to this verb

sonriente   smiling; **La Gioconda tiene una sonrisa bonita**   The Mona Lisa has a pretty smile.
la sonrisa   smile   **no perder la sonrisa**   not to lose a smile; keep smiling

For additional words and expressions related to this verb, see **reír** and **reírse.**

Get acquainted with what preposition goes with what verb on pages 669–677.

Regular **-ar** verb   to blow, to blow out

The Seven Simple Tenses		The Seven Compound Tenses	
Singular	Plural	Singular	Plural
1 presente de indicativo		8 perfecto de indicativo	
soplo	soplamos	he soplado	hemos soplado
soplas	sopláis	has soplado	habéis soplado
sopla	soplan	ha soplado	han soplado
2 imperfecto de indicativo		9 pluscuamperfecto de indicativo	
soplaba	soplábamos	había soplado	habíamos soplado
soplabas	soplabais	habías soplado	habíais soplado
soplaba	soplaban	había soplado	habían soplado
3 pretérito		10 pretérito anterior	
soplé	soplamos	hube soplado	hubimos soplado
soplaste	soplasteis	hubiste soplado	hubisteis soplado
sopló	soplaron	hubo soplado	hubieron soplado
4 futuro		11 futuro perfecto	
soplaré	soplaremos	habré soplado	habremos soplado
soplarás	soplaréis	habrás soplado	habréis soplado
soplará	soplarán	habrá soplado	habrán soplado
5 potencial simple		12 potencial compuesto	
soplaría	soplaríamos	habría soplado	habríamos soplado
soplarías	soplaríais	habrías soplado	habríais soplado
soplaría	soplarían	habría soplado	habrían soplado
6 presente de subjuntivo		13 perfecto de subjuntivo	
sople	soplemos	haya soplado	hayamos soplado
soples	sopléis	hayas soplado	hayáis soplado
sople	soplen	haya soplado	hayan soplado
7 imperfecto de subjuntivo		14 pluscuamperfecto de subjuntivo	
soplara	sopláramos	hubiera soplado	hubiéramos soplado
soplaras	soplarais	hubieras soplado	hubierais soplado
soplara	soplaran	hubiera soplado	hubieran soplado
OR		OR	
soplase	soplásemos	hubiese soplado	hubiésemos soplado
soplases	soplaseis	hubieses soplado	hubieseis soplado
soplase	soplasen	hubiese soplado	hubiesen soplado

S

imperativo

—	soplemos
sopla; no soples	**soplad; no sopléis**
sople	**soplen**

Words and expressions related to this verb
un soplamocos   a punch in the nose
una sopladura   air hole
un soplón, una soplona   tattletale
saber de qué lado sopla el viento
   to know which way the wind blows

un soplete atomizador   paint sprayer
un soplo   puff; **en un soplo**   in a jiffy
soplar a la policía   to tip off the police
soplar la vela   to blow out the candle
soplar con la boca   to blow with the mouth
el viento sopla   the wind blows

The subject pronouns are found on page 93.

587

to surprise, to astonish   Regular **-er** verb

The Seven Simple Tenses		The Seven Compound Tenses	
Singular	Plural	Singular	Plural
1 presente de indicativo		8 perfecto de indicativo	
sorprendo	**sorprendemos**	**he sorprendido**	**hemos sorprendido**
sorprendes	**sorprendéis**	**has sorprendido**	**habéis sorprendido**
sorprende	**sorprenden**	**ha sorprendido**	**han sorprendido**
2 imperfecto de indicativo		9 pluscuamperfecto de indicativo	
sorprendía	**sorprendíamos**	**había sorprendido**	**habíamos sorprendido**
sorprendías	**sorprendíais**	**habías sorprendido**	**habíais sorprendido**
sorprendía	**sorprendían**	**había sorprendido**	**habían sorprendido**
3 pretérito		10 pretérito anterior	
sorprendí	**sorprendimos**	**hube sorprendido**	**hubimos sorprendido**
sorprendiste	**sorprendisteis**	**hubiste sorprendido**	**hubisteis sorprendido**
sorprendió	**sorprendieron**	**hubo sorprendido**	**hubieron sorprendido**
4 futuro		11 futuro perfecto	
sorprenderé	**sorprenderemos**	**habré sorprendido**	**habremos sorprendido**
sorprenderás	**sorprenderéis**	**habrás sorprendido**	**habréis sorprendido**
sorprenderá	**sorprenderán**	**habrá sorprendido**	**habrán sorprendido**
5 potencial simple		12 potencial compuesto	
sorprendería	**sorprenderíamos**	**habría sorprendido**	**habríamos sorprendido**
sorprenderías	**sorprenderíais**	**habrías sorprendido**	**habríais sorprendido**
sorprendería	**sorprenderían**	**habría sorprendido**	**habrían sorprendido**
6 presente de subjuntivo		13 perfecto de subjuntivo	
sorprenda	**sorprendamos**	**haya sorprendido**	**hayamos sorprendido**
sorprendas	**sorprendáis**	**hayas sorprendido**	**hayáis sorprendido**
sorprenda	**sorprendan**	**haya sorprendido**	**hayan sorprendido**
7 imperfecto de subjuntivo		14 pluscuamperfecto de subjuntivo	
sorprendiera	**sorprendiéramos**	**hubiera sorprendido**	**hubiéramos sorprendido**
sorprendieras	**sorprendierais**	**hubieras sorprendido**	**hubierais sorprendido**
sorprendiera	**sorprendieran**	**hubiera sorprendido**	**hubieran sorprendido**
OR		OR	
sorprendiese	**sorprendiésemos**	**hubiese sorprendido**	**hubiésemos sorprendido**
sorprendieses	**sorprendieseis**	**hubieses sorprendido**	**hubieseis sorprendido**
sorprendiese	**sorprendiesen**	**hubiese sorprendido**	**hubiesen sorprendido**

imperativo

—	**sorprendamos**
sorprende; no sorprendas	**sorprended; no sorprendáis**
sorprenda	**sorprendan**

Words and expressions related to this verb

sorprender en el hecho   to catch in the act
una sorpresa   surprise
tomar por sorpresa   to take by surprise

coger de sorpresa   to take by surprise
sorprendente   surprising
sorprenderse   to be surprised, astonished

> Get your feet wet with verbs used in weather expressions on page 668.

The Seven Simple Tenses		The Seven Compound Tenses	

Singular	Plural	Singular	Plural
1 presente de indicativo		8 perfecto de indicativo	
sospecho	sospechamos	he sospechado	hemos sospechado
sospechas	sospecháis	has sospechado	habéis sospechado
sospecha	sospechan	ha sospechado	han sospechado
2 imperfecto de indicativo		9 pluscuamperfecto de indicativo	
sospechaba	sospechábamos	había sospechado	habíamos sospechado
sospechabas	sospechabais	habías sospechado	habíais sospechado
sospechaba	sospechaban	había sospechado	habían sospechado
3 pretérito		10 pretérito anterior	
sospeché	sospechamos	hube sospechado	hubimos sospechado
sospechaste	sospechasteis	hubiste sospechado	hubisteis sospechado
sospechó	sospecharon	hubo sospechado	hubieron sospechado
4 futuro		11 futuro perfecto	
sospecharé	sospecharemos	habré sospechado	habremos sospechado
sospecharás	sospecharéis	habrás sospechado	habréis sospechado
sospechará	sospecharán	habrá sospechado	habrán sospechado
5 potencial simple		12 potencial compuesto	
sospecharía	sospecharíamos	habría sospechado	habríamos sospechado
sospecharías	sospecharíais	habrías sospechado	habríais sospechado
sospecharía	sospecharían	habría sospechado	habrían sospechado
6 presente de subjuntivo		13 perfecto de subjuntivo	
sospeche	sospechemos	haya sospechado	hayamos sospechado
sospeches	sospechéis	hayas sospechado	hayáis sospechado
sospeche	sospechen	haya sospechado	hayan sospechado
7 imperfecto de subjuntivo		14 pluscuamperfecto de subjuntivo	
sospechara	sospecháramos	hubiera sospechado	hubiéramos sospechado
sospecharas	sospecharais	hubieras sospechado	hubierais sospechado
sospechara	sospecharan	hubiera sospechado	hubieran sospechado
OR		OR	
sospechase	sospechásemos	hubiese sospechado	hubiésemos sospechado
sospechases	sospechaseis	hubieses sospechado	hubieseis sospechado
sospechase	sospechasen	hubiese sospechado	hubiesen sospechado

S

imperativo	
—	sospechemos
sospecha; no sospeches	sospechad; no sospechéis
sospeche	sospechen

Words related to this verb
sospechar de   to suspect
sospechable   suspicious

la sospecha   suspicion, doubt
sospechoso, sospechosa   suspect

Do you need more drills? Have fun with the *501 Spanish Verbs* CD-ROM!

to sustain, to support, to maintain, to uphold   Irregular verb

The Seven Simple Tenses		The Seven Compound Tenses	
Singular	Plural	Singular	Plural
1 presente de indicativo		8 perfecto de indicativo	
sostengo	sostenemos	he sostenido	hemos sostenido
sostienes	sostenéis	has sostenido	habéis sostenido
sostiene	sostienen	ha sostenido	han sostenido
2 imperfecto de indicativo		9 pluscuamperfecto de indicativo	
sostenía	sosteníamos	había sostenido	habíamos sostenido
sostenías	sosteníais	habías sostenido	habíais sostenido
sostenía	sostenían	había sostenido	habían sostenido
3 pretérito		10 pretérito anterior	
sostuve	sostuvimos	hube sostenido	hubimos sostenido
sostuviste	sostuvisteis	hubiste sostenido	hubisteis sostenido
sostuvo	sostuvieron	hubo sostenido	hubieron sostenido
4 futuro		11 futuro perfecto	
sostendré	sostendremos	habré sostenido	habremos sostenido
sostendrás	sostendréis	habrás sostenido	habréis sostenido
sostendrá	sostendrán	habrá sostenido	habrán sostenido
5 potencial simple		12 potencial compuesto	
sostendría	sostendríamos	habría sostenido	habríamos sostenido
sostendrías	sostendríais	habrías sostenido	habríais sostenido
sostendría	sostendrían	habría sostenido	habrían sostenido
6 presente de subjuntivo		13 perfecto de subjuntivo	
sostenga	sostengamos	haya sostenido	hayamos sostenido
sostengas	sostengáis	hayas sostenido	hayáis sostenido
sostenga	sostengan	haya sostenido	hayan sostenido
7 imperfecto de subjuntivo		14 pluscuamperfecto de subjuntivo	
sostuviera	sostuviéramos	hubiera sostenido	hubiéramos sostenido
sostuvieras	sostuvierais	hubieras sostenido	hubierais sostenido
sostuviera	sostuvieran	hubiera sostenido	hubieran sostenido
OR		OR	
sostuviese	sostuviésemos	hubiese sostenido	hubiésemos sostenido
sostuvieses	sostuvieseis	hubieses sostenido	hubieseis sostenido
sostuviese	sostuviesen	hubiese sostenido	hubiesen sostenido

	imperativo	
—		sostengamos
sosten; no sostengas		sostened; no sostengáis
sostenga		sostengan

Words related to this verb

el sostén, el sostenimiento support, sustenance
sosteniente supporting, sustaining

sostenido, sostenida supported, sustained
el sostenedor, la sostenedora supporter
sostenerse to support or maintain oneself

For other words and expressions related to this verb, see **tener.**

Regular **-ir** verb

to go up, to come up, to climb, to rise,
to mount, to get on (a train, bus, etc.)

The Seven Simple Tenses		The Seven Compound Tenses	
Singular	Plural	Singular	Plural
1 presente de indicativo		8 perfecto de indicativo	
subo	subimos	he subido	hemos subido
subes	subís	has subido	habéis subido
sube	suben	ha subido	han subido
2 imperfecto de indicativo		9 pluscuamperfecto de indicativo	
subía	subíamos	había subido	habíamos subido
subías	subíais	habías subido	habíais subido
subía	subían	había subido	habían subido
3 pretérito		10 pretérito anterior	
subí	subimos	hube subido	hubimos subido
subiste	subisteis	hubiste subido	hubisteis subido
subió	subieron	hubo subido	hubieron subido
4 futuro		11 futuro perfecto	
subiré	subiremos	habré subido	habremos subido
subirás	subiréis	habrás subido	habréis subido
subirá	subirán	habrá subido	habrán subido
5 potencial simple		12 potencial compuesto	
subiría	subiríamos	habría subido	habríamos subido
subirías	subiríais	habrías subido	habríais subido
subiría	subirían	habría subido	habrían subido
6 presente de subjuntivo		13 perfecto de subjuntivo	
suba	subamos	haya subido	hayamos subido
subas	subáis	hayas subido	hayáis subido
suba	suban	haya subido	hayan subido
7 imperfecto de subjuntivo		14 pluscuamperfecto de subjuntivo	
subiera	subiéramos	hubiera subido	hubiéramos subido
subieras	subierais	hubieras subido	hubierais subido
subiera	subieran	hubiera subido	hubieran subido
OR		OR	
subiese	subiésemos	hubiese subido	hubiésemos subido
subieses	subieseis	hubieses subido	hubieseis subido
subiese	subiesen	hubiese subido	hubiesen subido

S

imperativo	
—	subamos
sube; no subas	subid; no subáis
suba	suban

Words related to this verb
subir a   to get on (a train, etc.)
subir pasajeros   to take on passengers
súbitamente, subitáneamente   all of a
    sudden, suddenly
la subida   ascent, increase

súbito, súbita   sudden
subirse a una escalera   to climb a ladder
Han subido los precios.   Prices have gone up.
subir la voz   to raise one's voice

The subject pronouns are found on page 93.

591

to underline, to underscore, to emphasize   Regular **-ar** verb

The Seven Simple Tenses		The Seven Compound Tenses	
Singular	Plural	Singular	Plural

1 presente de indicativo

		8 perfecto de indicativo	
subrayo	**subrayamos**	**he subrayado**	**hemos subrayado**
subrayas	**subrayáis**	**has subrayado**	**habéis subrayado**
subraya	**subrayan**	**ha subrayado**	**han subrayado**

2 imperfecto de indicativo

		9 pluscuamperfecto de indicativo	
subrayaba	**subrayábamos**	**había subrayado**	**habíamos subrayado**
subrayabas	**subrayabais**	**habías subrayado**	**habíais subrayado**
subrayaba	**subrayaban**	**había subrayado**	**habían subrayado**

3 pretérito

		10 pretérito anterior	
subrayé	**subrayamos**	**hube subrayado**	**hubimos subrayado**
subrayaste	**subrayasteis**	**hubiste subrayado**	**hubisteis subrayado**
subrayó	**subrayaron**	**hubo subrayado**	**hubieron subrayado**

4 futuro

		11 futuro perfecto	
subrayaré	**subrayaremos**	**habré subrayado**	**habremos subrayado**
subrayarás	**subrayaréis**	**habrás subrayado**	**habréis subrayado**
subrayará	**subrayarán**	**habrá subrayado**	**habrán subrayado**

5 potencial simple

		12 potencial compuesto	
subrayaría	**subrayaríamos**	**habría subrayado**	**habríamos subrayado**
subrayarías	**subrayaríais**	**habrías subrayado**	**habríais subrayado**
subrayaría	**subrayarían**	**habría subrayado**	**habrían subrayado**

6 presente de subjuntivo

		13 perfecto de subjuntivo	
subraye	**subrayemos**	**haya subrayado**	**hayamos subrayado**
subrayes	**subrayéis**	**hayas subrayado**	**hayáis subrayado**
subraye	**subrayen**	**haya subrayado**	**hayan subrayado**

7 imperfecto de subjuntivo

		14 pluscuamperfecto de subjuntivo	
subrayara	**subrayáramos**	**hubiera subrayado**	**hubiéramos subrayado**
subrayaras	**subrayarais**	**hubieras subrayado**	**hubierais subrayado**
subrayara	**subrayaran**	**hubiera subrayado**	**hubieran subrayado**
OR		OR	
subrayase	**subrayásemos**	**hubiese subrayado**	**hubiésemos subrayado**
subrayases	**subrayaseis**	**hubieses subrayado**	**hubieseis subrayado**
subrayase	**subrayasen**	**hubiese subrayado**	**hubiesen subrayado**

imperativo

—	**subrayemos**
subraya; no subrayes	**subrayad; no subrayéis**
subraye	**subrayen**

Words and expressions related to this verb
subrayado, subrayada underlined, underlining   **el papel rayado** lined paper
rayar to draw lines, to rule or line paper, to cross out   **rayos X** X-rays
un rayo de sol sunbeam; **un rayo lunar** moonbeam

Can't remember the Spanish verb you need?
Check the back pages of this book for the English-Spanish verb index!

Regular **-ir** verb; irregular past participle   to subscribe, to agree to, to sign

The Seven Simple Tenses		The Seven Compound Tenses	
Singular	Plural	Singular	Plural
1 presente de indicativo		8 perfecto de indicativo	
subscribo	**subscribimos**	**he subscrito**	**hemos subscrito**
subscribes	**subscribís**	**has subscrito**	**habéis subscrito**
subscribe	**subscriben**	**ha subscrito**	**han subscrito**
2 imperfecto de indicativo		9 pluscuamperfecto de indicativo	
subscribía	**subscribíamos**	**había subscrito**	**habíamos subscrito**
subscribías	**subscribíais**	**habías subscrito**	**habíais subscrito**
subscribía	**subscribían**	**había subscrito**	**habían subscrito**
3 pretérito		10 pretérito anterior	
subscribí	**subscribimos**	**hube subscrito**	**hubimos subscrito**
subscribiste	**subscribisteis**	**hubiste subscrito**	**hubisteis subscrito**
subscribió	**subscribieron**	**hubo subscrito**	**hubieron subscrito**
4 futuro		11 futuro perfecto	
subscribiré	**subscribiremos**	**habré subscrito**	**habremos subscrito**
subscribirás	**subscribiréis**	**habrás subscrito**	**habréis subscrito**
subscribirá	**subscribirán**	**habrá subscrito**	**habrán subscrito**
5 potencial simple		12 potencial compuesto	
subscribiría	**subscribiríamos**	**habría subscrito**	**habríamos subscrito**
subscribirías	**subscribiríais**	**habrías subscrito**	**habríais subscrito**
subscribiría	**subscribirían**	**habría subscrito**	**habrían subscrito**
6 presente de subjuntivo		13 perfecto de subjuntivo	
subscriba	**subscribamos**	**haya subscrito**	**hayamos subscrito**
subscribas	**subscribáis**	**hayas subscrito**	**hayáis subscrito**
subscriba	**subscriban**	**haya subscrito**	**hayan subscrito**
7 imperfecto de subjuntivo		14 pluscuamperfecto de subjuntivo	
subscribiera	**subscribiéramos**	**hubiera subscrito**	**hubiéramos subscrito**
subscribieras	**subscribierais**	**hubieras subscrito**	**hubierais subscrito**
subscribiera	**subscribieran**	**hubiera subscrito**	**hubieran subscrito**
OR		OR	
subscribiese	**subscribiésemos**	**hubiese subscrito**	**hubiésemos subscrito**
subscribieses	**subscribieseis**	**hubieses subscrito**	**hubieseis subscrito**
subscribiese	**subscribiesen**	**hubiese subscrito**	**hubiesen subscrito**

imperativo

—	**subscribamos**
subscribe; no subscribas	**subscribid; no subscribáis**
subscriba	**subscriban**

S

Words and expressions related to this verb
subscribirse a   to subscribe to (a magazine, etc.)   **subscriptor, subscriptora**   subscriber
la subscripción   subscription   **suscribir** (variant of **subscribir**)
subscrito, subscrita   subscribed, signed   to subscribe

For other words and expressions related to this verb, see **describir** and **escribir**.

The subject pronouns are found on page 93.
                                                                                            593

to suffer, to endure, to bear, to undergo   Regular **-ir** verb

The Seven Simple Tenses		The Seven Compound Tenses	
Singular	Plural	Singular	Plural
1 presente de indicativo		8 perfecto de indicativo	
sufro	**sufrimos**	**he sufrido**	**hemos sufrido**
sufres	**sufrís**	**has sufrido**	**habéis sufrido**
sufre	**sufren**	**ha sufrido**	**han sufrido**
2 imperfecto de indicativo		9 pluscuamperfecto de indicativo	
sufría	**sufríamos**	**había sufrido**	**habíamos sufrido**
sufrías	**sufríais**	**habías sufrido**	**habíais sufrido**
sufría	**sufrían**	**había sufrido**	**habían sufrido**
3 pretérito		10 pretérito anterior	
sufrí	**sufrimos**	**hube sufrido**	**hubimos sufrido**
sufriste	**sufristeis**	**hubiste sufrido**	**hubisteis sufrido**
sufrió	**sufrieron**	**hubo sufrido**	**hubieron sufrido**
4 futuro		11 futuro perfecto	
sufriré	**sufriremos**	**habré sufrido**	**habremos sufrido**
sufrirás	**sufriréis**	**habrás sufrido**	**habréis sufrido**
sufrirá	**sufrirán**	**habrá sufrido**	**habrán sufrido**
5 potencial simple		12 potencial compuesto	
sufriría	**sufriríamos**	**habría sufrido**	**habríamos sufrido**
sufrirías	**sufriríais**	**habrías sufrido**	**habríais sufrido**
sufriría	**sufrirían**	**habría sufrido**	**habrían sufrido**
6 presente de subjuntivo		13 perfecto de subjuntivo	
sufra	**suframos**	**haya sufrido**	**hayamos sufrido**
sufras	**sufráis**	**hayas sufrido**	**hayáis sufrido**
sufra	**sufran**	**haya sufrido**	**hayan sufrido**
7 imperfecto de subjuntivo		14 pluscuamperfecto de subjuntivo	
sufriera	**sufriéramos**	**hubiera sufrido**	**hubiéramos sufrido**
sufrieras	**sufrierais**	**hubieras sufrido**	**hubierais sufrido**
sufriera	**sufrieran**	**hubiera sufrido**	**hubieran sufrido**
OR		OR	
sufriese	**sufriésemos**	**hubiese sufrido**	**hubiésemos sufrido**
sufrieses	**sufrieseis**	**hubieses sufrido**	**hubieseis sufrido**
sufriese	**sufriesen**	**hubiese sufrido**	**hubiesen sufrido**

	imperativo	
—		**suframos**
sufre; no sufras		**sufrid; no sufráis**
sufra		**sufran**

Words and expressions related to this verb
el sufrimiento suffering
sufrible sufferable
insufrible insufferable
sufridor, sufridora suffering

sufrir una multa to be given a fine
sufrir un accidente to have an accident
sufrir una pérdida to suffer a loss

If you don't know the Spanish verb for the English verb you have in mind, look it up in the index on pages 682–706.

Regular **-ir** verb endings with stem change: to hint, to insinuate, to suggest
Tenses 1, 3, 6, 7, Imperative, Gerundio

The Seven Simple Tenses		The Seven Compound Tenses	
Singular	Plural	Singular	Plural
1 presente de indicativo		**8 perfecto de indicativo**	
sugiero	sugerimos	he sugerido	hemos sugerido
sugieres	sugerís	has sugerido	habéis sugerido
sugiere	sugieren	ha sugerido	han sugerido
2 imperfecto de indicativo		**9 pluscuamperfecto de indicativo**	
sugería	sugeríamos	había sugerido	habíamos sugerido
sugerías	sugeríais	habías sugerido	habíais sugerido
sugería	sugerían	había sugerido	habían sugerido
3 pretérito		**10 pretérito anterior**	
sugerí	sugerimos	hube sugerido	hubimos sugerido
sugeriste	sugeristeis	hubiste sugerido	hubisteis sugerido
sugirió	sugirieron	hubo sugerido	hubieron sugerido
4 futuro		**11 futuro perfecto**	
sugeriré	sugeriremos	habré sugerido	habremos sugerido
sugerirás	sugeriréis	habrás sugerido	habréis sugerido
sugerirá	sugerirán	habrá sugerido	habrán sugerido
5 potencial simple		**12 potencial compuesto**	
sugeriría	sugeriríamos	habría sugerido	habríamos sugerido
sugerirías	sugeriríais	habrías sugerido	habríais sugerido
sugeriría	sugerirían	habría sugerido	habrían sugerido
6 presente de subjuntivo		**13 perfecto de subjuntivo**	
sugiera	sugiramos	haya sugerido	hayamos sugerido
sugieras	sugiráis	hayas sugerido	hayáis sugerido
sugiera	sugieran	haya sugerido	hayan sugerido
7 imperfecto de subjuntivo		**14 pluscuamperfecto de subjuntivo**	
sugiriera	sugiriéramos	hubiera sugerido	hubiéramos sugerido
sugirieras	sugirierais	hubieras sugerido	hubierais sugerido
sugiriera	sugirieran	hubiera sugerido	hubieran sugerido
OR		OR	
sugiriese	sugiriésemos	hubiese sugerido	hubiésemos sugerido
sugirieses	sugirieseis	hubieses sugerido	hubieseis sugerido
sugiriese	sugiriesen	hubiese sugerido	hubiesen sugerido

imperativo	
—	sugiramos
sugiere; no sugieras	sugerid; no sugiráis
sugiera	sugieran

Words and expressions related to this verb
una sugestión, una sugerencia   suggestion   **sugestivo, sugestiva**   suggestive
sugestionable   easily influenced   **sugerente**   suggestive

Can't find the verb you're looking for?
Check the back pages of this book for a list of over 2,100 additional verbs!

The subject pronouns are found on page 93.   **595**

to submerge, to plunge, to immerse, to sink	Regular **-ir** verb endings with spelling change: **g** becomes **j** before **a** or **o**
The Seven Simple Tenses	The Seven Compound Tenses

Singular	Plural	Singular	Plural
1 presente de indicativo		**8 perfecto de indicativo**	
sumerjo	sumergimos	he sumergido	hemos sumergido
sumerges	sumergís	has sumergido	habéis sumergido
sumerge	sumergen	ha sumergido	han sumergido
2 imperfecto de indicativo		**9 pluscuamperfecto de indicativo**	
sumergía	sumergíamos	había sumergido	habíamos sumergido
sumergías	sumergíais	habías sumergido	habíais sumergido
sumergía	sumergían	había sumergido	habían sumergido
3 pretérito		**10 pretérito anterior**	
sumergí	sumergimos	hube sumergido	hubimos sumergido
sumergiste	sumergisteis	hubiste sumergido	hubisteis sumergido
sumergió	sumergieron	hubo sumergido	hubieron sumergido
4 futuro		**11 futuro perfecto**	
sumergiré	sumergiremos	habré sumergido	habremos sumergido
sumergirás	sumergiréis	habrás sumergido	habréis sumergido
sumergirá	sumergirán	habrá sumergido	habrán sumergido
5 potencial simple		**12 potencial compuesto**	
sumergiría	sumergiríamos	habría sumergido	habríamos sumergido
sumergirías	sumergiríais	habrías sumergido	habríais sumergido
sumergiría	sumergirían	habría sumergido	habrían sumergido
6 presente de subjuntivo		**13 perfecto de subjuntivo**	
sumerja	sumerjamos	haya sumergido	hayamos sumergido
sumerjas	sumerjáis	hayas sumergido	hayáis sumergido
sumerja	sumerjan	haya sumergido	hayan sumergido
7 imperfecto de subjuntivo		**14 pluscuamperfecto de subjuntivo**	
sumergiera	sumergiéramos	hubiera sumergido	hubiéramos sumergido
sumergieras	sumergierais	hubieras sumergido	hubierais sumergido
sumergiera	sumergieran	hubiera sumergido	hubieran sumergido
OR		OR	
sumergiese	sumergiésemos	hubiese sumergido	hubiésemos sumergido
sumergieses	sumergieseis	hubieses sumergido	hubieseis sumergido
sumergiese	sumergiesen	hubiese sumergido	hubiesen sumergido

	imperativo	
—		sumerjamos
sumerge; no sumerjas		sumergid; no sumerjáis
sumerja		sumerjan

Words related to this verb

el sumergimiento submersion, sinking   **la sumersión** submersion
el sumergible submarine   **emerger** to emerge

> If you want to see a sample English verb fully conjugated in all the tenses, check out pages 11 and 12.

The Seven Simple Tenses		The Seven Compound Tenses	
Singular	Plural	Singular	Plural
1 presente de indicativo		**8 perfecto de indicativo**	
supongo	suponemos	he supuesto	hemos supuesto
supones	suponéis	has supuesto	habéis supuesto
supone	suponen	ha supuesto	han supuesto
2 imperfecto de indicativo		**9 pluscuamperfecto de indicativo**	
suponía	suponíamos	había supuesto	habíamos supuesto
suponías	suponíais	habías supuesto	habíais supuesto
suponía	suponían	había supuesto	habían supuesto
3 pretérito		**10 pretérito anterior**	
supuse	supusimos	hube supuesto	hubimos supuesto
supusiste	supusisteis	hubiste supuesto	hubisteis supuesto
supuso	supusieron	hubo supuesto	hubieron supuesto
4 futuro		**11 futuro perfecto**	
supondré	supondremos	habré supuesto	habremos supuesto
supondrás	supondréis	habrás supuesto	habréis supuesto
supondrá	supondrán	habrá supuesto	habrán supuesto
5 potencial simple		**12 potencial compuesto**	
supondría	supondríamos	habría supuesto	habríamos supuesto
supondrías	supondríais	habrías supuesto	habríais supuesto
supondría	supondrían	habría supuesto	habrían supuesto
6 presente de subjuntivo		**13 perfecto de subjuntivo**	
suponga	supongamos	haya supuesto	hayamos supuesto
supongas	supongáis	hayas supuesto	hayáis supuesto
suponga	supongan	haya supuesto	hayan supuesto
7 imperfecto de subjuntivo		**14 pluscuamperfecto de subjuntivo**	
supusiera	supusiéramos	hubiera supuesto	hubiéramos supuesto
supusieras	supusierais	hubieras supuesto	hubierais supuesto
supusiera	supusieran	hubiera supuesto	hubieran supuesto
OR		OR	
supusiese	supusiésemos	hubiese supuesto	hubiésemos supuesto
supusieses	supusieseis	hubieses supuesto	hubieseis supuesto
supusiese	supusiesen	hubiese supuesto	hubiesen supuesto

S

imperativo

—	supongamos
supón; no supongas	suponed; no supongáis
suponga	supongan

Words related to this verb
un suponer, una suposición   supposition   **proponer**   to propose
poner   to put   **por supuesto**   of course

For additional words and expressions related to this verb, see **poner, ponerse,** and **componer.**

suprimir (459) Gerundio **suprimiendo** Part. pas. **suprimido** (**supreso,** *as an adj.*)

to suppress, to abolish, to cancel (in mathematics),
to eliminate, to delete

Regular **-ir** verb

The Seven Simple Tenses		The Seven Compound Tenses	
Singular	Plural	Singular	Plural
1 presente de indicativo		8 perfecto de indicativo	
suprimo	suprimios	he suprimido	hemos suprimido
suprimes	suprimís	has suprimido	habéis suprimido
suprime	suprimen	ha suprimido	han suprimido
2 imperfecto de indicativo		9 pluscuamperfecto de indicativo	
suprimía	suprimíamos	había suprimido	habíamos suprimido
suprimías	suprimíais	habías suprimido	habíais suprimido
suprimía	suprimían	había suprimido	habían suprimido
3 pretérito		10 pretérito anterior	
suprimí	suprimimos	hube suprimido	hubimos suprimido
suprimiste	suprimisteis	hubiste suprimido	hubisteis suprimido
suprimió	suprimieron	hubo suprimido	hubieron suprimido
4 futuro		11 futuro perfecto	
suprimiré	suprimiremos	habré suprimido	habremos suprimido
suprimirás	suprimiréis	habrás suprimido	habréis suprimido
suprimirá	suprimirán	habrá suprimido	habrán suprimido
5 potencial simple		12 potencial compuesto	
suprimiría	suprimiríamos	habría suprimido	habríamos suprimido
suprimirías	suprimiríais	habrías suprimido	habríais suprimido
suprimiría	suprimirían	habría suprimido	habrían suprimido
6 presente de subjuntivo		13 perfecto de subjuntivo	
suprima	suprimamos	haya suprimido	hayamos suprimido
suprimas	suprimáis	hayas suprimido	hayáis suprimido
suprima	supriman	haya suprimido	hayan suprimido
7 imperfecto de subjuntivo		14 pluscuamperfecto de subjuntivo	
suprimiera	suprimiéramos	hubiera suprimido	hubiéramos suprimido
suprimieras	suprimierais	hubieras suprimido	hubierais suprimido
suprimiera	suprimieran	hubiera suprimido	hubieran suprimido
OR		OR	
suprimiese	suprimiésemos	hubiese suprimido	hubiésemos suprimido
suprimieses	suprimieseis	hubieses suprimido	hubieseis suprimido
suprimiese	suprimiesen	hubiese suprimido	hubiesen suprimido

imperativo	
—	suprimamos
suprime; no suprimas	suprimid; no suprimáis
suprima	supriman

Words related to this verb
la supresión suppression
suprimido, suprimida suppressed

suprimible suppressible
supreso, supresa suppressed

Do you need more drills? Have fun with the *501 Spanish Verbs* CD-ROM!

Regular **-ir** verb endings with spelling change: **g** becomes **j** before **a** or **o**

to surge, to spout up, to spurt up, to spring up, to arise, to appear, to emerge, to loom up

The Seven Simple Tenses		The Seven Compound Tenses	
Singular	Plural	Singular	Plural
1 presente de indicativo		8 perfecto de indicativo	
surjo	**surgimos**	**he surgido**	**hemos surgido**
surges	**surgís**	**has surgido**	**habéis surgido**
surge	**surgen**	**ha surgido**	**han surgido**
2 imperfecto de indicativo		9 pluscuamperfecto de indicativo	
surgía	**surgíamos**	**había surgido**	**habíamos surgido**
surgías	**surgíais**	**habías surgido**	**habíais surgido**
surgía	**surgían**	**había surgido**	**habían surgido**
3 pretérito		10 pretérito anterior	
surgí	**surgimos**	**hube surgido**	**hubimos surgido**
surgiste	**surgisteis**	**hubiste surgido**	**hubisteis surgido**
surgió	**surgieron**	**hubo surgido**	**hubieron surgido**
4 futuro		11 futuro perfecto	
surgiré	**surgiremos**	**habré surgido**	**habremos surgido**
surgirás	**surgiréis**	**habrás surgido**	**habréis surgido**
surgirá	**surgirán**	**habrá surgido**	**habrán surgido**
5 potencial simple		12 potencial compuesto	
surgiría	**surgiríamos**	**habría surgido**	**habríamos surgido**
surgirías	**surgiríais**	**habrías surgido**	**habríais surgido**
surgiría	**surgirían**	**habría surgido**	**habrían surgido**
6 presente de subjuntivo		13 perfecto de subjuntivo	
surja	**surjamos**	**haya surgido**	**hayamos surgido**
surjas	**surjáis**	**hayas surgido**	**hayáis surgido**
surja	**surjan**	**haya surgido**	**hayan surgido**
7 imperfecto de subjuntivo		14 pluscuamperfecto de subjuntivo	
surgiera	**surgiéramos**	**hubiera surgido**	**hubiéramos surgido**
surgieras	**surgierais**	**hubieras surgido**	**hubierais surgido**
surgiera	**surgieran**	**hubiera surgido**	**hubieran surgido**
OR		OR	
surgiese	**surgiésemos**	**hubiese surgido**	**hubiésemos surgido**
surgieses	**surgieseis**	**hubieses surgido**	**hubieseis surgido**
surgiese	**surgiesen**	**hubiese surgido**	**hubiesen surgido**

S

imperativo

—	**surjamos**
surge; no surjas	**surgid; no surjáis**
surja	**surjan**

Words related to this verb

surgente   surging, salient   **el resurgimiento**   reappearance, recovery
resurgir   to reappear

Este muchacho es muy grande; surge entre los otros muchachos.
This boy is very big; he towers over the other boys.

surgir   also has the meaning of *to anchor* (nautical)
el surgidor, la surgidora   person who anchors

599

The subject pronouns are found on page 93.

to sigh Regular **-ar** verb

The Seven Simple Tenses		The Seven Compound Tenses	
Singular	Plural	Singular	Plural
1 presente de indicativo		8 perfecto de indicativo	
suspiro	**suspiramos**	**he suspirado**	**hemos suspirado**
suspiras	**suspiráis**	**has suspirado**	**habéis suspirado**
suspira	**suspiran**	**ha suspirado**	**han suspirado**
2 imperfecto de indicativo		9 pluscuamperfecto de indicativo	
suspiraba	**suspirábamos**	**había suspirado**	**habíamos suspirado**
suspirabas	**suspirabais**	**habías suspirado**	**habíais suspirado**
suspiraba	**suspiraban**	**había suspirado**	**habían suspirado**
3 pretérito		10 pretérito anterior	
suspiré	**suspiramos**	**hube suspirado**	**hubimos suspirado**
suspiraste	**suspirasteis**	**hubiste suspirado**	**hubisteis suspirado**
suspiró	**suspiraron**	**hubo suspirado**	**hubieron suspirado**
4 futuro		11 futuro perfecto	
suspiraré	**suspiraremos**	**habré suspirado**	**habremos suspirado**
suspirarás	**suspiraréis**	**habrás suspirado**	**habréis suspirado**
suspirará	**suspirarán**	**habrá suspirado**	**habrán suspirado**
5 potencial simple		12 potencial compuesto	
suspiraría	**suspiraríamos**	**habría suspirado**	**habríamos suspirado**
suspirarías	**suspiraríais**	**habrías suspirado**	**habríais suspirado**
suspiraría	**suspirarían**	**habría suspirado**	**habrían suspirado**
6 presente de subjuntivo		13 perfecto de subjuntivo	
suspire	**suspiremos**	**haya suspirado**	**hayamos suspirado**
suspires	**suspiréis**	**hayas suspirado**	**hayáis suspirado**
suspire	**suspiren**	**haya suspirado**	**hayan suspirado**
7 imperfecto de subjuntivo		14 pluscuamperfecto de subjuntivo	
suspirara	**suspiráramos**	**hubiera suspirado**	**hubiéramos suspirado**
suspiraras	**suspirarais**	**hubieras suspirado**	**hubierais suspirado**
suspirara	**suspiraran**	**hubiera suspirado**	**hubieran suspirado**
OR		OR	
suspirase	**suspirásemos**	**hubiese suspirado**	**hubiésemos suspirado**
suspirases	**suspiraseis**	**hubieses suspirado**	**hubieseis suspirado**
suspirase	**suspirasen**	**hubiese suspirado**	**hubiesen suspirado**

imperativo

—	**suspiremos**
suspira; no suspires	**suspirad; no suspiréis**
suspire	**suspiren**

Words and expressions related to this verb
suspirar por   to long for
el suspiro   sigh, breath; **exhalar el último**
  suspiro   to breathe one's last breath

el espíritu   spirit
exasperar   to exasperate
inspirar   to inspire, to inhale
la inspiración   inspiration

Don't miss the definitions of basic grammatical terms
with examples in English and Spanish on pages 33–44.

Regular **-er** endings in all tenses except   to pluck, to play (a stringed
Tenses 3 and 7; irregular Gerundio   musical instrument)

The Seven Simple Tenses   The Seven Compound Tenses

Singular	Plural	Singular	Plural
1 presente de indicativo		8 perfecto de indicativo	
taño	tañemos	he tañido	hemos tañido
tañes	tañéis	has tañido	habéis tañido
tañe	tañen	ha tañido	han tañido
2 imperfecto de indicativo		9 pluscuamperfecto de indicativo	
tañía	tañíamos	había tañido	habíamos tañido
tañías	tañíais	habías tañido	habíais tañido
tañía	tañían	había tañido	habían tañido
3 pretérito		10 pretérito anterior	
tañí	tañimos	hube tañido	hubimos tañido
tañiste	tañisteis	hubiste tañido	hubisteis tañido
tañó	tañeron	hubo tañido	hubieron tañido
4 futuro		11 futuro perfecto	
tañeré	tañeremos	habré tañido	habremos tañido
tañerás	tañeréis	habrás tañido	habréis tañido
tañerá	tañerán	habrá tañido	habrán tañido
5 potencial simple		12 potencial compuesto	
tañería	tañeríamos	habría tañido	habríamos tañido
tañerías	tañeríais	habrías tañido	habríais tañido
tañería	tañerían	habría tañido	habrían tañido
6 presente de subjuntivo		13 perfecto de subjuntivo	
taña	tañamos	haya tañido	hayamos tañido
tañas	tañáis	hayas tañido	hayáis tañido
taña	tañan	haya tañido	hayan tañido
7 imperfecto de subjuntivo		14 pluscuamperfecto de subjuntivo	
tañera	tañéramos	hubiera tañido	hubiéramos tañido
tañeras	tañerais	hubieras tañido	hubierais tañido
tañera	tañeran	hubiera tañido	hubieran tañido
OR		OR	
tañese	tañésemos	hubiese tañido	hubiésemos tañido
tañeses	tañeseis	hubieses tañido	hubieseis tañido
tañese	tañesen	hubiese tañido	hubiesen tañido

imperativo

—	tañamos
tañe; no tañas	tañed; no tañáis
taña	tañan

Words related to this verb
el tañido   sound, tone; twang of a stringed musical instrument;
  el tañimiento   plucking, strumming of a stringed musical instrument

Review the principal parts of important Spanish verbs on pages 9–10.

telefonear (463) Gerundio telefoneando Part. pas. telefoneado
to telephone Regular **-ar** verb

The Seven Simple Tenses		The Seven Compound Tenses	
Singular	Plural	Singular	Plural
1 presente de indicativo		8 perfecto de indicativo	
telefoneo	telefoneamos	he telefoneado	hemos telefoneado
telefoneas	telefoneáis	has telefoneado	habéis telefoneado
telefonea	telefonean	ha telefoneado	han telefoneado
2 imperfecto de indicativo		9 pluscuamperfecto de indicativo	
telefoneaba	telefoneábamos	había telefoneado	habíamos telefoneado
telefoneabas	telefoneabais	habías telefoneado	habíais telefoneado
telefoneaba	telefoneaban	había telefoneado	habían telefoneado
3 pretérito		10 pretérito anterior	
telefoneé	telefoneamos	hube telefoneado	hubimos telefoneado
telefoneaste	telefoneasteis	hubiste telefoneado	hubisteis telefoneado
telefoneó	telefonearon	hubo telefoneado	hubieron telefoneado
4 futuro		11 futuro perfecto	
telefonearé	telefonearemos	habré telefoneado	habremos telefoneado
telefonearás	telefonearéis	habrás telefoneado	habréis telefoneado
telefoneará	telefonearán	habrá telefoneado	habrán telefoneado
5 potencial simple		12 potencial compuesto	
telefonearía	telefonearíamos	habría telefoneado	habríamos telefoneado
telefonearías	telefonearíais	habrías telefoneado	habríais telefoneado
telefonearía	telefonearían	habría telefoneado	habrían telefoneado
6 presente de subjuntivo		13 perfecto de subjuntivo	
telefonee	telefoneemos	haya telefoneado	hayamos telefoneado
telefonees	telefoneéis	hayas telefoneado	hayáis telefoneado
telefonee	telefoneen	haya telefoneado	hayan telefoneado
7 imperfecto de subjuntivo		14 pluscuamperfecto de subjuntivo	
telefoneara	telefoneáramos	hubiera telefoneado	hubiéramos telefoneado
telefonearas	telefonearais	hubieras telefoneado	hubierais telefoneado
telefoneara	telefonearan	hubiera telefoneado	hubieran telefoneado
OR		OR	
telefonease	telefoneásemos	hubiese telefoneado	hubiésemos telefoneado
telefoneases	telefoneaseis	hubieses telefoneado	hubieseis telefoneado
telefonease	telefoneasen	hubiese telefoneado	hubiesen telefoneado

imperativo	
—	telefoneemos
telefonea; no telefonees	telefonead; no telefoneéis
telefonee	telefoneen

Words and expressions related to this verb
el teléfono telephone
telefonista telephone operator
telefónico, telefónica telephonic
marcar el número de teléfono to dial
  a telephone number
¡diga! hello! (when answering a phone)

la guía telefónica telephone book
la cabina telefónica telephone booth
el número de teléfono telephone number
por teléfono by telephone
una buscapersonas pager
un teléfono celular cell phone

Regular **-ar** verb endings with spelling change: **i** becomes   to telegraph, to cable
í on stressed syllable (see Tenses 1, 6, Imperative)

The Seven Simple Tenses		The Seven Compound Tenses	
Singular	Plural	Singular	Plural
1 presente de indicativo		8 perfecto de indicativo	
telegrafío	**telegrafiamos**	**he telegrafiado**	**hemos telegrafiado**
telegrafías	**telegrafiáis**	**has telegrafiado**	**habéis telegrafiado**
telegrafía	**telegrafían**	**ha telegrafiado**	**han telegrafiado**
2 imperfecto de indicativo		9 pluscuamperfecto de indicativo	
telegrafiaba	**telegrafiábamos**	**había telegrafiado**	**habíamos telegrafiado**
telegrafiabas	**telegrafiabais**	**habías telegrafiado**	**habíais telegrafiado**
telegrafiaba	**telegrafiaban**	**había telegrafiado**	**habían telegrafiado**
3 pretérito		10 pretérito anterior	
telegrafié	**telegrafiamos**	**hube telegrafiado**	**hubimos telegrafiado**
telegrafiaste	**telegrafiasteis**	**hubiste telegrafiado**	**hubisteis telegrafiado**
telegrafió	**telegrafiaron**	**hubo telegrafiado**	**hubieron telegrafiado**
4 futuro		11 futuro perfecto	
telegrafiaré	**telegrafiaremos**	**habré telegrafiado**	**habremos telegrafiado**
telegrafiarás	**telegrafiaréis**	**habrás telegrafiado**	**habréis telegrafiado**
telegrafiará	**telegrafiarán**	**habrá telegrafiado**	**habrán telegrafiado**
5 potencial simple		12 potencial compuesto	
telegrafiaría	**telegrafiaríamos**	**habría telegrafiado**	**habríamos telegrafiado**
telegrafiarías	**telegrafiaríais**	**habrías telegrafiado**	**habríais telegrafiado**
telegrafiaría	**telegrafiarían**	**habría telegrafiado**	**habrían telegrafiado**
6 presente de subjuntivo		13 perfecto de subjuntivo	
telegrafíe	**telegrafiemos**	**haya telegrafiado**	**hayamos telegrafiado**
telegrafíes	**telegrafiéis**	**hayas telegrafiado**	**hayáis telegrafiado**
telegrafíe	**telegrafíen**	**haya telegrafiado**	**hayan telegrafiado**
7 imperfecto de subjuntivo		14 pluscuamperfecto de subjuntivo	
telegrafiara	**telegrafiáramos**	**hubiera telegrafiado**	**hubiéramos telegrafiado**
telegrafiaras	**telegrafiarais**	**hubieras telegrafiado**	**hubierais telegrafiado**
telegrafiara	**telegrafiaran**	**hubiera telegrafiado**	**hubieran telegrafiado**
OR		OR	
telegrafiase	**telegrafiásemos**	**hubiese telegrafiado**	**hubiésemos telegrafiado**
telegrafiases	**telegrafiaseis**	**hubieses telegrafiado**	**hubieseis telegrafiado**
telegrafiase	**telegrafiasen**	**hubiese telegrafiado**	**hubiesen telegrafiado**

T

imperativo

—	**telegrafiemos**
telegrafía; no telegrafíes	**telegrafiad; no telegrafiéis**
telegrafíe	**telegrafíen**

Words and expressions related to this verb

el telégrafo   telegraph
el telegrama   telegram, cablegram
telegrafista   telegraph operator

la telegrafía   telegraphy
el telégrafo sin hilos   wireless telegraph
telegrafiar la intención   to telegraph (one's)
intentions

Do you need more drills? Have fun with the *501 Spanish Verbs* CD-ROM!

The subject pronouns are found on page 93.

603

to tremble, to quake, to quiver,
to shake, to shiver

Regular **-ar** verb endings with stem
change: Tenses 1, 6, Imperative

The Seven Simple Tenses | The Seven Compound Tenses

Singular	Plural	Singular	Plural
1 presente de indicativo		8 perfecto de indicativo	
tiemblo	**temblamos**	**he temblado**	**hemos temblado**
tiemblas	**tembláis**	**has temblado**	**habéis temblado**
tiembla	**tiemblan**	**ha temblado**	**han temblado**
2 imperfecto de indicativo		9 pluscuamperfecto de indicativo	
temblaba	**temblábamos**	**había temblado**	**habíamos temblado**
temblabas	**temblabais**	**habías temblado**	**habíais temblado**
temblaba	**temblaban**	**había temblado**	**habían temblado**
3 pretérito		10 pretérito anterior	
temblé	**temblamos**	**hube temblado**	**hubimos temblado**
temblaste	**temblasteis**	**hubiste temblado**	**hubisteis temblado**
tembló	**temblaron**	**hubo temblado**	**hubieron temblado**
4 futuro		11 futuro perfecto	
temblaré	**temblaremos**	**habré temblado**	**habremos temblado**
temblarás	**temblaréis**	**habrás temblado**	**habréis temblado**
temblará	**temblarán**	**habrá temblado**	**habrán temblado**
5 potencial simple		12 potencial compuesto	
temblaría	**temblaríamos**	**habría temblado**	**habríamos temblado**
temblarías	**temblaríais**	**habrías temblado**	**habríais temblado**
temblaría	**temblarían**	**habría temblado**	**habrían temblado**
6 presente de subjuntivo		13 perfecto de subjuntivo	
tiemble	**temblemos**	**haya temblado**	**hayamos temblado**
tiembles	**tembléis**	**hayas temblado**	**hayáis temblado**
tiemble	**tiemblen**	**haya temblado**	**hayan temblado**
7 imperfecto de subjuntivo		14 pluscuamperfecto de subjuntivo	
temblara	**tembláramos**	**hubiera temblado**	**hubiéramos temblado**
temblaras	**temblarais**	**hubieras temblado**	**hubierais temblado**
temblara	**temblaran**	**hubiera temblado**	**hubieran temblado**
OR		OR	
temblase	**temblásemos**	**hubiese temblado**	**hubiésemos temblado**
temblases	**temblaseis**	**hubieses temblado**	**hubieseis temblado**
temblase	**temblasen**	**hubiese temblado**	**hubiesen temblado**

imperativo

—	**temblemos**
tiembla; no tiembles	**temblad; no tembléis**
tiemble	**tiemblen**

Words and expressions related to this verb

temblante   trembling, shaking; **el temblante**   bracelet
el temblor   tremor, shaking; **temblón, temblona**   trembling
un temblor de tierra   earthquake; **un temblor de voz**   quivering of one's voice

---

If you want an explanation of meanings and uses of Spanish
and English verb tenses and moods, see pages 13–32.

The Seven Simple Tenses | The Seven Compound Tenses

Singular	Plural	Singular	Plural
1 presente de indicativo		**8 perfecto de indicativo**	
temo	tememos	he temido	hemos temido
temes	teméis	has temido	habéis temido
teme	temen	ha temido	han temido
2 imperfecto de indicativo		**9 pluscuamperfecto de indicativo**	
temía	temíamos	había temido	habíamos temido
temías	temíais	habías temido	habíais temido
temía	temían	había temido	habían temido
3 pretérito		**10 pretérito anterior**	
temí	temimos	hube temido	hubimos temido
temiste	temisteis	hubiste temido	hubisteis temido
temió	temieron	hubo temido	hubieron temido
4 futuro		**11 futuro perfecto**	
temeré	temeremos	habré temido	habremos temido
temerás	temeréis	habrás temido	habréis temido
temerá	temerán	habrá temido	habrán temido
5 potencial simple		**12 potencial compuesto**	
temería	temeríamos	habría temido	habríamos temido
temerías	temeríais	habrías temido	habríais temido
temería	temerían	habría temido	habrían temido
6 presente de subjuntivo		**13 perfecto de subjuntivo**	
tema	temamos	haya temido	hayamos temido
temas	temáis	hayas temido	hayáis temido
tema	teman	haya temido	hayan temido
7 imperfecto de subjuntivo		**14 pluscuamperfecto de subjuntivo**	
temiera	temiéramos	hubiera temido	hubiéramos temido
temieras	temierais	hubieras temido	hubierais temido
temiera	temieran	hubiera temido	hubieran temido
OR		OR	
temiese	temiésemos	hubiese temido	hubiésemos temido
temieses	temieseis	hubieses temido	hubieseis temido
temiese	temiesen	hubiese temido	hubiesen temido

	imperativo	
—		temamos
teme; no temas		temed; no temáis
tema		teman

Words and expressions related to this verb

temer + inf. to fear + inf.
temer por to fear for
temedor, temedora afraid, fearing
temedero, temedera dreadful, fearful
intimidar to intimidate

el temor fear
la temeridad temerity, daring
temeroso, temerosa fearful
sin temor a nada without fearing anything
tímido, tímida shy

Can't find the verb you're looking for?
Check the back pages of this book for a list of over 2,100 additional verbs!

tender (467) Gerundio **tendiendo** Part. pas. **tendido**

to extend, to offer, to stretch, to spread out, to hang out (washing)

Regular **-er** verb endings with stem change: Tenses 1, 6, Imperative

The Seven Simple Tenses		The Seven Compound Tenses	
Singular	Plural	Singular	Plural
1 presente de indicativo		8 perfecto de indicativo	
tiendo	tendemos	he tendido	hemos tendido
tiendes	tendéis	has tendido	habéis tendido
tiende	tienden	ha tendido	han tendido
2 imperfecto de indicativo		9 pluscuamperfecto de indicativo	
tendía	tendíamos	había tendido	habíamos tendido
tendías	tendíais	habías tendido	habíais tendido
tendía	tendían	había tendido	habían tendido
3 pretérito		10 pretérito anterior	
tendí	tendimos	hube tendido	hubimos tendido
tendiste	tendisteis	hubiste tendido	hubisteis tendido
tendió	tendieron	hubo tendido	hubieron tendido
4 futuro		11 futuro perfecto	
tenderé	tenderemos	habré tendido	habremos tendido
tenderás	tenderéis	habrás tendido	habréis tendido
tenderá	tenderán	habrá tendido	habrán tendido
5 potencial simple		12 potencial compuesto	
tendería	tenderíamos	habría tendido	habríamos tendido
tenderías	tenderíais	habrías tendido	habríais tendido
tendería	tenderían	habría tendido	habrían tendido
6 presente de subjuntivo		13 perfecto de subjuntivo	
tienda	tendamos	haya tendido	hayamos tendido
tiendas	tendáis	hayas tendido	hayáis tendido
tienda	tiendan	haya tendido	hayan tendido
7 imperfecto de subjuntivo		14 pluscuamperfecto de subjuntivo	
tendiera	tendiéramos	hubiera tendido	hubiéramos tendido
tendieras	tendierais	hubieras tendido	hubierais tendido
tendiera	tendieran	hubiera tendido	hubieran tendido
OR		OR	
tendiese	tendiésemos	hubiese tendido	hubiésemos tendido
tendieses	tendieseis	hubieses tendido	hubieseis tendido
tendiese	tendiesen	hubiese tendido	hubiesen tendido

imperativo	
—	tendamos
tiende; no tiendas	tended; no tendáis
tienda	tiendan

Words and expressions related to this verb

tender a + inf. to tend + inf.
un tendero, una tendera shopkeeper
un tenderete booth, stand (for selling merchandise)

una tienda shop, store; **tienda de pacotilla** junk store; **tienda de campaña** tent
una tienda de ultramarinos grocery store
una tendencia trend

Use the guide to Spanish pronunciation on pages 665–667.

606

Irregular verb   to have, to hold

The Seven Simple Tenses		The Seven Compound Tenses	
Singular	Plural	Singular	Plural
1 presente de indicativo		8 perfecto de indicativo	
tengo	tenemos	he tenido	hemos tenido
tienes	tenéis	has tenido	habéis tenido
tiene	tienen	ha tenido	han tenido
2 imperfecto de indicativo		9 pluscuamperfecto de indicativo	
tenía	teníamos	había tenido	habíamos tenido
tenías	teníais	habías tenido	habíais tenido
tenía	tenían	había tenido	habían tenido
3 pretérito		10 pretérito anterior	
tuve	tuvimos	hube tenido	hubimos tenido
tuviste	tuvisteis	hubiste tenido	hubisteis tenido
tuvo	tuvieron	hubo tenido	hubieron tenido
4 futuro		11 futuro perfecto	
tendré	tendremos	habré tenido	habremos tenido
tendrás	tendréis	habrás tenido	habréis tenido
tendrá	tendrán	habrá tenido	habrán tenido
5 potencial simple		12 potencial compuesto	
tendría	tendríamos	habría tenido	habríamos tenido
tendrías	tendríais	habrías tenido	habríais tenido
tendría	tendrían	habría tenido	habrían tenido
6 presente de subjuntivo		13 perfecto de subjuntivo	
tenga	tengamos	haya tenido	hayamos tenido
tengas	tengáis	hayas tenido	hayáis tenido
tenga	tengan	haya tenido	hayan tenido
7 imperfecto de subjuntivo		14 pluscuamperfecto de subjuntivo	
tuviera	tuviéramos	hubiera tenido	hubiéramos tenido
tuvieras	tuvierais	hubieras tenido	hubierais tenido
tuviera	tuvieran	hubiera tenido	hubieran tenido
OR		OR	
tuviese	tuviésemos	hubiese tenido	hubiésemos tenido
tuvieses	tuvieseis	hubieses tenido	hubieseis tenido
tuviese	tuviesen	hubiese tenido	hubiesen tenido

	imperativo	
—		tengamos
ten; no tengas		tened; no tengáis
tenga		tengan

AN ESSENTIAL
55 VERB

AN ESSENTIAL 55 VERB

Tener

Tener is one of the most important irregular verbs for beginning students.
It is used in a great number of idiomatic expressions and everyday situations.
Pay special attention to the stem changes!

Sentences using tener and related words

Tengo un dolor de muelas.
I have a toothache.

¿Tiene algo más barato?
Do you have something cheaper?

Aquí tiene usted nuestros pasaportes.
Here are our passports.

¿Tengo que trasbordar?
Do I have to transfer? (bus, train, etc.)

¡Tengo mucha hambre!
I'm very hungry!

Tenemos que salir.
We have to go out.

Aquí tiene el dinero.
Here is the money.

¿Cuántos años tienes?
How old are you?

Tengo diez y seis (or dieciséis) años.
I am sixteen years old.

—¿Qué tienes? ¿Qué tiene Ud.?
—What's the matter? What's the matter
with you?

—No tengo nada.
—There's nothing wrong. There's nothing the
matter with me.

Tengo ganas de tomar un helado.
I feel like having an ice cream.

Tengo mucho gusto en conocerle.
I am very glad to meet you.

Tenga la bondad de cerrar la puerta.
Please close the door.

El accidente tuvo lugar anoche.
The accident took place last night.

Tengo que estudiar.
I have to study.

Usted tiene razón.
You are right.

Proverbs

Anda despacio que tengo prisa.
Make haste slowly. (Easy does it.)

Aquellos son ricos, que tienen amigos.
Those who have friends are rich.

El que más tiene más quiere.
The more one has, the more one wants.

Words and expressions related to this verb

tener algo que hacer **to have something to do**

tener algo en la punta de la lengua **to have something on the tip of one's tongue**

tener apetito **to have an appetite**

tener cuidado **to be careful**

tener prisa **to be in a hurry**

tener hambre **to be hungry**

tener sed **to be thirsty**

tener frío **to be (feel) cold (persons)**

tener calor **to be (feel) warm (persons)**

tener dolor de cabeza **to have a headache**

tener dolor de estómago **to have a stomachache**

tener en cuenta **to take into account**

tener éxito **to be successful**

tener ganas de + inf. **to feel like + pres. part.**

tener gusto en + inf. **to be glad + inf.**

tener la bondad de **please, please be good enough to...**

tener la culpa de algo **to take the blame for something, to be to blame for something**

tener lugar **to take place**

tener más paciencia que Job **to have the patience of Job**

tener miedo de **to be afraid of**

tener mucha sed **to be (feel) very thirsty (persons)**

tener mucho que hacer **to have a lot to do**

tener por **to consider as**

tener que + inf. **to have + inf.**

tener que ver con **to have to do with**

tener razón **to be right**

tener sueño **to be (feel) sleepy**

tener suerte **to be lucky**

tener vergüenza de **to be ashamed of**

tenerse en pie **to stand**

retener **to retain**

T

Can't find the verb you're looking for?
Check the back pages of this book for a list of over 2,100 additional verbs!

to examine by touch, to feel with the fingers, to attempt, to try	Regular **-ar** verb endings with stem change: Tenses 1, 6, Imperative

The Seven Simple Tenses		The Seven Compound Tenses	
Singular	Plural	Singular	Plural
1 presente de indicativo		8 perfecto de indicativo	
tiento	tentamos	he tentado	hemos tentado
tientas	tentáis	has tentado	habéis tentado
tienta	tientan	ha tentado	han tentado
2 imperfecto de indicativo		9 pluscuamperfecto de indicativo	
tentaba	tentábamos	había tentado	habíamos tentado
tentabas	tentabais	habías tentado	habíais tentado
tentaba	tentaban	había tentado	habían tentado
3 pretérito		10 pretérito anterior	
tenté	tenamos	hube tentado	hubimos tentado
tentaste	tentasteis	hubiste tentado	hubisteis tentado
tentó	tentaron	hubo tentado	hubieron tentado
4 futuro		11 futuro perfecto	
tentaré	tentaremos	habré tentado	habremos tentado
tentarás	tentaréis	habrás tentado	habréis tentado
tentará	tentarán	habrá tentado	habrán tentado
5 potencial simple		12 potencial compuesto	
tentaría	tentaríamos	habría tentado	habríamos tentado
tentarías	tentaríais	habrías tentado	habríais tentado
tentaría	tentarían	habría tentado	habrían tentado
6 presente de subjuntivo		13 perfecto de subjuntivo	
tiente	tentemos	haya tentado	hayamos tentado
tientes	tentéis	hayas tentado	hayáis tentado
tiente	tienten	haya tentado	hayan tentado
7 imperfecto de subjuntivo		14 pluscuamperfecto de subjuntivo	
tentara	tentáramos	hubiera tentado	hubiéramos tentado
tentaras	tentarais	hubieras tentado	hubierais tentado
tentara	tentaran	hubiera tentado	hubieran tentado
OR		OR	
tentase	tentásemos	hubiese tentado	hubiésemos tentado
tentases	tentaseis	hubieses tentado	hubieseis tentado
tentase	tentasen	hubiese tentado	hubiesen tentado

imperativo	
—	tentemos
tienta; no tientes	tentad; no tentéis
tiente	tienten

Words and expressions related to this verb
tentar a uno a + inf. to tempt somebody + inf.
tentar al diablo to tempt the devil (to look for trouble)
el tentador the devil; **un tentador** tempter; **una tentadora** temptress
la tentación temptation; **una tentativa** attempt

If you want to see a sample English verb fully conjugated in all the tenses, check out pages 11 and 12.

Regular **-ar** verb   to end, to terminate, to finish

The Seven Simple Tenses		The Seven Compound Tenses	
Singular	Plural	Singular	Plural
1 presente de indicativo		8 perfecto de indicativo	
termino	terminamos	he terminado	hemos terminado
terminas	termináis	has terminado	habéis terminado
termina	terminan	ha terminado	han terminado
2 imperfecto de indicativo		9 pluscuamperfecto de indicativo	
terminaba	terminábamos	había terminado	habíamos terminado
terminabas	terminabais	habías terminado	habíais terminado
terminaba	terminaban	había terminado	habían terminado
3 pretérito		10 pretérito anterior	
terminé	terminamos	hube terminado	hubimos terminado
terminaste	terminasteis	hubiste terminado	hubisteis terminado
terminó	terminaron	hubo terminado	hubieron terminado
4 futuro		11 futuro perfecto	
terminaré	terminaremos	habré terminado	habremos terminado
terminarás	terminaréis	habrás terminado	habréis terminado
terminará	terminarán	habrá terminado	habrán terminado
5 potencial simple		12 potencial compuesto	
terminaría	terminaríamos	habría terminado	habríamos terminado
terminarías	terminaríais	habrías terminado	habríais terminado
terminaría	terminarían	habría terminado	habrían terminado
6 presente de subjuntivo		13 perfecto de subjuntivo	
termine	terminemos	haya terminado	hayamos terminado
termines	terminéis	hayas terminado	hayáis terminado
termine	terminen	haya terminado	hayan terminado
7 imperfecto de subjuntivo		14 pluscuamperfecto de subjuntivo	
terminara	termináramos	hubiera terminado	hubiéramos terminado
terminaras	terminarais	hubieras terminado	hubierais terminado
terminara	terminaran	hubiera terminado	hubieran terminado
OR		OR	
terminase	terminásemos	hubiese terminado	hubiésemos terminado
terminases	terminaseis	hubieses terminado	hubieseis terminado
terminase	terminasen	hubiese terminado	hubiesen terminado

	imperativo	
—		terminemos
termina; no termines		terminad; no terminéis
termine		terminen

Words and expressions related to this verb
la terminación termination, ending, completion
el término end, ending; term
en otros términos in other terms, in other words
determinar to determine

llevar a término to complete
estar en buenos términos con to be on
   good terms with
la terminal aérea air terminal
el terminal terminal (electrical or computer)

T

The subject pronouns are found on page 93.

611

to pull, to draw, to pitch (a ball), to
shoot (a gun), to throw, to fling

Regular **-ar** verb

The Seven Simple Tenses		The Seven Compound Tenses	
Singular	Plural	Singular	Plural
1 presente de indicativo		8 perfecto de indicativo	
tiro	**tiramos**	**he tirado**	**hemos tirado**
tiras	**tiráis**	**has tirado**	**habéis tirado**
tira	**tiran**	**ha tirado**	**han tirado**
2 imperfecto de indicativo		9 pluscuamperfecto de indicativo	
tiraba	**tirábamos**	**había tirado**	**habíamos tirado**
tirabas	**tirabais**	**habías tirado**	**habíais tirado**
tiraba	**tiraban**	**había tirado**	**habían tirado**
3 pretérito		10 pretérito anterior	
tiré	**tiramos**	**hube tirado**	**hubimos tirado**
tiraste	**tirasteis**	**hubiste tirado**	**hubisteis tirado**
tiró	**tiraron**	**hubo tirado**	**hubieron tirado**
4 futuro		11 futuro perfecto	
tiraré	**tiraremos**	**habré tirado**	**habremos tirado**
tirarás	**tiraréis**	**habrás tirado**	**habréis tirado**
tirará	**tirarán**	**habrá tirado**	**habrán tirado**
5 potencial simple		12 potencial compuesto	
tiraría	**tiraríamos**	**habría tirado**	**habríamos tirado**
tirarías	**tiraríais**	**habrías tirado**	**habríais tirado**
tiraría	**tirarían**	**habría tirado**	**habrían tirado**
6 presente de subjuntivo		13 perfecto de subjuntivo	
tire	**tiremos**	**haya tirado**	**hayamos tirado**
tires	**tiréis**	**hayas tirado**	**hayáis tirado**
tire	**tiren**	**haya tirado**	**hayan tirado**
7 imperfecto de subjuntivo		14 pluscuamperfecto de subjuntivo	
tirara	**tiráramos**	**hubiera tirado**	**hubiéramos tirado**
tiraras	**tirarais**	**hubieras tirado**	**hubierais tirado**
tirara	**tiraran**	**hubiera tirado**	**hubieran tirado**
OR		OR	
tirase	**tirásemos**	**hubiese tirado**	**hubiésemos tirado**
tirases	**tiraseis**	**hubieses tirado**	**hubieseis tirado**
tirase	**tirasen**	**hubiese tirado**	**hubiesen tirado**

	imperativo	
—		**tiremos**
tira; no tires		**tirad; no tiréis**
tire		**tiren**

Words and expressions related to this verb

tirar a   to shoot at

tirar una línea   to draw a line

a tiro   within reach; **a tiro de piedra**   within a stone's throw; **ni a tiros**   not for love nor money; **al tiro**   right away

tirar la toalla   to throw in the towel; **tirarse al agua**   to jump in the water

If you don't know the Spanish verb for the English verb you have in mind, look it up in the index on pages 682–706.

Regular **-ar** verb endings with spelling change: **c** becomes **qu** before **e**	to play (music or a musical instrument), to touch

The Seven Simple Tenses		The Seven Compound Tenses	
Singular	Plural	Singular	Plural
1 presente de indicativo		8 perfecto de indicativo	
toco	tocamos	he tocado	hemos tocado
tocas	tocáis	has tocado	habéis tocado
toca	tocan	ha tocado	han tocado
2 imperfecto de indicativo		9 pluscuamperfecto de indicativo	
tocaba	tocábamos	había tocado	habíamos tocado
tocabas	tocabais	habías tocado	habíais tocado
tocaba	tocaban	había tocado	habían tocado
3 pretérito		10 pretérito anterior	
toqué	tocamos	hube tocado	hubimos tocado
tocaste	tocasteis	hubiste tocado	hubisteis tocado
tocó	tocaron	hubo tocado	hubieron tocado
4 futuro		11 futuro perfecto	
tocaré	tocaremos	habré tocado	habremos tocado
tocarás	tocaréis	habrás tocado	habréis tocado
tocará	tocarán	habrá tocado	habrán tocado
5 potencial simple		12 potencial compuesto	
tocaría	tocaríamos	habría tocado	habríamos tocado
tocarías	tocaríais	habrías tocado	habríais tocado
tocaría	tocarían	habría tocado	habrían tocado
6 presente de subjuntivo		13 perfecto de subjuntivo	
toque	toquemos	haya tocado	hayamos tocado
toques	toquéis	hayas tocado	hayáis tocado
toque	toquen	haya tocado	hayan tocado
7 imperfecto de subjuntivo		14 pluscuamperfecto de subjuntivo	
tocara	tocáramos	hubiera tocado	hubiéramos tocado
tocaras	tocarais	hubieras tocado	hubierais tocado
tocara	tocaran	hubiera tocado	hubieran tocado
OR		OR	
tocase	tocásemos	hubiese tocado	hubiésemos tocado
tocases	tocaseis	hubieses tocado	hubieseis tocado
tocase	tocasen	hubiese tocado	hubiesen tocado

imperativo	
—	toquemos
toca; no toques	tocad; no toquéis
toque	toquen

Common idiomatic expressions using this verb

¿Sabe Ud. tocar el piano? Do you know how to play the piano?

Sí, yo sé tocar el piano. Yes, I know how to play the piano.

tocar a la puerta to knock on the door

Alguien toca a la puerta/Someone is knocking on (at) the door.

Don't confuse **tocar** with **jugar** (verb 282), which also means *to play*.

el tocadiscos record player

Aquel hombre está tocado. That man is crazy.

tocar a uno to be someone's turn; **Le toca a Juan.** It's John's turn.

The subject pronouns are found on page 93.

T

to take, to have (something to eat or drink)   Regular **-ar** verb

The Seven Simple Tenses		The Seven Compound Tenses	
Singular	Plural	Singular	Plural
1 presente de indicativo		8 perfecto de indicativo	
tomo	tomamos	he tomado	hemos tomado
tomas	tomáis	has tomado	habéis tomado
toma	toman	ha tomado	han tomado
2 imperfecto de indicativo		9 pluscuamperfecto de indicativo	
tomaba	tomábamos	había tomado	habíamos tomado
tomabas	tomabais	habías tomado	habíais tomado
tomaba	tomaban	había tomado	habían tomado
3 pretérito		10 pretérito anterior	
tomé	tomamos	hube tomado	hubimos tomado
tomaste	tomasteis	hubiste tomado	hubisteis tomado
tomó	tomaron	hubo tomado	hubieron tomado
4 futuro		11 futuro perfecto	
tomaré	tomaremos	habré tomado	habremos tomado
tomarás	tomaréis	habrás tomado	habréis tomado
tomará	tomarán	habrá tomado	habrán tomado
5 potencial simple		12 potencial compuesto	
tomaría	tomaríamos	habría tomado	habríamos tomado
tomarías	tomaríais	habrías tomado	habríais tomado
tomaría	tomarían	habría tomado	habrían tomado
6 presente de subjuntivo		13 perfecto de subjuntivo	
tome	tomemos	haya tomado	hayamos tomado
tomes	toméis	hayas tomado	hayáis tomado
tome	tomen	haya tomado	hayan tomado
7 imperfecto de subjuntivo		14 pluscuamperfecto de subjuntivo	
tomara	tomáramos	hubiera tomado	hubiéramos tomado
tomaras	tomarais	hubieras tomado	hubierais tomado
tomara	tomaran	hubiera tomado	hubieran tomado
OR		OR	
tomase	tomásemos	hubiese tomado	hubiésemos tomado
tomases	tomaseis	hubieses tomado	hubieseis tomado
tomase	tomasen	hubiese tomado	hubiesen tomado

imperativo	
—	tomemos
toma; no tomes	tomad; no toméis
tome	tomen

Tomar is an essential verb for beginning students of Spanish. It is useful in numerous idiomatic expressions and everyday situations.

Sentences using tomar and related words

¿A qué hora toma Ud. el desayuno?
At what time do you have breakfast?

Tomo el desayuno a las siete y media.
I have breakfast at seven thirty.

¿Qué toma Ud. en el desayuno?
What do you have for breakfast?

Mi amigo tomó el tren esta mañana
a las siete.
My friend took the train this morning
at seven o'clock.

¡Toma!
Here!

Tome, aquí tiene el dinero que le debo.
Here you are, here's the money I owe you.

Words and expressions related to this verb

tomar el tren **to catch/take the train**

tomar el sol **to take a sunbath**

tomar asiento **to take a seat**

tomar en cuenta **to consider**

tomar parte en **to take part in**

tomar por **to take for**

tomar el pelo a uno **to pull someone's leg** (el pelo/hair)

una tomadura de pelo **a joke**

una toma de sangre **blood sample**

T

Can't find the verb you're looking for?
Check the back pages of this book for a list of over 2,100 additional verbs!

The subject pronouns are found on page 93.

to toast, to tan, to roast (coffee) | Regular **-ar** verb endings with stem change: Tenses 1, 6, Imperative

The Seven Simple Tenses		The Seven Compound Tenses	
Singular	Plural	Singular	Plural
1 presente de indicativo		8 perfecto de indicativo	
tuesto	**tostamos**	**he tostado**	**hemos tostado**
tuestas	**tostáis**	**has tostado**	**habéis tostado**
tuesta	**tuestan**	**ha tostado**	**han tostado**
2 imperfecto de indicativo		9 pluscuamperfecto de indicativo	
tostaba	**tostábamos**	**había tostado**	**habíamos tostado**
tostabas	**tostabais**	**habías tostado**	**habíais tostado**
tostaba	**tostaban**	**había tostado**	**habían tostado**
3 pretérito		10 pretérito anterior	
tosté	**tostamos**	**hube tostado**	**hubimos tostado**
tostaste	**tostasteis**	**hubiste tostado**	**hubisteis tostado**
tostó	**tostaron**	**hubo tostado**	**hubieron tostado**
4 futuro		11 futuro perfecto	
tostaré	**tostaremos**	**habré tostado**	**habremos tostado**
tostarás	**tostaréis**	**habrás tostado**	**habréis tostado**
tostará	**tostarán**	**habrá tostado**	**habrán tostado**
5 potencial simple		12 potencial compuesto	
tostaría	**tostaríamos**	**habría tostado**	**habríamos tostado**
tostarías	**tostaríais**	**habrías tostado**	**habríais tostado**
tostaría	**tostarían**	**habría tostado**	**habrían tostado**
6 presente de subjuntivo		13 perfecto de subjuntivo	
tueste	**tostemos**	**haya tostado**	**hayamos tostado**
tuestes	**tostéis**	**hayas tostado**	**hayáis tostado**
tueste	**tuesten**	**haya tostado**	**hayan tostado**
7 imperfecto de subjuntivo		14 pluscuamperfecto de subjuntivo	
tostara	**tostáramos**	**hubiera tostado**	**hubiéramos tostado**
tostaras	**tostarais**	**hubieras tostado**	**hubierais tostado**
tostara	**tostaran**	**hubiera tostado**	**hubieran tostado**
OR		OR	
tostase	**tostásemos**	**hubiese tostado**	**hubiésemos tostado**
tostases	**tostaseis**	**hubieses tostado**	**hubieseis tostado**
tostase	**tostasen**	**hubiese tostado**	**hubiesen tostado**

imperativo	
—	**tostemos**
tuesta; no tuestes	**tostad; no tostéis**
tueste	**tuesten**

Words and expressions related to this verb
un tostador   toaster, toasting machine
pan tostado   toast, toasted bread; **una tostada**   piece of toast
el tostón   crouton; **dar el tostón a uno**   to get on someone's nerves
el tostadero de café   coffee roaster
dar la tostada a uno   to cheat someone

Regular **-ar** verb   to work, to labor

The Seven Simple Tenses		The Seven Compound Tenses	
Singular	Plural	Singular	Plural
1 presente de indicativo		8 perfecto de indicativo	
trabajo	**trabajamos**	**he trabajado**	**hemos trabajado**
trabajas	**trabajáis**	**has trabajado**	**habéis trabajado**
trabaja	**trabajan**	**ha trabajado**	**han trabajado**
2 imperfecto de indicativo		9 pluscuamperfecto de indicativo	
trabajaba	**trabajábamos**	**había trabajado**	**habíamos trabajado**
trabajabas	**trabajabais**	**habías trabajado**	**habíais trabajado**
trabajaba	**trabajaban**	**había trabajado**	**habían trabajado**
3 pretérito		10 pretérito anterior	
trabajé	**trabajamos**	**hube trabajado**	**hubimos trabajado**
trabajaste	**trabajasteis**	**hubiste trabajado**	**hubisteis trabajado**
trabajó	**trabajaron**	**hubo trabajado**	**hubieron trabajado**
4 futuro		11 futuro perfecto	
trabajaré	**trabajaremos**	**habré trabajado**	**habremos trabajado**
trabajarás	**trabajaréis**	**habrás trabajado**	**habréis trabajado**
trabajará	**trabajarán**	**habrá trabajado**	**habrán trabajado**
5 potencial simple		12 potencial compuesto	
trabajaría	**trabajaríamos**	**habría trabajado**	**habríamos trabajado**
trabajarías	**trabajaríais**	**habrías trabajado**	**habríais trabajado**
trabajaría	**trabajarían**	**habría trabajado**	**habrían trabajado**
6 presente de subjuntivo		13 perfecto de subjuntivo	
trabaje	**trabajemos**	**haya trabajado**	**hayamos trabajado**
trabajes	**trabajéis**	**hayas trabajado**	**hayáis trabajado**
trabaje	**trabajen**	**haya trabajado**	**hayan trabajado**
7 imperfecto de subjuntivo		14 pluscuamperfecto de subjuntivo	
trabajara	**trabajáramos**	**hubiera trabajado**	**hubiéramos trabajado**
trabajaras	**trabajarais**	**hubieras trabajado**	**hubierais trabajado**
trabajara	**trabajaran**	**hubiera trabajado**	**hubieran trabajado**
OR		OR	
trabajase	**trabajásemos**	**hubiese trabajado**	**hubiésemos trabajado**
trabajases	**trabajaseis**	**hubieses trabajado**	**hubieseis trabajado**
trabajase	**trabajasen**	**hubiese trabajado**	**hubiesen trabajado**

T

imperativo	
—	**trabajemos**
trabaja; no trabajes	**trabajad; no trabajéis**
trabaje	**trabajen**

Words and expressions related to this verb
el trabajo   work
trabajador, trabajadora   worker
trabajar de manos   to do manual work
el trabajo de media jornada   part-time
   employment

trabajar en + inf.   to strive + inf.
tener trabajo que hacer   to have work to do
trabajar a tiempo parcial   to work part-time
los trabajos forzados   hard labor

The subject pronouns are found on page 93.

617

traducir (476)

Gerundio **traduciendo**   Part. pas. **traducido**

to translate

Irregular in Tenses 3 and 7, regular **-ir** endings in all others; spelling change: **c** becomes **zc** before **a** or **o**

The Seven Simple Tenses		The Seven Compound Tenses	
Singular	Plural	Singular	Plural
1 presente de indicativo		8 perfecto de indicativo	
traduzco	traducimos	he traducido	hemos traducido
traduces	traducís	has traducido	habéis traducido
traduce	traducen	ha traducido	han traducido
2 imperfecto de indicativo		9 pluscuamperfecto de indicativo	
traducía	traducíamos	había traducido	habíamos traducido
traducías	traducíais	habías traducido	habíais traducido
traducía	traducían	había traducido	habían traducido
3 pretérito		10 pretérito anterior	
traduje	tradujimos	hube traducido	hubimos traducido
tradujiste	tradujisteis	hubiste traducido	hubisteis traducido
tradujo	tradujeron	hubo traducido	hubieron traducido
4 futuro		11 futuro perfecto	
traduciré	traduciremos	habré traducido	habremos traducido
traducirás	traduciréis	habrás traducido	habréis traducido
traducirá	traducirán	habrá traducido	habrán traducido
5 potencial simple		12 potencial compuesto	
traduciría	traduciríamos	habría traducido	habríamos traducido
traducirías	traduciríais	habrías traducido	habríais traducido
traduciría	traducirían	habría traducido	habrían traducido
6 presente de subjuntivo		13 perfecto de subjuntivo	
traduzca	traduzcamos	haya traducido	hayamos traducido
traduzcas	traduzcáis	hayas traducido	hayáis traducido
traduzca	traduzcan	haya traducido	hayan traducido
7 imperfecto de subjuntivo		14 pluscuamperfecto de subjuntivo	
tradujera	tradujéramos	hubiera traducido	hubiéramos traducido
tradujeras	tradujerais	hubieras traducido	hubierais traducido
tradujera	tradujeran	hubiera traducido	hubieran traducido
OR		OR	
tradujese	tradujésemos	hubiese traducido	hubiésemos traducido
tradujeses	tradujeseis	hubieses traducido	hubieseis traducido
tradujese	tradujesen	hubiese traducido	hubiesen traducido

imperativo	
—	traduzcamos
traduce; no traduzcas	traducid; no traduzcáis
traduzca	traduzcan

Words related to this verb

la traducción   translation
traducible   translatable
traductor, traductora   translator
traducir del inglés al español   to translate
    from English to Spanish

traducir del español al inglés   to translate
    from Spanish to English
una traducción fiel   a faithful translation
intraducible   untranslatable

Irregular verb   to bring

The Seven Simple Tenses		The Seven Compound Tenses	
Singular	Plural	Singular	Plural
1 presente de indicativo		8 perfecto de indicativo	
traigo	**traemos**	**he traído**	**hemos traído**
traes	**traéis**	**has traído**	**habéis traído**
trae	**traen**	**ha traído**	**han traído**
2 imperfecto de indicativo		9 pluscuamperfecto de indicativo	
traía	**traíamos**	**había traído**	**habíamos traído**
traías	**traíais**	**habías traído**	**habíais traído**
traía	**traían**	**había traído**	**habían traído**
3 pretérito		10 pretérito anterior	
traje	**trajimos**	**hube traído**	**hubimos traído**
trajiste	**trajisteis**	**hubiste traído**	**hubisteis traído**
trajo	**trajeron**	**hubo traído**	**hubieron traído**
4 futuro		11 futuro perfecto	
traeré	**traeremos**	**habré traído**	**habremos traído**
traerás	**traeréis**	**habrás traído**	**habréis traído**
traerá	**traerán**	**habrá traído**	**habrán traído**
5 potencial simple		12 potencial compuesto	
traería	**traeríamos**	**habría traído**	**habríamos traído**
traerías	**traeríais**	**habrías traído**	**habríais traído**
traería	**traerían**	**habría traído**	**habrían traído**
6 presente de subjuntivo		13 perfecto de subjuntivo	
traiga	**traigamos**	**haya traído**	**hayamos traído**
traigas	**traigáis**	**hayas traído**	**hayáis traído**
traiga	**traigan**	**haya traído**	**hayan traído**
7 imperfecto de subjuntivo		14 pluscuamperfecto de subjuntivo	
trajera	**trajéramos**	**hubiera traído**	**hubiéramos traído**
trajeras	**trajerais**	**hubieras traído**	**hubierais traído**
trajera	**trajeran**	**hubiera traído**	**hubieran traído**
OR		OR	
trajese	**trajésemos**	**hubiese traído**	**hubiésemos traído**
trajeses	**trajeseis**	**hubieses traído**	**hubieseis traído**
trajese	**trajesen**	**hubiese traído**	**hubiesen traído**

T

	imperativo	
—		**traigamos**
trae; no traigas		**traed; no traigáis**
traiga		**traigan**

AN ESSENTIAL 55 VERB

The subject pronouns are found on page 93.

AN ESSENTIAL 55 VERB

Traer

Traer is a very useful irregular verb for beginning students. It is used in a great number of idiomatic expressions and everyday situations. Pay special attention to the stem changes!

Sentences using traer

Tráigame una silla, por favor.
Bring me a chair, please.

¿Qué te trae por aquí?
What brings you here?

Words and expressions related to this verb

el traje **costume, dress, suit**

el traje de baño **bathing suit**

el traje hecho **ready-made suit**

el traje a la medida **tailor-made suit**

¡trae! ¡traiga! **Give it here! Give it to me!**

traer y llevar **to spread rumors**

contraer **to contract**

traer entre manos **to have in mind**

traer a la mente **to bring to mind**

trajear **to clothe**

traer buena suerte **to bring good luck**

traer mala suerte **to bring bad luck**

traer cola **to bring trouble**

Can't find the verb you're looking for?
Check the back pages of this book for a list of over 2,100 additional verbs!

Regular **-ar** verb   to try, to treat a subject

The Seven Simple Tenses		The Seven Compound Tenses	
Singular	Plural	Singular	Plural
1 presente de indicativo		8 perfecto de indicativo	
trato	tratamos	he tratado	hemos tratado
tratas	tratáis	has tratado	habéis tratado
trata	tratan	ha tratado	han tratado
2 imperfecto de indicativo		9 pluscuamperfecto de indicativo	
trataba	tratábamos	había tratado	habíamos tratado
tratabas	tratabais	habías tratado	habíais tratado
trataba	trataban	había tratado	habían tratado
3 pretérito		10 pretérito anterior	
traté	tratamos	hube tratado	hubimos tratado
trataste	tratasteis	hubiste tratado	hubisteis tratado
trató	trataron	hubo tratado	hubieron tratado
4 futuro		11 futuro perfecto	
trataré	trataremos	habré tratado	habremos tratado
tratarás	trataréis	habrás tratado	habréis tratado
tratará	tratarán	habrá tratado	habrán tratado
5 potencial simple		12 potencial compuesto	
trataría	trataríamos	habría tratado	habríamos tratado
tratarías	trataríais	habrías tratado	habríais tratado
trataría	tratarían	habría tratado	habrían tratado
6 presente de subjuntivo		13 perfecto de subjuntivo	
trate	tratemos	haya tratado	hayamos tratado
trates	tratéis	hayas tratado	hayáis tratado
trate	traten	haya tratado	hayan tratado
7 imperfecto de subjuntivo		14 pluscuamperfecto de subjuntivo	
tratara	tratáramos	hubiera tratado	hubiéramos tratado
trataras	tratarais	hubieras tratado	hubierais tratado
tratara	trataran	hubiera tratado	hubieran tratado
OR		OR	
tratase	tratásemos	hubiese tratado	hubiésemos tratado
tratases	trataseis	hubieses tratado	hubieseis tratado
tratase	tratasen	hubiese tratado	hubiesen tratado

	imperativo	
—		tratemos
trata; no trates		tratad; no tratéis
trate		traten

Words and expressions related to this verb

tratar de + inf.   to try + inf.
tratar con   to deal with
el trato   agreement; treatment
tratable   amiable, friendly

tratarse con   to have to do with
un tratado   treatise; treaty
¡Trato hecho!   It's a deal!
el tratamiento de textos   word processing

The subject pronouns are found on page 93.

tropezar (479)   Gerundio **tropezando**   Part. pas. **tropezado**

to stumble, to blunder   Regular **-ar** verb endings with stem change: Tenses 1, 6, Imperative; spelling change: **z** becomes **c** before **e**

The Seven Simple Tenses | The Seven Compound Tenses

Singular	Plural	Singular	Plural
1 presente de indicativo		8 perfecto de indicativo	
tropiezo	**tropezamos**	**he tropezado**	**hemos tropezado**
tropiezas	**tropezáis**	**has tropezado**	**habéis tropezado**
tropieza	**tropiezan**	**ha tropezado**	**han tropezado**
2 imperfecto de indicativo		9 pluscuamperfecto de indicativo	
tropezaba	**tropezábamos**	**había tropezado**	**habíamos tropezado**
tropezabas	**tropezabais**	**habías tropezado**	**habíais tropezado**
tropezaba	**tropezaban**	**había tropezado**	**habían tropezado**
3 pretérito		10 pretérito anterior	
tropecé	**tropezamos**	**hube tropezado**	**hubimos tropezado**
tropezaste	**tropezasteis**	**hubiste tropezado**	**hubisteis tropezado**
tropezó	**tropezaron**	**hubo tropezado**	**hubieron tropezado**
4 futuro		11 futuro perfecto	
tropezaré	**tropezaremos**	**habré tropezado**	**habremos tropezado**
tropezarás	**tropezaréis**	**habrás tropezado**	**habréis tropezado**
tropezará	**tropezarán**	**habrá tropezado**	**habrán tropezado**
5 potencial simple		12 potencial compuesto	
tropezaría	**tropezaríamos**	**habría tropezado**	**habríamos tropezado**
tropezarías	**tropezaríais**	**habrías tropezado**	**habríais tropezado**
tropezaría	**tropezarían**	**habría tropezado**	**habrían tropezado**
6 presente de subjuntivo		13 perfecto de subjuntivo	
tropiece	**tropecemos**	**haya tropezado**	**hayamos tropezado**
tropieces	**tropecéis**	**hayas tropezado**	**hayáis tropezado**
tropiece	**tropiecen**	**haya tropezado**	**hayan tropezado**
7 imperfecto de subjuntivo		14 pluscuamperfecto de subjuntivo	
tropezara	**tropezáramos**	**hubiera tropezado**	**hubiéramos tropezado**
tropezaras	**tropezarais**	**hubieras tropezado**	**hubierais tropezado**
tropezara	**tropezaran**	**hubiera tropezado**	**hubieran tropezado**
OR		OR	
tropezase	**tropezásemos**	**hubiese tropezado**	**hubiésemos tropezado**
tropezases	**tropezaseis**	**hubieses tropezado**	**hubieseis tropezado**
tropezase	**tropezasen**	**hubiese tropezado**	**hubiesen tropezado**

imperativo

—	**tropecemos**
tropieza; no tropieces	**tropezad; no tropecéis**
tropiece	**tropiecen**

Words and expressions related to this verb
tropezar con alguien   to run across someone, to meet someone unexpectedly
la tropezadura   stumbling
tropezador, tropezadora   tripper, stumbler
dar un tropezón   to trip, to stumble

Don't miss the definitions of basic grammatical terms with examples in English and Spanish on pages 33–44.

Regular **-ir** verb   to connect, to unite, to join, to bind, to attach

The Seven Simple Tenses		The Seven Compound Tenses	
Singular	Plural	Singular	Plural
1 presente de indicativo		8 perfecto de indicativo	
uno	unimos	he unido	hemos unido
unes	unís	has unido	habéis unido
une	unen	ha unido	han unido
2 imperfecto de indicativo		9 pluscuamperfecto de indicativo	
unía	uníamos	había unido	habíamos unido
unías	uníais	habías unido	habíais unido
unía	unían	había unido	habían unido
3 pretérito		10 pretérito anterior	
uní	unimos	hube unido	hubimos unido
uniste	unisteis	hubiste unido	hubisteis unido
unió	unieron	hubo unido	hubieron unido
4 futuro		11 futuro perfecto	
uniré	uniremos	habré unido	habremos unido
unirás	uniréis	habrás unido	habréis unido
unirá	unirán	habrá unido	habrán unido
5 potencial simple		12 potencial compuesto	
uniría	uniríamos	habría unido	habríamos unido
unirías	uniríais	habrías unido	habríais unido
uniría	unirían	habría unido	habrían unido
6 presente de subjuntivo		13 perfecto de subjuntivo	
una	unamos	haya unido	hayamos unido
unas	unáis	hayas unido	hayáis unido
una	unan	haya unido	hayan unido
7 imperfecto de subjuntivo		14 pluscuamperfecto de subjuntivo	
uniera	uniéramos	hubiera unido	hubiéramos unido
unieras	unierais	hubieras unido	hubierais unido
uniera	unieran	hubiera unido	hubieran unido
OR		OR	
uniese	uniésemos	hubiese unido	hubiésemos unido
unieses	unieseis	hubieses unido	hubieseis unido
uniese	uniesen	hubiese unido	hubiesen unido

imperativo	
—	unamos
une; no unas	unid; no unáis
una	unan

Words and expressions related to this verb
unido, unida   united
los Estados Unidos   the United States
la unión   union, agreement, harmony

unirse   to be united; to get married
La unión hace la fuerza   There is strength in unity.
las Naciones Unidas (ONU)   the United Nations (UN)

For other words and expressions related to this verb, see **reunirse.**

Check out the verb drills and verb tests with answers explained on pages 45–91.

to use, to employ, to wear   Regular **-ar** verb

The Seven Simple Tenses		The Seven Compound Tenses	
Singular	Plural	Singular	Plural
1 presente de indicativo		8 perfecto de indicativo	
uso	**usamos**	**he usado**	**hemos usado**
usas	**usáis**	**has usado**	**habéis usado**
usa	**usan**	**ha usado**	**han usado**
2 imperfecto de indicativo		9 pluscuamperfecto de indicativo	
usaba	**usábamos**	**había usado**	**habíamos usado**
usabas	**usabais**	**habías usado**	**habíais usado**
usaba	**usaban**	**había usado**	**habían usado**
3 pretérito		10 pretérito anterior	
usé	**usamos**	**hube usado**	**hubimos usado**
usaste	**usasteis**	**hubiste usado**	**hubisteis usado**
usó	**usaron**	**hubo usado**	**hubieron usado**
4 futuro		11 futuro perfecto	
usaré	**usaremos**	**habré usado**	**habremos usado**
usarás	**usaréis**	**habrás usado**	**habréis usado**
usará	**usarán**	**habrá usado**	**habrán usado**
5 potencial simple		12 potencial compuesto	
usaría	**usaríamos**	**habría usado**	**habríamos usado**
usarías	**usaríais**	**habrías usado**	**habríais usado**
usaría	**usarían**	**habría usado**	**habrían usado**
6 presente de subjuntivo		13 perfecto de subjuntivo	
use	**usemos**	**haya usado**	**hayamos usado**
uses	**uséis**	**hayas usado**	**hayáis usado**
use	**usen**	**haya usado**	**hayan usado**
7 imperfecto de subjuntivo		14 pluscuamperfecto de subjuntivo	
usara	**usáramos**	**hubiera usado**	**hubiéramos usado**
usaras	**usarais**	**hubieras usado**	**hubierais usado**
usara	**usaran**	**hubiera usado**	**hubieran usado**
OR		OR	
usase	**usásemos**	**hubiese usado**	**hubiésemos usado**
usases	**usaseis**	**hubieses usado**	**hubieseis usado**
usase	**usasen**	**hubiese usado**	**hubiesen usado**

imperativo	
—	**usemos**
usa; no uses	**usad; no uséis**
use	**usen**

Words and expressions related to this verb

¿Usa usted guantes?   Do you wear gloves?
el uso   use, usage
usado, usada   used
desusar   to disuse

en buen uso   in good condition
en uso   in use, in service
usar + inf.   to be used + inf.
desusarse   to be no longer in use

If you want an explanation of meanings and uses of Spanish
and English verb tenses and moods, see pages 13–32.

Regular **-ar** verb endings with spelling change: **z** becomes **c** before **e**   to utilize

The Seven Simple Tenses		The Seven Compound Tenses	
Singular	Plural	Singular	Plural
1 presente de indicativo		8 perfecto de indicativo	
utilizo	utilizamos	he utilizado	hemos utilizado
utilizas	utilizáis	has utilizado	habéis utilizado
utiliza	utilizan	ha utilizado	han utilizado
2 imperfecto de indicativo		9 pluscuamperfecto de indicativo	
utilizaba	utilizábamos	había utilizado	habíamos utilizado
utilizabas	utilizabais	habías utilizado	habíais utilizado
utilizaba	utilizaban	había utilizado	habían utilizado
3 pretérito		10 pretérito anterior	
utilicé	utilizamos	hube utilizado	hubimos utilizado
utilizaste	utilizasteis	hubiste utilizado	hubisteis utilizado
utilizó	utilizaron	hubo utilizado	hubieron utilizado
4 futuro		11 futuro perfecto	
utilizaré	utilizaremos	habré utilizado	habremos utilizado
utilizarás	utilizaréis	habrás utilizado	habréis utilizado
utilizará	utilizarán	habrá utilizado	habrán utilizado
5 potencial simple		12 potencial compuesto	
utilizaría	utilizaríamos	habría utilizado	habríamos utilizado
utilizarías	utilizaríais	habrías utilizado	habríais utilizado
utilizaría	utilizarían	habría utilizado	habrían utilizado
6 presente de subjuntivo		13 perfecto de subjuntivo	
utilice	utilicemos	haya utilizado	hayamos utilizado
utilices	utilicéis	hayas utilizado	hayáis utilizado
utilice	utilicen	haya utilizado	hayan utilizado
7 imperfecto de subjuntivo		14 pluscuamperfecto de subjuntivo	
utilizara	utilizáramos	hubiera utilizado	hubiéramos utilizado
utilizaras	utilizarais	hubieras utilizado	hubierais utilizado
utilizara	utilizaran	hubiera utilizado	hubieran utilizado
OR		OR	
utilizase	utilizásemos	hubiese utilizado	hubiésemos utilizado
utilizases	utilizaseis	hubieses utilizado	hubieseis utilizado
utilizase	utilizasen	hubiese utilizado	hubiesen utilizado

imperativo	
—	utilicemos
utiliza; no utilices	utilizad; no utilicéis
utilice	utilicen

Words and expressions related to this verb
la utilización utilization
utilizable usable, available
útil useful
el útil tool

la utilidad utility, usefulness
la utilidad pública public utility
ser útil to serve, to be useful
el programa de utilidad utility program

The subject pronouns are found on page 93.

to empty | Regular -ar verb endings with spelling change: **i** becomes **í** on stressed syllable (see Tenses 1, 6, Imperative)

The Seven Simple Tenses		The Seven Compound Tenses	
Singular	Plural	Singular	Plural
1 presente de indicativo		8 perfecto de indicativo	
vacío	vaciamos	he vaciado	hemos vaciado
vacías	vaciáis	has vaciado	habéis vaciado
vacía	vacían	ha vaciado	han vaciado
2 imperfecto de indicativo		9 pluscuamperfecto de indicativo	
vaciaba	vaciábamos	había vaciado	habíamos vaciado
vaciabas	vaciabais	habías vaciado	habíais vaciado
vaciaba	vaciaban	había vaciado	habían vaciado
3 pretérito		10 pretérito anterior	
vacié	vaciamos	hube vaciado	hubimos vaciado
vaciaste	vaciasteis	hubiste vaciado	hubisteis vaciado
vació	vaciaron	hubo vaciado	hubieron vaciado
4 futuro		11 futuro perfecto	
vaciaré	vaciaremos	habré vaciado	habremos vaciado
vaciarás	vaciaréis	habrás vaciado	habréis vaciado
vaciará	vaciarán	habrá vaciado	habrán vaciado
5 potencial simple		12 potencial compuesto	
vaciaría	vaciaríamos	habría vaciado	habríamos vaciado
vaciarías	vaciaríais	habrías vaciado	habríais vaciado
vaciaría	vaciarían	habría vaciado	habrían vaciado
6 presente de subjuntivo		13 perfecto de subjuntivo	
vacíe	vaciemos	haya vaciado	hayamos vaciado
vacíes	vaciéis	hayas vaciado	hayáis vaciado
vacíe	vacíen	haya vaciado	hayan vaciado
7 imperfecto de subjuntivo		14 pluscuamperfecto de subjuntivo	
vaciara	vaciáramos	hubiera vaciado	hubiéramos vaciado
vaciaras	vaciarais	hubieras vaciado	hubierais vaciado
vaciara	vaciaran	hubiera vaciado	hubieran vaciado
OR		OR	
vaciase	vaciásemos	hubiese vaciado	hubiésemos vaciado
vaciases	vaciaseis	hubieses vaciado	hubieseis vaciado
vaciase	vaciasen	hubiese vaciado	hubiesen vaciado

imperativo	
—	vaciemos
vacía; no vacíes	vaciad; no vaciéis
vacíe	vacíen

Words and expressions related to this verb
el vacío   void; vacancy; **un vacío de aire**   air pocket (aviation)
vacío, vacía   empty; **evacuar**   to evacuate
vacuo, vacua   empty

Don't miss the definitions of basic grammatical terms
with examples in English and Spanish on pages 33–44.

The Seven Simple Tenses		The Seven Compound Tenses	
Singular	Plural	Singular	Plural
1 presente de indicativo		8 perfecto de indicativo	
valgo	**valemos**	**he valido**	**hemos valido**
vales	**valéis**	**has valido**	**habéis valido**
vale	**valen**	**ha valido**	**han valido**
2 imperfecto de indicativo		9 pluscuamperfecto de indicativo	
valía	**valíamos**	**había valido**	**habíamos valido**
valías	**valíais**	**habías valido**	**habíais valido**
valía	**valían**	**había valido**	**habían valido**
3 pretérito		10 pretérito anterior	
valí	**valimos**	**hube valido**	**hubimos valido**
valiste	**valisteis**	**hubiste valido**	**hubisteis valido**
valió	**valieron**	**hubo valido**	**hubieron valido**
4 futuro		11 futuro perfecto	
valdré	**valdremos**	**habré valido**	**habremos valido**
valdrás	**valdréis**	**habrás valido**	**habréis valido**
valdrá	**valdrán**	**habrá valido**	**habrán valido**
5 potencial simple		12 potencial compuesto	
valdría	**valdríamos**	**habría valido**	**habríamos valido**
valdrías	**valdríais**	**habrías valido**	**habríais valido**
valdría	**valdrían**	**habría valido**	**habrían valido**
6 presente de subjuntivo		13 perfecto de subjuntivo	
valga	**valgamos**	**haya valido**	**hayamos valido**
valgas	**valgáis**	**hayas valido**	**hayáis valido**
valga	**valgan**	**haya valido**	**hayan valido**
7 imperfecto de subjuntivo		14 pluscuamperfecto de subjuntivo	
valiera	**valiéramos**	**hubiera valido**	**hubiéramos valido**
valieras	**valierais**	**hubieras valido**	**hubierais valido**
valiera	**valieran**	**hubiera valido**	**hubieran valido**
OR		OR	
valiese	**valiésemos**	**hubiese valido**	**hubiésemos valido**
valieses	**valieseis**	**hubieses valido**	**hubieseis valido**
valiese	**valiesen**	**hubiese valido**	**hubiesen valido**

V

	imperativo	
—		**valgamos**
val *or* **vale; no valgas**		**valed; no valgáis**
valga		**valgan**

Sentences using this verb and words related to it
Más vale pájaro en mano que ciento volando. A bird in the hand is worth two in the bush.
Más vale tarde que nunca. Better late than never.
el valor   value, price, valor
valor facial   face value
la valía   value, worth

valorar   to appraise, to increase the value
No vale la pena   It's not worth the trouble.
valeroso   courageous

The subject pronouns are found on page 93.   **627**

to stay awake, to guard, to watch over   Regular **-ar** verb

The Seven Simple Tenses		The Seven Compound Tenses	
Singular	Plural	Singular	Plural
1 presente de indicativo		8 perfecto de indicativo	
velo	velamos	he velado	hemos velado
velas	veláis	has velado	habéis velado
vela	velan	ha velado	han velado
2 imperfecto de indicativo		9 pluscuamperfecto de indicativo	
velaba	velábamos	había velado	habíamos velado
velabas	velabais	habías velado	habíais velado
velaba	velaban	había velado	habían velado
3 pretérito		10 pretérito anterior	
velé	velamos	hube velado	hubimos velado
velaste	velasteis	hubiste velado	hubisteis velado
veló	velaron	hubo velado	hubieron velado
4 futuro		11 futuro perfecto	
velaré	velaremos	habré velado	habremos velado
velarás	velaréis	habrás velado	habréis velado
velará	velarán	habrá velado	habrán velado
5 potencial simple		12 potencial compuesto	
velaría	velaríamos	habría velado	habríamos velado
velarías	velaríais	habrías velado	habríais velado
velaría	velarían	habría velado	habrían velado
6 presente de subjuntivo		13 perfecto de subjuntivo	
vele	velemos	haya velado	hayamos velado
veles	veléis	hayas velado	hayáis velado
vele	velen	haya velado	hayan velado
7 imperfecto de subjuntivo		14 pluscuamperfecto de subjuntivo	
velara	veláramos	hubiera velado	hubiéramos velado
velaras	velarais	hubieras velado	hubierais velado
velara	velaran	hubiera velado	hubieran velado
OR		OR	
velase	velásemos	hubiese velado	hubiésemos velado
velases	velaseis	hubieses velado	hubieseis velado
velase	velasen	hubiese velado	hubiesen velado

	imperativo	
—		velemos
vela; no veles		velad; no veléis
vele		velen

Words and expressions related to this verb
un velador   watchman, night guard; wooden candlestick
la vela   vigil; candle; **en vela**   without sleeping; **quedarse en velas**   to stay up (during the night)
velar a   to watch over (someone); **un velatorio**   wake
pasar la noche en vela   to toss and turn all night [or] to spend a sleepless night

Regular **-er** verb endings with spelling   to conquer, to overcome, to defeat
change: **c** becomes **z** before **a** or **o**

The Seven Simple Tenses		The Seven Compound Tenses	
Singular	Plural	Singular	Plural
1 presente de indicativo		8 perfecto de indicativo	
venzo	**vencemos**	**he vencido**	**hemos vencido**
vences	**vencéis**	**has vencido**	**habéis vencido**
vence	**vencen**	**ha vencido**	**han vencido**
2 imperfecto de indicativo		9 pluscuamperfecto de indicativo	
vencía	**vencíamos**	**había vencido**	**habíamos vencido**
vencías	**vencíais**	**habías vencido**	**habíais vencido**
vencía	**vencían**	**había vencido**	**habían vencido**
3 pretérito		10 pretérito anterior	
vencí	**vencimos**	**hube vencido**	**hubimos vencido**
venciste	**vencisteis**	**hubiste vencido**	**hubisteis vencido**
venció	**vencieron**	**hubo vencido**	**hubieron vencido**
4 futuro		11 futuro perfecto	
venceré	**venceremos**	**habré vencido**	**habremos vencido**
vencerás	**venceréis**	**habrás vencido**	**habréis vencido**
vencerá	**vencerán**	**habrá vencido**	**habrán vencido**
5 potencial simple		12 potencial compuesto	
vencería	**venceríamos**	**habría vencido**	**habríamos vencido**
vencerías	**venceríais**	**habrías vencido**	**habríais vencido**
vencería	**vencerían**	**habría vencido**	**habrían vencido**
6 presente de subjuntivo		13 perfecto de subjuntivo	
venza	**venzamos**	**haya vencido**	**hayamos vencido**
venzas	**venzáis**	**hayas vencido**	**hayáis vencido**
venza	**venzan**	**haya vencido**	**hayan vencido**
7 imperfecto de subjuntivo		14 pluscuamperfecto de subjuntivo	
venciera	**venciéramos**	**hubiera vencido**	**hubiéramos vencido**
vencieras	**vencierais**	**hubieras vencido**	**hubierais vencido**
venciera	**vencieran**	**hubiera vencido**	**hubieran vencido**
OR		OR	
venciese	**venciésemos**	**hubiese vencido**	**hubiésemos vencido**
vencieses	**vencieseis**	**hubieses vencido**	**hubieseis vencido**
venciese	**venciesen**	**hubiese vencido**	**hubiesen vencido**

V

imperativo	
—	**venzamos**
vence; no venzas	**venced; no venzáis**
venza	**venzan**

Words and expressions related to this verb

vencedor, vencedora   victor
vencible   conquerable
invencible   invincible

darse por vencido   to give in
vencerse   to control oneself
la invencibilidad   invincibility

See also **convencer.**

The subject pronouns are found on page 93.

to sell Regular **-er** verb

The Seven Simple Tenses		The Seven Compound Tenses	
Singular	Plural	Singular	Plural
1 presente de indicativo		8 perfecto de indicativo	
vendo	vendemos	he vendido	hemos vendido
vendes	vendéis	has vendido	habéis vendido
vende	venden	ha vendido	han vendido
2 imperfecto de indicativo		9 pluscuamperfecto de indicativo	
vendía	vendíamos	había vendido	habíamos vendido
vendías	vendíais	habías vendido	habíais vendido
vendía	vendían	había vendido	habían vendido
3 pretérito		10 pretérito anterior	
vendí	vendimos	hube vendido	hubimos vendido
vendiste	vendisteis	hubiste vendido	hubisteis vendido
vendió	vendieron	hubo vendido	hubieron vendido
4 futuro		11 futuro perfecto	
venderé	venderemos	habré vendido	habremos vendido
venderás	venderéis	habrás vendido	habréis vendido
venderá	venderán	habrá vendido	habrán vendido
5 potencial simple		12 potencial compuesto	
vendería	venderíamos	habría vendido	habríamos vendido
venderías	venderíais	habrías vendido	habríais vendido
vendería	venderían	habría vendido	habrían vendido
6 presente de subjuntivo		13 perfecto de subjuntivo	
venda	vendamos	haya vendido	hayamos vendido
vendas	vendáis	hayas vendido	hayáis vendido
venda	vendan	haya vendido	hayan vendido
7 imperfecto de subjuntivo		14 pluscuamperfecto de subjuntivo	
vendiera	vendiéramos	hubiera vendido	hubiéramos vendido
vendieras	vendierais	hubieras vendido	hubierais vendido
vendiera	vendieran	hubiera vendido	hubieran vendido
OR		OR	
vendiese	vendiésemos	hubiese vendido	hubiésemos vendido
vendieses	vendieseis	hubieses vendido	hubieseis vendido
vendiese	vendiesen	hubiese vendido	hubiesen vendido

	imperativo	
—		**vendamos**
vende; no vendas		**vended; no vendáis**
venda		**vendan**

Words and expressions related to this verb
vendedor, vendedora seller, sales person
la venta sale
el precio de venta selling price
Aquí se venden libros. Books are sold here.

vender a comisión to sell on commission
vender al contado to sell for cash
revender to resell
estar en venta to be on sale

Can't recognize an irregular verb form? Check out pages 678–681.

Irregular verb   to come

The Seven Simple Tenses | | The Seven Compound Tenses

Singular	Plural	Singular	Plural
1 presente de indicativo		8 perfecto de indicativo	
vengo	**venimos**	**he venido**	**hemos venido**
vienes	**venís**	**has venido**	**habéis venido**
viene	**vienen**	**ha venido**	**han venido**
2 imperfecto de indicativo		9 pluscuamperfecto de indicativo	
venía	**veníamos**	**había venido**	**habíamos venido**
venías	**veníais**	**habías venido**	**habíais venido**
venía	**venían**	**había venido**	**habían venido**
3 pretérito		10 pretérito anterior	
vine	**vinimos**	**hube venido**	**hubimos venido**
viniste	**vinisteis**	**hubiste venido**	**hubisteis venido**
vino	**vinieron**	**hubo venido**	**hubieron venido**
4 futuro		11 futuro perfecto	
vendré	**vendremos**	**habré venido**	**habremos venido**
vendrás	**vendréis**	**habrás venido**	**habréis venido**
vendrá	**vendrán**	**habrá venido**	**habrán venido**
5 potencial simple		12 potencial compuesto	
vendría	**vendríamos**	**habría venido**	**habríamos venido**
vendrías	**vendríais**	**habrías venido**	**habríais venido**
vendría	**vendrían**	**habría venido**	**habrían venido**
6 presente de subjuntivo		13 perfecto de subjuntivo	
venga	**vengamos**	**haya venido**	**hayamos venido**
vengas	**vengáis**	**hayas venido**	**hayáis venido**
venga	**vengan**	**haya venido**	**hayan venido**
7 imperfecto de subjuntivo		14 pluscuamperfecto de subjuntivo	
viniera	**viniéramos**	**hubiera venido**	**hubiéramos venido**
vinieras	**vinierais**	**hubieras venido**	**hubierais venido**
viniera	**vinieran**	**hubiera venido**	**hubieran venido**
OR		OR	
viniese	**viniésemos**	**hubiese venido**	**hubiésemos venido**
vinieses	**vinieseis**	**hubieses venido**	**hubieseis venido**
viniese	**viniesen**	**hubiese venido**	**hubiesen venido**

imperativo

—	**vengamos**
ven; no vengas	**venid; no vengáis**
venga	**vengan**

AN ESSENTIAL
55 VERB

AN ESSENTIAL 55 VERB

Venir

Venir is a very important irregular verb for beginning students. It is used in a great number of idiomatic expressions and everyday situations. Pay special attention to the stem changes!

Sentences using venir

La semana que viene voy a hacer un viaje.
Next week, I'm going to take a trip.

La señora González y su marido vienen de Venezuela.
Mrs. González and her husband come from (are from) Venezuela.

Prefiero quedarme en casa porque viene una tormenta.
I'd rather stay home because a storm is coming.

Words and expressions related to this verb

la venida **arrival, coming**

la semana que viene **next week**

el mes que viene **next month**

el porvenir **the future**

en lo porvenir **in the future**

venidero, venidera **future**

Venga lo que venga. **Come what may.**

Viene a ser lo mismo. **It amounts to the same thing.**

venir a las manos **to come to blows**

venir a buscar **to come for, to get**

venir a la mente **to come to mind**

venir a la cabeza **to come to mind**

venir a ser lo mismo **to amount to the same thing**

bienvenido, bienvenida **welcome**

dar la bienvenida a **to welcome**

¡Bienvenido! ¡Bienvenida! **Welcome!**

Can't find the verb you're looking for?
Check the back pages of this book for a list of over 2,100 additional verbs!

Irregular verb   to see

The Seven Simple Tenses		The Seven Compound Tenses	
Singular	Plural	Singular	Plural
1 presente de indicativo		**8 perfecto de indicativo**	
veo	vemos	he visto	hemos visto
ves	veis	has visto	habéis visto
ve	ven	ha visto	han visto
2 imperfecto de indicativo		**9 pluscuamperfecto de indicativo**	
veía	veíamos	había visto	habíamos visto
veías	veíais	habías visto	habíais visto
veía	veían	había visto	habían visto
3 pretérito		**10 pretérito anterior**	
vi	vimos	hube visto	hubimos visto
viste	visteis	hubiste visto	hubisteis visto
vio	vieron	hubo visto	hubieron visto
4 futuro		**11 futuro perfecto**	
veré	veremos	habré visto	habremos visto
verás	veréis	habrás visto	habréis visto
verá	verán	habrá visto	habrán visto
5 potencial simple		**12 potencial compuesto**	
vería	veríamos	habría visto	habríamos visto
verías	veríais	habrías visto	habríais visto
vería	verían	habría visto	habrían visto
6 presente de subjuntivo		**13 perfecto de subjuntivo**	
vea	veamos	haya visto	hayamos visto
veas	veáis	hayas visto	hayáis visto
vea	vean	haya visto	hayan visto
7 imperfecto de subjuntivo		**14 pluscuamperfecto de subjuntivo**	
viera	viéramos	hubiera visto	hubiéramos visto
vieras	vierais	hubieras visto	hubierais visto
viera	vieran	hubiera visto	hubieran visto
OR		OR	
viese	viésemos	hubiese visto	hubiésemos visto
vieses	vieseis	hubieses visto	hubieseis visto
viese	viesen	hubiese visto	hubiesen visto

V

imperativo	
—	veamos
ve; no veas	ved; no veáis
vea	vean

AN ESSENTIAL
55 VERB

AN ESSENTIAL 55 VERB

Ver is a very useful irregular verb for beginning students. It is used in a vast number of idiomatic expressions and everyday situations. Pay special attention to the stem changes!

Sentences using ver

Hay que verlo para creerlo.
You have to see it to believe it.

Está por ver.
It remains to be seen.

¿Vio Ud. el pájaro en el árbol?
Did you see the bird in the tree?

Proverbs

Ver es creer.
Seeing is believing.

De decir a hacer hay mucho que ver.
There is a great difference (much to see) between saying and doing.

Hasta que no lo veas, no lo creas.
Don't believe it until you see it.

Words and expressions related to this verb

la vista **sight, seeing, view, vision**

visto, vista **in view of**

a vista de pájaro **a bird's eye view**

vivir para ver **to live and learn**

a mi ver **in my opinion**

¡Ya se ve! **Of course! Certainly!**

¡A ver! **Let's see!**

¡Vamos a ver! **Let's see!**

no tener nada que ver con **to have nothing to do with**

la visión **vision**

visible **visible**

la visibilidad **visibility**

un vistazo **a glance**

echar un vistazo a **to take a look at**

verse las caras **to deal with it (have it out) face to face**

Can't remember the Spanish verb you need?
Check the back pages of this book for the English-Spanish verb index!

Regular **-ar** endings with spelling change:
c becomes **qu** before **e**

The Seven Simple Tenses		The Seven Compound Tenses	
Singular	Plural	Singular	Plural
1 presente de indicativo		8 perfecto de indicativo	
verifico	**verificamos**	**he verificado**	**hemos verificado**
verificas	**verificáis**	**has verificado**	**habéis verificado**
verifica	**verifican**	**ha verificado**	**han verificado**
2 inperfecto de indicativo		9 pluscuamperfecto de indicativo	
verificaba	**verificábamos**	**había verificado**	**habíamos verificado**
verificabas	**verificabais**	**habías verificado**	**habíais verificado**
verificaba	**verificaban**	**había verificado**	**habían verificado**
3 pretérito		10 pretérito anterior	
verifiqué	**verificamos**	**hube verificado**	**hubimos verificado**
verificaste	**verificasteis**	**hubiste verificado**	**hubisteis verificado**
verificó	**verificaron**	**hubo verificado**	**hubieron verificado**
4 futuro		11 futuro perfecto	
verificaré	**verificaremos**	**habré verificado**	**habremos verificado**
verificarás	**verificaréis**	**habrás verificado**	**habréis verificado**
verificará	**verificarán**	**habrá verificado**	**habrán verificado**
5 potencial simple		12 potencial compuesto	
verificaría	**verificaríamos**	**habría verificado**	**habríamos verificado**
verificarías	**verificaríais**	**habrías verificado**	**habríais verificado**
verificaría	**verificarían**	**habría verificado**	**habrían verificado**
6 presente de subjuntivo		13 perfecto de subjuntivo	
verifique	**verifiquemos**	**haya verificado**	**hayamos verificado**
verifiques	**verifiquéis**	**hayas verificado**	**hayáis verificado**
verifique	**verifiquen**	**haya verificado**	**hayan verificado**
7 imperfecto de subjuntivo		14 pluscuamperfecto de subjuntivo	
verificara	**verificáramos**	**hubiera verificado**	**hubiéramos verificado**
verificaras	**verificarais**	**hubieras verificado**	**hubierais verificado**
verificara	**verificaran**	**hubiera verificado**	**hubieran verificado**
OR		OR	
verificase	**verificásemos**	**hubiese verificado**	**hubiésemos verificado**
verificases	**verificaseis**	**hubieses verificado**	**hubieseis verificado**
verificase	**verificasen**	**hubiese verificado**	**hubiesen verificado**

imperativo	
—	**verifiquemos**
verifica; no verifiques	**verificad; no verifiquéis**
verifique	**verifiquen**

Words and expressions related to this verb
la verificación   verification, checking
el verificador, la verificadora   inspector

verificador, verificadora   verifying
verificarse   to come true, take place

to dress oneself,
to get dressed

Reflexive verb; regular **-ir** verb endings with stem
change: Tenses 1, 3, 6, 7, Imperative, Gerundio

The Seven Simple Tenses

The Seven Compound Tenses

Singular	Plural	Singular	Plural
1 presente de indicativo		**8 perfecto de indicativo**	
me visto	nos vestimos	me he vestido	nos hemos vestido
te vistes	os vestís	te has vestido	os habéis vestido
se viste	se visten	se ha vestido	se han vestido
2 imperfecto de indicativo		**9 pluscuamperfecto de indicativo**	
me vestía	nos vestíamos	me había vestido	nos habíamos vestido
te vestías	os vestíais	te habías vestido	os habíais vestido
se vestía	se vestían	se había vestido	se habían vestido
3 pretérito		**10 pretérito anterior**	
me vestí	nos vestimos	me hube vestido	nos hubimos vestido
te vestiste	os vestisteis	te hubiste vestido	os hubisteis vestido
se vistió	se vistieron	se hubo vestido	se hubieron vestido
4 futuro		**11 futuro perfecto**	
me vestiré	nos vestiremos	me habré vestido	nos habremos vestido
te vestirás	os vestiréis	te habrás vestido	os habréis vestido
se vestirá	se vestirán	se habrá vestido	se habrán vestido
5 potencial simple		**12 potencial compuesto**	
me vestiría	nos vestiríamos	me habría vestido	nos habríamos vestido
te vestirías	os vestiríais	te habrías vestido	os habríais vestido
se vestiría	se vestirían	se habría vestido	se habrían vestido
6 presente de subjuntivo		**13 perfecto de subjuntivo**	
me vista	nos vistamos	me haya vestido	nos hayamos vestido
te vistas	os vistáis	te hayas vestido	os hayáis vestido
se vista	se vistan	se haya vestido	se hayan vestido
7 imperfecto de subjuntivo		**14 pluscuamperfecto de subjuntivo**	
me vistiera	nos vistiéramos	me hubiera vestido	nos hubiéramos vestido
te vistieras	os vistierais	te hubieras vestido	os hubierais vestido
se vistiera	se vistieran	se hubiera vestido	se hubieran vestido
OR		OR	
me vistiese	nos vistiésemos	me hubiese vestido	nos hubiésemos vestido
te vistieses	os vistieseis	te hubieses vestido	os hubieseis vestido
se vistiese	se vistiesen	se hubiese vestido	se hubiesen vestido

imperativo	
—	vistámonos; no nos vistamos
vístete; no te vistas	vestíos; no os vistáis
vístase; no se vista	vístanse; no se vistan

Words and expressions related to this verb

vestir to clothe, to dress
desvestirse to undress oneself, to get
  undressed
el vestido clothing, clothes, dress
vestidos usados secondhand clothing

bien vestido well-dressed
vestir de uniforme to dress in uniform
vestir de blanco to dress in white
el vestuario wardrobe; cloakroom
la vestimenta clothes, garments

The Seven Simple Tenses		The Seven Compound Tenses

Singular	Plural	Singular	Plural
1 presente de indicativo		8 perfecto de indicativo	
viajo	**viajamos**	**he viajado**	**hemos viajado**
viajas	**viajáis**	**has viajado**	**habéis viajado**
viaja	**viajan**	**ha viajado**	**han viajado**
2 imperfecto de indicativo		9 pluscuamperfecto de indicativo	
viajaba	**viajábamos**	**había viajado**	**habíamos viajado**
viajabas	**viajabais**	**habías viajado**	**habíais viajado**
viajaba	**viajaban**	**había viajado**	**habían viajado**
3 pretérito		10 pretérito anterior	
viajé	**viajamos**	**hube viajado**	**hubimos viajado**
viajaste	**viajasteis**	**hubiste viajado**	**hubisteis viajado**
viajó	**viajaron**	**hubo viajado**	**hubieron viajado**
4 futuro		11 futuro perfecto	
viajaré	**viajaremos**	**habré viajado**	**habremos viajado**
viajarás	**viajaréis**	**habrás viajado**	**habréis viajado**
viajará	**viajarán**	**habrá viajado**	**habrán viajado**
5 potencial simple		12 potencial compuesto	
viajaría	**viajaríamos**	**habría viajado**	**habríamos viajado**
viajarías	**viajaríais**	**habrías viajado**	**habríais viajado**
viajaría	**viajarían**	**habría viajado**	**habrían viajado**
6 presente de subjuntivo		13 perfecto de subjuntivo	
viaje	**viajemos**	**haya viajado**	**hayamos viajado**
viajes	**viajéis**	**hayas viajado**	**hayáis viajado**
viaje	**viajen**	**haya viajado**	**hayan viajado**
7 imperfecto de subjuntivo		14 pluscuamperfecto de subjuntivo	
viajara	**viajáramos**	**hubiera viajado**	**hubiéramos viajado**
viajaras	**viajarais**	**hubieras viajado**	**hubierais viajado**
viajara	**viajaran**	**hubiera viajado**	**hubieran viajado**
OR		OR	
viajase	**viajásemos**	**hubiese viajado**	**hubiésemos viajado**
viajases	**viajaseis**	**hubieses viajado**	**hubieseis viajado**
viajase	**viajasen**	**hubiese viajado**	**hubiesen viajado**

	imperativo	
—		**viajemos**
viaja; no viajes		**viajad; no viajéis**
viaje		**viajen**

Words and expressions related to this verb

el viaje trip	**¡Buen viaje!** Have a good trip!
hacer un viaje to take a trip	**un viaje de negocios** business trip
un viaje de ida y vuelta round trip	**un viaje redondo** round trip
viajero, viajera traveler	**viajes espaciales** space travel
el viaje de novios honeymoon	**el viaje de recreo** pleasure trip

V

Do you need more drills? Have fun with the *501 Spanish Verbs* CD-ROM!

The subject pronouns are found on page 93.

to watch (over), to keep guard, to look out for   Regular **-ar** verb

The Seven Simple Tenses		The Seven Compound Tenses	
Singular	Plural	Singular	Plural
1 presente de indicativo		8 perfecto de indicativo	
vigilo	vigilamos	he vigilado	hemos vigilado
vigilas	vigiláis	has vigilado	habéis vigilado
vigila	vigilan	ha vigilado	han vigilado
2 imperfecto de indicativo		9 pluscuamperfecto de indicativo	
vigilaba	vigilábamos	había vigilado	habíamos vigilado
vigilabas	vigilabais	habías vigilado	habíais vigilado
vigilaba	vigilaban	había vigilado	habían vigilado
3 pretérito		10 pretérito anterior	
vigilé	vigilamos	hube vigilado	hubimos vigilado
vigilaste	vigilasteis	hubiste vigilado	hubisteis vigilado
vigiló	vigilaron	hubo vigilado	hubieron vigilado
4 futuro		11 futuro perfecto	
vigilaré	vigilaremos	habré vigilado	habremos vigilado
vigilarás	vigilaréis	habrás vigilado	habréis vigilado
vigilará	vigilarán	habrá vigilado	habrán vigilado
5 potencial simple		12 potencial compuesto	
vigilaría	vigilaríamos	habría vigilado	habríamos vigilado
vigilarías	vigilaríais	habrías vigilado	habríais vigilado
vigilaría	vigilarían	habría vigilado	habrían vigilado
6 presente de subjuntivo		13 perfecto de subjuntivo	
vigile	vigilemos	haya vigilado	hayamos vigilado
vigiles	vigiléis	hayas vigilado	hayáis vigilado
vigile	vigilen	haya vigilado	hayan vigilado
7 imperfecto de subjuntivo		14 pluscuamperfecto de subjuntivo	
vigilara	vigiláramos	hubiera vigilado	hubiéramos vigilado
vigilaras	vigilarais	hubieras vigilado	hubierais vigilado
vigilara	vigilaran	hubiera vigilado	hubieran vigilado
OR		OR	
vigilase	vigilásemos	hubiese vigilado	hubiésemos vigilado
vigilases	vigilaseis	hubieses vigilado	hubieseis vigilado
vigilase	vigilasen	hubiese vigilado	hubiesen vigilado

imperativo	
—	**vigilemos**
vigila; no vigiles	**vigilad; no vigiléis**
vigile	**vigilen**

Words and expressions related to this verb

vigilar de cerca   to keep a close watch on
el, la vigilante   vigilante; vigilant, wakeful
la vigilancia   vigilance, watchfulness, surveillance

vigilantemente   vigilantly
vigilar sobre *or* **por**   to watch over
comer de vigilia   to abstain from meat
vigilante de noche   night watchman

The Seven Simple Tenses		The Seven Compound Tenses	
Singular	Plural	Singular	Plural
1 presente de indicativo		8 perfecto de indicativo	
visito	**visitamos**	**he visitado**	**hemos visitado**
visitas	**visitáis**	**has visitado**	**habéis visitado**
visita	**visitan**	**ha visitado**	**han visitado**
2 imperfecto de indicativo		9 pluscuamperfecto de indicativo	
visitaba	**visitábamos**	**había visitado**	**habíamos visitado**
visitabas	**visitabais**	**habías visitado**	**habíais visitado**
visitaba	**visitaban**	**había visitado**	**habían visitado**
3 pretérito		10 pretérito anterior	
visité	**visitamos**	**hube visitado**	**hubimos visitado**
visitaste	**visitasteis**	**hubiste visitado**	**hubisteis visitado**
visitó	**visitaron**	**hubo visitado**	**hubieron visitado**
4 futuro		11 futuro perfecto	
visitaré	**visitaremos**	**habré visitado**	**habremos visitado**
visitarás	**visitaréis**	**habrás visitado**	**habréis visitado**
visitará	**visitarán**	**habrá visitado**	**habrán visitado**
5 potencial simple		12 potencial compuesto	
visitaría	**visitaríamos**	**habría visitado**	**habríamos visitado**
visitarías	**visitaríais**	**habrías visitado**	**habríais visitado**
visitaría	**visitarían**	**habría visitado**	**habrían visitado**
6 presente de subjuntivo		13 perfecto de subjuntivo	
visite	**visitemos**	**haya visitado**	**hayamos visitado**
visites	**visitéis**	**hayas visitado**	**hayáis visitado**
visite	**visiten**	**haya visitado**	**hayan visitado**
7 imperfecto de subjuntivo		14 pluscuamperfecto de subjuntivo	
visitara	**visitáramos**	**hubiera visitado**	**hubiéramos visitado**
visitaras	**visitarais**	**hubieras visitado**	**hubierais visitado**
visitara	**visitaran**	**hubiera visitado**	**hubieran visitado**
OR		OR	
visitase	**visitásemos**	**hubiese visitado**	**hubiésemos visitado**
visitases	**visitaseis**	**hubieses visitado**	**hubieseis visitado**
visitase	**visitasen**	**hubiese visitado**	**hubiesen visitado**

V

imperativo	
—	**visitemos**
visita; no visites	**visitad; no visitéis**
visite	**visiten**

Words and expressions related to this verb

una visita visit   **una visitación** visitation
visitante visitor   **pagar la visita** to return a visit
visitarse to visit one another   **tener visita** to have company
hacer una visita to pay a call, a visit   **una visita acompañada** guided tour

Can't recognize an irregular verb form? Check out pages 678–681.

The subject pronouns are found on page 93.

vivir (495)

Gerundio **viviendo**

Part. pas. **vivido**

to live

The Seven Simple Tenses		The Seven Compound Tenses	
Singular	Plural	Singular	Plural
1 presente de indicativo		8 perfecto de indicativo	
vivo	vivimos	he vivido	hemos vivido
vives	vivís	has vivido	habéis vivido
vive	viven	ha vivido	han vivido
2 imperfecto de indicativo		9 pluscuamperfecto de indicativo	
vivía	vivíamos	había vivido	habíamos vivido
vivías	vivíais	habías vivido	habíais vivido
vivía	vivían	había vivido	habían vivido
3 pretérito		10 pretérito anterior	
viví	vivimos	hube vivido	hubimos vivido
viviste	vivisteis	hubiste vivido	hubisteis vivido
vivió	vivieron	hubo vivido	hubieron vivido
4 futuro		11 futuro perfecto	
viviré	viviremos	habré vivido	habremos vivido
vivirás	viviréis	habrás vivido	habréis vivido
vivirá	vivirán	habrá vivido	habrán vivido
5 potencial simple		12 potencial compuesto	
viviría	viviríamos	habría vivido	habríamos vivido
vivirías	viviríais	habrías vivido	habríais vivido
viviría	vivirían	habría vivido	habrían vivido
6 presente de subjuntivo		13 perfecto de subjuntivo	
viva	vivamos	haya vivido	hayamos vivido
vivas	viváis	hayas vivido	hayáis vivido
viva	vivan	haya vivido	hayan vivido
7 imperfecto de subjuntivo		14 pluscuamperfecto de subjuntivo	
viviera	viviéramos	hubiera vivido	hubiéramos vivido
vivieras	vivierais	hubieras vivido	hubierais vivido
viviera	vivieran	hubiera vivido	hubieran vivido
OR		OR	
viviese	viviésemos	hubiese vivido	hubiésemos vivido
vivieses	vivieseis	hubieses vivido	hubieseis vivido
viviese	viviesen	hubiese vivido	hubiesen vivido

imperativo	
—	vivamos
vive; no vivas	vivid; no viváis
viva	vivan

AN ESSENTIAL
55 VERB

AN ESSENTIAL
55 VERB

Vivir

Vivir is a very useful regular –ir verb for beginning students. It is used in a vast number of idiomatic expressions and everyday situations.

Sentences using vivir

Vivimos en esta casa desde hace veinte años.
We have been living in this house for twenty years.

Tenemos con que vivir.
We have enough to live on.

Proverb

Comer para vivir y no vivir para comer.
One should eat to live and not live to eat.

Words and expressions related to this verb

vivo, viva **living**

sin vida **lifeless**

vivir de **to live on**

la vida **life**

en vida **living, alive**

estar en vida **to be alive**

ganarse la vida **to earn one's living**

una lengua viva **a living language**

vivir del aire **to live on thin air**

vivir para ver **to live and learn (live to see)**

vivir a oscuras **to live in ignorance**

revivir **to revive**

vivir bien **to live well**

¿Quién vive? **Who goes there?**

¡Viva la reina! **Long live the queen!**

¡Viva el rey! **Long live the king!**

¡La vida es así! **That's life!**

V

Can't find the verb you're looking for?
Check the back pages of this book for a list of over 2,100 additional verbs!

The subject pronouns are found on page 93.

to fly | Regular **-ar** verb endings with stem change: Tenses 1, 6, Imperative

The Seven Simple Tenses		The Seven Compound Tenses	
Singular	Plural	Singular	Plural
1 presente de indicativo		8 perfecto de indicativo	
vuelo	volamos	he volado	hemos volado
vuelas	voláis	has volado	habéis volado
vuela	vuelan	ha volado	han volado
2 imperfecto de indicativo		9 pluscuamperfecto de indicativo	
volaba	volábamos	había volado	habíamos volado
volabas	volabais	habías volado	habíais volado
volaba	volaban	había volado	habían volado
3 pretérito		10 pretérito anterior	
volé	volamos	hube volado	hubimos volado
volaste	volasteis	hubiste volado	hubisteis volado
voló	volaron	hubo volado	hubieron volado
4 futuro		11 futuro perfecto	
volaré	volaremos	habré volado	habremos volado
volarás	volaréis	habrás volado	habréis volado
volará	volarán	habrá volado	habrán volado
5 potencial simple		12 potencial compuesto	
volaría	volaríamos	habría volado	habríamos volado
volarías	volaríais	habrías volado	habríais volado
volaría	volarían	habría volado	habrían volado
6 presente de subjuntivo		13 perfecto de subjuntivo	
vuele	volemos	haya volado	hayamos volado
vueles	voléis	hayas volado	hayáis volado
vuele	vuelen	haya volado	hayan volado
7 imperfecto de subjuntivo		14 pluscuamperfecto de subjuntivo	
volara	voláramos	hubiera volado	hubiéramos volado
volaras	volarais	hubieras volado	hubierais volado
volara	volaran	hubiera volado	hubieran volado
OR		OR	
volase	volásemos	hubiese volado	hubiésemos volado
volases	volaseis	hubieses volado	hubieseis volado
volase	volasen	hubiese volado	hubiesen volado

imperativo	
—	volemos
vuela; no vueles	volad; no voléis
vuele	vuelen

Words and expressions related to this verb
el **vuelo**   flight
Más vale pájaro en mano que ciento volando   A bird in the hand is worth two in the bush.
Las horas vuelan   The hours go flying by.   **¡Como vuela el tiempo!**   How time flies!
volear   to volley (a ball); **el voleo**   volley
el **volante**   steering wheel

Don't forget to study the section on defective and impersonal verbs. It's right after this main list.

Regular **-er** verb endings with stem change: to return, to go back
Tenses 1, 6, Imperative, Past Participle

The Seven Simple Tenses		The Seven Compound Tenses	
Singular	Plural	Singular	Plural
1 presente de indicativo		8 perfecto de indicativo	
vuelvo	**volvemos**	**he vuelto**	**hemos vuelto**
vuelves	**volvéis**	**has vuelto**	**habéis vuelto**
vuelve	**vuelven**	**ha vuelto**	**han vuelto**
2 imperfecto de indicativo		9 pluscuamperfecto de indicativo	
volvía	**volvíamos**	**había vuelto**	**habíamos vuelto**
volvías	**volvíais**	**habías vuelto**	**habíais vuelto**
volvía	**volvían**	**había vuelto**	**habían vuelto**
3 pretérito		10 pretérito anterior	
volví	**volvimos**	**hube vuelto**	**hubimos vuelto**
volviste	**volvisteis**	**hubiste vuelto**	**hubisteis vuelto**
volvió	**volvieron**	**hubo vuelto**	**hubieron vuelto**
4 futuro		11 futuro perfecto	
volveré	**volveremos**	**habré vuelto**	**habremos vuelto**
volverás	**volveréis**	**habrás vuelto**	**habréis vuelto**
volverá	**volverán**	**habrá vuelto**	**habrán vuelto**
5 potencial simple		12 potencial compuesto	
volvería	**volveríamos**	**habría vuelto**	**habríamos vuelto**
volverías	**volveríais**	**habrías vuelto**	**habríais vuelto**
volvería	**volverían**	**habría vuelto**	**habrían vuelto**
6 presente de subjuntivo		13 perfecto de subjuntivo	
vuelva	**volvamos**	**haya vuelto**	**hayamos vuelto**
vuelvas	**volváis**	**hayas vuelto**	**hayáis vuelto**
vuelva	**vuelvan**	**haya vuelto**	**hayan vuelto**
7 imperfecto de subjuntivo		14 pluscuamperfecto de subjuntivo	
volviera	**volviéramos**	**hubiera vuelto**	**hubiéramos vuelto**
volvieras	**volvierais**	**hubieras vuelto**	**hubierais vuelto**
volviera	**volvieran**	**hubiera vuelto**	**hubieran vuelto**
OR		OR	
volviese	**volviésemos**	**hubiese vuelto**	**hubiésemos vuelto**
volvieses	**volvieseis**	**hubieses vuelto**	**hubieseis vuelto**
volviese	**volviesen**	**hubiese vuelto**	**hubiesen vuelto**

V

imperativo

—	**volvamos**
vuelve; no vuelvas	**volved; no volváis**
vuelva	**vuelvan**

AN ESSENTIAL
55 VERB

The subject pronouns are found on page 93.

Volver

Volver is a very useful –er verb for beginning students. It is used in a vast number of idiomatic expressions and everyday situations. Be careful to make the stem change in Tenses 1 and 6, as well as the imperative and past participle.

Sentences using volver

¿A qué hora vuelve Ud. a casa?
At what time are you going back home?

¿Cuándo podré volver?
When may I return?

Vuelve la página, por favor.
Turn the page, please.

Words and expressions related to this verb

volver en sí **to regain consciousness, to come to**

volver sobre sus pasos **to retrace one's steps**

volver atrás **to turn back**

una vuelta **a turn, revolution, turning**

dar una vuelta **to take a stroll**

volverse triste **to become sad**

un revólver **revolver, pistol**

revolver **to revolve, shake (up), to turn around**

volver con las manos vacías **to return empty-handed**

volverse **to turn (oneself) around**

volverse loco **to go mad**

devolver un artículo **to return an article**

devolver **to return, go back**

Can't remember the Spanish verb you need?
Check the back pages of this book for the English-Spanish verb index!

Regular **-ar** verb   to vote, to vow

The Seven Simple Tenses		The Seven Compound Tenses	
Singular	Plural	Singular	Plural
1 presente de indicativo		8 perfecto de indicativo	
voto	**votamos**	**he votado**	**hemos votado**
votas	**votáis**	**has votado**	**habéis votado**
vota	**votan**	**ha votado**	**han votado**
2 imperfecto de indicativo		9 pluscuamperfecto de indicativo	
votaba	**votábamos**	**había votado**	**habíamos votado**
votabas	**votabais**	**habías votado**	**habíais votado**
votaba	**votaban**	**había votado**	**habían votado**
3 pretérito		10 pretérito anterior	
voté	**votamos**	**hube votado**	**hubimos votado**
votaste	**votasteis**	**hubiste votado**	**hubisteis votado**
votó	**votaron**	**hubo votado**	**hubieron votado**
4 futuro		11 futuro perfecto	
votaré	**votaremos**	**habré votado**	**habremos votado**
votarás	**votaréis**	**habrás votado**	**habréis votado**
votará	**votarán**	**habrá votado**	**habrán votado**
5 potencial simple		12 potencial compuesto	
votaría	**votaríamos**	**habría votado**	**habríamos votado**
votarías	**votaríais**	**habrías votado**	**habríais votado**
votaría	**votarían**	**habría votado**	**habrían votado**
6 presente de subjuntivo		13 perfecto de subjuntivo	
vote	**votemos**	**haya votado**	**hayamos votado**
votes	**votéis**	**hayas votado**	**hayáis votado**
vote	**voten**	**haya votado**	**hayan votado**
7 imperfecto de subjuntivo		14 pluscuamperfecto de subjuntivo	
votara	**votáramos**	**hubiera votado**	**hubiéramos votado**
votaras	**votarais**	**hubieras votado**	**hubierais votado**
votara	**votaran**	**hubiera votado**	**hubieran votado**
OR		OR	
votase	**votásemos**	**hubiese votado**	**hubiésemos votado**
votases	**votaseis**	**hubieses votado**	**hubieseis votado**
votase	**votasen**	**hubiese votado**	**hubiesen votado**

imperativo	
—	**votemos**
vota; no votes	**votad; no votéis**
vote	**voten**

Words and expressions related to this verb
votar en pro   to vote for; **votar en contra**   to vote against
el votador, la votadora   voter
el voto   vote, vow; **voto de gracias**   vote of thanks; **voto activo**   right to vote;
   voto de confianza   vote of confidence; **echar votos**   to curse, to swear
la votación   voting; **la votación a mano alzada**   voting by show of hands
la votación secreta   secret ballot

Get acquainted with what preposition goes with what verb on pages 669–677.

The subject pronouns are found on page 93.   **645**

yacer (499) Gerundio yaciendo Part. pas. yacido

to lie down, to be lying down, to lie in a grave	Regular **-er** verb endings; spelling change (see Tenses 1, 6, and Imperative)

The Seven Simple Tenses	The Seven Compound Tenses

Singular	Plural	Singular	Plural
1 presente de indicativo		**8 perfecto de indicativo**	
yazco or **yazgo** or **yago**	**yacemos**	**he yacido**	**hemos yacido**
yaces	**yacéis**	**has yacido**	**habéis yacido**
yace	**yacen**	**ha yacido**	**han yacido**
2 imperfecto de indicativo		**9 pluscuamperfecto de indicativo**	
yacía	**yacíamos**	**había yacido**	**habíamos yacido**
yacías	**yacíais**	**habías yacido**	**habíais yacido**
yacía	**yacían**	**había yacido**	**habían yacido**
3 pretérito		**10 pretérito anterior**	
yací	**yacimos**	**hube yacido**	**hubimos yacido**
yaciste	**yacisteis**	**hubiste yacido**	**hubisteis yacido**
yació	**yacieron**	**hubo yacido**	**hubieron yacido**
4 futuro		**11 futuro perfecto**	
yaceré	**yaceremos**	**habré yacido**	**habremos yacido**
yacerás	**yaceréis**	**habrás yacido**	**habréis yacido**
yacerá	**yacerán**	**habrá yacido**	**habrán yacido**
5 potencial simple		**12 potencial compuesto**	
yacería	**yaceríamos**	**habría yacido**	**habríamos yacido**
yacerías	**yaceríais**	**habrías yacido**	**habríais yacido**
yacería	**yacerían**	**habría yacido**	**habrían yacido**
6 presente de subjuntivo		**13 perfecto de subjuntivo**	
yazca or **yazga** or **yaga**	**yazcamos** or **yazgamos** or **yagamos**	**haya yacido**	**hayamos yacido**
yazcas or **yazgas** or **yagas**	**yazcáis** or **yazgáis** or **yagáis**	**hayas yacido**	**hayáis yacido**
yazca or **yazga** or **yaga**	**yazcan** or **yazgan** or **yagan**	**haya yacido**	**hayan yacido**
7 imperfecto de subjuntivo		**14 pluscuamperfecto de subjuntivo**	
yaciera	**yaciéramos**	**hubiera yacido**	**hubiéramos yacido**
yacieras	**yacierais**	**hubieras yacido**	**hubierais yacido**
yaciera	**yacieran**	**hubiera yacido**	**hubieran yacido**
OR		OR	
yaciese	**yaciésemos**	**hubiese yacido**	**hubiésemos yacido**
yacieses	**yacieseis**	**hubieses yacido**	**hubieseis yacido**
yaciese	**yaciesen**	**hubiese yacido**	**hubiesen yacido**

imperativo

—	**yazcamos** or **yazgamos** or **yagamos**
yaz or **yace; no yazcas**	**yaced; no yazcáis**
yazca or **yazga** or **yaga**	**yazcan** or **yazgan** or **yagan**

Words and expressions related to this verb
la yacija bed, couch; grave, tomb
el yacimiento mineral deposit

Aquí yace don Juan Here lies Don Juan.
una estatua yacente statue lying in state (usually on a catafalque)

Regular **-ar** verb   to buzz, to hum, to flutter around

The Seven Simple Tenses		The Seven Compound Tenses	
Singular	Plural	Singular	Plural
1 presente de indicativo		8 perfecto de indicativo	
zumbo	zumbamos	he zumbado	hemos zumbado
zumbas	zumbáis	has zumbado	habéis zumbado
zumba	zumban	ha zumbado	han zumbado
2 imperfecto de indicativo		9 pluscuamperfecto de indicativo	
zumbaba	zumbábamos	había zumbado	habíamos zumbado
zumbabas	zumbabais	habías zumbado	habíais zumbado
zumbaba	zumbaban	había zumbado	habían zumbado
3 pretérito		10 pretérito anterior	
zumbé	zumbamos	hube zumbado	hubimos zumbado
zumbaste	zumbasteis	hubiste zumbado	hubisteis zumbado
zumbó	zumbaron	hubo zumbado	hubieron zumbado
4 futuro		11 futuro perfecto	
zumbaré	zumbaremos	habré zumbado	habremos zumbado
zumbarás	zumbaréis	habrás zumbado	habréis zumbado
zumbará	zumbarán	habrá zumbado	habrán zumbado
5 potencial simple		12 potencial compuesto	
zumbaría	zumbaríamos	habría zumbado	habríamos zumbado
zumbarías	zumbaríais	habrías zumbado	habríais zumbado
zumbaría	zumbarían	habría zumbado	habrían zumbado
6 presente de subjuntivo		13 perfecto de subjuntivo	
zumbe	zumbemos	haya zumbado	hayamos zumbado
zumbes	zumbéis	hayas zumbado	hayáis zumbado
zumbe	zumben	haya zumbado	hayan zumbado
7 imperfecto de subjuntivo		14 pluscuamperfecto de subjuntivo	
zumbara	zumbáramos	hubiera zumbado	hubiéramos zumbado
zumbaras	zumbarais	hubieras zumbado	hubierais zumbado
zumbara	zumbaran	hubiera zumbado	hubieran zumbado
OR		OR	
zumbase	zumbásemos	hubiese zumbado	hubiésemos zumbado
zumbases	zumbaseis	hubieses zumbado	hubieseis zumbado
zumbase	zumbasen	hubiese zumbado	hubiesen zumbado

imperativo	
—	zumbemos
zumba; no zumbes	zumbad; no zumbéis
zumbe	zumben

Words and expressions related to this verb

Me zumban los cincuenta años.   I am close
   to fifty years old.
zumbarse de   to make fun of
zumbar una bofetada   to give a hard slap
Bala que zumba no mata.   A bullet that
   buzzes doesn't kill.

un zumbo, un zumbido   buzz, hum; **un
   zumbido de ocupado**   busy signal of a
   telephone
un zumbador   buzzer

Y
Z

to darn, to mend

Regular -ir verb endings with spelling change: c becomes z before a or o

The Seven Simple Tenses		The Seven Compound Tenses	
Singular	Plural	Singular	Plural
1 presente de indicativo		8 perfecto de indicativo	
zurzo	zurcimos	he zurcido	hemos zurcido
zurces	zurcís	has zurcido	habéis zurcido
zurce	zurcen	ha zurcido	han zurcido
2 imperfecto de indicativo		9 pluscuamperfecto de indicativo	
zurcía	zurcíamos	había zurcido	habíamos zurcido
zurcías	zurcíais	habías zurcido	habíais zurcido
zurcía	zurcían	había zurcido	habían zurcido
3 pretérito		10 pretérito anterior	
zurcí	zurcimos	hube zurcido	hubimos zurcido
zurciste	zurcisteis	hubiste zurcido	hubisteis zurcido
zurció	zurcieron	hubo zurcido	hubieron zurcido
4 futuro		11 futuro perfecto	
zurciré	zurciremos	habré zurcido	habremos zurcido
zurcirás	zurciréis	habrás zurcido	habréis zurcido
zurcirá	zurcirán	habrá zurcido	habrán zurcido
5 potencial simple		12 potencial compuesto	
zurciría	zurciríamos	habría zurcido	habríamos zurcido
zurcirías	zurciríais	habrías zurcido	habríais zurcido
zurciría	zurcirían	habría zurcido	habrían zurcido
6 presente de subjuntivo		13 perfecto de subjuntivo	
zurza	zurzamos	haya zurcido	hayamos zurcido
zurzas	zurzáis	hayas zurcido	hayáis zurcido
zurza	zurzan	haya zurcido	hayan zurcido
7 imperfecto de subjuntivo		14 pluscuamperfecto de subjuntivo	
zurciera	zurciéramos	hubiera zurcido	hubiéramos zurcido
zurcieras	zurcierais	hubieras zurcido	hubierais zurcido
zurciera	zurcieran	hubiera zurcido	hubieran zurcido
OR		OR	
zurciese	zurciésemos	hubiese zurcido	hubiésemos zurcido
zurcieses	zurcieseis	hubieses zurcido	hubieseis zurcido
zurciese	zurciesen	hubiese zurcido	hubiesen zurcido

imperativo	
—	zurzamos
zurce; no zurzas	zurcid; no zurzáis
zurza	zurzan

Words related to this verb
la zurcidura darning, mending
zurcido, zurcida darned, mended

un huevo de zurcir darning ball (egg)
la aguja de zurcir darning needle

Don't forget to study the section on defective and impersonal verbs. It's right after this main list.

Appendixes

Defective and impersonal verbs

Gerundio **aboliendo**   Part. pas. **abolido**   **abolir**

Regular **-ir** verb endings

to abolish

The Seven Simple Tenses		The Seven Compound Tenses	
Singular	Plural	Singular	Plural
1 presente de indicativo		8 perfecto de indicativo	
—	abolimos	he abolido	hemos abolido
—	abolís	has abolido	habéis abolido
—	—	ha abolido	han abolido
2 imperfecto de indicativo		9 pluscuamperfecto de indicativo	
abolía	abolíamos	había abolido	habíamos abolido
abolías	abolíais	habías abolido	habíais abolido
abolía	abolían	había abolido	habían abolido
3 pretérito		10 pretérito anterior	
abolí	abolimos	hube abolido	hubimos abolido
aboliste	abolisteis	hubiste abolido	hubisteis abolido
abolió	abolieron	hubo abolido	hubieron abolido
4 futuro		11 futuro perfecto	
aboliré	aboliremos	habré abolido	habremos abolido
abolirás	aboliréis	habrás abolido	habréis abolido
abolirá	abolirán	habrá abolido	habrán abolido
5 potencial simple		12 potencial compuesto	
aboliría	aboliríamos	habría abolido	habríamos abolido
abolirías	aboliríais	habrías abolido	habríais abolido
aboliría	abolirían	habría abolido	habrían abolido
6 presente de subjuntivo		13 perfecto de subjuntivo	
Not in use		haya abolido	hayamos abolido
		hayas abolido	hayáis abolido
7 imperfecto de subjuntivo		haya abolido	hayan abolido
aboliera	aboliéramos		
abolieras	abolierais	14 pluscuamperfecto de subjuntivo	
aboliera	abolieran	hubiera abolido	hubiéramos abolido
OR		hubieras abolido	hubierais abolido
aboliese	aboliésemos	hubiera abolido	hubieran abolido
abolieses	abolieseis	OR	
aboliese	aboliesen	hubiese abolido	hubiésemos abolido
		hubieses abolido	hubieseis abolido
		hubiese abolido	hubiesen abolido

imperativo	
—	—
—	abolid
—	—

Abolir is a defective verb.

bastar	Gerundio **bastando**	Part. pas. **bastado**
to be enough, to be sufficient, to suffice		Regular **-ar** verb

The Seven Simple Tenses		The Seven Compound Tenses	
Singular	Plural	Singular	Plural
1 presente de indicativo		8 perfecto de indicativo	
basta	**bastan**	**ha bastado**	**han bastado**
2 imperfecto de indicativo		9 pluscuamperfecto de indicativo	
bastaba	**bastaban**	**había bastado**	**habían bastado**
3 pretérito		10 pretérito anterior	
bastó	**bastaron**	**hubo bastado**	**hubieron bastado**
4 futuro		11 futuro perfecto	
bastará	**bastarán**	**habré bastado**	**habrán bastado**
5 potencial simple		12 potencial compuesto	
bastaría	**bastarían**	**habría bastado**	**habrían bastado**
6 presente de subjuntivo		13 perfecto de subjuntivo	
que baste	**que basten**	**haya bastado**	**hayan bastado**
7 imperfecto de subjuntivo		14 pluscuamperfecto de subjuntivo	
que bastara	**que bastaran**	**hubiera bastado**	**hubieran bastado**
OR		OR	
que bastase	**que bastasen**	**hubiese bastado**	**hubiesen bastado**

imperativo

¡Que baste!   **¡Que basten!**

Common expression related to this verb
¡Basta!   Enough! That will do!
This is an impersonal verb and it is used mainly in the third person singular and plural.
It is a regular **ar** verb and can be conjugated in all the persons.

Regular **-ar** verb endings with stem　　　　to cost
change: Tenses 1, 6, Imperative

The Seven Simple Tenses		The Seven Compound Tenses	
Singular	Plural	Singular	Plural
1　presente de indicativo		8　perfecto de indicativo	
cuesta	**cuestan**	**ha costado**	**han costado**
2　imperfecto de indicativo		9　pluscuamperfecto de indicativo	
costaba	**costaban**	**había costado**	**habían costado**
3　pretérito		10　pretérito anterior	
costó	**costaron**	**hubo costado**	**hubieron costado**
4　futuro		11　futuro perfecto	
costará	**costarán**	**habrá costado**	**habrán costado**
5　potencial simple		12　potencial compuesto	
costaría	**costarían**	**habría costado**	**habrían costado**
6　presente de subjuntivo		13　perfecto de subjuntivo	
que cueste	**que cuesten**	**que haya costado**	**que hayan costado**
7　imperfecto de subjuntivo		14　pluscuamperfecto de subjuntivo	
que costara	**que costaran**	**que hubiera costado**	**que hubieran costado**
OR		OR	
que costase	**que costasen**	**que hubiese costado**	**que hubiesen costado**

imperativo
¡Que cueste!　　　　　　**¡Que cuesten!**

Sentences using this verb and words and expressions related to it
—**¿Cuánto cuesta este libro?**　　　　**Cuesta + inf.**　It is difficult to . . .
—**Cuesta diez euros.**　　　　　　　　**Cuesta creerlo.**　It's difficult to believe it.

costoso, costosa　costly, expensive　　　**costar un ojo de la cara**　to be very expensive
el costo　price, cost　　　　　　　　　　(to cost an arm and a leg)
el costo de la vida　the cost of living　　**cueste lo que cueste**　at any cost
costear　to finance

Defective and impersonal verbs　**653**

embaír

Gerundio **embayendo**   Part. pas. **embaído**

to trick, to deceive   Irregular verb

The Seven Simple Tenses		The Seven Compound Tenses	
Singular	Plural	Singular	Plural
1 presente de indicativo		8 perfecto de indicativo	
—	embaímos	he embaído	hemos embaído
—	embaís	has embaído	habéis embaído
—	—	ha embaído	han embaído
2 imperfecto de indicativo		9 pluscuamperfecto de indicativo	
embaía	embaíamos	había embaído	habíamos embaído
embaías	embaíais	habías embaído	habíais embaído
embaía	embaían	había embaído	habían embaído
3 pretérito		10 pretérito anterior	
embaí	embaímos	hube embaído	hubimos embaído
embaíste	embaísteis	hubiste embaído	hubisteis embaído
embayó	embayeron	hubo embaído	hubieron embaído
4 futuro		11 futuro perfecto	
embairé	embairemos	habré embaído	habremos embaído
embairás	embairéis	habrás embaído	habréis embaído
embairá	embairán	habrá embaído	habrán embaído
5 potencial simple		12 potencial compuesto	
embairía	embairíamos	habría embaído	habríamos embaído
embairías	embairíais	habrías embaído	habríais embaído
embairía	embairían	habría embaído	habrían embaído
7 imperfecto de subjuntivo		13 perfecto de subjuntivo	
embayera	embayéramos	haya embaído	hayamos embaído
embayeras	embayerais	hayas embaído	hayáis embaído
embayera	embayeran	haya embaído	hayan embaído
OR			
embayese	embayésemos	14 pluscuamperfecto de subjuntivo	
embayeses	embayeseis	hubiera embaído	hubiéramos embaído
embayese	embayesen	hubieras embaído	hubierais embaído
		hubiera embaído	hubieran embaído
		OR	
		hubiese embaído	hubiésemos embaído
		hubieses embaído	hubieseis embaído
		hubiese embaído	hubiesen embaído

imperativo

—	—
—	embaíd
—	—

Embaír is a defective verb. It is used only in the tenses given above.

Gerundio **encantando**   Part. pas. **encantado**   **encantar**

Regular **-ar** verb endings   to delight, to love, to bewitch

The Seven Simple Tenses		The Seven Compound Tenses	
Singular	Plural	Singular	Plural
1 presente de indicativo		8 perfecto de indicativo	
encanta	**encantan**	**ha encantado**	**han encantado**
2 imperfecto de indicativo		9 pluscuamperfecto de indicativo	
encantaba	**encantaban**	**había encantado**	**habían encantado**
3 pretérito		10 pretérito anterior	
encantó	**encantaron**	**hubo encantado**	**hubieron encantado**
4 futuro		11 futuro perfecto	
encantará	**encantarán**	**habrá encantado**	**habrán encantado**
5 potencial simple		12 potencial compuesto	
encantaría	**encantarían**	**habría encantado**	**habrían encantado**
6 presente de subjuntivo		13 perfecto de subjuntivo	
encante	**encanten**	**haya encantado**	**hayan encantado**
7 imperfecto de subjuntivo		14 pluscuamperfecto de subjuntivo	
encantara	**encantaran**	**hubiera encantado**	**hubieran encantado**
OR		OR	
encantase	**encantasen**	**hubiese encantado**	**hubiesen encantado**

imperativo

Singular
¡Que me encante!   **¡Que nos encante!**
¡Que te encante!   **¡Que os encante!**
¡Que le encante!   **¡Que les encante!**

Plural
¡Que me encanten!   **¡Que nos encanten!**
¡Que te encanten!   **¡Que os encanten!**
¡Que le encanten!   **¡Que les encanten!**

Words and expressions related to this verb
encantado, encantada   delighted, enchanted
encantador, encantadora   delightful
¡Encantado!   Pleased/delighted to meet you!
Me encanta ir a caballo.   I love to go horseback riding. (Horseback riding is delightful to me.)
Nos encantan los chocolates.   We love chocolates. (Chocolates are delightful to us.)

This verb is commonly used in the third person singular or plural, as in the above examples. See also **gustar**, which is used in a similar way.

Defective and impersonal verbs   655

gustar	Gerundio **gustando**	Part. pas. **gustado**
to be pleasing (to), to like		Regular **-ar** verb

The Seven Simple Tenses		The Seven Compound Tenses	
Singular	Plural	Singular	Plural
1 presente de indicativo		8 perfecto de indicativo	
gusta	**gustan**	**ha gustado**	**han gustado**
2 imperfecto de indicativo		9 pluscuamperfecto de indicativo	
gustaba	**gustaban**	**había gustado**	**habían gustado**
3 pretérito		10 pretérito anterior	
gustó	**gustaron**	**hubo gustado**	**hubieron gustado**
4 futuro		11 futuro perfecto	
gustará	**gustarán**	**habrá gustado**	**habrán gustado**
5 potencial simple		12 potencial compuesto	
gustaría	**gustarían**	**habría gustado**	**habrían gustado**
6 presente de subjuntivo		13 perfecto de subjuntivo	
que guste	**que gusten**	**que haya gustado**	**que hayan gustado**
7 imperfecto de subjuntivo		14 pluscuamperfecto de subjuntivo	
que gustara	**que gustaran**	**que hubiera gustado**	**que hubieran gustado**
OR		OR	
que gustase	**que gustasen**	**que hubiese gustado**	**que hubiesen gustado**

imperativo

¡Que guste!   ¡Que gusten!

AN ESSENTIAL 55 VERB

Gustar is an essential regular –ar verb for beginning students of Spanish. It is used in many everyday expressions and situations. Please note that this verb is commonly used in the third person singular or plural, as in the examples below.

(a) Essentially, the verb **gustar** means *to be pleasing to...*

(b) In English, we say, for example, *I like ice cream.* In Spanish, we say **Me gusta el helado**; that is to say, "Ice cream is pleasing to me (Literally: To me, ice cream is pleasing)."

(c) In English, the thing that you like is the direct object. In Spanish, the thing that you like is the subject. Also, in Spanish, the person who likes the thing is the indirect object: to me, to you, etc. For example: "**A Roberto le gusta el helado**/Robert likes ice cream (Literally: "To Robert, ice cream is pleasing to him)."

(d) In Spanish, therefore, the verb **gustar** is used in the third person, either in the singular or plural, when you talk about something that you like—something that is pleasing to you. Therefore, the verb form must agree with the subject; if the thing that is liked is singular, the verb is third person singular: **Me gusta el café**/I like coffee. If the thing that is liked is plural, the verb **gustar** is third person plural: "**Me gustan el café y la leche**/I like coffee and milk (Literally: Coffee and milk are pleasing to me)."

(e) When you mention the person or the persons who like something, you must use the preposition **a** in front of the person. You must also use the indirect object pronoun that is associated with the person: **A los muchachos y a las muchachas les gusta jugar**/Boys and girls like to play. (Literally: To boys and girls, to play is pleasing to them.)

Sentences using gustar and related words

Me gusta el café. I like coffee.

Me gusta leer. I like to read.

Te gusta leer. You (*familiar*) like to read.

Me gustan la leche y el café. I like milk and coffee.

A María le gustan los dulces. Mary likes candy.

A José y a Elena les gustan los deportes. Joseph and Helen like sports.

Nos gustan mucho las películas policíacas. We like detective movies very much.

Me gustaría un pastel. I would like a pastry.

A Felipe le gusta el helado. Philip likes ice cream.

A las chicas les gustó la película. The girls liked the movie.

Nos gustó el cuento. We liked the story.

A mi amigo le gustaron los chocolates. My friend liked the chocolates.

Words and expressions related to this verb

el gusto taste, pleasure, liking

gustoso, gustosa tasty, pleasing

dar gusto to please

tener gusto en to be glad to

to freeze

Regular **-ar** verb endings with stem change: Tenses 1, 6; Imperative

The Seven Simple Tenses	The Seven Compound Tenses
Singular Plural	Singular Plural
1 presente de indicativo **hiela** OR **está helando**	8 perfecto de indicativo **ha helado**
2 imperfecto de indicativo **helaba** OR **estaba helando**	9 pluscuamperfecto de indicativo **había helado**
3 pretérito **heló**	10 pretérito anterior **hubo helado**
4 futuro **helará**	11 futuro perfecto **habrá helado**
5 potencial simple **helaría**	12 potencial compuesto **habría helado**
6 presente de subjuntivo **hiele**	13 perfecto de subjuntivo **haya helado**
7 imperfecto de subjuntivo **helara** OR **helase**	14 pluscuamperfecto de subjuntivo **hubiera helado** OR **hubiese helado**

imperativo
¡Que hiele! (Let it freeze!)

Words and expressions related to this verb
la helada   frost (**helada blanca**/hoarfrost)
el hielo   ice
el helado   ice cream; sherbet (**el sorbete**)
la heladería   ice cream shop

la heladora   ice cream machine
el heladero   ice cream man (ice cream vendor)
romper el hielo   to break the ice

This verb is presented here in the third person singular referring to the weather. It can be used as a personal verb in the three persons of the singular and plural. The verb is then conjugated like a regular **-ar** type verb. Remember that when the vowel **e** in the stem is stressed, it changes to **ie**, as in the verb **pensar** among the 501 verbs in this book.

Regular **-ar** verb   to matter, to be important

The Seven Simple Tenses		The Seven Compound Tenses	
Singular	Plural	Singular	Plural
1 presente de indicativo		8 perfecto de indicativo	
importa	**importan**	**ha importado**	**han importado**
2 imperfecto de indicativo		9 pluscuamperfecto de indicativo	
importaba	**importaban**	**había importado**	**habían importado**
3 pretérito		10 pretérito anterior	
importó	**importaron**	**hubo importado**	**hubieron importado**
4 futuro		11 futuro perfecto	
importará	**importarán**	**habrá importado**	**habrán importado**
5 potencial simple		12 potencial compuesto	
importaría	**importarían**	**habría importado**	**habrían importado**
6 presente de subjuntivo		13 perfecto de subjuntivo	
que importe	**que importen**	**que haya importado**	**que hayan importado**
7 imperfecto de subjuntivo		14 pluscuamperfecto de subjuntivo	
que importara	**que importaran**	**que hubiera importado**	**que hubieran importado**
OR		OR	
que importase	**que importasen**	**que hubiese importado**	**que hubiesen importado**

imperativo

¡Que importe!   **¡Que importen!**

Words and expressions related to this verb
No importa.   It does not matter.
Eso no importa.   That does not matter.
No me importaría.   It wouldn't matter to me.
la importancia   importance
importante   important

dar importancia a   to value
de gran importancia   of great importance
darse importancia   to be pretentious
¿Qué importa?   What difference does it make?

This verb can be conjugated regularly in all the persons but it is used most commonly as an impersonal verb in the third person.

Defective and impersonal verbs   659

llover

to rain

Regular **-er** verb endings with stem
change: Tenses 1, 6; Imperative

The Seven Simple Tenses	The Seven Compound Tenses
Singular Plural	Singular Plural
1 presente de indicativo **llueve** OR **está lloviendo**	8 perfecto de indicativo **ha llovido**
2 imperfecto de indicativo **llovía** OR **estaba lloviendo**	9 pluscuamperfecto de indicativo **había llovido**
3 pretérito **llovió**	10 pretérito anterior **hubo llovido**
4 futuro **lloverá**	11 futuro perfecto **habrá llovido**
5 potencial simple **llovería**	12 potencial compuesto **habría llovido**
6 presente de subjuntivo **llueva**	13 perfecto de subjuntivo **haya llovido**
7 imperfecto de subjuntivo **lloviera** OR **lloviese**	14 pluscuamperfecto de subjuntivo **hubiera llovido** OR **hubiese llovido**

imperativo
¡Que llueva!   Let it rain!

Words and expressions related to this verb
la lluvia rain
lluvioso, lluviosa rainy
llover a cántaros to rain in torrents
llueva o no rain or shine

la llovizna drizzle
llover chuzos to rain canes (cats and dogs)
tiempo lluvioso rainy weather
lloviznar to drizzle

Regular **-ar** verb endings with stem
change: Tenses 1, 6; Imperative

to snow

The Seven Simple Tenses	The Seven Compound Tenses
Singular Plural	Singular Plural
1 presente de indicativo **nieva** OR **está nevando**	8 perfecto de indicativo **ha nevado**
2 imperfecto de indicativo **nevaba** OR **estaba nevando**	9 pluscuamperfecto de indicativo **había nevado**
3 pretérito **nevó**	10 pretérito anterior **hubo nevado**
4 futuro **nevará**	11 futuro perfecto **habrá nevado**
5 potencial simple **nevaría**	12 potencial compuesto **habría nevado**
6 presente de subjuntivo **nieve**	13 perfecto de subjuntivo **haya nevado**
7 imperfecto de subjuntivo **nevara** OR **nevase**	14 pluscuamperfecto de subjuntivo **hubiera nevado** OR **hubiese nevado**

imperativo
¡Que nieve!   Let it snow!

Words and expressions related to this verb
la nieve   snow
    Me gusta la nieve.   I like snow.
nevado, nevada   snowy, snow covered
la nevada   snowfall; the state of Nevada, U.S.A.
¿Hay mucha nieve aquí en el invierno?   Is there much snow here in winter?

la nevera   refrigerator
un copo de nieve   snowflake
una bola de nieve   snowball

Defective and impersonal verbs   **661**

ocurrir

Gerundio ocurriendo **Part. pas. ocurrido**

to occur, to happen

The Seven Simple Tenses		The Seven Compound Tenses	
Singular	Plural	Singular	Plural
1 presente de indicativo		8 perfecto de indicativo	
ocurre	**ocurren**	**ha ocurrido**	**han ocurrido**
2 imperfecto de indicativo		9 pluscuamperfecto de indicativo	
ocurría	**ocurrían**	**había ocurrido**	**habían ocurrido**
3 pretérito		10 pretérito anterior	
ocurrió	**ocurrieron**	**hubo ocurrido**	**hubieron ocurrido**
4 futuro		11 futuro perfecto	
ocurrirá	**ocurrirán**	**habrá ocurrido**	**habrán ocurrido**
5 potencial simple		12 potencial compuesto	
ocurriría	**ocurrirían**	**habría ocurrido**	**habrían ocurrido**
6 presente de subjuntivo		13 perfecto de subjuntivo	
ocurra	**ocurran**	**haya ocurrido**	**hayan ocurrido**
7 imperfecto de subjuntivo		14 pluscuamperfecto de subjuntivo	
ocurriera	**ocurrieran**	**hubiera ocurrido**	**hubieran ocurrido**
OR		OR	
ocurriese	**ocurriesen**	**hubiese ocurrido**	**hubiesen ocurrido**

imperativo

¡Que ocurra! **¡Que ocurran!**
Let it occur! Let them occur!

Words related to this verb
ocurrente   occurring; funny, witty, humorous
la ocurrencia   occurrence, happening, event; witticism

This verb is generally used in the third person singular and plural.

Regular **-er** verb endings with stem change: Tenses 1 and 6	to be accustomed to, to be in the habit of, to have the custom of
The Seven Simple Tenses	The Seven Compound Tenses

Singular	Plural	Singular	Plural
1 presente de indicativo		**8 perfecto de indicativo**	
suelo	**solemos**	**he solido**	**hemos solido**
sueles	**soléis**	**has solido**	**habéis solido**
suele	**suelen**	**ha solido**	**han solido**
2 imperfecto de indicativo		**9 pluscuamperfecto de indicativo**	
solía	**solíamos**	**había solido**	**habíamos solido**
solías	**solíais**	**habías solido**	**habíais solido**
solía	**solían**	**había solido**	**habían solido**
3 pretérito		**10 pretérito anterior**	
solí	**solimos**	**hube solido**	**hubimos solido**
soliste	**solisteis**	**hubiste solido**	**hubisteis solido**
solió	**solieron**	**hubo solido**	**hubieron solido**
4 futuro		**11 futuro perfecto**	
[not in use]		[not in use]	
5 potencial simple		**12 potencial compuesto**	
[not in use]		[not in use]	
6 presente de subjuntivo		**13 perfecto de subjuntivo**	
suela	**solamos**	**haya solido**	**hayamos solido**
suelas	**soláis**	**hayas solido**	**hayáis solido**
suela	**suelan**	**haya solido**	**hayan solido**
7 imperfecto de subjuntivo		**14 pluscuamperfecto de subjuntivo**	
soliera	**soliéramos**	**hubiera solido**	**hubiéramos solido**
solieras	**solierais**	**hubieras solido**	**hubierais solido**
soliera	**solieran**	**hubiera solido**	**hubieran solido**
OR		OR	
soliese	**soliésemos**	**hubiese solido**	**hubiésemos solido**
solieses	**solieseis**	**hubieses solido**	**hubieseis solido**
soliese	**soliesen**	**hubiese solido**	**hubiesen solido**

imperativo
[not in use]

This verb is defective and it is used primarily in the five simple tenses given above. When used, it is followed by an infinitive.

suceder

Gerundio **sucediendo**   Part. pas. **sucedido**

to happen

The Seven Simple Tenses		The Seven Compound Tenses	
Singular	Plural	Singular	Plural
1 presente de indicativo		8 perfecto de indicativo	
sucede	**suceden**	**ha sucedido**	**han sucedido**
2 imperfecto de indicativo		9 pluscuamperfecto de indicativo	
sucedía	**sucedían**	**había sucedido**	**habían sucedido**
3 pretérito		10 pretérito anterior	
sucedió	**sucedieron**	**hubo sucedido**	**hubieron sucedido**
4 futuro		11 futuro perfecto	
sucederá	**sucederán**	**habrá sucedido**	**habrán sucedido**
5 potencial simple		12 potencial compuesto	
sucedería	**sucederían**	**habría sucedido**	**habrían sucedido**
6 presente de subjuntivo		13 perfecto de subjuntivo	
suceda	**sucedan**	**haya sucedido**	**hayan sucedido**
7 imperfecto de subjuntivo		14 pluscuamperfecto de subjuntivo	
sucediera	**sucedieran**	**hubiera sucedido**	**hubieran sucedido**
OR		OR	
sucediese	**sucediesen**	**hubiese sucedido**	**hubiesen sucedido**

imperativo

¡Que suceda!   **¡Que sucedan!**
Let it happen!   Let them happen!

Words and expressions related to this verb
suceder a   to succeed to (a high position, etc.)
suceder con   to happen to

un sucedido   event, happening
sucediente   succeeding, following

Suceda lo que sucediere.   Come what may.
The verb form **sucediere** is the future subjunctive. For the formation and use of the future subjunctive, see page 30.

The verb **suceder** is usually used impersonally. However, if you wish to use it to mean *to succeed,* conjugate it like **deber.** To express *to succeed (to be successful in something),* many people use **tener éxito. See tener**.

664   **Defective and impersonal verbs**

Basic guide to Spanish pronunciation

The purpose of this guide is to help you pronounce Spanish words as correctly as possible so you can communicate effectively. It is not intended to perfect your pronunciation of Spanish; that is accomplished by imitating correct spoken Spanish, which you must hear from persons who pronounce Spanish accurately.

Latin American pronunciation is generally the same as you will hear in many regions of Spain, but there are some areas where Castilian pronunciation is dominant. For example, the letter c before e or i and the letter z are pronounced *th*, as in the English word *thin*, and the double (ll) is similar to the sound in the English word *million*. This is something you should be aware of in case you are visiting those areas of Spain where you will hear those sounds.

The simple rule of stressed vowel sounds in Spanish is as follows:

1. When a word ends in a vowel, n, or s, you must stress the vowel that *precedes* the last vowel or final syllable. For example, you should stress the first syllable in casa and comen, but you should stress the second syllable (-me-) in comemos because the word ends in the letter s and -me- is the next to last syllable.
2. When a word ends in a consonant other than n or s, you must stress the last vowel in the word. For example, you should stress -lor in calor, -bril in abril, -roz in arroz, and -lud in salud.
3. When the pronunciation of a word does not follow the above two rules, you must write an accent mark over the vowel that is stressed. The only way to know this is to hear the word pronounced accurately so you will know whether or not an accent mark is needed. For example, the last syllable of jabón is stressed, even though you would expect the stress to fall on the vowel that precedes it. That is why there is an accent on –bón. The word árbol has an accent over the a in the first syllable because normally one would stress the vowel in the last syllable. However, the stress falls on ár- instead of –bol.

An accent mark is written over a vowel at times to distinguish the meaning between two words that are spelled identically. Examples:

sí (yes)	él (he)	ése (that one)
si (if)	el (the)	ese libro (that book)

In some Spanish-speaking countries, the simple vowel e is at times pronounced open or closed and it can sound like *ay* in the English word *say* or *eh* as in the English word *egg*. In other countries, the final s in a word is not pronounced. This does not mean that one pronunciation is wrong and the other is correct. These are simply regional differences that have come about over decades and centuries of change. In fact, the meaning of a particular word may sometimes vary from place to place.

Now, become familiar with the following pronunciation guide. Remember that the approximate pronunciations in English serve only as a guide to pronouncing the Spanish.

Guide to Spanish Pronunciation

Approximate pronunciation

Sound	Spanish Word	English Word (Approximate sound)
Vowel, semivowel, and diphthong sounds		
a	l*a*	f*a*ther
ai	b*ai*le	*eye*
ay	h*ay*	*eye*
au	*au*la	c*ow*
e	l*e*	l*e*t
ei	r*ei*no	th*ey*
ey	l*ey*	th*ey*
i	t*i*	s*ee*
o	y*o*	*o*rder
oi	*oi*go	t*oy*
oy	est*oy*	t*oy*
u	t*u*	t*oo*
ya	env*ia*r	*y*ard
ya	*ya*	*y*ard
ye	t*ie*ne	*y*es
ye	*ye*ndo	*y*es
yo	*io*do	*y*ore
yo	*yo*do	*y*ore
yu	v*iu*da	*you*
yu	*yu*go	*you*
wa	c*ua*ndo	*w*ant
we	b*ue*no	*way*
wi	s*ui*zo	w*ee*k
wo	c*uo*ta	*w*oke

Other sounds

Sound	Spanish Word	English Word (Approximate sound)
h	*j*usto	*h*elp
h	*g*eneral	*h*elp
h	*g*igante	*h*elp

Note: The letter *h* in a Spanish word is not pronounced.

Sound	Spanish Word	English Word (Approximate sound)
y	*y*o	*y*es
y	*ll*ave	*y*es

Approximate pronunciation

Sound	Spanish Word	English Word (Approximate sound)
Consonant sounds		
b	*bien*	*b*oy
b	*v*a	*b*oy
d	*d*ar	*th*is
f	*f*alda	*f*an
g	*g*ato	*g*ap
g	*g*oma	*g*ap
g	*g*usto	*g*ap
k	*c*asa	*c*ap
k	*c*ulpa	*c*ap
k	*qu*e	*c*ap
k	*qu*ito	*c*ap
l	*l*a	*l*ard
m	*m*e	*m*ay
n	*n*o	*n*o
ñ	ni*ñ*o	ca*ny*on
p	*p*apá	*p*apa
r	pe*r*o	Ap*r*il
rr	pe*rr*o	bu*rr*, g*r-r-r*
s	*s*opa	*s*oft
s	*c*ero	*s*oft
s	*c*ita	*s*oft
s	*z*umo	*s*oft
t	*t*u	si*t*
ch	mu*ch*o	*ch*urch
Triphthong sounds		
yai	env*iái*s	*yi*pe
yau	m*iau*	m*eow*
yei	env*iéi*s	*yea*
wai	g*uai*na	*wi*se
wai	Urug*uay*	*wi*se
wau	g*uau*	*wow*
wei	contin*uéi*s	*wai*t
wei	b*uey*	*wai*t

Weather expressions using verbs

Weather expressions using hacer and hay

¿Qué tiempo hace?   What is the weather like?
Hace buen tiempo.   The weather is good.
Hace calor.   It is warm (hot).
Hace fresco hoy.   It is cool today.
Hace frío.   It is cold.
Hace mal tiempo.   The weather is bad.
Hace sol.   It is sunny.
Hace viento.   It is windy.
¿Qué tiempo hacía cuando usted salió esta mañana?   What was the
    weather like when you went out this morning?
Hacía mucho frío ayer por la noche.   It was very cold yesterday evening.
Hacía mucho viento.   It was very windy.
¿Qué tiempo hará mañana?   What will the weather be like tomorrow?
Se dice que hará mucho calor.   They say it will be very hot.
Hay lodo.   It is muddy.   Había lodo.   It was muddy.
Hay luna.   The moon is shining or There is moonlight.   Había luna ayer
    por la noche.   There was moonlight yesterday evening.
¿Hay mucha nieve aquí en el invierno?   Is there much snow here in winter?
Hay neblina.   It is foggy.   Había mucha neblina.   It was very foggy.
Hay polvo.   It is dusty.   Había mucho polvo.   It was very dusty.

Other weather expressions using other verbs

Está lloviendo ahora.   It is raining now.
Está nevando.   It is snowing.
Esta mañana llovía cuando tomé el autobús.   This morning it was raining
    when I took the bus.
Estaba lloviendo cuando tomé el autobús.   It was raining when I took the
    bus.
Estaba nevando cuando me desperté.   It was snowing when I woke up.
¿Nieva mucho aquí en el invierno?   Does it snow much here in winter?
Las estrellas brillan.   The stars are shining.
¿Le gusta a usted la lluvia?   Do you like rain?
¿Le gusta a usted la nieve?   Do you like snow?
Sí. Me gusta la lluvia y me gusta la nieve.   Yes, I like rain and I like snow.
Pero no me gustan los días ventosos.   But I don't like windy days.
El viento sopla.   The wind blows.
El cielo está cubierto hoy.   The sky is overcast today.

Verbs with prepositions

Spanish verbs are used with certain prepositions or no preposition at all. At times, the preposition used with a particular verb changes the meaning entirely, e.g., **contar** means *to count, to relate,* or *to tell;* **contar con** means *to rely on, to count on.*

When you look up a verb among the 501 to find its verb forms (or in the section of Over 2,100 Spanish Verbs Conjugated Like Model Verbs), also consult all the categories given below so that you will learn what preposition that verb requires, if any.

The following are used frequently in Spanish readings and in conversation.

A. *Verbs of motion take the prep. a + inf.*

apresurarse a   to hasten to, to hurry to
dirigirse a   to go to, to go toward
ir a   to go to
regresar a   to return to
salir a   to go out to
venir a   to come to
volver a   to return to

> Examples:
> *Me apresuré a tomar el tren.*   I hurried to take the train.
> *El profesor se dirigió a abrir la puerta.*   The teacher went to open the door.
> *María fue a comer.*   Mary went to eat.

B. *The following verbs take the prep. a + inf.*

acertar a   to happen to
acostumbrarse a   to become used to, to become accustomed to
aficionarse a hacer algo   to become fond of doing something
alcanzar a   to succeed in (doing something)
aprender a   to learn to, to learn how to
aspirar a   to aspire to
atreverse a   to dare to
ayudar a (hacer algo)   to help to
comenzar a   to begin to
condenar a   to condemn to
convidar a   to invite to
decidirse a   to decide to
dedicarse a   to devote oneself to
detenerse a   to pause to, to stop to
disponerse a   to get ready to
echarse a   to begin to, to start to

empezar a   to begin to, to start to
enseñar a   to teach to
exponerse a   to run the risk of
invitar a   to invite to
negarse a   to refuse to
obligar a   to oblige to, to obligate to
ponerse a   to begin to, to start to
prepararse a   to prepare (oneself) to
principiar a   to begin to, to start to
resignarse a   to resign oneself to
resolverse a   to make up one's mind to
someter a   to submit to, to subdue to
venir a   to end up by
volver a   to (do something) again

Examples:
Me acostumbré a estudiar mis lecciones todas las noches.   I became used
   to studying my lessons every evening.
No me atreví a responder.   I did not dare to answer.
El hombre comenzó a llorar.   The man began to cry.
Me dispuse a salir.   I got ready to go out.
Me eché a llorar.   I began to cry.
El señor Gómez se negó a ir.   Mr. Gómez refused to go.
Juana se puso a correr.   Jane began to run.
El muchacho volvió a jugar.   The boy played again.

C. *The following verbs take the prep. a + noun (or pronoun if that is the required dependent element)*

acercarse a   to approach
acostumbrarse a   to become accustomed to, to become used to
aficionarse a   to become fond of
asemejarse a   to resemble, to look like
asistir a   to attend, to be present at
asomarse a   to appear at
cuidar a alguien   to take care of someone
dar a   to face, to overlook, to look out upon, to look out over
dedicarse a   to devote oneself to
echar una carta al correo   to mail, to post a letter
echar la culpa a alguien   to blame someone, to put the blame on someone
jugar a   to play (a game, sport, cards)
llegar a ser   to become
llevar a cabo   to carry out, to accomplish
oler a   to smell of, to smell like
parecerse a   to resemble, to look like
querer a   to love

saber a   to taste of, to taste like, to have the flavor of
ser aficionado a   to be fond of, to be a fan of
sonar a   to sound like
subir a   to get on, to get into (a bus, a train, a vehicle)
tocarle a una persona   to be a person's turn

Examples:
Nos acercamos a la ciudad.   We are approaching the city.
Una muchacha bonita se asomó a la puerta.   A pretty girl appeared at
  the door.
Mi cuarto da al jardín.   My room faces the garden.
Me dedico a mis estudios.   I devote myself to my studies.
Enrique llegó a ser profesor de matemáticas.   Henry became a
  mathematics teacher.
Jorge llevó a cabo sus responsabilidades.   George carried out his
  responsibilities.
Mi hermano se parece a mi padre y yo me parezco a mi madre.   My brother
  resembles my father and I resemble my mother.
Quiero a mi patria.   I love my country.
Soy aficionado a los deportes.   I am fond of sports.
Subí al tren.   I got on the train.
Le toca a Juan.   It is John's turn.

D. *The following verbs take the prep. con + inf.*

amenazar con   to threaten to
contar con   to count on, to rely on
contentarse con   to be satisfied with
soñar con   to dream of, to dream about

Examples:
Cuento con tener éxito.   I am counting on being successful.
Me contento con quedarme en casa.   I am satisfied with staying at home.
Sueño con ir a Chile.   I dream of going to Chile.

E. *The following verbs take the prep. con + noun (or pronoun if that is the required dependent element)*

acabar con   to finish, to put an end to, to make an end of, to finish off
casarse con   to marry, to get married to
conformarse con   to put up with
contar con   to count on, to rely on
contentarse con   to be satisfied with
cumplir con   to fulfill
dar con   to meet, to find, to come upon
encontrarse con   to run into, to meet by chance
entenderse con   to come to an understanding with
meterse con   to pick a quarrel with

quedarse con   to keep, to hold on to
soñar con   to dream of, to dream about
tropezar con   to come upon, to run across unexpectedly, to run into

Examples:
José se casó con Ana.   Joseph married Anna.
Me conformo con tus ideas.   I put up with your ideas.
Contamos con nuestros padres.   We count on our parents.
Me contento con poco dinero.   I am satisfied with little money.
Siempre cumplo con mi promesa.   I always fulfill my promise.
Anoche di con mis amigos en el cine.   Last night I met my friends at the movies.
Ayer por la tarde me encontré con un amigo mío.   Yesterday afternoon I ran into a friend of mine.
Me quedo con el dinero.   I am keeping the money; I am holding on to the money.
Sueño con un verano agradable.   I am dreaming of a pleasant summer.

F. *The following verbs take the prep. de + inf.*

acabar de   to have just
acordarse de   to remember to
alegrarse de   to be glad to
arrepentirse de   to repent
cansarse de   to become tired of
cesar de   to cease, to stop
dejar de   to stop, to fail to
encargarse de   to take charge of
haber de   *see* verb 257.
ocuparse de   to be busy with, to attend to
olvidarse de   to forget to
tratar de   to try to
tratarse de   to be a question of

Examples:
Guillermo acaba de llegar.   William has just arrived.
Felipe acababa de partir.   Philip had just left.
Me alegro de hablarle.   I am glad to talk to you.
Me canso de esperar el autobús.   I'm getting tired of waiting for the bus.
Cesó de llover.   It stopped raining.
Jaime dejó de escribir la redacción.   James failed to write the composition.
Mi padre se ocupa de preparar la comida. My father is busy preparing the meal.
Andrés se olvidó de estudiar.   Andrew forgot to study.
Siempre trato de hacer un buen trabajo.   I always try to do a good job.
Se trata de abstenerse.   It is a question of abstaining.

abusar de   to abuse, to overindulge in
acordarse de   to remember
alejarse de   to go away from
apartarse de   to keep away from
apoderarse de   to take possession of
aprovecharse de   to take advantage of
bajar de   to get out of, to descend from, to get off
burlarse de   to make fun of
cambiar de   to change (trains, buses, clothes, etc.)
cansarse de   to become tired of
carecer de   to lack
compadecerse de   to feel sorry for, to pity, to sympathize with
constar de   to consist of
cuidar de algo   to take care of something
depender de   to depend on
despedirse de   to say good-bye to, to take leave of
despojarse de   to take off (clothing)
disfrutar de   to enjoy
enamorarse de   to fall in love with
encogerse de hombros   to shrug one's shoulders
enterarse de   to find out about
fiarse de alguien   to trust someone
gozar de algo   to enjoy something
ocuparse de   to be busy with, to attend to
oír hablar de   to hear of, to hear about
olvidarse de   to forget
pensar de   to think of (**pensar de** is used when asking for an opinion)
perder de vista   to lose sight of
ponerse de acuerdo   to come to an agreement
preocuparse de   to worry about, to be concerned about
quejarse de   to complain about
reírse de   to laugh at
saber de memoria   to know by heart, to memorize
salir de   to go out of, to leave from
servir de   to serve as
servirse de   to make use of, to use
tratarse de   to be a question of, to deal with

Examples:
Me acuerdo de aquel hombre.   I remember that man.
Vamos a aprovecharnos de esta oportunidad.   Let's take advantage of this
   opportunity.

Después de bajar del tren, fui a comer.   After getting off the train, I went to eat.

Todos los días cambio de ropa.   Every day I change my clothes.

Me canso de este trabajo.   I am getting tired of this work.

Esta composición carece de calidad.   This composition lacks quality.

Me compadezco de ese pobre hombre.   I pity that poor man.

Ahora tengo que despedirme de usted.   Now I have to say good-bye.

Eduardo se enamoró de Carmen.   Edward fell in love with Carmen.

Mi madre se ocupa de mi padre que está enfermo.   My mother is busy with my father who is sick.

Oí hablar de la boda de Anita.   I heard about Anita's wedding.

Carlos se olvidó del aniversario de sus padres.   Charles forgot about his parents' anniversary.

¿Qué piensa Ud. de nuestro profesor de español?   What do you think of our Spanish teacher?

¡Mira! ¡El mono se ríe de nosotros!   Look! The monkey is laughing at us.

Siempre salgo de casa a las ocho de la mañana.   I always leave (from, go out of) the house at eight in the morning.

En nuestro club, Cristóbal sirve de presidente.   In our club, Christopher serves as president.

H. *The following verbs generally take the prep. en + inf.*

acabar en   to end in

complacerse en   to be pleased to, to delight in

consentir en   to consent to

convenir en   to agree to, to agree on

empeñarse en   to persist in, to insist on

esforzarse en   to strive for, to force onself to, to try hard to

insistir en   to insist on

quedar en   to agree to, to agree on

tardar en   to be late (to delay) in

Examples:

La señora Pardo consintió en asistir a la conferencia.   Mrs. Pardo consented to attending the meeting.

El muchacho se empeñó en salir.   The boy insisted on going out.

Mis amigos insistieron en venir a verme.   My friends insisted on coming to see me.

El avión tardó en llegar.   The plane was late in arriving.

I. *The following verbs generally take the prep. en + noun (or pronoun if that is the required dependent element)*

apoyarse en   to lean against, to lean on

confiar en   to rely on, to trust in

consistir en   to consist of

convertirse en   to become, to convert to
entrar en   to enter (into), to go into
fijarse en   to stare at, to notice, to take notice, to observe
meterse en   to get involved in, to plunge into
pensar en   to think of, to think about [**pensar en** is used when asking or when stating what or whom a person is thinking of]
ponerse en camino   to set out, to start out
reparar en   to notice, to observe
volver en sí   to regain consciousness, to be oneself again

Examples:

Me apoyé en la puerta.   I leaned against the door.
Entré en el restaurante.   I entered (I went into) the restaurant.
¿En qué piensa Ud.?   What are you thinking of?
Pienso en mi trabajo.   I am thinking of my work.
¿En quién piensa Ud.?   Whom are you thinking of?
Pienso en mi madre.   I am thinking of my mother.
¿En quiénes piensa Ud.?   Whom are you thinking of?
Pienso en mis padres.   I am thinking of my parents.

J. The following verbs generally take the prep. por + inf., noun, pronoun, adj., if that is the required dependent element

acabar por   to end up by
dar por   to consider, to regard as
darse por   to pretend (to be something), to think oneself (to be something)
estar por   to be in favor of
interesarse por   to take an interest in
pasar por   to be considered as
preguntar por   to ask for, to inquire about
tener por   to consider something, to have an opinion on something
tomar por   to take someone for

Examples:

Domingo acabó por casarse con Elena.   Dominic finally ended up by marrying Helen.
¿Mi libro de español? Lo doy por perdido.   My Spanish book? I consider it lost.
La señorita López se da por actriz.   Miss López pretends to be an actress.
Estamos por quedarnos en casa esta noche.   We are in favor of staying at home this evening.
El señor Pizarro pasa por experto.   Mr. Pizarro is considered an expert.
Pregunto por el señor Pardo. ¿Está en casa?   I am asking for Mr. Pardo. Is he at home?

K. Verb + NO PREPOSITION + inf. *The following verbs do not ordinarily take a preposition when followed by an infinitive*

deber + inf.   must, ought to
Debo hacer mis lecciones.   I must (ought to) do my lessons.

dejar + inf.   to allow to, to let
Mi madre me dejó salir.   My mother allowed me to go out.
Dejé caer mi libro.   I dropped my book (I let my book fall).

desear + inf.   to desire to, to wish to
Deseo tomar un café.   I wish to have a cup of coffee.

esperar + inf.   to expect to, to hope to
Espero ir a la América del Sur este invierno.   I expect to go to South America this winter.

hacer + inf.   to do, to make, to have something made or done
Tú me haces llorar.   You make me cry.
Mi padre hace construir una casita.   My father is having a small house built [by someone].

> Note that the use of *hacer + inf.* can be described as the "causative (causal)" use of *hacer* when there is an inf. directly after. it. The construction *hacer + inf.* indicates that something is being made or being done by someone. Further examples: *hacer firmar*/to have (something) signed (by someone); *hacer confesar*/to have (someone) confess or to make (someone) confess. This causative use of *hacer* is used in a verb tense that is needed + inf. form of the verb which tells what action is being done or being made: *Mi padre hizo construir una casita*/My father had a little house built; *Le haré confesar*/I shall make him confess; *El señor López lo hizo firmar la carta*/Mr. López made him sign the letter.

necesitar + inf.   to need
Necesito pasar una hora en la biblioteca.   I need to spend an hour in the library.

oír + inf.   to hear
Le oí entrar por la ventana.   I heard him enter through the window.
He oído hablar de su buena fortuna.   I have heard (talk) about your good fortune.
He oído decir que la señora Sierra está enferma.   I have heard (tell) that Mrs. Sierra is sick.

pensar + inf.   to intend to, to plan to
Pienso hacer un viaje a México.   I plan to take a trip to Mexico.

poder + inf.   to be able to, can
Puedo venir a verle a la una.   I can come to see you at one o'clock.

preferir + inf.   to prefer
Prefiero quedarme en casa esta noche.   I prefer to stay at home this evening.

prometer + inf.   to promise
Prometo venir a verle a las ocho.   I promise to come to see you at eight o'clock.

querer + inf. to want to, to wish to
Quiero comer ahora. I want to eat now.
¿Qué quiere decir este muchacho? What does this boy mean?

saber + inf. to know how to
¿Sabe Ud. nadar? Do you know how to swim?
Sí, yo sé nadar. Yes, I know how to swim.

ver + inf. to see
Veo venir el tren. I see the train coming.

L. *The following verbs do not ordinarily require a preposition, whereas in English a preposition is used*

agradecer to thank for, to be thankful (to someone) for (something)
Le agradecí su paciencia. I thanked him for his patience.

aprovechar to take advantage of
¿No quiere Ud. aprovechar la oportunidad? Don't you want to take advantage of the opportunity?

buscar to look for, to search for
Busco mi libro. I am looking for my book.

esuchar to listen to
Escucho la música. I am listening to the music.

esperar to wait for
Espero el autobús. I am waiting for the bus.

guardar cama to stay in bed
La semana pasada guardé cama. Last week I stayed in bed.

lograr to succeed in
El alumno logró hacerlo. The pupil succeeded in doing it.

mirar to look at
Miro el cielo. I am looking at the sky.

pagar to pay for
Pagué los billetes. I paid for the tickets.

pedir to ask for
Pido un libro. I am asking for a book.

soler + inf. to be accustomed to, to be in the habit of
(Yo) suelo acompañar a mis amigos en el autobús. I am in the habit of accompanying my friends on the bus.

Index of common irregular Spanish verb forms identified by infinitives

The purpose of this index is to help you identify those verb forms that cannot be readily identified because they are irregular in some way. For example, if you come across the verb form *fui* (which is very common) in your Spanish readings, this index will tell you that *fui* is a form of *ir* or *ser*. Then you look up *ir* and *ser* in this book and you will find that verb form on the page where all the forms of *ir* and *ser* are given.

Verb forms whose first three or four letters are the same as the infinitive have not been included because they can easily be identified by referring to the alphabetical listing of the 501 verbs in this book.

After you find the verb of an irregular verb form, if it is not given among the 501 verbs, consult the list of Over 2,100 Spanish Verbs Conjugated Like Model Verbs, which begins on page 707.

A

abierto   abrir
acierto, *etc.*   acertar
acuerdo, *etc.*   acordar
acuesto, *etc.*   acostarse
alce, *etc.*   alzar
andes   andar
anduve, *etc.*   andar
apruebo, *etc.*   aprobar
ase, *etc.*   asir
asgo, *etc.*   asir
ataque, *etc.*   atacar
ate, *etc.*   atar

C

cabré, *etc.*   caber
caí, *etc.*   caer
caía, *etc.*   caer
caigo, *etc.*   caer
calce, *etc.*   calzar
caliento, *etc.*   calentar
cayera, *etc.*   caer
cierro, *etc.*   cerrar
cojo, *etc.*   coger
colija, *etc.*   colegir
consigo, *etc.*   conseguir
cuece, *etc.*   cocer
cuelgo, *etc.*   colgar
cuento, *etc.*   contar
cuesta, *etc.*   costar (Def. and Imp.)

cuezo, *etc.*   cocer
cupe, *etc.*   caber
cupiera, *etc.*   caber

D

da, *etc.*   dar
dad   dar
das   dar
dé   dar
demos   dar
den   dar
des   dar
di, *etc.*   dar, decir
dice, *etc.*   decir
diciendo   decir
dicho   decir
diera, *etc.*   dar
diese, *etc.*   dar
digo, *etc.*   decir
dije, *etc.*   decir
dimos, *etc.*   dar
dio   dar
diré, *etc.*   decir
diría, *etc.*   decir
diste   dar
doy   dar
duelo, *etc.*   doler
duermo, *etc.*   dormir
durmamos   dormir
durmiendo   dormir

E

eliges, *etc.*   elegir
eligiendo   elegir
eligiera, *etc.*   elegir
elijo, *etc.*   elegir
era, *etc.*   ser
eres   ser
es   ser
estoy   estar
estuve, *etc.*   estar
exija, *etc.*   exigir

F

fíe, *etc.*   fiar
finja, *etc.*   fingir
fío, *etc.*   fiar
friego, *etc.*   fregar
friendo   freír
friera, *etc.*   freír
frío, *etc.*   freír
frito   freír
fue, *etc.*   ir, ser
fuera, *etc.*   ir, ser
fuese, *etc.*   ir, ser
fui, *etc.*   ir, ser

G

gima, *etc.*   gemir
gimiendo   gemir
gimiera, *etc.*   gemir
gimiese, *etc.*   gemir
gimo, *etc.*   gemir
goce, *etc.*   gozar
gocé   gozar

H

ha   haber
había, *etc.*   haber
habré, *etc.*   haber
haga, *etc.*   hacer
hago, *etc.*   hacer
han   haber
haría, *etc.*   hacer
has   haber
haya, *etc.*   haber
haz   hacer
he   haber
hecho   hacer

hemos   haber
hice, *etc.*   hacer
hiciera, *etc.*   hacer
hiciese, *etc.*   hacer
hiela   helar (Def. and Imp.)
hiele   helar (Def. and Imp.)
hiera, *etc.*   herir
hiero, *etc.*   herir
hiramos   herir
hiriendo   herir
hiriera, *etc.*   herir
hiriese, *etc.*   herir
hizo   hacer
hube, *etc.*   haber
hubiera, *etc.*   haber
hubiese, *etc.*   haber
huela, *etc.*   oler
huelo, *etc.*   oler
huya, *etc.*   huir
huyendo   huir
huyera, *etc.*   huir
huyese, *etc.*   huir
huyo, *etc.*   huir

I

iba, *etc.*   ir
id   ir
ido   ir
idos   irse
irgo, *etc.*   erguir
irguiendo   erguir
irguiera, *etc.*   erguir
irguiese, *etc.*   erguir

J

juego, *etc.*   jugar
juegue, *etc.*   jugar

L

lea, *etc.*   leer
leído   leer
leo, *etc.*   leer
leyendo   leer
leyera, *etc.*   leer
leyese, *etc.*   leer
llueva   llover (Def. and Imp.)
llueve   llover (Def. and Imp.)

M

mida, *etc.*   medir
midiendo   medir
midiera, *etc.*   medir
midiese, *etc.*   medir
mido, *etc.*   medir
mienta, *etc.*   mentir
miento, *etc.*   mentir
mintiendo   mentir
mintiera, *etc.*   mentir
mintiese, *etc.*   mentir
muerda, *etc.*   morder
muerdo, *etc.*   morder
muero, *etc.*   morir
muerto   morir
muestre, *etc.*   mostrar
muestro, *etc.*   mostrar
mueva, *etc.*   mover
muevo, *etc.*   mover
muramos   morir
muriendo   morir
muriera, *etc.*   morir
muriese, *etc.*   morir

N

nazca, *etc.*   nacer
nazco   nacer
niego, *etc.*   negar
niegue, *etc.*   negar
nieva   nevar (Def. and Imp.)
nieve   nevar (Def. and Imp.)

O

oíd   oír
oiga, *etc.*   oír
oigo, *etc.*   oír
oliendo   oler
oliera, *etc.*   oler
oliese, *etc.*   oler
oye, *etc.*   oír
oyendo   oír
oyera, *etc.*   oír
oyese, *etc.*   oír

P

pida, *etc.*   pedir
pidamos   pedir
pidiendo   pedir
pidiera, *etc.*   pedir

pidiese, *etc.*   pedir
pido, *etc.*   pedir
pienso, *etc.*   pensar
pierda, *etc.*   perder
pierdo, *etc.*   perder
plegue   placer
plugo   placer
pluguiera   placer
pluguieron   placer
pluguiese   placer
ponga, *etc.*   poner
pongámonos   ponerse
ponte   ponerse
pruebe, *etc.*   probar
pruebo, *etc.*   probar
pude, *etc.*   poder
pudiendo   poder
pudiera, *etc.*   poder
pudiese, *etc.*   poder
puedo, *etc.*   poder
puesto   poner
puse, *etc.*   poner
pusiera, *etc.*   poner
pusiese, *etc.*   poner

Q

quepo, *etc.*   caber
quiebro   quebrar
quiero, *etc.*   querer
quise, *etc.*   querer
quisiera, *etc.*   querer
quisiese, *etc.*   querer

R

raí, *etc.*   raer
raía, *etc.*   raer
raiga, *etc.*   raer
raigo, *etc.*   raer
rayendo   raer
rayera, *etc.*   raer
rayese, *etc.*   raer
ría, *etc.*   reír
riamos   reír
riego, *etc.*   regar
riendo   reír
riera, *etc.*   reír
riese, *etc.*   reír
riña, *etc.*   reñir
riñendo   reñir

riñera, *etc.*   reñir
riñese, *etc.*   reñir
riño, *etc.*   reñir
río, *etc.*   reír
roto   romper
ruego, *etc.*   rogar
ruegue, *etc.*   rogar

S
sal, salgo, *etc.*   salir
saque, *etc.*   sacar
sé   saber, ser
sea, *etc.*   ser
sed   ser
sepa, *etc.*   saber
seque, *etc.*   secar
sido   ser
siendo   ser
siento, *etc.*   sentar, sentir
sigo, *etc.*   seguir
siguiendo   seguir
siguiera, *etc.*   seguir
siguiese, *etc.*   seguir
sintiendo   sentir
sintiera, *etc.*   sentir
sintiese, *etc.*   sentir
sintió   sentir
sirviendo   servir
sirvo, *etc.*   servir
sois   ser
somos   ser
son   ser
soy   ser
suela, *etc.*   soler (Def. and Imp.)
suelo, *etc.*   soler (Def. and Imp.)
suelto, *etc.*   soltar
sueno, *etc.*   sonar
sueño, *etc.*   soñar
supe, *etc.*   saber
supiera, *etc.*   saber
supiese, *etc.*   saber
surja, *etc.*   surgir

T
ten, tengo   tener
tiemblo, *etc.*   temblar
tiendo, *etc.*   tender
tienes, *etc.*   tener
tiento, *etc.*   tentar
toque, *etc.*   tocar

traigo, *etc.*   traer
traje, *etc.*   traer
tuesto, *etc.*   tostar
tuve, *etc.*   tener

U
uno, *etc.*   unir

V
va   ir
vais   ir
val, valgo, *etc.*   valer
vámonos   irse
vamos   ir
van   ir
vas   ir
vaya, *etc.*   ir
ve   ir, ver
vea, *etc.*   ver
ved   ver
ven   venir, ver
vendré, *etc.*   venir
venga, vengo   venir
veo, *etc.*   ver
ves   ver
vete   irse
vi   ver
viendo   ver
viene, *etc.*   venir
viera, *etc.*   ver
viese, *etc.*   ver
vimos, *etc.*   ver
vine, *etc.*   venir
vio   ver
viste   ver, vestir
vistiendo   vestir
vistiéndose   vestirse
vistiese   vestirse
visto   ver, vestir
voy   ir
vuelo, *etc.*   volar
vuelto   volver
vuelvo, *etc.*   volver

Y
yaz   yacer
yazco, *etc.*   yacer
yendo   ir
yergo, *etc.*   erguir
yerro, *etc.*   errar

English-Spanish verb index

The purpose of this index is to give you instant access to the Spanish verb for the English verb you have in mind to use. This saves you time if you do not have a standard English-Spanish dictionary handy.

When you find the Spanish verb you need, look up the form of the model verb that has a similar conjugation (*e.g.*, to alarm is alarmar, which is conjugated like verb 54, which is amar). If there is no verb number listed (*e.g.*, abrir) that means that the Spanish verb is one of the 501 model verbs. If you see "Def. and Imp." instead of a verb number, look in the list of defective and impersonal verbs. It's right after the main verb listing.

The preposition *to* in front of the English verb has been omitted.

A

abandon abandonar (473)
abandon desamparar (342)
abandon desertar (11)
abdicate abdicar (99)
abduct abducir (132)
abhor aborrecer (344)
abjure abjurar (284)
abnegate abnegar (327)
abolish abolir (Def. and Imp.)
abominate abominar (107)
abound abundar (39)
abrogate abrogar (421)
absolve absolver
absorb absorber (128)
abstain abstenerse
abstract abstraer (477)
abuse abusar (25)
abuse maltratar (478)
accede acceder (128)
accelerate apresurar (64)
acelerar
accentuate acentuar (141)
accept aceptar
acclaim aclamar
acclimatize aclimatar (308)
accommodate acomodar (259)
accompany acompañar
accumulate acaudalar (259)
accumulate acumular (85)
accumulate amontonar (107)
accumulate cumular (259)

accuse culpar (332)
accuse acusar
ache doler
achieve lograr (29)
acquire adquirir
acquit absolver
act actuar (141)
act foolishly disparatar (308)
act foolishly tontear (206)
activate activar (288)
adapt adaptar (11)
adapt oneself amoldarse (39, 289)
add adicionar (54)
add añadir
add up sumar (54)
adhere adherir (435)
adjudge adjudicar (424)
adjust ajustar (259)
adjust arreglar
administrate administrar (215)
admire admirar
admit admitir
adopt adoptar
adore adorar
adorn adornar (54)
adorn ornamentar (11)
adorn ornar (249)
adulate adular (259)
advance anticipar (332)
advance adelantar
advance avanzar
advise asesorar (409)
advise avisar (340)
advise aconsejar
affect afectar (11)

affirm afirmar (243)
afflict afligir (188)
Africanize africanizar (339)
age envejecer (344)
aggravate exacerbar (9)
aggravate agravar
agitate agitar
agree acceder (128)
agree asentir (370)
agree concertar (352)
agree concurrir (495)
agree acordarse
agree (upon) acordar
agree to pactar (11)
agree to transigir con (188)
aid ayudar
aim apuntar (11)
alarm alarmar (54)
alert alertar (11)
alienate alienar (249)
alleviate aliviar (232)
alleviate mitigar (341)
allow consentir (435)
allow dejar
alter alterar (409)
alternate alternar (107)
amass (a fortune) amasar (2)
amaze asombrar (113)
amaze pasmar (54)
ambush emboscar (424)
amend enmendar (352)
Americanize americanizar (339)
amplify amplificar (117)
amuse divertir (370, 194)
amuse entretener (468)

be delinquent delinquir
be delirious delirar (409)
be disdainful desdeñarse
  (88)
be displeased disgustarse
  (250, 289)
be enough bastar (Def.
  and Imp.)
be frightened, scared
  asustarse
be hindered embarazarse
  (339, 289)
be ignorant of ignorar
be important importar
  (Def. and Imp.)
be in danger peligrar (259)
be in discord desacordar
  (19)
be in fashion estilarse (289)
be in need of carecer de
  (333)
be in the habit of soler
  (Def. and Imp.)
be incumbent upon
  incumbir (353)
be interested in interesarse
be lacking faltar
be left over sobrar (409)
be mischievous travesear
  (175)
be mistaken aberrar (54)
be mistaken equivocarse
be moved emocionarse
  (355, 289)
be negligent descuidarse
  (153)
be obstinate, stubborn
  obstinarse (289)
be overloaded with cargarse
  de (111, 112)
be pleasing (to) gustar
  (Def. and Imp.)
be plentiful abundar (39)
be proud enorgullecerse
  (344, 102)
be reborn renacer (323)
be rejuvenated
  rejuvenecerse (344, 102)
be seasick marearse (175,
  289)
be shipwrecked naufragar
  (341)
be shipwrecked zozobrar
  (259)
be silent callarse
be startled sobresaltarse
  (427, 289)

be titled, called titularse
  (289)
be understood entenderse
  (214)
be upset afligirse (188, 8)
be urgent urgir (188)
be vaccinated vacunarse
  (114, 289)
be worth valer
bear aguantar (54)
beat batir (1)
beat machar (306)
beat pegar
beat again rebatir (1)
beautify embellecer (344)
become devenir (488)
become a member asociarse
  (232, 289)
become a widow, widower
  enviudar (39)
become accustomed to
  acostumbrarse (22, 289)
become accustomed to
  habituarse (141, 289)
become affiliated afiliarse
  (232, 289)
become angry enfadarse
become angry enojarse
become conceited infatuarse
  (141, 289)
become damaged dañarse
  (88)
become empty vaciarse
  (483, 289)
become famous afamarse
  (112)
become flattened chafarse
  (289)
become fond apegarse
  (341, 289)
become fond of aficionarse
  a (338)
become fond of encariñarse
  (213, 289)
become forgetful
  desacordarse (20)
become frightened
  acobardarse (39, 289)
become independent
  independizarse (339, 289)
become involved envolverse
  (219, 80)
become involved implicarse
  (424, 289)
become night oscurecer
  (344)

become pregnant
  embarazarse (339, 289)
become rich enriquecerse
  (344, 102)
become sunburned tostarse
  (289, 474)
become tired cansarse
become vacant vacar (424)
become void caducar
  (424)
beg mendigar (341)
beg rogar
begin entablar (259)
begin iniciar (383)
begin empezar
begin principiar
behave actuar (141)
behave comportarse (11,
  289)
behave portarse (11, 289)
behave childishly niñear
  (206)
belch eructar (54)
believe creer
bellow rugir (188)
bend doblegar (341)
bend on your knees
  arrodillarse (261, 289)
benefit beneficiar (232)
bequeath dotar (11)
bequeath legar (341)
besiege sitiar (232)
bet apostar (474)
betray traicionar (107)
bewilder atolondrar (409)
bifurcate bifurcarse (424,
  289)
bill facturar (409)
bind aligar (421)
bind atar (308)
bind encuadernar (107)
bind liar (256)
bind trabar (54)
bite morder
blame culpar (332)
blame oneself culparse
  (189)
blaspheme blasfemar
  (247)
blaze llamear (206)
bleach blanquear (206)
bleed desangrar (409)
bleed sangrar (215)
bless bendecir
blind cegar (327)
blind obcecar (99)
blink parpadear (206)

cause   causar   (481)
cause   ocasionar   (355)
cause   suscitar   (308)
cease   cesar   (235)
cede   ceder   (413)
celebrate   solemnizar   (339)
celebrate   celebrar
celebrate (mass)   oficiar   (57)
censure   censurar   (72)
center   centrar   (259)
centralize   centralizar
   (339)
certify   certificar
challenge   desafiar   (256)
challenge   retar   (254)
change   alterar   (409)
change   modificar   (424)
change   permutar   (308)
change   cambiar
change residence
   trasladarse   (289)
characterize   caracterizar
charge   cobrar   (259)
charm   encantar   (Def. and
   Imp.)
chase   cazar   (81)
chase away   zapear   (206)
chastise   castigar   (341)
chat   dialogar   (341)
chat   charlar
chat   platicar
chat (Internet)   chatear
   (175)
chatter   charlar   (259)
chatter   garlar   (259)
cheat   estafar   (259)
cheat   timar   (231)
cheat   truhanear   (206)
check   comprobar   (378)
check   revisar   (2)
check, verify   chequear
   (175)
cheer on   jalear   (206)
cheer up   reconfortar   (11)
chew   mascar   (99)
chew   masticar   (99)
chew   ronchar   (225)
chill   enfriar   (218)
chisel   cincelar   (259)
choose   optar   (11)
choose   seleccionar   (355)
choose   escoger
circulate   circular   (71)
cite   citar
civilize   civilizar   (90)
clamp   abrazar
clap hands   palmear   (206)

clarify   aclarar   (409)
clarify   clarificar   (117)
clarify   esclarecer   (344)
clarify   aclarar
classify   acopiar   (106)
classify   calificar   (117)
classify   clasificar   (117)
clean   limpiar
clean oneself   limpiarse
cleanse   lustrar   (215)
clear   desembarazar   (339)
clear   despejar   (86)
clear up   escampar   (332)
climb   escalar   (259)
climb   trepar   (332)
clip   tundir   (346)
clog   atorar   (409)
close   obturar   (284)
close   cerrar
close halfway   entrecerrar
   (116)
clothe   arropar   (332)
clothe   envestir   (491)
clothe   vestir   (491)
cloud   nublar   (259)
clown around   monear
   (206)
coagulate   coagular   (259)
coagulate   cuajar   (86)
coexist   coexistir   (495)
coincide   coincidir   (60)
collaborate   colaborar
   (409)
collate   compaginar   (107)
collect   acopiar   (106)
collect   coleccionar   (107)
collect   recolectar   (11)
collect   colegir
collect   recoger
collect (money)   colectar
   (11)
collide   chocar   (424)
color   colorar   (32)
color   colorear   (175)
comb one's hair   peinarse
combat   combatir   (1)
combine   combinar   (107)
combine   fusionar   (107)
come   advenir   (488)
come   venir
come apart   separarse
   (289, 437)
come from   provenir   (488)
come in   ingresar   (2)
come to the rescue   acudir
comfort   confortar   (11)
comfort   desahogar   (341)

comfort   reconfortar   (11)
command   capitanear
   (175)
command   comandar   (109)
command   mandar   (259)
commemorate   conmemorar
   (409)
commemorate   solemnizar
   (339)
commence   comenzar
commend   encomendar
   (352)
comment   comentar   (109)
comment   glosar   (2)
commit   cometer   (91)
commit perjury   perjurar
   (284)
commit suicide   suicidarse
   (39, 289)
communicate   comunicar
   (234)
compare   comparar   (342)
compare   contraponer
   (364)
compare   equiparar   (342)
compensate   compensar   (2)
compete   competir   (411)
compile   compilar   (259)
compile   recopilar   (259)
complain   quejarse
complete   completar   (308)
complete   acabar
complicate   complicar   (76)
compliment   obsequiar
   (228)
compose   componer
compress   comprimir   (267)
compute   computar   (279)
computerize   informatizar
   (339)
conceal   esconder   (413)
conceal   ocultar   (11)
concede   conceder   (413)
conceive   concebir   (349)
conceive   ingeniar   (232)
concentrate   concentrar
   (215)
conclude   concluir   (268)
concur   concurrir   (495)
condemn   condenar   (114)
condemn   justiciar   (57)
conduct   conducir
confess   confesar
confide   fiar
confine   confinar   (107)
confirm   confirmar   (243)
confiscate   confiscar   (99)

cut segar (327)
cut tallar (261)
cut cortar
cut around retajar (86)
cut into pieces trocear (206)
cut into decentar (352)
cut off capar (332)
cut short truncar (424)

D

damage averiar (256)
damage damnificar (424)
damage dañar (109)
damage deteriorar (409)
damage lesionar (355)
damage maleficiar (383)
damage perjudicar (424)
dampen humedecer (344)
dance danzar (81)
dance bailar
dare desafiar (256)
dare atreverse
dare osar
darken ensombrecer (344)
darken obscurecer (333)
darn zurcir
date (a letter, an account) datar (308)
daydream fantasear (206)
daze aturdir (60)
dazzle deslumbrar (259)
dazzle ofuscar (99)
dazzle relumbrar (51)
deactivate desactivar (259)
deaden amortiguar (83)
deafen ensordecer (344)
deal traficar (424)
debate cuestionar (473)
debate debatir (407)
decant trasegar (327)
deceive engañar (213)
deceive mistificar (424)
deceive oneself engañarse (88)
decide decidir
decipher descifrar (409)
declaim declamar (54)
declare alegar (341)
declare declarar
decline declinar (107)
decline desmedrar (259)
decorate decorar (32)
decorate ornar (249)
decree decretar (308)
dedicate dedicar (424)
deduce deducir (132)

deduct deducir (132)
deepen ahondar (41)
defame difamar (54)
defame infamar (54)
defame oprobiar (232)
defeat derrotar (308)
defeat vencer
defend amparar (409)
defend defender
defer aplazar (339)
defer deferir (370)
defer diferir (370)
define definir (346)
deform afear (54)
deform deformar (244)
defraud defraudar (39)
defrost descongelar (259)
defy afrontar (109)
degrade degradar (39)
dehumanize deshumanizar (339)
dehydrate deshidratar (308)
delay atrasar (2)
delay demorar (409)
delay dilatar (308)
delay retrasar
delegate delegar (341)
delegate legar (341)
deliberate deliberar (409)
delight encantar (Def. and Imp.)
delineate delinear (175)
deliver entregar
delve into cavar (9)
demand demandar (199)
demarcate demarcar (424)
demolish arrasar (2)
demolish demoler (321)
demonstrate demostrar
denigrate denigrar (409)
denominate denominar (107)
denote denotar (11)
denounce delatar (308)
denounce denunciar
deny denegar (327)
deny negar
deny oneself abnegarse (289, 327)
depart partir
depend depender
depend on atenerse
depict figurar (72)
depilate depilar (259)
deplore deplorar (32)
depopulate despoblar (209)

deport deportar (11)
depose destronar (355)
deposit depositar (259)
deposit (money) ingresar (2)
depreciate depreciar (383)
depreciate desvalorar (409)
depreciate desvalorizar (47)
depress agobiar (232)
depress deprimir (267)
deprive privar (288)
derive derivar (259)
derogate derogar (421)
descend descender (354)
descend bajar
describe describir
desert desertar (11)
deserve merecer
design diseñar (213)
design dibujar
designate designar (114)
desire desear
desist desistir (495)
despise despreciar (57)
despise vilipendiar (232)
destine destinar (107)
destroy arruinar (107)
destroy destruir
detach despegar
detail detallar (261)
detain arrestar (54)
detain detener
deteriorate empeorarse (409, 289)
determine determinar (470)
detest aborrecer (344)
detest detestar (250)
dethrone destronar (355)
detonate detonar (355)
detoxify desintoxicar (424)
devaluate devaluar (141)
devalue desvalorar (409)
devalue desvalorizar (47)
devalue devaluar (141)
develop desarrollar (261)
deviate desviar (218)
devote oneself dedicarse
devour devorar (409)
diagnose diagnosticar (424)
diaper empañar (213)
dictate dictar (11)
die fallecer (344)

die morir
differ diferir (370)
differ discrepar (332)
differ disentir (435)
differentiate diferenciar (57)
dig zahondar (336)
dig a ditch zanjar (86)
digest digerir (370)
digress divagar (341)
dilate dilatar (308)
dilute aguar (83)
dilute diluir (271)
dilute jetar (308)
dim amortiguar (83)
diminish disminuir (271)
diminish minimizar (339)
diminish minorar (409)
dine cenar
direct adiestrar (352)
direct dirigir
dirty ensuciar (383)
disable inhabilitar (308)
disable tullecer (333)
disable tullir (97)
disagree discrepar (332)
disagree divergir (188)
disappear desaparecer (59)
disarm desarmar (54)
disarrange desordenar (338)
disarticulate desarticular (71)
disassemble desensamblar (259)
discard descartar (11)
discern divisar (2)
discharge despedir (349, 178)
discipline disciplinar (107)
disclose revelar (259)
disconcert desconcertar (352)
disconnect desconectar (259)
disconnect desenchufar (259)
discontinue descontinuar (141)
discontinue discontinuar (141)
discount descontar (138)
discourage desanimar (54)
discourage descorazonar (355)
discourage desesperar (227)

discourse discursar (25)
discover atinar (107)
discover descubrir
discredit desacreditar (308)
discredit desvalorar (409)
discriminate discriminar (107)
discuss discutir
disdain desdeñar (213)
disembark desembarcar (424)
disenchant desencantar (109)
disfigure desfigurar (409)
disgrace deshonrar (409)
dishearten descorazonar (355)
dishonor deshonrar (409)
disillusion desengañar (213)
disillusion desilusionar (355)
disinfect desinfectar (259)
disinherit desheredar (39)
disintegrate desintegrar (409)
dismantle desmantelar (259)
dismantle desmontar (11)
dismiss despedir (349, 178)
dismiss destituir (271)
dismount desmontar (11)
disobey desobedecer (328)
disorganize desorganizar (339)
dispense dispensar
disperse dispersar (2)
display visualizar (339)
displease disgustar (250)
dispose disponer (364)
dispossess desposeer (152)
disprove desmentir (312)
disqualify descalificar (117)
disrobe desarropar (332)
dissemble disimular (71)
disseminate diseminar (107)
dissent disentir (435)
dissipate disipar (332)
dissolve derretir (349)
dissolve diluir (271)
dissolve disolver (321)
dissolve jetar (308)
dissuade disuadir (346)
distill destilar (259)
distinguish diferenciar (57)

distinguish distinguir
distort tergiversar (2)
distract distraer (477)
distract divertir (370, 194)
distress afligir (188)
distress atormentar (11)
distribute distribuir (264)
distribute repartir
disturb descomponer (364)
disturb disturbar (9)
disturb perturbar (9)
disturb turbar (9)
disunite desunir (480)
dive zambullir (97)
diverge divergir (188)
diversify diversificar (424)
divert desviar (218)
divide compartir (346)
divide dividir (346)
divide into syllables silabear (175)
divine adivinar
divulge divulgar (341)
do hacer
document documentar (11)
domesticate domesticar (424)
dominate dominar (107)
donate donar (355)
dot jalonar (355)
dot puntar (494)
doubt dudar
download (Internet) descargar (111)
download (Internet) telecargar (111)
doze dormitar (308)
drag arrastrar (215)
dramatize dramatizar (339)
draw diseñar (213)
draw figurar (72)
draw trazar (81)
draw lines, sketch linear (175)
draw near aproximarse (289)
draw near acercarse
dream soñar
drench calar (259)
drench empapar (342)
dress oneself vestirse
dress up acicalarse (259, 289)
dribble (sports) driblar (259)

689

forecast   pronosticar   (424)
forego   abnegar   (327)
foresee   prever   (489)
foreshadow   prefigurar
   (284)
foretell   hadar   (324)
foretell   ominar   (107)
foretell   pronosticar   (424)
foretell   vaticinar   (470)
foretell   adivinar
forge   forjar   (86)
forget   olvidar
fork   bifurcarse   (424, 289)
form   formar
formalize   formalizar   (339)
formulate   formular   (71)
fortify   fortalecer   (344)
found   fundar   (39)
fracture   fracturar   (409)
fragment   fragmentar   (11)
free   liberar   (409)
free   libertar   (11)
freeze   congelar   (259)
freeze   helar   (Def. and
   Imp.)
frequent   frecuentar   (11)
fret   apurarse
frighten   aterrorizar   (339)
frighten   espantar   (109)
frustrate   frustrar   (215)
fry   freír
fry lightly   sofreír   (404)
fulfill   cumplir
fumigate   fumigar   (341)
function   funcionar
furnish   amueblar   (259)
furnish   habilitar   (308)
furnish   suministrar   (215)

G

gage   calibrar   (259)
Gallicize   afrancesar   (2)
gallop   galopar   (54)
galvanize   galvanizar   (339)
gather   acopiar   (106)
gather   amontonar   (107)
gather   agregar
gather   recoger
gather around   aglomerarse
   (409, 289)
generalize   generalizar
   (339)
generate   generar   (215)
gesticulate   gesticular   (259)
gesture   gesticular   (259)
get a doctorate   doctorarse
   (409, 289)

get along well with
   simpatizar con   (339)
get away from   alejarse de
   (86, 289)
get burned   asurarse   (112)
get cold   enfriarse   (256,
   289)
get cozy   acurrucarse
   (424, 289)
get dark   atardecer   (344)
   (3rd person only)
get dark   oscurecer   (344)
get divorced   divorciarse
get engaged or married
   desposarse   (2, 289)
get excited, enthusiastic
   entusiasmarse   (54, 289)
get into debt   endeudarse
   (39, 289)
get late   atardecer   (344)
   (3rd person only)
get married   casarse
get ready   alistarse   (11,
   289)
get revenge   vengarse   (341,
   289)
get sick, ill   enfermarse
get thin   adelgazar   (339)
get tipsy   alumbrarse
get up   levantarse
get up early   madrugar
   (341)
get used to   acostumbrarse
   (22, 289)
get wet   mojarse
gild   dorar   (32)
give   donar   (355)
give   dar
give a little more   yapar
   (332)
give as a present, gift
   regalar
give asylum   asilar   (259)
give back   restituir   (264)
give birth   parir   (495)
give up   capitular   (259)
give up   claudicar   (424)
glide   planear   (206)
glitter   destellar   (261)
glorify   ensalzar   (339)
glorify   exaltar   (11)
glorify   glorificar   (424)
gloss   glosar   (2)
glow   arder   (63)
glow   resplandecer   (344)
gnaw   carcomer   (128)
gnaw   remorder   (318)

gnaw   tascar   (99)
go   ir
go away   irse
go away   marcharse
go backwards   recular   (71)
go beyond the limits
   translimitar   (254)
go crazy   enloquecerse
   (344, 102)
go down   abajar, bajar
   (86)
go forward   adelantarse
go in the direction of
   rumbar a   (54)
go on a pilgrimage, journey
   peregrinar   (107)
go round   tornear   (206)
go round, turn   versar   (25)
go through   atravesar   (352)
go to bed   acostarse
go toward   dirigirse a   (188,
   8)
go up   subir
go without   abnegarse
   (289, 327)
gobble down   zampar
   (332)
gobble up   soplarse   (289,
   448)
gossip   chismear   (259)
govern   regir   (203)
govern   gobernar
graduate   graduarse   (141,
   289)
graduate in   licenciarse   (57,
   289)
grant   impartir   (495)
grant   otorgar   (421)
grasp   empuñar   (213)
grasp   prender   (63)
grasp   agarrar
grasp   asir
grasp   coger
gratify   contentar   (109)
gravitate   gravitar   (254)
graze   rasar   (2)
grease   engrasar   (2)
grieve   afligirse   (188, 8)
grieve   apurarse
grieve   gemir
grimace   gesticular   (259)
grind   moler   (321)
grind   triturar   (72)
grip   apretar   (352)
group   agrupar
grow   crecer
grow tired   aburrirse

increase   acrecentar   (352)
increase   acrecer   (151)
increase   aumentar   (317)
increase   engrandecer   (344)
increase   incrementar   (11)
increase   multiplicar   (424)
increase   agrandar
increase in value   valorar   (54, 409)
increase in value   valorear   (54, 206)
increase production   bonificar   (117)
inculcate   inculcar   (424)
incur   incurrir   (495)
indemnify   indemnizar   (339)
indent   dentar   (352)
indicate   indicar
indispose   indisponer   (364)
individualize   individualizar   (339)
induce   inducir
induce a liking for   aficionar   (338)
indulge oneself   regalarse   (401, 289)
industrialize   industrializar   (339)
infect   infectar   (11)
infer   inferir   (400)
infiltrate   infiltrar   (215)
inflame   inflamar   (54)
inflate   hinchar   (306)
inflate   inflar   (259)
inflict   infligir   (188)
influence   influenciar   (383)
influence   influir
inform   avisar   (340)
inform   enterar   (215)
inform   informar   (244)
inform   noticiar   (383)
inform   notificar   (117)
inform oneself   informarse
infringe   infringir   (188)
infuriate   enfurecer   (344)
infuriate   ensañar   (213)
infuriate   indignar   (107)
ingest   ingerir   (435)
inhabit   habitar
inhale   aspirar   (29)
inhale   inhalar   (259)
inherit   heredar
inhibit   cohibir   (382)
inhibit   inhibir   (353)
initial   rubricar   (424)

initiate   iniciar   (383)
inject   inyectar   (11)
injure   agraviar   (54)
injure   damnificar   (424)
injure   dañar   (109)
injure   injuriar   (232)
injure   llagar   (298)
injure   maleficiar   (383)
innovate   innovar   (259)
inoculate   inocular   (71)
inquire   inquirir   (33)
inscribe   inscribir
insert   insertar   (11)
insinuate   insinuar   (141)
insist   insistir
inspect   inspeccionar   (355)
inspire   alentar   (352)
inspire   inspirar   (29)
install   instalar   (259)
instigate   instigar   (341)
institute   instituir   (264)
instruct   adiestrar   (352)
instruct   instruir   (271)
insult   denigrar   (409)
insult   injuriar   (232)
insult   insultar   (11)
insult   ofender   (63)
insult each other   trabarse de palabras   (289)
integrate   integrar   (259)
intellectualize   intelectualizar   (339)
intend to   pretender   (63)
intensify   intensificar   (424)
intercalate   intercalar   (259)
intercede   interceder   (63)
intercept   atajar   (86)
intercept   interceptar   (11)
interchange   intercambiar   (232)
interconnect   interconectar   (11)
interfere   entrometerse   (444, 102)
interfere   interferir   (435)
interlace   entrelazar   (339)
intermingle   entremezclar   (259)
intern   internar   (107)
interpose   interponer   (364)
interpret   deletrear   (206)
interpret   interpretar   (376)
interpret   trujamanear   (206)
interrogate   interrogar   (297)
interrupt   atajar   (86)

interrupt   interrumpir   (452)
intertwine   entrelazar   (339)
intervene   intervenir   (488)
interview   entrevistar   (494)
intimidate   intimidar   (199)
intoxicate   intoxicar   (424)
intrigue   intrigar   (341)
introduce   involucrar   (259)
introduce   introducir
intuit   intuir   (271)
inundate   inundar   (39)
invade   invadir   (60)
invalidate   invalidar   (39)
invent   ingeniar   (232)
invent   inventar   (279)
invert   invertir   (370)
invest (as a title)   investir   (349)
invest money   invertir   (370)
investigate   curiosear   (175)
investigate   investigar   (421)
investigate   averiguar
invite   convidar   (39)
invite   invitar
invoice   facturar   (409)
invoke   invocar   (424)
involve   involucrar   (259)
iron   planchar   (225)
irradiate   irradiar   (232)
irrigate   irrigar   (341)
irrigate   sorregar   (327)
irritate   chinchar   (259)
irritate   enfadar   (210)
irritate   enojar   (212)
irritate   irritar   (279)
isolate   aislar   (218)
Italianize   italianizar   (339)

J

jest   bufonearse   (348)
join   acoplar   (259)
join   afiliarse   (232, 289)
join   anudar   (39)
join   ensamblar   (259)
join   trabar   (54)
join   juntar
join (a group)   incorporarse   (409, 289)
joke   bromear   (206)
joke   bufonearse   (348)
journey   transitar   (254)
joust   justar   (11)
judge   sentenciar   (57)
judge   juzgar

jump   brincar   (430)
jump   saltar
justify   justificar   (117)
juxtapose   yuxtaponer
   (364)

K

keep   guardar   (259)
keep awake   desvelar   (259)
keep away from   apartarse
   (11, 289)
kick   patalear   (206)
kick   patear   (206)
kick (a ball)   pelotear   (175)
kidnap   secuestrar   (409)
kill   matar
kill off   rematar   (308)
kiss   besar   (235)
knead   amasar   (2)
knead   sobar   (54)
kneel down   hincarse   (424,
   289)
knife   acuchillar
knit   tricotar   (254)
knit (eyebrows)   fruncir
   (501)
knock down   revolcar   (19,
   424)
knock down   tumbar   (9)
knock down   varear   (175)
knock down   abatir
know   conocer
know   saber

L

label   rotular   (71)
lacerate   lacerar   (409)
lack   carecer de   (333)
laicize   laicizar   (339)
lament   lamentar   (11)
laminate   laminar   (107)
lance   alanzar   (286)
lance   lancear   (175)
land   aterrizar   (47)
last   durar   (409)
last a long time   perdurar
   (215)
lather   enjabonar   (355)
lather   jabonar   (473)
laugh   reír
laugh   reírse
launch   botar
launch   lanzar
lay aside   deponer   (364)
lay the foundation   cimentar
   (352)
lay waste   yermar   (54)

lead   encabezar   (339)
lead   conducir
leaf through   hojear   (175)
lean   ladear   (206)
lean on/upon   reclinarse
   en/sobre   (289)
lean out   asomarse   (112)
learn   aprender
lease   arrendar   (352)
leave   partir
leave   salir
legislate   legislar   (259)
legitimize   legitimar   (54)
lend   prestar
lengthen   alargar   (421)
lessen   achicar   (424)
lessen   apocar   (99)
let go   largar   (341)
let go   soltar   (209)
level   aplanar   (107)
level   arrasar   (2)
level   nivelar   (259)
liberate   emancipar   (332)
liberate   independizar
   (339)
liberate   liberar   (409)
liberate   libertar   (11)
lick   lamer   (91)
lie   mentir
lie down   acostarse
lie down   yacer
lift   alzar
lift   levantar
light up   esclarecer   (344)
like   gustar   (Def. and
   Imp.)
limit   limitar   (308)
line up   enfilar   (259)
liquefy   licuar   (141)
liquefy   liquidar   (39)
liquidate   liquidar   (39)
list   catalogar   (341)
listen (to)   escuchar
litigate   litigar   (341)
live   vivir
live together   convivir
   (495)
load   cargar
loaf   cantonear   (54)
loaf   gandulear   (206)
loaf   haraganear
loaf   vaguear   (206)
loathe   repugnar   (107)
localize   localizar   (81)
locate   localizar   (81)
locate   situar   (141)
locate   ubicar   (424)

lock   candar   (109)
lodge   alojar   (86)
lodge   hospedar   (39)
long for   anhelar   (259)
long for   apetecer   (59)
look   mirar
look after   atender   (164)
look at oneself, each other
   mirarse
look at over again   remirar
   (314)
look for   buscar
loosen   aflojar   (86)
loosen   zafar   (54)
lose   perder
lose hope   desesperarse
   (227, 289)
lose interest   desinteresarse
   (277)
lose one's appetite
   desganarse   (289)
lose one's patience
   impacientarse   (11, 289)
lose the habit of
   desacostumbrarse   (259,
   289)
lose weight   adelgazar
   (339)
lose weight   enflaquecer
   (344)
love   encantar   (Def. and
   Imp.)
love   amar
lower   rebajar   (86)
lower   bajar
lubricate   lubricar   (469)
lunch   almorzar

M

macerate   macerar
   (409)
magnetize   magnetizar
   (339)
magnify   magnificar
   (424)
maintain   mantener
make   hacer
make a bad marriage
   malcasarse   (112)
make a pact   pactar
   (11)
make a speech   discursar
   (25)
make a speech   perorar
   (409)
make a will, testament
   testar   (54)
make agile   agilitar
   (11)

make an appointment citar
make an effort esforzarse
(49, 289)
make angry despechar
(225)
make bitter amargar (341)
make breathless desalentar
(103)
make cheaper abaratar
(308)
make cheese quesear (175)
make clear clarar (16)
make deeper ahondar (41)
make even nivelar (259)
make eyes at galantear
(175)
make famous afamar (54)
make frequent use of trillar
(259)
make known divulgar (341)
make legal formalizar
(339)
make old envejecer (344)
make one's debut debutar
(308)
make ready aprestar (376)
make sad entristecer (344)
make someone crazy alocar
(472)
make sour agriar (54)
make ugly afear (54)
make uneven desnivelar
(259)
make uniform uniformar
(244)
make untidy desaliñar
(213)
make untidy desarreglar
(259)
make up (one's face)
pintarse
make use of aprovechar
(66)
make use of utilizarse
(289, 482)
make worse empeorar
(409)
maltreat maltratar (478)
manage gestionar (355)
manage manejar
manage regir (203)
manifest manifestar (352)
manipulate manipular (71)
manufacture confeccionar
(107)
manufacture manufacturar
(284)

marinate adobar (259)
mark jalonar (355)
mark marcar
mark again remarcar
(305)
mark with an accent
acentuar (141)
mark with buoys abalizar
(339)
martyr martirizar (339)
marvel at maravillarse
(261, 289)
mash majar (86)
massage sobar (54)
match emparejar (86)
match equiparar (342)
match parear (175)
materialize materializar
(339)
matter importar (Def. and
Imp.)
mature madurar (409)
maul machucar (424)
measure acompasar (347)
measure medir
meddle entrometerse
(444, 102)
mediate mediar (232)
meditate meditar (254)
melt derretir (349)
melt fundir (60)
mend coser (128)
mend remendar (352)
mend zurcir
mention mencionar
mention mentar (352)
merge fusionar (107)
merit merecer
metamorphose
metamorfosear (175)
methodize metodizar
(339)
migrate trashumar (54)
mine minar (107)
mislead descaminar
(107)
mislead despistar (250)
mistake equivocar (220)
mistrust desconfiar (256)
misunderstand malentender
(164)
mitigate mitigar (341)
mix amasar (2)
mix mezclar (259)
mix together barajar (86)
mix up embarullar (261)
mix up triscar (99)

mobilize movilizar (339)
mock chufar (259)
mock escarnecer (344)
model modelar (259)
moderate moderar (409)
modernize actualizar
(339)
modernize modernizar
(339)
modify modificar (424)
modulate modular (71)
moisten humedecer (344)
monkey around monear
(206)
moralize moralizar (339)
mortgage hipotecar (424)
mortify macerar (409)
mortify mortificar (424)
motivate motivar (9)
mount montar
move abalar (54)
move conmover (321)
move mover
move mudarse
move ahead adelantarse
move near arrimarse (54,
289)
move out desalojar (165)
move to new land
trashumar (54)
mow segar (327)
muddle embarullar (261)
muffle amortiguar (83)
muffle ensordecer (344)
muffle silenciar (57)
multiply multiplicar (424)
mumble chistar
mummify momificar (424)
murder asesinar (107)
murmur murmurar (72)
murmur susurrar (54)
mutilate mutilar (71)
mutter murmurar (72)

N

nail clavar (54)
name nombrar (113)
name llamar
narrate narrar (215)
narrate relatar (308)
narrow estrachar (200)
nationalize nacionalizar
(90)
naturalize naturalizar (90)
navigate navegar
need faltar
need necesitar

periphrase   perifrasear (175)
perish   perecer   (344)
permit   dejar
permit   permitir
perpetrate a crime   perpetrar (409)
perpetuate   perpetuar   (141)
persevere   perseverar   (409)
persist   empeñarse   (213, 289)
persist   persistir   (74)
personalize   personalizar (339)
personify   personalizar   (339)
personify   personificar (424)
perspire   sudar   (54)
perspire   transpirar   (314)
persuade   persuadir   (346)
pertain   pertenecer
pervert   pervertir   (410)
pest   acosar   (2)
pester   fastidiar   (232)
photocopy   fotocopiar (106)
photograph   fotografiar (464)
pierce   picar   (424)
pierce   traspasar   (347)
pile up   amontonar   (107)
pile up   hacinar   (107)
pillage   saquear   (206)
pilot   pilotar   (54)
pilot   pilotear   (54)
place in front   anteponer (364)
plague   plagar   (341)
plait   trenzar   (81)
plan   planear   (206)
plan   planificar   (424)
plant   plantar   (109)
plate (with silver or gold)   chapar   (332)
play (game, sport)   jugar
play (music)   tocar
play piano   teclear   (206)
play the lead in   protagonizar   (339)
please   complacer   (361)
please   contentar   (109)
please   agradar
please   placer
pleat   plegar   (327, 341)
plot   conspirar   (314)
plot   intrigar   (341)
plot   tramar   (54)

plot   urdir   (346)
plow   arar   (54)
plow   laborar   (409)
plow   surcar   (424)
pluck   tañer
plug   obturar   (284)
plug   taponar   (355)
plug in   enchufar   (54)
plunge   zambullir   (97)
plunge into water   zapuzar (81)
pluralize   pluralizar   (339)
pocket   embolsar   (2)
pocket a ball in billiards   trucar   (424)
point   apuntar   (11)
point out   mencionar
point out   mostrar
poison   atosigar   (341)
poison   envenenar   (107)
poison   intoxicar   (424)
polemicize   polemizar (339)
polish   alisar   (2)
polish   bruñir   (255)
polish   limar   (231)
polish   lustrar   (215)
polish   sutilizar   (339)
polish   pulir
polish again   repulir   (386)
politicize   politizar   (339)
ponder   cavilar   (259)
pontificate   pontificar (424)
popularize   popularizar (339)
popularize   vulgarizar (339)
populate   poblar   (474)
pose   posar   (481)
possess   poseer
postpone   aplazar   (339)
postpone   diferir   (370)
postpone   posponer   (364)
postulate   postular   (71)
pound   golpetear   (175)
pound   macear   (175)
pound   machacar   (424)
pour   verter   (354)
practice   ejercitar   (308)
practice   practicar
praise   alabar   (259)
praise   exaltar   (11)
praise   glorificar   (424)
praise   loar   (259)
prattle   charlar   (259)
prattle   garlar   (259)

pray   orar   (32)
pray   rezar   (53)
preach   sermonear   (175)
preach   predicar
precede   preceder   (63)
precipitate   precipitar (254)
predestine   predestinar (107)
predetermine   predeterminar (107)
predict   augurar   (409)
predict   ominar   (107)
predict   pronosticar   (424)
predict   vaticinar   (470)
predict   predecir
predispose   predisponer (364)
predominate   predominar (107)
prefabricate   prefabricar (424)
prefer   preferir
prefigure   prefigurar   (284)
preheat   precalentar   (352)
prejudge   prejuzgar   (341)
premeditate   premeditar (308)
prepare   aparar   (342)
prepare   aprestar   (376)
prepare   preparar
prepare onself   prepararse
presage   presagiar   (232)
prescribe   prescribir   (224)
present   presentar
preserve   conservar   (9)
preserve   preservar   (288)
preside over   presidir   (60)
press   oprimir   (267)
press   prensar   (2)
pressure   presionar   (355)
presume   presumir   (267)
presuppose   presuponer (364)
pretend   aparentar   (11)
pretend   simular   (71)
prevail   prevaler   (484)
prevail, take root   prevalecer (344)
price   cotizar   (339)
print   estampar   (332)
probe   sondar   (39)
proceed   proceder   (413)
proclaim   proclamar
produce   generar   (215)
produce   producir
profane   profanar   (107)

698   **English-Spanish verb index**

profess profesar (403)
program programar (54)
progress progresar (235)
progress adelantar
prohibit vedar (54)
prohibit prohibir
project proyectar (11)
proliferate proliferar (409)
prolong prolongar (341)
promise prometer (444)
promote promover (321)
promulgate promulgar
  (341)
pronounce pronunciar
propagate propagar (341)
propel impulsar (2)
propose proponer (364)
proscribe proscribir (224)
prosecute procesar (403)
prosper prosperar (227)
protect abrigar (297)
protect amparar (409)
protect escudar (39)
protect proteger
protest protestar (308)
protrude descollar (138)
prove constatar (309)
provide deparar (342)
provide proporcionar
  (107)
provide proveer (152)
provide for needs subvenir
  (488)
provoke provocar (99)
provoke suscitar (308)
prowl rondar (215)
publish editar (254)
publish publicar (99)
pull arrastrar (215)
pull jalar (259)
pull tirar
pull out desfijar (241)
pulse pulsar (25)
pulverize pulverizar (339)
punctuate puntuar (141)
puncture picar (424)
puncture punchar (306)
punish castigar (341)
punish sancionar (107)
purge purgar (341)
purify apurar (67)
purify purificar (424)
purse (lips) fruncir (501)
pursue acosar (2)
pursue perseguir (432)
push empujar (86)
put colocar

put poner
put a seal or stamp on
  timbrar (22)
put at a disadvantage
  desfavorecer (344)
put away arrinconar (107)
put back remeter (444)
put back reponer (364)
put before preponer (364)
put down posar (481)
put in charge encargar
  (111)
put in order ordenar
put into meter (444)
put on (clothing) ponerse
put on makeup maquillarse
  (289)
put on weight engordar
  (54)
put out of order desajustar
  (250)
put to bed acostar (21)
putrefy pudrir

Q

quarrel camorrear (54)
quiet acallar (261)
quiet quietar (308)
quiet sedar (54)
quiet sosegar (327)

R

radiate radiar (232)
raffle sortear (206)
rage rabiar (106)
rain llover (Def. and Imp.)
raise realzar (339)
raise remontar (317)
raise erguir
raise prices encarecer
  (344)
rake rastrillar (261)
ramify ramificarse (424,
  289)
ransom rescatar (308)
ratify ratificar (424)
ration racionar (107)
rationalize racionalizar
  (339)
raze arrasar (2)
raze rasar (2)
reach arribar (9)
reach alcanzar
react reaccionar (355)
reactivate reactivar (259)
read leer
reaffirm reafirmar (243)

realize acatar (11)
realize realizar
reanimate reanimar (107)
reappear reaparecer (59)
rear educar (424)
rearm rearmar (54)
reason argüir (264)
reason (out) razonar (355)
reassume reasumir (495)
reassure reasegurar (72)
rebel rebelarse (259, 289)
rebound rebotar (308)
rebound resaltar (427)
rebroadcast retransmitir
  (30)
rebuild reconstruir (264)
recapitulate recapitular (71)
receive recibir
receive hospitably acoger
  (123)
recite recitar (254)
reclaim reclamar (15)
recline reclinar (107)
recognize reconocer
recoil recular (71)
recommend recomendar
recompense gratificar (424)
recompense recompensar
  (2)
reconcile avenir (488)
reconcile reconciliar
  (232)
reconcile reconciliarse
  (232, 289)
reconsider repensar
  (352)
reconstitute reconstituir
  (271)
reconstruct reconstruir
  (264)
recover recobrar
  (259)
recover recuperar
  (227)
recover reponerse
  (364, 102)
recriminate
  recriminar (107)
recruit reclutar (308)
rectify rectificar
  (424)
recuperate recuperar (227)
recycle reciclar (259)
recycle recircular
  (71)
redo rehacer (260)
redouble redoblar (259)
reduce abreviar (232)
reduce achicar (424)
reduce acortar (11)

revert revertir (34)
review repasar (347)
review rever (489)
review revisar (2)
revise enmendar (352)
revise rever (489)
revise revisar (2)
revive reanimar (107)
revive revivir (495)
revoke abrogar (421)
revoke revocar
revolt rebelarse (259, 289)
revolutionize revolucionar (355)
revolve revolver
reward gratificar (424)
reward premiar (232)
reward recompensar (2)
rhyme rimar (54)
ridicule escarnecer (344)
ridicule ridiculizar (339)
ridicule burlarse
rinse enjuagar (298)
rip rasgar (341)
ripen madurar (409)
ripple ondear (206)
risk arriesgar (341)
risk aventurarse (48)
rival emular (259)
rival rivalizar (339)
roam vagabundear (463)
roam vagar (341)
roar rugir (188)
roast asar (2)
rob hurtar (11)
rob saltear (206)
rob robar
roll liar (256)
roll rodar (474)
roll rular (71)
roll up enrollar (261)
roll up sleeve, pants remangar (341)
root up arrancar
rot pudrir
rotate rotar (308)
round off redondear (206)
row bogar (421)
row remar (54)
rub frotar (498)
rub gratar (249)
rub together transfregar (327)
ruin arruinar (107)
ruin desbaratar (109)
ruin destrozar (339)
ruin hundir (60)

ruin malear (206)
rule regir (203)
ruminate rumiar (62)
run correr
run (street) desembocar (424)
run away fugarse (341, 289)
run to someone's aide acorrer (148)
rush apresurarse
rush about trajinar (107)
rust oxidar (39)

S

sack saquear (206)
sacrifice sacrificar (117)
sadden apenar (107)
saddle ensillar (261)
sail zarpar (332)
sail navegar
salivate salivar (288)
salt salar (71)
salute saludar
sample catar (308)
sanction sancionar (107)
satirize satirizar (339)
satisfy satisfacer
saturate saturar (284)
sauté sofreír (404)
save librar (259)
save salvar (288)
save ahorrar
savor paladear (206)
savor saborear (206)
saw serrar (116)
say decir
say good-bye to despedirse
say stupid things gansear (175)
scare espantar (109)
scare away zapear (206)
scatter esparcir
scheme intrigar (341)
scheme urdir (346)
scold regañar (213)
scold reñir
scorch chamuscar (99)
score goals golear (206)
scrape raspar (332)
scrape rozar (81)
scrape raer
scratch arañar (213)
scratch rascar (99)
scratch rozar (81)
scream chillar (259)
screech ulular (259)

scribble emborronar (54)
scribble garabatear (463)
scrub fregar
scrutinize escudriñar (213)
sculpt esculpir (157)
seal sellar (261)
search carefully rebuscar (99)
season aderezar (339)
season adobar (259)
season aliñar (213)
season condimentar (11)
season salpimentar (352)
season sazonar (355)
seat asentar (352)
second secundar (39)
secularize secularizar (339)
secure sujetar (308)
seduce seducir (381)
see ver
seek buscar
seem parecer
segment segmentar (11)
segregate segregar (421)
seize empuñar (213)
seize prender (63)
seize agarrar
seize asir
seize coger
select seleccionar (355)
sell vender
send despachar (225)
send enviar
send over and over again remandar (259)
sense intuir (271)
sentence someone sentenciar (57)
separate desunir (480)
separate separarse (289, 437)
separate separar
serve servir
serve in the army militar (308)
set aside apartar (11)
set down asentar (352)
set on fire incendiar (106)
set on fire inflamar (54)
set on fire abrasar
settle saldar (54)
sew coser (128)
shake abalar (54)
shake menear (206)

shake   retemblar   (352)
shake   sacudir
shake about   zarandar   (54, 41)
shake about   zarandear   (54, 206)
shame   avergonzar
share   compartir   (346)
shatter   estrellar   (261)
shave   afeitar   (35)
shave (one's beard)   rasurarse   (292)
shave oneself   afeitarse
shear   trasquilar   (259)
shear   tundir   (346)
shelter   abrigar   (297)
shelter   albergar   (341)
shelter   cobijar   (54)
shield   blindar   (39)
shield   escudar   (39)
shine   brillar   (259)
shine   lucir   (495) (before a or o, c becomes zc in Tenses 1, 6 and imperative)
shine   relucir   (495) (before a or o, c becomes zc in Tenses 1, 6 and imperative)
shine   resplandecer   (344)
shiver   tiritar   (308)
shock   escandalizar   (339)
shoe   calzar
shoot   disparar   (409)
shoot   fusilar   (259)
shoot at   abalear   (206)
shoplift   ladronear   (206)
shorten   abreviar   (232)
shorten   achicar   (424)
shorten   acortar   (11)
shout   rugir   (188)
shout   vocear   (206)
shout   vociferar   (227)
shout   gritar
shovel   palear   (206)
show   manifestar   (352)
show   mostrar
show off   alardear   (54)
show off   farolear   (54)
show off   garbear   (175)
show off   ostentar   (11)
shower oneself   ducharse
shriek   chillar   (259)
shuffle   barajar   (86)
shut   clausurar   (409)
sift   tamizar   (339)
sigh   suspirar
sign   signar   (114)
sign   firmar

sign on   enrolar   (259)
signal   señalar
signify   significar
silence   acallar   (261)
silence   silenciar   (57)
simplify   simplificar   (117)
simulate   simular   (71)
sin   pecar   (424)
sing   cantar
sing in tune   entonar   (355)
sing softly   cantalear   (54)
sing softly   canturrear   (232)
sing to sleep   arrullar   (261)
singe   chamuscar   (99)
single out   singularizar   (339)
sink   sumir   (459)
sink in   hincar   (424)
sip   sorber   (91)
sit down   sentarse
situate   situar   (141)
situate   ubicar   (424)
skate   patinar   (107)
sketch   trazar   (81)
ski   esquiar
skid   patinar   (107)
skim   hojear   (175)
skip   brincar   (430)
slacken   aflojar   (86)
slander   calumniar   (232)
slander   difamar   (54)
slander   infamar   (54)
slap   cachetear   (206)
slap   sopapear   (206)
slap in the face   abofetear   (54)
slap in the face   acachetear   (54)
slash   acuchillar
sleep   dormir
slice   tajar   (86)
slice   tronzar   (81)
slice (meat)   trinchar   (54)
slide   patinar   (107)
slow down   retardar   (199)
smash   destrozar   (339)
smash   estrellar   (261)
smash   quebrar   (352)
smell   apestar   (11)
smell   olfatear   (206)
smell   oler
smile   sonreír
smoke   humear   (175)
smoke   fumar
smooth   alisar   (2)

smooth   aplanar   (107)
smooth   limar   (231)
smooth   suavizar   (339)
snatch   arrebatar   (308)
sneeze   estornudar   (39)
sniff   olfatear   (206)
sniff   ventar   (352)
snitch   sisar   (9)
snooze   dormitar   (308)
snore   roncar   (424)
snow   nevar   (Def. and Imp.)
snow heavily   ventiscar   (424)
snow lightly   neviscar   (424)
soak   empapar   (342)
soak   remojar   (239)
soak in   embeber   (91)
soap   enjabonar   (355)
soap   jabonar   (473)
sob   sollozar
soften   ablandar   (41)
soften   ablandecer   (344)
soften   endulzar   (339)
soften   suavizar   (339)
soil   ensuciar   (383)
solder   soldar   (209)
solve   solucionar   (355)
soothe   apaciguar   (83)
soothe   aplacar   (424)
soothe   sedar   (54)
sound   sondar   (39)
sound   sonar
sow   sembrar   (352)
spank   zurrar   (54)
spark   chispear   (175)
sparkle   chispear   (175)
sparkle   destellar   (261)
speak   hablar
spear   lancear   (175)
specialize   especializarse   (339, 289)
specify   particularizar   (339)
specify   precisar   (2)
speed   acelerar
speed up   acelerar   (409)
spell   deletrear   (206)
spend (time)   pasar
spend the summer   veranear   (463)
spew   gormar   (244)
spill   derramar   (259)
spin   girar   (215)
spit   escupir   (346)
splash   salpicar   (424)

English-Spanish verb index

703

suspect maliciar (383)
suspect sospechar
suspend suspender (91)
sustain sostener
swallow tragar (421)
swallow soft food without
 chewing papar (332)
swear jurar
sweat sudar (54)
sweat transpirar (314)
sweep barrer
sweeten endulzar (339)
swell hinchar (306)
swim nadar
swindle estafar (259)
swindle timar (231)
swirl (snow) ventiscar
 (424)
symbolize simbolizar
 (339)
synchronize sincronizar
 (339)
systematize metodizar
 (339)
systematize sistematizar
 (339)

T

take (food) tomar
take a long time tardar
 (199)
take a walk pasearse
take advantage
 aprovecharse
take care of custodiar
 (232)
take care of oneself cuidarse
take courses cursar (2)
take hold of aferrarse
 (352, 289)
take in ingerir (435)
take notice fijarse
take off (airplane) despegar
take off (clothing) quitarse
take off shoes descalzar
 (339)
take on asumir (267)
take out sacar
take place supervenir (488)
take possession of
 adueñarse (213, 289)
take power, possession
 apoderarse
take refuge asilar (259)
take refuge refugiarse
 (232, 289)
take root arraigar (341)

talk hablar
talk foolishly disparatar
 (308)
talk nonsense necear (206)
tally tarjar (86)
tame domesticar (424)
tan broncear
tangle enredar (39)
tap one's feet zapatear
 (463)
taste catar (308)
taste paladear (206)
taste saborear (206)
teach instruir (271)
teach enseñar
tear lacerar (409)
tear rasgar (341)
tear off desgajar (54)
tear shreds trizar (81)
tear to pieces despedazar
 (339)
tease embromar (54)
teethe dentar (352)
telegraph telegrafiar
telephone telefonear
televise televisar (2)
tell contar
terminate terminar
terrify aterrorizar (339)
test ensayar (54)
test, try probar
testify testificar (117)
thank agradecer
thaw descongelar (259)
theorize teorizar (339)
think pensar
think over recapacitar
 (308)
think up idear (175)
threaten amenazar (339)
throw disparar (409)
throw arrojar
throw echar
throw lanzar
throw (away) botar
throw back, repel relanzar
 (286)
thunder tronar (474)
tidy aliñar (213)
tie aligar (421)
tie amarrar (409)
tie atar (308)
tie empatar (308)
tie liar (256)
tie knots anudar (39)
tie together anudar (39)
tie together enlazar (339)

tighten estrachar (200)
tile tejar (86)
till laborar (409)
tilt ladear (206)
tint colorear (175)
tint tintar (254)
title titular (71)
toast tostar
toast again retostar (474)
tolerate tolerar (227)
torture atormentar (11)
torture torturar (72)
totter titubear (175)
touch palpar (332)
touch tocar
tow remolcar (424)
trace trazar (81)
trade comerciar (57)
traffic traficar (424)
train adiestrar (352)
train capacitar (308)
train ejercitar (308)
train entrenar (107)
trample pisotear (175)
trample pisar
trample down atropellar
 (261)
tranquilize tranquilizar
 (339)
transact tramitar (254)
transcend trascender (354)
transcribe transcribir
 (224)
transfer transferir (370)
transfer transponer (364)
transfer trasferir (370)
transfer trasladar (215)
transform transformar
 (244)
transgress infringir (188)
translate traducir
translate over again
 retraducir (476)
transmigrate transmigrar
 (273)
transmit transmitir (30)
transplant trasplantar (11)
transport acarrear (206)
transport transportar
 (427)
travel transitar (254)
travel viajar
tread on pisar
treat attentively agasajar
 (86)
tremble retemblar (352)
tremble temblar

English-Spanish verb index

warm (up) calentar
warm up acalorar (409)
warn alertar (11)
warn avisar (340)
warn prevenir (488)
warn advertir
wash enjabonar (355)
wash lavar
wash again relavar
  (288)
wash oneself again relavarse
  (289)
wash onself lavarse
waste derrochar (225)
waste desperdiciar (57)
waste malgastar (250)
waste gastar
watch acechar (200)
watch (over) vigilar
watch over velar
water regar
water (eyes) lagrimear
  (206)
weaken desfallecer (344)
wear llevar
wear out deteriorar (409)
weave tejer (91)
weep lagrimar (231)
weep lagrimear (206)
weep llorar
weigh pesar (25)
weigh sopesar (2)
weigh again repesar (25)
weigh anchor zarpar
  (332)

weigh down sobrecargar
  (111)
welcome acoger (123)
weld soldar (209)
westernize occidentalizar
  (339)
whimper lloriquear
  (206)
whine lloriquear (206)
whip fustigar (341)
whirl up in the air
  revolotear (206)
whisper chuchear (259)
whisper rechistar (250)
whisper susurrar (54)
whistle chiflar (259)
whistle silbar (9)
whiten blanquear (206)
widen ampliar (256)
wiggle menear (206)
win ganar
wink guiñar (213)
wink parpadear (206)
wink pestañear (206)
wipe out aniquilar (259)
wish desear
wish querer
withdraw from apartarse
  (11, 289)
wobble bambolear (206)
wolf down soplarse (289,
  448)
work laborar (409)
work labrar (409)
work obrar (113)

work trabajar
work hard afanarse (289)
worry inquietar (308)
worry remorder (318)
worry turbar (9)
worry apurarse
worry preocuparse
worry excessively
  torturarse (289)
worsen empeorarse (409,
  289)
wound lesionar (355)
wound llagar (298)
wound herir
wound by gunshot abalear
  (206)
wound with words zaherir
  (263)
wrap up envolver
wreck desbaratar (109)
wring out exprimir (267)
wrinkle arrugar (341)
write escribir
write off amortizar (339)
wrong agraviar (54)

X

x-ray radiografiar (256)

Y

yawn bostezar
yearn anhelar (259)
yield ceder (413)
yoke uncir (501)

Over 2,100 Spanish verbs conjugated like model verbs

The number after each verb is the page number in this book where a model verb is shown fully conjugated. At times there are two page references; for example, sonarse (to blow one's nose) is conjugated like sonar (verb 445) because the o in the stem changes to ue and it is like lavarse (verb 289), which is a reflexive -ar type verb, as is sonarse. Don't forget to use the reflexive pronouns with reflexive verbs. Consult the entry **reflexive pronoun and reflexive verb** in the section on definitions of basic grammatical terms with examples beginning on page 33. If you see "Def. and Imp." instead of a verb number, look in the list of defective and impersonal verbs. It's right after the main verb listing.

Note: The English definitions are a guide to the most common meanings. In some cases we have also included a preposition when it is likely that you will use it along with the verb. There are obviously many more definitions for the verbs in this list. Think of the definitions as a way to make sure that you're looking up the right word!

A

abajar, bajar   to go down (86)

abalanzar   to balance (81)

abalanzarse   to hurl oneself (81)

abalar   to move, shake (54)

abalear   to shoot at, to wound or kill by gunshot (206)

abalizar   to mark with buoys (339)

abanar   to cool with a fan (249)

abandonar   to abandon (473)

abanicar   to fan (117)

abaratar   to make cheaper, reduce prices (308)

abdicar   to abdicate (99)

abducir   to abduct (132)

aberrar   to err, be mistaken (54)

abjurar   to abjure, renounce (284)

ablandar   to soften (41)

ablandecer   to soften (344)

abnegar   to abnegate, forego (327)

abnegarse   to go without, deny oneself (289, 327)

abofetear   to slap in the face (54)

abominar   to abominate (107)

abonar   to buy a subscription (54)

abonarse   to subscribe oneself (54, 289)

abordar   to board (54)

aborrecer   to abhor, detest (344)

abotonarse   to button up (355, 289)

abreviar   to reduce, shorten (232)

abrigar   to shelter, protect (297)

abrochar   to button up, fasten (259)

abrogar   to abrogate, revoke, annul (421)

abrumar, brumar   to crush, oppress, overwhelm (247)

absorber   to absorb (128)

abstraer   to abstract (477)

abundar   to abound, be plentiful (39)

abusar   to abuse (25)

acachetear   to slap in the face (54)

acaecer   to happen (344) (3rd person only)

acallar   to silence, quiet, hush, pacify, calm down (261)

acalorar   to warm up (409)

acamar   to flatten (54)

acampar   to camp (332)

acaparar   to buy up, hoard (342)

acariciar   to caress (57)

acarrear   to transport, cause (206)

acatar   to obey, respect the law, notice, realize (11)

acatarrarse   to catch a cold (409, 289)

acaudalar   to accumulate (259)

acceder   to accede, agree (128)

accidentar   to have an accident, be hurt or injured (11)

acechar   to watch, spy on (200)

acelerar   to speed up, expedite (409)

acentuar   to accentuate, mark with an accent   (141)

achicar   to reduce, lessen, shorten   (424)

acicalarse   to dress up, spruce up   (259, 289)

aclarar   to clarify, explain   (409)

aclimatar   to acclimatize   (308)

acobardarse   to become frightened, turn cowardly   (39, 289)

acoger   to receive hospitably, welcome   (123)

acometer   to attack, undertake, overcome   (444)

acomodar   to accommodate, arrange, hire   (259)

acompasar   to measure   (347)

acomplejarse   to suffer from a complex   (86, 289)

acongojarse   to be anguished   (86, 289)

acontecer   to happen, occur   (43) (3rd person only)

acopiar   to classify, collect, gather   (106)

acoplar   to connect, join, couple   (259)

acorrer   to run to someone's aide, help, assist   (148)

acortar   to shorten, reduce   (11)

acosar   to harass, pursue, pest   (2)

acostar   to put to bed   (21)

acostumbrarse   to become accustomed, get used to   (22, 289)

acrecentar   to increase   (352)

acrecer   to augment, increase   (151)

activar   to activate   (288)

actualizar   to modernize, bring up to date   (339)

actuar   to act, behave   (141)

acumular   to accumulate   (85)

acurrucarse   to curl up, get cozy   (424, 289)

adaptar   to adapt   (11)

adelgazar   to lose weight, get thin   (339)

aderezar   to season, flavor, embellish   (339)

adherir   to adhere, stick on   (435)

adicionar   to add   (54)

adiestrar   to train, instruct, direct   (352)

adjudicar   to award, adjudge   (424)

administrar   to administrate   (215)

adobar   to season, flavor, marinate   (259)

adornar   to adorn   (54)

adscribir   to ascribe, assign, attribute   (224)

adueñarse   to take possession of   (213, 289)

adular   to adulate, flatter   (259)

advenir   to arrive, come   (488)

afamar   to make famous   (54)

afamarse   to become famous   (112)

afanarse   to work hard, strive   (259, 289)

afear   to deform, make ugly   (54)

afectar   to affect   (11)

afeitar   to shave   (35)

aferrarse   to take hold of, stick to   (352, 289)

afianzar   to fasten   (286)

aficionar   to induce a liking for   (338)

aficionarse a   to become fond of   (338)

afiliarse   to join, become affiliated   (232, 289)

afinar   to tune (instrument), perfect, refine   (107)

afirmar   to affirm, assert   (243)

afligir   to afflict, distress   (188)

afligirse   to grieve, be upset   (188, 8)

aflojar   to loosen, slacken, let go   (86)

afluir   to flow   (264)

afrancesar   to Gallicize   (2)

africanizar   to Africanize   (339)

afrontar   to confront, face, defy   (109)

agacharse   to stoop, crouch   (225, 289)

agasajar   to treat attentively   (86)

agilitar   to make agile, empower, facilitate   (11)

aglomerarse   to crowd, gather around   (409, 289)

agobiar   to overwhelm, oppress, depress   (232)

agraviar   to wrong, injure, offend   (54)

agriar   to make sour   (54)

aguantar   to bear, endure   (54)

aguar   to dilute   (83)

ahogarse   to drown   (289, 421)

ahondar   to deepen, make deeper   (41)

ahuyentar   to drive or chase away   (11)

aislar   to isolate   (218)

ajustar   to adjust, fit   (259)

alabar   to praise   (259)

alambrar   to fence with wire   (51)

alanzar   to lance   (286)

alardear   to boast, brag, show off   (54)

alargar   to lengthen   (421)

alarmar   to alarm   (54)

albergar   to shelter   (341)

alborotar   to stir up, arouse, incite   (11)

alegar   to contend, state, declare   (341)

alejarse de   to get away from   (86, 289)

alentar   to breathe; encourage, inspire   (352)

alertar   to alert, warn   (11)

alienar   to alienate   (249)

aligar   to bind, tie   (421)

alimentar   to feed, nourish   (291)

aliñar   to straighten, tidy, season   (213)

alisar   to smooth, polish   (2)

alistarse   to enroll, enlist, get ready   (11, 289)

aliviar   to alleviate, ease   (232)

almacenar   to store   (114)

alocar   to make someone crazy   (472)

alojar   to lodge, give accommodation to   (86)

alterar   to alter, change (409)

alternar   to alternate (107)

amargar   to make bitter (341)

amarrar   to fasten, tie (409)

amasar   to knead, mix, amass (a fortune) (2)

amenazar   to threaten (339)

americanizar   to Americanize (339)

amoldarse   to adapt oneself, conform (39, 289)

amonestar   to reprimand (11)

amontonar   to pile up, gather, accumulate (107)

amortiguar   to muffle, deaden, dim (83)

amortizar   to write off, pay off (339)

amparar   to protect, defend (409)

ampliar   to widen, extend (256)

amplificar   to amplify, enlarge (117)

amueblar   to furnish (259)

analizar   to analyze (90)

anglicanizar   to anglicize (339)

anhelar   to long for, yearn (259)

animar   to animate (54)

aniquilar   to annihilate, wipe out (259)

anotar   to annotate, write notes about (54)

anteponer   to place in front, place before (364)

anticipar   to anticipate, bring forward, advance (332)

anudar   to tie knots, tie together, join (39)

anular   to annul (259)

apaciguar   to pacify, calm, soothe (83)

aparar   to prepare (342)

aparcar   to park (424)

aparentar   to feign, pretend, assume (11)

apartar   to remove, set aside (11)

apartarse   to keep away from, withdraw from (11, 289)

apasionar   to excite, enthuse (107)

apedrear   to stone, attack (206)

apegarse   to become fond, become attached to (341, 289)

apenar   to sadden (107)

apestar   to stink, smell, annoy (11)

apetecer   to crave for, long for (59)

aplacar   to appease, calm, soothe (424)

aplanar   to flatten, smooth, level (107)

aplastar   to crash, overwhelm (250)

aplazar   to postpone, defer (339)

aplicar   to apply (99)

aplicarse   to apply oneself (424, 289)

apocar   to lessen, reduce (99)

apoderar   to empower (61)

aportar   to bring, contribute, furnish (11)

apostar   to bet, wager (474)

apoyar   to support (453)

aprehender   to apprehend (63)

aprestar   to make ready, prepare (376)

apresurar   to accelerate, hurry (64)

apretar   to grip, press (352)

apropiar   to appropriate money, adapt (106)

aprovechar   to make use of (66)

aproximar   to approach, bring close or move near (107)

aproximarse   to draw near, approach (107, 289)

apuntar   to aim, point (11)

apurar   to purify, exhaust, consume (67)

arabizar   to Arabize (339)

arañar   to scratch (213)

arar   to plow (54)

archivar   to file (259)

arder   to burn, glow (63)

argüir   to argue, reason (264)

armar   to arm (54)

arraigar   to take root, establish (341)

arrasar   to level, flatten, demolish, raze (2)

arrastrar   to pull, drag, drag down (215)

arrebatar   to snatch, carry off (308)

arrendar   to lease, let, rent, hire (352)

arrepentirse de   to repent for, regret (436)

arrestar   to arrest, detain (250)

arribar   to arrive, reach (9)

arriesgar   to risk, venture (341)

arrimar   to bring, draw near (54)

arrimarse   to bring close or move near (54, 289)

arrinconar   to corner, put away, ignore (107)

arrodillarse   to bend on your knees (261, 289)

arropar   to clothe, wrap up (332)

arrugar   to wrinkle, crease (341)

arruinar   to ruin, destroy (107)

arrullar   to lull or sing to sleep (261)

asaltar   to assault, attack (427)

asar   to roast (2)

asentar   to seat, set down (352)

asentir   to assent, agree (370)

asesinar   to assassinate, murder (107)

asesorar   to advise, consult (409)

aseverar   to assert (409)

asfixiar   to asphyxiate, suffocate (232)

asignar   to assign, apportion, give (114)

asilar   to give or grant asylum, take refuge (259)

asociarse   to associate, become a member (232, 289)

asomar to appear slowly (as through an opening) (473)

asomarse to lean out, look out (as out of a window) (112)

asombrar to amaze, astonish (113)

asombrarse de to be astonished, surprised at (409, 289)

aspirar to breathe in, inhale (29)

asumir to assume, take on (267)

asurarse to get burned (112)

atajar to intercept, halt, interrupt (86)

atar to bind, tie (308)

atardecer to get late, dark (344) (3rd person only)

atascar to obstruct, block (424)

atender to look after, attend to, pay attention (164)

atentar to attempt (11)

aterrizar to land (47)

aterrorizar to terrify, frighten (339)

atestiguar to attest (83)

atinar to find, discover, hit upon (107)

atolondrar to bewilder (409)

atontar to stun, confuse (11)

atorar to obstruct, clog, stop up (409)

atormentar to torture, trouble, distress (11)

atosigar to poison (341)

atracar to hold up, assault (424)

atrapar to catch (332)

atrasar to retard, delay, slow down (2)

atravesar to cross, cross over, go through (352)

atribuir to attribute (264)

atropellar to trample down, run over, knock down (261)

aturdir to daze, stun, bewilder, confuse (60)

augurar to augur, predict (409)

aumentar to augment, increase (317)

ausentarse to be absent, absent oneself (11, 289)

autorizar to authorize (90)

avalar to guarantee, be the guarantor of (259)

avenir to reconcile (488)

aventurarse to venture, risk (48)

avergonzarse to be ashamed (82, 289)

averiar to damage, spoil, break (256)

avisar to advise, inform, warn, notify (340)

avivar to spur on, brighten, arouse (9)

ayunar to fast, go without food (171)

azuzar to stir up, arouse, incite (339)

B

balancear to balance, rock, vacillate (175)

balbucir to stammer (386)

bambolear to wobble (206)

bañar to bathe (88)

barajar to shuffle, mix together, quarrel (86)

basar to base, support, be based, rely on (2)

bastar to be enough, be sufficient, suffice (Def. and Imp.)

batallar to fight, battle, struggle (261)

batir to beat, whip (1)

beneficiar to benefit, sell at a discount (232)

besar to kiss (235)

bifurcarse to bifurcate, fork, branch (424, 289)

blanquear to whiten, bleach (206)

blasfemar to blaspheme, curse (247)

blindar to armor, shield (39)

bloquear to blockade, block, obstruct (206)

bogar to row (421)

bombardear to bombard, bomb (206)

bonificar to increase production (117)

boxear to box (206)

bregar to fight, brawl (341)

brillar to shine (259)

brincar to bounce, jump, skip (430)

brindar to offer, invite, drink a toast (54)

bromear to joke, jest (206)

brotar to bud, sprout, break out (308)

brumar, abrumar to crush, oppress, overwhelm (247)

bruñir to polish, burnish (255)

bufonearse to jest, joke (348)

burbujear to bubble (54)

C

cabecear to nod one's head when sleepy (54)

cachar to break into pieces (200)

cachetear to slap (206)

caducar to become void, expire (a right, passport) (424)

calar to drench, soak (259)

calcar to trace, copy (424)

calcular to calculate (259)

calibrar to calibrate, gage, measure (259)

calificar to assess, rate, classify (117)

calmar to calm (54)

calmarse to calm (oneself) down (54, 289)

calumniar to slander (232)

camorrear to quarrel (54)

cancelar to cancel, strike out (54)

candar to lock (109)

cantalear to hum, sing softly (54)

cantonear to idle, loaf, wander about (54)

canturrear to sing softly (232)

capacitar to train, equip, train oneself, be competent (308)

capar to castrate, cut off (332)

capitanear   to command, captain   (175)

capitular   to capitulate, surrender, give up   (259)

captar   to capture, win trust   (54)

capturar   to capture, apprehend   (409)

caracterizarse   to be characterized or distinguished   (339, 289)

carcajear   to burst out laughing   (54)

carcomer   to eat away, gnaw   (128)

carecer de   to be in need of, to lack   (333)

cargarse de   to be overloaded with   (111, 112)

castigar   to chastise, punish   (341)

castrar   to castrate, to dry a wound   (54)

catalogar   to catalog, list   (341)

catar   to sample, taste   (308)

causar   to cause   (481)

cautivar   to capture, captivate, charm   (288)

cavar   to dig, delve into   (9)

cavilar   to ponder   (259)

cazar   to hunt, chase   (81)

ceder   to cede, yield   (413)

cegar   to blind, block up, to grow blind   (327)

censurar   to censure   (72)

centralizar   to centralize   (339)

centrar   to center, focus   (259)

cercar   to fence in, enclose   (12)

cesar   to cease, stop   (235)

chafar   to crease, crumple (clothes)   (259)

chafarse   to become flattened   (289)

chamar   to barter, exchange   (54)

chamuscar   to singe, scorch   (99)

chapar   to cover, plate with silver or gold   (332)

charlar   to chatter, prattle   (259)

chascar   to crunch   (99)

chatear   to chat (Internet)   (175)

chequear   to check, verify   (175)

chiflar   to whistle, blow a whistle   (259)

chillar   to scream, shriek   (259)

chinchar   to annoy, irritate   (259)

chismear   to gossip   (259)

chispear   to spark, sparkle   (175)

chocar   to collide, crash   (424)

chuchear   to whisper   (259)

chufar   to mock   (259)

cicatrizar   to heal   (339)

cifrar   to encode   (259)

cimentar   to consolidate, lay the foundation   (352)

cincelar   to chisel, carve   (259)

circular   to circulate, move   (71)

civilizar   to civilize, become civilized   (90)

clamar   to cry out, wail   (15)

clarar   to make clear, explain   (16)

clarificar   to clarify   (117)

clasificar   to classify   (117)

claudicar   to give up, back down   (424)

clausurar   to bring to a close, shut   (409)

clavar   to nail   (54)

coagular   to coagulate   (259)

cobijar   to cover, shelter   (54)

cobrar   to cash, charge   (259)

cocer   to cook   (321, 486)

codear   to elbow, nudge   (54)

coexistir   to coexist   (495)

cohibir   to inhibit, restrain   (382)

coincidir   to coincide, agree   (60)

colaborar   to collaborate, contribute   (409)

colar   to filter, strain   (474)

colear   to wag, move   (54)

coleccionar   to collect   (107)

colectar   to collect (money)   (11)

colorar   to color, give color to   (32)

colorear   to color, tint   (175)

comandar   to command   (109)

combatir   to combat, fight   (1)

combinar   to combine   (107)

comentar   to comment   (109)

comerciar   to trade, deal   (57)

cometer   to commit, entrust   (91)

compaginar   to arrange in order, collate   (107)

comparar   to compare   (342)

compartir   to divide, share   (346)

compensar   to compensate, indemnify   (2)

competir   to compete, contest   (411)

compilar   to compile   (259)

complacer   to please   (361)

completar   to complete   (308)

complicar   to complicate   (76)

comportarse   to behave   (11, 289)

comprimir   to compress   (267)

comprobar   to check, verify   (378)

computar   to compute, calculate   (279)

comunicar   to communicate   (234)

concebir   to conceive, imagine   (349)

conceder   to concede   (413)

concentrar   to concentrate   (215)

concertar   to arrange, agree   (352)

concluir   to conclude   (268)

concurrir   to agree, attend, concur   (495)

condenar   to condemn (114)

condimentar   to season (11)

conectar   to connect   (11)

confeccionar   to manufacture (107)

confiar   to trust, entrust (240)

confinar   to confine, border (107)

confirmar   to confirm (243)

confiscar   to confiscate (99)

confluir   to converge   (271)

conformar   to conform (244)

confortar   to comfort, console, cheer   (11)

confrontar   to confront   (11)

confundir   to confuse, perplex   (60)

congelar   to congeal, freeze (259)

congestionar   to congest (107)

congratular   to congratulate, rejoice   (259)

conjugar   to conjugate (297)

conmemorar   to commemorate, celebrate (409)

conmover   to move, touch (321)

connotar   to connote, imply (308)

conquistar   to conquer, win (250)

consagrar   to consecrate, devote   (259)

consentir   to consent, allow (435)

conservar   to conserve, preserve, keep   (9)

considerar   to consider (227)

consistir   to consist of, be composed of   (495)

consolar   to console   (138)

consolidar   to consolidate (39)

conspirar   to conspire, plot (314)

constar   to be clear, consistent   (109)

constatar   to prove, verify (309)

constiparse   to catch a cold (332, 289)

consultar   to consult   (308)

consumir   to consume, use up   (267)

contagiar   to give or spread (a disease, enthusiasm, hate) (232)

contaminar   to contaminate, pollute, corrupt   (107)

contemplar   to contemplate, meditate   (259)

contentar   to gratify, please (109)

contentarse   to be contented (11, 289)

contradecir (past part. contradicho)   to contradict (302)

contraer   to contract, shorten, catch   (477)

contrapesar   to counterbalance   (2)

contraponer   to compare, contrast   (364)

contrariar   to oppose, go against, contradict   (256)

contrarrestar   to counteract, block, stop   (250)

contrastar   to contrast (250)

contratar   to contract, engage, hire   (478)

controlar   to control   (259)

convalecer   to convalesce (333)

conversar   to converse (340)

convidar   to invite   (39)

convivir   to live together (495)

cooperar   to cooperate (409)

coordinar   to coordinate (107)

copiar   to copy   (106)

coquetear   to flirt   (175)

coronar   to crown, queen (107)

corresponder   to correspond (413)

corromper   to corrupt (422)

coser   to sew, mend   (128)

costar   to cost   (Def. and Imp.)

costear   to finance   (175)

cotizar   to quote, price (339)

criticar   to criticize   (117)

cuajar   to coagulate, congeal, curdle   (86)

cuestionar   to debate, discuss (473)

culpar   to blame, accuse (332)

culparse   to blame oneself (189)

cultivar   to cultivate, grow (288)

cumplimentar   to congratulate   (11)

cumular   to accumulate (259)

curar   to cure   (72)

curiosear   to pry, investigate, snoop   (175)

cursar   to study, take courses (2)

custodiar   to guard, take care of   (232)

D

damnificar   to damage, harm, injure   (424)

dañar   to damage, injure (109)

dañarse   to become damaged, injured   (88)

danzar   to dance   (81)

datar   to date (a letter, an account)   (308)

debatir   to debate   (407)

debutar   to make one's debut, open (a play)   (308)

decantar   to exaggerate, pour off   (109)

decentar   to cut into, begin cutting   (352)

declamar   to declaim, recite (54)

declinar   to decline, get weak (107)

decorar   to decorate   (32)

decretar   to decree, resolve (308)

dedicar   to dedicate   (424)

deducir   to deduce, infer, deduct   (132)

deferir   to defer, delegate
(370)

definir   to define   (346)

deformar   to deform   (244)

defraudar   to deceive,
deprive, defraud   (39)

degradar   to demote,
degrade, reduce in rank
(39)

delatar   to denounce, accuse
(308)

delegar   to delegate   (341)

deletrear   to spell, interpret
(206)

deliberar   to deliberate,
ponder, confer   (409)

delinear   to draw, delineate,
design   (175)

delirar   to be delirious, talk
nonsense   (409)

demandar   to demand,
petition, sue   (199)

demarcar   to demarcate,
delimit   (424)

demoler   to demolish, pull
down   (321)

demorar   to delay   (409)

denegar   to deny, refuse
(327)

denigrar   to denigrate,
disparage, insult   (409)

denominar   to denominate,
name   (107)

denotar   to denote   (11)

dentar   to teethe, provide
with teeth; indent   (352)

deparar   to provide, supply
(342)

departir   to converse   (346)

depilar   to depilate, remove
hair   (259)

deplorar   to deplore   (32)

deponer   to lay aside, put
aside   (364)

deportar   to deport, exile
(11)

depositar   to deposit, place,
put   (259)

depreciar   to depreciate
(383)

deprimir   to depress   (267)

derivar   to incline, drift,
derive   (259)

derogar   to derogate, abolish
(421)

derramar   to spill   (259)

derretir   to melt, dissolve
(349)

derrochar   to squander,
waste   (225)

derrotar   to defeat   (308)

desabrigar   to uncover,
undress, deprive of
protection   (341)

desacomodar   to
inconvenience, bother   (39)

desacordar   to be in discord
(19)

desacordarse   to become
forgetful   (20)

desacostumbrarse   to lose
the habit of, to break oneself
of the habit of   (259, 289)

desacreditar   to discredit,
disgrace   (308)

desactivar   to deactivate
(259)

desafiar   to challenge, dare,
oppose   (256)

desahogar   to comfort, ease
(341)

desajustar   to put out of
order, disarrange   (250)

desalentar   to make
breathless, put out of breath
(103)

desaliñar   to make untidy,
crease   (213)

desalojar   to move out,
vacate   (165)

desamparar   to abandon,
forsake   (342)

desangrar   to bleed, bleed
dry, drain, empty   (409)

desanimar   to discourage
(54)

desaparecer   to disappear
(59)

desapreciar   to
underestimate   (62)

desaprender   to unlearn
(63)

desarmar   to disarm, take
apart   (54)

desarraigar   to uproot,
extirpate, expel   (341)

desarreglar   to make untidy,
disarrange   (259)

desarrollar   to develop
(261)

desarropar   to undress,
disrobe   (332)

desarticular   to disarticulate
(71)

desayudar   to hinder, impede
(84)

desbaratar   to ruin, wreck,
spoil   109)

desbordar   to overflow
(39)

descalificar   to disqualify
(117)

descalzar   to take off shoes
(339)

descambiar   to cancel an
exchange   (106)

descaminar   to mislead, lead
astray   (107)

descargar   to unload; to
download (Internet)   (111)

descartar   to discard, put
aside   (11)

descender   to descend, go
down   (354)

descifrar   to decipher,
decode, make out   (409)

descolgar   to unhook, take
down from a hanging
position   (125)

descollar   to protrude, stand
out   (138)

descomponer   to disarrange,
disrupt, disturb   (364)

desconcertar   to disconcert,
upset   (352)

desconectar   to disconnect,
switch off   (259)

desconfiar   to distrust,
mistrust   (256)

descongelar   to thaw, defrost,
unfreeze   (259)

desconocer   to not know,
not recognize   (134)

descontar   to discount,
deduct, disregard   (138)

descontinuar   to
discontinue, cease,
suspend   (141)

descorazonar   to
discourage, dishearten
(355)

descorchar   to uncork
(306)

descuidar   to neglect,
forget   (39)

descuidarse   to be
negligent, careless
(153)

desdecir   to fall short
of, not live up to   (368)

desdeñar   to disdain, scorn (213)

desdeñarse   to be disdainful (88)

desechar   to reject (200)

desembalar   to unpack (259)

desembarazar   to clear, get rid of obstacles (339)

desembarcar   to disembark, unload (424)

desembocar   to flow (river), run (street) (424)

desempacar   to unpack, unwrap (424)

desencantar   to disenchant (109)

desenchufar   to unplug, disconnect (259)

desengañar   to disillusion (213)

desenlazar   to unfasten, untie, unravel (lit.) (339)

desenrollar   to unroll, unwind (261)

desensamblar   to disassemble (259)

desenterrar   to exhume, unearth (352)

desenvolver   to unwrap (497)

desequilibrar   to throw off balance, unbalance (259)

desertar   to desert, abandon (11)

desesperar   to discourage, exasperate (227)

desesperarse   to become or get desperate, lose hope (227, 289)

desfallecer   to weaken, faint (344)

desfavorecer   to put at a disadvantage, not to flatter or suit (344)

desfigurar   to disfigure (409)

desfijar   to pull out, unfix (241)

desfilar   to parade (259)

desflorar   to deflower (300)

desgajar   to rip off, tear off (54)

desganarse   to lose one's appetite (289)

desheredar   to disinherit (39)

deshidratar   to dehydrate (308)

deshinchar   to reduce swelling (306)

deshonrar   to dishonor, disgrace (409)

deshumanizar   to dehumanize (339)

designar   to designate (114)

desilusionar   to disillusion (355)

desinfectar   to disinfect (259)

desinflamar   to reduce swelling or inflammation (54)

desintegrar   to disintegrate, break up, split (409)

desinteresarse   to lose interest (277)

desintoxicar   to detoxify (424)

desistir   to desist, stop, give up (495)

deslumbrar   to dazzle, blind, overwhelm (259)

desmantelar   to dismantle (259)

desmayarse   to faint, swoon (453, 289)

desmedrar   to decline, deteriorate (259)

desmentir   to disprove, prove false (312)

desmontar   to dismount, dismantle (11)

desnivelar   to make uneven, tilt (259)

desnudar   to undress, strip (324)

desnudarse   to undress oneself (289)

desobedecer   to disobey (328)

desocupar   to vacate (332)

desoír   to ignore, not listen (334)

desordenar   to disarrange (338)

desorganizar   to disorganize (339)

desorientar   to confuse, mislead (11)

despachar   to complete, see to, send (225)

despechar   to vex, make angry or resentful (225)

despedazar   to break, tear to pieces (339)

despedir   to dismiss, fire, discharge (349, 178)

despejar   to clear, clear up (weather) (86)

desperdiciar   to waste, squander (57)

despertar   to wake up (someone) (352, 181)

despistar   to lead astray, mislead (250)

desplegar   to unfold, spread out, unfurl (327)

despoblar   to depopulate, lay waste, clear (209)

desposarse   to get engaged or married (2, 289)

desposeer   to dispossess (152)

despreciar   to despise, scorn, snub (57)

despreocuparse   to stop worrying, forget, neglect (372)

despuntar   to blunt (11)

destacar   to highlight, stand out (424)

destapar   to uncork, open, uncover (332)

destellar   to flash, sparkle, glitter (261)

desterrar   to banish, exile (352)

destilar   to distill, exude, filter (259)

destinar   to destine, intend, send, earmark (107)

destituir   to dismiss, discharge, deprive (271)

destornillar   to unscrew (261)

destronar   to dethrone, overthrow, depose (355)

destrozar   to break, tear, smash, ruin (339)

desunir   to separate, disunite (480)

desvalorar   to devalue, depreciate, discredit (409)

desvalorizar   to depreciate, devalue (47)

desvelar   to keep awake (259)

desviar   to divert, deviate (218)

detallar   to detail, specify, sell retail (261)

deteriorar   to damage, spoil, wear out (409)

determinar   to determine, set, decide (470)

detestar   to detest (250)

detonar   to detonate, explode (355)

devaluar   to devaluate, devalue (141)

devastar   to devastate (250)

devenir   to happen, come about, become (488)

devorar   to devour, consume, squander (409)

diagnosticar   to diagnose (424)

dialogar   to converse, chat (341)

dictar   to dictate (11)

difamar   to defame, slander (54)

diferenciar   to differentiate, distinguish, differ (57)

diferir   to differ, defer, postpone, delay (370)

digerir   to digest (370)

dilatar   to dilate, expand, delay, spread (308)

diluir   to dilute, dissolve, weaken (271)

dirigirse a   to go to, toward (188, 8)

disciplinar   to discipline, teach (107)

discontinuar   to discontinue, cease (141)

discrepar   to differ, disagree (332)

discriminar   to distinguish, discriminate (107)

discursar   to discourse, make a speech (25)

diseminar   to disseminate, spread (107)

diseñar   to design, draw (213)

disentir   to dissent, differ (435)

disgustar   to annoy, displease (250)

disgustarse   to be displeased, annoyed (250, 289)

disimular   to cover up, dissemble, pretend (71)

disipar   to dissipate, squander, dispel (332)

disminuir   to diminish (271)

disolver   to dissolve (321)

disparar   to fire, shoot, throw (409)

disparatar   to talk or act foolishly (308)

dispersar   to disperse (2)

disponer   to lay out, arrange, dispose (364)

distraer   to distract (477)

distribuir   to distribute (264)

disturbar   to disturb (9)

disuadir   to dissuade (346)

divagar   to digress, wander (341)

divergir   to diverge, disagree, differ (188)

diversificar   to diversify (424)

divertir   to amuse, distract, entertain (370, 194)

dividir   to divide (346)

divisar   to discern, make out (2)

divulgar   to divulge, make known (341)

doblar   to fold, turn, dub (259)

doblegar   to fold, bend (341)

doctorarse   to get a doctorate (409, 289)

doctrinar   to teach (107)

documentar   to document (11)

domesticar   to domesticate, tame, subdue (424)

dominar   to dominate (107)

donar   to donate, give (355)

dorar   to gild, cover with gold (32)

dormitar   to doze, snooze (308)

dotar   to endow, bequeath, give a dowry (11)

dramatizar   to dramatize (339)

driblar   to dribble (sports) (259)

duplicar   to duplicate, copy (424)

durar   to last, continue (409)

E

economizar   to economize on (339)

edificar   to build, construct, erect (424)

editar   to publish (254)

educar   to educate, instruct, rear, bring up (424)

efectuar   to effect, carry out (141)

ejemplificar   to exemplify, illustrate (424)

ejercitar   to exercise, practice, train (308)

elaborar   to elaborate; manufacture (93)

electrificar   to electrify (424)

electrizar   to electrify (339)

elevar   to elevate, ennoble (259)

eliminar   to eliminate (107)

elogiar   to eulogize, praise (232)

elucidar   to elucidate, explain (39)

eludir   to elude, avoid (60)

emanar   to emanate, flow (107)

emancipar   to emancipate, liberate (332)

embalar   to pack (259)

embarazarse   to be hindered, become pregnant (339, 289)

embarcar   to embark, go on board (99)

embargar   to impede, hamper (341)

embarullar   to muddle, mix up, bungle (261)

embeber   to soak in, soak up, suck in, imbibe (91)

embelesar   to fascinate, enthrall (2)

embellecer   to beautify, embellish (344)

embocar   to cram down food, gulp down (424)

embolsar   to pocket (2)

emborronar   to scribble (54)

emboscar   to ambush (424)

embotellar   to bottle, jam
(261)

embrollar   to confuse,
embroil   (261)

embromar   to tease, banter at
(54)

embutir   to stuff, cram   (60)

emerger   to emerge   (123)

emigrar   to emigrate   (273)

emitir   to emit, send forth
(346)

emocionarse   to be moved,
be touched inside   (355,
289)

empacar   to pack   (424)

empanar   to bread   (107)

empañar   to diaper, swaddle
(213)

empapar   to drench, soak
(342)

empaquetar   to pack, wrap
(308)

emparejar   to match, pair off
(86)

empatar   to tie, be equal
(308)

empeñarse   to strive,
endeavor, persist   (213,
289)

empeorar   to make worse,
become worse   (409)

empeorarse   to worsen,
deteriorate   (409, 289)

emprender   to undertake,
start   (63)

empujar   to push   (86)

empuñar   to grasp, seize
(213)

emular   to emulate, rival
(259)

enamorar   to enamor, inspire
love   (54)

enamorarse de   to fall in
love   (289)

enardecer   to ignite, set
aflame   (344)

encabezar   to head, lead
(339)

encantar   to charm, cast a
spell on, love, be delighted
with   (Def. and Imp.)

encarcelar   to imprison
(259)

encarecer   to raise prices
(344)

encargar   to put in charge,
entrust   (111)

encariñarse   to become fond
of   (213, 289)

enchufar   to connect, plug in
(54)

encomendar   to commend,
entrust   (352)

encuadernar   to bind   (107)

encubrir   to hide, conceal
(495)

endeudarse   to get into debt
(39, 289)

endosar   to endorse   (2)

endulzar   to sweeten, soften
(339)

enervar   to enervate, weaken
(9)

enfadar   to anger, irritate
(210)

enfilar   to line up, put in a
line   (259)

enflaquecer   to lose weight,
slim down   (344)

enfocar   to focus   (424)

enfrentar   to confront, face
(11)

enfriar   to cool, chill   (218)

enfriarse   to get cold, catch a
cold   (256, 289)

enfurecer   to make furious,
infuriate   (344)

engañar   to deceive   (213)

engañarse   to deceive
oneself, be mistaken   (88)

engordar   to fatten, grow fat,
put on weight   (54)

engrandecer   to increase,
enhance, exaggerate   (344)

engrasar   to grease, oil   (2)

enjabonar   to soap, wash,
lather   (355)

enjaular   to cage, imprison
(259)

enjuagar   to rinse   (298)

enlazar   to tie together,
connect   (339)

enloquecerse   to go crazy or
mad, become enchanted with
(344, 102)

enmendar   to amend, revise,
correct   (352)

ennoblecer   to ennoble
(344)

enojar   to annoy, irritate
(212)

enorgullecerse   to be proud
(344, 102)

enredar   to tangle, entangle,
confuse   (39)

enriquecerse   to become
rich, prosper   (344, 102)

enrojecerse   to blush, turn
red   (344, 102)

enrolar   to sign on, enlist
(259)

enrollar   to wind, roll up
(261)

ensalzar   to exalt, glorify
(339)

ensamblar   to connect, join
(259)

ensañar   to infuriate, enrage
(213)

ensangrentar   to stain with
blood, shed blood   (352)

ensayar   to test, try, rehearse
(54)

ensillar   to saddle   (261)

ensolver   to include, reduce,
condense   (497)

ensombrecer   to darken,
overshadow, eclipse   (344)

ensordecer   to deafen, muffle
(344)

ensuciar   to dirty, soil, stain
(383)

entablar   to begin, start   (259)

entenderse   to understand
each other, be understood
(214)

enterar   to inform   (215)

enterarse de   to find out
about   (289)

enterrar   to bury, inter;
forget   (116)

entonar   to sing in tune,
harmonize   (355)

entreabrir   to open halfway,
ajar   (495)

entrecerrar   to close
halfway, ajar   (116)

entregarse   to surrender, give
in   (216, 289)

entrelazar   to intertwine,
interlace   (339)

entremezclar   to intermingle
(259)

entrenar   to train   (107)

entreoír   to half-hear, hear
vaguely   (334)

entretener   to entertain,
amuse   (468)

entretenerse   to amuse
oneself   (77)

entrever   to catch a glimpse (489)

entrevistar   to interview (494)

entristecer   to make sad (344)

entrometerse   to meddle, interfere (444, 102)

entusiasmarse   to get excited, enthusiastic (54, 289)

enumerar   to enumerate (409)

envejecer   to age, make old (344)

envenenar   to poison (107)

envestir   to clothe (491)

envidiar   to envy (232)

enviudar   to become a widow, widower (39)

envolverse   to become involved (219, 80)

equilibrar   to balance (259)

equipar   to equip (332)

equiparar   to compare, match, make equal (342)

equivaler   to equal (484)

equivocar   to mistake (220)

erradicar   to eradicate, uproot (424)

erigir   to erect, build, construct (188)

eructar   to belch, burp (54)

esbozar   to sketch (81)

escalar   to climb (259)

escampar   to clear up (332)

escandalizar   to shock (339)

escapar   to escape (332)

escarnecer   to ridicule, mock (344)

esclarecer   to light up, clarify (344)

esconder   to conceal, hide (413)

esconderse   to hide oneself (413, 80)

escudar   to shield, protect (39)

escudriñar   to scrutinize, examine (213)

esculpir   to sculpt, carve, engrave (157)

escupir   to spit (346)

esforzar   to strengthen, encourage (49)

esforzarse   to make an effort (49, 289)

espantar   to frighten, scare (109)

especializarse   to specialize (339, 289)

espiar   to spy on (256)

espirar   to breathe out, exhale (409)

esposar   to handcuff (340)

esquivar   to avoid, evade (259)

estacionar   to station, park (a vehicle) (355)

estafar   to swindle, cheat (259)

estallar   to burst, explode, break out (261)

estampar   to print, stamp, emboss, engrave (332)

estereotipar   to stereotype (332)

estigmatizar   to stigmatize, brand (339)

estilarse   to be in fashion, in use (289)

estimular   to stimulate, encourage (259)

estirar   to stretch, extend (409)

estorbar   to obstruct, hinder, bother (9)

estornudar   to sneeze (39)

estrachar   to narrow, tighten (200)

estrangular   to strangle (259)

estrellar   to smash, shatter (261)

estructurar   to structure, organize (284)

evadir   to evade, avoid (60)

evaluar   to evaluate, assess (141)

evaporar   to evaporate, disappear (409)

evaporizar   to vaporize (339)

evitar   to avoid (254)

evocar   to evoke, recall (424)

evolucionar   to evolve (107)

exacerbar   to exacerbate, aggravate (9)

exagerar   to exaggerate (259)

exaltar   to glorify, extol, praise (11)

examinar   to examine (107)

exasperar   to exasperate (227)

excitar   to excite, stimulate (254)

exclamar   to exclaim (54)

excluir   to exclude (268)

excusar   to excuse (25)

exhalar   to exhale (261)

exhibir   to exhibit, display (353)

existir   to exist (276)

expedir   to expedite (349)

experimentar   to experience (11)

explorar   to explore (32)

exponer   to expose (364)

exportar   to export (109)

exprimir   to squeeze, wring out (267)

expulsar   to expel, drive out (2)

extender   to extend (354)

extinguir   to extinguish (193)

extirpar   to extirpate (332)

extraer   to extract, draw out (477)

extrañar   to surprise (213)

F

facilitar   to facilitate (238)

facturar   to invoice, bill (409)

fallar   to trump, fail (261)

fallecer   to die (344)

falsear   to falsify, misrepresent (206)

falsificar   to falsify, forge (424)

familiarizar   to familiarize (339)

familiarizarse   to familiarize oneself with (339, 289)

fantasear   to daydream (206)

farolear   to boast, brag, show off (54)

fascinar   to fascinate (107)

fastidiar   to annoy, pester (232)

fatigar   to fatigue, tire (421)

favorecer to favor, improve the appearance of (344)
fecundar to fertilize (39)
fermentar to ferment (11)
fertilizar to fertilize (339)
figurar to depict, draw, represent (72)
figurarse to imagine (72, 289)
fijar to fix, fasten (241)
filmar to film, shoot (54)
filtrar to filter (259)
finalizar to finish, conclude (339)
financiar to finance (57)
florecer to bloom (344)
flotar to float (308)
fluctuar to fluctuate, rise and fall (141)
fluir to flow (271)
fomentar to foment, stir up, promote (11)
forjar to forge, form, make, invent (86)
formalizar to formalize, make legal (339)
formular to formulate (71)
fortalecer to fortify (344)
forzar to force (49)
fotocopiar to photocopy (106)
fotografiar to photograph (464)
fraccionar to break up (355)
fracturar to fracture, break, rupture (409)
fragmentar to fragment (11)
frecuentar to frequent (11)
frenar to brake (107)
frotar to rub (498)
fruncir to knit (eyebrows); to purse (lips) (501)
frustrar to frustrate (215)
fugarse to flee, run away (341, 289)
fumigar to fumigate (341)
fundar to found, establish, build (39)
fundir to melt, cast, join, go out (bulb) (60)
fusilar to shoot (259)
fusionar to combine, merge (107)
fustigar to whip (341)

G

galantear to woo, make eyes at (175)
galopar to gallop (54)
galvanizar to galvanize (339)
gandulear to idle, loaf (206)
gansear to say, do stupid things (175)
garabatear to scribble (463)
garbear to show off (175)
garlar to chatter, prattle (259)
gatear to crawl (175)
generalizar to generalize (339)
generar to generate, produce (215)
gesticular to gesture, grimace, gesticulate (259)
gestionar to negotiate, manage (355)
girar to turn around, spin (215)
glorificar to glorify, praise (424)
glosar to glose, comment (2)
golear to score goals (206)
golpear to crush, hit, strike (175)
golpetear to pound, hammer (175)
gorgotear to gurgle, bubble (206)
gorjear to warble, gurgle (206)
gormar to vomit, spew (244)
gotear to drip (206)
grabar to engrave (249)
graduarse to graduate (141, 289)
granizar to hail (339)
gratar to brush, rub (249)
gratificar to recompense, reward (424)
gravar to burden (249)
gravitar to gravitate (254)
guardar to keep, guard, save (259)
guerrear to war, fight (175)
guiñar to wink (213)

guipar to notice, see (54)
guisar to cook (25)
gustar to be pleasing (to), to like (Def. and Imp.)

H

habilitar to qualify, furnish, equip (308)
habituarse to become accustomed to (141, 289)
hacinar to pile up, stack (107)
hadar to foretell (324)
halagar to flatter (341)
halar to haul, tow (259)
hambrear to starve (206)
haraganear to idle, loaf (206)
hay (See haber) (verb 257)
heder to stink (354)
helar to freeze (Def. and Imp.)
hender to split, crack (164)
hervir to boil (370)
hidratar to hydrate (308)
hincar to sink, drive in (424)
hincarse to kneel down, sink (424, 289)
hinchar to swell, inflate, blow up (306)
hipnotizar to hypnotize (339)
hipotecar to mortgage (424)
hispanizar to hispanicize (339)
hojear to skim, leaf through (175)
holgar to rest, be idle (125)
homenajear to pay homage to (175)
honrar to honor (32)
hornear to bake (206)
hospedar to lodge, put up (39)
humear to smoke, steam (175)
humedecer to dampen, moisten (344)
humillar to humiliate, humble (261)
hundir to sink, ruin (60)
hurtar to rob, steal (11)

I

idealizar to idealize (339)

idear to think up, invent (175)

identificar to identify (117)

idolatrar to idolize (259)

igualar to equal, equalize, even out (259)

iluminar to illuminate (107)

ilusionar to fascinate (248)

ilusionarse to have illusions (289)

ilustrar to illustrate; enlighten, explain (215)

imaginar to imagine (107)

imbuir to imbue (264)

imitar to imitate (254)

impacientarse to lose one's patience (11, 289)

impartir to grant, concede (495)

implicar to implicate (424)

implicarse to become involved (424, 289)

implorar to implore (300)

imponer to impose (364)

importar to matter, be important (Def. and Imp.)

importunar to bother, importune (107)

imprecar to curse, imprecate (424)

impresionar to impress (107)

improvisar to improvise (2)

impugnar to refute, impugn, contest (107)

impulsar to drive, impale, to propel (2)

imputar to charge with, impute (308)

inaugurar to inaugurate, open (409)

incendiar to set on fire (106)

incitar to incite (279)

inclinar to incline, tilt (107)

incomodar to bother, inconvenience (39)

incorporar to incorporate, help someone sit up (in bed) (409)

incorporarse to join (a group), sit up (in bed) (409, 289)

incrementar to increase, augment (11)

incrustar to encrust, inlay (250)

inculcar to inculcate (424)

incumbir to be incumbent upon, be the duty, obligation of (353)

incurrir to incur, commit (495)

indemnizar to indemnify, compensate (339)

independizar to liberate, emancipate (339)

independizarse to become independent (339, 289)

indignar to infuriate, anger (107)

indisponer to upset, indispose (364)

individualizar to individualize, make personal (339)

industrializar to industrialize (339)

infamar to defame, slander, discredit (54)

infatuarse to become conceited (141, 289)

infectar to infect (11)

inferir to infer (400)

infiltrar to infiltrate (215)

inflamar to set on fire, inflame, arouse (54)

inflar to inflate, blow up (259)

infligir to inflict (188)

influenciar to influence (383)

informar to inform (244)

informatizar to computerize (339)

infringir to infringe, transgress, break (188)

ingeniar to invent, conceive, think up (232)

ingerir to ingest, take in, consume (435)

ingresar to come in, enter, enroll, register; deposit (money) (2)

inhabilitar to disable, incapacitate, disqualify (308)

inhalar to inhale (259)

inhibir to inhibit (353)

iniciar to initiate, begin (383)

injuriar to offend, insult, injure (232)

inmergir to immerse (188)

inmolar to immolate, sacrifice (259)

inmovilizar to immobilize, paralyze (339)

inmunizar to immunize (339)

innovar to innovate (259)

inocular to inoculate (71)

inquietar to disturb, worry, trouble (308)

inquirir to inquire, investigate (33)

insertar to insert, include (11)

insinuar to insinuate, hint (141)

inspeccionar to inspect, examine (355)

inspirar to inspire (29)

instalar to install, fit out, settle (259)

instar to urge, press (11)

instaurar to establish, set up (409)

instigar to instigate, stir up (341)

instituir to institute, found (264)

instruir to instruct, teach (271)

instrumentar to orchestrate (11)

insubordinar to stir up (107)

insultar to insult (11)

integrar to integrate, compose, make up (259)

intelectualizar to intellectualize (339)

intensificar to intensify (424)

intentar to try, attempt (11)

intercalar to insert, intercalate (259)

intercambiar to interchange, exchange (232)

interceder to intercede (63)

interceptar to intercept (11)

Over 2,100 Spanish verbs

interconectar   to interconnect, hook up   (11)
interferir   to interfere   (435)
internar   to intern, commit   (107)
interpelar   to appeal, implore   (259)
interponer   to interpose   (364)
interpretar   to interpret   (376)
interrogar   to interrogate, question   (297)
interrumpir   to interrupt, block   (452)
intervenir   to intervene, interfere, participate   (488)
intimidar   to intimidate   (199)
intoxicar   to poison, intoxicate   (424)
intrigar   to intrigue, plot, scheme   (341)
intuir   to intuit, sense   (271)
inundar   to flood, inundate   (39)
invadir   to invade, trespass   (60)
invalidar   to invalidate   (39)
inventar   to invent   (279)
invertir   to invert, turn upside down; invest money   (370)
investigar   to investigate   (421)
investir   to invest (as a title), endow   (349)
invocar   to appeal, call upon, invoke   (424)
involucrar   to involve, introduce, bring in   (259)
inyectar   to inject   (11)
irradiar   to irradiate   (232)
irrigar   to irrigate   (341)
irritar   to irritate   (279)
italianizar   to Italianize   (339)
izar   to hoist   (339)

J

jabonar   to soap, lather   (473)
jacarear   to annoy; to roam the streets at night making merry   (206)
jactarse   to boast, brag   (48)
jadear   to pant   (206)

jalar   to pull   (259)
jalear   to encourage, cheer on   (206)
jalonar   to mark, stake out, dot   (355)
jamar   to eat   (54)
jarapotear   to stuff with drugs, medicines   (206)
jerarquizar   to arrange hierarchically, to hierarchize   (339)
jetar   to dilute, dissolve   (308)
jipar   to hiccup   (332)
jubilar   to retire   (259)
justar   to joust, tilt   (11)
justiciar   to condemn, execute   (57)
justificar   to justify   (117)

L

laborar   to work, till, plow   (409)
labrar   to work, carve, bring about   (409)
lacerar   to lacerate, tear, damage   (409)
lactar   to nurse, breast-feed   (11)
ladear   to lean, tilt, incline   (206)
ladrar   to bark   (54)
ladrillar   to brick   (261)
ladronear   to shoplift   (206)
lagrimar   to cry, weep, shed tears   (231)
lagrimear   to water (eyes), weep   (206)
laicizar   to laicize   (339)
lamentar   to lament   (11)
lamer   to lick   (91)
laminar   to laminate   (107)
lancear   to spear, lance   (175)
largar   to let go, release, loosen, give   (341)
laurear   to crown with laurels, honor   (175)
legar   to delegate, bequeath   (341)
legislar   to legislate   (259)
legitimar   to legitimize   (54)
lesionar   to damage, wound   (355)
liar   to tie, bind, roll   (256)
liberar   to liberate, free, release   (409)

libertar   to liberate, free, release   (11)
librar   to save, rescue, release   (259)
licenciarse   to graduate in   (57, 289)
licuar   to liquefy   (141)
lidiar   to fight, combat, fight bulls   (232)
limar   to file, polish, smooth   (231)
limitar   to limit, reduce, border on   (308)
linear   to draw lines, sketch   (175)
liquidar   to liquefy, liquidate, sell off   (39)
litigar   to litigate, dispute   (341)
llagar   to injure, hurt, wound   (298)
llamear   to blaze, flame   (206)
lloriquear   to whimper, whine   (206)
llover   to rain   (Def. and Imp.)
lloviznar   to drizzle   (288)
loar   to praise   (259)
localizar   to localize, locate, find   (81)
lograr   to achieve, attain, get   (29)
lubricar   to lubricate   (469)
lucir   to shine   (495) (before a or o, c becomes zc in Tenses 1, 6 and imperative)
lustrar   to polish, cleanse   (215)

M

macear   to hammer, pound   (175)
macerar   to macerate, mortify   (409)
machacar   to pound, crush   (424)
machar   to beat, crush   (306)
machucar   to crush, bruise, maul   (424)
madrugar   to get up early   (341)
madurar   to mature, ripen   (409)
magnetizar   to magnetize, hypnotize   (339)

magnificar   to magnify
(424)

magullar   to batter, bruise
(261)

majar   to crush, mash   (86)

malcasarse   to make a bad
marriage   (112)

malear   to ruin, spoil   (206)

maleficiar   to damage, harm,
injure   (383)

malentender   to misunderstand   (164)

malgastar   to squander,
waste   (250)

maliciar   to fear, suspect
(383)

maltratar   to maltreat, abuse
(478)

mamar   to suck, nurse
(54)

manar   to flow, run, spring
(107)

manchar   to spot, stain, blot
(306)

mandar   to command, order
(259)

manifestar   to demonstrate,
show, manifest   (352)

manipular   to manipulate
(71)

manufacturar   to
manufacture   (284)

maquillarse   to put on
makeup   (289)

maravillarse   to marvel at,
be amazed   (261, 289)

marearse   to feel dizzy, be
seasick   (175, 289)

martillar   to hammer   (261)

martirizar   to martyr, torture
(339)

mascar   to chew, masticate
(99)

masticar   to chew, masticate
(99)

materializar   to materialize
(339)

matricular   to register, get
registered   (71)

mediar   to mediate, intercede
(232)

meditar   to meditate   (254)

mendigar   to beg   (341)

menear   to move, shake,
wiggle   (206)

mentar   to mention, name
(352)

merendar   to have a snack,
refreshment   (352)

metamorfosear   to
metamorphose, change
(175)

meter   to put in, into   (444)

metodizar   to organize,
systematize, methodize
(339)

mezclar   to mix   (259)

militar   to serve in the army
(308)

mimar   to pamper, spoil,
indulge   (314)

minar   to mine, bore, tunnel
through, undermine   (107)

minimizar   to reduce, lessen,
diminish   (339)

minorar   to diminish, lessen,
reduce   (409)

mistificar   to falsify, trick,
deceive   (424)

mitigar   to mitigate, allay,
alleviate   (341)

modelar   to model, pattern,
shape   (259)

moderar   to moderate,
control   (409)

modernizar   to modernize
(339)

modificar   to modify, change
(424)

modular   to modulate   (71)

moler   to grind, crush, mill
(321)

molestar   to bother, annoy
(250)

momificar   to mummify
(424)

monear   to clown (monkey)
around   (206)

moralizar   to moralize   (339)

morar   to reside, dwell
(409)

mortificar   to mortify,
humiliate, wound, hurt
(424)

motivar   to motivate   (9)

movilizar   to mobilize
(339)

multicopiar   to duplicate
(232)

multiplicar   to multiply,
increase   (424)

murmurar   to murmur,
mutter   (72)

mutilar   to mutilate   (71)

N

nacionalizar   to nationalize,
naturalize   (90)

narrar   to narrate   (215)

naturalizar   to naturalize
(90)

naufragar   to sink, be
wrecked, shipwrecked
(341)

nausear   to feel nauseated,
sick   (206)

necear   to talk nonsense
(206)

negociar   to negotiate   (383)

nevar   to snow   (Def. and
Imp.)

neviscar   to snow lightly
(424)

niñear   to behave childishly
(206)

nivelar   to level, make even
(259)

nombrar   to name, appoint
(113)

normalizar   to normalize,
restore to normal   (339)

notar   to note   (308)

noticiar   to inform, notify
(383)

notificar   to notify, inform
(117)

nublar   to cloud, mar   (259)

numerar   to number   (227)

nutrir   to feed, nourish
(346)

O

obcecar   to blind   (99)

objetar   to object
(308)

objetivar   to objectify
(9)

obligar   to oblige,
compel   (341)

obliterar   to obliterate,
erase   (227)

obrar   to build, work
(113)

obscurecer   to darken
(333)

obsequiar   to entertain,
compliment   (228)

obsesionar   to obsess
(355)

obstaculizar   to hinder,
obstruct, block   (339)

obstar   to obstruct,
impede, hinder   (215)

obstinarse   to be obstinate, stubborn   (289)

obstruir   to obstruct, to block   (264)

obturar   to plug, close, fill   (284)

ocasionar   to occasion, cause, jeopardize   (355)

occidentalizar   to westernize   (339)

ocluir   to occlude, shut   (271)

ocultar   to hide, conceal   (11)

ocurrir   to occur, happen   (Def. and Imp.)

odiar   to hate   (232)

ofender   to offend, insult   (63)

oficiar   to officiate, celebrate (mass)   (57)

ofuscar   to dazzle   (99)

ojear   to eye, stare at   (175)

olfatear   to smell, sniff   (206)

ominar   to predict, foretell, forecast   (107)

omitir   to omit   (30)

ondear   to undulate, wave, ripple   (206)

ondular   to undulate, wind   (71)

operar   to operate   (227)

opinar   to opine, think, have an opinion   (107)

oprimir   to oppress, press, squeeze   (267)

oprobiar   to defame, revile, disgrace   (232)

optar   to opt, choose   (11)

optimar   to optimize   (54)

optimizar   to optimize   (81)

orar   to pray   (32)

orientar   to orient, guide, direct, position   (11)

originar   to originate, give rise to, cause   (107)

orillar   to edge, trim, go around, settle   (261)

ornamentar   to ornament, adorn   (11)

ornar   to adorn, decorate   (249)

orquestar   to orchestrate   (250)

oscilar   to oscillate, swing   (71)

oscurecer   to get dark, become night   (344)

ostentar   to show, show off, flaunt   (11)

otorgar   to grant, concede   (421)

oxidar   to oxidize, rust   (39)

P

pacificar   to pacify, calm   (424)

pactar   to agree to, come to an agreement, make a pact   (11)

padecer   to suffer, endure   (333)

paginar   to paginate   (107)

palabrear   to chat   (175)

paladear   to savor, taste, relish   (206)

palatalizar   to palatalize   (339)

palear   to shovel   (206)

paliar   to palliate   (232)

palidecer   to turn pale   (344)

palmear   to clap hands   (206)

palpar   to feel, touch   (332)

palpitar   to palpitate, beat, throb   (254)

papar   to swallow soft food without chewing   (332)

parafrasear   to paraphrase   (175)

paralizar   to paralyze   (339)

parear   to pair, match   (175)

parir   to give birth   (495)

parodiar   to parody   (232)

parpadear   to blink, wink   (206)

parquear   to park   (206)

participar   to participate   (332)

particularizar   to specify, particularize   (339)

pasmar   to leave flabbergasted, astound, astonish, amaze   (54)

patalear   to kick   (206)

patear   to kick   (206)

patentar   to patent   (11)

patinar   to skate, skid, slide   (107)

patrullar   to patrol   (261)

pausar   to pause   (25)

pecar   to sin   (424)

pedalear   to pedal   (206)

pelar   to peel   (259)

pelear   to fight   (206)

peligrar   to be in danger, be threatened   (259)

pelotear   to kick (a ball); audit   (175)

penalizar   to penalize   (339)

pender   to hang   (63)

penetrar   to penetrate   (215)

pensionar   to pension   (107)

perdurar   to last a long time   (215)

perecer   to perish   (344)

peregrinar   to go on a pilgrimage, journey   (107)

perfeccionar   to perfect, improve, brush up (knowledge)   (355)

perforar   to perforate, pierce   (409)

perfumar   to perfume   (247)

perifrasear   to periphrase   (175)

perjudicar   to damage, harm   (424)

perjurar   to commit perjury   (284)

permanecer   to remain, stay   (323)

permutar   to exchange, change, swap   (308)

perorar   to make or deliver a speech   (409)

perpetrar   to perpetrate a crime   (409)

perpetuar   to perpetuate   (141)

perseguir   to pursue   (432)

perseverar   to persevere, continue   (409)

persistir   to persist   (74)

personalizar   to personalize, personify, embody   (339)

personificar   to personify   (424)

persuadir   to persuade   (346)

perturbar   to disturb, upset, become upset   (9)

pervertir   to pervert, corrupt   (410)

pesar   to weigh   (25)

pescar   to fish   (99)

pestañear   to wink, blink   (206)

picar   to prick, puncture, pierce   (424)

pilotar   to pilot   (54)

pilotear   to pilot   (54)
pisotear   to trample   (175)
plagar   to infest, plague   (341)
planchar   to iron   (225)
planear   to plan, design, glide   (206)
planificar   to plan   (424)
plantar   to plant   (109)
plantear   to expound, set forth, state   (206)
plegar   to fold, pleat   (327, 341)
pluralizar   to pluralize, use the plural   (339)
poblar   to populate   (474)
polemizar   to polemicize, argue   (339)
politizar   to politicize   (339)
pontificar   to pontificate   (424)
popularizar   to popularize   (339)
portarse   to behave   (11, 289)
posar   to pose, put, lay down   (481)
posponer   to postpone   (364)
postular   to postulate, request, demand, be a candidate for   (71)
precalentar   to preheat   (352)
preceder   to precede   (63)
preciar   to appraise, value   (62)
preciarse   to brag about oneself   (289)
precipitar   to precipitate   (254)
precisar   to specify   (2)
predestinar   to predestine   (107)
predeterminar   to predetermine   (107)
predisponer   to predispose   (364)
predominar   to predominate   (107)
prefabricar   to prefabricate   (424)
prefigurar   to foreshadow, prefigure   (284)
prejuzgar   to prejudge   (341)
premeditar   to premeditate   (308)

premiar   to reward, give award, a prize   (232)
prender   to seize, grasp, catch   (63)
prensar   to press   (2)
preponer   to put before   (364)
presagiar   to presage, portend, forebode   (232)
prescribir   to prescribe   (224)
preservar   to preserve   (288)
presidir   to preside over, chair   (60)
presionar   to pressure, push   (355)
presumir   to presume, be presumptuous   (267)
presuponer   to presuppose   (364)
pretender   to seek, try for, want, intend to   (63)
prevalecer   to prevail, take root   (344)
prevaler   to prevail   (484)
prevenir   to warn   (488)
prever   to foresee   (489)
privar   to deprive   (288)
proceder   to proceed   (413)
procesar   to prosecute   (403)
procurar   to endeavor, try, strive for   (72)
profanar   to profane, desecrate   (107)
proferir   to utter, say   (370)
profesar   to profess   (403)
programar   to program   (54)
progresar   to progress   (235)
proliferar   to proliferate   (409)
prolongar   to prolong   (341)
prometer   to promise   (444)
promover   to promote, cause   (321)
promulgar   to promulgate, announce   (341)
pronosticar   to forecast, foretell, predict   (424)
propagar   to propagate, spread   (341)
proponer   to propose   (364)
proporcionar   to furnish, supply, provide   (107)

proscribir   to proscribe, banish   (224)
proseguir   to continue, follow up, proceed   (432)
prosperar   to prosper   (227)
protagonizar   to play the lead in, star   (339)
protestar   to protest   (308)
proveer   to provide, supply   (152)
provenir   to originate, come from   (488)
provocar   to provoke   (99)
proyectar   to project, plan, throw   (11)
publicar   to publish, issue   (99)
pugnar   to fight   (54)
pujar   to struggle   (54)
pulsar   to pulse, throb   (25)
pulverizar   to pulverize, shatter   (339)
punchar   to pierce, puncture   (306)
puntar   to dot   (494)
puntualizar   to arrange, fix, settle   (339)
puntuar   to punctuate, mark, grade   (141)
purgar   to purge, clean, purify   (341)
purificar   to purify, cleanse   (424)

Q

quebrar   to break, smash   (352)
querellarse   to file a legal complaint, bring suit against   (261, 289)
quesear   to make cheese   (175)
quietar   to quiet, calm   (308)
quietarse   to calm oneself   (289)
quillotrar   to incite, excite   (259)
quimerizar   to have fanciful ideas   (81)

R

rabiar   to rage   (106)
racionalizar   to rationalize   (339)
racionar   to ration   (107)

radiar   to radiate   (232)
radiografiar   to x-ray   (256)
ramificarse   to ramify, branch out   (424, 289)
rasar   to graze, skim, raze   (2)
rascar   to scratch, itch   (99)
rasgar   to rip, tear   (341)
raspar   to scrape   (332)
rastrillar   to rake   (261)
rasurarse   to shave (one's beard)   (292)
ratificar   to ratify   (424)
rayar   to rule, underline, cross, strike out   (453)
razonar   to reason (out)   (355)
reaccionar   to react   (355)
reactivar   to reactivate   (259)
reafirmar   to reaffirm, reassert   (243)
realzar   to raise, highlight, enhance   (339)
reanimar   to reanimate, revive   (107)
reaparecer   to reappear   (59)
rearmar   to rearm   (54)
reasegurar   to reassure, reinsure   (72)
reasumir   to resume, reassume   (495)
reatar   to tie again, retie   (308)
rebajar   to lower, reduce, bring down   (86)
rebatir   to knock down again, beat again   (1)
rebelarse   to rebel, revolt   (259, 289)
rebotar   to bounce, rebound   (308)
rebuscar   to search carefully, search into   (99)
recaer   to fall again, back, relapse   (101)
recalentar   to reheat, warm up, warm over   (103)
recapacitar   to think over, consider   (308)
recapitular   to recapitulate   (71)
recargar   to reload, overload   (111)
rechazar   to reject, repel   (81)

rechistar   to whisper   (250)
reciclar   to recycle   (259)
recircular   to recycle, distribute   (71)
recitar   to recite   (254)
reclamar   to reclaim, claim, demand, protest   (15)
reclinar   to recline, lean   (107)
reclinarse en/sobre   to lean on/upon   (289)
recluir   to shut, lock in (away), imprison   (271)
reclutar   to recruit   (308)
recobrar   to recover, regain, get back   (259)
recolectar   to harvest, collect   (11)
recompensar   to reward, recompense   (2)
reconciliar   to reconcile   (232)
reconciliarse   to reconcile   (232, 289)
reconfortar   to comfort, cheer up   (11)
reconstituir   to reconstitute   (271)
reconstruir   to rebuild, reconstruct   (264)
reconvenir   to reprimand, rebuke   (488)
recopilar   to compile   (259)
recorrer   to go, travel, cover (distance)   (148)
recortar   to cut, trim   (149)
recrear   to amuse, entertain   (175)
recrearse   to amuse, entertain oneself   (289)
recriminar   to recriminate   (107)
rectificar   to rectify, right a wrong, correct   (424)
recular   to recoil, go backwards   (71)
recuperar   to recuperate, recover   (227)
recuperar   to recuperate, retrieve, recover   (409)
recurrir   to turn to, appeal to, resort to   (495)
redactar   to edit   (215)
redoblar   to intensify, redouble   (259)
redondear   to round off   (206)

reduplicar   to intensify, redouble, reduplicate   (424)
reeditar   to reprint, publish again   (254)
reelegir   to reelect, elect again   (203)
reembolsar   to reimburse, repay   (2)
reemplazar   to replace   (339)
refinar   to refine   (107)
reflejar   to reflect   (86)
reflexionar   to reflect   (107)
reformar   to reform, alter, revise   (244)
reforzar   to reinforce, strengthen   (49)
refrescar   to refresh, cool, revive, brush up   (424)
refrigerar   to cool, refrigerate, refresh   (409)
refugiarse   to take refuge, shelter   (232, 289)
refunfuñar   to grumble, growl   (213)
regalarse   to indulge oneself   (401, 289)
regañar   to scold   (213)
regenerar   to regenerate   (409)
regir   to govern, rule, manage   (203)
registrar   to register, record, examine   (215)
rehacer   to do over, redo   (260)
rehuir   to avoid, shun   (264)
rehusar   to refuse   (481)
reinar   to reign, rule   (107)
reinstalar   to reinstate, reinstall   (259)
reintegrar   to reimburse, refund   (259)
reiterar   to reiterate, repeat   (72)
rejuvenecerse   to be rejuvenated   (344, 102)
relacionar   to relate   (355)
relajarse   to relax   (86, 289)
relanzar   to throw back, repel   (286)
relatar   to relate, narrate   (308)
relavar   to wash again   (288)
relavarse   to wash oneself again   (289)

releer   to reread, read again   (290)

relegar   to relegate   (341)

relucir   to shine, glitter, gleam   (495) (before a or o, c becomes zc in Tenses 1, 6 and imperative)

relumbrar   to dazzle, sparkle   (51)

remandar   to send over and over again   (259)

remangar   to turn, roll up sleeve, pants   (341)

remar   to row   (54)

remarcar   to mark again   (305)

rematar   to kill off, terminate, finish off   (308)

remediar   to remedy   (232)

remedir   to remeasure   (309)

rememorar   to remember   (32)

remendar   to mend   (352)

remeter   to put back   (444)

remirar   to look at over again   (314)

remojar   to soak   (239)

remolcar   to tow   (424)

remontar   to elevate, raise; frighten away   (317)

remorder   to worry, gnaw   (318)

remover   to remove, take away; move   (321)

remunerar   to remunerate, pay   (409)

renacer   to be born again, be reborn   (323)

rendir   to defeat, surrender   (349)

renegar   to renege, deny; abhor   (327)

renovar   to renew, renovate   (209)

rentar   to yield, produce, rent   (11)

renunciar   to renounce   (383)

reorganizar   to reorganize   (339)

repararse   to restrain oneself   (409, 289)

repasar   to review, go over again   (347)

repeler   to repulse, repel, throw out   (91)

repensar   to rethink, reconsider   (352)

repesar   to weigh again   (25)

repintar   to repaint   (358)

replantar   to replant   (109)

replicar   to retort, reply   (99)

reponer   to put back   (364)

reponerse   to recover, get over   (364, 102)

reposar   to rest, lie, be buried   (2)

represar   to repress, hold back   (376)

representar   to represent   (375)

reprimir   to repress   (267)

reprobar   to reprove, fail in an exam   (378)

reprochar   to reproach   (200)

reprocharse   to reproach   (200, 289)

reproducir   to reproduce   (381)

repudiar   to repudiate   (232)

repugnar   to loathe, detest, disgust   (107)

repulir   to polish again   (386)

repulsar   to repulse, reject   (2)

reputar   to deem, consider, repute   (308)

requemar   to burn again, overcook   (389)

requerir   to require   (370)

resaltar   to bounce, rebound   (427)

resaludar   to return someone's greeting   (428)

rescatar   to ransom, rescue   (308)

rescindir   to cancel, rescind, annul   (60)

resentirse   to feel the effects   (435, 8)

reservar   to reserve   (288)

resfriarse   to catch a cold   (256, 289)

residir   to reside, live   (60)

resignarse   to resign oneself   (107, 289)

resistir   to resist   (74)

resonar   to resound, ring   (209)

respetar   to respect   (54)

respirar   to breathe, respire   (227)

resplandecer   to shine, blaze, glow   (344)

restaurar   to restore   (259)

restituir   to refund, give back   (264)

resucitar   to resuscitate, bring back to life   (254)

resultar   to result   (427)

resumir   to summarize, sum up   (480)

resurgir   to resurge, spring up again   (460)

retacar   to hit twice (a ball)   (76)

retajar   to cut around   (86)

retar   to challenge   (254)

retardar   to retard, slow down   (199)

retemblar   to shake, tremble   (352)

retener   to retain   (468)

retocar   to touch up, retouch   (472)

retorcer   to twist   (321, 486)

retostar   to toast again   (474)

retraducir   to translate over again   (476)

retraer   to bring again, bring back   (477)

retransmitir   to retransmit, rebroadcast   (30)

retratar   to paint a portrait   (478)

retribuir   to repay, reward   (264)

retrotraer   to antedate, date back   (477)

reunificar   to reunify   (424)

revalorar   to revalue   (409)

revalorizar   to revalue   (339)

revelar   to reveal, disclose   (259)

revender   to resell   (487)

reventar   to burst, explode   (352)

rever   to review, revise   (489)

reverberar   to reverberate, be reflected   (409)

reverter   to overflow   (354)

revertir   to revert   (34)
revisar   to revise, check, review   (2)
revivir   to revive   (495)
revolar   to fly again   (496)
revolcar   to knock down   (19, 424)
revolcarse   to wallow, roll about   (21, 19, 424)
revolotear   to whirl up in the air   (206)
revolucionar   to revolutionize   (355)
rezar   to pray   (53)
ridiculizar   to ridicule   (339)
rimar   to rhyme   (54)
rivalizar   to rival   (339)
rizar   to curl   (339)
rociar   to spray, sprinkle   (62)
rodar   to roll   (474)
rodear   to surround   (206)
rodearse de   to surround oneself with   (206, 289)
roncar   to snore   (424)
ronchar   to crunch, chew   (225)
rondar   to patrol, prowl   215)
rotar   to rotate   (308)
rotular   to label   (71)
rozar   to scrape, scratch, rub   (81)
rubricar   to initial, sign and seal   (424)
rugir   to roar, bellow, shout   (188)
rular   to roll   (71)
rumbar a   to go in the direction of   (54)
rumiar   to ruminate, meditate   (62)

S

saborear   to savor, taste, relish   (206)
sacrificar   to sacrifice   (117)
salar   to salt, season with salt   (71)
saldar   to settle, pay a debt   (54)
salivar   to salivate   (288)
salpicar   to splash   (424)
salpimentar   to season   (352)

saltear   to hold up, rob   (206)
salvar   to save, rescue   (288)
sanar   to cure, heal   (54)
sancionar   to sanction, authorize; punish   (107)
sangrar   to bleed   (215)
sangrarse   to be bled   (215, 289)
saquear   to pillage, loot, sack   (206)
satirizar   to satirize   (339)
saturar   to saturate   (284)
sazonar   to season, flavor   (355)
secuestrar   to confiscate, kidnap, hijack   (409)
secularizar   to secularize   (339)
secundar   to second, support   (39)
sedar   to soothe, quiet   (54)
seducir   to seduce   (381)
segar   to cut, mow   (327)
segmentar   to segment   (11)
segregar   to segregate   (421)
seleccionar   to select, choose   (355)
sellar   to seal, stamp   (261)
sembrar   to sow   (352)
semejar   to resemble   (86)
sentenciar   to sentence someone; judge   (57)
separarse   to separate, come apart   (289, 437)
sepultar   to bury   (427)
sermonear   to preach, lecture   (175)
serrar   to saw   (116)
signar   to sign   (114)
signarse   to cross oneself   (289)
silabear   to pronounce syllable by syllable, divide into syllables   (175)
silbar   to whistle   (9)
silenciar   to muffle, silence   (57)
simbolizar   to symbolize   (339)
simpatizar con   to get along well with   (339)
simplificar   to simplify   (117)

simular   to simulate, feign, pretend   (71)
sincronizar   to synchronize   (339)
singularizar   to single out, distinguish   (339)
sintonizar   to tune   (339)
sisar   to snitch   (9)
sistematizar   to systematize   (339)
sitiar   to besiege   (232)
situar   to situate, place, locate   (141)
sobar   to knead, massage, rub, slap   (54)
sobornar   to bribe   (107)
sobrar   to have, be left over   (409)
sobrecargar   to overload, weigh down   (111)
sobreexcitar   to overexcite   (308)
sobreexponer   to overexpose   (364)
sobregirar   to overdraw   (107)
sobrepasar   to surpass, exceed   (2)
sobreponer   to superimpose   (364)
sobresalir   to stand out, excel   (426)
sobresaltar   to attack, startle   (427)
sobresaltarse   to be startled   (427, 289)
sobrevenir   to supervene, occur later   (488)
sobrevivir   to survive   (495)
sofreír   to sauté, fry lightly   (404)
soldar   to solder, weld   (209)
solemnizar   to celebrate, commemorate   (339)
soler   to be accustomed to, be in the habit of, have the custom of   (Def. and Imp.)
soltar   to let go, release   (209)
solucionar   to solve, resolve   (355)
sonarse (las narices)   to blow (one's nose)   (445, 289)
sondar   to sound, investigate probe   (39)

sonorizar   to voice (phonetics) (339)

sonrojarse   to blush (86, 289)

sonrosarse   to blush, turn pink (2, 289)

sopapear   to slap (206)

sopesar   to weigh, examine (2)

soplarse   to gobble up, wolf down (289, 448)

soportar   to support, endure, put up with (427)

sorber   to sip (91)

sorregar   to irrigate (327)

sortear   to raffle; avoid, dodge (206)

sosegar   to quiet, calm down (327)

soterrar   to bury; hide (352)

suavizar   to smooth, soften (339)

subarrendar   to sublet, sublease (352)

subastar   to auction (54)

sublimar   to exalt (54)

subordinar   to subordinate (338)

subsistir   to subsist (74)

substituir   to substitute (264)

substraer   to subtract, take away, remove (477)

subvencionar   to subsidize (311)

subvenir   to provide for needs (488)

subvertir   to subvert, disturb (263)

subyugar   to subjugate, captivate (325)

suceder   to happen (Def. and Imp.)

sudar   to sweat, perspire (54)

suicidarse   to commit suicide (39, 289)

sujetar   to secure, fasten; subdue, subject (308)

sumar   to add, add up (54)

suministrar   to furnish, provide, supply (215)

sumir   to sink, submerge (459)

superar   to surpass, exceed (54)

superponer   to superpose (364)

supervenir   to happen, take place (488)

suplantar   to supplant, take the place of (109)

suplicar   to supplicate, entreat, implore (117)

surcar   to plow (424)

surfear   to surf (Internet) *slang* (206)

surtir   to supply, stock, provide (346)

suscitar   to provoke, cause, arouse (308)

suscribir   to subscribe (454)

suspender   to suspend, hang (91)

sustituir   to substitute (271)

sustraer   to subtract, take away (477)

susurrar   to murmur, whisper (54)

sutilizar   to file, refine, polish, taper (339)

T

tacar   to mark, stain (472)

tachar   to cross out, strike out, eliminate (200)

tajar   to slice, carve, chop (86)

talar   to fell, cut down (54)

tallar   to carve, engrave, cut (261)

tambalear   to stagger (206)

tamborear   to drum, beat, pitter-patter (rain) (175)

tamizar   to sift (339)

tapar   to cover (332)

tapiar   to wall up, wall in (232)

tapizar   to upholster, hang tapestry (339)

taponar   to plug, stop up (355)

tardar   to take a long time (199)

tarjar   to tally (86)

tartamudear   to stammer, stutter (206)

tascar   to gnaw, nibble (99)

teclear   play piano, type; to run one's fingers over piano or typewriter keys (206)

tejar   to tile (86)

tejer   to weave (91)

telecargar   to download (Internet) (111)

teledirigir   to operate by remote control (188)

teleguiar   to guide by remote control (256)

televisar   to televise (2)

teñir   to dye, stain (408)

teorizar   to theorize (339)

tergiversar   to distort, twist, misrepresent (2)

testar   to make a will, testament (54)

testificar   to testify, bear witness (117)

timar   to cheat, swindle (231)

timarse con   to flirt with (289)

timbrar   to put a seal or stamp on (22)

tintar   to tint, dye (254)

tipificar   to standardize, typify (424)

tiranizar   to tyrannize (339)

tiritar   to shiver (308)

titubear   to stagger, totter, hesitate (175)

titular   to title, entitle (71)

titularse   to be titled, called (289)

tolerar   to tolerate (227)

tontear   to act foolishly (206)

torcer   to twist (321, 486)

tornar   to turn (288)

tornear   to go round (206)

torturar   to torture (72)

torturarse   to worry excessively (289)

toser   to cough (91)

tostarse   to become sunburned (289, 474)

trabar   to bind, join, lock (54)

trabarse de palabras   to insult each other (289)

traficar   to deal, trade, traffic (424)

tragar   to swallow (421)

traicionar   to betray (107)

trajinar   to rush about (107)

tramar   to plot   (54)

tramitar   to negotiate, transact   (254)

trancar   to stride along   (424)

tranquilizar   to tranquilize   (339)

transcribir   to transcribe   (224)

transcurrir   to pass, elapse (time)   (495)

transferir   to transfer   (370)

transformar   to transform   (244)

transfregar   to rub together   (327)

transigir con   to agree to   (188)

transitar   to journey, travel   (254)

translimitar   to go beyond the limits   (254)

transmigrar   to transmigrate   (273)

transmitir   to transmit   (30)

transpirar   to perspire, sweat   (314)

transponer   to transfer   (364)

transportar   to transport   (427)

tranzar   to break off, cut off; braid   (81)

trascender   to transcend   (354)

trascolar   to filter, strain   (474)

trascolarse   to percolate   (289, 474)

trascordarse   to remember incorrectly, forget   (20)

trasegar   to decant   (327)

trasferir   to transfer   (370)

trashumar   to migrate, move to new land   (54)

trasladar   to transfer, move   (215)

trasladarse   to move, change residence   (289)

traspasar   to pierce   (347)

trasplantar   to transplant   (11)

trasquilar   to shear, clip, crop (hair)   (259)

trastornar   to turn upside down, upset, disturb   (54)

trasvolar   to fly over, fly across   (496)

tratarse de   to be a question of   (289, 478)

travesar   to cross, cross over, go through   (79)

travesear   to be mischievous   (175)

trazar   to trace, draw, sketch   (81)

trenzar   to braid, plait   (81)

trepar   to climb, mount   (332)

tributar   to pay tribute   (215)

tricotar   to knit   (254)

trillar   to make frequent use of   (259)

trinar   to trill, warble   (107)

trinchar   to slice (meat)   (54)

triplicar   to triplicate, triple   (424)

triscar   to mix up   (99)

triturar   to crush, grind   (72)

triunfar   to triumph   (54)

trizar   to tear to shreds   (81)

trocar   to exchange   (19, 424)

trocear   to cut into pieces   (206)

trompicar   to trip, stumble   (424)

tronar   to thunder   (474)

tronchar   to crack, split   (54)

tronzar   to slice   (81)

trotar   to trot   (478)

trucar   to pocket a ball in billiards   (424)

truhanear   to cheat, trick   (206)

trujamanear   to interpret   (206)

truncar   to truncate, cut short, down   (424)

tullecer   to cripple, disable   (333)

tullir   to cripple, disable   (97)

tumbar   to knock down, knock over, overthrow   (9)

tundir   to clip, shear; beat, thrash   (346)

turbar   to disturb, upset, worry   (9)

tutear   to use the tú form with someone   (206)

tutearse   to use the tú form with each other   (206, 289)

U

ubicar   to locate, situate   (424)

ufanarse de   to boast of   (88)

ultimar   to finish off   (107)

ultrajar   to outrage   (86)

ulular   to ululate, howl, screech, hoot   (259)

uncir   to yoke   (501)

undular   to undulate   (71)

ungir   to anoint   (188)

unificar   to unify   (117)

uniformar   to make uniform, standardize   (244)

untar   to apply ointment, spread butter on   (371)

urbanizar   to urbanize, develop, educate   (339)

urdir   to scheme, plot   (346)

urgir   to urge, be urgent   (188)

usurpar   to usurp, encroach   (332)

utilizarse   to use, make use of   (289, 482)

V

vacar   to become vacant   (424)

vaciarse   to become empty   (483, 289)

vacilar   to vacillate   (115)

vacunar   to vaccinate   (114)

vacunarse   to be vaccinated   (114, 289)

vagabundear   to roam, idle, loaf   (463)

vagar   to roam, wander   (341)

vaguear   to idle, loaf   (206)

validar   to validate   (39)

vallar   to fence in, barricade   (261)

valorar   to value, increase in value   (54, 409)

valorear   to value, increase in value   (54, 206)

valorizar   to value   (339)

valsar to waltz (25)
varear to knock, beat down (175)
variar to vary (483)
vaticinar to vaticinate, prophesy, predict, foretell (470)
vedar to prohibit, forbid (54)
vendar to bandage (54)
venerar to venerate, revere (409)
vengar to avenge (421)
vengarse to get revenge (341, 289)
ventar to sniff, scent; blow (wind) (352)
ventilar to ventilate (71)
ventiscar to snow heavily, blow (blizzard), swirl (snow) (424)
veranear to spend the summer (463)
versar to go round, turn (25)
versificar to versify, write verses (117)
verter to pour (354)
vestir to clothe (491)
vibrar to vibrate (259)
vilipendiar to vilify, despise (232)

vincular to relate, connect (71)
vindicar to vindicate (424)
violar to violate, rape (259)
visar to visa, examine and endorse (25)
visualizar to visualize, display (339)
vituperar to reprehend, applaud (409)
vocalizar to vocalize (81)
vocear to shout, cry out (206)
vociferar to vociferate, shout (227)
volcar to overturn, turn over, tilt (424, 496)
voltear to turn over, roll over (206)
vomitar to vomit (254)
vulgarizar to popularize, vulgarize (339)

Y

yapar to give a little more, add a tip (332)
yermar to strip, lay waste (54)
yuxtaponer to juxtapose (364)

Z

zafar to loosen, untie (54)
zafarse de to escape from, get out of (54, 289)
zaherir to wound with words, reproach, reprimand (263)
zahondar to dig (336)
zambullir to dive, plunge (97)
zampar to stuff, cram food down one's throat, gobble down (332)
zanjar to dig a ditch (86)
zapatear to tap one's feet (463)
zapear to chase away, scare away (206)
zapuzar to plunge into water (81)
zarandar to shake about (54, 41)
zarandear to shake about (54, 206)
zarpar to weigh anchor, sail (332)
zozobrar to be shipwrecked, capsize (259)
zunchar to fasten with a band (306)
zurrar to spank, wallop (54)

Over 2,100 Spanish verbs

Minimum Systems Requirement for the Flash Standalone Executable

Windows:
- Pentium II or higher recommended
- Windows 98, ME, NT4, 2000, XP
- 64 MB of installed RAM, 128 MB recommended
- 1024 × 768 color display

Apple:
- Power Macintosh Power PC processor (G3 or higher recommended)
- Mac OS® X 10.2–10.4 64 MB of installed RAM
- 128 MB recommended
- CD-ROM drive
- 1024 × 768 color display

Launching Instructions for the PC

Windows Users:
Insert the CD-ROM into your CD-ROM drive. The application should start in a few moments. If it doesn't, follow the steps below.

1. Click on the Start button on the Desktop and select Run.
2. Type "D:/501Verbs" (where D is the letter of your CD-ROM drive).
3. Click OK.

Launching Instructions for the Mac

Macintosh Users:
The CD will open to the desktop automatically when inserted into the CD drive. Double click the 501 Verbs Flash icon to launch the program.